Oracle Web Services Manager
Securing Your Web Services

Sitaraman Lakshminarayanan

BIRMINGHAM - MUMBAI

Oracle Web Services Manager
Securing Your Web Services

First published: June 2008

Production Reference: 1020608

Published by Packt Publishing Ltd.
32 Lincoln Road
Olton
Birmingham, B27 6PA, UK.

ISBN 978-1-847193-83-4

www.packtpub.com

Cover Image by Nilesh R. Mohite (nilpreet2000@yahoo.co.in)

Credits

Author

Sitaraman Lakshminarayanan

Reviewers

Marc Chanliau

Rajesh Warrier

Acquisition Editor

Bansari Barot

Technical Editor

Usha Iyer

Editorial Team Leader

Mithil Kulkarni

Project Manager

Abhijeet Deobhakta

Project Coordinator

Lata Basantani

Indexer

Hemangini Bari

Proofreader

Cathy Cumberlidge

Production Coordinator

Shantanu Zagade

Cover Work

Shantanu Zagade

About the Author

Sitaraman Lakshminarayanan is an Enterprise Architect with over 11 years of IT experience in implementing software solutions based on Microsoft and Java platforms. His area of interest is in enterprise architecture, application integration and information security, and he specializes in identity and access management, web services and SOA. He is a co-author of ASP.NET Security (Wrox publications) and has presented at regional and international conferences on web services security and identity management.

I thank my wife, Vijaya for her exceptional support in finishing this book on time in the midst of her new job and a new addition to our family. I thank my mother for her constant love and support. I am grateful to the reviewers who provided valuable help to ensure content accuracy. I appreciate the help from the Packt Publishing team, especially Usha Iyer for reviewing and editing, Lata Basantani for coordinating the work between myself, the reviewers and the editorial team.

I dedicate this book to my late mother-in-law,
who wished me success in every step of my career since I met her.

About the Reviewers

Marc Chanliau has over 30 years' experience in the software industry including systems engineering, project and product management. Marc is currently responsible for the product management of platform security and web services security for Oracle's Fusion Middleware. Marc has been closely involved with XML standards development over the last 8 years, in particular SAML, WS-security, and WS-Policy. Marc holds an MS in Linguistics from the University of Paris (Jussieu).

> I would like to thank all the developers and quality-assurance engineers of Oracle Web Services Manager for providing an amazing SOA and web services security tool that is being used by many customers worldwide.

Rajesh Warrier, currently working as one of the lead system architects in Emirates Group IT, has around 10 years, experience in the industry, working with companies like Sun Microsystems. Rajesh has been responsible for architecting and designing many mission-critical enterprise applications using cutting edge technologies, and is currently working as an architect and mentor for the new generation cargo system for Emirates airlines, developed completely using JEE. He has also reviewed another Packt book, Service Oriented Java Business Integration by Binildas C.A.

Table of Content

Preface

Oracle Web Services Manager, a component of SOA Suite from Oracle is a web services security and monitoring product that helps organizations not only to define and enforce security policies, but also to define and enforce the service level agreements. One of the key components of Service Oriented Architecture is security, and this book will be useful for those who are implementing SOA or for those who just want to manage and secure their web services.

This book not only describes the need for and the standards of web services security, but also how to implement them with Oracle WSM. It contains detailed examples on how to secure and monitor web services using Oracle WSM with explanations on the internals of WS-* security standards. It also describes how to customize Oracle WSM and how to plan for high availability.

What This Book Covers

Chapter 1 gives an in-depth overview of web services security from a business point of view, describing the security challenges in a web services environment, why traditional network security isn't enough, and how to measure the ROI on web services security.

Chapter 2 discusses the architecture of web services security including the various interoperable standards, challenges in implementing web services security in .NET and Java applications, and the need for centralized policy definition and enforcement. It also discusses the need to integrate with existing single sign-on systems and provides an overview of Oracle Web Services Manager.

Chapter 3 discusses the architecture of Oracle Web Services Manager. In this chapter, we explore the various components of Oracle WSM, such as gateway, agent, policy management, routing, monitoring, etc.

Chapter 4 talks in-depth about how to implement authentication and authorization in web services using Oracle WSM. It explains how to define security policy and protect web services with a detailed step-by-step example. Once you learn to authenticate and authorize web services requests, the next step is to protect the confidentiality of the message.

Chapter 5 discusses in-depth about encryption and decryption in web services and how to implement them using Oracle WSM with a detailed step-by-step example. This chapter also discusses how to test using a Microsoft .NET application and Oracle WSM test pages.

Chapter 6 addresses the most important part of web services security: digital signature. In this chapter, you will learn how to define security policy to digitally sign and verify SOAP messages with a detailed step-by-step example. This chapter also discusses how to test using Microsoft .NET application and Oracle WSM test pages.

Chapter 7 discusses the internals of Oracle WSM policy manager and how to implement a custom policy with an example scenario and a step-by-step description. No matter what features the Oracle WSM product offers, there may be reasons why you might want to implement certain custom security policies.

Chapter 8 discusses the deployment strategy, database options, high availability requirements and various options to deploy Oracle WSM. It is important that Oracle WSM is highly available to meet business needs.

Chapter 9 discusses the requirements to monitor the availability of Oracle WSM, how to define and monitor the service level agreements, performance metrics, etc.

Chapters 10 and *11* discuss the internals of XML encryption and XML signature standards and how they are used within WS-* security. We walk through with example SOAP messages and explain how encryption and signature are implemented.

Chapter 12 discusses how to combine both digital signature and encryption to ensure both confidentiality and integrity of the message. In this chapter, we will discuss how to implement sign and encrypt in Oracle WSM with a step-by-step example.

Chapter 13 concludes the book with a discussion on Enterprise Security — web services and single sign-on and the need to bridge the gap between SSO products such as Oracle Access Manager and Oracle WSM with the introduction to security token service. We also discuss the integrated security architecture.

What You Need for This Book

You need Oracle Web Services Manager stand alone or the SOA Suite. This can be installed in Windows or Unix platform.

Who is This Book for

This book mainly targets developers, architects and technical managers with expertise in developing and deploying web services. The readers are expected to have a basic understanding of web services, and also development and deployment of web services.

Conventions

In this book, you will find a number of styles of text that distinguish between different kinds of information. Here are some examples of these styles, and an explanation of their meaning.

There are two styles for code. Code words in text are shown as follows: "We can include other contexts through the use of the `include` directive."

A block of code will be set as follows:

```xml
<?xml version="1.0" encoding="utf-8"?>
<soap:Envelope xmlns:soap="http://schemas.xmlsoap.org/soap/envelope/"
xmlns:xsi="http://www.w3.org/2001/XMLSchema-instance" xmlns:
xsd="http://www.w3.org/2001/XMLSchema">
```

Any command-line input and output is written as follows:

wsmadmin.bat start

New terms and **important words** are introduced in a bold-type font. Words that you see on the screen, in menus or dialog boxes for example, appear in our text like this: "clicking the **Next** button moves you to the next screen".

Reader Feedback

Feedback from our readers is always welcome. Let us know what you think about this book, what you liked or may have disliked. Reader feedback is important for us to develop titles that you really get the most out of.

To send us general feedback, simply drop an email to feedback@packtpub.com, making sure to mention the book title in the subject of your message.

If there is a book that you need and would like to see us publish, please send us a note in the **SUGGEST A TITLE** form on www.packtpub.com or email suggest@packtpub.com.

If there is a topic that you have expertise in and you are interested in either writing or contributing to a book, see our author guide on www.packtpub.com/authors.

Customer Support

Now that you are the proud owner of a Packt book, we have a number of things to help you to get the most from your purchase.

Downloading the Example Code for the Book

Visit `http://www.packtpub.com/files/code/3834_Code.zip` to directly download the example code.

The downloadable files contain instructions on how to use them.

Errata

Although we have taken every care to ensure the accuracy of our contents, mistakes do happen. If you find a mistake in one of our books—maybe a mistake in text or code—we would be grateful if you would report this to us. By doing this you can save other readers from frustration, and help to improve subsequent versions of this book. If you find any errata, report them by visiting `http://www.packtpub.com/support`, selecting your book, clicking on the **Submit Errata** link, and entering the details of your errata. Once your errata are verified, your submission will be accepted and the errata are added to the list of existing errata. The existing errata can be viewed by selecting your title from `http://www.packtpub.com/support`.

Questions

You can contact us at `questions@packtpub.com` if you are having a problem with some aspect of the book, and we will do our best to address it.

1
Introduction to Web Services Security

Web services have become an integral part of software development and with the increased adoption of Service Oriented Architecture, business functionalities are being exposed as services within and outside the organization. While web services can expedite the integration process, business owners also need to understand the risk of Service Oriented Architecture from the security point of view and should make every attempt to mitigate that risk. This chapter will give an introduction to web services security—the need for it, what the security options are, and will even give a look quickly into the return on investment in web services security.

The Need for Web Services Security

Application integrations have gone through different phases from traditional file transfer to distributed systems, such as Distributed Component Object Model (DCOM) or Common Object Request Broker Architecture (CORBA) to the current platform independent standards based on Web Services (SOAP). Web services expedite the process of integrating different applications in different platforms without changing much of the underlying business process.

While web services can help the business, the data which was accessible only to that application is now available for integration with any other application. This leads to security concerns in exposing business functionality as web services. The most common questions asked by service providers and consumers in web services architecture regarding security are:

- Service provider:
    - How secure is the data being exchanged? How do I control access to the service?

- How do I ensure the confidentiality and integrity of the message, while still maintaining the interoperability benefits of web services?
- How do I manage the enhancements and fixes to the service without affecting the consumers?
- How do I monitor the performance of the service, its availability, and so on? (various parameters of Service Level Agreement)

- Consumers:
  - How do I access multiple web services with their own unique security requirements?
  - How can I decouple the service invocation from the client application so that I can switch to a different service without affecting the client application?

There are some questions that are common to both service providers and service consumers, such as:

- How can I externalize the security so that I need not worry about various security implementations for the underlying business application or service?
- How can I define and enforce the governance around publishing web services, consuming service, security, and so on?

Security Challenges in a Web Services Environment

Web services actually expose the data and the business process without the need to have access to the user interface of that application. The security requirements in the web service environment can be best illustrated by an example.

Consider a scenario where a bank acquires information about its customer including a Social Security Number to open a credit card account. One critical requirement to open a credit card account is to have certain minimum credit history. The business process can be defined as:

- Obtain the customer's personal information, including Social Security Number.
- Perform credit check with an external agency via web service.
- Upon the approval of credit history, open the credit card account.

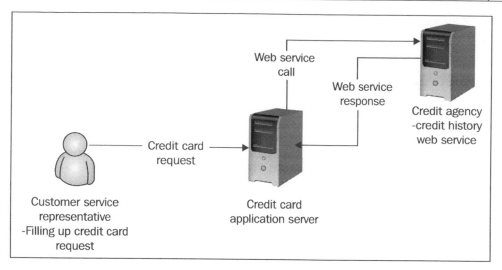

The picture shows the interaction between different systems. From the picture, it is clear that the security at the front end layer, that is at the application layer alone, is not enough.

When there is critical business information exchanged within web services, the service should:

- Identify the service consumer: Authentication
- Validate that the service consumer is authorized to access the service: Authorization
- Protect the message integrity: Signature
- Protect the confidential data: Encryption
- Track who accessed and when: Auditing

The Need for Identity Propagation from Calling Application to Web Services

Security at the application layer can show the pages for which the user has the privileges to view. It can even control the operations allowed on that web page, such as Add, Modify, Delete, and so on. This is typically done by means of a web access management product such as Oracle Access Manager. However, the application actually does certain operations on behalf of the user, such as accessing the database, accessing web services, and so on. Consider the scenario where the user at the travel department of your company makes travel reservations. The user will login to the application and when the user actually makes the reservation, the application makes the web service calls to reserve the tickets and charge the credit card. In this scenario, the web application has the following capabilities (but not limited to):

- Accept credit card information
- Charge the credit card
- Make the reservation

In the above scenario, the application layer can only protect the information based on the user who logged in, and can only protect someone from accessing a web page that they are not supposed to. However, the application needs to call a few web services to complete the travel reservation. In that scenario, the challenges are:

- How do I propagate the identity of the logged-in user to the web services? How do I translate the SSO token that was established when the user logged into the system to one of the security tokens required by the web service provider?
- How do I add any additional information to the web service request so that the service provider can authenticate and authorize the request?
- How do I enforce security that may be different for different services without writing security-specific code within my application?

Since the web services are easily accessible, it is important to make sure that it is very well secured, not only to protect the confidentiality and integrity, but also to allow access only to the authorized users. The following figure shows the reason why web layer security is not enough for database application.

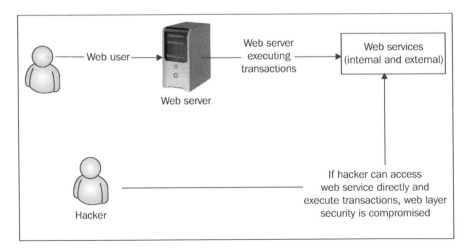

The next section looks at why network security isn't sufficient, and also provides an overview of different web service security components.

Why HTTPS Based Security Is Not Enough

One common security practice is to implement network level security, such as **HTTPS** for transport layer security. Secure Socket Layer (SSL) is the de-facto standard way of communicating over HTTP, commonly used as HTTPS, so that the data is encrypted over the network between the client (for example, web service consumer) and the web server (for example, web service provider). While HTTPS offers transport layer security by encrypting the data over the wire, it does not validate the user actually accessing the URL by default. HTTPS only assures the clients (consumers) that they are talking to the legitimate web site (by means of digital certificate). However, there is an option available to validate the client—by means of client certificate validation. In this case, the client application has to attach the client certificate while invoking the HTTPS URL, and the web server can validate the authenticity of the client certificate before actually granting access to the URL. HTTPS with the client certificate validation will ensure that the server knows exactly who the consumer is.

In our example application scenario, one easy way to enforce secure access to the web service is to enable HTTPS along with client certificate validation between the web service provider and the web service consumer. The following diagram shows how the web service is given access only to a trusted organization, and the intruder is prevented from accessing the web service.

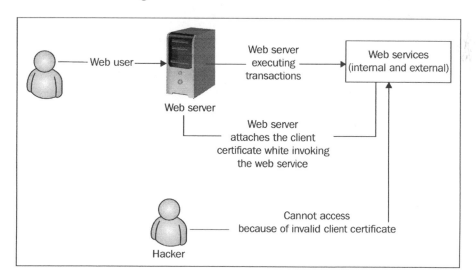

Certain network level security such as HTTPS, client certificate validation can be applied even to web services. However, each has its own pros and cons, and a detailed discussion is beyond the scope of this book. We will describe the network level security for web services in depth here:

Network level security	Description	What it doesn't do for web services
HTTPS (SSL)	It creates a secure connection with server and thus encrypts the data transmitted over the network.	HTTPS access alone does not validate the client/consumer of the web service.
HTTPS (SSL) with Mutual Authentication	It encrypts the data over the network after performing client certificate validation.	Even though it can encrypt and identify the client or the consumer, it does not ensure the integrity of the message that actually left the server.

While network level security is a great place to start, for web services to secure the transaction at the network layer, the data or the message itself should be protected once the message leaves or reaches the destination. The next section will provide an overview of the different components of web services security, and why it is important to address them.

Components of Web Services Security

The various components of web services security are:

Authentication

Authentication is the process of verifying the credentials of the user accessing the system. Webservices should authenticate the user requesting the service before it can execute the request. Without any proper identification of the user, it will be impossible to perform an audit of any unauthorized access.

Authorization

Authorization is the process of validating who has access to what before granting access to perform an operation. Web services security should not only authenticate the user, but should also validate if the user has enough privileges to perform the operation.

Confidentiality

Web services exchange critical business information in XML; certain information can be confidential and it should be protected from any intruder or unauthorized access. XML messages should be encrypted by the service, or the consumer, depending on the sensitivity of the message being exchanged.

Integrity

Since web services exchange XML messages, the integrity of the message should be ensured. Message integrity can be ensured by means of digital signature. Digitally signing the XML messages in the web services can ensure that the message was not tampered by the intruder in transit.

Return on Investment

Investment in security is not easily quantifiable as any other IT system investment. While there is a technology component to the security implementation, it is often the risk that the business is willing to take that drives the security implementation, and securing the web services is no different.

Implementing web services security does require certain investment, either in terms of buying an off-the-shelf product such as Oracle Web Service Manager, or implementing a custom security framework across all the web services and the clients. In either case, the investment should be justified for the business owners. While calculating the ROI on web services security implementation, the following factors should be considered from the business stand point:

- How much of the confidential data is being exposed on services?
- Is it fine not to have any data integrity checks on those web service messages?
- What would be the business impact? Lost monetary value, lost productivity, reputation, and so on.
- Should the service authenticate the user? Is it okay for anyone to access this service?
- Is it okay for everyone to perform all the operations exposed by the service?
- Is it required to satisfy any government regulations?

If the business owners decide to make sure that the web services should be secured, then the IT department should consider the following while defining the ROI:

- How many web services are deployed in a single server, or multiple servers?
- Is there a potential for many more services in the future?
- Are those services in different platforms such as Microsoft .NET and Java?
- Are there any web services behind the firewall that need to be exposed to external vendors?

When there are many web services in different platforms, and that require the understanding of multiple authentication tokens, encryption, signature and so on, the cost of custom development and maintenance of security should be considered and compared with the cost of the product and its performance benefits.

Summary

This chapter gives an introduction to why web services should be secured in an organization and explains the different components of web services security that should be addressed. The next chapter will describe the various standards in web services security, the importance of centralized policy manager, and will also explain the web services security from an architect's point of view.

2
Web Services Security— Architectural Overview

Integrating applications and business processes across various platforms is made easier with web services and it is important that the web services security be considered as an integral part of the organization's web services initiative. As the organization evolves and exposes or integrates with many web services, the management of security policies and enforcement across all the applications can get cumbersome. One way to overcome the challenge is to externalize the security to another application such as Oracle Web Services Manager. In this chapter, we will discuss the need for centralized management of web services, policy definition and policy enforcement with a quick introduction to Oracle Web Services Manager.

Overview of XML Security Standards

Web services is nothing but a set of **XML** messages that are exchanged between software applications in various platforms to provide a better integration platform for a distributed environment. Since its adoption to facilitate faster integration of disparate business processes, requirement for interoperable security definitions has become imminent. In this section, we will take a closer look at why existing security implementations such as SSL are not sufficient, and the need for standards such as **WS-Security**.

Closer Look at SOAP Messages

Consider the example of an online ecommerce web site where you pay for the shopping using credit or debit card. The online ecommerce web site leverages web services to talk to the payment gateway to process the transactions. A typical SOAP message under this scenario for charging a credit card would look like:

```
<?xml version="1.0" encoding="utf-8"?>
<soap:Envelope xmlns:soap="http://schemas.xmlsoap.org/soap/envelope/"
xmlns:xsi="http://www.w3.org/2001/XMLSchema-instance" xmlns:
xsd="http://www.w3.org/2001/XMLSchema">
  <soap:Body>
    <ChargeToCreditCard xmlns="http://tempuri.org/">
      <CreditCardNumber>309192281120999</ CreditCardNumber >
      <Amount>10</ Amount >
    </ ChargeToCreditCard >
  </soap:Body>
</soap:Envelope>
```

The SOAP message above consists of a SOAP envelope that includes a SOAP header and a SOAP body. The SOAP body contains the actual message that the SOAP header is provided with to add any additional processing information that the application can extend to. In the above example, SOAP body contains the information to charge the credit card and the SOAP header does not have any additional information.

The above payment gateway web service, if invoked as such without SSL, causes the SOAP message described to be actually visible for anyone who can sniff the network traffic. Even with SSL, the content is accessible as there is no authentication or authorization of the request. In order to effectively protect the customer information and the business, the web service should:

- Authenticate the user
- Encrypt the SOAP body message
- Digitally sign the SOAP body message

Let's take a closer look at each one of these security measures and explore how it can be done without any interoperability requirements. Then we will describe the need for WS-security standards.

Authentication

Authentication is the process of validating the credentials such as username and password. In the previous example, if the payment gateway web service were to be protected with a username and password, the client, i.e. the ecommerce web site, has to send the username and password in the web service request. Now the question arises as to how the username and password is to be sent in the web service SOAP request. One possible option is:

- Payment gateway web service can request username and password in the SOAP header.

- Client application, i.e. the ecommerce web site, has to construct the SOAP header with username and password and attach it to SOAP envelope/web service request.

- Payment gateway will parse the SOAP header and validate the username and password.

The sample SOAP message with username and password as a custom SOAP header would look like:

```
<?xml version="1.0" encoding="utf-8"?>
<soap:Envelope xmlns:soap="http://schemas.xmlsoap.org/soap/envelope/"
xmlns:xsi="http://www.w3.org/2001/XMLSchema-instance" xmlns:
xsd="http://www.w3.org/2001/XMLSchema">
  <soap:Header>
    <CustomSoapHeader xmlns="http://tempuri.org/">
      <UserID>eCommerceClient</UserID>
      <Password>electronics</Password>
    </CustomSoapHeader>
  </soap:Header>
  <soap:Body>
    <ChargeToCreditCard xmlns="http://tempuri.org/">
      <CreditCardNumber>309192281120999</ CreditCardNumber >
      <Amount>10</ Amount >
    </ ChargeToCreditCard >
  </soap:Body>
</soap:Envelope>
```

In the example SOAP message, the payment gateway can only accept username and password, and validate if (and only if) specified in the specified SOAP header. The drawbacks of sending username and password in a custom SOAP header are:

- Each service provider will come up with their own custom SOAP header with different names, such as uid, username, password, etc.

- The service provider has to communicate various token types for each service.

- Applications that are accessing multiple services have to deal with attaching credentials in different formats for different services.

- Maintenance of both service and the client application becomes unmanageable when there are multiple services.

The above drawbacks make a good case for creating interoperable standards for describing authentication information. WS-security standards have incorporated several token profiles to support a wide variety of authentication mechanisms, such as username and password, Kerberos, SAML, etc.

Let us assume that the payment gateway web service is modified to accept username and password as per the WS-security standards; then the SOAP message would look like:

```
<?xml version="1.0" encoding="utf-8"?>
<soap:Envelope xmlns:soap="http://schemas.xmlsoap.org/soap/envelope/"
xmlns:xsi="http://www.w3.org/2001/XMLSchema-instance" xmlns:
xsd=http://www.w3.org/2001/XMLSchema
xmlns:S11="http://docs.oasis-open.org/wss/oasis-wss-wssecurity-secext-
1.1.xsd ">
    <S11:Header>
          <wsse:Security>
                  <wsse:UsernameToken>
                          <wsse:Username>eCommerceClient</wsse:Username>
                          <wsse:Password>electronics</wsse:Password>
                  </wsse:UsernameToken>
          </wsse:Security>
    </S11:Header>
   <soap:Body>
    <ChargeToCreditCard xmlns="http://tempuri.org/">
      <CreditCardNumber>309192281120999</ CreditCardNumber >
      <Amount>10</ Amount >
    </ ChargeToCreditCard >
   </soap:Body>
 </soap:Envelope>
```

When service providers can accept the username and password, as per WS-Security standards, it becomes easier for both providers and consumers to implement the security in a standard, as opposed to custom implementations that are specific to a service provider or consumer.

In the next section we will explore the importance of WS-security standards for exchanging encryption information.

Confidentiality

The SOAP message that the payment gateway web service receives with the credit card information should be encrypted to protect the customer information. The SOAP message without encryption would look like:

```xml
<?xml version="1.0" encoding="utf-8"?>
<soap:Envelope xmlns:soap="http://schemas.xmlsoap.org/soap/envelope/"
xmlns:xsi="http://www.w3.org/2001/XMLSchema-instance" xmlns:
xsd=http://www.w3.org/2001/XMLSchema
xmlns:S11="http://docs.oasis-open.org/wss/oasis-wss-wssecurity-secext-
1.1.xsd ">
    <S11:Header>
          <wsse:Security>
                <wsse:UsernameToken>
                      <wsse:Username>eCommerceClient</wsse:Username>
                      <wsse:Password>electronics</wsse:Password>
                </wsse:UsernameToken>
          </wsse:Security>
    </S11:Header>
  <soap:Body>
    <ChargeToCreditCard xmlns="http://tempuri.org/">
      <CreditCardNumber>309192281120999</ CreditCardNumber >
      <Amount>10</ Amount >
    </ ChargeToCreditCard >
  </soap:Body>
</soap:Envelope>
```

The traditional way of encrypting is to use a shared secret key. In this case, the secret key is shared between the service provider and the consumer, and the information is encrypted. Let's consider the case where the payment gateway web service requires the credit card number to be encrypted using Triple DES algorithm and the encryption key is already shared between the consumer and the service provider. The SOAP message with an encrypted credit card number will look like:

```xml
<?xml version="1.0" encoding="utf-8"?>
<soap:Envelope xmlns:soap="http://schemas.xmlsoap.org/soap/envelope/"
xmlns:xsi="http://www.w3.org/2001/XMLSchema-instance" xmlns:
xsd=http://www.w3.org/2001/XMLSchema
xmlns:S11="http://docs.oasis-open.org/wss/oasis-wss-wssecurity-secext-
1.1.xsd ">
    <S11:Header>
          <wsse:Security>
                <wsse:UsernameToken>
                      <wsse:Username>eCommerceClient</wsse:Username>
                      <wsse:Password>electronics</wsse:Password>
```

```
              </wsse:UsernameToken>
          </wsse:Security>
      </S11:Header>
    <soap:Body>
      <ChargeToCreditCard xmlns="http://tempuri.org/">
        <CreditCardNumber>AEB123XY231ENCRYPTED</ CreditCardNumber >
        <Amount>10</ Amount >
      </ ChargeToCreditCard >
    </soap:Body>
  </soap:Envelope>
```

In the above example, we only talk about exchanging credit card numbers and the SOAP message looks pretty simple. But in reality, the XML data that are exchanged are far more complicated as it has to describe necessary information for that business transaction.

In the above SOAP message, the service provider makes the following assumptions:

- The data in CreditCardNumber XML element is an encrypted value.
- The encryption algorithm is Triple DES.
- The encryption key is the one that is exchanged between the service provider and the consumer.

The challenges associated with the above approach for sending encryption information are:

- The service provider has to explain which data elements are encrypted and the algorithm, key, etc. too.
- The service provider has to give a new key for each consumer.
- The service provider has to differentiate the SOAP messages for each consumer by means of some identifier for using different encryption keys.
- The challenges are the same when service encrypts the response message and the consumer has to decrypt the information.

The challenges are the same or more complicated even when a different algorithm such as Public Key–Private Key is used to encrypt data in web services.

Since it is all XML data that is exchanged in web services, the recipient of the encrypted message has to know the basic information about encrypted data, such as:

- What data (i.e. XML) elements are encrypted?
- What is the algorithm used to encrypt the data?

- Is encryption based on shared secret (symmetric) or public-private key (asymmetric)?

- Where is the encryption key if it is exchanged along with the data?

WS-security standards adopted the XML encryption standards from W3C to represent the encrypted data information. The SOAP message below describes that the CreditCard element data is encrypted using Triple DES as per WS-security/ XML encryption standards.

```xml
<?xml version="1.0" encoding="utf-8"?>
<soap:Envelope xmlns:soap="http://schemas.xmlsoap.org/soap/envelope/"
xmlns:xsi="http://www.w3.org/2001/XMLSchema-instance" xmlns:
xsd=http://www.w3.org/2001/XMLSchema
xmlns:S11="http://docs.oasis-open.org/wss/oasis-wss-wssecurity-secext-
1.1.xsd ">
    <S11:Header>
          <wsse:Security>
                <wsse:UsernameToken>
                       <wsse:Username>eCommerceClient</wsse:Username>
                       <wsse:Password>electronics</wsse:Password>
                </wsse:UsernameToken>
          </wsse:Security>
    </S11:Header>
  <soap:Body>
    <ChargeToCreditCard xmlns="http://tempuri.org/">
    <EncryptedData xmlns="http://www.w3.org/2001/04/xmlenc#"
Type="http://www.w3.org/2001/04/xmlenc#Element" ID="ED">
      <EncryptionMethod Algorithm="http://www.w3.org/2001/04/
xmlenc#tripledes-cbc" />
      <ds:KeyInfo xmlns:ds="http://www.w3.org/2000/09/xmldsig#">
        <ds:KeyName>Test</ds:KeyName>
      </ds:KeyInfo>
      <CipherData xmlns="http://www.w3.org/2001/04/xmlenc#">
        <CipherValue> 0qn/Au2bWIZNJsM3I/7nkk0Tv0OSUbh8c=</CipherValue>
      </CipherData>
    </EncryptedData>
      <Amount>10</ Amount >
    </ ChargeToCreditCard >
  </soap:Body>
</soap:Envelope>
```

In the SOAP message above shown the `EncryptionMethod` clearly explains that it is a Triple DES algorithm and that `KeyName` is an identifier to get the key name. One should also note that the `EncryptedData` element has an attribute called `Type` that shows that the data that was encrypted was an XML element. What that means is, you can also encrypt the entire XML document, i.e. the entire SOAP message, if required. This flexibility is mainly there to address any performance constraints that we might have on large SOAP messages. (Encryption is a fairly expensive CPU intensive task.)

The above SOAP message is an example for representing encryption information in an interoperable manner and it also demonstrates that WS-security addresses by adopting XML encryption standards from W3C. In the next section, we will explore the need for interoperable standards to ensure the integrity of the message.

Integrity

Authenticating the consumer ensures that a valid user is accessing the service and encrypting the information will keep it confidential. However, the recipient of the message should ensure that the message was not modified by anyone or replaced with a different encrypted data.

A SOAP message that was sent to the payment gateway with the credit card Number encrypted using the public key of the payment provider, would look like:

```xml
<?xml version="1.0" encoding="utf-8"?>
<soap:Envelope xmlns:soap="http://schemas.xmlsoap.org/soap/envelope/"
xmlns:xsi="http://www.w3.org/2001/XMLSchema-instance" xmlns:
xsd=http://www.w3.org/2001/XMLSchema
xmlns:S11="http://docs.oasis-open.org/wss/oasis-wss-wssecurity-secext-
1.1.xsd ">
  <soap:Body>
    <ChargeToCreditCard xmlns="http://tempuri.org/">
    <EncryptedData xmlns="http://www.w3.org/2001/04/xmlenc#"
            Type="http://www.w3.org/2001/04/xmlenc#Element" ID="ED">
      <EncryptionMethod Algorithm=
            "http://www.w3.org/2001/04/xmlenc#RSA" />
      <ds:KeyInfo xmlns:ds="http://www.w3.org/2000/09/xmldsig#">
        <ds:KeyName>Test</ds:KeyName>
      </ds:KeyInfo>
      <CipherData xmlns="http://www.w3.org/2001/04/xmlenc#">
        <CipherValue> Oqn/Au2bWIZNJsM3I/7nkk0Tv0OSUbh8c=</CipherValue>
      </CipherData>
    </EncryptedData>
      <Amount>10</ Amount >
    </ ChargeToCreditCard >
  </soap:Body>
</soap:Envelope>
```

Since the above message is encrypted using the public key of the payment gateway, anyone can get access to the same public key (if it's made public so that other business partners can access it easily) and can send the encrypted message.

The SOAP message below is also encrypted with the same public key and even the same credit card information is encrypted. So any intruder can actually replace the encrypted portion of the message and replace the credit card number.

In the SOAP message below, the `CipherValue` is actually different, which could map to any other valid credit card number.

```
<?xml version="1.0" encoding="utf-8"?>
<soap:Envelope xmlns:soap="http://schemas.xmlsoap.org/soap/envelope/"
xmlns:xsi="http://www.w3.org/2001/XMLSchema-instance" xmlns:
xsd=http://www.w3.org/2001/XMLSchema
xmlns:S11="http://docs.oasis-open.org/wss/oasis-wss-wssecurity-secext-
1.1.xsd ">
  <soap:Body>
    <ChargeToCreditCard xmlns="http://tempuri.org/">
    <EncryptedData xmlns="http://www.w3.org/2001/04/xmlenc#"
            Type="http://www.w3.org/2001/04/xmlenc#Element" ID="ED">
      <EncryptionMethod Algorithm=
            "http://www.w3.org/2001/04/xmlenc#RSA" />
      <ds:KeyInfo xmlns:ds="http://www.w3.org/2000/09/xmldsig#">
        <ds:KeyName>Test</ds:KeyName>
      </ds:KeyInfo>
      <CipherData xmlns="http://www.w3.org/2001/04/xmlenc#">
        <CipherValue> afaf3234234kjkadfa==</CipherValue>
      </CipherData>
    </EncryptedData>
      <Amount>10</ Amount >
    </ ChargeToCreditCard >
  </soap:Body>
</soap:Envelope>
```

Payment gateway has to ensure that the message was not tampered with or altered by anyone, and hence requires digital signatures to sign the message before it is actually encrypted.

The way digital signatures work is by first creating a one way hash (digest) of the message and then encrypting the hash value using the private key of the sender. The recipient will recalculate the hash value and encrypt using the public key to compare the value.

In the payment gateway example, in order to protect the integrity of the message, the credit card number and the amount should be digitally signed first and then encrypted to protect the confidentiality of the message. Now the signed and encrypted message would look like:

```xml
<?xml version="1.0" encoding="utf-8"?>
<soap:Envelope xmlns:soap="http://schemas.xmlsoap.org/soap/envelope/"
xmlns:xsi="http://www.w3.org/2001/XMLSchema-instance" xmlns:
xsd=http://www.w3.org/2001/XMLSchema
xmlns:S11="http://docs.oasis-open.org/wss/oasis-wss-wssecurity-secext-
1.1.xsd ">
  <soap:Body>
    <ChargeToCreditCard xmlns="http://tempuri.org/">
    <EncryptedData xmlns="http://www.w3.org/2001/04/xmlenc#"
            Type="http://www.w3.org/2001/04/xmlenc#Element" ID="ED">
      <EncryptionMethod Algorithm=
              "http://www.w3.org/2001/04/xmlenc#RSA" />
      <ds:KeyInfo xmlns:ds="http://www.w3.org/2000/09/xmldsig#">
        <ds:KeyName>Test</ds:KeyName>
      </ds:KeyInfo>
      <CipherData xmlns="http://www.w3.org/2001/04/xmlenc#">
        <CipherValue> 0qn/Au2bWIZNJsM3I/7nkk0Tv0OSUbh8c=</CipherValue>
      </CipherData>
    </EncryptedData>
      <Amount>10</ Amount >
    </ ChargeToCreditCard >
    <Signature xmlns="http://www.w3.org/2000/09/xmldsig#">
      <SignedInfo>
        <CanonicalizationMethod Algorithm=
                "http://www.w3.org/TR/2001/REC-xml-c14n-20010315" />
        <SignatureMethod Algorithm=
                "http://www.w3.org/2000/09/xmldsig#rsa-sha1" />
        <Reference URI="#xpointer(/)">
          <Transforms>
            <Transform Algorithm="http://www.w3.org/2000/09/
                xmldsig#enveloped-signature" />
          </Transforms>
          <DigestMethod Algorithm=
                "http://www.w3.org/2000/09/xmldsig#sha1" />
          <DigestValue>AZ/q/WCsODcM0tfcoGzGgraVxxk=</DigestValue>
        </Reference>
      </SignedInfo>
  <SignatureValue> gv0s0cFlboSSbF/PlnMQw9ygH6+E6msSX8c=</SignatureValue>
        <KeyInfo>
          <KeyValue xmlns="http://www.w3.org/2000/09/xmldsig#">
```

```
              <RSAKeyValue>
<Modulus>fFnoomEnyk10=</Modulus>
              <Exponent>AQAB</Exponent>
              </RSAKeyValue>
            </KeyValue>
          </KeyInfo>
        </Signature>
      </soap:Body>
    </soap:Envelope>
```

In the SOAP message above, the entire SOAP body is digitally signed and then the credit card number information is encrypted. The DigestValue will not match when the data is tampered with or replaced with other encrypted data.

In the SOAP message above, the most commonly asked questions about digital signatures are:

- What is the hash algorithm used?
- What is the hash value?
- What data is hashed?
- What is the information regarding the public key?

The XML signature specification from W3C addresses the interoperability concerns around exchanging signed XML messages, thus addressing the above mentioned questions. Based on the SOAP message above, it is clear that the hash algorithm used is "sha1", the hash value is represented by the DigestValue element and that the KeyValue element describes the public key. The XML signature standards from W3C are now incorporated in WS-security to ensure the integrity of the message.

Overview of WS-Security Standards

In the last section, we explored how the XML encryption and XML signature address the interoperability requirements around exchanging encrypted or digitally-signed messages. In web services, all the messages are XML messages. Hence, the WS-security standards from Oasis addresses the encryption and signature requirements by incorporating the XML encryption and XML signature specifications from W3C. WS-security standards also include security token profiles, such as username, Kerberos, SAML, and X.509 to address the need for security token (authentication and authorization). In this section, we will take a closer look at WS-*security standards.

Implementing WS-*Security in Applications

WS-security standards are a way to represent security information. Each application has to leverage its native API or external product to actually implement the WS-security standards.

Consider for example, a web service that requires the client to authenticate using a username and password. In this case, the web service will receive the SOAP message with the username and password. The web service has to perform the actual validation of username and password against a database, or LDAP directory, or other data store. The detailed steps to perform the authentication are:

- Service will accept the SOAP message.
- Service will parse the SOAP message to obtain the username and password.
- Service will validate the username and password against a data store such as LDAP or RDBMS.

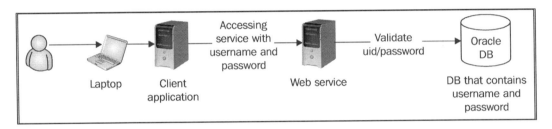

Now let's consider the case where the client application has to talk to two different web services, each requiring different usernames and passwords to authenticate to the service. The following figure shows the client and service interaction.

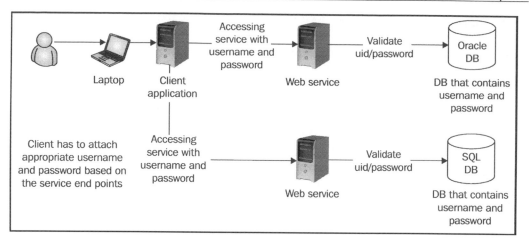

In the above diagram, the client application has to perform the following actions:

- Identify which service end point is being invoked.
- Look up the username and password from a configuration file or database.
- Attach the username and password to the appropriate web service.
- Invoke the web service.

The complexity grows as the client application talks to many services that require different usernames and passwords to authenticate. On the service provider side, the complexity increases with multiple web services using different databases for authenticating credentials. It also increases the security risk by not maintaining credentials in one place, and the cost of enforcing security best practice increases due to duplicating efforts across multiple services and databases.

If you thought that authentication itself is complicating your web services security implementation, think about implementing encryption or digital signatures.

Consider the example of payment gateway service provider that requires the incoming message to be encrypted using the public key of the payment gateway. Web service has to perform the following operations:

1. Look up the private key based on a certain key identifier
2. Decrypt the message.

Now if the web service is encrypting the response message back to the consumer, it has to encrypt with the public key of the client application. Now the service provider has to perform the following operations:

- Look up the public key based on some identifier.
- Encrypt the message with appropriate public key.

Consider the following diagram where you have two internal web services and one external web service being accessed by one or more applications.

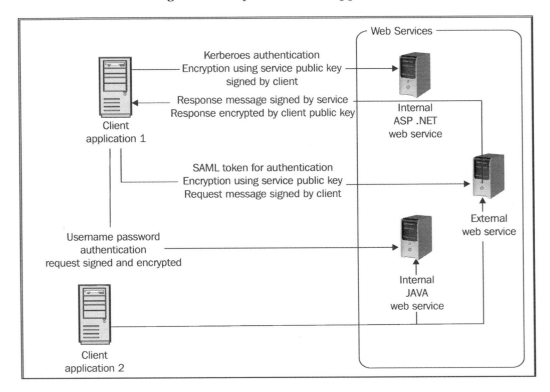

In the diagram above, the two internal web services have to:

- Enforce two types of authentication — **username/password** and **Kerberos.**
- Verify digital signatures from two different clients.
- Encrypt response message from one of the web services.

With one **external web service** each client has to:

- Be accessed from two different clients.
- Implement the security policy, such as service public key certificates.
- Deal with any changes in security policy.

Both the service provider and the consumer, which are business applications, now have to deal with a lot of security implementation, and that creates a challenge in terms of design, development, deployment, and maintenance.

Now imagine having multiple client applications having to deal with multiple services. Both the client and the service has to deal with the same challenge of enforcing the security policy. This leads to the need for centralized management of web services security, which is discussed in the next section.

Centralized Management of WS-*Security

One of the main reasons for the faster adoption of web services is its support for interoperability and ease of integration, without worrying about firewall or sticking to one particular technology or standard. Security should not be a hindrance to the adoption of services, even with standards such as WS-security. In this section, we will discuss the need for centralizing the web services security operations and the benefits of centralizing them.

The Need for Centralizing WS-*Security Operations

The service providers (web service providers) should fully leverage the WS-security standards and should be able to accept and process multiple authentication tokens, different encryption algorithms, flexibility in what data is signed and what data is encrypted, etc. The service consumers also should send the necessary security tokens and perform the required encryption and signature, as required by the service provider.

The implementations of WS-security components, such as encryption, signature, Kerberos token, username token, etc. are available in both .NET and Java platform. However, the developers have to spend time configuring security within each application they write, and it becomes an administrative nightmare when it comes to managing web services security across a variety of applications in various platforms. The complexity increases when SSL is required for a certain web service (providers or consumers).

In order to perform all these operations, each web service has to maintain multiple public keys and private keys all over the organization. It becomes unmanageable when a key is lost, stolen or expired and needs to be updated across all the servers. Based on the challenges described, there is a strong need to centralize the WS-security operations in one place (e.g. Oracle Web Services Manager).

Benefits of Centralizing Web Services Security Operations

While it is apparent that the web services security operations should be centralized, there are more benefits in centralizing the security operations:

- Developers need not implement security in each web service or client application.
- Administrators can define the security policy, i.e. what data should be encrypted, signed, what type of authentication tokens are accepted, etc.
- Security operations are moved away from the core service or consumer application.
- It draws an inherent benefit of increasing the performance by moving the security to another process or server.

In order to centralize the web service security operation, organization, should either custom implement the security operations or adopta web services security product, such as Oracle Web Services Manager. In the next section, we will briefly talk about this product.

Introduction to Oracle Web Services Manager

In the last section we explored the importance of centralizing the web services security operations. However, any custom implementation would be too expensive to develop and maintain, especially with the fast-growing changes in the web services standards and WS security standards. In this section, we will take a took at the Oracle Web Services Manager product to secure the web services.

Oracle Web Services Manager can actually centralize the security operation by merely acting as a gateway for all your services, and the Oracle WSM product will perform all the security operations. Oracle WSM brings the benefit of:

- Centralizing security operations
- Defining different policies for different web services
- Creating policy templates that can be applied over a set of services
- Enhanced logging capability for troubleshooting
- Flexible auditing mechanism to track the performance
- Strong integration with Oracle Access Manager and Siteminder
- Flexible architecture for easy customization
- Monitor web service operations, security operations, etc.
- Manage the web services deployment
- Generate reports about web services performance, usage, etc.

Oracle Web Services Manager can actually reduce the security development effort and can offload the security processing to another server.

Summary

In a service oriented architecture, security should be included right from the design, and the services should support all the WS-security standards, and should be flexible enough to adapt to any new standards. The security architecture should be flexible enough that all the security operations can be offloaded to another process with the possibility of customizations to support any specific requirements. Products such as Oracle Web Services Manager can help implement the web services security and centralize the policy for web services with the flexibility for customization to support any custom security requirements. In the next chapter, we will take a closer look at the architecture of Oracle Web Services Manager.

3
Architecture Overview of Oracle WSM

The service oriented architecture using web services has a strong need to secure the web services and to monitor the web services infrastructure. The security infrastructure for web services should address authentication, authorization, confidentiality, integrity and non-repudiation, and should also support the interoperability standards. The SOA (using web services) infrastructure should also have the ability to monitor the availability of services to provide timely and on-demand reports about the success and failure of various service operations. Oracle Web Services Manager is the web services security and monitoring product from Oracle that addresses both the security and monitoring aspect of the web services infrastructure. Oracle WSM supports WS-security standards to effectively secure the web services, and the product itself is designed with greater flexibility to support any new standard or even write custom extensions. In the first two chapters, we talked about the need for web services security and in this chapter, we will take a closer look at the architecture of Oracle Web Services Manager.

Oracle WSM Architecture

In a service-oriented architecture using web services, organizations can expose their service offerings as web services and their business partners can consume their services to create business solutions. A good example would be a HR System which can integrate with a background check service provided by an external organization to perform a background check before an applicant is hired or offered a job.

In the previous example, web services are exposed by the background check service provider and the service is consumed by many organizations (HR systems of various organizations). In order to effectively maintain the defined service level agreements and also to ensure that only authorized organizations can invoke the service, and still ensure confidentiality and integrity of the data, the service provider exposing web services should:

- Externalize the security implementation.
- Centralize the security definitions or policies, i.e. what type of authentication tokens are accepted, what data elements are encrypted, etc.
- Change the security definition without having to redeploy any code or not affecting the actual service implementation.
- Integrate with existing infrastructure such as LDAP compliant directory or access management products.
- Monitor the web service for performance and availability.
- Expose service to business partners outside the firewall.

On the other hand, the service consumers should also have the flexibility to:

- Adhere to the appropriate security policy of the service provider.
- Externalize the security implementation.
- Flexible enough to Change security implementation or adapt to the service provider's new security policies.

Oracle Web Services Manager addresses the above mentioned requirement, and the architecture of Oracle WSM consists of:

- Oracle WSM Gateway: proxy-based approach to separate the security enforcement from the web service.
- Oracle WSM Policy Manager: Policy manager to define the web services policy.
- Oracle WSM Server Agents: Enforces security policy at the service end.
- Oracle WSM Client Agents: Adheres to the service policy defined by attaching appropriate tokens or performing encryption or signature.
- Oracle WSM Monitor: To monitor the performance, service level agreements, etc.

Oracle WSM Policy Manager

Securing a web service involves one of the many steps, such as authentication, authorization, encryption, decryption, signature generation, signature verification, etc. It is easy to manage when the security is not complicated and there is only a handful of services. It becomes unmanageable when the number of services increases or the complexity of the security, such as multiple authentication token, verifying incoming signature vs signing outgoing message, etc. increases. The Policy Manager component of Oracle WSM not only centralizes the security policy administration, but also makes it easy to attach existing policies to new services.

Overview of Oracle WSM Policy Manager

The web services security has various components, such as authentication, authorization, confidentiality, integrity and non-repudiation. Each of these components can have multiple ways to perform the operation, i.e. authentication can happen based on username and password, or based on SAML token, etc. Let's take a brief look at individual components and then describe how Oracle WSM can help in addressing the security requirements.

Authentication

By definition, it is a process of validating the user's credentials, i.e. who they say they are matches with who they are. The credentials can either be what they know, such as username and password, or what they have, such as a digital certificate issued by a trusted authority, or what they are, i.e. biometric information.

In the context of web services, the service provider should be able to authenticate the consumer based on the information that is presented as a part of the web service message. The information can be username and password, or a SAML token, or another SSO token or any other custom or other token type. Whatever the information is, it needs to be extracted and validated.

The service provider should be able to support multiple token types for authentication, and should also be able to integrate with various data stores within the organization, such as the LDAP compliant directory or another access management system to validate the credentials.

Authorization

Authorization or access control is the means of granting access to a specific resource (such as invoking the web service) for the authenticated user. The authenticated user should have the necessary privileges to perform the requested action.

In the web services world, the service provider should be able to validate that the authenticated user has the privileges to invoke the service. It is usually done either by validating whether the user belongs to a particular role or by validating the user's attributes, such as title that has a value of "Hiring Manager".

Confidentiality

Confidentiality is nothing but ensuring the privacy. In the web services world, the message should be encrypted so that no one other than the intended recipient can see the message.

The web service provider or consumer should be able to handle both encryption and decryption, i.e:

- Decrypt incoming SOAP message for certain web services
- Encrypt the response message

Integrity and Non-Repudiation

In the web service world it is important to ensure that the message is not altered during the transit, and that can be accomplished by digitally signing the message. Digital signature also creates a unique time stamp and validates the sender, thus providing a mechanism to establish non-repudiation. The web service provider or consumer should be able to:

- Validate incoming SOAP message signatures for certain web services.
- Sign a response message for certain web services.
- Sign and encrypt certain response messages.

Web services security requirements include token translation, i.e. converting one authentication token to another authentication token, and transport level security such as SSL too.

A heavily used web services architecture would require a flexible security management product that can externalize the security implementation with a flexibility to support these requirements, and any other custom requirements. Oracle WSM can let you define the security policies and attach it to web services. It also provides a flexible architecture that supports various token formats, authentication stores and is even customizable to meet any unique security need.

Oracle WSM Policy Manager consists of pipeline templates which are made up of different policy steps. Two key pipeline templates are Request Pipeline and Response Pipeline. Each of them consists of its own policy steps to process the request and response message.

Note: PreRequest and PostRequest pipleline templates will be removed in the future version of Oracle WSM.

Policy Steps and Pipeline Templates

Oracle WSM Policy Manager comprises Request and Response pipeline templates, which in turn consist of a set of policy steps. Policy steps are nothing but individual operations, such as authentication, authorization, encryption, and signature. With reference to the use case described in the earlier section, the various policy steps are as shown in the next figure:

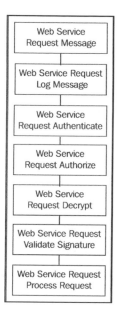

The previous diagram shows the Request pipeline template with the policy steps.

The policy steps described are generic policy steps. However, in actual implementation, the authentication can be against any LDAP compliant directory, and the authorization can be against any LDAP compliant directory or custom data store.

Consider for instance, two web services exposed by consumer electronics corporation and each of them require authentication against the file system. All the response messages are digitally signed. To summarize, the requirements are:

- Two web services exposed by the organization
- Two web services require authentication against file system
- Response messages are digitally signed
- Web services security is enforced by Oracle WSM

There are a couple of ways in which the policy can be defined and enforced by Oracle WSM.

Option 1: Individual Policy Definition for Each Web Service

One option is to define an individual policy for each web service and configure the request and response steps. In this option, the administrator will modify each policy for the web service and will then configure the Active Directory Authentication step during Request processing and sign the message on the Response processing.

The following screenshot shows the policy steps configured for each service.

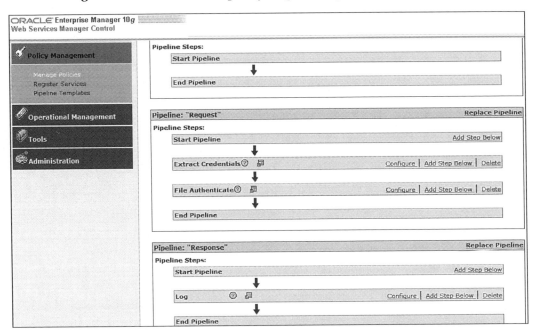

In the previous screenshot, the **Request** pipeline is configured to authenticate based on the users in the file system, and the **Response** pipeline is configured to sign the message.

In this approach, the administrator has to configure the Request pipeline for each web service and has to follow the steps correctly.

Option 2: Pipeline Templates

The other alternative to the above solution is to actually define the Request and Response pipeline template with policy steps, and even configure the policy steps. Once the pipeline templates are created, the administrator has to just modify each policy for the web service and replace the Request pipeline with the appropriate pipeline.

In this example, a Request pipeline template called "FileAuth" is created with both **Extract Credentials** and **File Authentication** steps.

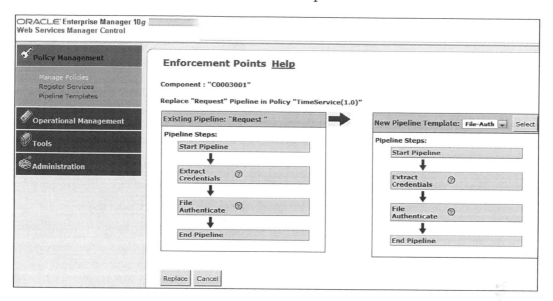

The previous screenshot show the process of replacing the default **Request** pipeline for a policy with **FileAuth Request** pipeline, with steps that are already configured.

Relationship Between Policy and Service

Oracle WSM Policy Manager consists of policies to actually secure the web service. But that policies should be attached to the web service to actually enforce the security. In order to do that, the service should be registered first in Oracle WSM. Once the service is registered, a default policy is created. The default policy can then be replaced with an appropriate policy or the pipeline templates.

Oracle WSM Gateway

Oracle WSM Gateway is a self-contained module that provides protocol mediation and service end point virtualization. It can also enforce security when the client invokes the web service exposed through the gateway. The consumers of the web service can identify the web services by means of its end point URL. While a web service can be developed in Java or .NET, the URL can be virtualized by means of registering the web service within the Oracle WSM Gateway. What Oracle WSM Gateway provides is a way to virtualize the end point, thus making a highly load-balanced environment available.

Oracle WSM Gateway is no different than a traffic cop (or a security officer) from a security perspective. Oracle WSM Gateway features are:

- Perform security checks on the SOAP message
    - Inspects all the SOAP messages, as per the defined policies.

- Protocol translation
    - Transforms the HTTP request to a JMS or MQ type of request.
    - Transforms data from one format to another, if required.

- Message routing

    - Routes messages to the appropriate end point, based on the content.
    - Routing can even be dynamic, based on XPATH expressions.

The importance of Oracle WSM gateway architecture can be best explained in the context of use cases and they are:

- Proxy, or exposing internal service to external business partner, or outside of intranet
- Transport protocol translation
- Content routing
- Security policy

Proxy, or Exposing Internal Service to External Business Partner, or Outside of Intranet

It is not uncommon for business partners to request access to internal service and at the same time it is not uncommon for organizations to host services internally and make it available to extranet via proxy architecture. One typical example is reverse proxy architecture for web sites. Organizations can build and deploy web sites internally within their protected security zone and have a reverse proxy appliance to rewrite the URL and make it available to the external users. While a similar concept applies for web services, it is not exactly the same architecture because there is no URL rewrite in this case.

The following are the reasons why an internal service should be made available to extranet:

- Web service developed and hosted by one business unit is required by another business unit, but both of them are in different data centres without a dedicated network connection.
- Internally hosted service is a key component in enabling the process automation and needs to be exposed to the extranet.
    - Example: A consumer electronics organization typically takes orders through its own web site and has now decided to accept orders from other online portals, and it is needed to expose web services to external business partners.
- Security concerns may prevent an organization from deploying web services on its public network, and hence it is deployed internally and made available via proxy.

In the following figure, the Oracle WSM Gateway exposes the internal web service to an external customer. The **Oracle WSM Gateway** is accessible from the internet and the gateway then internally forwards the request to one or many internal web services.

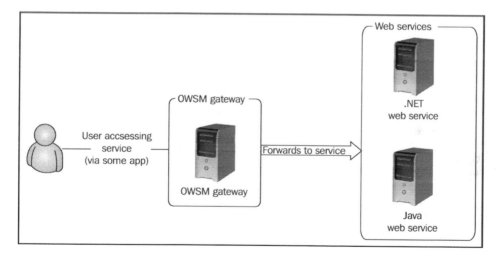

Transport Protocol Translation

The key advantage of the Service Oriented Architecture (SOA) is that we can expose the existing business process as services so that it can be better integrated with other applications and business partners. It does not mean that the existing technology should be shut down and everything should be based on web services. There are instances where internal implementation of a business process may be based on a set of internal protocols, such as MQ Series, JMS, etc. In a SOA, the architecture should create the flexibility to integrate with existing technology infrastructure, and at the same time, should adhere to the industry standards for interoperability. Let's walk through a case study to examine this in more detail.

Consider our earlier example of consumer electronics corporation which was accepting orders only from its own web site. Here the architecture was designed in such a way that once the order is placed, a message is sent to a MQ Series message queue, so that another application can process the transaction. The following figure describes the current architecture of consumer electronics corporation that leverages the MQ Series.

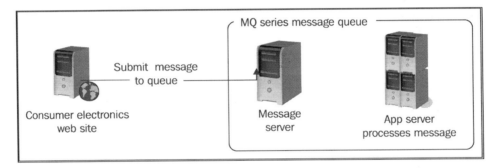

In this example, when the business decides to expand to receive orders from other business partners, such as online portals, it can either rewrite the application based on web services or create a web service gateway to translate the message to MQ Series so that the underlying architecture or process remains unchanged. The following figure describes how the **B2B Online Portal** can place an order via web service and the web service (gateway) then internally translates to an MQ Series request.

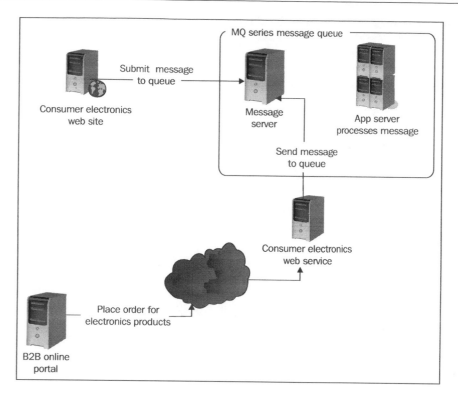

Protocol translation is also applicable for outgoing messages to be translated into web services protocol. This is a nice feature from Oracle WSM on its gateway architecture where you can leverage the existing applications and infrastructure, and still expose business process as services.

Content Routing

Web service end points can expose the business process as a service. However, when there are too many services exposed to business partners, it may become unmanageable from a deployment and security perspective. Consider our example of consumer electronics corporation which accepts orders from an online B2B portal. Now let's consider the following use case:

- Electronics company accepts orders for cameras, camcorders and TVs, both from its web site and from its business partners.

- Each order type is sent to a different MQ Series message queue for processing.

- In order to enable B2B Portal integration, three new web services are developed for each order type.

In the above scenario, the electronics company can either expose all the three web services to the B2B partners, or can expose just one service which then routes the message. The latter has the following advantages:

- Only one web service to be exposed to the gateway/extranet.
- Security should only be enforced on one service.
- It's easy to communicate with business partners to access one service with a different message type for each order.
- Oracle WSM Gateway can then route the message to the appropriate service internally, based on the content.

Summary

In this chapter, we discussed the Oracle WSM architecture and how services, policies, pipeline templates, policy steps and gateway are related. We also discussed the importance of gateway architecture. In the following chapters, we will explore certain individual security steps in detail, to understand how to configure the web services security.

4

Authentication and Authorization of Web Services Using Oracle WSM

The first step in protecting web services is to authenticate and authorize the web service requests. Authentication in web services is the process of verifying that the user has valid credentials to access the web services and authorization is the process of validating that the authenticated user has appropriate privileges to access the web services. Besides restricting access to users with valid credentials and proper privileges, Oracle WSM can track who accessed which service and when — to provide detailed audit trails. In this chapter, we will explore how Oracle Web Services Manager can be leveraged to authenticate and authorize the web services requests.

Oracle WSM: Authentication and Authorization

Oracle Web Services Manager can authenticate the web services request by validating the credentials against a data store. The credentials (e.g. username and password, SAML token, certificate, etc.) that are attached to the web services will be validated against the data store, such as the file system, databases, active directory and any LDAP compliant directory. Once authentication is successful, the next step is to perform authorization by validating the username against a set of pre-defined groups which have access to the web service.

The following figure shows the process where the user accesses an application which acts as a client for the web service. The client application then attaches the username and password to make the web service request. The username and password are then validated against file system or LDAP directory by Oracle WSM, either using the gateway or the agent.

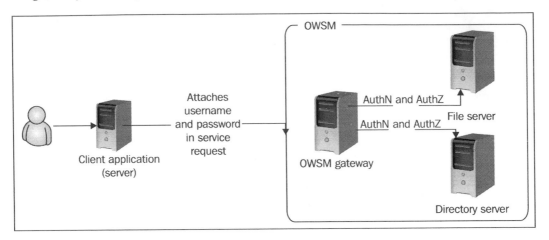

The authentication and authorization against different directory stores can be configured using Oracle WSM policy steps. Oracle Web Services Manager has predefined policy steps for:

- File Authenticate and Authorize
- Active Directory Authenticate and Authorize
- LDAP Authenticate and Authorize

In the previous figure, the **Oracle WSM Gateway** is used to protect the web services and externalize the security. In order to authenticate and authorize requests to web services, the web services can be registered within the gateway and the request pipeline of gateway will validate the credentials and authorize the access before it forwards the request to the actual web service provider. The gateway steps for authentication and authorization can be summarized as:

- Log incoming request (optional)
- Extract credentials (get the credentials from the SOAP message or HTTP header)
- Authenticate (file authenticate, active directory authenticate, etc.)
- Authorize (file authorize, active directory authorize, etc.)
- Request is forwarded to the web service provider

The response from the web service also follows through a similar response pipeline where you can implement the log, encryption of response, or signing, or response, etc. While it is not required to implement any steps in the response pipeline, there should be a response pipeline even if it's doing nothing.

Oracle WSM: File Authenticate and Authorize

Oracle Web Services Manager can authenticate the web services requests against a file that has the list of usernames and passwords. In this example, the username and password information are part of the SOAP message, however one can also send a username and password as HTTP header, or it can be any XML data that is a part of the web services message. While file-based authentication can easily be compromised, it is often used as a jump start or testing process to validate the authentication and authorization process.

Authentication and authorization of web service requests against a file requires three main steps, and these are described below. There is a default log step which will log all the request and response messages, and you can also include that log step at any point to log messages:

- Extract Credentials
- File Authenticate
- File Authorize

The first step to authenticate a web service request against a password file (file authenticate) is to extract the username and password credentials from the SOAP message. The client application attaches the username and password to the SOAP message, as per the UserName token profile, which is described later in this chapter.

In the policy to authenticate the web service against the file, add the step in the request process to extract credentials. Since this is a web service request, as opposed to HTTP post, configure the **Credentials location** to **WS-BASIC** (refer to the following screenshot).

Note: WS-BASIC means that it is WS-security compliant. WS-security is the oasis specification that specifies how security tokens are inserted as a part of the SOAP message. In other words, WS-BASIC means that the username and password can be found in the SOAP message, as per the username token profile of the WS-security specification.

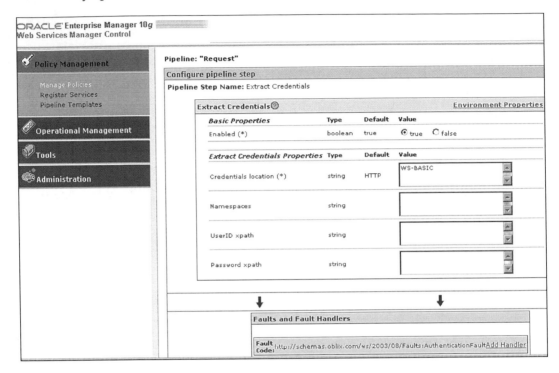

Once the credentials are extracted, the next step is to validate them against the file. The default implementation of the Oracle WSM File Authenticate requires the username and password to be in a comma separated format and the password should be the hash value using a MD5 or SHA1 algorithm.

In order to authenticate the credentials against the data store, the next step is to configure the **File Authenticate** step in Oracle WSM. In this step, the options are straightforward. We have to configure the location of the password file and the hash algorithm format as either **md5** or **SHA1** (see the next screenshot).

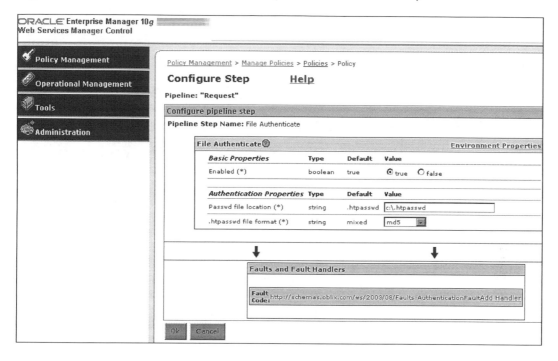

The sample file with username and password is:

```
bob:{MD5}jK2x5HPF1b3NIjcmjdlDNA==
```

Note: You can use the wsmadmin tool provided as part of Oracle WSM (standalone or SOA suite). Type: `wsmadmin md5encode bob password c;\.htpasswd`

Now that the authentication steps are configured, the next step is to configure the authorization policy step to ensure that only valid users can access the web service. For the file authorization method, it is no different than the file authenticate method i.e. even the user-to-role mappings are kept in the file.

The following figure shows the **File Authorize** policy step. In this step, we have to define the location of the XML file that contains the users to roles mapping, and also the list of roles that should be allowed to access the service.

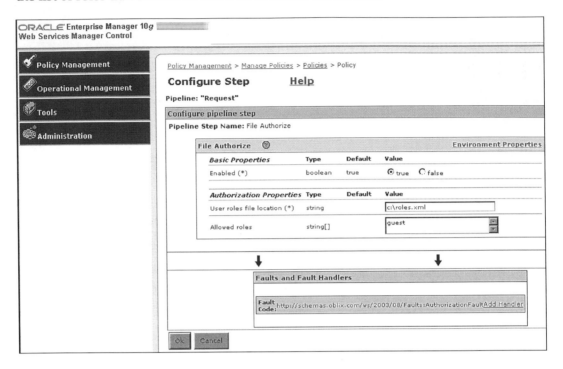

The roles XML file should look like:

```
<?xml version='1.0' encoding='utf-8'?>
<UserRoles>
  <user username="joe" roles="guest"/>
  <user username="Bob" roles="Admin,guest"/>
</UserRoles>
```

In the previous XML file, the list of roles the user belongs to are defined as a value of `roles element` and is `comma` separated.

Now that we have completed the steps to extract credentials, authenticate the request and also authorize the request, the next step is to save the policy steps and commit the policy changes. Once the policy is committed, any request to that web service would require a username and password, and that user should have necessary privileges to access the service.

Oracle WSM: Active Directory Authenticate and Authorize

In the previous section, we discussed authenticating and authorizing web service requests against a file. Though it's an easy start, security based on a file system can be easily compromised and will be tough to maintain. Authentication and authorization of web services are better handled when integrated with a native LDAP directory, such as active directory, so that the AD administrator can manage users and group membership. In this section, we will discuss how to authenticate and authorize web service requests against an active directory.

Active-directory-based authentication and authorization of web service requests involves the same steps as file-based-authentication and authorization, and they are:

- Extract Credentials
- Active Directory Authenticate
- Active Directory Authorize

The first step towards active-directory-based authentication and authorization is to extract the username and password credentials from the SOAP message. This step is the same for both file-based-authentication and active-directory-based authentication. The next screenshot describes how the **Extract Credentials** steps should be configured.

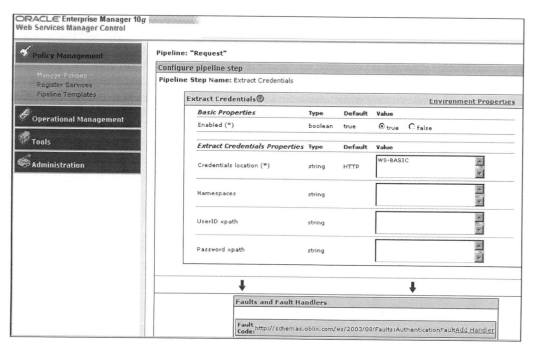

In the **Extract Credentials** step, the **Credentials location** should be changed to **WS-BASIC** since it is a web service invocation.

The second step is to authenticate the web service request against the active directory data store. Well, we know that the credentials i.e. username and password are attached to the SOAP message. Once the credentials are extracted from the SOAP message, we then have to define the following in order to authenticate the user against the active directory:

- Name of the active directory server
- Ports on which to communicate (both plain text and SSL)
- Base distinguished name under which the user can be found
- Active directory domain name
- User attribute that uniquely identifies the user.

This information is then configured in the **Active Directory Authenticate** policy step.

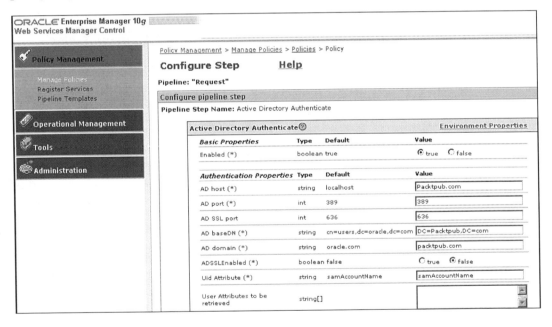

In the previous figure, the sample **Active Directory Authenticate** policy step is configured to validate the user against:

- Packtpub active directory at **Packtpub.com**
- Listening on port **389** and **636**
- With the domain name of **packtpub.com**

- The user can be found under **DC=Packtpub, DC=com**
- The unique user id attribute is **samAccountName**

Once this policy step is configured, the username and password will be validated against the packtpub active directory.

The next step is to ensure that only valid users can access the web service by defining the Active Directory Authorize policy step. In this step, Oracle WSM will validate the authenticated user against the configured groups and will be granted access only if the user belongs to one of those groups. The following screen capture shows how the **Active Directory Authorize** step is configured.

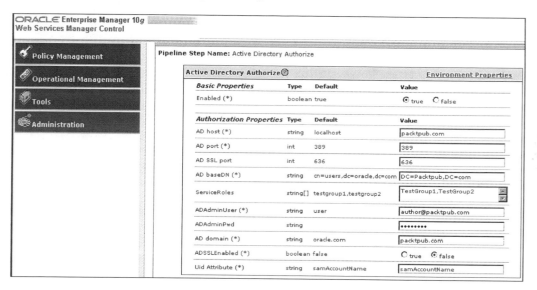

In the previous figure, the AD Authorize policy step is configured to protect against **TestGroup1** and **TestGroup2**. In the This step, you should also define the service account that can bind to the active directory.

Note: The **AD baseDN** should be a root distinguished name under which both users and groups are defined. Technically, users can be in a different container to the groups, but in the AD Authorize policy step, the **AD baseDN** should be the root of both the user's and group's container.

Once the AD Authenticate and Authorize steps are configured, the next step is to save the policy steps and then commit the policy. When the web service request is made with the appropriate username and password that belong to TestGroup1 or TestGroup2, they will be either granted or denied access to the service.

In the next section, we will take a closer look at what policy templates are and how they can be used in defining policy steps.

Oracle WSM: Policy Template

Policy templates are reusable policy steps that can be created once and used across multiple policies. It is not uncommon to have a similar sequence of steps to perform operations such as authentication, authorization, signature verification, etc. Instead of defining the same steps over and over again in each policy, it can be defined as a policy template in one place and then used when defining each policy step.

In the previous sections, we discussed authenticating users against an active directory. Imagine that each service should be authenticated against the same active directory; one has to define the same steps of Extract Credentials and AD authenticate across each policy. While Extract Credentials and AD Authenticate are mandatory, there is also an optional logging step that may be required to help troubleshoot the application. In the overall, the administrator has to:

- Create the log step and specify what information should be logged.
- Create the Extract Credentials steps in each policy and define if it is WS-BASIC or not.
- Create the AD Authenticate step and define the same AD user DN, uid attribute, etc.

When these steps are repeated across all services, it increases the administrative overhead and can also cause increase in the chances of manual data entry errors.

Defining the policy template for AD Authenticate for your environment would be ideal so that the default request template can be replaced with this new template. In order to define the policy template, the administrator has to go to the **Pipeline Templates** section and then create a new template.

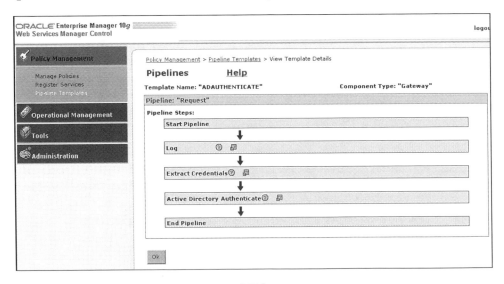

In the previous figure, a new request pipeline template named **ADAUTHENTICATE** has been defined. Defining the pipeline template is exactly the same as configuring the steps in policy in the request pipeline section.

In this example, we defined a template that will:

- **Log** the request.
- **Extract Credentials** with WS-BASIC.
- Authenticate the user against the active directory using samaccountname as uid attribute.

Once this template is defined, in the policy section, when you want to authenticate the request against the active directory, you can replace the default request pipeline template with the ADAUTHENTICATE pipeline template.

In the previous figure, the default **Request** pipeline is replaced with the ADAUTHENTICATE pipeline template.

Note: Once the template is chosen, it can then be modified to add any additional steps, and that will not affect the actual template.

Oracle WSM: Sample Application AD Authentication

The previous sections described the various options and steps involved in authenticating web service requests. In this section, we will create a sample Microsoft .NET client application that will access a web service whose security is managed by Oracle Web Service Manager for authenticating the requests.

Since this book assumes that the readers are familiar with the creation of web services, we will leave out the details of web service creation. We will be using the sample web service that comes with Oracle WSM product installation.

We will divide this section into two components; one is to ensure that the web service is protected by Oracle WSM and the other component is the creation of the .NET client application.

Web Service Security Policy

In order to secure the web service, it should be defined within Oracle WSM and then the policy will be attached and modified to protect the web service. Three high level steps are required to protect a web service using Oracle WSM, and they are:

- Register the web services with Oracle WSM.
- Create and define the security policy.
- Commit the policy.

Registering The Web Service with Oracle WSM

The first step in securing the web service is to register the web service with Oracle WSM as a part of a gateway. In order to register the web service, one has to have the service WSDL URL handy. In our sample, we will be using the time service that comes with the Oracle WSM installation. You can download and install Oracle Web Service Manager from `http://download.oracle.com/otn/nt/ias/101310/soa_windows_x86_ws_mgr_101310.zip` Once the Oracle WSM is installed, you can start the Oracle WSM from the `bin` directory of the installation folder by entering

wsmadmin.bat start.

Once the Oracle WSM is started, you can access it via browser by typing

`http://localhost:3115/ccore` The default username and password is admin/oracle.

You can now view the Time Service at:

> `http://owsm.packtpub.com:3115/ccore/TimeService.wsdl`

The following steps describe how to register the service.

Login to Oracle Web Service Manager Console at:

> `http://owsm.packtpub.com:3115/ccore`

Click on **Policy Management** and then **Register Services**, you will see the list of gateways that are available, as shown in the next screen capture.

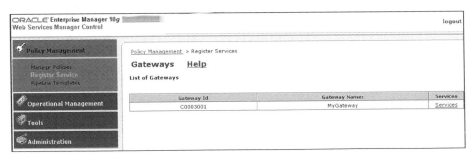

On the right side of the screen, if you click on the **Services** hyperlink, you will see the list of registered services.

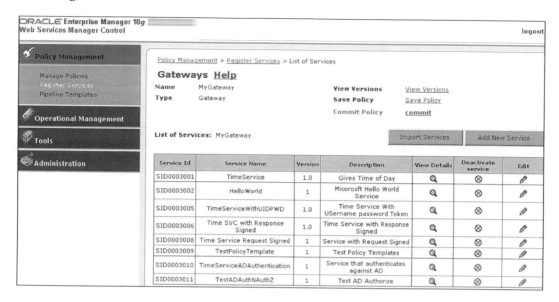

In order to add a new service, click on **Add New Service** from the right side panel (refer to the previous screenshot).

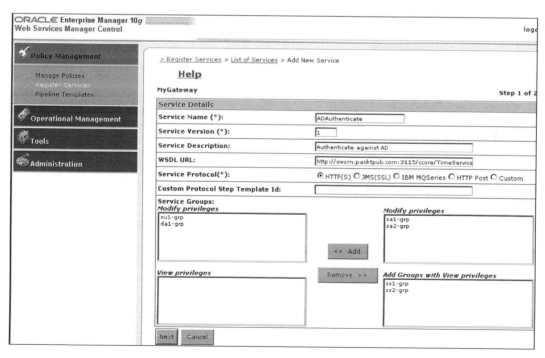

The previous screen shows the details that can be added while adding the new service. The * after each label makes those fields mandatory. The screen asks for typical information such as:

- Name of the service
- Version of the service
- Any description of the service
- **WSDL URL** of the service
- Protocol in which the service will accept messages

It also asks for additional information, such as **Service Groups**, groups that are part of Oracle WSM who have the right to view and who have the right to update.

In our example, we are registering a time service that will authenticate users against the active directory. The time service is registered with the following information:

- Name of service: ADAuthenticate
- Service version: 1
- Service description: Time service that will authenticate users against AD
- WSDL URL: `http://owsm.packtpub.com:3115/ccore/TimeService.wsdl`
- Service protocol: HTTP(S)
- Service groups: Select the default that has full permissions

Once the information is filled out, click **Next** on **New Service** registration. This will take you to the next screen which will display the actual **URL** of the service (refer to the next screenshot).

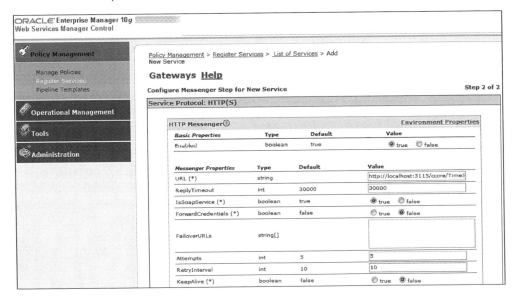

The URL in this page comes from the WSDL URL. You just have to make sure that the service is enabled and find out whether it is SOAP service or not.

You can then click **Finish** to register the service. Once you click **Finish**, the Oracle WSM internally generates a new service ID, and now the client applications can use that service ID to communicate (refer to the following screenshot).

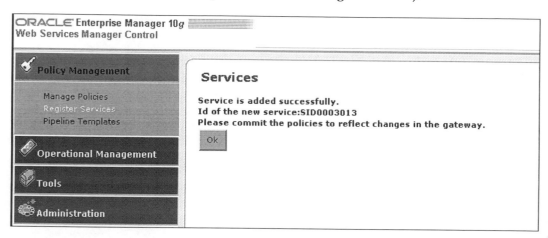

The previous figure shows that Oracle WSM registered the time service and created a new service ID as **SID00003013**.

Click **OK** to get back to the main screen that lists all the services.

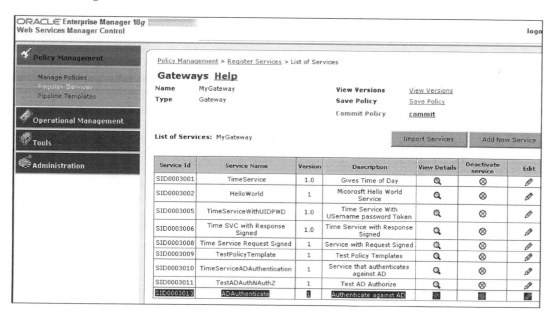

The previous figure shows all the services. The highlighted one is the **ADAuthenticate** service that was just registered.

We have only added the new service which hasn't been committed yet. The previous figure shows the **Commit Policy** in red and you can now click on that to commit the policy.

Creating The Security Policy

In the previous section, we learnt how to register the service and commit the policy. Once a service is registered and committed, it is associated with a default policy without any security. You can actually view the associated policy from **Policy Management**. In order to view the policy, you can click on **Policy Management** and then **Manage Policies**. This will bring you to the screen with the gateway information and a hyperlink for policies.

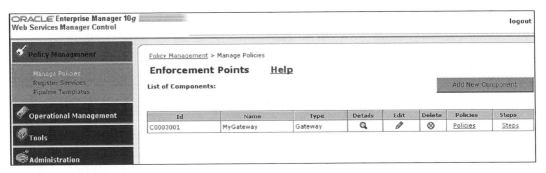

You can then click on **Policies** to view all the policies and you will see the **ADAuthenticate** policy that is created by default (refer to the following screenshot).

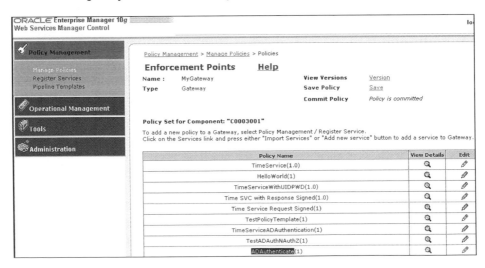

At this point, a dummy policy is attached to the newly registered ADAuthenticate service without any security. Any application that can call this web service will not be forced to provide the username and password.

In order to enforce the authentication policy, you have to edit it to make sure that Oracle WSM checks whether the SOAP message request has a valid username and password. You can now click on the **Edit** button to edit the policy, and a new screen is shown (refer to the following screen capture).

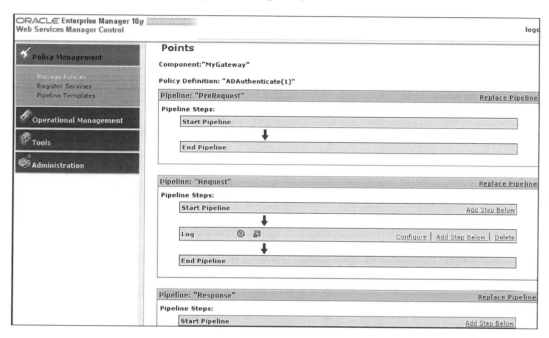

The Oracle WSM web service policy goes through four pipelines where the message can be manipulated or security can be enforced. In the previous figure, you can see the **Pipelines** for **PreRequest**, **Request**, **Response** and **PostResponse**. Typically it's the **Request** and **Response** pipeline that is often used to either validate the incoming message (authentication, authorization, encryption, and signature) or perform security on the outgoing message. Note: **PreRequest** and **PostReponse** will be disabled in future releases.

In our case, we need to validate the username and password in the incoming message against the active directory before the client application is given access to the service. In order to authenticate the request, we need to configure the request pipeline and add the **Extract Credentials** step and **AD Authenticate** step.

We can add the **Extract Credentials** step by clicking on the **Add Step Below** hyperlink under the **Log** step. Once you click the **Add Step Below**, you can then select the **Extract Credentials** from the dropdown and click **OK** (refer to the following screenshot).

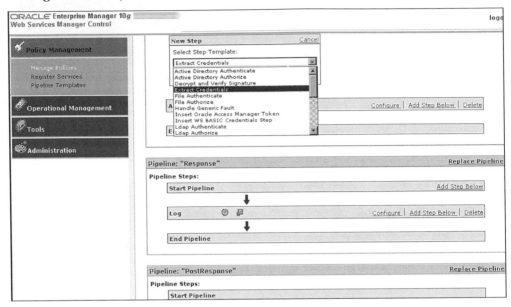

Once you click **OK**, the **Extract Credentials** step is added below the **Log** step in the **Request** pipeline, and it will look as shown in the following screenshot.

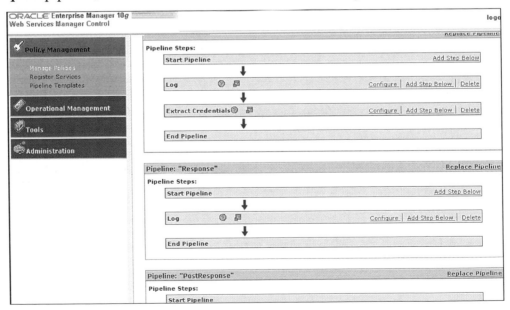

Once the **Extract Credentials** step is added, you can configure the step to modify the default values by clicking on the **Configure** hyperlink. Once you click on the **Configure** hyperlink, you will see the default values which can be replaced as shown in the following screenshot.

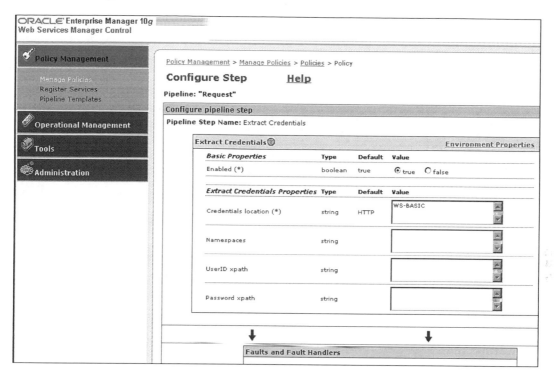

In the previous figure, the **Credentials location** is now changed to **WS-BASIC**. Since we set the service as "SOAP service" during the registration, the username and password that will be sent can be obtained from the SOAP message. You can now click **OK**; you can add the next step.

Now that the credentials are extracted, we need to validate them by adding the **AD Authenticate** step. You can now click on the **Add Step Below** under **Extract Credentials** and select **AD Authenticate** from the dropdown as shown in the following screen capture.

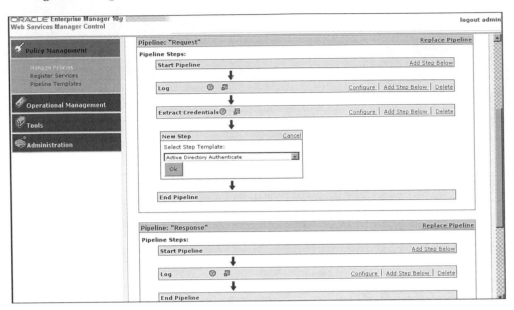

Once you click **OK**, **AD Authenticate** is added below the **Extract Credentials** (refer to the following screenshot).

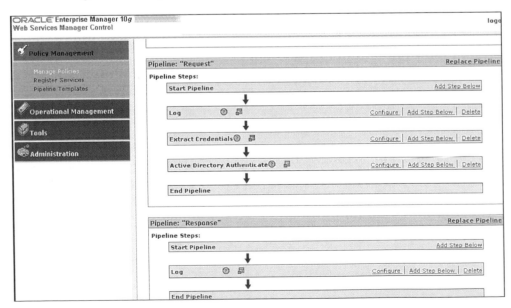

Now we have to modify the default values with the actual active directory server name, domain name, username attribute in active directory, the **OU** under which the user can be found.

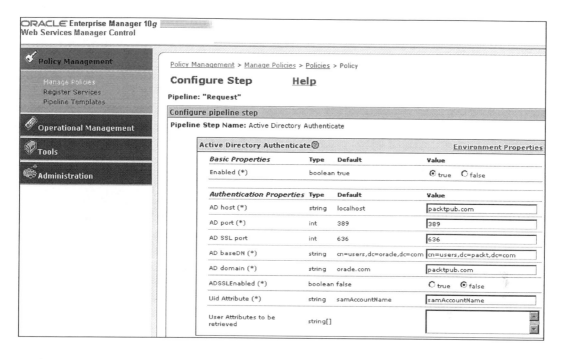

In the previous figure, the fields that are mandatory are marked with **(*)** and we have the following values populated as:

- **AD host**: active directory server name: **packtpub.com**

- **AD port**: active directory port: **389**

- **AD SSL port**: secure port where the communication happens over secure channel: **636**

- **AD baseDN**: DN under which users can be found: **cn=users**, **dc=packtpub**, **dc=com**

- **AD domain**: domain name of AD: **packtpub.com**

- **ADSSLEnabled**: **true** or **false** to specify if AD can support secure communication: **false**

- **Uid Attribute**: unique attribute that uniquely identifies the user: **samAccountName**

- **User Attributes to be retrieved**: any additional user data to be retrieved: **none**

Now you can click OK and finish updating the policy.

Commit The Policy

You still have to commit the policy before it can take effect. Once the policy is committed, all the requests to time service will require a valid username and password. In the next section, we will describe how to use Microsoft .NET Windows Forms as a client application to access the web service with the username and password attached to the web service request.

Oracle WSM Test Page as Client Application

In order to test the policy that was just defined (file based authentication or active directory authentication), one has to write a client application that will invoke the web service with appropriate credentials. While writing client applications is certainly possible, Oracle WSM ships with its own test page where you can perform certain basic tests. In this section, we will explore how to use the test page to test the web services that validate the user's credentials (authentication) and grant access to valid users (authorization).

The **Tools** menu from the Oracle WSM has the **Test Page** link. The following figure shows what the test page looks like:

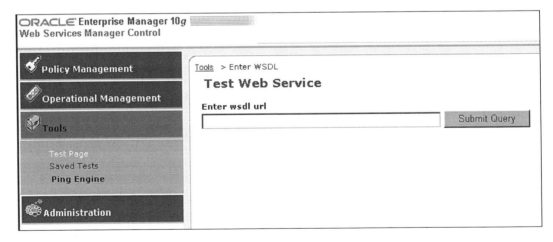

You can enter the WSDL (Web Services Description Language) here and click **Submit Query**. This will take you to the next screen where you can enter the username and password.

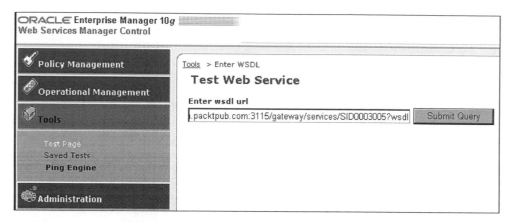

The WSDL entered in the previous screenshot is the WSDL for the time service where the policy requires the client to provide appropriate credentials (username and password). It will validate if the user has the privilege to access the web service. Once you click on **Submit Query**, the next screen will appear as shown in the following screenshot.

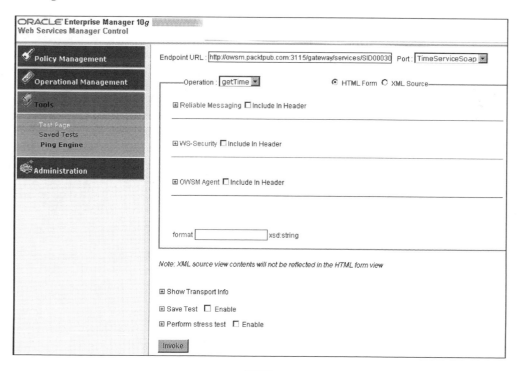

You can enter the **User Name** and **Password** under **WS-Security**. Remember that we chose WS-BASIC while configuring the policy, which will send the username and password as per the WS-security specification. There is also an option to save the test and **Perform stress test**, etc. When you click **Invoke**, the web service will be invoked, the credentials will be validated, and the response message will be displayed as shown in the following screen capture.

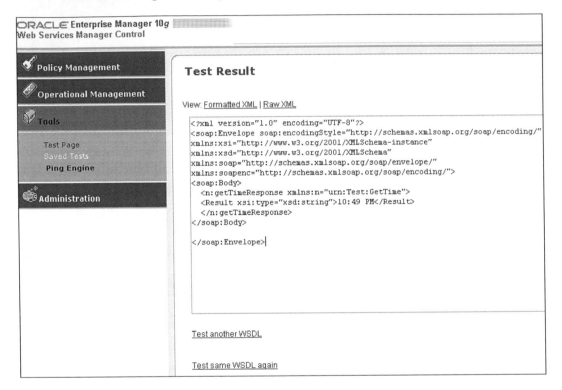

While the Oracle WSM test page is an excellent tool to test web service policies, you can also write a client application to test the web services. In the next section we will describe how to use Microsoft .NET to create a client application which will invoke the web service with a username and password.

Microsoft .NET Client Application

Now that the web service has been registered with Oracle WSM and the policy has been updated to make sure that only authenticated users can access the web service, let's take a look at how can we build a client application that attaches the username and password to the web service request. In this example, we will create a Windows Forms application using Microsoft Visual Studio 2005 and Microsoft Web Services Enhancements Toolkit 3.0.

In order to create the Microsoft Windows Forms project, open Visual Studio 2005 and click on **File** and then on **New Project** (refer to the following screenshot).

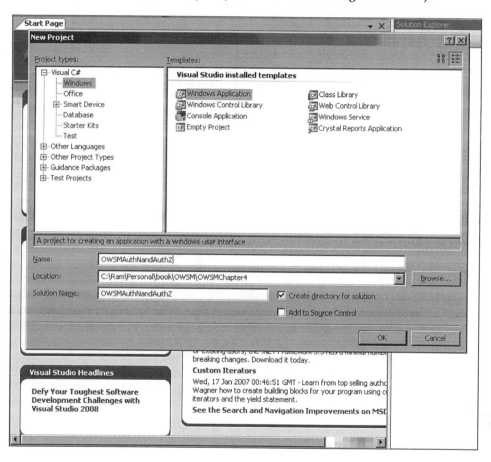

In the previous figure, the new **Windows Application** project is being opened with C# as the language.

The **Windows Application** will be accompanied by a basic windows form. You can then add text boxes, buttons, and labels to capture the **username**, **password**, error and to invoke the web service.

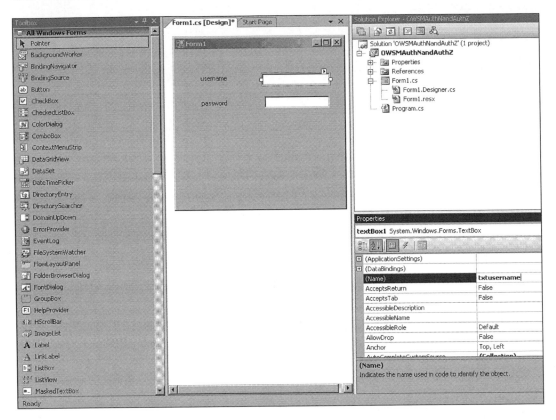

The text boxes are named as **txtusername** and **txtpassword**.

The next step is to add the web services enhancements 3.0 assembly as a reference (refer to the next screenshot).

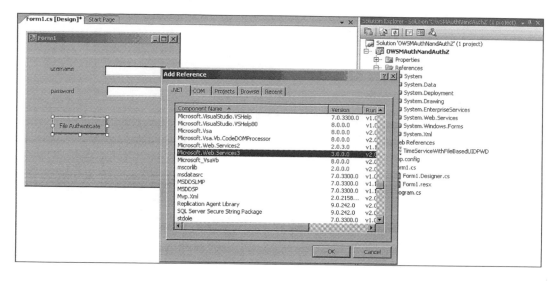

Once **WSE 3.0** is added as reference, we can add the WSDL URL as the web reference by right-clicking on the **Web Reference** section. The following figure shows how to add WSDL as a web reference.

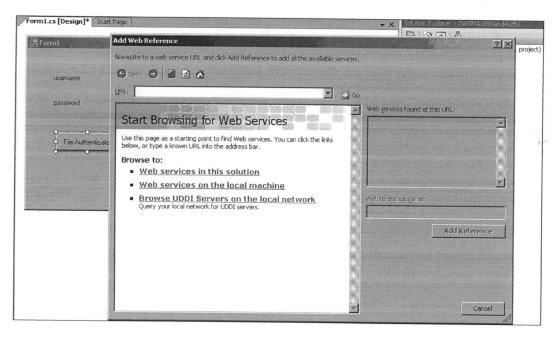

In the **URL** box, you can now type the WSDL URL. This time the URL should point to the service ID of the web service in Oracle WSM (refer to the following screen capture).

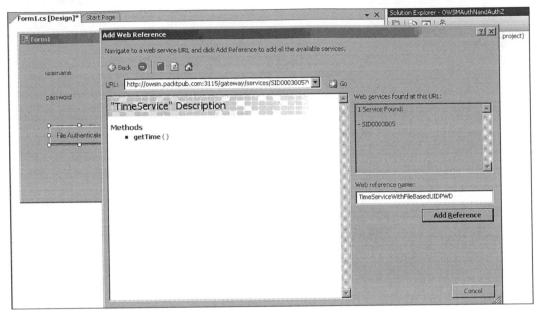

In the **Web reference name**, you can enter any name.

Now that the WSE 3.0 assembly reference has been added and the web service reference also has been added, it is time to write code to call the web service with a username and password. In the application, we have a button that can invoke the web service. We can now write code on the button click event.

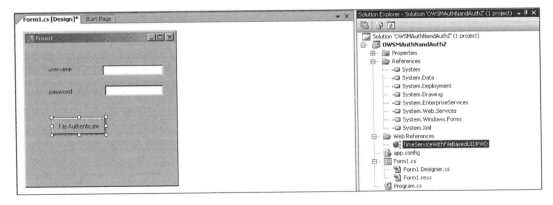

Double-click on the button so that it opens up the code behind page where the web service call can be made.

In order to call the web service with a username and password, the following needs to happen:

Create an instance of the proxy class that is WSE enabled.

```
                TimeServiceWithFileBasedUIDPWD.
   TimeServiceWse _timeserviceproxy = new OWSMAuthNandAuthZ.
   TimeServiceWithFileBasedUIDPWD.TimeServiceWse();
```

The next step is to create the UsernameTokenProvider with the username and password.

```
                UsernameTokenProvider _usernametoken = new UsernameTokenPro
   vider(username, password);
```

The username and password comes from the text boxes. The next step is to set the token to the proxy's client credential.

```
                //Set the username token to the Client Credential of the
                    Proxy Object_timeserviceproxy.SetClientCredential
                    (_usernametoken.GetToken());
```

Once the credentials are attached, the next step is to create the policy object and attach the UserNameOvertransportAssertion.

```
                //Create instance of Policy Object
                Policy webServiceClientPolicy = new Policy();
                //Create the username Over Transport Assertion
                // This assertion will send username and password
                    in SOAP message webServiceClientPolicy.Assertions.
                    Add(new UsernameOverTransportAssertion());
```

The policy object is then attached to the web service proxy.

```
                // Apply the policy to the SOAP message exchange.
                _timeserviceproxy.SetPolicy(webServiceClientPolicy);
```

The complete code will look like this:

```
                //Get the username and password from screen
                string username = txtusername.Text;
                string password = txtpassword.Text;
                //Create the WSE enabled Proxy object
                TimeServiceWithFileBasedUIDPWD.
   TimeServiceWse _timeserviceproxy = new OWSMAuthNandAuthZ.
   TimeServiceWithFileBasedUIDPWD.TimeServiceWse();
                //Create the Username Token Provider object with username
```

and password

```
        UsernameTokenProvider _usernametoken =
                new UsernameTokenProvider(username, password);
    //Set the username token to the Client Credential of the
        Proxy Object_timeserviceproxy.SetClientCredential
        (_usernametoken.GetToken());
    //Create instance of Policy Object
    Policy webServiceClientPolicy = new Policy();
    //Create the username Over Transport Assertion
    // This assertion will send username and password
        in SOAP message webServiceClientPolicy.Assertions.
        Add(new UsernameOverTransportAssertion());
    // Apply the policy to the SOAP message exchange.
    _timeserviceproxy.SetPolicy(webServiceClientPolicy);
    _timeserviceproxy.getTime("AnyString");
```

Now when you compile and run this project, and enter a valid username and password that exists in the directory, you will see the time as shown in the following screenshot:

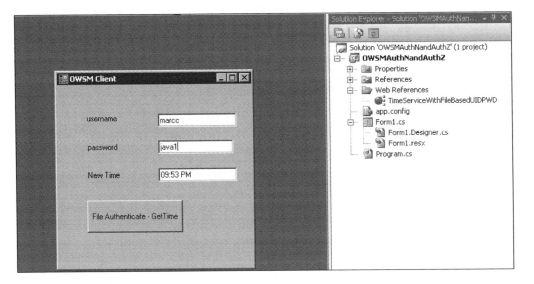

Summary

In this chapter, we learnt to protect a web service with a username and password, and also wrote a client application that can attach the username and password in the web service call. In the next chapter, we will learn how to encrypt and decrypt SOAP messages.

5

Encrypting and Decrypting Messages in Oracle WSM

Encryption and decryption are key components of web services which protect the confidentiality of the data being exchanged. In order to encrypt and decrypt messages in web services, each service should know what key should be used to encrypt and to decrypt the message, the algorithm, what part of the message should be encrypted, etc. As organizations deploy more web services that require encryption or decryption, management of the key and related policies for encryption get tough to maintain. Oracle Web Services Manager addresses those issues by centrally managing and enforcing the encryption and decryption policies, including the key management. In this chapter, we will take a closer look at how we can leverage Oracle WSM to protect the confidentiality of the messages.

Overview of Encryption and Decryption

Encryption is the process of masking the data from plain text to derive at cipher text (encrypted data). Decryption is the process of deriving the plain text from the cipher text. The process of encrypting and decrypting depends on the type of encryption and the type of algorithm. There are actually two types of encryption:

Symmetric Cryptography

In symmetric encryption, plain text is converted into encrypted text using an encryption key. In order to decrypt the encrypted data, the same encryption key should be used. This is called "secret key cryptography" or "symmetric cryptography".

```
Plain Text + secret Key (Encryption Operation) = Cipher Text
Cipher Text + secret Key (Decryption Operation) = Plain Text
```

In symmetric cryptography there are various algorithms, such as DES, Triple DES, AES, Blowfish, etc.

Asymmetric Cryptography

In **Asymmetric** cryptography encryption, there are actually two keys involved. One key is used to encrypt the data and the other key is used to decrypt the data. This is also called public key cryptography. Let us consider, for example, that Alice wants to send a confidential message to Bob:

- Alice will encrypt the data using Bob's public key.
- Bob will receive the message and decrypt using his private key.

The idea is that anyone who wants to send an encrypted message to Bob can actually encrypt the data using Bob's public key.

Asymmetric cryptography is also used to digitally sign the message to ensure the integrity of the message. When Alice wants to send a message to Bob and wants to ensure that no one will tamper with the message in transit:

- Alice will digitally sign the message using Alice's private key.
- Bob will receive the message and validate the signature using Alice's public key.

When a message is digitally signed, a message digest (unique value for each message) is calculated using a digest algorithm such as MD5 or SHA1, and that value is then encrypted using Alice's private key. When Bob receives the message, he recalculates the digest again using the same algorithm and encrypts using Alice's public key, and then compares it with the one that was sent. If the values differ, we can be sure that the data was tampered in transit.

In asymmetric cryptography, there are various algorithms such as RSA, DSA, and Elliptic Curve Cryptography (ECC).

Oracle WSM and Encryption

In order to protect the confidential data in web services, the data should be encrypted. From the last two sections we understand that in order to encrypt and decrypt data, one has to know the type of encryption, the algorithm and the encryption key. In the web services scenario, where there can be multiple services in an organization, each service should know:

- What data elements are encrypted or to be encrypted
- What the encryption algorithm is
- Where the encryption key is or how to obtain one

It becomes increasingly difficult to manage the encryption and decryption policies for web services as more and more services are being deployed. **Oracle WSM** can help address these issues by centrally managing the policies where it can define the encryption and decryption processes for the incoming and outgoing **SOAP** messages.

Encryption and Decryption with Oracle WSM

In the web services scenario, the Oracle WSM gateway or the agent should be able to decrypt the incoming message and encrypt the outgoing message. In order to encrypt the outgoing message using an asymmetric algorithm, Oracle WSM has to know:

- Location of the key store that contains the public key
- Password to the key store
- Key store type—either JKS or PKCS (JKS: Java Key Store, PKCS: Public Key Crypto System. Both are used to store the public/private key)
- Alias to identify the public key
- Encryption algorithm—Triple DES, AES, etc.
- Key transport algorithm
- Encrypted content
- Namespace or XPATh info to encrypt specific data (XPath is used to query XML document to get XML element(s) and attributes)

In order to decrypt the incoming message, Oracle WSM has to know:

- Location of the key store that contains the private key
- Password to the key store
- Key store type
- Alias to the private key
- Password to access the private key

Now if you read the previous bullet points again, you will notice the key difference about the information required by Oracle WSM for encryption and decryption. They key difference is that for encryption, Oracle WSM requires the encryption algorithm and key transport algorithm, and for decryption, it requires only the private key password and does not require any information regarding the algorithm.

This is the advantage of Oracle WSM implementing the industry standards, such as the WS-security that encompasses XML encryption. The following screenshot shows the information that Oracle WSM requires to perform the encryption of the response message.

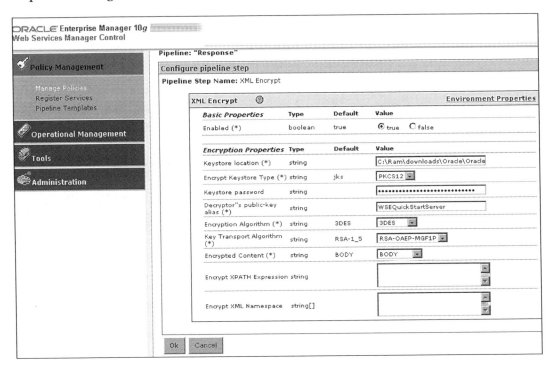

We know that the **Keystore location, password, Keystore Type, alias** are required to access the key store to retrieve the public key information. The **Encrypted Content** lets you choose which part of the SOAP message is to be encrypted, the **Encrypt XPATH Expression string** lets you specify the Xpath expression to specify XML elements or attributes to be encrypted. However, what is the deal with **Encryption Algorithm** and **Key Transport Algorithm**, and other parameters?

Encryption Algorithm

Encryption algorithm is used to specify the symmetric key encryption algorithm, such as Triple DES, AES, Rijndeal, etc. This is actually used to encrypt the SOAP message, and in this case, the body of the message (specified as part of the encrypted content parameter). When encrypted, the SOAP body is actually encrypted using the Triple DES algorithm.

Note: Public key encryption is usually CPU intensive and encrypting large XML documents using public key will affect the performance of the system. Hence it is not uncommon to encrypt the SOAP body using a secret key (symmetric cryptography) and then encrypt the "key" with the public key.

Key Transport Algorithm

The previous section described that the encryption algorithm parameter in Oracle WSM is used to encrypt the SOAP message. In order to decrypt the message, the recipient should know the encryption key. The obvious question then is how is the encryption key information transported?

The encryption key can be transported outside of Oracle WSM and the client can decrypt using their own tools or the encryption key itself can be encrypted. If you are wondering how encrypting the encryption key is going to help with transporting the encryption key, the working when Oracle WSM is configured to encrypt the response message is as follows:

- SOAP Message (in this case, Body) is encrypted using triple DES algorithm
- Encryption key is generated at run time
- Using the specified key transport algorithm, encryption key is encrypted with the public key
- Encrypted encryption key is transported with SOAP message (EncryptedKey element)

Internal Working of the XML Encrypt Policy Step

Now that we know about the XML encrypt policy step and the options that are available within the policy step, let's take a look at how it internally works when the SOAP message is transferred in an encrypted format. This will help us understand the importance of each option and how it is related.

The sample XML message show how the SOAP body is encrypted.

```
<soap:Body>
        <xenc:EncryptedData xmlns="http://www.w3.org/2001/04/
        xmlenc#" xmlns:xenc="http://www.w3.org/2001/04/
        xmlenc#" Type="http://www.w3.org/2001/04/xmlenc#Content"
        Id="_63BQq2iUOIn6m00ZkQ2F0A22">
                <xenc:EncryptionMethod Algorithm=
                "http://www.w3.org/2001/04/xmlenc#tripledes-cbc"/>
                <xenc:CipherData>
                                <xenc:CipherValue>**EncryptedDa
                                taVneQADWk=</xenc:CipherValue>
                </xenc:CipherData>
        </xenc:EncryptedData>
</soap:Body>
```

If you look at the message, the EncryptedData element has a client element called EncryptionMethod that specifies the algorithm as triple DES. The CipherValue element contains the encrypted SOAP body. The encryption key is encrypted and transported along with the SOAP message, and it is referenced by EncryptedKey and is part of the SOAP header. The following message shows the SOAP header value that contains the EncryptedKey element:

```
<xenc:EncryptedKey xmlns=
"http://www.w3.org/2001/04/xmlenc#" xmlns:
xenc="http://www.w3.org/2001/04/xmlenc#">
        <xenc:EncryptionMethod Algorithm=
        "http://www.w3.org/2001/04/xmlenc#rsa-oaep-mgf1p">
            <dsig:DigestMethod Algorithm=
            "http://www.w3.org/2000/09/xmldsig#sha1" xmlns:
            dsig="http://www.w3.org/2000/09/xmldsig#"/>
            </xenc:EncryptionMethod>
            <dsig:KeyInfo xmlns:dsig=
            "http://www.w3.org/2000/09/xmldsig#">
                <wsse:SecurityTokenReference
                xmlns="http://docs.oasis-open.org/
                wss/2004/01/oasis-200401-wss-wssecurity-
                secext-1.0.xsd">
                    <wsse:Reference URI="#a2XD1JG7keBavISVs
                    j2HxLw22" ValueType="http://docs.oasis
                    -open.org/wss/2004/01/oasis-200401-wss-
                    x509-token-profile-1.0#X509v3"/>
                    </wsse:SecurityTokenReference>
            </dsig:KeyInfo>
            <xenc:CipherData>
                <xenc:CipherValue>**encrypted key value/
                SDqW4WKY15/7w=</xenc:CipherValue>
```

```
        </xenc:CipherData>
        <xenc:ReferenceList>
            <xenc:DataReference URI=
            "#_63BQq2iUOIn6m00ZkQ2F0A22"/>
        </xenc:ReferenceList>
    </xenc:EncryptedKey>
```

In the previous sample message, the EncryptedKey element represents information about the encrypted encryption key and is a reference to what data is encrypted using that encryption key. In other words, the EncryptedKey element contains:

- EncryptionMethod element to describe what algorithm is used to encrypt the encryption key.

- CipherData and CipherValue elements contain the actual encrypted data (encrypted encryption key)

- KeyInfo element gives information about the key, and in this case, it's public key.

So far the elements above describe the key, the algorithm, and the location of the encrypted encryption key. The DataReference element, a part of ReferenceList element, contains a list of references that point to the **EncryptedData** element, which contains the actual data that is encrypted.

In a nutshell, when Oracle WSM encrypts the portion of the SOAP message (in this case, SOAP body) here is what happens internally:

- Symmetric encryption key is generated at random.

- SOAP body is encrypted using triple DES algorithm with the encryption key.

- The encrypted data (CipherValue) and algorithm (EncryptionMethod) are represented as a part of the EncryptedData element.

- EncryptedData is identified with Id attribute.

- The encryption key is then encrypted using RSA OAEP algorithm (Optimal Asymmetric Encryption Padding, i.e. message is OAEP encoded and then encrypted with RSA algorithm)

- The **encrypted encryption key** is represented by the **EncryptedKey** element along with the algorithm, the key information and the cipher text (encrypted value of encryption key).

- The relationship between the EncrypedData element and EncryptedKey is established by the DataReference element that is a part of the EncryptedKey.

Once the client application receives the SOAP message, it can decrypt the data using the information that is available within the XML message. During the decryption process, the client application, that is aware of WS-security standards, can easily understand from the XML message that:

- The encrypted data in the EncryptedData element is encrypted using triple DES.
- The key information is available within the EncryptedKey element.

Once the client application understands the various elements, it will then:

- Decrypt the encryption key using its private key
  (from the EncryptedKey element).
- Use the encryption key to then decrypt the SOAP message.

In the next section, we will explore how to leverage Oracle WSM to encrypt and decrypt messages with a sample application.

Oracle WSM Sample Application Overview

In order to demonstrate the capability of encryption and decryption within Oracle WSM we will deploy a web service within Oracle WSM and configure the policy to protect the web service. The idea is to demonstrate both encryption and decryption using Oracle WSM, so in our sample we will have Oracle WSM:

- Enforce that the incoming SOAP message should be encrypted.
- Decrypt the incoming SOAP message (request).
- Enforce that the outgoing SOAP message should be encrypted.
- Encrypt the outgoing SOAP message (response).

In order to have a complete demo sample, we will also a develop a client application using Microsoft .NET, and the client application will:

- Encrypt the outgoing message.
- Decrypt the incoming message.

Since the web service development is outside the scope of this book, we will leverage the existing web service that comes with Oracle WSM installation, the time service. The time service takes the format as an input string, but it doesn't really matter what data is entered, and you will get a response with actual time. The sample application will demonstrate how to use:

- Microsoft .NET application to encrypt the SOAP request (i.e. body of the SOAP message, the format string).
- Oracle WSM to decrypt incoming SOAP message.
- Oracle WSM to encrypt the response message that contains the actual time value.
- Microsoft .NET application to decrypt the SOAP response (the actual time in the SOAP body).
- Both the client and Oracle WSM will use the WSEQuickStartServer key that ships with Microsoft WSE 3.0.

In the next section, we will explore how to configure the Oracle WSM policy to encrypt and decrypt messages in detail.

Oracle WSM Encryption and Decryption Policy

In order to protect a web service within Oracle WSM, the first step is to register the web service within Oracle WSM and then edit the policy associated with it. The following steps describe how to register the service.

Login to Oracle Web Service Manager Console at:

```
http://owsm.packtpub.com:3115/ccore
```

Click on **Policy Management** and then **Register Services**. You will see the list of **Gateways** that are available, as shown in the following screenshot.

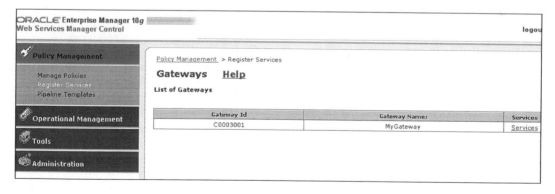

On the right side of the screen, if you click on the **Services** hyperlink, you will see the list of registered services (refer to the following screenshot).

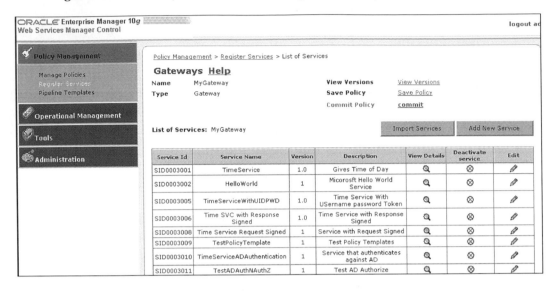

In order to add a new service, click on **Add New Service** from the right side panel.

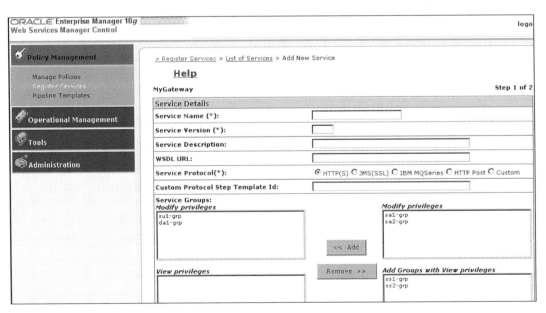

The previous screen capture describes the details that can be added while adding the new service. The * after each label makes those fields mandatory. The screen asks for typical information such as:

- Name of the service
- Version of the service
- Any description of the service
- WSDL URL of the service
- Protocol in which the service will accept messages

It also asks for additional information such as **Service Groups**, the Oracle WSM groups that has previleges to view and edit.

In our example, we are registering the time service that will authenticate users against active directory. The time service is registered with the following information:

- Name of service: EncryptionDecryptionSample
- Service Version: 1
- Service Description: Encrypt and decrypt SOAP message
- WSDL URL: `http://owsm.packtpub.com:3115/ccore/TimeService.wsdl`
- Service Protocol: HTTP(S)
- Service Groups: Select the default that has full permissions

Once the information is filled out, click **Next** on **New Service** registration. This will take you to the next screen which will display the actual URL of the service (see the following screenshot).

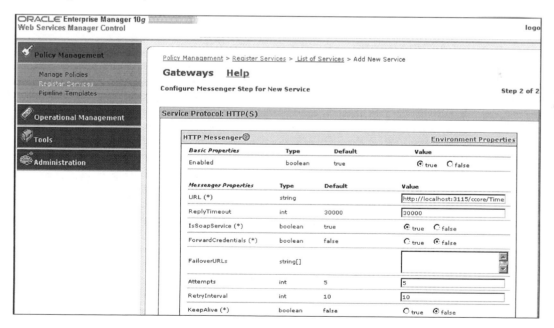

The URL in this page comes from the WSDL which contains the actual web service code (i.e. in this case, the JSP page). You just have to make sure that the service is enabled and also check if it is Soap service or not.

You can then click **Finish** to register the service. Once you click **Finish**, the Oracle WSM internally generates a new service ID and now the client applications can use that service ID to communicate.

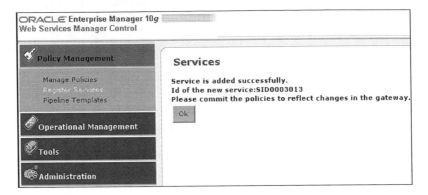

The previous screenshot show that Oracle WSM registered the time service and created a new Service ID.

Click **OK** to get back to the main screen that lists all the services.

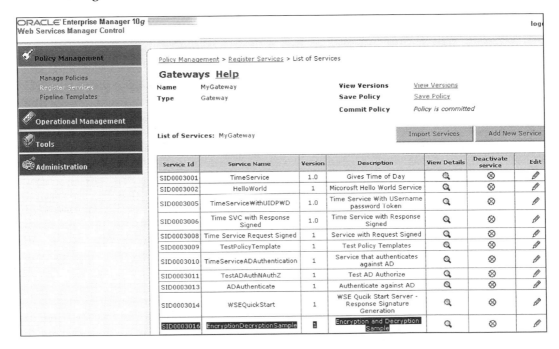

The previous screenshot shows all the services. The highlighted one is the **EncryptDecrypt** service that was just registered.

We have only added the new service, but it hasn't been committed yet. The previous figure shows the **Commit Policy** in red and you can now click on that to commit the policy. Policy steps are not saved until it is actually committed.

Creating the Security Policy

In the previous section, we learnt how to register the service and commit the policy. Once a service is registered and committed, it is associated with a default policy without any security. In order to view the policy, you can click on **Policy Management** and then **Manage Policies**. This will bring you to the screen with the **Gateway** information and a hyperlink for **Policies** (see the following screen capture).

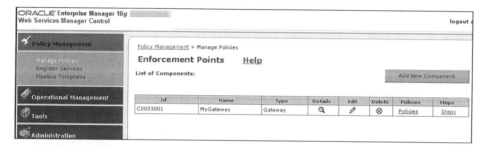

You can then click on **Policies** to see all the policies, and you will see the `EncryptDecrypt` policy that is created by default (see the following screenshot).

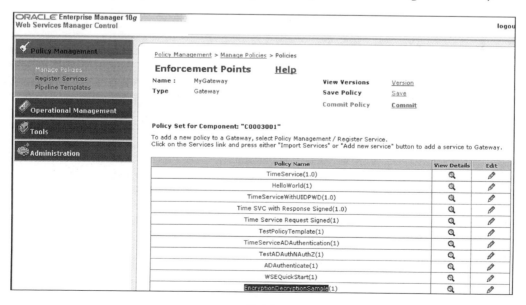

At this point, a dummy policy is attached to the newly registered EncryptDecrypt service without any security. Any application can now call this web service without the request or response message being encrypted.

In order to enforce the encryption and decryption policy, you have to edit this policy. This is done to make sure that the Oracle WSM checks the SOAP message request to enforce encryption, and that the response message is encrypted. When you click on the **Edit** button on the policy, the default policy steps are described, as shown in the following screenshot.

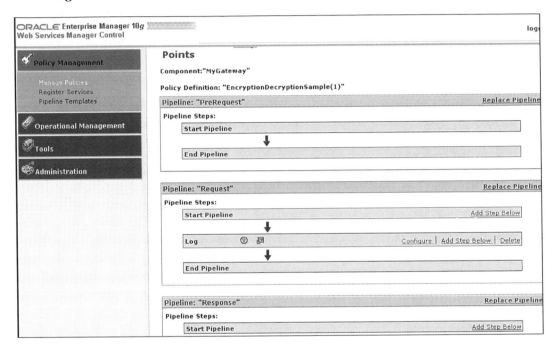

In order to decrypt the SOAP Request, the **Request** pipeline should be modified to include the **XML Decrypt** policy step. In order to add the new policy step, click on **Add Step Below** under the **Log** step and select the **XML Decrypt** policy step from the dropdown.

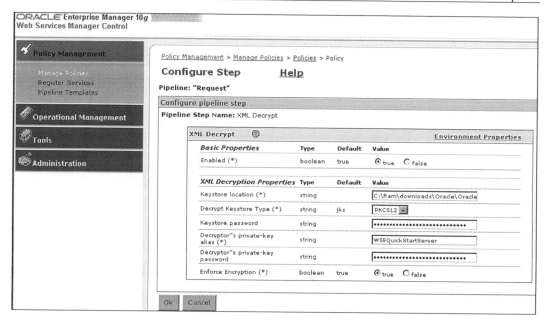

The previous figure shows the **XML Decrypt** policy step that describes:

- Location of the key store, i.e. key store location that points to PKCS 12 certificate file

- Keystore Type i.e. PKCS12

- Keystore password i.e. in this case it is `test123`

- Private Key Alias, i.e WSEQucikStartServer

- Password to access the private key i.e. in this case `test123`

- Enforce Encryption option is **true** to make sure that the incoming message is encrypted

Note: The **WSEQuickStartServer** key that ships with Microsoft WSE does not have an alias (i.e. friendly name) and it is not straightforward to convert to a **PKCS12** key store. Here are the steps to create the **PKCS12**:

- Import the certificate into Microsoft certificate key store by just double clicking on the certificate file and follow the prompts

- Modify to enter the friendly name, i.e. alias

- Click **Export** to export with private key and save to a location

- Install Firefox browser

- Import the certificate from the **Advanced Security** tab of Firefox

- Export the certificate and save as PKCS12 file.

Once all the information is entered at the **XML Decrypt** policy step, click **OK** to return to the **Policy** screen.

Now that we have configured the **Request** pipeline to enforce encryption and can also decrypt the message, the next step is to configure encrypting the response message.

From the policy definition of **Encrypt Decrypt**, we should add steps to encrypt the response message.

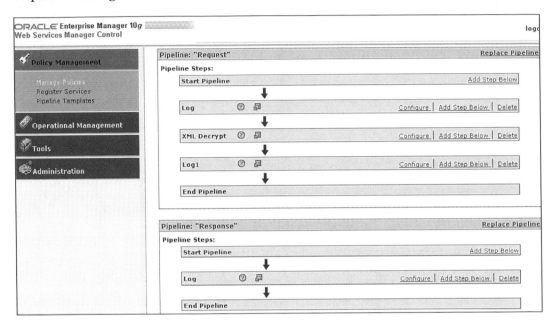

The response pipeline has the **Log** step configured, and now we have to add the XML encrypt policy step under the **Log** step. We can now click on the **Add step below** under the **Log** the step of response pipeline and select **XML Encrypt** from the list of policy steps. The **XML Encrypt** policy step would look like the following screenshot:

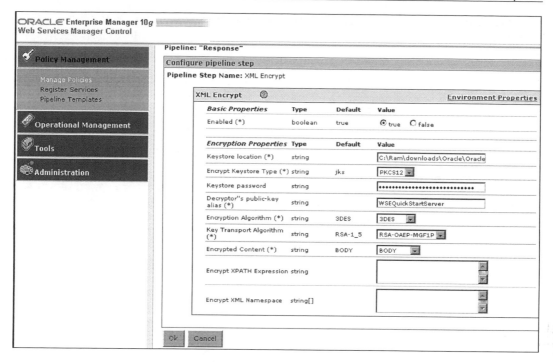

The previous figure describes the details of the XML Encrypt policy step. Before we enter the details, we should know:

- What algorithm are we going to use to encrypt the data?
- What algorithm are we going to use to encrypt the encryptionkey?

In this sample, we have configured to use the same **WSEQuickStartServer PKCS12** key store, and we have selected triple DES for the encryption of data and RSA OAEP to encrypt the encryption key.

Note: RSA OAEP is chosen because Microsoft WSE 3.0 by default can only understand RSA OAEP.

Once the details are entered, you can click **OK** and then save the policy. Once the policy is committed, the policy steps for EncryptDecrypt would look like the following screenshot.

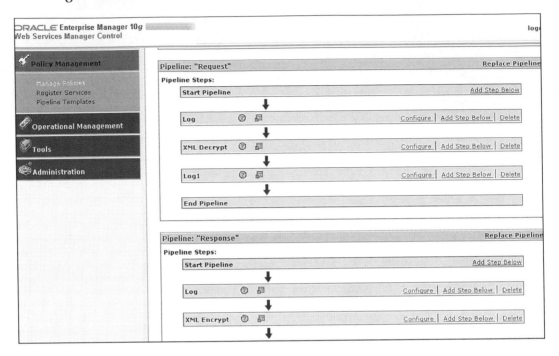

In the previous figure, you can see the **Log** steps configured twice for both request and Response pipelines. This is to capture the data before and after request and response so that you can take a look at how the data looked before the policy step and how it looks after the policy step.

Now that we have configured the Oracle WSM to decrypt the SOAP request and encrypt the SOAP response, we should create the client application which can actually encrypt the SOAP request and decrypt the response to show the actual time. We will take a look at how to use Oracle WSM test page and Microsoft .NET to test the web service policy where the request message is encrypted and the response message is decrypted to view the time.

Oracle WSM Test Page as Client Application

The EncryptDecrypt example policy that was described in the earlier section requires that the web service request should be encrypted. The web service URL for the time service after it is registered within Oracle WSM (where the Encrypt Decrypt policy was applied) is `http://owsm.packtpub.com:3115/gateway/services/SID0003016?WSDL`. Since the web service policy requires that the SOAP request should be encrypted, you cannot really use the test page from Oracle WSM where the request message is encrypted. However, you can still use Oracle WSM to simulate the behavior. Here is how it works:

- You take the WSDL of the web service that you just registered within Oracle WSM (SID0003016?WSDL).
- Register that WSDL in Oracle WSM.
- Now a new WSDL URL is generated by Oracle WSM (SID0003031?WSDL).
- Define the policy in such a way that you include the XML Encrypt policy step in the request pipeline.
- Now you invoke the newly generated WSDL from the test page.
- SOAP request to our original web service (SID0003016?WSDL) is now encrypted.

Let's go through the steps to test our EncryptDecrypt policy. The first step is to register the SID0003016 web service within Oracle WSM and the new service URL will be created, as shown in the following screenshot. (Note: you would follow the normal process of clicking on **Services** and enter SID0003016?WSDL)

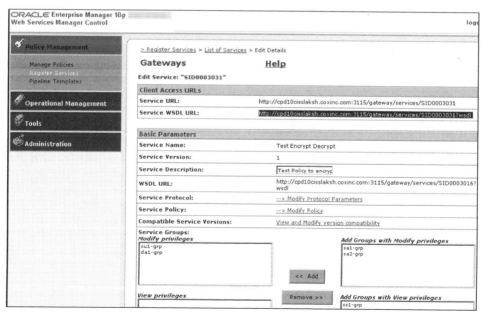

Once the web service is registered, it generates a new WSDL which is identified as `http://owsm.packtpub.com:3115/gateway/services/SID0003031?WSDL` and the service is registered as **Test Encrypt Decrypt**.

Now that the service is registered, you can edit the policy to define the request pipeline. Since this web service will simply call our original web service, we will implement the **XML Encrypt** policy in the **Request** pipeline to encrypt the web service request, as shown in the next screen capture.

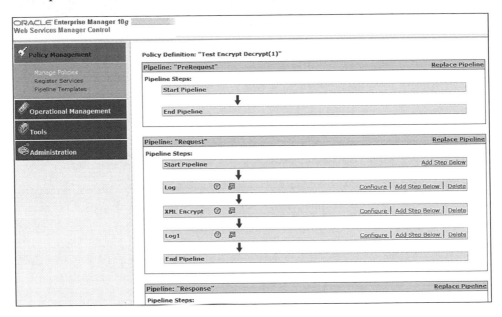

Now that the policy is defined and committed, we can now test the web service from the test page.

In the test page, you can enter the location of the WSDL as `http://owsm.packtpub.com:3115/gateway/services/SID0003031?WSDL` (see the following screenshot).

Now you can click on **Submit Query** and then check the **Save Test** page button and enter the **Description** to save the test page (refer to the following screen capture).

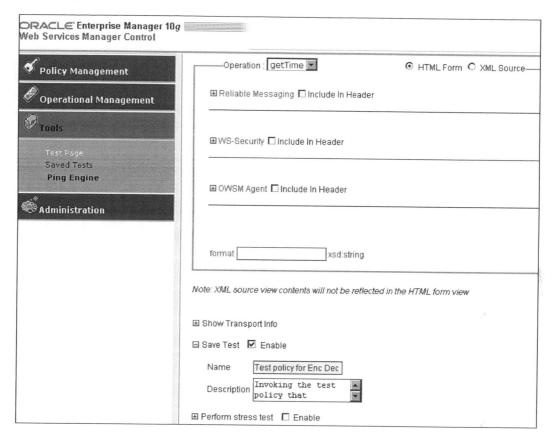

You can now click on the **Invoke** button, which will invoke the SID0003031 web service. The policy defined in SID0003031 will encrypt the SOAP request for SID0003016 and the policy for SID0003016 will first decrypt the SOAP request and then will generate the encrypted SOAP response message, as shown in the following screenshot.

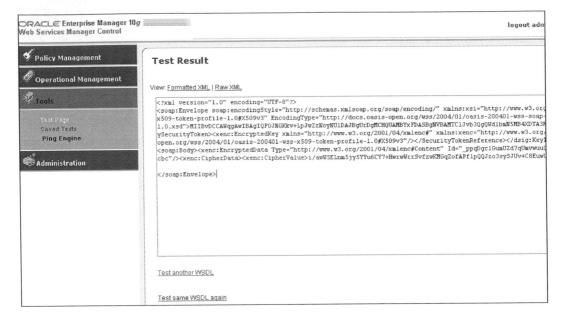

You can actually verify that the request to SID0003016 (original web service) is encrypted by looking at the **Message Logs** under **Operational Management** as shown in the following screen capture.

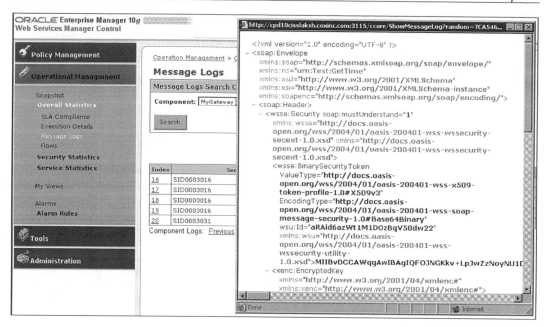

We are using Oracle WSM Policy to actually test our previous policy, but it also brings up a point—that you can implement security for any outgoing web service (especially to external organizations or applications) within Oracle WSM Gateway without having to install and configure any client agents. This design also brings in the following advantages:

- You can virtualize the web services.

- You can centralize the security for all external web services interaction.

- You can even implement identity propagation and translation (security token service):

    ○ Example: If you want to invoke Amazon web service which requires a SAML token, you can register that within Oracle WSM and in the policy. First validate the username and password, and then attach SAML or any other token on the request pipeline.

Microsoft .NET Client Application

The client application is a Windows Forms application written using Microsoft Visual Studio 2005 with Microsoft WSE 3.0. The first step in creating client application is to create a Windows Forms application called OWSMEcnryptionDecryption. The following screenshot shows how to create the Windows Forms application (as described in last chapter).

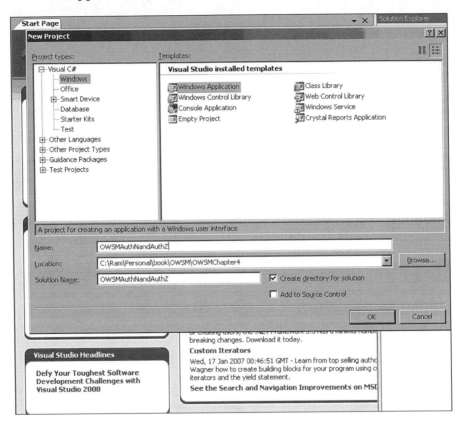

Once you click **OK**, the Windows Forms application is created with a default form.

Since we are going to invoke the time web service with input data, we will add a text box to enter any random input data (refer to the following screen capture) and a button to invoke the web service. We will also add another text box to show error messages, if any.

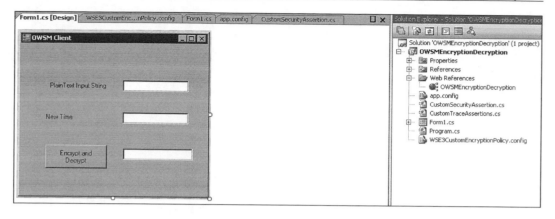

Now we should add the Microsoft WSE 3.0 as a reference before we can create the proxy class. You can add the WSE reference by selecting **Add Reference** from the project and then selecting **Microsoft.Web.Services3**.

Now that WSE 3.0 is added, we can then add a web reference to the web service to create the proxy object. It can be added by right-clicking on the **Add Web Reference** and then entering the WSDL URL, and then clicking **OK** to generate the proxy.

So far we have:

- Created the Windows Forms application
- Added reference to WSE 3.0
- Created the web service proxy

The next step is to configure and write code to perform the encryption and decryption. Though it is beyond the scope of this book to explain in detail how to configure policy and write custom policy assertions, we will take a high level overview of how Microsoft .NET and WSE 3.0 can be used to encrypt and decrypt SOAP messages.

With Microsoft .NET and WSE 3.0, the web services security can be applied through:

- Policy configuration for certain frequently-used security configurations, or;
- Custom assertion in combination with the policy to perform all other security operations.

Since our example focuses only on encrypting the request and decrypting the response, we will have to write a custom policy assertion. This is done so that the SOAP messages can be interpreted both during request and response cycle to perform encryption or decryption. The next step is to write the custom assertion that will:

- Encrypt the outgoing message
- Decrypt the incoming message

At a high level, the custom assertion inherits from SecurityPolicyAssertion class, and has methods such as CreateClientOutputFilter and CreateClientInputFilter which can be overrriden to perform any operation at the client side. In our sample, we have created two new classes called CustomSecurityClientInputFilter and CustomSecurityClientOutputFilter to perform any data processing on a request or response.

The CustomSecurityClientOutputFilter is derived from SendSecurityFilter and has a method called SecureMessage which can be overridden to perform the encryption.

The CustomSecurityClientInputFilter is derived from ReceiveSecurityFilter and has a method called ValidateMessageSecurity which can be overridden to decrypt the message.

The custom security assertion code would look like:

```
public override SoapFilter CreateClientOutputFilter(
                        FilterCreationContext context)
{
   // return null;
    //Encrypt outgoing msg
    return new CustomSecurityClientOutputFilter(this);
}
public override SoapFilter CreateClientInputFilter(
                        FilterCreationContext context)
{
//Decrypt incoming data
        return new CustomSecurityClientInputFilter(this);
}
```

The CreateClientOutputFilter and CreateClientInputFilter are overwritten to perform the encryption or decryption. The SecureMessage of CustomSecurityClientOutputFilter is invoked during the outbound transaction and the ValidateMessageSecurity of CustomSecurityClientIputFIlter is invoked during the inbound transaction.

Once the custom security is written, it should then be added to the policy. In order to create the policy, you can click on **Add New Item** and then select the configuration file. Then name your policy file as `WSE3CustomEncryptionPolicy.config`, as shown in the next screen capture:

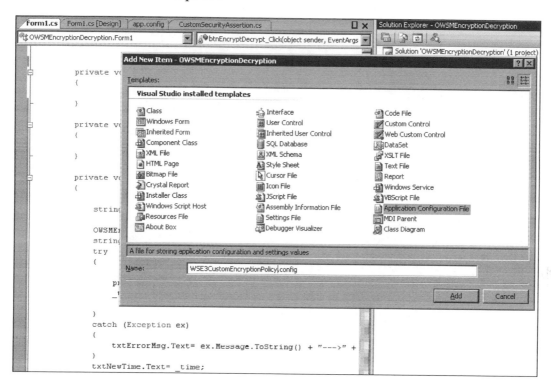

Once the policy file is added, replace the value with the following code:

```
<policies   xmlns="http://schemas.microsoft.com/wse/2005/06/
policy">
  <extensions>
    <extension name="CustomSecurityAssertion" type="OWSMEncryption
Decryption.CustomSecurityAssertion, OWSMEncryptionDecryption" />
  </extensions>
  <policy name="ServicePolicy">
    <CustomSecurityAssertion >
      <clientToken>
        <x509
          storeLocation="CurrentUser"
          storeName="My"
          findValue="CN=WSE2QuickStartClient"
          findType="FindBySubjectDistinguishedName" />
```

```
        </clientToken>
        <serviceToken>
          <x509
            storeLocation="LocalMachine"
            storeName="My"
            findValue="CN=WSE2QuickStartServer"
            findType="FindBySubjectDistinguishedName" />
        </serviceToken>
      </CustomSecurityAssertion >
    </policy>
  </policies>
```

The previous policy information describes the location of the certificate along with a policy name. Once the policy is added, it should be included with the application configuration file so that the policy can be loaded at run time. The app.config can be replaced with the following to include the custom assertion extensions and policy extensions.

```
<?xml version="1.0" encoding="utf-8" ?>
<configuration>
    <configSections>
        <sectionGroup name="applicationSettings" type="System.
        Configuration.ApplicationSettingsGroup, System,
        Version=2.0.0.0, Culture=neutral,
        PublicKeyToken=b77a5c561934e089" >
            <section name="OWSMEncryptionDecryption.Properties.
            Settings" type="System.Configuration.
            ClientSettingsSection, System, Version=2.0.0.0,
            Culture=neutral, PublicKeyToken=b77a5c561934e089"
            requirePermission="false" />
        </sectionGroup>
        <section name="microsoft.web.services3" type="Microsoft.Web.
        Services3.Configuration.WebServicesConfiguration, Microsoft.
        Web.Services3, Version=3.0.0.0, Culture=neutral,
        PublicKeyToken=31bf3856ad364e35" />
    </configSections>
    <applicationSettings>
        <OWSMEncryptionDecryption.Properties.Settings>
            <setting name="OWSMEncryptionDecryption_
                            OWSMEncryptionDecryption_TimeService"
                serializeAs="String">
                <value>http://owsm.packtpub.com:3115/gateway/
                            services/SID0003016</value>
            </setting>
        </OWSMEncryptionDecryption.Properties.Settings>
```

```
    </applicationSettings>
  <microsoft.web.services3>
    <policy fileName="..\..\WSE3CustomEncryptionPolicy.config" />
  </microsoft.web.services3>
</configuration>
```

The policy file has been created, application configuration has been modified, and the custom assertion has been written. We can now write the code for the button click event to invoke the web service and attach the policy, so that the request can be encrypted and response can be decrypted.

The button click code is straightforward. All it does is:

- Gather input from the text boxes
- Instantiate the web service proxy with a WSE enabled extension
- Attach the service policy to the proxy
- Invoke the method

The code will look like:

```
string TextThatWillbeEncrypted = txtInputString.Text;
OWSMEncryptionDecryption.TimeServiceWse proxy =
new global::OWSMEncryptionDecryption.
OWSMEncryptionDecryption.TimeServiceWse();
string _time = "";
try
{
    proxy.SetPolicy("ServicePolicy");
    _time = proxy.getTime(TextThatWillbeEncrypted);
}
catch (Exception ex)
{
    txtErrorMsg.Text= ex.Message.ToString() + "--->" +
    ex.InnerException.Message.ToString();
}
txtNewTime.Text= _time;
```

If the configurations are correct, you will have the new time in the text box when you run the application.

Summary

In this chapter, we learnt how to configure Oracle WSM to decrypt the incoming SOAP message and encrypt the response messages. Though encryption can protect the confidentiality of the message, the security is stronger when combined with a digital signature. In this case, the message is digitally signed first and then encrypted. In the next chapter, we will discuss how to digitally sign and verify the SOAP messages.

6

Digitally Signing and Verifying Messages in Web Services

Confidentiality and integrity are two critical components of web services. In the last chapter, we discussed how support for encryption and decryption in web services addressed the confidentiality issue. While confidentiality can be ensured by means of encryption, the encrypted data can still be overwritten and the integrity of the message can be compromised. It is equally important to protect the integrity of the message, and digital signatures can help protect the integrity of the message. In this chapter, I will describe in detail how to digitally sign and verify messages in web services using Oracle Web Services Manager.

Overview of Digital Signatures

In the web services scenario, XML messages are exchanged between the client application and the web services. Certain messages contain critical business information and, therefore, the integrity of the message should be ensured. Ensuring the integrity of the message is not a new concept, it has been there for a long time. The concept is to make sure that the data was not tampered with in transit between the sender and the receiver.

Consider, for example, that Alice and Bob are exchanging emails that are critical to business. Alice wants to make sure that Bob receives the correct email that she sent and no one else tampered with or modified the email in between. In order to ensure the integrity of the message, Alice digitally signs the message using her private key, and when Bob receives the message, he will check to make sure that the signature is still valid before he can trust or read the email.

What is this digital signature? And how does it prove that no one else tampered with the data? When a message is digitally signed, it basically follows these steps:

- Create a digest value of the message (a unique string value for the message using a SHA1 or MD5 algorithm).
- Encrypt the digest value using the private key, known only to the sender.
- Exchange the message along with the encrypted digest value.

Note: MD5 and SHA1 are message digest algorithms to calculate the digest value. The digest or hash value is nothing but a non-reversible unique string for any given data, i.e. the digest value will change even if a space is added or removed. SHA1 produces a 160 bit digest value, while MD5 produces a 128 bit value.

When Bob receives the message, his first task is to validate the signature. Validation of signature goes through a sequence of steps:

- Create a digest value of the message again using the same algorithm.
- Encrypt the digest value using the public key of Alice (obtained out of band or part of message, etc.)
- Validate to make sure that the digest value encrypted using the public key matches the one that was sent by Alice.
- Since the public key is known or exchanged along with the message, Bob can check the validity of the certificate itself.

Note: Digital certificates are issued by a trusted party such as Verisign. When a certificate is compromised, you can cancel the certificate, which will invalidate the public key.

Once the signature is verified, Bob can trust that the message was not tampered with by anyone else. He can also validate the certificate to make sure that it is not expired or revoked, and also to ensure that no one actually tampered with the private key of Alice.

Digital Signatures in Web Services

In the last section, we learnt about digital signatures. Since web services are all about interoperability, digital-signature-related information is represented in an industry standard format called XML Signature (standardized by W3C). The following are the key data elements that are represented in an interoperable manner by XML Signature:

- What data (what part of SOAP message) is digitally signed?
- What hash algorithm (MD5 or SHA1) is used to create the digest value?
- What signature algorithm is used?
- Information about the certificate or key.

In the next section, we will describe how the Oracle Web Services Manager can help generate and verify signatures in web services.

Signature Generation Using Oracle WSM

Oracle Web Services Manager can centrally manage the security policy, including digital signature generation. One of the greatest advantages in using Oracle WSM to digitally sign messages is that the policy information and the **digital certificate** information are centrally stored and managed.

An organization can have many web services and some of them might exchange certain business critical information and require that the messages be digitally signed. Oracle WSM will play a key role when different web services have different requirements to sign the message or when it is required to take certain actions before or after signing the message. Oracle WSM can be used to configure the signature at each web service level and that reduces the burden of deploying certificates across multiple systems. In this section, we will discuss more about how to digitally sign the response message of the web service using Oracle WSM.

Sign Message Policy Step

As a quick refresher, in Oracle WSM, each web service is registered within a gateway or an agent and a policy is attached to each web service. The policy steps are divided mainly into request pipeline template and response pipeline template, where different policies can be applied for request or response message processing. In this section, I will describe how to configure the policy for a response pipeline template to digitally sign the response message. (Note: Pipeline templates are reusable templates that can be applied across various policies and are described in detail in Chapter 3)

Note: It is assumed that the web service is registered within a gateway and a detailed example will be described later in this chapter.

In the response pipeline, we can add a policy step called **Sign Message** to digitally sign the message. In order to digitally sign a message, the key components that are required are:

- Private key store
- Private key password
- The part of SOAP message that is being signed
- The signature algorithm being used

The following screenshot describes the "**Sign Message**" policy step with certain values populated.

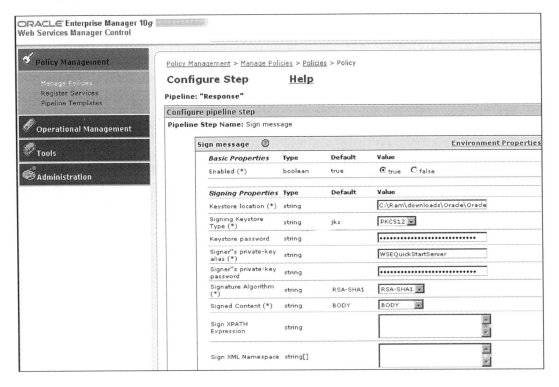

In the previous screenshot, the values that are populated are:

- **Keystore location**—The location where the private key file is located.
- **Keystore type**—Whether or not it is **PKCS12** or **JKS**.
- **Keystore password**—The password to the keystore.
- **Signer's private-key alias**—The alias to gain access to the private key from the keystore.

- **Signer's private-key password**—The password to access the private key.
- **Signed Content**—Whether the **BODY** or envelope of the SOAP message should be signed.

The above information is a part of a policy that is attached to the time service which will sign the response message. As per the information that is shown in the screenshot, the **BODY** of the SOAP message response will be digitally signed using the **SHA1** as the digest algorithm, and **PKCS12** key store. Once the message is signed, the SOAP message will look like:

```
<?xml version="1.0" encoding="UTF-8"?>
<soap:Envelope soap:encodingStyle="http://schemas.xmlsoap.org/
soap/encoding/" xmlns:xsi="http://www.w3.org/2001/XMLSchema-
instance" xmlns:xsd="http://www.w3.org/2001/XMLSchema" xmlns:
soap="http://schemas.xmlsoap.org/soap/envelope/" xmlns:
soapenc="http://schemas.xmlsoap.org/soap/encoding/">
    <soap:Header>
        <wsse:Security xmlns:wsse="http://docs.oasis-open.
        org/wss/2004/01/oasis-200401-wss-wssecurity-secext-
        1.0.xsd" xmlns="http://docs.oasis-open.org/
        wss/2004/01/oasis-200401-wss-wssecurity-secext-1.0.xsd"
        soap:mustUnderstand="1">
            <wsse:BinarySecurityToken ValueType="http://docs.
            oasis-open.org/wss/2004/01/oasis-200401-wss-
            x509-token-profile-1.0#X509v3"
            EncodingType="http://docs.oasis-open.
            org/wss/2004/01/oasis-200401-wss-soap-message-
            security-1.0#Base64Binary" wsu:Id="_
            VLL9yEsi09I9f5ihwae21Q22" xmlns:wsu="http://docs.
            oasis-open.org/wss/2004/01/oasis-200401-wss-
            wssecurity-utility-1.0.xsd">SecurityTOkenoKE2ZA==<
            /wsse:BinarySecurityToken>
            <dsig:Signature xmlns="http://www.w3.org/2000/09/
            xmldsig#" xmlns:dsig="http://www.w3.org/2000/09/
            xmldsig#">
                <dsig:SignedInfo>
                    <dsig:CanonicalizationMethod
                    Algorithm="http://www.w3.org/2001/10/
                    xml-exc-c14n#"/>
                    <dsig:SignatureMethod
                    Algorithm="http://www.w3.org/2000/09/
                    xmldsig#rsa-sha1"/>
                    <dsig:Reference URI="#ishUwYWW2AAthrx
                    hlpv1CA22">
                        <dsig:Transforms>
                            <dsig:Transform
Algorithm="http://www.w3.org/2001/10/xml-exc-c14n#"/>
```

```
                                        </dsig:Transforms>
                                        <dsig:DigestMethod
        Algorithm="http://www.w3.org/2000/09/xmldsig#sha1"/>
                                        <dsig:DigestValue>ynuqANuYM3qzh
        dTnGOLT7SMxWHY=</dsig:DigestValue>
                                    </dsig:Reference>
                                    <dsig:Reference URI="#UljvWiL8yjedImz
                                    6zy0pHQ22">
                                        <dsig:Transforms>
                                            <dsig:Transform
        Algorithm="http://www.w3.org/2001/10/xml-exc-c14n#"/>
                                        </dsig:Transforms>
                                        <dsig:DigestMethod
        Algorithm="http://www.w3.org/2000/09/xmldsig#sha1"/>
                                        <dsig:DigestValue>9ZebvrbVYLiPZ
        v1BaVLDaLJVhwo=</dsig:DigestValue>
                                    </dsig:Reference>
                                </dsig:SignedInfo>
                                <dsig:SignatureValue>QqmUUZDLNeLpAEFXndiBLk=
        </dsig:SignatureValue>
                                <dsig:KeyInfo>
                                    <wsse:SecurityTokenReference
        xmlns="http://docs.oasis-open.org/wss/2004/01/oasis-200401-wss-
        wssecurity-secext-1.0.xsd" wsu:Id="_7vjdWs1ABULkiLeE7Y4lAg22"
        xmlns:wsu="http://docs.oasis-open.org/wss/2004/01/oasis-200401-
        wss-wssecurity-utility-1.0.xsd">
                                        <wsse:Reference URI="#_
        VLL9yEsi09I9f5ihwae2lQ22"/>
                                    </wsse:SecurityTokenReference>
                                </dsig:KeyInfo>
                            </dsig:Signature>
                            <wsu:Timestamp xmlns:wsu="http://docs.oasis-open.
        org/wss/2004/01/oasis-200401-wss-wssecurity-utility-1.0.xsd"
        xmlns="http://docs.oasis-open.org/wss/2004/01/oasis-200401-wss-
        wssecurity-utility-1.0.xsd" wsu:Id="UljvWiL8yjedImz6zy0pHQ22">
                                <wsu:Created>2007-11-16T15:13:48Z</wsu:
        Created>
                            </wsu:Timestamp>
                        </wsse:Security>
                </soap:Header>
                <soap:Body wsu:Id="ishUwYWW2AAthrxhlpv1CA22" xmlns:wsu="http://
        docs.oasis-open.org/wss/2004/01/oasis-200401-wss-wssecurity-
        utility-1.0.xsd">
                    <n:getTimeResponse xmlns:n="urn:Test:GetTime">
                        <Result xsi:type="xsd:string">10:13 AM</Result>
                    </n:getTimeResponse>
                </soap:Body>
        </soap:Envelope>
```

Internals of Sign Message Policy Step

The example XML message is nothing but the SOAP response message that is digitally signed by Oracle WSM. The parameters that are selected or that can be selected will affect the message output and hence it is important to understand how Oracle WSM assembles the digitally signed message.

First of all, Oracle WSM was configured to sign the SOAP body message, which in our example is the actual time from the server. In the above example, the SOAP body is referenced by the identifier `ishUwYWW2AAthrxhlpv1CA22`. Only the SOAP body message should be digitally signed. We understand that in the signature generation process, we should first calculate the digest value of the message and then encrypt the digest value. In the sample XML, there are a few components which are worth explaining.

Reference Element

The `Reference` element describes what part of the message is hashed and what digest algorithm is used to create the hash value and any transformations applied before the digest was calculated.

Let's consider a portion of our signed response message and in the message below, we will notice that the `DigestMethod` is `SHA1` and, that the `DigestValue` is also embedded.

```
<dsig:Reference URI="#ishUwYWW2AAthrxhlpv1CA22">
    <dsig:Transforms>
        <dsig:Transform Algorithm="http://
        www.w3.org/2001/10/xml-exc-c14n#"/>
    </dsig:Transforms>
    <dsig:DigestMethod Algorithm="http://www.
    w3.org/2000/09/xmldsig#sha1"/>
    <dsig:DigestValue>ynuqANuYM3qzhdTnGOLT7SMxWH
    Y=</dsig:DigestValue>
</dsig:Reference>
```

In the above example, there is also an element called `Transforms` which contains a list of transform elements. The `Transform` element describes what transformation is applied to the XML message before the digest is calculated. In our example, the **Exclusive Canonicalization** transformation is used.

Note: Since the digest values can differ even when a space is added or removed, canonicalization transformation will transform the data to an accepted format before the digest is calculated.

SignedInfo Element

The SignedInfo element describes the actual signature algorithm and a list of references that contain the digest value of the message. In our case, the signature algorithm is rsa-sha1 and it also contains a reference to the SOAP Body element (Id attribute of the SOAP Body element). In our example of signed SOAP response message, there are actually two reference elements: one that refers to the SOAP Body and an other that refers to the Timestamp element. The SignatureMethod element describes the actual signature algorithm used.

Signature

The Signature element is the root element that describes the digital signature. It contains the SignedInfo element, SignatureValue and the KeyInfo element. The SignatureValue element contains the actual signature value and the KeyInfo element contains information about the certificate.

Signature Generation and Verification Example

In an earlier section, we learnt how the sign message policy step can be configured to digitally sign the message and also the internals of how Oracle WSM creates the signed SOAP response message. In this section, we will walk through the signature generation and verification process within Oracle WSM by means of an example.

In this example, we will have the same time web service which will be registered within Oracle WSM Gateway. Oracle WSM will validate the incoming signed SOAP message and then will respond with a signed SOAP message. In this example we will demonstrate how:

- To register web service with Oracle WSM
- Oracle WSM can be configured to validate the signature in SOAP request
- A Microsoft .NET application can digitally sign the SOAP request
- Oracle WSM can be configured to sign the response SOAP message
- A Microsoft .NET application can validate the signature of the SOAP message

Registering Web Service with Oracle WSM

In order to protect a web service within Oracle WSM, the first step is to register the web service within Oracle WSM and then edit the policy associated with it. The following steps describe how to register the service:

Login to Oracle Web Service Manager Console at:

```
http://owsm.packtpub.com:3115/ccore
```

Click on **Policy Management** and then **Manage Services**; you will see the **List of Gateways** that are available as shown in the following screenshot.

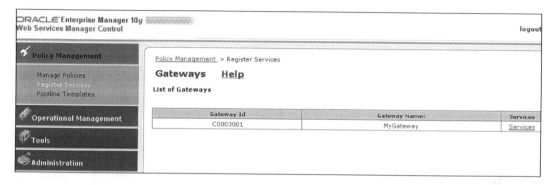

On the right side of the screen, if you click on the **Services** hyperlink, you will see the list of registered services (refer to the following screenshot).

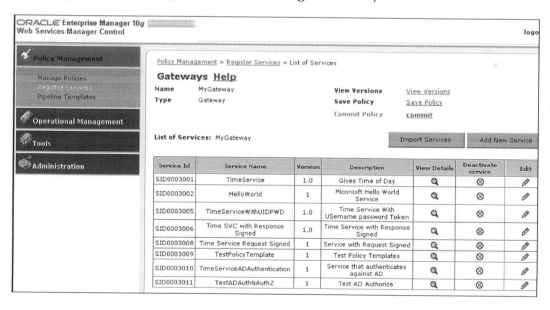

In order to add a new service, click on **Add New Service** on the right side panel.

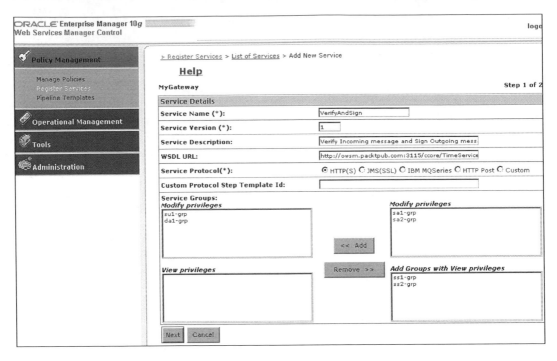

The previous screenshot show the details that can be added while adding the new service. The * after each label makes those fields mandatory. The screen asks for typical information such as:

- Name of the service
- Version of the service
- Any description of the service
- **WSDL URL** of the service
- Protocol in which service will accept messages

It also asks for additional information such as **Service Groups**, groups that are part of Oracle WSM with the right to view and with the right to update.

In our example, we are registering time service that will validate the signature of the web service request and then will sign the response message. The time service is registered with the following information:

- Service Name: VerifyAndSign

- Service Version: 1

- Service Description: Verify Incoming message and Sign Outgoing message

- WSDL URL: `http://owsm.packtpub.com:3115/ccore/TimeService.wsdl`

- Service Protocol: HTTP(S)

- Service Groups: Select the default that has full permissions

Once the information is filled out, click **Next** on **New Service** registration. This will take you to the next screen which will display the actual **URL** of the service (refer to the following screenshot).

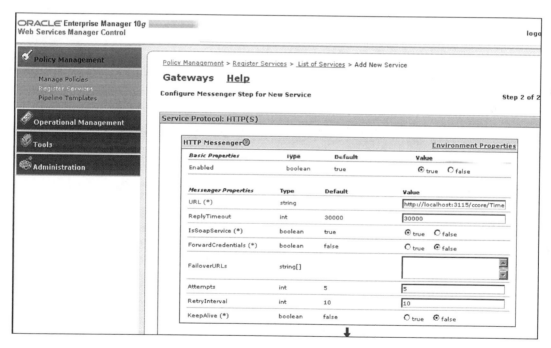

The URL in this page comes from the WSDL URL. You just have to make sure that the service is enabled and check if it is SOAP service or not.

You can then click **Finish** to register the service. Once you click **Finish**, the Oracle WSM internally generates a new service ID and now the client applications can use that service ID to communicate.

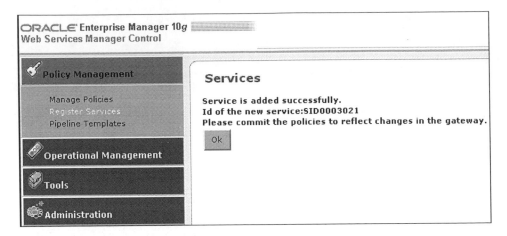

The previous screenshot show that the Oracle WSM registered the time service and created a new service ID.

Click **OK** to get back to the main screen that lists all the services.

We have only added the new service, but it hasn't been committed yet. You can now click **OK** to commit the policy.

Signature Verification by Oracle WSM

Oracle Web Services Manager can actually validate the signature in the incoming i.e. request SOAP message. By using Oracle WSM to validate the signature, organizations can actually centralize the policy enforcement and also the public key management. As organizations deploy more web services that are accessed by other divisions and business partners, managing the signature verification process might become tedious, as with each new consumer, the certificate information should be maintained. Oracle WSM can address such issues by centralizing those operations. In this section I will describe how to configure Oracle WSM policy to validate the signature of the SOAP request message.

In order to view the policy, you can click on **Policy Management** and then **Manage Policies**. This will bring you to the screen with the gateway information and a hyperlink for policies (see the following screen capture).

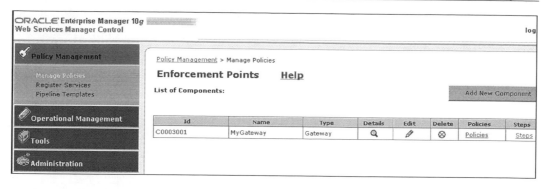

You can then click on **Policies** to see all the policies and you will see the
VerifyAndSign policy too that is created by default.

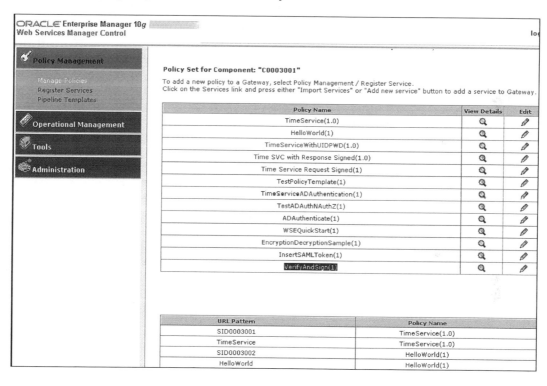

A default policy is attached to the service. We can now click **Edit** to edit the policy. When you click **Edit**, you will see the policy steps as shown in the following screenshot.

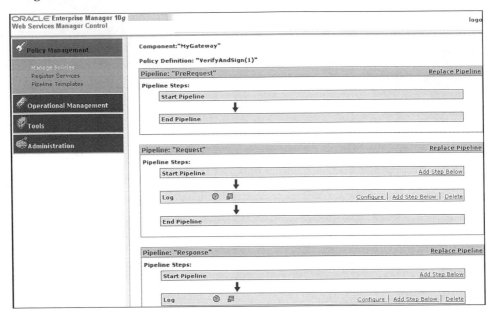

In this section, we want to configure the **Request** pipeline to validate the signature of the incoming SOAP message. In order to validate the signature, click **Add Step Below** to add the **Verify Signature** policy step as shown in the following screenshot.

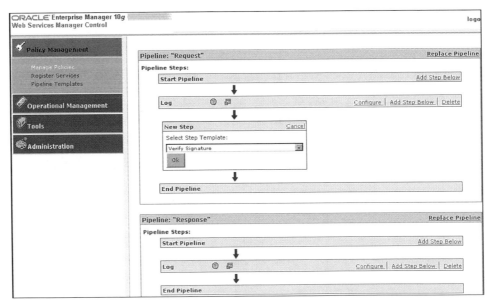

Once you click **OK,** the verify signature policy step is added, but that policy step should be configured. If you click on the **Configure** button on the verify signature policy step, it will take you to the screen where you can configure the verify signature policy information as shown in the following screen capture.

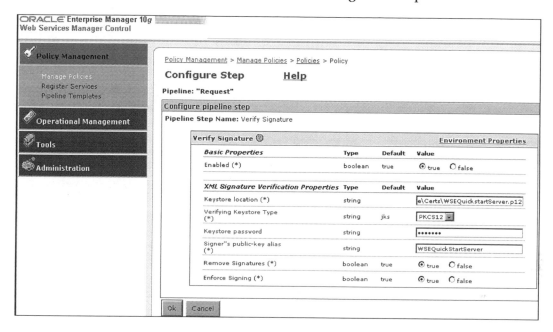

In the previous screenshot, I configured **Verify Signature** policy steps with:

- Location of the key store
- Key store type as **PKCS12**
- Password of the key store
- Public key alias in the key store
- Set **Remove Signatures** to **true** to remove the digital signature after the signature validation
- **Enforce Signing** is set to **true** to make sure that the incoming requests are signed

Note: In order to generate a PKCS12 key store from certificate that is installed already in Microsoft certificate services, you should first export the certificate (with or without private key) and then import that certificate in FireFox (Advanced option) and then export back to PKCS12.

Once the verify signature policy has been configured and saved (Commit Policy), the policy would enforce that any request for the time service with the particular service ID be digitally signed.

Signature Generation by Oracle WSM

In the last section, we discussed how to digitally sign a web service request by Microsoft .NET application and how to validate the signature by Oracle WSM. In this section, we will discuss how to digitally sign the web service response message. In the earlier section, we discussed how to register the service and how to attach the verify signature policy step to the request pipeline.

In order to digitally sign the response message, the response pipeline of the policy should be modified to include the sign message policy step. The policy with the request pipeline that is already configured to verify signature would look like:

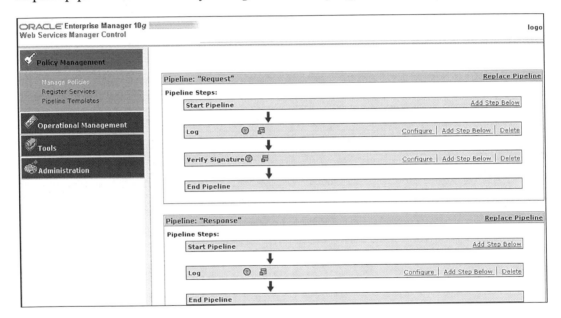

Now we have to add the step in the **Response** pipeline to actually sign the response message. In order to add the policy step, click on **Add Step Below** and then select the **Sign Message** policy step. Once the Sign Message policy step is added, it can then be configured, as shown in the following screenshot, to include the appropriate key store location for the public key to digitally sign the message.

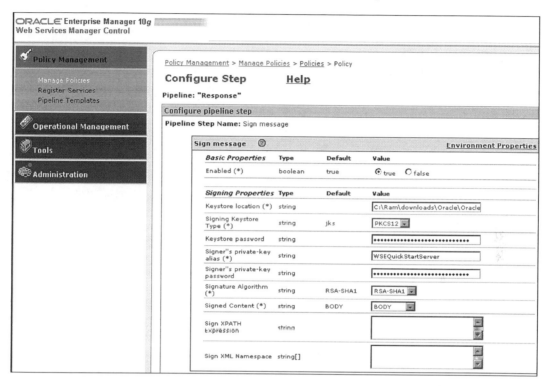

In the previous figure, the location of the key store that has the private key, along with the **Keystore password**, alias and part of message to be signed are specified.

Once the policy is created, it would look like:

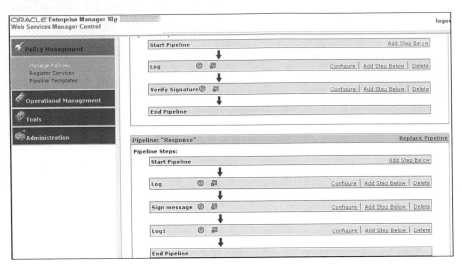

In the previous screenshot, the **Response** pipeline has two log steps—one to log the message before digitally signing and one to log the message after digitally signing the message. In this sample, we are using the same WSEQuickStartServer certificate to sign the message.

Once the policy is saved, the response message will be digitally signed. The client application (Microsoft .NET) can be configured to validate the signature.

Oracle WSM Test Page as Client Application

Oracle WSM comes with its own test page where you can test the web service and the security policy associated with the web service. In this example, we will show how to test the web service policy that was just deployed and which digitally signs the response message.

You can get to the test page from the **Tools** menu.

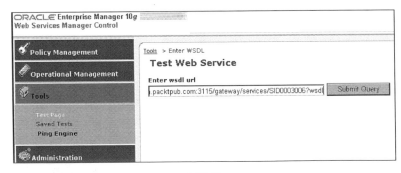

In the WSDL URL text box, enter the WSDL URL and then click on **Submit Query**. It will come up with a window to enter any credentials (username and password) and specify if that should be sent in the HTTP header or as a part of the SOAP message. It also has an option to save the test as shown in the following screen capture.

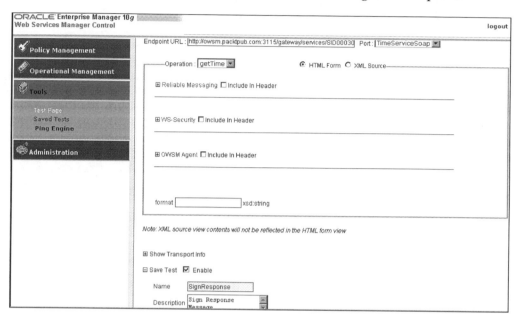

You can give a name for the test and any description and then click **Invoke**. When you click the **Invoke** button, the web service is invoked and the test is also saved. In our example, once the web service is invoked, the security policy is applied and the response message is digitally signed as shown in the next screenshot.

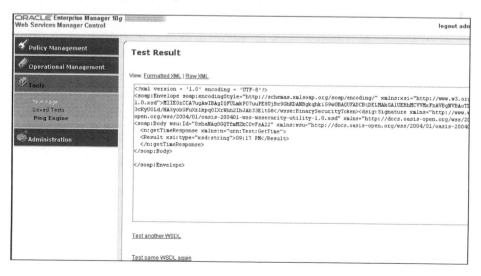

In the next example, you will see how to create a client application in Microsoft .NET to perform the signature generation and validation.

Microsoft .NET Client Application

The client application is a Windows Forms application written using Microsoft Visual Studio 2005 with Microsoft WSE 3.0. The first step in creating a client application is to create a Windows Forms application called **SignatureGenerationValidationSample**. The following is a screenshot on how to create the Windows Forms application (as described in last chapter).

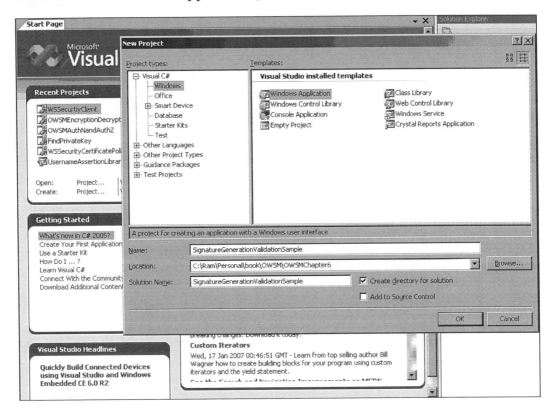

Once you click **OK**, the Windows Forms application is created with a default form.

Since we are going to invoke the time web service with input data, we will add a text box to enter any random input data and a button to invoke the web service. We will also add another text box to show the **Error** message if any (refer to the following screenshot).

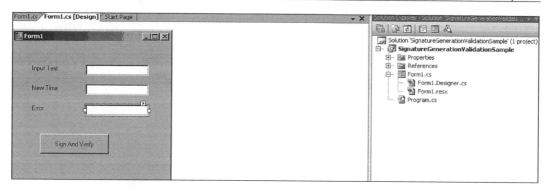

Now we should add the Microsoft WSE 3.0 as a reference before we can create the proxy class. You can add the WSE reference by selecting **Add Reference** from the project and then selecting Microsoft.Web.Services3.

Now that WSE3 is added, we can add a web reference to the web service to create the proxy object. It can be added by right-clicking on the **Add Web Reference** and then entering the WSDL URL and clicking **OK** to generate the proxy.

So far we have:

- Created the Windows Forms application
- Added a reference to WSE3.0
- Created the web service proxy

The next step is to configure and write code to digitally sign the message. Though it is beyond the scope of this book to explain in detail how to configure policy and write custom policy assertions, we will take a high level overview of how Microsoft .NET and WSE 3.0 can be used to sign and verify SOAP messages.

With Microsoft .NET 3.0 and WSE 3.0, the web services security can be applied either through:

- Policy configuration for certain frequently-used security configurations
- Custom assertion in combination with policy to perform all other security operations

Since our example focuses only on signing the request and validating the response, we will have to write a custom policy assertion so that SOAP messages can be interpreted both during request and response cycles to perform signature generation and validation. The next step is to write the custom assertion that will:

- Sign the outgoing message
- Verify the incoming message

At a high level, the custom assertion inherits from SecurityPolicyAssertion class and has methods such as CreateClientOutputFilter and CreateClientInputFilter that can be overridden to perform any operation at the client side. In our sample, we have created two new classes called CustomSecurityClientInputFilter and CustomSecurityClientOutputFilter to perform any data processing on request or response.

The CustomSecurityClientOutputFilter is derived from SendSecurityFilter and has a method called SecureMessage which can be overridden to digitally sign the message.

The CustomSecurityClientInputFilter is derived from ReceiveSecurityFilter and has a method called ValidateMessageSecurity which can be overridden to validate the signature of the message.

The custom security assertion code would look like:

```
        public override SoapFilter CreateClientOutputFilter(
                        FilterCreationContext context)
        {
           // return null;
            //Encrypt outgoing msg
            return new CustomSecurityClientOutputFilter(this);
        }
        public override SoapFilter CreateClientInputFilter(
                        FilterCreationContext context)
        {
//Decrypt incoming data
            return new CustomSecurityClientInputFilter(this);
        }
```

The CreateClientOutputFilter and CreateClientInputFilter are overwritten to perform the signature generation or validation. The SecureMessage of CustomSecurityClientOutputFilter is invoked during the outbound transaction and the ValidateMessageSecurity of CustomSecurityClientIputFIlter is invoked during the inbound transaction.

Once the custom security is written, it should then be added to the policy. In order to create the policy, you can click on **Add New Item** and then select the configuration file, then name your policy file as WSE3CustomSignaturePolicy.config as shown in the following screen capture:

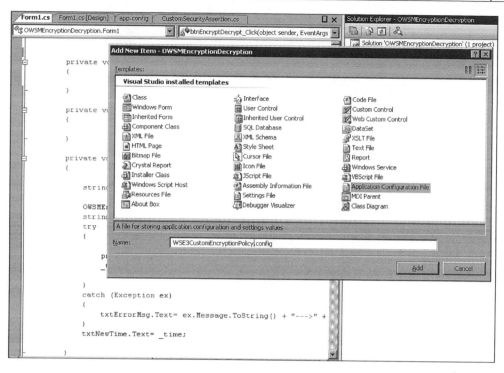

Once the policy file is added, replace the value with the following code:

```
<policies  xmlns="http://schemas.microsoft.com/wse/2005/06/
policy">
  <extensions>
    <extension name="CustomSecurityAssertion" type="Sign
atureGenerationValidationSample.CustomSecurityAssertion,
SignatureGenerationValidationSample" />
  </extensions>
  <policy name="ServicePolicy">
    <CustomSecurityAssertion >
      <clientToken>
        <x509
          storeLocation="CurrentUser"
          storeName="My"
          findValue="CN=WSE2QuickStartClient"
          findType="FindBySubjectDistinguishedName" />
      </clientToken>
      <serviceToken>
        <x509
          storeLocation="LocalMachine"
          storeName="My"
```

```
            findValue="CN=WSE2QuickStartServer"
            findType="FindBySubjectDistinguishedName" />
        </serviceToken>
      </CustomSecurityAssertion >
    </policy>
  </policies>
```

The policy information above describes the location of the certificate along with a policy name. Once the policy is added, it should be included with the application configuration file so that the policy can be loaded at run time. The app.config can be replaced with the following to include the custom assertion extensions and the policy extensions.

```xml
<?xml version="1.0" encoding="utf-8" ?>
<configuration>
    <configSections>
        <sectionGroup name="applicationSettings" type="System.
Configuration.ApplicationSettingsGroup, System, Version=2.0.0.0,
Culture=neutral, PublicKeyToken=b77a5c561934e089" >
            <section name="WSSecurtiyClient.Properties.Settings"
type="System.Configuration.ClientSettingsSection, System,
Version=2.0.0.0, Culture=neutral, PublicKeyToken=b77a5c561934e089
"
requirePermission="false" />
            <section name="SignatureGenerationValidationS
ample.Properties.Settings" type="System.Configuration.
ClientSettingsSection, System, Version=2.0.0.0, Culture=neutral,
PublicKeyToken=b77a5c561934e089" requirePermission="false" />
        </sectionGroup>
      <section name="microsoft.web.services3" type="Microsoft.Web.
Services3.Configuration.WebServicesConfiguration, Microsoft.Web.
Services3, Version=3.0.0.0, Culture=neutral, PublicKeyToken=31bf38
56ad364e35" />
    </configSections>
    <applicationSettings>
        <SignatureGenerationValidationSample.Properties.Settings>
            <setting name="SignatureGenerationValidationSample_
SignAndVerify_TimeService"
                serializeAs="String">
                <value>http://cpd10cisslaksh.coxinc.com:3115/
gateway/services/SID0003021</value>
            </setting>
        </SignatureGenerationValidationSample.Properties.Settings>
    </applicationSettings>
```

```
<microsoft.web.services3>
  <policy fileName="..\..\WSE3CustomSignaturePolicy.config" />
</microsoft.web.services3>
</configuration>
```

Now that the policy file is created, application configuration is modified, and custom assertion is written, we can write the code for the button click event to invoke the web service and attach the policy so that the request can be encrypted and response can be decrypted.

The button click code is straightforward. All it does is:

- Gather input from the text boxes
- Instantiate the web service proxy with a WSE enabled extension
- Attach the service policy to the proxy
- Invoke the method

The code will look like:

```
string _Inputdata = txtInput.Text;
string _Newtime="";
string _error = "";
try
{
    SignAndVerify.TimeServiceWse _Proxy =
new SignatureGenerationValidationSample.SignAndVerify.
TimeServiceWse();
    _Proxy.SetPolicy("ServicePolicy");
    _Newtime = _Proxy.getTime(_Inputdata);
}
catch (Exception ex)
{
    txtError.Text = "";
    _error = ex.Message.ToString();
}
txtNewTime.Text = _Newtime;
txtError.Text = _error;
```

If the configurations are correct, you will find the new time in the text box when you run the application.

Summary

In this chapter, we discussed the importance of digital signatures and how Oracle WSM can be leveraged to digitally sign and verify the messages to ensure the integrity of the message. With digital signatures, especially in validating signatures, each application has to maintain the public key information from each business partner and that will eventually become a tedious task by itself. Oracle WSM can help address such issues by centrally managing the keys and the related policy. In the next few chapters, we will explore how Oracle WSM will be deployed in a real world scenario and how Oracle WSM can help address the security issues and, at the same time, how it is highly available and scalable.

7
Oracle WSM Custom Policy Step

Organizations can externalize their web services security policy definition and enforcement to Oracle Web Services Manager so that the web services' service developers can concentrate on adding business functionality to the services. While Oracle WSM can help define and enforce WS-security policies, there are times where you need to perform additional processing that is not supported by Oracle WSM out of the box, such as validating the IP address of the client invoking the web service or validating custom authentication tokens generated by another identity management product. Under those circumstances, you can implement a custom policy step to address those challenges. Instead of performing those customizations at individual web service provider or consumer level, one can add a custom policy step to Oracle WSM and still derive the benefits of centralizing all the security operations and externalizing security from the application code. In this chapter, we will take a look at how to implement a custom policy step in Oracle WSM.

Overview of Oracle WSM Policy Steps

The web services security policies that can be defined within Oracle WSM are a collection of various policy steps. Policy steps are nothing but Java code that extends the AbstractStep class and has its own implementation. The policy step that performs active directory authentication has its own Java class that extends the AbstractStep with the implementation to authenticate the username and password against the active directory.

In Oracle WSM, you can see the list of policy steps that are available when you click on the **Steps** link from the **Manage Policies** tab on the left side. The following screenshot shows the main screen when you click on **Manage Policies**.

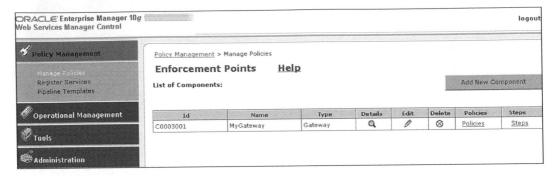

When you click on the **Steps** link, you will see the list of all the policy steps that are available by default with Oracle WSM (refer to the following screenshot).

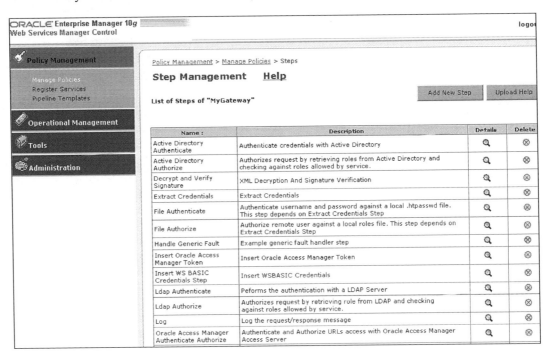

When defining a security policy for a web service, you will select one or more of these policy steps to create a policy. For instance, if you want to authenticate users against an active directory and then verify a signature, you will use the following policy steps:

- **Extract Credentials**
- **Active Directory Authenticate**
- Verify Signature

In the example above, each policy step performs a set of actions. The **Extract Credentials** will extract the username and password from the SOAP header, the **Active Directory Authenticate** will authenticate the user against active directory and the Verify Signature will validate the incoming digital signature.

While Oracle WSM is shipped with a set of known policy steps, you may have requirements that are not met by the existing policy steps, such as authenticating the username and password that were sent as a part of **UserNameToken**, or authenticating based on the information available in the HTTP header variables, or you may want to modify the request or response messages, etc. When Oracle WSM policy steps don't meet your requirements, you can always implement your own custom policy step that can still be added to list of the steps and included within a policy to secure the web services. In the next section, we will take a closer look at what it takes to implement a custom policy step.

Implementing a Custom Policy Step

Oracle WSM policy step comprises the following components:

- Java class that extends the `AbstractStep` class and implements the `execute` method
- Step template XML file with unique identifier, name and other parameters that are required for the step
- Deployment of custom policy step

The Java class that extends the `AbstractStep` class contains the actual code to execute when the custom policy step is invoked. However, if you want to provide any inputs while adding that policy step to the policy, that information is represented in the step template so that the administrator can add the appropriate values while configuring the policy step. Once the custom policy step implementation is ready and compiled, it needs to be deployed within Oracle WSM and the step template will be used to add the new step. In the next section, we will discuss extending the `AbstractStep` class to develop the custom policy step.

Extending the AbstractStep Class

In order to implement the custom step, you have to implement the execute method which is a part of the com.cfluent.policysteps.sdk.AbstractStep class. You can also override the Init method to add any specific initialization code for the custom policy step, and you can override the destroy method to perform any clean up.

When you actually implement the execute method, you have to keep in mind the following characteristics of the execute method:

- The execute method is the entry point for the custom policy step.
- The execute method returns an object of type IResult.
- The execute method can throw an exception of type Fault (com.cfluent. policysteps.sdk.Fault).

The sample code below shows a simple custom policy step that extends the AbstractStep and has implemented the execute method. The execute method implementation in this example is nothing but creating the Result object and setting the Result status to succeeded. The code will give an overview of various methods in the custom policy step.

```
public class PacktpubCustomStep extends AbstractStep{
      public PacktpubCustomStep() {
    }
    public void init() throws IllegalStateException {
        // nothing to initialize
    }
    public void destroy() {
        // do nothing
    }
/* Custom policy step execute method implementation
*/
    public IResult execute(IMessageContext messageContext) throws
Fault {
        Result result = new Result();
        result.setStatus(IResult.SUCCEEDED); //initialize result
    return result;
    }
}
```

The result object type that the execute method returns has three main states, such as:

- IResult.FAILED
- IResult.SUCCEEDED
- IResult.SUSPENDED

Like the name indicates, each state describes the state of the custom policy step execution as either "failed" or "succeeded" or "suspended".

Now that the `AbstractStep` has been extended and the custom policy step code has been written, the next step is to create the step template XML file.

Deploying the Custom Policy Step

The custom policy step Java code should be compiled and converted as a jar file, and then it should be deployed. In order to compile the above Java program you should include the necessary JAR files, and then compile and create the new JAR file with a custom policy step. Once the custom policy step JAR file is created, it should be copied to `ORACLE_HOME/owsm/lib/custom`

Once the JAR files are copied, the Oracle WSM should be restarted for the new JAR file to take effect.

Step Template XML File Creation

Once the custom policy step extension code has been written, the next step is to deploy the code. As a part of the deployment process, create a step template XML file and upload them into Oracle Web Service Manager so that it can appear as one of the possible policy steps when you are ready to define the Policy to protect your web service.

The step template is nothing but an XML file that contains information such as:

- Name: Name of the step template.
- Id: A unique identifier for the step template.
- Package: Name of the Java package that will be executed when the policy step is invoked.
- Description: Description of the custom policy step.
- Implementation: Class name of the actual implementation that will be invoked when this step is executed.
- PropertyDefinitions: Contains a list of property definition sets.
- PropertyDefinitionSet: Contains a list of property definitions.
- PropertyDefinition: Contains information such as description, whether or not enabled, and any default value.

The sample XML file below describes the step template for the custom policy step that contains the above-mentioned information.

```xml
<csw:StepTemplate xmlns:csw="http://schemas.confluentsw.com/
ws/2004/07/policy" name="Packtpub Basic Custom Policy Step"
package="customsteps" timestamp="Oct 31, 2005 05:00:00 PM" version="1"
id="118970813">
    <csw:Description>PacktPub Sample Custom Policy Step -Basic Version
</csw:Description>
    <csw:Implementation>customsteps.PacktpubCustomStep</csw:
Implementation>
    <csw:PropertyDefinitions>
        <csw:PropertyDefinitionSet name="Basic Properties">
            <csw:PropertyDefinition name="Enabled"
type="boolean">
                <csw:Description>If set to true, this step is
enabled</csw:Description>
                <csw:DefaultValue>
                    <csw:Absolute>true</csw:Absolute>
                </csw:DefaultValue>
            </csw:PropertyDefinition>
        </csw:PropertyDefinitionSet>
    </csw:PropertyDefinitions>
</csw:StepTemplate>
```

The above XML file is the step template for the packtpub custom policy step. The XML file contains information such as:

- id: Unique template Id as 118970813
- name: Packtpub Basic Custom Policy Step
- package: customsteps
- Implementation: customsteps.PacktpubCustomstep

Once the step template is uploaded into Oracle WSM by clicking the **Add New Step** button (Navigate from **Manage Policies**, to click on **Steps** and then **Add New Step**), the policy step is available to be used in any policy. The following screenshot shows that the **Packtpub Basic Custom Policy Step** is available as one of the possible policy steps when you are defining a new policy for the web service.

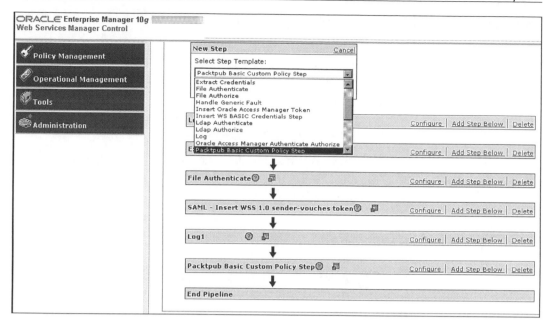

Once you select the packtpub policy step, and click on the **Configure** tab, you will see the description of the packtpub policy step along with the property definitions that we included in the step template XML. The following screenshot shows the Packtpub custom step configuration window.

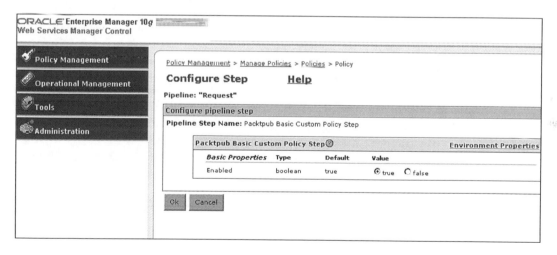

The description and the details that you see in the screenshot actually came from the step template XML that was uploaded.

Once the custom policy step is configured, the policy can be committed. You can then run a test to check if your customization actually took effect or not.

So far we have seen a very simple custom policy step that goes through the process of creating the custom implementation, deploying the JAR file, defining the step template and adding the new policy step as a part of the policy. While the above custom policy step just simply returns success without performing any action, you can write code to perform your custom implementations.

In the next section, we will walk through a detailed example of creating a custom policy step that will restrict access to the service only from a specified IP address, and will only give access to the configured web service method name.

Custom Policy Step Example: Restrict Access Based on IP Address to the Specified Method

In the last section, we walked through the steps to create and deploy a basic custom policy step. In this section, we will walk through an example of custom policy step which we will restrict access to the specific IP address and to the specific web service method.

Oracle Web Service Manager can only protect the web services and can enforce access control policies for the entire web service. However, Oracle WSM cannot restrict access only to specific web service methods within one web service. Also, there is no policy step available that will restrict access to web services based on the IP address. In this section, we will create a custom policy step that will:

- Grant access only to the specific web service method.
- Grant access only to the specific IP address.

In order for the custom policy step to restrict access based on an IP address, and only to a specific web service method, the custom policy step should know about:

- What web service method is allowed access for the specified policy?
- What IP address is a valid IP address that can be allowed to access the web service?
- What web service method is currently being invoked by the client application?
- What is the IP address of the client application?

The above questions can be categorized into two different sets. One set of questions are the configurable values within the policy step, i.e. what IP address is allowed access and what web service method can be executed, and what other set of values are available when the policy step is executed, i.e. which method is currently being executed and from where (IP address) the web service is being invoked.

The custom policy step has to simply take the configured parameter values from the policy step and compare that against the values that are available when the policy step is being executed. If they both match, the authorization is successful, otherwise access is denied.

In order to implement the above scenario, the custom policy step should consist of:

- Custom policy step Java code that extends the AbstractStep class and implements the execute method.
- Define the step template with parameters such as IP address and the web service method name.

Extending the AbstractStep

The CustomStep class extends the AbstractStep class and implements the execute method. This example is different from the previous example because here we will have to validate the IP address of the client application and the web service method name being invoked against the one that will be configured during the policy creation. The "shell" of the customstep class will look like:

```java
public class CustomStep extends AbstractStep{
    private static String CLASSNAME = CustomStep.class.getName();
    private static ILogger LOGGER = LogManager.getLogger(CLASSNAME);
    private String allowedIpAddress = null;
    private String allowedRoleName = null;
    private String protectedServiceMethodName = null;

    public CustomStep() {
    }
    public void init() throws IllegalStateException {
        // nothing to initialize
    }
    public void destroy() {
        // do nothing
    }

    /**
```

```
    * This is the main method which will validate that the request is
coming from
    * the correct IP Address and has permission to access the
specified metod.
    */
    public IResult execute(IMessageContext messageContext) throws
Fault {
        LOGGER.entering(CLASSNAME, "execute");

        Result result = new Result();
        result.setStatus(IResult.FAILED); //initialize result
    return result;
}
}
```

In the above example, the `execute` method was just returning the `Result` object with the status as **Failed**. However, we need to add functionality to the code to:

- Execute the policy step only during the request pipeline.
- Retrieve the IP address of the remote host.
- Retrieve the web service method name being executed.

In order to add the additional functionality, it is important to know where to get that information from. The `execute` method of the custom policy step has a parameter of type `IMessageContext`.

While `IMessageContext` has various methods and fields, for our example, we are interested in knowing how to retrieve:

- Current processing stage
- Remote host IP address
- Web service method name being executed

The following code snippets describe how to get the remote host IP address, web service method name, etc.

```
        String processingStage = messageContext.getProcessingStage();
```

The `getProcessingStage` method will return the processing state information. You can then compare this with the static fields of the `IMessageContext` to find out if the processing is at request or response stage.

```
        boolean isRequest =
                (IMessageContext.STAGE_REQUEST.equals(messageContext.
getProcessingStage()) ||
                IMessageContext.STAGE_PREREQUEST.
equals(messageContext.getProcessingStage()));
```

The previous code snippet compares the value returned from `getProcessingStage` with the static fields `STAGE_REQUEST` and `STAGE_PREREQUEST`.

The following code snippet will return the web service method name being executed and also the remote host IP address.

```
MessageContext msgCtxt = (MessageContext) messageContext;
    String _MethodName = msgCtxt.getRequest().getMethodName();
LOGGER.log(Level.INFO, "Writing Allowed IP Addr before creating
SOAP header " + msgCtxt.getRemoteAddr() );
```

Now that we have added functionality to retrieve the remote host IP address and the web service method name, we now have to define and get the IP address is that allowed to access, and the web service method that is granted access to the client.

We have to first define the IP address and the web service method name as configurable parameters in the policy step. This can be done by creating the step template XML file with both the IP address and web service method name as parameters. The step template XML file will also include the unique template ID, name, implementation class, etc. The following is the step template XML file.

```
<csw:StepTemplate xmlns:csw="http://schemas.confluentsw.
com/ws/2004/07/policy" name="Custom authenticate step"
package="customsteps" timestamp="Oct 31, 2005 05:00:00 PM" version="1"
id="118970810">
    <csw:Description>Custom step that authenticates the user against
the credentials entered here. This step requires Extract credentials
to be present before it in the request pipeline.</csw:Description>
    <csw:Implementation>customsteps.CustomStep</csw:Implementation>
    <csw:PropertyDefinitions>
        <csw:PropertyDefinitionSet name="Basic Properties">
            <csw:PropertyDefinition name="Enabled"
type="boolean">
                <csw:Description>If set to true, this step is
enabled</csw:Description>
                <csw:DefaultValue>
                    <csw:Absolute>true</csw:Absolute>
                </csw:DefaultValue>
            </csw:PropertyDefinition>
        </csw:PropertyDefinitionSet>
        <csw:PropertyDefinitionSet name="Custom Access Rules">
            <csw:PropertyDefinition name="IpAddress"
type="string" isRequired="true">
                <csw:DisplayName>IpAddress</csw:DisplayName>
                <csw:Description>IP Address that is allowed
access</csw:Description>
                <csw:DefaultValue>
                    <csw:Absolute>192.168.0.1</csw:Absolute>
                </csw:DefaultValue>
```

```
            </csw:PropertyDefinition>
            <csw:PropertyDefinition name="ServiceMethodName"
type="string" isRequired="true">
                    <csw:DisplayName>ServiceMethodName</csw:
DisplayName>
                    <csw:Description>Service Method Name that is
Protected (Secured)</csw:Description>
                    <csw:DefaultValue>
                            <csw:Absolute>getTime</csw:Absolute>
                    </csw:DefaultValue>
            </csw:PropertyDefinition>
        </csw:PropertyDefinitionSet>
    </csw:PropertyDefinitions>
</csw:StepTemplate>
```

In the example above, there are two property definitions: one for the IpAddress and another for ServiceMethodName. Once this template is uploaded and added as a new step, these properties will be available to be configured when defining the policy.

The following screenshot shows the list of available parameters that can be configured once the custom policy step is added to the web service policy.

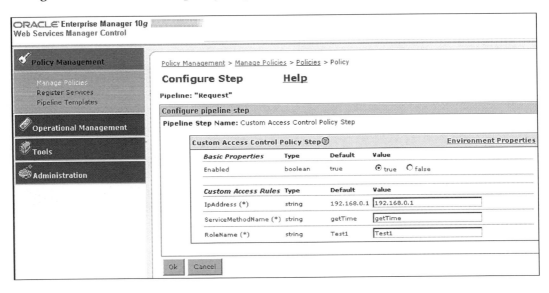

Now the next step is to make sure that the custom policy step code can read the values that are configured during the policy creation. In order for the custom code to read the values, the code should have the method (properties) defined with the same name as the one used in the step template XML file.

In our example, the step template XML had two property definitions, one called as IpAddress and the other called as ServiceMethodName.

```
<csw:PropertyDefinitionSet name="Custom Access Rules">
        <csw:PropertyDefinition name="IpAddress"
type="string" isRequired="true">
                <csw:DisplayName>IpAddress</csw:DisplayName>
                <csw:Description>IP Address that is allowed
access</csw:Description>
                <csw:DefaultValue>
                        <csw:Absolute>192.168.0.1</csw:Absolute>
                </csw:DefaultValue>
        </csw:PropertyDefinition>
        <csw:PropertyDefinition name="ServiceMethodName"
type="string" isRequired="true">
                <csw:DisplayName>ServiceMethodName</csw:
DisplayName>
                <csw:Description>Service Method Name that is
Protected (Secured)</csw:Description>
                <csw:DefaultValue>
                        <csw:Absolute>getTime</csw:Absolute>
                </csw:DefaultValue>
        </csw:PropertyDefinition>
    </csw:PropertyDefinitionSet>
```

The custom policy step code should have the get and set methods that have the same name as the one defined in the name attribute of the PropertyDefiniton element. In our example, the IpAddress and ServiceMethodName are the names that are defined in the step template. The custom policy code should have getIpAddress, setIpAddress, getServiceMethodName, setServiceMethodName to retrieve the values that will be configured during the policy creation. The following examples describe the get and set methods:

```
public String getIpAddress() {
    return allowedIpAddress;
}
public void setIpAddress(String IpAddress) {
    this.allowedIpAddress = IpAddress;
}
public String getServiceMethodName() {
    return protectedServiceMethodName;
}
public void setServiceMethodName(String serviceMethodName) {
    this.protectedServiceMethodName = serviceMethodName;
}
```

Now that we have retrieved the remote host IP address and the web service method name being executed, and also the configured values from the policy, we now have to compare those values to find out if they are the same. The following code describes how the two `IpAddress` values and the web service method names are compared and the result object is set accordingly.

```
        if (allowedIpAddress.equals(msgCtxt.getRemoteAddr()) && _
MethodName.equals(protectedServiceMethodName) )
                {
                        result.setStatus(IResult.SUCCEEDED);
                }
        else
                {

    msgCtxt.getInvocationStatus().setAuthorizationStatus(InvocationSta
tus.FAILED);

                }
```

Now that we have looked at the various components of writing and deploying custom policy step, let's take a minute to summarize the steps to develop the custom policy step. In a nutshell one has to:

- Design the custom policy and decide how many parameters will be accepted and their data types.
- Write a Java code that extends the `AbstractStep`.
- Implement the `execute` method.
- Override `Init` and `Destroy` if required.
- Create the step template XML file that contains the property names for the parameters.
- Add properties (methods) that match property name with the appropriate data type.
- Complete the execute method.
- Compile the Java code.
- Create the JAR file.
- Copy the JAR file to `/owsm/lib/custom`.
- Upload the step template XML file.
- Create or modify policy and include the policy step appropriately.
- Test the web service and ensure that the custom policy is invoked.

The example below shows the complete custom policy step code that does the following:

- Execute only during the request processing stage.
- Get the remote host IP address and the executing web service method name.
- Get the parameter values entered during the policy creation.
- Compare the remote host IP address with the configured value and compare the executing web service method name with the configured value.
- Return the result object with appropriate status.

```
/*
 * CustomStep.java
 *
 * This custom policy step performs authorizatio check to ensure
 * that the service is invoked from a specific IP Address and
 * only the specified web service method.
 *
 */
package customsteps;

import com.cfluent.ccore.util.logging.*;
import com.cfluent.pipelineengine.container.MessageContext;
import com.cfluent.policysteps.sdk.*;
import java.io.ByteArrayOutputStream;
import java.util.Locale;
import javax.xml.soap.SOAPFactory;

import org.apache.axis.message.SOAPEnvelope;
import org.apache.axis.message.SOAPHeaderElement;

public class CustomStep extends AbstractStep{
    private static String CLASSNAME = CustomStep.class.getName();
    private static ILogger LOGGER = LogManager.getLogger(CLASSNAME);
    private String allowedIpAddress = null;
    private String allowedRoleName = null;
    private String protectedServiceMethodName = null;

    public CustomStep() {
    }
    public void init() throws IllegalStateException {
        // nothing to initialize
    }
    public void destroy() {
        // do nothing
```

```
        }
    /**
     * This is the main method which will validate that the request is
coming from
     * the correct IP Address and has permission to access the
specified metod.
     */
    public IResult execute(IMessageContext messageContext) throws
Fault {
        LOGGER.entering(CLASSNAME, "execute");

        Result result = new Result();
        result.setStatus(IResult.FAILED); //initialize result

        String processingStage = messageContext.getProcessingStage();
        LOGGER.log(Level.INFO, "Processing stage is " +
processingStage);
        boolean isRequest =
                (IMessageContext.STAGE_REQUEST.equals(messageContext.
getProcessingStage()) ||
                IMessageContext.STAGE_PREREQUEST.
equals(messageContext.getProcessingStage()));

    //Execute the step Only when its a Request pipeline else return
success
        if(!isRequest) {
            result.setStatus(IResult.SUCCEEDED);
            return result;
        }

        MessageContext msgCtxt = (MessageContext) messageContext;
            String _MethodName = msgCtxt.getRequest().getMethodName();
        LOGGER.log(Level.INFO, "Writing Allowed IP Addr before
creating SOAP header " + allowedIpAddress );
        LOGGER.log(Level.INFO, "Writing Allowed IP Addr before creating
SOAP header " + msgCtxt.getRemoteAddr() );

            if (allowedIpAddress.equals(msgCtxt.getRemoteAddr()) && _
MethodName.equals(protectedServiceMethodName) )

                {
                        result.setStatus(IResult.SUCCEEDED);

                }
        else
                {
                        msgCtxt.getInvocationStatus().setAuthorization
Status(InvocationStatus.FAILED);

                }
```

```
// Set the result to SUCCESS
//result.setStatus(IResult.SUCCEEDED);
return result;
    }

    public String getIpAddress() {
        return allowedIpAddress;
    }

    public void setIpAddress(String IpAddress) {
        this.allowedIpAddress = IpAddress;
        LOGGER.log(Level.INFO, "IP Address is.. " + allowedIpAddress);
    }

    public String getServiceMethodName() {
        return protectedServiceMethodName;
    }

    public void setServiceMethodName(String serviceMethodName) {
        this.protectedServiceMethodName = serviceMethodName;
    }

    public String getRoleName() {
        return allowedRoleName;
    }

    public void setRoleName(String roleName) {
        this.allowedRoleName = roleName;
    }
}
```

Now that the custom policy step code is created, the next step is to compile the code. In order to compile the above code, you need to include the following JAR files:

```
/owsm/lib/extlib/saaj.jar
/owsm/lib/extlib/axis.jar
/owsm/lib/coresv-4.0.jar
```

Once the CustomStep.java is compiled, the CustomAuthenticationStep.JAR file can be created and copied to /owsm/lib/custom/CustomAuthenticationStep.jar. The **ant** build file is attached along with the source code for this chapter.

Testing the Custom Policy Step

Once the custom policy step is deployed and the step template is uploaded, the custom policy step is available to be included in any policy step. Let's take an existing web service policy and add the new custom policy step so that only specific IP addresses are allowed access to the web service method that is configured.

In order to enforce the custom authorization rules, edit the policy for the web service and in the **Request** Pipeline, click **Add Step Below** to select the custom policy step which is to be added to the policy (refer to the following screenshot).

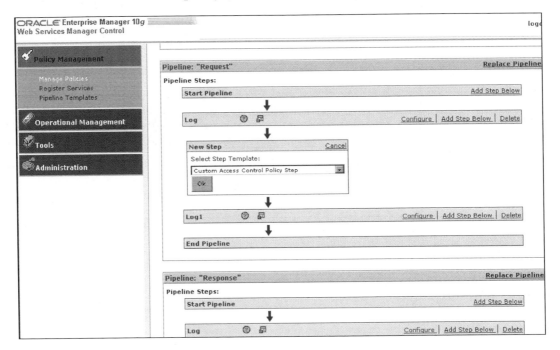

Once you click **Ok**, you will see that the custom policy step is added to the policy as shown in the following screen capture.

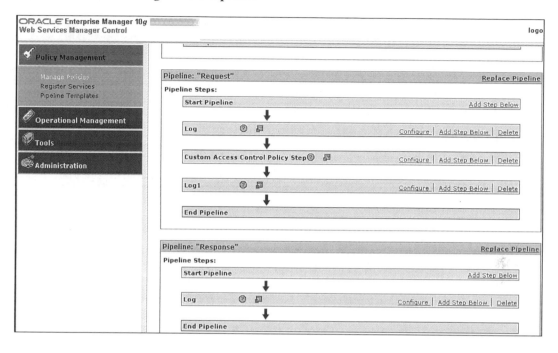

Now you can click on the **Configure** button to enter the **IpAddress** value and the web service method name. When you click **Configure**, you will see the screen to enter the IP address and web service method name as shown in the following screen capture.

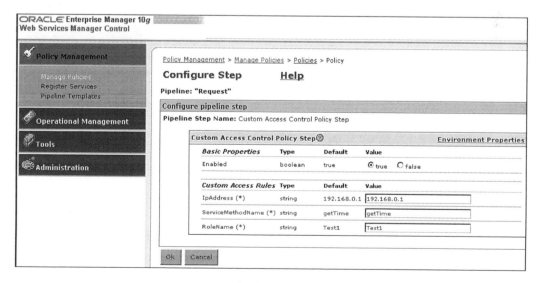

Once you click **Ok** and then save the policy, the new custom step is added to the policy.

In order to test the custom policy step, go to the **Tools** section and then select **Test Page** and enter the WSDL for the service. When you invoke this service, it will grant access only if the configured IP address and the remote host address matches, and also the configured web service method name and the method being invoked matches. If the custom policy step executes successfully you will get the web service response message.

In the above example, we discussed in detail about how to create the custom policy code, how to deploy the jar file and also how to create the step template XML file. The source code is attached with this chapter and the jar file can be deployed to get a quick start on the custom policy step.

Summary

In this chapter, we took a closer look at how to add a custom policy step to enforce any custom authentication or authorization rules. Custom policy steps can be built to address any type of customization that is not directly addressed by Oracle WSM, such as validating **UserNameToken**, validating IP address of the consumer, etc. Oracle Web Service Manager can be used to externalize the web service security policy definition and enforcement so that the web service and the consumer applications are relieved from performing the underlying security functionalities.

8

Deployment Architecture

Oracle Web Services Manager enforces the security policies for web services and it is critical that the Oracle WSM components are highly available and scalable to meet any service level agreements. In order to design a highly available and scalable architecture, one has to understand the various components of Oracle WSM and how they can be deployed individually or in combination to meet the requirements. In this chapter, I will discuss the various components of Oracle WSM and how they can be deployed to ensure high availability and scalability.

Oracle WSM Components

The main functionality of the Oracle Web Services Manager is to give the administrator the ability to define the security policy, define service level agreements, and configure Oracle WSM to enforce security policy and to monitor the SLA. In order to perform the above functions, the Oracle WSM leverages few of its internal components, such as:

- Policy Manager — Used to register web services, define the security policy, etc.
- Policy Enforcement Point — EP will enforce the security policy deployed either as a gateway or as an agent.
- Oracle WSM Monitor — To monitor the events and SLAs, etc.
- Oracle WSM Database — Where all the policy data and configurations are stored.
- Web Services Manager UI Control — Web UI to administer the Oracle WSM.

In the deployment of Oracle WSM, both the scalability and high availability should be considered.

Addressing Oracle WSM Scalability

Oracle Web Services Manager can be deployed to handle a growing web services environment, and the components of Oracle WSM can be deployed on one or many computers to handle the demand. In addressing the scalability of Oracle WSM, the first and foremost is the policy enforcement point. The policy enforcement point can be either a Oracle WSM gateway or an agent. The agents, i.e. server agents or client agents, can be attached to the application platform (client or server) to maximize the performance of PEP. The Oracle WSM gateways can also be deployed in different servers and each talking to the same policy manager to aggregate a certain set of services with one set of gateways to maximize the performance and also to address the high availability and SLAs. The PEP can be deployed across many computers to distribute the load to increase the performance.

While PEP can be deployed to optimize the performance of enforcing the security, the policy manager can also be deployed across multiple computers, and behind a load balancer to ensure high availability and to optimize performance to register and define web services policies.

Note: When load balancer is used in front of the policy manager, the load balancer should be configured to have the "sticky bit" on so that it maintains the session with a particular Oracle WSM component on the same server for the same client request.

Addressing High Availability

Oracle Web Services Manager should be deployed in such a way that it is highly available to meet the customer requirements, which in some cases may be 24 by 7. The simple answer to high availability is to configure the Oracle WSM components behind a load balancer. In order to configure Oracle WSM behind a load balancer, the Oracle WSM components should be installed and configured in a specific order on multiple machines, as described in this section.

In a typical load balanced configuration, you would deploy Oracle WSM components on two different hosts and then configure the load balancer to send the requests to those two hosts. However, with Oracle WSM, you have to handle the component ID, which is unique to each Oracle WSM installation. In order to have Oracle WSM load balanced, the component ID should be unique when the request goes to any of the Oracle WSM installations. The following steps describe how to configure Oracle WSM in a load balanced environment.

Installation

The first step is to install the Oracle WSM components on three different hosts:

- Install Oracle WSM components on Host1
- Install Oracle WSM components on Host2
- Install Oracle WSM components on Host3
- Configure load balancer to send requests to Host1 and Host2

We will use Host1 and Host2 behind the load balancer which contains the Oracle WSM policy manager of the Oracle WSM gateway. The Host3 will contain the Oracle WSM monitor and the Oracle WSM web services manager control. The following diagram shows the overview of the Oracle WSM highly available architecture.

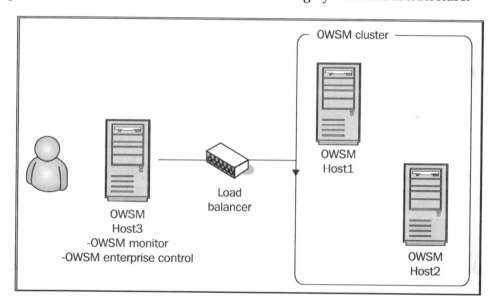

Once the Oracle WSM components are installed on all the three hosts, the Host3 which contains the web services manager control should be configured to talk to the load balancer (so that the requests go to Host1 or Host2).

On the Host3, you should edit the `ui-config-installer.properties` file to specify the host name of the load balancer. The following configuration changes should be made on the `ui-config-installer.properties` file.

Open the `ui-config-installer.properties` file under `ORACLE_HOME/owsm/config/ccore/`.

Add or modify the following properties to change the host name and port number:

- `Ui.pm.server.httphost` — Host name of the load balancer which manages the Oracle WSM policy manager.
- `Ui.pm.server.httpport` — Port number of the load balancer which maps to Oracle WSM policy manager.

Once you modify the properties file, you should run the following commands to deploy the solution.

```
Wsmadmin deploy control
```

Disabling Unnecessary Components

It is clear from the previous figure that each host only needs a few components, but each Oracle WSM default installation comes up with all the necessary components. From the previous figure, we need the following configuration:

- Host1 — Oracle WSM policy manager and gateway
- Host2 — Oracle WSM policy manager and gateway
- Host3 — Oracle WSM monitor and web services manager control

So in all the three hosts, we should remove the components that are not required, and you can do that by using the following commands in each environment.

Host1 and Host2:

On Host1 and Host2 we need only the Oracle WSM policy manager and gateway. We need to uninstall the monitor and the web services manager control and you can do that by running the following commands on each host.

```
wsmadmin undeploy monitor
wsmadmin undeploy control
```

Host3:

On Host3 you need to uninstall the policy manager and the gateway. You can do that by running the following commands.

```
wsmadmin undeploy policymanager
wsmadmin undeploy gateway
```

Note: It is not necessary to deploy both the policy manager and gateway on the same host. You can have multiple gateways talking to the same policy manager. Typically the load is on the gateway and not on the policy manager. Deploying policy manager and gateway on two different machines will also make it more secure. In order to remove the policy manager from a host, you can undeploy policy manager using the `wsmadmin` command. The following figure shows how you can have two gateways and one policy manager and one monitor/UI control.

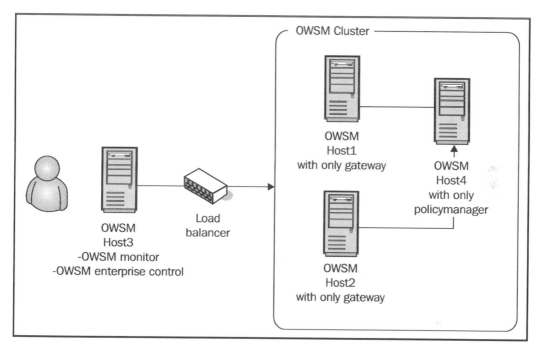

Mapping Component ID on Host1 and Host2

When you invoke Oracle WSM from Host3, which points to one of the Oracle WSM on Host1 or Host2 via the load balancer, you need to make sure that both hosts have the same component ID for the gateway. You can register a gateway by connecting to the Oracle WSM policy manager from Host3 through the web services manager control. When you register a gateway, it will generate a component id and will also ask for the URL of the component. When asked for the URL of the component, enter the load balancer URL. Once registered, the component ID is generated.

Now we need to make sure that the same component ID is in the `gateway-config-installer.properties` file on both Host1 and Host2. The `gateway-config-installer.properties` can be found at `ORACLE_HOME/owsm/config/gateway/`.

Make sure that the property `gateway.component.id` is the one that you just generated, otherwise replace the value with the one you just generated.

Example: `gateway.component.id =C0003001`

Once the changes are made, you need to deploy the gateway by executing the following command:

`wsmadmin deploy gateway`

Configuring Oracle WSM Monitor on Host3

Now that Host1 and Host2 have Oracle WSM gateway and policy manager, and Host3 has the Oracle WSM monitor, we need to configure Oracle WSM monitor on Host3 to monitor for events on both Host1 and Host2. You can edit the gateway properties on each host and modify the `cfluent.monitor.rmi.host` and `cfluent.monitor.rmi.port` values to map to Host3 where the Oracle WSM monitor is deployed.

Summary

Oracle Web Services Manager is designed to be scalable to address the growing web services environment and can be highly available by configuring behind a load balancer. In this chapter, we took a closer look at how to create a clustered Oracle WSM deployment and how easy it is to horizontally scale the Oracle WSM components.

Oracle WSM Runtime-Monitoring

9

Oracle Web Service Manager enforces security policies for the web service and hence it is critical to know about ongoing security violation, authentication failure, authorization failures, any delay in service, etc. Oracle WSM is a critical component of SOA infrastructure and requires appropriate auditing and monitoring to proactively address any service failures or security violations. In this chapter, we will discuss in detail how to manage the Oracle WSM environment from an operation point of view, i.e. how the monitoring works.

Oracle WSM Operational Management

Oracle Web Service Manager not only enforces the security policies for the web services, but also virtualizes the web service end points (vaguely like reverse proxy where you can access intranet web applications from outside of a corporate network). So when Oracle WSM is down or not operational, it's not just the security that is affected but also the service operations (that may or may not have any security attached to it). On the other hand, if you have a lot of web services, you can register them in Oracle WSM, which not only virtualizes the web service end points, but also monitors the health of the web services. It is important to monitor the various operations and statistics of the Oracle WSM to proactively address any operational issues. Oracle WSM has built-in functionality to monitor:

- Overall Statistics
- Security Statistics
- Service Statistics

Oracle Web Services Manager can also let you create custom views for the administrator to select and view certain statistics for all or few services. The administrator can also create **alarms** to notify them in case of any failure that the administrator is they'd be interested in.

Oracle WSM collects the statistics data at the gateway and at the agents which are then transferred to the Oracle WSM monitor, where the data is persisted to a database and then displayed as a report or pie chart view. Since the data regarding all the statistics can be huge, the it is automatically purged every 100 minutes. If you choose to keep the data for a longer period of time, you should modify the `monitor.aggregator.measurementStore.WindowSize` and then redeploy the Oracle WSM.

In the following sections, we will discuss each statistics in detail and also discuss how to create custom views and alarms.

Oracle WSM Overall Statistics

To begin with, administrators need to know the overall behaviour or statistics of Oracle Web Services Manager that will give more information about:

- Overall failures
- Authentication failures
- Service failures
- Overall latency
- Authorization failures
- Service latency

In Oracle WSM, you can go to **Operational Management** and click on **Snapshot** to get the overall statistics of all the web services in one place. Before you click on **Operational Management**, go to the **Test Page** under **Tools** and invoke a few web services with valid credentials and invalid credentials so that Oracle WSM can collect all the relevant data to display the report as shown in the following screenshot.

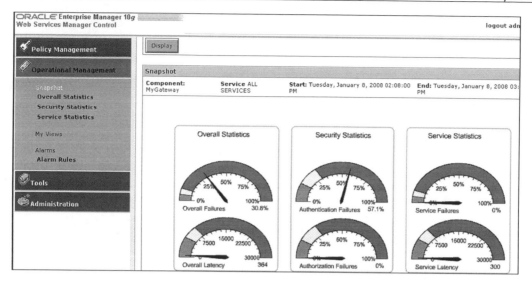

The figure above gives complete statistics such as 30% **Overall Failures** and 50% **Authentication Failures**.

Once you identify that there are some failures, you may want to know which service operations did not meet the service level agreements. Oracle WSM gives the flexibility to define the SLA values and the administrators can actually monitor individual services that failed, or did not meet the latency requirements as shown in the following screenshot.

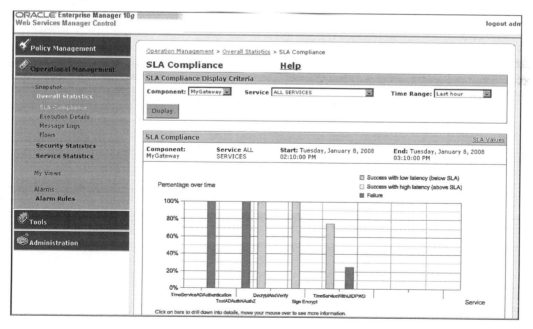

You can navigate to the **SLA Compliance** section from **Operational Management** by clicking on **Snapshot, Overall Statistics,** and then **SLA Compliance**. You can also modify the SLA values by clicking on the **SLA Values** hyperlink. You can also move the mouse over it to get more detailed information.

Now that you were able to monitor whether or not the web services meet the service level agreements defined, you can actually see the details of the web service execution by clicking on the **Execution Details** tab on the left-hand side menu. In the following screenshot, you can see the execution details for all the web services, where it indicates:

- **Latency** in milliseconds
- **Execution successful**
- Execution failure
- **SLA Assured Latency**

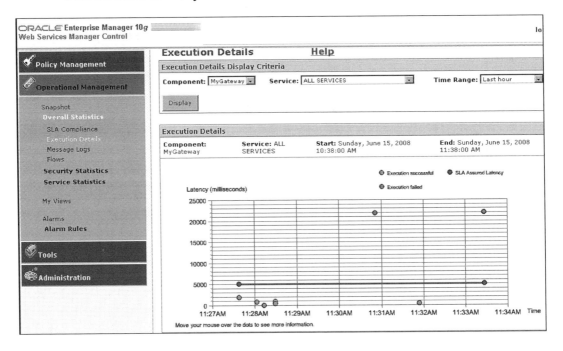

Once you are able to see the **Execution Details**, and if you are curious about execution success or execution failure and would like to see the message logs, you can click on the **Message Logs** from the left-side menu. This will take you to the list of message logs that was logged as shown in the following screenshot.

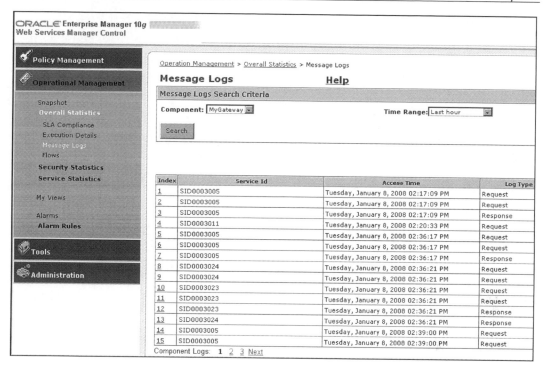

In the screenshot, you can see the list of message logs and you can click on the hyperlinks for individual services to look at request or response operations. In order to view the logs here, you should have added log steps in the Request or Response pipelines.

The overall statistics helps in maintaining the services as per the SLA. However, it is also critical to monitor the security statistics such as authentication failures and authorization failures to monitor any security failure or security breaches. In the next section, we will discuss more about the security statistics.

Oracle WSM Security Statistics

The operation management feature of Oracle WSM can also monitor the security statistics for the authentication and authorization failures. It is important to know how many web services failed at the authentication or authorization step. This will help address a couple of things:

- Service failure due to wrong credential or access privilege.
- Security breach, where an intruder is trying to access the system.

The administrator can navigate to **Security Statistics, Access Control** from the **Operational Management** to get a complete view of access control violations for all the services. When you click on **Access Control** from the left-side menu, you can see a bar diagram as shown in the following screenshot, which describes the percentage of **Access Denied**.

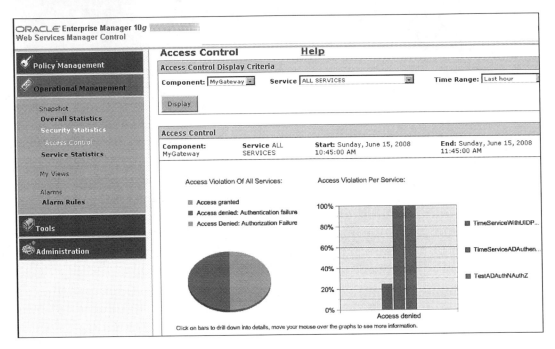

From the screenshot, you can get a clear picture of what percentage of each service were denied access, either because of improper authentication credentials or authorization privileges. You can also move the mouse over the pie chart to get the details.

Oracle WSM Service Statistics

While it is important to understand the overall statistics and the security statistics, it is also important to know how often a particular service is being invoked and what the overall latency for each service is. Oracle Web Services Manager can actually keep track of each service invocation and the latency.

One can navigate to **Service Statistics** from **Operational Management** and then click on **Latency Variance** to find out the minimum and maximum latency for each service during a particular period of time as shown in the following screenshot.

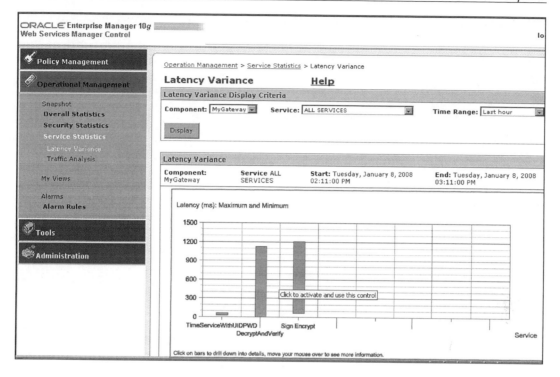

The figure shows the minimum and maximum latency for the services invoked in the last hour.

Both developers and administrators are also interested in finding out how often the web services were invoked in a particular period of time. You can navigate to the **Traffic Analysis** link to find out:

- How often a service was invoked in a particular time period.
- **Number of Bytes per Service** in a particular time period.

The following screen capture shows the traffic details of the services.

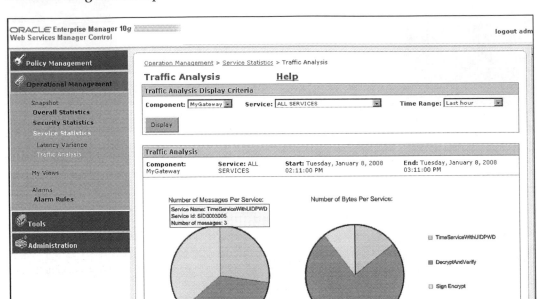

While Oracle WSM has various statistics built in and one can navigate to find out overall statistics or security statistics, it also has an option to create custom views. In the next the section, we will explore how to create custom these.

Oracle WSM Custom Views

Oracle Web Services Manager maintains the statistics of all the services, and the snapshot view can help give a complete overview of all the services deployed in an organization. However, it is tedious to go through multiple levels to find out details of a particular service or a set of services that an administrator or developer may be interested in. Oracle Web Services Manager has an option to create custom views where an administrator can select only a set of services, either critical for business or the one he is responsible for, and can monitor the activities of those services.

One can create a new view from the **My Views** section under **Operational Management**, as shown in the following screen capture.

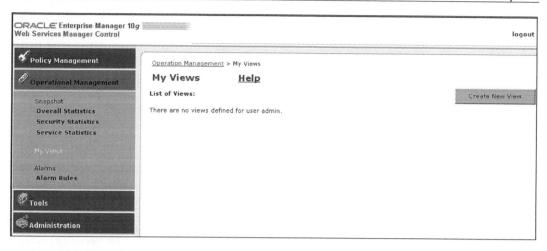

Once you click on the **Create New View** button, you can then create a new view that only has a limited number of services you are interested in. You can also select what statistics data you would be interested in and the time interval. The following screenshot shows the **Create New View** screen.

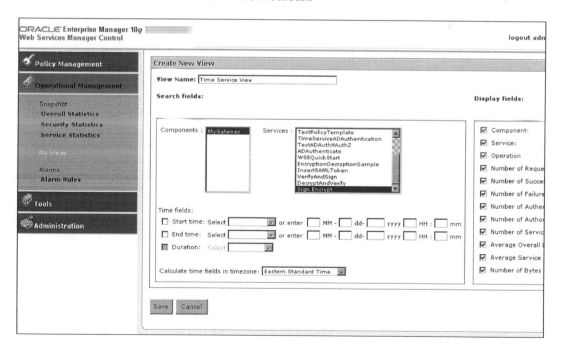

Once the services are selected and appropriate statistics data that you are interested in are selected, you can click **Save**. Once the new view is created, it will show up in the My Views section as shown in the following screenshot.

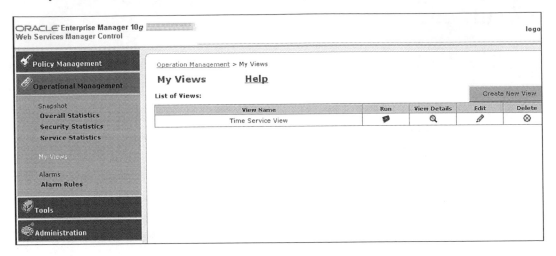

You can now click on the **Run** button to actually run the custom view to get the statistics as shown in the following screenshot.

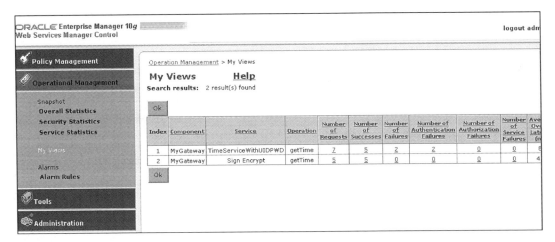

In the screenshot, you can actually see all the statistics data, such as the **Number of Requests**, successes, failures, authentication failures, authorization failures, service failures, etc. You can actually click on the hyperlinks to get the individual details, such as **Success, Failure**, latency of each service invocation, as shown in the following screenshot.

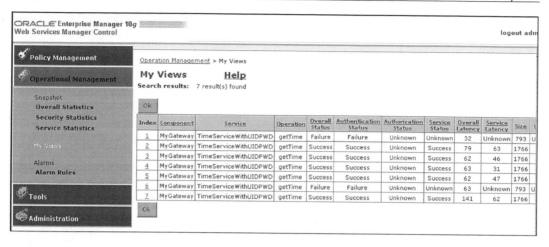

From the this screen, you can actually navigate to the message log to see the details of the message or even troubleshoot reasons for failure.

The view is created with the option called "Aggregated" which will give the total number of requests, successes, failures, etc. for each service, and you can click on each service to find out individual details about latency, success, failure, etc. However, you can also get to the details by creating the view with the option of **Atomic** as shown in the following screen capture.

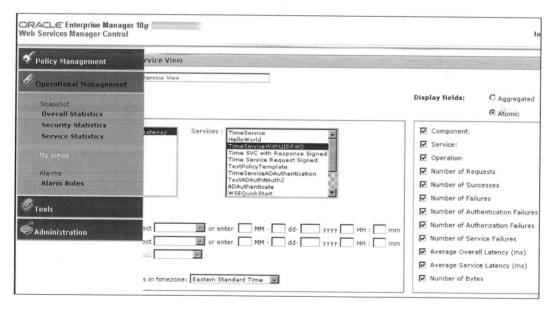

In the screenshot, the **Atomic** view is selected. Once you save and run the view, you will get all the details of the individual services directly as shown in the following screen capture (as opposed to an aggregated view).

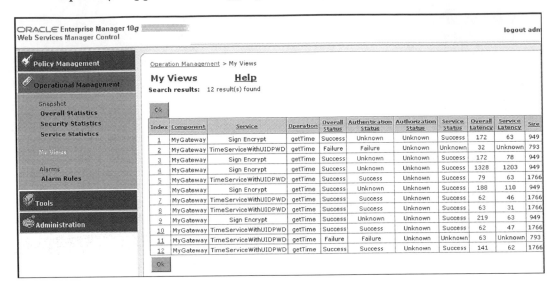

The custom view comes in handy when you want to monitor the statistics of a few services that you are interested in. However, this still gives all the information and you have to identify if there was any latency variation or security failure. Another way is to capture the details when there are any violations such as latency greater than 30, or security failures. In the next section, we will discuss alarms in detail.

Oracle WSM Alarms

Alarms are another alternative way to identify any service failure or any other type of issue. Instead of looking through the snapshot view or custom view and then looking through all the messages or services, you can actually get notified only when there is an issue such as latency variation, authentication failure, etc.

Administrators can actually define various types of alarms. When the conditions are met, the alarm is raised. You can then click on **Alarms** from **Operational Management** to find out what alarms were created in the last hour as shown in the following screenshot.

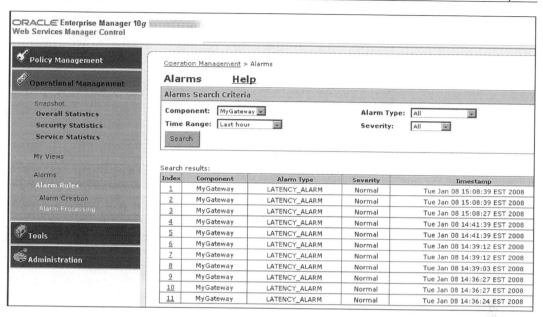

The screenshot describes all the messages that triggered the latency alarm. In order to view the alarms, one has to actually define an alarm by clicking on **Alarm Creation**. Once you click on **Alarm Creation**, you can enter the details along with **Measurement Type** as shown in the following screen capture.

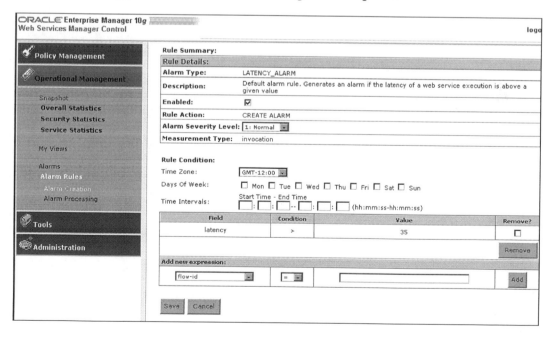

In the screenshot, the latency alarm will be triggered when the latency is greater than 35. You will be able to view the triggered alarms from the **Alarms** menu. You can also configure **Alarm Processing**, where you can trigger an external action such as email or other notification when an alarm is triggered. One of the options for the action is the ability to raise the SNMP events. When you raise SNMP events you can actually integrate the monitoring of Oracle WSM with other products such as Microsoft Operations Manager, HP Open View, etc.

Summary

In this chapter, we were able to discuss the various statistics that Oracle WSM captures and the ways in which those statistics are presented. It is important to define the service level agreement and monitor if any service violates that SLA. Also, it is important to monitor the security statistics to prevent any unauthorized access. For a larger deployment, the alarms and alarm processing comes in very handy so that the administrators can be notified when there is a problem. Oracle Web Services Manager provides the statistics to proactively monitor the service operations and the administrators and SOA architects should leverage that in their applications.

10
XML Encryption

XML encryption is a W3C standard that is now part of WS-security specification (with certain extensions for WS-security) which addresses the interoperability concerns in encryption and decryption. In Chapter 5, we discussed how Oracle Web Services Manager can encrypt and decrypt web service messages. While it is easy to configure Oracle WSM to encrypt and decrypt messages, it will be helpful if one can understand the internal details of how the encrypted XML message is formatted. Understanding the internals of XML Encryption in WS-security will help you relate to certain parameters that you select in the Oracle WSM policy steps to perform encryption or decryption. In web services, the encrypted XML is represented in an interoperable standard format, such as XML encryption. In this chapter, we will take a closer look at XML encryption standard from W3C.

XML Encryption and Web Services

Confidentiality in web services is ensured by encrypting the confidential data in the web service messages. Encryption is nothing but a process of applying an algorithm using an encryption key over the plain text to create the cipher text (encrypted data). While this sounds simple, applications need to know the algorithm used to encrypt the data, how the encrypted data is represented in the final output, etc. Traditional applications tend to encrypt the entire message even if there is only one piece of information that is confidential. They also require both the sender and the recipient to use the same software, such as PGP (Pretty Good Privacy), for encryption and decryption.

In the web services world, it is not practical to force everyone to use one set of programs to encrypt or decrypt messages, and it may not be necessary to encrypt the entire message every time a piece of confidential data needs to be protected (encrypted). The ideal solution would be to:

- Encrypt only portions of the XML that needs to be encrypted.
- Service provider and consumer should not be tied to the same set of programs to encrypt and decrypt.

In order for anyone who has the appropriate keys to decrypt the data, the encrypted data should be represented in such a way that the application can determine:

- Where the encrypted data is placed inside the XML message.
- What encryption algorithm is used to encrypt the data.
- Any other cryptographic parameters.

The said requirements are addressed by the XML encryption specification from W3C where the XML encryption schema describes how the encrypted data can be represented. We will take a closer look at XML encryption in the next section.

XML Encryption Schema

By definition, the XML encryption schema is nothing but an XML schema that outlines how the encrypted data can be described in an XML format. Any application that can understand the XML encryption schema should be able to encrypt and display data as per the schema, and should also be able to decrypt the data. The following example XML represents encrypted data in the XML format.

```
<xenc:EncryptedData xmlns="http://www.w3.org/2001/04/xmlenc#"
xmlns:xenc="http://www.w3.org/2001/04/xmlenc#" Type="http://www.
w3.org/2001/04/xmlenc#Element" Id="ED">
    <xenc:EncryptionMethod Algorithm="http://www.w3.org/2001/04/
xmlenc#tripledes-cbc"/>
    <dsig:KeyInfo xmlns:dsig="http://www.w3.org/2000/09/xmldsig#">
      <dsig:KeyName>EncryptedElementWithSymmKey</dsig:KeyName>
    </dsig:KeyInfo>
    <xenc:CipherData>        <xenc:CipherValue>nrNckdqE5O1CCZkjA0RM9
s7mOYv8t4QUJ/tE1ONdfUe8zWaXeJuDYAl5dQ4Ypfpu</xenc:CipherValue>
    </xenc:CipherData>
  </xenc:EncryptedData>
```

In the example, the encrypted data is represented by the `CipherValue` XML element and the algorithm used, which is **Triple DES,** represented by `EncryptionMethod` XML element. `EncryptedData` XML element represents all the information together such as `EncryptionMethod` to describe the algorithm, `KeyInfo` to describe the symmetric key information, `CipherData` to represent the cipher text or encrypted text.

This example describes a symmetric key encryption scenario where both the sender and recipient are aware of the encryption key (communicated over phone or other means). The asymmetric key encryption addresses the key exchange problem by encrypting the data using the public key of the recipient, and the recipient can decrypt the data using the private key, known only to the recipient.

Encrypting the data using a public key is usually not recommended for high volume transactions as it is CPU intensive. Instead, a combination of symmetric and public key methods are used, as follows:

- Symmetric key is generated at random.

- Plain text data is encrypted using the symmetric key.

- Symmetric key (also called encryption key) is then encrypted using the public key of recipient.

The mentioned process can be easily translated to the XML encryption schema by means of the `EncryptedKey` XML element. The following example XML message describes how the EncryptedKey is represented.

```
<xenc:EncryptedData xmlns="http://www.w3.org/2001/04/xmlenc#"
    xmlns:xenc="http://www.w3.org/2001/04/xmlenc#"
    Type="http://www.w3.org/2001/04/xmlenc#Content" Id="Lock">
<xenc:EncryptionMethod Algorithm="http://www.w3.org/2001/04/
xmlenc#tripledes-cbc"/>
<dsig:KeyInfo xmlns:dsig="http://www.w3.org/2000/09/xmldsig#">
<xenc:EncryptedKey xmlns="http://www.w3.org/2001/04/xmlenc#"
    xmlns:xenc="http://www.w3.org/2001/04/xmlenc#" Id="EK">
<xenc:EncryptionMethod Algorithm="http://www.w3.org/2001/04/
xmlenc#rsa-1_5"/>
<dsig:KeyInfo xmlns:dsig="http://www.w3.org/2000/09/xmldsig#">
  <dsig:X509Data>
    <dsig:X509Certificate>MIICajCCAdMCBD3RhNAwDQYJKoZIhvcNA</dsig:
X509Certificate>
  </dsig:X509Data>
  </dsig:KeyInfo>
<xenc:CipherData>
    <xenc:CipherValue>WIRgk=</xenc:CipherValue>
```

```
</xenc:CipherData>
<xenc:ReferenceList>
   <dsig:DataReference URI="#Lock"/>
</xenc:ReferenceList>
</xenc:EncryptedKey>
</dsig:KeyInfo>
<xenc:CipherData>
<xenc:CipherValue>/cpa26ZsDr1AF8</xenc:CipherValue>
</xenc:CipherData>
</xenc:EncryptedData>
```

This XML message is a very good example of how flexible the XML encryption schema is. From the two examples shown, it is clear that the XML encryption schema is comprised of two key XML elements, `EncryptedData` and `EncryptedKey`, which we will explore in detail in the following sections.

EncryptedData

`EncryptedData` element represents the encrypted data information so that the recipient can actually decrypt the data. The following example shows the `EncryptedData` element that describes the information about the encrypted data.

```
<xenc:EncryptedData xmlns="http://www.w3.org/2001/04/xmlenc#"
xmlns:xenc="http://www.w3.org/2001/04/xmlenc#" Type="http://www.
w3.org/2001/04/xmlenc#Element" Id="ED">
   <xenc:EncryptionMethod Algorithm="http://www.w3.org/2001/04/
xmlenc#tripledes-cbc"/>
   <dsig:KeyInfo xmlns:dsig="http://www.w3.org/2000/09/xmldsig#">
     <dsig:KeyName>EncryptedElementWithSymmKey</dsig:KeyName>
   </dsig:KeyInfo>
   <xenc:CipherData>        <xenc:CipherValue>nrNckdqE5O1CCZkjA0RM9
s7mOYv8t4QUJ/tE1ONdfUe8zWaXeJuDYAl5dQ4Ypfpu</xenc:CipherValue>
   </xenc:CipherData>
   </xenc:EncryptedData>
```

In this example, `EncryptedData` element consists of various key information required to decrypt the data, such as:

- `EncryptionMethod`: XML element that describes that the algorithm is Triple DES.

- `KeyInfo`: XML element that describes the `KeyName` so that the recipient can use it to derive the actual symmetric key.

- `CipherData`: XML element that contains the `CipherValue` element, which is the actual encrypted data.

The `EncryptedData` element is actually derived from `EncryptedType` XML element and the structure of `EncryptedType` (or its instance `EncryptedData`) is:

```
<complexType name='EncryptedType' abstract='true'>
  <sequence>
  <element name='EncryptionMethod' type='xenc:EncryptionMethodType'
minOccurs='0'/>
  <element ref='ds:KeyInfo' minOccurs='0'/>
  <element ref='xenc:CipherData'/>
  <element ref='xenc:EncryptionProperties' minOccurs='0'/>
  </sequence>
  <attribute name='Id' type='ID' use='optional'/>
  <attribute name='Type' type='anyURI' use='optional'/>
  <attribute name='MimeType' type='string' use='optional'/>
  <attribute name='Encoding' type='anyURI' use='optional'/>
</complexType>
```

The `EncryptedType` schema shown describes:

- `Id` attribute: Uniquely identifies the `EncryptedData` or `EncryptedKey` element in the document.

- `Type`, `MimeType` and `Encoding` attributes: These optional attributes describe the encrypted text. In our example, the plain text that was encrypted was an XML element. It is represented by `Type = http://www.w3.org/2001/04/xmlenc#Element`.

- `EncryptionMethod` element: This describes the algorithm used to encrypt the data. This element is of a type called `EncryptionMethodType` which is described later.

- `CipherData` element: This describes the encrypted text, i.e. the cipher text.

- `KeyInfo` element: This describes the encryption key used to encrypt the data.

EncryptionMethodType

The `EncryptionMethod` element described in the `EncryptedType` schema is of a data type called `EncryptionMethodType`. The `EncryptionMethodType` data type describes the information about the encryption method, such as algorithm and any other additional parameters based on the type, algorithm.

The `EncryptionMethodType` element should be generic enough to support both symmetric and asymmetric algorithms, and the schema is described as:

```
<complexType name='EncryptionMethodType' mixed='true'>
  <sequence>
    <element name='KeySize' minOccurs='0' type='xenc:KeySizeType'/>
    <element name='OAEPparams' minOccurs='0' type='base64Binary'/>
```

```
            <any namespace='##other' minOccurs='0' maxOccurs='unbounded'/>
        </sequence>
        <attribute name='Algorithm' type='anyURI' use='required'/>
    </complexType>
```

EncryptionMethodType Schema

The `Algorithm` attribute in the schema shown describes the encryption algorithm used. In our example, the algorithm used is Triple DES as shown in the following code..

```
<xenc:EncryptionMethod Algorithm="http://www.w3.org/2001/04/
xmlenc#tripledes-cbc"/>
```

Besides the `Algorithm` attribute, the `EncryptionMethod` can also have child elements such as `KeySize`, OAEP parameters, and any other additional elements. The OAEP parameters and any other XML elements are based on the value of the `Algorithm URI` attribute. For instance, the presence of `KeySize` element would make the schema invalid if the `Algorithm` attribute did not permit the `KeySize` element.

CipherData Element

The `CipherData` element is the one that actually describes the information regarding the cipher text. The typical encryption process is nothing but:

```
Plain Text + Encryption Algorithm = Cipher Text.
```

The cipher text is required in order to decrypt to obtain the plain text information. In the XML world, the `CipherData` element represents the information about cipher text, and the schema is described as:

```
<element name='CipherData' type='xenc:CipherDataType'/>
  <complexType name='CipherDataType'>
    <choice>
      <element name='CipherValue' type='base64Binary'/>
      <element ref='xenc:CipherReference'/>
    </choice>
  </complexType>
```

As you can see from the schema, the `CipherData` element can either contain the `CipherValue` element or a reference to the cipher value by means of `CipherReference`. (Note: the `choice` element is an XML syntax to make a selection among the list of choices.)

`CipherValue` element describes the encrypted text in base64 binary and the `CipherReference` element is a reference to URI where the cipher text can be found. In our `EncryptedData` example, the cipher text is represented by `CipherValue` element in **base64** binary format as shown in the following code.

```
<xenc:CipherData>          <xenc:CipherValue>nrNckdqE5O1CCZkjA0RM9s7mOYv
8t4QUJ/tE1ONdfUe8zWaXeJuDYA15dQ4Ypfpu</xenc:CipherValue>
     </xenc:CipherData>
```

EncryptedKey Element

The `EncryptedData` element describes information about the cipher text, algorithm and the encryption key. When the encryption key is a symmetric key, both the sender and recipient should share the encryption key in an out of band mechanism. It will become increasingly difficult to share the encryption key when there are too many consumers accessing a web service that contains the encrypted information. It will also be a security risk to share the same encryption key across all the consumers. One possible way to address the key distribution is to encrypt the symmetric encryption key and the process would be:

- Symmetric key is generated at run time.
- Plain text is encrypted using the symmetric encryption key.
- Encryption key is then encrypted using the public key of the recipient.
- Encrypted encryption key is distributed along with the XML message (i.e. EncryptedKey).

Like `EncryptedData` element, the `EncryptedKey` element is also derived from the `EncryptedType` element. The `EncryptedKey` element represents the information about the encryption key in an encrypted format, along with additional information that is required to decrypt the `EncryptedData` element using the encryption key. The `EncryptedKey` element schema is described as:

```
<element name='EncryptedKey' type='xenc:EncryptedKeyType'/>
<complexType name='EncryptedKeyType'>
  <complexContent>
    <extension base='xenc:EncryptedType'>
      <sequence>
        <element ref='xenc:ReferenceList' minOccurs='0'/>
        <element name='CarriedKeyName' type='string' minOccurs='0'/>
      </sequence>
      <attribute name='Recipient' type='string' use='optional'/>
    </extension>
  </complexContent>
</complexType>
```

The `EncryptedKey` schema has the same elements and attributes as the `EncryptedData` element, with additional information such as `ReferenceList`, `CarriedKeyName` and `Recipient`.

The optional `ReferenceList` element can contain a list of references to data and keys that are encrypted using the enclosed encryption key. The `CarriedKeyName` and `Recipient` are also optional elements that can carry a friendly key name and any specific hint about the encryption key respectively.

KeyInfo Element

In order to decrypt the `EncryptedData` or `EncryptedKey` element, the recipient has to know about the encryption key. The recipient may already know about the encryption key, in which case there may not be any need to exchange the `KeyInfo` element. However, when the recipient does not know about the encryption key, the `KeyInfo` element can provide the necessary information so that recipient can decrypt the message.

In the case of symmetric key encryption, the recipient should know something about the encryption key in order to decrypt the `EncryptedData` element. In this case, the sender can attach a friendly `KeyName` as a part of the `KeyInfo` element as shown in the following code:

```
<dsig:KeyInfo xmlns:dsig="http://www.w3.org/2000/09/xmldsig#">
  <dsig:KeyName>TestKeyname</dsig:KeyName>
</dsig:KeyInfo>
```

In case of asymmetric key encryption, the sender can send information about the X509 certificate. The `KeyInfo` element schema is described as:

```
<element name="KeyInfo" type="ds:KeyInfoType"/>
<complexType name="KeyInfoType" mixed="true">
  <choice maxOccurs="unbounded">
    <element ref="ds:KeyName"/>
    <element ref="ds:KeyValue"/>
    <element ref="ds:RetrievalMethod"/>
    <element ref="ds:X509Data"/>
    <element ref="ds:PGPData"/>
    <element ref="ds:SPKIData"/>
    <element ref="ds:MgmtData"/>
    <any processContents="lax" namespace="##other"/>
    <!-- (1,1) elements from (0,unbounded) namespaces -->
  </choice>
  <attribute name="Id" type="ID" use="optional"/>
</complexType>
```

Summary

The XML encryption schema addresses the interoperability issues in exchanging encrypted data and it adds a lot of value as a part of the WS-security specification. In the web services world, the confidential data is protected by encrypting the data and representing, as per XML encryption schema. In this chapter, we took a closer look at XML encryption schema, how the different elements are organized, represented and how they are linked together.

11
XML Signature

In any data exchange, the integrity of the message is very important—especially the ones that involve business critical data where any data changed by an intruder can affect the day-to-day business. One way to ensure that no one else tampered with the message (integrity) is to digitally sign the message. While digital signatures are not new, traditionally applications used tools such as PGP (pretty good privacy) to sign and verify messages. The drawback of PGP, or any other tool, is that it requires both the sender and recipient to use the same tool to sign and verify messages, which is a bottleneck in the web services world. In the web services world, the sender and recipient should be able to use any software tool and any algorithm they like to generate and verify messages, as long as the signed messages are represented in an industry standard way. XML signature is an interoperable industry standard from W3C that addresses how the digitally-signed messages are represented or described in an XML format. Oracle WSM can digitally sign and verify the web service messages. In this chapter, we will take a closer look at XML signature specification from W3C.

XML Signature and Web Services

The integrity of data can only be ensured by creating a digest of the message and then encrypting the digest value, i.e. digitally signing the message. Now in order for the recipient to validate the signature, the recipient has to know:

- What parts of the message were digitally signed.
- What digest algorithm was used.
- Where the encrypted digest value is.
- What algorithm was used to encrypt the digest value.

In the web services world, it is not feasible to communicate where the digest values are described in the XML message, what algorithm is used to create the digest, etc. All the information that is required for the recipient to successfully validate the digital signature should be described in such a way that any recipient is able to validate the signature.

The XML signature specification from W3C addresses how the digital signature information is represented in an extensible mark up language format so that the recipient can understand:

- What parts of the XML message are digitally signed.
- What digest algorithm was used to create the digest value.
- What algorithm was used to digitally sign the message.
- Where is the key information is located within the XML message.

The XML signature schema describes the syntax about how the digital signature information should be described in an XML document and how it fits within the WS-security framework to ensure the integrity of messages. In the next section, we will describe in detail the XML signature schema and how it is used in WS-security to represent the signature.

XML Signature Schema

The XML signature schema is a W3C standard that describes how the digital signature information is represented in an XML document. XML signature schema can not only describe the digital signature of an XML element or XML element content, but also an image or an externally-referenced entity. In any case, the recipient of the XML signature message has to know:

- Data that is being signed.
- Digest value of that data.
- Digest algorithm used.
- Digital signature information, such as signature value, key information.

The digitally-signed message that adheres to the XML signature schema always starts with a **signature** XML element which contains the following main child elements:

- SignedInfo
- SignatureValue
- KeyInfo
- Object

The mentioned XML elements can have there own child elements that can specify additional instructions to process the digitally-signed message. The following figure shows an overview of the XML signature schema with the signature element as the root element and its child elements. The figure also shows the order in which those elements appear, which is very important, as described in the XML signature schema.

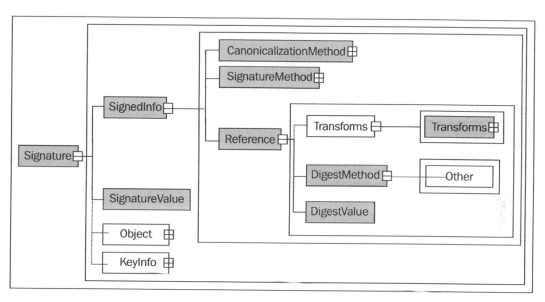

When the digital signature is applied on the web service message, the signature element is inserted, which contains the reference to the data that is signed along with digest value, signature value and key information, as shown by the following code.

```
<?xml version="1.0" encoding="UTF-8"?>
<soap:Envelope soap:encodingStyle="http://schemas.xmlsoap.org/
soap/encoding/" xmlns:xsi="http://www.w3.org/2001/XMLSchema-
instance" xmlns:xsd="http://www.w3.org/2001/XMLSchema" xmlns:
soap="http://schemas.xmlsoap.org/soap/envelope/" xmlns:
soapenc="http://schemas.xmlsoap.org/soap/encoding/">
    <soap:Header>
        <wsse:Security xmlns:wsse="http://docs.oasis-open.
org/wss/2004/01/oasis-200401-wss-wssecurity-secext-1.0.xsd"
xmlns="http://docs.oasis-open.org/wss/2004/01/oasis-200401-wss-
wssecurity-secext-1.0.xsd" soap:mustUnderstand="1">
            <wsse:BinarySecurityToken ValueType="http://docs.
```

```
oasis-open.org/wss/2004/01/oasis-200401-wss-x509-token-profile-
1.0#X509v3" EncodingType="http://docs.oasis-open.org/wss/2004/01/
oasis-200401-wss-soap-message-security-1.0#Base64Binary" wsu:
Id="_VLL9yEsi09I9f5ihwae2lQ22" xmlns:wsu="http://docs.oasis-open.
org/wss/2004/01/oasis-200401-wss-wssecurity-utility-1.0.xsd">Secur
ityTOkenoKE2ZA==</wsse:BinarySecurityToken>
                    <dsig:Signature xmlns="http://www.w3.org/2000/09/
xmldsig#" xmlns:dsig="http://www.w3.org/2000/09/xmldsig#">
                      <dsig:SignedInfo>
                        <dsig:CanonicalizationMethod
Algorithm="http://www.w3.org/2001/10/xml-exc-c14n#"/>
                        <dsig:SignatureMethod
Algorithm="http://www.w3.org/2000/09/xmldsig#rsa-sha1"/>
                        <dsig:Reference URI="#ishUwYWW2AAthrx
hlpv1CA22">
                          <dsig:Transforms>
                            <dsig:Transform
Algorithm="http://www.w3.org/2001/10/xml-exc-c14n#"/>
                          </dsig:Transforms>
                          <dsig:DigestMethod
Algorithm="http://www.w3.org/2000/09/xmldsig#sha1"/>
                          <dsig:DigestValue>ynuqANuYM3qzh
dTnGOLT7SMxWHY=</dsig:DigestValue>
                        </dsig:Reference>
                        <dsig:Reference URI="#UljvWiL8yjedImz
6zy0pHQ22">
                          <dsig:Transforms>
                            <dsig:Transform
Algorithm="http://www.w3.org/2001/10/xml-exc-c14n#"/>
                          </dsig:Transforms>
                          <dsig:DigestMethod
Algorithm="http://www.w3.org/2000/09/xmldsig#sha1"/>
                          <dsig:DigestValue>9ZebvrbVYLiPZ
v1BaVLDaLJVhwo=</dsig:DigestValue>
                        </dsig:Reference>
                      </dsig:SignedInfo>
                      <dsig:SignatureValue>QqmUUZDLNeLpAEFXndiBLk=
</dsig:SignatureValue>
                      <dsig:KeyInfo>
                        <wsse:SecurityTokenReference
xmlns="http://docs.oasis-open.org/wss/2004/01/oasis-200401-wss-
wssecurity-secext-1.0.xsd" wsu:Id="_7vjdWs1ABULkiLeE7Y4lAg22"
xmlns:wsu="http://docs.oasis-open.org/wss/2004/01/oasis-200401-
wss-wssecurity-utility-1.0.xsd">
```

```
                                    <wsse:Reference URI="#_
VLL9yEsi09I9f5ihwae2lQ22"/>
                           </wsse:SecurityTokenReference>
                    </dsig:KeyInfo>
             </dsig:Signature>
             <wsu:Timestamp xmlns:wsu="http://docs.oasis-open.
org/wss/2004/01/oasis-200401-wss-wssecurity-utility-1.0.xsd"
xmlns="http://docs.oasis-open.org/wss/2004/01/oasis-200401-wss-
wssecurity-utility-1.0.xsd" wsu:Id="UljvWiL8yjedImz6zy0pHQ22">
                     <wsu:Created>2007-11-16T15:13:48Z</wsu:
Created>
             </wsu:Timestamp>
        </wsse:Security>
    </soap:Header>
    <soap:Body wsu:Id="ishUwYWW2AAthrxhlpv1CA22" xmlns:wsu="http://
docs.oasis-open.org/wss/2004/01/oasis-200401-wss-wssecurity-
utility-1.0.xsd">
         <n:getTimeResponse xmlns:n="urn:Test:GetTime">
             <Result xsi:type="xsd:string">10:13 AM</Result>
         </n:getTimeResponse>
    </soap:Body>
</soap:Envelope>
```

The above example is taken from Chapter 6 where the web service response was digitally signed. In this chapter, we will be talking a closer look at the Signature element. In order to understand how the Signature element was formed and how the options that you select in the Oracle WSM signature policy step can affect the signed message, we will take a closer look at the XML signature schema elements in detail.

Signature Element

The Signature element is the root XML element, as per the XML signature schema that contains information such as:

- **SignedInfo**—Information about which data elements were signed and the transformations that were applied before the digest value was generated.

- **SignatureValue**—Base 64 encoded digital signature value.

- **KeyInfo**—Optional element that describes the key that was used to sign the message.

- **Object**—Optional element which can embed the actual data object itself, if required.

- **Id**—Id attribute that uniquely identifies the signature element inside the XML document.

The **Signature** element schema can be described as:

```
<element name="Signature" type="ds:SignatureType"/>
<complexType name="SignatureType">
  <sequence>
    <element ref="ds:SignedInfo"/>
    <element ref="ds:SignatureValue"/>
    <element ref="ds:KeyInfo" minOccurs="0"/>
    <element ref="ds:Object" minOccurs="0" maxOccurs="unbounded"/>
  </sequence>
  <attribute name="Id" type="ID" use="optional"/>
</complexType>
```

SignedInfo Element

`SignedInfo` element contains the maximum information about the digital signature such as the reference to the data being signed, list of transformations applied to the data, digest value, etc. The `SignedInfo` element schema is described as:

```
<element name="SignedInfo" type="ds:SignedInfoType"/>
  <complexType name="SignedInfoType">
    <sequence>
      <element ref="ds:CanonicalizationMethod"/>
      <element ref="ds:SignatureMethod"/>
      <element ref="ds:Reference" maxOccurs="unbounded"/>
    </sequence>
    <attribute name="Id" type="ID" use="optional"/>
  </complexType>
```

The `SignedInfo` element contains:

- **CanonicalizationMethod**: Element that describes the canonicalization algorithm that is applied. There are actually four types of canonicalization algorithms—C14n, C14n with comments, exclusive C14n, and exclusive C14n with comments.

- **SignatureMethod**: It describes the signature algorithm used, along with any additional information about the algorithm.

- **Reference**: The `Reference` element holds references to the data element and its associated digest value.

Reference Element

The `Reference` element that is a part of the `SignedInfo` element contains the digest value of the data being signed along with a list of transformations that were applied to the data. The `Reference` element schema is described as:

```
<element name="Reference" type="ds:ReferenceType"/>
  <complexType name="ReferenceType">
    <sequence>
      <element ref="ds:Transforms" minOccurs="0"/>
      <element ref="ds:DigestMethod"/>
      <element ref="ds:DigestValue"/>
    </sequence>
    <attribute name="Id" type="ID" use="optional"/>
    <attribute name="URI" type="anyURI" use="optional"/>
    <attribute name="Type" type="anyURI" use="optional"/>
  </complexType>
```

The `Reference` element typically describes the digest value and the digest method that is used to create the digest value. It also describes the data upon which the digest algorithm is applied and the list of transformations that were applied. In the `Reference` element schema:

- `URI` attribute describes the reference to the data that is being digitally signed.

- `Transforms` element describes the list of transformations that are applied to the data. One can apply XSL transformation or any other transformation to derive the actual data from the referenced URI.

- `DigestMethod` element describes the algorithm used to create the digest value.

- `DigestValue` element is the Base 64 encoded digest value.

The following example shows the `Reference` element, which is a part of the web service response message that was digitally signed.

```
<dsig:Reference URI="#UljvWiL8yjedImz6zy0pHQ22">
                    <dsig:Transforms>
                            <dsig:Transform
Algorithm="http://www.w3.org/2001/10/xml-exc-c14n#"/>
                    </dsig:Transforms>
                    <dsig:DigestMethod
Algorithm="http://www.w3.org/2000/09/xmldsig#sha1"/>
                    <dsig:DigestValue>9ZebvrbVYLiPZ
v1BaVLDaLJVhwo=</dsig:DigestValue>
            </dsig:Reference>
        </dsig:SignedInfo>
```

In the example, the URI value `UljvWiL8yjedImz6zy0pHQ22` points to the data within the web service message. The `Transforms` element contains `Transform` element that describes the exclusive C14 algorithm as described by the following code.

```
<dsig:Transforms>
    <dsig:Transform
Algorithm="http://www.w3.org/2001/10/xml-exc-c14n#"/>
    </dsig:Transforms>
```

What this means is that exclusive canonical transformation is applied to the data referenced by the URI, and then the digest algorithm is applied. The `DigestMethod` shows that it is a SHA1 algorithm and the actual digest value is described in the `DigestValue` element.

Transforms Element

The `Transforms` element contains a list of transformations that are applied to the data before the digest value is calculated. The Transforms schema is described as:

```
<element name="Transforms" type="ds:TransformsType"/>
<complexType name="TransformsType">
  <sequence>
    <element ref="ds:Transform" maxOccurs="unbounded"/>
  </sequence>
</complexType>
<element name="Transform" type="ds:TransformType"/>
<complexType name="TransformType" mixed="true">
  <choice minOccurs="0" maxOccurs="unbounded">
    <any namespace="##other" processContents="lax"/>
    <!-- (1,1) elements from (0,unbounded) namespaces -->
    <element name="XPath" type="string"/>
  </choice>
  <attribute name="Algorithm" type="anyURI" use="required"/>
</complexType>
```

The digest value is unique on the data that is applied. So when the recipient has to validate the signature, the digest algorithm should be applied over the same data to get the exact digest value.

Consider, for example, that the web service response (or request) message can have a lot of information and there may be only a portion of the XML message that is critical for the business to ensure the message integrity. In this case, either XSL transformation or Xpath can be applied to select only a portion of the message.

KeyInfo Element

In order to verify the digital signature, the recipient should have access to the sender's public key. The sender can either send the actual public key itself as a part the XML signature message, or can send enough information to derive the key. In either case, web services that contain the digitally-signed message should contain information about the sender's public key. The KeyInfo element schema is described as:

```
<element name="KeyInfo" type="ds:KeyInfoType"/>
<complexType name="KeyInfoType" mixed="true">
  <choice maxOccurs="unbounded">
    <element ref="ds:KeyName"/>
    <element ref="ds:KeyValue"/>
    <element ref="ds:RetrievalMethod"/>
    <element ref="ds:X509Data"/>
    <element ref="ds:PGPData"/>
    <element ref="ds:SPKIData"/>
    <element ref="ds:MgmtData"/>
    <any processContents="lax" namespace="##other"/>
    <!-- (1,1) elements from (0,unbounded) namespaces -->
  </choice>
  <attribute name="Id" type="ID" use="optional"/>
</complexType>
```

It is very clear from the KeyInfo element schema that the X509 certificate data itself can be sent as a part of the X509Data element or just a reference to the certificate can be sent as a part of the KeyName element.

Summary

The XML signature specification from W3C addresses the interoperability challenges in exchanging the digital signature information between two different applications. In this chapter, we looked at different components of the XML signature and how they are related to each other in forming a meaningful XML signature message. XML signature is widely used in web services security as a mechanism to ensure the integrity of the message. In the previous chapter, we discussed XML encryption and the interoperable standard to exchange the encrypted information. Both XML encryption and XML signature play a significant part in web services security, either individually or in combination. In the next chapter, we will discuss in detail how to sign and encrypt the web service message in one transaction.

12
Sign and Encrypt

In the earlier chapters, we learned how Oracle Web Services Manager can be leveraged to digitally sign and encrypt messages to ensure the integrity and confidentiality of the data. But at times it is necessary to sign and encrypt the same message and in this chapter, we will discuss how to sign and encrypt using Oracle Web Services Manager.

Overview of Sign and Encrypt

Let's consider the example of a web service which accepts credit card details to charge to that credit card and that is being consumed by an online electronics web site. In this type of transaction it is important to ensure that the:

- Credit card number, expiration date, amount, etc, were sent from an authorized consumer, i.e. electronics web site, and the data was not modified by any one other than the electronics company.
- Credit card details are kept confidential over the wire.

In order to ensure that the credit card data was not modified by anyone other than the electronics company web site, the message should be digitally signed, and in order to ensure the confidentiality of the credit card details, the message should be encrypted. While we have discussed how to digitally sign and encrypt the message, we have not explored which one should happen first.

While signature and encryption can happen in any order, it is important to understand the impact of the order in which the signature and encryption are applied. In our example, we can either encrypt the credit card details and then sign the encrypted data or sign the credit card details and then encrypt the data.

When the credit card information is encrypted first and the encrypted data is then digitally signed, the digital signature is applied over the encrypted data, not on the actual credit card details. In other words, the signature only ensures that the encrypted data is not tampered with, but it does not ensure the integrity of the actual plain text, i.e. credit card details.

Now when the credit card information is signed first and then encrypted, it ensures that no one else tampered with the original credit card details and that the information is also kept confidential by means of encryption.

In Oracle Web Services Manager, there is a built-in policy step called "sign and encrypt" which will digitally sign the message first and then perform the encryption. In the next section, we will describe in detail how to configure the policy for a web service to sign and encrypt, and also a policy for web services to decrypt and verify a signature.

Signing and Encrypting Message

In Oracle Web Services Manager, it is easy to sign and encrypt the SOAP messages in just one policy step. Let's consider an example where you want to access an external web service, and the request should be digitally signed first and then encrypted. In this case, the sign and encrypt policy step can be added in the request pipeline so that the messages are digitally signed and then encrypted. The following screenshot shows how the **Sign Message And Encrypt** step can be added to the **Request** pipeline.

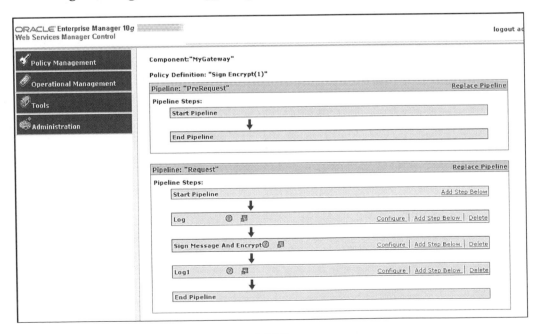

Now if you click to configure the **Sign Message And Encrypt** policy step, you have to enter two sets of information:

- One set of information to digitally sign the message
- Another set of information to encrypt the signed message

In the following screenshot, you can see how to configure the **Sign Message And Encrypt** policy step.

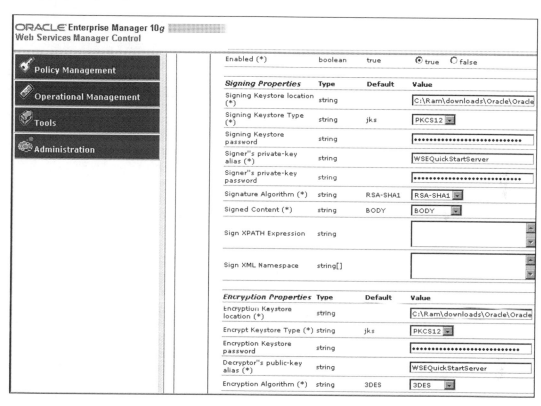

The **Signing Properties** information is used to digitally sign the data. In this case, you have to enter the **PKCS12** key store location and password along with the password to access the private key. A private key is required as the data will be digitally signed.

The Encryption Properties information is used to encrypt the message. In this case, you have to enter the key store location, keystore type, public key from keystore file and the algorithm used to encrypt the data.

The following steps happen within the sign and encrypt step when Oracle WSM digitally signs the message and then encrypts the data.

- The request message is first digitally signed.
  - Message is digitally hashed first.
  - Digitally signed using the sender's private key.
- The signature is then encrypted.
  - A new symmetric key is generated at run time.
  - The signature element (digital signature data) is then encrypted using the symmetric key.
  - The encrypted symmetric key is then encrypted using the public key of the recipient.
- The EncryptedData element is then sent along with the message.

Once Oracle WSM receives the signed and encrypted message, it can then decrypt the message and validate the signature before proceeding further, and Oracle WSM will perform the following steps:

- The SOAP message will decrypt the encrypted data first using the private key of the recipient.
- The digital signature is regenerated using the public key of the recipient.
- The signature value is compared and validated with the one that was decrypted.

In the following sample XML message, the web service request to get the time is first digitally signed and then encrypted. The SOAP body message now contains the encrypted value. But before the SOAP body was encrypted, it was digitally signed and attached to the SOAP header.

```
<?xml version="1.0" encoding="UTF-8"?>
<soap:Envelope xmlns:soap="http://schemas.xmlsoap.org/soap/envelope/"
xmlns:ns="urn:Test:GetTime" xmlns:xsd="http://www.w3.org/2001/
XMLSchema" xmlns:xsi="http://www.w3.org/2001/XMLSchema-instance"
xmlns:soapenc="http://schemas.xmlsoap.org/soap/encoding/">
    <soap:Header>
        <wsse:Security soap:mustUnderstand="1" xmlns:wsse="http://
docs.oasis-open.org/wss/2004/01/oasis-200401-wss-wssecurity-secext-
1.0.xsd" xmlns="http://docs.oasis-open.org/wss/2004/01/oasis-200401-
wss-wssecurity-secext-1.0.xsd">
            <wsse:BinarySecurityToken ValueType="http://docs.
oasis-open.org/wss/2004/01/oasis-200401-wss-x509-ten-profile-
1.0#X509v3" EncodingType="http://docs.oasis-open.org/wss/2004/01/
oasis-200401-wss-soap-message-security-1.0#Base64Binary" wsu:Id="
```

```
aZlTmJt9p7wCfugDdlGweDA22" xmlns:wsu="http://docs.oasis-open.org/
wss/2004/01/oasis-200401-wss-wssecurity-utility-1.0.xsd">oKE2ZA==</
wsse:BinarySecurityToken>
                    <xenc:EncryptedKey xmlns="http://www.w3.org/2001/04/
xmlenc#" xmlns:xenc="http://www.w3.org/2001/04/xmlenc#">
                        <xenc:EncryptionMethod Algorithm="http://www.
w3.org/2001/04/xmlenc#rsa-1_5"/>
                        <dsig:KeyInfo xmlns:dsig="http://www.
w3.org/2000/09/xmldsig#">
                            <SecurityTokenReference xmlns="http://
docs.oasis-open.org/wss/2004/01/oasis-200401-wss-wssecurity-secext-
1.0.xsd">
                                <Reference URI="#aZlTmJt9p7wCfug
DdlGweDA22" ValueType="http://docs.oasis-open.org/wss/2004/01/oasis-
200401-wss-x509-token-profile-1.0#X509v3"/>
                            </SecurityTokenReference>
                        </dsig:KeyInfo>
                        <xenc:CipherData>
                            <xenc:CipherValue>jXyDqgTC0DvyXkS7lz+Qq1
P2MMG4G5W5zy4D3K2s+S2b7o=</xenc:CipherValue>
                        </xenc:CipherData>
                        <xenc:ReferenceList>
                            <xenc:DataReference URI="#_
4LDVnkQFr3DlbkZFa91f2w22"/>
                        </xenc:ReferenceList>
                    </xenc:EncryptedKey>
                    <wsse:BinarySecurityToken ValueType="http://docs.
oasis-open.org/wss/2004/01/oasis-200401-wss-x509-token-profile-
1.0#X509v3" EncodingType="http://docs.oasis-open.org/wss/2004/01/
oasis-200401-wss-soap-message-security-1.0#Base64Binary" wsu:Id="_
w4lpzuDj1hb1czr0ptHCeg22" xmlns:wsu="http://docs.oasis-open.org/
wss/2004/01/oasis-200401-wss-wssecurity-utility-1.0.xsd"\KE2ZA==</
wsse:BinarySecurityToken>
                    <dsig:Signature xmlns="http://www.w3.org/2000/09/
xmldsig#" xmlns:dsig="http://www.w3.org/2000/09/xmldsig#">
                        <dsig:SignedInfo>
                            <dsig:CanonicalizationMethod
Algorithm="http://www.w3.org/2001/10/xml-exc-c14n#"/>
                            <dsig:SignatureMethod Algorithm="http://
www.w3.org/2000/09/xmldsig#rsa-sha1"/>
                            <dsig:Reference URI="#BUHXr0pEKOjsguyWzr
KrHA22">
                                <dsig:Transforms>
                                    <dsig:Transform
Algorithm="http://www.w3.org/2001/10/xml-exc-c14n#"/>
                                </dsig:Transforms>
                                <dsig:DigestMethod
```

```
Algorithm="http://www.w3.org/2000/09/xmldsig#sha1"/>
                                <dsig:DigestValue>DLzrUyWQmjl+Hjh
z9ZEomPOLeaU=</dsig:DigestValue>
                            </dsig:Reference>
                            <dsig:Reference URI="#wdETzbUTVeZq50drbm
Wcsw22">
                                <dsig:Transforms>
                                    <dsig:Transform
Algorithm="http://www.w3.org/2001/10/xml-exc-c14n#"/>
                                </dsig:Transforms>
                                <dsig:DigestMethod
Algorithm="http://www.w3.org/2000/09/xmldsig#sha1"/>
                                <dsig:DigestValue>OPseOpadhqa8VsB
HaH+ZLyPwG1g=</dsig:DigestValue>
                            </dsig:Reference>
                        </dsig:SignedInfo>
                        <dsig:SignatureValue>MWlJjuHw6y0L9YdEtclgYykuN
AtjEcScJK8l4y4ooAe+N4=</dsig:SignatureValue>
                        <dsig:KeyInfo>
                            <SecurityTokenReference wsu:Id="_
wfQx1sqYwS1KqOfQ0DPd9Q22" xmlns="http://docs.oasis-open.org/
wss/2004/01/oasis-200401-wss-wssecurity-secext-1.0.xsd" xmlns:
wsu="http://docs.oasis-open.org/wss/2004/01/oasis-200401-wss-
wssecurity-utility-1.0.xsd">
                                <Reference URI="#_
w4lpzuDj1hb1czr0ptHCeg22"/>
                            </SecurityTokenReference>
                        </dsig:KeyInfo>
                    </dsig:Signature>
                    <wsu:Timestamp wsu:Id="wdETzbUTVeZq50drbmWcsw22"
xmlns:wsu="http://docs.oasis-open.org/wss/2004/01/oasis-200401-
wss-wssecurity-utility-1.0.xsd" xmlns="http://docs.oasis-open.org/
wss/2004/01/oasis-200401-wss-wssecurity-utility-1.0.xsd">
                            <wsu:Created>2007-12-04T02:49:19Z</wsu:
Created>
                    </wsu:Timestamp>
            </wsse:Security>
    </soap:Header>
    <soap:Body soap:encodingStyle="http://schemas.xmlsoap.org/soap/
encoding/" wsu:Id="BUHXr0pEKOjsguyWzrKrHA22" xmlns:wsu="http://docs.
oasis-open.org/wss/2004/01/oasis-200401-wss-wssecurity-utility-
1.0.xsd">
            <xenc:EncryptedData Type="http://www.w3.org/2001/04/
xmlenc#Content" Id="_4LDVnkQFr3DlbkZFa91f2w22" xmlns="http://www.
w3.org/2001/04/xmlenc#" xmlns:xenc="http://www.w3.org/2001/04/
xmlenc#">
```

```
                <xenc:EncryptionMethod Algorithm="http://www.
w3.org/2001/04/xmlenc#tripledes-cbc"/>
                <xenc:CipherData>
                    <xenc:CipherValue>\kzSqksyBm0e6LpxIDxYkJ+jccr
ldMuupLRYkqwIzasMTJ6rzVsfirYlQpaSUiJCq/SfyvOLiWLkPeEJlxmPig6o=</xenc:
CipherValue>
                </xenc:CipherData>
            </xenc:EncryptedData>
        </soap:Body>
</soap:Envelope>
```

Once the web services receive the above SOAP message, it will first decrypt it and then calculate the digital signature to find the match. Once the signature value matches, it is assumed that the data was not tampered with by anyone else. With Oracle WSM it is also easy to configure the decrypt and verify policy step to decrypt the message and then validate the signature. We will take a look at how to leverage Oracle WSM to both sign and encrypt and also to decrypt, and verify, in the next section with an example.

Sign and Encrypt by Example

In the web services world, it is not uncommon to exchange messages that are confidential, and at the same time, the integrity of the message should be protected. When both signature and encryption are involved, both the web service and the consumer application should be capable enough to sign, encrypt, decrypt and verify signatures. In this section, we will explore in detail how Oracle Web Services Manager can be leveraged to sign and encrypt, and also to decrypt and verify signature.

Example Overview

The example that we will be using in this chapter is the same time web service where the web service request is digitally signed and then encrypted. The web service will decrypt the data and then will validate the signature before processing the request. This can be summarized as:

- Time web service will validate if the incoming SOAP request is digitally signed and encrypted.
- Decrypt the message.
- Validate the signature of the decrypted data.

Consumer application (client application) will:

- Digitally sign the SOAP body of the request.
- Encrypt the SOAP body.

In this example, we will not be using any Microsoft application as a client application. We will use Oracle WSM to actually sign and encrypt the SOAP request to the time web service. By doing this, we will also be showing how Oracle WSM can be leveraged to centralize security operations of an external web service.

Time Web Service: Decrypt and Verify Signature

The web service, time service in our example, is configured to expect that the incoming SOAP request is digitally signed and then encrypted. The service should be able to decrypt and then validate the signature before the request is processed. Such configuration can be done easily with Oracle WSM by adding the Decrypt and Verify Signature policy step to the request message.

Once the web service is registered within Oracle Web Service Manager Gateway, the policy attached to the service can be modified to include the decrypt and verify signature. Let's consider for instance that the **Service ID** that was generated for this web service is SID0030256; the policy for this service can be modified to include the **Decrypt and Verify Signature** step (refer to the following screenshot).

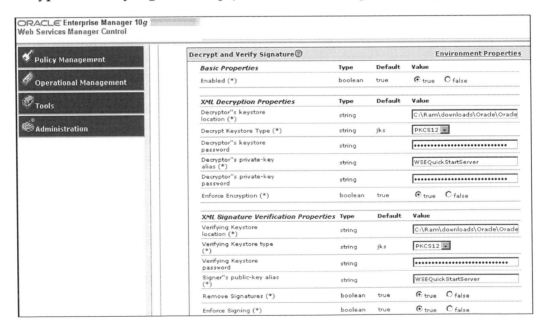

In the figure, the decrypt and verify signature policy step is enabled and the SOAP request decrypted using the **PKCS12** certificate found at the specified location (Decryptor keystore location), with the keystore password of **test123**. The **Enforce Encryption** option describes that the encryption should be enforced.

The **XML Signature Verification Properties** section contains information about the location of the certificate, keystore password and the type of key store. This section also has the option to strictly enforce a signature and can also remove a signature value after validation.

Now that we have configured Oracle WSM to decrypt and verify the signature of an incoming SOAP message, we can now explore how Oracle WSM can be configured to sign and encrypt SOAP requests. The web service URL that is expecting a signed and encrypted SOAP request is `http://owsm.packtpub.com:3115/gateway/services/SID00256?WSDL`

Beauty of Oracle WSM Gateway: Sign And Encrypt by Oracle WSM

A client application such as Microsoft .NET or Java should digitally sign the SOAP message and encrypt before invoking the web service. However, in order to sign and encrypt a SOAP message, the client application should:

- Manage the private key of the client organization/application.
- Manage the public key of the service provider organization.

When an organization is digitally signing all SOAP messages, and when there are multiple client applications, it becomes a challenge and a security risk to manage the private key deployment across all the applications.

With Oracle Web Services Manager, service consumer organization can centrally manage all the security policies of the web services that it interacts with. This provides a scalable architecture where all the client applications can interact with Oracle WSM Gateway and the gateway can enforce the security policy. The following diagram show the architecture where Oracle WSM is used in both service provider and service consumer ends.

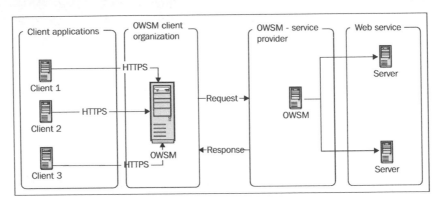

In the diagram, the client applications at the service consumer end talk to Oracle WSM Gateway over HTTPS and the Oracle WSM talks to the web service at the service provider end. The Oracle WSM at the service provider will enforce the security policies before the service is executed.

Note: Instead of the gateways, you can either use Oracle WSM client agents or any other third party software that supports WS-security standards (e.g. WSE from Microsoft, Glassfish from Sun, etc.)

In our example, the time web service is protected by Oracle WSM which will enforce the security policy that the incoming SOAP request should be digitally signed and encrypted. The following steps describe how Oracle WSM can be leveraged at both service provider and consumer side to enforce security policy to access the time service.

Service Provider:

- Web service is deployed inside the application server.
- Web service is registered with Oracle Web Services Manager Gateway.
- Policy is modified to decrypt and validate signature.
- The new URL (Service ID of Oracle WSM) is published to the consumer. (In our example it will be `http://owsm.packtpub.com:3115/gateway/services/SID00256?WSDL`)

Service Consumer:

- Service consumer is also using Oracle Web Services Manager.
- The WSDL URL is registered within Oracle WSM.
- Oracle WSM will create another URL with the service ID.
- Policy is modified to sign the message and then encrypt:
    - The Request policy step is modified to include the sign and encrypt policy step.
- Client application such as .NET or Java will invoke the new web service URL (for example, it could be SID00259?WSDL).

Note: In this example, this can be tested within the same Oracle WSM installation.

Sign And Encrypt Policy

The web service URL is registered within Oracle WSM and then the policy is modified to sign and encrypt the message. The web service URL, `http://owsm.packtpub.com:3115/gateway/services/SID00256?WSDL` is now registered within Oracle WSM. The Request policy step of the web service policy in Oracle WSM is modified to include the **Sign and Encrypt** policy step. The following screenshot shows the steps to include the **Sign and Encrypt** policy step.

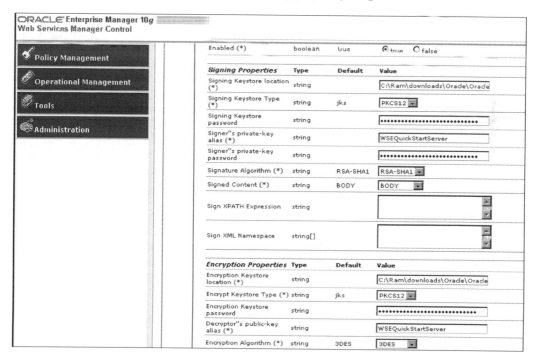

In the figure, the **Signing Properties** section has the key store location, the key store type, the password of the key store and the private key to digitally sign the message entries. The **Encryption Properties** section contains the information regarding the public key of the service provider, key store, and the password to encrypt the message.

Once the policy is created, when a client application makes the request, Oracle WSM will sign and encrypt the SOAP request message. The client application invokes the web service (in our example you can actually use Test Page from the Tools section by entering the WSDL URL and then just clicking invoke) invokes the web service:

- Client application invokes the new WSDL URL that points to the Oracle WSM Gateway.

- Oracle WSM Gateway will invoke the Request policy step and will sign and encrypt the message.

- Since the time web service URL is registered within Oracle WSM Gateway, the client gateway will invoke the time web service, which is signed and encrypted.

- Oracle WSM at the service provider will decrypt and validate the signature

- The request is passed to the actual time web service.

- Time web service will respond with the actual time.

Summary

In this chapter, we described two different things: one is how to digitally sign and encrypt the message (and decrypt and verify the signature); and also how Oracle WSM can be used at the consumer side to enforce or attach the required security credentials before invoking the web service.

13
Enterprise Security — Web Services and SSO

Web services security addresses the concerns regarding authentication, authorization, confidentiality and integrity, and Oracle Web Services Manager makes it easier to implement security in web services. However, in any organization, web services security is not the only security solution; it's probably one of the many security solutions they might have. Many times you have multiple LDAP directories, multiple authentication data stores, web access management (SSO) solutions, etc. When deploying the web services security solution, one should consider the enterprise security to provide an integrated security solution. In this chapter, we will take a closer look at the integrated web services security solution.

Web Services Security Components

By now you must be familiar with various components of web services security, such as authentication, authorization, encryption and signature. Before web services were widely adopted in organizations, there were different flavors of security systems that could authenticate and authorize users. Most of the authentication and authorization systems leverage LDAP compliant directory stores, such as Active Directory, Sun One, Novell eDirectory, etc. However there are systems that authenticate users against a traditional database such as Oracle or SQL Server. Authorization is either implemented as role-based access control, where role/group information is stored in the LDAP directory, or a custom implementation where user's privileges are checked against certain attributes or permissions.

Now with the advent of web services, the same user or system can be authenticated against existing credential store (be it database or active directory or eDirectory, etc.) before they can gain access to the web services. In order to reduce the support cost and leverage investment in an existing credential store, web services security components, i.e. authentication and authorization should be integrated with existing enterprise security systems. In the next few sections we will discuss:

- Leveraging investment in existing credential stores i.e. directories and databases.
- Integrating with access management solutions.
- Security token service.
- Integrated web services security architecture.

Authentication, Authorization and Credential Stores

Before web services were even introduced in the organization, there were various systems that authenticate and authorize users against a credential store, typically an LDAP compliant directory or database. Applications that take advantage of existing credential store, to authenticate its users now have to face the challenge of authenticating users who need access to its web services.

Oracle Web Services Manager supports various authentication options, including authenticating users against a file, active directory, or any other LDAP compliant directory. Maintaining a separate directory or file system to authenticate users to gain access to web services will become an additional maintenance effort.

In order to reduce the cost of maintaining a list of separate credential stores for each web service that is registered within Oracle WSM, it can actually authenticate users against existing credential stores, such as active directory or any other LDAP compliant directory. If an application is authenticating its users against a database and would like to authenticate the web services as well against the database, a custom authentication mechanism can be written to authenticate against the database.

Note: When organizations have different LDAP directories and databases as their credential stores, they can all be combined to form a virtual directory tree using any virtual directory product such as Oracle Virtual Directory, Radiant Logic, Symlabs, etc. Once a virtual directory layer is created, Oracle WSM can authenticate against that directory (all virtual directory products expose LDAP v3 compliant interface). Virtual directory topic is outside the scope of this book.

Integrating with Web Access Management Solution

Web access management solutions are deployed primarily to:

- Provide a single sign-on experience to end users.

- Centrally manage resources and their access policies to enforce better access control.

While the access management product eliminates multiple username and passwords and centralizes access control enforcement, they are mainly intended for web applications. On the other hand, web services were being deployed to integrate better with existing applications. The security of the web services was often left to be implemented either with the web service provider or with a web service security product such as Oracle Web Services Manager. What makes it more interesting is that the web services were being invoked from the web applications that are protected by web access management products.

Let's take a closer look at how the web access management products enforce access control for web applications. A Typical web access management product has the following components:

- Policy server to manage the access policies.

- Policy enforcement point where the access policies are enforced.

A typical policy enforcement point is usually an ISAPI filter or agent sitting on the web server which will:

- Intercept the request to web application.

- Validate if the user is authorized to access or not.

- Validate if the user is authenticated, if it requires authorization.

- Present the user with a login page, if he is not authenticated.

- Validate the credentials the user has entered against the data store

- Create an encrypted cookie (i.e. single sign on cookie).

- Validate whether the user is authorized to access the requested resource (i.e.: web page).

- Allow the user to perform the action (e.g: view the page) if user has privileges.

A web services security product such as Oracle WSM also performs similar steps to make sure that the user has enough privileges before the web service operation is performed. Oracle WSM will:

- Extract credentials from the web service message (typically from SOAP header).
- Validate the credentials.
- Validate if the user has appropriate privileges to perform the operation.
- Allow the web service operation, if yes.

Now let's take a closer look at where a web service is invoked from a web application. In this case, the web application is protected (i.e. security is enforced) by a web access management product. Let's consider an example where a credit card payment web service is invoked from a shopping web site (or a customer update web service is invoked from a CRM application). In order to effectively secure both the web application and the web service, both should authenticate, i.e. validate the end user before any operation is allowed. The web application is protected by the web access management product, which will validate the user credential and then create a SSO token (i.e. cookie). The challenge is that when the web service is invoked on a button click from the web application, the web service has to authenticate (or identify) the end user and not the server/web application that is making the web service call. It can be easily addressed by using the SSO token to authenticate the web service access.

Authentication based on the SSO token (i.e. SSO cookie) actually leverages the existing investment in web access management platforms and also provides a means to centralize the access policies for web services as well. When SSO token is used to authenticate the web services, the various interactions that happen between the user, the web application, web access management, and Oracle WSM are:

- Web application protected by Web Access Management (WAM) product such as Oracle Access Manager (or Siteminder).
- User enters credentials (username and password).
- WAM product will validate the credentials.
- WAM product will create the SSO token (i.e. SSO cookie).
- Web service is invoked by the web application (on an event such as button click, form post, etc.)
- Oracle WSM client agent (or custom code) will insert the SSO token in the SOAP message.
- Oracle WSM will validate the SSO token using WAM SDK (this will ensure that the SSO token is valid and that the user has permission to access the web service).

Let's take a closer look at the architecture that leverages both Oracle WSM and Oracle Access Manager (or Siteminder) in the same organization to protect the web applications and web services. In this scenario, the various steps involved to enforce the access control will be:

- Install and configure web access management product.
- Configure the resource policies for the web application.
- Install and configure Oracle Web Services Manager.
- Configure the gateway, policy, etc.
- Install the Oracle WSM client agent on the client application (or a custom written one):
  - Client agent would insert the SSO token in the SOAP message.
- Install web access management SDK where the Oracle WSM is installed:
  - SDK and custom code would let you validate the SSO token against the web access management platform.

The various advantages of using SSO token to authenticate the web services are:

- Web service provider can authenticate the actual end user, not the web application that is acting as service consumer.
- Access policies can be configured within the web access management product itself (thus removing any additional access policy maintenance within Oracle WSM).

However, the disadvantages to using SSO token to authenticate web services are:

- Authentication is not based on any interoperable standards.
- Client applications that cannot provide the SSO token will be unable to consume the web service.
- Solution is only limited to the same internet domain and requires Oracle WSM and Oracle Access Manager.

The disadvantages actually introduce the challenge in integrating the web access management system with the web services security product, such as Oracle WSM, for authentication and authorization. In the next section we will look at how to overcome the challenge by means of Security Token Service.

Security Token Service: Bridging the GAP between WAM and Oracle WSM

One of the key challenges in integrating Oracle WSM with Oracle Access Manager (or any other web access management product) is that the each client (i.e. web service consumer) should have Oracle WSM client agent to insert the SSO token, and it does not provide any flexibility for web services to be consumed by someone who does not support Oracle WSM client agents.

The tight integration between Oracle WSM and web access management reduces the flexibility of expanding the service adoption with applications within organizations that cannot provide SSO cookie (Oracle Access Manager). One way to overcome this challenge is to break the tight integration and make it loosely coupled, but still support industry standards such as **Security Assertion Markup Language (SAML)**.

SAML is the interoperable industry standard that is widely used to federate identities across organizational boundaries. Web services security specification also adopted SAML as one of the authentication token profiles, and it is also supported by Oracle Web Services Manager.

In Oracle Web Services Manager, you can configure the authentication step to validate the SAML token, or you can write custom steps to validate any other token profiles that are part of WS-security. Once Oracle WSM authenticates, it can then authorize the users against Active Directory or any other directory store.

Now we know that web access management creates SSO token to track the authenticated users and Oracle WSM can authenticate based on SAML token profile (or other token profiles such as **UserName** token), we can integrate leverage Oracle WSM to convert the SSO token to SAML token and let the web services authenticate using SAML token.

Security token service gives flexibility to convert one token format to another format, so that it can bridge the gap between web access management systems and web services security products, such as Oracle WSM. The following figure show the interaction between user, web access management, STS and Oracle WSM.

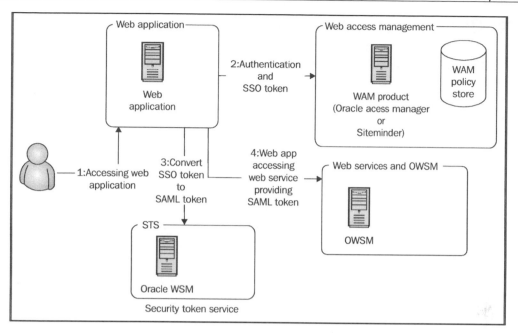

The figure show that Oracle WSM is used a security token service to convert the Web Access Management SSO token to a SAML token. SAML token is used by another Oracle WSM gateway or agent or native application to authenticate access to the web service. The advantages of using security token service are:

- Centralizes the token translation in one place (SAML 1.1 to SAML 2.0, SSO token to SAML, etc.)

- Gives flexibility for Oracle WSM to accept SAML and other types of token format without requiring all the clients to send the SSO token in a custom SOAP extension.

- End user identity is flown from web access management to Oracle WSM (e.g. John Doe login with "JDoe" and password; web access management creates a SSO token; Oracle WSM understands John Doe by means of SAML with JDoe as identifier, or UserName token with JDoe as identifier).

- Web applications can be protected by WAM products such as Siteminder, Sun Java Access Manager, Oracle Access Manager, etc.

You can use Oracle WSM just as a token service to convert tokens from SSO tokens (OAM or Siteminder) to SAML or any other tokens.

Integrated Security Architecture

Enterprise security architecture design should consider passing the end user identifier across all the layers, such as web application to back-end components, to web services, etc. The architecture design should also keep in mind the interoperability, and having a service to broker the authentication types should be an integral part of enterprise security architecture. The integrated security architecture design should consider having security token service to bridge the gap between web access management product and Oracle WSM. In this section, we will explore in detail how to use Oracle WSM to issue SAML tokens.

While security token service is based on WS-Trust specification, there are times where there is a need to convert from one token format to another token format when Oracle Web Services Manager is the only WS-Security product in the organization. In this section, we will take a closer look at Oracle WSM to issue SAML tokens.

Consider the scenario where your organization has Oracle Web Services Manager and your web application should access a web service outside of your organization (e.g. Amazon web service) that requires a SAML token profile to authenticate the user. The user interactions can be described as:

- User will authenticate with username and password to the web application.
- Web application has to invoke external web service.
- Web service requires a SAML token with user information.

While authenticating the user to the web application can be handled by custom or web access management products, Oracle WSM can be used to invoke the web service by attaching the SAML token profile. In order for Oracle WSM to issue a SAML token, we have to work around the way web services are imported into Oracle WSM. In an ideal situation, the external web service will be registered within Oracle WSM Gateway or agent, and the client application or client agent would be required to attach the SAML token.

Here we would like to demonstrate that Oracle WSM can be used to issue a SAML token without using client agents. In this case, we can do the following within Oracle WSM to issue the SAML token:

- Register the external web service within Oracle WSM gateway.
- Oracle WSM gateway will now create a new URL with a new WSDL description.

- Policy can be configured as:

    ° The first step of Request pipeline can extract credential and validate username and password.

    ° The last step of Request pipeline can be configured to insert SAML token profile.

Now the client application will invoke the internal Oracle WSM WSDL URL with their internal username and password. Oracle WSM will validate the username and password, and then attach a SAML token while accessing the external web service.

Integrated security architecture that bridges the gap between WAM and Oracle WSM will increase the security of the enterprise applications by passing the end user information across the application boundaries.

Summary

Web services security products such as Oracle WSM are focused on externalizing the security operations from the web service providers and consumers. Enterprise architecture should leverage products such as Oracle WSM to externalize the security operations such as authentication, authorization, encryption and signature, and at the same time support industry standards such as SAML for authentication. This chapter focused on integrating Oracle WSM with existing web access management products with or without using security token service. This book focused on how to use Oracle Web Services Manager to authenticate and authorize access to web services and also to protect the confidentiality and integrity of messages.

Index

About Packt Publishing

Packt, pronounced 'packed', published its first book "*Mastering phpMyAdmin for Effective MySQL Management*" in April 2004 and subsequently continued to specialize in publishing highly focused books on specific technologies and solutions.

Our books and publications share the experiences of your fellow IT professionals in adapting and customizing today's systems, applications, and frameworks. Our solution based books give you the knowledge and power to customize the software and technologies you're using to get the job done. Packt books are more specific and less general than the IT books you have seen in the past. Our unique business model allows us to bring you more focused information, giving you more of what you need to know, and less of what you don't.

Packt is a modern, yet unique publishing company, which focuses on producing quality, cutting-edge books for communities of developers, administrators, and newbies alike. For more information, please visit our website: www.packtpub.com.

Writing for Packt

We welcome all inquiries from people who are interested in authoring. Book proposals should be sent to authors@packtpub.com. If your book idea is still at an early stage and you would like to discuss it first before writing a formal book proposal, contact us; one of our commissioning editors will get in touch with you.

We're not just looking for published authors; if you have strong technical skills but no writing experience, our experienced editors can help you develop a writing career, or simply get some additional reward for your expertise.

Service Oriented Java Business Integration

ISBN: 978-1-847194-40-4   Paperback: 414 pages

Enterprise Service Bus integration solutions for Java developers

1. Vendor-independent integration of components and services through JBI explained with real-world examples

2. Hands-on guidance to ESB-based Integration of loosely coupled, pluggable services

3. Enterprise Integration Patterns (EIP) in action, in code

4. ESB integration solutions using Apache open-source tools

SOA Approach to Integration

ISBN: 1-904811-17-5   Paperback: 300 pages

XML, Web services, ESB, and BPEL in real-world SOA projects

1. Service-Oriented Architectures and SOA approach to integration

2. SOA architectural design and domain-specific models

3. Common Integration Patterns and how they can be best solved using Web services, BPEL and Enterprise Service Bus (ESB)

4. Concepts behind SOA standards, security, transactions, and how to efficiently work with XML

Please visit **www.PacktPub.com** for information on our titles

SOA and WS-BPEL

ISBN: 1-847192-70-X   Paperback: 250 pages

Composing Service-Oriented Architecture Solutions
with PHP and Open-Source ActiveBPEL

1. Build Web Services with PHP

2. Combine PHP Web Services into orchestrations
   with WS-BPEL

3. Use better WS-BPEL to enable parallel
   processing and asynchronous communication

4. Simplify WS-BPEL development with free
   graphical tool ActiveBPEL Designer

Business Process Execution Language for Web Services 2nd Edition

ISBN: 1904811817   Paperback: 350 pages

An Architects and Developers Guide to BPEL
and BPEL4WS

1. Architecture, syntax, development and
   composition of Business Processes and Services
   using BPEL

2. Advanced BPEL features such as compensation,
   concurrency, links, scopes, events, dynamic
   partner links, and correlations

3. Oracle BPEL Process Manager and BPEL
   Designer Microsoft BizTalk Server as
   a BPEL server

2494378

Made in the USA

MASTERING

MICROSOFT EXCHANGE 2000 SERVER

MASTERING™

MICROSOFT®
EXCHANGE 2000
SERVER

Barry Gerber

SYBEX®

San Francisco • Paris • Düsseldorf • Soest • London

Associate Publisher: Jordan Gold
Contracts and Licensing Manager: Kristine
    O'Callaghan
Acquisitions Editor: Maureen Adams
Developmental Editor: Tom Cirtin
Editor: Argosy
Production Editor: Argosy
Technical Editor: Ed Crowley
Book Designers: Patrick Dintino, Catalin Dulfu, Franz
    Baumhackl
Graphic Illustrator: Argosy
Electronic Publishing Specialist: Argosy
Proofreader: Argosy
Indexer: Ted Laux
Cover Designer: Design Site
Cover Illustrator/Photographer: Sergie Loobkoff

To Jane, my wife, best friend, and the best long-term care ombudsman the state of California has ever had, for reminding me in so many ways that technology should serve and not control humanity

ACKNOWLEDGMENTS

Microsoft's Exchange Server has come a long way since its first release in 1996. Keeping up with all the changes and tracking through all the beta and pre-release versions of Exchange 4.0, 5.0, and 5.5 was an adventure with all the peaks and dips of a world-class roller-coaster ride. Equally adventuresome was the production of this edition, which delves feet first into all the exciting new features of Windows 2000 Server and Exchange 2000 Server. Without the help and support of a number of fine people, Mastering Microsoft Exchange 2000 Server would never have happened.

Deepest thanks to the marketing folks at Microsoft and Microsoft's public relations support firm, Waggner Edstrom, for their early encouragement and continuing assistance in opening doors that I never even knew existed.

Words really cannot express both my indebtedness to and respect for the Exchange Server development teams I've worked with over the past six years. I'll never forget the patience they showed with my seemingly endless and not always well-articulated questions, especially as product delivery deadlines approached. My Exchange Book e-mail folder overflows with helpful, timely, and just-in-time responses from them all: Behrooz Chitsaz, Ken Ewert, Karim Battish, August Hahn, David Johnson, Bill Kilcullen, Eric Lockard, Mark Ledsome, David Lemson, Steve Masters, Tom McCann, Ramez Naam, Jim Reitz, Todd Roberts, Rob Sanfilippo, Elaine Sharp, Rob Shurtleff, Aaron Snow, Bill Sorinsin, Paul Waszkiewicz, Jeff Wilkes, and Rusty Williams.

Finally, my heartfelt and everlasting thanks to the team of editors who kept me honest and articulate through all editions of the book. John Read at Sybex listened to my ideas for the first edition and helped shape them into the book *Mastering Microsoft Exchange Server 4*. Peter Kuhns, Neil Edde, and Maureen Adams most ably managed editorial development on the other editions of the book. Tom Cirtin handled editorial development for this book, and he did so with intelligence and grace under considerable pressure. As I have done many times in e-mail, I welcome this opportunity to thank him once again for his help. Maureen Adams, Lorraine Fry, Ben Miller, Chad Mack, and Susan Berge were responsible for editorial production for the Exchange 4, 5, and 5.5 books. Cecelia Musselman and Krista Hansing took over this task for this book. Like Tom, they have made my job easier and have made it look like I'm a far better writer than I am. I'd also like to thank Argosy, the production team for this book. And last, but far from least, thanks to the technical editors who have kept me honest and on target: Eric Lockard (Exchange 4), Rob Sanfilippo (Exchange 5 and 5.5 first edition), Don Fuller (Exchange 5.5 second edition), and Ed Crowley (this book). I appreciate the help each has given.

Thanks to everyone for all your help. Whatever errors of fact or judgment remain are mine and mine alone.

Barry Gerber (bg@bgerber.com)
Los Angeles, California

CONTENTS AT A GLANCE

CONTENTS

PART IV • BASIC EXCHANGE 2000 SERVER ADMINISTRATION

PART V • EXPANDING AN EXCHANGE SERVER ORGANIZATION

INTRODUCTION

I wrote this book because I want to share the excitement that I feel about the future of electronic messaging in general and, in particular, about Exchange 2000 Server and its constant companion, Windows 2000 Server. I also want to help you determine whether there is a place for Exchange in your organization and, if so, to provide the information that you'll need to set up an Exchange system of your own.

Your explorations of Exchange 2000 Server will open many new doors in the area of electronic communications. And, while you're learning about and working with Exchange in this book, I'll also help you build valuable Windows 2000 Server skills.

What's So Exciting about Exchange 2000 Server?

Exchange Server 5.5 was one of the most powerful, extensible, scalable, easy-to-use, and manageable electronic messaging back ends on the market. Exchange 2000 Server retained all of 5.5's best features and added new ones. In building Exchange 2000 Server, Microsoft changed the way most legacy features are implemented, used, and managed. These changes combined with Exchange 2000's new features allow Microsoft to retain a strong set of bragging rights in the electronic messaging world.

Much of the change in Exchange 2000 Server relates to its very tight integration with Windows 2000 Server. Exchange 5.5's directory service was the model for Windows 2000 Server's Active Directory. Active Directory is an industrial-strength directory service providing users and computers with information about and access to network services and resources. Information about Exchange 2000 Server recipients and services is integrated into Active Directory.

Additionally, unlike with Exchange 5.x, Exchange 2000 depends on Windows 2000's Internet Information Server for its base Simple Mail Transfer Protocol (SMTP) mail transmission services and Network News Transfer Protocol (NNTP) newsgroup services. Although management of these services is based in Exchange 2000 Server, once that product is installed on a computer, the services continue to be Windows 2000 Server services. Underlying both SMTP and NNTP is Microsoft's new virtual server technology, which supports multiple SMTP or NNTP services on a single server.

Virtual servers also now support version 3 of the Post Office Protocol (POP3) and version 4 of the Internet Message Access Protocol (IMAP4), both available since Exchange Server 5.5. Unlike SMTP and NNTP, however, POP3 and IMAP4 are native Exchange Server services. POP3 enables nonproprietary, lightweight client access to Exchange Server messages. IMAP4 adds key features missing in the POP3 protocol, such as access to folders other than the Inbox. Each of these employs the same virtual server technology as SMTP and NNTP server. Any POP3 or IMAP4 client, whether running in MS Windows, Macintosh, any flavor of Unix, or another operating system, can access Exchange Server to send and receive messages. Furthermore, POP3 and IMAP4 clients, such as Qualcomm's Eudora, Netscape's mail client, the University of Washington's Pine, or Microsoft's Outlook (POP3 only) or Outlook Express (POP3 and IMAP4), are easier to manage and demand fewer workstation resources than the standard Microsoft Outlook client. As a result, they can be run with less intervention by information technology staff on lower-end workstations.

The Hypertext Transfer Protocol (HTTP), another Exchange 5.5 veteran, makes possible Web browser access to Exchange Server-based mailboxes, public folders, and calendars. HTTP is built on Internet Information Server and virtual server technology. Microsoft uses the term *Outlook Web Access* (*OWA*) to refer to its support for HTTP in Exchange. Like POP3 and IMAP4 clients, Web browsers are both nonproprietary and lighter in weight than Outlook clients. As a result, users and their organizations realize the same benefits that they get with POP3 or IMAP4 clients, while using a client that is on virtually every desktop. HTTP support also enables controlled and selective access to Exchange Server environments by anonymous users. Finally, Exchange 2000's implementation of HTTP makes it easier than it ever has been for users and developers to access messages and other items in Exchange mailboxes and public folders.

Like SMTP and NNTP, Lightweight Directory Access Protocol (LDAP) services have moved from Exchange to Windows 2000, with LDAP becoming a key protocol for users and managers of Active Directory. On the messaging side, LDAP supports user access to e-mail address and other information stored in Active Directory. Exchange Server users with LDAP-enabled POP3, IMAP4, and OWA clients can find e-mail addresses in the Exchange directory from anywhere in the world. This adds an unprecedented and most welcome level of user friendliness to the POP3 and IMAP4 world as well as to OWA.

Exchange 2000 Server's information storage technology has changed drastically. Multiple mailbox and public information store databases can be created. Databases can be larger, and each database can be managed separately. Any information store database can be taken offline for cleanup, backup, and restore operations without affecting users' capability to access remaining online databases. Novice and seasoned application developers will be especially impressed with Microsoft's introduction of file-based access to Exchange mailbox and public stores. This permits easy access to mailboxes, public folders, and other public information stores with applications ranging from Microsoft's Word to Visual Basic and C++.

Exchange 2000 Server splits Exchange 5.5 and earlier sites into administrative groups and routing groups. Exchange administrators can distribute management responsibilities by delegating control over specific administrative groups to different Windows 2000 security groups. Administrative groups hold servers, system policies, public folders, routing groups, and other objects. However, routing groups, which contain servers linked by high-bandwidth networks, do not have to exist in the same administrative group as the servers that they contain. In addition, servers can be moved between administrative groups and system policies, and public folders can exist in any administrative group, further extending the Exchange administrator's ability to distribute responsibility for managing specific components of Exchange 2000 Server.

Speaking of management Windows 2000's Microsoft Management Console (MMC) technology makes Windows 2000/Exchange 2000 administration easier and more intuitive. Based on the familiar object-oriented, tree technology of Microsoft's latest Windows file and directory browsers, MMC snap-ins enable focused, efficient management of everything from users and computers to Windows and Internet domains, to Exchange server and the wide array of services that it supports.

With these and an impressive array of other features, Exchange 2000 Server can help your organization move smoothly and productively into the world of electronic messaging.

What You Need to Run Exchange Server

Exchange 2000 Server is a complex product with a remarkably easy-to-use interface for administration and management. All of this complexity and parallel ease of use requires an industrial-strength computer. The minimum server computer suggested here is for testing, learning about, and evaluating the product. It's also enough for a small, noncritical installation. However, as I discuss in the book, when the server moves into critical production environments, where it will be accessed by large numbers of users, you'll need to beef up its hardware and add a number of fault-tolerant capabilities. On the client side, with the broad range of clients available for Exchange, the machines now on desktops in most organizations should be more than adequate.

At a minimum, to test, learn about, and evaluate Exchange Server you'll need the following:

- Either Microsoft Exchange 2000 Server and any version of Windows 2000 Server, or Microsoft Exchange 2000 Enterprise Server and Windows 2000 Advanced or Datacenter Server. For all versions of Windows 2000, the Windows 2000 Service Pack 1 or later is required.

- A 500MHz Pentium III-based PC with 256MB of RAM (if the computer is also a Windows 2000 domain controller) or 128MB of RAM (if the computer is not a Windows 2000 domain controller), and two 9 GB disk drives. This allows you to complete exercises involving a single Exchange server.

- A minimum of three additional computers in the class just described. This allows you to complete exercises involving multiple computers in multiple administrative groups and Windows 2000 Server domains.

- Tape backup hardware.

- A local area network (preferably connected to the Internet).

- At least one 400MHz Pentium II or equivalent computer, with 32MB of memory running Microsoft Windows 95 or later (Windows 2000 Professional preferred).

How This Book Is Organized

I've divided this book into 6 parts, 18 chapters, and an appendix. As you proceed through the book, you'll move from basic concepts to several increasingly more complex levels of hands-on implementation.

This book won't work well for practitioners of the timeworn ritual of chapter hopping. I've taken great pains to write an integrated book on Windows 2000 Server and Exchange 2000 Server. Unless you already have considerable experience with these products, to get the maximum value out of this book, you'll need to track through the chapters in order. Readers like to send me questions by e-mail. About 25 percent of the why-doesn't-it-work questions that I receive can be answered by, "Because you didn't do what I suggested in Chapter so-and-so."

However, if you're in a hurry to get your hands dirty, start with Part II, "Installation" (Chapters 7 and 8); Part III, "The Outlook Client" (Chapters 9 and 10), and Part IV, "Basic Exchange 2000 Server Administration" (Chapters 11 and 12). These chapters will help you get a Windows 2000 server, an Exchange 2000 server, and an Outlook client up and running. As long as you're not planning to put your quickie server into production immediately, there should be no harm done. Before going into production, I strongly suggest that you explore other parts of this book. Here's a little guide to what's in other chapters:

Chapter 1 "Introducing Exchange 2000 Server," through Chapter 4, "Exchange 2000 Server Architecture": Key Windows 2000 Server and Exchange 2000 Server concepts

Chapter 5 "Designing a New Exchange 2000 System": Step-by-step planning for an Exchange 2000 deployment

Chapter 6 "Upgrading to Windows 2000 Server and Exchange 2000 Server": Planning and deployment strategies for existing Windows NT 4 and Exchange 5.5 environments

Chapter 13 "Managing Exchange 2000 Internet Services" (SMTP messaging), and Chapter 14, "Managing Exchange 2000 Services for Internet Clients": Internet mail server support and Internet client server technologies (POP3, IMAP4, HTTP, NNTP, and LDAP)

Chapter 15 "Installing and Managing Additional Exchange 2000 Servers": Adding Exchange servers to an organization (in the same administrative group, in new administrative groups, and in new Windows 2000 Server domains)

Chapter 16 "Connecting to Foreign Messaging Systems": Connecting to other messaging systems (including X.400 and Microsoft Mail for PC networks)

Chapter 17 "Advanced Exchange Server Management": Advanced Exchange features and topics (including advanced security, message tracking, Exchange organization-wide settings, and troubleshooting)

Chapter 18 "Building, Using, and Managing Outlook Forms Designer Applications": Developing applications based on Outlook forms

Conventions Used in This Book

I've included many notes in this book. Generally, they are positioned below the material to which they refer. There are three kinds of notes: notes, tips, and warnings.

 NOTE Notes give you information pertinent to the procedure or topic being discussed.

 TIP Tips indicate practical hints that might make your work easier.

WARNING Warnings alert you to potential problems that you might encounter while using the program.

Remember, Exchange is designed to help your organization do what it does better, more efficiently, and with greater productivity. Have fun, be productive, and prosper!

PART I

Understanding and Planning

This part of the book focuses on concepts and features of Microsoft's Exchange 2000 Server client/server electronic messaging system. It is designed to provide you with the underlying knowledge that you'll need when you tackle Exchange 2000 Server installation, administration, and management later in this book.

Chapter 1, "Introducing Exchange 2000 Server," presents some basic information about Exchange 2000 Server products, helping you optimize the value of these products in your organization. Chapter 2, "2000: A Magic Number?" looks in some detail at the similarities and differences between Windows 2000 Server and Windows NT Server 4; this chapter also examines the differences between Exchange 2000 Server and Exchange Server 5.5, assisting you in focusing your learning efforts if you're an old hand at NT 4 and Exchange 5.5. Chapter 3, "Two Key Architectural Components of Windows 2000 Server," attempts to break through the hype and vagaries promulgated by early technical treatises on Windows 2000, giving you a head start on the road to Windows 2000/Exchange 2000 competency. Chapter 4, "Exchange 2000 Server Architecture," focuses on the architecture of Exchange 2000, an understanding of which is essential to successful Exchange 2000 implementation. Chapter 5, "Designing a New Exchange 2000 System," covers Windows 2000 and Exchange 2000 system planning and design, facilitating your initial use of these complex products in your organization. Chapter 6, "Upgrading to Windows 2000 Server and Exchange 20000 Server," looks at the planning and design issues involved in bringing Windows 2000 and Exchange 2000 to existing Windows NT/Exchange 5.5 environments, again easing the introduction of these products in your organization.

CHAPTER **1**

Introducing Exchange 2000 Server

Microsoft's Exchange 2000 client/server electronic messaging system is a major player in what I call the "electronic messaging" decade. Exchange 2000 lets people work together in a variety of productivity-enhancing ways. It is one of the most exciting, innovative, and promising software products that I've ever seen.

Unlike its predecessor, Exchange Server 5.5, Exchange 2000 Server is tightly integrated into the Windows 2000 Server environment: You can't talk about Exchange 2000 Server without talking about Windows 2000 Server. This chapter concentrates on Exchange 2000 Server, but when we leave the safe confines of this introductory chapter, hardly a paragraph will go by without mention of Windows 2000 Server.

A Confusing Array of Terms

Before we move on, let me clarify some of the terms that I'll be using. I'll use *Windows 2000 Server* to refer to the entire line of Windows 2000 server products. I'll use the names of the individual Windows 2000 Server products when referring specifically to one of them—for example, *Windows 2000 Advanced Server*. I'll follow the same conventions for Windows NT Server 4.

When I use the word *Exchange* or the words *Exchange system*, I'm talking about the whole Exchange 2000 Server client/server system.

Exchange Server refers to just the Exchange 2000 Server product (Server or Enterprise Edition), and an *Exchange server* is any computer running the Exchange 2000 Server product.

Got that? Okay, explain it to me.

Exchange 2000 Server and the Electronic Messaging Decade

Electronic messaging is more than e-mail. It involves the use of an underlying messaging infrastructure (addresses, routing, and so on) to build applications that are based on cooperative tasking, whether by humans or computers. We can expect the years 1996 to 2005 to be the decade of electronic messaging *(electronic messaging)*, when store-and-forward–based messaging systems and real-time interactive technologies will complement each other to produce wildly imaginative business, entertainment, and educational applications with high pay-off potential.

Microsoft's Exchange Server products have played and will continue to play a key role in electronic messaging. Exchange 2000 Server is one of the most powerful, extensible, scalable, easy-to-use, and manageable electronic messaging back ends currently on the market. Combined with Microsoft's excellent Outlook clients, Internet-based clients from Microsoft and other vendors, and third-party or home-grown applications, Exchange 2000 Server can help your organization move smoothly and productively into the electronic messaging decade.

In writing this book, I was guided by three goals:

- To share the excitement that I feel about both the promise of electronic messaging and the Exchange 2000 client/server system

- To help you decide if there's a place for Exchange 2000 Server in your organization

- To provide information and teach you skills that you'll need to plan for and implement Exchange 2000 Server systems of any size and shape

The rest of this chapter introduces you to the Exchange 2000 client/server system. We start with a quick look at several of the neat ways that you can use Exchange for e-mail and more, and then we focus on some of Exchange's key characteristics and capabilities. This is just an introduction, so don't worry if you don't understand everything completely by the end of this chapter. Everything that we discuss here we also will cover in more detail later in the book.

Exchange 2000 Server Applications

I dare you not to get excited about electronic messaging and Exchange 2000 Server as you read this section. Just look at what's possible, and imagine what you could do with all this potential.

Exchange supports a range of e-mail protocols, including Microsoft's own proprietary Mail Application Program Interface (MAPI), as well as the Internet standard protocols Post Office Protocol version 3 (POP3) and the often overlooked Internet Message Access Protocol version 4 (IMAP4). But that's just the tip of the iceberg. Exchange servers can host user and organizational calendars, e-mail–enabled contact lists, to-do lists, notes, and other data. Users can access all this data using standard personal computer-based e-mail clients, Web browsers, and even those tiny personal digital assistants (PDAs) that are all the rage today.

Exchange servers are also great places to build and support custom applications. You can build simple applications using existing products such as Microsoft Word or Excel. If your application needs are more complex, you can turn to Exchange-based forms. And, if you've got the need, time, and skills, you can build applications using programming languages such as Java, Visual Basic, or C++. Finally, you can use the built-in sorting and searching capabilities of Exchange public folders to build some pretty powerful applications.

E-Mail Is Only the Beginning

Together, Exchange 2000 Server and its clients perform a variety of messaging-based functions. These include e-mail, message routing, scheduling, and support for several types of custom applications. Certainly, e-mail is a key feature of any messaging system, and the Outlook Calendar is by far better than previous versions of Microsoft's appointment and meeting-scheduling software. (Figures 1.1 and 1.2 show the Outlook 2000 client Inbox and Calendar for Windows in action.) Take a look at Figures 1.3, 1.4, and 1.5 for a glimpse of the Internet-based POP3, IMAP4, and Web browser clients that you can use with Exchange 2000 Server.

FIGURE 1.1

The Outlook 2000 client for Windows Inbox

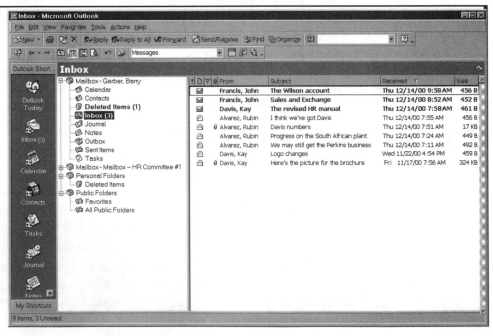

FIGURE 1.2

The Outlook 2000 client Windows Calendar

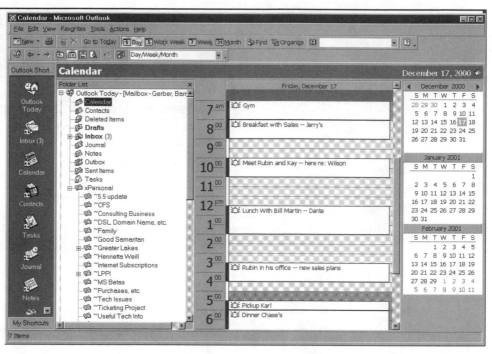

FIGURE 1.3

Qualcomm's Eudora Pro 3.0 POP3-compliant client accesses mail stored on an Exchange server.

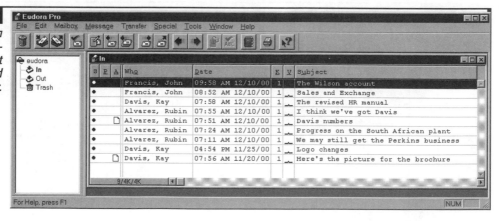

FIGURE 1.4

Microsoft's Outlook Express IMAP4 client function accesses messages and folders on an Exchange server.

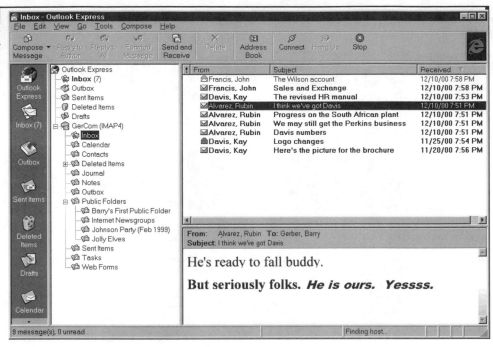

FIGURE 1.5

Microsoft's Internet Explorer Web browser accesses mail stored on an Exchange 2000 server.

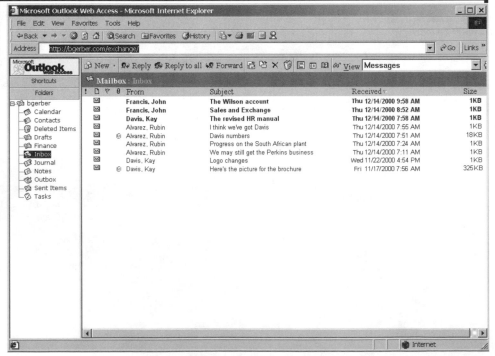

E-mail clients are exciting and sexy, but to get the most out of Exchange 2000 Server, you need to throw away any preconceptions you have that messaging packages are only for e-mail and scheduling. The really exciting applications are not those that use simple e-mail or scheduling, but those that are based on the routing capabilities of messaging systems. These applications bring people and computers together for cooperative work.

So what do these hot apps look like? Let's start with the simplest and move toward the more complex.

Change Is the Name of the Game

Some of the marvelous user interfaces that you see in Figures 1.1 through 1.5 may look very different by the time you read this book. Software development and marketing is running at hyperspeed, especially in the world of electronic communications. Updates and even major revisions hit the market at a breakneck pace. The Internet makes it even easier for vendors to market and deliver their wares. New pieces and parts of applications appear almost daily for manual or totally automatic download and installation.

The basic architecture of Exchange 2000 Server and its clients is unlikely to change much over the next year or so, but the outward appearance of user interfaces is much more likely to change. As far as Exchange goes, plan for change as a way of life. Keep an open mind and at least one eye on Microsoft's Exchange-oriented Web pages.

I will admit that I sometimes long for the days of yearly or less-frequent updates on low-density 5¼-inch floppies. In the long run, however, all of this hyperactivity will prove a good thing. Our requirements will find their way *into* products faster, and bugs will find their way *out* of products faster.

Just a Step beyond Mail

You're probably familiar with e-mail *attachments*—those word processing, spreadsheet, and other work files that you can drop into messages. Attachments are a simple way to move work files to the people who need to see them.

Sure, you could send your files on diskette or tell people where on the network they can find and download the files. But e-mail attachments let you make the files available to others with a click of their mouse buttons: Recipients just double-click on an icon, and the attachment opens in the original application that produced it (if your correspondent has access to the application, of course).

Using attachments offers the added advantage of putting the files and accompanying messages right in the faces of those who need to see them. This leaves less room for excuses such as "Oh, I forgot" or "The dog ate the diskette."

As great as attachments can be, they have one real weakness: The minute that an attachment leaves your Outbox, it's out of date. If you do further work on the original file, that work is not reflected in the copy that you sent to others. If someone then edits a copy of the attached file, it's totally out of sync with the original and all other copies. Getting everything synchronized again can involve tedious hours or days of manually comparing different versions and cutting and pasting them to create one master document.

Exchange offers several ways to avoid this problem. One of the simplest is the *attachment link* or *shortcut:* Instead of putting the actual file into a message, you put in a link to the file (see Figure 1.6), which can be stored anywhere on the network. The real kicker is that the file can also be stored in Exchange public folders (more about these in the section "Applications Using Exchange Public Folders," later in this chapter). When someone double-clicks on an attachment link icon, the linked file opens. Everyone who receives the message works with the same linked attachment, so everyone reads and can modify the same file. Of course, your users will have to learn to live with the fact that only one person can edit an application file at a time. Most modern end user apps warn the user of this fact and allow the user to open a read-only copy of the file. Third-party applications offer tighter document checkout control (see Appendix A "Cool Third-Party Applications for Exchange Server and Outlook Clients.")

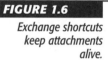

FIGURE 1.6

Exchange shortcuts keep attachments alive.

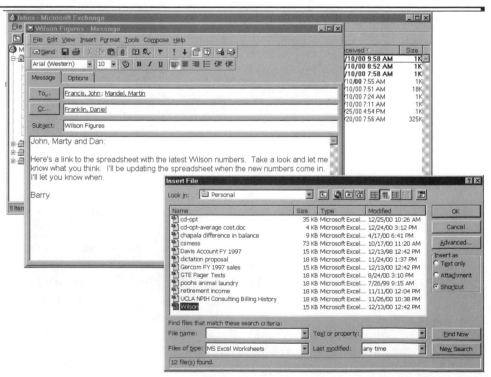

Off-the-Shelf Messaging-Enabled Applications

Here's another way to guard against dead work files: Microsoft Windows enables messaging in many word processing and spreadsheet applications. For example, when you install the Outlook client on your computer, Microsoft's Office products such as Word and Excel are electronic messaging-enabled. You can select Send or Route options from the app's File menu; this pops up a routing slip. You then add addresses to the slip from your Outlook client's address book, select the routing method that you want to use, and assign a right-to-modify level for the route. Finally, you ship your work off to others with just a click of the Route button.

Figure 1.7 shows how all of this works. Although it's simple, application-based messaging can significantly improve user productivity and speed up a range of business processes.

FIGURE 1.7

Microsoft Word 97 includes messaging-enabled functions for sending and routing.

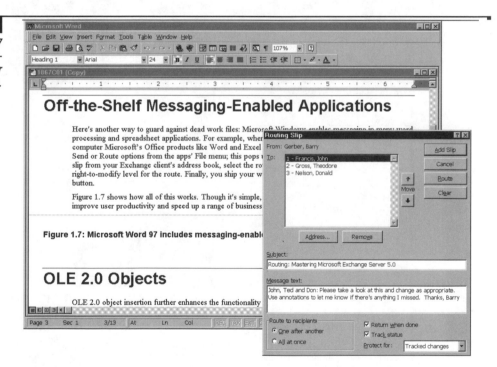

OLE 2.0 Objects

OLE 2.0 object insertion further enhances the functionality of the Exchange messaging system. Take a close look at Figure 1.8. Yes, the message includes an Excel spreadsheet and chart. The person who sent the message simply selected Object from the Insert menu that appears on every Exchange message. The Outlook client then inserted a blank Excel spreadsheet into the message as an OLE 2.0 object. Having received the message, we can see the spreadsheet as an item in the message, as shown in the figure. When we double-click on the spreadsheet, Excel is launched and Excel's menus and toolbars replace those of the message (see Figure 1.9). In essence, the message becomes Excel.

The Excel spreadsheet is fully editable. Although Excel must be available to your recipients, they don't have to launch it to read and work on the spreadsheet. Even if your recipients don't have Excel, they can still view the contents of the spreadsheet, although they won't be able to work on it. (That is, even if they don't have the app, they can still view the object when they open the message.)

FIGURE 1.8

With OLE 2.0 objects, sophisticated messaging-enabled applications are easy to build.

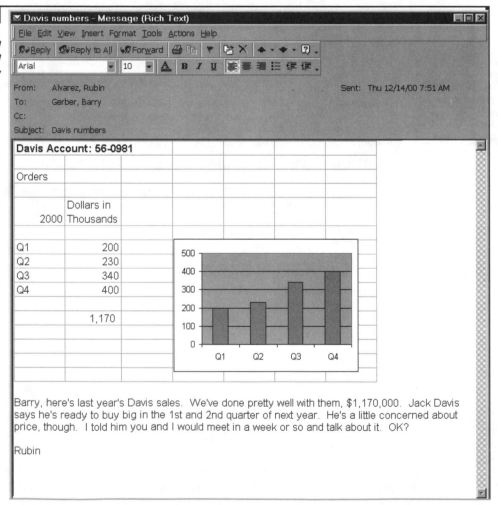

FIGURE 1.9

Double-clicking on an OLE 2.0-embedded Excel spreadsheet in a message enables Excel menus and toolbars.

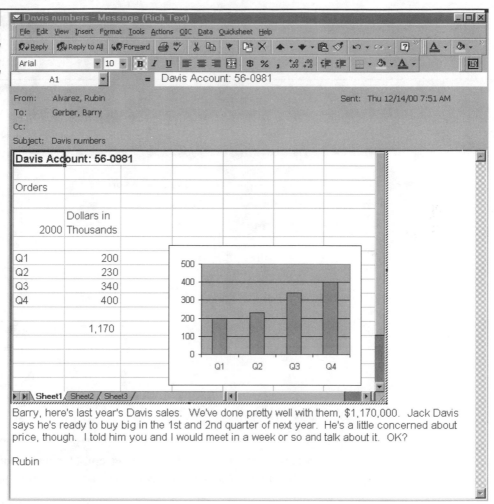

Electronic Forms

Exchange 2000 Server supports Outlook Forms Designer (OFD). You can use OFD to build information-gathering forms containing a number of the bells and whistles that you're accustomed to in Windows applications. These include drop-down list boxes, check boxes, fill-in text forms, tab dialog controls, and radio buttons (see Figure 1.10).

OFD, which is easy enough for nontechnical types to use, includes a variety of messaging-oriented fields and actions. For example, you can choose to include a preaddressed To field in a form so that users of the form can easily mail it off to the appropriate recipient. (The preaddressed To field for the form shown in Figure 1.10 is on the page with the tab marked Message.) When you've designed a form, you can make it available to all users or select users, who can access the completed form simply by selecting it while in an Outlook client.

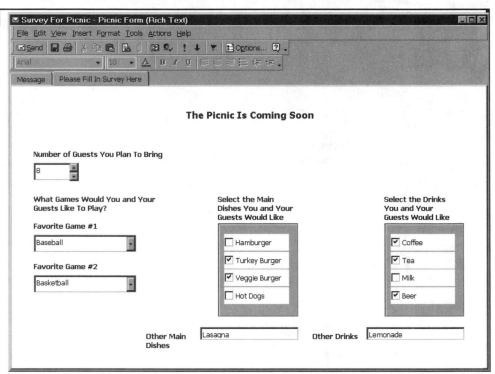

FIGURE 1.10

Electronic forms turn messages into structured information-gathering tools.

I discuss OFD further in Chapter 18, "Building, Using, and Managing Outlook Forms Designer Applications." That chapter also includes a nice hands-on exercise using OFD.

Applications Built on APIs

If all this functionality isn't enough, you can go to the heart of Exchange Server and use its *application programming interface (API)*. Exchange Server supports both the Simple and Extended versions of Microsoft's Windows-based Mail Application Program Interface (MAPI). It also supports the X.400-oriented, platform-independent Common Mail Call (CMC) APIs, which have functions similar to those of Simple MAPI. Using Simple MAPI or CMC, you can build applications that use electronic messaging addresses behind the scenes to route data between users and programs. Extended

MAPI lets you get deeper into Exchange's storage and electronic messaging address books to create virtually any messaging-enabled application that you can imagine.

These custom-built applications may involve some level of automation, such as performing regular updates of your company's price lists for trading partners or sending a weekly multimedia message from the president to employees at your organization. Building apps based on MAPI or CMC requires someone with programming skills in languages such as Visual Basic or C++, and this is beyond the scope of this book.

Applications Using Exchange Public Folders

As you'll discover later in this chapter and in chapters to come, Exchange Server supports mailboxes and private and public folders. All of these can hold messages and any kind of computer application or data file. Mailboxes and private folders are the places where Exchange users store and manage their messages and files. Public folders are for common access to messages and files. Files can be dragged from file access interfaces, such as Explorer in Microsoft's Windows 98, NT 4, and Windows 2000, and can be dropped into mailboxes or private or public folders. If you begin thinking of mailboxes and private and public folders as a messaging-enabled extension of Explorer, you'll have a fairly clear picture of Microsoft's vision of the future as to how an operating system organizes and displays stored information.

You can set up sorting rules for a mailbox or a private or public folder so that items in the folder are organized by a range of attributes, such as the name of the sender or creator of the item, or the date that the item arrived or was placed in the folder. Items in a mailbox or private or public folder can be sorted by conversation threads. You can also put applications built on existing products such as Word or Excel, or with Exchange or Outlook Forms Designer, server scripting, or the API set into mailboxes and private or public folders. In mailboxes and private folders, these applications are fun for one, but in public folders, where they are accessed by many people, they can replace the tons of maddening paper-based processes that abound in every organization.

If all this isn't already enough, Exchange is very much Internet-aware. With Exchange 2000 Server, you can publish all or selected public folders on the Internet, where they become accessible with a simple Internet browser. You can limit Internet access to public folders to only users who have access under Windows 2000 Server's security system, or you can open public folders to anyone on the Internet. Just think about it: Internet-enabled public folders let you put information on the Internet without the fuss and bother of Web site design and development. Any item can be placed on the Internet by simply adding a message to a public folder.

Before we leave public folder applications, I want to mention one more option: Exchange 2000 Server enables you to bring any or all of those Usenet Internet newsgroups to your public folder environment. With their Outlook clients, users then can read and reply to newsgroup items just as though they were using a standard newsgroup reader application. Exchange Server comes with all the tools that you need to do this. All you need is an Internet connection, access to a host computer that can provide you with a feed of newsgroup messages, and a set of rules about which groups to exclude. (Remember, this is where the infamous alt.sex newsgroups live.)

A New Era For Exchange-Oriented Web Application Developers

Though it's beyond the scope of this book I must say something about the fantastic new programming options enabled by Microsoft's exposing Exchange 2000 Server's Information Store through the Windows 2000 file system and the Web. Using a variety of built-in and custom file system, HTML, and other commands, it's possible to program sophisticated custom applications with third-party products and Microsoft proprietary products ranging from Word to Visual Basic and C++. For an excellent introduction to this exciting new development opportunity, see Mindy Martin, *Programming Collaborative Web Applications with Microsoft Exchange 2000 Server* (Microsoft Press, 2000).

Some Exchange 2000 Server Basics

It's important to get a handle on some of Exchange's key characteristics and capabilities. When you do, you'll better appreciate the depth and breadth of Microsoft's efforts in developing Exchange, and you'll be better prepared for the rest of this book. In this section, we'll take a look at these topics:

- Exchange as a client/server system
- The Outlook client
- Exchange Server's dependency on Microsoft's Windows 2000 Server
- Exchange Server's object orientation
- Exchange Server scalability
- Exchange Server security
- Exchange Server and other electronic messaging systems
- Third-party applications for Exchange Server

Taken together, Exchange 2000 Server's attributes make it a powerful, flexible, and extensible platform, capable of meeting the needs of small and large enterprises alike.

Exchange 2000 Server as a Client/Server System

The term *client/server* has been overused and overworked. To put it simply, there are two kinds of networked applications: shared-file and client/server.

Shared-File Applications

Early networked applications were all based on *shared-file* systems. The network shell that let you load your word processor from a network server also allowed you to read from and write to files stored on a server. At the time, this was the easiest and most natural way to grow networked applications.

Microsoft Mail for PC Networks is a shared-file application. You run Windows, OS/2, DOS, or Macintosh front ends, which send and receive messages by accessing files on a Microsoft Mail for PC Networks post office that resides on a network file server. The front end and your PC do all the work; the server is passive. Figure 1.11 shows a typical Microsoft Mail for PC Networks setup.

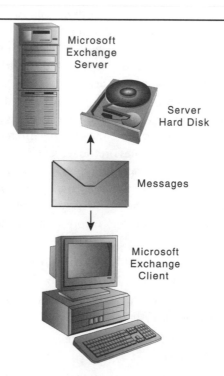

FIGURE 1.11

Microsoft Mail for PC Networks is a typical shared-file electronic messaging system.

Microsoft
Exchange
Server

Server
Hard Disk

Messages

Microsoft
Exchange
Client

Easy as it was to develop, this architecture leads to some serious problems in today's networked computing world:

- Changing the underlying structure of the server file system is difficult because you have to change both the server and the client.

- System security is always compromised because users must have read and write permissions for the whole server file system, which includes all other users' message files. Things are so bad that a naive or malicious user can actually destroy shared-file system databases in some cases.

- Network traffic is high because the front end must constantly access indexes and hunt around the server's file system for user messages.

- Because the user workstation writes directly to shared files, the server-based files can be destroyed if workstation hardware or software stops functioning for some unexpected reason.

Shared-file applications are in decline. Sure, plenty of *legacy* (that is, out-of-date) apps will probably live on for the data processing equivalent of eternity, but client/server systems have quickly supplanted the shared-file model. This is especially true in the world of electronic messaging.

Client/Server Applications

Though they have some limitations of their own, client/server applications overcome the shortcomings of shared-file apps. So, today, networked applications increasingly are based on the client/server model. The server is an active partner in client/server applications. Clients tell servers what they want done, and if security requirements are met, servers do what they are asked.

Processes running on a server find and ship data to processes running on a client. When a client process sends data, a server receives it and writes it to server-based files. Server processes can do more than simply interact with client processes. For example, they can compact data files on the server or—as they do on Exchange Server— automatically reply to incoming messages to let people know, for instance, that you're going to be out of the office for a period of time. Figure 1.12 shows how Exchange implements the client/server model.

Client/server applications are strong in all the areas in which shared-file apps are weak:

- Changing the underlying structure of the server file system is easier than with shared-file systems because only the server processes access the file system.

- System security can be much tighter, again because only the server processes access the file system.

- Network traffic is lighter because all the work of file access is done by the server, on the server.

- Because server processes are the only ones that access server data, breakdowns of user workstation hardware or software are less likely to spoil data. With appropriate transaction logging features, client/server systems can even protect against server hardware or software malfunctions.

FIGURE 1.12

Microsoft Exchange is based on the client/server model.

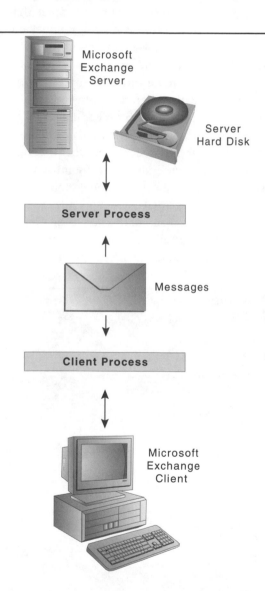

Microsoft Exchange Server

Server Hard Disk

Server Process

Messages

Client Process

Microsoft Exchange Client

As good as the client/server model is, it does have some general drawbacks. Client/server apps require more computing horsepower, especially on the server side. With Exchange, you should plan to start with very fast Pentium machines, lots of RAM, and plenty of hard disk capacity—and expect to grow from there.

Client/server applications are more complex than shared-file apps. This is partly because of the nature of the client/server model and partly because of the tendency of client/server apps to be newer and thus filled with all kinds of great capabilities that you won't find in shared-file applications. Generally, you're safe in assuming that you'll need to devote more and more sophisticated human resources to managing a client/server application than to tending to a similar one based on shared files.

The good news is that Microsoft has done a lot to reduce the management load and to make it easier for someone who isn't a computer scientist to administer an Exchange system. I've looked at many client/server messaging systems, and I can say without any doubt that Exchange is absolutely the easiest to administer, even in its slightly more complex 2000 implementation. Exchange 2000 Server includes a set of graphical user interfaces (GUIs) that organize the processes of management very nicely. With these interfaces, you can do everything from adding users to assessing the health of your messaging system. In Figure 1.13, I'm using the Windows 2000 Server Active Directory Users and Computers interface to modify an Exchange user's mailbox.

FIGURE 1.13

Managing an Exchange user's mailbox in the Active Directory Users and Computers interface

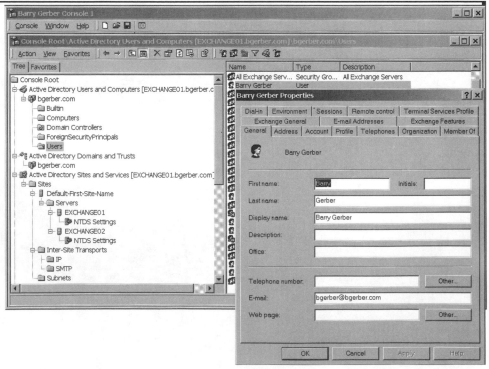

A Quick Take on the Outlook Client

As should be clear from our look at some of its applications earlier in this chapter, the Outlook client is the sexy part of Exchange. This is where the action is, the view screen for the backroom bits and bytes of Exchange Server. Although this book is mostly about Exchange Server, you can't implement an Exchange system without the clients. So, we'll spend some time on the Outlook client in various places in this book. Meanwhile, let's discuss some client basics.

Information Storage

The client stores information in one of two places on an Exchange 2000 server: a mailbox store or a public store. Each has a different purpose and function. Furthermore, an Outlook client can have personal folders, which reside outside the Exchange Server environment.

Mailbox Stores and Mailboxes

Mailbox stores contain individual Exchange 2000 Server user mailboxes. Mailboxes can send and receive messages. Although you can share their contents with others, mailboxes generally hold items to which you alone have access. You access mailboxes using an Exchange client or Internet-based clients such as the POP3 and IMAP4 clients built into Microsoft's Outlook Express.

You can add folders to a mailbox to help you organize your messages. If you have the rights to other mailboxes, you can open them in your Exchange client as well.

Public Stores and Public Folders

Public folder stores stores contain, you guessed it, public folders, which hold items that you want others to see. Users whom you authorize can create public folders and then drag and drop anything that they want into them. Public folders can also be nested, and rules can be applied to them.

Public folders are key to the organization-wide implementation of Exchange. Some, all, or none of an Exchange server's public folders can be automatically replicated to other Exchange servers. This lets you post items to public folders on one Exchange server and have them quickly and painlessly appear on any combination of the Exchange servers in your system. Even without replication, users all over your organization can access public folders.

Personal Folders: Another Place for Clients to Store Information

Outlook has personal folders that reside outside the Exchange Server on local or network hard disks. Personal folders may or may not have the send and receive capabilities of mailboxes. You can create as many personal folders as you want, and a personal folder can hold as many subfolders as you want. Like the folders that you add to mailboxes, personal folders help you organize information. You can drag and drop messages between folders. Using *rules* (discussed in the section "Rules," later in this chapter) you can direct incoming mail into any of your personal folders.

Sharing Information

You can share information with others by sending it to them or placing it in public folders for them to retrieve on their own. You can drop messages, word processing documents, other work files, and even whole applications into public folders. You can use public folders to implement many of the kinds of applications that I mentioned at the beginning of this chapter.

For example, instead of electronically routing a draft word processing document to a bunch of colleagues, you can just drop it into a public folder. Then you can send e-mail to your colleagues asking them to look at the document and even to edit it right there in the public folder.

Organizing Information

Creating a set of personal and public folders and then dropping messages in them is a simple way to organize information. More sophisticated approaches include the use of rules, views, and the Exchange client's Finder.

Rules

As a user, you can set up a range of *rules* to move mail from your Inbox into personal or public folders. For example, you might want to move all the messages from your boss into a folder marked "Urgent." Rules can be based on anything from the sender of a message to its contents. Depending on its type, a rule may run on the Exchange server or on the client. The Outlook client doesn't have to be running for server-based rules to execute.

Views

Exchange messages can have numerous attributes. These include the obvious, such as sender, subject, and date received, as well as less common information, including the sender's company, the last author, and the number of words. You can build views of messages using almost any combination of attributes and a variety of sorting schemes. Then you can apply a particular view to a folder to specially organize the messages that it contains.

The Finder

You can use the Outlook client Finder to search all folders or a single folder for messages from or to specific correspondents; messages with specific information in the subject field or message body, or attachments to messages; and even messages received between specific dates or of a specific size.

Exchange 2000 Server's Dependency on Windows 2000 Server

Exchange 2000 Server runs only on specific versions of Windows 2000 Server. It won't run on Windows NT Server, Windows 2000 Professional, or Windows 98.

Among operating systems, Windows 2000 Server is the new kid on the block. As a longtime Windows NT Server user, I initially faced Windows 2000 Server with more than a little fear and foreboding. That was then, however. Now I am a confirmed Windows 2000 Server user and supporter. My personal workstation is a Windows 2000 Server-based machine, and all my servers but one run Windows 2000 Server. (The one holdout is a NetWare server that I use to ensure that Windows 2000 Server and Windows-based software work with Novell's IPX/SPX.)

It took me about two weeks to get comfortable with Windows 2000 Server, and it took a month or so to become totally productive with it. What sets Windows 2000 Server apart from all other operating systems for workstations and servers is Microsoft Windows. Windows 2000, whether the workstation or server version, *is* Microsoft Windows. If you can use Windows 98, you can get started using Windows 2000 Server in no time. You'll have to learn how to accomplish various server-related tasks, but once you figure out how to do a task, the Windows graphical user interface greatly simplifies performing almost any task. Networking with Windows 2000 Server is pretty much a breeze if you understand a few basic concepts, and running apps on top of Windows 2000 Server is a piece of cake. Figure 1.14 shows one of my Windows 2000 Server/Exchange Server desktops with some Windows 2000 Server and Exchange 2000 Server management applications running. This shouldn't be foreign territory for any Windows aficionado.

Windows 2000 Server is chock-full of features that make it an especially attractive operating system. One of these is its very usable and functional implementation of Microsoft's domain-based security system. Domains have names—mine is called bgerber.com—and include Windows 2000 servers, Windows 2000, and Windows NT workstations, and all flavors of other Windows- and DOS-based machines. Although there are a number of ways to approach domain structure and security, the general rule is that the members of a domain can use any resource that they have been given permission to use in the domain—disk files, printers, and so on—no matter where these resources reside. Exchange 2000 Server depends on Windows 2000 Server domain structure and security for its security.

In Chapter 2, "2000: A Magic Number"; Chapter 3, "Two Key Architectural Components of Windows 2000 Server"; and Chapter 6, "Upgrading to Windows 2000 Server and Exchange 2000 Server," you'll read a lot more about Window 2000 Server and what you need to know about it to run Exchange Server. You'll install Windows 2000 Server in Chapter 7, "Installing Windows 2000 Server."

FIGURE 1.14

On the surface, Windows 2000 Server is just plain old Microsoft Windows.

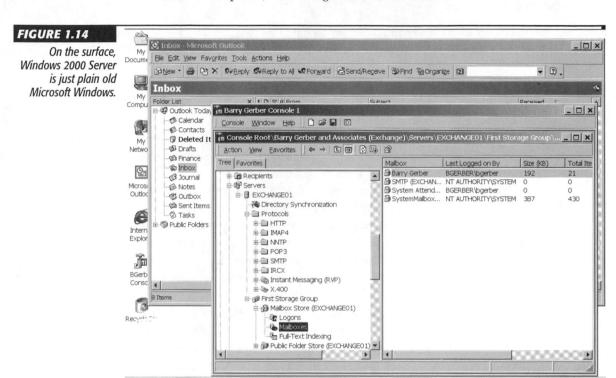

Exchange 2000 Server's Object Orientation

Exchange is a classic example of an *object-oriented* system. Figure 1.15 shows the main tool for managing an Exchange 2000 Server organization, Exchange System Manager. Take a look at all those items on the tree on the left side of the tool, such as Barry Gerber and Associates (Exchange), Servers, EXCHANGE01, Protocols, and First Storage Group. Each of these is an *object*. Each object has attributes and can interact with other objects in specific ways. Exchange objects can hold other objects, serving as what Microsoft calls *containers*.

FIGURE 1.15

*Exchange 2000
Server's object orienta-
tion is evident in the
Exchange System
Manager tool.*

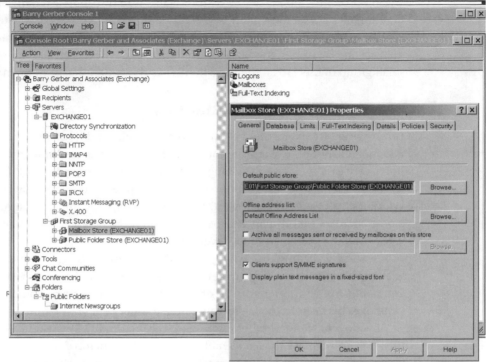

Barry Gerber and Associates is the name of my consulting business; it is the equivalent of a company name such as IBM or TRW. This top-level object is called the *organization*. The Barry Gerber and Associates organization contains all the objects below it.

Servers is the container that holds the individual servers in the Barry Gerber and
Associates enterprise hierarchy. Right now, there's only one server in the Servers container, EXCHANGE01, but just you wait.

The First Storage Group object contains mailbox and public stores; remember those
from earlier in this chapter?

Take a look at the dialog box on the right side of Figure 1.15. It shows the properties or attributes of the mailbox store. Objects have attributes. The attributes of a
mailbox store object are puny compared to those of a Windows 2000 Server/Exchange
2000 Server user: Compare this to the number of tabs on the user object back in Figure 1.13.

Object orientation makes it easy for Microsoft to distribute Exchange 2000 Server's functionality and management, and it makes it easy for you to administer an Exchange Server environment. For example, based on my security clearances, I can manage any set of Windows 2000 Server/Exchange 2000 Server users, from only a small group of users to all the users in my Windows 2000 Server domain.

Exchange 2000 Server Scalability

Exchange 2000 Server scales very well both vertically and horizontally. Windows 2000 Server runs on top of computers based on single and multiple Intel processors, so it's very easy to scale an Exchange server upward to more powerful hardware when increased user loads make additional computing power necessary. You can also cluster Windows 2000 Server/Exchange 2000 Servers so that they mirror each other in a fault-tolerant way and share the load placed on them by users. This is another way to vertically scale Exchange 2000 Server systems.

If vertical scalability isn't what you need, horizontal scaling is also a breeze with Exchange Server. You can set up a new Exchange server and quickly get its directory and public folders in sync with all or some of your other servers. You can even move mailboxes between Exchange servers with a few clicks of your left mouse button.

How do you know whether it's time to scale up or out? Microsoft has an answer for this, too: You can use the load simulation tools that Microsoft provides to simulate a range of different user loads on your server hardware. By analyzing the results of your tests, you'll get some idea of the messaging loads that you can expect a server to handle in a production environment.

Exchange 2000 Server Security

Exchange 2000 Server security starts with Windows 2000 Server's security system. Several different Windows 2000 Server security structure options are available; the one that's right for you depends mostly on the size and structure of your organization and the department that supports Exchange 2000 Server. In all cases, the idea is to select a security model that puts the lightest burden on users and system administrators while still appropriately barring unauthorized users from messaging and other system resources. (More on this in Chapters 7 and 8, "Installing Exchange 2000 Server.")

Windows 2000 Server also audits security. It can let you know when a user tries to add, delete, or access system resources.

The security of Exchange 2000 Server is enhanced in several ways beyond the Windows 2000 Server operating system's security. Access to Exchange Server objects such as public folders can be limited by the owner of the object. Data encryption on the server and client protects messages and other Exchange resources from eavesdropping by those with server or workstation access. Digital signatures prove the authenticity of a message. Even traffic between servers can be encrypted.

Exchange 2000 Server and Other Electronic Messaging Systems

The world of electronic messaging is far from a single-standard nirvana. A good electronic messaging system must connect to and communicate with a variety of other messaging systems. Microsoft has done a nice job of providing Exchange 2000 Server with key links, called *connectors,* to other systems, including Exchange 5.5 servers. The company has also built some cross-system message-content translators into Exchange 2000 Server that work automatically and very effectively. With these translators, you're less likely to send a message containing, say, a beautiful embedded image that can't be viewed by some or all of the message's recipients.

In the case of Microsoft's legacy messaging systems—Microsoft Mail for PC Networks and Microsoft Mail for AppleTalk Networks—you have an option beyond connectivity. You can choose to migrate users to Exchange. Migration utilities for other messaging systems such as Lotus cc:Mail are also provided with Exchange.

The following sections describe the most prominent messaging systems in use today.

Exchange Server 5.5

Exchange 2000 Server wouldn't be much of a connectivity product if it couldn't link with its predecessor, Exchange Server 5.5. It can, as you'll see in Chapter 6.

X.400

A fully standards-compatible X.400 service is built into Exchange Server. It can be used to access foreign X.400 messaging systems and to link groups of Exchange 2000 Servers. The 1984 and 1988 standards for X.400 are supported, as discussed in detail in Chapter 16, "Connecting to Other Foreign Messaging Systems."

SMTP

In league with Windows 2000 Server, Exchange 2000 Server supports the Simple Message Transport Protocol (SMTP) service. Unlike the old Microsoft Mail for PC Networks SMTP gateway, this implementation is a full-fledged SMTP host system capable of relaying messages and resolving addresses, while supporting several Enhanced SMPT (ESMTP) commands. UUencode/UUdecode and Multipurpose Internet Mail Extensions (MIME) message-content standards are also supported. So, after you've moved your users from MS Mail for PCs to Exchange 2000 Server, you won't hear any more of those vexing complaints about the meaningless MIME-source attachments that users get because the SMTP gateway was incapable of converting them back to their original binary format.

Microsoft Mail for PC Networks

A built-in connector makes Microsoft Mail for PC Networks 3.x (MS Mail 3.x) post offices look like Exchange 2000 servers to Outlook clients, and vice versa. If connectivity isn't enough, you can transfer MS Mail 3.x users to Exchange with a supplied migration tool. If all this is too much, Exchange clients can directly access MS Mail 3.x post offices. Thus, you can keep your MS Mail 3.x post offices, at least until you've got Exchange 2000 Server running the way you want and have moved everyone off the legacy mail system. I'll talk about MS Mail for PC Networks connectivity in Chapter 16.

Microsoft Mail for AppleTalk Networks

Connectivity for Microsoft Mail for AppleTalk Networks systems is also provided by a connector built into Exchange. When connectivity isn't enough, Mail for AppleTalk users can be migrated to Exchange Server. We'll look at MS Mail for AppleTalk Networks in Chapter 16.

cc:Mail

If Lotus cc:Mail is running in your shop, you'll be happy to hear that Exchange 2000 Server comes with tools to connect and migrate users to Exchange. Never let it be said that Microsoft doesn't care about users of IBM/Lotus products. At least there's a way to pull them into the MS camp.

Lotus Notes

Exchange 2000 Server also includes a connector for Lotus Notes. With this connector, Exchange and Notes clients can see each other's address directories and can exchange mail.

Other Messaging Systems

Gateways are available for links to other messaging systems such as Notes, PROFS, SNADS, fax, and MCI Mail. Both Microsoft and third parties build and support these gateways. You can even extend the benefit of these gateways to your MS Mail users.

Third-Party Applications for Exchange 2000 Server

Exchange Server has been around for some time now. This time has given third-party application providers time to develop an exciting range of add-on products. These include sophisticated products that enhance Exchange in such areas as document management, work flow, system backup, system management, faxing, security, virus control, wireless access, and application development.

At various places in this book, I'll spend some time discussing one of these third-party applications. For example, in Chapters 7 and 8, I talk about Exchange 2000 Server-specific backup products; in Chapter 17, I focus on apps for controlling those pesky viruses right inside Exchange Server. Appendix A, "Cool Third-Party Applications for Exchange/Outlook Clients and Exchange Server," contains a fairly exhaustive list of third-party apps for Exchange Server.

Summary

Microsoft Exchange 2000 Server represents a significant upgrade over previous versions, and contains features that position it as the premier messaging package for this age of electronic messaging. Even experienced Exchange Server 5.5 administrators will need to digest the information in this book to become proficient with Exchange 2000 Server.

For starters, Microsoft Exchange 2000 Server is closely tied to Windows 2000 Server —in fact, it won't run on Windows NT Server. Nonetheless, it is capable of messaging with a variety of legacy systems, as well as systems from other vendors. If all that isn't enough, you can use Exchange Server's APIs to build custom applications. Furthermore, Exchange 2000 Server scales both vertically and horizontally to grow with the needs of your enterprise.

Outlook 2000, Exchange's *native* e-mail client, provides a large variety of features for sending, receiving, and organizing mail messages using mailboxes, public and personal folders, and rules for automatically sorting and classifying e-mail. Furthermore, its e-mail functions are only part of the picture. Scheduling and contact management are big parts of Exchange 2000 Server's features. But perhaps most impressive is its capability of dynamically linking documents that are sent as e-mail attachments. Outlook can also import documents as OLE 2.0 objects into e-mail messages from other applications, while maintaining the formatting and editing features of the original application.

Now that you've gotten a taste of the features and functions of Exchange 2000 Server, it's time to learn about its constant companion, Windows 2000 Server. Read on to learn about this subject in Chapter 2.

CHAPTER <u>2</u>

2000: A Magic Number?

1999 will probably be best remembered as the year of the Y2K anxiety attack. Everyone and their sisters worried about the impact on computing systems of the early use of two digits to represent the YY part of the date in programming code. But when the calendar rolled over to 12:01:01 A.M. on January 1, 2000, precious little happened—largely because of the months of intensive work fixing millions of lines of ancient code.

On the upside, Y2K brought us a slew of new and mostly improved products from Microsoft. The first to hit the streets was the Windows line: Windows 2000 Professional, Server, and Advanced Server. Windows 2000 Datacenter Server followed several months later. On overall evaluation, I must admit that although there aren't any totally new technologies in the Windows 2000 product line, this represents a major step forward for Microsoft. Active Directory and the new Windows 2000 security system alone bring Windows server products into parity with products such as Novell's NetWare, which, along with Banyan's Vines, brought network-wide directory services to PC-based systems a number of years ago.

Exchange 2000 Server is another Y2K product of significance from Microsoft. However, Exchange 2000 is much more an evolutionary than revolutionary product. Some of the most significant pieces of Exchange Server 5.x, such as Exchange directory services, are now gone, having been extensively updated and integrated into the Windows 2000 server line. Furthermore, Exchange Server 5.x management functionality has been integrated into Windows 2000 server. This is good because you can now more easily parcel out electronic messaging management functions to different people or groups. It's not so good because Exchange Server 5.x's all-in-one-place Administrator program is gone, replaced by a seemingly dizzying array of disparate Windows 2000 management tools, officially called *Microsoft Management Console snap-ins*.

One of my goals in writing this book is to facilitate your entry into the new and sometimes daunting world of Windows 2000/Exchange 2000. As the last two paragraphs indicate, I certainly have my work cut out for me.

 WARNING You might be tempted to bypass this chapter because it seems to concentrate extensively on comparisons between Windows 2000 Server and Windows NT Server 4, as well as comparisons between Exchange 2000 Server and Exchange Server 5.5. "After all," you might say, "I'm new to both Windows 2000 Server and Exchange 2000 Server. What do I need with all this comparison stuff?" My advice? Read this chapter. It contains a great deal of introductory information about both Windows 2000 Server and Exchange 2000 Server. The few minutes that you'll spend reading it will not only give you the lowdown on the relationship between the two products, but it also will provide a strong base for the chapters to come. Try it! You'll like it! I promise.

Windows 2000 Server: What's New, What Isn't?

"Wait a minute!" you say. "Isn't this a book about Exchange 2000 Server? Why are we starting right off talking about Windows 2000 Server?" The answer is quite simple.

Windows 2000 Server and Exchange 2000 Server are so tightly integrated that we really can't talk about one without talking about the other—and Windows 2000 Server must come first. That doesn't mean that you need to be an expert in every aspect of Windows 2000 Server to implement and support Exchange 2000 Server. However, you will need a solid grounding in a number of aspects of Windows 2000 Server. Therefore, I'm going to spend a fair amount of time in this book covering information that Exchange 2000 Server planners, designers, administrators, and managers need to know about Windows 2000 Server to do their jobs successfully.

As you can see in Figure 2.1, on the surface, Windows 2000 looks a lot like Windows 98. But that's just the surface. Under the Windows 2000 GUI is an extremely powerful operating system designed to cover everything from the end-user desktop to the very high-end mainframe-oriented server environment.

FIGURE 2.1

*On the surface,
Windows 2000 looks
like Windows 98.*

Windows 2000 is actually four different products, three of which are server products. Each offers a different level of computing capacity and features. I'll talk about these in the section "The Four Flavors of Windows 2000," later in this chapter. Windows 2000 Server is a wonderfully well thought-out amalgam of existing technologies, many of which are new to the Windows server environment or are used in new ways in Windows 2000 Server. Some of these technologies were imported without change into Windows 2000 Server. We'll take a look at the Windows 2000 product line later in this chapter. Let's begin with a discussion of what's new and what isn't in Windows 2000 Server when it is compared to its predecessor, Windows NT Server 4.

Key New Features of Windows 2000 Server

As you'll discover throughout this chapter, Windows 2000 Server is somewhat like a bride at a wedding, wearing something old, something new, something borrowed, and something blue.

First, let's examine the *old*. Some functionality in Windows 2000 Server remains unchanged from NT Server 4. For example, the Control Panel still exists, albeit with fewer applets on display because some functionality formerly in the Control Panel has moved elsewhere in Windows 2000 Server. After you find the new homes for this functionality, you'll see that a number of other functions are performed exactly as in NT Server 4. For example, you no longer access the Open Database Connectivity (ODBC) interface through the Control Panel. Instead, you start the applet through the Administrative Tools menu. For all this change, however, the ODBC interface itself is exactly the same in Windows 2000 as in Windows NT. In addition, you still manage the Windows 2000 Server desktop environment in pretty much the same way as with NT Server 4. More on this comes in the section "What Hasn't Changed in Windows 2000 Server?"

Very little in Windows 2000 Server is really *new*. What is new is the code that implements this massive operating system, and the mixture of old and borrowed functionality to create an exciting operating system with much greater capability and capacity than Windows NT Server.

Microsoft borrowed heavily from itself and from Unix in creating Windows 2000 Server. From Unix came such things as the integration of the Domain Name System (DNS) into the Windows 2000 Server operating system. From the Unix world (if not exactly from Unix), Microsoft borrowed the Kerberos authentication system to beef up Windows 2000 Server security. From Banyan's Vines and Novell's NetWare—as well as one of my favorite products, Exchange Server 5.x—Microsoft borrowed the components upon which it built the very core of Windows 2000 Server, Active Directory. If you know Exchange 5.5's directory service, you'll find that Windows 2000

Server's Active Directory offers few surprises. Given this borrowing, you shouldn't be surprised to learn that certain queries against Active Directory are done using the Lightweight Directory Access Protocol (LDAP), which was used to query the Exchange 5.5 directory service. Also borrowed from Exchange 5.5 are sites and folder replication. Sites enable you to effectively link network segments over high- or low-bandwidth networks. Folder replication, in league with site links, lets users locally access network-based files, no matter how low the bandwidth is connecting their network to the rest of the network.

Finally comes something *blue*. I'm glad this one comes last because I have sort of a lame joke to tell here. It goes like this: As you know, Windows 2000 Server is based on NT Server, and NT Server is based on OS/2 (remember that one?). OS/2 was developed jointly by Microsoft and IBM and then was taken over by IBM. Of course, IBM has long been referred to as—drum roll—*Big Blue*. Yea, I know.

All joking aside, despite being based mostly in old and borrowed technologies, Windows 2000 Server is a very different beast than Windows NT Server. Let's take a look at some of Windows 2000 Server's new features. Then we'll spend a little time on what hasn't changed.

Windows 2000 Server Active Directory and Security

Before we move on to the Windows 2000 Server product line, we need to take a quick look at Windows 2000 Active Directory and security. I could write a whole book on these two exciting features, and I'll discuss them in much more detail in Chapters 3, "Two Key Architectural Components of Windows 2000 Server"; 6, "Upgrading to Windows 2000 Server and Exchange 2000 Server"; 7, "Installing Windows 2000 Server"; 8, "Installing Exchange 2000 Server"; 11, "Managing Exchange Users, Distribution Groups, and Contacts"; and 17, "Advanced Exchange Server Management." For now, let me give you a quick overview of Windows 2000 Active Directory and security.

Active Directory is a grand repository for information about such entities as users, domains, computers, domain controllers, shared resources (such as files and printers), and security. Active Directory lets you log into very large domains and use resources across the domain with ease. All objects in Active Directory are protected by a security system based on Kerberos, an industry-standard secret-key encryption network authentication protocol developed at the Massachusetts Institute of Technology. (For more on Kerberos, see http://web.mit.edu/kerberos/www./.) Windows 2000 Server controls who can see each object in Active Directory, what attributes each user can see, and what actions a user can perform on an object. The Windows 2000 permissions model is richer and more complex under the hood than NT's, but it's quite easy to manage at the user interface level. Windows 2000 group policies are also a significant improvement over NT 4's policies: For example, they enable you to set a range of policies for users and computers, determine what software can be installed on a computer, and tie the application of specific policies to Windows 2000 security groups.

Figure 2.2 shows the three major tools (Microsoft Management Console snap-ins) for Active Directory management: Active Directory Users and Computers, Active Directory Domains and Trusts, and Active Directory Sites and Services. Figure 2.2 shows the Properties dialog box for my Windows 2000 user account.

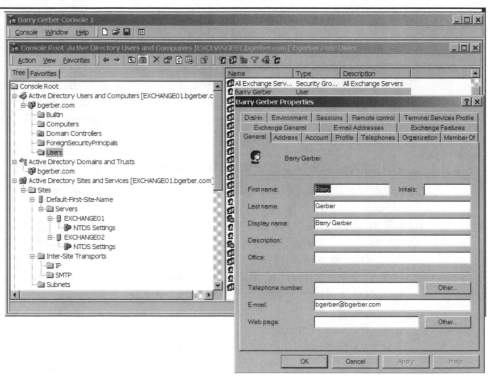

FIGURE 2.2

The three major tools for managing Windows 2000 Server Active Directory plus the Properties dialog box for a Windows 2000 user.

What's neat about the Windows 2000 User Properties dialog box is that it brings together functionality in the Windows NT 4 User Manager for Domains (the Account, Profile, and Terminal Services tabs, for example) and the Exchange 5.5 Administrator (the Exchange General and E-mail Addresses tabs, for example).

In fact, if you know Exchange 5.5, a lot of what you see in Active Directory should be quite familiar. The Properties dialog box in Figure 2.2 has a lot of the qualities of the Exchange 5.5 recipient mailbox Properties dialog box (see Figure 2.3).

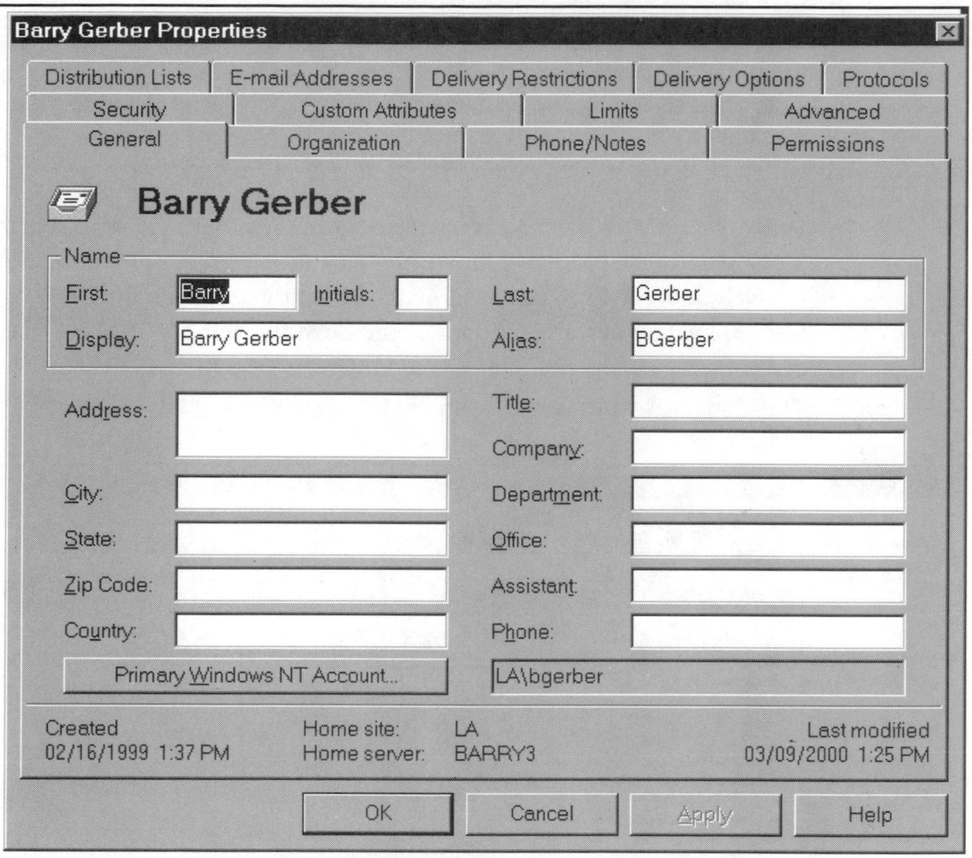

FIGURE 2.3

*Similarities exist
between the Properties
dialog box for a
Windows 2000 user
account and the
Exchange 5.5 Mailbox
Properties dialog box.*

Barry Gerber Properties ☒

Distribution Lists	E-mail Addresses	Delivery Restrictions	Delivery Options	Protocols
Security	Custom Attributes		Limits	Advanced
General	Organization		Phone/Notes	Permissions

📧 **Barry Gerber**

┌─ Name ──
First: `Barry`   Initials: ` `   Last: `Gerber`
Display: `Barry Gerber`   Alias: `BGerber`
└───

Address: ` `   Title: ` `

Company: ` `

City: ` `   Department: ` `

State: ` `   Office: ` `

Zip Code: ` `   Assistant: ` `

Country: ` `   Phone: ` `

[Primary Windows NT Account...]   `LA\bgerber`

Created   Home site: LA   Last modified
02/16/1999 1:37 PM   Home server: BARRY3   03/09/2000 1:25 PM

[OK]   [Cancel]   [Apply]   [Help]

Exchange 5.5 users will also find the Active Directory Sites and Services snap-in
familiar—at least, the *Sites* part. Sites were used in Exchange 5.5 to integrate networks
connected by slower non-LAN networking technologies into the overall Exchange
environment. They ensure that continuous, high-speed connections aren't required
for networks in the same organization to remain connected. Well, Microsoft has
moved this sites technology from Exchange to Windows 2000 Server. Microsoft
implemented sites in Windows 2000 Server to make it possible to build large, single-
domain Windows networks even if some segments of those networks were connected
by relatively slow wide-area links. Servers can share Active Directory information and
even files through site links. This is a major change in emphasis for Microsoft networking, and one that we'll revisit many times in this book.

NOTE All of this Windows 2000 Server site stuff doesn't let Exchange 2000 Server managers off the hook. They'll still need to set up routing groups, the equivalent of Exchange 5.5 sites, and implement Exchange 2000 Server connectors between routing groups.

Let's take a quick look at Active Directory from the user's view point of view. Figure 2.4 illustrates the process of browsing available resources using the Windows 2000 equivalent of NT 4's Explorer. In Active Directory in this figure, I've located user Barry Gerber; by right-clicking his name, I can open this user's Web home page (if he has one) or send him mail. If I select Send Mail, my default e-mail client—Outlook 2000, in my case—will open, and then I do everything as though I was in Outlook.

FIGURE 2.4

Active Directory from the end user perspective

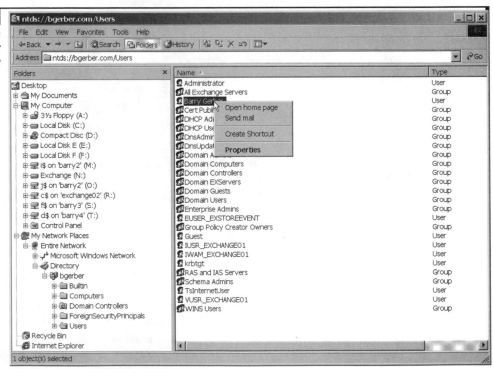

Of course, I can still send e-mail to Barry directly from Outlook without finding him in the Active Directory tree. The point here is that, with Active Directory, users can quickly and easily find just about anything that they might need in a networked computing environment.

Windows 2000 Server: E-Mail Not Included

I should point out that, with one exception, e-mail services are not built into the Windows 2000 Server product line. All the e-mail–related stuff that we've just looked in Active Directory doesn't exist until you install Exchange 2000 Server in a Windows 2000 domain. Unlike the Unix operating system, which comes with a working, if primitive, electronic messaging capability, Windows 2000 Server is almost mail-less without Exchange 2000. Well, maybe that's a bit of an overstatement. Although SMTP mail send and receive services do come with Windows 2000, standard Exchange mailbox services and POP3 and IMAP4 messaging servers are available only after Exchange 2000 is installed in a domain.

How about third-party alternatives to Exchange 2000 Server for Windows 2000 Server? There appear to be no technical barriers to third parties building their own fully functional messaging systems for Windows 2000 Server that use Windows 2000 Server's basic SMTP services.

The Domain Name System, the Lightweight Directory Access Protocol, and Other Internet Protocols

Before we move on to talk about the Windows 2000 Server product line, let's talk a bit about the role of two Windows 2000 Server services: the Domain Name System (DNS) and the Lightweight Directory Access Protocol (LDAP). Old Exchange Server 5.x hands should know both of these intimately. Just as the concepts behind Active Directory were borrowed from Exchange 5.5, Microsoft also borrowed heavily from its use of DNS in relation to Exchange Server 5.x and its implementation of LDAP in Exchange Server 5.x.

NT 4 could get along quite well without DNS. You installed DNS mainly to locally support Internet name resolution—the conversion of external computer names to IP addresses, and vice versa. Although you could use DNS for local name resolution, it was usually done using NetBEUI or the Windows Internet Name Service (WINS), which resolves Microsoft NetBIOS workstation names to IP addresses.

Windows 2000 Server Active Directory can't run without DNS. As do Unix systems, Windows 2000 Server uses DNS to resolve internal as well as external computer names to IP addresses, and vice versa. Windows 2000 Servers still support native NetBEUI networking, although you have to jump through a few more hoops than with NT 4 to install it. WINS is still supported on Windows 2000 Servers, but only for legacy NT and other operating systems. The goal in a pure Windows 2000 Server/Workstation network is for all name resolution services to be done by DNS. Put in other terms, to find the IP address of a computer on a Windows 2000 Server network, a computer should query a Windows 2000 server running DNS.

These concepts are pretty easy to understand. However, you might scratch your head more than once trying to figure out why a Windows 2000 server computer can't talk to an NT 4 computer on your network. The reason is very likely that you've never installed NetBEUI on the Windows 2000 server. How do I know this? I've just about scratched off all the hair on the left side of my head.

A great feature of Windows 2000 Server DNS is that it can run in dynamic mode. In this mode, you can use the Dynamic Host Configuration Protocol (DHCP) to assign IP addresses to computers on your network and still have the more or less randomly assigned address correctly associated with the appropriate workstation name in the DNS.

What Happened to Those Backup Domain Controllers?

Within a Windows NT Server 4 domain, you could have one primary and one or more secondary domain controllers. Domain controllers were the founts of network resource and security knowledge in NT 4 networks. If a primary domain controller crashed, the remaining secondary controllers held an election, and one of them became the primary domain controller. That has all changed in Windows 2000 Server. All domain controllers in a Windows 2000 Server network are *primary*, to use an NT 4 term. You and Windows 2000 Server don't need to worry about failed controllers, or how and if a backup controller gets quickly and properly promoted to primary controller status. Everybody's equal.

Now let's look quickly at the Lightweight Directory Access Protocol (LDAP). LDAP was used in Exchange 5.5 to access information in the Exchange directory. That's also exactly what it's used for in Windows 2000 Server, except that the target is Active Directory, not the no longer existent Exchange directory. Security willing, you can still search for e-mail addresses using an LDAP-compliant client. But, with Windows 2000 Server/Exchange 2000 Server, you're searching Windows 2000 Server's Active Directory, not the Exchange directory.

NOTE LDAP names use the X.500 format. The native Exchange Server address of a mailbox, for example, is in X.500 format (c = US; a = ; p = bgerber; o = LA; s = Gerber; g = Barry). Active Directory also supports Internet RFC 822 names (bg@bgerber.com), HTTP (Web) URL names (http://bgerber.com), and Microsoft UNC names (\\server1\share1). Of course, LDAP is used only to access LDAP names. Other technologies are used to access RFC 882, HTTP and UNC names.

Two key Internet protocols that were once the exclusive province of Exchange 5.5—the Simple Mail Transport Protocol (SMTP) and the Network News Transport Protocol (NNTP)—are now supported right inside Windows 2000. SMTP is used to replicate information across Windows 2000 sites. NNTP support is finally where it belongs: in the operating system. That doesn't mean that Exchange 2000 Server makes no use of these protocols, however. SMTP supports everything from Internet messaging to cross-server public folder replication in Exchange 2000, and NNTP is still supported through Exchange public folders.

Enough new stuff! Let's move on to the unchanged aspects of Windows 2000 Server.

NOTE Well, maybe I should mention one more thing before we move on. New to Windows 2000 Server is support for a fairly wide range of peripheral devices never supported by NT Server 4. Essentially, this includes pretty much the full range of devices supported by Windows 98, including support for DVD ROM and Universal Serial Bus (USB) devices. I love it; I'm running a USB video camera on one of my Windows 2000 Advanced Server computers.

What Hasn't Changed in Windows 2000 Server?

A great deal of the functionality in NT Server 4 was imported directly into Windows 2000 Server. Although the code underlying this functionality may have changed somewhat, the user interface is often exactly or nearly the same.

Active Directory has brought many changes to resource management and security, but you can still access a lot of network resources in the same way that you did using NT Server 4. For example, you can still map a network drive using the familiar drive-mapping interface that you know and love from NT Server 4. Well, I should qualify that: The interface looks a little more artsy and "Webbish," but it works just like the interface in NT Server 4. In addition, you can still use the Printers icon on the Settings submenu of the Start menu to add and manage printers.

You still manage your desktop by right-clicking on it; the same holds true for the Taskbar, for you Task Manager aficionados. Aside from some Windows 98-related changes, the Windows 2000 Server desktop looks pretty much like the NT Server 4 desktop. For example, the Taskbar works just as it does in NT Server 4; it just looks like the Windows 98 Taskbar and shares that Taskbar's enhanced functionality.

Although you can run the old NT 4 (Windows 95) Explorer using the Start menu's Run option, Explorer is no longer a default Start menu option. Given this state of affairs, you'll probably find yourself using the My Computer desktop icon to browse your computer and the network, including Active Directory. My Computer is a little different from Explorer, but you should be pretty comfortable using it, as long as you disable Web content in folders and click the Folders button on My Computer's Standard toolbar.

As I mentioned earlier, although some functions no longer occupy a prominent place in the Windows 2000 Server Control Panel, when you find them, they function pretty much as they did in NT Server 4. For example, the Open Database Connectivity (ODBC) applet icon is no longer available when you open the Control Panel. Where is it? It's on the Administrative Tools submenu of the Start menu and is called Data Sources (ODBC). Of course, technically, ODBC is still on the Control Panel because there's an Administrative Tools icon on the Control Panel. You just have to remember to click open Administrative Tools to see ODBC.

On the other hand, some old functions are actually easier to find. For example, although there's still a Network icon on the Control Panel, now called Network and Dial-up Connections, you can find the same icon on the Start Menu's Settings submenu in Windows 2000 Server. You can also right-click My Network Places on your desktop and select Properties from the menu that pops up. I can't tell you how much time these little enhancements have saved me. I access the Network configuration applet several times a day, and with Windows 2000 Server, I no longer have to go to the Control Panel to open it.

Even some things that may seem new to you really aren't. As Figure 2.2 illustrates, you'll be using a number of new tools—Microsoft Management Console snap-ins, to be precise—to manage your Windows 2000 Server environment. However, while the tools are new, Microsoft Management Console (MMC), the place where you snap-in and run these tools (the master window in Figure 2.2, titled Barry Gerber Console 1), is far from new. MMC has been used since the dawn of the NT Server 4 Option Pack to manage such NT Server add-ons as Internet Information Server.

As you can see, a lot hasn't changed between NT Server 4 and Windows 2000 Server. And I've only skimmed the surface here, focusing on the kinds of functionality that is key to really basic Windows 2000 Server management. As you work with Windows 2000 Server, you discover lots more under the hood that's pure NT 4 Server.

Windows 2000 Server and NT 4 Server: A Summary of Major Differences and Similarities

After reading about Windows 2000 Server in this section, you've probably got a fair picture of key differences and similarities between Microsoft's new server product line and its older NT 4 Server products. Let me quickly summarize these and emphasize their significance.

Active Directory and Kerberos-based security are the most important additions to the Windows 2000 Server product line. Active Directory with Kerberos security provides a new way to organize, protect, and access network resources. Large, single-domain networks now are not only possible, but highly desirable. The Active Directory tree and Windows 2000's new security model make it easy for managers to administer all or part of an organization's resources and for users to access all or part of those resources.

With Active Directory taking center stage in Windows 2000 Server, you use the Active Directory Users and Computers tool to create new users and manage existing users. NT Server's User Manager for Domains is a thing of the past. NT Server's Server Manager has been replaced by this and other tools.

Windows 2000 Server supports native NetBEUI, but you have to make a much more conscious decision to install it than with NT 4. If you, like I, have been cheating by running NetBEUI in nonrouted networks, you'll have to be sure to manually install NetBEUI, bite the bullet and install WINS, or move to a full DNS-supported network naming environment. I recommend the DNS route.

As for the similarities between Windows 2000 Server and NT Server 4, when your first Window 2000 Server initially starts up, you should find its basic user interface quite familiar, especially if you've worked with Windows 98. Much in the basic Windows interface was borrowed from older Windows products. Also, although you may have to search a bit to find it, you'll often discover that functionality available in NT 4 Server has familiar user interfaces in Windows 2000 Server.

Now let's take a look at the different products bearing the Windows 2000 name and see how they compare to the NT Server 4 product line.

The Four Flavors of Windows 2000

Windows 2000 is packaged as four separate products: Windows 2000 Professional, a workstation product, and three versions of Windows 2000 Server: Windows 2000 Server, Windows 2000 Advanced Server, and Windows 2000 Datacenter Server. As I mentioned earlier, I'll use the term *Windows 2000 Server* when I refer to the three server products collectively. Let's begin with a look at the various flavors of Windows 2000 and see how they relate to the various NT Server 4 products.

Windows 2000 Professional

Windows 2000 Professional is the end-user desktop version of Windows 2000. The neatest thing about Professional is its capability to take full advantage of the services offered in a Windows 2000 server environment. For example, a Professional workstation can make full use of Active Directory services and Windows 2000 security. Neither Windows NT Workstation nor Windows 95/98 can fully participate as members of a Windows 2000 domain.

Microsoft has positioned Windows 2000 Professional as the desktop operating system of choice in business computing environments; it replaces NT Workstation 4. For the home user, Microsoft recommends Windows Millennium, or Windows Me, the replacement for Windows 98. If you're establishing a new Windows-based system in a business setting, Windows 2000 Professional should be the product of choice. I'd even recommend that you cheat and put Professional on every computer you touch, including any computers you use at home. That way, you'll be able to connect to Windows 2000 Server systems and enjoy all the benefits that they offer.

Windows 2000 Server

Microsoft has positioned Windows 2000 Server similarly to Window NT Server 4. However, unlike NT Server 4, on which you can run Exchange Server 5.x Enterprise Edition, you can't run Exchange 2000 Enterprise Server on Windows 2000 Server. For that, you'll need Windows 2000 Advanced Server or Datacenter Server. The standard edition of Exchange 2000, Exchange 2000 Server, will run on Windows 2000 Server.

Windows 2000 Server fully supports Active Directory and Windows 2000 security. It can run on computers with one to four processors and up to 4GB of random access memory (RAM). Microsoft recommends using Windows 2000 Server to support file and print sharing, small databases, moderate throughput World Wide Web services, and the group (nonenterprise) mail services available in the standard edition Exchange 2000 product, Exchange 2000 Server.

If you're interested in price, Windows 2000 Server is priced at about the same level as Windows NT Server. With 25 client licenses, Windows 2000 Server has a street price at this writing of about $1,400.

Windows 2000 Advanced Server

Windows 2000 Advanced Server is the middle-level product in the Windows 2000 Server line. It runs on machines with up to eight processors and up to 8GB of RAM. In many ways, Advanced Server is very much like NT Server 4 Enterprise Edition.

Windows 2000 Advanced Server has a couple of really neat built-in features. The first is two-node server clustering. Server clustering in Advanced Server lets you build two-computer redundant systems, where one computer can take over if the other fails. In many cases, clustered servers, having the same data stored on their disks, can also service heavy client loads more efficiently and quickly.

Windows 2000 Advanced Server also allows for up to 32-node network load balancing. Essentially, this capability distributes incoming requests for individual TCP/IP services across a group of servers. This is especially useful in networks that support high-demand Internet applications.

According to Microsoft, Advanced Server is the place to run hefty database and Internet applications as well as Exchange 2000 Enterprise Server. In fact, in the same way that SQL Server Enterprise Editions 6 and 7 require NT Server 4 Enterprise Edition or Windows 2000 Advanced Server, Exchange 2000 Enterprise Server won't even install on anything less than Windows 2000 Advanced Server.

Windows 2000 Advanced Server sells at about the same price as NT Server 4 Enterprise Edition. The street price at this writing is about $3,300 with 25 client licenses.

Windows 2000 Datacenter Server

Windows 2000 Datacenter Server is the steamroller of Windows 2000 Server products. It's the monster server for highest-demand applications, and Microsoft has never offered a product of this capacity: It can run on computers with up to 32 processors and up to 64GB of RAM. Wow! It also supports up to 4-node clustering and 32-node network load balancing.

Microsoft recommends Datacenter Server for really heavy-duty database and Internet applications. It's also the place to run Exchange 2000 Enterprise Server if you've got lots of users.

Microsoft also suggests that you use Datacenter Server to consolidate existing Windows NT domains. You'll remember that Windows 2000 Server was designed with a very different concept of domains in mind. Simply put, domains can be much larger in terms of resources and users than with Windows NT 4. Microsoft encourages new adopters of its Windows 2000 Server products to think in terms of big domains—

really big domains—and it strongly advises that those converting from NT 4 to Windows 2000 Server should consolidate domains. In many cases, Microsoft argues, all you really need with Windows 2000 Server is one overarching domain.

As of this writing, Microsoft hadn't announced pricing for Datacenter Server.

Now we're ready to take a look at Exchange 2000 Server.

Exchange 2000 Server: What's New, What Isn't?

Well, we're finally in Exchange 2000 Server territory. You'll find that the time we've given to Windows 2000 Server was far from wasted. Let's jump right into the similarities and differences between Exchange Server 5.x and Exchange 2000 Server. Then we'll take a look at the two products in the Exchange 2000 line: Exchange 2000 Server and Exchange 2000 Enterprise Server.

Unlike the section on what's new in Windows 2000 Server, I'm going to mix the new and the old in one section. Hopefully this will cut down on some frustration, especially if you're an Exchange Server 5.5 user, because so much of what's old is hidden behind a set of new doors. If I don't open those doors in addition to showing them to you, and instead make you wait for a section on what's not changed in Exchange 2000 Server, you're going to hate me by the end of the chapter!

In many ways, Exchange 2000 Server is new for what has been removed rather than for what has been added. Exchange 5.5 directory services have been replaced by Windows 2000 Server Active Directory services. Exchange Server 5.5 sites have been replaced by routing groups. These changes have led to a number of changes in the user interfaces that you use to manage Exchange 2000 Server. Much of what previously was managed in Exchange Server 5.5's Administrator program is now managed either in Active Directory interfaces or in an array of Windows 2000 Server-based Microsoft Management Console snap-ins for Exchange 2000 Server.

If you're looking for really new stuff in Exchange 2000 Server, you'll have to turn to things such as storage groups, instant messaging services, and Exchange 2000 Conferencing Server. So, let's take a look at what's new, by this definition, in Exchange 2000 Server.

Bye, Bye Exchange Directory Services

As I noted earlier, Microsoft beefed up and extended Exchange 5.5's directory services and then turned it into Windows 2000 Server's Active Directory. So, some of the things that you previously did in Exchange Server 5.5 user interfaces, you now do in an Active Directory interface. For example, you use an Active Directory user interface to enable a Windows 2000 user's mailbox and to create what used to be called *custom recipients* (now *contacts*) and *distribution lists* (now *distribution groups*).

Figure 2.5 illustrates the process of adding a new Exchange 2000 Server distribution group to my Windows 2000 Active Directory. I'm creating this group in exactly the same place as I'd create a Windows 2000 Server security group. You should know local and global security groups from NT Server 4.

FIGURE 2.5

Creating an Exchange 2000 Server distribution group in Windows 2000 Server's Active Directory

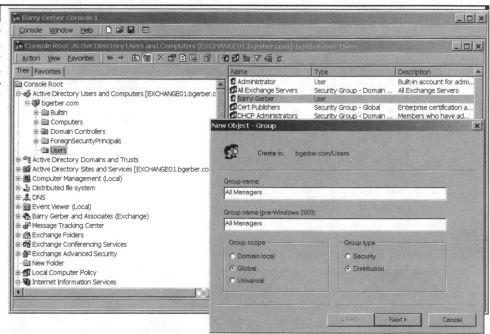

One of the major differences between a distribution group and a Windows 2000 Server security group is that one has an attribute identifying it as a distribution group and the other has an attribute identifying it as a security group. When an address list (the global address list, for example) is created and updated on an Exchange 2000 server, all eligible Active Directory groups with the distribution group attribute are included in that address list.

Figure 2.6 shows the dialog box for managing an Exchange 2000 Server distribution group. I opened it by double-clicking on the All Managers row in the window just in back of the All Managers dialog box. You add e-mail addresses to the distribution group on the Members property page and then add the distribution group to other distribution groups on the Member Of property page. We'll get into the creation of Exchange 2000 Server recipients later in Chapters 11, "Managing Exchange Users, Distribution Groups, and Contacts," and 12, "Managing the Exchange Server Hierarchy and Core Components." For now, I hope you're beginning to see how important it is to know how to use and manage Active Directory to manage Exchange 2000 recipient objects.

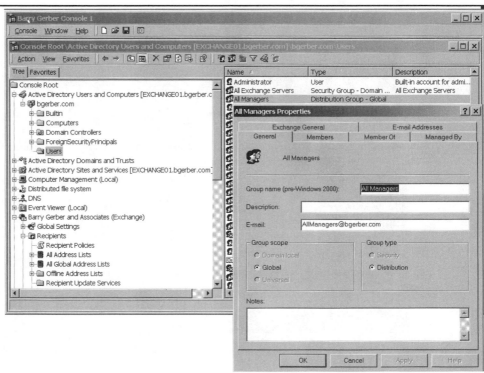

FIGURE 2.6

Managing an Exchange 2000 Server distribution group

Just so you don't get the idea that all recipient management is done in the Active Directory snap-in, take a look at Figure 2.7. Here, I'm using an Exchange 2000 Server snap-in for Microsoft Management Console to view and manage the default domain addresses assigned to recipients in my Exchange 2000 system. For example, I can edit my default SMTP (Internet mail) domain address @bgerber.com.

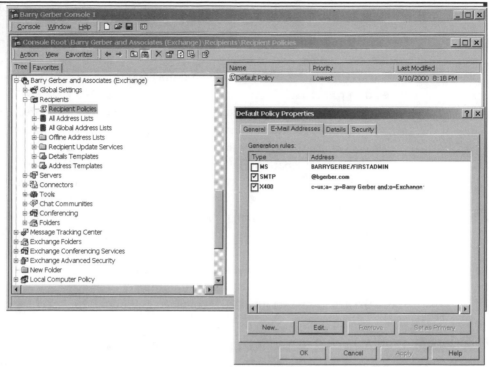

FIGURE 2.7

Managing recipient policies using an Exchange 2000 Server Microsoft Management Console snap-in

It's important to realize that, although I'm using an interface other than an Active Directory snap-in to manage these recipient objects, the objects and attributes that I'm managing still live in Active Directory. For the most part, Microsoft has very carefully isolated interfaces related to Exchange 2000 Server to assure that they show up in logical places. It makes sense to manage user mailboxes, distribution groups, and custom recipients in the Active Directory interface. It doesn't make sense to manage generic recipient attributes such as default e-mail domain names in the Active Directory Users and Computers interface.

Look at some of the other objects in the container called Recipients in the Barry Gerber and Associates (Exchange) container. Many of these should be familiar to Exchange Server 5.5 users, such as the address list and template objects.

Bye, Bye Exchange Server Sites

Exchange Server 5.5 users will remember Exchange Server 5.5 sites as a tool both for allowing lower-bandwidth network links between servers in the same Exchange organization and for implementing distributed administrative access to groups of Exchange servers in the same organization. Say that you had an office in Los Angeles and one in New York, and all you had for a link between the two was a T1 line. With Exchange Server 5.5, it would be best to put each of the offices in its own Exchange site and connect the two sites using some sort of site connector. Site connectors didn't require continuous, high-speed connectivity to keep Exchange 5.5 directories and public folders synchronized. They communicate primarily using X.400- or SMTP-based data protocols.

Just as Exchange site connectors allowed geographically distributed Exchange 5.5 servers to participate in the same Exchange organization, Windows 2000 Server site connectors are key to building larger Windows 2000 Server domains. No longer do you have to create separate domains just because your servers are separated by low-bandwidth networks. Just link your Windows 2000 sites into a single domain using Windows 2000 Server sites.

Exchange Server 5.5 allowed for multiple redundant connectors between sites and for setting priorities between site connectors based on the bandwidth available on different connectors. Thus, you could use a T1 line for your daily site link, but specify that a DSL or even dial-up link should be used if the T1 were not be available. Windows 2000 Server sites allow for similar site link prioritization options. See Figure 2.8 for a view of the Active Directory user interface for managing Windows 2000 Server sites.

FIGURE 2.8

Managing Windows 2000 Server sites using the Active Directory Sites and Services Microsoft Management Console snap-in

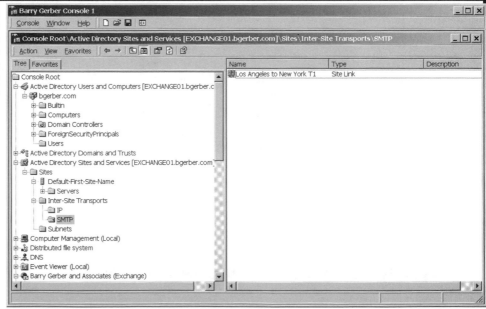

Exchange 2000 servers separated by lower bandwidth can still be grouped and connected to compensate for lower-bandwidth wide-area links. You don't use Windows 2000 Server sites. Instead, you use what are called in Exchange 2000 Server *message routing groups*. After you're over the different naming convention, all is pretty much the same, including how you set up and use Exchange connectors. Distributed administration of groups of Exchange servers is not implemented in routing groups. Rather, Exchange 2000 administrative groups support distributed management. In Exchange 2000 message routing and distributed management have been separated, which, as many Exchange 5.5 administrators will attest, is a very good thing. Lots more on all of this comes in later chapters.

"New" User Interfaces

Exchange 2000 Server is chock-full of new user interfaces. Well, maybe that's a bit of an exaggeration. The interfaces aren't always all that new. Where they're located is. Borrowing an analogy from earlier in this chapter, the doors are new. What's behind them is pretty much the same. Let me talk a bit about some of the "new" interfaces that we haven't already covered.

Figure 2.9 shows the user interface for Exchange 2000 provided by the Exchange System Manager snap-in. Exchange 5.5 users will recognize a number of familiar management functions. From top to bottom, you deal here with Exchange organization-wide (global) property settings, property settings relating to Exchange 2000 recipients, server management (which includes the management of a range of Internet and other protocols), and Exchange 2000 Server storage groups.

FIGURE 2.9

The Exchange System Manager Microsoft Management Console snap-in

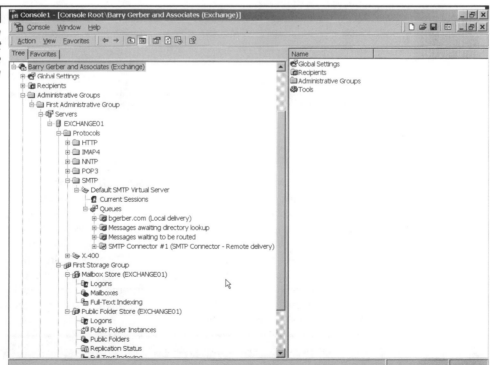

Services for both Network News Transfer Protocol (NNTP) and Simple Mail Transfer Protocol (SMTP) are installed when you install Windows 2000 Server. Both are required if you're going to install Exchange 2000 Server. Before you install Exchange 2000 Server, these two interfaces live in the Internet Information Server snap-in (see Figure 2.10). After you install Exchange 2000, the interfaces move to the Exchange container shown in Figure 2.9. It took me a while to realize this and, thus, to find these interfaces after I installed Exchange 2000 Server.

FIGURE 2.10

The NNTP and SMTP interfaces can be found in the Internet Information Services interface before Exchange 2000 Server is installed.

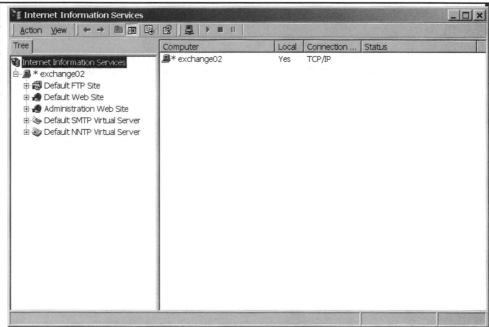

 NOTE As a Windows 2000 Server service, the Simple Mail Transfer Protocol is used to send messages to and receive them from external Internet e-mail systems; the Network News Transfer Protocol supports those neat to nasty Internet newsgroups. Both of these services can function just fine without Exchange 2000 Server. When Exchange 2000 Server is installed, SMTP services are modified to provide Exchange 2000 Server mailbox users with Internet message transfer functionality, and NNTP services are enhanced to allow Exchange 2000 users to see select newsgroups in Exchange 2000 Server public folders. As you'll see in Chapters 13, "Managing Exchange Internet Services," and 14, "Managing Exchange 2000 Services for Internet Clients," both services are significantly enhanced when Exchange 2000 Server is installed.

Now take a look at Figure 2.11, which shows the organization-wide System Manager user interface for Exchange Server 2000. You actually saw this interface back in Figure 2.7 and 2.9. I've just expanded it a bit here so that you can see a lot more of what's inside the container. Again, old hands at Exchange Server 5.5 will recognize a wide range of interfaces formerly found in the Exchange Server Administrator.

FIGURE 2.11

The organization-wide system manager user interface for Exchange Server 2000

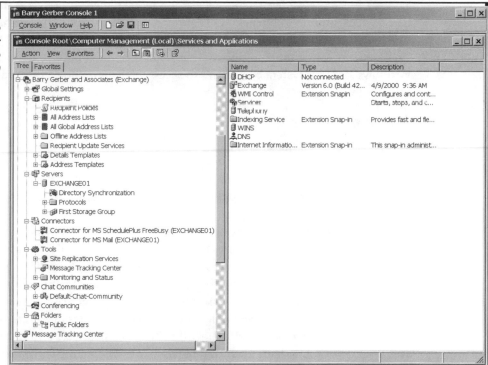

Notice the last container visible in Figure 2.11, the Message Tracking Center. It occupies the same level in the Microsoft Management Console hierarchy as the Barry Gerber and Associates (Exchange) organization-wide container. You'll notice that the tracking center is also visible in the Tools container within the Barry Gerber and Associates (Exchange) container. This is one of the neat capabilities of Microsoft Management Console. Not only do many containers (and their user interfaces) live within other containers, but they also can exist independently of those containers. I was able to install a separate instance of message tracking outside the Exchange 2000 Server System Manager container. This way, to get to message tracking, I don't need to drill down into the System Manager container to find it.

Other New Stuff

As should be clear by now, from an Exchange administrator's perspective and in general, basic administration hasn't changed all that much with Exchange 2000 Server. After you figure out where you have to go to do whatever you previously did in the Exchange Server Administrator program, doing it is much like doing it in Exchange Server 5.5. There are a few really new features in Exchange, although even they borrow from existing technologies. These are storage groups, instant messaging, and Conference Server. A couple of other features come pretty close to qualifying as radically new, including support for Exchange mailboxes and public folders through the Windows 2000 file system commands to access the information store and fully indexed text searches.

Storage Groups

Storage groups (see Figure 2.9) are new to Exchange 2000 Server. Exchange Server 5.5 allowed for one private store and one public store per server. Exchange 2000 Server lets you create your own groups of information stores, called *storage groups*. It also gives you the capability to group up to six private and public information store databases within a single storage group.

In Exchange 2000 Server, private information stores are called *mailbox stores*, and public information stores answer to the name *public stores*. All the storage groups in an Exchange 2000 Server installation are contained in the *information store*. Storage groups enable you to organize mailboxes and public folders logically—departmentally, for example—across your organization. This helps you manage multiple mailbox and public information stores; additionally, you can back up and restore information store databases independently. This makes backups and restores faster and also allows you to back up or restore one information store database while other databases are still accessible to users.

 NOTE While we're on the subject of backup, guess what? Using Windows 2000 Server's built-in backup software, you can now back up and restore individual Exchange 2000 Server mailboxes. And, not only can you restore a whole mailbox, but you also can restore just one or a few messages in a mailbox. That alone is worth the price of admission for some Exchange Server 5.5 administrators.

Instant Messaging and Conferencing Server

Instant messaging enables users to know who's online and then lets them send messages to one or more of those people. Information about available users is provided by an instant messaging virtual server based on Exchange 2000 Server. The virtual server can also route messages to appropriate users. Messages aren't stored on the Exchange 2000 server; instead, instant messaging delivers messages in real-time, and the user's experience is much like participating in an Internet chat group. You can open instant messaging to the Internet or enable it only for your organization's intranet.

Exchange 2000 Conferencing Server is a neat application that supports real-time multimedia (data, voice, and video) interaction between users. Conferencing Server includes support for application sharing, chat services, whiteboards, and file transfer. Users can schedule conferences in advance with the calendar services supported by Exchange Server 2000. Administrators can control conferencing bandwidth allocation and can determine who is allowed to participate in conferences. Conferencing Server supports load balancing and fail-over. Although you can use any T.120-compliant client, Microsoft's client of choice for Conference Server is NetMeeting.

Neither instant messaging nor Conferencing Server are brand new conceptually. Both were born of earlier Microsoft technologies. Instant messaging was first developed for use with Microsoft's ISP service, MSN. Conferencing Server adds significant server-based functionally to the long-lived, though constantly improved, NetMeeting platform.

 NOTE I need to at least make note of the Exchange chat service. It enables real-time interaction between users through the Internet Relay Chat (IRC) and Extended Internet Relay Chat (IRCX) protocols. The Exchange chat service is not new to Exchange Server 2000—it was implemented in Exchange Server 5.5.

File System Support and Full-Text Indexing

There's no question that Exchange 2000's support for file system access to certain Exchange objects qualifies as really new to Exchange 2000 Server. This is pretty neat stuff, as you can see in Figure 2.12. In this figure, I'm using the My Computer browser to look at my e-mail. Exchange 2000 Server adds a network drive to your file and resource browser that points to the Exchange information store. Based on your security privileges, you can march through this drive using a GUI-based file interface such as My Computer or command-line utilities such as DIR, looking at different mailboxes and public folders. You can even set up backups against all or selected objects on this drive. And, file system access opens a whole range of Exchange-based application development options using products ranging from Microsoft and third-party word processing programs to sophisticated applications developed in Visual Basic and C++.

FIGURE 2.12

Exploring the Exchange 2000 Server information store using the My Computer browser

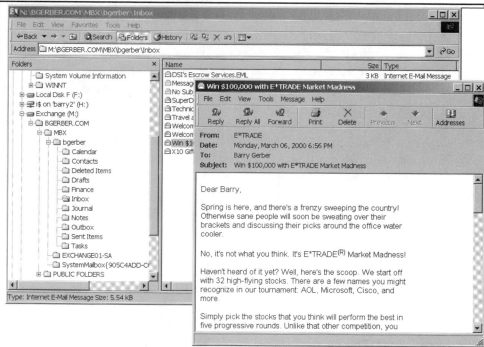

Built-in full-text indexing is another really new addition to Exchange 2000 Server. This feature significantly speeds up searches for specific text in Exchange messages. Full-text indexing can be extended to message attachments, making it possible to search attachment content for the first time.

Exchange 2000 Server and Exchange Server 5.5: A Summary of Major Differences and Similarities

Exchange 2000 Server is an evolutionary product. Features such as directory services and Exchange sites migrated over to Windows 2000 Server as Active Directory and Windows 2000 Server sites. Even though sites migrated to Windows 2000 Server, they're of no use to Exchange 2000 Server administrators, who still need to manage links between server groups connected by lower-bandwidth networks.

Exchange Server 5.5 administrators will require some time to get accustomed to the fact that the functionality of the singular Exchange Server 5.5 Administrator user interface has been divided into a set of logical but quite different Microsoft Management Console snap-ins. This book is dedicated in part to opening and explicating this maze of new interfaces for both old Exchange Server 5.5 hands and those new to Exchange Server with version 2000.

Some features are new to Exchange Server 2000, even though most of it at least conceptually was derived from earlier Microsoft products. Instant Messaging and Exchange 2000 Conferencing Server add valuable real-time user interaction to an already powerful store-and-forward electronic messaging environment.

Really new to Exchange Server 2000 are storage groups, file system access to Exchange mailbox and public stores, and full-text indexing. Storage groups enable you to put multiple mailbox and public folder databases on an Exchange 2000 server, and they make it easier to manage multiple mailbox and public folder databases. File system access command support lets you explore the Exchange 2000 Server world from your My Computer browser. Full-text indexing speeds up searches through Exchange messages while adding the capability to search attachments.

Now let's take a quick look at the Exchange Server 2000 product line.

Getting a Handle on Exchange 2000 Server Versions

Unlike the Windows 2000 product line, there are only two versions of Exchange 2000 Server: Exchange 2000 Server and Exchange 2000 Enterprise Server. Table 1.1 shows some of the similarities and differences between the two products.

TABLE 1.1: FEATURES OF EXCHANGE 2000 SERVER AND EXCHANGE 2000 ENTERPRISE SERVER

Feature	Server	Enterprise Server
Storage	Limited to 16GB	Unlimited
Multiple database support	No	Yes
Connectivity to other systems	Yes	Yes
X.400 connector	No	Yes
Instant messaging	Yes	Yes
Chat service	No	Yes
Windows clustering support	No	Yes

The key differences between the Server and Enterprise versions of Exchange 2000 Server relate to the amount of storage available and support for multiple storage groups (databases), X.400 connectivity, Exchange Server chat services, and Windows 2000 Server fail-safe clustering capabilities. Both products include Internet mail, Microsoft legacy mail system connectivity, and instant messaging. Conferencing Server is a separate option.

As I noted earlier in this chapter, Exchange 2000 Server will run on Windows 2000 Server. Windows 2000 Advanced Server or Datacenter Server is required for Exchange 2000 Enterprise Server. Exchange 2000 Server has a street price of about $1,200 with five user licenses. Enterprise Server goes for around $6,600 with 25 user licenses. Conference Server is a separate product that sells for about $4,700.

Planning: There's Really No Choice But to Do It

I've always been a big advocate of planning for software installations. With Windows 2000 Server and Exchange 2000 Server, not planning is sure death. For example, to set up your Windows 2000 Server domain or domains without planning is to invite misery of the worst kind. To install Exchange 2000 Server before your domain model is clearly established almost assures that you'll spend double, triple, or even quadruple the time fixing things after the fact.

We'll talk about domain planning later in great detail, especially in Chapter 5, "Designing a New Exchange 2000 System," and Chapter 6 "Upgrading to Windows 2000 Server and Exchange 2000 Server." Suffice it to say that Microsoft designed both Windows 2000 and Exchange 2000 with a certain organizational model in mind. Windows 2000 Server is flexible, but there are some things that you can't change without totally reinstalling it. Your domain structure is one of these things. You can add domains to an existing domain structure, and you can even create a new and separate domain structure. But you can't delete your master domain and start over, and you can't rename your domain. Although these domains need not cement your Internet mail-addressing scheme, it's a lot easier if you can keep your Windows 2000 Server domains and Internet messaging domains in sync.

A number of the chapters in this part of the book touch on planning. Bypass them at your peril. 'Nuff said.

End User Support Is Easy

So, how do you feel about Exchange 2000 Server and its constant companion, Windows 2000 Server? Ready to move on? Discouraged? If you're feeling a bit daunted, don't give up quite yet. For all the newness and complexity in Microsoft's new Windows and Exchange products, Exchange 2000 Server and Windows 2000 Server are conquerable. Both products offer the end user a comfortable and often better working environment than did their predecessors.

Unless they're using Windows 2000 Professional on their workstations, end users will hardly realize that they're using new server operating and electronic messaging systems. Logging into the network will look pretty much the same, and so will accessing file shares and printers. If they're using Outlook, POP3, or IMAP4 e-mail clients, all will appear almost exactly the same. Only users accessing Exchange 2000 server through Outlook Web Access—that is, using their Web browser—will experience a noticeable difference. And that will be a pleasant experience, as Figure 2.13 shows.

FIGURE 2.13

Exchange 2000 Server's implementation of Outlook Web Access

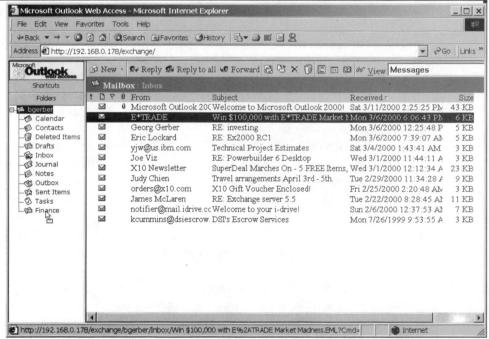

I mean, look at that interface! It looks almost like the Outlook 2000 client. And take a close look at what I'm doing in this figure. Yes, I'm dragging a message from my Inbox and dropping it into a folder that I created a minute ago while in the Web interface. Is that cool, or what?

The bottom line is that you're going to have to stretch some to get your arms around Windows 2000 Server and Exchange 2000 Server. The good news is that you won't have to worry much about supporting users as they access what's on these server products. And, there are even a few really nice rewards for users, including the new Outlook Web Access support offered by Exchange 2000 Server. Wonderful world!

In the next chapter, I'll spend a little time discussing earlier books on Windows 2000 Server and showing you how almost all of them have managed to ignore some key information that you need to get started with Windows 2000 and Exchange 2000. Join me.

Summary

Exchange 2000 Server is an integral part of Windows 2000 Server. As with other systems (Unix comes immediately to mind), with Windows 2000 Server and Exchange 2000 Server, it's often difficult to tell where the operating system leaves off and the electronic messaging system begins. Integration has its price: It demands very careful planning, and after you've implemented Windows and Exchange 2000, it will keep you or those with whom you work hopping from one interface to the other to create and manage the myriad objects required to make a complex electronic messaging system work.

Windows 2000 Server is an evolutionary product featuring Active Directory, Microsoft's first system-wide user and resource directory borrowed in part from earlier implementations of Exchange, much stronger reliance on Internet standards (including DNS and LDAP), and advanced security based on Kerberos. Much of Windows 2000 hasn't changed, from the Windows 98 GUI look and feel, to starting network drive mapping from the Explorer (My Computer) Tools menu. With Windows 2000 Server, size does matter. Three server versions exist; in order of potential capacity and system redundancy, they are Server, Advanced Server, and Datacenter Server.

Exchange 2000 Server is also more of an evolutionary than revolutionary product. With a good portion of Exchange 5.5's innards appropriated for use in Windows 2000 Server, Exchange 2000 is somewhat less than it was in former incarnations. Maintenance of most recipients is done in Active Directory interfaces, not Exchange 2000 interfaces. Basic SMTP and NNTP services are provided by Windows 2000. Exchange 2000 sports a fair number of new features, including storage groups, integrated instant messaging, conference services, and file system access to Exchange mailboxes and public folders. Exchange comes in two sizes, Exchange 2000 Server and Exchange 2000 Enterprise Server. The former, best suited to smaller electronic messaging environments, runs on all flavors of Windows 2000 Server. The Enterprise edition requires Advanced Server or Datacenter Server.

The best news regarding Microsoft's new Windows and Exchange products is for end users. Combined, the two products promise end users better access to the precious data and information stored in Windows server-based computing environments.

We're not finished with Windows 2000, not by a long shot. In Chapter 3, we'll look in more detail at Windows 2000's Active Directory and networking. Exchange 2000 Server is so dependent on these that you have to get a good handle on them before you can move on to Exchange itself.

CHAPTER **3**

Two Key Architectural Components of Windows 2000 Server

L ike most people, when a new computing technology comes on the scene, I turn to whatever documentation I can find. Sometimes, although it's hard to admit it, the best documentation comes from the vendor of the new technology. I'm not saying that vendor documentation is perfect, but it can be pretty okay. Other times, especially as more and more people come to understand the technology, third-party sources produce the best technology. That shouldn't be such a surprise, because vendors are good at telling you what their products should do and how to implement those products at the basic level. Over time, however, third-party sources, such as the people who write books for Sybex, often come to better understand a product and its strengths and weaknesses far better than the product's vendor.

In spite of my protestations to the contrary in earlier chapters, Windows 2000 Server—and Exchange 2000 Server, for that matter—are new technologies from the user's perspective. Understanding them takes time and effort. So, I can guarantee that you're going to see a lot of books that remind you of those famous Escher drawings. You know, the ones in which a guy is walking up a set of stairs that suddenly seem to be going down. That certainly has been my experience with the current crop of books on Windows 2000 Server. You know what I mean. You start reading something and are sure that it is going to help you with what you need to do, and then suddenly the topic veers off 180+ degrees, leaving you without a solution and less time to find one.

In this chapter, I'll cover the two biggest problems that I encountered in my early work with Windows 2000 Server. These relate to the architectures of Active Directory and Windows 2000 Server networking. Along the way, I'll vent some of the frustration that I've experienced trying to use the other available documentation. Join me in the next section, and we'll see how well I'm able to advance mankind's understanding of Active Directory. (Well, I suppose that mankind is a pretty big target; I'd really be happy just to clarify a few things for you.) After that, I'll tackle the issues surrounding Windows 2000 Server network architecture.

What You Need to Know about Active Directory Right Now

Hands down, Active Directory is the most important piece of Windows 2000 Server architecture that you need to understand. Almost everything in Windows 2000 Server revolves around Active Directory.

There's a lot to know about Active Directory. I'm not going to tell you everything that you need to know in great detail in this chapter. Rather, my goal here is to expose you to key concepts that will arm you for coming chapters and for your first experiences with Active Directory. In later chapters, I'll get into the nitty-gritty detail that you'll need to make your Windows 2000 Server and Exchange 2000 Server environments work.

Active Directory Isn't the Whole House

You shouldn't let my emphasis here on Active Directory as the linchpin of Window 2000 Server architecture lead you to believe that Active Directory is all there is. For example, Windows 2000 Server's file system, NT File System 5 (NTFS 5), is a pretty impressive piece of work. Along with all the neat stuff imported from NT Server, including full integration of distributed file system technology, the file system is tightly integrated with Active Directory. In addition, NTFS 5 includes built-in disk quotas, file defragmentation, and file/subdirectory encryption.

Another key piece of Windows 2000 Server architecture is site-based routing and folder replication. Borrowed from Exchange Server 5.5, site-based routing and folder replication enable Windows 2000 servers to live anywhere that they need to and to communicate with other computers on a Windows 2000 Server network using whatever bandwidth technology is available and affordable. As I've said before—and will say again before this chapter ends—site-based routing and folder replication are key to large, single-domain Windows 2000 Server networks.

That's not all the new architecture, but hopefully it reinforces the idea that although Active Directory is the foundation and the framework of Windows 2000 Server architecture, it is not the entire building.

Active Directory: Five Major Architectural Components

Here's the story in a nutshell: To begin understanding Active Directory, you need to understand five of its key components: namespaces, forests, trees, domains, and objects. Every instance of Active Directory is a namespace. An Active Directory namespace encompasses one and only one forest. A forest consists of one or more trees. Trees include one or more domains. Each domain lives on its own server or set of servers. How you use forests, trees, and domains depends at least in part on how your organization is structured. All the resources in an Active Directory namespace—forests, trees, domains, users, printers, files, and so on—are objects. Objects are often containers that can hold other objects. For example, a domain is a container that can hold, among other things, subdomains.

In practical terms, if you use a Microsoft Management Console Active Directory snap-in to manage a specific Active Directory, you will see all the domains and subobjects in the forest that are supported by that Active Directory, no matter which specific computer or set of computers any particular domain resides on. Figure 2.2, back in Chapter 2, "2000: A Magic Number?" shows the major Active Directory snap-ins in action.

Pretty simple huh? Tell it to the authors of most of the Windows 2000 Server documentation that I've seen. It took me days to figure out what all this stuff is about, and I know Active Directory from its days as Exchange Server 5.5's directory service. Anyway, I'll try to short-circuit the learning process just a bit for you here. Let's look at each of Active Directory's components in more detail.

NOTE Virtually every book I've read on Windows 2000 Server that doesn't come from Microsoft presents the same view of Active Directory: a long, dry dissertation with few, if any, illustrations. These works almost always stop before I'm satisfied. Microsoft does a somewhat better job, although even that documentation occasionally contains unclear and even contradictory information. Active Directory can be daunting. It's my guess that a lot of authors grabbed the documentation that Microsoft provided with the beta version of Windows 2000 Server and more or less regurgitated it in one form or another in their early chapters on Active Directory. I sense that they didn't experiment much with the product at this point and thus really didn't appreciate how important hands-on experience is in telling the story of this new way of organizing Microsoft networks.

Namespaces

Like all directories, Active Directory is at heart a namespace with subnamespaces and subsubnamespaces and sub-sub-sub.... Well, you get the point. A directory namespace is the place that holds the names of objects. You look in a namespace to find an object and whatever other information you need to use an object. Namespaces are hierarchical in nature. As noted previously, the Microsoft Management Console snapins that we explored in Chapter 2 graphically present a variety of views of the Windows 2000 Server Active Directory namespace.

It's important to note that, in a very real sense, namespaces are concepts, not visible entities. What you see in Microsoft Management Console are the various objects that exist in the Active Directory namespace. You really don't see the namespace, per se; you see a very nice representation of Active Directory itself, which is the container for all the objects in the Active Directory namespace. Of course, all of this doesn't mean that understanding the concept of namespaces isn't important to understanding Windows 2000 Server's Active Directory. *Au contraire.* Without a clear understanding of namespaces, you'll never master Active Directory. (Also, all of this doesn't mean that I and others won't slip occasionally and refer to the Active Directory namespace as though it were a real container for names.)

Let's start with an example of a namespace. The Internet Domain Name System (DNS) is a namespace. Its major function is to tie natural-language names to IP addresses because the TCP/IP protocol uses IP addresses for intercomputer communication, not the natural-language names that we're all more comfortable with.

At the top of the DNS hierarchy is a large, essentially container that holds all the top-level Internet names, including com, edu, and mil. This container is often represented by a dot. Within each of these top-level Internet subnamespaces are the subdomains or subsubnamespaces that are for a specific organization, such as microsoft or bgerber. The DNS namespace nests increasingly lower until a specific computer or cluster of computers is identified. Sometimes a specific computer will actually be included in the namespace—as in web1, for example. Sometimes no computer is named, as is often the case with Web sites. See Figure 3.1 for a glimpse at a very small piece of the DNS namespace—my own real-world Web site bgerber.com.

FIGURE 3.1

A small piece of the Domain Name System hierarchy

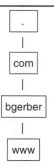

When a program such as a Web browser goes hunting for a specific Web site, it asks an Internet domain name server for a specific domain object, such as www.bgerber.com. The domain name server looks up the requested name in its table. If it finds a match, it then looks up the IP address of that name, such as 216.132.83.21, and sends the IP address back to the browser. This is called *resolving* the domain name into an IP address. The Web browser then uses the IP address to find and talk to the Web server. The IP address belongs to the Web server computer or possibly to a cluster of computers.

I should point out that www.bgerber.com is a distinguished name. I'm not saying that www.bgerber.com is distinguished in the way that a gray-haired gentleman of

60 years might be distinguished. I'm using the term in its namespace sense to indicate that www.bgerber.com identifies a unique object in the DNS namespace. An object in a directory must have distinguished name, or it is useless.

Active Directory's namespace functions in a manner quite similar to the DNS namespace. In fact, when some names are resolved in a Windows 2000 Server network—for example, the names of internal computers running the Windows 2000 operating system—DNS is used exactly as it is used on the Internet.

Like DNS, the Active Directory namespace has a structure and specific ways of identifying objects. As noted in Chapter 2, four different naming conventions are used in Active Directory: Lightweight Directory Access Protocol (LDAP), Internet RFC 822 (DNS), Hypertext Transfer Protocol (HTTP) URLs, and Microsoft's Universal Naming Convention (UNC). Also, like DNS, clients query Active Directory for whatever lower-level identifiers are required to access a specific network resource, such as a computer, a printer, a user, a user mailbox, a security policy, a domain, and so on.

Active Directory Helps Make Windows 2000 Server Industrial Strength

For the record, all the stuff in your Active Directory is represented in what is called the *schema*. The *stuff* is officially called *objects*. Objects represent everything from Windows 2000 user accounts to Exchange 2000 mailboxes You can look at the schema and, if you know what you're doing, edit it.

One of the problems with Windows NT server is its somewhat limited capability to support extensive numbers of users and other resources in a domain. One NT domain allows for about 40,000 resource objects, about 20,000 of which can be users. That may seem like a lot until your organization starts growing and you've got lots of users, files, printers, and workstations to support. Then you want lots more. With NT Server, the solution is to create multiple domains to handle lots of resources.

Active Directory supports up to 1 million objects. That's a lot! The main thing that you should carry away from this is that you no longer need to think multiple domains when structuring your Windows 2000 Server networking environment. For this and other reasons, Microsoft encourages you to think small when it comes to the number of Windows 2000 domains that you create. In fact, in most cases, Microsoft's favorite number for domains is 1. I'll talk more on this in Chapters 5, "Designing a New Exchange 2000 System"; 6, "Upgrading to Windows 2000 Server and Exchange 2000 Server"; and 7, "Installing Windows 2000 Server."

Forests, Trees, Domains, and Objects

As mentioned earlier, Windows 2000 Server domains are contained in trees, which are contained in forests. A forest can contain one or more trees. Any given Active Directory namespace covers only one forest. In other words, a forest and a specific Active Directory namespace have contiguous boundaries.

Figure 3.2 shows an Active Directory structure based on a namespace with a forest that contains a single tree. The correct name for such a structure is a *single contiguous namespace*. Everything in my organization is a subentity of the top-level or root-level Windows 2000 Server domain, bgerber.com. The domains below bgerber.com are called *child domains*. Single contiguous namespace Active Directory structures model organizations that can be represented as a single hierarchical entity. These entities can be small, such as bgerber.com, or quite large, such as microsoft.com or us.gov. All the domains in Figure 3.2 make up the single tree in the Active Directory namespace.

FIGURE 3.2

An Active Directory structure based on a single root tree or single contiguous namespace model

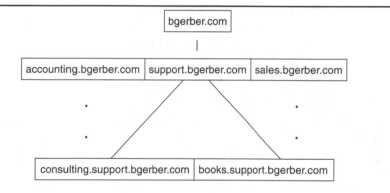

Microsoft encourages that, if at all possible, you seriously consider creating one large single tree domain like the one in Figure 3.2. Assuming that there are no organizational reasons why you can't do this, how do you create one big, happy domain if some of your Windows 2000 Servers are on low-bandwidth links? As I mentioned in passing in Chapter 2 and in the previous sidebar, "Active Directory Isn't the Whole House," you use the site connector and folder replication technology that Windows 2000 Server borrowed from Exchange Server 5.5.

TIP The Active Directory naming choices that you make within your organization need have no impact on how your organization looks to the outside world. Your organization can be `killandplunder.com` internally and `worldlover.com` to the Internet. That doesn't mean that you might not want to use the same name domain name internally and externally, though. In fact, that's often a very good idea. Again, planning is the key. As long as you know where you want to go both internally and externally, you'll build the right structure from the beginning. If you don't have a road map, watch out. There's nothing less fun than fixing naming decisions down the road. We'll spend more time on naming issues in Chapters 5 and 6.

Now, let's say that you've got a more complex organizational structure and you need to preserve that structure in your Active Directory. Then you need a namespace with a forest that contains multiple trees or domains. Such namespaces are called *noncontiguous namespaces* because each tree in the forest is independent of the others. There are no unbroken lines from one tree to the other.

In Figure 3.3, you see an organization—let's call it Eat The World, Inc.—that just can't get everything into one root tree. This organization needs four root trees because Eat The World, Inc., really consists of four distinct organizational entities. Note that I've included just the top level of each root tree. Be assured, however, that each of the four trees has a full set of subtrees, just like `bgerber.com` in Figure 3.2.

FIGURE 3.3

An Active Directory namespace based on a forest of root trees or a noncontiguous namespace model

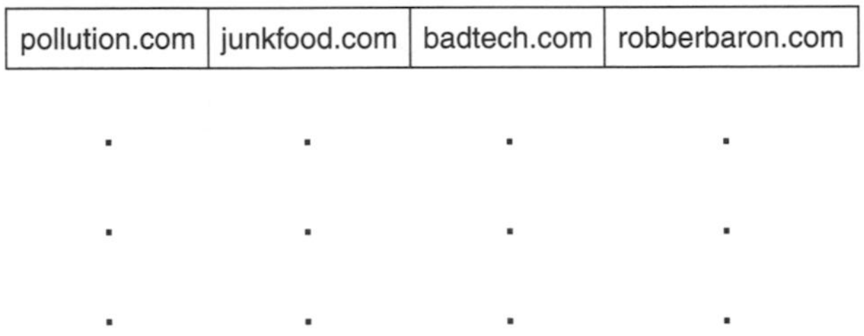

pollution.com	junkfood.com	badtech.com	robberbaron.com

Eat The World, Inc., is the result of the buyout fever that has struck the modern world. For a range of political, economic, and organizational reasons, the various operating units within Eat The World, Inc., just can't function happily within a single top-down hierarchy. Each unit of Eat The World, Inc., requires its own tree or Windows 2000 Server domain.

Now let's say that Eat The World, Inc., buys another company. This one, destroy-all.com, is such a deviant organization that even the folks who run Eat The World, Inc., can't stomach it being in the same forest as their other blighted trees. Figure 3.4 shows the structure required to make this organizational decision work.

FIGURE 3.4

*An Active Directory
noncontiguous name-
space based on two
forests of root trees*

```
|------------------------------- Forest 1 ------------------------------------| |---- Forest 2 ---|
```

| pollution.com | junkfood.com | badtech.com | robberbaron.com | destroyall.com |

The key here is to understand that both Forest 1 and Forest 2 have their own Active Directory structure and namespace—more specifically, they have their own *schema*. Each forest must be viewed independently in any Microsoft Management Console Active Directory snap-in. For example, if you open the Active Directory Users and Computers Microsoft Management Console snap-in on any computer that is a member of a domain in Forest 1, you'll be able to manage anywhere from none to all four of the domains in that forest, depending on security. If you open the same interface on a computer that is a member of the one and only domain in Forest 2, you'll be able to manage the domain destroyall.com if you have the correct security privileges.

I can just hear you. "Okay, so now I think I understand this namespace, forest, tree, and domain stuff. What's next?"

My first answer is that so much depends on Active Directory and its key components that without a good understanding of it and them, you're bound to make some serious mistakes. For example, if you don't get your domains and forests in order before you start planning and designing your Windows 2000 Server setup, you could face the misery of either combining domains in a forest or moving a domain from one forest to another. These are not easy tasks.

Furthermore, the domains represented by trees play a major role in Windows 2000 Server security. As with Windows NT Server 4 (and 3.51, for that matter), domains are at the heart of Windows 2000 Server network security. A domain is a security boundary. As with NT Server, users log into domains. When a user logs into a domain, internal security willing, that user can access any resource in the domain.

Windows 2000 Server automatically sets up trust relationships between a root domain and its child domains, such as between bgerber.com and accounting.bgerber.com in Figure 3.2. Windows 2000 Server also automatically sets up trusts between domains in a non-contiguous namespace (see Figure 3.3). These trusts are transitive, meaning that because all child domains in the forest have trust relationships with the root domain, they also have trusts with each other. So, you don't have to do anything to give all users access to all resources in all child domains in a root domain. Of course, you do have to do something to allow or prevent a user in one domain from accessing specific resources in another domain.

You can even access resources in other forests (see Figure 3.4). To do this, you must manually establish trusts between domains in each forest just as you establish trusts between domains in the same forest.

Now let's talk a bit more about objects. Objects in Active Directory are the resources that you work with. In a sense, they represent the real stuff that you work with in Active Directory. Forests, trees, and domains are objects. Like all objects, Active Directory objects have attributes that define them. For example, users have first, last, and middle name attributes. Files have name, security, and sharing attributes, to name but a few.

I won't go into detail about all the issues relating to objects. Suffice it to say that Active Directory objects are the result of a very disciplined implementation of object-oriented programming design by Microsoft. As an Active Directory user, you don't need to understand object-oriented programming. You just need to appreciate the role that objects play in making Active Directory a real-world repository for all the services and functionality required to run and manage a complex operating system.

Global Catalogs and Organizational Units

Before we leave namespaces, forests, trees, domains, and objects, I should mention two other Windows 2000 Server objects: Global Catalogs and organizational units.

Every domain has a Global Catalog, which contains all the Active Directory information for its host domain. A Global Catalog also contains partial information for all the objects in other domains in the forest. This partial information is at least adequate to ensure that the object exists in the particular domain. A domain's Global Catalog allows for faster extra-domain searches because a search for an object in another domain doesn't require time-consuming cross-domain network access and right-to-search authentication.

Organizational units are used to group objects within a domain. They're a nice way to create domainlike substructures when you want to assign different tasks or security rights to different persons or groups within a domain. Rights and privileges in an organizational unit apply only within the unit, not to the domain as a whole. Organizational units require much less overhead than domains. They help you reach Microsoft's new goal of keeping everything in one domain, if at all possible. I'll discuss these neat little tools further in Chapter 11, "Managing Exchange Users, Distribution Groups, and Contacts," Chapter 15, "Installing and Managing Additional Exchange 2000 Servers," and Chapter 16, "Connecting to Other Foreign Messaging Systems."

Active Directory Is Real Stuff

To conclude this section, let's talk just a bit about what Active Directory is from a bits-and-bytes point of view. First, as should be quite obvious by now, Active Directory is a database. It's a grandly scaled, extensible collection of carefully architected and organized fields that represent the attributes of everything from usernames to Exchange mailboxes to security policies.

But Active Directory is something more—something without which the database would be nothing but a bucket of useless bits. Active Directory consists of the computer programs (*services*) that fill it with data and that take data from it so that a Windows 2000 Server network can operate smoothly and with high-level security.

These programs include a collection of services that come with Windows 2000 Server, such as the Net Logon service, which supports pass-through authentication of logon events for computers in a domain. The Net Logon service uses information in Active Directory to perform its authentication tasks.

Active Directory-oriented services can also be developed to support applications that run on Windows 2000 Server. The Exchange Routing Engine that moves messages between Exchange servers and to external messaging components is an example of such a service. The Routing Engine uses routing information stored in Active Directory to figure out where and even when to send messages.

It is even possible for end-user organizations to add their own objects to the Active Directory schema. These objects are then available to support programs that perform tasks customized to the needs of the organization. Although you've got to know a lot more than I will tell you in this book to do so, you can develop some pretty nifty messaging applications using hooks into the Exchange 2000 Server system and home-grown Active Directory objects.

So, does all this Active Directory stuff make sense? Obviously, you don't know everything about Active Directory at this point, but you should know enough to think rationally about how you'll design your Windows 2000 Server environment. Hold that thought. We'll get to planning and design in Chapters 5 and 6.

What You Need to Know about Windows 2000 Server Network Architecture

As I mentioned in Chapter 2, one of the keys to understanding Windows 2000 Server networking is the much lower emphasis placed on Microsoft's older NetBEUI protocol and the WINS service. You really have to dig into the Windows 2000 Server installation process to install NetBEUI, and, if the truth be known, Microsoft would like to kill NetBEUI as a Windows 2000 Server-supported networking protocol as quickly as possible. WINS is a somewhat more favored but still second-class networking citizen. It, too, is destined to die a slower but no less sure death than NetBEUI. Both protocols are there to support legacy Windows server and workstation products.

The key function of NetBEUI and WINS is to help one computer on a network find and communicate with another computer on the same network. Each Microsoft Windows computer (including each Windows 2000 computer, by the way) has what is called a *NetBIOS name*. NetBIOS names are ones that show up in network neighborhood in Windows Explorer.

The remainder of this section describes NetBEUI and WINS, and discusses a better option that I discovered through experimentation.

Understanding NetBIOS, NetBEUI, and WINS

IBM developed the NetBIOS protocol for use in early PC networks. The protocol describes how computers on a network talk to each other. Key to this description is the concept of a NetBIOS name. Every computer on a NetBIOS network has its own unique NetBIOS name. NetBIOS was designed for early local area networks in which every network node was located on the same physical wire. NetBIOS data packets can't travel between routed networks. NetBEUI is an enhanced version of NetBIOS, also developed by IBM, which more than anything else defines the arrangement of information in a network data packet. Microsoft adopted both NetBIOS and NetBEUI for its network operating systems. Between NetBIOS and NetBEUI, NetBEUI is the current protocol of choice.

With the growing popularity of the TCP/IP protocol, which allows packets to pass from network to network over routers, Microsoft worked out a way to allow Windows computers to communicate over TCP/IP instead of NetBEUI. This required some way of resolving a NetBIOS computer name into a TCP/IP address. To answer this need, Microsoft designed the Windows Internet Naming Service (WINS) (also often called *NetBIOS over TCP/IP*). WINS is essentially a namespace that links NetBIOS computer names with IP addresses.

Let's focus on NetBEUI for a bit. Those of you with massive routed NT Server networks have probably all but stamped out that cockroach NetBEUI. However, I'll bet that a lot of you still rely on the protocol—maybe even without knowing it. Historically, NetBEUI was either automatically installed or was readily offered as an option when you installed one flavor or another of Windows. Even if you've installed TCP/IP and WINS, and NetBEUI is also installed, I'll bet that some communications on your network still depend on NetBEUI.

I've ceased to be surprised to find NetBEUI lurking somewhere on a network. For example, one consulting client called me in to figure out why some workstations that it had just installed couldn't get to the organization's Exchange server. I should note that these were the first workstations in the organization to be placed on a separate, routed network segment. The Exchange server supported only NetBEUI. The new workstations supported only NetBEUI. The organization hadn't changed its networking protocols to accommodate these other-side-of-the-router workstations. After we installed WINS on the network and TCP/IP on the routed workstations, all was fine.

Here's lesson one: Before you even touch a Windows 2000 Server installation CD, make sure that you know what protocols are running where on your network. If you think that the problems you had with NetBEUI in the past were a pain, wait until you see what it's like living in a world where you have to make a very conscious choice to install NetBEUI, but your mind hasn't fully absorbed the fact. It is kind of like going from driving an automatic to driving a shift car. Sometimes you almost forget the clutch and shifter.

So what does all this have to do with your life? Well, I wish I had a dollar for every book that I've read on Windows 2000 Server that assured me everything would be just fine when I installed a second domain controller in a domain if I just had my network set up in order. And, just what does *in order* mean? Among other things, it means that your existing Windows 2000 domain controller and the new Windows 2000 server that is to become a domain controller must be capable of talking to each other. This sounds simple, but the only way to really make it simple is to give up on NetBEUI and WINS, as you'll soon see.

Maybe information about getting my network in order was buried somewhere in one of those 1,000-page tomes, but I sure couldn't find it—and that includes Microsoft's own documentation and books. Maybe the authors of these documents say nothing because, as I discovered after a good deal of experimentation, you have to do precious little to add a new domain controller to an existing domain. For me, that's not a good excuse. Even what some believe to be obvious must be stated clearly. This is especially true when readers come to a particular piece of technology armed with varying amounts of experience. My extensive experience with Windows NT Server 4 and Exchange 5.5 led me to one set of conclusions on this topic. Others' experiences might lead them to other conclusions. Those with no experience at all are unlikely to see the "obvious," no matter how well it's not stated. (That's a joke.)

Windows 2000 Servers Are Domain Controller Chameleons

To understand the difference between NT 4 and Windows 2000 servers, it's important to understand that Windows NT Server 4 servers were either standalone servers or primary or secondary domain controllers. You created a domain controller while installing the NT 4 operating system. A domain controller could not revert to standalone status, and a standalone server could not become a domain controller.

When you install a Windows 2000 server, you don't even have the option of making it a domain controller. Windows 2000 standalone servers become domain controllers after they are fully installed and up and running. Somewhat like a magician, you can promote a Windows 2000 server to domain controller status at any time, and you can demote it back to standalone server status at any time. You can perform this metamorphosis as many times as you want or need to.

An Alternative: Using DNS and DHCP

You can use NetBEUI to enable communication between a Windows 2000 domain controller and a standalone server, although you do have to remember to install it. You can also use WINS for this purpose. A third option is available as well (I'll discuss that soon), but based on the substandard documentation previously available to me, I thought that I needed to use NetBEUI or WINS when I promoted a standalone server to domain controller status in an existing Windows 2000 domain. Windows 2000 servers, standalone or not, have standard NetBIOS names just like NT 4 servers. So, I assumed that I needed to make some use of NetBEUI or WINS to enable the standalone server to find the existing domain controller.

I didn't want to turn to the bewhiskered NetBEUI. So, using WINS in combination with other applications, I managed to cobble together a complex contraption and was actually able to promote my server to a domain controller. However, as I later discovered at great pain, through seemingly endless hours of experimentation, I really didn't need WINS or NetBEUI at all. All I needed was the Domain Name System (DNS) and Windows 2000's Dynamic Host Configuration Protocol (DHCP).

As I mentioned previously in the section "Active Directory: Five Major Architectural Components," the native computer naming system on Windows 2000 Server networks is DNS. That's the same DNS that served as an example of a namespace earlier in this chapter. To get started, a standalone Windows 2000 server that is to be promoted to a domain controller in an existing domain needs both an IP address of its own and the IP address of its DNS server. The standalone server needs an IP address so that it can communicate with other computers on the network, specifically the existing domain controller. It needs a DNS server so that it can find the domain controller, connect to it, and be authenticated by it so that it can join the domain as a new domain controller.

Although you can manually set the parameters discussed previously, Windows 2000 Server lets you automate the whole process using DHCP. DHCP not only can assign an IP address to the new computer, but it also can give your new computer the IP address of the DNS server that it should use. Then (and this is really neat), when your new Windows 2000 server is up and running, Windows 2000 Server DHCP can even dynamically register your new computer in the existing domain controller's DNS. This process is called *dynamic DNS*. You don't even have to make a manual entry for the computer in the DNS. You can reserve specific IP addresses in DHCP so that you're sure that a server will get the same address each time it boots up.

The even neater thing is that, like earlier Windows products, a Windows 2000 Server is ready to use DHCP immediately after standalone server installation is completed. So, as long as DHCP is properly set up on your existing domain controller or another Windows 2000 server on your network, you don't have to do anything to promote a standalone server to domain controller status except run the domain controller promotion program on it.

My goal in this section is not to make you an expert in adding domain controllers to Windows 2000 Server networks. We'll do that in Chapters 7 and 15, and we'll use Dynamic DNS to install a standalone server that will become our first Exchange server. Instead, my goal is to give you a sense of the changes in Windows 2000 Server networking compared to NT Server 4 networking.

Summary

Windows 2000 Server's Active Directory is central to both Windows 2000 and Exchange 2000. Active Directory is a namespace like the Internet standard Domain Name System (DNS). Active Directory is a repository for virtually all the information about users and resources (files, printers, and so on) available on a network.

Key to Active Directory creation and management are forests, trees, and domains. Forests are the top-level containers in Windows 2000 environments. A forest can contain one or more trees. Trees contain one or more domains. Domain objects in the same forest can communicate with each other automatically because transitive trust relationships are created between the domains by default. Domains in different forests require that trust relationships be specifically set up before objects within them can communicate with each other.

Windows 2000 Server networking is based on DNS. The legacy Windows NT server networking protocols, NetBEUI and WINS, are available but are totally unnecessary in Windows 2000 networks. Windows 2000's preferred networking approach is IP supported by Dynamic DNS, which combines DHCP and DNS to deliver IP address and other information to a computer and to place the computer in the network's DNS.

That should be enough of Windows 2000 Server for a bit. Now let's move on to Exchange 2000 Server and take a look at its architecture.

CHAPTER 4

Exchange 2000 Server Architecture

Exchange is a client/server electronic messaging system. In this chapter, we'll take a close look at the Exchange 2000 Server-relevant architecture of Windows 2000 Server, as well as the architectures of both the Exchange 2000 server and client systems. We'll also see how the Exchange server and clients interact from an architectural perspective.

This is an important chapter because it exposes you to a range of Exchange terminology that you'll find useful later. It also gives you a sense of how the whole Exchange system hangs together and works. Remember that virtually all the architectural components that we discuss here are, in whole or in part, real program code running somewhere on a Windows 2000 server or an Exchange 2000 server or client machine.

Key Exchange 2000 Server Organizing Components

Every system, whether social, biological, or computer, needs a set of organizing components. Without these components, you'll have a devil of a time understanding or working with the system. Here's a highly simplified example using social organizations. We think of social organizations as having groups, and groups as having individual members. When we attempt to work within social organizations, it's very important to remember those groups because people often learn to behave and actually behave as group members, not as individual persons.

Exchange 2000 Server has its own set of key organizing components. These are borrowed from Exchange Server 5.5, but a lot happened to 5.5 on the way to 2000. Let's take a look at the organizing components of Exchange Server. We'll start with Exchange Server 5.5 and then see how these components were or were not modified in Exchange 2000 Server.

The key organizing components of Exchange Server 5.5 include organizations, sites, messaging servers, and message recipients (objects that can at least receive messages). In 5.5, these four components formed a hierarchy:

- Organizations contained sites.
- Sites contained messaging servers.
- Messaging servers contained message recipients.

An Exchange organization encompassed an Exchange Server 5.5 system that was a collection of servers in one or more sites. Think of an Exchange organization as Exchange Server 5.5's *forest*, in Windows 2000 Server parlance. Recipients in 5.5 included mailboxes, distribution lists, custom addresses (e-mail addresses outside the

Exchange system) and public folders. Figure 4.1 shows the organizing components of Exchange Server 5.5.

FIGURE 4.1

Exchange Server 5.5's organizing components

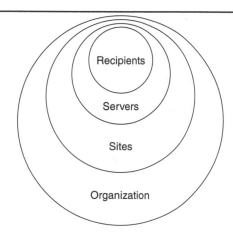

All is not quite so simple with Exchange 2000 Server. All four of the organizational components are still around, but although most have retained homes in Exchange 2000 Server, a few have moved at least in part to Windows 2000 Server. Exchange organizations, messaging servers, and public folders (the only type of message recipients that remain organizationally in Exchange) are a part of Exchange 2000 Server.

Sites are now a part of Windows 2000 Server, where they function similarly to the way they did in Exchange 5.5. However, they no longer have anything to do with Exchange. In Exchange Server 2000, administrative groups and routing groups replace sites. I'll talk more about administrative groups soon; I discussed routing groups back in Chapter 2, "2000: A Magic Number?"

The four types of recipients in Exchange 2000 are these:

- Exchange users (mailbox-enabled users and mail-enabled users)
- Distribution groups or mail-enabled groups (distribution lists in Exchange 5.5)
- Contacts (custom recipients in Exchange 5.5)
- Public folders

A mailbox-enabled user is a Windows 2000 user with an Exchange mailbox. A mail-enabled user is a Windows 2000 user who has no Exchange mailbox, but who does have an address in a foreign messaging system. See Figure 4.2 for a graphic representation of this state of affairs.

FIGURE 4.2

*Exchange 2000
Server's organizing
components with a lit-
tle help from Windows
2000 Server*

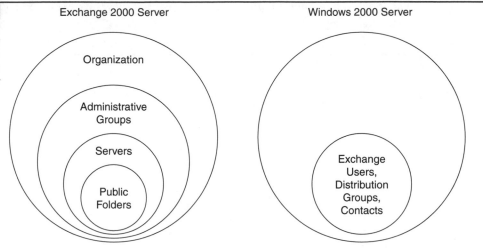

Exchange 2000 Server

Organization

Administrative
Groups

Servers

Public
Folders

Windows 2000 Server

Exchange
Users,
Distribution
Groups,
Contacts

"Wow!" you say, "That's a pretty bifurcated messaging mess." It's really not all that
bad. If you're an old hand at Exchange, all you have to do is readjust your thinking
about recipients. Recipients are still very important to Exchange 2000 Server, no matter where they live. So, for the sake of this discussion, let's agree to treat all four kinds
of recipients together. We probably shouldn't try to shoehorn them into the
Exchange 2000 Server organizational hierarchy, but we can still talk about them in
the same breath as the hierarchy.

You can see the hierarchy in Exchange Server 5.5's Administrator program. Figure
4.3 shows the hierarchy of one Exchange organization in the 5.5 Administrator program. GerCom is the name of the Exchange organization. LA is the name of the
Exchange site. The Exchange servers are called EXCHLA01 and EXCHLA02. All recipients in a site can be viewed in the Recipients container at the bottom of the screen.
You can see all four kinds of recipients in the Recipients container, mailboxes (Easton,
David), distribution lists (Dead Letter Manag...), custom recipients (Franklin, Marsha),
and public folders (Johnson Party (Fe...).

FIGURE 4.3

*The Exchange Server
5.5 hierarchy as
viewed through
the Exchange
Administrator program*

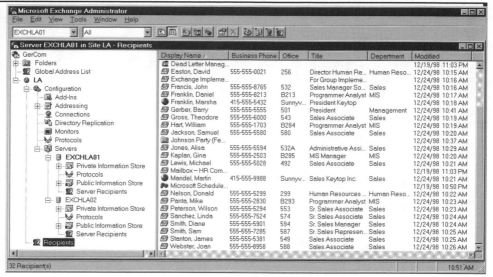

In Exchange Server 5.5, mailboxes resided on one and only one Exchange server. So, if you looked in the container labeled Server Recipients under any of the Exchange servers in Figure 4.3, you'd see the mailboxes that resided on that server. When you set up an Exchange Server 5.5 mailbox, you could designate the Exchange server where the mailbox would live. Public folders also lived on an Exchange 5.5 server, although they could be replicated to other servers. Exchange Server 5.5 distribution lists and custom recipients lived only in the Exchange directory, which could be replicated across Exchange Server 5.5 servers. Hold these thoughts. The good news is that most of this is still true with Exchange 2000 Server.

Figure 4.4 shows how my Exchange 2000 environment looks in the Exchange 2000 Server System Manager snap-in for Windows 2000 Server's Microsoft Management Console. My organization (Barry Gerber and Associates) includes my administrative groups (there's only one right now, First Administrative Group). My administrative group includes my Exchange servers (again, only one right now, EXCHANGE01), and my Exchange server contains a public store that includes public folders. To work on public folders, I click Public Folder Instances, right-click the folder that I want to administer, and open up its properties.

"Wait," you say. "Can't I do the same thing with mailboxes in the mailbox store right above the public store?" Nope. To administer mailboxes, you must use the Active Directory Users and Computers snap-in. That's why I say that recipients other than public folders are organizationally part of Windows 2000 Server.

FIGURE 4.4

The Exchange 2000 server hierarchy as viewed through the Exchange Server System Manager snap-in for Windows 2000 Server's Microsoft Management Console

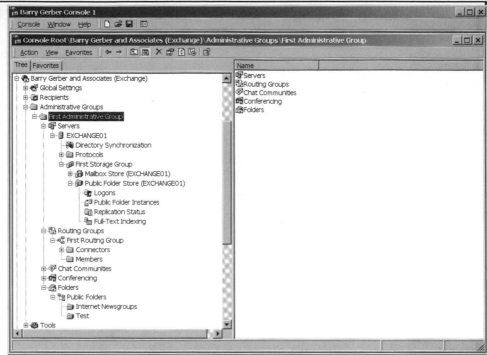

 WARNING If you've just installed Exchange 2000 Server, your Exchange system manager snap-in won't look anything like the one in Figure 4.4. It'll look a lot more like the one in Figure 1.15, in Chapter 1, "Introducing Exchange 2000 Server." You'll see a lot of the same stuff, but it won't be organized under administrative groups. You actually have to choose to view Administrative Groups before you can work with them. If you're accustomed to Exchange Server 5.5, where your first site was displayed automatically, you'll probably have more trouble adjusting to this new reality than a new Exchange 2000 Server user would. For now, don't worry about all of this. We're talking architecture here. We'll talk in Chapter 12, "Managing the Exchange Server Hierarchy and Core Components," about displaying administrative group containers, and in Chapter 15, "Installing and Managing Additional Exchange Servers," we'll create some new administrative group containers.

There is no container for recipients in the Exchange snap-in. "Wait," you say once again. "What about the container called Recipients that's just above Administrative Groups in Figure 4.4?" Well, that's a container for organization-wide recipient attributes such as addressing. You won't find mailboxes, distribution groups, contacts, and public folders there. Go to the public store in the Exchange system manager to administer public folders. Go to Windows 2000's Active Directory Users and Groups snap-in to administer Exchange users, distribution groups, and contacts.

 TIP For many Exchange components, you can assign management permissions at the component level. For example, you can create administrative groups for different departments in your organization and can assign different users management rights for each administrative group.

Figure 4.5 shows what's in the Users folder in the Active Directory Users and Groups snap-in. Barry Gerber in the right pane is a user. Users are Windows 2000 Server users. They have accounts that allow them to log into domains and access resources based on their permissions. You can mailbox-enable a Windows 2000 user while or after creating the user. You manage mailboxes when you manage the users with whom they are associated.

In Figure 4.5, All Managers is a distribution group; Joe W. Blow, about two-thirds down in the right pane, is a contact.

FIGURE 4.5

Viewing Exchange 2000 Server recipients with the Active Directory Users and Computers snap-in for Microsoft Management Console

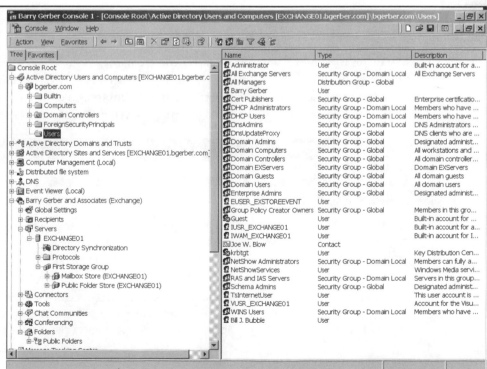

Not everything has changed with Exchange 2000 Server. For example, when you mailbox-enable a user, you still specify which Exchange 2000 server it will reside on. Public folders still reside on a single Exchange server and can be replicated to other Exchange servers. You can still see the mailboxes that reside on each server by looking in the server's mailbox store EXCHANGE01\First Storage Group\Mailbox Store (EXCHANGE01) in Figure 4.4. Now, you can even see which public folders exist on a given Exchange server, EXCHANGE01\First Storage Group\Public Folder Store (EXCHANGE01) in Figure 4.4. And, distribution groups (formerly distribution lists) and contacts (formerly custom recipients) continue to live only in a directory, but now it's Active Directory instead of the Exchange Server 5.5 directory.

So, in summary, Exchange 2000 Server includes four organizing components:

- Organizations
- Administrative groups
- Servers
- Recipients:
    - Exchange users
    - Distribution groups
    - Contacts
    - Public folders

Mailboxes live on Exchange 2000 servers and are managed in Active Directory. Distribution groups and contacts live on Windows 2000 Servers in Active Directory and are managed using Active Directory-specific management tools. Public folders live on Exchange 2000 servers and are managed using Exchange-specific management tools.

Does an Object Live on Exchange 2000 Server, on Windows 2000 Server, or on Both?

What follows is very important. It will help you understand the difference between objects that live only in Windows 2000 Server's Active Directory and objects that live both in Active Directory and someplace else, such as, Exchange 2000 Server. I strongly suggest you read what follows very carefully.

The first thing to understand is that all objects have a presence in the Active Directory namespace. Their attributes live in Active Directory. Some objects, such as distribution groups and contacts, live only in Active Directory. Some objects also have a presence in

Continued

CONTINUED

other places. For example, mailboxes live both on Windows 2000 servers in Active Directory and on Exchange 2000 servers.

When you manage the attributes of an object, such as a mailbox, you work in Active Directory. When you change attributes, you work solely in Active Directory because the attributes are stored in Active Directory. On the other hand, when you delete a mailbox, you still work in Active Directory to request the deletion, but your work affects both Windows 2000 Server and Exchange 2000 Server. The mailbox object with all its attributes is deleted from the Active Directory namespace. At the same time, the actual physical mailbox is deleted from the Exchange server.

Make sense? Good. Remembering this distinction will see you through many a dark and stormy night.

Exchange 2000 Server Core Components

We're now ready to look at some other key components of Exchange 2000 Server. These are not key organizing components; rather, these components provide the core functionality of Exchange 2000 Server.

Exchange Server 5.5 has four core components:

- Information Store
- Directory
- Message Transfer Agent
- System Attendant

Except for the directory, which is now Windows 2000 Server's Active Directory, the other three components remain, although one of the three has a new name:

- Information Store
- Routing Engine
- System Attendant

Let's tackle these three core components of Exchange 200 Server.

Information Store

Although it still has the same name as in Exchange 5.5, the Exchange 2000 Information Store (IS) can do lots more than the 5.5 Information Store could. We'll talk about the neat new features in a bit. First, I need to be sure that you have a firm grounding in the Exchange 2000's new Information Store.

Like Active Directory, the IS is a database—actually, a collection of databases—and a Windows 2000 Server program or, more correctly, *service* (see Figure 4.6). The IS is a grand container for what are called *storage groups*. Exchange 2000 Server—the lower-end product in the Exchange 2000 Server product line—supports one storage group per server installation. Top-of-the-product-line Exchange 2000 Enterprise Server allows for one or more storage groups per server installation, although you're limited to about four storage groups per server unless you're using the new 64-bit Windows 2000 products. All the storage groups in an Exchange organization constitute the Information Store. Each storage group can contain one or more databases. Two types of databases exist: mailbox stores and public stores. A storage group can contain one or more public stores. You can separately administer, back up, and restore individual databases, which allows for much better information store management and performance than was possible with Exchange Server 5.5.

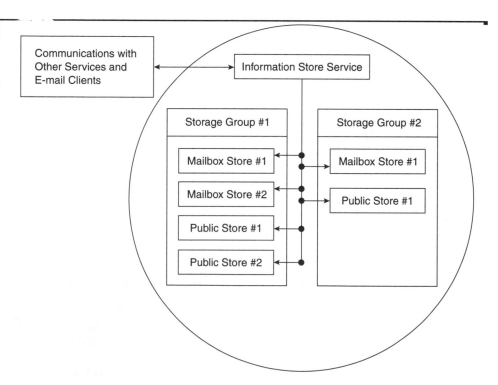

FIGURE 4.6

The Information Store is a collection of mailbox and public folder databases managed by the Information Store service.

To balance network loads and to reduce access costs, public folders can be replicated in whole or in part to other Exchange servers. Additionally, to lighten the load on servers with mailboxes, you can place public folders on separate Exchange servers and direct clients to those servers when they need access to public folders.

The IS service is a link between the IS databases and other components of Exchange Server. It performs a number of functions. Among other things, it receives incoming mail from and delivers outgoing mail to the Exchange 2000 Server Routing Engine and message transfer agents for other e-mail systems, notifies clients of the arrival of new mail, looks up addresses in Active Directory, and creates directory entries for public folders.

Now let's take a look at some other neat new features of the Information Store. As I pointed out in a previous chapter, you can actually do Internet publishing from Exchange 2000 Server public folders. Exchange 2000 folders support the Multipurpose Internet Mail Extension (MIME) protocol. MIME lets you send messages through the Internet and preserve their content type. Put simply, you can specify that an attachment to a message is in Microsoft Word format. When you open the document, Word opens and you can do anything with the document that you can do in Word.

Additionally, you can place actual HTML pages or Microsoft Active Server Pages (ASP) in Exchange folders. Web pages can include standard Exchange functionality such as calendars and custom Exchange applications. You can replicate these folders to other Exchange 2000 servers. Users can access these folders and pages through your Microsoft Internet Information Server, just as they'd access files through the same server. Microsoft claims that Web performance is better from public folders than from the file system.

Aside from the Internet, Exchange 2000's IS supports what Microsoft calls the *Installable File System* (IFS). IFS enables you to map Exchange 2000 Server mailbox and public stores as you would disk drives. You can then use the Windows Explorer or an instance of the command line to access these folders and their contents just as you'd access file folders and their contents. You can double-click messages and see them in the same message viewing form as is available in the Exchange-compatible messaging client installed on your computer. You can even back up mailboxes and public folders and their contents just as though they were part of your Exchange server's file system. In addition, you can restore any message within a backed-up mailbox or public folder. So, with IFS you no longer have to worry about the complexities of restoring an entire information store just to retrieve one message for one user.

The Routing Engine

The Routing Engine (RE) performs two basic routing functions. First, it routes messages between its server and other Exchange servers. Second, it routes messages between its server and Exchange connectors for foreign messaging systems. Figure 4.7 shows the RE in action. Let's look at the RE's various tasks in a bit more detail.

FIGURE 4.7

Each Exchange server's routing engine moves messages to other LAN- and WAN-connected Exchange servers.

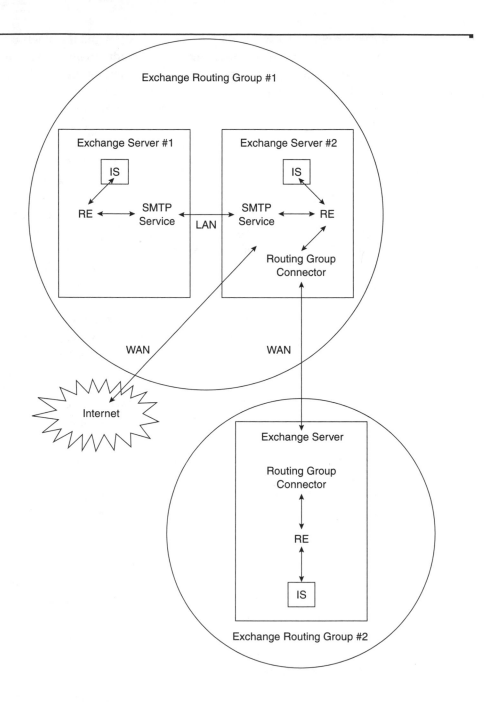

You'll remember that SMTP is the native protocol for Exchange 2000 Server. You probably also remember that Windows 2000 Server comes with a basic SMTP server (service) that is enhanced when Exchange 2000 is installed. Within an Exchange 2000 routing group, the RE routes messages between its server's IS and its server's SMTP service. The SMTP service then sends the messages to the appropriate Exchange server's SMTP service. (See Exchange Server #1 in Exchange Routing Group #1 in Figure 4.7.)

When it routes messages to Exchange servers located in different Exchange 2000 Server routing groups in the same Exchange organization, the RE gets help from Exchange 2000 Server connectors, discussed in the section "Exchange Connectors," later in this chapter. In Figure 4.7, the Routing Group Connector is being used to move messages between Exchange Routing Group #1 and Exchange Routing Group #2.

When the Exchange RE routes messages to Internet-based messaging systems, it uses the same SMTP service used to route messages internally (see Figure 4.7). Optionally, you can enhance the SMTP service with the Exchange SMTP Connector. Among other things, the SMTP Connector supports Internet message transfer using dialup links. I'll discuss the SMTP Connector in Chapter 15.

Connectors aren't optional for communicating with foreign messaging systems other than Internet systems. For example, the RE needs help from the X.400 Connector to link to route messages to X.400 messaging systems.

The System Attendant

Other Exchange Server components cannot run without the System Attendant (SA); it's the first Exchange component to activate on startup and the last to stop on shutdown. The SA performs a range of functions which are key to Exchange Server's operation. Let's take a closer look at each of these functions:

The SA helps other servers monitor network connections to its server. The System Attendant receives and replies to network link integrity messages from other Exchange servers. These servers know that something is wrong—either with the network link or the System Attendant's own server—if they fail to receive these replies.

The SA monitors for and corrects Exchange-related Active Directory inconsistencies on its server. The SA automatically checks the consistency of its copy of the Exchange-relevant entries in Active Directory against similar entries in the Active Directories of other Exchange servers in its Windows 2000 Server site. If it finds inconsistencies, the SA attempts to reconcile and fix them.

The SA collects message-tracking data for its server. The SA logs data about sent messages, which can be used for tracking a message's status and the route that it traveled once sent. This capability is especially useful when used in conjunction with similar data gathered by the SAs on other Exchange servers.

The SA builds Windows 2000 Server routing group-based message routing tables for its server. Like any network, an Exchange Server network needs *routing tables*, which are used specifically for routing messages. The SA interacts with Active Directory to build tables that the RE uses to route messages to servers in its routing group.

The SA triggers the generation of foreign electronic messaging addresses for recipients on its server. The SA generates X.400, SMTP, Microsoft Mail, and cc:Mail addresses by default. When gateways are installed, the SA generates gateway-specific e-mail addresses for users. When creating addresses, the SA interacts with Active Directory.

The SA participates in certain security functions. Security in Exchange is very good. An Exchange mailbox can use both digital signatures and encryption. The SA is involved in enabling and disabling these two components of Exchange security. To do this, it interacts with the *Key Management Service,* which is described in the next section.

Optional Exchange 2000 Server Components

You'll remember from the section "Getting a Handle on Exchange 2000 Server Versions," in Chapter 2, that there are two flavors of Exchange 2000 Server: the Server and Enterprise editions. Exchange 2000 Enterprise Server comes with the all the components discussed here, except gateways. Exchange 2000 Server edition includes all the components but the X.400 Connector and Internet Chat protocol.

You can at least start up Exchange 2000 Server without any of these components. That is why I call them *optional components*, not necessarily because you have to pay extra to get them. However, as you'll see, the components significantly enhance the functionality of the product, so you'll very likely use a number of them. Optional components include these:

- Microsoft Management Console snap-ins for Exchange 2000 Server
- The Directory Synchronization Agent
- The Key Management service
- Event Management service

- Microsoft Search (full-text indexing) service
- Exchange Internet protocol servers:
  - Outlook Web Access Server
  - Post Office Protocol V3 (POP3) Server
  - Internet Message Access Protocol V4 (IMAP4) Server
  - Network News Transfer Protocol Server
  - Extended Internet Relay Chat (IRCX) Server
  - Rendezvous Protocol (RVP) Server
- Exchange connectors:
  - Routing Group Connector
  - Simple Message Transfer Protocol (SMTP) Connector
  - Active Directory Connector
  - X.400 Connector
  - Connector for Microsoft Mail
  - Schedule+ Free/Busy Connector
  - Connector for cc:Mail
  - Other Legacy Messaging System Connectors
- Exchange gateways

Microsoft Management Console Snap-ins for Exchange 2000 Server

You saw examples of the Microsoft Management Console snap-ins for Exchange 2000 Server in action in Chapter 2 and in Figure 4.4 in this chapter, and you'll get to know them very well as we move along. The main point that I want to make here is that the snap-ins are *home.* They're where you go whenever you need to do almost anything with Exchange Server, from creating and managing users to linking with other Exchange servers or foreign mail systems, to monitoring the activities on your server. The snap-ins are a set of points from which you can manage anything, whether it's one Exchange server or your entire Exchange organization.

The snap-ins are home in another way, too: When you figure out which snap-in you need for a particular management task, they're easy. Soon after you start using the snap-ins, you'll feel about it the same way you feel about that comfortable old chair in the den. Really!

The Directory Synchronization Agent

The Directory Synchronization Agent (DXA) lets you create address books that include addresses from outside your Exchange system. It also enables you to send Exchange Server address information to other electronic messaging systems. It sends directory update information to and receives it from Microsoft Mail for PC Networks 3.*x* systems.

The DXA uses the Microsoft Mail 3.*x* Directory Synchronization Protocol, so any foreign, non-Microsoft electronic messaging system that is compatible with this protocol is fair game for cross-system directory synchronization.

The Key Management Service

Exchange 2000 Server supports public/private key encryption and digital signatures within an Exchange organization and, in certain situations, when communicating outside an Exchange organization. These help ensure the authenticity of a message and the person sending it. Exchange Server's Key Management service supports these services. With this component in place and running, Exchange client users can create secure messages.

The Event Management Service

The Event Management service supports event driven, server-based applications developed for Exchange Server 5.5. Event-driven applications perform a set of custom actions when something happens on an Exchange server, such as when a message from a specific sender arrives.

The Microsoft Search (Full-Text Indexing) Service

Microsoft has implemented a new service called Microsoft Search that enables you to fully index text in certain BackOffice applications. This service comes with such products as SQL Server 7 and Exchange 2000 Server enhances this service. Full-text indexing significantly increases the speed of searches within Exchange 2000 Server objects, such as messages.

Exchange Internet Protocol Access Components

Exchange 2000 Server comes with a set of six Internet protocol servers. These let you extend the reach of Exchange users beyond Microsoft's very good, but proprietary, electronic messaging protocol MAPI. The six servers are Hypertext Transmission Protocol (HTTP), which supports Outlook Web Access (OWA); Post Office Protocol

(POP3), Internet Message Access Protocol (IMAP4); Network News Transfer Protocol (NNTP), Extended Internet Relay Chat (IRCX); and Rendezvous Protocol (RVP).

HTTP (Outlook Web Access)

HTTP is the core protocol that supports Web access. Outlook Web Access uses the HTTP protocol to give users access to everything in their Exchange mailboxes, as well as items in public folders, using a Web browser such as Microsoft Internet Explorer or Netscape Navigator. On the server side, OWA is supported by Windows 2000 Server's Internet Information Server.

POP3 Server

Exchange Server's POP3 server gives users with standard POP3 e-mail clients, such as Eudora or the mail clients in both Microsoft Internet Explorer and Netscape Navigator, limited access to their Exchange mailboxes. Users can download mail from their Exchange Inboxes, but that's all. Users have no direct access to other personal or public information stores or to their schedules. This is due to limitations in the POP3 protocol itself, not in Microsoft's implementation of the protocol.

IMAP4 Server

The Exchange IMAP4 server goes one better than POP3, adding access to folders in addition to the Exchange Inbox. With IMAP4, folders and their contents can remain on the Exchange server, be downloaded to the computer running your IMAP4 client, or both. You can keep Exchange Server-based folders and their contents in sync with the folders on an IMAP4 client.

NNTP Server

The NNTP server lets you bring all those exciting Usenet newsgroups into your Exchange server's public folders, where your users can read and respond to them with the same e-mail clients that they use to read other public folders.

 NOTE Wondering what happened to Exchange Server 5.5's Lightweight Directory Access Protocol (LDAP) server? It just moved uptown. As I noted in Chapter 2 and Chapter 3, "Two Key Architectural Components of Windows 2000 Server," it's now a Windows 2000 Server service. Now, when a messaging client needs LDAP information, it queries Windows 2000 Server's LDAP service.

Extended Internet Relay Chat and Rendezvous Protocol (RVP)

Exchange 2000 Server brings two new servers to the table: the Extended Internet Relay Chat (IRCX) and the Rendezvous Protocol (RVP) servers. Both of these servers are based on existing or draft Internet standards. They support real-time interaction between users.

Exchange Connectors

Exchange servers, whether the 5.5 or 2000 flavor, need to talk to each other for a variety of reasons:

- To transfer messages and other information internally between Exchange servers

- To transfer messages between Exchange Server and foreign messaging systems

- To replicate e-mail addresses and other information between Exchange servers and foreign messaging systems

The native communication protocol for Exchange 2000 servers is the Simple Message Transfer Protocol (SMTP). Microsoft's Remote Procedure Call (RPC) protocol, Exchange 5.5's key interserver protocol, is supported on Exchange 2000 servers, but only to allow them to communicate "natively" with Exchange Server 5.5 systems.

The Exchange system allows for different communication methods, depending on the nature of the network connecting Exchange servers. When Exchange servers are linked by high-bandwidth, reliable, continuous networks, they can communicate with no intervening connectors.

However, when Exchange servers are connected by lower-bandwidth, perhaps less reliable, and maybe even noncontinuous (dial-up, for example) networks, Exchange connectors are required. Connectors not only establish the communications protocols to be used to link Exchange servers, but they also let you monitor and even schedule connections. You can even set priorities for some connectors, forcing Exchange to pick the highest-bandwidth or lowest-cost connection when multiple connectors link the same Exchange servers or foreign messaging systems.

To manage lower-bandwidth links, you first put all your servers with high-bandwidth, reliable, continuous connections into routing groups. You create one routing group per collection of well-connected servers. Then you link routing groups using Exchange connectors.

In addition to inter-Exchange server communications, Exchange servers also need to communicate with foreign messaging systems such as Internet mail systems to transfer messages. Specific Exchange connectors are available for many of these links.

For other foreign messaging system links, third-party gateways must be used. I discuss gateways in the section "Exchange Gateways," later in this chapter.

So, just what is the function of an Exchange connector? Well, basically, it allows you to set parameters compatible with the protocol the connector supports. For example, to exchange messages, addressing and other information with legacy Microsoft Mail or cc:Mail systems, you need to set up and configure the appropriate Exchange connector for either of these systems.

Okay, now we can talk about the Exchange connectors. There are a number of different Exchange connectors, including the Routing Group Connector, the Active Directory Connector, the X.400 Connector, the Simple Message Transfer Protocol (SMTP) Connector, the Microsoft Mail Connector, the Schedule+ Free/Busy Connector, and the cc:Mail Connector. Let's look at each of these connectors.

Routing Group Connector

The Routing Group Connector is the preferred connector for linking Exchange 2000 Server routing groups. It is quite similar to Exchange Server 5.5's Site Connector. You can also use the SMTP Connector or the X.400 Connector to link routing groups. The advantage of the Routing Group Connector is that it's easy to configure and supports multiple (redundant) links between the same two routing groups. The Routing Group Connector uses SMTP, so it preserves the native communications mode of Exchange 2000 Server. The Routing Group Connector is one of the Exchange connector options shown in Figure 4.7.

Active Directory Connector

This connector is new with Exchange 2000 Server and is used primarily to link Exchange 2000 Server and Exchange Server 5.5 systems. It keeps Active Directory and Exchange Server 5.5's directory in sync. As soon as you've converted all your 5.5 servers to Exchange 2000 Server, you won't need the Active Directory Connector any longer.

SMTP Connector

The Exchange Server 5.5 Internet Mail Service supported both the transfer of messages to Internet-based messaging systems and the linking of Exchange sites. In Exchange 2000, the Windows 2000 SMTP service handles Internet messaging. The Exchange 2000 SMTP Connector isn't required for standard Internet messaging. Rather, it is used to enhance Internet messaging. For example, the SMTP Connector supports a range of options for dialup connections to SMTP smart hosts that act as relay servers for incoming and outgoing Internet-bound messages. The SMTP Connector also supports inter-routing group connections, much as Exchange 5.5's Internet Mail Service supported inter-site connections.

X.400 Connector

The X.400 Connector is used to link Exchange servers to foreign X.400 systems for user message exchange. The X.400 Connector is fully compliant with all the 1984 and 1988 X.400 transport and message content standards.

The X.400 Connector can ride on top of TCP/IP, Microsoft Remote Access Server (RAS), or X.25 networking services. The X.400 Connector can also be used to link Exchange routing groups. It would be an Exchange connector in Figure 4.7.

Connector for Microsoft Mail

You have two post office-wide options for dealing with legacy systems running Microsoft Mail 3.*x* for PC Networks. Either you can move entire post offices and their user mailboxes to Exchange Server using migration tools that come with Exchange Server, or you can link the legacy systems to Exchange Server, providing recipients on all sides with transparent access to each other. The Connnector for Microsoft Mail (CMM) supports the latter option.

The CMM creates and interacts with a shadow (emulated) Microsoft Mail post office on the Exchange server. Exchange sends and receives mail through the CMM using this shadow, which looks like an Exchange server to users on the Exchange side and looks like a Microsoft Mail 3.*x* post office to users on the MS Mail side. Microsoft Mail's EXTERNAL.EXE program, or a version of EXTERNAL.EXE that runs as an NT or Windows 2000 service, is used to transfer mail between the shadow and the real MS Mail post office. Connections can be either synchronous or asynchronous. If it can bear the traffic, you need only one MMC to link all your MS Mail post offices to the Exchange world.

Before we leave the CMM, I want to be sure that you're aware of a third option for users of legacy Microsoft Mail for PC networks systems. This one requires neither whole post office migration nor use of the CMM. On a user-by-user basis, you can connect a user's Exchange client directly to both the user's Microsoft Mail and Exchange mailboxes. This lets the user send and receive messages from both the Microsoft Mail and Exchange systems. This option is best when you haven't got the time or other resources to migrate everyone in a Microsoft Mail post office to an Exchange server or to deal with the intricacies of the CMM.

Schedule+ Free/Busy Connector

Microsoft Schedule+ lets Exchange and Microsoft Mail users set up meetings with each other. It uses a graphical user interface to show, in aggregate fashion, the times available to users selected for a meeting. This information is available on Exchange servers and in Microsoft Mail for PC Networks post offices. The Free/Busy Connector, which is an extension of the MMC, lets Exchange servers and Microsoft Mail post offices share schedule information.

Connector for cc:Mail

The Connector for cc:Mail works a lot like the Microsoft Mail Connector. It enables Exchange Server users to continue accessing messages in their Lotus cc:Mail post office. Like the Connector for Microsoft Mail, the Connector for cc:Mail is ideally suited to keeping access to a legacy mail system alive during migration to Exchange Server.

Other Legacy Messaging System Connectors

Exchange 2000 Server comes with connectors for other foreign messaging systems. These include Lotus Notes and Novell GroupWise. These connectors function similarly to the connectors for Microsoft Mail and cc:Mail.

Exchange Gateways

Exchange Server supports X.400 and SMTP mail natively and provides connectors to other messaging systems such as Microsoft Mail. To access other systems, you'll need *gateways*. Exchange Server gateways don't resemble the clunky DOS gateways used with such products as Microsoft Mail 3.*x*. Like the rest of Exchange Server, they run as processes on NT Server. As long as gateway developers know what they're doing (and that's sometimes a big assumption), gateways tend to be stable, robust, and fast.

Gateways are available for such services as IBM's, PROFS and SNADS, and fax, as well as for pagers and voicemail. Microsoft produces some gateways, and third parties offer others. Keep in touch with Microsoft and the trade press for details.

Clients for Exchange

As I've noted before, the real fun of Exchange is on the client side. That's where you get to see the business end of Exchange, from "simple" e-mail to complex, home-grown messaging-enabled applications. Exchange client components include these:

- Outlook
- Internet browser
- POP3 and IMAP4

- Conferencing
- Chat and instant messaging
- Schedule+
- Microsoft Outlook Forms Designer forms
- Custom client-based applications

Here's a quick look at the Exchange client components from an architectural perspective.

The Outlook Client

An Outlook client provides full access to all the client features that Exchange 2000 offers. This includes everything from folders and messages in your mailbox to items in public folders, to rules-based message management, to encrypted and digitally signed messages.

You receive, transmit, and access messages in the Outlook client. It's your window on your mailbox and on public folders. Earlier versions of Exchange Server came with a variety of clients, including those for Macintosh, MS DOS, and Windows 3.1. As these clients worked with Exchange Server 5.5, they will work with Exchange 2000 Server.

The Outlook 2000 client ships with Microsoft Office 2000. There are also Outlook 97 and 98 versions. Outlook nicely integrates electronic messaging, scheduling, and contact and task management with a whole bunch of other functions, including electronic journaling of every message that you read or file that you open. Take a look at Figures 1.1 and 1.2, in Chapter 1, for a refresher on Outlook's user interface.

Outlook modifies your Exchange mailbox, adding new folders for things such as your schedule, contacts, and tasks. More importantly, it uses a differently structured schedule database, so if you've still got Microsoft Mail users lurking in your organization, you must decide whether you're going to use the older Microsoft Mail-based Schedule+ or Outlook for scheduling and contact/task management.

The Internet Browser Client

As I noted in Chapter 1, Exchange 2000 Server provides significantly improved support for Internet browser access to Exchange mailboxes and public folders. Using an Internet browser such as Microsoft's Internet Explorer 5 or later, you'll surf the folders in your mailbox and your public folders store almost exactly as you would with a true Outlook client.

POP3 and IMAP4 Clients

Microsoft Internet Explorer 4 and later come with Outlook Express. This lighter-weight client supports both POP3 and IMAP4 server access. The regular Outlook product line includes support only for POP3.

You can also find a number of POP3 and IMAP4 clients from third-party vendors. In addition to products such as Netscape's Communicator and Qualcomm's Eudora for Macs, Unix, and PCs, some of the most interesting of these clients run on hand-held systems such as Palm's Palm products. Armed with a package like Actual Software's IMAP4-capable MultiMail and a wireless Palm device, you can access, respond to, and manage your e-mail anywhere, at any time.

Conferencing Clients

Exchange 2000 Server includes an optional multimedia conferencing server. This server supports standard audio and video services, as well as the kinds of services familiar to users of Microsoft's NetMeeting client. Exchange 2000 Servers host and manage meetings, including the bandwidth required for conferences. Additionally, Exchange 2000 Servers support a centralized conference session reservation system.

Chat and Instant Messaging Clients

Both chat and instant messaging services support real-time interaction between users. Chat services let you enter into live group discussions. Instant messaging services enable you to communicate one-to-one with another user. Exchange 2000 Server supports these services in a variety of ways. For example, you create chat communities on Exchange 2000 servers. Users then access these communities using standard chat and instant messaging clients.

Schedule+ Clients

Schedule+ is a messaging-enabled application that includes scheduling, planning, and contact-management features. Version 7.5, the version that comes with Exchange Server, is a serious update of the original version, which was labeled "version 1.0" (Microsoft has a knack for skipping version numbers). Most of the improvements lie in the way that it handles features such as schedule viewing, printing, and creating to-do lists, and less in the program's already pretty decent collaborative-scheduling function.

Microsoft Outlook Forms Designer Forms

Users and developers can create forms with the Outlook Forms Designer, a component of the Outlook client. Forms created with the designer can be used for a range of tasks, including the collection of data, and can have drop-down pick lists, multiple-choice selections, action buttons, and other useful attributes.

Forms created in the Microsoft Outlook Forms Designer can be stored on Exchange servers and made available to all or select users. With their Outlook clients, these users can send a form to specific recipients as messages, or post it in public folders for others to access. Forms users can manually collate data collected in forms. Or, with the right programming, data can be automatically extracted from forms and processed. (Look back at Figure 1.10, in Chapter 1, for a glimpse into the wonderful world of electronic forms.)

Custom Client-Based Applications

Aside from the Microsoft Outlook Forms Designer, there are a variety of ways to build client-based applications using Exchange Server's messaging capabilities:

- Microsoft's versions 95, 97, and 2000 stable of applications (Word, Excel, and so on) include some nice collaborative tools and easy-to-use routing-slip capabilities based on Exchange messaging. Applications from other vendors also incorporate these capabilities.

- You can turn an Exchange message into any OLE 2–compliant application just by inserting an object from the app into the message.

- You can write programs that use Simple and Extended MAPI hooks or the X.400-oriented Common Mail Call APIs supported by Exchange Server.

- You can develop programs that use Exchange 2000's new file-based and Internet-based mailbox and public folder access capabilities.

Summary

Exchange Server organizing components give hierarchical structure to your entire Exchange system. The Exchange hierarchy begins with your Exchange organization. Organizations contain administrative groups. Administrative groups contain Exchange servers. Recipients are the lowest rung of the Exchange 2000 hierarchy ladder. Four types of Exchange recipients exist: Exchange users, distribution groups, contacts, and public folders. All four of these have a virtual presence in Windows 2000's

Active Directory. The mailboxes of mailbox-enabled Exchange users and public folders reside physically on Exchange servers. Distribution groups and contacts are only Active Directory objects.

Core Exchange components include the Information Store, Routing Engine, and System Attendant. Each Exchange server sports one instance of each of these components. An Information Store can have one or more storage groups, depending on whether you're using the Standard or Enterprise edition of Exchange Server. Storage groups can contain one or more mailbox stores and one or more public stores. The Routing Engine moves messages between Exchange servers and between Exchange servers and Exchange connectors. The System Attendant is responsible for a range of monitoring, security, and system maintenance tasks.

Exchange 2000 Server comes with a dizzying array of optional components, components that aren't required to start up Exchange server but that significantly enhance the Exchange environment. There are optional components for managing your Exchange organization and individual Exchange servers, keeping Exchange addresses in sync with foreign messaging system addresses, providing industrial-strength security for Exchange messaging and other services, doing full-text indexing of Exchange server content, servicing a wide range of Internet protocols, and connecting Exchange servers to each other and to foreign messaging systems.

Exchange clients come in a wide variety of sizes and shapes. The Outlook client is most tightly integrated with the whole Exchange system; the Internet-based Outlook Web Access client comes in a close second. In addition, users can access messages on their Exchange servers using Internet standard POP3 or IMAP4 clients. Exchange 2000 Server also supports Internet standard conferencing and chat clients. Legacy Schedule+ calendaring information is available to Schedule+ and Outlook client users. Finally, Outlook electronic forms and custom applications can serve as clients for data stored on Exchange 2000 Servers.

The first four chapters of this book were designed to give you a firm grounding in Windows 2000 and Exchange 2000 Server architecture and concepts. With this information under your belt, you're now ready to move into the very important area of preinstallation planning, which is the topic of the next chapter. I strongly urge you not to skip Chapter 5: It not only provides you with some key information on planning, but it also discusses technical issues that have not been discussed and that will not be discussed anywhere else in this book.

CHAPTER 5

Designing a New Exchange 2000 System

FEATURING:

Whether your system will be based on a single Exchange server in a single physical location and an Exchange 2000 administrative group, or hundreds of Exchange servers spread out over multiple locations and administrative groups, you need to consider a number of design issues before implementation. This chapter presents a stepped planning model based loosely on a model developed by Microsoft. Tracking and retracking through these steps will help your organization decide where it wants to go with electronic messaging and how it can get there with Exchange. I can tell you from lots of experience that this process really works. Generally, I've found that I can gather any required information and generate a fairly complex first-draft plan, complete with a most convincing executive summary, in a month or so.

This chapter isn't just about design, though. It also offers practical information about Exchange 2000 Server and how it works. For example, you'll find detailed information about Exchange's network connection options: what they do and which networking topologies and protocols support them. Information like this is central to designing and implementing an Exchange system, and it's not found anywhere else in this book.

This is a long chapter covering a great deal of information in detail. Just as you wouldn't try to implement a complex Exchange system in one day, you shouldn't try to plow through this chapter in one hour.

 NOTE This chapter doesn't cover upgrading Exchange Server 5.5 systems to Windows 2000 Server and Exchange 2000 Server. You'll find information on this matter in the next chapter. However, even if your immediate goal is an upgrade, I strongly suggest that you first carefully read this chapter.

Here, then, are the steps that I suggest you follow in designing your Exchange 2000 Server system:

1. Assign planning, design, and management responsibilities to staff.

2. Assess user needs.

3. Study your organization's geographic profile.

4. Assess your organization's network.

5. Establish naming conventions.

6. Select a Microsoft networking domain model.

7. Define administrative group boundaries.

8. Define routing group boundaries.

9. Plan routing group links.

10. Plan servers and internal connections to them.

11. Plan connections to other systems.

12. Validate and optimize your design.

Roll out the plan.

These 13 steps fit nicely into four categories. The first has to do with assigning responsibilities for planning, design, and management of your Exchange 2000 system. The second category includes the steps that you need to take related to analysis of user and technical needs. The third category helps you tackle the complex tasks involved in network planning. The last category focuses on the actual rollout of your Exchange system.

Now let's discuss each of these steps in more detail. This discussion builds upon the 13-step process presented by Microsoft in the Exchange documentation and other Microsoft publications, but it is far from a word-for-word regurgitation. Therefore, you should blame me—not Microsoft—if you encounter any problems from following the advice I give in this chapter. (Of course, if this stuff helps in any way, you should send the fruit baskets and such to *me*.)

Exchange Design Is Iterative, Not Linear

Throughout this chapter, remember that designing an Exchange system is not a linear process, but an iterative one. You'll find yourself coming back to each of the steps to gather new information, to reinterpret information that you've already gathered, and to collect even more information based on those reinterpretations. New information will likely lead to design changes and further iterations. Even after you've fully implemented your Exchange 2000 Server system, you'll return to steps in the design process as problems arise or as your organization changes.

Within reason, the more iterations that you go through, the better your final design will be. But take care not to use iteration as a route to procrastination. Whatever you do, start running Exchange 2000—if only in a limited test environment—as soon as you can.

Assigning Accountabilities for Planning, Design, and Management

You'll need two ensure that two sets of specific responsibilities are assigned to staff. First, you'll need to assign a set of responsibilities related mostly to planning and design. Then you'll need to assign a second set of responsibilities that deal with ongoing management of key aspects of your Exchange 2000 Server system when it is in place.

Assign Responsibilities for Planning and Design

Microsoft has identified 14 different roles that must be filled in planning, designing, and, to some extent, implementing and operating an Exchange 2000 Server system. That doesn't mean that you'll need 14 staff members to fill these roles, but it does mean that you'll need to assign each of these roles to a staff member. If you're the only staff member, good luck!

Here's a list of the 14 roles and their related responsibilities.

Product Manager:

- Sets objectives
- Manages external relationships
- Sets the budget

Program Manager:

- Has overall responsibility for Microsoft Exchange network design and implementation
- Specifies Exchange messaging system functional requirements

Exchange Engineer: Determines technical configuration of all components of Exchange servers

Testing and QA Engineer: Ensures that the Exchange messaging system conforms to functional requirements and corporate standards

Operations Developer: Develops procedures, policies, and programs that monitor and control the Exchange network

Technical Consultant: Provides consulting services and problem resolution for internal business units

Training Developer: Develops training materials and documentation used by users and technical support personnel

Rollout Planner:

- Determines the most efficient way to roll out Exchange servers and accompanying Window 2000 Servers
- Minimizes deployment costs
- Promotes efficient implementation

Migration Planner: Determines the work needed to migrate from an existing messaging system to Exchange 2000 Server

Implementation Manager: Manages the implementation of Exchange 2000 servers and associated components

End-User Technical Support Technician: Provides user support for Exchange-related problems and questions

Messaging Transport Operations Engineer: Maintains, operates, and repairs the Exchange server environment after installation

Marketing and Consumer Relations Manager: Develops and carries out the Exchange rollout marketing program (product demonstrations, newsletters, pilot site coordination, and so on)

Financial Controller:

- Monitors financial aspects of the project
- Tracks expenses against budget allocations

If you've ever implemented an information systems project, the generic versions of these roles should be quite familiar to you, even if you've never thought specifically and in great detail about each of them. The key point here is that you're much more likely to successfully roll out your new Exchange 2000 Server system if you ensure that each of these 14 roles is properly filled. As we go through the planning and design process, think about these roles and how you might fill them.

Assign Responsibilities for Day-to-Day Management

When your Exchange 2000 Server system has been implemented, you'll need to fill six roles that support your system. Again, you might assign each of these roles to a separate person or combine them in one or two persons. These six roles are listed here along with the responsibilities associated with them.

User Management: Administers at least Exchange 2000 Server aspects of Windows 2000 Server Active Directory, such as creation and management of recipients (Exchange users, distribution groups, and contacts)

Administrative Group Management: Administers select pieces of the Exchange 2000 Server environment based on organizational or security requirements

Routing Groups Management: Administers the routing groups created to allow for Exchange 2000 Server connectivity across lower-bandwidth networks

Public Folder Management: Administers Exchange 2000 Server public folder hierarchy

Application Development Management: Administers development of Exchange 2000 Server-related add-on applications

Real-time Collaboration Management: Administers chat, online conferencing, instant messaging, and other unified messaging components in Exchange 2000 Server environment

This list is based on a list of four roles provided by Microsoft. I've taken some liberties with that list, separating Administrative Group and Routing Group management and adding Application Development Management.

As with the set of 14 roles illustrated in the preceding section, as we go through the planning and design process, think about these roles and how you might fill them.

Performing a Needs Assessment

A needs assessment is a two-part process. First, you must understand the current state of affairs in some detail. Then, using your knowledge about what is currently in place, you must come up with an analysis of need that focuses both on keeping the best of what is and developing new approaches where required. You should perform a needs assessments on areas relating to these categories:

- Users
- Geography
- Data networks

You'll probably find that assessing user needs will be the most difficult because you're dealing almost exclusively with people and their perceptions of their needs and those of your organization. You should focus on the fact that, in addition to being an e-mail system, Exchange is a platform for a range of collaborative applications. You also should remember that user needs and wants have significant costs in time, money, and computer and network capacity.

A geographical needs assessment focuses on what is where in buildings, cities, states, and countries. You need to know what kind of computing and networking hardware and software you've got, and then you need to determine what, if any, changes must be made to ensure that everyone in your organization can participate in your Exchange system at a reasonably optimal level.

Exchange is nothing without quality network links from workstation to server and from server to server. Your network needs assessment should deal with several issues. The first is the location and nature of your network connections. The second relates to the bandwidth on your network, and the third relates to network reliability.

Assess User Needs

Here you're interested in who needs what, when they need it, and how you'll provide it. You'll want to get a handle on the programming, software, hardware, MIS systems, systems support, and training resources that will be required to satisfy user needs.

Remember that Exchange is an electronic messaging package, not just an e-mail product. Users may need specific electronic messaging-enabled applications. Depending on what users have in mind, application development can be a real resource hog. Also remember that, in some cases, hardware and software may require new workstations, not just new servers.

Be prepared to give users a clear idea of what Exchange can do. You don't need to get technical with most users; just give them a view of Exchange from the end user's perspective. Take another look at the first two sections of Chapter 1, "Introducing Exchange 2000 Server," to see how you might organize your presentation. And don't forget newer Exchange services such as chat, conferencing, and instant messaging. These could drastically change how you do business.

Keep in mind that one of the biggest mistakes that most people make when implementing a system is to ignore or give only passing attention to this step. Knowing as much as you can about what the users require up-front means that you'll have an easier time during implementation. For example, imagine that you don't know from the get-go that your organization could benefit significantly from a particular custom-programmed electronic messaging-enabled application. You'd go ahead and implement Exchange as an e-mail system with only the resources such an implementation requires. You'd get your Exchange system up, and it would be perking along just fine when, maybe three months later, some user comes up with this great idea for an electronic messaging-enabled app. Boink! Suddenly you have to tell management that you need a few programmers and maybe more hardware to implement this idea that nobody thought of four or five months ago. I'll leave the rest to your imagination.

NOTE Regardless of what you find out in your user needs assessment, add a fudge factor in favor of more hardware and support personnel. Exchange has so many capabilities that you can be sure your users will find all kinds of ways to challenge whatever resources you make available. Depending on your users and their ability to get away with unplanned demands for resources, fudging by as much as 25 percent is reasonable.

Suffice it to say that a user needs assessment is the single most important part of the Exchange design process. Therefore, we'll cover it in more detail than the other 13 Exchange design steps.

Questions to Ask

You'll want to answer a number of questions during your user needs assessment. Here are the major ones:

1. What kinds of users (for example, managers, salespeople, clerical staff, lawyers, doctors) does my organization have, and what do they think they want from the new Exchange system?

2. What sorts of electronic messaging services are different groups of users likely to need (for example, e-mail, calendars and scheduling, public folders, specially designed applications)?

3. Which specially designed applications can be developed by users, and which must be developed by MIS personnel?

4. Do all users need every capability from day one, or can implementation be phased in, perhaps based on user groupings?

5. What sorts of demands will users (or groups of users) put on your Exchange servers? Much of the information in this category can be used with Microsoft's Exchange server load simulation program to predict expected server load and project server hardware and networking requirements.

   - How many mailboxes will you create per server?
   - How many messages will the typical user send per day?
   - How many messages will the typical user receive per day?
   - How frequently will users send messages...
     - to others on their server?
     - to others in their routing group?
     - to others in each of the other routing groups in your organization?

- to others outside your organization? (Be sure to break this down by the different kinds of external connections you'll have; see steps 9 and 11.)
- How often will users read messages in their mailboxes?
- How often will users read messages in public folders?
- How often will users move messages to personal folders stored locally and on the network?
- How often will users move messages to public folders?
- How big will the messages be? What percentage will be 1K, 2K, 4K, 10K with attachments, or 100K with attachments?

6. What level of message delivery service will users want and need? This should be stated in hours or minutes between the time a message is sent and received. You'll need to specify this for both internal and external communications.

7. What sorts of hardware and software resources (for example, computers, operating systems, Outlook client licenses) will different groups of users need to implement Exchange on the client side?

8. What kinds of training will be required for users or groups of users?

9. What sorts of MIS resources will be required to support user needs?

Study Your Organization's Geographic Profile

You need a list of all the geographical units in your organization. Here you should think not only in terms of cities, states, and countries, but also in-city and even in-building locations. Start at the top and work your way down. At this point, diagrams are important. Draw maps and building layouts.

This is the time to gather information on the workstations and servers you've got in each location. You'll want to know how many run each of the different kinds of operating systems in your organization. Operating systems to watch for include these:

- Windows 2000 Workstation and Server
- Windows NT Workstation and Server
- Novell NetWare 3.*x,* 4.*x,* and 5.*x* Servers, and NetWare IPX/SPX workstations
- Windows 95/98
- Windows 3.1*x*
- MS-DOS
- Apple Macintosh

- Unix workstations by type of operating system
- Banyan VINES servers and workstations
- Workstations used remotely

If you've got hardware and software inventories for these machines, your job will be a lot easier. If you're looking for an automatic inventorying system, check out Microsoft's Systems Management Server. Not only can you use it to gather workstation and server hardware information automatically, but it also can help you install Outlook clients throughout your organization. You can use all the information that you collect about workstations and servers to determine who's ready for Exchange and how many Outlook client licenses you'll have to buy.

As you gather information in other steps, begin to look at it in the context of your geographic profile. For example, you'll want to meld geographic information with what you've found out about user needs and user groupings.

More on User Workstations

Most user workstations are underpowered. That's a pretty strong statement, but I stand by it. I limped along for quite some time on a substandard 400MHz Pentium II workstation with 128MB of memory. Then I moved up to an 800MHz dual Pentium III processor and 512MB of RAM. (Yes, 512MB of RAM.) When I ran Windows 2000 on my old, underpowered sleepwalker, it was all I could do to keep my word processor, a spreadsheet, and my e-mail software open at the same time. If I opened anything else, the machine started thrashing around so much between RAM and virtual memory that it slowed to a nearly useless crawl.

With my new system and Windows 2000, I can run word processing programs, spreadsheet programs, and Exchange together without wasting precious time to switch among them. And I still have plenty of horsepower left for all those tasks that I used to do with paper because I couldn't bring up the applications fast enough when I needed them. At will, I can now simultaneously open (or keep open) such apps as an accounting package and Microsoft Word, Excel, Project, Outlook, and PowerPoint. With all that computer power, I'm also no longer reluctant to run other key programs—say, Internet Web browsers or Windows 2000 Control Panel applets—at the drop of a hat.

Here's the bottom line: I've had my new system for less than a year. By my estimates, the productivity increase that I've experienced in that time has already paid back the cost of the system's purchase.

Continued

CONTINUED

Maybe all your users don't need a dual 800MHz Pentium system with Windows 2000 Server and 512MB of RAM. However, as you start assessing user needs, don't let the dismal state of your organization's stable of workstations stop you and your users from reaching for the stars as you think about potential applications for Exchange. You'll notice that I talk here about my Windows 2000 desktop system, not my Windows 95 or 98 system. I strongly urge you to consider starting with or moving to at least the Windows 2000 Professional workstation product for desktop business computing. Yes, I said "at least." When I said I run Windows 2000 on my workstation, I meant Windows 2000 Advanced Server, not Professional.

Assess Your Organization's Network

In this step, you just want to know what your network looks like now. This isn't the place to get into what kinds of networking you'll need; that comes later. You need to answer four key questions here: What's connected to what, and how? (Okay, if you're counting, that's two questions.) How much bandwidth have we got on each network? Finally, how reliable are our networks?

What's Connected to What, and How?

Generally, in answering these questions, you should start at the top of your organization and work down to the domain or server level. For each link, name the physical connection, the networking topology, and the networking protocols running on the connection. (For example, physical connection = local hardwire, networking topology = 100BaseT Ethernet, networking protocols = NetBEUI, TCP/IP, IPX/SPX, SNA.) This information, especially when combined with the information you've collected in steps 1 and 2, will prove valuable as you start to plan for the Exchange connectivity that you'll need.

In looking at your organization's network, don't forget about connections to the outside world. Do you have connections to the Internet, to X.400 messaging systems, or to trading partners?

How Much Bandwidth Have You Got on Each Network?

Although bandwidth begins with network topology (type of connection), such as 100BaseT, T1, and DSL, it doesn't stop there. You need to know how much of your network topology's theoretical bandwidth is actually available.

To assess the actual bandwidth on each of your networks, you'll need some help from a network monitoring tool. If your networks are Windows 2000- or NT-based, you can try using the performance monitoring tools that come with these operating systems to get a handle on traffic. For Windows NT, select Start Menu ➢ Programs ➢ Administrative Tools ➢ Performance Monitor. For Windows 2000, select Start Menu ➢ Programs ➢ Administrative Tools ➢ Performance.

Microsoft's Systems Management Server has some pretty good network monitoring capabilities, too. For NetWare systems, try one of the many software-based network traffic monitors out there. A lot of modern network hubs, switches, and such also come with excellent network-monitoring software. If you're flush with cash, go for a hardware-based monitor, such as Network Associates' Sniffer.

What you want here is a chart that tells you, on average, how much of a network's bandwidth is available during each of the 24 hours in a day. You'll have to take several samples to get reliable data, but it's worth it. A warning light should go on in your head if you're already using more than, say, 40 percent of the available bandwidth on any network during daytime hours and you're not already running a heavy-duty messaging system such as Exchange. With that kind of scenario, you just might have to make some changes in the network before installing Exchange. We'll talk about those changes later; for now, be sure to collect this data on available bandwidth and incorporate it into your organizational maps.

How Reliable Are Your Networks?

Having a reliable network is an important issue. Increasingly in corporate America, there is strong pressure to centralize network servers. Centralization makes good economic sense. If all network servers are in one place, one set of staff can support and monitor them, assuring 7-day-a-week, 24-hour-a-day uptime.

Of course, 7-day, 24-hour server availability is useless if the networks that people use to get to the servers are unreliable. I've seen this little scenario play itself out in several organizations: They centralize the servers, the network fails, users can't get to their now mission-critical e-mail and other data, responsible IS planners are roundly criticized, and lower-level IS personnel are even more heavily criticized or fired. Grrr!

Here's the bottom line: Don't make your users work on unreliable networks. If your networks can't come close to matching the reliability of your servers, put the servers closer to their users. The little extra that it costs to manage decentralized servers is worth the access insurance that it buys. Sure, get those networks up to par, but don't risk your Exchange implementation on centralized servers before a reliable network is in place to support them.

Planning Your Network Configuration

Although it takes but a few words to say, planning your network configuration will take you on a long and winding road. In the process, you'll need to do the following:

- Establish naming conventions for objects in your Exchange server hierarchy
- Select a Microsoft networking domain model
- Define administrative group boundaries
- Define routing group boundaries
- Plan routing group links
- Plan servers and internal connections to them
- Plan connections to other systems
- Validate and optimize your design

You need to establish naming conventions for your Exchange organization, administrative groups, servers, and recipients. Some of these names depend on how you name Windows 2000 objects, while others have no dependency on the operating system. The Windows 2000 domain model that you choose will significantly impact how your Exchange servers interact, especially from a security standpoint.

Administrative groups replace the security groupings function of Exchange 5.5's sites. How you set their boundaries depends heavily on how you want to parcel out responsibility for Exchange server management in your organization. Routing groups replace the server-to-server communication functionality of Exchange 5.5. Clear, technically appropriate routing group boundaries and links are essential to smooth wide-area exchange of messages and other information between servers in Exchange 2000 environments.

The servers where you install Exchange 2000 must have adequate capacity. Even if you plan for servers of very high capacity, you should consider distributing user mailboxes across multiple servers to increase performance; you also should consider setting user storage quotas to ensure adequate disk capacity over time. In addition, you should be sure that your servers are protected against low-level and catastrophic glitches by such things as fault-tolerant hardware, uninterruptible power supplies, and a reliable tape backup system. Finally, you should ensure that users have adequate bandwidth to access messages and other objects on your Exchange servers.

If you need to link to public messaging services such as the Internet or the X.400 system, you'll need to think about the Exchange connectors that support these services. If you need to access third-party messaging systems such as cc:Mail or SNADS, you'll have to factor connectors or gateways for these into your plans.

Finally, when key aspects of your Exchange system are in place, you need to test them to be sure that they work at all. Then you'll need to ensure that they work up to whatever performance and other standards you need to meet.

Okay, let's start our trip down that long and winding road.

Establish Naming Conventions

Here you set some criteria for naming the four key Exchange organizational components: your organization, administrative groups, servers, and recipients. Your goal should be to establish a logical and consistent set of naming conventions that fit in well with your real-world organizational structure and culture.

Naming the Organization, Administrative Groups, and Servers

Here's one easy and usually safe naming convention that you can use:

- Organization = master company name (for example, Barry Gerber and Associates)
- Administrative Group = a geographic location or a department (for example, Los Angeles or Sales)
- Server = generic naming (for example, EXCHANGE01)

Names for organizations and administrative groups can be up to 256 characters long, but I strongly suggest that you keep names to around 32 characters, just so that you can see them in the tree of the Exchange 2000 Server System Manager. Server names are set when you install Windows 2000 Server. They are limited to a maximum of 63 characters, but you should limit them to 15 characters if pre-Windows 2000 clients will access them.

For most names, almost any character is permitted. However, for organization, administrative groups, and server names, I strongly suggest you use only the 26 uppercase and lowercase letters of the alphabet, and the numerals 0 through 9. Don't use spaces, underscores, or any accented letters.

Naming Recipient Mailboxes

You'll also need some criteria for naming mailboxes. There are four key names for each Exchange mailbox: the first name, the last name, the display name, and the alias name. Mailbox administrators create and modify these names in the Windows 2000 Active Directory Users and Computers Microsoft Management Console snap-in.

The first and last names are entered when creating the user's Windows 2000 login account. The display name is created from the first and last name (as well as the middle name, if present). The alias name is created from the user's Windows 2000 logon name, which is entered when the user's Windows 2000 account is created.

The first and last names and the display name are Windows 2000 objects that are also used by Exchange. The alias is an Exchange object that is used in forming some Exchange e-mail addresses.

You can change the default rules for constructing mailbox names, and you can manually change these names. In Figure 5.1, you can see the first and last names as well as the display name for my Exchange 2000 mailbox. Figure 5.2 shows the alias name for my mailbox.

FIGURE 5.1

*Display names are cre-
ated using first and
last names when a
Windows 2000 user
account is created.*

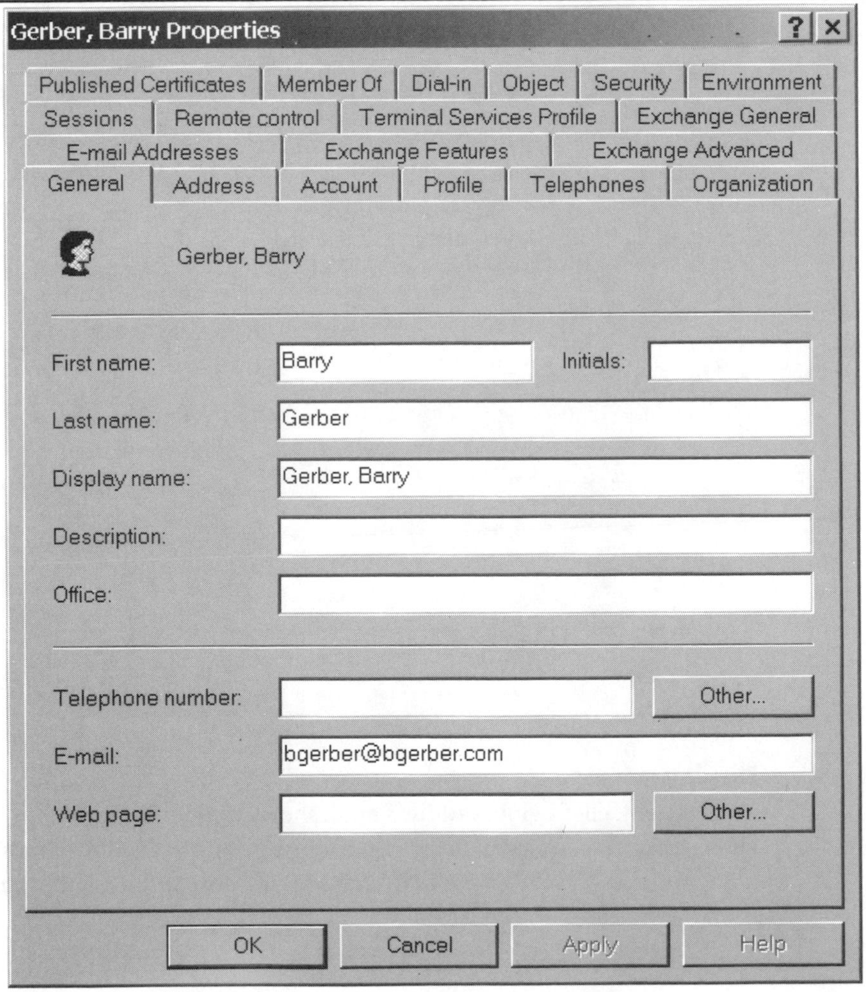

Gerber, Barry Properties

| Published Certificates | Member Of | Dial-in | Object | Security | Environment |

| Sessions | Remote control | Terminal Services Profile | Exchange General |

| E-mail Addresses | Exchange Features | Exchange Advanced |

| General | Address | Account | Profile | Telephones | Organization |

Gerber, Barry

First name: Barry   Initials:

Last name: Gerber

Display name: Gerber, Barry

Description:

Office:

Telephone number: Other...

E-mail: bgerber@bgerber.com

Web page: Other...

OK   Cancel   Apply   Help

FIGURE 5.2

The alias name for an Exchange 2000 mailbox

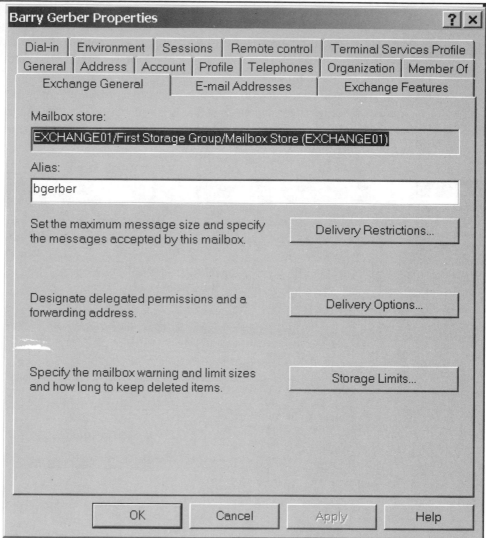

Display Names

The Outlook client global address book shows the display name for each mailbox (see Figure 5.3). You'll need to decide on a convention for display names. You've got two basic options: *first-name-space-last-name* (as in John Smith) or *last-name-comma-space-*

first-name (as in Smith, John). You can also set up custom defaults. You can change the defaults at any time, but the change applies only to newly created mailboxes. Fortunately, there's a way to automatically change the display names of old mailboxes; I'll show you how in Chapter 11, "Managing Exchange Users, Distribution Groups, and Contacts."

Display names can be up to 256 characters long. Display names are only a convenience—they're not a part of the mailbox's e-message address. However, they are the way in which Exchange users find the people they want to communicate with, so don't scrimp when setting them up. You might even want to include department names or titles in display names so that users aren't faced with ambiguous selections, as they might be if they encountered a list of 25 recipients named John Smith.

Practically speaking, display name lengths should be limited only by your users' willingness to read through lots of stuff to find the mailbox they're looking for.

FIGURE 5.3

The Exchange client global address book shows each mailbox's display name.

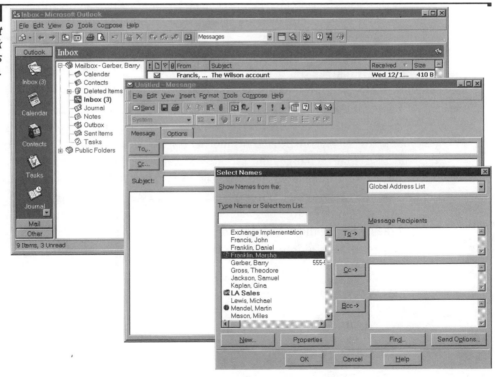

Full-blown religious arguments have sprung up around the metaphysics of display name conventions. I'll leave the decision to you, although I prefer the convention of Smith, John.

WARNING Something as apparently simple as changing the default order of last and first name in display names isn't all that simple with Exchange 2000. In Exchange Server 5.5, you made the change in the Exchange Administrator program. With Windows 2000/Exchange 2000 Server, you have to edit the Active Directory Schema. Why? Display names aren't just for Exchange mailboxes anymore. They're also used whenever end users or system administrators go looking for a specific Windows 2000 Server user in Active Directory. That's why it's an Active Directory issue. Editing Active Directory is somewhat akin to editing the Windows registry. It's not a job for amateurs, and it's a job that may be done by someone not directly involved in day-to-day Exchange 2000 Server management. In addition, the decision to change the display name default for an Active Directory namespace is no longer simply an Exchange Server issue. It's an organization-wide issue because changes impact more than electronic messaging.

Alias Names

For some messaging systems, the user's mailbox is identified by an alias name, which is part of the mailbox's address. Either Exchange itself or the gateway for the foreign mail system constructs an address using the alias. For other messaging systems, the mailbox name is constructed from other information. Figure 5.4 shows the two addresses that Exchange built for me by default for the Internet and for X.400. My Internet addresses use the alias bgerber, in my case. X.400 addresses do not use the alias. Instead, they use the full first and last name attributes of the user.

Aliases can be up to 63 characters long. That's too long, of course, because some people in foreign messaging systems will have to type in the alias as part of an electronic messaging address. Try to keep aliases short—10 characters is long enough.

FIGURE 5.4

Exchange Server uses the mailbox alias or the first and last names to construct e-mail addresses.

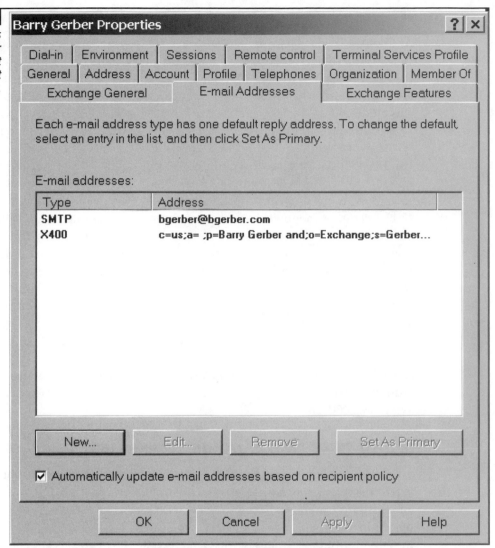

For some foreign messaging system addressing schemes, Exchange must remove illegal characters and shorten the alias to meet maximum character-length requirements. For example, underscores become question marks in X.400 addresses. Do all you can to ensure that aliases are constructed using less-esoteric characters.

Alias naming conventions are a religious issue, too, so you'll get no recommendations from me.

Select a Microsoft Networking Domain Model

As I noted in earlier chapters, particularly in Chapter 3, "Two Key Architectural Components of Windows 2000 Server," Microsoft much wants you to strongly consider using a single root Windows 2000 domain model for your network. You can still create child domains (subdomains) and control access to various network resources using this model.

Aside from certain security requirements, one of the main reasons for multidomain NT networks was the difficulty of building single domains that crossed lower-bandwidth links. Microsoft has outfitted Windows 2000 with such features as sites and site connectors to deal with this issue. Unless you've got some strong security requirements, the single-root domain model really makes the most sense.

If it works for your organization, you can even use your Internet domain name for your Windows 2000 root domain. I've done this by naming my Windows 2000 root domain bgerber.com, which is the same as my Internet domain name. This greatly simplifies Exchange server installation, although you'll need to be especially careful to protect any internal resources that shouldn't be accessible on the Internet. If you want to use a separate name for your Windows 2000 root domain, then do so, by all means. You can still use your Internet domain name for external Exchange messaging.

This is not the last you'll see of Windows 2000 domains in this book. Chapter 6, "Upgrading to Windows 2000 Server and Exchange 2000 Server," includes a discussion of the role of domains in a Windows 2000/Exchange 2000 upgrade. Chapter 7, "Installing Windows 2000 Server," focuses on domains in the installation of new Windows 2000 servers.

Define Administrative Group Boundaries

Administrative groups play a couple of roles. First, they can be used to control administrative access to your Exchange server environment. You can set permissions on an administrative group so that only certain users can manage the servers and other objects in the group. Second, you create routing groups, which we'll discuss next, inside administrative groups in what are called Routing Groups containers. When Exchange 2000 server is installed, one administrative group is created, and within that group, one Routing Groups container is created.

The administrative group structure of your Exchange Server environment will probably depend to some extent on the structure of your organization. If you want a particular group, such as a department, to manage its own Exchange server environment, you would create an administrative group, put the department's Exchange server(s) in the administrative group, and assign permissions to manage the group to the appropriate Windows 2000 users or group.

If you want, you can create administrative groups solely for the purpose of managing message routing. In this case, administrative groups become a convenient way to group together like Exchange servers and control routing between them.

By default, one administrative group is created in a domain when you install Exchange. You can add more administrative groups to a domain as needed.

Define Routing Group Boundaries

When defining routing group boundaries, you should keep a couple of things in mind. First, Exchange routing groups and Microsoft network domains are related. Second, all the Exchange servers in a routing group should have certain networking capabilities.

Remember as you read the rest of this section that you must create routing groups. You create routing groups inside an administrative group in a Routing Group container.

Required Networking Capabilities

With the right security in place, the moment that an Exchange server starts running, it automatically begins communicating with other Exchange servers. Initially, these communications are mostly related to swapping messages. You can also replicate public folders across Exchange servers.

You don't have to do a thing to start inter-Exchange server communications—they just happen. The first time this happens, you'll jump for joy, especially if you're accustomed to those old-fashioned e-mail systems such as Microsoft Mail, with all their gizmo gateways, dirsync machines, and such.

You create routing groups and add Exchange servers to them to ensure that servers linked by adequate bandwidth networks communicate optimally—basically, at the highest speeds possible without any intervention on the network side other than controls built into the networking hardware and software.

You then create inter-routing group connectors to ensure the integrity and reliability of links between servers on networks with less than optimal bandwidth. For example, routing group connectors let you schedule connections where required, and some even let you build redundant links so that the failure of one link doesn't stop inter-server communications.

Because users in a routing group often have some affinity for each other, you can usually expect higher user messaging and folder replication traffic between servers in one routing group than between servers in different routing groups.

All this intra-routing-group/interserver network traffic requires that Exchange servers in a routing group be connected by a high-bandwidth dedicated network, but high bandwidth isn't absolute. For example, from Exchange's perspective, a 155Mbps ATM link isn't high-bandwidth if you're eating up 154.9Mbps sending continuous streams of video images. There are no hard and fast rules here, but any physical network that can provide Exchange with 512Kbps of bandwidth most of the time should be adequate. Lower bandwidths can work in cases where messaging traffic is light and public folder replication is nonexistent or kept to a bare minimum. Physical networks capable of delivering at least this kind of dedicated bandwidth include faster Frame Relay and satellite, full T1, microwave, DSL, T3, Ethernet, Token Ring, Fast Ethernet, FDDI, ATM, and SONET.

Consider DSL

Digital Subscriber Line (DSL) networking is finally available in many locales in the United States. DSL is a variable-bandwidth networking topology. Bandwidth ranges from as little as 64Kbps through T1. Compared to most other higher-bandwidth technologies, DSL is inexpensive: I currently pay $199 per month for a 384Kbps always-on business-oriented symmetrical DSL Internet link with multiple IP addresses. This link supports my Exchange Server connection to Internet mail as well as a lot of other Internet-based functionality, such as an FTP service, a Web server, and a time sync service. As we'll see in Chapter 15, "Installing and Managing Additional Exchange 2000 Servers," always-on links offer distinct advantages when you're connecting Exchange Server to the Internet.

Plan Routing Group Links

As I noted previously, you link routing groups by running one or more Exchange connectors on Exchange servers in each routing group. There's no need for each Exchange server in a routing group to run its own connectors; one Exchange server can serve all the inter-routing group needs of all Exchange servers in a routing group. However, if a routing group has two or more Exchange servers, it often makes sense to run routing group connectors on multiple servers. This improves performance and, if you use different network links for each connector, allows for redundant links between routing groups.

Routing Group Link Options

You can connect routing groups either *directly* or *indirectly*. Direct connections are point-to-point connections between servers; indirect links pass through foreign electronic messaging systems. Both direct and indirect connections use SMTP messages to move user communications and public folder replication information between Exchange servers in different routing groups. With direct connections, the servers talk directly to each other. With indirect connections, the servers communicate by sending messages through a mediating messaging system. Exchange 2000 server allows for indirect routing group connection options using either a public X.400 service or the Internet mail service.

 NOTE I use the terms *connection* and *link* to refer to two very different things. In the previous paragraph, they refer to the way servers *communicate* with each other, whether directly or indirectly. In other places in this book, *connection* and *link* refer to actual *physical and protocol-level networking options*, such as Ethernet, TCP/IP, and X.400. I tried without success to find another word to modify the terms *direct* and *indirect*.

When connecting Exchange routing groups, you get to choose among three connector options:

- Routing group connector (direct link only)
- X.400 connector (direct or indirect link)
- SMTP connector (direct or indirect link)

Let's look at each of these in more detail.

The Routing Group Connector

Of all the Exchange connectors, the routing group connector is the fastest and simplest to set up and manage. In addition, of all the ways to link routing groups, the routing group connector is most similar to the automatic, built-in links between Exchange servers in the same routing group. Like built-in links, the routing group connector moves messages and folder replication information between Exchange 2000 servers using Exchange's standard SMTP messaging format. The major difference is that the routing group connector allows for scheduling connections, optionally transmitting messages with large attachments at different times than smaller messages, providing redundant links, and prioritizing multiple routing group connections based on the bandwidth available for each connection.

The routing group connector requires a continuous network. It doesn't support dial-up links, and it's best suited to Exchange inter-routing group connections with heavy user loads and public folder replication duties. If you already have a wide area network with adequate bandwidth in place, the routing group connector can be especially attractive because you don't need to add any networking infrastructure to support the connector. Of course, if you're expecting heavy cross-routing group network loads, you'll need high-bandwidth network connections such as those provided by topologies such as T1, Ethernet, Token Ring, T3, Fast Ethernet, FDDI, ATM, and SONET. When you begin considering the higher-capacity networking topologies listed here to link routing groups, you might want to go one step further and merge the routing groups to take advantage of Exchange Server's higher performance intrarouting group communications.

The X.400 Connector

Microsoft recommends that the X.400 connector be used primarily for connecting to and exchanging messages with foreign X.400 messaging systems. Microsoft recommends the X.400 connector for direct or indirect routing group links only when an X.400 networking infrastructure is already in place.

The X.400 connector can run on top of three different networking protocols: TCP/IP, OSI TP0 (X.25), and Microsoft's Remote Access Service (RAS). The X.400 connector can support dial-up links between Exchange servers. With its support for RAS dial-up connectivity, the X.400 connector is one alternative to Exchange 5.5's dynamic remote access connector, which doesn't exist in Exchange 2000 Server.

You can schedule X.400 routing group links. This allows you to take advantage of lower off-hours connection costs. You also can schedule transmission of messages with large attachments for different hours than messages without attachments or with smaller attachments.

The X.400 connector is a bit slower than the routing group connector, both because it must translate to and from the X.400 format when that format is used for inter-routing group communications, and because there's some extra networking overhead involved in X.400 communications.

Cost considerations lead most organizations to opt for lower, sublocal area network bandwidth links to public X.400 providers. That's fine, but it means that indirect routing group links should be used mostly for low-traffic routing group connections and to provide redundant links for routing groups already connected by higher-bandwidth direct links.

The SMTP Connector

As I noted in Chapter 4, the main function of the SMTP connector, the Internet Mail Service in Exchange 5.5, is to add functionality to the SMTP service that is native to

Windows 2000 Server. This service enables standard Internet send and receive messaging services for a Windows 2000 Server/Exchange 2000 Server. We'll talk about SMTP services and using the SMTP connector for Internet mail in Chapter 13, "Managing Exchange 2000 Internet Services."

The SMTP connector also lets you link routing groups. You can use standard TCP/IP links or dial-up links with the SMTP connector. As with the X.400 connector, you can schedule connectivity with the X.400 connector and separately schedule transmission of messages with large attachments.

 NOTE   Just to be sure we've got things straight, let's go over terminology. The routing group connector allows for scheduling connections, optionally transmitting messages with large attachments at different times than smaller messages, providing redundant links, and prioritizing multiple routing group connections based on the bandwidth available for each connection. The X.400 and SMTP connectors support only the first two options.

Plan Servers and Internal Connections to Them

There's quite a bit to do in planning your servers and user links. You must decide what kinds of hardware to use for each of your Exchange servers. Then you'll need to think through some policies relating to storage. After that, you must figure out how to back up the servers. Then you must make sure you've got adequate bandwidth on your local networks to keep Exchange happy; if you don't have it, you've got to decide how to get it. Finally, before you go on to the next step in the Exchange design process, you must think about remote users and how you'll connect them to Exchange.

Designing Your Exchange Servers

The intricacies of Exchange Server design and fine-tuning could occupy a whole book; you'll have to experiment here. Fortunately, Microsoft doesn't leave you out in the cold when it comes to this experimentation. The company provides a couple of applications for testing the capacity of hardware that is a candidate to run Exchange 2000 Server. These are called LoadSim and, at least at the time of this writing, Medusa.

LoadSim is an updated version of the LoadSim product that was used with Exchange Server 5.5. Medusa is a fancy new product that is still in development at the time of this writing. You can find the two products in the Exchange 2000 Server Resource Kit.

Because LoadSim is fairly well set, I'll focus on it here. LoadSim tests your server hardware (CPU, disk drives, RAM) and network capacity by simulating messaging loads on an Exchange 2000 Server.

To begin your experimentation, install Windows 2000 Server and Exchange 2000 Server, and then run LoadSim. Next, take out that set of user-demand numbers that you put together when you did your user needs assessment. Plug those numbers into LoadSim, and run it against a reasonable Exchange server machine—say, an 800MHz Pentium III or Xeon machine with 512MB of memory and at least two 9GB SCSI hard drives. Don't run LoadSim on your Exchange server. Instead, run it on a separate 600MHz or better Pentium-based Windows 2000 Pro workstation with at least 256MB of memory. And don't try to simulate more than 200 users on one LoadSim machine. If you don't follow these guidelines, LoadSim may not be capable of generating the loads that you've asked it to, and you could be led to believe that your Exchange server hardware is adequate, when it's not.

In selecting servers for Exchange, my rule is always to go for the biggest guns that you can afford, commensurate with expected user loads. After working a while now with Windows 2000 Server and Exchange 2000 Server, I've got my own ideas about server sizing. My monster machine of the week would be a dual Intel Pentium III or Xeon 800MHz or greater computer with 1GB of random access memory (RAM) and a hardware RAID 5 disk capacity of at least 30GB. Such a computer should be capable of handling upwards of 1,000 average Exchange 2000 Server users, network bandwidth willing. If you're going to get into chat, instant messaging, and conferencing services, you'll need more horsepower. I'd go for a second server to support these.

While I'm in recommendation mode, let me talk about other software that might run your Exchange 2000 server. If you can afford the hardware, it's best to run Exchange 2000 on a Windows 2000 server that is not also a domain controller. Unlike Exchange 5.5, which might benefit from running on an NT 4 domain controller, Exchange 2000 not only doesn't benefit from running on a domain controller, but it actually suffers as it competes with Active Directory and other CPU/disk-intensive software that runs on a Windows 2000 Server domain controller.

If you had to gulp a few times after reading my recommendations for a production Exchange 2000 server, don't worry. You can get by with less horsepower, especially if you need to support fewer users. In my experience, Windows 2000 Server alone requires more memory than NT Server 4, so don't cheap out on memory. Go for a minimum of 512MB, even in a server with a 500 or so MHz Pentium III.

If you do decide to go with less costly or less powerful hardware, I strongly suggest that you go with SCSI disk drives over Enhanced IDE drives. Enhanced IDE drives are nice, but for production Exchange Servers, I prefer SCSI drives. They're fast and tend to be more reliable than IDE drives over the long haul. For best performance, choose ultrawide SCSI drives.

Server Fault Tolerance

The more fault tolerance you can build into your Exchange server hardware, the better you and your users will sleep at night. Almost nothing is worse than losing even one user's e-mail messages. Here are a few steps that you can take to improve server fault tolerance.

Look for systems with error-correcting RAM memory. On the disk side, consider multiple SCSI controllers or RAID level 5 technologies. Many machines are now available with two or more redundant power supplies. In some cases, you can swap out failed RAID drives and power supplies without even bringing down your system. Also be sure to consider Microsoft's Windows 2000 Advanced and Datacenter Server editions, which let you set up clusters of Windows 2000/Exchange 2000 servers that mirror each other, with server A generally being capable of quickly and automatically replacing server B in case server B fails.

When you're comfortable with the basic design of your servers, you need to plan for uninterruptible power supplies (UPSs). I consider a UPS to be part of a server, not an add-on. UPSs are cheap, given the peace of mind that they can bring. In spite of Windows 2000 Server and Exchange 2000 Server's capability of recovering from most disastrous events, you don't want to tempt fate and risk damage to your organization's precious electronic messaging data. Get enough UPSs to serve the power needs of each server, and get a UPS that comes with software to gracefully shut down your servers if power stays off for an extended period. I'll talk more about UPSs in Chapter 7.

Setting Exchange Server Storage Policies

You'll need to start thinking now about how you'll manage user storage on each server. Storage management gives you more control over how much of what is stored on Exchange server disks, and it helps you remain within your server disk budget. You'll want to answer several disk management policy questions, including these:

- Do you want some or all of your users to store messages in personal folders on a workstation or non-Exchange networked disk drives, instead of in their Exchange server-based mailboxes?

- For those who will use their Exchange server mailboxes, do you want to limit the amount of storage that they can use?

- Do you want to impose limits on the storage used by public folders?

- If you have public folders containing messages that lose value with time (for example, messages from Internet lists or Usenet news feeds) do you want Exchange to automatically delete messages from these folders based on message age?

- Will you implement Exchange Server's capability to save deleted messages for a designated period of time? This is a neat capability because users can recover messages that they accidentally deleted. However, all those "deleted" messages can take up lots of disk space.

You can base your answers to most of these questions on the results of your user needs assessment, although you're bound to make adjustments as you pass through iterations of the design process. Also note that while it's tempting to force users to store messages in personal folders on local or non-Exchange networked disk drives to save on Exchange server disk, you then run the risk that key user messages won't get backed up. As the ever-present "they" say, "You pays your money and you takes your chances."

Backing Up Your Exchange Servers

When you know what your Exchange servers and networks will look like, you can begin thinking about backing up your servers. You need to use backup software that is especially designed for Exchange's client/server transaction-oriented architecture. Such software enables you to back up an Exchange server's information store without shutting down Exchange processes and, thus, closing off user access to the server. The software communicates with Exchange's information store service to ensure that the databases that it is responsible for are fully backed up. I'll talk more about the fine points of Exchange backup in Chapter 8, "Installing Exchange 2000 Server."

Windows 2000 Server's own backup program has add-ons to do a proper backup of Exchange servers. Other Windows 2000 Server backup vendors, such as Computer Associates' ArcServeIT (`http://www.cai.com/`) and Veritas Software's Backup Exec (`http://www.veritas.com/`), have released add-ons to their products that can properly back up Exchange 2000 Server. These products add better backup scheduling, easier-to-use logs, multiple server backup from a single instance of the backup program, quicker and easier restore of backed up data, and disaster recovery options.

You can back up an Exchange server either locally or over the network. When you back it up over the network, you can run the backup from another Windows 2000/Exchange server or from a Windows 2000-only server.

For Exchange servers with lots of disk space (5GB or more) and slow network links to potential backup servers (less than 100Mbps), I strongly suggest that you bypass the networked server backup option and do the backup locally on and from the

Exchange server itself. You'll have to spend some money on a backup device and software for the Exchange server, but you'll get it back in available bandwidth and faster backups. Available bandwidth means that other network-dependent tasks—and there are lots of those on a Window 2000/Exchange 2000 network—run faster. Faster backups mean shorter periods of that awful feeling you get when important data is not yet on tape.

Whether you back up over the network or locally, don't skimp on backup hardware. You're going to *add* hard disk storage to your Exchange server, not take it away. Go for high-capacity 4mm, 8mm, or DLT tape backup systems. Think about tape autoloaders, those neat gizmos that give one or more tape drives automatic access to anything from a few tapes to hundreds of them.

Don't forget those personal folders stored on user workstations. You have to decide who will be responsible for backing them up: Exchange staff, other MIS staff, or users themselves. The technology for centralized workstation backup is readily available. For example, agents for most third-party Windows 2000 Server backup products let you back up all or part of specific user workstations.

While you're at it, don't forget Windows 2000 server backup. If you have Windows 2000 servers that don't support Exchange, you'll need to back them up, too. You can back up a Windows 2000 server over the network, but if the servers have lots of disk space, consider the same local backup strategy for non-Exchange Windows 2000 servers that I suggested for Exchange servers.

Networking Your Exchange Users

When you've got your server design down, you'll need to think about how to connect users to your Exchange servers. It's usually a no-brainer for local connections, although you'll want to be sure that you've got enough bandwidth to move the stuff that Exchange makes available to your users. For example, a message I put together with a very simple embedded color screen capture is 855K. The graphic looks impressive, and it let me make a point that I never could have made without it. Still, I wouldn't want my recipients to get it over a 33.3Kbps or 56Kbps connection.

If you're concerned about LAN bandwidth, you can do a couple things. First, get rid of those slower networks. Dump 4Mbps Token Ring and Arcnet networks. (Are there still Arcnet networks?) You might also want to consider upgrading 10BaseT networks to 100BaseT. Second, segment your LANs to reduce the number of users on any segment. In this situation, you might even put multiple network adapters in your Exchange server, one for each segment or group of segments. And do take a look at faster networking technologies such as 100Mbps Ethernet, those really neat networking switches that can replace routers and significantly improve network backbone performance, and the latest switched Fast Ethernet hubs that bring switching to workstation connectivity. Yes, any of these options will cost your organization some bucks, but they're likely to be bucks well spent. Just as with user workstations, slow technologies don't get used, and the benefits of the applications that you're trying to run on top of them are lost.

Don't forget remote Exchange users. Many users need to keep in touch when they're away from the office, whether at home or on the road. Remote users can connect to a Windows 2000 server by way of its Remote Access Server. The RAS gives users the equivalent of a hard-wired connection, so for them it's more or less like being on the office LAN. The major difference is that they probably won't stay connected all the time—they'll connect to send and receive messages, and the rest of the time they'll work offline.

Remote users also can connect to their Exchange servers by way of direct TCP/IP links through an Internet Service Provider (ISP). And don't forget the Internet-based POP3, IMAP4, and Web browser-based client options that are supported by Exchange Server. With their lighterweight demands on workstation resources, they could be just what the doctor ordered for your remote users.

We'll talk more about how to implement remote Exchange links in Chapter 17, "Advanced Exchange Server Management." At this point, you need to think about how many users will likely need a RAS connection to each site at one time. If it's just one or two, you can set up a couple of modems on an Exchange or Windows 2000 server and let users dial in to those. If you expect lots of users, you might want to consider setting up a separate Windows 2000 server dedicated to dial-in connections. Remember that one Windows 2000 server with the right hardware can support up to 256 dial-in RAS connections.

If users will be connecting to their Exchange servers over the Internet, you'll need an Internet connection of adequate bandwidth to support them. Unless you have just a few users who need Internet access, think at least T1 bandwidth.

Plan Connections to Other Systems

As John Donne almost said, "No organization is an island." In fact, not only is no organization an island today, but no organization can *afford* to be an island. With the electronic messaging decade upon us, electronic messaging will increasingly become the primary means of communicating and doing business. Consider connections to systems outside your organization to be necessities, not niceties.

Connection Options

Exchange organizations can be connected directly to foreign X.400 systems, Internet mail systems, and legacy Microsoft Mail, Lotus cc:Mail and Notes, and GroupWise systems. Legacy system links can include not just message exchange, but synchronization of Exchange and legacy address directories as well. With optional gateways from Microsoft and third-party vendors, you can connect to such systems as IBM PROFS and fax devices.

Exchange connections to foreign X.400 systems use the X.400 connector. Such connections can be either continuous and permanent or dial-up, and they can use any of the X.400 connector networking options listed previously in Step 9 (plan routing group links). The SMTP connector can use a continuous and permanent or dial-up TCP/IP link to the Internet. Third-party gateways use a range of networking protocols; contact your gateway vendor for specifics. The Connector for Microsoft Mail can run on top of almost anything, including TCP/IP, IPX/SPX, NetBEUI, X.25, voice lines, and RAS. The Exchange Directory Synchronization Agent mentioned in Chapter 3 lets you keep Exchange and legacy Microsoft messaging systems in sync. It uses the same networking protocols as the Connector for Microsoft Mail.

In planning, don't underplay the importance of X.400 connections, especially if your company communicates with organizations outside the United States. The X.400 suite includes the Electronic Document Interchange (EDI) standard, which supports electronic commerce by providing secure communications when you use your messaging system to, say, purchase products and services. Yes, you can secure your Internet mail communications, but X.400 isn't dead yet.

You need only one Exchange connector to link an entire Exchange organization to a foreign messaging system. And as long as inter-routing group links are in place, a single foreign messaging system connector can send and receive messages for an entire organization.

Connect or Migrate?

Now is the time to decide whether it's better to migrate users from legacy systems to Exchange Server, or to wait and just link them to Exchange Server using various connectors, gateways, or even direct individual workstation connections in the case of Microsoft Mail. The number of users to be migrated, the kinds of messaging systems that they use, and the size of your own technical and training staff will play a big role in this decision.

If you do decide to migrate users, you should determine exactly which messaging systems you'll be migrating your users from: Microsoft Mail, Lotus cc:Mail, Lotus Notes, Novell GroupWise, IBM PROFS, Verimation Memo, DEC All-in-One, and so on. Next, you should figure out what kinds of tools, if any, exist that can help you migrate users from each messaging system to Exchange. For example, Exchange includes a nice migration application for Microsoft Mail users. When you know what kinds of migration tools are available, you must set a timetable for migration. Finally, you must determine whether, based on your timetable, you should link other messaging systems to Exchange before you've migrated all users in them to Exchange.

If you choose to migrate users to Exchange, be aware that you can create new user Windows 2000 accounts and Exchange 2000 mailboxes from text data files. If your legacy messaging system lets you output user information to a file, and if you've got someone around who can write a program to ensure that all the information Exchange needs is in the file in the right format and order, you should certainly consider using this time-saving migration option. I'll talk more about migration in Chapter 17.

Migrating from Exchange 5.5 to Exchange 2000

I must mention one other migration scenario. Technically, transitioning from Exchange 5.5 to Exchange 2000 is a migration. As with other migrations, there is planning to do, and Microsoft provides a set of useful tools to smooth your migration. That's especially nice because an Exchange 5.5 migration involves not just Exchange 2000, but Windows 2000 Server as well. We'll begin delving into this piece of the migration puzzle in the next chapter. Oh, for the days when we Exchange Server types were the ones forcing everyone else to migrate!

Validate and Optimize Your Design

Validation means ensuring that you've got a system that guarantees message delivery, integrity, and security. It also means making sure that the system you've designed is versatile enough to handle the range of documents, messaging formats, and applications that your organization needs. *Optimization* is a balancing act in which you try to build the fastest, most stable, and most reliable systems that you can while still meeting organizational requirements and keeping costs down.

Guaranteed Delivery

Guaranteed message delivery comes with reliable Windows 2000 and Exchange 2000 servers and reliable internal and external networks. To increase the likelihood of guaranteed delivery, go for as much server fault tolerance and networking redundancy as your organization can afford. Use high-quality server and networking hardware and software inside your organization; buy outside networking services from stable, experienced, and well-established providers. Monitor the health of your networks, and be prepared to fix problems quickly. During the validation phase, send messages of all kinds through all your connections, and then check to see if they arrive intact. When problems arise, use Exchange's own message-tracking tools to catch up with wayward messages, and take advantage of Exchange's network and system-monitoring tools to discover why a message didn't get through.

Reliability is only one side of guaranteed message delivery. You also need Exchange servers that are sufficiently fast and networks that have the bandwidth to move messages quickly enough to meet maximum delivery time parameters. If you've specified that all messages should be delivered to all internal users within five minutes, for example, now's the time to see if your Exchange system is capable of performing up to spec. If not, you must either increase your permissible maximum delivery times or, depending on the source of the problem, come up with speedier servers or higher-bandwidth networks.

Message Integrity

Message integrity means that messages arrive in the same form as they were transmitted. Problems with message integrity often can be traced to mismatched binary message-part encoding and decoding. For example, a binary attachment to a message bound for the Internet is UUencoded by the sender, while the receiver expects MIME encoding. As you'll see later, in Chapter 13, there are lots of ways to set encoding parameters in Exchange to help avoid problems like this.

Message Security

In Exchange 5 and greater, RSA encryption and public keys both work within a single Exchange organization and can be enabled to work across Exchange organizations. For messages destined for foreign electronic messaging systems, Exchange Server implements a set of encryption and authentication standards: NTLM encryption, TLS encryption, SASL clear-text authentication, and Secure MIME. (More on these comes in Chapter 17.)

You can try to validate message security on your own or with the help of a certified electronic data processing auditor. If security is important to your organization, I strongly recommend the latter.

System Versatility

Exchange's internal message formatting, along with formatting available in X.400 and Internet mail, means that you'll be able to send documents of almost any type, containing virtually anything from text to last night's Letterman show. But be sure to validate that everything you need is there and works.

On the applications side, you've got all the app development environments mentioned in Chapter 1, as well as applications such as Microsoft's Schedule+ and Outlook. Exchange Server is a very popular product, so plenty of Exchange-based applications enabled with electronic messaging applications are already available from third-party vendors; many more are in development. Keep your eyes open for the latest "killer" Exchange apps.

Optimization

When you've done everything to ensure guaranteed message delivery, message integrity, and security, as well as system versatility, it's time for *optimization*. You optimize your design by checking out alternatives that may help improve your Exchange system. The basic question is, can you do it better, faster, and easier? For example, you might want to consider implementing support for X.400 messaging, even though your organization has no current need for it, simply because competitors are moving toward it.

Optimization can also focus on reducing costs without compromising the quality of your system. For example, you might want to come up with lower-cost options for connecting Exchange routing groups or for realizing network redundancy.

Rolling Out the Plan

Rollout doesn't mean dropping a whole Exchange system on your organization at once. It means making Exchange available to specific systems people and users according to a carefully thought-out schedule. You should also go through a testing phase with specific users.

You might start your rollout in MIS—maybe just with yourself, if you're part of MIS. Next, you might move on to samples of users based on the groupings that you uncovered in your user-needs assessment. Then move steadily onward until all users are up and running in Exchange. The key is to get Exchange out to all users as fast as possible without crashing your organization. (Here I'm referring to your *real* organization, not your Exchange organization.)

Remember that rollout is an integral part of the Exchange design process. As you step through your rollout plans, be ready to change your design. If something doesn't work, change it now. Don't let things pile up to the point that change becomes virtually impossible.

Whether you're in a test or production rollout phase, be sure to keep users in the loop. Get them committed to Exchange. Let them know if and when they're going to see the new Exchange client or other clients supported by Exchange Server. Explain to them how they can use whatever client you plan to provide them both to do what they're already doing and to get other tasks done. This is where user training comes in.

Keep MIS staff involved and informed as well. An Exchange installation and implementation is a big deal for an MIS department. Over time, I'll bet that just about everyone in MIS will get involved with Exchange. MIS staff should understand and welcome Exchange, not see it as a threat to their jobs. Train MIS personnel as data processing colleagues rather than just end users. You don't have to tell everyone in MIS everything there is to know about Exchange—they can buy this book for that purpose (hint, hint). But be sure to talk to them about both server and client basics from a more technical perspective.

Summary

Designing a new Exchange system is neither easy nor fast. You must complete several steps and then track back to ensure that you've taken each step's impact on other steps into account. Moving through this iterative process while covering each of the steps in painstaking detail ensures that your Exchange system will function pretty much as expected from the get go and that costly redesign is kept to a minimum.

One of the most important steps in the design process is the allocation of responsibility for very specific stages of the design and implementation process. This should be the first step in the design process. It ensures that the right people with the right skills and knowledge are in place, and that they are clearly in charge of and must account for their particular piece of the design puzzle.

Needs assessments are another key to effective Exchange system design. You must perform assessments of user need, the geographic distribution of your organization and its computing and networking resources, and your data network. Needs assessments focus on not only what is required as new, but also on what of the old can be preserved.

Exchange 2000 Server is a network-dependent, network-intensive system. You need to establish a consistent set of conventions for naming your Exchange organization, administrative groups, servers, and recipients. You must choose a Windows 2000 networking model that fits well with your organization's geographical distribution and business structures. You must define the boundaries of Exchange administrative groups, the administrative units into which you break your Exchange organization. As with domain models, geographic distribution and business structures may be key to setting these boundaries. If required, you must define boundaries for Exchange routing groups and determine how your routing groups will communicate across wide area networks.

Next, you must design your Exchange servers, paying attention to performance, storage capacity, reliability, backup, and networking users to your servers. When you've designed your Exchange server environment, you must deal with connecting your servers to other messaging systems, both public and private. Here you must select from among available Exchange connectors and gateways. As your Exchange network becomes a reality, you must ensure, through exhaustive testing, that everything works as planned and up to whatever performance, reliability, and other standards you must adhere to.

Finally, you need to develop a plan for rolling out your Exchange system when everything is ready and has been tested. You shouldn't expect everything to be perfect on first rollout. However, if you've adhered to the design steps laid out in this chapter, your rollout experience should be a fairly pleasant one.

In the next chapter, I'll talk about upgrading from NT 4 Server to Windows 2000 Server, and from Exchange Server 5.5 to Exchange 2000 Server. Even if you don't need to do an upgrade, I encourage you to read the next chapter. Thinking through the upgrade process will help you better understand the inner workings of Windows 2000 Server and Exchange 2000 Server.

CHAPTER <u>6</u>

Upgrading to Windows 2000 Server and Exchange 2000 Server

FEATURING:

"**W**elcome to Hell!" That's the first title that I wanted to use for this chapter. As a thoroughly immersed Windows NT/ Exchange 5.5 "expert," the idea of upgrading to Windows 2000 Server *and* Exchange 2000 Server seemed nothing short of a nightmare. The more I read and experimented in my hardware lab, the more convinced I became that the nightmare would be long and very, very scary. I'm not fully over my fears yet, but I can tell you two things: First, it's really okay to be scared, and you should be, at least just a bit. Second, it's not as bad as you may think right now, the previous comments to the contrary notwithstanding.

I'm going to try to help you avoid some of the anxiety that I felt about upgrading. Even so, you might need help from other authors, especially on the NT upgrade side. On this subject, take a look at the books *Microsoft Windows 2000 Server Administrator's Companion*, by Charlie Russel and Sharon Crawford (Microsoft Press, 2000), and *Mastering Windows 2000 Server*, by Mark Minasi, et al (Sybex, 2000.) Also, be sure to read the Exchange 2000 Server docs on upgrades. They do a pretty good job of laying out your options for both NT Server and Exchange 2000 Server upgrades.

Much of what I talk about here depends on your knowledge of topics covered in the first five chapters. If you've skipped to here because you just couldn't wait to get into the knotty issues related to upgrading, you're soon going to be even more anxious than I was when I first confronted the subject. If you haven't already done so, go back and at least look carefully at Chapter 2, "2000: A Magic Number?"; Chapter 3, "Two Key Architectural Components of Windows 2000 Server"; Chapter 4, "Exchange 2000 Server Architecture," and Chapter 5, "Designing a New Exchange 2000 System."

Upgrading from Windows NT Server 4 to Windows 2000 Server

Upgrading an NT 4 server to a Windows 2000 server isn't all that difficult. The real issue is the networking context in which that server lives. If you've got only one NT 4 server in your network, it's a no-brainer. Upgrade the thing to Windows 2000! However, if your network includes several NT 4 servers performing a variety of functions, you've got to do some careful planning.

When upgrading from NT Server 4 to Windows 2000 Server, you need to do the following:

- Specify how you will translate your NT Server 4 domain structure into a Windows 2000 Server domain structure
- Select appropriate Windows 2000 Server versions
- Specify the strategy that you will use to upgrade your NT 4 servers

WARNING You'll notice that I don't mention NT 3.51 here. There's a very good reason for that. NT 3.51 doesn't do too well in a Windows 2000 environment. What should you do? Upgrade 3.51 servers to NT Server 4, or shut them down forever.

Specifying a Windows 2000 Server Domain Structure

Before you can decide on a Window 2000 domain model, you need to understand your existing domain structure well. Then you can focus on selecting a Windows 2000 domain structure. Let me start by refreshing your memory on NT Server 4 domains and trust relationships. After that, I'll describe the process of documenting your domain structure and its components.

NT Server 4 Domains

Microsoft NT Server 4 networks are built around *domains*. An NT Server 4 network can have one or many domains, each of which is a logically separate entity. A resource in a Microsoft network can belong to one and only one domain.

Generally, domain users log in to domains, not the individual machines in a domain. Domains can make life easier both for users and for system managers. Users don't have to remember more than one password to access any resource in the domain (unless it is protected by a special password). System managers can centrally create and administer user accounts for the domain.

Domains also make interserver communications easy. If servers live in the same domain, each has to log in to the domain only once to communicate with all other servers in the domain—unless, of course, a special password is required for specific communications.

Domains require *domain controllers,* which is where

- NT administrators:
  - Create and manage accounts for domain users
  - Set access rights for domain resources
- The NT Server 4 operating system:
  - Stores user account information for the domain
  - Stores resource access rights for the domain
  - Authenticates domain users
  - Enforces access rights for domain resources

Of all the resources in an NT Server 4 network domain, only NT 4 servers can be domain controllers; although every NT server needn't be a domain controller, every domain controller *must* be an NT server.

Every NT Server 4 domain requires one primary domain controller. Good practice dictates at least one backup domain controller per domain.

NT Server 4 Cross-Domain Trusts

When one NT Server 4 domain (called the *trusting* domain) trusts another (the *trusted* domain), it accepts the other domain's authentication of a user or server. The user or server doesn't have to log in to the trusting domain to access its resources; one login to a trusted domain is enough to access all available resources in a trusting domain, unless access to a resource is specifically limited by a special password.

Figure 6.1 shows how cross-domain trust relationships make it easier for users and servers to access resources across an NT Server 4 network. The users and servers in domain B (the trusted domain) can access resources in domain A (the trusting domain) without using additional passwords. Note that the figure's arrowhead points *to* the trusted domain and *away* from the trusting domain.

NT Server 4 trusts are not only good for users; they're just what the doctor ordered for busy system administrators as well. Trusts expand the reach of administrators in creating and maintaining user accounts. After setting up a trust relationship between domains, an administrator with appropriate permissions in the trusting domain can, in one fell swoop, create a user in one domain and give that user access to all other trusting domains.

FIGURE 6.1

NT Server 4 trust relationships open a network to users.

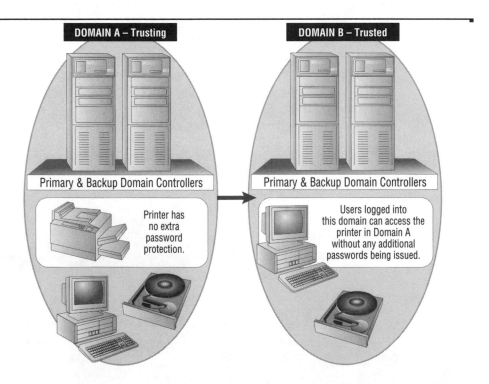

DOMAIN A – Trusting   DOMAIN B – Trusted

Primary & Backup Domain Controllers   Primary & Backup Domain Controllers

Printer has no extra password protection.

Users logged into this domain can access the printer in Domain A without any additional passwords being issued.

Trust relationships have all kinds of implications for the way users and systems managers operate day to day. For example, with the right kind of trust relationship and security rights, an administrator can manage an Exchange 5.5 organization not on a domain-by-domain basis, but from a multidomain or network-wide perspective.

Also, NT Server 4 trust relationships are key to cross-domain interaction between Exchange 5.5 servers. With the appropriate trust relationships and rights in place, Exchange 5.5 servers in different domains can interact to exchange messages and to cross-replicate directories and public folders.

 NOTE A good deal of NT Server 4 networking found its way into Windows 2000 Server networking. Domains remain and function pretty much as they did in NT Server 4, at least from a security perspective. Cross-domain trusts are still with us, although as I noted in Chapter 3, trusts are automatically created between parent and child domains.

Documenting Your Existing Domain Structure

With a little bit of background about NT Server 4 domains and trusts under your belt, you're now ready to tackle the first step in an upgrade from NT Server 4 to Windows 2000 Server, specifying exactly what type of NT Server 4 domain model you have. Microsoft defines four NT Server 4 domain models:

- Single-domain model
- Single-master domain model
- Multiple-master domain model
- Complete trust domain model

The following discussion of NT Server 4 domain models should help clarify these domain models.

The Single-Domain Model

Single-domain systems have no need for trust relationships because there is only one isolated domain. (See Figure 6.2 for a graphical depiction of a network with a single domain.) The NT Server 4 single-domain model is usually used when there is no organizational or technical need for a segmented network.

FIGURE 6.2

*A network based on
the single-domain
model*

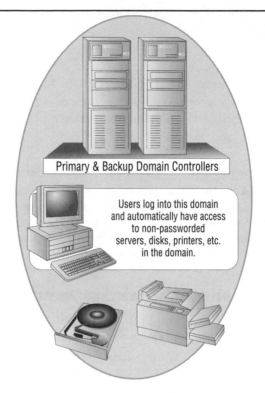

Primary & Backup Domain Controllers

Users log into this domain
and automatically have access
to non-passworded
servers, disks, printers, etc.
in the domain.

The Single-Master Domain Model

Single-master domain systems include one administrative domain and one or more resource domains where servers and workstations are located. The master domain handles all security tasks. It is a trusted domain, while all other domains are trusting. Users are in the master domain; resources such as servers, workstations, and printers are in the resource domain. (See Figure 6.3 for a diagram of a master-domain system.)

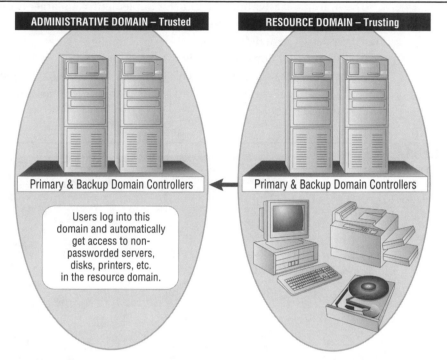

FIGURE 6.3

A network based on the master-domain model

ADMINISTRATIVE DOMAIN – Trusted

RESOURCE DOMAIN – Trusting

Primary & Backup Domain Controllers

Primary & Backup Domain Controllers

Users log into this domain and automatically get access to non-passworded servers, disks, printers, etc. in the resource domain.

The single-master domain model is deployed in organizations that need to segment resources (say, by department or geographically) and that have a centralized MIS department. Each department or geographical unit can have its own domain, while MIS administers from the master domain.

The Multiple-Master Domain Model

Multiple-master domain systems have two or more master domains and two or more resource domains. Each master domain is responsible for some portion of users based on a logical segmenting factor, such as the first letter of the user's last name, or the geographical breakdown of the company. Each resource domain trusts all the master domains. Figure 6.4 depicts the multiple-master domain model. Here the master domains trust each other and are trusted by both of the resource domains. This is not required, however; each master domain can be trusted by one or a set of resource domains. In the figure, for example, Administrative Domain #1 could be trusted only by Resource Domain #1, while Administrative Domain #2 could be trusted by both resource domains.

Often two-way trusts are implemented between the master domains. That way, system administrators with appropriate rights are able to create new users, and so on, in any master domain as needed.

The multiple-master domain model is implemented in larger organizations that need to segment both resources and MIS administration. Resource domains are often based on departmental divisions.

Multiple-master domains also allow MIS administration to divide the task of managing domains into smaller units. This tends to reduce the likelihood of error and lets large multinational organizations spread the management tasks across geographical and sociopolitical boundaries.

FIGURE 6.4

A network based on the multiple-master domain model

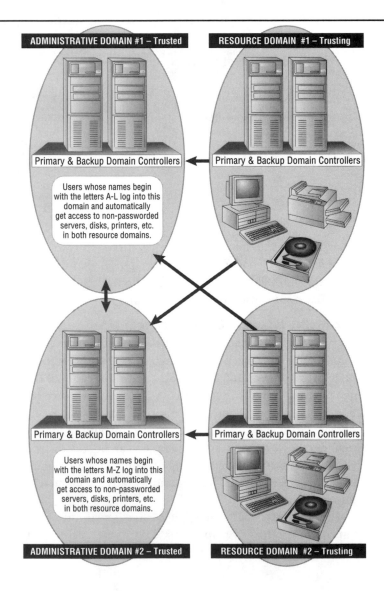

The Complete Trust Domain Model

Complete trust domain systems consist of several domains; each domain handles its own security administration. Because this model has no master domains, all domains must be both trusted and trusting. Figure 6.5 shows a system based on the complete trust domain model.

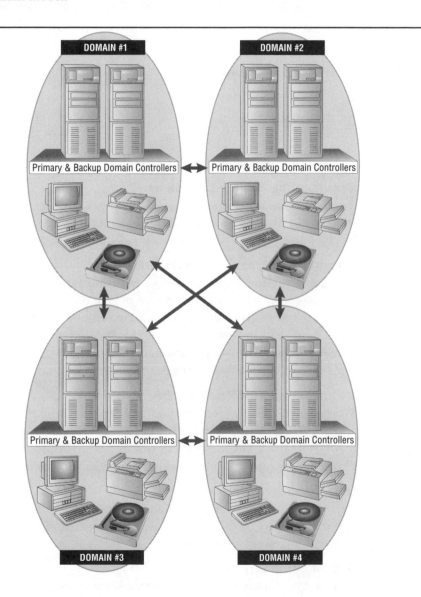

FIGURE 6.5

A network based on the complete trust domain model

Complete trust domain systems are implemented when an organization lacks central MIS administration and is segmented in some way, such as by department. Each department becomes a domain, and control of the domain is in the hands of the department.

Documenting Your NT Server 4 Domain Components

You must document the following components in your existing NT Server 4 domains:

- Domain controllers
- Types of domains
- Trust relationships
- Namespace(s)
- Servers

The following discussion explains what to document and why.

Documenting Domain Controllers

You must know where your domain controllers are, which are primary domain controllers (PDCs), and which are backup domain controllers (BDCs). As you upgrade an NT domain to Windows 2000, you'll usually first upgrade the PDC in the domain.

Documenting Types of Domain Structures

Whether you plan to retain or alter your existing domain structure during the upgrade process, you must know which of your domains are account domains and which are resource domains. If you want to retain your existing domain structure, you'll need to know what you're retaining. If you want to upgrade to a different domain structure, you'll need to know what you have so that you can match it to the types of domain structures available in Windows 2000 Server.

Documenting Trust Relationships

Trust relationships are preserved during an upgrade from NT to Windows 2000 networking. If only so that you know what you're dragging over to your new environment, you must know what's what with trust relationships. If you revise your domain structure during an upgrade, you must know how trust relationships may change.

Documenting Namespaces

Carefully document both your NT and DNS domain naming structures. You can't rename Windows 2000 domains after they're created, and you can't have duplicate names in a Windows 2000 network.

Documenting Servers

Knowing your NT servers is an important key to a successful Windows 2000 networking upgrade. Which servers are functioning as DHCP, WINS, or DNS servers? Which are application servers, such as Exchange servers, SQL servers, or Internet proxy servers? Don't forget other operating systems. Do you have NetWare or Unix servers? Do you have any NT 3.51 servers?

You'll need to be especially careful about your DNS servers. As I noted in Chapters 2 and 3, DNS is not an option in Windows 2000 Server. It is *the* way Windows 2000 computers resolve computer names to IP addresses. Windows 2000 Server supports WINS, but Microsoft wants you to get rid of it as soon as possible after an upgrade.

You'll also want to decide which computers will run DNS. If DNS ran on a separate server from your NT domain controllers, you'll probably want to take Microsoft's advice and run it on your Windows 2000 domain controllers. DNS is an integral part of the Windows 2000 Server operating system. You don't want to degrade the performance of your Windows 2000 domain controllers by requiring that they cross your networks to get DNS information.

Do you have Exchange 5.5 servers that are running on NT Server 4 domain controllers? If so, you might want to consider running Exchange 2000 Server on Windows 2000 servers that are not domain controllers, for performance reasons.

If you have NetWare servers, do you want to synchronize Novell's Novell Directory Services with Active Directory? How will your Windows 2000 and Unix servers interact with regard to DNS and file and printer sharing? NT 3.51 servers must be upgraded to NT Server 4.

 WARNING While you're at it, you should actually count the number of instances of each of the four components discussed in this section. It's one thing to say, "I have trust relationships or application servers or WINS servers." It's quite another thing to say, "I have 25 trust relationships, 6 DNS servers, or 6 Exchange 5.5 servers, or 200 Exchange 5.5 servers." Counting gives you a concrete indication of the work ahead of you, in terms of both planning and implementation. It helps you estimate the load that an upgrade will put on your staff or any consultants that you might bring in.

Window 2000 Mixed and Native Mode

Before moving on to Windows 2000 domain structures, let's talk about Windows 2000 Server domain modes. When you create a new Windows 2000 Server domain by installing Windows 2000 from scratch or by upgrading an NT Server 4 server, the domain is set to mixed mode.

In mixed mode, Windows 2000 domain controllers can communicate with NT 4 domain controllers in the same or other domains. Cross-domain trusts work like they do in NT 4 domain networks. Windows 2000 domain controllers emulate NT 4 domain controllers when interacting with NT 4 domain controllers. Additionally, NT 4 domain controller emulation allows for free replication of user and other information between Windows 2000 and NT 4 domain controllers.

You must leave a Windows 2000 domain in mixed mode until your last NT 4 server domain controller is gone. Then you'll want to switch it to native mode.

Once in native mode, Windows 2000 domains soar. They can support up to one million objects per domain, as opposed to 40,000 in mixed mode. They can also support multiple Active Directory masters, several new kinds of security groups, nested groups, full cross-domain administration, and Kerberos-only authentication. Additionally, as you may remember, in the previous section "NT Server 4 Cross-Domain Trusts," Windows 2000 Server automatically sets up trusts between domains in the same forest. This happens only after you switch a domain to native mode.

For now, just in case you stumble on the fatal mode-switching button, note that once you've made the switch, there's no going back except by starting all over again. Once a Windows 2000 domain is in native mode, NT 4 servers can't interact with Window 2000 servers. So, don't click that button until you're absolutely ready. For your edification, Figure 6.6 shows the button. At this point, you should think of Figure 6.6 like you think of the skull and crossbones on poison bottles. It's your warning about a bad place that you don't want to go.

FIGURE 6.6

Avoid the Change Mode button until all NT Server 4 domain controllers have been upgraded to Windows 2000 Server.

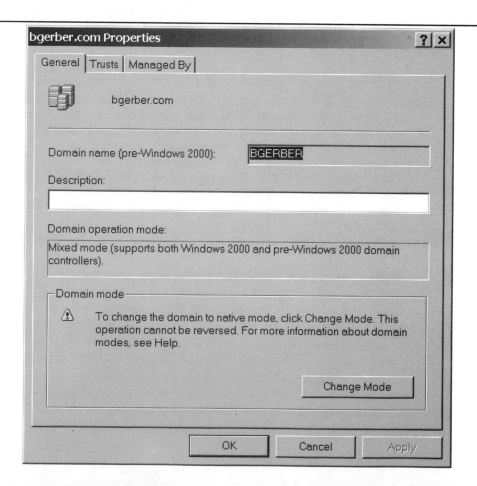

How Windows 2000 and NT 4 Domains Get and Stay in Sync

When you upgrade an NT 4 domain controller to a Windows 2000 domain controller, Active Directory is automatically populated with user and other information from the NT domain controller. While a Windows 2000 domain is in mixed mode, NT 4 and Windows 2000 domain controllers are capable of automatically cross-replicating user and other resource information.

When a domain is running in mixed mode, you should always make changes, such as adding a new user, on the Windows 2000/Active Directory side. Then you'll be assured that Active Directory gets everything it needs and replicates whatever information NT 4 domain controllers need.

Choosing a Windows 2000 Server Domain Structure

Let's look at upgrade scenarios as they might be implemented, given one or another NT server domain structure. If you need a refresher on Windows 2000 domain structuring, take a look at Chapter 3.

 NOTE As you're selecting a domain model, you should also be thinking about your Active Directory namespace. How will you name the domain or domains that you create? Will you use existing names or create new ones? How will you realize your plans in hardware? What type of hardware do you need in terms of horsepower, disk space, and RAM? See the sections in the last chapter that focus on these issues.

Upgrading the NT Single-Domain Model

A single-domain model can readily be upgraded to a Windows 2000 system with an Active Directory that has a single contiguous namespace. The single NT domain becomes the root domain in Active Directory. The neat thing is that, unlike with your NT domain, when the upgrade is complete, you can use Windows 2000 organizational units to organize user accounts and resources, and then hand off responsibility for administering suborganizational units to others. For more on organizational units, see the sidebar "Global Catalogs and Organizational Units," in Chapter 3.

Upgrading the Single-Master Domain Model

With a single-master-domain model, you upgrade the administrative domain to become the root domain in a single contiguous namespace Active Directory and add the resource domains as child domains. Take a look at Figure 3.2 in Chapter 3 for a graphic refresher on this approach.

If your organizational and networking structure allows, you can even consolidate the child domains into the root domain after you've fully upgraded the domain and switched to native mode. Then you can use organizational units to play the role that resource domains played in your NT server network. You can even reorganize your resources within your new organizational units. This is the real power of Windows 2000 Server.

Upgrading the Multiple-Master Domain Model

No matter how you may want your Windows 2000 domain structure to look in the end, a multiple-master domain network should first be upgraded to a noncontiguous Active Directory namespace. This means that each master domain becomes a root domain in Active Directory. See Figure 3.3 in Chapter 3 for an example of a noncontiguous namespace.

After upgrading your multiple-master domain and switching it to native mode, you should very seriously consider converting it to a single-domain structure. As I noted in Chapters 2 and 3, Microsoft has gone out of its way to make it easier for you to build large-scale, single-root domain (contiguous namespace) networks. For example, Windows 2000 Server sites let you effectively connect segments of your network linked by lower-bandwidth networking topologies, and Windows 2000 Server supports enough user accounts and other objects to keep most organizations happy well into the next millennium. You can use Windows 2000 Server organizational units to retain whatever organizational, security, or administrative separateness you need, while simplifying your entire network and making managing it much, much easier.

Upgrading the Complete Trust Domain Model

The complete trust domain model can be upgraded in a variety of ways, depending on your needs. You can take the same approach as with the multiple-master domain model, starting with a multiple-root domain, noncontiguous namespace. Then you can consolidate all into a single-root domain, contiguous namespace after you've completed the upgrade and switched to native mode.

You can also make one domain the root domain and the other domains child domains. This can be the end of your domain structuring, or you can then do as you might with a single-master domain model, consolidating the child domains into the root domain and possibly re-creating child domain functionality with organizational units.

If organizational, economic, or political need dictates, you can retain the multiple-master structure in Windows 2000 by locating each domain in a separate forest. (See Figure 3.4, in Chapter 3, for an example of a multiforest Widows 2000 network.) This is the most extreme approach, and it pretty much guarantees significantly greater administrative costs. However, if ya gotta do it, ya gotta do it.

Structural Domains

If you're upgrading a multiple-master or complete trust domain, you might want to consider using what Microsoft calls a *structural domain*. A structural domain has no users or other resources. It is the root directory within which you create child domains as you upgrade each of your NT domains. Using a structural domain lets you establish a single-root tree, contiguous namespace while making no particular NT 4 domain the root domain. It also helps simplify and make Active Directory replication more efficient. Structural domains are often simply named "." (*dot*, in Internet parlance).

Windows 2000 Sites and Organizational Units

When you've selected a Windows 2000 domain model, you're ready to think about two subcomponents of Windows 2000 domains: sites and organizational units.

Windows 2000 sites group together computers on the same LAN. Site boundaries can cross Windows 2000 domains, trees, and even forests. Sites are used by Active Directory in authentication and replication. Windows 2000 site connectors let you connect sites without concern for the lower-bandwidth network links between them.

Active Directory throttles down replication to sites, to account for lower bandwidth connections. During authentication, Active Directory directs each workstation to domain controllers that are in the same site as the workstation. All of this nicely supports lower-bandwidth intersite links.

Two types of intersite transports are available in Windows 2000:

- Point-to-point low-speed synchronous (continuous) links based on Microsoft's remote procedure call (RPC) protocol connections
- SMTP messaging-based links

If a Windows 2000 domain crosses two or more sites, you can use only a point-to-point synchronous RPC-based link to connect the sites. You can use SMTP messaging-based links for communications between two or more domains, each of which is located in a different site.

From a planning perspective, you must determine whether you need sites. If you do, you'll need to review existing bandwidth and plan for more, if necessary. We've already discussed organizational units (OUs) to some extent in Chapter 3 and in the preceding section, "Choosing a Windows 2000 Server Domain Structure." Here I just want to remind you that you need to consider how you'll use OUs to organize users and other resources, and to delegate management responsibilities.

Selecting from Among Windows 2000 Server Versions

Now that you know what your Windows 2000 Server domain structure will look like, it's time to decide on the Windows 2000 Server version or versions you'll need. The good news is that your choices are pretty limited and depend mostly on both the version of Exchange 2000 that you plan to install and the expected server loads.

As I noted in Chapter 2, three versions of Windows 2000 Server exist: Server Edition, Advanced Server Edition, and Datacenter Server Edition. These are listed in order of increasing capability to handle server loads and the number of servers that can be clustered. (See Chapter 2 for more on load-handling capacity and clustering.)

Chapter 2 also discussed the two versions of Exchange Server: Server Edition and Enterprise Edition. (Check out Chapter 2 for the differences between these two products.)

You may install Exchange 2000 Server Edition on any version of Windows 2000 Server. You'll probably install it on Windows 2000 Server Edition, although you could install it on Windows 2000 Advanced Server or Datacenter Server, if you need the added load-handling capacity or server-clustering capabilities offered by either of these products.

Checking the Readiness of Your NT Server 4 System

You need to be sure that the hardware and software on each NT 4 server that you plan to upgrade is Windows 2000 Server-ready. When you install Windows 2000 Server, you'll be told about any incompatibilities between Windows 2000 and your existing hardware and software. That's nice, but just a bit too late. The last thing that you want to do is to get everything ready for an upgrade and then find out that your server's hardware or software isn't up to snuff for Windows 2000 Server.

Fortunately, Microsoft has an answer. You can download the Windows 2000 Readiness Analyzer from Microsoft's Windows 2000 site; the URL at the time of this writing was `http://www.microsoft.com/windows2000/upgrade/compat/default.asp`.

You can run the analyzer at any time before you do an upgrade. The tool checks your hardware and software and gives you a list like the one in Figure 6.7.

FIGURE 6.7

List of incompatible hardware and software provided by Microsoft's Windows 2000 Readiness Analyzer

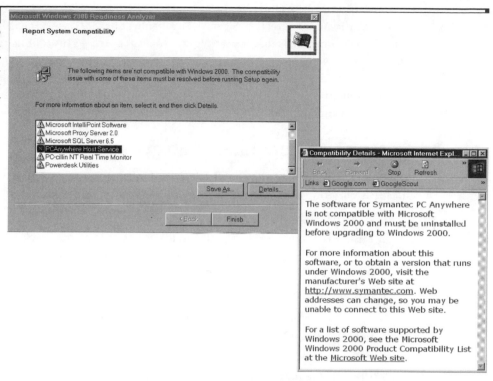

Problematic hardware and software are listed with icons indicating the severity of the incompatibility. The yellow triangle with an exclamation mark in it indicates products that are incompatible in their existing form; remove these at your discretion. The red circle with an X in it indicates hardware or software that absolutely must be removed before Windows 2000 is installed. As you can see in Figure 6.7, you can get detailed information on any particular item listed in the Readiness Analyzer.

In addition to checking hardware and software compatibility, you need to make sure that hardware on servers to be upgraded is adequate to handle the load that Windows 2000 Server will put on them. If necessary, consider adding memory or disk space, or even upgrading to new server hardware before the upgrade from NT 4 to Windows 2000. Also, if you have low-capacity NT 4/Exchange 5.5 servers that are also domain controllers, you might want to consider demoting them to non-domain-controller servers after you've upgraded to Windows 2000 Server. I'll talk more about domain controller promotion and demotion in the next chapter.

You can take a look at my hardware suggestions in the previous chapter. Also, check out the Active Directory Sizer tool available at `http://www.microsoft.com/windows2000/downloads/deployment/sizer/default.asp`. This tool helps you estimate the hardware capacity that you'll need to deploy Active Directory in your organization. The Sizer tool's estimates are based on your organization's profile, domain information, and site topology. You must gather the information and enter it manually into the Sizer, but I think you'll find the time and effort well spent.

A Windows 2000 Upgrade Strategy

When you've completed all the tasks described in the preceding section, you must specify a Windows 2000 upgrade strategy. Here are some suggestions:

1. Schedule upgrades at the least intrusive times.

2. Ensure that every existing NT 4 domain has at least one backup domain controller. That way, if an upgrade fails, you'll always be able to fall back to the backup domain controller to keep the domain running.

3. Synchronize all backup domain controllers with the primary domain controller.

4. Take one backup domain controller offline to act as a backup in case your upgrade fails, and to be sure that it isn't corrupted during the upgrade.

5. Back up each NT 4 server to tape just before upgrading it. Test each backup.

6. Upgrade the primary domain controller in any NT domain first.

7. Upgrade backup domain controllers as soon as possible.

8. For upgrades of multiple-master or complete trust domains, create the new root domain before upgrading. Do this on a new computer, and add a Windows 2000 domain controller or two. Then upgrade the NT 4 primary domain controller to act as a Windows 2000 domain controller for a new child domain.

9. Upgrade other servers and workstations as time permits, but as quickly as possible. Existing workstations and non-domain-controller servers needn't be updated immediately. Only after you've installed Windows 2000 will servers and workstations be capable of taking full advantage of Active Directory services.

PART

I

Understanding
and Planning

Active Directory Migration Tool

Microsoft has designed a pretty neat tool, called *Active Directory Migration Tool* (ADMT), to help you move smoothly from NT 4 to Windows 2000. You can use ADMT to migrate users, groups, computers, and Exchange information from NT 4 server environments to Active Directory. You can also use ADMT to ensure that correct file permissions are set on your new Windows 2000 systems. In addition, you can use ADMT to issue reports that help you uncover potential problems in the migration and see how well your migration is going. You can even roll back a piece of your migration, if you discover problems.

If that's not enough to whet your appetite, ADMT features a nice wizard that makes migration process even easier.

ADMT is a Microsoft Management Console snap-in, but it doesn't come with Windows 2000 Server. You'll have to download it. As of this writing, ADMT is available at `http://www.microsoft.com/windows2000/downloads/deployment/admt/default.asp`. If you can't find it there, do a search on the Microsoft Web site for "ADMT," "Active Directory Migration Tool," or "Active Directory Migration Wizard."

We'll spend more time with ADMT in the next section, "Upgrading from Exchange Server 5.5 to Exchange 2000 Server."

At this point, you're almost ready to undertake an upgrade to Windows 2000 Server. However, you'll first need to consider exactly how your Windows 2000 Server upgrade relates to upgrades that you will do from Exchange 5.5 to Exchange 2000. So, don't do anything yet. Read the rest of this chapter first. In the next section, on upgrading Exchange 5.5 to Exchange 2000, I'll talk even more about the Windows 2000 upgrade process and give more detail on Windows 2000 upgrade strategies.

In the next chapter, we'll actually do a Windows 2000 installation. We won't actually do any upgrades, because of the numerous flavors of existing NT Server 4 systems. However, in Chapter 7, "Installing Windows 2000 Server," I will show you the interfaces where you choose to build a particular kind of Windows 2000 domain structure.

Upgrading from Exchange Server 5.5 to Exchange 2000 Server

Upgrading to Exchange 2000 Server is fairly straightforward after you've done your Windows 2000 Server upgrade. Exchange 2000 adds a fair amount of functionality to a Windows 2000 server, but the most important additions (at least, from an upgrade perspective) are those made to Active Directory. Your major tasks when upgrading from Exchange 5.5 revolve around ensuring that Active Directory is correctly populated with Exchange 5.5 directory objects.

Preparing Active Directory for Exchange 2000 Server

Unlike Exchange 5.5, Exchange 2000 Server does not have a directory of its own. As I noted in Chapters 2 and 3, Microsoft "stole" the Exchange 5.5 directory, improved it, and turned it into Windows 2000 Server's Active Directory.

Exchange 2000 Server uses Active Directory pretty much as Exchange 5.5 used its own directory service. When Exchange 2000 Server is installed on a Windows 2000 server, a number of Exchange-specific objects and attributes are added to the Active Directory schema. If you're doing a new installation of both Windows and Exchange 2000, you really don't need to worry about anything beyond ensuring that the new schema objects get installed.

However, if you're doing an upgrade, you must make sure that your Exchange 5.5 directory objects and attributes get moved into the new Active Directory Exchange-specific objects and attributes. In Microsoft's terminology, you must *populate Active Directory*. Active Directory is populated when both NT 4's user account information and Exchange 5.5's recipient-related directory information reside in Active Directory.

As you'll see in a bit, the Exchange upgrade process is pretty simple when you can upgrade your entire network to Windows 2000 Server and Exchange 2000 Server in a very short time—like in one night. Upgrades become more complex when your network is so large that upgrading will take several days, weeks, or even months. At that point, you must plan very carefully to ensure that NT 4 and Windows 2000 servers as well as Exchange 5.5 and 2000 servers can coexist. That means, more than anything else, that key Windows 2000 domains remain in mixed mode and that you use the Windows 2000 tools designed to keep Exchange 5.5/2000 information in sync.

Using Active Directory Connector

We really can't go any further until I talk about one of the primary tools for synchronizing Exchange 5.5 and 2000 information, the Active Directory Connector (ADC). Before you can install Exchange 2000, you must install and run the ADC that comes with Exchange 2000. ADC lets you replicate Exchange-relevant recipient and other configuration information between Exchange 5.5 and 2000 servers. As you'll soon see, this information can be used in the process of populating both the Windows 2000 and Exchange 2000 sides of Active Directory.

You must manually install the ADC. After the ADC is installed, you should make changes on the Exchange 2000 side and let those changes replicate to the Exchange

5.5 side. This ensures that Active Directory receives all the rich Exchange 2000 information it needs and that Exchange 5.5 servers get what they need. As you'll remember, this is the same procedure that I advised you to follow when making changes in Windows 2000/NT 4 mixed-mode networks.

ADC runs on Windows 2000 servers. It can run on a Windows 2000 server even before Exchange 2000 has been installed. You can run ADC just to do a one-time move of Exchange 5.5 directory information to Active Directory, and you can also use ADC to keep Exchange 5.5 directory information in sync with Exchange 2000 (Active Directory) on an ongoing basis. ADC works whether a domain is running in mixed or native mode.

The good news with ADC is that, as an Exchange 5.5 administrator, you should have little trouble understanding, installing, or running it. ADC is very similar to Exchange 5.5's directory synchronization connector for Microsoft Mail-type systems. The main difference is that you will need to set up what are called *connection agreements*. Connection agreements support synchronization of user and configuration information between Exchange Server 5.5's directory service and Active Directory.

One of the most important lessons that you should carry away from this section is that Exchange 2000 Server installation isn't always intuitive and that it's a bit more complex than you might be used to. You don't upgrade from Exchange 5.5 to Exchange 2000 simply by running the installation program from the Exchange 2000 CD-ROM disk. You have to get your Exchange 5.5 directory and your Windows 2000 Active Directory in sync before you install Exchange 2000 Server. That's where the ADC comes in.

NOTE A stripped-down version of Active Directory Connector comes with Windows 2000 Server. You'll find it on the Windows 2000 Server installation CD in \valueadd\msft\mgmt\adc. Like the version that comes with Exchange 2000 Server, this version allows you to synchronize mailbox information from the Exchange 5.5 directory to Active Directory. It doesn't support synchronization of configuration information, however. The Windows 2000 version of ADC was designed to let you populate Active Directory in a new Windows 2000 domain with user information from Exchange 5.5's directory. This information is used to create your Windows 2000 users. You can use the Windows 2000 ADC before purchasing Exchange 2000 Server. If you already own Exchange 2000 Server, you can just use the version of ADC that comes with that product. It can do all that the Windows 2000 version can do and synchronize configuration information between Exchange 5.5 and 2000. If some of this is a bit unclear right now, not to worry. Soon it'll all make perfect sense.

A Simple Upgrade for Starters

Even if your upgrade scenario doesn't involve the sort of simple upgrade described here, I very strongly encourage you to read this section because it will give you a sense of the issues that you need to deal with, no matter what your upgrade scenario. Upgrades from Exchange 5.5 to 2000 aren't always as intuitive as you might expect. A little grounding in the upgrade process based on a simple example will prepare you for both the intuitive and the nonintuitive aspects of an upgrade.

Let's look at the simplest possible upgrade first. Imagine that you've got an NT 4 server functioning as the primary domain controller in a small network in which the only other NT server is a backup domain controller. Exchange 5.5 is installed on the primary domain controller. How do you upgrade the primary domain controller to Windows 2000 Server and Exchange 2000 Server? You'll need to complete four tasks:

1. Change the LDAP port on your NT 4/Exchange 5.5 server

2. Upgrade your NT 4 server to Windows 2000 Server

3. Run the version of Active Directory Connector that comes with Exchange 2000 Server

4. Upgrade your Exchange 5.5 server to Exchange 2000 Server

Changing the LDAP Port Number on Your NT 4/Exchange 5.5 Server

First you must change the existing Exchange 5.5 Lightweight Directory Access Protocol (LDAP) port on your server to something other than the default of 389. As I noted in Chapter 3, unlike NT 4, Windows 2000 uses LDAP as a key Active Directory communication protocol. When you upgrade the server to Windows 2000 Server, Windows 2000 takes port 389 as its own port. After the upgrade to Windows 2000 Server and until the upgrade to Exchange 2000 is completed, Exchange 5.5 needs an LDAP port of its own.

It took me a while to figure out where to change the Exchange 5.5 LDAP port number. So, to save you the pain I went through, here's how to do it. First, you need to find an available port: Run `netstat -an | more` at a command prompt, pressing any key every time you see More at the bottom of the screen. You'll see a list of IP addresses, followed by a colon and a number. The number after the colon is a port number. Any port in the list is in use. Any port number not in the list is available. Your best bet is a port in the range of 1001 to 1009. These ports have not been given a specific assignment by the authority that assigns ports.

Now you're ready to change the port:

1. In the left pane of the Exchange 5.5 Administrator program, expand a site. Then expand the site's Configuration container and click the Protocols container.

2. In the Protocols container, double-click LDAP (Directory) Site Defaults to open the LDAP configuration dialog box.

3. On the General tab of the dialog box, change the LDAP port to 1005 or another available port.

4. When you've finished changing the LDAP port number, click OK and then restart the server.

Upgrading your NT Server 4 to Windows 2000 Server

Next, you do the NT Server 4 to Windows 2000 Server upgrade. That's pretty straightforward. The upgrade moves NT 4 user and other information to Active Directory. However, an upgrade to Windows 2000 Server doesn't move Exchange 5.5 directory service user and other mail-specific information (objects and their attributes) to Active Directory.

Furthermore, even an upgrade to Exchange 2000 Server doesn't move Exchange 5.5 directory service information to Active Directory. This is the nonintuitive part of the upgrade from Exchange 5.5 to Exchange 2000 that I mentioned in the section "Using Active Directory Connector," earlier in this chapter. *Before* you upgrade to Exchange 2000, you must *manually intervene* to move directory service information to Active Directory. No matter how you upgrade to Exchange 2000, you must perform this manual task.

The previous paragraph is extremely important. If you don't understand the point of the paragraph, I guarantee that you will experience nothing but misery trying to do an Exchange upgrade and understanding the rest of this chapter.

"So," you may be asking, "you've told me elsewhere that Exchange 2000 modifies Active Directory's schema to allow for the new objects and attributes that Exchange 2000 requires. How do I manually move Exchange 5.5 directory service information to Active Directory *before* installing Exchange 2000? There's no place in Active Directory for the information to go."

As you might have guessed, there is an answer. When you install the Active Directory Connector, the Active Directory schema is extended to allow for most of the Exchange-specific object/attribute information required by Exchange 2000 Server. The schema extension also covers all the information that the ADC will move between the Exchange 5.5 directory and Active Directory. When you install Exchange 2000 itself, the schema is further extended to include additional Exchange-specific object/attribute information.

Upgrading Your Exchange 5.5 Server to Exchange 2000 Server

When ADC has completed its synchronization tasks, you're ready to upgrade to Exchange 2000 Server. Well, maybe almost ready.

First, be sure that you've installed at least Service Pack 3 on your Exchange 5.5 server. You can't upgrade 5.5 to 2000 with anything less than SP3 installed.

Second, if you don't have full security privileges for the Windows 2000 Active Directory and domain where Exchange 2000 Server will be installed during the upgrade, you'll need a little help from your friends before you can do the upgrade. You'll need to ask whoever is responsible for Active Directory or domain maintenance to run the Exchange 2000 Server setup program with two special switches at a command prompt. Let's take a quick look at these two special switches: *ForestPrep* and *DomainPrep*.

When the Exchange setup program is executed with the ForestPrep switch, it adds the Exchange 2000 Server-relevant nonuser/recipient objects that weren't added to the Active Directory schema when you installed the Active Directory Connector that comes with Exchange 2000. When setup is executed with the DomainPrep switch, it identifies a recipient update server for the domain and adds permissions within the domain required by Exchange 2000. Each of these programs need to be run only once in a given forest or domain, respectively.

ForestPrep and DomainPrep are part of the Exchange 2000 Server installation process. If you have rights to alter the Active Directory schema and have administrator privileges in the domain where you're installing Exchange 2000 Server, you don't need to run setup with the ForestPrep and DomainPrep switches separately. They run as part of your Exchange 2000 Server installation. If neither ForestPrep nor Domain-Prep has been run before you attempt to install Exchange 2000, and if you don't have the required permissions for Active Directory or in the domain, Exchange 2000 will not install.

For more on the two Exchange 2000 setup program switches, their location on the Exchange 2000 Server CD-ROM, and the process of running setup with the switches, see Chapter 8, "Installing Exchange 2000 Server."

 NOTE The capability to run the Exchange 2000 Server setup program with the Forest-Prep and DomainPrep switches allows organizations to distribute responsibility for managing a Windows 2000/Exchange 2000 environment among different IS staff groups. The group that manages Active Directory runs ForestPrep. The group that manages a particular domain runs DomainPrep. The Exchange group installs Exchange 2000 Server, without needing security access to run either ForestPrep or DomainPrep.

Okay, so now you're finally ready to upgrade the simple system that I've been discussing to Exchange 2000 Server. If the system represents your world, consider yourself lucky, and do the upgrade. If your NT 4/Exchange 5.5 system is more complex, read on and discover the joys of Active Directory population strategies.

Strategies for Populating Active Directory

Although you might have to approach things a little differently, any Exchange upgrade is going to be pretty much like the simple upgrade discussed previously. Populating Active Directory with NT and Exchange 5.5 information is the hairiest part of any Windows 2000/Exchange 2000 upgrade. Microsoft has identified five strategies that you might use to populate Active Directory. These strategies are based mostly on assumptions about the size and breadth of your Windows network, on the NT domain structure that you're coming from, and on the Windows 2000 domain structure that you're planning to implement.

For all the fire and brimstone that may be thrown from the volcano, Microsoft's five Active Directory population strategies are designed to accomplish nothing more than what was done in the second and third steps of the preceding section's simple upgrade procedure: to replicate NT 4 information and Exchange 5.5's directory information to Active Directory.

Remember that none of these strategies includes installing or upgrading to Exchange 2000 Server. That comes right after you've completed all of the steps in any of the five strategies. Let's look at Microsoft's five strategies in a little detail.

Active Directory Population Strategy #1

The first two Active Directory population strategies are accomplished using a single Windows 2000 Server domain. In the first strategy, you create a Windows 2000 Server domain by upgrading an NT domain controller to a Windows 2000 Server domain controller. In the second strategy, you create a Windows 2000 Server domain by installing Windows 2000 Server from scratch. Here's the first strategy (see Figure 6.8):

1. Upgrade an NT 4 domain controller to Windows 2000 Server.

2. Synchronize Exchange 5.5 with the new Windows 2000 Active Directory using Active Directory Connector.

This is a pretty simple strategy. You upgrade an NT 4 server to Windows 2000 Server. Then you set up Active Directory Connection agreements to bring over Exchange-specific information from one or more Exchange 5.5 servers. When the information you need has been pulled over, you're ready to upgrade your Exchange 5.5 servers.

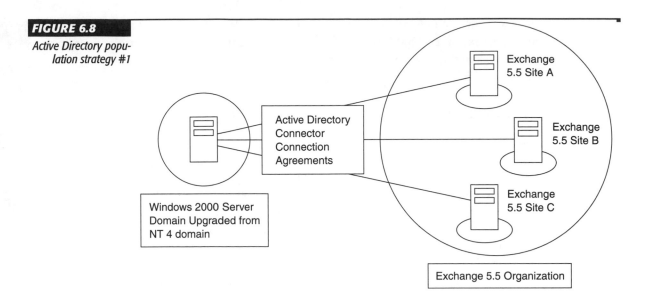

FIGURE 6.8

*Active Directory popu-
lation strategy #1*

Active Directory Population Strategy #2

In this strategy, you create a Windows 2000 domain without having to upgrade any NT servers. Active Directory population is accomplished manually after your new Windows 2000 Server is installed:

1. Install Windows 2000 Server from scratch, thus creating a new Windows 2000 Server domain.

2. Use the Active Directory Migration Tool to clone Windows 2000 accounts into Active Directory on the new Windows 2000 server.

3. Synchronize Exchange 5.5 with the new Windows 2000 Active Directory using the Active Directory Connector.

Figure 6.9 shows the second Active Directory population strategy in graphic form. The numbers in Figure 6.9 correspond to the numbers in this list. This numbering scheme is used in the rest of the figures showing Active Directory population strategies.

You'll remember Active Directory Migration Tool (ADMT) from the sidebar "Active Directory Migration Tool," earlier in this chapter. This tool allows you to pull NT Server information from one or more NT servers and then bring it into Active Directory.

After you've completed the three steps in this strategy, you can upgrade Exchange 5.5 or install Exchange 2000 immediately. You can also upgrade your NT servers and the domains that they occupy when you're ready.

FIGURE 6.9

Active Directory popu-lation strategy #2

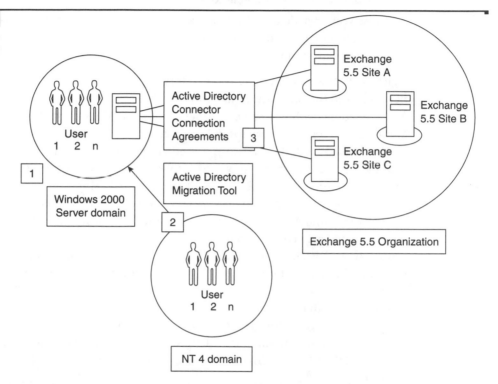

Active Directory Population Strategy #3

The first two Active Directory population strategies used a single Windows 2000 domain. The next two strategies use two domains. A new domain is created from scratch to hold either Exchange 5.5 or NT 4 information. A second domain in the same forest is created either from scratch or as a result of an NT 4 upgrade. This domain holds whatever information, Exchange 5.5 or NT 4, isn't in the first domain. Because the two domains are in the same forest, they're in the same Active Directory. You then merge the Exchange 5.5 and NT 4 information for each user in the Active Directory to create a fully functioning user. Here's the third Active Directory popula-tion strategy:

1. Install Windows 2000 Server from scratch, thereby creating a new Windows 2000 Server domain.

2. Synchronize Exchange 5.5 with Active Directory on the new Windows 2000 server using Active Directory Connector, thereby creating disabled user objects that contain Exchange information.

3. Upgrade each NT 4 user account domain as time allows.

4. As you upgrade an NT domain and its users, use the Active Directory Account Cleanup Wizard to merge the Active Directory Connector-created accounts with upgraded accounts.

Figure 6.10 shows the third Active Directory population strategy. This strategy adds a new player to the game, the Active Directory Cleanup Wizard (ADCUW). The ADCUW comes with Exchange 2000 Server. You'll find it on the Windows 2000 Start Menu under Programs ➤ Microsoft Exchange.

The ADCUW is designed to bring together Exchange 5.5 and NT 4 information about a user that has found its way to Active Directory. Here's how it accomplishes this task: All information about an NT 4 user is stored using a unique security identifier (SID). Each user's SID is an index that represents the user. When information is synchronized into Active Directory, wherever it comes from, the NT 4 SID is preserved. So, when Exchange 5.5 information for a user comes into Active Directory by way of Active Directory Connector, the user's NT 4 SID is stored along with the Exchange 5.5 information. When NT 4 information for the same user comes into Active Directory by way of an upgrade or Active Directory Migration Tool, the user's SID is stored with the information.

The ADCUW goes through Active Directory, matching NT 4 information with Exchange 5.5 information. It uses each user's SID to make the match. When a match is made, ADCUW firmly links NT 4 and Exchange 5.5 information for a user in Active Directory.

So, in this strategy, you first use Active Directory Connector to bring Exchange 5.5 information into Active Directory on a newly installed Windows 2000 Server. Then, after you upgrade each NT domain to a Windows 2000 Server domain, which brings NT 4 information into Active Directory, you use ADCUW to merge the two kinds of information in Active Directory.

Until you upgrade an NT 4 domain, the Exchange 5.5 information lies in a dormant or disabled object. With the upgrade, an enabled user object is created for each user in the upgraded NT 4 domain. ADCUW merges the disabled and enabled objects, creating fully functional Active Directory users.

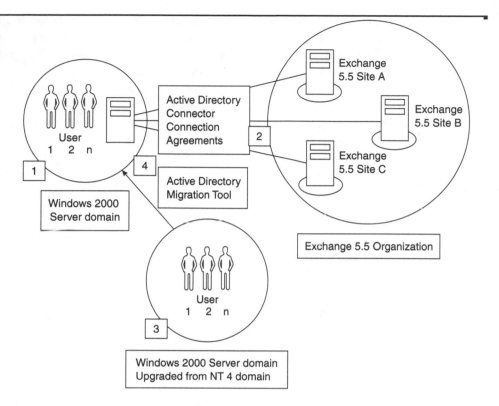

FIGURE 6.10

Active Directory population strategy #3

Active Directory Population Strategy #4

This strategy is similar to the third strategy, but you don't create the second domain by upgrading an NT 4 domain controller. Instead you use Active Directory Migration Tool to clone accounts from the NT 4 domain into a transition domain:

1. Install Windows 2000 Server from scratch, thereby creating a new Windows 2000 Server domain.

2. Synchronize Exchange 5.5 with Active Directory on the new Windows 2000 server using Active Directory Connector, thereby creating disabled user objects that contain Exchange information.

3. Create a transition Windows 2000 Server domain, and use the Active Directory Migration Tool to clone Windows NT user accounts into Active Directory in the transition domain.

4. Use the Active Directory Account Cleanup Wizard to merge the Active Directory Connector-created accounts with cloned accounts.

See Figure 6.11 for a graphic view of the fourth directory population strategy. Here's how it works: In this strategy, you create two domains in the same forest by installing Windows 2000 Server from scratch on two different computers. Then you use the Active Directory Connector to create disabled Exchange 5.5 user information in the first domain. You also use the Active Directory Migration Tool to clone NT 4 users into the second (transition) domain. Because the two domains are in the same forest (Active Directory), you can then run the Active Directory Account Cleanup Wizard to merge Exchange 5.5 and NT 4 information.

FIGURE 6.11

Active Directory population strategy #4

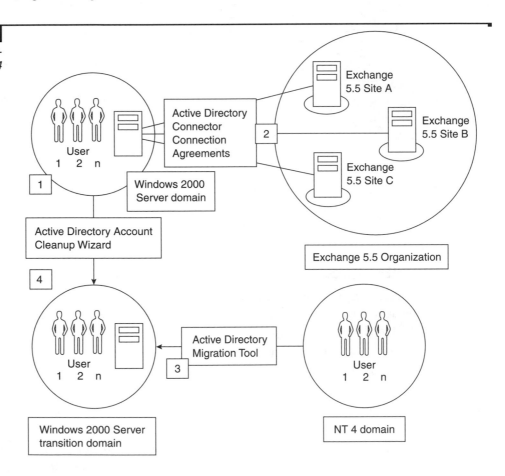

PART

I

Understanding
and Planning

Active Directory Population Strategy #5

This is the last strategy for populating Active Directory. Like the first two strategies, this one uses a single Windows 2000 Server domain:

1. Install Windows 2000 Server from scratch, thereby creating a new Windows 2000 Server domain.

2. Synchronize Exchange 5.5 with Active Directory on the new Windows 2000 server using Active Directory Connector, thereby creating disabled user objects that contain Exchange information.

3. Enable the user objects created from Exchange 5.5 information in Active Directory by the Active Directory Connector.

4. Use the Active Directory Migration Tool to match user objects in the new Windows 2000 domain's Active Directory to existing NT 4 accounts.

Figure 6.12 shows the fifth Active Directory population strategy. In this strategy, you enable the user objects created from your Exchange 5.5 environment by the Active Directory Connector. Because user objects have been enabled, NT 4 information is merged with Exchange 5.5 information in Active Directory through the use of the Active Directory Migration Tool.

You enable a disabled user object through the Active Directory Users and Computers snap-in for the Microsoft Management Console. Find the user in the Users subcontainer; right-click the user, and select Enable Account. That's it. (You can also enable user objects by updating the Active Directory schema, but that is something you don't want to get into unless you really know what you're doing.)

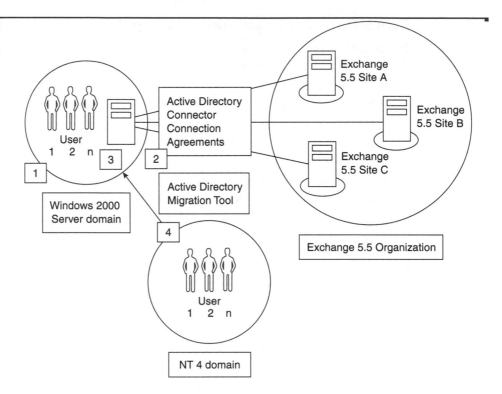

Do You Need a Group Management Domain?

Before we finish with Active Directory population strategies, we should talk about one other issue. Exchange 5.5 distribution lists can be used to send messages to a group of recipients. They can also be used to control access to Exchange resources such as public folders. If you use distribution lists for this latter function, you might have a bit of a problem in Exchange 2000 Server.

With Exchange 2000 Server, you can control access to Exchange resources only by using Windows 2000 universal security groups. When you run the Active Directory Connector with a connection agreement between an Exchange 5.5 server and a Windows 2000 domain in native mode, Exchange 5.5 distribution lists serving an access control function in Exchange 5.5 become universal security groups in Windows 2000. As such, you can use these groups for Exchange 2000 Server access control.

Unfortunately, universal security groups are available only when a Windows 2000 domain is running in native mode. So, if you're all switched to native mode, all is well. If you're not, you'll have to run what Microsoft calls a *group management domain*.

A group management domain is a Windows 2000 Server domain running in native mode.

Remember that you need a group management domain only if you want to continue using distribution list-like management of access to Exchange resources. You could also use Windows 2000 local or global domain groups. Note, however, that using local or global groups for this function requires more time and effort, and may require more involvement by Windows 2000 networking managers outside your group of Exchange managers.

If you opt for a group management domain, you'll need to set up a Windows 2000 server domain and switch it to native mode. Before you upgrade any Exchange 5.5 servers, you'll also need to set up one or more Active Directory Connector connection agreements between your new Windows 2000 group management domain and NT 4 domains containing the Exchange 5.5 servers.

If you decide to use the fourth Active Directory population strategy and you can switch the transition server domain to native mode, you're in luck. You can use the transition domain as your group management domain.

Exchange Server 5.5 Upgrade Strategies

Now that I've discussed Active Directory population in detail, you should be ready to think seriously about upgrading from Exchange 5.5 to Exchange 2000, and you're also ready to look at Exchange 5.5 upgrade strategies. Microsoft has identified three basic upgrade strategies: an in-place upgrade, a move-mailbox upgrade, and a leapfrog upgrade.

All these strategies assume that you've taken into account the need to properly populate Active Directory with NT 4 and Exchange 5.5 information. Let's look a bit at each upgrade strategy.

An In-place Upgrade

If your existing Exchange 5.5 hardware is powerful enough to support Windows 2000 Server and Exchange 2000 Server, you can do an in-place upgrade. We've talked a lot about this sort of upgrade, so I won't spend a lot of time on it. Basically, you take your Exchange 5.5 server offline and upgrade it first to Windows 2000 Server, populate Active Directory, and then upgrade Exchange 5.5 to Exchange 2000. You can employ this strategy whether you have one or many Exchange 5.5 servers.

When you do an in-place upgrade, you don't have the option of installing additional components such as the Exchange 2000 chat or conferencing services. However, after you've completed your in-place upgrade, you can go back and install additional components to your heart's content.

A Move-Mailbox Upgrade

If you're concerned about the capacity of your existing Exchange 5.5 servers or want to minimize the chances of an upgrade failure, try a move-mailbox upgrade. First, you create a new Windows 2000 Server, populate Active Directory, and ensure that the Exchange version of Active Directory Connector is up and running. Then you install Exchange 2000 Server in the same Exchange 5.5 site as the Exchange 5.5 server whose mailboxes you want to move. Finally, you move user mailboxes from the Exchange 5.5 server to your new Exchange 2000 server. This approach will work with one or many Exchange 5.5 servers.

This is a very neat option. If the old Exchange 5.5 server is still running, it will even direct users to the new server automatically, and user profiles will be automatically updated. All this happens because your new Exchange 2000 server and the server from which you moved the mailboxes are in the same Exchange 5.5 organization. As far as the old server is concerned, your users have just moved to a new Exchange 5.5 server. What could be easier?

Moving public folders is about as easy as moving mailboxes. Just replicate public folders on Exchange 5.5 servers to your new Exchange 2000 server. Then remove the instances of the folders on the 5.5 servers. Users will be automatically directed to the public folders on your new server.

A Leapfrog Upgrade

A leapfrog upgrade is much like a move-mailbox upgrade in that it is quick and fairly low risk. There is one major difference, though. With the move-mailbox upgrade you use new hardware for all your new Windows 2000/Exchange 2000 servers. With the leapfrog method, you use a new server to hold mailboxes while you upgrade your existing servers.

Basically, you set up a Windows 2000/Exchange 2000 server just as you do with the move-mailboxes method. Then you move the mailboxes and public folders from an Exchange 5.5 server and upgrade it to Windows 2000 and Exchange 2000. When the upgraded server is up and running, you move the mailboxes and folders back to it. Depending on your need and the capacity of your new server, you can upgrade one or many Exchange 5.5 servers in the same time period.

Exchange 5.5/2000 Coexistence

All three of the upgrade strategies in this section can include a period in which Exchange 5.5 and Exchange 2000 servers coexist in the same site or organization. In most cases, coexistence is required only long enough to upgrade all Exchange 5.5 servers to 2000 status. However, I can imagine scenarios in which coexistence is a long-term thing. For example, your Exchange 5.5 organization might include some sites that lack adequate technical or financial resources to permit an upgrade to Windows 2000 and Exchange 2000. The nice thing about the upgrade paths that Microsoft has architected for Exchange is that everything will work pretty well, whether short- or long-term coexistence is necessary.

However, aside from all the caveats that I've already dropped on you, there is one thing more that you need to deal with: You can expect the upgrade process to move relatively slowly. You shouldn't upgrade an Exchange 5.5 server to Windows 2000 Server and stop there. There will be a conflict between the SMTP service provided by 5.5's Internet Mail Service and Windows 2000 Server's native SMTP service. If you need to upgrade Exchange 5.5 servers to Windows 2000 and then let them sit for a while, be sure that SMTP services are provided either by your Windows 2000/Exchange 2000 servers or by Exchange 5.5 servers not yet upgraded to Windows 2000.

What Happens and Doesn't Happen During an Exchange Upgrade?

Active Directory is the center of an upgrade from Exchange 5.5 to Exchange 2000. You should be pretty clear on what happens to Active Directory during an upgrade. However, other things do happen. Let's look at some of the things that happen and some that don't.

When you upgrade your first Exchange 5.5 server to Exchange 2000 server, the Exchange 2000 site replication service (SRS) is installed. SRS is also installed when you upgrade any Exchange 5.5 directory replication bridgehead server. SRS makes an Exchange 2000 server look just like an Exchange 5.5 server that supports intersite and intrasite directory replication. The Exchange version of the Active Directory Connector isn't enough to keep a 5.5 directory in full sync with Active Directory. SRS supplements the Active Directory Connector's functionality.

Exchange 5.5 connectors are updated to Exchange 2000 versions, when an Exchange 2000 version is available. If a required connector is not available, you'll need to continue to run an Exchange 5.5 bridgehead server with the 5.5 version of the connector. With the bridgehead server integrated into your Exchange 2000 environment, you'll continue to enjoy the benefits of the old connector. Of course, as with any purely Exchange 5.5 feature, you'll have to manage the bridgehead server and connector using the Exchange 5.5 Administrator program.

Some Exchange 5.5 features may require additional attention after an upgrade. For example, in certain circumstances, Outlook Web Access, the Web server-based service that lets users access their Exchange mailboxes with a Web browser, may need tweaking after an upgrade. The same is true for the Exchange 5.5 Chat service. (See the Exchange 2000 Server documentation for more on what you may need to do regarding the Outlook Web Access and chat services, and for information on other Exchange 5.5 components that may need additional work after an upgrade.)

Summary

Whew! That really was hell. Just kidding. (I think.) In this chapter, we focused on upgrade issues. First, we took a long, hard look at the upgrade process from NT Server 4 to Windows 2000 Server. Then we walked the upgrade path from Exchange Server 5.5 to Exchange 2000 Server. We discovered that Exchange 2000 upgrades are intimately linked to Windows 2000 upgrades.

Upgrades from NT 4 to Windows 2000 begin with a clear mapping between your current NT 4 domain structure and your future Windows 2000 domain structure. There is nothing to stop you from mapping any of the four NT 4 domain models to a nearly parallel Windows 2000 domain model. However, the preferred approach is to create a single Windows 2000 domain that incorporates all your NT 4 domains. Windows 2000 includes features that make this process easier, such as sites and organizational units.

You must do several tasks in preparation for an NT 4 to Windows 2000 upgrade:

1. You must select from the three flavors of Windows 2000 Server: Server, Advanced Server, and Datacenter Server. You must select carefully, remembering that the version of Exchange 2000 Server that you plan to install must be compatible with the version of Windows 2000 Server that you install.

2. You must ensure that your server's hardware is adequate to support the Windows 2000 software that you'll be installing and that all the software on the server is compatible with Windows 2000.

3. You must draw up an upgrade plan that takes into account the specifics of your NT Server 4 environment, the Windows 2000 domain model that you're shooting for, and the process of getting from NT 4 to Windows 2000 without risking a large amount of downtime.

Before you actually upgrade from Exchange Server 5.5 to Exchange 2000 Server, you need to select an appropriate strategy for populating your Windows 2000 Active Directory with information from your Exchange 5.5 system. After you've done this, you need to implement the strategy by synchronizing your Exchange 5.5 server's directory with your Windows 2000 server's Active Directory. You use the Active Directory Connector (ADC) to accomplish this task. If you can upgrade all your Exchange 5.5 servers to Exchange 2000 in a single night, you'll just use the ADC to get the Exchange 5.5 directory and Active Directory in sync; then turn off the ADC. If your Exchange upgrade will take longer, you'll leave the ADC in place and allow it to keep your remaining Exchange 5.5 servers in sync with your Exchange 2000 environment.

When Active Directory has been populated, you're ready to actually upgrade your Exchange 5.5 servers to Exchange 2000. Before you do the upgrade, however, you need to develop a strategy for the upgrade. Three basic strategies are available:

In-place　An in-place upgrade is the simplest conceptually and practically. You simply run the upgrade program on each Exchange 5.5 server.

Move-mailbox　With a move-mailbox upgrade, you install Exchange 2000 on a new server and use built-in Exchange 2000 tools to move user mailboxes from the Exchange 5.5 server to the Exchange 2000 server. Move-mailbox upgrades are best when you need to replace your existing Exchange 5.5 hardware with newer, more powerful hardware.

Leapfrog　In a leapfrog upgrade, you first do a move-mailbox upgrade, but, instead of discarding the old Exchange 5.5 server, you make it the next move-mailbox upgrade server. Leapfrog upgrades are ideally suited to a situation in which you don't want to do in-place upgrades, but your existing Exchange 5.5 hardware has adequate capacity.

Now we're ready to move on to the hands-on part of this book where we'll begin by installing and using Windows 2000 Server and Exchange 2000 Server. Even though Chapters 7 and 8 don't include specific upgrade information, you should read both chapters carefully. Why? See the introduction to Part II, "Installation."

PART II

Installation

Microsoft Exchange 2000 Server runs on top of Microsoft's Windows 2000 Server. In this part, we'll discuss how to install both products, protect them and their users against hardware crashes, and build a basic networking environment to support them. Chapter 7, "Installing Windows 2000 Server," focuses on installing and configuring Windows 2000 Server, setting up an uninterruptible power supply, and backing up. Chapter 8, "Installing Exchange 2000 Server," provides the details on Exchange 2000 Server installation and security.

If you need to upgrade from NT Server 4 to Windows 2000 Server and from Exchange Server 5.5 to Exchange 2000 Server, this part of the book is for you, too. Much of what you'll have to do when upgrading is covered in the next two chapters. You can get started upgrading by just inserting the Windows 2000 Server or Exchange 2000 Server CD and then following the onscreen instructions. However, you'll need to read Chapters 7 and 8 to fully understand what you're doing during the upgrades. Of course, I'm assuming that you've already read Chapter 6, "Upgrading to Windows 2000 Server and Exchange 2000 Server."

CHAPTER <u>7</u>

Installing Windows 2000 Server

FEATURING:

This is a dual-purpose chapter. First, it's designed to help you install a Windows 2000 Server as a domain controller that fully supports network login, access to various resources, DHCP, and DNS. Second, this chapter is designed to help you install a standalone Windows 2000 Server. It assumes that you will install a Windows 2000 domain controller first and then, in conjunction with reading Chapter 8, "Installing Exchange 2000 Server," install a standalone server on which you will install and run Exchange 2000 Server. I have tried to construct this chapter so that you know when I'm talking about installing a domain controller and when I'm talking about installing a standalone server. (I use warning notes to call your attention to critical points at which you'll take one path if installing a domain controller and another path if installing a standalone server.)

 NOTE   This is ultimately a book about Exchange 2000 Server. So, it's not possible for me to cover everything about Windows 2000 Server in great detail. You should find two books on this subject most useful: *Microsoft Windows 2000 Server Administrator's Companion*, by Charlie Russel and Sharon Crawford (Microsoft Press, 2000), and *Mastering Windows 2000 Server*, by Mark Minasi, et al (Sybex, 2000).

In this chapter, I'm presuming that you'll be installing Windows 2000 Server on a computer with nothing on it that you want to preserve. For example, I assume that you don't need to upgrade an NT 4 server or Windows 98 workstation to Windows 2000 Server and preserve the software that you've installed under the existing operating system. If you need to upgrade an NT 4 server, see Chapter 6, "Upgrading to Windows 2000 Server and Exchange 2000 Server." If you need to upgrade from a workstation product to Windows 2000 Server, check out the Windows 2000 Server documentation.

Windows 2000 Server installation is a multistep process. These steps are listed at the start of this chapter, and we'll look at each of these steps in detail.

 WARNING   As I mentioned in Chapter 1, "Introducing Exchange 2000 Server," things are likely to change by the time you read this book. The Internet and the high-speed, high-pressure marketing and software delivery channels that it has fostered make unending, unpredictable, and incredibly quick software modification not only possible, but also economically necessary for vendors. Before you install Windows 2000 Server, check the Web to be sure that a new service pack isn't available for the product or that you don't have to do something new and special when installing Windows 2000 Server, if you plan to install Exchange 2000 Server. The best Web sites are www.microsoft.com/windows2000 and www.microsoft.com/exchange for updates. You can also update Windows 2000 directly over the Internet. Just select the Windows Update option on the Start menu. The system can even check for new updates and let you know when an update is available. This is a really neat capability.

Have you ever gone on the Alice in Wonderland ride at Disneyland? It starts by taking you down a rabbit hole, with Alice saying, "Here we gooooooooooooooooooooo." That extended "go" fades away toward the end, adding to the ride's excitement and sense of entering the unknown. Like Alice, we're about to embark on a wild and exciting adventure. I promise to do all I can to make our hands-on trip through Windows and Exchange 2000 interesting, productive, and fun—but a little less bumpy, arbitrary, and confusing than Alice's sojourn through Wonderland. Let's go.

Setting Up Server Hardware

Setting up the hardware is a pretty straightforward process. First, you pick a server platform and outfit it with various components. Then you test its memory, disk drives, and other hardware to ensure that everything is working well.

Windows 2000 Server is much easier to install than NT 4 from a hardware perspective. Running on a modern plug-and-play PCI bus-based computer, with PCI adapters and its own Windows 98-like plug-and-play capabilities, 2000 Server automatically recognizes and installs hardware drivers. In such an environment, you'll rarely have to manually configure video, SCSI, modem, or other adapters. That alone is almost worth the price of admission to Windows 2000 Server.

 WARNING Throughout this chapter and in Chapter 8, I assume that the first Windows 2000 server that you will install will be a domain controller. I also assume that you will not run Exchange 2000 Server on this computer. When we get to Chapter 8, we'll install Exchange on another Windows 2000 server, a standalone Windows 2000 server that isn't a domain controller. If you're hard-pressed for hardware, for testing purposes, you can try installing Exchange on a Windows 2000 domain controller. However, I join Microsoft in strongly recommending against doing this in a production environment, no matter how powerful you might think your computing hardware is. In this chapter, you'll learn how to install Windows 2000 as both a domain controller and a standalone server. I'll use a warning note like this one at the beginning of sections of this chapter where you should do things differently depending on whether you're installing a domain controller or a standalone server.

Getting Server Components in Order

In Chapter 5, "Designing a New Exchange 2000 System," I wrote of my computer of choice for running Exchange 2000 Server: an 800MHz Pentium III or Xeon machine with 512MB of memory and at least two 9GB SCSI hard drives. That's pretty much my recommendation for an Exchange-less Windows 2000 domain controller in a serious networked computing environment. Ideally, I'd like to see you use a dual-processor machine with 1GB of RAM memory and at least 20GB of RAID 5 disk storage for your domain controller.

If you're just going to test Windows 2000 and promise not to put your test configuration into production, you can use a somewhat lesser hunk of hardware than the one that I tout. I'd recommend at a minimum a 500MHz Pentium PC with 512MB of RAM and a 9GB to 10GB IDE or SCSI hard disk. I suggest that you outfit your system with a high-resolution VGA display adapter, at least a 17-inch monitor, a 24x-speed or faster CD-ROM drive, two or more serial ports, two or more USB ports, a mouse, and one or more network adapters.

Regarding the serial and USB port, you'll need one serial or USB port to interface your Windows 2000 server to an uninterruptible power supply (UPS). You also might want to use a serial port for a mouse. However, if you plan to provide Microsoft's Remote Access Server (RAS) connections for your Windows 2000 Server users, use a PS/2 mouse port to free a serial port for RAS. If you need a lot of RAS ports, look at multiport boards from companies such as Digi International (http://www.dgii.com/).

What to Buy

Microsoft publishes a hardware compatibility list for its Windows products. The HCL lists the components that work with Windows 2000 Server and other Windows-based operating systems. You can find this list on the Web at http://www.microsoft.com/hcl/default.asp. Before you buy anything, consult this guide.

One crucial bit of advice: Don't be cheap! The newspapers in Los Angeles and most big cities are full of ads for what seem to be unbelievably inexpensive components such as SIMMS, DIMMs, disk drives, motherboards, and CPUs. Don't bite. Trust me on this one: I've been through the mill with cheap, flaky components. Windows 2000 Server all by itself can beat the living daylights out of a computer. Add Exchange 2000 Server, and you'll pay back in your own sweat and time every penny and then some that you saved by buying cheap. Buy from stable, long-lived vendors at reasonable but not fairy-tale prices. RAM for a Windows 2000 Server should always be ECC-type. They cost a little more but are worth the money.

'Nuff said.

Testing Key Components

The networking services provided by a Windows 2000 server are critical applications. You should also consider fault-tolerant hardware, as discussed in Chapter 2, "2000: A Magic Number?" and Chapter 5. But even before you consider this option, you should be sure that everything in your server is working properly. You'll want to test five key components as soon as your server is in-house: memory, hard disks, CD-ROM drives, SCSI controllers, and network adapters.

Good memory and disk tests are time-consuming. Testing out the high-end computer that I recommend could take a week or more. Don't let that deter you, though. You want to be sure that you've got a solid platform under your organization—if for no other reason than that you'll sleep better at night.

During Windows 2000 Server installation, the system is automatically configured for a variety of hardware options, so you should be sure that all your hardware is working during the installation process. For this reason, you'll want to test your CD-ROM drive, SCSI controllers, and network adapters before installing Windows 2000 Server. Be sure to test all these together to be sure that no IRQ, I/O address, or DMA conflicts occur, although this should be less of a problem if your computer and adapters support plug-and-play hardware.

It should go without saying, but I'll say it anyway: Don't consider your testing phase finished until all components pass the tests you set out for them. Now let's start testing:

Testing memory   Because the quick boot-up memory test on Intel-based PCs cannot find most memory problems, use Touchstone Software's Checkit (http://www.checkit.com/) or PC-Doctor's PC-Doctor for DOS (http://www.pc-doctor.com/) to test memory. You should run either of these programs from DOS with no memory manager present, and run the complete suite of tests in slow rather than quick mode.

Testing hard disks   There are two kinds of software-based hard disk testers: those that write one pattern all over the disk and then read to see whether the pattern was written correctly (MS-DOS's SCANDISK is such a tester), and those that write a range of patterns and test to see whether each was properly written. You'll want a multipattern tester because it is more likely to find the bit-based problems on a disk. SpinRite from Gibson Research (http://grc.com/default.htm) is a good multipattern tester that can find and declare off-limits any bad areas on disk that the manufacturer didn't catch.

Testing CD-ROM drives   I test my CD-ROM drives in DOS using MSCDEX.EXE and the DOS driver for the drive. If I can do a directory on a

CD-ROM in the drive that I'm testing and copy a file or two from the CD-ROM, I assume that it's working well enough to move on to Windows 2000 installation.

Testing SCSI controllers   If you've tested your hard drives as suggested previously, you've also tested their controllers, at least in isolation from other adapters. Just be sure to run your tests again with active CD-ROM drives and network cards to ensure that no adapter conflicts are lurking in the background just waiting to mess up your Windows 2000 Server installation.

Testing network adapters   I never install a machine that will be networked without making sure that it can attach in MS-DOS mode to a server. I use Microsoft's NDIS drivers.

 TIP   If you've got enough hardware, you might want to run your RAM and disk tests simultaneously. This will cut down on testing time.

Installing Windows 2000 Server Software

As with setting up hardware, installing Windows 2000 Server is fairly straightforward. If you've read Part I, "Understanding and Planning," you should encounter no surprises. We'll go through all the steps that you'll take to get Windows 2000 Server up and running.

I'd love to show you all the screens that you'll see during installation; however, because no operating system is yet in place, there's no way to capture these screens. Rest assured that each step discussed here parallels a screen that you'll see during installation. Later in this chapter—after we've got Windows 2000 Server installed—I'll show you enough setup screens to make up for the early deficit.

 TIP   My first encounter with the Windows 2000 Server documentation was pretty scary. I nearly panicked when I saw nothing about choosing whether a new server was to be a domain controller or a standalone server. After all, this was a major and irrevocable decision point in the installation of an NT 4 server. My discomfort subsided when I realized that Windows 2000 servers become domain controllers *after*, not during, initial installation. So, relax and track through the initial installation process with me. After that, we'll turn our newly installed server into a domain controller.

Starting the Installation

Now I'm going to discuss how to install Windows 2000 Advanced Server. If you're installing the Server or Datacenter Server edition, your experience will be pretty much the same as what I show you here. To make things a bit easier, I'll refer to the product that we're installing as *Windows 2000 Server*.

Windows 2000 Server comes on a CD-ROM. If your computer can boot from a CD-ROM drive, insert the CD in the CD-ROM drive, and boot your computer. The Windows 2000 Setup program will start automatically.

If you can't boot from your CD-ROM drive, you'll need to boot from a disk. You can make boot disks by running MAKEBOOT.EXE, which resides in the \BOOTDISK directory on the Windows 2000 Server CD. Boot your computer with the first setup disk in the computer's disk drive.

On bootup, the installation program will start, and you're off to the races. The first notable thing you'll see is a blue screen with "Windows 2000 Setup" displayed in white letters. At the bottom of the screen, you'll see the message "Setup is loading files," along with text in parentheses indicating which file is being loaded. Windows 2000 is loading files into RAM memory at this point. These files support a variety of disk drives, CD ROM drives, SCSI and RAID devices, video adapters, file systems, and so on. Windows 2000 will use these drivers during the setup phase. All this takes some time, so be patient.

Next you have the option of setting up Windows 2000, repairing an existing Windows 2000 installation, or quitting Setup. Select the first option to begin installation. When the licensing dialog box pops up, page down through the licensing agreement and then press F8 to agree to the conditions of the license. F8 doesn't show up on the screen until you've paged all the way down to the end of the license.

Preparing Disk Partitions

Next, Setup shows you the unpartitioned space on the hard disk drives that it detected and asks how you want to set up your partitions and where you want to install Windows 2000 Server. If you've worked with NT 4 or DOS disk partitions, what follows should be pretty familiar. You can choose to set up partitions of any size, up to the capacity of a disk drive. I recommend setting up a partition between 8GB and 9GB for the Windows 2000 Server operating system.

For now, you need to worry about only the primary partition that Windows 2000 Server will be installed on. You can take care of other partitions later using Windows 2000's Disk Management application. I'll talk more about this application in the section "Configuring Unallocated Disk Space," later in this chapter.

Choose to install in the default partition or to create a new partition. If you select the first option, installation will begin immediately. If you pick the second option, you'll see a new screen that lets you select the size of the partition and create it.

Now comes the $64,000 question: Do you want to format the partition as a file allocation table (FAT) or NTFS (Windows 2000 NT File System v.5) partition? I format all my Windows 2000 Server operating system partitions in NTFS format. NTFS is far more fault-tolerant than FAT and is far more secure. Furthermore, Active Directory runs only on NTFS. In addition, unlike the past, when FAT files access was faster than NTFS file access, performance is now comparable between the two file systems. My own opinions notwithstanding, choose the format that you want and press the Enter key. Setup displays a little gauge showing formatting progress. Formatting takes quite a bit of time and may continue quite a bit longer after the gauge shows 99 percent complete.

Next, Setup begins copying files from the CD-ROM to the partition that you designated. After copying the files, Setup tells you that it has finished this phase of installation and reboots your computer.

Setup's Installation Wizard

Upon reboot, Windows 2000 Setup runs through some basic text startup screens. Soon Setup goes into graphical user interface mode and runs some more setup routines, asking you to "Please wait."

Then Setup brings up a wizard to guide you through the next phase of Windows 2000 Server installation. The wizard looks a lot like the installation wizards that come with a range of products designed for the Windows operating system. It leads you through a hardware detection/device installation phase, the selection of a number of important options for installation, the installation of Windows 2000 networking, and a bunch of other housekeeping chores.

The sections that follow guide you through the various phases of Windows 2000 Server installation. They're keyed to the installation wizard; click Next on the wizard to move on to the next phase of installation.

Detection of Hardware Devices and Installation of Appropriate Drivers

I'm sure that you, like I, often turned green with envy when Windows 9x users installed their operating system and new hardware without so much as a passing worry about interrupts, I/O memory addresses, and all that stuff. Well, Windows 2000 brings plug-and-play to the high-end server world, and you're going to love it.

In the next phase of installation, the wizard kicks off a hardware device detection process. As you watch the little progress gauge turn bluer and bluer, you're participating in one of the miracles of the twenty-first century. Windows 2000's device detection code finds all relevant hardware devices—keyboards, mouse devices, display adapters, network adapters, USB-connected devices, and so on—and installs drivers for them from the vast array of files cached on the CD. If the right driver isn't present, you're given the chance to load it from alternative media.

Regional Settings

The next step in the installation process involves selecting appropriate regional settings. These include the locale setting; language settings (Windows 2000 can handle multiple languages); formats for numbers, currency, time, and date; and keyboard layout.

Generally, the default settings work fine if you're in the United States or if you're using a CD with a localized version of Windows 2000.

Name and Organization

If you've ever installed a Windows product before, you've filled in this screen. Enter you name (or whatever name your organization wants in the name field). Enter whatever is appropriate in the Company field, or leave it blank. Here you're just entering identifying information. This information is often used in installing other software, such as Microsoft Office. It has nothing to do with how your computer or domain will be named.

Licensing Information

Next, the wizard requests licensing information. Select the licensing type that you've paid for, per server or per seat, and enter any required values. Heed the wizard's warning to use the License Manager in the Administrative Tools program group to set the number of client licenses purchased after your Windows 2000 server is up and running. If you don't, users and other systems won't be able to connect to the server.

Naming Your Windows 2000 Server

The wizard next asks you to name your Windows 2000 server and offers a suggested name. If you like the name, fine. If not, change it. If you'll be running Exchange 2000 on this server, the name should follow the Exchange Server naming scheme that you developed based on discussions in Chapter 5. If this server won't be running Exchange on this server, use whatever naming scheme you've chosen for non-Exchange servers.

I'm naming my first server BG01. Following my own advice, this server won't run Exchange 2000; it'll be a domain controller running Active Directory, DHCP, and DNS. That's more than enough for one server.

The name can be up to 63 characters long. If this computer will interact with non-Windows 2000 clients, the name should be 15 characters or less in length.

You're also asked for a password for the Administrator account on this server. Enter the password and confirm the password by re-entering it. Passwords can be up to 14 characters long.

Selecting Components

Next the wizard shows you a page for selecting the components that you want to install. Figure 7.1 shows a portion of this page.

FIGURE 7.1

Using the Setup Wizard's Windows Components page to select Windows 2000 Server components to be installed

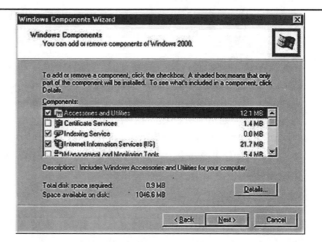

Explore the Windows Components page to see what the options are all about. Just be sure to select Management and Monitoring Tools. Also select Networking Services by checking its little white box. However, if you're installing Exchange 2000 on this server, and if this server will not be a domain controller, don't install DNS, DHCP, or WINS. Select Networking Services and click Details to deselect these three services.

If you're installing Exchange 2000 on this server, select Internet Information Server by clicking on its box. Then click Details and select Network News Transport Protocol (NNTP). Exchange 2000 Server won't install if NNTP isn't installed.

⚠ **TIP** If you ever need to install additional components after you have completed initial installation, just put the Windows 2000 Server CD-ROM in your CD drive and follow the directions for installing add-on components. This feature is pretty neat, and you usually don't even have to reboot your computer after add-on installation.

Modem Dialing Information

If Windows 2000 detected a modem in your computer, you'll be asked to enter basic dialing information. If there's no modem, you won't see this wizard page.

Installing Windows 2000 Networking

Windows 2000 Server is nothing without networking. First, networking software is installed. Then the wizard takes you into the network installation portion of the Setup process. You're asked if you want typical or custom settings.

- If you're installing the first domain controller in your domain, select the custom settings.
- If you've already set up a domain controller and are installing a standalone server for Exchange 2000, select the typical settings.

Custom settings let you put in IP address, DNS, and other information. You have to do this for at least the first DHCP server on your network. Typical settings assume that there is already a DHCP server on your network and that you want the server you're installing to use the DHCP server to get IP address, DNS, and other information.

If you select typical settings, click Next and you'll be taken to the Workgroup or Domain page of the Windows 2000 Server Setup Wizard. For information on how to use this page, go to the next section, "Specifying Whether You Want the Computer to Be a Member of a Domain."

After you've chosen custom settings and clicked Next, the wizard shows you its Networking Components page. Figure 7.2 shows this page. You can use this page to install additional networking components such as the NetBEUI or IPX/SPX networking protocols. (Click Install.) You can also use this page to modify settings for existing components.

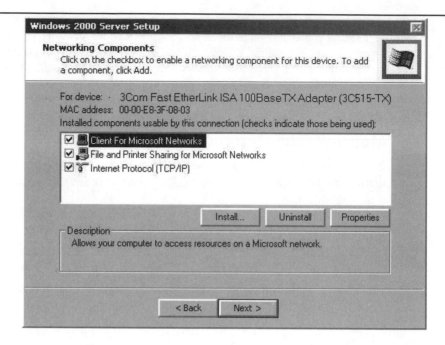

Unless you have a good reason for doing otherwise, leave all settings but Internet Protocol (TCP/IP) at their default levels. Click Internet Protocol (TCP/IP) and click Properties. Use the Internet Protocols (TCP/IP) dialog box that pops up to set an IP address, address mask, gateway router, and DNS servers for your new server.

If your server will be connected to the Internet, use an IP address and address mask, a gateway router, and DNS servers as assigned by your ISP. You should also include the IP address of the server that you're installing now in the DNS server list. If you have only one ISP-assigned DNS server, which is unlikely, add your new server's IP address in the Alternate DNS field. If both DNS server fields are full, click Advanced on the Internet Protocols (TCP/IP) dialog box. Add the IP address on the DNS page of the Advanced TCP/IP Settings dialog box that pops up.

If your server won't be connected to the Internet, use an IP address and address mask, a gateway router, and DNS servers as assigned by your organization's networking authority. If your organization doesn't have a networking authority, select your IP address from one of the standard test IP address ranges, such as 192.168.0.10. For this address, use a mask of 255.255.255.0. Don't enter an address for the gateway router, and set your first DNS server to the same address as you've assigned to your new server, such as 192.168.0.10.

Specifying Whether You Want the Computer to Be a Member of a Domain

Next, the Setup Wizard shows you a page where you can specify the domain status of your new server. Figure 7.3 shows this page.

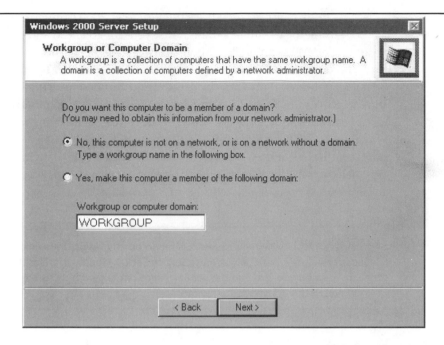

FIGURE 7.3

Using the Setup Wizard's Workgroup or Computer Domain page to set the domain status of a new Windows 2000 server

If you're installing the first domain controller in your domain, be sure that the first option is selected as it is in Figure 7.3. Then delete the name in the Workgroup or Computer Domain field. After installation, you'll convert this computer to a domain controller.

If you're installing a standalone server, select the option Yes, Make This Computer a Member of the Following Domain. Then, enter the pre-Windows 2000 name of your domain. My domain is called BGERBER. When you click Next, the Join Computer to Domain dialog box pops up and requests a username and password. Enter the name of an account that belongs to the Domain Admins group (for example, Administrator) and that account's password. There will be a little pause while your new server uses DHCP to obtain an IP address from your domain controller and then requests that it be allowed to join the domain. When all this is done, your new server will have been assigned the IP address that you reserved for it and will be a full-fledged member of the domain. You should find its name in the Computers container of the Active Directory Computers and Users snap-in in your Microsoft Management Console.

Installation and Up and Running at Last

At this point, Setup copies the files needed for your installation from the CD-ROM to your server's hard disk. Then it installs the Start menu for your server, registers installed components, saves settings, and removes temporary files created during the install. Setup then lets you know that the installation was successful and invites you to click Finish. The server reboots and, lo and behold, your Windows 2000 server is up and running. Press the familiar Ctrl+Alt+Delete keys, and log in as Administrator.

After a bit of churning, you'll see the Windows 2000 Configure Your Server Wizard. We'll be using the wizard in a bit, but first you can go ahead and do some manual cleanup work. You can fiddle with your display adapter's video resolution, if necessary, and do any other housekeeping chores that you'd like. To modify display adapter resolution, right-click the desktop and choose Properties ➤ Settings. If you have to reboot, the Configure Your Server Wizard will open on startup.

At last, you get your reward. It may seem anticlimactic, however. All that work and what do you get? The Microsoft Windows 98 desktop, that's what! Heck, you've probably seen that a hundred times. No bells? No whistles? No dancing bears? Nothing—just plain vanilla Windows 98 front-ending one of the most powerful multitasking, multithreaded operating systems in the world. Enjoy!

WARNING After your server has rebooted after initial installation of Windows 2000 Server, you'll need to apply at least Service Pack 1. See the note at the beginning of this chapter on how to find and download service packs, and how to check for other updates to Windows 2000 Server.

Promoting a Standalone Server to Domain Controller Status

WARNING If this server is to be a domain controller complete this section. If this server is to be standalone server, then read this section, but do not do the hands-on tasks.

Now we get to perform a task that's new to Windows 2000 Server. We're going to turn our server into a domain controller. For the record, in Windows 2000 parlance, we are going to *promote* our server to domain controller status. As I mentioned at the beginning of this section, unlike with NT 4, in which you must make irrevocable domain controller decisions during initial installation, you create Windows 2000 domain controllers after initial installation.

When you get used to this little fact of life, you'll actually come to love the concept. Why? Well, first you can promote a standalone server to domain controller status at any time. And, drum roll/rim shot, you can demote a domain controller back to standalone server status any time. As Pooh's friend, Eeyore, learned, you can put the little deflated balloon into the pot and take it out as many times as you like. (If you haven't read A.A. Milne's original Pooh stories, I strongly recommend them to you.

They recall a pre-high-tech world in which people and animals lived by simple wits and caring thoughts. What a nice respite from the edge-of-the-knife-blade lives most of us lead today!)

Oh yes. Back to the edge of the knife blade. Let's turn our newly installed server into a Windows 2000 domain controller. Now here's the neat part: You accomplish this task by installing Active Directory on your server. Here's how.

If the Configure Your Server Wizard is still open and running, wait just a second. If the wizard isn't running, start it as follows: Start Menu ➤ Administrative Tools ➤ Configure Your Server. When the wizard is running, click Active Directory. Figure 7.4 shows the wizard.

FIGURE 7.4

The Configure Your Server Wizard

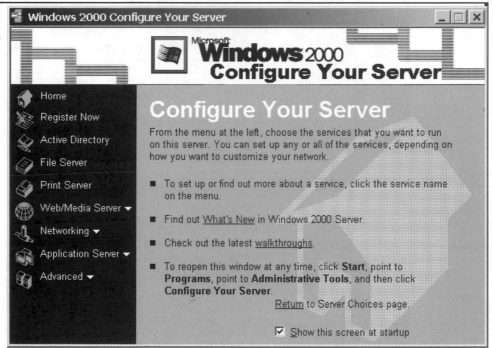

This brings up the Active Directory Management page. Figure 7.5 shows the first part of this page, and Figure 7.6 shows the portion of the page revealed after scrolling down. I call this the Active Directory Management page because, after you install Active Directory, you can go here to start managing Active Directory user accounts and groups. There are easier ways to accomplish this task, but you might find this page useful in the early going.

FIGURE 7.5

*The Active Directory
Management page*

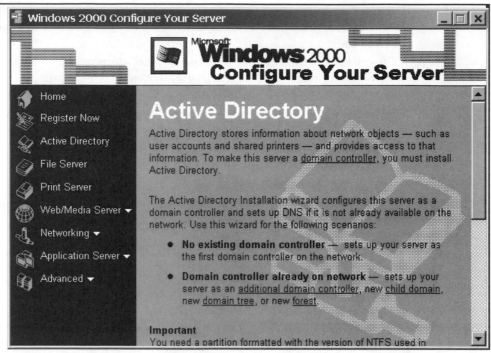

FIGURE 7.6

*The rest of the Active
Directory Management
page*

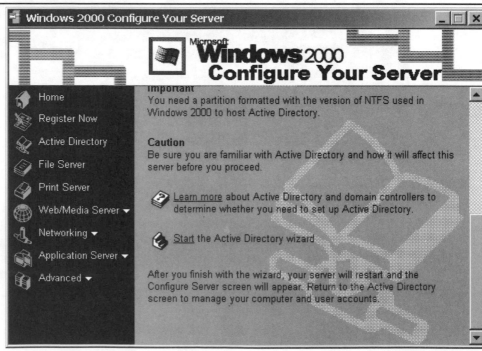

Next, click Start the Active Directory Wizard. (See Figure 7.6.) This starts the Active Directory Installation Wizard shown in Figure 7.7.

FIGURE 7.7

The Active Directory Installation Wizard

NOTE You can also start the Active Directory Installation Wizard by typing **dcpromo** into the dialog box that pops up when you select Start Menu ➢ Run. If your server isn't yet a domain controller, you'll see the Active Directory Installation Wizard, and you'll be offered the opportunity to promote your server to a domain controller. To protect you from accidentally demoting a domain controller back to a standalone server and losing your Active Directory and much more, demotion can be done only with the version of Active Directory Installation Wizard invoked by running dcpromo. You can't demote a server by running the Active Directory Installation Wizard through the Configure Your Server Wizard.

Now, let's step through the domain controller promotion process. Click Next on the Active Directory Installation Wizard to see the Domain Controller Type page, shown in Figure 7.8. This is the page you will come to know and love: This is where you create new forests, domains, and child domains. If you've read the earlier chapters of this book, all these terms will make eminent sense. If not, I strongly advise that you go back and look at Chapter 2; Chapter 3, "Two Key Architectural Components of Windows 2000 Server"; and Chapter 5. If you don't, you're going to get pretty lost pretty fast.

We are going to create a new forest and a new domain in that forest. So, be sure that the first option on the page is checked, as it is in Figure 7.8.

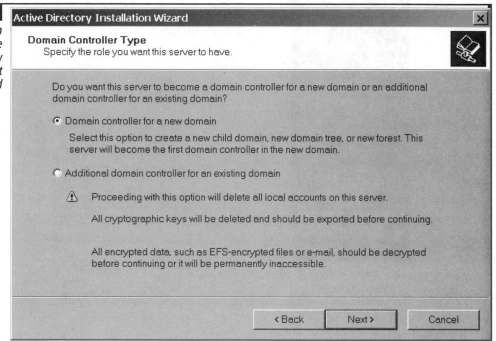

FIGURE 7.8

Using the Domain Controller Type page to specify that a new domain in a new forest is to be created

The next page of the Active Directory Installation Wizard lets you specify whether you want to create a new domain tree (a root domain) or a child domain in an existing tree. Again we're doing a new root domain, so we select the first option. See Figure 7.9.

FIGURE 7.9

Using the Create Tree or Child Domain page to specify that a new root domain is to be created

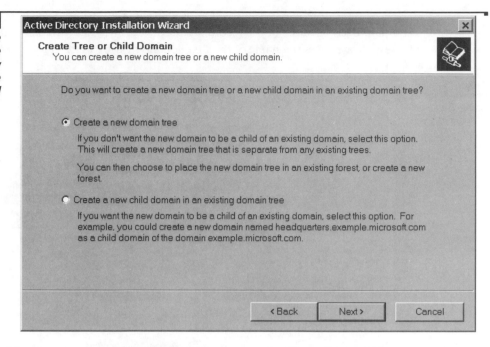

The Create or Join Forest page comes up next. See Figure 7.10. We want to create a new forest, so select the first option.

FIGURE 7.10

Using the Create or Join Forest page to specify that a new forest is to be created

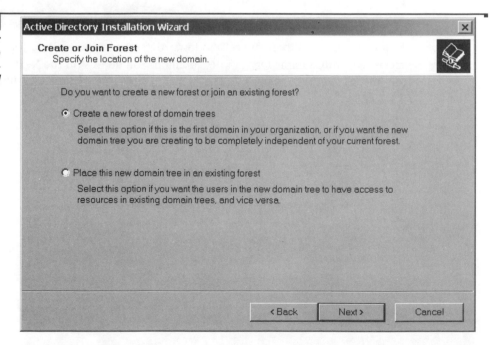

Next you specify the name of the new domain. In Figure 7.11, I've chosen to call my domain bgerber.com. For the record, the new forest will have the same name. A new forest always takes the name of the first domain in the forest.

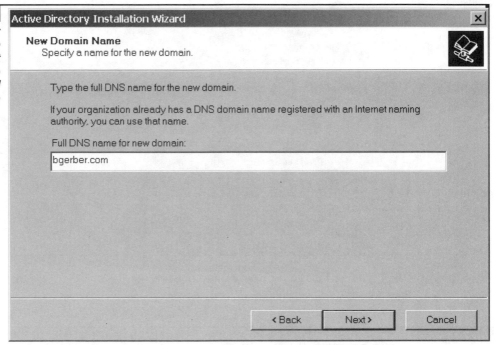

FIGURE 7.11

Using the Create or New Domain Name page to specify that the new domain is to be named bgerber.com

To retain compatibility with pre-Windows 2000 servers and workstation, you need to specify a NetBIOS name for your new domain. You do this on the Next Active Directory Installation Wizard page. In Figure 7.14, I've set my domain's NetBIOS name to BGERBER.

FIGURE 7.12

Using the NetBIOS Domain Name page to specify that the new NetBIOS domain name is to be BGERBER

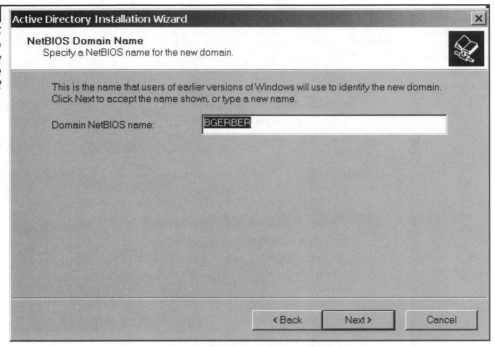

Active Directory Installation Wizard

NetBIOS Domain Name
Specify a NetBIOS name for the new domain.

This is the name that users of earlier versions of Windows will use to identify the new domain. Click Next to accept the name shown, or type a new name.

Domain NetBIOS name: BGERBER

< Back   Next >   Cancel

Next you must specify some disk directories. First, you need to set the directories where the Active Directory database and its logs will be stored (see Figure 12.13). For performance's sake, it's best to put the database on one disk drive and the logs on another. Second, you must specify where the domain's public files will be stored. These include scripts and user and machine policies. Public files are stored in a directory named SYSVOL (see Figure 12.14).

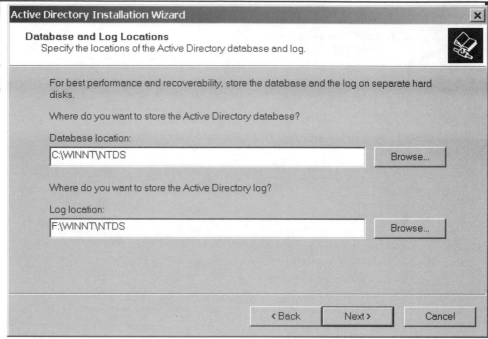

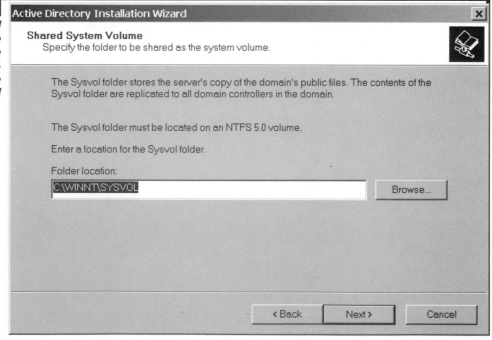

Next you'll see a little message box that tells you that the wizard could not contact the DNS for your domain and that asks you to confirm your DNS configuration or install DNS. Although it sounds like something is wrong, don't worry. Just click OK, and you'll see the Active Directory Installation Wizard page shown in Figure 7.15. After berating you for not installing DNS or at least not installing it properly, the wizard generously offers to install DNS for you. Take it up on its offer.

FIGURE 7.15

Using the Configure DNS page to specify that DNS is to be installed along with Active Directory

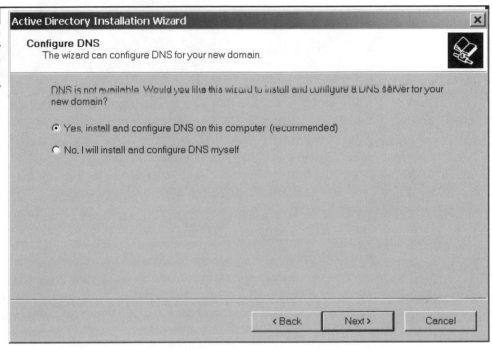

The Permissions page is used to indicate whether you want your domain to support legacy NT Server permissions. See Figure 7.16. Select the first option unless you're sure that users and groups will never have to access programs dependent on NT 4 permissions.

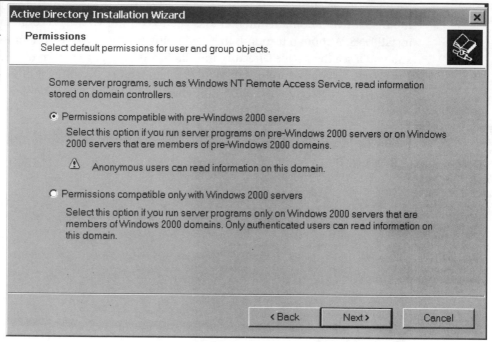

Windows 2000 Server has a variety of boot options. The concept is the same as with Windows 95 and 98 when you press the F8 key. But the options are more serverlike. One of the boot options allows you to restore Active Directory. You need to enter a password to run this option. You create this password on the next Active Directory Installation Wizard page, as shown in Figure 7.17. Be sure to record this password; you won't be able to perform a restore without it.

FIGURE 7.17

Using the Directory Services Restore Mode Administrator Password page to specify a password for a Directory Services restore boot

Active Directory Installation Wizard   ✕

Directory Services Restore Mode Administrator Password
Specify an Administrator password to use when starting the computer in Directory Services Restore Mode.

Type and confirm the password you want to assign to this server's Administrator account, to be used when the computer is started in Directory Services Restore Mode.

Password: [********]

Confirm password: [********]

     < Back   Next >   Cancel

You're just about done. Installation is ready to start. The Summary page shown in Figure 7.18 shows you what's about to happen. You can make any necessary changes by clicking Back as many times as needed to get to the page you need to change. Click Next to begin installation.

FIGURE 7.18

The Summary page shows how Active Directory will be installed.

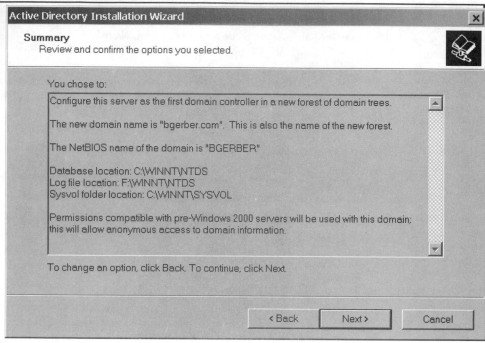

You'll grow to know and love the image in Figure 7.19. Active Directory installation isn't the fastest thing in the world. As long as that little pencil is writing, you're okay. If it stops, you've got trouble. In all the Active Directory installations I've done, I've never seen a stalled pencil, though, so, don't worry too much about failure here.

FIGURE 7.19

A little animated pencil assures you that the installation of Active Directory is proceeding well.

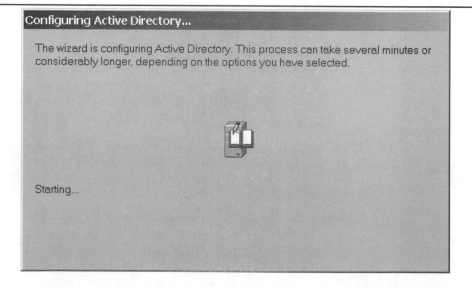

When all is done, you'll see the page in Figure 7.20. Click Finish, and you've completed promotion of your server to domain controller status. Well, almost: You have to reboot the computer for all the changes to take effect.

FIGURE 7.20

Active Directory has been successfully installed, and the server is now a Windows 2000 Server domain controller.

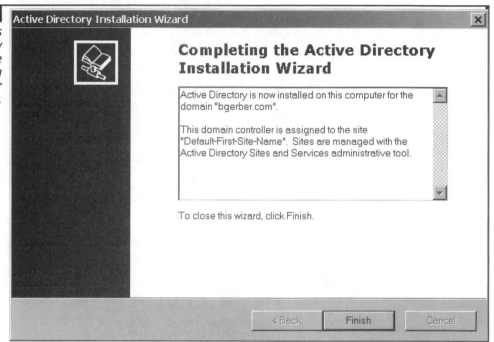

Using Microsoft Management Console

 WARNING   If this server is a domain controller, complete this section. If this server is a standalone server on which you'll install Exchange 2000 Server, read through this section, but don't try to do the hands-on setup work. We'll set up Microsoft Management Console for your Exchange server in the next chapter.

You've just installed some pretty neat software. To view the fruits of your labor, you'll need to use some of the tools that Microsoft provides with Windows 2000 Server. You can find most of these tools in Start Menu ➤ Programs ➤ Administrative Tools. (See Figure 7.21.) The items on the menu pretty much speak for themselves. You'll get to know a number of them in a bit more detail before the end of this chapter.

FIGURE 7.21

*Windows 2000 Server's
Administrative
Tools menu*

- Active Directory Domains and Trusts
- Active Directory Sites and Services
- Active Directory Users and Computers
- Component Services
- Computer Management
- Configure Your Server
- Connection Manager Administration Kit
- Data Sources (ODBC)
- DHCP
- Distributed File System
- DNS
- Domain Controller Security Policy
- Domain Security Policy
- Event Viewer
- Internet Authentication Service
- Internet Services Manager
- Licensing
- Local Security Policy
- Network Monitor
- Performance
- QoS Admission Control
- Routing and Remote Access
- Server Extensions Administrator
- Services
- Telnet Server Administration
- WINS

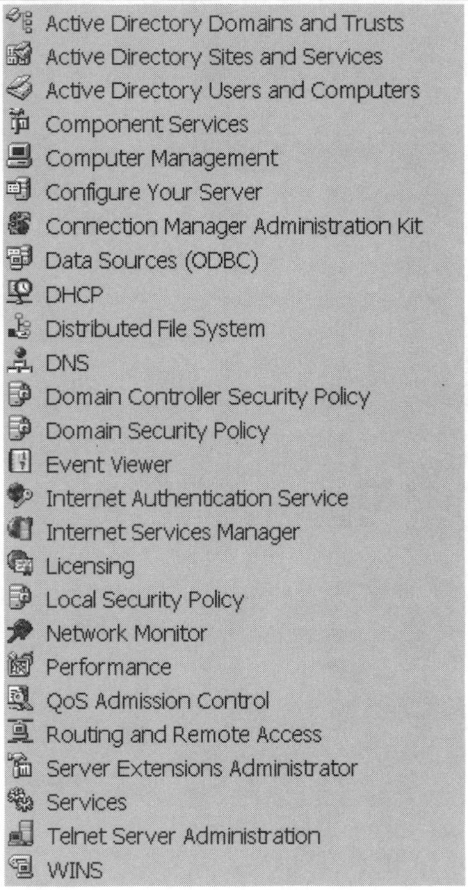

If you've had any experience with NT 4, the Administrative Tools menu should look somewhat familiar. You're probably wondering where things such as User Manager for Domains and Server Manager have gone, but DHCP, DNS, Event Viewer, and WINS should be old friends. Licensing, an old pal from the Control Panel, continues to live there and on the Administrative Tools menu. The Services applet has moved from the Control Panel to Administrative Tools.

The Administrative Tools menu is one way to get to many of the tools that you'll need to manage your Windows 2000 servers. But, it's not the only way and, for many tasks, is not the easiest way.

Unless you've got a real aversion to it, you're going to want to start using Microsoft Management Console (MMC). MMC is a container into which you can add a wide range of management snap-ins. If you've managed Internet Information Server 4 or Microsoft Transaction Server in an NT 4 environment, you already know MMC—at least, in an earlier incarnation. Figure 7.22 shows IIS 4/Microsoft Transaction Server's MMC. Figure 7.23 shows Windows 2000 Server's MMC. No snap-ins have been installed in the Windows 2000 MMC. We'll do that soon.

FIGURE 7.22

Microsoft Management Console for Internet Information Server 4 and Microsoft Transaction Server

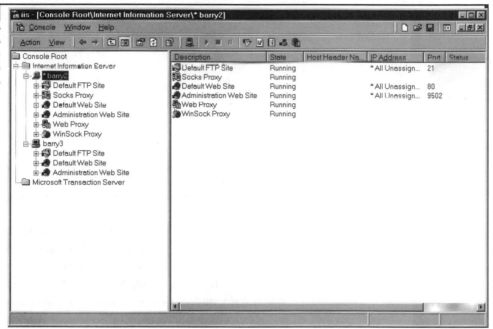

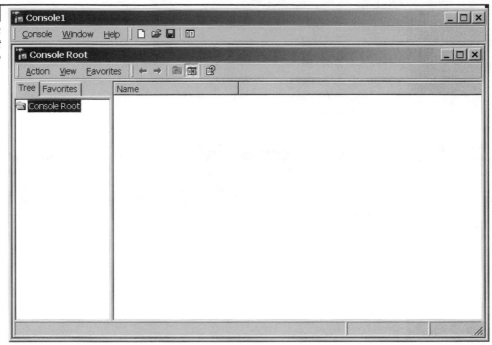

Let's focus on the Windows 2000 MMC shown in Figure 7.23. Each MMC can hold many instances of a snap-in, although this make sense only if each snap-in of the same kind is for a different entity in your Windows 2000 Server world (for example, a separate snap-in for managing each of two remote Windows 2000 servers). You can have as many MMCs as you want, and you can mix and match MMCs to your heart's content. You save each MMC under a different name, and you can open one or more MMCs at any time. You might want to use different MMCs to manage Active Directory, your local computer, and Exchange 2000, for example.

To open a new console, select Program Menu ➤ Run; type **MMC** into the Open field, and click OK. To add a snap-in to MMC, just select Console ➤ Add/Remove Snap-in. This opens the Add/Remove Snap-in dialog box shown in Figure 7.24. Click Add to open the Add Standalone Snap-in dialog box (see Figure 7.25).

FIGURE 7.24

Preparing to add a snap-in to a new instance of Microsoft Management Console

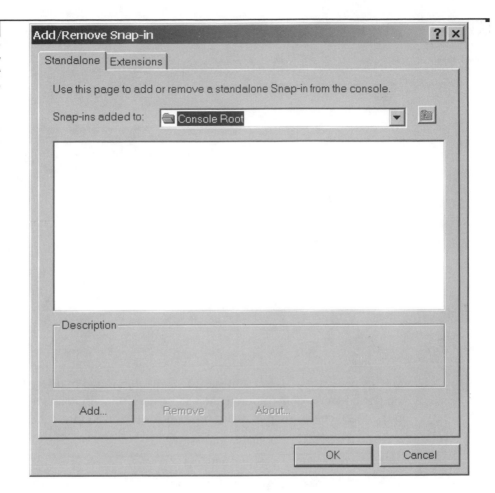

FIGURE 7.25

*Adding a snap-in to a
new instance of
Microsoft Management
Console*

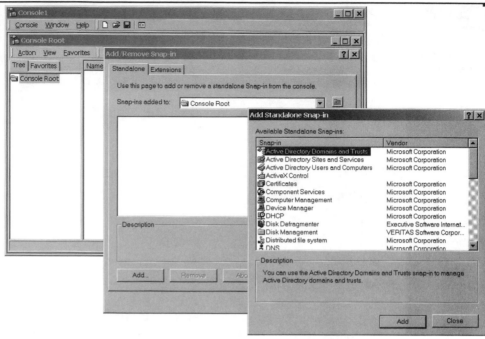

To add a new snap-in, select it in the Add Standalone Snap-in dialog box, and click Add. When you're done, close the Add Standalone Snap-in dialog box, and click OK on the Add/Remove Snap-in dialog box. Go ahead and add the following snap-ins:

- Active Directory Domains and Trusts
- Active Directory Sites and Services
- Active Directory Users and Computers
- Computer Management (for your local computer)
- DHCP
- DNS
- Event Viewer (for your local computer)

What's this *local computer* stuff? If you're a fugitive from NT 4, you'll remember that both Server Manager and Event Viewer let you partially manage activities on computers other than your own. You did this within the Server Manager or Event Viewer for your local computer. Windows 2000 Server offers the same capability and more, but by using an instance of Computer Manager for each computer that you want to manage. Here you only set up a snap-in on the server you just installed, for the server you just installed, your *local server*. But, if they existed and you needed to manage them, you could also have set up Computer Management snap-ins for other servers and managed those servers from the same instance of MMC. As you'll see, this snap-in does lots more than NT's Server Manager, but it's Windows 2000's way of providing remote computer management similar to what you had with NT 4.

The same goes for Event Viewer. The instance of the Event Viewer snap-in that you just installed lets you view the event logs on your local server. You can also install instances of the Event Viewer snap-in for other servers that you need to manage and to which you have access.

Now size the two MMC windows so that they look like the MMC shown in Figure 7.26. Save this particular instance of MMC by selecting Save As from the File menu. Then, when you need it, just select Start Menu ➢ Programs ➢ Administrative Tools and the name under which you saved this MMC.

Okay, we're ready to use MMC to do some preliminary exploring and a bit of serious work. Let's start by looking at Active Directory.

FIGURE 7.26

An instance of MMC ready for use

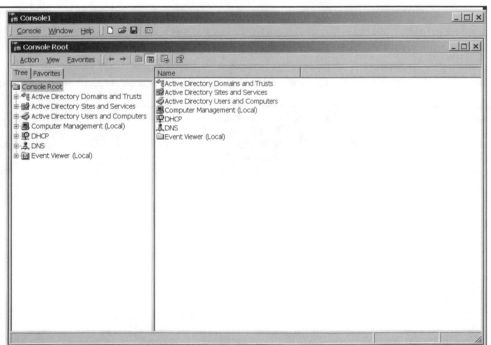

A Quick Look at Active Directory

 WARNING If the server is a domain controller, read this section and complete the hands-on part. If this server is a standalone server, read through this section, but don't do the hands-on part. Remember my discussions in Chapters 5 and 6 on division of responsibility for Windows 2000 and Exchange 2000 management? If your organization won't let you touch Active Directory, then much of this section either will be hands-off or will have to happen on a test server. I do encourage you to go the test-server route. Even if you'll never touch Active Directory in the real world, you need to understand it and how it works to do an effective job as an Exchange 2000 system manager.

I've talked much about Active Directory in this book. Given its central role, I can think of no better place to start our exploration of Windows 2000 Server. For now, we'll concentrate on users and computers, so open the tree for Active Directory Users and Computers. Figure 7.27 shows the domain container (mine is bgerber.com) and its five default subcontainers. The Builtin container holds security groups created during installation. Any computers in your domain are placed in the Computers container—that is, any computers except for domain controllers. These live in the Domain Controllers container. Because there is one and only one computer in your new domain and it is a domain controller, you should see nothing in the Computers container and just your new computer in the Domain Controllers container.

FIGURE 7.27

The Active Directory Users and Computers domain container and default subcontainers

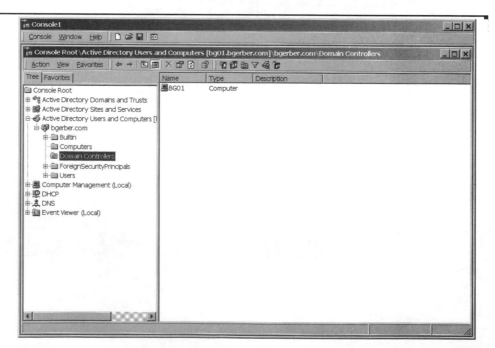

The ForeignSecurityPrincipals container holds security information for domains other than the current domain. These can be domains in the same forest or in another forest. Because you currently have only one domain, you shouldn't see anything in this container.

You will come to know and love the Users container. This is where you create users and, after Exchange 2000 is installed, Exchange users, contacts, and distribution groups. This is the Windows 2000 Server equivalent of NT 4's User Manager for Domains. Figure 7.28 shows the Users container on my newly installed server. NT Server 4 users should have no difficulty identifying most of the users and groups in the container.

FIGURE 7.28
The Active Directory Users and Computer Users container

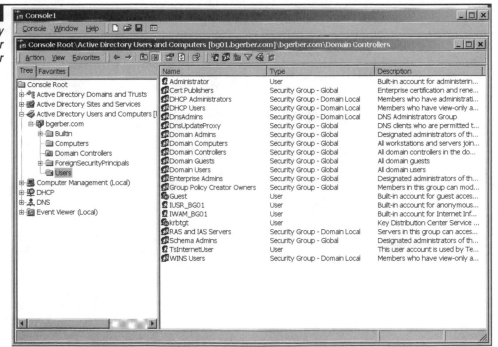

Here's how to create a new user. Right-click the Users container. Then select New ➢ User from the pop-up menu. See Figure 7.29. On the New Object User Wizard, shown in Figure 7.30, fill in the First Name, Initials, and Last Name fields. The Full Name field is automatically filled in (you can edit it, if you want). Next, enter the User logon name. The pre-Windows 2000 (NT) logon name is filled in automatically (you can edit it, if you need to).

NOTE Instead of right-clicking on objects in your MMC to view and select from your options, you can use the Action menu (see Figure 7.29). Just select an object and open the Action menu to see your options.

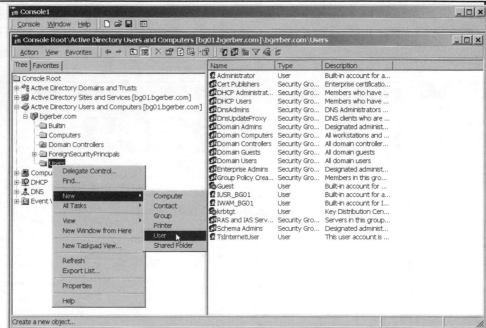

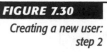

FIGURE 7.30

*Creating a new user:
step 2*

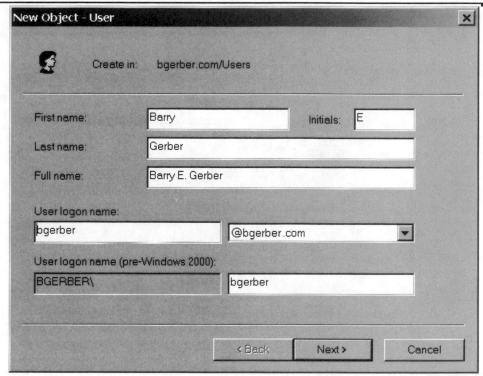

Click Next, and enter a password and select any special options relating to the password (see Figure 7.31). Finally, review the information presented in the dialog box in Figure 7.32, and click Finish. Your new user shows up at the end of the list in the right pane of MMC. To get the list in the correct alphabetical order, click the gray column header labeled Name in the pane at the right.

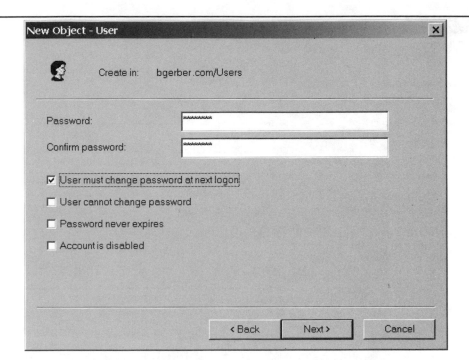

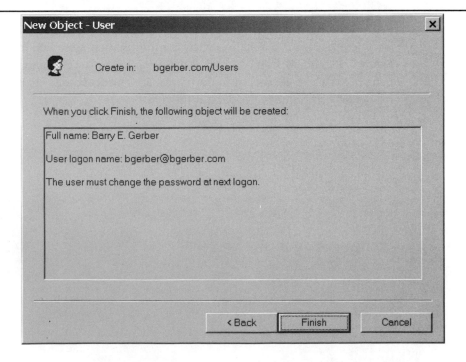

The new user account that you just created for yourself will be able to log into your domain and function with minimal rights. Windows 2000 Server comes equipped with some of the very best security features around. We'll talk about some of them in later chapters. Suffice it to say that you'll need to spend some time working out the details of you security system and implementing it.

Don't give your account any more rights than you would give a standard user. That way, you'll be able to test to see whether a particular setup, such as Outlook client access to an Exchange 2000 server, works for a typical user. When you need to do administrator-like tasks, log in as Administrator or as a user with just enough rights to complete a specific task. You can also use the Run As feature of Windows 2000 to run an application as a user with adequate rights to run the application. For example, to run a saved MMC as Administrator, when you're logged in to a different Windows 2000 account, find and right-click Start menu ➤ Programs ➤ Administrative Tools and then the name of the saved MMC. Then select Run As from the pop-up menu. Enter the username, password, and Windows domain on the Run As Another User dialog box, and click OK to start the MMC.

Configuring DHCP and Dynamic DNS

This section covers three tasks relating to DHCP and DNS:

- Configuring DHCP to automatically assign IP addresses to computers on your network

- Enabling Dynamic DNS

- Configuring DHCP to automatically assign fixed IP addresses to computers on your network

Each of these topics is discussed next.

Configuring DHCP to Automatically Assign IP Addresses to Computers on Your Network

 WARNING If this server is a standalone server, read through this section, but don't do the hands-on part. If the server is a domain controller, read the section and complete the hands-on part.

Windows 2000 networking is based on the TCP/IP protocol. Every workstation or server in your Windows 2000 network requires at least one IP address. You can manually assign these addresses, or you can use the Dynamic Host Configuration Protocol (DHCP) to automatically assign the addresses. Addresses are leased to a computer for a given period of time (usually several days). When the lease is up, the computer needs to re-lease an IP address. Unless you reserve an address for a specific computer, the computer may get a different IP address.

Open the DHCP tree in your MMC and select the DHCP container for your computer (see Figure 7.33). One of the nice things about Windows 2000 is the way in which it pretty much tells you what you need to do to configure any particular component. You can see what I mean in the right pane of Figure 7.33. Let's do as instructed in Figure 7.33.

FIGURE 7.33

The DHCP container for a Windows 2000 server

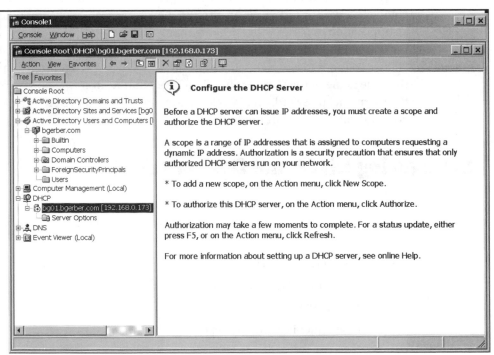

A scope is a range of addresses for DHCP to lease out. Scopes can also contain information about routers, DNS servers, and other things. One DHCP server can support many scopes. To create your new scope, select Action ➢ New Scope to start the New Scope Wizard. Click Next, and give your new scope a name, as I have in Figure 7.34. Then click Next and enter an address range and subnet mask information. See Figure 7.35. If you're not sure about all of this, check with your network management group. If your Windows 2000 network will be isolated from your organization's network and the Internet, you can use the values in Figure 7.34.

FIGURE 7.34

Naming a DHCP scope

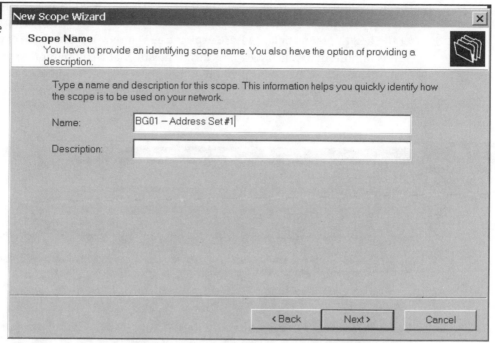

FIGURE 7.35

Entering address range and subnet mask information for a DHCP scope

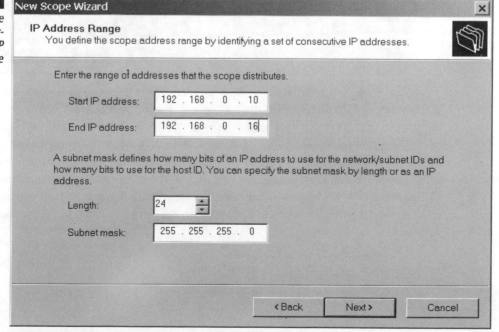

The next wizard page enables you to tell DHCP to exclude addresses in the range that you just gave it. For the time being, you probably don't need to use this page. Next, set the length of time before a lease expires (see Figure 7.36). This lease expiration stuff is important to remember. Basically, it means that a computer that gets its IP address from a DHCP address pool might not get the same IP address every time that its lease expires. In a bit, I'll show you how to guarantee that a computer gets the same address every time.

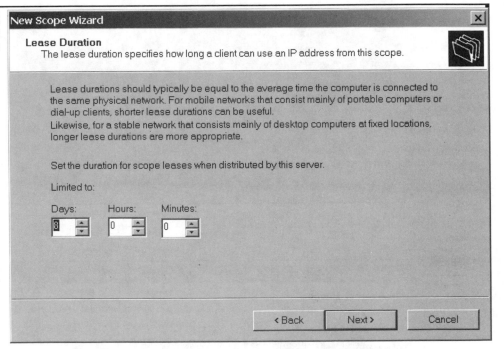

FIGURE 7.36

Setting lease duration time for a DHCP scope

You'll then be offered an opportunity to set the addresses of gateway routers, DNS servers, and so on that should be given to a computer along with its IP address (see Figure 7.37). This is a very nice feature of DHCP. With it, you don't have to manually configure each computer on your network with this information. Giving out an IP address lease is only part of the DHCP service. Automatically handing out router, DNS, and other information ensures that, without any manual intervention on your part, a computer will be capable of communicating not only within the narrow confines of its physical network, but also with the world outside that network.

FIGURE 7.37

Opting to set router, DNS, and other options for a DHCP scope

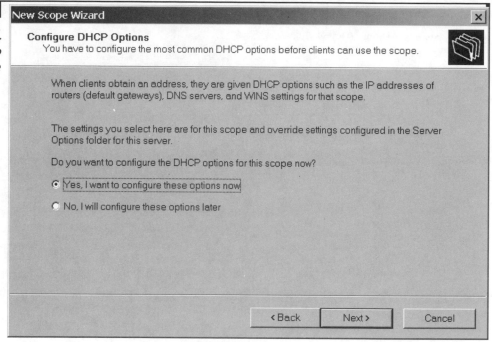

Assuming that you've opted to configure DHCP scope options, you'll see the two wizard pages in Figures 7.38 and 7.39. On the Router (Default Gateway) page, enter the address or addresses of routers that let computers access IP addresses other than those on their physical network. I'm adding the address 192.168.0.49. Be sure to click Add after you've entered an address.

FIGURE 7.38

*Entering router infor-
mation for a DHCP
scope*

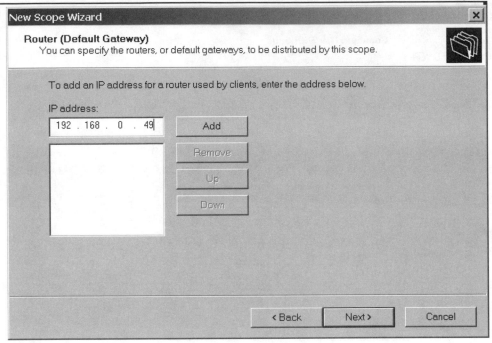

On the Domain Name and DNS Servers page, enter the name of the domain that you
want affixed to the computer's name to create a full domain name and the addresses
of one or more DNS servers. As you can see in Figure 7.39, I'm using bgerber.com for
the parent domain for this DHCP scope. So, if I go looking for a computer called
BG04, the assumption in DNS is that I'm looking for a computer with a full name of
BG04.bgerber.com. In the DNS Server IP Address field, I'm adding the IP address of
my one and only domain controller server, the very one that I'm configuring right
now. That way, all new computers on the network will get the address as the DNS
server.

FIGURE 7.39

Entering parent domain and DNS server information for a DHCP scope

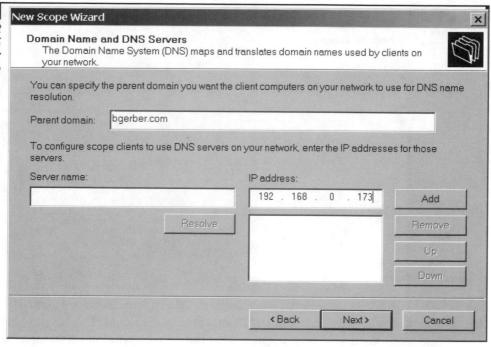

So, what if I add or remove routers or DNS servers over time? That's the real beauty of DHCP. I just go in and add or remove the addresses in DHCP; from that point on, all computers get the new addresses when their leases are renewed.

The next wizard page enables you to configure your Windows Internet Naming Service (WINS) setup. If you need WINS, as you will if you're going to integrate with NT Server 4 networks, I'll leave it to you to do the setup.

On the next wizard page, you can choose whether to activate the DHCP scope that you just created (see Figure 7.40). Activate it and click Next. You're just about done! Click Finish on the last wizard page.

FIGURE 7.40

Choosing to activate a DHCP scope

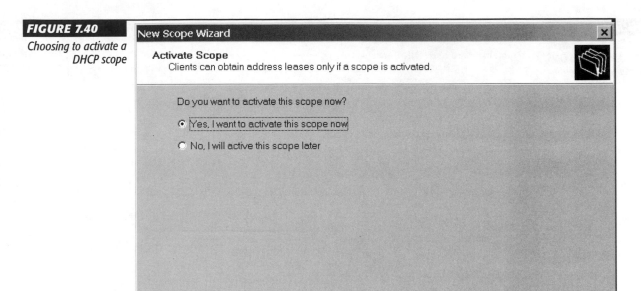

Figure 7.41 shows what you'll see next. True to form, Windows 2000 tells you that you must authorize your DHCP server before it can run. This is a nice security touch, ensuring that servers (services) don't run on your Windows 2000 server without explicit authorization. Notice that the little arrow on the computer icon on the DCHP container for your server is pointing down and is red. That's how Window 2000 signals you that a server process isn't running.

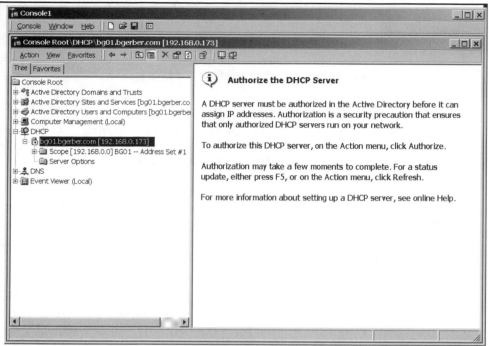

FIGURE 7.41

A DHCP server ready to be authorized

To authorize your DHCP server, follow the instructions in the right pane of your MMC: select Action ➢ Authorize. Wait a bit and then select Refresh from the Action menu. The little arrow turns green and points up. All is well.

Turning On Dynamic DNS

 WARNING If this server is a standalone server, you can skip this section. If this server is at least your first domain controller, read and complete the hands-on part of this section. If you don't complete this task, your Exchange 2000 Server will not become a part of your DNS domain and will thus not be available to users trying to open their mailboxes or to other servers trying to send mail to your Exchange server.

The Domain Name System (DNS) contains the names of computers, called hosts, and the IP addresses associated with them. Traditionally, you make manual entries into DNS for each computer in your network. Manual entry is not only time-consuming, but it also doesn't work when you're using DHCP. If a computer can get a different IP address from DHCP every time its address lease expires, your manual DNS entry is no longer correct.

Enter Dynamic DNS. It lets you assign IP addresses to servers and workstations using DHCP, and then have DNS entries for them created and updated dynamically in your DNS namespace. Even if a server or workstation is assigned a different IP address when its address lease expires, Dynamic DNS ensures that the computer and its current IP address get properly placed in your DNS system.

 NOTE   Dynamic DNS is based on a standard promulgated by the Internet Engineering Task Force. The standard can be found in Request for Comment (RFC) 2136, "Dynamic Updates in the Domain Name System (DNS Updates)."

Here's how to turn on Dynamic DNS. You'll remember that DNS was installed during initial installation. Not only was it installed, but it was configured at the basic level, as Figure 7.42 makes abundantly clear. The domain bgerber.com was created along with a domain called simply "." or *dot*. I discussed the dot domain in Chapter 3, in the section "Active Directory: Five Major Architectural Components." In addition, BG01, my new server, was added to the zone bgerber.com and was linked with the IP address 192.168.0.173. At this point on BG01 I could open a command prompt and type in **ping bg01** or **ping bg01.bgerber.com** and get a response. And I didn't have to do a thing.

FIGURE 7.42

A DNS zone created during initial installation of Windows 2000 Server

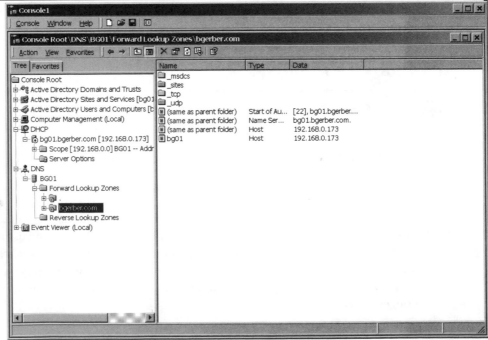

To turn on Dynamic DNS, right-click your DNS domain container. Mine is the high-lighted container called bgerber.com in Figure 7.42. Then select Properties. On the Properties dialog box for your DNS domain container, select Yes from the Allow Dynamic Updates drop-down list (see Figure 7.43).

FIGURE 7.43

Activating Dynamic DNS

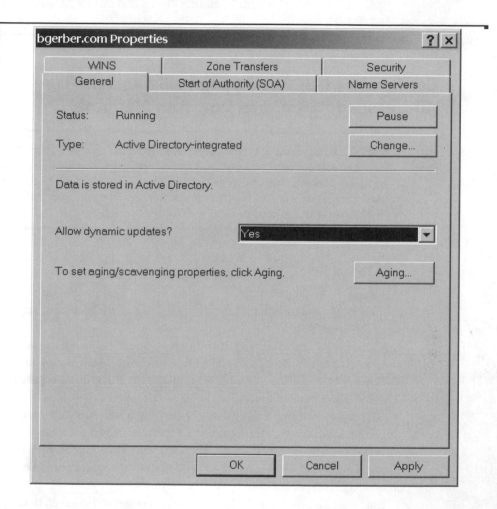

That's it. Dynamic DNS is on and ready to do its thing. The next time a new computer with its DNS client enabled logs into your new network, not only will it get all the information that DHCP has to offer, but it also will be automatically registered in the DNS. By default, all newly installed modern Microsoft Windows clients are configured to use DHCP, so you don't have to do a thing after installation to enable DHCP. Amazing! All this used to require such manual drudgery.

NOTE You can configure Dynamic DNS to work with pre-Windows 2000 clients such as NT or Windows 95/98 clients. Right-click your DHCP scope, and select Properties. Then tab over to the DNS page on the Properties dialog box that pops up. Select the option Always Update DNS and Enable Updates for DNS Clients That Do Not Support Dynamic Updates, and click OK.

Configuring DHCP to Dynamically Assign Fixed IP Addresses to Computers on Your Network

 NOTE If this server is a standalone server, you can skip this section. If this server is at least your first domain controller, read and complete the hands-on part of this section. If you don't complete this task, your Exchange 2000 Server will not become a part of your DNS domain and will thus not be available to users trying to open their mailboxes, or to other servers trying to send mail to your Exchange server.

In Chapter 8, you'll install a Windows 2000 standalone server and then install Exchange 2000 Server on it. Before installing Windows 2000 on your soon-to-be Exchange server, you must set up your domain so that the new server can easily enter your network. You can do that right here using a special capability of DHCP called *address reservation*.

Address reservation allows DHCP to automatically allocate the same IP address to a server each time the computer's address lease expires. That way, your Exchange server will always have the same IP address. And, everything is done on the DHCP server side. You don't have to touch the client.

Address reservations are important especially when outside servers need to find your Exchange server's address. It takes a few minutes to a few days for a new DNS entry to propagate across the Internet. So, if your Exchange server's IP address changed every day, servers trying to send mail to the server could be out of touch for an unacceptable period of time.

You could assign a hard IP address to your new server. However, that would mean you'd have to go through hell and high water any time you needed to change that address. With a DHCP address reservation, all you have to do is remove the reservation and run a program called IPCONFIG.EXE on the server with the lease to release the old address. At that point, you've reclaimed the address and can use it for any other purpose.

Okay, let's get going. I assume here that you have access to the Administrator account for your domain controller. If you don't, someone else will have to do the following. Go to your domain controller. As you may remember my domain controller is called BG01. Log in as Administrator.

Here's how to set up a DHCP reservation. Start up your Microsoft Management Console (MMC), and click open the DHCP container until it looks like the one in Figure 7.44. Now, do what the right pane of the Reservations subcontainer says: Select New Reservation from the Action menu.

FIGURE 7.44

Ready to create a new DHCP IP address reservation using the Microsoft Management Console DHCP snap-in

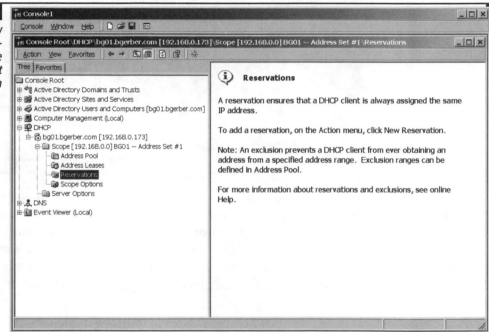

This brings up the New Reservation dialog box shown in Figure 7.45. Give the reservation a name, and enter the IP address that you want to assign to your new server.

FIGURE 7.45

Creating a new DHCP
IP address reservation

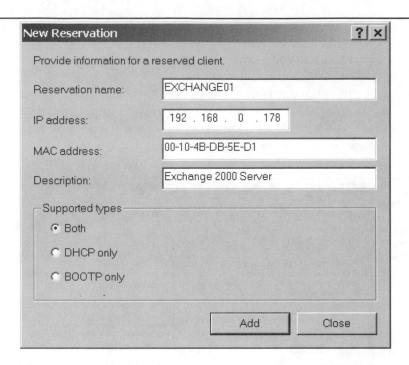

Next type in the Media Access Control (MAC) address of the network adapter to which you want to assign the address. The MAC address is a unique address that's burned into each network adapter when it is manufactured. An international standard ensures that no network adapter, no matter who makes it, will have the same MAC address as any other network adapter. That's how DHCP knows which machine to give the reserved address to when contacted by a bevy of IP address hungry computers.

How do you find out the MAC address of a network adapter? Good question. For some adapters, the MAC address is actually on a little sticker on the adapter or on the box that the adapter came in. Additionally, most adapters come with a configuration utility that can be run under MS DOS. Among other things, the utility tells you the MAC address of the adapter. For example, 3Com's 3C90x line of adapters comes with a program called 3C90XCFG.EXE. When you boot up under DOS (including with a Windows 98 boot disk) and run 3C90XCFG.EXE, the first screen shows you the MAC address (called Node Address here). If, by some chance, before you install Windows 2000 on the computer, it is up and running under Windows 2000 (or NT 4), you can open a command prompt and type **IPCONFIG -ALL | MORE**. The MAC address is listed as the physical address, usually on the first screen right under the description of the adapter itself. Copy the address exactly as you see it, including the dashes. On

Windows 95 and 98 computers, run WINIPCFG from an MS DOS prompt. The MAC address is in the Adapter Address field.

It may seem like a heck of a lot of work to find an adapter's MAC address. Actually, it's quite simple, and when you see how Dynamic DNS simplifies network management, you'll agree that it's worth the little extra work required to obtain the address.

Next, if you want, you can enter some text in the New Reservation box's Description field, and click Add. Leave Supported Types set to Both. When the address has been created, your Reservations container should look something like the one in Figure 7.46. The router, DNS servers, and DNS domain name information that you set in the section "Configuring DHCP and Dynamic DNS," earlier in this chapter, should have been inherited by the reservation (see the right pane in Figure 7.46).

FIGURE 7.46

The newly created IP address reservation, complete with inherited router, DNS server, and domain name information

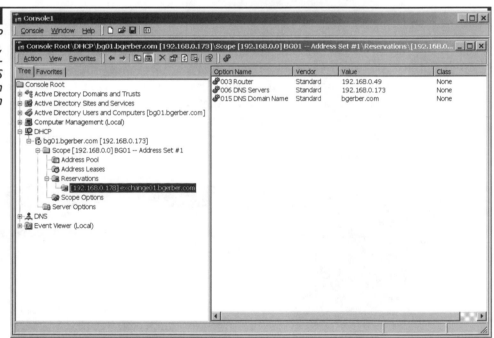

That's it. Your DHCP server is configured to provide your Exchange server a fixed IP address when you install it in the next chapter. And, remember, because you've turned Dynamic DNS on, your server will also be automatically registered in your domain DNS. That's about as easy as it gets.

TIP You can use DHCP address reservations for any computer that is part of your network. This includes most domain controllers. The only computers on your network that must absolutely have fixed addresses assigned to their network adapters when Windows 2000 Server is installed are domain controllers that serve as DHCP servers. For safety, you should be sure that there are at least two DHCP servers on any network segment. You don't want your network to be without an IP address if your one and only DHCP server fails. When you set up additional DHCP servers, remember that, except for reserved addresses, the specific IP addresses in each server's address pool(s) must be unique.

Configuring Unallocated Disk Space

Now let's get to some tasks that directly impact your server. If you installed more than one hard disk drive in your server, or if the volume that you installed Windows 2000 Server on is smaller than the disk drive on which the boot partition resides, you need to set up and format remaining unallocated disk space.

We'll use another snap-in to do this task. It's located in the Computer Management (Local) snap-in of the MMC that you created earlier. Open the snap-in's tree, and select the Disk Management folder. If you have one or more disk drives that haven't been set up, in a moment or two you'll see the Write Signature and Upgrade Disk Wizard, shown in Figure 7.47.

FIGURE 7.47

The Write Signature and Upgrade Disk Wizard

This wizard performs a couple simple tasks. First, it writes a signature on whatever new physical disks you select, creating an empty basic disk. A disk's signature is used to store information about it in the Windows 2000 registry. After the signature is written, the wizard upgrades the basic disk to a dynamic disk.

Dynamic disks are new to Windows 2000 Server. You can do a number of things with them, including mirroring, setting up various levels of Redundant Array of Independent Disk (RAID) storage, spanning across multiple physical drives, or striping a volume across multiple drives for better performance. You can do most of these tasks without rebooting your server. Add to this the capability to set up a Computer Management snap-in for servers other than your local one, and you've got a tremendous amount of control over storage on your Windows 2000 network.

 WARNING Although software implementation of the redundant storage solutions discussed previously works just fine, you should strongly consider implementing these solutions in hardware. Hardware implementations include smart disk controllers that do work that must be done by software run on your server's CPU. Software-based redundant storage solutions can significantly affect performance by placing a heavy load on a computer's CPU.

Back to the wizard. Click Next, and you're offered the opportunity to select the physical disks on which you want to write a signature (see Figure 7.48). Because I have only one new physical disk in my new server, the wizard offers me only the opportunity to write a signature on it.

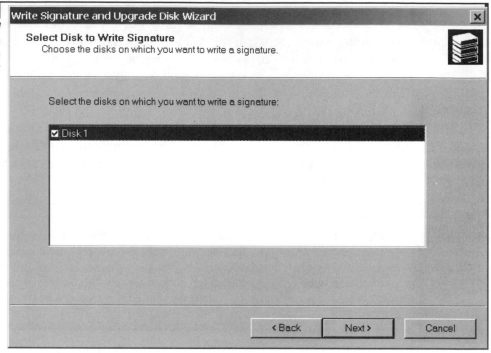

When you click Next, the signature is quickly written on the disk, and the disk becomes a basic disk. Then the Select Disks to Upgrade Wizard page is displayed. Your disk should already be selected for upgrade to dynamic disk status. Click Next once more, and on the final page, accept the wizard's offer to upgrade your disk to a dynamic disk.

When the wizard is finished, your server's disk configuration shows up in the right pane of the MMC. Figure 7.49 shows my disk set up after processing by the wizard. In the top pane on the right side is a list of my current volumes. Because no volumes have been created on my new disk, only one volume is displayed; this is the boot volume created during Windows 2000 Server installation.

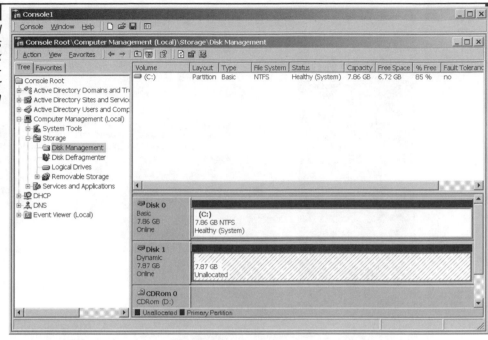

My disks are displayed graphically in the lower pane on the right side. There you see my first disk with its healthy NTFS partition. Disk 1 is the disk that was just processed by the Write Signature and Upgrade Disk Wizard. It's now ready for me to create one or more new volumes on it.

To start creating volumes, right-click your unallocated physical disk space and select Create Volume. This starts the Create Volume Wizard, shown in Figure 7.50. Click Next on the wizard to select the type of volume that you want to create (see Figure 7.51). Assuming that you've installed but one disk, you'll be offered only the option of creating a simple volume.

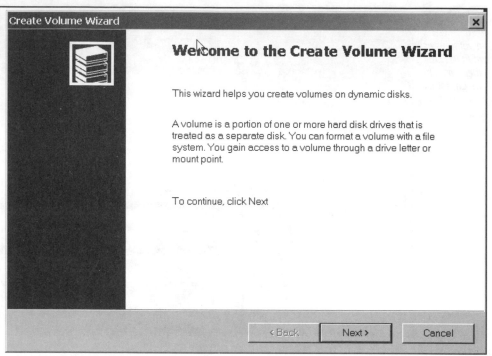

FIGURE 7.50

Starting up the Create Volume Wizard

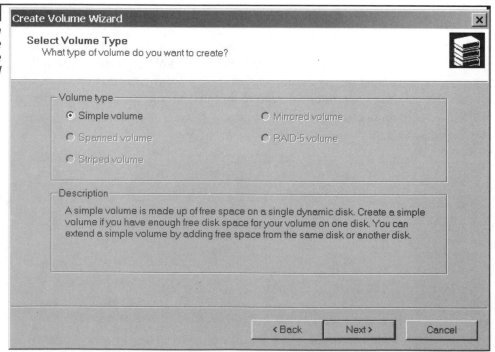

FIGURE 7.51

Accepting the creation of a simple volume using the Create Volume Wizard

On the next wizard page, you select the disks to be included in a volume and set the size that you want the volume to be. In Figure 7.52, my single unallocated disk has been automatically selected, and I've accepted the default option to use all the space on the disk for the new volume. If you have unallocated space available on multiple physical disks, you can create volumes that span as many or few of those disks as you want.

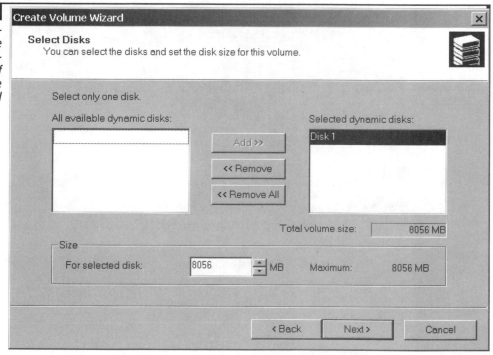

FIGURE 7.52

Accepting default values for the disk to be included in a new volume and the size of the volume using the Create Volume Wizard

On the next wizard page shown in Figure 7.53, you assign a drive letter or mount point for your new volume. Drive letters are old stuff. Mount points, borrowed from the Unix operating system, are new to Windows 2000 Server. Mount points finally let you create volumes unlimited by the number of available drive letters. I've chosen to assign a drive letter to my new volume.

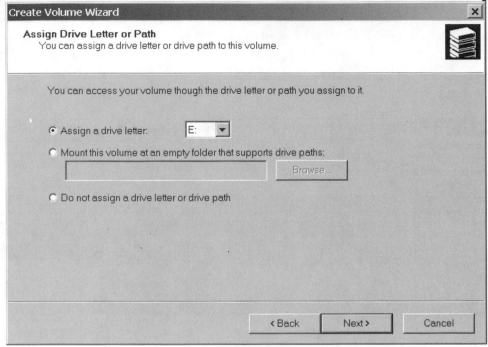

You select formatting parameters for your volume using the next wizard page (see Figure 7.54). I've chosen to format my new volume with the NTFS file system, I've accepted the default allocation unit size, and I've labeled my volume LocalDisk E. You can't go wrong for now following my lead.

FIGURE 7.54

Selecting formatting parameters for a new volume using the Create Volume Wizard

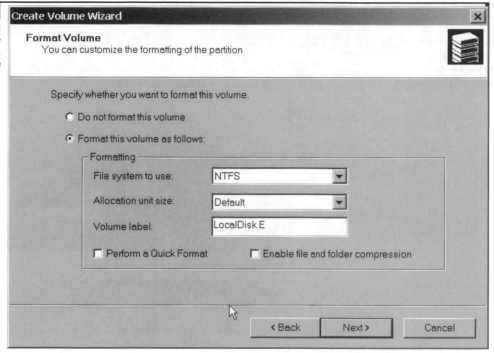

Finally, the wizard shows you what it's about to do. Click Finish, and the wizard begins formatting your new volume. This takes some time. When it has finished its work, the wizard tells you that your computer needs to be rebooted. Go ahead and reboot.

When your server has finished rebooting, the right pane of \Computer Management (Local)\Storage\Disk Management in your MMC should look something like the one in Figure 7.55. Your new volume has been created and is in a healthy state. What else could you ask for?

FIGURE 7.55

*A newly created vol-
ume as shown in the
Disk Management sub-
folder of the Computer
Management snap-in*

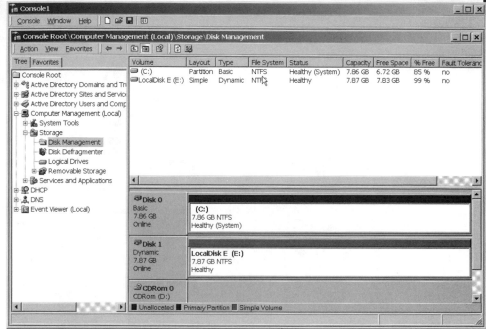

You create volumes on dynamic disks. As with NT Server 4, you create partitions on what
are now called basic disks. Notice that in Figure 7.55, the C volume is on a basic disk.
This basic disk has a single partition that takes up all the space on the physical disk. If
you have extra space on your first physical disk, you can create additional partitions on
it, just as you can create volumes on a dynamic disk. Creating a partition is much like
creating a volume, so I won't provide specific instructions here. To start creating a partition, right-click on unallocated space on a basic disk and select Create Partition.

Don't Forget Shutdown

Like all good operating systems, Windows 2000 Server must be shut down; you should
never just turn off a Windows 2000 server. Windows 2000 Server buffers a lot of data
to RAM before writing it to disk. Although the writes from RAM are done quickly, on a
busy server there's always data waiting in the buffers. A graceful shutdown ensures that
this data is all written out to disk. To shut down a server, click the Start menu icon and
select Shutdown. You can select from three options: Shut Down, Restart, or Log Off. If
you pick Shut Down, don't turn off the computer until you see a message telling you
that it's okay to do so. Modern computers will actually power themselves off when the
server has completed all shutdown tasks.

Installing an Uninterruptible Power Supply

An uninterruptible power supply (UPS) takes power from the wall socket and feeds it to a battery to keep it charged. The UPS continuously feeds power from its battery to your computer through internal power-conversion circuitry. When power from the wall socket fails, the UPS battery continues to supply power to your computer, letting it run until wall-socked power returns or the battery is exhausted and, if so configured, shutting down the computer before UPS battery power is exhausted.

UPSs with Universal Serial Bus (USB) connectors are also available. These offer an attractive alternative to the finicky RS-232 connection of a UPS to your server.

As I noted in Chapter 5, a UPS should be considered part of your Windows 2000 Server installation. Let's install one right away.

The UPS Itself

Buy a UPS with "online" circuitry; these tend to be the best and most responsive in power outages. This also should be one that can be controlled by a Windows 2000 server, so it should be equipped with an RS-232 port that you connect by a cable to one of the server's serial ports. Get the RS-232 cable from the UPS's vendor, if at all possible; then you won't have to mess with that old devil known as RS-232 interfacing.

Windows 2000 Server's built-in UPS software listens to the UPS and can shut down the server gracefully, just as if you'd done it manually. Get a UPS that can detect and signal both a wall socket power failure and a low battery. With low-battery information available, Windows 2000 Server doesn't have to begin a shutdown immediately on power failure. If AC power returns before the low-battery signal, no shutdown needs to occur at all.

 WARNING Be sure to put each of your Windows 2000 servers on its own UPS. Most UPSs usually have one serial port and can thus automatically shut down only a single server. If you need a UPS for multiple servers, take a look at the ones that include Ethernet ports and that include Simple Network Monitoring Protocol (SNMP)-related software.

Configuring UPS Support

To configure UPS support in Windows 2000 Server, select Start ➤ Settings ➤ Control Panel, and double-click Power Options. This opens the Power Options Properties dialog box. The first three pages on this dialog box are for managing your computer's use of power. The fourth page, shown on the left side of Figure 7.56, is for UPS management.

American Power Conversion (APC) created custom user interfaces and default settings for its UPS product line. These were in the initial Windows 2000 release. Other manufacturers are sure to follow with their own interfaces. For now, owners of UPSs from other manufacturers can use a generic interface and set of defaults.

To select a UPS to configure, click Select on the Power Options Properties dialog box to open the UPC Selection dialog box. In Figure 7.56, I've chosen to set up an APC Backup-UPS model. To select the generic interface and defaults, select Generic from the Select Manufacturer drop-down list on the UPS Selection dialog box. Click Finish on the UPS Selection dialog box when you're done choosing a UPS model.

FIGURE 7.56

Selecting an interface and default settings for a UPS

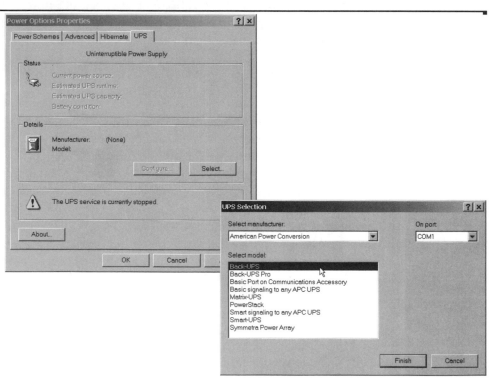

Next, click Configure on the Power Options Properties dialog box to open the UPS Configuration dialog box (see the right side of Figure 7.57). Unless you have reason to do otherwise, accept the defaults for notifications.

What's a Notification?

Windows 2000 Server notifications are sent to the desktops of a specific list of computers or users. By default, notifications go to the user Administrator on the computer. To add users to this list, you must run a sort of secret program, SRVMGR.EXE. To run it, select Start ➢ Run, and enter **srvmgr.exe** in the Open field. Then select Computer ➢ Properties, and click Alerts. Use the resultant Alerts dialog box to add computers or users that are to receive alerts. The interface is pretty primitive, offering no dialog box for selecting computers and users, so, you'll need to know the names of the computers you want to add. NT Server 4 users will recognize SRVMGR.EXE as a stripped-down version of NT 4's Server Manager program.

I strongly suggest that you set a critical alarm and specify a file to run when the critical alarm fires and before your server is shut down. Be sure to allow lots of time for a smooth shutdown before the battery is likely to run out. The two-minute default setting for Minutes on Battery Before Critical Alarm should be fine. You want to be sure that the server doesn't crash due to lack of battery power before all buffered data has been written to your server's databases. You'll want to put a UPS on all your Windows 2000 server, including the ones that run Exchange 2000.

In Figure 7.57, I've told Windows 2000 Server to execute a batch file, END.BAT, before shutting down. This particular file deletes some temporary files that one of my applications writes and closes, but it leaves them on disk until the application itself is closed.

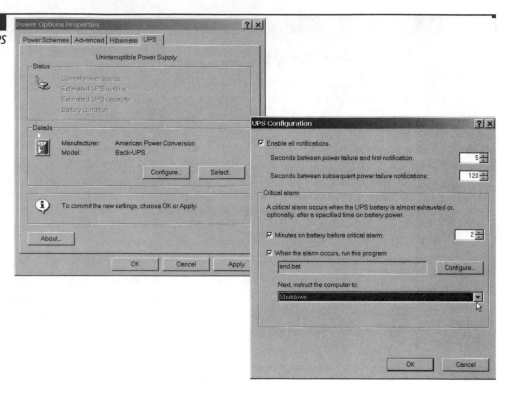

FIGURE 7.57

Configuring a UPS

That's it. Press OK to exit the two dialog boxes shown in Figure 7.57, and your UPS is configured.

 TIP Of course, you need to test your UPS regularly. Do the tests during off-hours, and warn users that you'll be taking the system down. Testing is simple: Just cut power to the UPS and make sure that everything goes as expected. Be sure to let the test go far enough for battery power to run out and for the UPS service to shut down the server. When testing, you should shut down key Windows 2000 services, especially Exchange 2000 services. If the UPS fails, you don't want to run the risk of destroying key Windows 2000 services-supported databases.

Some UPSs come with special software for Windows 2000 Server. This software replaces the UPS software that comes with Windows 2000 Server, providing such enhanced features as scheduled periodic testing of the UPS and monitoring of power quantity and quality over time. This software doesn't add much to the cost of a UPS, and it's well worth having.

Setting Up a Windows 2000 Server Backup

As I mentioned in Chapter 5, a variety of products are available for backing up Windows 2000 Server. The product comes with its own backup software, which is quite functional for local server backup if you're not using a tape autoloader. It's important to get some sort of backup going immediately on your Windows 2000 server, so let's get Windows 2000 Server's own backup program up and running right now.

Hardware

Okay, let me say it right at the start: Don't use anything other than 4mm, 8mm, or DLT SCSI-compatible tape drives. Forget those awful third-floppy minicartridge thingies that take forever to back up a byte of information to low-capacity tape cartridges. And don't mess with those fancy new units that use gigantic but relatively low-capacity (and high-priced) 3M cartridges. Stick with the proven, working, relatively inexpensive 4mm, 8mm, or DLT tape technologies. Whatever technology you decide on, go for more rather than less capacity. You'll need it sooner, rather than later.

If you have a larger computing environment, take a serious look at tape systems with autoloaders that allow you to put many tapes online at the same time. These save you from having to manually insert tapes into a drive when it's time to change to a new tape either because the tape change cycle dictates or because you've filled the tape sooner than expected. All this ensures that data gets backed up when it should, not the next morning after you and all your users have arrived at the office.

Installing a SCSI tape backup unit is easy. Just install an appropriate SCSI adapter and plug in the drive, being sure that your SCSI chain is properly terminated. You can use the same SCSI controller that you use for your disk drives, although you'll get better backup throughput if you use a separate controller for the tape drive, or at least a separate channel on the controller. Also be sure to use the shortest SCSI cables you can: When a SCSI cable chain (including the cable inside your computer that supports internal disk drives) gets too long, you'll start experiencing some pretty crazy data glitches on your disks and tape drives.

 TIP Windows 2000 Server comes with device drivers for a wide range of tape drives. The correct driver should be installed automatically the first time you boot with your new tape drive installed. If you need to provide a driver that Windows 2000 doesn't have, you'll be offered the opportunity after new tape hardware has been discovered.

Setting Up a Basic Backup

Our real interest in backups comes with Exchange 2000 Server. However, we're not ready to tackle Exchange backup right now. Nevertheless, you should have a backup in place immediately. So, right now I'll take you through a simple backup scenario using Windows 2000 Server's Backup program. In the next chapter, I'll show you how to back up Exchange Server.

We're going to schedule our backup, so we need to be sure that Windows 2000's Task Scheduler is running. In your MMC, go to \Computer Management (Local)\ Services and Applications\Services. Find Task Scheduler, and double-click it. Set startup type to Automatic, and click Start. When the service has started, click OK.

To open the Windows 2000 Server backup program, select Start ➤ Programs ➤ Accessories ➤ System Tools ➤ Backup. This is the Backup dialog box, shown in Figure 7.58. You can manually set up backups; that's what the Backup, Restore, and Schedule Jobs tabs are for. You can also use wizards to set up backup and restore jobs, and you can use a wizard to guide you through creation of an emergency repair disk here. Emergency repair disks are useful in restoring your system if key data becomes lost. You should create an emergency repair disk on a regular basis every time there is a change in your system, such as when you install a system update.

FIGURE 7.58

The Windows 2000 Server Backup dialog box

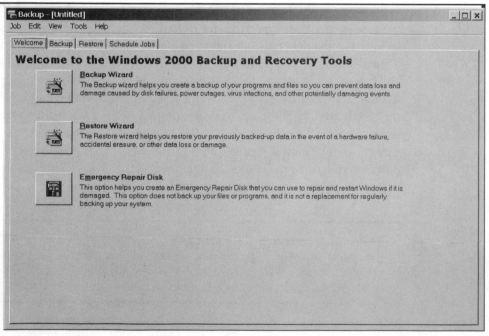

Let's set up a backup using the Backup Wizard. Click the Backup Wizard button to bring up the wizard (see Figure 7.59). Click Next for the What to Back Up wizard page shown in Figure 7.60. As you can see, you can choose to back up everything on your computer, selected files and disks on your computer or on the network, or system state data. The latter is useful if you're planning a change on your computer that might change the machine's registry or Active Directory schema. Restoring system state data lets you return your computer to its prechange state without having to restore an entire drive. System state data can be backed up and restored only on the local computer. Ensure that the default option, Back Up Everything on My Computer, is selected; then click Next. On the Where to Store the Backup page (see Figure 7.61), be sure that the correct backup media type is selected (mine is 4mm DDS). Because this is your first backup, leave New Media selected. When you have created one or more backups, the Backup media or file name drop-down list will show the tapes that contain these backups. Oh yes, be sure that there's a blank or newly erased tape in your tape drive.

 TIP Note that you can back up to disk as well as tape. You might find this capability useful for backing up a key set of files on a regular basis throughout the day.

FIGURE 7.59

The Windows 2000 Server Backup Wizard

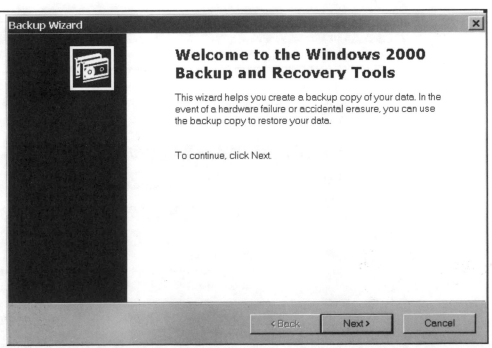

Backup Wizard

Welcome to the Windows 2000 Backup and Recovery Tools

This wizard helps you create a backup copy of your data. In the event of a hardware failure or accidental erasure, you can use the backup copy to restore your data.

To continue, click Next.

< Back   Next >   Cancel

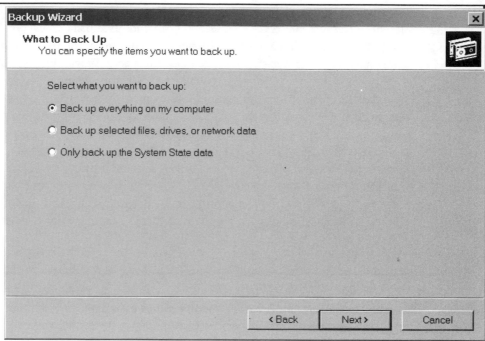

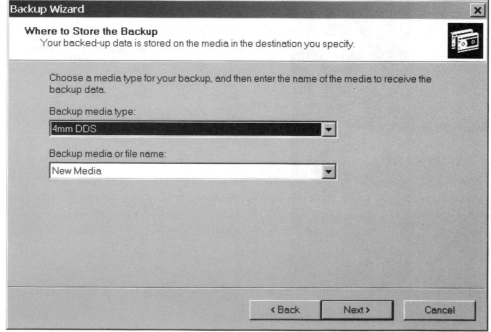

Click Next, and you'll see a page like the one in Figure 7.62. This page summarizes the backup as it stands at this point. But you don't have to stop here. By clicking the Advanced button, you can set up some more interesting and valuable options. Go ahead, click Advanced to bring up the first of the advanced options wizard pages (see Figure 7.63). Here you choose the type of backup that you want. This includes the way that you want files to be backed up and whether you want to back up files that have been migrated to near-line media. This second option is necessary now that Windows 2000 Server can move less-used files from disk to other media such as tape and bring them back if someone tries to use them.

You have five options for the way that you want files backed up:

Normal backup   Backs up all files that have been selected and marks them as having been backed up (clears or turns off what is called the *archive bit* for each file). When a file is changed or a new file is created, its archive bit is set to indicate that it is a candidate for backup.

Differential backup   Backs up all files with their archive bit set and does not clear the archive bit.

Incremental backup   Backs up all files with their archive bit set and clears the archive bit.

Copy backup   Backs up all selected files, but doesn't clear the archive bit.

Daily backup   Backs up all selected files that have been modified on the day of the backup, but doesn't clear the archive bit.

There's no need to back up every file every night. The usual practice is to back up an entire disk once a week (normal backup) and then to perform either a differential or incremental backup every other day of the week. Differential backups grow larger every day because you're backing up everything that changed on all previous days, plus whatever changed on the day of the backup. Incremental backups are smaller because you back up only what changed on the day of the backup. Differential back-ups are easier to restore because you need to restore only from the last normal backup and the last differential backup to fully restore a disk drive. With incremental back-ups, you must restore the last normal backup and all incremental backups done since the normal backup. Take your pick, depending on the issues raised previously and the capacity of your tape backup hardware. I'll leave it to you to decide whether you can benefit from copy and daily backups.

FIGURE 7.62

The Backup Wizard presents its backup plan and offers an opportunity to set advanced options.

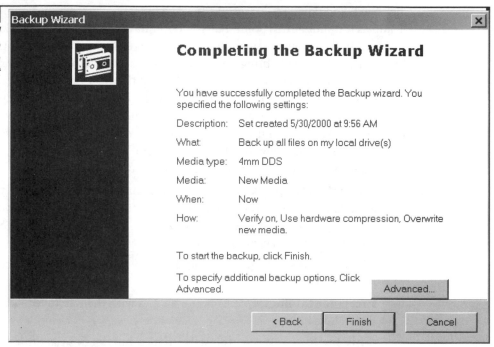

FIGURE 7.63

Using the Windows 2000 Server Backup Wizard to select the type of backup to be performed

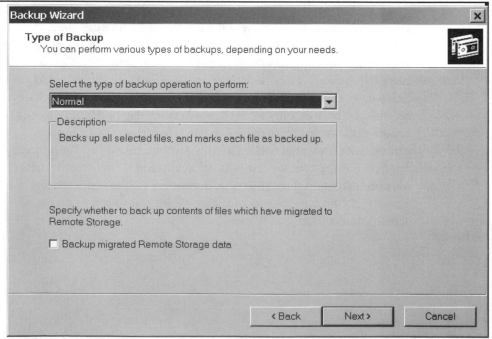

You use the next wizard page shown in Figure 7.64 to specify whether data should be verified after backup and whether hardware compression is to be used. Always select the first option. Select the second option, Use Hardware Compression, If Available, if you're sure that you'll always have the same kind of drive available to read the compressed data.

FIGURE 7.64

Using the Windows 2000 Server Backup Wizard to determine whether data verification and hardware compression should be used

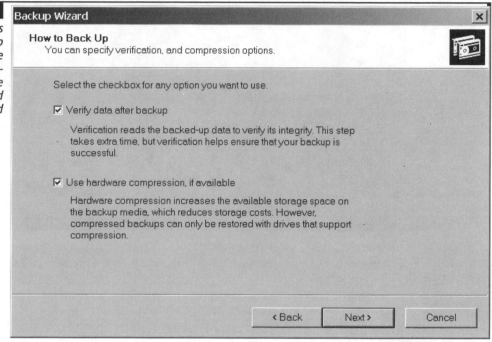

The Media Options wizard page in Figure 7.65 lets you choose whether to append to the tape or overwrite it. In a normal backup, you're offered only the option of replacing data on the media. You can also restrict access to the tape to only someone logged in as Administrator or the person setting up the backup.

FIGURE 7.65

Using the Windows 2000 Server Backup Wizard to specify whether the tape can be overwritten and who can access the tape

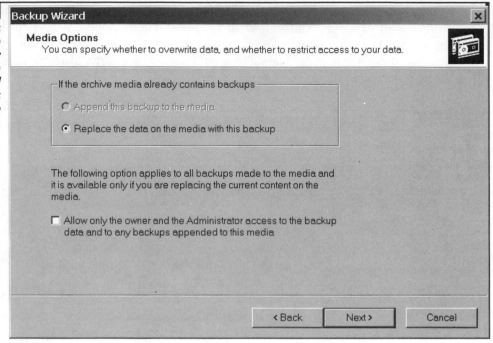

You use the Backup Label Wizard page, shown in Figure 7.66, to label both the backup and the tape. The tape label (media label) shows up on the drop-down list in Figure 7.61.

FIGURE 7.66

*Using the Windows
2000 Server Backup
Wizard to label the
backup and the tape*

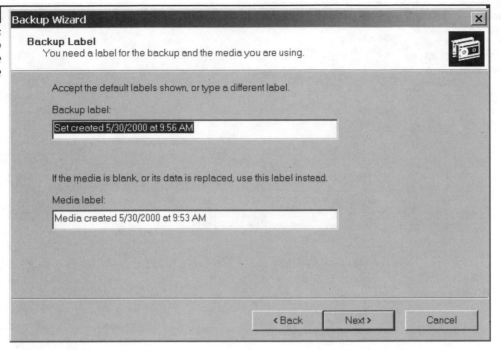

The final advanced option enables you to run your backup immediately or schedule it
to run one or more times (see Figure 7.67). Leave the default setting of Now to run the
backup immediately. Select Later to schedule your backup. Enter a job name and click
Set Schedule. This pops up the Set Account Information dialog box shown in Figure
7.68. Accept the default, or enter a Windows 2000 account to run the backup under.
This account should at least belong to the Backup Operators security group in the
\Active Directory Users and Computers\Built-in container.

FIGURE 7.67

Using the Windows 2000 Server Backup Wizard to back up immediately or on a schedule

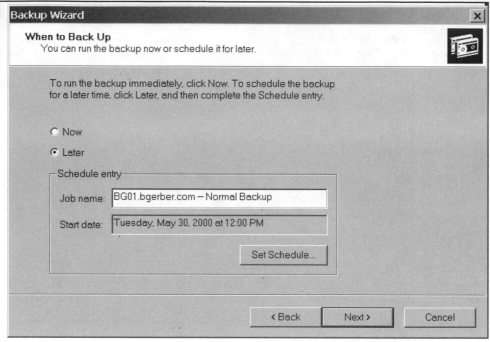

FIGURE 7.68

Using the Windows 2000 Server Backup Wizard to enter a Windows 2000 account to run the backup under

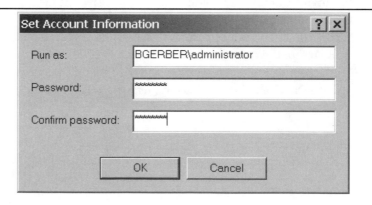

The Schedule Job dialog box comes up next (see Figure 7.69). It enables you to do some pretty fancy scheduling. I've selected to run my normal backup every Friday at midnight. Click OK when you're done scheduling, and then click Next on the When to Back Up wizard page. The final Backup Wizard page shows you the backup plan (see Figure 7.70). Click Finish to close the wizard and implement your scheduled backup.

FIGURE 7.69

Using the Windows 2000 Server Backup Wizard to schedule a backup

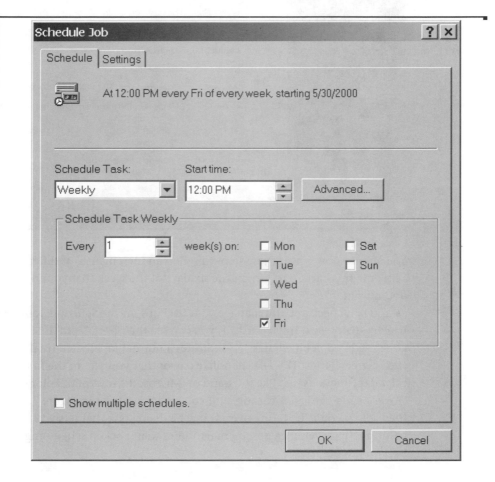

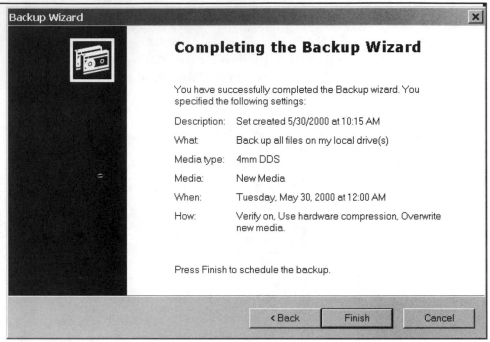

You should now repeat these steps to set up an incremental or differential backup. Schedule this backup to run on the six days of the week that your normal backup doesn't run.

You can check out and manage your backups on the Schedule Jobs page of the Backup dialog box. In Figure 7.71, you can see the normal and differential jobs that I've scheduled. A blue letter "N" indicates a normal job. Differential jobs are marked with a green letter "D." That handlike cursor that you see on the first Friday in the calendar functions just like the hand on Microsoft's Internet Explorer Web browser. Hover over a particular backup, and you see its name, as in Figure 7.71. If you click the backup you're hovering over, you get a dialog box that lets you manage the backup. This is better by several magnitudes than backup scheduling with NT 4's Backup program.

FIGURE 7.71

Managing scheduled backups with on the Schedule Jobs page of the Backup dialog box

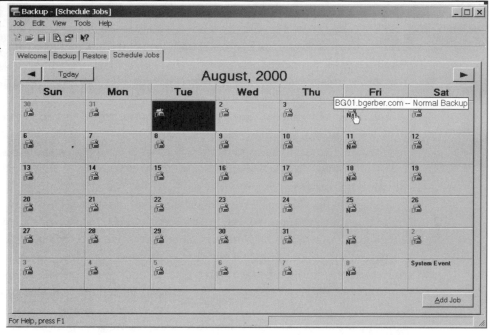

Use the Restore Wizard to restore some data from your backup. After our little trip through the Backup Wizard, you should find it pretty easy to use. You've probably heard this before, but I'll say it anyway: Be sure to do test restores frequently. A perfectly executed backup scheme isn't worth anything if you can't restore what you've backed up.

NOTE Consider third-party backup solutions for Windows 2000 Server. These offer a range of options not available in Windows 2000 Server's backup program. They can, for example, backup system state and registry data on remote computers. See Appendix A, "Cool Third-Party Applications for Exchange Server and Outlook Clients " for information on some very nice third-party backup products for Exchange 2000 Server that also have much to offer when used to back up Windows 2000 Server.

Summary

This chapter covers the installation of both Windows 2000 domain controllers and Windows 2000 standalone servers. Domain controllers make Windows 2000 networks happen. Standalone servers are the workhorses of your network, hosting applications such as Exchange 2000 Server.

Before installing the Windows 2000 Server operating system on any computer, you need to ensure that your hardware ducks are in a row. Your server hardware should have adequate capacity to support the Windows 2000 and application functionality that you require. You also should exhaustively test your hardware to ensure that it is functioning properly.

The actual installation of Windows 2000 server software is fairly easy. This is especially true if you've prepared well by tracking through the planning steps described in Chapter 5. If you're familiar with NT Server 4, you'll need to adjust your thinking a bit to deal with such things as Active Directory forests and trees, as well as the fact that domain controllers come into being after, not during, installation.

After your Windows 2000 server is installed, you can turn to managing it. Microsoft Management Console (MMC) is the home for a range of snap-in Windows 2000 management tools. For example, you use the Active Directory Users and Computers MMC snap-in to create and manage users.

Dynamic DNS is central to Windows 2000 networking. Working in tandem with DHCP, it enables you to install new servers and workstations without having to worry about assigning IP addresses or other TCP/IP-related parameters to the new computer during installation. Both Dynamic DNS and DHCP are managed within MMC.

When you install Windows 2000 Server, a disk partition is created to hold the operating system. You partition any remaining disk space using the Computer Management MMC snap-in (Disk Management container) and disk management wizards, which size, create, and format partitions. You can also use functionality provided in the Disk Management folder to set up a range of software-based fault-tolerant disk options such as RAID 5.

After your Windows 2000 server is up and running, it's time to ensure its reliability and stability. You must install and configure an uninterruptible power supply and set up your tape backup. Both of these tasks can be accomplished using software built into Windows 2000 or enhanced software from various third-party vendors.

With Windows 2000 Server in place, we can now move on to installing Exchange 2000 Server itself. Here we goooooooooooooooooooooooo (fade toward the end). You didn't think our trip to Wonderland was over, did you?

CHAPTER 8

Installing Exchange 2000 Server

This will be a fun chapter. After all the theory, concepts, and planning and installation of Windows 2000 Server, we're actually going to get an Exchange server up and running. Installing an Exchange server is a four-step process. First, you install Windows 2000 Server in standalone mode. Second, you prepare to install Exchange 2000 Server. Third, you actually install Exchange. Fourth, you do some key housekeeping chores when installation is complete. After you've completed these tasks, you're ready to create an Exchange mailbox and set up a backup of your Exchange server. We'll take on these two tasks here as well. Let's get to work.

Installing a Windows 2000 Standalone Server

Before you install Windows 2000 Server, you need to verify that you've got the right hardware and that your hardware is functioning properly. Then you need to be sure which version of Windows 2000 you're going to install and where you're going to install it.

Verifying Server Hardware

Unless you're running a really basic test machine, I'm assuming that you've got that 800MHz Pentium III or Xeon machine with 512MB of memory and at least two 9GB SCSI hard drives that I recommended back in Chapter 5, "Designing a New Exchange 2000 Server." If you're setting up a heavy-duty Exchange system, consider upping memory to 1GB, adding a second processor, and using RAID 5 disk storage, again as recommended in Chapter 5. You should also have installed a UPS and a 4mm, 8mm, or DLT SCSI tape backup device. Be sure to test your hardware, as suggested in Chapter 7, "Installing Windows 2000 Server."

What to Install Where

In what follows, I assume that you're installing Exchange 2000 on a standalone server—that is, a server that is not a Windows 2000 domain controller. That means that I assume that, at the very least, two things are true:

1. You have already installed Windows 2000 Server on a computer and have promoted the server to domain controller status, as per Chapter 7.

2. You will install another copy of Windows 2000 Server on another computer without promoting this server to domain controller status, also as per Chapter 7.

The first server is your domain controller. You'll install Exchange 2000 Server on the second computer. To avoid performance problems when you attempt to run Exchange 2000 on a Windows 2000 domain controller, I strongly recommend against installing Exchange 2000 on a domain controller. So, I won't discuss doing that here in detail. If you absolutely must do this, just promote your second server to domain controller status and proceed from there. In this chapter, I will mention anything special that you need to do if you do choose the domain controller route.

If you're going to install Exchange 2000 Server edition, you should install Windows 2000 Server. If you need Exchange 2000 Server Enterprise Edition, install Windows 2000 Advanced Server or Windows 2000 Datacenter Server.

Installing Windows 2000 Server

It is time to install Windows 2000 Server on your soon-to-be Exchange server. I carefully constructed Chapter 7 so that you could use it to install a domain controller or a standalone server. So, please do use it to install the standalone server that will become your Exchange 2000 Server. Let me re-emphasize several points here that are also made in Chapter 7 regarding installing Windows 2000 Server on a computer that will support Exchange 2000 Server:

- Install the Network News Transport Protocol when you install Windows 2000 Server.
- Don't install DHCP or DNS on your server.
- Be sure that you have set up DHCP and Dynamic DNS on your domain controller, as specified in Chapter 7.
- Set your new server to join your Windows 2000 Server domain when asked during installation whether you want to join a domain or a workgroup.
- Don't promote your server to a domain controller.
- When you're all done installing your new server, make sure that it is capable of joining your domain. Using the Microsoft Management Console that you created in Chapter 7, you should see your server in \Active Directory Users and Computers\Computers and in the DNS container for your domain.

Okay, now go ahead and install Windows 2000 Server. When you're finished, I'll meet you in the next section.

Getting Ready to Install Exchange 2000 Server

Yay! Your Windows 2000 standalone server is installed. Now you're ready to begin preparing to install Exchange 2000. You'll have to do the following:

1. Ensure that all aspects of security are properly set up.

2. Gather some information.

Security Issues

You'll need to consider three security issues. These relate to the following:

- Ensuring that you've enabled security appropriately for the Windows 2000 Server domain model that you're working under
- Logging into your Exchange server under an appropriate account
- Setting privileges relating to who can administer a specific Exchange 2000 component

Domain Security

If you're installing Exchange Server in a single contiguous namespace domain (also called a *single-root tree domain*) as defined in Chapter 3, "Two Key Architectural Components of Windows 2000 Server," you won't have to take any special steps before installation. If your Exchange Server will operate in a noncontiguous namespace domain (*forest of root trees domain*), as defined in Chapter 3, you may have to set up the required cross-domain trusts. Your first time through this chapter, you should be working in a single contiguous namespace domain, and you shouldn't have to worry about cross-domain trusts. Later in this book, you'll get into installing multiple Exchange servers in multiple domains. Then you'll need to think about cross-domain trusts.

Installation Security

To install Exchange 2000 Server, you must be logged into an account that is a member of the following Windows 2000 security groups:

- Domain Admins
- Enterprise Admins
- Schema Admins

The Administrator account that's created when you install Windows 2000 Server on your domain controller belongs to all these groups. If you have access to this account, use it to install Exchange 2000.

 TIP Throughout this chapter, I talk about logging into your domain on a particular server using the domain administrator account, Administrator. I also talk about logging directly into a particular server using the server's Administrator account. Here's how to do both of these: To log into your domain on a particular server, such as your Exchange server, using the domain Administrator account, first press Ctrl+Alt+Del and then click Options on the Log On to Windows dialog box. Select your domain from the drop-down list. Then enter the account name **Administrator** and its password, and click OK. To log directly into your Exchange server, select its name from the drop-down list, type in the username **Administrator** and its password, and click OK.

If your organization divides responsibility for Active Directory and Exchange Server between two groups, you can still install Exchange 2000. However, before you can install Exchange, you'll have to ask the Active Directory folks—the ones with access to an account that is a member of all three of the previous groups—to run the Exchange 2000 Server setup program with a couple switches at a command prompt.

The setup program is on the Exchange 2000 Server CD-ROM in the directory \setup\i386. The switches are called *ForestPrep and DomainPrep*. The full commands are: \SETUP\I386\SETUP.EXE /ForestPrep and \SETUP\I386\ SETUP.EXE /DomainPrep. I'll refer to running the setup program with one of these switches simply as ForestPrep or DomainPrep.

ForestPrep should be run before DomainPrep. Run ForestPrep on a domain controller logged in as a domain administrator. Run DomainPrep on the computer where you plan to install Exchange 2000 Server logged into the domain as a domain administrator.

ForestPrep extends the Active Directory schema, adding Exchange 2000 Server-relevant objects. DomainPrep identifies an Exchange 2000 Server that will act as the recipient update server for the domain, and it adds permissions within the domain required by Exchange 2000. A recipient update server uses Active Directory information from Windows 2000 Server accounts with mailboxes to keep Exchange 2000 e-mail addresses and address lists up-to-date.

After ForestPrep and DomainPrep have been run, you can install Exchange 2000 using an account that belongs to the Domain Admins and Enterprise Admins groups.

NOTE When you install Exchange 2000 Server under the domain Administrator account, ForestPrep and DomainPrep run as part of the installation. You don't need to run them before running the Exchange 2000 installation itself.

Component Management Security

You can set extensive security permissions for most Windows 2000 Server objects. Exchange 2000 Server objects are no different. On installation, the account installing Exchange 2000 gets full access to Exchange objects. You can play with rights on objects to control who can access and manage different Exchange objects. In this way, you can remove permissions installed by default and give select Exchange permissions to other accounts or security groups. For example, if you create multiple Exchange administrative groups (see Chapter 4, "Exchange 2000 Server Architecture"), you can assign different accounts rights to manage different Exchange objects.

Whatever you decide to do with component security in the future, it's a good idea to set up a Windows 2000 group that has specific rights to administer one or more Exchange servers and their components. Then, when you need to give someone these rights, all you have to do is add them to the Exchange administration group.

If you expect to be the one and only Exchange administrator, and if you can operate using the domain controller's Administrator account, then you probably can get by without an Exchange administration group. Even in such a case, however, I strongly recommend that you explore the use of an Exchange administration group. If nothing else, you'll learn quite a bit about Windows 2000 and Exchange 2000 security in the process.

NOTE In various sections of this book, this being one, you may not be able to accomplish some of the tasks that I ask you to perform because you don't have the required Windows 2000 Server permissions. This often happens in organizations in which operating system management is the responsibility of one group while management of a specific application, such as Exchange, is the responsibility of another group. In such a case, you can ask whoever manages the operating system either to grant you the rights you need or to do the task for you.

To perform the following tasks, you should be logged into your domain on your domain controller under an account with Administrator privileges.

We'll create the Exchange administration group in a bit. First, however, we need to create a Windows 2000 user account that will be added to the group. I don't want you to use the account that you created for yourself in the last chapter, because we're saving that one to test a typical Exchange user's experience. So, create a new account with the name ExAd, followed by your first initial and last name. (My account will be named ExAdBGerber.) For specific instructions on creating a new account, see Chapter 7.

Okay, now you can create your Exchange administration group. Call it Exchange Admins. Use the Microsoft Management Console (MMC) that you created in Chapter 7. Right-click the container \Active Directory Users and Computers\Users, and select New ➤ Group. This brings up the New Object— Group dialog box shown in Figure 8.1. Type in the Group Name. The pre-Windows 2000 group name is filled in automatically. Make sure that Global is selected for Group Scope and that Security is selected for Group Type. Click OK.

 TIP To open an MMC that you've saved, select Start Menu ➤ Programs ➤ Administrative Tools ➤ name_of_MMC, where name_of_MMC is the name that you used to save the MMC.

FIGURE 8.1

Setting up a global security group for Exchange Server administration

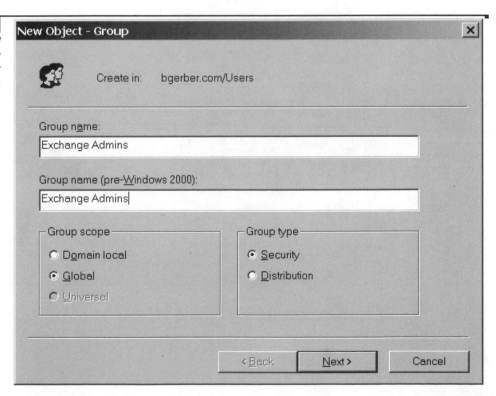

Now, find your new group in the right pane of the Users container, and double-click it. Add a description as I have in Figure 8.2. Finally, tab over to the Members property page (see Figure 8.3), add the user that you just created to your new group, and click OK.

After Exchange 2000 Server has been installed, you'll be able to grant your group the proper permissions. I'll cover that process later in this chapter in the section "Granting Permissions for the Exchange Administration Group to Manage Exchange Server."

FIGURE 8.2

Adding a description for the Exchange Server Administrative group

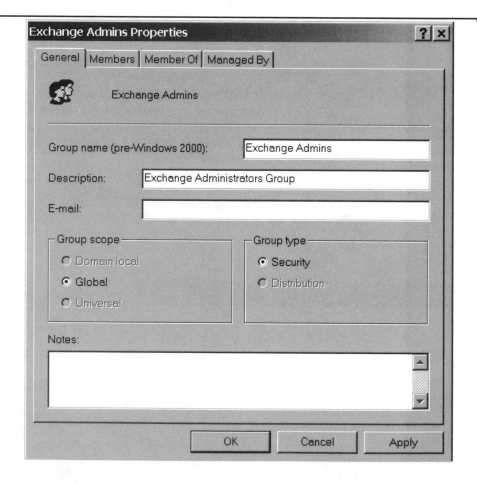

FIGURE 8.3

Adding a Windows 2000 Server account to the Exchange Admins global security group

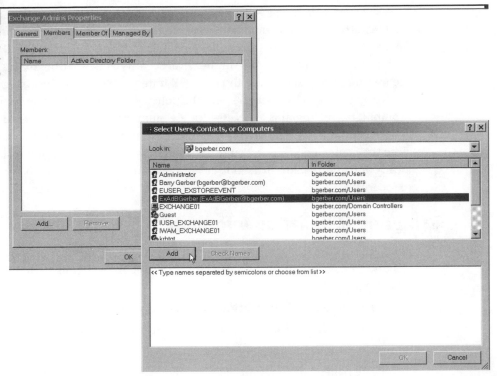

 WARNING   If you installed Exchange on a standalone Windows 2000 Server, you can move on to the next section because the hands-on tasks that immediately follow won't even work. If you installed Exchange on a Windows 2000 domain controller, you must read and do the hands-on tasks immediately below, or what follows in the next section won't work for you.

If you installed Exchange 2000 Server on a domain controller, you must give logon locally permissions to the ExAd Windows 2000 account that you created just a bit ago. If you don't do that, this user will be able to administer Exchange only from another workstation or server and only after the Exchange management tools have been installed on that workstation or server. For now, I want you to administer Exchange on your Exchange server so let's give your ExAd account logon locally permissions.

Select Start ➤ Programs ➤ Administrative Tools ➤ Domain Controller Security Policy. Open the Security Settings container, then open the Local Policies container, and finally click the User Rights Assignment container. In the right pane, find and double-click Log On Locally; click Add on the Local Security Policy Setting dialog box. Add the user that you just created, and press OK until you've exited the dialog boxes that you've opened. Finally, to implement the policy you've just added, at a command prompt (Start ➤ Programs ➤ Accessories ➤ Command Prompt) type **secedit /refreshpolicy machine_policy /enforce**. When this program is finished running, close the command prompt. You're done granting your new user permission to log on locally and you've had a little look at Windows 2000 Server's policy-based approach to security.

Gathering Installation Information

The Exchange 2000 Server Setup program will give you a number of options. To respond to these options, you'll need some specific information, including the following:

- The product identification number for your copy of Exchange 2000 Server
- A list of the Exchange Server components that you want to install
- The path where Exchange Server is to be installed
- The name that you want to give your Exchange organization
- The Windows 2000 Server account to be granted Exchange administrative rights

Let's look at each of these in a bit more detail.

Product Identification Number

You'll be asked to enter a product identification number. This is on the Exchange 2000 Server CD-ROM product case.

What Will Be Installed?

As with most programs installed in Microsoft Windows environments, you'll be able to choose which Exchange 2000 Server components you want to install. Options include these:

- Microsoft Exchange 2000 [install]
- Microsoft Exchange Messaging and Collaboration Services [install]
    - Microsoft Exchange MSMail Connector
    - Microsoft Exchange Connector for Lotus cc:Mail

- Microsoft Exchange Connector for Lotus Notes
- Microsoft Exchange Connector for Novell GroupWise
- Microsoft Exchange Conference Management Service
- Microsoft Exchange Key Management Service
- Microsoft Exchange System Management Tools [install]
  - Microsoft Exchange 5.5 Administrator
- Microsoft Exchange Chat Service
- Microsoft Exchange T.120 MCU Conference Service
- Microsoft Exchange Instant Messaging Service

Check out Chapter 4 for more on these components. I suggest that you install components marked *[install]* in this list. These are the basic components required to run and manage Exchange server. The good news is that you can install additional components at any time.

The Installation Path

The Setup program defaults to the path C:\EXCHSRVR. Unless there's some reason that you don't want to use this path (for example, to install Exchange Server on another drive), accept the default.

Exchange Organization Name

The Exchange organization name is the top item in the Exchange organizing hierarchy. You should have decided on a name back in Chapter 5.

Windows 2000 Server Account to be Granted Exchange Administrative Rights

As with the recipient update server, if you're installing Exchange as Administrator or its equivalent, you won't need this information. The installation program will assume that you want the account that you're installing under to receive Exchange administrative rights. On the other hand, if someone has to run ForestPrep for you, that person will be asked for an account name when running the program.

Running the Exchange 2000 Server Setup Program

At last! Insert the Exchange 2000 Server CD-ROM into your CD-ROM drive. The Exchange 2000 Server startup program should open (see Figure 8.4). If the application doesn't open, run `\SETUP\I386\SETUP.EXE` from the CD-ROM.

 NOTE Microsoft just loves to change user interfaces. Sometimes the changes are just cosmetic; sometimes they are more than that. I don't expect that the Exchange-related user interfaces shown in the figures in this chapter and later chapters will look much different from the ones that you'll be working with. In my experience, even when there are major differences, you can still usually figure out what to do.

You can use the startup program to do various things, including installing Exchange 2000 Server. When the program is running, select Exchange Server Setup from the menu.

FIGURE 8.4

The Exchange 2000 Server CD-ROM startup application

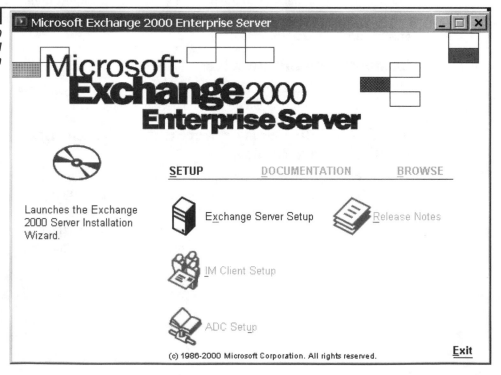

This brings up the Microsoft Exchange 2000 Installation Wizard. Click Next and indicate your agreement with the End-User Licensing Agreement. On the next wizard page, enter the product identification number and click Next for the Component Selection Wizard page (see Figure 8.5). As with most software, you have three basic installation options: minimum, typical, and custom. Select the typical option to install the components that I mentioned in the previous section.

You also pick the drive or drives on which to install Exchange 2000 on this wizard page. As you can see, I've chosen to install Exchange on the second drive that I installed and set up back in the last chapter.

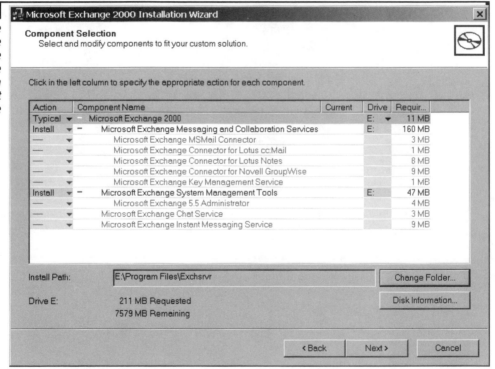

FIGURE 8.5

Selecting Exchange 2000 features to be installed using the Microsoft Exchange 2000 Installation Wizard's Component Selection page

Next, as you can see in Figure 8.6, you're asked whether you want to create a new Exchange Organization or join an existing Exchange Server 5.5 Organization. Pick the second option if you have a 5.5 system and want to begin your migration to Exchange 2000 by setting up a 2000 server in the 5.5 system. See Chapter 6, "Upgrading to Windows 2000 Server and Exchange 2000 Server," for more on upgrade/migration issues related to moving from version 5.5 to 2000. We're installing a new Exchange 2000 system here, so be sure that the first option is selected.

FIGURE 8.6

Choosing to create a new Exchange 2000 organization using the Microsoft Exchange 2000 Installation Wizard's Installation Type page

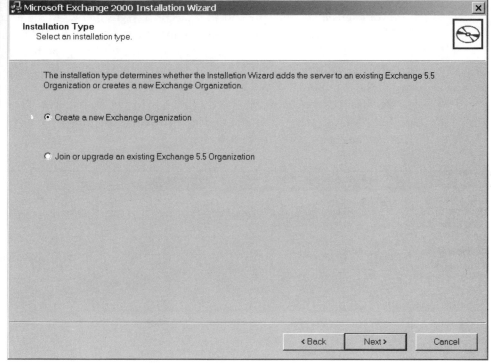

On the following Wizard page, you're asked to name your new Exchange 2000 organization. Enter a name as I have in Figure 8.7.

FIGURE 8.7

Entering a name for a new Exchange 2000 organization using the Microsoft Exchange 2000 Installation Wizard's Organization Name page

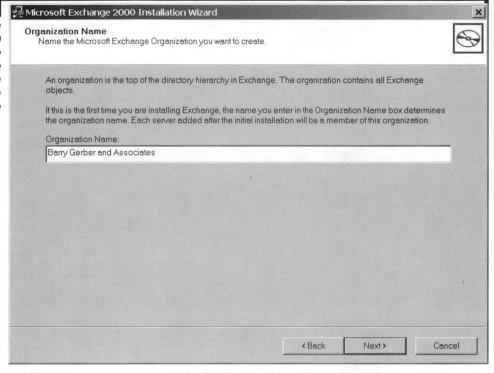

On the next wizard page, you're asked to agree to Exchange 2000 Server's per-seat-only licensing (see Figure 8.8). If you don't agree, it's all over. So, unless you've decided to abandon the product, be sure that the first option is selected, and click Next for the Component Summary Wizard page (see Figure 8.9). This page shows you which Exchange features will be installed. If all is well, click Next; if not, back up to the Component Selection page and alter your selection.

FIGURE 8.8

Accepting Exchange 2000's per-seat licensing policy using the Microsoft Exchange 2000 Installation Wizard's Licensing Agreement page

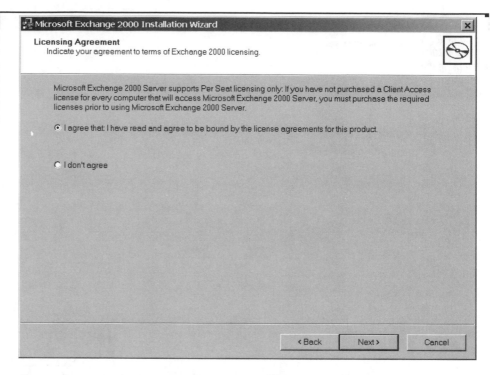

FIGURE 8.9

Reviewing the Exchange 2000 features to be installed using the Microsoft Exchange 2000 Installation Wizard's Component Summary page

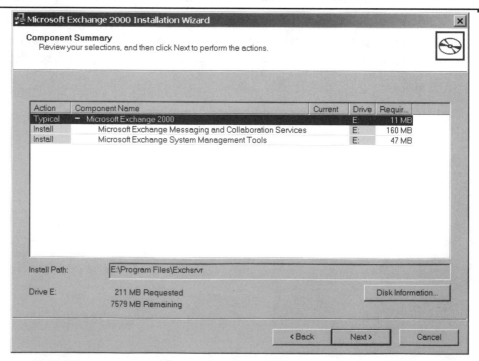

At this point, you're pretty much done with the Installation Wizard. Installation more or less starts, as you can see in Figure 8.10. I say "more or less" because, as that little dialog box in Figure 8.10 indicates, the wizard needs to tell you that members of the security group Pre-Windows 2000 Compatible Access will see Exchange distribution list members that are hidden. If you're concerned about all of this, do what the dialog box says, and remove any users that might be in the group. For more on distribution lists (groups), see Chapter 4. After fully absorbing the dialog box's message, Click OK, and installation starts in earnest (see Figure 8.11).

FIGURE 8.10

Exchange 2000 Server installation stops temporarily to warn that hidden distribution list members will be seen by members of the Pre-Windows 2000 Compatible Access security group.

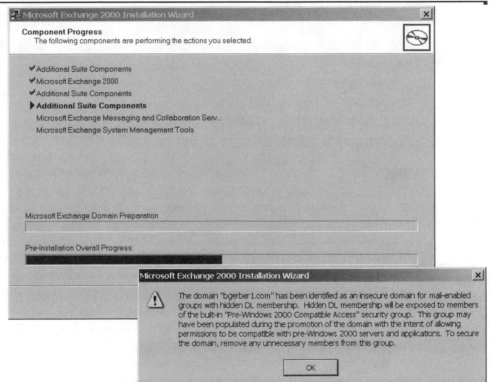

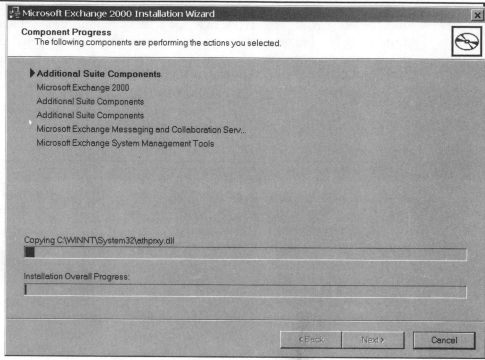

If you're installing Exchange 2000 Server with the correct permissions, both Forest-Prep and DomainPrep run silently as part of the installation process. ForestPrep needs no input, so it just runs when its time comes. You can tell that ForestPrep is running when the wizard tells you that it's updating the Active Directory schema (see Figure 8.12). This is coffee break time in the extreme. Things can be so slow that, after watching the Active Directory schema update progress meters for a while, you might have difficulty distinguishing between the frozen image in Figure 8.12 and the real-world meters on your screen.

Because you're creating a new organization, DomainPrep assumes quite logically that you want your new Exchange server to act as the update server, and it needs no input from you to set up Exchange-related permissions.

FIGURE 8.12

The ForestPrep progress meters move with deliberate slowness.

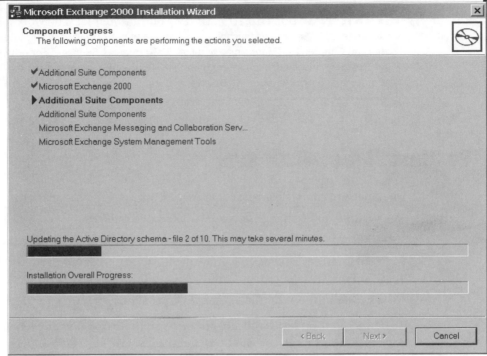

When ForestPrep is done, the wizard goes on to install lots of files on your server. Then it does some registry tricks and starts up the Exchange 2000 services.

When all is done, the final wizard page congratulates you on successful installation of Exchange 2000 and asks you to click Finish to close the wizard. After the wizard closes, exit the Exchange 2000 Server startup program, and you're done. Well, it would be more appropriate to say that *you're* done, but your server isn't. It'll grind away for a while setting everything up. The server spends a good deal of its time futzing around with the information store. Just let it do its thing.

If you want to watch what's going on, right-click the Windows 2000 Taskbar (the one with the Start Menu button) and select Task Manager from the pop-up menu. Tab over to the Processes page, and click CPU. That sorts the tasks running on your computer by percent of CPU used. Notice that STORE.EXE is a busy little beaver. That's the Exchange information store process. When System Idle Process consumes a steady 98 or so percent of CPU capacity, the Exchange services have finished their post-installation tasks. Now you have some post-installation stuff to take care of yourself.

WARNING Don't expect messaging outside your local network to work when Exchange 2000 Server has finished installing. We won't actually activate Internet messaging until Chapter 13, "Managing Exchange 2000 Internet Services." For now, you want to get Exchange installed, experiment with the Outlook messaging client, and learn how to administer a basic Exchange 2000 Server system.

Postinstallation Activities

You'll need to complete a series of tasks immediately after installation:

- Check out Exchange server's Windows program group.
- Ensure that all required Exchange Server processes are up and running.
- Ensure that Exchange communications are working properly (by using the Microsoft Management Console to do a little administrative work).
- Set permissions for the Exchange Server administration group.

It's best to do these tasks while logged into your domain on your Exchange server as a domain administrator. You can do all but the last task logged directly into your Exchange server as Administrator. (See the note earlier in this chapter in the section "Installation Security," if you need help with these two types of logons.)

Exchange 2000 Server's Windows Program Group

Select Start ➤ Programs ➤ Microsoft Exchange to view the programs installed with Exchange 2000 Server (see Figure 8.13).

You can find out more about Active Directory Cleanup Wizard in Chapter 6. This wizard is used in certain Exchange 5.5 to Exchange 2000 upgrade scenarios.

Active Directory Users and Computers is in this program group to make it easy for you to run the application used to set up user mailboxes, distribution groups, and contacts.

FIGURE 8.13

Viewing programs in the Microsoft Exchange program group

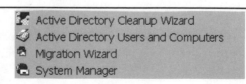

The Migration Wizard helps you transition from other messaging system to Exchange 2000 Server. It works with a wide range of systems, including Microsoft Mail, Lotus cc:Mail and Notes, and Novell GroupWise.

System Manager is a standalone version of the snap-in that you use to manage much of your Exchange 2000 Server environment. You'll see a lot more of this application throughout this book.

Verifying That Exchange Server Services Are Running

Now you need to make sure that all Exchange Server services are running. If they're not, you'll have to do some troubleshooting. Before you can check out the Exchange services, you'll need to set up a Microsoft Management Console on your Exchange server.

Setting Up a Microsoft Management Console on Your Exchange Server

You can use the instructions in Chapter 7 to set up your MMC. The MMC should include at least the following snap-ins

- Active Directory Users and Computers
- Computer Management
- Event Viewer

Before you create your MMC, be sure that you understand the following information:

When creating your MMC, you should be logged into your domain as Administrator on your Exchange server. If you're not permitted to do this, then you'll have to log into the Exchange server itself as Administrator. If you have to do the latter, you will be able to usefully add only the snap-ins for Computer Management and Event Viewer. You'll be able to add but not use the Active Directory Users and Computers snap-in.

Now, go back to Chapter 7 and set up the MMC following the instructions in the section "Using Microsoft Management Console." If you're permitted to log in as domain administrator, do so and add the Active Directory Users and Computers snap-in as well as the Computer Management and Event Viewer snap-ins. If you're not permitted to log in as domain administrator, log into your Exchange server as administrator and install the Computer Management and Event Viewer snap-ins. Then join me in the next section.

Are the Services Running?

Using the MMC that you've just created for your Exchange server, find and click on the Services container in \Computer Management (Local)\Services and Applications. The right pane of your Services container should look something like the one in Figure 8.14. I've scrolled up the right pane so that you can see the Exchange-specific services. For more on these services, see Chapter 4. Be sure that the Exchange services in your Services container are in the same state as the ones in Figure 8.14. If they are, your Exchange services are correctly up and running.

FIGURE 8.14

The Services container with Exchange 2000 Server services displayed

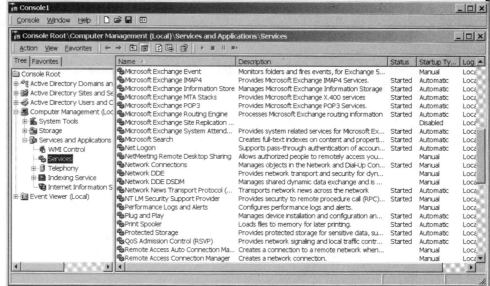

Troubleshooting Problems with Services

If some or all of the Exchange Server processes that should be running aren't, first take a look at the Windows 2000 Server Application Event Log using the Event Viewer. In your MMC, click on the Application container in \Computer Management (Local)\System Tools\Event Viewer. Look for events related to Exchange Server marked with an icon showing a white X on a red background—these indicate serious problems such as failure to start a service. Click on the event to open the Event Properties dialog box that shows details of the event. If you find a problem that you think you can handle, try to fix it; otherwise, check with Microsoft regarding the event.

TIP You may not have to contact Microsoft directly, if you have a problem that is represented in the Event Viewer. Windows 2000 Server includes a neat new feature. If you see an Internet URL on the Event Properties dialog box, you can click it to try to get some additional help through the Internet.

You can also try shutting down the server and rebooting it. If that doesn't fix things, try to start nonrunning Exchange processes manually. To do this, double-click on a service in the Services container (see Figure 8.14), and then click the Start button on the Properties dialog box that opens. Your Windows 2000 server will chug away for a bit, and then the service should start up—along with any other services that this service depends on.

Setting Up Microsoft Management Console for Exchange 2000 Server

At this point, you need to set up the MMC on your Exchange server for Exchange 2000 Server management. You need to do this for two reasons. First, you want to be sure that your Exchange server's various components are capable of communicating with client processes. Second, to set permissions for the Exchange Server administration group (Exchange Admins) that you created a while back, you'll need the Exchange System Manager snap-in that you're about to add to MMC. If you need to, check out Chapter 7 for a review of MMC and adding snap-ins.

To ensure that you can do some of the tasks in the next sections, be sure that you're logged into your domain on your Exchange server as Administrator. You can also add the snap-in while logged directly into your Exchange server as Administrator, but you won't be able to do many of the tasks in the next section.

To add the Exchange System Manager snap-in, select Add/Remove Snap-in from the MMC's Console menu. Click Add on the Standalone page of the Add/Remove Snap-in dialog box. You'll see a number of Exchange-oriented snap-ins. We are going to work with just one of these; in later chapters, we'll talk about the other snap-ins. Select the Exchange System snap-in from the Add Standalone Snap-in dialog box, and click Add.

Be sure that the option Any Writable Domain Controller is selected on the Change Domain Controller dialog box. Here you're selecting the domain controller to which any additions, deletions, or edits you make to your Exchange environment will be written. You might select a specific controller as opposed to any writable domain controller, for a variety of reasons. For example, you might want to write to a controller that runs on a massively fault-tolerant computer to ensure that changes you make are very reliably entered into your domain's Active Directory. Or, you might want to pick a controller that is on the same local area network as the Exchange server you're managing. For now, any writable domain controller is a good choice. When you're done with the Change Domain Controller dialog box, click OK.

The snap-in should now show up in the Add/Remove Snap-in dialog box. Close the Add Standalone Snap-in dialog box by clicking Close, and then click OK on the Add/Remove Snap-in dialog box. At this point, your MMC should look something like the one in Figure 8.15.

The snap-in shows the Exchange organization created during Exchange 2000 installation. As you'll remember, during installation I named my organization Barry Gerber and Associates.

The Exchange System snap-in is the same as the System Manager on the Start ➢ Programs ➢ Microsoft Exchange menu (see Figure 8.13). That's why I call the snap-in Exchange System Manager.

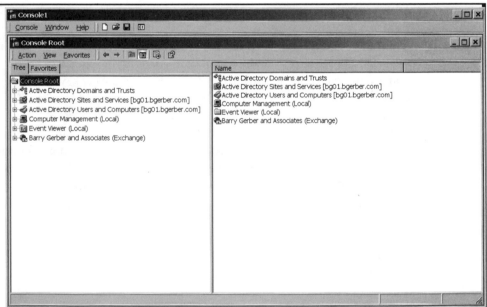

FIGURE 8.15

Microsoft Management Console with the Exchange System Manager snap-in installed

You've seen the Exchange System Manager in earlier chapters. Now you'll actually start using it. Just to get a feel for how it works, click open the Exchange System Manager and then click open the Servers container so that your MMC looks like the one in Figure 8.16. Exchange Server 5.5 users will be happy to see a somewhat familiar environment.

FIGURE 8.16

The Exchange System Manager snap-in open to reveal some of its subcontainers

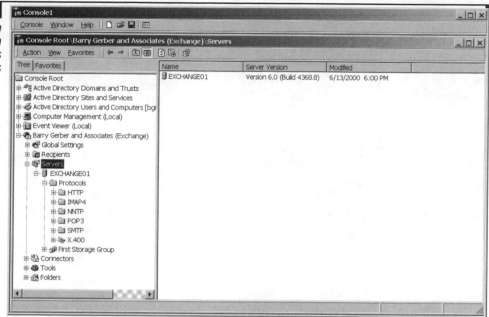

Just for fun, right-click your Exchange server (EXCHANGE01, in my case), and select Properties to open the Exchange Server Properties dialog box shown in Figure 8.17. Again, Exchange 5.5 users should find at least some of what they see on this dialog box familiar. I'll talk a lot more about what you see here in later chapters. For now, I just want to help familiarize you with the Exchange System Manager snap-in. Go ahead and muck about a bit in the snap-in. Just be careful not to add or delete anything at this point, and be sure to close the Properties dialog box. I'll be waiting right here when you're done.

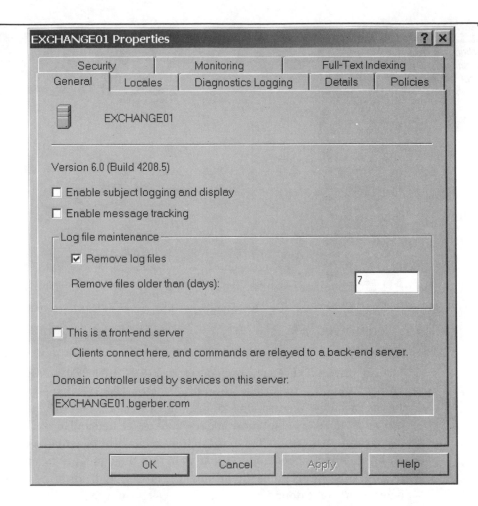

Running Exchange System Manager Remotely

As long as you have the right security permissions, you can run Exchange System Manager and other Exchange-specific applications from any networked Windows 2000 workstation or server. This is convenient because you won't have to keep running to an Exchange server to administer it.

You must install the Exchange Management Tools on a Windows 2000 computer in the Exchange server's domain or in a domain trusted by the server's domain. To install

Continued

CONTINUED

Exchange System Manager, run the Exchange 2000 Server Setup program on the computer from which you want to run Exchange System Manager. Select the Custom installation option, and select only the Microsoft Exchange System Management Tools for installation. When Exchange System Manager is installed, snap it into a Microsoft Management Console, and you're off and running. If you wanted to do the tasks in the next section on your domain controller, you would have to install the management tools on the domain controller.

Granting Permission for the Exchange Administration Group to Manage Exchange Server

Now you're ready to give members of your Exchange administration group, Exchange Admins, permissions to administer Exchange. You should be logged into your domain on your Exchange server as Administrator. Assuming that you're still in Exchange System Manager in your MMC, right-click the Manager's root container and select Delegate Control. (My root container is called Barry Gerber and Associates [Exchange] in Figures 8.15 and 8.16.) This brings up the Exchange Administration Delegation Wizard.

Click Next to see the Users or Groups page of the wizard, shown in Figure 8.18. Use the Browse button to select your Exchange Admins group. The Role field's drop-down list gives you a choice of three roles:

- Exchange View Only Administrator
- Exchange Administrator
- Exchange Full Administrator

As its name implies, View Only Administrator permits no editing of Exchange parameters. Exchange Administrator allows for viewing and editing of most Exchange parameters. Excluded are things such as the capability to change permissions. Exchange Full Administrator has complete control over the Exchange 2000 Server environment.

FIGURE 8.18

Granting the Exchange Admins group permissions to administer Exchange 2000 Server Organization

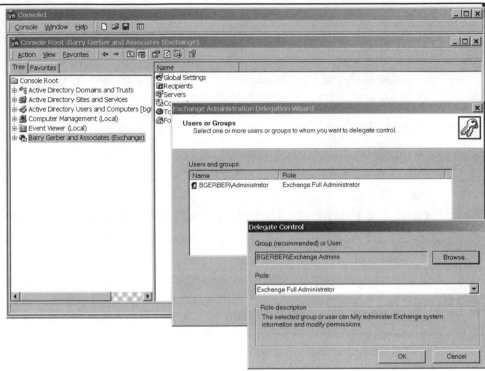

Select Exchange Full Administrator from the drop-down list, and click OK. Then click Next and then Finish on the last page of the Exchange Administrator Delegation Wizard.

The permissions that you've given to Exchange Admins cascade down through all of the subcontainers under the Exchange System Manager root container for your Exchange Organization. This means that Exchange Admins have management rights in all the existing subcontainers and any new subcontainers you create.

You can go a step further and grant one or more other groups permissions in the subcontainers of the Exchange System Manager root container. In this way, you can assign rights to manage pieces of your Exchange Organization to different individuals or groups. This is especially useful when you begin creating Exchange administrative group subcontainers that contain pieces of your Exchange organizational hierarchy you want others to be able to manage. See Chapter 4 for more on administrative groups.

TIP If you want to see the permissions that you've granted to the Exchange Admins group, select Advanced Features from the View menu in the Console Root window of your MMC. Then right-click on the Exchange System Manager's root container and select Properties. Tab over to the Security page and find and click on the Exchange Admins group. The Permissions field shows the rights you've granted to Exchange Admins. If you hadn't selected Advanced Features, you wouldn't have seen the Security page. Shades of Exchange 5.5's Show Permissions Page for All Objects option.

Now for the moment of truth. Log out of your Windows 2000 Server, and log back in to your domain on your Exchange server as the special Exchange administrator account you created. (My account was named ExAdBGerber.) When you're logged in, set up a Microsoft Management Console with the following snap-ins:

- Active Directory Users and Computers
- Computer Management
- Event Viewer
- Exchange System Manager

If you've set up everything as I've advised, including adding your ExAd account to the Exchange Admins account, you should be able to open Exchange System Manager without any error messages. You should also be able to add and then delete a new storage group by right-clicking on your Exchange server container in the Exchange System Manager's Servers container. In Figure 8.19, I'm adding the new storage group. To delete the new storage group, right-click it and select Delete from the pop-up menu.

FIGURE 8.19

Adding a new storage group to an Exchange Server using a Windows 2000 Server account that was added to a Windows 2000 Server security group, delegated authority to manage an Exchange 2000 Server Organization

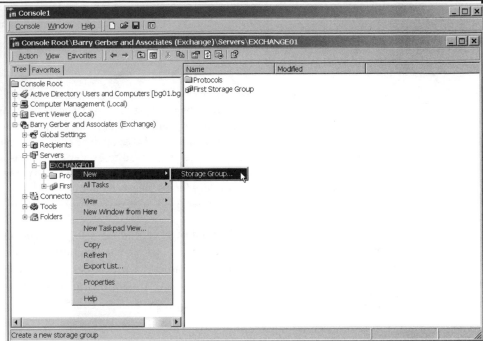

Now, while still logged into your ExAd account, try to use the Active Directory Users and Computers snap-in to add a new user or create a new mailbox. This can't be done. That's because this account is not authorized to fully manage Active Directory user accounts. An account that is authorized to change permissions, such as the domain controller's Administrator account, would have to give the permissions required to fully manage users in Active Directory to the ExAd account.

However, and this is a *big* however, by virtue of its membership in the group Exchange Admins, and by virtue of the fact that you delegated full Exchange administration privileges to Exchange Admins, your ExAd account *does* have full edit control over Exchange-relevant objects in Active Directory Users and Computers. Although it doesn't have permissions to create mailboxes, distribution groups, or contacts, it can edit the Exchange-specific attributes of these.

NOTE That wizard for delegating control of Exchange components is pretty neat, huh? Well, you should know that it is just a specialized version of the Windows 2000 wizard for delegating control. To see the Windows 2000 wizard, in your MMC, right-click your domain name in the Active Directory Users and Computers container. Then select Delegate Control from the pop-up menu, and there's the Windows 2000 Server wizard. This is where you'd give permissions to fully manage users to the ExAd account, if you wanted to.

Mailbox-Enabling a Windows 2000 User

The next two chapters of this book deal with the Microsoft Outlook e-mail client. To use the client, you'll need an Exchange 2000 mailbox—or more correctly, you'll need to mailbox-enable your Windows 2000 user account. This is the account that you created back in Chapter 7. Mine is called bgerber.

To start, log into your domain on your domain controller as Administrator. Open your MMC; find your account in the \Active Directory Users and Computers\Users container, and right-click it. Then select Exchange Tasks from the pop-up menu.

This brings up the Exchange Task Wizard. Click Next to move to the Available Tasks Wizard page, shown in Figure 8.20. Be sure that Create Mailbox is selected, and click Next. The Create Mailbox Wizard page then offers default options for the mailbox's alias and the Exchange server and mailbox store on the server where the mailbox will be created (see Figure 8.21). Accept the defaults. In later chapters, we'll play with other available options.

FIGURE 8.20

Choosing to create a new mailbox using the Exchange Task Wizard

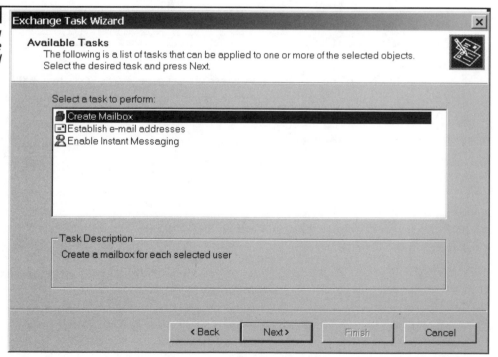

FIGURE 8.21

*Accepting default
options for a mailbox
using the Exchange
Task Wizard*

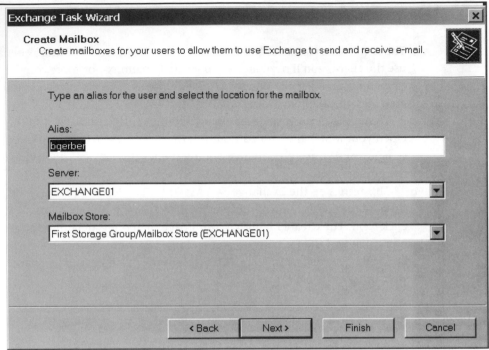

Click Next, and the Task in Progress Wizard page shows Exchange 2000 Server's progress in creating the new mailbox (see Figure 8.22). When the task has completed, click Finish.

FIGURE 8.22

Monitoring the mailbox creation task progress using the Exchange Task Wizard

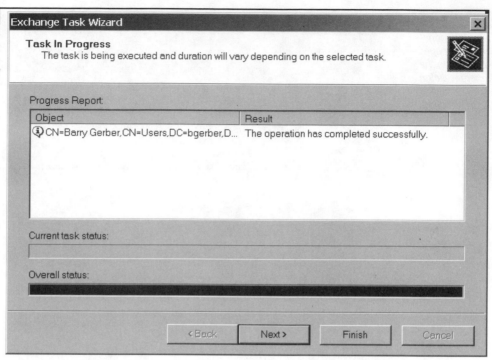

Next, right-click your account in \Active Directory Users and Computer\Users and select Properties from the pop-up menu. As Figure 8.23 shows, during creation of the new mailbox, several new Exchange-based pages were added to the Properties dialog box for the account. We'll delve into these new pages in great detail in later chapters.

FIGURE 8.23

Several new Exchange-based property pages were added to the User Properties dialog box during mailbox creation.

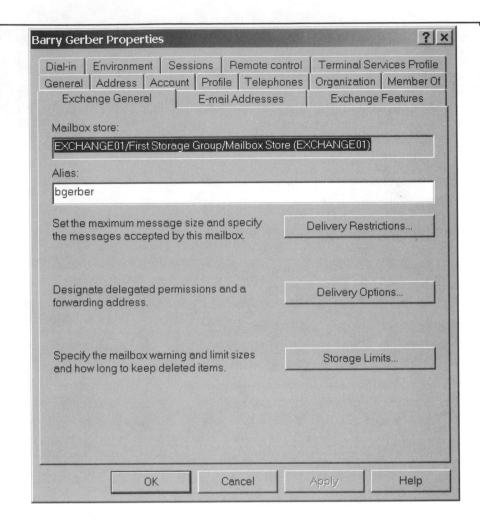

Now, before we leave all this management stuff, log back in using your ExAd account. Open your MMC and find your account in the \Active Directory Users and Computer\Users container. Double-click it, and check out the new Exchange-specific pages on the Properties dialog box. Notice that this user has considerable edit capability on these pages, just as I promised back in the last section. We'll get into these in later chapters.

That's it. Your Exchange server is installed and ready to use. Now you need to set up a backup regimen for the server.

Backing Up Exchange 2000 Server

Now, let's set up a backup for our Exchange 2000 Server. We're going to use the Windows 2000 Server Backup application. When you install Exchange 2000 Server, Exchange-based application program interfaces (APIs) are installed for backup. Windows 2000 Server Backup takes advantage of these APIs to let you access and properly back up your Exchange 2000 server.

I'm going to move through this pretty fast because I already discussed the Backup application in Chapter 7. To perform the backup, you can log into your domain on your Exchange server as Administrator or into the server itself as Administrator. Select Start menu ➢ Programs ➢ Accessories ➢ System Tools ➢ Backup to run the Backup application. This brings up the Backup Wizard. Click to the next wizard page called What to Back Up (see Figure 8.24). Select Back Up Selected Files, Drives, or Network Data, and click Next. On The Items to Back Up Wizard, select the Microsoft Information Store, as I have in Figure 8.25.

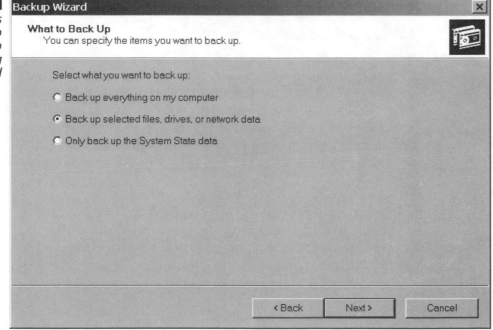

FIGURE 8.25

*Selecting Exchange
components to be
backed up by the
Windows 2000 Server
Backup program using
the Backup Wizard*

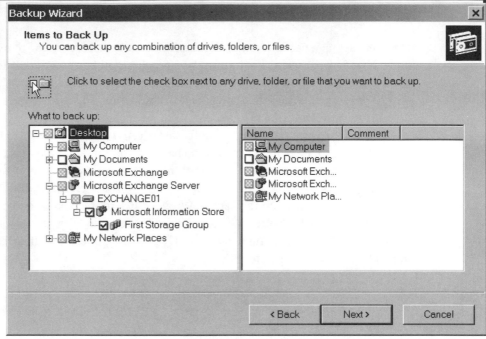

Click Next, and confirm the media type and media name for your backup setup, as shown in Figure 8.26. Click Next; on the Completing the Backup Wizard page (see Figure 8.27), click Advanced and, among other things, schedule your backup. Check out Chapter 7 for details on scheduling a backup. Be sure to schedule a normal backup and a set of either incremental or differential backups.

FIGURE 8.26

Confirming media type and media name to be used by the Windows 2000 Server Backup program using the Backup Wizard

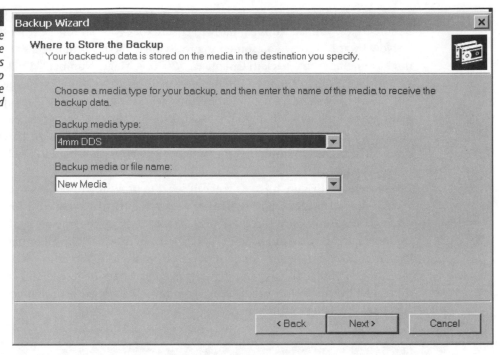

FIGURE 8.27

Using the Backup Wizard's Completing the Backup page to select Advance options, including backup job scheduling

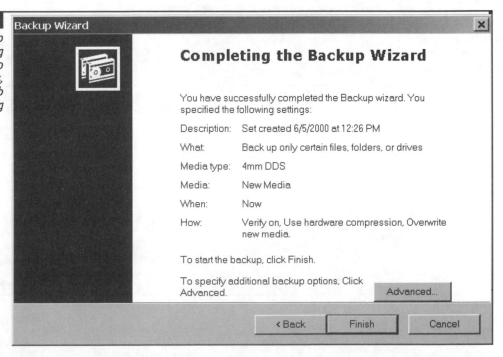

To see the logs for your backups, select Reports from the Backup program's Tools menu. Be sure to test your backups regularly to ensure that you can restore from them.

Now I want to show you something really neat about Exchange 2000 Server. You might remember that back in Chapter 2, "2000: A Magic Number?" I talked about file system access support that essentially lets you interact with the Exchange information store using standard command prompt features such as DIR. This capability really comes in handy when you're backing up Exchange 2000 Server. Not only can you use command prompt features, but you also can use certain GUI-based applications, such as the My Computer file browser. The browser is used in the Exchange Backup program.

Take a look at Figure 8.28. As you can see, I'm browsing my M: drive on the Backup Wizard's Items to Back Up page. This drive is actually the Exchange information store on my computer. As you can see, I've chosen to back up the one piece of mail in my Exchange mailbox. With Exchange 2000, you can now back up all or part of your Exchange 2000 mailboxes. No need to restore your entire server to get back that one piece of e-mail that one user accidentally deleted. That's neat, no? You can play with this capability a bit. However, because you haven't accessed your mailbox yet, you won't see anything in this area yet.

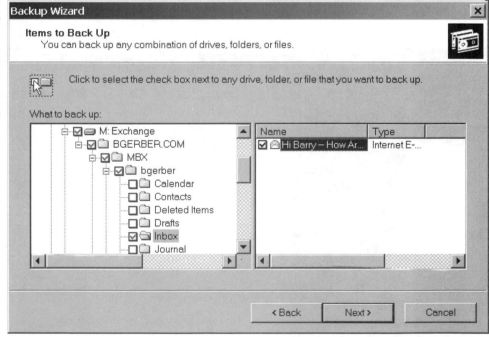

FIGURE 8.28

Selecting individual Exchange 2000 mailboxes or mailbox folders to be backed up by the Windows 2000 Server Backup program using the Backup Wizard

WARNING Now that you've got a basic backup regimen in place, don't forget to back up your Exchange server's disk drives. See Chapter 7 for details on setting up basic disk drive backups.

Any vendor can splice into the application-programming interface that Windows 2000 Server Backup uses when it does an online backup of the Exchange information store. A number of vendors have done just that, including Computer Associates (ArcServeIT; http://www.cai.com), Legato Systems (Legato Networker for Windows NT; http://www.legato.com), and Veritas (Backup Exec; http://www.veritas.com). Third-party backup solutions add value beyond Windows 2000 Server's own built-in backup program. For example, they can do the following:

- Let you easily and efficiently back up multiple servers and even other workstations on the network, including registry and system state information
- Support online Exchange Server backup as well as online backup of other application services such as Oracle or Microsoft SQL Server
- Make scheduling and monitoring the whole backup process very easy
- Can send you e-mail containing information about the most recent backup

Summary

You must take care of a number of preliminaries before actually installing Exchange 2000 Server. You must set up and test your server hardware, including disk drives and a tape backup system. Then you must install the correct version of Windows 2000 Server on a standalone server and ensure that it is capable of joining its domain.

When Windows 2000 is installed, you need to do some tasks before installing Exchange 2000:

1. Ensure that security matters have been taken into account, including setting up any cross-domain trusts and establishing a security group to manage your soon-to-be Exchange server

2. Gather information that you will need when installing your Exchange server, including where on your server's disk drives you want to install Exchange, the Exchange components that you want to install, and the name that you want to use for your Exchange organization

After all the preparation, Exchange server installation is a piece of cake. An installation wizard guides you through the process. The only thing that you might find distasteful is the long waits while certain steps in the process take place, such as Active Directory schema updating.

After Exchange 2000 Server is installed, you must check to ensure that Exchange services are running and that you can communicate with your server. To do this, you need to create a Microsoft Management Console (MMC) and add basic plug-ins as well as the Exchange System Manager. With the System Manager installed, you can grant your Exchange security group permissions to manage your Exchange server and begin managing the server. One of your first Exchange management steps should be to add a new mailbox. Finally, you should be sure to set up backup for your Exchange server.

Now that you have a mailbox, it's time to use it. In the next couple chapters, I'll introduce you to Microsoft's Outlook e-mail client. First I'll show you how to set up Outlook so that users can install it preconfigured from a centralized server. Then I'll spend some time helping you get familiar with Outlook from an end user's perspective.

PART III

The Outlook Client

Exchange Server is a pretty nifty little gadget. But without clients, it's nothing more than fancy technology. Although this is a book on Exchange Server, we need to spend a little time talking about the Outlook client. This section is devoted to that discussion.

In Chapter 9, "Installing Outlook 2000 from a Customized Server Image," we'll take an administrative perspective as we focus on the Outlook 2000 client for Windows that is part of the Office 2000 Suite. We'll cover installation of the clients, both on a server and from the server, onto user workstations. In Chapter 10, "A Quick Overview of Outlook 2000," we'll take a look at the Outlook 2000 client for Windows from the user's perspective. We'll take a quick tour of Outlook's menus to get comfortable with the impressive functionality that Microsoft has built into the client.

CHAPTER 9

Installing Outlook 2000 from a Customized Server Image

Exchange Server has been around for more than five years. In that time, Microsoft has generated a slew of new and increasingly improved Exchange clients:

- Original DOS, Windows 3.x, Windows 95, and Windows NT clients that came with Exchange Server 4 and 5
- Exchange client for Macintosh
- Windows 95 and Windows NT Outlook client that came with Office 97
- Windows 95 and Windows NT Outlook client that came with Exchange Server 5.5
- Outlook 98 client
- Outlook 2000 client
- The Outlook Web Access (Web browser-based client)

In addition to these Exchange clients, which provide access to the full range of Exchange Server capabilities, Exchange Server also supports POP3 and IMAP4 clients from Microsoft and other vendors. I'll focus here on the current native Exchange Server client, Outlook 2000, and reserve discussion of the POP3 and IMAP4 clients for Chapter 14, "Managing Exchange 2000 Services for Internet Clients."

In this chapter, we'll cover installation of Outlook 2000. First we'll tackle customizing Outlook 2000 for installation from a network server onto user workstations. Then we'll install Outlook 2000 on an individual workstation using our custom server-based setup. If you need to install any of the older Exchange Server clients, get your hands on the third edition of this book, or check out the docs that come with the client that you need to install.

 NOTE   "Wait," you say, "setting up server-based installations isn't my thing. I want to get started using Outlook 2000 right away." If that's you, go ahead and install Office 2000 or just Outlook 2000 directly on your workstation. Pop in the Office 2000 CD-ROM, and follow the online installation instructions. You might want to take a look at the last section in this chapter, "Installing the Outlook 2000 Client on a Workstation," before you begin installation. When you're done, flip over to Chapter 10, "A Quick Overview of Outlook 2000," for a look at Outlook 2000 in action.

Customizing Outlook 2000 for Installation on User Workstations

If you've ever attempted to customize the installation of older Office products for Windows and you're still certifiably *sane*, you'll really appreciate the new Windows installer for Office 2000 products such as Outlook 2000. Installations of past Office components used the infamous Acme Setup program. Bad old Acme required endless lines of text instructions to copy program files, set Windows registry entries, and do whatever else was required to get Office programs on a user's computer.

Office 2000 Windows installer technology replaces Acme Setup. All the default data required to install each Office 2000 product resides in a relational database with the extension MSI, for Microsoft Installer. Data to uniquely customize an Office 2000 installation—data you create that overrides or adds to default settings— is stored in relational databases with the extension MST, for Microsoft Transform. Not only is data in these files used to set up basic and custom installations, but it's also used to update and repair existing installations. You can even install apps or parts of apps so that they aren't actually placed on a user's hard disk until they are used for the first time.

All things considered, we IS types are the winners here. Customizing installations is easier and, to a fair extent, Office 2000 reduces day-to-day maintenance because it is self-healing in a variety of ways.

 TIP   For more on Windows installer technology, take a look at the *Microsoft Office 2000 Resource Kit*, from Microsoft Press (1999).

In this chapter, we're going to focus on building the MST databases required to deliver customized versions of Outlook 2000 to a user's desktop. Then we'll manually run a customized installation of Office 2000 on a workstation. I'll leave it to you to deal with automatic delivery of the software to the user hard disks. There are several ways to accomplish this end:

- Automating the execution of the customized installation program through a batch file or an NT or Windows 2000 logon script

- Automating the customized installation using Microsoft's Systems Management Server (SMS), or other systems management tools such as Intel LANDesk (http://www.intel.com) or HP OpenView Desktop Administrator (http://www.hp.com)

- Burning and running a CD-ROM or DVD that executes the customized installation program

The following approaches won't work with the method I'm discussing here, but they will also get Outlook installed on user workstations:

- Use Norton Ghost (http://www.symantec.com) to create a hard disk image of a model end-user drive, with everything from the operating system to Outlook and other applications preinstalled; then automatically write the image to each new hard disk
- Use a product such as wINSTALL (http://www.install.com) to create an image of Office 2000 or Outlook 2000 and install it on user workstations

Check the Office 2000 Resource Kit for more on these options.

 NOTE Windows 2000 Server comes with a new and exciting feature, Remote Installation Services (RIS). RIS installs Windows 2000 Professional, the workstation version of Windows 2000, along with any set of end-user applications that you desire. You can script a RIS installation, or you can install a hard disk image as with Norton Ghost.

Installing Office 2000 on an Administrative Installation Point

Before you can customize an Office 2000 installation, you first must install a copy of Office 2000 on a server. This copy of Office 2000 is installed on what is officially called an *administrative installation point*.

Creating an Administrative Installation Point

An administrative installation point is a shared folder on a Windows 95, 98, NT, or 2000 computer. You can put an administrative installation point on your Exchange server for testing, but I suggest that you use another NT or Windows 2000 server in production mode. Office 2000 installations can eat up a lot of server resources, resources better dedicated to running Exchange Server.

You'll need about 550MB of free disk space to install Office 2000 on an installation point. So, don't move on to the next paragraph until you've located a disk drive with sufficient space.

To create a shared folder, in NT Explorer or Windows 2000 My computer, find the folder you want to share in the left pane, and click it. Then, with your mouse pointer in Explorer's right pane, right-click and select New ➤ Folder. Name the folder something like Off2000. Because the Office 2000 setup program runs under MS-DOS on

Windows 95/98 machines, keep the name of the directory at or under eight characters. If you don't, the setup program will fail with a command-line error.

To share your new folder, right-click it and select Sharing from the menu that pops up. Next click the Permissions button on the Properties dialog box for your folder. In the Access Through Share Permissions dialog box, change the Everyone group's permissions to Read; add the NT or Windows 2000 group Administrators, and give it Full Control permissions (see Figure 9.1).

That's it! Now you can install Office 2000 on the administrative installation point.

FIGURE 9.1

Setting up a share for an administrative installation point

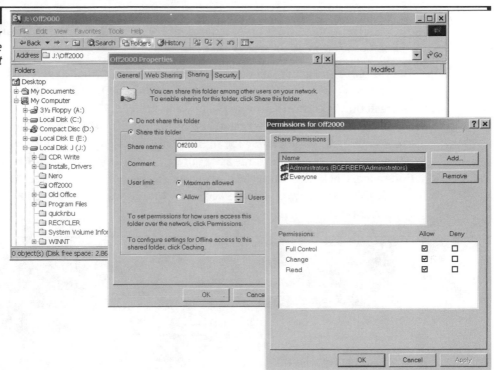

Installing Office 2000 on an Administrative Installation Point

Before we begin our installation, I need to make three points:

- I want to be sure you understand that we are not installing Office 2000 on this computer so that we can use it for word processing, e-mail, spreadsheets, or so on. We're installing it so that we can customize it and make it available for installation on the workstations of others.

- Although we will install all of Office 2000, if you purchase a separate copy of Outlook 2000, you can install it just as we are here.

- You must purchase a workstation license for each workstation on which one or more Office 2000 components is installed. Check with Microsoft or a reseller for information on licensing plans and prices.

To install Office 2000 on an administrative installation point, follow these steps:

1. Put the CD-ROM disk labeled Office 2000 Disc 1 into the CD-ROM drive on the server where you want to do the installation.

2. Open a Command Prompt (for Windows 2000, Start Menu ➢ Programs ➢ Accessories ➢ Command Prompt or, for Windows NT, Start Menu ➢ Programs ➢ Command Prompt).

3. In the Command Prompt, change over to your CD-ROM's root directory, and type **setup.exe /a data1.msi**.

The file data1.msi is the MSI database that comes with Office 2000. When you type the previous command, you're telling setup.exe to use this file for all the default Office 2000 application settings.

The installer for Office 2000 starts up in administrative mode (see Figure 9.2). Enter the default organization name for all installations from this administrative installation point. This can be the same as or different from your Exchange Server organization name. Click Next, and read and agree to the license terms. Then click Next and specify the share that you just created as the location where Office 2000 should be installed (as I'm doing in Figure 9.3).

FIGURE 9.2

The Installer for Office 2000 in administrative mode

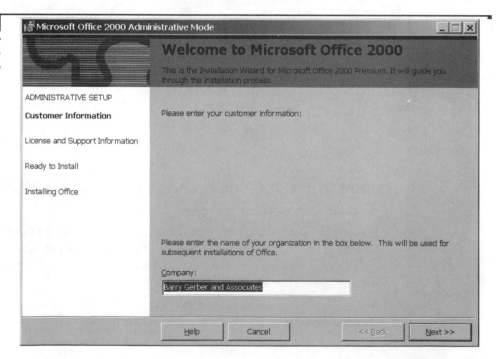

FIGURE 9.3

Specifying where Office 2000 should be installed

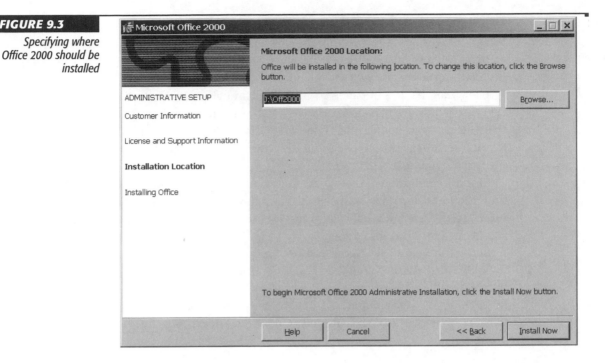

Finally, click Install Now, and Windows installer takes off. (Well, *takes off* may be a bit of an exaggeration. Let's say runs...and runs...and runs...and....) Fear not, though. You'll have to do this only once for each custom installation that you need to set up. For small to middle-sized organizations, that usually means once.

Customizing Outlook 2000

Before you can customize the installation of Office 2000 that you just placed on your new administrative installation point, you must install the Office 2000 Custom Installation Wizard. The wizard comes with the Office 2000 Resource Kit that I mentioned earlier in this chapter. To install the wizard and a whole bunch of other neat tools and docs, put the Office 2000 Resource Kit CD-ROM into your CD-ROM drive and track through the auto-run Resource Kit installation program.

Getting Started with the Custom Installation Wizard

When installation is finished, run the Custom Installation Wizard: Start Menu ➢ Programs ➢ Microsoft Office Tools ➢ Microsoft Office 2000 Resource Kit Tools ➢ Custom Installation Wizard. Whew!

The wizard has lots of panels to guide you through customization of Office 2000. Let's take a look at key panels, especially as they relate to Outlook 2000. I'll assume that you can any handle panels that I don't discuss here without any input from me. If you have any questions, check out the Office 2000 Resource Kit or Microsoft's Web site (http://www.microsoft.com).

In the second panel of the wizard, you select the MSI file that holds the default settings for your Office 2000 installations. In Figure 9.4, I'm pointing the Custom Installation Wizard to the file data1.msi on the administrative installation point where I just installed Office 2000.

In the third panel (see Figure 9.5), accept the default option Do Not Open an Existing MST File. Because you haven't yet customized the configuration for this administrative installation point, there are no MST files to open. You want to create a new MST file. If you were coming back to modify a custom configuration, you would select Open an Existing MST File and do your modifications using it as your starting point.

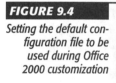

FIGURE 9.4

Setting the default configuration file to be used during Office 2000 customization

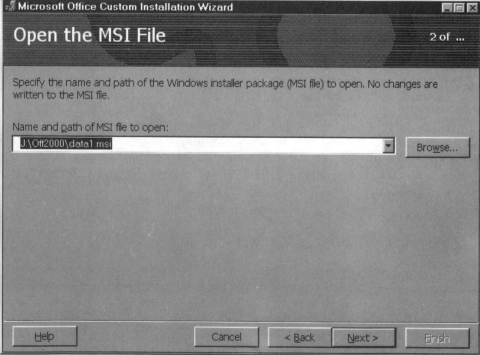

FIGURE 9.5

*Telling the Custom
Installation Wizard to
use a new file for the
current customization
session*

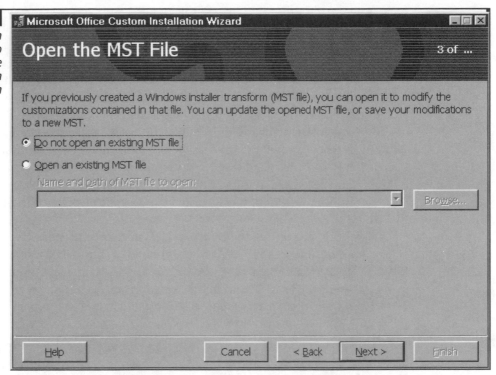

Use the fourth panel of the wizard to specify the name of the new MST file that you'll use for this customization session. Keep the name less than eight characters so that it's available to Windows 95/98 workstations. Try CUSTOM01.MST.

On the fifth Wizard panel, you set the default directory to be used when Office 2000 applications are installed – for example, D:\Program Files\ Microsoft Office or <Program Files>\Microsoft Office. <Program Files> tells the installer to put Office 2000 components into the first directory named Program Files that it encounters on a user's workstation. If users are likely to have multiple Program Files directories, and if you care which one Office 2000 apps are installed in, use the full path, including the hard disk drive letter, to force installation on a particular drive.

On the fifth wizard panel, you can also change the name of the organization for this custom installation. If you don't change the organization name, the one that you entered when you installed Office 2000 on your administrative installation point will be used. This is the place where you can specify organization names such as Accounting or Los Angeles Office.

The sixth wizard panel lets you choose which legacy Office applications should be removed when the new Office 2000 components are installed. It's good policy to remove all the old Office stuff before installing the latest and greatest Office apps. To do so, select Remove the Following Versions of Microsoft Office Applications and uncheck any that you want to keep. If you accept the default option Default Setup Behavior, the Office 2000 installer will ask if it should remove old Office applications if they exist on a workstation. If you want to do a silent installation with no queries from the installer and no input from a human, and if your workstations have old Office products on them, then you don't want the default here.

Panel seven of the Custom Installation Wizard is full of neat options (see Figure 9.6). This is where you tell the installation program whether to install various Office 2000 features, and where and when to install them. You can choose to install features on users' hard disks or on network drives, or to run them from CD-ROM. You also can decide if you want installation of all or some features to be deferred until a user first tries to run them.

In Figure 9.7, you can see the various feature installation state options that you can choose from in panel 7. The Not Available option tells the installer not to install the feature at all. Any of these state options can be applied at any level in the feature list, including at the top level. If you choose the Not Available option for an entire Office 2000 application, that application won't be installed.

FIGURE 9.6

Setting feature installation states

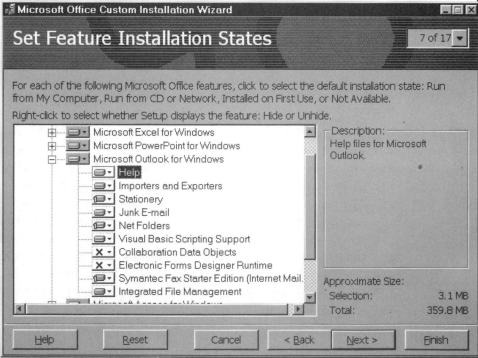

The Outlook Client

FIGURE 9.7

*Feature installation
state options*

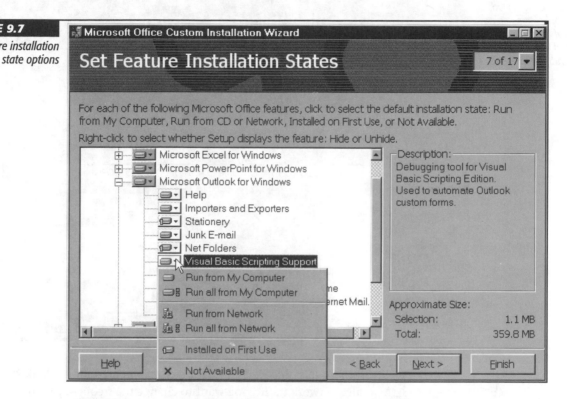

Customizing Outlook 2000 with an OPS File

The eighth wizard panel shown in Figure 9.8 is an important one. To understand this panel's function, you must understand how Office 2000 application installations are customized.

As you'll see in a bit, many important Outlook settings can be modified right in the Custom Installation Wizard. But there are other options that you can only customize using what is called a *profile*. Just to prevent a little confusion, these profiles have nothing to do with either Microsoft operating system profiles or the Outlook profiles that I'll discuss in the next chapter.

You customize all the major Office 2000 applications with a single profile file. To create a profile, you first install and run each Office 2000 application that you want to customize, changing its custom configuration settings to suit your needs. Then you run the Office 2000 Resource Kit's Office Profile Wizard on the same computer. This wizard processes your custom settings and creates an Office application settings profile file with the extension OPS. This file is then used by the installer to customize the settings for Office 2000 applications when they are installed on a user's workstation.

FIGURE 9.8

*Selecting an Office
application settings
profile, which will be
used to customize an
Outlook installation*

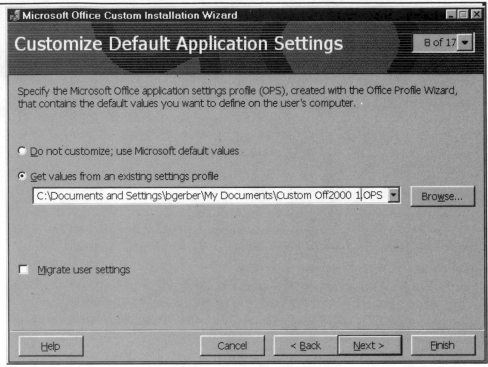

Let's walk quickly through this process, as it might be implemented for Outlook 2000. Let's say that, to reduce network traffic, you want to change the frequency with which Outlook checks the Exchange Server for new e-mail. You'd run Outlook on a workstation, bring up the Options menu, and change the mail check frequency. Then you'd close Outlook and run the Profile Wizard to convert the custom configuration for that instance of Outlook 2000 into the OPS file format. Finally, you'd use the Profile Wizard to save the converted configuration into an OPS file, which then can be used to customize all installations of Outlook 2000.

The only pain in all this is that you have to install Outlook and other Office 2000 applications that you're interested in to generate a custom OPS profile. On the other hand, this is heaven compared to the hoops that you had to jump through to create and edit profiles for earlier Office products.

TIP The first time I ran the Profile Wizard, I forgot to note where the wizard stored the OPS file it had created. I spent a fair amount of time looking for the file and quietly cursing. The Profile Wizard shows the path where it saves each OPS file. Be sure to write down the path. The wizard saves OPS files in your personal folder. For Windows 2000, that's `C:\Documents and Settings\WINDOWS2000_USERNAME\My Documents`, where WINDOWS2000_USERNAME is the Windows 2000 Server account that you were logged in under when you ran the Profile Wizard. For NT, the OPS file is saved in `C:\WINNT\ Profiles\<NT_USERNAME>\Personal`.

Now back to the eighth Custom Installation Wizard panel. You use this panel, shown in Figure 9.8, to specify whether you want to use default configuration profiles for the various Office 2000 applications, or whether you want to use a custom OPS file that you've created.

In Figure 9.8, I've chosen to use a custom OPS file that I created. Note that there is room here for only one OPS file. As I pointed out earlier, for a given installation, all the custom profile settings for Office 2000 applications that can be optimized using an OPS file must reside in one and only one OPS file. This file is incorporated right into the MST database file. This means that, unlike older Office customization processes, you don't need to keep track of the location of separate profile files.

If you check Migrate User Settings on panel 8 of the Custom Installation Wizard, the installer will retain each user's Office 97 settings where they exist. This option is automatically disabled when you select Get Values from an Existing Settings Profile. That's because you'll likely want to leave the settings in your new OPS file in place and not replace them with older settings.

 TIP You can control which applications and registry settings the Profile Wizard includes in an OPS file. To do so, edit the file PROFLWIZ.INI. This file can usually be found in \PRO-GRAM FILES\ORKTOOLS\TOOLBOX\TOOLS\OFFICE PROFILE WIZARD.

Continuing On with the Custom Installation Wizard

The ninth wizard panel lets you request that non-Office 2000 files be installed along with the regular Office 2000 application files. You could use this to install special templates or sample data files used in your organization, such as Word or Excel files. You use panel 10 to add registry entries during the Office 2000 installation. You might use this to modify a standard Office 2000 registry entry.

The eleventh of the Custom Installation Wizard's panels lets you specify which Office 2000 program icons are displayed. In panel 12, you can create a list of all servers that have a copy of the administrative installation point and its contents. Users can then install from any of these installation points. One of these alternative servers is used when the original installation server is not available and a workstation needs to repair itself, access Office 2000 files set to run from a server, or install new software set for installation on first use.

Use wizard panel 13 to specify other programs to run after Office 2000 installation is completed. This might include a setup program to install other applications or modify applications that you've already installed. See the Office 2000 Resource Kit for some interesting options, including one in which you modify Outlook settings using an application called NEWPROF.EXE.

More Outlook Customization Options

Panel 14 is just for Outlook; you can set a range of Outlook options in this panel (see Figure 9.9). As you set these options, you are building what is called an *Outlook profile*. As I noted earlier, this is something very different from an OPS profile or a Windows system profile.

You use Outlook profiles to set the types of e-mail systems that a user can access and many of the parameters associated with those systems. As you'll see at the end of this chapter, one user can have multiple profiles, each of which allows for access to different mail systems or parts of a single mail system.

Let's take a brief tour of panel 14. You use the drop-down menu that's open in Figure 9.9 to select the master configuration for the Outlook profile that you'll create. Your options are Exchange Server-oriented-with-Internet (Corporate or Workgroup Settings) or Internet-oriented (Internet Only Settings). Because we're focusing on Exchange Server here, select the Corporate or Workgroup option.

Figure 9.9 shows the General property settings for an Outlook profile. The profile name is used to identify this particular profile. If a user has multiple Outlook profiles, this is the name that the user picks when selecting which profile to use when starting Outlook.

FIGURE 9.9

Setting Outlook profile configuration parameters

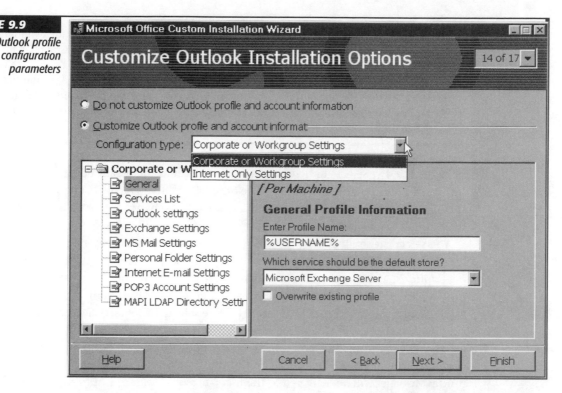

I've entered %USERNAME% in the Enter Profile Name field in Figure 9.9. USERNAME is an operating system environment variable. In the NT and Windows 2000 operating systems, USERNAME is a system environment variable that contains a user's NT/Windows 2000 username, which is what you type in before your password to log into your NT/Windows 2000 account. In Windows 95/98, you can set USERNAME or any other environment variable to whatever you want in a logon script or in the AUTOEXEC.BAT file. The command to create the environment variable USERNAME and set it to BGERBER is set USERNAME = BGERBER.

Why the percent signs in %USERNAME%? When an environment variable is used in setting Outlook 2000 profile parameters, it is prefixed and suffixed with a percent sign.

This is a wonderful new feature of Outlook 2000 profile configuration. In the past, you had to enter a constant in the Profile Name field or leave it blank, which then required that the user enter a profile name upon initially running Outlook. Now you can enter a variable from which the installer takes the name of the profile.

WARNING If you need to set USERNAME as an environment variable for Windows 95/98 workstations, use AUTOEXEC.BAT if only one user will log into the workstation. If the workstation will have more than one user, use a unique logon script for each user. There is one and only one AUTOEXEC.BAT on a workstation; it runs when the workstation first boots up. Anyone logging into the workstation will have the same USERNAME if you use AUTOEXEC.BAT to set USERNAME. If you use a unique logon script for each workstation user, then each user will get her or his own USERNAME.

In Figure 9.9, I've selected Microsoft Exchange Server as the default location for the storage of messages and other items. The other alternative on the drop-down menu is Personal Folders. Personal folders are stored outside Exchange Server on a user's own hard disk or on the network.

You select the services to be installed with Outlook from among the properties listed under Services List. Services support different kinds of mail systems and other neat options. The Exchange Server, Microsoft Mail, and Internet e-mail services give the user access to—you guessed it—Exchange Server, Microsoft Mail, and Internet e-mail systems. As you can see in Figure 9.10, I've selected Exchange Server, Personal Folders, and the Microsoft LDAP Directory. If you select Personal Folders, you're saying that the users' mailbox and other Outlook folders and their contents should be stored not on your Exchange server, but in the users' personal folders, wherever they reside. Messages will be delivered to the users' personal folders, not to their mailboxes on your Exchange server.

 WARNING If you select a mail service, be sure to configure it in the appropriate place in panel 14. If you don't, your users will be asked all kinds of confusing questions about parameters for any unconfigured mail services when they start up Outlook 2000 for the first time. Of course, if you have knowledgeable users or plan to provide training or cheat-sheets, you can ignore this note.

FIGURE 9.10

Selecting Outlook services to be installed

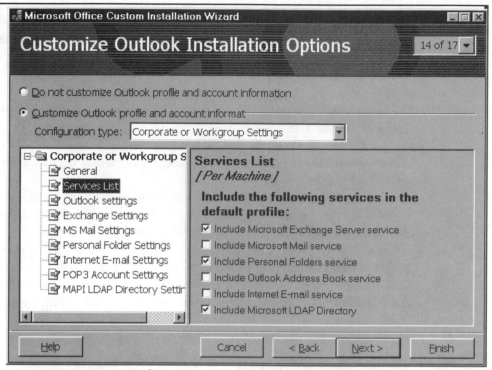

The Personal Folders service provides the user with the capability to store messages and other items locally. However, because of previous selections, these personal folders are just for drag-and-drop storage. Messages will be delivered to the users' Exchange Server-based mailbox, not to these personal folders. Other Outlook features such as scheduling or contact management will be in the user's Exchange Server mailbox, not in personal folders. To get all that stuff in personal folders, I would have had to select the Personal Folders as the default store back in Figure 9.9.

The Outlook Address Book service is pretty much a holdover from past versions of Outlook. Outlook's contact management feature is a far better place to store personal e-mail addresses, so select this option only if you're upgrading from a previous version of Outlook.

The Microsoft LDAP Directory service is neat. As you'll learn in Chapter 14, the Lightweight Directory Access Protocol (LDAP) is a way to access information about e-mail addresses and such from servers anywhere on the Internet. Windows 2000 Server supports LDAP for lookup of Exchange 2000 Server recipients, but this service is more about LDAP on other Internet-based servers. A bunch of these servers just sit out there collecting names, e-mail addresses, and so on. When you search for an e-mail address by a person's name, your Outlook client firsts looks locally at your contacts and at addresses on your Exchange servers. If it doesn't find the name there, it goes out to one of the big LDAP servers in the sky. Amazingly, it often finds the name that you're looking for. Unless your corporate policy runs contrary to this sort of stuff, do include the LDAP service in your Outlook installations.

Continuing our climb down the tree of Outlook custom installation options, the Outlook Settings properties relate to providing access to Outlook forms through a Web server. For a refresher on forms, see the section "Microsoft Outlook Forms Designer Forms" in Chapter 4, "Exchange 2000 Server Architecture." We'll get into all this later. For now, just remember that you can control Internet-based access to Outlook forms right here.

Move on down to Exchange Settings. This is an important one. As you can see in Figure 9.11, I've entered %USERNAME% as the name for user mailboxes. Again, each user's mailbox will get the name stored in the USERNAME environment variable on his or her computer. I've specified my server EXCHANGE01 as the server that the user should connect to when Outlook first runs. As the text in Figure 9.11 indicates, if you have multiple Exchange servers, you can enter the name of any one of them here, and the user will be directed to his or her own server automatically by the Exchange Server system.

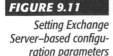

FIGURE 9.11

Setting Exchange Server–based configuration parameters

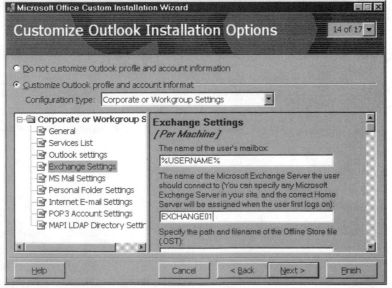

Figure 9.12 shows your other Exchange Server options. Users can make a local copy of their Exchange mailbox and the Exchange address book. This is most useful if the installation is on a laptop, but it's also comforting to have these files on a fixed workstation's hard disk in case network connectivity is lost. You can specify the path where the offline mailbox and address book files are stored, or you can leave these options blank and these two files will be stored in the user's NT- or Windows 2000-based personal folder.

FIGURE 9.12

Setting Exchange Server–based configuration parameters, continued

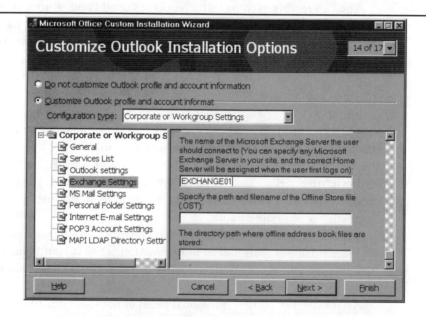

We can cover the other options on panel 14 quickly. Use the MS Mail Settings properties to preset a passel of parameters such as the path to the MS Mail server, the name of the user's mailbox, and the connection type. If you're an MS Mail aficionado, all this will make sense to you.

The Personal Folders Settings options enable you to specify the name of the file that contains personal folders and the type of encryption to be used on personal folders. The last three options on panel 14—Internet E-Mail Settings, POP3 Account Settings, and MAPI LDAP Directory Settings—are used to specify parameters for these Internet-oriented services. If you know what's what in regard to Internet services, you should be able to use what you've learned here to modify these settings. If Internet services are still a bit of a mystery to you, you'll be better able to tackle these settings after you read Chapter 13, "Managing Exchange 2000 Internet Services," and Chapter 14.

Finishing Up with the Custom Installation Wizard

Wizard panel 15 is used to customize Internet Explorer. To install Outlook 2000, Internet Explorer 4.01 or greater must be installed on the user's workstation. IE is used to support such things as Outlook 2000's extended encryption options. The Office 2000 Resource Kit comes with a copy of the Internet Explorer Administration Kit. Click Customize on panel 15, and the kit runs. Then you can customize the version of IE 5 that's installed with Office 2000 to your heart's content.

You can modify existing setup properties or add and remove new ones with panel 16. For example, you can change the default language used during the installation process (see Figure 9.13). Two options on this panel relate directly to Outlook 2000: OUTLOOKASDEFAULTAPP and OutlookConfiguration. As you can see in Figure 9.13, by double clicking OUTLOOKASDEFAULTAPP, you can choose how the installer handles making Outlook 2000 components the default application on a user's workstation.

OutlookConfiguration does the same for the Outlook master configuration. You can choose Corporate or Workgroup, Internet Only, or Ask User When Outlook First Runs. You'll remember that we set this option back on the Custom Installation Wizard's eighth panel. What you do on the 16th panel overrides any other settings that you've made, so if you select another option here, it (not the option that you set in panel 8) becomes the default.

Wizard Panel 15 contains a lot of interesting options. For example, if you want to force the user's workstation to reboot after setup is complete, which you might if this were to be a totally noninteractive installation of Office 2000, just set REBOOT to Force.

That's it! Click Finish on the final panel of the Custom Installation Wizard, and you're done customizing your Office 2000 installation. The wizard will save your MST file to your administrative installation point.

You must do one more thing before running a test installation: You must specify at least one command-line argument for Office 2000's SETUP.EXE program. This argument specifies which custom MST file or files should be used by SETUP.EXE. These arguments are set in the Office 2000 SETUP.INI file in the root of your administrative installation point. Then when a user double-clicks SETUP.EXE in your OFFICE 2000 share, or when SETUP.EXE is run in a batch file or logon script, the program includes your custom settings and any other options that you've specified on the command line.

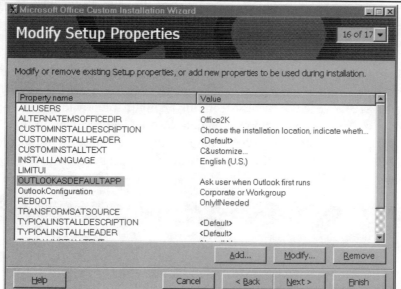

FIGURE 9.13

Modifying Setup properties

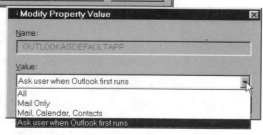

 WARNING When you edit the Office 2000 SETUP.INI file to add the name of your MST file, be very, very sure to uncomment (remove the semicolon before) the MST section header [MST]. If you don't, your MST file won't be applied during installation.

Using Windows Explorer, find the file SETUP.INI in the root of your administrative installation point. As you'll remember, mine is the shared folder OFF2000. Double-click SETUP.INI to open it in Window's Notepad app. Add a line like the one that follows to the [MST] section of the file:

```
MST1=\\EXCHANGE01\Off2000\custom01.mst
```

This tells the SETUP.EXE program to use the database CUSTOM01.MST located on my Exchange server EXCHANGE01 in the share OFF2000 when it installs Office 2000 from this administrative installation point. Also, as I warned earlier, be sure to remove the semicolon in front of [MST], or your MST file won't be included in the installation and all your work will be for naught.

You can do lots more to enhance the installation of Office 2000. For example, you can add command-line parameters directly to the SETUP.EXE command that cause the installation to proceed without requiring any user input and without displaying any output. For example, you could run setup like this: `setup.exe /qn+`, where /qn+ tells SETUP.EXE to run silently, requiring no input and providing no output except for a notice that the installation has completed. You'd especially want to do this if you were going to install Office 2000 components using one of the automatic methods that I discussed early in this chapter, such as running it from an NT or Windows 2000 logon script. Check out the Office 2000 Resource Kit for more on all this.

Watch Those SETUP.EXE Command-Line Arguments

Be careful about using direct command-line parameters with SETUP.EXE. Just before the Custom Installation Wizard terminates, it offers a sample command line that looks something like this: `setup.exe TRANSFORMS=J:\Off2000\custom01.MST /qn+`. You already know what /qn+ does. The TRANSFORMS parameter points the Office 2000 installer to the MST file to be used to customize the installation. If you know that users already have their J drive mapped, you should pick a drive letter that you know is available to users.

You might be tempted to create a batch file with this command on the administrative installation point and have users run it to install Office 2000. If this command is run on the workstation where you installed Office 2000 on the administrative installation point, all will be fine. `J:` directs the workstation to the correct path for the installation point. However, if this command is run on any other workstation, it won't work, unless the `net use` command is run before SETUP.EXE in the same batch file to map the drive letter J to the share containing the installation point, which is \\EXCHANGE01\Off2000, in my case.

The next command in the batch file after the `net use` command should be `J:` to ensure that the workstation is on the right drive to run SETUP.EXE. If you do map the drive before running SETUP.EXE, remember to unmap the drive letter after SETUP.EXE runs using the `net use /delete` option. Here's an example:

```
net use J: \\EXCHANGE01\OFF2000
J:
setup.exe TRANSFORMS=J:\Off2000\custom01.MST /qn+. /qn+
net use J: /delete
```

If you're not sure about the syntax for the `net use` command, just type **net use /?** at the command prompt.

Installing the Outlook 2000 Client on a Workstation

First, let me offer a bit of advice on where to install Outlook. Remember, from this point forward and all through Chapter 10, you're trying to replicate an end user's experience with Outlook. So, install the product in a typical end user environment. Install Outlook on a Windows 95/98 or Windows 2000 Professional workstation, not on a Windows 2000 domain controller or Exchange 2000 server. To install on the latter two systems, you'll need to mess too much with user permissions and will deviate too much from a standard user's experience.

Installing Outlook on a Windows 2000 Professional Workstation or Standalone Server

Each Windows 2000 Professional workstation or standalone server has a security group called Power Users. When you add a user to the Power Users group, you allow that user to sidestep Windows 2000 security for applications that have not been optimized for the Windows 2000 environment, or, as Microsoft calls them, *legacy applications*. For applications that are fully compliant with Windows 2000, the Power Users kludge isn't necessary. Of course, you can't stop using it until all applications on a computer are fully compliant.

Outlook 2000 is a legacy application. If you want to install Outlook on a Windows 2000 Professional workstation or a standalone Windows 2000 server, you must add the personal account that you created in Chapter 7, "Installing Windows 2000 Server," to the local group Power Users on the workstation or server. Here's how: Log in to your domain on the Windows 2000 Professional or standalone server computer as Administrator. Select Start Menu ≻ Settings ≻ Control Panel, double-click Administrative Tools and then double-click Computer Management. Next, find and select the container \System Tools\Local Users and Groups\Groups. Double-click the Power Users group. On the Power Users Properties dialog box, click Add. On the Select Users or Groups dialog box that pops up, select your domain from the Look In drop-down list. Then select your personal account, click Add, and click OK on the Power Users Properties dialog box. That's it.

You can accomplish the same end by creating a domain-based global group. A good name for the group is Power Users. Then add the group instead of the user to the workstation or server's Power Users group. To give a domain user Power User access on any Windows 2000 Professional or standalone server computer in the domain, add the user to the Power Users domain group. This approach is especially useful if you want to clone Windows 2000 Professional workstations from a disk image created by a program such as Norton Ghost. Just put the Power Users global group into the Power Users group on the workstation that you plan to use to create the disk image.

Continued

CONTINUED

One last point: If multiple users on a Windows 2000 workstation or standalone server must be capable of accessing Outlook, you need to take special precautions when installing Outlook. You must install it on the computer while logged into the computer's own Administrator account or into the domain Administrator account. If you're logged in as any other user, the install will work only for that user.

Okay, now let's start installing Outlook. From your workstation, log into your Windows 2000 domain using the personal account that you created back in Chapter 7. My account is named bgerber. From a workstation that doesn't have Office 2000 installed on it, open Windows 95's Explorer, or Windows 98 or 2000's My Computer. Find and open Network Neighborhood inside Explorer. Then find the server with your Office 2000 administrative installation point, and click the installation point, \\EXCHANGE01\OFF2000, in my case. Find SETUP.EXE and double-click it.

After several minutes, the setup wizard starts, gives you a few installation options, and begins installation. When the installation is done, your computer will reboot, your system settings will be updated, and Office 2000 installation will run to completion.

At this point, Office 2000 is in place, and Outlook 2000 and any of the other Office 2000 components that you installed should run like a charm with little or no intervention on your part. We'll actually run Outlook 2000 for the first time in the next chapter.

That's it for workstation installation. Not much, huh? That's because of all the work you did preparing everything with the Custom Installation Wizard.

Summary

Installing Office 2000 (or only Outlook 2000) on a server for others to install is a fairly complex process. First you need to install the product on a server on an administrative installation point on a server. Then you customize your Office 2000 programs using the Office 2000 Custom Installation Wizard that comes in the Microsoft Office 2000 Resource Kit. The Custom Installation Wizard allows for a fair amount of customization, including setting a default Exchange server and a variable that specifies a unique user account for first and subsequent logins to Exchange server.

You might not be able to do all the customization that you need with the Custom Installation Wizard. You can further customize your Office 2000 installation by creating an Office 2000 profile and then converting that profile into an OPS file. You create the profile by accessing a copy of Outlook 2000 (or any other Office 2000 application) on a workstation. After you've modified such attributes as the frequency Outlook 2000 checks for e-mail messages, you use the Office 2000 Resource Kit's Office Profile Wizard to create the OPS file.

After you've customized the copy of Outlook or all of Office 2000 on your administrative installation point, installation on any workstation is fairly easy. You need to ensure that certain security matters have been taken care of. If your installation plans include Windows 2000 Professional workstations, security preparations include adding anyone who will do an installation to the Power Users group on each Windows 2000 Professional computer.

Now we're ready to explore Outlook 2000. If you will, please flip a couple of pages and join me in the next chapter.

CHAPTER **10**
<u>**10**</u>

A Quick Overview of Outlook 2000

Because the focus of this book is on Exchange 2000 Server, I really don't have a lot of time for the client side of things. My goal here is to provide you with enough information to use Outlook 2000 in your explorations of Exchange 2000 Server from this point forward. For lots more on Outlook, see the book *Mastering Microsoft Outlook 2000, Premium Edition*, by Gini Courter and Annette Marquis (Sybex Inc., 2000).

In spite of the limited time that we can devote to Outlook 2000, we're still going to cover quite a bit of territory in this chapter. We'll set up a new Outlook 2000 client, send and receive a message, continue the exploration of Outlook profiles that we began in the last chapter, create a new public folder, and take a quick tour of some Outlook 2000 menus. That's quite a handful, so let's get started.

Before We Begin...

As you go along, remember that this is exactly the experience that an end user will have when starting and using Outlook 2000 for the first time. Try to think like a nontechnical user throughout this chapter. This will help you come up with ideas for special instructions or other help that you might want to give your users. As will become more obvious as you move through the rest of this chapter, it's much easier on your users if you do some of the preliminary setup work that I discussed in the last chapter.

I'm assuming that you'll use the Windows 2000 account that you created for yourself. If you expect to have new users who will be logging into their Windows 2000 accounts for the first time to set up and use their Outlook clients, you'll need to provide each user with whatever password information will be needed to log in. This will depend on the options that you select when creating each account.

Starting Up a Newly Installed Client

In the last chapter, you installed Outlook 2000 on an administrative installation point and then installed a customized copy of Outlook 2000 onto a workstation from the installation point. Now you're ready to use Outlook.

Log into your Windows 2000 domain using the personal account that you created back in Chapter 7, "Installing Windows 2000 Server." Mine is bgerber.

When you're logged in, to start Outlook 2000, find the desktop icon labeled Microsoft Outlook and double-click it. The Outlook 2000 client should open right up in your Exchange mailbox if you did the following:

- Mailbox-enabled your personal Windows 2000 user account back in Chapter 8, "Installing Exchange 2000 Server"

- Installed the Outlook client on a workstation while logged in as yourself, as per my instructions at the end of Chapter 9, "Installing Outlook 2000 from a Customized Server Image"

- Are now logged into your Windows 2000 domain on your workstation using the personal account that you created in Chapter 7

- Modified your Outlook client as I suggested in the last chapter

If things don't seem to be working as advertised, welcome to the club. It took me several iterations of the installation customization steps in Chapter 9 to get Outlook to behave as I expected it to.

This is Square One (Square One? Don't ask; you'll understand in a bit.): Check to make sure that your custom MST file is indeed in the shared directory that is your administrative installation point. If it's not there, then either you saved it somewhere else while running the Custom Installation Wizard, or the wizard never saved it. If the file is missing, you can look for it with Explorer or just rerun the wizard and create a new MST file. Be sure to save the file in your administrative installation point.

If your MST file is there, rerun the wizard, open the MST file, and check to make sure that all the custom settings you set up are there. If anything is missing, add it back and save the changed MST file.

When you're sure about your MST file, run SETUP.EXE from your administrative installation point, and choose to remove Office 2000 from your workstation. After everything is removed, run SETUP.EXE again and reinstall Office 2000. If all is well, Outlook 2000 should act as indicated. If not—you guessed it—back to Square One. All I can say is, given the time that it takes to uninstall, reboot, and reinstall Office 2000, you'll find that patience is a real virtue as you work the kinks out of your custom installation.

Okay, your Outlook 2000 client is finally up and running as expected. Figure 10.1 shows what the client looks like when starting up for the first time. Of course, depending on a variety of things, your client might look somewhat different. We'll fix that in the next section.

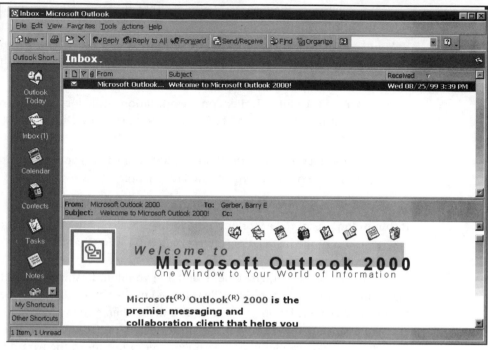

FIGURE 10.1

The Outlook 2000 client immediately after installation

Sending and Receiving a Message with an Outlook 2000 Client

Your client window is probably kind of small and scrunchy, so go ahead and enlarge it until it looks like the one in Figure 10.1. Now let's do some quick reconfiguring to make the client really useful.

If you can't see the toolbar just under the Outlook 2000 menu bar, select Standard and then Advanced from the View menu's Toolbar submenu. If you're accustomed to the left pane from the older Exchange clients that shows your folders, select Folder List from the View menu, or click the Folder List button on the Advanced toolbar. Then turn off the Outlook bar by deselecting it on the View menu. Finally, turn off the preview pane by deselecting it on the View menu or by clicking the Preview Pane button on the Advanced toolbar. When you're done, your Outlook 2000 client should look like the one in Figure 10.2.

If some of the configuration options that I've asked you to make clash horribly with your own aesthetic or practical values, feel free to change them when you're done with this chapter. But do wait until then, or you'll have a devil of a time tracking through what is to come.

FIGURE 10.2

Outlook 2000 configured according to Gerber's aesthetic and practical view of electronic messaging GUIs

Folder List Button   Preview Pane Button   Advanced Toolbar   Standard Toolbar

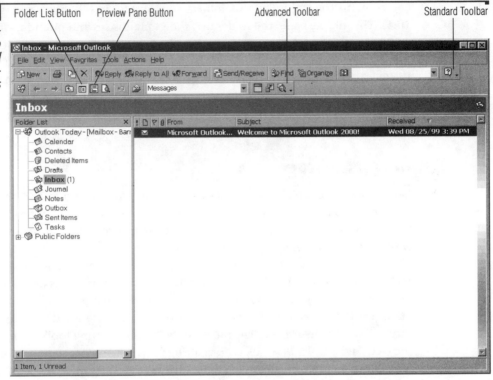

Now you should be able to see all seven of the client's default column titles. These include the following:

Exclamation mark: Message importance

Sheet of paper: Type of message

Flag: Status of messages marked for follow-up

Paperclip: Message attachments

From: Who sent the message

Subject: What the sender says the message is about

Received: The date and time that the message was received by the Exchange Server

Outlook remembers the window size that you've set when you exit. Every time you run the client, the window will be set to that size. Outlook is divided into two resizable panes (three, if you activate the folder list). The left pane, called the *Outlook bar*, contains the major Outlook folders, plus any folders that you add (see Figure 10.1). The middle pane, the folder list, shows mailboxes and public and personal folders in a hierarchical arrangement (see Figure 10.2). The right pane, the message items pane, displays the messages contained in the folder that has been selected in the Outlook bar or folder list (see Figure 10.2). And, if you've turned on the preview pane, you'll see a pane below the message items pane that automatically displays the contents of whatever message is selected in the message items pane (see the bottom half of Figure 10.1).

Sending a Message

Before we start, double-click the message from Microsoft Outlook 2000 in the message items pane. Read it, enjoy it, close it, and then delete it by clicking the big X on the Standard toolbar. Good, now we have a totally empty message items pane to work with—more of Gerber's aesthetic and practical values.

Let's start by sending ourselves a message. Click the New Mail Message button on the Standard toolbar (see Figure 10.2 for the icon's location). This opens a New Message window like the one in Figure 10.3. If you don't see the Standard toolbar for managing messages in the New Message window, select Standard from the Toolbar submenu on the message's View menu. If the text-formatting toolbar isn't visible in the New Message window, select Formatting from the Toolbar submenu on the message's View menu. Your client will remember that you've turned on these toolbars and will present them on every new message window.

FIGURE 10.3

An Outlook client's New Message window

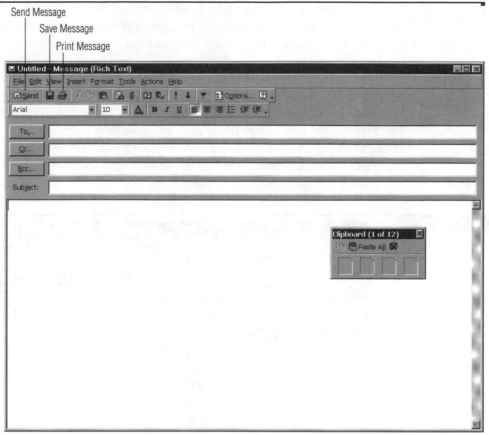

If you really want a thrill, select Clipboard from the View menu's Toolbar submenu. This is new to Office 2000. The Office 2000 Clipboard is really multiple clipboards: up to 12. So, you can copy different stuff to each clipboard and then paste whatever you need from whichever clipboard. If you don't like the floating version of the Clipboard, just drag it up to the toolbars section above the message, and it'll turn into a toolbar.

If you didn't know that you were in an Outlook client, you just might think you were running a word processing application. The top of the screen includes drop-down menus and a number of icons that you've probably seen in your Windows-based word processor. These enable you to produce very rich messages that can include text in different fonts, sizes, formats, and colors, as well as variously formatted paragraphs and lists.

The New Message window starts to look more e-messagy just below the Formatting toolbar. This is where you enter the address of the recipient(s) of your message. Click To; this brings up the Outlook Address Book (Select Names) dialog box (see Figure 10.4).

Notice in Figure 10.4 that I've clicked open the drop-down list of address lists and selected the Global Address List. It holds addresses for all unhidden recipients in your Exchange organization. We'll talk about hidden and unhidden recipients in Chapter 12, "Managing the Exchange Server Hierarchy and Core Components." The All Address Lists container and its subcontainers let you quickly find a type of address. You'll usually want to store your own addresses, such as personal Internet mail addresses, in an Outlook Contacts List.

FIGURE 10.4

The Outlook Address Book

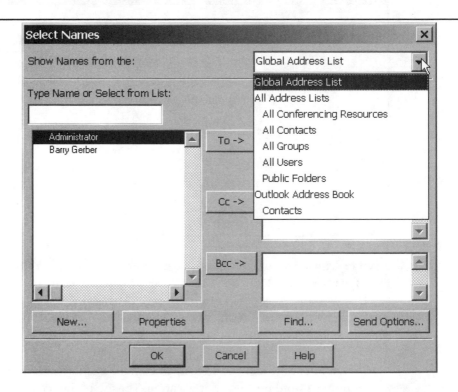

Because you'll be sending this message to yourself, click your name in the Global Address List. Then click To and OK in the Select Names dialog box. This returns you to your message (see Figure 10.5).

FIGURE 10.5

Composing a new
Outlook message

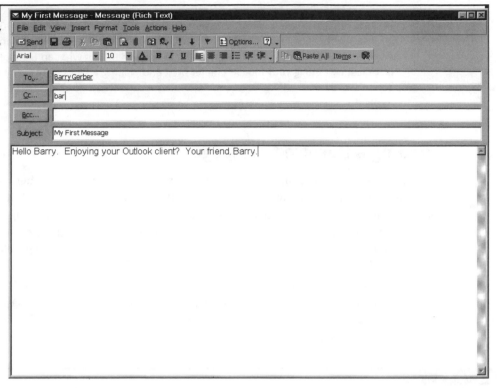

Now move to the Subject field, using either your mouse or the Tab key. Type in some text for a subject title. Next, move to the Message field and type in a message. Now place the text cursor in the Cc (carbon copy) field of your message. Type in the first few letters of your first name. Don't do anything else in the Cc field; you'll see why we did all this in just a bit.

 NOTE "Hey," you might be saying, "why are names are in first name/last name order (Barry Gerber). I want them to be in reverse order, with the last name first followed by a comma and a space and then the first name (Gerber, Barry)." Exchange 5.5 users are probably already thinking about the Exchange Administrator's Tools menu with its Options choice. That's where you previously set the display name format. Well, that's true no more, and for good reason. Now, to set this option, you must set the display name not just for e-mail, but for Windows 2000 users as a whole. The display name now shows up in a bunch of places, including Active Directory itself. You must change Active Directory attributes to change the default first name/last name order for display name. I'll talk more about how you do this in Chapter 12.

Now click the Send button on the Standard toolbar. In a second or two, the message should show up in your Inbox.

NOTE A few of the icons on the main Outlook client window in Figures 10.6 and 10.7 are labeled for your information. The rest of the icons are not terribly important right now. Anyway, as with most Windows apps, you can always find out what an Outlook client icon is for just by putting your mouse pointer on it and waiting a second for a tiny information box to show up.

Reading a Received Message

Let's take a look at your newly received message. Double-click anywhere on the message line in the Inbox window (see Figure 10.6) to open it. Figure 10.7 shows the open message. Take a look at the Cc field—notice how your Outlook client figured out your name from the few letters that you typed in while composing the message. Entering partial names into message address fields can save time compared with clicking the To button and finding names in the Address Book. Separate partial names in address fields with semicolons. If you enter a partial name that's not in the Address Book, or one that appears in more than one display name or alias name, the client will offer you a chance to change what you've entered or to pick from a list of all recipients containing the partial name.

FIGURE 10.6

The new message shows up in the Outlook 2000 client's Inbox.

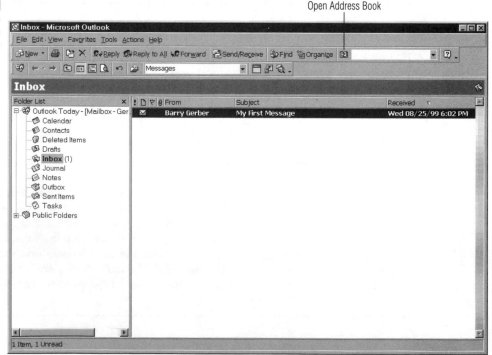

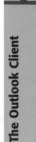

FIGURE 10.7

A received Exchange message

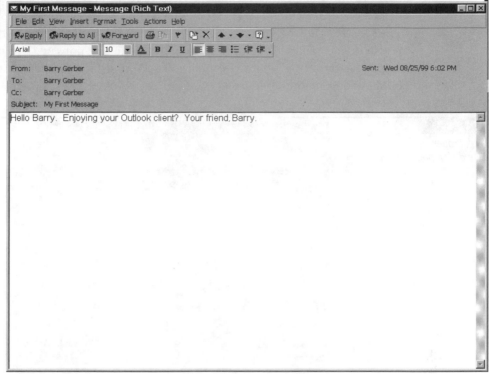

I won't go into detail about the message's Standard toolbar icons here; check out Figure 10.7 for specifics. If you don't see the toolbar in your message, select Standard from the Toolbar submenu on the message's View menu.

Outlook Profiles Continued

Back in Chapter 9, we customized an Outlook profile using the Office 2000 Custom Installation Wizard. I promised that we'd pick up on the topic in this chapter. This time, instead of dealing with Outlook profiles in the abstract, we'll take a hands-on look at them using our Outlook 2000 client.

You'll remember that profiles determine what e-mail system you can access and provide you with special features such as personal folders and special address books.

Each Outlook 2000 user can have one or many personal Outlook profiles. You can set up different Outlook profiles so that each allows access to a different Exchange mailbox, or to one or more Internet mail services, or to a combination of an Exchange mailbox and Internet mail services, or you name it.

Be sure that Outlook 2000 is closed. Then right-click the Microsoft Outlook icon on your desktop and select Properties from the menu that pops up. This opens your Outlook Properties dialog box (see Figure 10.8). Your default profile is displayed. We'll talk about default profiles in a bit.

FIGURE 10.8

The Outlook Properties dialog box

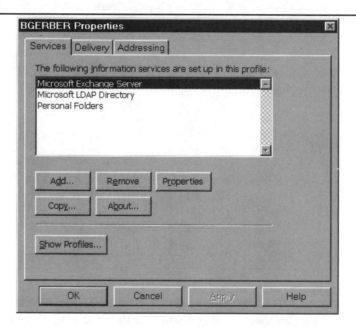

Click Show Profiles to open a dialog box for managing your profiles. Figure 10.9 shows this dialog box. To add a profile, click Add. This opens the Microsoft Outlook Setup Wizard (see Figure 10.10). Let's step through the wizard.

FIGURE 10.9

The Outlook profiles properties dialog box

FIGURE 10.10

The Microsoft Outlook Setup Wizard

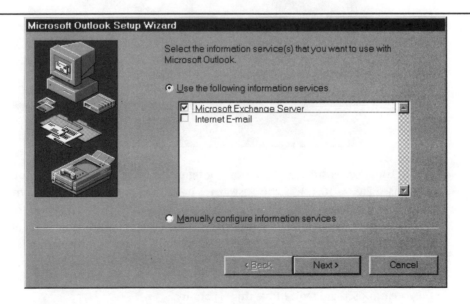

You use the first panel of the Outlook Setup Wizard to select the e-mail system or systems that you want to access through your new profile. Select Microsoft Exchange Server. When you're an Outlook profile wizard in your own right, you can bypass the wizard by selecting Manually Configure Information Services at the bottom of the first panel.

In the second wizard panel, you name your profile (refer to Figure 10.11). I'm naming my new profile BarryGerber (you'll see why in just a bit). In the next panel of the Outlook Setup Wizard, you indicate the Exchange server and mailbox that you want to use (see Figure 10.12). I've created a new mailbox called BGerber2 for this profile. You can enter either the mailbox name or the display name for the mailbox in the Mailbox field.

FIGURE 10.11

Naming a new Outlook profile

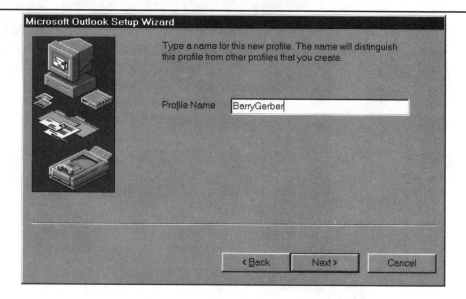

The next wizard panel lets you configure your profile to support mobile computers (see Figure 10.13). If you answer yes here, the profile will support synchronizing your Exchange Server-based folders for e-mail, contacts, to-do lists, and so on, to local files on your computer's hard disk. Then, when you're at home or in an airplane and not connected to the network, you'll still be able to access your Outlook messages, contacts, and so on. A yes answer also enables you to compose e-mail messages while you're not connected to the network. When you reconnect, the messages that you've composed are sent. I love this capability.

FIGURE 10.12

Specifying the Exchange server and mailbox for the new profile

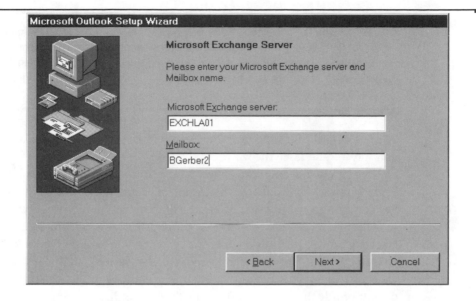

FIGURE 10.13

Setting the new profile to support folder synchronization

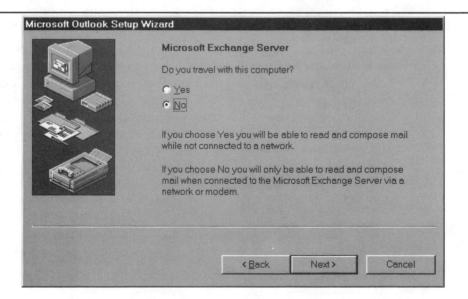

TIP If you're concerned about how your users will access their e-mail, contacts, and similar items if your network goes down, consider enabling folder synchronization on their fixed workstations. That way, if the network crashes, users can still open Outlook and use whatever folders they've synchronized. We'll talk more on picking folders to be synchronized later in this chapter.

The last wizard panel tells you what services have been installed. Click Finish to save your profile and leave the wizard.

Now let's take a look at your new profile. After you click Finish on the Outlook Setup Wizard, you should see the Outlook Profiles Manager (refer back to Figure 10.9). Before you do anything else, notice the drop-down menu at the bottom of the Outlook Profiles Manager (see Figure 10.9). You use it to select which profile you want to be active (in this case, the default profile) when you start up Outlook. If you need to change the default profile, then before starting Outlook, right-click the Microsoft Outlook icon on your desktop, bring up the Outlook profiles manager, and select the default profile that you want from the drop-down list. When you start up Outlook, the profile that you choose will control your Outlook session. Later in this chapter, I'll show you how to force Outlook to ask you which profile to use when it starts up.

Okay, now, double-click your new profile; you should see the Properties dialog box for your profile. Figure 10.14 shows the Properties dialog box for my new profile. You use the Services property page of this dialog box to view and alter existing services and to add services such as personal folders or support for Internet mail or for the Internet's Lightweight Directory Access Protocol. You can also remove services. The Delivery property page on the dialog box lets you specify where messages should be delivered for this profile, such as into an Exchange mailbox or into private folders, if they exist. Use the Addressing property page to specify the order in which Outlook should search contact lists and address books when it's looking up addresses for e-mail that you're composing.

FIGURE 10.14

The dialog box for a specific profile

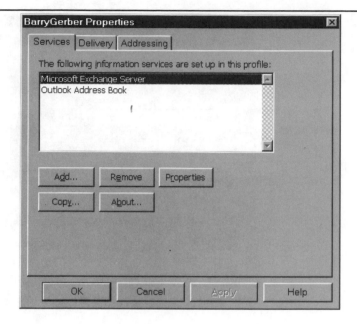

I'll leave it to you to explore most of these profile configuration options. Let's focus here on Exchange Server properties. Double-click the Exchange Server service. Figure 10.15 shows the General property page of the Exchange Server properties dialog box. Here you can indicate whether you want your Outlook 2000 client to automatically detect whether it can connect to your Exchange server or default to an offline or network-based connectivity mode. You also can set the timeout period after which Outlook will assume that it can't connect to your Exchange server and will open in offline mode.

You can also use the General property page of the Exchange Server properties dialog box to check whether your Exchange server and mailbox are available. Just delete and retype all or part of what's in the Microsoft Exchange Server or Mailbox field. At this point, your mailbox name will no longer be underlined. Then click Check Name. If all is well and Outlook can connect to your Exchange server and your mailbox, your mailbox name will again be underlined. This is a very useful way to check connectivity when you're setting up a new Exchange Server/Outlook 2000 user.

FIGURE 10.15

*The Exchange Server
properties dialog box*

On the Advanced property page, you can open additional mailboxes so that you can access them in Outlook at the same time as your own mailbox. You can also use the Advanced property page to set encryption options for different kinds of connectivity, choose the kind of network security that you'll use, and set up offline access to synchronized folders. We'll look at the latter capability later in this chapter. I'll let you work through the other options on your own.

The Dial-Up Networking property page is used to specify parameters for direct dial-up connectivity between your Outlook client and your Exchange server. This is different from dialing up to your network or to an Internet Service Provider and then using a generic NetBEUI or TCP/IP link to connect to your Exchange server and other applications such as a Web server. With Windows 2000, I encourage TCP/IP links, as should be no surprise if you've read Chapter 2, "2000: A Magic Number?"; Chapter 3, "Two Key Architectural Components of Windows 2000 Server"; Chapter 5, "Designing a New Exchange 2000 System"; Chapter 6, "Upgrading to Windows 2000 Server and Exchange 2000 Server"; and Chapter 7.

You can use the Remote Mail property page to designate how Outlook will act when it contacts your Exchange server through a direct dial-up connection that you've set up on the Dial-Up Networking property page. For example, you can download only message headers (sender, subject, date, time, and so on) and then choose which messages to download in their entirety. I'll leave it to you to follow through on direct dial-up networking and remote mail settings.

Creating a New Public Folder

Exchange public folders are created by mailbox users in their clients. For coming chapters, we're going to need a public folder or two, so I'll show you how to create one now.

Open your Outlook client and make sure that the folder list is displayed. Next, double-click Public Folders in the folder list, or click the plus icon just in front of Public Folders. Do the same for the All Public Folders subfolder. Your client window should look something like the one in Figure 10.16. (Notice that the little plus sign becomes a minus sign when a folder is expanded to show the folders within it.)

FIGURE 10.16

The top-level folder for public folders and two default subfolders

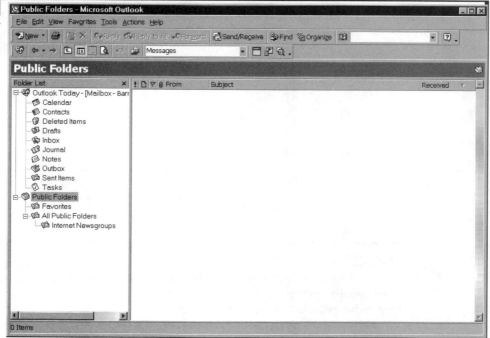

You've opened the top-level folder for public folders, which contains two subfolders: Favorites and All Public Folders. The All Public Folders folder has one subfolder, Internet Newsgroups. If your Exchange organization has a large number of public folders, you can drag the ones that you use a lot to your Favorites subfolder. This makes them easier to find. Folders in the Favorites folder are also the only ones that are available when you work offline without a connection to your Exchange server.

You create new public folders in the folder All Public Folders, so click All Public Folders and then select New ➤ Folder from your Outlook client's File menu. This brings up the Create New Folder dialog box (see Figure 10.17). Enter a name for the folder; I've given mine the somewhat unimaginative name Barry's First Public Folder. When you're done, click OK.

If you're told that you don't have sufficient permissions to create the folder, you'll need to give yourself those permissions in the Exchange System Manager.

FIGURE 10.17

Naming a new folder

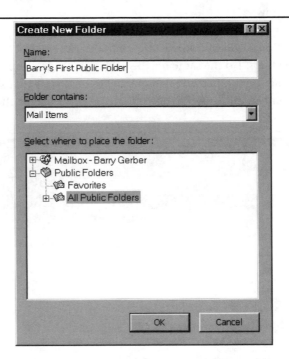

NOTE Have you noticed that public folder Internet Newsgroups? It was created when I installed Exchange Server back in Chapter 8. It holds Usenet (Internet-based) and local newsgroups and their messages. I'll talk more about newsgroups in Chapter 14, "Managing Exchange 2000 Services for Internet Clients."

The new public folder now shows up under the All Public Folders hierarchy (see Figure 10.18). If you can't see the full name of your new folder, make the folder list a little wider.

Now right-click your new folder and select Properties from the pop-up menu. This brings up the Properties dialog box for the folder, shown in Figure 10.19.

FIGURE 10.18

The new folder in the
All Public Folders
hierarchy

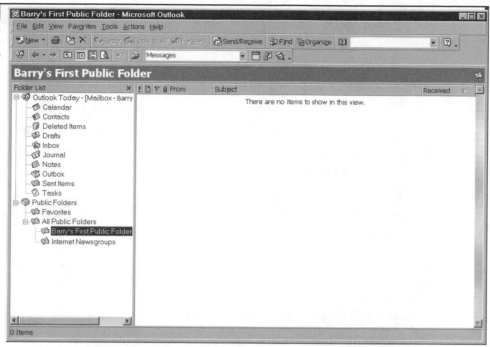

FIGURE 10.19

The Outlook client's
Properties dialog box
for a public folder

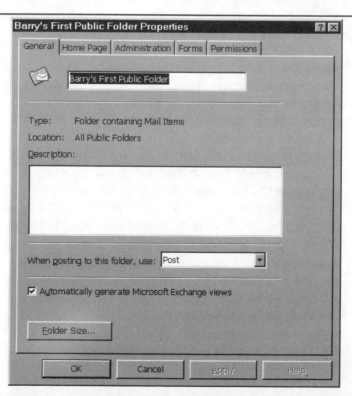

We're not going to spend a lot of time with this dialog box. Among other things, mailbox owners use public folder Properties dialog boxes to do the following:

- Add a description for other mailbox owners who access the folder
- Make the folder available on the Internet
- Set up views of the folder based on specific column title bars
- Set up some administrative rules on folder characteristics, access, and such
- Manage those neat electronic forms that I'll talk about in Chaper 18, "Building, Using, and Managing Outlook forms Designer Applications"
- Set permissions for using the folder

Go ahead and look around in the Properties dialog box. When you're done, click Cancel, unless you've made some changes. If you have, then click OK to save your changes.

 NOTE You create and manage private folders inside mailboxes in the same way that you create and manage public folders. 'Nuff said.

Using Outlook 2000's E-Mail Menus

To conclude this chapter, we'll take a quick tour of the e-mail menus for the main window of an Outlook 2000 client. These menus apply to Outlook's Deleted Items, Drafts, Inbox, and Outbox folders.

My goal here is merely to highlight the capabilities of Outlook as an e-mail client, not to teach you how to use all the options on the Outlook e-mail menus. To save time, I'll skip over obvious items that you should know about from using other Windows applications, such as the File menu's Page Setup, Print Preview, and Print options, or the Edit menu's Cut, Copy, and Paste options. And I won't be discussing the menus for new and received messages here, partly because some of what's in them was covered as we looked at message menus earlier in this chapter, and partly because I don't want to turn this into a full-blown tutorial on Outlook clients.

NOTE Menus for non-e-mail folders created by Outlook in a mailbox have a lot in common with their e-mail brethren. However, they also have their own special options. For example, the Calendar folder's File menu includes an option to save your calendar as a Web page for viewing by others. I'll leave to you the joy of discovering all the neat non-e-mail folder options.

The File Menu

The Outlook 2000 File menu is shown in Figure 10.20. If you see a little downward-pointing double arrow at the bottom of the menu, it means that all the selections on the menu aren't being displayed. To display all selections, wait a second or two, or move your mouse pointer over the double arrow and click it. The menu will bloom open, and you'll see all of the menu's options.

FIGURE 10.20

The File menu of an Outlook client's main window

New	▶
Open	▶
Close All Items	
Save As...	
Save Attachments	▶
Folder	▶
Share	▶
Import and Export...	
Archive...	
Page Setup	▶
Print Preview	
Print... Ctrl+P	
Exit	
Exit and Log Off	

New

The New submenu on the Outlook 2000 File menu holds a whole bunch of exciting options. Here you can start a new message or enter a new item for Outlook's Calendar, Contact Manager, Task List, Journal, or Notes Folder. You can also select forms or templates to use in messages, or you can even create a new folder.

A number of functions on the New submenu can also be initiated by clicking a button (for example, the New Mail Message button on the main Toolbar), or by right-clicking an object and selecting an option (for example, to create a new subfolder).

Open

The File menu Open option in most applications is pretty boring, but this is not the case with Outlook 2000. Of course, you can open (display) messages in a folder by highlighting them and selecting the Selected Items option on the Open submenu. But what's really interesting is the option that lets you open certain folders in another user's mailbox. Assuming that you've been given rights to do so, you can open one or more of the following folders in another's mailbox: Inbox, Calendar, Contacts, Journal, Notes, or Tasks. I often use this option to make calendar folders for scheduling rooms and other resources available to Exchange Server users.

 TIP To allow someone to access one of your folders, right-click the folder and select Properties from the pop-up menu. Select the Permissions property page, click Add, and select the user's name from the Outlook Address Book.

Close All Items

If you have a number of messages open, click Close All Items to close all of them.

Save As

This works pretty much like Save As for files. However, it lets you save an item in a folder as a text file, as an Outlook message file, or as an Outlook template. If the item in a folder is an application file, such as a Word document, you can save it to disk as an application file.

Save Attachments

If a message contains attachments such as spreadsheet files, you can use the Save Attachments submenu to select the attachments that you want and save them to disk.

Folder

Use the Folder submenu to create subfolders; to copy, move, delete, rename, or check the properties of the selected folder; or to add a public folder to the Favorites folder. (See Figure 10.16 and related text for more on the Favorites folder.) The Folders submenu is also the place to go if you want to copy the design of one folder to another folder. Folder designs include such things as the attributes of messages that are displayed in the columns of a folder and specifications for the way messages are sorted in a folder.

Share

You can share folders that are not in your mailbox—in other words, *private folders*—with anyone you can communicate with by e-mail. The person you want to share with must have installed the Net Folders option that comes with Outlook 98 and 2000. To share a folder, locate the folder that you want to share and click it. Then select Share ➢ This Folder from the File menu. A wizard guides you through the folder-sharing process. When you're done, those you're sharing with are informed by an e-mail message that sharing is enabled for the folder and are told how to share the folder. It's all done through e-mail and is pretty nifty.

Import and Export

Use the Import and Export options to input data into Outlook 2000 from a range of applications such as cc:Mail, Eudora or Netscape mail, ACT!, ECCO, Schedule+, or Sidekick. You can also import data in standard VCARD format (for Outlook 2000 Contacts), or standard iCalendar or vCalendar format (for Outlook 2000 Calendar). Items in a folder can be exported in a variety of file formats, including comma-delimited and Access and Excel format. Import and Export operates on the currently selected folder.

Archive

You can save Exchange server storage space by moving Outlook folder contents to a Personal Folders archive file. Use the Archive option to customize the archiving process to your heart's content.

Properties

Mailboxes, folders, and messages all have properties. Select the message or folder whose properties you want to see, and then click Properties. You can also see the properties of most Outlook objects by right-clicking the object and selecting the properties option on the menu that pops up.

Exit, and Exit and Log Off

Select Exit to leave Exchange while remaining logged in to all information services. You'll use this option when you want to close Outlook 2000 but still want to run other applications that use your information services. Choose Exit and Log Off to leave Outlook and log off all information services.

The Edit Menu

The Outlook client's Edit menu is shown in Figure 10.21. You use this menu to move and copy folders, mark messages as read or unread, and set up categories that you can use to classify messages.

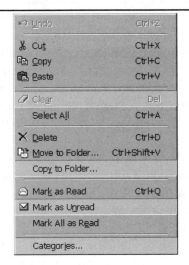

Move to Folder and Copy to Folder

You can use these menu options to copy or move an item or a set of items from the currently selected folder to another folder. You can also move items by highlighting them, right-clicking them, and selecting Move to Folder from the menu that pops up. In addition, you can simply drag highlighted items from one folder to another to move them. If you hold down the Ctrl key while dragging, the items are copied to the second folder instead of being moved to it.

Mark as Read, Mark as Unread, and Mark All as Read

When a message has not been read, its subject line as seen in a folder appears in bold type. When a message has been read, its subject line is in plain type. Select the messages for which you want to change the read status, and then click either of the first two options on the menu as appropriate. Choosing Mark All as Read will mark all messages in the open folder as having been read, regardless of which lines are selected.

Categories

You can place messages in one or more categories. Categories are used like key words when you search for messages. To categorize one or more messages, select the messages that you want to categorize in the Message Items pane, and click Categories on the Edit menu. Then check off the categories that you want to use for the message on the Categories dialog box that pops up. You can add new categories by clicking Master Category List on the Categories dialog box.

The View Menu

The Outlook client's View menu is shown in Figure 10.22. This is where you can set up a custom view of your mailbox and turn the Outlook Bar and Folder List on and off. You can also choose to preview messages in two different formats when you select them, and turn toolbars and the informational status bar on or off.

FIGURE 10.22

The View menu of the Outlook client's main window

Current View	▶
Go To	▶
Outlook Bar	
Folder List	
Preview Pane	
AutoPreview	
Expand/Collapse Groups	▶
Toolbars	▶
✓ Status Bar	

Current View

The Current View submenu lets you view the messages in a folder in a range of interesting ways. For example, with the AutoPreview option selected, the first several lines of each unread message are displayed just below each message's standard message header. AutoPreview saves you time because you don't have to open each unread message to view its contents and decide whether you need to give it your immediate attention. Among other things, Current View submenu options let you see only the last seven days of messages or to sort messages by conversation topic or sender. As you'll see in a bit, you can create your own views that are then available under the Current View submenu.

The Current View submenu also lets you customize your view of the currently selected folder by adding columns (such as Message Size) to the view, or by sorting and grouping by one or more columns (such as Sender or Message Importance). And, if that weren't enough, you can format the columns that are displayed in a folder and design your own custom views.

Outlook Bar and Folder List

You'll remember the Outlook Bar and Folder List from earlier discussions in this chapter (see Figures 10.1 and 10.2 and related text). You turn the bars on and off here.

Preview Pane

The preview pane is a window just below the pane containing messages. The currently highlighted message is displayed in the preview pane window so that you don't have to open the message to see what's in it. Click the Preview Pane button on the View menu to turn the preview pane on or off.

AutoPreview

The View menu's AutoPreview option shows you each message and the first several lines of each message. AutoPreview differs from the preview pane in that the former shows you all messages in a single pane (message header followed by content), while the latter shows you the message header in the standard message pane and the content in the preview pane.

Expand/Collapse Groups

If you've set up group-by-options capabilities for columns in a folder, you can use this menu item to expand or collapse the grouped views. As with hierarchies in Outlook 2000's Folder List, groupings that can be expanded are shown with a little plus sign to their left. Expanded groupings have a minus sign in front of them. You can click the pluses and minuses to open and close groupings instead of using the Expand/ Collapse Groups option.

Toolbars

Use the Toolbars submenu to turn Outlook's Standard, Advanced, Remote, and Web toolbars on or off. The Standard toolbar is just below the Menu bar on the Outlook client. The Remote toolbar is used when you connect to your Exchange server with a modem without a direct LAN connection. You can also customize toolbars by adding or removing commands from them and setting a variety of formatting options for them.

Status Bar

The status bar is at the bottom of the Outlook client's main window. It provides information about the contents of whatever folder is displayed in the window. Back in Figure 10.6, the status bar reads "1 Item, 1 Unread."

The Favorites Menu

This one is a little weird, from my perspective. It's the same view menu that you see on Microsoft's Internet Explorer. It shows your favorite Internet sites. When you select a site from the Favorites menu, the message pane (your Inbox, for example) turns into a Web browser.

At first, I thought this was the neatest thing. After the novelty wore off, however, I stopped using the Favorites menu. The Web browser in Outlook doesn't have the same functionality as Internet Explorer. For example, you can't open multiple browser windows simultaneously, and once you click any folder in the folder list, your capability to return to the Web page that you were viewing in Outlook's Web browser is severely limited.

The Tools Menu

The Outlook client's Tools menu is shown in Figure 10.23. You can use the Tools menu to initiate mail transmission and reception for your Exchange and other mailboxes, and to synchronize your Exchange mailbox and selected public folders with a copy of both on your computer. The Tools menu is also the place to set up remote (dial-up) access to your Exchange server, find and organize messages in folders, and set up rules for the automatic handling of incoming and outgoing messages. Finally, the Tools menu lets you empty your Deleted Items folder, work with forms, modify Exchange and other e-mail services, set a wide range of options, and customize toolbars and menus.

Send, Send/Receive

Send does just what it says: It sends any messages in your Outbox. Send/Receive lets you send to and receive mail from all your currently defined mail services, or pick a service to send to and receive from.

Synchronize

When you work offline with your Outlook client, you can have an image of your online Exchange Server/Outlook client environment, including items stored in folders in your mailbox and in public folders. That image is stored in a file outside your

Exchange server. What's included in that file is determined by your folder synchronization setup. You keep this image up-to-date by synchronizing it with your online environment. You can use this file and its contents whenever you're not connected to the network, whether on a laptop or your stationary workstation.

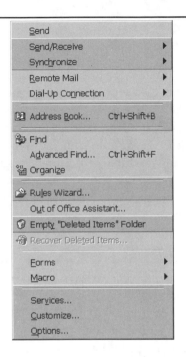

FIGURE 10.23

The Tools menu of the Outlook client's main window

You can synchronize when connected remotely or when connected directly to the network, as you might do with a laptop. If you're connected remotely by modem and your connection isn't too expensive, you can fire off a synchronization nightly or even set synchronization to happen every few minutes. If you're using a laptop on the road, when you return to the office with your folders full of new items, you can update your online environment by synchronizing it with your offline file. If any messages are waiting to be sent in your Outbox, they're sent out through your server, and any messages waiting for you on the server are copied to your offline folders.

Here's how to set up offline folder synchronization. If you didn't select this option during installation of Outlook 2000 or when setting up a new profile, you must set it up now. Select Services on the Tools menu. Double-click Microsoft Exchange Server on the Services dialog box. This brings up the Microsoft Exchange Server dialog box shown in Figure 10.24. Tab over to the Advanced property page. Click Enable Offline Use. Then set the directory where your offline folder file will be stored. If you're not automatically asked for the name and location of the file, click the Offline Folder File Settings button right next to Enable Offline Use. Finally, click OK until you've closed the Services dialog box.

FIGURE 10.24

Turning on offline folder synchronization and setting the location of the file to hold offline folders

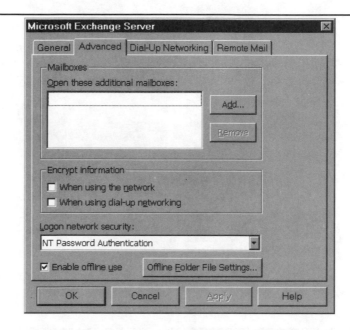

Next you must specify which of your Outlook/Exchange private and public folders should be synchronized. You can do this in two different ways:

- Right-click any folder and select Properties. Tab over to the Synchronization property page in the resultant Properties dialog box, and then select When Offline or Online from the page.

- Select Tools ➤ Synchronize ➤ Offline Folder Settings. Then select the folders that you want to synchronize from the tree on the Offline Folder Settings dialog box (see Figure 10.25).

The second option is new to Outlook 2000. It alone is worth the price of admission if you're a heavy offline folder synchronizer. You must go through the first option for every folder you want to synchronize. It's a pain, trust me. With the second option, you just check off the folders that you want to synchronize from the tree, and that's it. Thanks, Microsoft.

FIGURE 10.25

Selecting Outlook folders for offline synchronization

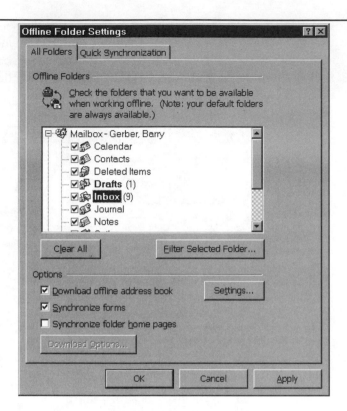

 WARNING The Offline Folder File Settings option on the Advanced property page of the Microsoft Exchange Server dialog box (Figure 10.24) is quite different from the Offline Folders option (Figure 10.25). The former lets you select the directory where the file that holds your offline folders will be stored. The latter lets you select which folders will be synchronized for offline use. What a difference a word or two makes.

Next use the Synchronize option on the Tools menu to ensure that your online and offline Outlook client environments are the same. The menu includes a small submenu that lets you synchronize all folders or only the currently selected folder. This submenu also enables you to download the current copy of the offline address book that is used when you're not directly connected to your Exchange server. I'll discuss the offline address book in Chapter 17, "Advanced Exchange Server Management."

TIP When setting people up to use an Outlook client at home, I often ask them to bring their workstation to the office. I connect the workstation to the network and then set up and perform a synchronization of all folders. For users with big mailboxes, this method is especially nice because those users don't have to run the first and most time-consuming synchronization when connected at home at 56.6Kbps or even at higher DSL speeds. And don't forget those public folders. Any public folder that you drag into the Favorites folder under Public Folders will be copied during synchronization if you've selected the folder for synchronization.

Remote Mail

Remote mail lets you set your client to do such things as periodically dial up your Exchange server to pick up message headers or messages. The interface is pretty self-explanatory, so have fun.

Dial-up Connection

You manage and activate NT/Windows 2000 Remote Access Service links to Internet Service Providers and to your Exchange server here.

Address Book

Select the Address Book menu item to see and work with the Address Book. Because you can easily access the Address Book when composing a message, you're most likely to select it from here when you want to add an item to your Personal Address Book. (You can also bring up the Address Book by pressing Ctrl+Shift+B or by clicking the Address Book icon in your Outlook client's main window.)

Find and Advanced Find

The Find option on the Tools menu opens a quick search pane on Outlook 2000. The pane applies to messages and other items in the currently selected folder. Type in what you want to find and click Find Now; Outlook shows you messages with the text in the From, Subject, and Message Body fields.

Advanced Find opens an impressive GUI that lets you specify multiple find criteria, including those in the Find command. Advanced Find adds such filters as who the message was sent to; times, such as sent time or received time; items with or without attachments; and so on. You name it, Outlook 2000 has got it.

Organize

You can organize any folder in a variety of ways by selecting the Organize option on the Tools menu while the folder is selected. Like Find, Organize uses a pane on the Outlook 2000 GUI. You can move messages from the currently selected folder to other folders, set Outlook to display messages in the folder from different senders in different colors, and change the current view that is used with the folder.

Rules Wizard

The Rules Wizard is a very nice rules-based agent with a helpful graphical user interface. When installed, Exchange Server and Outlook 2000 can perform a wide range of functions with mail that comes into your Inbox—for example, putting the mail into another folder, forwarding a message to another address, or performing a custom action that deals with the message. All these tasks can be based on various properties of the messages, from the sender to the occurrence of specific text in the subject line or body of the message.

Out of Office Assistant

The Out of Office Assistant is another neat GUI-based agent that you can use to send an auto-reply message telling people that you're out of the office—and letting them know what the consequences might be (for example, that you won't be getting to your mail until a specific date). The Out of Office Assistant generates only one message to a specific message originator during the time you're away from the office. If the original message is sent to an Exchange Server distribution group, the Out of Office Assistant generates out-of-office messages for the list's members, provided that the option has been selected on the Exchange Advanced property page of the distribution group. The services of the Inbox Assistant are also available as you set up out-of-office message scenarios.

Empty "Deleted Items" Folder

This one's obvious. The key here is that nothing is permanently deleted until it is removed from the Deleted Items folder. The Empty Deleted Items Folder option clears the Deleted Items folder of all deleted messages. With Exchange 2000 Server, even that may not be the end of "deleted" items because you can set up Exchange server so that items that are deleted from an Outlook user's Deleted Items folder remain on the Exchange server for a set period of time. I'll talk more in a later chapter on setting up Exchange Server to hold on to deleted items.

Recover Deleted Items

To recover deleted items, click the Deleted Items folder and select Recover Deleted Items from the Tools menu. You'll be offered a list of items that can be recovered. Highlight the ones that you want, and click the little envelope on the Recover Deleted Items window. Be sure to note the date of the item that you're recovering, because the item is silently recovered to your Deleted Items folder. If that folder is full of yet-to-be-deleted items, you might have a difficult time finding the recovered item if you don't know its date. This works best, of course, if your Deleted Items folder is sorted by the default received date.

Forms

I talked a bit about electronic forms back in Chapter 1, "Introducing Exchange 2000 Server" (see Figure 1.10 and surrounding text). I'll go into much more detail about them in Chapter 18. You use the Forms submenu to select existing forms and to create new ones.

Macro

Using Visual Basic for Applications, you can create macros to do various tasks in your Outlook 2000 client. You create and execute macros from the Macro submenu.

Services

You use the Services option to add, modify, or delete information services.

Customize

This option lets you customize toolbars and menus.

Options

The Options item is where users can override many of the default settings. It's also the place to give permission to other recipients to send messages on behalf of yourself, as well as myriad other neat functions.

While we're on Options, I'll keep a promise. Earlier in this chapter, I promised to show you how to get Outlook 2000 to prompt you for the Outlook profile to use when it starts up. Here's how.

Select Options from the Tools menu, and use the Tab key to move to the Mail Services properties page (see Figure 10.26). Click Prompt for a Profile to Be Used. That's it.

FIGURE 10.26

Setting Outlook 2000 to prompt on startup for the Outlook profile to be used

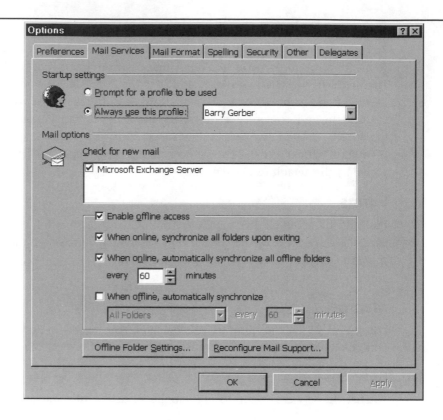

The Actions Menu

The Outlook client's Actions menu is shown in Figure 10.27. You use the Actions menu to start composing, reply to or forward a message, quickly find certain messages, and block junk mail.

FIGURE 10.27

The Actions menu of the Outlook client's main window

New Mail Message

Select New Mail Message to compose a message in a new message window. Clicking the New Mail Message icon in the main window or pressing Ctrl+N has the same effect.

New Mail Message Using

You can create messages with a variety of look and feel options. These range from plain old text messages to messages that use one of the cool-looking pieces of electronic stationery that comes with Outlook 2000.

Find All

Need to quickly find messages similar to the one you're reading? Highlight a message and select Related Messages or Messages from Sender on the Find All menu.

Junk E-Mail

Outlook 2000 has the capability to deal with junk and pornographic messages. You manage this feature here.

Reply and Reply to All

Use the Reply or Reply to All options to answer a selected or open received message. You can reply either just to the person who sent the message (Reply) or to all its recipients (Reply to All). When working with an open received message, you'll find it far easier to use the message's own Reply and Reply to All icons, which appear on the message's toolbar (see Figure 10.7). You can also use keyboard alternatives: Ctrl+R for Reply to Sender, or Ctrl+Shift+R for Reply to All.

Forward

The Forward option sends a copy of a received message to one or more other recipients; Ctrl+F is the keyboard alternative. As with replies, it's easier to use the Forward icon on the toolbar of an open received message (see Figure 10.7).

Summary

Outlook 2000 is a pretty user-friendly electronic-messaging client with lots of bells and whistles, such as calendaring capabilities, contacts, and a notepad. When Outlook 2000 is installed properly on a server, as in Chapter 9, a user can easily install Outlook and begin using it without having to respond to a single installation query.

Creating, composing, and reading Outlook messages is a very straightforward task. The Outlook address book, which includes Exchange mailboxes, distribution groups, contacts, and public folders, simplifies the e-mail addressing process. As with managing messages, basic public folder creation and management is an easy task, most of which can be done right in the Outlook client.

Among other things, Outlook profiles allow a single user to access a range of mail accounts with ease. Each user may have one or more Outlook profiles. When creating an Outlook profile, you can choose to access messaging services such as Exchange Server and Internet. You can also include personal folders and specific kinds of address books in a profile. By selecting a profile when Outlook 2000 starts, you choose which set of messaging services and other features will be available during your Outlook session.

The Outlook 2000 menu structure is complex, but it's easy to use when you're clear on what certain menu items do. Exchange 2000 Server brings several significant enhancements to the Outlook 2000 menu structure. One of these gives an Outlook user the capability to recover items that were accidentally deleted.

This concludes the part of this book dedicated to the Outlook 2000 client. Now we're ready to get into Exchange 2000 Server management. We'll start small in the next part, focusing on the Exchange server that you created in Chapter 8. Then, later in the book, we'll move on to larger, multiserver, multidomain Exchange 2000 environments.

PART IV

Basic Exchange 2000 Server Administration

So you've got Exchange Server up and running, and you've got the Outlook clients under your belt. Although you used it a little back in Chapter 8, "Installing Exchange 2000 Server," you now need to get comfortable with Microsoft Management Console, some of its snap-ins, and how these are used to administer and manage Exchange 2000 Server. In Chapter 11, "Managing Exchange Users, Distribution Groups, and Contacts," we'll focus on the Active Directory Users and Computers Microsoft Management Console snap-in and using it to administer and manage three recipient components in the Exchange 2000 Server hierarchy: users, distribution groups, and contacts. In Chapter 12, "Managing the Exchange Server Hierarchy and Core Components," we'll focus on managing the rest of Exchange Server's hierarchy and core components primarily by using the Exchange System Manager MMC snap-in.

CHAPTER <u>11</u>

Managing Exchange Users, Distribution Groups, and Contacts

FEATURING:

This chapter and the next walk you through lots of menus, dialog boxes, and pages for setting properties of one kind or another. I think you'll find it useful to track through everything once and set some specific Exchange Server parameters when appropriate. When you need to come back to a particular section, it should be relatively easy to find. Just remember that this chapter deals with the management of all Exchange recipients but public folders, while Chapter 12, "Managing the Exchange 2000 Server Hierarchy and Core Components," covers objects in the Exchange hierarchy, including the four core Exchange components and public folders.

 WARNING Throughout this chapter, you need to be logged onto your network as a user with adequate permissions to perform a particular task. I'll be logged in as a domain administrator so that I can show you every aspect of recipient management. If you can do that, great. If not, then you'll need to work with someone who can so that you can complete tasks such as creating users and their mailboxes. You should also try out the ExAd-First_Initial_Last_Name account that you created back in Chapter 8, "Installing Exchange 2000 Server." You'll find it has considerable control over the Exchange environment because it belongs to the Exchange Admins group to which you delegated Exchange organizational control in Chapter 8.

An Overview of the Active Directory Users and Computers Snap-in

You use the Active Directory Users and Computers (ADUC) snap-in to create new Exchange 2000 Server mailboxes, distribution groups, and contacts. The ADUC snap-in lives in the Microsoft Management Console (MMC). Before we tackle ADUC, let's spend a little time talking about MMC itself.

Microsoft Management Console

The Microsoft Management Console is a generic container that can hold one or many specialized management applications (snap-ins) for a wide range of programs that run on Windows 2000 servers. MMC centralizes system management in a single interface.

In designing MMC and its snap-ins, Microsoft sought to create a more object-oriented environment. In addition to pre-Windows 2000 drop-down menus, MMC snap-ins include menus that pop open when an object is right-clicked. For example, with Exchange 5.5, you chose to create a new mailbox by selecting New Mailbox from the Exchange Administrator program's File drop-down menu (see Figure 11.1).

FIGURE 11.1

Using Exchange Server 5.5's Administrator program to choose to create a mailbox

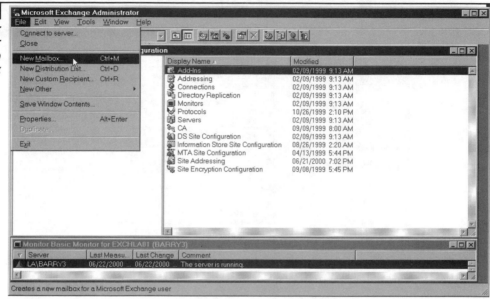

With Exchange 2000, however, you don't create new mailboxes: You mailbox-enable a Windows 2000 user account. We'll get into all this in the section "Managing Exchange Users," later in this chapter. You have the option to mailbox-enable a user account while creating the account. But, let's say that you didn't, for some reason. There are two ways to start mailbox-enabling a user account. You can select the user account and then select Exchange Tasks from the Active Directory Users and Computers snap-in Actions menu (see Figure 11.2), or you can right-click the user and select Exchange Tasks (see Figure 11.3). The Exchange Task Wizard helps you do such tasks as mailbox-enabling a user account or mailbox-disabling a user account.

FIGURE 11.2

Using the Action menu on the Active Directory Users and Computers snap-in to begin mailbox-enabling a user account

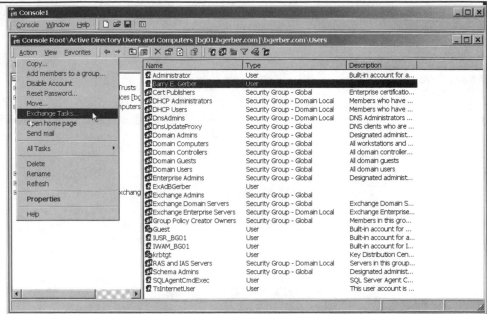

FIGURE 11.3

Right-clicking a user in the Active Directory Users and Computers snap-in to start creating a new mailbox

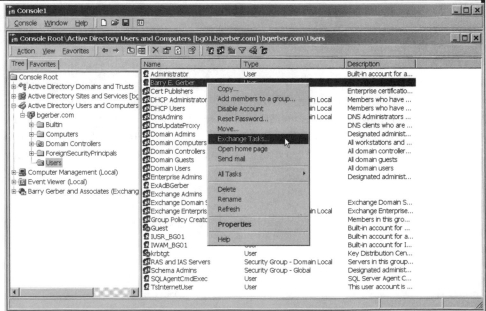

In addition to this seemingly minor change related to MMC snap-in design, Microsoft has renamed and even redesigned some of Exchange Server's key components. So, before you can even look on the Action menu or right-click an object, you're going to have to find the object. As we move through the world of Exchange 2000 Server management, I'll try to alert you to the changes between 5.5 and 2000, and point you quickly to the object that you need to complete a specific task. I'll use the right-click method throughout this book, but you can always turn to the Action menu if you're more comfortable.

Why Do I Have to Use That *+@#!% MMC?

It appears that not everyone loves the Microsoft Management Console. Focus groups and general user comments have not always been favorable to this new Microsoft tool. So what else is new? I really like MMC because it lets me put all my management tools in one place. Sure, many key snap-ins are available as standalone programs in the same place that your saved MMCs reside, in Start Menu ➤ Programs ➤ Administrative Tools. But I really don't like ripping through a bunch of menus every time I need to administer or manage a server component. As the number of programs administered and managed through MMC grows, this one program/one management app madness is only going to get worse. I don't even do the Start Menu dance to get to my main MMC. I put a shortcut to it on my desktop, and now I'm one double-click away from all my beloved tools. In this book, MMC rules. MMC haters will have to go elsewhere for solace.

Getting Comfortable with the Active Directory Users and Computers Snap-in

You used ADUC for some simple tasks back in Chapter 7, "Installing Windows 2000 Server," and Chapter 8. However, that was a closely guided experience. Now I want to give you a grounding in the snap-in so that you can work with it more creatively. In the process, I'll also be exposing you to some of the standard features of all MMC snap-ins. As my discussion of ADUC proceeds, track along on Figure 11.3 and on the MMC that you created back in Chapter 8.

First, notice that each snap-in that you add to an MMC occupies one row in the Console Root. In the left pane in Figure 11.3, the snap-ins are as follows:

- Active Directory Domains and Trusts
- Active Directory Sites and Services

- Active Directory Users and Computers
- Computer Management (Local)
- Event Viewer (Local)
- Barry Gerber and Associates (Exchange)

You can open any snap-in or its subcontainers by double-clicking it or by clicking on the plus sign just to the left of the snap-in or a subcontainer. In Figure 11.3, Active Directory Users and Computers is open to show some of its subcontainers.

All Active Directory-oriented snap-ins use the Windows 2000 domain for internal organization. In Figure 11.3, there is one domain in Active Directory User and Computers, bgerber.com. Within each domain are subcontainers that hold various components relevant to the function of the snap-in. The subcontainers within an Active Directory Users and Computers snap-in include, but are not limited to, these:

- Builtin
- Computers
- Domain Controllers
- ForeignSecurityPrincipals
- Users

The Builtin container holds local Windows 2000 groups essential to the operation of the domain. These include groups such as Administrators, Backup Operators, and Users. Nondomain controller computers are held in the Computers container, while domain controllers find a home in the Domain Controllers container. Security information relating to other domains is held in the ForeignSecurityPrincipals container.

System- and user-created groups and user accounts live in the Users container, at least in simple systems. Technically, users and groups can live in any container in ADUC. You'll probably want to leave default users and groups in the Users container and create new users and groups in that container. However, if your system is complex, you might want to create organizational unit containers to better organize your users and groups and to allow you to distribute administrative responsibility. To create an organizational unit, right-click on your domain in ADUC and select New ➢ Organizational Unit.

It could probably go without saying, but I'm going to say it anyway. The right pane always shows what's in the selected container in the left pane. In Figure 11.3, the Users container has been selected, and the users and groups in the container are displayed in the right pane.

TIP The columns in the right pane of any container show attributes of the objects in the container. Some containers show only a few of the many attributes available for a container: The Users container is one. To show more columns, select the container and select Choose Columns from the snap-in's View menu. This brings up a dialog box that you can use to add columns to the right pane.

As I noted previously, you initiate tasks relating to a specific object in a container either by selecting the task from the Action menu or by right-clicking the object and selecting the task from the pop-up menu. As its name implies, the Action menu is the place you go for just about everything. Even the Refresh command, to update whatever is in the right and left panes, is in the Action menu, not in its familiar pre-Windows 2000 location in the View menu. As you'll see in a bit, the View menu is important, but not for something as mundane as refreshing your view of a window.

The Favorites menu and tab, both in the upper-left portion of Figure 11.3, work just like Favorites in Microsoft's Internet Explorer and Outlook. You use the Favorites menu to select a specific container for inclusion on the Favorites tab. Then you can use the Tab key to move to Favorites and see just your favorite containers. With Internet Explorer and Outlook, the Favorites option is a shortcut to often-used Web URLs. With MMC snap-ins, the option is a shortcut to often-used containers. In Figure 11.4, I've added the Active Directory Users and Computers User container and Exchange System Manager to my Favorites.

FIGURE 11.4

The Active Directory Users and Computers Users container and Exchange System Manager as MMC favorites

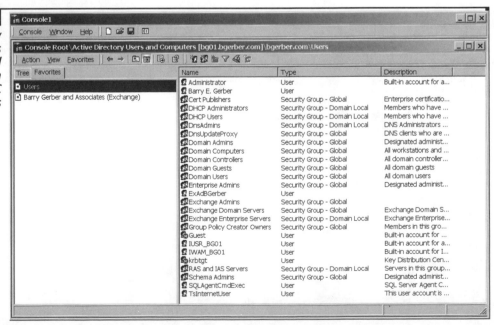

Preliminary Settings

Now that you have some Active Directory Users and Computer snap-in basics under your belt, you're almost ready to use the snap-in. Before you start, however, you'll need to set a parameter for ADUC and ensure that you're happy with a couple of formats used when e-mail addresses are created for new users.

Turning On Advanced Features

The Active Directory Users and Computers container is like a chameleon. In its default mode, you see the containers shown in Figure 11.3. When you turn on what are called Advanced Features, the chameleon figuratively turns a very different color. You not only see additional containers within a domain container, but you see a lot of additional attributes for many objects. These additional containers and attributes allow you to do a range of neat tasks that are otherwise unavailable in the default mode.

Okay, let's turn on Advanced Features. This is a no-brainer. On your MMC, while in any container in ADUC, Select View ➢ Advanced Features. As Figure 11.5 shows, three new containers become visible:

- LostAndFound
- Microsoft Exchange System Objects
- System

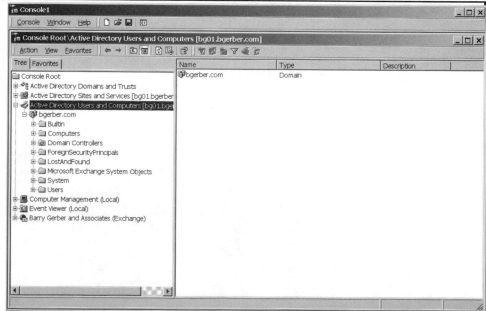

FIGURE 11.5

Active Directory Users and Computers with Advanced Features turned on

LostAndFound is a place where objects that have become detached from their home container are placed. Microsoft Exchange System Objects holds system-created public folders and users. System is where a range of Windows 2000 system objects are represented, from default domain policy to IP security, to policies. Now, don't get too excited about these three containers; you really can't do much within them other than find something in them or move them somewhere else.

The real power of the Advanced Features setting is in the attributes of objects that it exposes. Here's an example: Figure 11.6 shows the dialog box for my Windows 2000 user account with Advanced Features turned off. Figure 11.7 shows the same dialog box with Advanced Features activated.

FIGURE 11.6

The dialog box for a Windows 2000 user account without Advanced Features

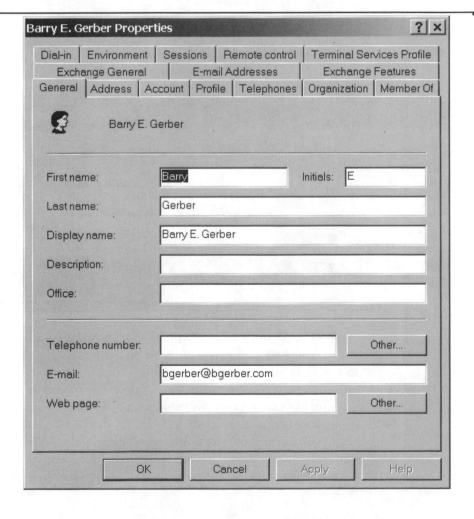

Barry E. Gerber Properties

Tabs: Published Certificates | Member Of | Dial-in | Object | Security | Environment
Sessions | Remote control | Terminal Services Profile | Exchange General
E-mail Addresses | Exchange Features | Exchange Advanced
General | Address | Account | Profile | Telephones | Organization

Barry E. Gerber

First name: Barry   Initials: E

Last name: Gerber

Display name: Barry E. Gerber

Description:

Office:

Telephone number: Other...

E-mail: bgerber@bgerber.com

Web page: Other...

OK   Cancel   Apply   Help

Figure 11.6 may be daunting enough with its 15 tabs. Add Advanced Features, and you've got another 4 tabs, for a total of 19. Yipes!

Not to worry. We'll talk about the Exchange-related tabs in both figures in some detail before this chapter comes to an end. For now, just appreciate that without Advanced Features, you won't see the Published Certificates, Object, Security, and Exchange Advanced tabs.

Now that you've turned on ADUC Advanced Features, I'd like to be sure that your MMC opens with Advanced Features activated. To do this, close your MMC. When you're asked whether you want to save your MMC console settings, click Yes. Now, as long as you don't turn off Advanced Features and resave your settings, every time you open your MMC console, Advanced Features will be turned on.

 WARNING Mark this page in your copy of this book by folding over the corner. As you move into later chapters, I'll ask you to do something that requires Advanced Features without necessarily telling you that it's an advanced feature. If this ever happens, hopefully you will remember this page and come back here. How do I know this? A good deal of the e-mail that I have received from readers in the past regarding doing one task or another in Exchange Server 5.5 was motivated by the fact that they forgot to do the equivalent of setting Advanced Features in the Exchange 5.5 Administrator program. For Exchange 5.5 aficionados, it was Tools ➤ Options ➤ Permissions ➤ Show Permissions page for all objects.

Default E-Mail Address Formats

There are two defaults for e-mail addresses that you should consider now. The first has to do with the format of display names, as these were defined in Chapter 5, "Designing a New Exchange 2000 System." The second default has to do with the format of e-mail addresses, such as @bgerber.com. You may change either of these at any time. However, it is best to get things straight now, so take a moment to peruse the next two sections.

Setting the Default Format for Display Names

The display name is the one that a user sees when looking for an e-mail address in the Outlook address book or when looking for a user in Active Directory. With Exchange Server 5.5, setting the default format for a user's display name (Martha E. Jones vs. Jones, Martha E., for example) was a very simple task. You chose Options from the Tool menu and then selected the format or set up a custom format.

With Exchange 5.5 and NT 4, e-mail and user display names were essentially two different things stored in two different places. With Exchange 2000 and Windows 2000, e-mail and operating system display names are the same thing. The display name is created when the user's Windows 2000 account is created. You can change a display name in ADUC, but the default format for the display name must be set in the Active Directory schema.

Messing with Active Directory's schema is akin to messing with a server or workstation's registry, but it's a thousand times more dangerous because you can affect a whole Windows 2000 forest, not just one computer. That said, I'm going to show you how to change the default display name format (first_name first_letter_of_middle_ name period last_name) by editing Active Directory. Be careful! Of course, if you're happy with the default, you can just follow along here without doing anything, for a lesson in the fun and games of Active Directory editing.

First, you must install a program called ADSI Edit (for Active Directory Service Interfaces Edit). You'll use this program to change the default display name format. ADSI Edit is one of a number of support tools that you install from your Windows 2000 Server CD-ROM disk. To install the support tools, find and double-click \support\tools\setup.exe on the CD. Follow the simple directions for installation.

When the support tools are installed, you're ready to use ADSI Edit. Select Start Menu ➤ Programs ➤ Windows 2000 Support Tools ➤ Tools ➤ ADSI Edit. In a second or so, you should see a window something like the one in Figure 11.8.

FIGURE 11.8

ADSI Edit as it appears when it starts up

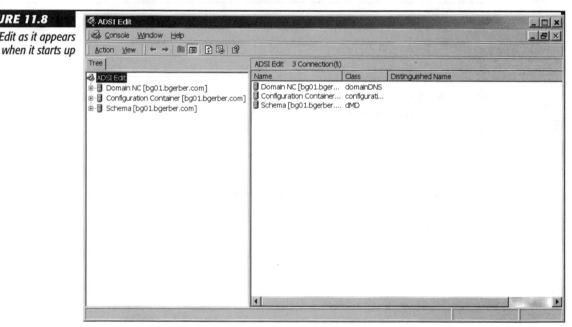

Now, click open Configuration Container and its subcontainers until your ADSI Edit window looks like the one in Figure 11.9. Select the correct language container. CN=409 is for English. Find the object user-Display in the right pane, and double-click it (see Figure 11.10). Select createDialog from the Select a Property to View drop-down list, as in Figure 11.10. Then enter **%<sn>, %<givenName>** in the Edit Attribute field. This will cause the surname (last name) to appear first, followed by a comma and then by the givenName (first name). Click Set and then OK.

FIGURE 11.9

Accessing the appropriate ADSI Edit language subcontainer

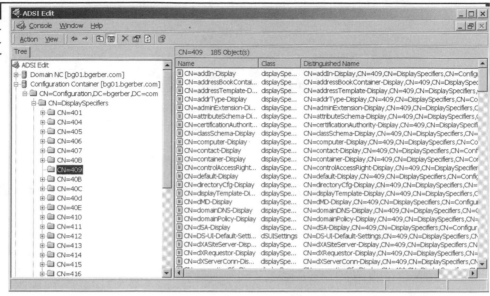

FIGURE 11.10

Editing the Active Directory schema to change the format of the Windows 2000/Exchange 2000 display name

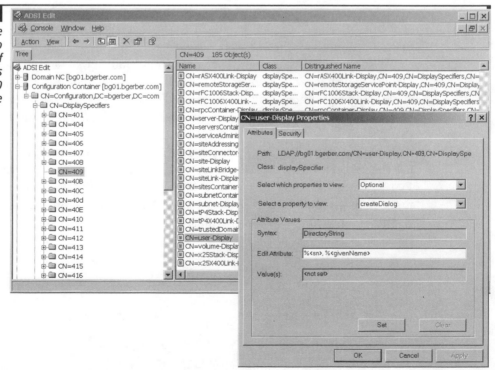

ADSI Edit is an MMC snap-in. After you've installed the Windows 2000 support tools, you can add ADSI Edit to your MMC. After you add ADSI Edit to your MMC, you need to connect to Active Directory. With ADSI Edit highlighted, select Action ➢ Connect To. Be sure to select Configuration Container from the Naming Context drop-down list on the Connection dialog box. Click OK, and your ADSI Edit snap-in will have full access to the same Configuration container that you used previously when running ADSI Edit from the Start menu.

For the record, ADSI Edit gives you access to your Active Directory's schema by way of the Lightweight Directory Access Protocol (LDAP). LDAP has come a long way since its first implementation in Exchange Server 5.5.

Setting the Default Format for Organizational E-mail Addresses

When you installed your Exchange server (assuming that you followed the directions in Chapter 8), two addressing defaults were created for your Exchange organization: one for SMTP (Internet) and one for X.400. These addressing defaults are contained within what is called the *default recipient policy*. The SMTP addressing default is appended to each Exchange user's alias name to create the user's full SMTP address. For example, my organizational SMTP addressing default is @bgerber.com; my e-mail address then becomes bgerber@bgerber.com. See Figure 11.11, which shows the E-mail Addresses property page of the Properties dialog box for user bgerber. Exchange Server uses first and last names, along with the X.400 addressing default, to a create full X.400 address for each user.

You can change either of the two addressing defaults. Use caution here, however, because any changes that you make should be based on addresses that you have or expect to get in the real world. For example, if you already have a registered Internet domain name, you may want to change your SMTP addressing default to reflect that name.

To change addressing defaults, open your Exchange System Manager until it looks like the one in Figure 11.12. Find and click Recipient Policies. Keep tracking on Figure 11.12. Locate the Default Policy object in the right pane, and double-click it. Tab over to the E-mail Addresses property page on the Default Policy Properties dialog box.

There you see the addressing defaults. To change either addressing default, double-click it and make your changes.

FIGURE 11.11

*A user's Exchange
e-mail addresses, as
shown on the user's
Properties dialog box*

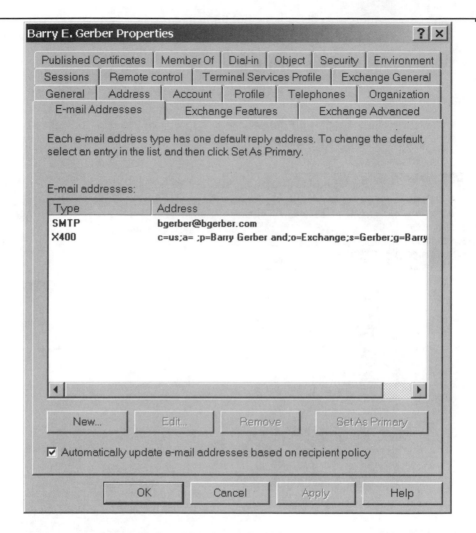

In addition to changing the addressing default for an organization, you can add policies for specific types of Exchange recipients. As you begin to develop a multi-server Exchange hierarchy, you can develop additional recipient policies for specific types of Exchange recipients that apply to specific Exchange servers. This lets you create different addressing defaults for different servers.

Addressing defaults are not limited to the SMTP and X.400. When you install a new Exchange connector or gateway (for cc:Mail or MS Mail, for example,) Exchange generates addressing defaults the new messaging system.

If you change or add an addressing default, you don't have to manually change all existing recipient addresses. Exchange can regenerate addressing entries for all recipients.

We're done with the preliminaries. Now we're ready to begin working with Exchange recipients.

FIGURE 11.12

The Default Policy Properties dialog box is used to change the addressing default for an Exchange organization.

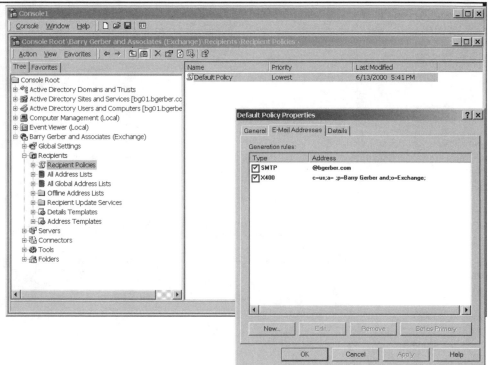

Managing Exchange Recipients

If you're familiar with Exchange Server 5.5, a lot of what follows should make sense. However, because Windows 2000 and Exchange 2000 take an object-oriented approach to system management, you often have to start and complete a specific task in a different way in Exchange 2000.

In this section, we'll focus on managing three of the four Exchange recipient types:

- Users who may be either *mailbox-enabled* or *mail-enabled*
- Distribution groups, also called *mail-enabled groups*
- Contacts

In the next chapter, we'll work with public folders. Why not deal with public folders in this chapter? As I've mentioned before, you work with mailboxes, distribution groups, and contacts in Active Directory Users and Computers, while you work with public folders in Exchange System Manager. We'll deal in great detail with Exchange System Manager in the next chapter, and I'd like to wait until we get there to get into public folder management.

Now let's move on to managing each type of Exchange recipient. As we look at Exchange users, distribution groups, and contacts, we'll first focus on creating one of these objects and then on the details of further managing it. You've already created a mailbox, so the creation section will be relatively brief.

At the end of this section, I'll show you how to search for Exchange recipients. As your Exchange organization grows, I guarantee that you'll find this capability more useful.

Managing Exchange Users

As I noted in the previous section, there are two types of Exchange users: mailbox-enabled users and mail-enabled users. A mailbox-enabled user has a mailbox in your Exchange system and can send and receive messages from that mailbox. A mail-enabled user has no mailbox in your Exchange system. Rather, a mail-enabled user has an e-mail address outside your Exchange system. A mail-enabled user can log onto your Windows 2000 network and act as any other Windows 2000 user. However, such a user must send and receive messages in another messaging system. When a mailbox-enabled user sends a message to a mail-enabled user, Exchange sends the message to the mail-enabled user's external e-mail address.

Mail-enabled users are new to Exchange. They make it easy to deal with Windows 2000 users who want to use an external e-mail account.

Don't confuse mail-enabled users with contacts (custom recipients in Exchange 5.5). Contacts point to addresses that are external to your Exchange system, just like mail-enabled users. However, that's all they do. There is no Windows 2000 user connected with a contact.

To start, I'll show you how to create and manage a new mailbox-enabled user. After that, I'll show you how to create and manage a mail-enabled user.

 NOTE You'll notice that I use the term *user* here rather than *user account*. An Exchange user is a Windows 2000 user account that has been either mailbox- or mail-enabled. At times, I also use the word *user* in place of *user account*. You shouldn't have any problem recognizing my use of this bit of shorthand.

Creating and Managing Mailbox-Enabled Users

This is a pretty complex section. Creating a mailbox-enabled user is a piece of cake, but managing one isn't so easy. Because a mailbox-enabled user is both a Windows 2000 and an Exchange 2000 user, the management interface for such a user is full of mind-boggling and sometimes diverting detail. You'll spend a good deal of time in this section doing hands-on tasks, but you'll also devote considerable effort to understanding the dizzying array of management options available for mailbox-enabled users.

Creating a Mailbox-Enabled User

Let's create a mailbox-enabled user for Jane Dough, a securities consultant for a major multinational conglomerate. Because Jane doesn't exist as a user, we'll first have to create her user account to mailbox-enable that account.

To start, right-click on the Users container and select New ➢ User from the pop-up menu. The New Object – User dialog box opens (see Figure 11.13). Fill in your user's first name, initials, and last name. Each field that you're filling in contains a *property*, or, more specifically, an *attribute* of the user. The user's full name is automatically created. Notice in Figure 11.13 that the system uses the last_name, first_name format for display names that I created back in the section "Setting the Default Format for Display Names." Finally, enter a user logon name. The pre-Windows 2000 name is automatically created.

FIGURE 11.13

Using the New Object – User dialog box to create a new user account

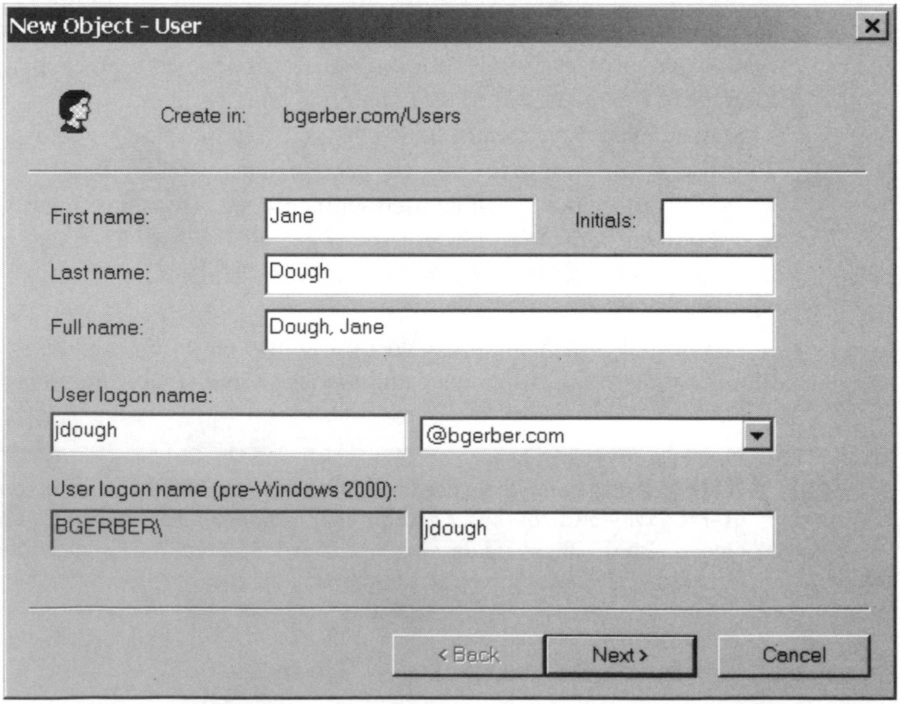

Click Next and enter a password for the user. Click Next again, and view and accept
the creation of an Exchange mailbox (see Figure 11.14). This is where you choose to
mailbox-enable or not mailbox-enable this user. Note that you can change the
default mailbox alias and select the server and mailbox store on which the mailbox
will be created. Click Next and then Finish on the last page of the New Object –
User dialog box.

FIGURE 11.14

*Mailbox-enabling a
new user*

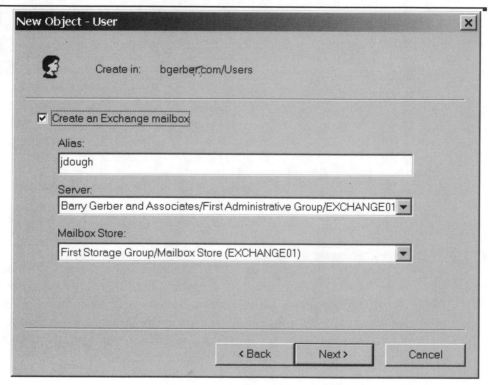

Find your new user in the Users container, and double-click it (see Figure 11.15). This
opens the Properties dialog box for your new user.

FIGURE 11.15

The Properties dialog
box for a new user

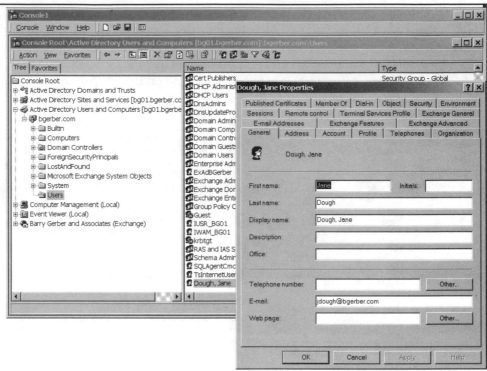

FIGURE 11.15

The Properties dialog box for a new user

You don't have to create a new user account and mailbox-enable the user at the same time. You can deselect the Create an Exchange Mailbox option on the New Object – User dialog box shown in Figure 11.14, create the user account, and then mailbox-enable the user later. To mailbox-enable an existing user account, right-click the account in the Users container, and select Exchange Tasks. A wizard will then guide you through the mailbox-enabling process.

TIP When a user account has been mailbox-enabled, how do you get rid of the mailbox? Just open the Exchange Task Wizard and select Delete Mailbox. To delete a user account, whether it's mailbox-enabled or not, select it and either press the Delete key or right-click it and select Delete from the menu that pops up.

Managing Mailbox-Enabled Users

Okay, now let's take a tour of the user Properties dialog box shown in Figure 11.15. Before we begin that tour, I need to talk a bit about the property pages on the dialog box that are relevant to Exchange and those that are not.

Exchange-Relevant Property Pages

Exchange-relevant means that a property page contains e-mail-specific attributes, attributes that provide information about a user that other users can view, or attributes that are necessary to the proper functioning of the electronic-messaging environment.

E-mail–specific attributes are attributes relating directly to a mailbox-enabled user's mailbox. These include limits on what can be stored in the mailbox, who can access it, and such. E-mail–specific property pages in Figure 11.15 include these:

- E-mail Addresses
- Exchange Features
- Exchange General
- Exchange Advanced

Attributes that provide information about a user that other users can view are attributes that an Outlook user can view. Figure 11.16 shows the Properties dialog box for user Jane Dough that opens when you click on her name in the Address Book that is part of the Outlook client. See Chapter 10, "A Quick Overview of Outlook 2000," for a refresher on the Address Book.

FIGURE 11.16

*Viewing user attributes
in the Outlook
Address Book*

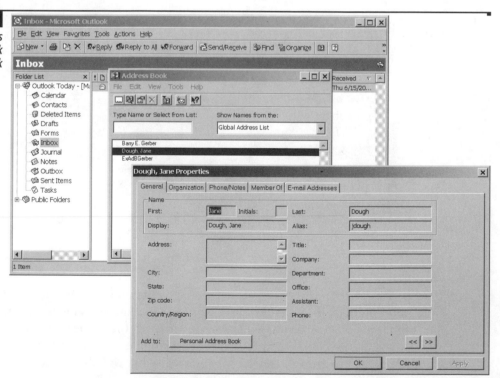

The General tab, which you can see in detail, and the other four tabs, which you can't see in detail, include a great deal of the information that is administered and managed on various property pages of the user Properties dialog box shown in Figure 11.15. Information carries over to the Outlook Address Book properties dialog box (Figure 11.16) from the following property pages on the user Properties dialog box (Figure 11.15):

- General
- Address
- Telephones
- Organization
- Member Of

Users can view the attributes of other users in another place. Active Directory shows up as a part of your network hierarchy in Windows 2000 networks (see Figure 11.17). By finding and double-clicking a user in Active Directory, a user can see many of the basic attributes of other users.

FIGURE 11.17

Viewing user attributes as a user in Active Directory

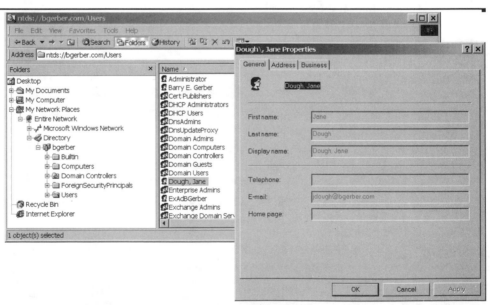

So, as an Exchange 2000 Server manager, you should focus on 9 of the 19 property pages on the user Properties dialog box. Does that mean that you don't have to worry about the other 10 pages? No such luck. Although these pages focus heavily on Windows 2000 account attributes, you will need to understand some of them so that you can either use them when necessary or ask a Windows 2000 Server person to set up certain attributes for you. These pages, which have *attributes that are necessary to the proper functioning of the electronic messaging environment*, include these:

- Account
- Profile
- Published Certificates
- Security
- Environment

All right! Now, let's move on to the 14 Exchange-specific property pages on the user Properties dialog box. We'll look at each property page in the order specified here. After I discuss the 14 Exchange-specific property pages, I'll quickly discuss the remaining five property pages on the user Properties dialog box.

E-mail–Specific Property Pages

Exchange 5.5 administrators will find most of the mailbox management user interfaces that they are accustomed to in the four e-mail–specific property pages. A number of property pages were displayed on Exchange 5.5's mailbox dialog box. To avoid property page mania, Exchange 2000 adds only four e-mail–specific property pages to the user Properties dialog box. Two of these pages, Exchange General and Exchange Advanced, contain buttons that open seven additional property pages. Let's take a look at the four e-mail–specific property pages on the Windows 2000 user Properties dialog box.

E-mail Addresses

The E-mail Addresses property page shows a mailbox's addresses for different types of messaging systems (see Figure 11.11). As I noted in the previous section "Setting the Default Format for Organizational E-mail Addresses," two addressing defaults are created by default when you install Exchange 2000 Server: SMTP and X.400. These addressing defaults are then used to generate specific addresses for each recipient.

Using the E-mail Addresses property page, you can add a new address or manually change or even remove an existing address. For example, I sometimes give certain users a second SMTP address that includes their specific department. Adding, modifying, or removing addresses manually is fun, but not for those new to Exchange 2000, both because it's a little dangerous to play with addresses and because it's sometimes not enough to just add, change, or remove the address. You may also have to do some things in other areas within Exchange and maybe even in external systems. I'll talk about all this stuff in Chapter 17, "Advanced Exchange Server Management."

You can also use the E-mail Addresses property page to set an address of a particular type as the primary address. The primary address is the one that appears in the

From field of a message. It is also the return address for replies to the message. You need two addresses of the same type to change the primary address. In the case of my second SMTP address example, I leave the system-generated address as the primary address.

Exchange Features

You use the Exchange Features properties page to enable and disable features such as instant messaging. If a feature has properties, you can view and modify them here. The only feature that you're likely to find on this properties page if you've followed the installation instructions in Chapter 8 is instant messaging.

Exchange General

Now, click over to the Exchange General property page. The store holding the mailbox is shown in the Mailbox Store field (see the left side of Figure 11.18). You can't change the mailbox store here; you have to move a mailbox to change its store. We'll get into moving mailboxes in the next chapter.

The alias for the user's mailbox is shown immediately after the name of the mailbox store. You can change the alias here, but that won't change the aliases used in Exchange addresses that have already been generated for this mailbox. The change will affect any addresses added in the future.

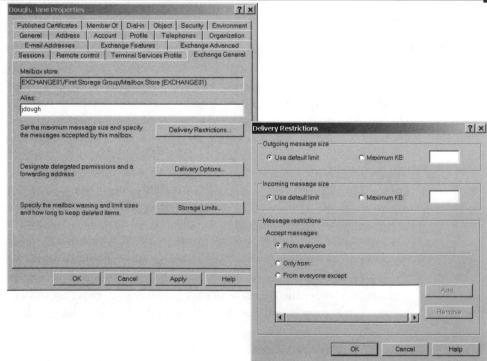

FIGURE 11.18

The Exchange General property page and its Delivery Restrictions property page that is opened by clicking the Delivery Restrictions button

Delivery Restrictions, Delivery Options, and Storage Limits

The three buttons on the Exchange General property page open additional property pages. These pages enable you to set a range of attributes relating to messages and permissions.

Delivery Restrictions

Sending and receiving messages takes network bandwidth. You can control bandwidth usage by setting limits on the size of messages that a user can send and receive. As you can see on the right side of Figure 11.18, you can choose to use the default limit for sent and received messages, or set a specific limit for the mailbox. I'll talk about setting default size options in the next chapter.

In addition to setting message size limits, you can restrict the message senders from whom a mailbox can receive messages. The default, as you can see in Figure 11.18, is to accept messages from everyone. In the alternative, you can choose to allow the mailbox to receive messages from a specific list of senders or from all senders but a specific list. You must choose the senders from users, groups, and computers in your Active Directory. So, you can't use message restriction options to control messages from outside your Exchange organization, unless you enter a specific address as a contact in your Active Directory and then select that address.

Delivery Options

Figure 11.19 shows the Delivery Options property page. This one's pretty neat. You can grant another user permission to send messages on behalf of this mailbox. The From field in Send on Behalf messages identifies both the person sending the message and the individual on whose behalf the message was sent. Can you imagine going through and setting Send on Behalf options for each user? Whew! But don't worry: Users can do it for themselves using their Exchange clients.

FIGURE 11.19

Using the Delivery Options property page to give other recipients special rights to a mailbox, to set a forwarding address, and to limit the number of recipients that a mailbox can send messages to at one time

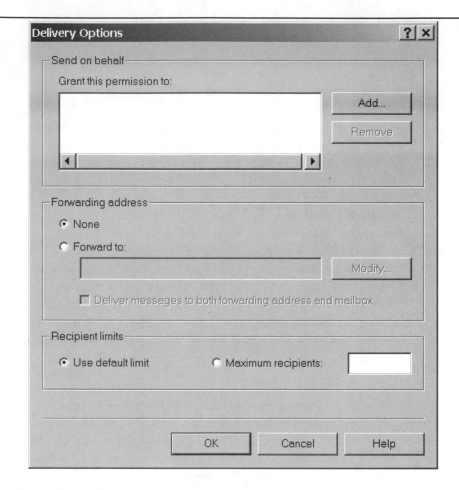

The forwarding address option is new to Exchange 2000 and is a very welcome addition. Before Exchange 2000, users had to set up forwarding in their Outlook clients. They can still do this, but Exchange administrators now have the option of setting the forwarding address, which, if nothing else, means that forwarding from Exchange environments should be more accurate.

As with message restrictions in the last section, you can forward to an address only in your Active Directory. So, you have to enter a custom address for addresses outside your Active Directory. Even so, this little addition is almost worth the price of admission to Exchange 2000 Server.

Some organizations have their mass mailers. These are people who write a message and then send it to everyone that they can find on their corporate address list, either by picking everyone's name or by using one or more distribution lists. The Recipients Limits option on the Deliver Options property page lets you limit the number of recipients that a mailbox user can send a message to. In computing this limit, a distribution group is not equal to one recipient. Instead, it is equal to all the recipients on the list. This is a nice way to cut down on all that spamming on your system. The default is a whopping 5,000 recipients. I'll show you how to change the default in next chapter.

Storage Limits

Use the Storage Limits options to either accept the store's default maximum size limits—you'll learn how to set the default in the next chapter—or set specific maximum limits for the mailbox. As shown in Figure 11.20, you can use any or all of three options when setting limits. The mailbox user gets a warning when the first limit is reached and then on a specific schedule thereafter until storage drops below the limit. I'll show you how to set the warning message schedule in the next chapter.

When the second limit is reached, the mailbox can no longer send mail. It still can receive mail, however, because you might not want those who send messages getting a bunch of bounced message notifications just because a mailbox user is a resource hog. The third limit prevents reception as well as sending of messages. This option is useful when a user will be out of the office for an extended period and you don't want that person's mailbox to fill with gobs of unanswered messages.

FIGURE 11.20

Using the Storage Limits property page to limit the amount of disk space available to a mailbox and determine how deleted but retained items are handled

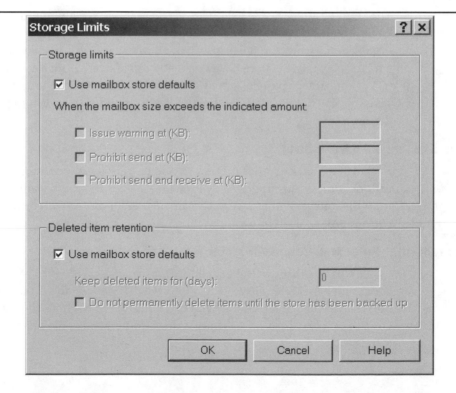

Exchange 5.5 brought a great new concept to Microsoft messaging: deleted item retention. Essentially, when a user deletes messages from the Deleted Items folder, the messages no longer show up in the folder, but they are retained in the Exchange server message store for a specific time. Using an Outlook 2000 client, a user can retrieve "deleted" messages not yet deleted from the store. I'll show you how to set default deleted item retention parameters in the next chapter. You can use the Storage Limits property page to set retention parameters for a specific mailbox. You can set the number of days that deleted items are kept on the mailbox's Exchange server before they are automatically and finally deleted, or you can specify that items should not be deleted until the store in which they are located has been backed up.

Exchange Advanced

The Exchange Advanced properties page brings together a number of Exchange 2000 attributes that you may need to modify (see Figure 11.21). Exchange 5.5 refugees will be happy to see that they can manage many of their favorite Exchange attributes using this page. Let's look at these attributes in the order they appear on the page.

The Simple Display Name

The Simple Display Name field is especially useful in certain multilingual Exchange environments. Exchange clients and the Exchange System Manager show the simple display name when the full display name can't be properly displayed. For example, if a full display name is stored in a double-byte character set such as Chinese Traditional or Korean, and if a particular copy of the client or the Exchange System Manager isn't set to display the character set, the simple display name is shown in place of the full display name.

Hide from Exchange Address Lists

Select Hide from Exchange Address Lists to prevent a mailbox from showing up in the various address lists supported by Exchange. Generally, you'll want to hide a mailbox from the Address Book to protect a particular mailbox's privacy or when it is used by custom-programmed applications rather than by human users.

Downgrade High-Priority Mail Bound for X.400

Check this box to prevent the mailbox from sending X.400 mail at high priority. If the mailbox user attempts to send a message destined for an X.400 system at high priority, the Exchange Server downgrades the priority to Normal. You use this option to ensure that messages to X.400 mail systems conform with the older 1984 X.400 standard.

FIGURE 11.21

*The Exchange
Advanced
property page*

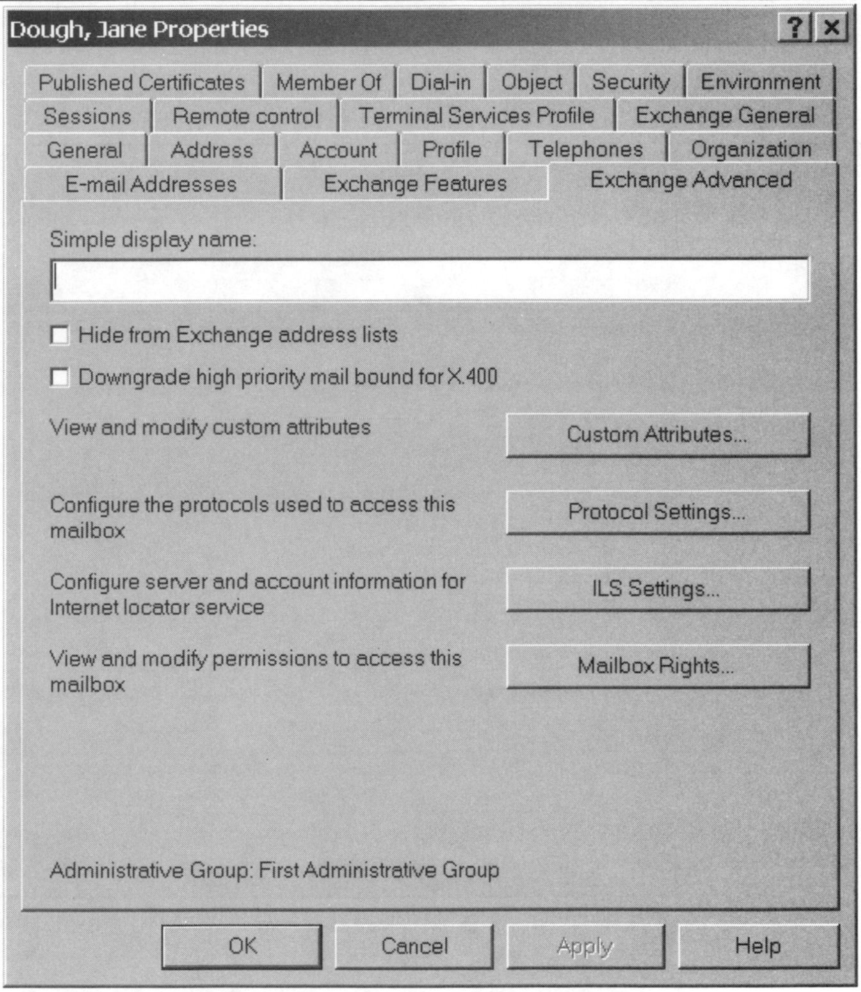

Dough, Jane Properties   ? X

| Published Certificates | Member Of | Dial-in | Object | Security | Environment |

| Sessions | Remote control | Terminal Services Profile | Exchange General |

| General | Address | Account | Profile | Telephones | Organization |

| E-mail Addresses | Exchange Features | Exchange Advanced |

Simple display name:

☐ Hide from Exchange address lists

☐ Downgrade high priority mail bound for X.400

View and modify custom attributes   Custom Attributes...

Configure the protocols used to access this
mailbox   Protocol Settings...

Configure server and account information for
Internet locator service   ILS Settings...

View and modify permissions to access this
mailbox   Mailbox Rights...

Administrative Group: First Administrative Group

OK   Cancel   Apply   Help

Custom Attributes, Protocol Settings, ILS Settings, and Mailbox Rights

Now let's focus on the subproperty pages on the Exchange Advanced properties page
that you view by clicking the button bearing their names.

Custom Attributes

You use the Custom Attributes property page shown in Figure 11.22 to fill in custom
information for a mailbox. For example, you can use one of the custom fields to hold
the Employee ID for the user of the mailbox. You would, of course, use the same custom field for the same item for each user's mailbox. You can rename the attributes,

but it requires digging deeply into Active Directory. I talk a little about how you go about digging in Chapter 14, "Managing Exchange 2000 Services for Internet Clients."

FIGURE 11.22

Setting custom attributes for a mailbox

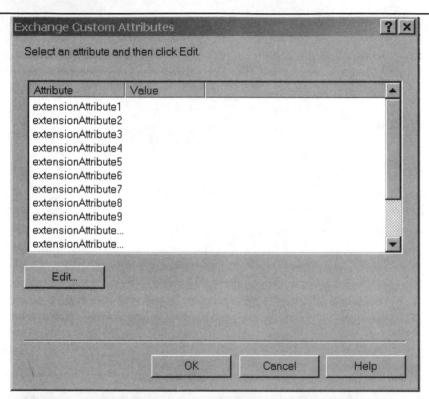

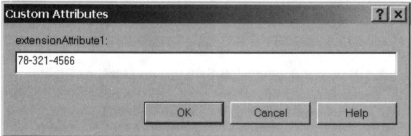

Protocol Settings

Exchange 2000 Server comes with a bunch of Internet-oriented features. You use the Protocols property page to enable and set attributes for three of these features for a mailbox. I've devoted Chapter 14 to these new features. Here I'll give you the most basic of introductions.

The three Internet protocols supported by Exchange 2000 Server and managed on the Protocol Setting properties page are these:

- HTTP (Web) lets mailbox users access their Exchange server with an Internet browser, for example, to read their e-mail. *HTTP* is an acronym for Hypertext Transfer Protocol.

- IMAP4 (Mail) provides access to Exchange server messages and folders through the Internet Message Access Protocol version 4.

- POP3 (Mail) support lets a mailbox user read and, with the help of the SMTP e-mail protocol, send mail through Exchange server using a Post Office Protocol version 3 (POP3)–compliant client, such as Microsoft's Outlook or Outlook Express or Qualcomm's Eudora.

ILS Settings

Microsoft's Internet Locator Service (ILS) is designed to make it easier for users to find each other so that they can hold electronic discussions or conferences. You enter information about the mailbox user's ILS server and account on the dialog box that pops up when you click ILS Settings. ILS runs as a Windows 2000 service.

Mailbox Rights

You use the Mailbox Rights property page to establish or change permissions for the mailbox. Figure 11.23 shows the default mailbox access permissions granted to the user for whom the mailbox is created. SELF is an Active Directory-wide group—that is, it is not limited to any specific domain in Active Directory. SELF has a range of rights, including Exchange-specific rights. When a user is created, that user is added to the group. Members of the group SELF get the default mailbox permissions shown in Figure 11.23 by virtue of belonging to the group. These permissions apply only to the user's mailbox, not to all mailboxes.

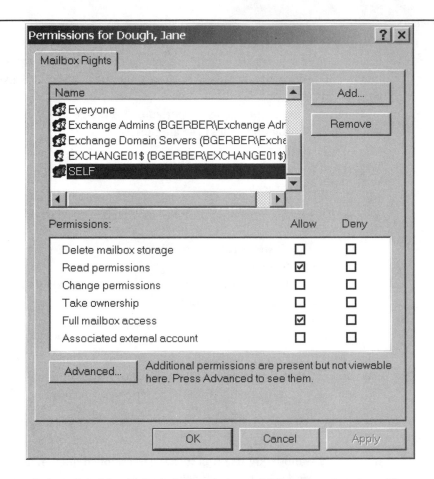

The permissions listed in the Permissions box are fairly self-explanatory. However, to be sure that we're all on the same page, here's a list of the permissions and a brief explanation of their functions:

Delete mailbox storage   If allowed, the user or group may delete the mailbox itself.

Read permissions   The user or group can read the permissions granted to the mailbox.

Change permissions   The user or group can change mailbox permissions.

Take ownership   The user or group can take ownership of the mailbox.

Full mailbox access   The user or group can access the mailbox and all its contents, including all subfolders.

Associated external account   The account, which is a Windows 2000 Server account outside of the Windows 2000 forest where your Exchange system resides, may access the mailbox.

 TIP   If you see only the group SELF on the Mailbox Rights property page, that's because the user's mailbox has yet to be created. Yeah, I know, Exchange said it was creating the mailbox, but it lied. The mailbox isn't created until the first message is sent to the user. So, to see all the groups that have permissions on the mailbox, just send a message to the user and then close and reopen the Mailbox Rights property page. In the alternative, if you sent yourself a message back in Chapter 10, look at the Mailbox Rights property page for your mailbox.

Scroll through the Name field at the top of the Mailbox Rights property page, and find and select the group Exchange Admins. You'll notice that the group has permissions that allow it to fully administer the mailbox, but not to access the messages in it. Those permissions were inherited from the permissions set on the Exchange organizational container (Barry Gerber and Associates) when you delegated control to Exchange Admins back in Chapter 8.

You probably won't need to grant others permissions to a mailbox very often. As I noted in Chapter 10, users can grant others access to all or part of their mailboxes right inside Outlook. So, why might you want to give others permissions to a mailbox? One reason would be to create a shared mailbox. Maybe you want people to send help desk-type messages to a mailbox and then have several staff members access the mailbox to read the messages and resolve problems. Or, a specific department might want to collaborate using a common mailbox. You could do these sorts of tasks using a secure public folder, but a mailbox might work better in some cases.

So, to give other users permissions to access a mailbox, click Add on the Mailbox Rights property page. Then use the Select Users, Computers, or Groups dialog box to pick the users or groups allowed access to the mailbox (see Figure 11.24).

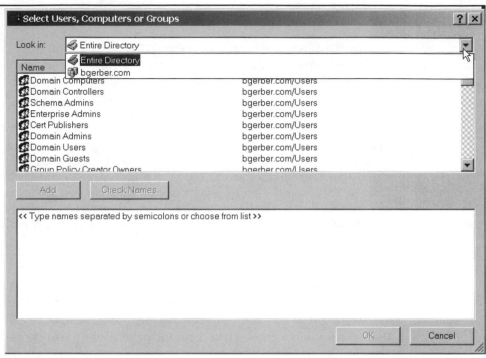

The Look In field at the top of the Select Users, Computers, or Groups dialog box lets you pick from all users, groups, and computers in your Active Directory (entire directory) or in a specific domain. The dialog box opens showing the entire directory. Select a specific domain from the drop-down list. I suggest that you look in a specific domain unless you're not sure which domain a user or group resides in. When you look at the entire directory, you'll see a bunch of objects that will make little sense to you, unless you're a Windows 2000 security maven. For example, the group SELF is visible when you look at the entire directory, but you really shouldn't be messing with it.

In some cases, clicking Advanced on a Rights Property page will allow you to give an object additional permissions. If this option is available for a user or group, a message shows up to the right of the Advanced button, as it does for the group SELF in Figure 11.23. As Figure 11.25 shows, you can actually change the user or group to whom the permissions are granted, and you can choose how the permissions are to be applied. If an object has inherited permissions that were set higher up in the Exchange hierarchy, you'll find that the Change button and the Apply Onto field are grayed out and therefore unchangeable. Check this out by selecting Exchange Admins and clicking Advanced on the Permissions property page. See Figure 11.23 for the location of the Advanced button.

FIGURE 11.25

Using the Object property page to select the objects to which permissions will apply

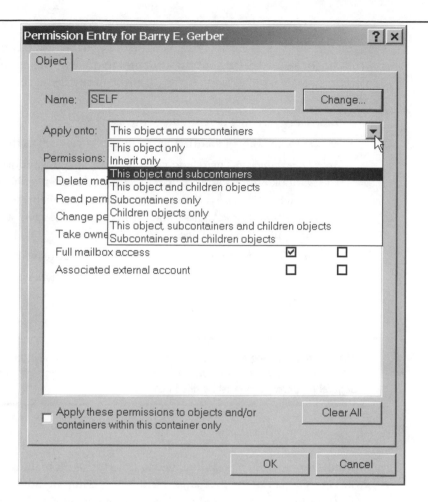

Property Pages That Provide Information Useful to Users

Now let's turn to the property pages that aren't e-mail-specific and that include information that end users will encounter in one place or another as they move through your Exchange and Windows 2000 system. I think that Exchange managers are more attuned than Windows 2000 administrators to users and both how they perceive this information and how they might use it. Additionally, Exchange administrators managed this information in Exchange 5.5. Therefore, I believe that Exchange managers should administer this information. Let's take a brief walk through these property pages.

General

As you can see back in Figure 11.15, you use the General property page to set basic attributes for a user. Leaving out the attributes that I discussed in the previous section "Creating a Mailbox-Enabled User," the General properties page includes the following attributes:

Description   A brief description of the user.

Office   Some way of identifying the user's office, such as the office number.

Telephone number   The telephone number that you want other users to see in the Outlook Address Book. Click Other to add more telephone numbers for the user to Active Directory. These numbers are not available to other users through the Outlook Address Book. You could make them available through custom applications that access Active Directory.

E-mail   The user's SMTP address, automatically displayed in this field.

Web page   The user's Web page. The Other button works as it does for telephone number.

 TIP When creating a new account and mailbox, you don't have to fill in every last lovin' field on every property page. Only the First and Last names and logon name fields on the General property page must be filled in.

Address

The Address properties page is designed to hold the user's mailing address. These attributes were part of the Exchange 5.5 directory. They are now standard Windows 2000 attributes. As I mentioned previously, I still believe that Exchange 2000 managers should support this property page.

Telephones

As you might expect, you manage a user's telephone numbers on the Telephones property page. The page has room for five phone numbers. The defaults are these:

- Home
- Pager
- Mobile
- Fax
- IP Phone (an Internet IP address-based phone)

You can change the defaults.

The Telephones property page also includes a text box for notes. Exchange 5.5 managers will be happy to see that this pretty much keeps intact the content of the Phone/Notes property page of the Exchange 5.5 mailbox Properties dialog box.

Organization

You use the Organization property page to record information about the user's status in your organization's hierarchy. See Jane Dough's Organization property page on the left side of Figure 11.26. Here you can set the following user information:

- Title
- Department
- Company
- Manager

You can also view the names of the individuals who directly report to the user. Jane Dough has no direct reports. However, she does have a manager: me. If you look at my Organizational property page on the right side of Figure 11.26, you'll see that she is listed in the Direct Reports box. That's because I've set myself as her manager on her Organization property page.

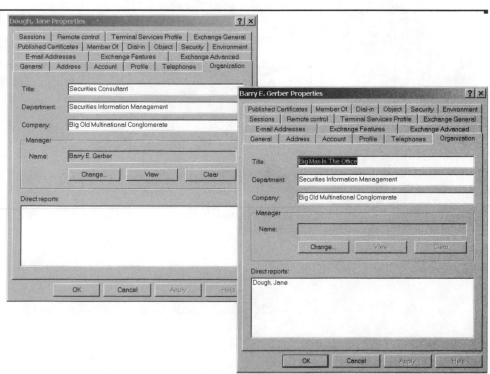

FIGURE 11.26

Using the Organization property page to show a user's place in an organization's corporate hierarchy

This is a big improvement over Exchange 5.5's Organization property page. With 5.5, you had to jump through too many hoops to produce essentially the same information that you see here. Of course, neither 5.5 or 2000 works if you've got one of those dysfunctional organizations where people are expected to serve multiple masters. That's a joke, sort of.

Member Of

The Member Of property page is used to add users to groups. You can add users to security groups or to distribution groups. You don't have any distribution groups yet, so you can't do it now; in Figure 11.27, however, I'm adding Jane Dough's mailbox to a distribution list that I sneakily created while you were otherwise occupied. I just tabbed over to the Member Of property page, clicked Add, double-clicked the group Sneakily Created Distribution Group, and clicked OK on the Select Groups dialog box. We'll get into creating distribution groups later in this chapter in the section "Managing Distribution Groups."

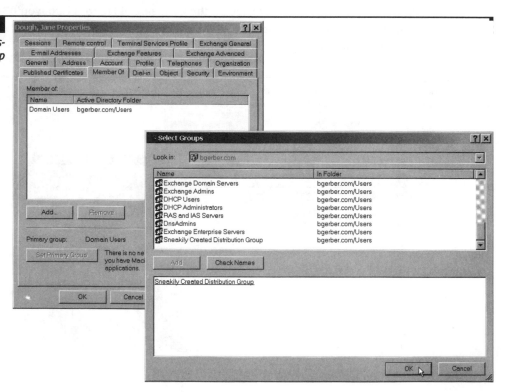

FIGURE 11.27

Adding a user to a distribution group

Property Pages Essential to the Proper Functioning of Exchange

A number of property pages contain an attribute here or an attribute there that you'll need to be aware of when managing mailbox-enabled users. I discuss these next.

Account

A good deal of the contents of the Account property page appeared in NT 4's User Manager for domains. Much of advanced security functionality, such as the kind of encryption used for the password, is also managed on the Account property page. As should be obvious in Figure 11.28, much of what's on this page relates to Windows 2000 security. The page is important for Exchange 2000 managers, mainly because it is where the user logon name is managed.

Don't be fooled by that @bgerber.com following my logon name in Figure 11.28. It refers to the domain I log into, not my e-mail address.

FIGURE 11.28

The Account property page is used to manage a range of Windows 2000 security options.

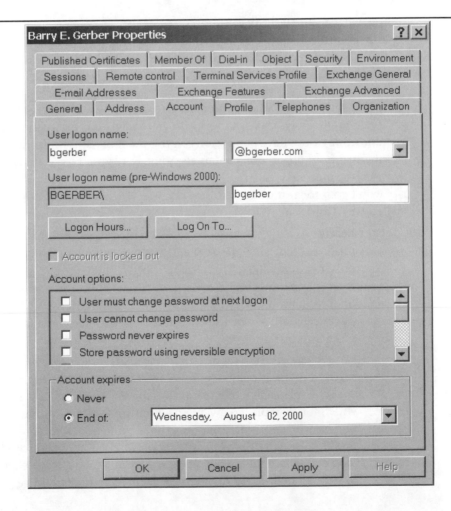

Profile

The Profile property page is another page imported pretty much intact from NT 4's User Manager. As an Exchange manager, your main interest in this page is likely to be in the script that is run when a user logs on to your Windows 2000 network. Some programs, such as the third-party application Profile Maker, need to run when the user first logs on. Profile Maker ensures that a user's Exchange profile (see Chapter 10) is properly created and remains as the Exchange administrator wants it to be. You can run a program such as Profile Maker in the logon script. (See Appendix A, "Cool Third-Party Applications for Exchange Server and Outlook Clients," for more on Profile Maker.)

Oh yes, just for the record, the *Profile* in *Profile Maker* has nothing to do with the name of this property page.

Published Certificates

You can view the security certificates that have been assigned to the user on the Published Certificates property page. If and when you get into Exchange Advanced Security, you'll see the certificates for this service on this property page.

Security

You should treat the Security property page as you would the registry on your server or Active Directory. Make changes with great care. You can see in Figure 11.29 that a number of groups have permissions on this mailbox. Most of those permissions were inherited from upper-level containers. Some were granted specifically for the user when the user was created.

I won't go into great detail here, but I do want to talk about a couple of permissions, Receive As and Send As:

- Receive As allows the user or group granted the right for a mailbox to open the mailbox inside an Outlook client. The user or group member operates out of his or her own mailbox. That person can read messages in any mailbox to which receive as permission has been granted, but this user cannot send messages. To open a mailbox, use the Tools ➤ Services ➤ Microsoft Exchange Server ➤ Advanced (tab) ➤ Open These Additional Mailboxes option. See Chapter 10 for more information.

- Send As allows the user or group granted the right for a mailbox to send messages from other mailboxes to which that person has rights so that it appears that the messages came from the Send As mailbox. This right can be useful when, for example, you want an administrative aide to send messages from his or her own mailbox that appear to have come from a corporate mailbox (such as President at Barry Gerber and Associates). The right is exercised inside the Outlook mailbox of the user by using the From field, which is exposed by selecting View ➤ From Field on any message. Send As rights should be granted with care.

They can be dangerous in the wrong hands, such as when a disgruntled employee sends out a nasty message that appears to have come from some innocent person's mailbox.

FIGURE 11.29

Using the Security property page to modify permissions on the user object as a whole

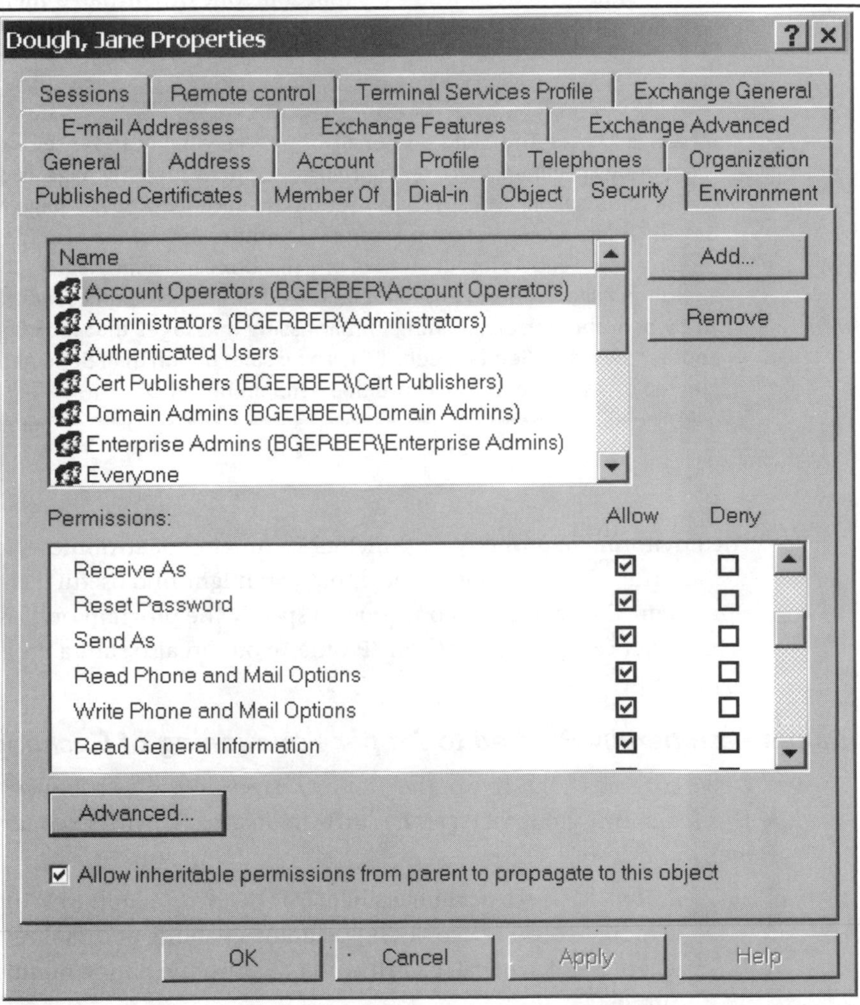

You may be wondering why send as and receive as permissions are granted on the Security property page and not on the Exchange Advanced/Mailbox Rights property page. Exchange 2000 was designed to better protect user mailboxes from the prying eyes of rogue Exchange administrators than Exchange 5.5 did. As I noted back in the section "Mailbox Rights," Exchange administrators (for example, members of the Exchange Admins group that we created back in Chapter 8) aren't given access to user messages. And, although Exchange administrators can administer mailbox rights, they cannot administer the Security property page that contains receive as and send as permissions. Only a user with permissions to change objects in the Active Directory Users and Computers User container can modify attributes on the Security property page. There's nothing to stop someone from giving such permissions to the group Exchange Admins. The key point is that someone other than a member of that group must grant the permissions.

 WARNING The Send on Behalf Of option, which can be set by a user in Outlook client or by an administrator on the Delivery Options property page, is quite different from the Send As option, which you can set on the Security property page for a user. Send on Behalf Of lets a user send a message for another user while also identifying the actual sending user. Send As lets the user of one mailbox send a message as though it came from another mailbox, without any hint that the other mailbox didn't send the message itself. If you worry about users sending embarrassing messages that look like they came from another user, then Send on Behalf Of is a far safer option than Send As. If both options are granted to a user, Send As will override Send on Behalf Of.

Environment

The Environment property page includes a number of attributes relating to Windows 2000 startup. The only one of these that you might find useful has to do with starting a program when a user logs on. You can specify the program on this page. As I pointed out earlier in the section "Profile," you can also start a program in the user's logon script.

Property Pages Peripherally Related to Proper Functioning of Exchange

We've covered all but five of the property pages on the user Properties dialog box. This remaining group of pages has little to do directly with Exchange server. I'll cover them quickly.

Dial-in You set parameters here for the user's dial-in to Windows 2000's Remote Access Service (RAS), including enabling or disabling dial-in, and whether RAS will call back the user at a specific phone number for security purposes.

Object This page contains information about the user as an object. This includes the object's class, its fully qualified domain name, the dates that it was created and modified, and the object's initial and current update sequence number, which tell you how many times the object was updated.

Terminal Services Profile This is where you set a home directory to be used when the user logs on through a Windows 2000 terminal server session and gives permission to actually log on to terminal server.

Remote Control   You set the capability for another to remotely view and control the user's terminal server session here.

Session   This is another terminal server-oriented property page where you set session termination and reconnection parameters.

Creating and Managing Mail-Enabled Users

As you'll remember, a mail-enabled user is a Window 2000 user with an external e-mail address, a user without an Exchange mailbox. Exchange routes messages sent by a mailbox-enabled user to the mail-enabled user's external e-mail address.

Mail-enabled users are a lot like mailbox-enabled users. So, I'm going to move quickly through this section, pointing out only differences between the two types of Windows 2000 users.

Creating a Mail-Enabled User

To create a mail-enabled user, create a user just as you did in the section "Creating a Mailbox-Enabled User," earlier in this chapter, but don't accept the creation of an Exchange mailbox. Then, when the user has been created, right-click the user and select Exchange Tasks. This opens the Exchange Task Wizard. Click over to the Available Tasks page, shown in Figure 11.30, and select Establish E-mail Addresses. Then click Next to move to the next wizard page, Establish E-mail Addresses.

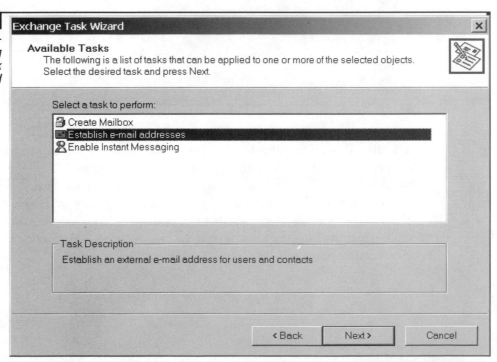

FIGURE 11.30

Choosing to mail-enable a user using the Exchange Task Wizard

You use the Establish E-mail Addresses page of the Exchange Task Wizard shown in Figure 11.31 to add an e-mail address for your mail-enabled user. You're offered an alias for the user, an opportunity to enter the user's e-mail address and select an Exchange administrative group where the user will be managed. To enter the e-mail address, click Modify.

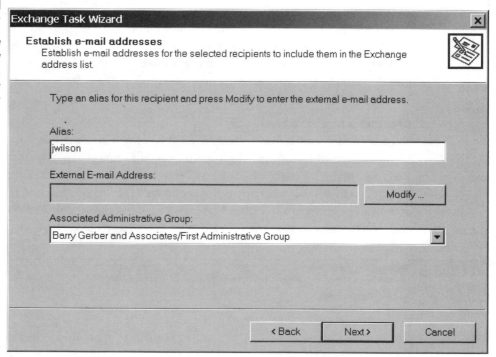

This opens the New E-mail Address dialog box, shown in Figure 11.32. Select the type of address that you're going to enter (I'm selecting SMTP Address). Click OK to open the properties dialog box for the type of address you want to create. In my case the Internet Address Properties dialog box opens (see Figure 11.33). Enter the address for your mail-enabled user. You can use the Advanced property page shown in Figure 11.34 to override default settings that you've made on your Exchange server regarding Internet mail. We'll get into all this stuff in Chapter 13, "Managing Exchange 2000 Internet Services."

FIGURE 11.32

Using the New E-mail Address dialog box to specify the kind of e-mail address to be created for a mail-enabled user

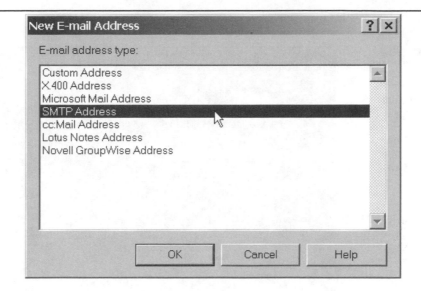

FIGURE 11.33

Using the Internet Address Properties dialog box General property page to enter the e-mail address for a mail-enabled user with an SMTP address

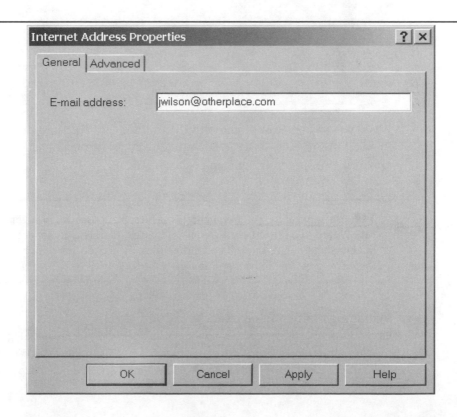

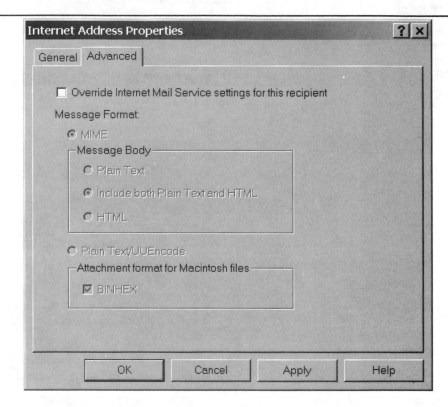

When you've finished working with the address, click Next and then click Finish on the final wizard page. That's it. You've created your first mail-enabled user. Now let's move on to management of mail-enabled users.

 TIP At some point, you may need to mail-disable a user. To do so, open the Exchange Task Wizard and select Delete E-mail Addresses. To delete a user account, whether it's mail-enabled or not, select it and either press the Delete key or right-click it and select Delete from the menu that pops up.

Managing Mail-Enabled Users

Find and double-click the mail-enabled user that you just created. Figure 11.35 shows the Properties dialog box for my new user, John Wilson. Because Wilson is a Windows 2000 user, all of his property pages but the e-mail-specific pages are exactly the same as they are for a mailbox-enabled user. Even the e-mail-specific pages are quite similar to those for a mailbox-enabled user. So, this is going to be a very quick trip.

The Exchange General property page for mail-enabled users is a combination of the Exchange General page for mailbox-enabled users and the Delivery Restrictions subproperty page of the Exchange General property page for mailbox-enabled users. Wow! That's a mouthful, but it should make sense. For a refresher, take a look at Figure 11.35 and the section "Managing Mailbox-Enabled Users (especially Figure 11.18), earlier in this chapter.

FIGURE 11.35

*The Exchange General
property page for a
mail-enabled user*

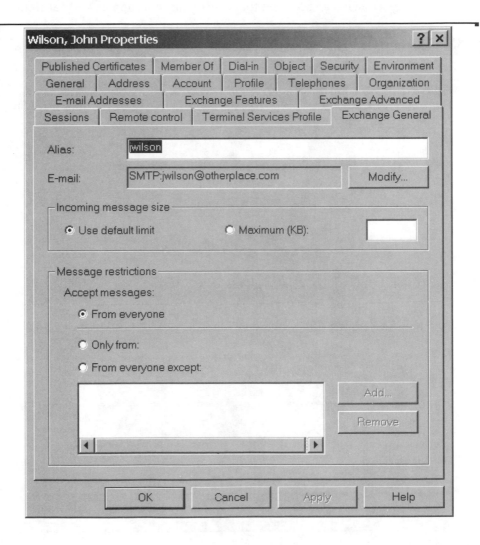

The Exchange Advanced property page, shown in Figure 11.36, contains one field that needs some explaining, Use MAPI Rich Text Format. If this option is selected for an Exchange mail-enabled user, messages sent to the user by mailbox-enabled users can contain such attributes as color, bold, and italic text. By default, mailbox-enabled users send messages to mail-enabled users in plain text. Of course, the mail-enabled user's messaging system or e-mail client must support messages with MAPI attributes for all this to work. We'll encounter this field again when dealing with Exchange contacts, later in this chapter. That's because both mail-enabled users and contacts have external e-mail addresses that may or may not support MAPI attributes.

FIGURE 11.36

The Use MAPI Rich Text Format option is unique to Exchange recipients with external e-mail addresses.

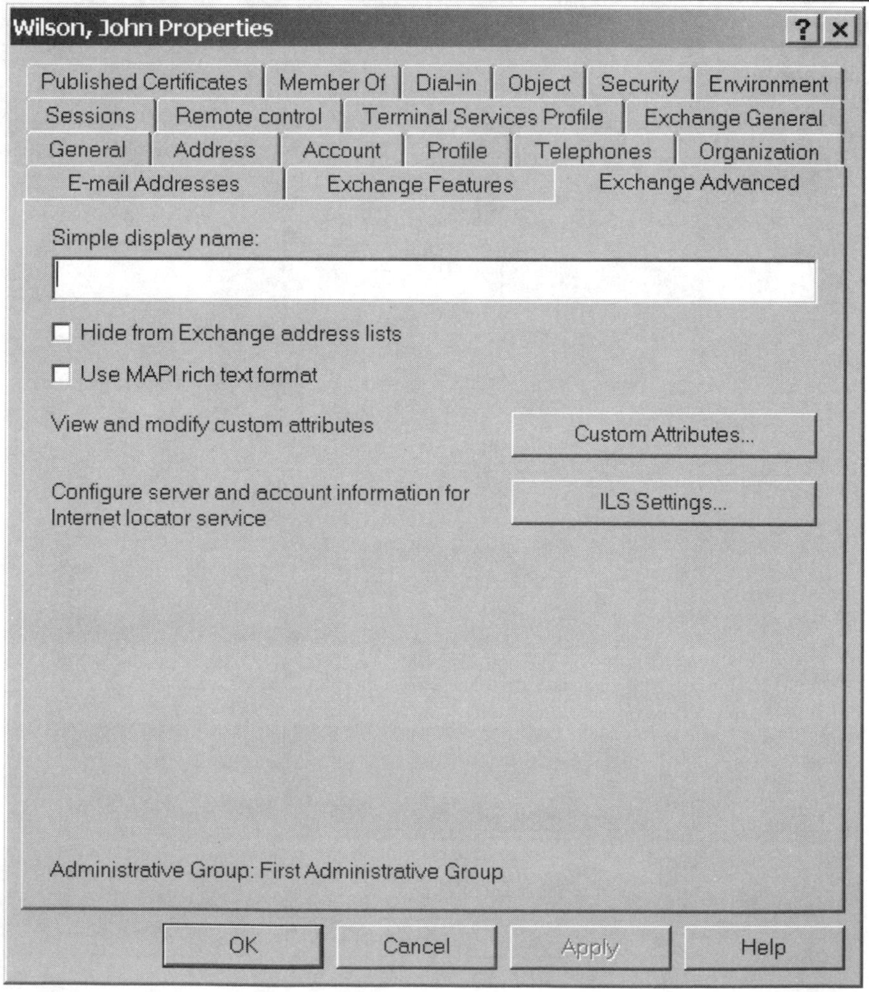

Creating and Managing Distribution Groups

Distribution groups, also known as mail-enabled groups, are used to group together all four types of Exchange recipients: users, contacts, public folders, and even other distribution groups. They are the equivalent of Exchange 5.5's distribution lists.

Creating a Distribution Group

To create a new distribution group, known as a *distribution list* in Exchange 5.5, and also known as a *mail-enabled group* in Exchange 2000, right-click the Users container in Active Directory Users and Computers then select New ➤ Group. This pops up the New Object – Group dialog box, shown in Figure 11.37.

FIGURE 11.37

Using the New Object – Group dialog box to create a new distribution group

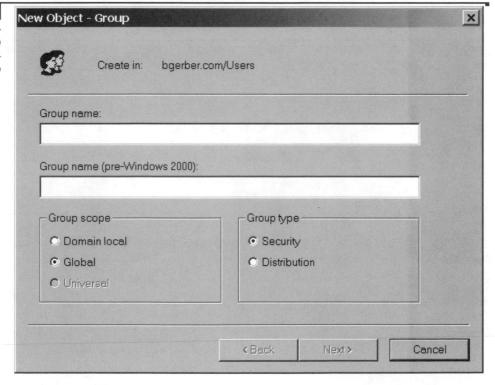

Figure 11.37 shows you how the dialog box looks immediately upon opening. This dialog box is used to create both security and distribution groups. You can create three kinds of groups: domain local, global, and universal. You can create a universal security group only after you've set your domain to native mode. (See Chapter 6,

"Upgrading to Windows 2000 Server and Exchange 2000 Server," for more on mixed- and native-mode domains.) That's why Universal is grayed out in Figure 11.37, where the default group type is Security.

Universal groups, new to Windows 2000, make more sense than the local domain and global groups of NT 4, which are carried over to Windows 2000 for the sake of compatibility. Local groups hold users and global groups. Global groups exist simply to hold users and be included in local groups. It's kind of strange. A universal group can hold users or other groups. That's so much less complex. NT 4 domain controllers are incapable of dealing with the deep nesting of universal groups. That's why they're not available in mixed mode for security groups.

Okay, now select Distribution as the group type and name your group. I chose Managers for the name of my group. Things should look pretty much as they do in Figure 11.38. Notice that distribution groups can be universal.

FIGURE 11.38

Naming a new distribution group and specifying its scope

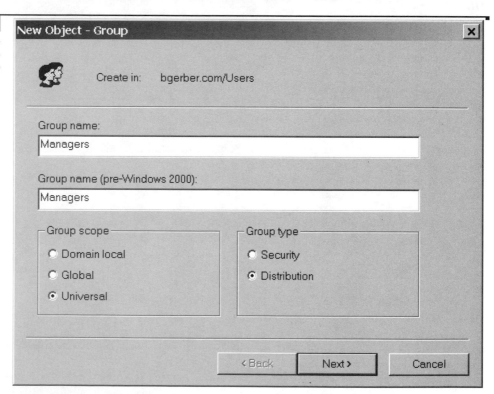

On the next dialog box property page, you're offered the opportunity to create an e-mail address for your distribution group (see Figure 11.39). Accept the default, and

click Next. The last dialog box property page shows you what is about to happen.
Click Finish to create your new distribution group.

FIGURE 11.39

*Accepting creation of
an e-mail address and
the location for the
address*

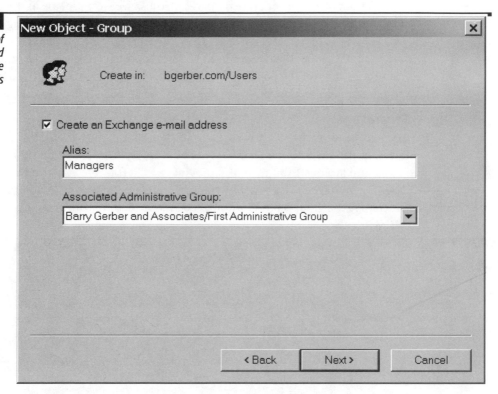

Any Windows 2000 Group Can Be Mail-Enabled or Mail-Disabled

You can mail-enable any group, including a security group. As with a distribution group, when you create a security group, you're asked whether you want to give it an e-mail address. To e-mail–enable a group, right-click it and select Exchange Tasks from the pop-up menu. Using the Exchange Task Wizard that pops up, select Establish an E-mail Address, and complete the wizard.

To mail-disable a group, use the Delete E-mail Addresses option on the Exchange Task Wizard. To delete a distribution group, select it and press the Delete key, or right-click it and select Delete from the pop-up menu.

Managing Distribution Groups

In the section on managing mailbox-enabled users, you had a fair amount of exposure to the format of a range of property pages. Because we were looking at the user Properties dialog box, we explored pages of varying relevance to the functioning of Exchange 2000 Server. In this section, we're going to move pretty quickly through the distribution group Properties dialog box, both because there are far fewer pages and because you've seen some of the pages already. If I skip a page, the page has the same format and function as the same page on the mailbox-enabled user Properties dialog box.

General

To open the Properties dialog box for your new distribution group, find and double-click it in the Users container. The General property page shows naming, descriptive, e-mail, and group attributes. It also provides a field for notes. As you can see in Figure 11.40, if you have the right permissions (remember, I'm a domain administrator), you can change the group's pre-Windows 2000 name, description, and e-mail address.

FIGURE 11.40

Using the General property page to view and edit the basic attributes of a distribution group

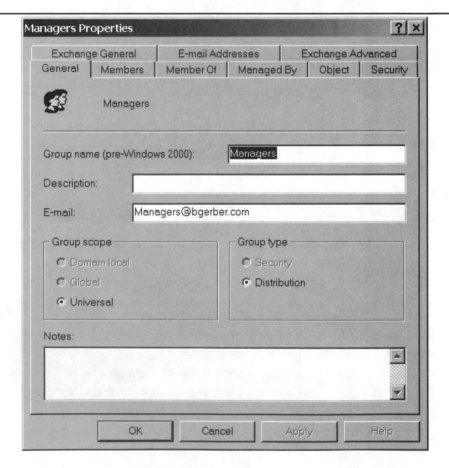

Members

You use the Members property page to add recipients to a distribution group. In Figure 11.41, I'm adding our friend Jane Dough to the Managers list. I know, she wasn't a manager back in the section where I talked about the user property page, Organization, but now she is. Hey, what can I say, she's a really good worker and rises quickly through the organizational hierarchy.

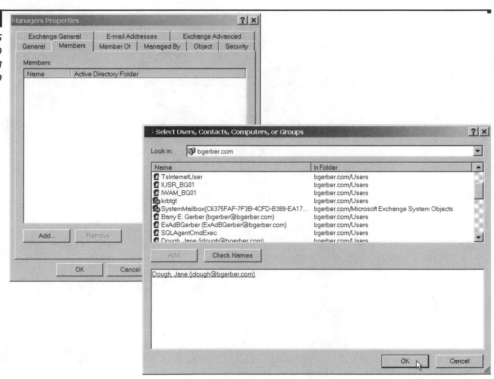

FIGURE 11.41

Using the Members property page to add a user to a distribution group

Distribution groups can contain public folders, the only recipient that we are not covering in this chapter. They're a hot topic for the next chapter, however. To add a public folder to a distribution group, right-click the group and select Add Exchange Public Folders from the pop-up menu. This brings up a dialog box that you can use to pick the folders that you want to include in the list.

Member Of

The Member Of property page shows you the security and distribution groups to which your distribution group belongs. If you have adequate rights, you can add your distribution group to other distribution groups right here. You don't have to open the other group and use its Members property page.

The manager of a distribution group can add and remove group members right inside their Outlook client. In Figure 11.42, using the Managed By property page, I've made Jane Dough the manager of the Managers distribution list. I did this by clicking Change and selecting the manager from the Select Users, Contacts, or Groups dialog box that popped up. The office, address, and phone information that I entered for Jane Dough automatically fills the fields on the property page. I entered only her phone number here, so that's all that shows.

FIGURE 11.42

Using the Managed By property page to give a user permission to manage a distribution group from an Outlook client

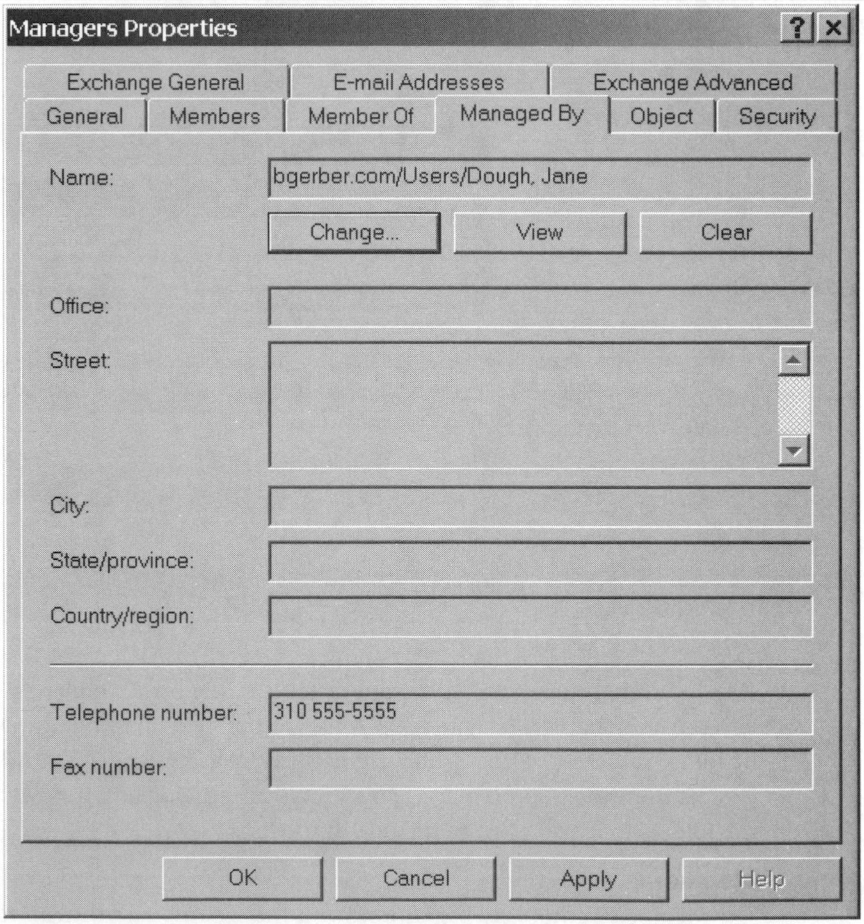

The View button is neat. Click it, and the Properties dialog box for the manager opens. In this case, Jane Dough's user Properties dialog box opens.

Exchange General

The Exchange General property page looks a lot like a combination of several user and Exchange mailbox pages that we looked at back in the section "Managing Exchange Mailbox-Enabled Users." However, it'll be easier for both of us if I show you the page, rather than write a thousand words and refer you back to previous sections of this chapter. So, take look at Figure 11.43.

Unlike mailboxes, distribution lists don't have different size limits for incoming and outgoing messages. That's because distribution groups almost always receive messages. The limits that you set are for outgoing messages only. You saw everything else on this page in the section "Managing Exchange Mailbox-Enabled Users," so I'll leave it to you to give meaning to the rest of this property page.

FIGURE 11.43

Using the Exchange General property page to manage a distribution group's alias, display name, outgoing message size limits, and message restrictions

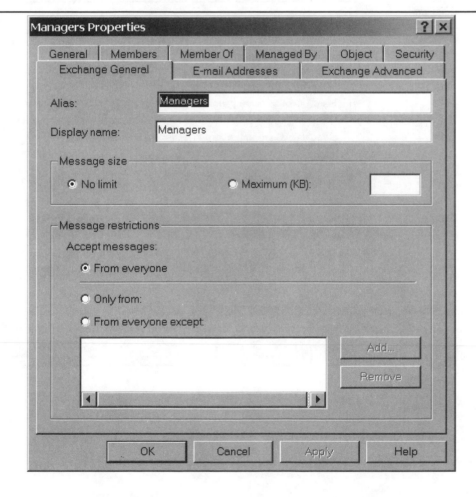

Exchange Advanced

As you can see in Figure 11.44, distribution groups have much thinner Exchange Advanced property pages than mailboxes. However, there are a number of attributes on this page that you haven't seen before. So, let's dive into this page. I'll talk only about fields that I haven't already discussed in this chapter.

FIGURE 11.44

Using the Exchange Advanced property page to manage a distribution group's visibility, out-of-office messaging, reporting responsibilities, and custom attributes

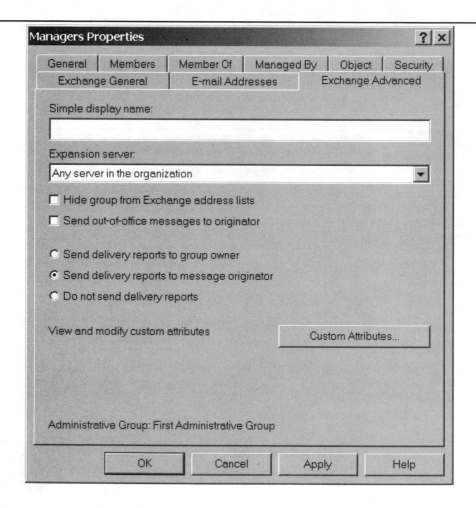

Expansion Server

Distribution groups must be *expanded*—that is, the members of the group must be identified and an efficient route to each group member must be determined. Expansion is done on an Exchange server in the organization; if a distribution group is large (with thousands of users), you may want to specify an expansion server for it that is less busy. For smaller lists, you don't have to change the Any Server in the Organization default.

Other Exchange Advanced Options

You can set a number of additional options on the Advanced property page. You can hide a group from address lists, control how out-of-office messages are sent for a distribution group, specify to whom reports will be sent, and enter information relating to a group's custom attributes.

Hide group from Exchange address lists   This one should be obvious.

Send out-of-office messages to originator   An out-of-office message goes to the sender of a message to the distribution group if even one member of the group has set up an out-of-office message.

Send delivery reports to group owner   This sends notification to the owner of the distribution group when a message sent to the list has requested a delivery notification message or when the message is undeliverable.

Send delivery reports to message originator   This sends, to the message originator, delivery notification or undeliverable message information for each member of the distribution group. If this option is not selected, delivery notifications and nondelivery messages are sent to the message originator for the list as a whole. If a distribution group member is hidden from Exchange address lists, to protect the secrecy of hidden members, delivery notification and undeliverable information messages are sent for the group, not its individual members.

Do not send delivery reports   You can select only one of the previous two options or this option. If you want no delivery reports, select this one.

Custom Attributes   Clicking Custom Attributes opens the same Exchange Custom Attributes dialog box shown in Figure 11.22. The same attributes apply to mailboxes, distribution groups, and contacts. So, if you've staked out an attribute to represent a specific variable for mailboxes such as employee number, you can't use it for something else for distribution groups or contacts.

Hiding Distribution Group Members from Exchange Address Lists

The Exchange 5.5 Advanced property page included an option for hiding the members of a group from the Exchange address book. This is a nice feature if you want users to see a distribution group in Exchange 2000 address lists but don't want them to see the membership of the group. So, how do you do it in Exchange 2000? Run the Exchange Task Wizard (right-click on the group and select Exchange Tasks) and select Hide Membership.

Creating and Managing Contacts

Contacts are essentially aliases for recipients in foreign messaging systems. Their equivalent in Exchange 5.5 is the custom recipient. Contacts are helpful when a lot of people in your organization need to communicate with users of external messaging systems. If a user or two need such communication, you don't need to create an Exchange contact. Each user can set up a contact in his or her Outlook Address Book.

 NOTE You might be wondering how contacts differ from mail-enabled users. Both have external e-mail addresses. Neither has an Exchange mailbox. However, mail-enabled users have Windows 2000 accounts; contacts don't.

Creating a Contact

To create a contact, right-click the \Active Directory Users and Computers\Users container and select New ➤ Contact from the menu that pops up.

As with mailboxes and distribution groups, you use a dialog box, the New Object – Contact dialog box, to create a new contact. Figure 11.45 shows the first property page of the dialog box. When you fill in the user's first name, middle initials, and last name, the full name is automatically generated. Of course, you may edit the full name. You manually enter the display name.

Because I'm creating a contact for my e-mail address at my Internet Service Provider, Deltanet, I'm careful to note that in the display name. This way, users are less likely to pick the wrong address when sending messages to me. Of course, you usually wouldn't create a contact for an Exchange mailbox-enabled user like me.

FIGURE 11.45

*Using the New Object –
Contact dialog box to
enter the naming
attributes of a new
contact*

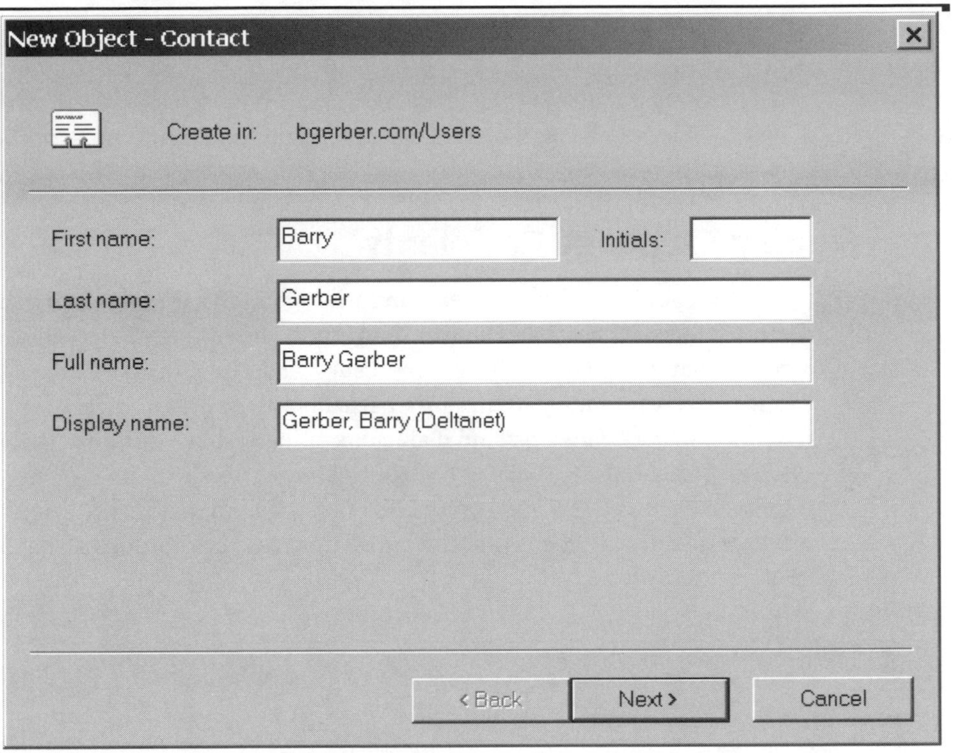

New Object - Contact   ⊠

Create in: bgerber.com/Users

First name: Barry   Initials:

Last name: Gerber

Full name: Barry Gerber

Display name: Gerber, Barry (Deltanet)

                              < Back   Next >   Cancel

The next dialog box property page is exactly the same as the Establish E-mail
Addresses page of the Exchange Task Wizard, shown in Figure 11.31. Check out that
figure and surrounding text for details on entering an e-mail address for your new
contact.

When you're done entering the contact's address, click OK. You'll see the address
that you entered in the E-mail field of the New Object – Contact dialog box property
page. Click Next, and the dialog box tells you what it's going to do. Click Finish, and
your new contact is created.

 TIP To delete a contact, select it and either press Delete or right-click it and select
Delete from the pop-up menu.

Managing Contacts

A contact is very much like a mail-enabled user from a management perspective. Based on my discussion of mail-enabled user property pages in the section "Managing Mail-Enabled Users," earlier in this chapter, you should find none of the contact property pages foreign.

Finding Exchange Recipients

Now that you know how to create and manage Exchange users, distribution groups, and contacts, I'll bet you'll be swimming in Exchange recipients before long. That means that your \Active Directory Users and Computers\Users container is going to fill up to the point that finding a particular user or set of users is a royal pain. Enter Windows 2000's fantastic Find dialog box enhanced by your installation of Exchange Server. You can use this dialog box to search the Users container or any container in Active Directory Users and Groups. To open the Find dialog box, select Find from the Action menu. This opens the Find Users, Contacts, and Groups dialog box, shown in Figure 11.46.

FIGURE 11.46

Using the Find dialog box to search for objects that begin with specific text

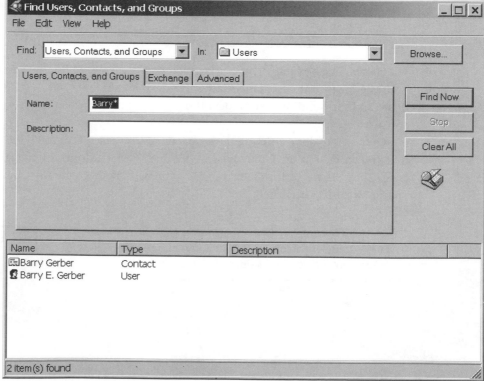

In Figure 11.46, I'm searching in the Users container for any object that begins with *Barry*. Two objects were found: my mailbox-enabled user object (type: User) and my mail-enabled user object (type: Contact). You can double-click any found object and open its Properties dialog box.

You can select other types of objects to be found by using the Find drop-down list in the upper-left corner of the dialog box. Other choices include computers, printers, Windows 2000 organizational units, and Exchange recipients. Each selection on the drop-down list has its own set of property pages.

The Exchange Recipients option is shown in Figure 11.47. It has three Exchange-oriented property pages. The Storage property page lets you further qualify your search by looking for recipients on a particular Exchange server and in a particular mailbox store on the server. Figure 11.48 shows how you can use the Advanced property page on the Find Exchange Recipients dialog box to further qualify your search by looking for specific values for specific user attributes. These are not just Exchange attributes, but all available Windows 2000 user attributes.

FIGURE 11.47

Using the Find dialog box to refine a search to include or exclude specific Exchange recipient objects

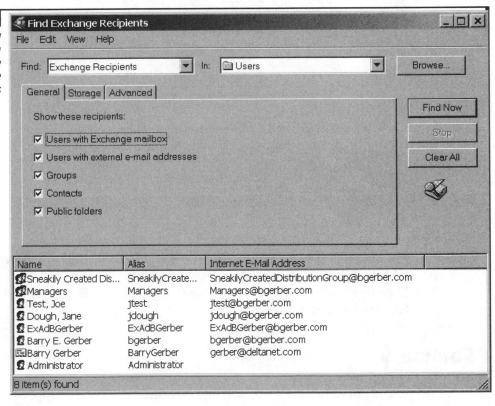

FIGURE 11.48

Using the Find dialog box to refine a search to include or exclude specific user attributes

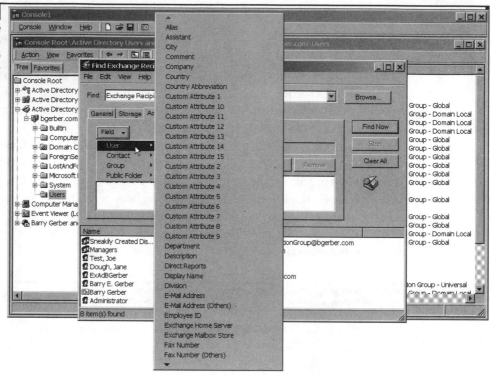

Now, flip back to Figure 11.46. The Exchange tab lets you confine your search to one or more of the following:

- Mailbox-enabled users
- Mail-enabled users
- Groups
- Contacts

The Advanced property page works like the one on the Exchange Recipients Advanced property page, shown in Figure 11.48.

Pretty neat, huh? The Find dialog box is a real improvement over Exchange 5.5's Find Recipients dialog box.

Summary

You've just completed the basic course on management of Exchange users, distribution groups, and contacts. In Chapter 17, I'll cover some advanced techniques for managing these recipients. Meanwhile, here's a quick summary of this chapter.

Before you start managing Exchange Server recipients, you should do three things. First, you need to become familiar with both Microsoft Management Console (MMC) and the Active Directory Users and Computers snap-in (ADUC) for MMC. Second, you should ensure that the formats used for Windows 2000/Exchange 2000 user display names is set as you want them to be. Third, you need to make certain that the addressing defaults for your Exchange organization are as you want them to be.

Three types of Exchange Server recipients are managed with the ADUC. These are users, distribution groups, and contacts.

Two types of users exist: mailbox-enabled users and mail-enabled users. Mailbox-enabled users are Windows 2000 users with Exchange mailboxes. Mail-enabled users are Windows 2000 users without mailboxes, but with e-mail addresses in foreign messaging systems.

Distribution groups are collections of Exchange recipients. A copy of a message addressed to a distribution group goes to each member of the group.

Contacts are non-Windows 2000 users with e-mail addresses that are located in foreign messaging systems. The main difference between mail-enabled users and contacts is that mail-enabled users have Exchange mailboxes, while contacts do not. Contacts are totally foreign to both your Windows 2000 and Exchange 2000 environments.

When you create an Exchange user, distribution group, or contact, you name it, set any required security parameters, specify where it is to reside in your Exchange hierarchy, and set available messaging attributes such as alias and e-mail address. Managing an Exchange user, distribution group, or contact is largely a matter of finding the right property page on the Properties dialog box for the object and manipulating the attributes on the page. Users, distribution groups, and contacts have similar property pages. Generally, you use these property pages to set display names, aliases, and e-mail addresses, as well as to restrict what can be received from whom and to limit the size of incoming and outgoing messages. When modifying restrictions and limits for individual recipients, you're essentially choosing to override Exchange server-based defaults.

When you start creating Exchange users, distribution groups, and contacts, it gets increasingly difficult to find these recipients in Active Directory. The search feature of ADUC makes this task much easier. You can find Exchange recipients based on their type and on a wide range of Windows 2000 and Exchange 2000 attributes.

In the next chapter, we'll continue our exploration of basic Exchange Server management. We'll focus on the management of Exchange Server's hierarchy and core components. This includes the last of the Exchange recipients, public folders, and all the other aspects of the hierarchy, including the organization, administrative groups, and servers.

CHAPTER 12

Managing the Exchange Server Hierarchy and Core Components

After completing the last chapter, you should have a firm grounding in the use of the Active Directory Users and Computers snap-in to manage Exchange users, distribution groups, and contacts. Now I want to show you how to use the Exchange 2000's System Manager to administer the Exchange Server hierarchy and core components. As in the last chapter, I'll focus mainly on the basics here, saving advanced administration and management for later chapters.

 NOTE As you've probably already discovered, some types of property pages are very similar, no matter where you encounter them. The Security page is a good example. From this point on, if we've already covered the subject matter of a particular property page, I'll skip over it without comment. I'll still let you know when we're bypassing material that we'll cover in later chapters, though. Therefore, if I don't say anything at all about a specific property page or property, I'm assuming that you already know how to deal with it. Check back to earlier discussions for specifics.

The Exchange Server Hierarchy

You'll remember from Chapter 4, "Exchange 2000 Server Architecture," that the Exchange 2000 Server hierarchy includes the following components:

- The organization
- Administrative groups
- Servers
- Recipients

In the last chapter, we talked a good deal about three kinds of recipients: Exchange users, distribution groups, and contacts. Here we'll focus on the organization, administrative groups, and servers. We'll also cover the last of the four recipient types: public folders.

Open your Microsoft Management Console (MMC) and click open the main subcontainers in Exchange System Manager so that it looks like the one in Figure 12.1.

FIGURE 12.1

Exchange System Manager, ready to administer and manage the Exchange hierarchy

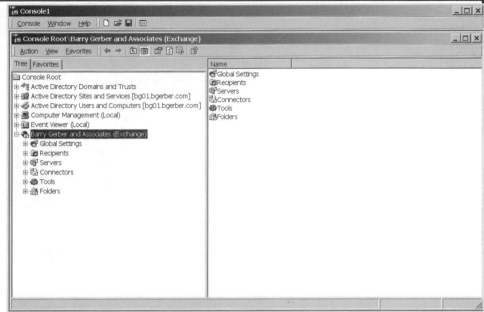

"Wait," I can hear you saying, *"this* is the Exchange hierarchy? Where are administrative groups?" Good eyes. You have to turn on the display of administrative groups. Right-click your Exchange organization—my organization is called Barry Gerber and Associates (Exchange)—and select Properties from the pop-up menu. This brings up the organization Properties dialog box, shown in Figure 12.2. Select Display Administrative Groups. Click OK to close the dialog box. Exit your MMC and open it again.

 WARNING If you have or expect to have Exchange 5.5 servers in your Exchange organization, don't click Change Mode on the organization dialog box shown in Figure 12.2. Native Exchange mode is a nice place to be, but not until all your Exchange servers are running Exchange 2000 Server. My Exchange organization has no Exchange 5.5 servers, so I've already set my organization to native mode.

Setting an Exchange organization to native mode is not the same as setting a Windows 2000 domain to native mode. The two are totally unrelated. As I mentioned in Chapter 6, "Upgrading to Windows 2000 Server and Exchange 2000 Server," you set a domain to native mode when you no longer need to support NT 4 servers, when all your servers are Windows 2000 servers. You set an organization to native mode when you no longer need to support Exchange 5.5 servers, when all of your servers are Exchange 2000 servers.

FIGURE 12.2

Using the organization Properties dialog box to display administrative groups

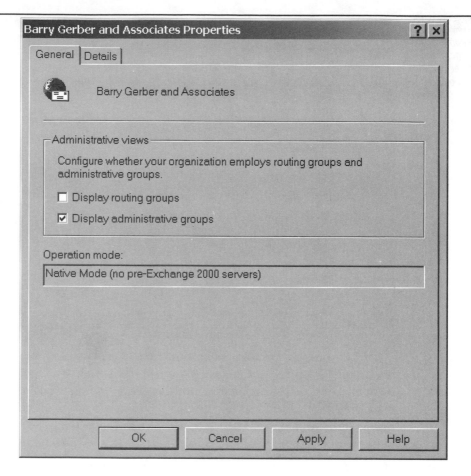

Your System Manager should now look like the one in Figure 12.3. As we move along, refer back to this figure if you need help in finding a particular object in the Exchange hierarchy.

PART

IV

Basic Exchange 2000
Server Administration

FIGURE 12.3

Exchange System Manager, with administrative groups displayed

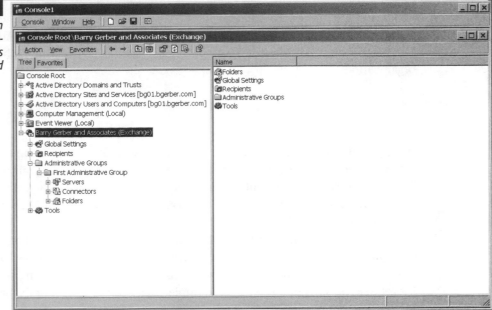

Managing the Organization

As it was in Exchange 5.5, the organization is the topmost rung on the Exchange 2000 hierarchy. More than anything else, it is a holding tank for other Exchange objects. We'll talk specifically about these objects in this and later chapters. There isn't a heck of a lot that you need to do in relation to your organization; the Properties dialog box in Figure 12.2 is almost all you have. The Details property page of the dialog box shows when the organization was created and when changes were last made, and it allows for free-form text notes.

Two interesting options appear on the menu that pops up when you right-click your organization: Delegate Control and Export List.

Delegate Control opens the Exchange Administration Delegation Wizard. You used this wizard back in Chapter 8, "Installing Exchange 2000 Server," to give the group Exchange Admins permission to manage your Exchange organization. We'll talk about it again when we get into administrative groups in the next section.

The Export List option appears on most MMC pages. Selecting it enables you to save a list of objects in a container to a tab- or comma-delimited file. All the attributes of the object that are visible in the container are saved to the file. As I noted in the last chapter, you expose hidden attributes in a container by selecting Choose

Columns from a snap-in's View menu. Exporting object attributes can be useful when you need to modify Active Directory data or use Active Directory data in an external application, such as a database. We'll get into all of this in Chapter 17, "Advanced Exchange Server Management." For now, that's it for managing your Exchange organization.

Managing Administrative Groups

Administrative groups are containers for Exchange servers, connectors, public folder trees, policies, routing groups, conferencing services, and chat communities. A group can hold one or more of these Exchange objects. On installation of your first Exchange 2000 server, a default administrative group is created, called First Administrative Group. It includes containers for servers, connectors, and public folders (see Figure 12.3).

You use administrative groups to isolate a specific set of Exchange objects so that management responsibilities can be assigned to different Windows 2000 groups or users. You use system policies within administrative groups. System policies make it easy to apply a set of attributes to multiple objects, such as a set of Exchange servers. Let's look more closely at administrative group models and system policies.

Administrative Group Models

Three basic administrative group models exist:

- Decentralized
- Centralized
- Mixed

As the names of these models imply, administrative groups enable you to build an Exchange management infrastructure that fits the hierarchical or geographic structure of your organization. Let's look at each model in more detail.

Decentralized

You use the decentralized administrative group model when you want to parcel out full responsibility for administering different segments of your Exchange system to different groups. For example, you might want to give one group full responsibility for your Exchange system in the United States, and another group full responsibility for your European Exchange system.

To do this, you'd create two administrative groups, one for the United States and one for Europe. Then you'd put all the Exchange objects (servers, public folders, policies, routing groups, and so on) for each geographical region in the appropriate administrative group. Finally, you would delegate control for each administrative group to the appropriate groups or users for each geographical area. Delegating control is done just as you did it in Chapter 8, when you delegated control of your Exchange organization to the group Exchange Admins. To begin, right-click the appropriate administrative group and select Delegate Control from the pop-up menu.

This model has political advantages in some organizations. It also works well where high-bandwidth network connections aren't available between geographically distributed offices.

This model will likely seem familiar to Exchange 5.5 administrators. It is the way Exchange 5.5 sites were used.

Centralized

In a centralized administrative group structure, you would use one or very few administrative groups. You would use the groups more to distribute the workload among a centralized staff than to distribute responsibility among organizationally decentralized staff, as you would with decentralized administrative groups.

This model is especially effective for small to medium organizations. It also works in large organizations, though it works best when high-bandwidth connections exist between distributed offices.

Mixed

A mixed-mode administrative group environment includes either a centralized or a decentralized model, plus administrative groups for specific Exchange objects that you don't want managed by the centralized or decentralized managers. For example, you might want to consolidate control of Exchange policies in one group, while leaving all the rest of Exchange management to a decentralized set of Exchange managers at your organization's branch offices.

To do this, you would create an administrative group for each of your branch offices, leaving out policy objects. Then you would delegate control for each decentralized administrative group to the appropriate Windows 2000 groups or users. Next you would create an administrative group for policy management, add a policy container, and delegate control to the users or groups that you want to manage Exchange policies.

Using Organizational Units to Distribute Responsibility for Users, Groups, Contacts, and Computer Objects

You can also distribute responsibility for administering Active Directory user, group, contact, and computer objects among different users or groups in your organization. To do this, you create one or more Windows 2000 organizational units in Active Directory using the Active Directory Users and Computers snap-in (right-click the domain container and select New Organizational Unit from the pop-up menu). Your organizational units can parallel your administrative groups in focus and membership, or they can have an entirely different focus and membership. When your organizational units are in place, you can move pre-existing users, groups, contacts, or computers into the appropriate organizational unit and delegate control for each unit to the appropriate groups or users.

Right now you have one Exchange server and a very simple Windows 2000/Exchange 2000 environment, so, there isn't a lot you can do with Exchange administrative groups. However, as you add Exchange servers to your Exchange organization in Chapter 15, "Installing and Managing Additional Exchange 2000 Servers," you'll be able to make very good use of administrative groups. For now, we'll use our single administrative group to organize our Exchange hierarchy.

Exchange System Policies

Exchange policies are a quick way to assign properties to groups of Exchange objects. These are generally the same properties that you can assign to individual objects using a Properties dialog box. You create policies and then apply them to the appropriate objects.

Two basic types of Exchange policies exist:

- Recipient
- System

As you'll remember from the last chapter, recipient policies relate to how e-mail addresses are generated for one or more types of Exchange recipients. Recipient policies are managed in the Recipients container of your Exchange organization. System policies are managed in administrative groups. Administrative groups must be displayed before you can use system policies.

Three types of system policies exist:

- Server
- Mailbox store
- Public store

I'll discuss each of these in the next sections.

Servers

Servers constitute the third level of the Exchange 2000 hierarchy. Their major function is to hold mailbox and public stores that make up one of Exchange's core components, the Information Store.

In Figure 12.4, I've expanded my administrative group to show key containers for my one and only server, EXCHANGE01. The server supports a range of protocols, as well as a storage group that includes a mailbox store and a public store. We'll get into storage groups later in this chapter, in the section "The Information Store."

FIGURE 12.4

Exchange System Manager, with the Servers container expanded

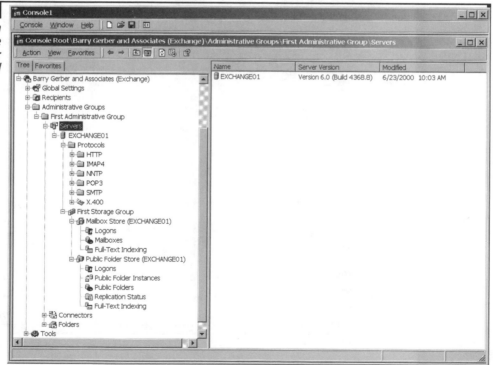

Server Properties

Let's start by looking at the properties of Exchange servers that we can manipulate. Right-click your server—mine is named EXCHANGE01—and select Properties from the pop-up menu. This opens the server Properties dialog box, shown in Figure 12.5.

Because they should be familiar to you, I'll skip the Details and Security pages. We'll deal with server policies later, in the section, "Creating and Managing Server Policies," and we'll cover full-text indexing in the section "The Information Store." Let's look at the remaining property pages of this dialog box.

FIGURE 12.5

The server Properties dialog box with its general property page exposed

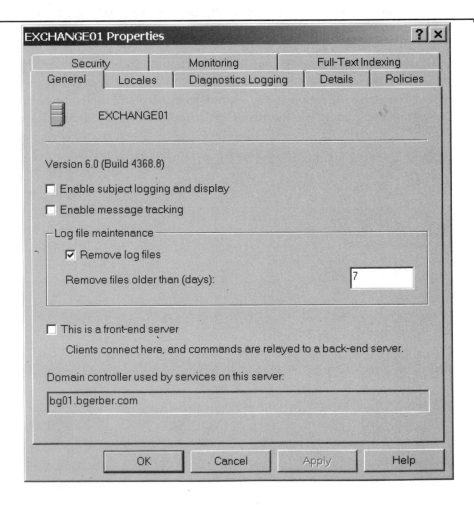

General

You use the General property page, shown in Figure 12.5, to enable and disable logging and message tracking, to set log file deletion parameters, and to specify whether the server is a front- or back-end server for certain Internet-based services. I discuss each of these next.

Enable Subject Logging and Display

When tracking messages (see the next subsection), you can choose to have the subject line of each message included in the tracking log and displayed when you're tracking the message. It can be helpful when tracking messages to see the subject. However, some might consider viewing subject lines to be an invasion of privacy. Also, storing the subject of each message takes disk space. Depending on how long you keep your tracking logs, this could create a disk storage problem.

Enable Message Tracking

If the Enable Message Tracking check box is selected, a daily log file is kept on all messages that the information store handles. Exchange Server's Message Tracking Center (which I'll talk about in Chapter 17) uses these log files to help you figure out what might have happened to wayward messages. You can track messages to foreign messaging systems up to the point of successful delivery. You can't track what happened to such messages inside the foreign messaging system.

Often, you'll use this feature to satisfy a user's request about what happened to a message. I suggest that you enable message tracking right now and start building the log files. If you want to play with the Message Tracking Center after something is in the log files, open the Tools container in Exchange System Manager, right-click Message Tracking Center, and select All Tasks ➤ Track Message from the pop-up menu.

Log File Maintenance

You can't track messages if the log for the day they were sent has been deleted. So, you must time log file deletion with this in mind. For now, it's pretty safe to accept the default that message-tracking log files more than seven days old should be deleted. If you back up your server regularly using the backup cycle that I suggested in Chapter 7, "Installing Windows 2000 Server," and Chapter 8, seven days should be fine. You'll always be able to restore recent log files from your backup if you need them.

By the way, deleting log files (in fact, performing most scheduled activities) is the job of the System Attendant service. You'll remember that the SA is one of the core components of Exchange Server.

This Is a Front-End Server

With Exchange 5.5, the Information Store (IS) took care of both mailbox and public folder databases and Internet client access protocols such as Post Office Protocol v3 (POP3), Internet Message Access Protocol version 4 (IMAP4), Network News Transfer Protocol (NNTP), and Outlook Web Access (OWA). The IS also managed Microsoft's non–Internet-oriented Messaging Application Programming Interface (MAPI) client access protocol. The IS managed MAPI communications directly and communicated with Internet Information Server (IIS) to accomplish its Internet protocol access tasks.

With Exchange 2000, the IS continues to handle MAPI access. However, the Internet client access protocols are managed by IIS. A front-end Exchange server handles communication between IIS and back-end Exchange server information stores. A front-end server still has at least a basic IS. You can create mailboxes in it or not, as you want.

This new front-end/back-end server technology is a very good idea because it reduces the load on Exchange servers by moving management of Internet access protocols to IIS. It also makes it very easy for a user to access a single front-end server to get to an Exchange mailbox or, when the the protocol supports it, a public folder using a POP3, IMAP4, NNTP, or OWA client.

For now, don't check This Is A Front-End Server. In Chapter 14, "Managing Exchange 2000 Services for Internet Clients" I'll talk more about Internet clients and front- and back-end servers.

Domain Controller Used by Services on This Server

This box shows the domain controller that controls access to Windows 2000 logon, as well as Windows 2000 and Exchange 2000 authentication and access to Active Directory and shared resources.

Locales

Users of Outlook clients can select a locale-specific format for the display of such things as currency, time, and date. The options that they can choose from are set on the server Locales property page (see Figure 12.6). To add country-specific locale information, click Add and select the locales from the Add Locale dialog box. Remove locales with the Remove button.

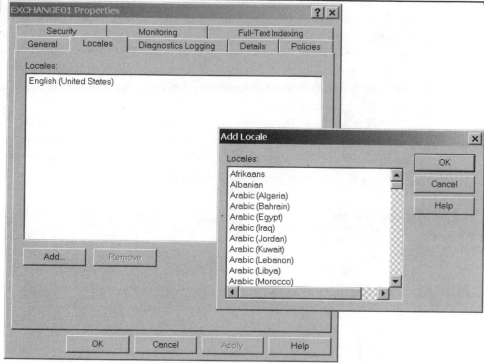

FIGURE 12.6

Using the Locales property page to add country-specific currency, time, and date display options to a server

Diagnostics Logging

Exchange Server writes diagnostic information to Windows 2000 Server's event logs. You should keep an eye on the Application and System Event logs to be sure that Exchange's services are up and functioning properly. You'll find them in the MMC snap-in\Computer Management (Local) under System Tools\Event Viewer.

Some Exchange server logging is enabled by default. You use the Diagnostics Logging property page to specify additional items to log and the depth of logging to be done for each. Most of the time, you'll enable more extensive diagnostics logging when you think you've got a problem. In many cases, technical support folks at Microsoft or another group will tell you what they want logged and then will ask you to turn it on. However, it's still worth knowing how to use the Diagnostics Logging page, so let's try it.

When you first select the Diagnostics Logging property page, it looks pretty sparse. All you see are the name of the server; a tree listing several cryptic names that you might correctly assume represent Exchange Server objects; and, at the bottom, some unselected logging-level options.

You can set diagnostic logging options for most services at the root level, except for the Information Store, MSExchangeIS. Double-clicking MSExchangeIS (or clicking the plus sign in front of MSExchangeIS) opens a list of system, public, and private information store services (see Figure 12.7).

When you click a service in the left Services pane, the right pane shows the specific items within the service that can be logged. Figure 12.7 shows some of the diagnostic items for the MSExchangeIS (Information Store) private service.

You can set a logging option for any item in the right pane by clicking the item and then selecting an option in the Logging Level area at the bottom of the property page. (In Figure 12.7, I've chosen a medium level of logging for the use of the Send As permission that I discussed in the last chapter.)

FIGURE 12.7

Using the Diagnostics Logging property page to set additional Exchange Server logging options

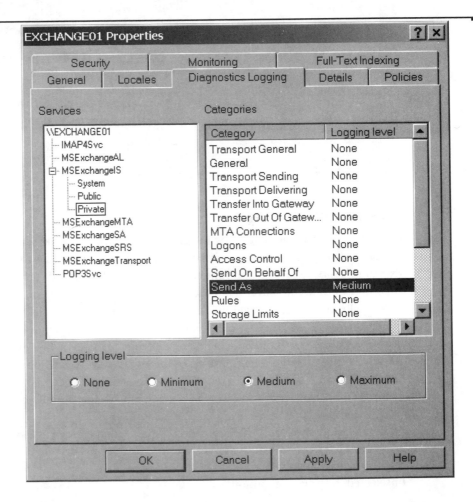

To set the same logging level for a group of items, just use the standard Microsoft Windows selection options: Ctrl+mouse clicks for noncontiguous items, and Shift+mouse clicks for contiguous items.

WARNING   Use diagnostics logging with care and as a short-term debugging tool. It can eat disk space faster than you can say *Exchange Server,* especially when you set logging levels to Maximum. If the disk happens to be the one where your Exchange server's databases or logs reside, Exchange Server might not have enough disk space to run, and it will shut itself down. Diagnostics logging writes information to the Windows 2000 Server Application event log. You can view the log and limit the amount of information written to it using the Event Viewer application (Start menu ➤ Programs ➤ Administrative Tools ➤ Event Viewer).

Monitoring

Server monitors are really impressive. They watch over Exchange servers, their resources, and the services running on them. One server monitor can operate on one or more of the servers in an Exchange organization. You can set up multiple monitors on a server.

Monitors have both warning and critical state criteria. You can set up notifications to trigger when warning or critical states having been reached. You can set up monitoring so that you're notified by e-mail when a warning or critical state threshold is reached on one or more of your servers. You can also set up monitoring so that a script executes when there's a problem. A script can be any executable program file or batch file. Scripts can send console messages to you or a group of Exchange administrators, or they can communicate by another method, such as a pager. Scripts are especially valuable when your Exchange system is in a state in which it can't send e-mail.

Server monitors are important. You should get comfortable with them right away.

Exchange comes with a default monitor, called Default Microsoft Exchange Services in Figure 12.8. As you can see on the Default Microsoft Exchange Services dialog box in Figure 12.8, the monitor checks the status of a range of key Exchange services. Notice the Critical State column on the Monitoring property page. That's not the current state of the Exchange services; it's the state at which the monitor goes critical. That is, the monitor goes into a critical state when one or more services are not running (stopped).

To check the status of your monitors, open the monitor by double-clicking it on the Monitoring property page, as I have done in Figure 12.8. This opens a dialog box for the monitor, Default Microsoft Exchange Services in Figure 12.8. Note on the Default Microsoft Exchange Services dialog box that all the services being monitored are running fine. You can also view the status of your server and its monitors in the Status subcontainer of the Tools container, shown in the lower-left corner of Figure 12.8. I'll talk more about the Status subcontainer in the upcoming section "Viewing Server Status."

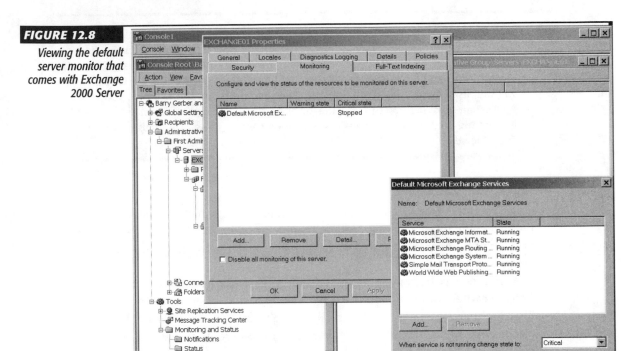

FIGURE 12.8

Viewing the default server monitor that comes with Exchange 2000 Server

Creating a New Server Monitor

Let's create a new monitor. Close the Default Microsoft Exchange Services monitor dialog box, if it's open. Then click Add on the Monitoring property page. The Add Resource dialog box, shown in Figure 12.9, includes a list of resources that you can monitor. Each monitor can monitor one of these resource sets. There can be only one of each resource monitor on a server per specific resource. For example, there can be only one SMTP queue growth monitor, but there can be (really *must* be) a free disk space monitor for each disk drive.

FIGURE 12.9

*Using the Add
Resource dialog box to
select the type of mon-
itor to be created*

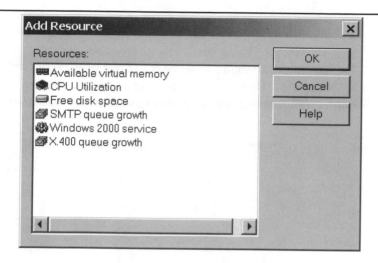

Here's a quick overview of the resource monitors available:

Available Virtual Memory   This is the disk-based paging memory used by Windows 2000 services and programs to gain memory beyond the physical RAM memory in a computer. You don't want virtual memory to run too low—say, below 25 percent—as a rule of thumb.

CPU Utilization   CPU utilization above 90 percent for a sustained period (10 minutes) indicates either a problem on your server or inadequate capacity to run the installed services.

Free Disk Space   I like to have at least 1GB available on all of my Exchange server disks.

SMTP Queue Growth   Remember from Chapter 4 that SMTP is the communication protocol of Exchange server-to-server communications. Interserver e-mail messages and other information, such as public folder replication information, pass through SMTP queues. If queues continue to grow for 20 minutes, you've usually got a local or network communication problem.

Windows 2000 Service   This innocent item lets you monitor as many Exchange and non-Exchange services as you want. It's a good idea to monitor non-Exchange services that Exchange Server depends on. For example, users cannot access their mailboxes with a Web browser unless the Internet Information Server's World Wide Web Publishing Service is up and running.

X.400 Queue Growth   This one works the same way as the SMTP queue growth monitor.

Okay, back to the monitor we're creating. It's always a good idea to monitor available disk space, so let's set up a free disk space monitor. Select the disk space option from the Add Resource dialog box, and click OK. This opens the Disk Space Thresholds dialog box, shown in Figure 12.10. Select a drive to be monitored, set warning and critical state remaining space thresholds, and click OK. You need to do a separate free disk space monitor for each disk on your server that you want to monitor.

FIGURE 12.10

Using the Disk Space Thresholds dialog box to configure a free disk space monitor

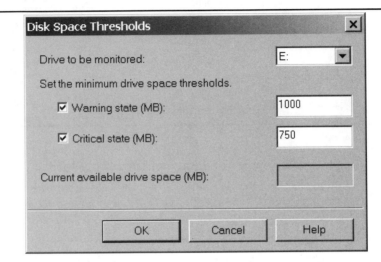

Viewing Server Status

As I mentioned previously, you check the status of a server in the Status subcontainer of the Tools container. In Figure 12.11, you can see the general status of the server in the right pane of the MMC snap-in. The server is in fine shape—or, as Exchange puts it, it is *available*. By double-clicking the server, I opened the ECHANGE01 Properties dialog box (see Figure 12.11), which looks pretty much like the Monitoring property page in Figure 12.8, except for the addition of the free disk space monitor.

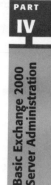

FIGURE 12.11

*Viewing a server's
monitoring status*

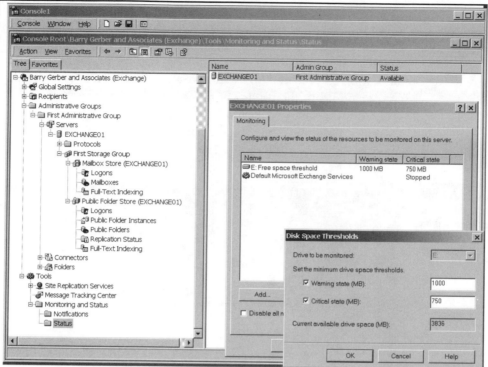

Double-clicking a monitor opens its dialog box. In Figure 12.11, I've opened the Disk Space Thresholds dialog box that not only shows me what thresholds I've set and allows me to change them, but also shows the amount of disk space remaining on my E drive. This is where you'd go to check out a problem on your server.

"Ah," you say, "but how do I know there is a problem on my server?" Funny you should ask. One answer is that you regularly do exactly what we just did. You look at your servers and their monitors. For my second answer, you'll have to join me in the next section. See ya.

Setting Up Notifications

Notifications let you know when something is amiss in serverland. You can create e-mail notifications or notifications that run scripts. Here's how.

Setting Up E-mail Notifications

You set up e-mail and other monitoring notifications in the Notifications container (see Figure 12.11, lower-left corner, for the location of this container). It's important to remember that what you're doing here is setting up a notification, not a monitor. A notification uses the monitors that have been created on the Monitoring page of a server or automatic monitoring of connectors. It doesn't create any new monitors.

To create an e-mail notification, right-click the Notifications container and select New ➤ E-mail Notification from the pop-up menu. Use the resultant Properties dialog box to set up the notification (see Figure 12.12).

FIGURE 12.12

Using the notification Properties dialog box to create a new notification

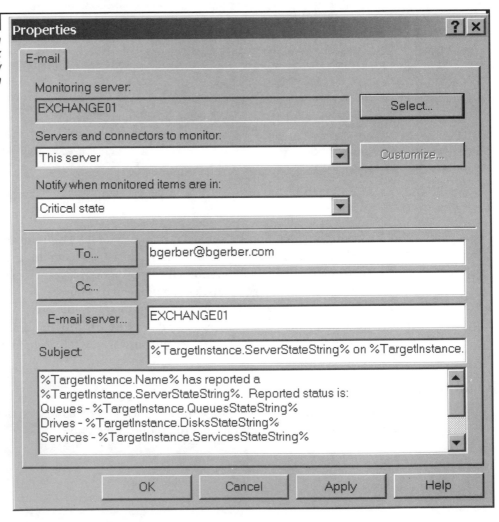

The monitoring server is the server where the notification you're setting up runs. It's called a *monitoring server* because it watches the status of all the monitors on all the servers that the notification includes. We have only one server right now, so we'll run our notification on that server. However, you really don't want to run a notification on the server that it is going to be watching. If something goes wrong with the server, it may not be capable of running the notification. It's best to set up a cross-server notification plan so that a server runs notifications for one or more other servers, not itself.

You use the Servers and Connectors to Monitor field to select the monitors that the notification will watch. Your options include these:

- This server
- All servers
- Any server in the routing group
- All connectors
- Any connector in the routing group
- Custom list of servers
- Custom list of connectors

As I hinted previously, connectors are monitored by default. In other words, you don't have to set up connector monitors; Exchange just starts monitoring connectors upon creation. We'll return to connector monitoring and notifications when we get into Internet messaging in Chapter 13, "Managing Exchange 2000 Internet Services," and we'll cover installing, managing, and connecting additional Exchange servers in Chapter 15.

Use the Customize button, shown in Figure 12.12, to set up a custom list of servers or connectors. Notice that you can set up a notification for servers or connectors, not for both.

The next field, Notify When Monitored Items Are In, lets you select the state when an e-mail notification is triggered. Your choices are critical state and warning state, and they relate to the way you've set state thresholds on your monitor.

Select the user or distribution group to which notifications will be sent using the To and Cc fields. Specify the Exchange server to be used to send the messages using the E-mail Server field.

The Subject and Message Content fields contain variables and constants that form the subject line and body of the notification message to be sent. You can modify these two fields, although you should make any modifications with care.

When you're done with your notification, click OK. Then be sure that the notification appears in the right pane of your MMC.

Setting Up Scripted Notifications

A scripted notification runs a program or batch file when a specific state occurs on one or more servers. For example, you can run a program that notifies your pager of a problem—or, more simply, you can set up a batch file that notifies a user or group about a problem by sending a Windows 2000 console message. A console message shows up on the desktop of whatever user or group it is sent to. Console messages are generated with the command net send. For example, I could include the following line in a batch file and then select the batch file as the script to be run by a notification:

Net send /bgerber EXCHANGE01 has reached a critical state. Please check it out.

To set up a scripted notification, right-click the Notifications container and select New ➤ Script notification. The dialog box for a new scripted notification is pretty much like the one for an e-mail notification. Basically, script-oriented fields replace e-mail–oriented fields. There's a field for the path to the script and the script filename, as well as a field for any command-line arguments to be included when the script file is run.

 TIP   There is another way to monitor Exchange services and take limited but effective action, depending on the status of a service. It involves setting specific recovery actions to be taken by a server when a service becomes unavailable. Actions include attempting to restart a service or to reboot the server that a service runs on. You can even set a series of increasingly more drastic actions for a service that's in trouble. I discuss this option for monitoring services in Chapter 14, in the section "Exchange 2000 Virtual Servers Are Not Just for SMTP."

I'll leave it to you to come up with other neat ideas for implementing script-based notifications.

 TIP   You can also use Windows 2000 performance logs and alerts to monitor your Exchange server. Hundreds of Exchange-related counters are available, ranging from message queue size growth to number of messages submitted by users per minute, to authentication failures for the Internet mail protocols POP3 and IMAP4. In addition, there are lots of counters for the Windows 2000 side of your server. These include everything from CPU usage to disk access times, to network logon errors. For more on all this, see the books *Mastering Windows 2000 Server*, by Mark Minasi, et al. (Sybex, 2000), and *Microsoft Windows 2000 Server Administrator's Companion*, by Charlie Russel and Sharon Crawford (Microsoft Press, 2000).

Creating and Managing Server Policies

Before we start, let me reiterate a point that I made earlier: Exchange policies are designed to make it easy for you to apply a set of properties to a group of objects—recipients, servers, mailbox stores, and public stores—without having to open the dialog box for each object (100 servers, for example). What we're about to do is kind of meaningless right now because we have only one server. However, it's important that you understand Exchange policies, and now is as good a time as any for that to happen. We'll return to Exchange policies in Chapter 15, when you begin adding servers to your Exchange organization.

To create a new server policy, right-click your administrative group (it should be called First Administrative Group) and select New ➤ System Policy Container from the pop-up menu. Then locate the System Policies container that was just created in your administrative group container, right-click it, and select New ➤ Server policy.

This opens the New Policy dialog box, shown in Figure 12.13. At this writing, I am able to create server policies only for the General property page of the server dialog box. So, I've chosen that page and clicked OK.

PART

IV

Basic Exchange 2000
Server Administration

FIGURE 12.13

Using the New Policy dialog box to select the property pages to be included in a new policy

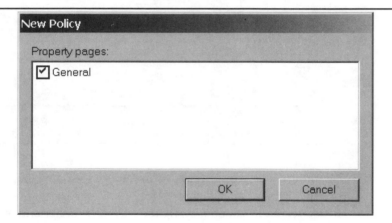

This opens the Properties dialog box that you use to create a new server policy. Give your policy a name using the General property page. I've "creatively" called mine Server Policy #1.

Next tab over to the Policy (General) property page (see Figure 12.14). Compare Figure 12.14 with Figure 12.5: They are essentially the same, but the property page for server policies does not include the front-end server option. This option needs to be set with some refinement. The key difference between these two property pages is that when I use the General property page for a server (see Figure 12.5), I'm able to set properties for only that server. When I use the General property page for server policies (see Figure 12.14), I can change properties for as many servers as I want.

FIGURE 12.14

Using the server policy Properties dialog box to specify how specific properties should be handled under a new policy

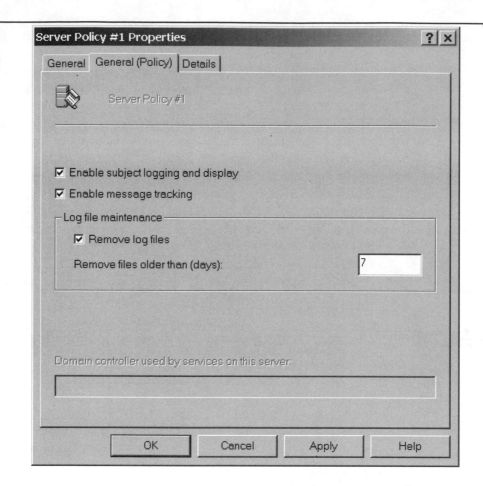

Fill in the dialog box and click OK. When you're done, your MMC should look something like the one in Figure 12.15.

To add servers to your policy, right-click on the policy and select Add Server from the pop-up menu. Just for fun, add your one-and-only Exchange server. If you had more servers, of course, you could add all or some of them to this policy. You can create as many policies as you need to ensure that all your servers have the appropriate policy applied to them.

FIGURE 12.15

*Choosing to add a
server to a policy*

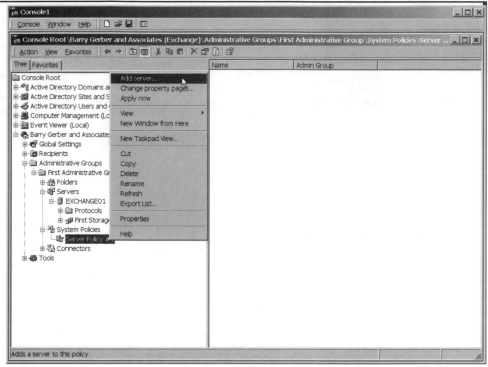

When you're done, you should see your server in the container for the policy that
you just created. It's a subcontainer of the System Policies container. Double-click
your server open, and you'll see the server Properties dialog box, shown in Figure
12.5. However, properties controlled by the policy are grayed out because they can't
be altered (see Figure 12.16). While your server Properties dialog box is open, tab over
to the Policies dialog box; miracle of all miracles, your new policy shows in the Policies field (see Figure 12.17).

FIGURE 12.16

The server Properties dialog box after a server policy has been applied to a server

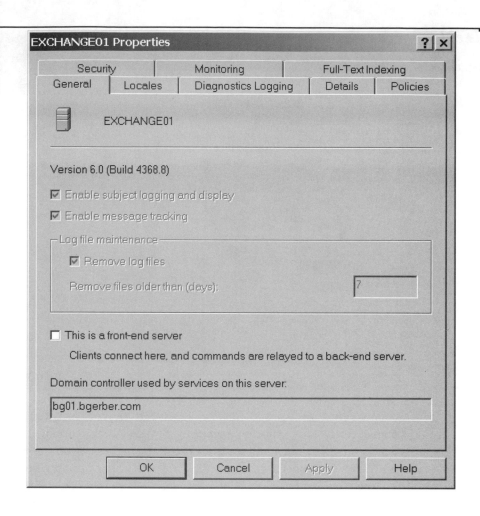

FIGURE 12.17

The Policies property
page shows a newly
added server policy.

Creating and Managing Public Folders

Okay, we're ready to tackle the last of the four recipient types, public folders. When
we've completed our look at public folders, we'll also have completed our look at
basic management of the Exchange hierarchy.

Creating a Public Folder

Back in Chapter 10, "A Quick Overview of Outlook 2000," we created a public folder
using the Outlook client. I named my public folder Barry's First Public Folder. You can
see it in the Public Folders container on the lower-left side of Figure 12.18.

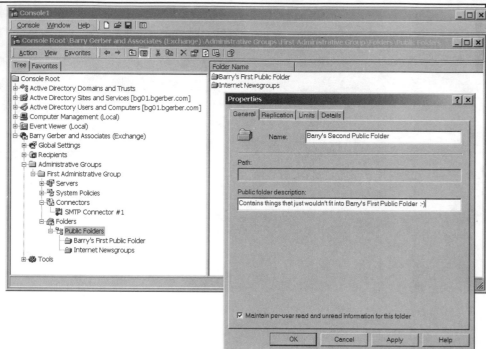

In Exchange 5.5, you could create a folder only using an e-mail client. You couldn't create one in the Administrator program. Exchange 2000 lets you create public folders in Exchange System Manager as an Exchange administrator. That's what I'm doing on the right side of Figure 12.18. I right-clicked the Public Folders container and selected New ➢ Public Folder from the pop-up menu to bring up the new public folder Properties dialog box. Let's take a look at the key property pages on this dialog box.

General

You use the General property page, shown in Figure 12.18, to name your folder and enter a description of the folder. The Path field will show where the folder is located in the Public Folder hierarchy after it has been created. If Maintain Per-User Read and Unread Information for This Folder is selected, a user will see items in the folder that he or she has read in non-bold text. If this option is not selected, all items show in bold text whether read or not.

Replication

This is a very important property page because it is used to manage replication of folders between this server and other Exchange servers. Replication enables you to put copies of the same folder on multiple Exchange servers. It is very useful either for local load balancing or to limit wide area network traffic and improve performance by placing copies of folders in routing groups at geographically distant sites.

Important as replication is, we're not ready for it. We'll tackle it in Chapter 15 after we have some servers to replicate to.

Limits

You've seen limits property pages before. This one is interesting, as you can see in Figure 12.19. Let's look at each of the three types of limits on this page.

Storage Limits   Similar to mailboxes, you can set points at which warnings are sent, and posting to the folder is prohibited. You can also set a maximum posted item size. If you want you can choose to use the default storage limits settings for the public store where the folder resides.

Deletion Setting   As with mailboxes, you can set the maximum number of days that a deleted item will be kept for recovery before being totally deleted. If you deselect Use Public Store Defaults, you'll be able to enter a number of days that deleted items should be retained. If you don't want items retained at all, set number of days to 0.

Age Limits   This is the number of days that an item in the folder lives before being deleted. This is a very useful tool for controlling storage usage.

FIGURE 12.19

Using the Limits property page to set storage, deletion, and aging limits for a public folder

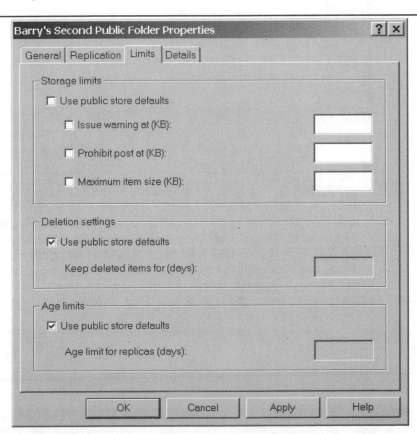

When you're finished creating your public folder, click OK and admire your handiwork in the Public Folders container. See Figure 12.20 for my admirable handiwork.

FIGURE 12.20 *A new public folder takes its place in the Public Folders container.*	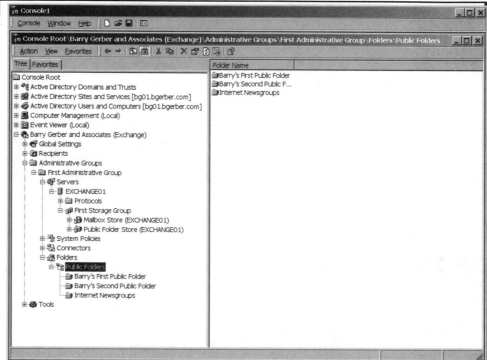

 WARNING By default, the Windows 2000 group Everyone has rights to create folders in the Public Folder container. This right extends to both top-level folders (folders within and just below the Public Folder container) and subfolders within top-level folders. If you want to alter this right, right-click the Public Folders container and select Properties. Use the Security tab on the Public Folders Properties dialog box to add or remove users and groups or their rights on the Public Folders container. Even if you don't want to change the default, I strongly recommend that you take a look at the Security tab. Many of the permissions on it are specific to public folders and, therefore, are quite different from the permissions for other types of Exchange recipients.

Managing Public Folders

You set a number of public folder management parameters while creating your public folder in the previous section. A good deal of public folder management has to do with replication and limits. However, there is more to public folder life than replication and limits. Let's take a look at some of the public folder management options available to you.

You need to open the Properties dialog box for your new folder. To do this, right-click your folder and select Properties from the pop-up menu. Figure 12.21 shows the Properties dialog box for my new folder; you've seen most of these pages before. We need to talk at least a bit about the General, Exchange General, Exchange Advanced, Permissions, and Member Of property pages.

PART

IV

Basic Exchange 2000 Server Administration

FIGURE 12.21

The public folder Properties dialog box, with the General property page showing

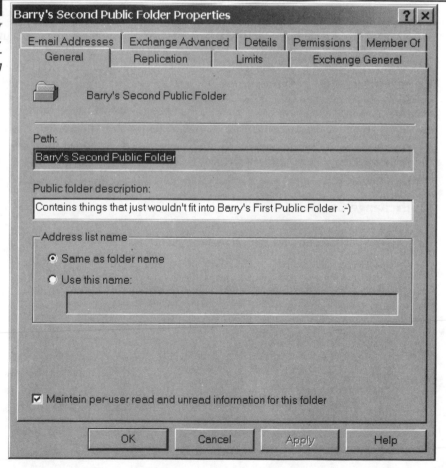

General

The only thing on this page that wasn't on the General property page of the dialog box that you used to create the folder (see Figure 12.18) is the Address List Name field. Before I explain this field, I need to fill you in a bit on e-mail–enabled public folders.

Public folders created in the Public Folders tree—that is, inside the Public Folders container—are automatically e-mail–enabled. This means that they are assigned e-mail addresses. That is why the dialog box in Figure 12.21 has an E-mail Addresses property page. E-mail–enabled public folders can receive and even send messages. You send a message from a public folder by having the permissions send on behalf of or send as on the folder, and using the From field in an Outlook message. (I discussed these permissions in Chapter 11, "Managing Exchange Users, Distribution Groups, and Contacts.")

 NOTE As you'll see later in this chapter, not all public folders are automatically e-mail–enabled. You can actually create additional public folder trees that are parallel to the Public Folders tree. Folders created in these trees are not automatically e-mail–enabled.

Okay, back to the Address List Name field in Figure 12.21. You can use this field to have Exchange display a different name for the folder in Exchange's address lists than the name you gave the folder when you created it. That's it for the Address List Name field, but do keep the concept of e-mail-enabled public folders firmly in place in your mind. As you'll soon see, not all public folders are automatically e-mail–enabled.

Exchange General

This page is very much like the Exchange General property page for a mailbox. It has buttons for opening property pages for delivery restrictions (size of incoming and outgoing messages, and which recipients messages will be received from) and delivery options (delegate send on behalf of permissions and set a forwarding address). These pages look and behave just like the same pages for a mailbox (see Chapter 11, Figures 11.18 and 11.19).

Exchange Advanced

The Exchange Advanced property page is similar to the same page for a mailbox (see Chapter 11, Figure 11.21). You can use it to set a simple display name and to unhide and hide a public folder from Exchange address lists. By default, a new public folder is hidden from address lists. You must deselect Hide from Exchange Address Lists to expose it to the address lists.

The Exchange Advanced property page contains a Custom Attributes button. Click it to enter custom information for this recipient (see Chapter 11, Figure 11.22).

Permissions

The Permissions property page for a public folder includes a range of security options. As you can see in Figure 12.22, these options cover client permissions, directory rights, and administrative rights. I cover each of these next.

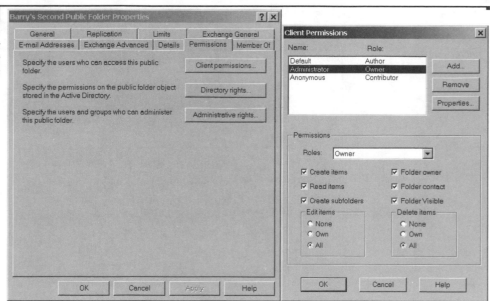

FIGURE 12.22

A public folder's Permissions property page and its Client Permissions dialog box

Client Permissions

The right side of Figure 12.22 shows the Client Permissions dialog box. As in Exchange 5.5, you use the Client Permissions dialog box to assign specific folder access rights to Exchange users and distribution groups, who can then work with a public folder using their Outlook clients. For emphasis, let me restate what I just said in a somewhat different form: You grant public folder access permissions to Exchange recipients, not Windows 2000 users and groups. Once access to a public folder is granted, Exchange recipients access the folder in their Outlook client while connected to their mailbox.

For a graphic reinforcement of this point, click Add on the Client Permissions dialog box to start adding a new user or group that will have access to this public folder. This action opens a dialog box that looks very much like the Outlook Address Book

PART

IV

Basic Exchange 2000
Server Administration

that you use to select recipients to send a message to, not the dialog box that you use to select Windows 2000 users and groups (see Figure 12.23). 'Nuff said. Click Cancel to get out of the Add Users dialog box.

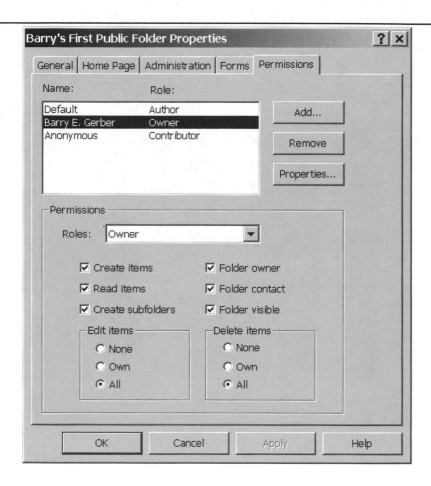

Now flip your eyes back to Figure 12.22. Because I created the public folder in Exchange System Manager while logged in as the domain administrator, Administrator is given the role of Owner. As Figure 12.22 shows, the owner of a public folder has complete control over the folder.

"Wait!" you exclaim, "Administrator is not an Exchange recipient. It's a Windows 2000 user account. That violates the rule that you so elegantly posited in the paragraph before last." So sue me. Seriously, though, because the creator is the default owner of a public folder, what other choice does Exchange have than to make the

Windows 2000 user Administrator the owner of this public folder? This seeming
anomaly arises because Exchange 2000 lets Windows 2000 users who are not
Exchange users create public folders in Exchange System Manager. As I noted previously, in Exchange 5.5, you could only create public folders in an Outlook client as a
user with an Exchange mailbox, meaning that only an Exchange user could ever be
the default owner of a new public folder. That's all changed in Exchange 2000, and
Windows 2000 users can be public folder creators and owners. All this proves the rule
that for every rule, there's an exception.

If a user has the correct permissions on a public folder, that user can change access
permissions on the folder for other users. Permissions on a public folder can be modified in two places. They can be modified from within the Outlook client using the
Permissions property page for a public folder (see Figure 12.24). Permissions can also
be modified using the Client Permissions dialog box that is available in Exchange System Manager (see Figure 12.22). Which of these you use depends on your security
rights. If you are an Exchange user with no extraordinary permissions who is an
owner of a public folder, you manage permissions on the folder in Outlook using the
Permissions property page for a public folder, shown in Figure 12.24. If you're a user
with Exchange administrative rights, for example, if you're a member of the group
Exchange Admins that we created back in Chapter 8, you can change permissions on
any public folder using the Client Permissions dialog box shown in Figure 12.22.

FIGURE 12.24

*The Permissions prop-
erty page for a public
folder, as seen from
within the Outlook
client*

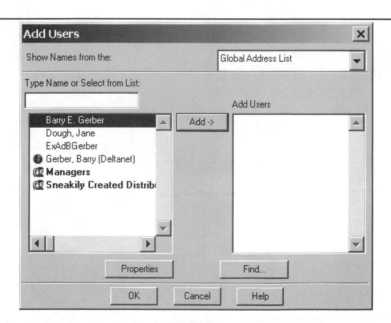

The permission *folder contact* (see Figure 12.22) is especially interesting. A folder contact receives notifications about the folder (for example, a warning that the folder's storage limits have been exceeded or that a conflict has occurred in folder replication). A folder contact is also the person whom users should ask for permissions to access to the folder. You could set things up so that a folder contact is not a folder owner. This means that a contact may have to ask a folder owner or an Exchange administrator to give a particular Exchange user access to the folder using one either the client Permissions dialog box in Figure 12.22 or the Permissions property page in Figure 12.24.

There is a group named Default that includes all Exchange recipients not separately added to the Name list box. When the folder is created, this group is automatically given the default role of Author. As Figure 12.25 shows, Authors don't own the folder and can't create subfolders. Also note that Authors can edit and delete only their own folder items.

FIGURE 12.25

The permissions granted to the Role Author on the Client Permissions dialog box

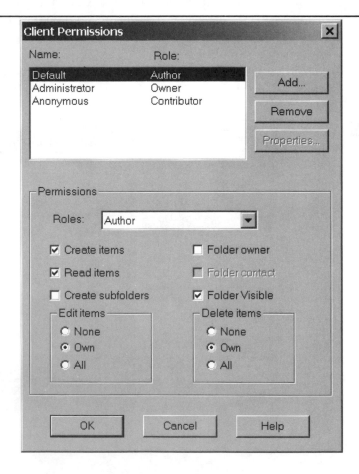

Microsoft has come up with several interesting roles—including Owner, Publishing Editor, Editor, Publishing Author, Author, Nonediting Author, Reviewer, Contributor, and Custom—each with a different combination of client permissions. I'll leave it to you to check out the specific permissions assigned to each of these roles. And, I'll leave it to you to explore your options regarding public folder access permissions. Generally, the default settings work fine for most folders.

 NOTE Wondering about that Anonymous user in Figure 12.22, 12.24, and 12.25? You set access rights to a public folder for users who don't have Exchange mailboxes through the Anonymous user. When such users access a public folder, for example, with an Internet browser, the rights granted to the Anonymous user control what they can do with the folder.

Directory Rights

Okay, back to Figure 12.22. Users and groups with appropriate permission at the directory rights level can change properties of a public folder object in Active Directory. The Directory Rights property page that pops up when you click Directory Rights is the same as the Security property page for other Exchange recipients (see Chapter 11, Figure 11.29 and related text). That's why public folders don't have a Security property page.

Administrative Rights

Administrative rights are permissions to manage a public folder using Exchange System Manager. Click Administrative Rights to open the Administrative Rights property page. As you can see in Figure 12.26, permissions include rights to modify the public folder access control list and the public folder administrative access control. These rights include permission to use the Directory Rights property page and the Administrative Rights property page, the very page that I'm talking about right now. Permissions also include the right to set deleted item retention time and space quotas for the public folder. You had the option of exercising both of these rights on the Limits page when you created your public folder earlier in this chapter.

Note in Figure 12.26 that our old friend, the group Exchange Admins, has full administrative rights to this folder. That's because we delegated control to the group at the Exchange organizational level back in Chapter 8 and because the rights granted at the organizational level were inherited by this public folder object.

Let me conclude this section by pointing out that administrative rights are granted to Windows 2000 users and groups, not Exchange 2000 users and distribution groups. Among other things, this means that any users or group members who need to exercise administrative rights must do it in Exchange System Manager, not in their mailboxes.

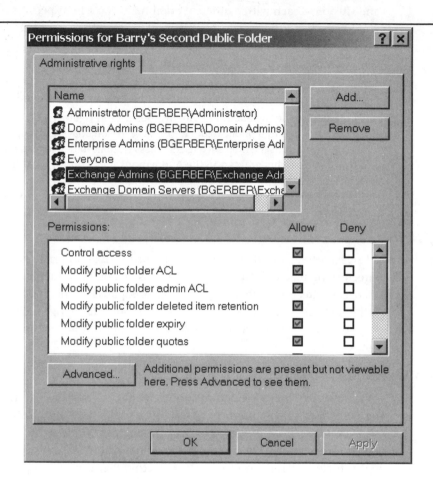

Member Of

I don't need to say a lot about the Member Of property page on the public folder Properties dialog box in Figure 12.22. I just want to call your attention to it so that I can point out that public folders, just like other Exchange recipients, can belong to security and distribution groups. When you send a message to a distribution group that includes a public folder, the message appears in the folder.

Exchange Core Components

We're now ready to take on Exchange 2000's three core components:

- The Information Store
- The Routing Engine
- The System Attendant

The Information Store holds mailboxes and public folders. We'll give these thorough coverage in this chapter. The Routing Engine helps move messages from one Exchange server to another and out to foreign messaging systems. We'll spend a little time on the Routing Engine here and more time later when we have connections to foreign messaging systems (Chapter 13 and Chapter 16, "Connecting to Other Foreign Messaging Systems") and multiple Exchange servers that need to communicate with each other (Chapter 15). The System Attendant performs a range of housekeeping tasks that keep Exchange running smoothly and efficiently. We'll cover the minimal control that you have over the System Attendant in this chapter.

For more information on the function of these components and how they fit into the Exchange system, check out Chapter 4. Okay, let's take a look at each of Exchange's core components.

The Information Store

The Information Store on an Exchange server is composed of storage groups. The Information Store has no physical being in Exchange System Manager other than in its storage groups. That's why there is no Information Store container in Figure 12.27, which shows the one and only storage group that is the Information Store on my Exchange server EXCHANGE01.

FIGURE 12.27

The Exchange Information Store is composed of storage groups.

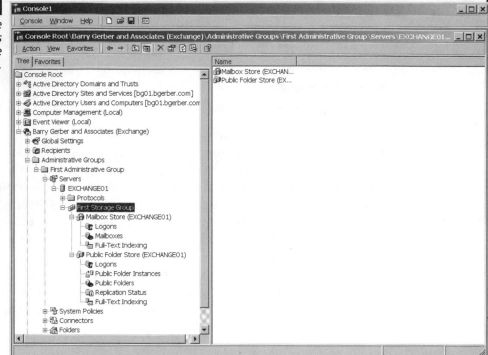

FIGURE 12.27

The Exchange Information Store is composed of storage groups.

A storage group is supported by an instance of Microsoft's Extensible Storage Engine (ESE). A storage group can contain one or more databases. Databases, also called *stores*, can contain either mailboxes or public folders, but not both. Figure 12.27 shows the mailbox store and public store in my server's storage group. Each database is made up of two files, an .EDB file and an .STM file. The .EDB file holds rich-text messages like the ones generated by Outlook and message header information (From, To, Cc, Time Sent, Subject, and so on). The .STM (for "streaming") file contains Internet content in pure Multipurpose Internet Mail Extensions (MIME) format. MIME supports everything from rich-text–like formatted text with bolding and color to multimedia audio and video content. A message with MIME content is divided into header information, which goes to the .EDB file, and other content, which is stored in the .STM file. The ESE seamlessly stores content into and delivers content from the .EDB and .STM files as needed.

A storage group has a set of transaction log files. Data destined for a particular database is quickly and dirtily written to a log file. Then, as time allows, the data is transferred into the database file. Transfer to the database file is significantly slower than the write to the transaction log file because a number of issues such as data indexing must be attended to. Log files are designed to speedily move data from RAM memory to disk, both to ensure against hardware failure and to improve performance in the early stages of committing data to disk.

Exchange 2000 Server supports one storage group per server. Exchange 2000 Enterprise Server supports multiple storage groups on each server. Enterprise Server supports up to 16 storage groups per server. Fifteen of these function as standard storage groups. One of them is used for database restoration and recovery. Because of architectural limitations related to memory management, a 32-bit platform can support four to six storage groups, one of which must be reserved for restoration and recovery. This will change when 64-bit versions of Windows and Exchange become available. You should then be able to use as many storage groups as Exchange's architecture allows.

Each storage group can support up to six databases. Each database in a storage group can reside on the same or different physical disk drives. With Exchange 2000 Server, the maximum size of a database is limited to 16GB, as with Exchange 5.5. There is no limit on database size with Enterprise Server. However, practically speaking, databases larger than 200GB don't work well. So, you'll want to use multiple storage groups and databases to handle large numbers of mailboxes, not one gigantic database. If your needs exceed the capacity of a single server, of course, you can create more storage groups and databases on other Exchange servers. By keeping database size at a reasonable level, you avoid single points of failure, you can distribute database load across multiple disk drives, and you can maintain databases separately. Independent maintenance of databases—backing up or restoring one database while the others remain online and continue to function, for example—is one of the really important bonuses of Exchange 2000.

With all of this in mind, you should be more than ready to get into Information Store management.

Creating and Managing Storage Groups

As should be pretty obvious by now, you create and manage storage groups in Exchange System Manager. So, be sure that you've got your MMC open and that your Exchange System Manager looks something like the one in Figure 12.27.

Creating a Storage Group

To create a new storage group on your Exchange server, right-click on the server and select New ➤ Storage Group. This opens the storage group Properties dialog box. Here's a quick take on your options on this dialog box (see Figure 12.28).

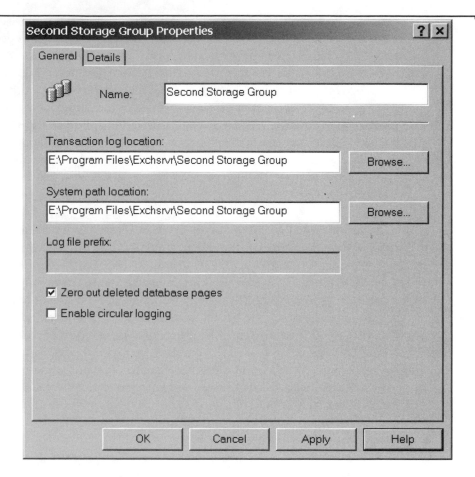

Name The name of your new storage group.

Transaction Log Location The disk drive and path where the group's transaction logs should be stored. You can change the suggested location or at any time after the store is created.

System Path Location The disk drive and path where the group's temporary and recovered files will reside. You can change this location as well.

Log File Prefix The default prefix assigned to each log file. This is a view-only field visible after group is created.

Zero Out Deleted Database Pages Checking this box improves security, but it does cost some in server performance.

Enable Circular Logging When circular logging is disabled for a storage group, a new log file is opened every time the 5MB limit for a log file is reached. When

PART

IV

Basic Exchange 2000
Server Administration

circular logging is enabled, log files are overwritten when the 5MB limit is reached. This saves disk space, but you can't recover changes to databases in a storage group after the last backup because the required log files are no longer available. I suggest that you leave circular logging disabled and rely on Windows 2000's backup program or an Exchange-aware third-party backup program to take care of pruning transaction logs. After backing up a storage group using a full or incremental backup, Exchange-aware backup programs delete transaction log files if all the data in them has been transferred to the database.

When you're finished with the storage group Properties dialog box, click OK.

Managing Storage Groups

Your new storage group should show up in the left pane of your MMC (see the left side of Figure 12.29). Right-click on the new storage group and select Properties to open the Properties dialog box for the group (see the right side of Figure 12.29). Notice that you still have control over file placement, zeroing of database pages and circular logging. That's pretty much the extent of your ability to manage storage groups.

FIGURE 12.29

A new storage group and its Properties dialog box

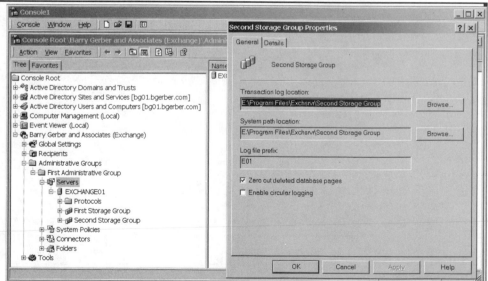

Creating and Managing Mailbox Stores

Storage groups are really shells for mailbox and public stores. Stores are the really fun part of the Information Store. So, we should get right to creating and managing stores. We'll start with mailbox stores.

Creating a Mailbox Store

We could create a new mailbox store in our first storage group, but, just for fun, let's put it in the storage group that we just created. Right-click your new storage group, and select New ➤ Mailbox Store from the pop-up menu. This opens the mailbox store Properties dialog box, shown in Figure 12.30. Right now, we need to look at the General, Database, and Limits property pages. We'll look at the Full-Text Indexing page later.

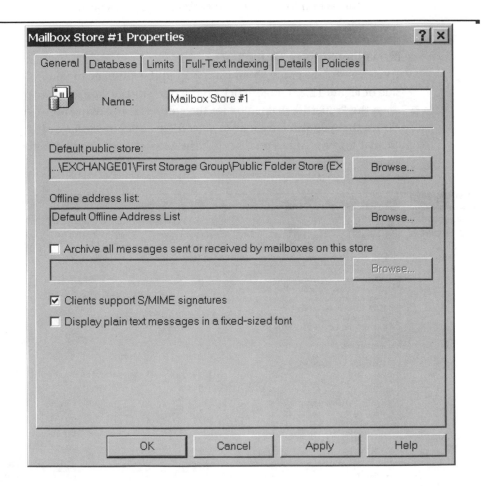

General

Most of the properties on the General property page require a fair amount of explanation, so we're going to spend a little more time then we usually spend on General pages.

Use the Name field to specify a name for your mailbox store. This is the name that will appear in Exchange System Manager. Naming conventions for mailbox stores depend on how you plan to use them. You might want to create different stores for different user groups. You could create one store for clerical personnel, another for salespeople, and another for top management. You could name each store for the group that it supports. Then you could set the attributes of each store differently. For example, you might set different storage limits on each store, or you might use different security measures for digital signatures. On the other hand, you might decide to use mailbox stores to distribute loads across your organization. You could still set different attributes for different stores, but you would probably use generic names for the stores, as I have in Figure 12.30. The choice is yours.

You're probably staring at the Default public store field on the General property page in disbelief. I know I did when I first saw it. I mean, why does a mailbox store need a default public store? The answer is simpler than you might imagine. Every mailbox store needs to be associated with the default public store on an Exchange server. The default public store on my Exchange server is named Public Folder Store (EXCHANGE01) in Figure 12.27. There is one default public store on a server, and that store is created when Exchange is installed. A mailbox store can be associated with the default public store on its own server or on any Exchange server in the organization. The public folder store associated with a mailbox store is the public folder store that users of mailboxes in the mailbox store see when using an Outlook or IMAP4 client. Figure 12.31 should help make all this clearer. If more Exchange servers existed in my Exchange organization, their default public folder stores would also show up in the Select Public Store dialog box. By the way, I opened the Select Public Store dialog box by clicking the Browse button to the right of the Default Public Store field.

FIGURE 12.31

Using the Select Public Store dialog box to choose the default public store to be associated with a mailbox store

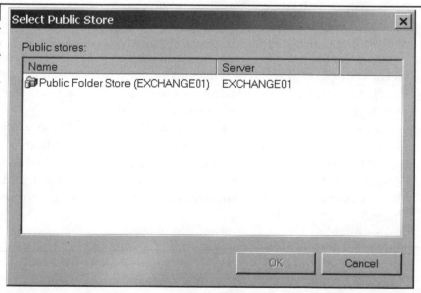

An offline address list is a list of Exchange recipients that is used to select message recipients when a user runs Outlook while disconnected from his or her Exchange server. Offline address lists are most useful when a user is incapable of connecting to an Exchange server, such as when in-flight on an airplane. Offline address lists reside in the organizational Recipients container in Exchange System Manager. A default list is created when Exchange is installed, and it shows all unhidden Exchange recipients. You can create a new address list and use it here. We'll get into address list in Chapter 17. For now, just accept the default.

If you've been bugged by someone in high places in your organization for a way to check on Exchange messages sent and received by users, Exchange 2000 has a nice but just a little bit scary solution. It's all in that innocent Archive All Messages Sent or Received by Mailboxes on This Store Field. Click the check box and then click Browse to select any Exchange user, distribution group, contact, or public folder where you'd like all messages archived to. If you pick a mailbox-enabled user or distribution group, copies of all messages show up in the user's or users' Inbox. If you select a mail-enabled user or contact, copies of the messages are sent to the mail-enabled user's or the contact's external e-mail address. If you select a public folder, copies of the messages are placed in the public folder.

There are two drawbacks to this capability. First, someone needs to carefully consider the privacy issues related to archiving. Second, you must consider disk space issues. A message is actually stored only once in a mailbox store, no matter how many recipients it has. Each recipient gets a pointer to the single instance of the message. The message is deleted when the last pointer is deleted. So, if you don't clear your archives, you'll be keeping a copy of every message ever sent or received by a mailbox in the mailbox store forever. Also, if you archive to mailboxes or public folders on a different mailbox store, there will be one copy of the message in the original store and one in the archive store.

Secure Multipurpose Internet Mail Extensions (S/MIME) signatures provide a secure way of sending e-mail over the Internet. We'll talk more about S/MIME signatures in Chapter 17. Check the box if the e-mail client used in your organization supports S/MIME. Outlook 98 or later supports this protocol.

Plain-text messages are messages that don't include the rich formatting attributes of messages sent through e-mail clients such as Outlook. Typically, they are received from the Internet. If the Display Plain Text Messages in a Fixed-Sized Font option is selected, e-mail clients will be instructed to use a nonproportional screen type font. This ensures that lists and diagrams display properly without the user having to change the display font of a message.

Database

Compared to the General property page, the Database page is pretty simple, as you can see in Figure 12.32. To start, you select the disk drive and path to use for both the Exchange database (.EDB file) and the Exchange streaming database (.STM file).

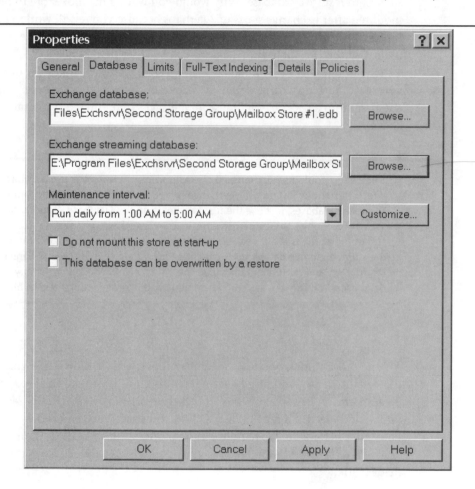

FIGURE 12.32

Using the Database property page to set file location, maintenance, and other properties for a new mailbox store

Mailbox store maintenance is an automatic process that includes checking to see whether mailboxes have exceeded their storage limits and managing deleted messages. You set parameters for these maintenance processes on the Limits property page, which I discuss in the next section. You set the schedule under which these processes are executed in the Maintenance Interval field. It's best to let your server perform maintenance in off-hours. You can select a schedule from the drop-down list or create a customized maintenance schedule by clicking Customize.

A store is offline if it isn't mounted. A dismounted store is not available to its users. Typically, you dismount a store when you want to do manual maintenance on it, such as to restore a database. Why would you want a mailbox store to remain dismounted after Exchange starts up? Perhaps because you're still working on fixing a problem with the store, or perhaps to control when a particular store is available to users. Use the Do Not Mount This Store at Start-up field as needed.

You should select This Database Can Be Overwritten by a Restore only when you've exhausted all other means of recovering a damaged database. If you recover a database from a backup, you'll lose all messages that entered the database since the backup.

 TIP You could use Exchange 5.5's Optimizer program to move databases to different directories and drives on your Exchange server. Exchange 2000 has no Optimizer program. To move databases, first use the first two fields on the Database property page (see Figure 12.32) to change the directory where you want the Exchange database or Exchange streaming database to be stored. After you've made these changes, you must dismount the storage group's databases (right-click each database in its original directory and select Dismount), and then manually move the databases to the new directory and mount the databases. You can use this same technique with storage groups and public stores.

Limits

Among other things, you use the Limits property page, shown in Figure 12.33, to set the default storage and deleted item retention limits for your mailbox store. These defaults are applied to a mailbox in the store unless you specifically set alternative limits for it. See Chapter 11 (Figure 11.20 and related text) for more on setting alternative limits for a mailbox and for more on the limit options in Figure 12.33. Unless you plan to set storage limits for each mailbox, be sure not to leave the storage limits fields blank.

FIGURE 12.33

Using the Limits property page to set storage and deleted items parameters for a mailbox store

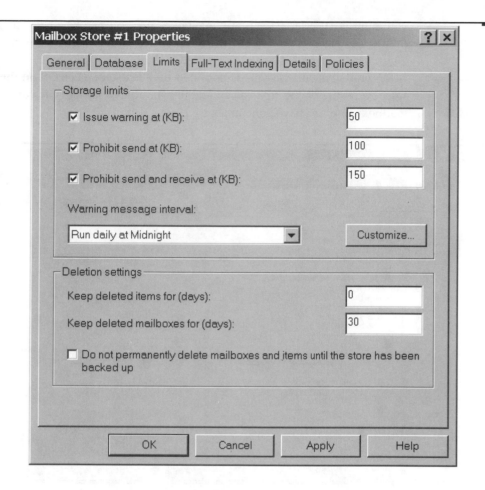

Mailbox Store #1 Properties

General | Database | Limits | Full-Text Indexing | Details | Policies

Storage limits

☑ Issue warning at (KB):   50

☑ Prohibit send at (KB):   100

☑ Prohibit send and receive at (KB):   150

Warning message interval:

Run daily at Midnight   ▾   Customize...

Deletion settings

Keep deleted items for (days):   0

Keep deleted mailboxes for (days):   30

☐ Do not permanently delete mailboxes and items until the store has been backed up

OK   Cancel   Apply   Help

Note that, in addition to setting a default value for deleted item retention—Keep Deleted Items for (Days)—you can set a retention period for deleted mailboxes.

You set the schedule for checking to see whether any mailboxes have exceeded their storage limits on the Database property page that I discussed in the last section. You set the schedule for sending warning messages using the Warning Message Interval field on the Limits property page. Any mailboxes that have exceeded their storage limits receive an appropriate message.

No matter what deleted items and mailbox retention schedule you set, you can also instruct Exchange to not permanently delete items or mailboxes until they have been backed up (Do Not Permanently Delete Mailboxes and Items Until the Store Has Been Backed Up). This is a nice option that you'd be wise to check no matter what schedule you've set, but especially if you've set retention times of 0 days. This way, you're sure that deleted items and mailboxes are protected by a backup. Checking this option also protects you against the unlikely situation in which your backups fail for a number of days greater than the retention periods that you've set.

When you're done setting up your new mailbox store, click OK on the mailbox store Properties dialog box. You should now be able to see and click open your new mailbox store, as I have done in Figure 12.34.

FIGURE 12.34

*Viewing a newly cre-
ated mailbox store*

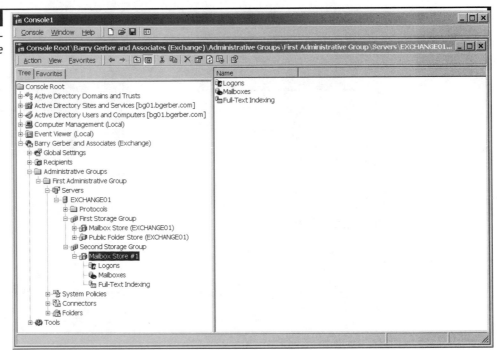

Now create a new mailbox-enabled Exchange user following the instructions in Chapter 11. When you get to the point where you can set parameters for the creation of a new mailbox, open the drop-down list for the Mailbox Store field. You really should-n't be too surprised to see not only the default mailbox store created when Exchange was installed, but also your new store. Just as I promised in Chapter 11, this is how you create a mailbox in a mailbox store other than the default store. Anyway, create the user's mailbox in your new mailbox store. We'll make use of this user soon.

Managing Mailbox Stores

Because you've created a new mailbox store, you already know a heck of lot about mailbox store management. The properties that you set while creating your new mailbox store can be altered by opening the Properties dialog box for the store. Just right-click the store and select Properties from the pop-up menu. As we move through this section, when appropriate, I'll show you how to use the remaining property pages on the mailbox store Properties dialog box. We'll look at the following:

- Mounting and dismounting a mailbox store
- Implementing full-text indexing on a mailbox store
- Monitoring mailbox logons and resource use
- Setting policies for a mailbox store

Mounting and Dismounting Mailbox Stores

To mount or dismount a mailbox store, right-click on the store and select Dismount Store, if the store is mounted, or Mount Store, if the store is dismounted. Remember that you dismount stores mostly to do maintenance on them.

Implementing Full-Text Indexing on a Mailbox Store

Exchange 2000 Server comes with a really neat capability: full-text indexing of mailbox and public stores. Yes, every word in a store can be indexed to greatly speed up user searches for specific words or phrases. Full-text indexing comes at a price in storage requirements and demands on server capacity, but it is something that you'll almost always want to turn on. To turn it on for your new mailbox store, right-click the store and select Create Full-Text Index. Use the dialog box that pops up to set the location for the index catalog (see Figure 12.35).

FIGURE 12.35

Setting the location of the catalog for a mailbox store's full-text index

You now have to populate your new index with information. To do this, right-click your mailbox store and select Start Full Population from the pop-up menu (see Figure 12.36). The Start Incremental Population option enables you to manually start an update of your index at any time. When your index is initially populated, you can fully rebuild the index manually at any time by selecting the Start Full Population option.

FIGURE 12.36

*Starting full population
of a mailbox store's
full-text index*

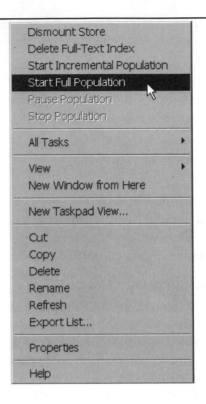

Manual population and updating of a full-text index may be some people's idea of
fun, but for me it's a royal pain. You can schedule automatic full and incremental
population of your index using the Properties dialog box for your mailbox store.
Open the dialog box and tab over to the Full-Text Indexing property page. Figure
12.37 shows this page.

FIGURE 12.37

*Using the Full-Text
Indexing property
page to set up auto-
matic population of a
full-text index*

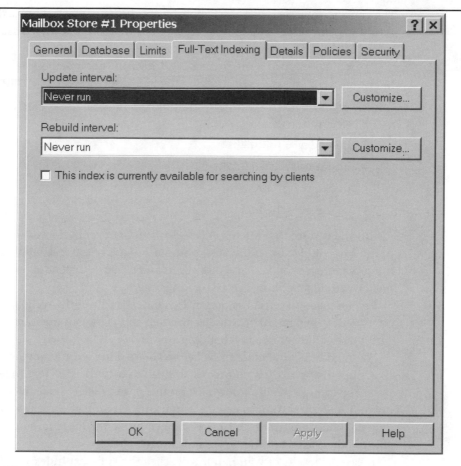

The update interval is the frequency at which text in new items in the mailbox store is added to the index. Options on the drop-down list include these:

- Never run
- Run daily at 10:00 P.M.
- Run daily at 1:00 A.M.
- Run daily at 3:00 A.M.
- Run every hour
- Always run

You can also set a customized schedule by clicking Customize. Notice that Microsoft is trying to encourage you to run indexing during off-hours. That's because it takes up lots of CPU cycles and disk accesses.

The rebuild interval is the frequency with which the index is totally reconstructed. Microsoft recommends reconstructing the index once a week to ensure total accuracy. Rebuild intervals on the drop-down list include these:

- Never run
- Run Friday at midnight
- Run Saturday at midnight
- Run Sunday at midnight
- Use custom schedule

Again, you can see that Microsoft is really bending over backwards to encourage you to run full re-indexing in the most off-hours. That's because rebuilding the index is intensive in terms of CPU and disk access and because, depending on the size of your mailbox store, rebuilding can take a long time.

Be sure that you select the option This Index Is Currently Available for Searching by Clients. When might you disable indexed access to your mailbox store? Well, for sure when you're manually rebuilding your index.

You need to do one more thing before you're done setting up your index. Open the Properties dialog box for your server, and tab over to the Full-Text Indexing property page. You can use the drop-down list on this page to select how much of the resources on your server you want to devote to indexing. Options include minimum, low, high, and maximum amounts. The fewer resources used, the more resources will be available to other tasks, but the slower indexing will be.

To see the results of your handiwork, click the Full-Text Indexing subcontainer of your new mailbox store. Your MMC should look something like the one in Figure 12.38. If it doesn't look like any indexing has happened, select Refresh from the Action menu. If it still doesn't look like anything happened, manually start another full population. After a bit, select Refresh again. That should do it. Of course, there should be messages in your mailbox store to index or none of this will be much fun.

FIGURE 12.38

*Checking full-text
indexing progress in
the Full-Text Indexing
container*

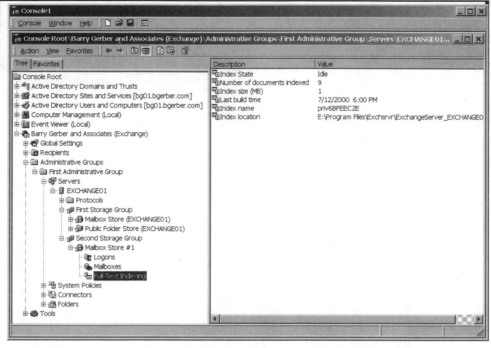

Monitoring Mailbox Logon and Resource Usage

If you need to know when particular users last logged on to their mailboxes or last
accessed the Exchange system and with which client, look in the Logons container
shown in Figure 12.39. Mark Test is the mail-enabled user that I created at the end of
the section "Creating a Mailbox Store." The other two users support SMTP and system
services for the mailbox store. The client 5.0.2819.0, used by our friend Mark, is a version of Outlook 2000.

FIGURE 12.39

Monitoring user logons to mailboxes in a mailbox store in the Logons container

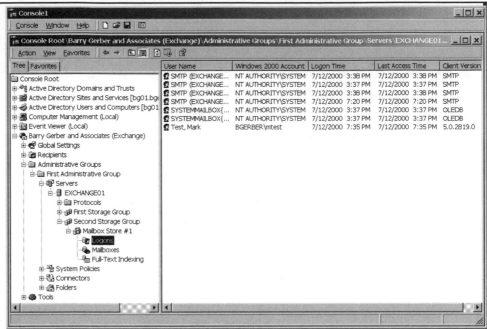

Want to know how many messages a user has in a mailbox or how much storage a mailbox is taking up? Look in the Mailboxes container (see Figure 12.40). I've met some Exchange 5.5 administrators who would give their left arm to be able to save the contents of the 5.5 Administrator's Logons container to a file. Why? They wanted to process the file to determine which users hadn't logged onto their mailboxes since a certain date. Then they wanted to check to find out if it was okay to delete the mailboxes of such users. Well, all you 5.5 refugees can save the contents of the Logons container just as you can save the contents of any MMC container. Just right-click the container and select Export List from the pop-up menu. Then just follow the online instructions to create a tab- or comma-delimited file with one row for each user that includes the data for all the columns visible in the container. For more on Export List, see the section "Managing the Organization," earlier in this chapter.

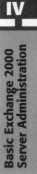

FIGURE 12.40

*Monitoring use of
mailbox resources in
mailbox store in the
Mailboxes container*

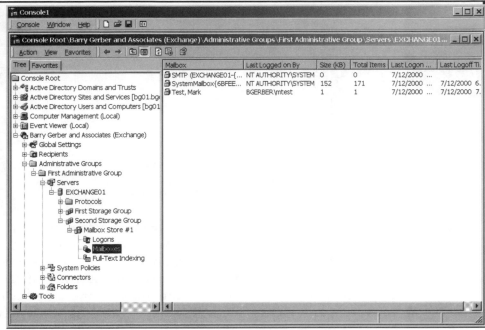

Setting Policies for a Mailbox Store

You'll remember that Exchange policies apply properties to groups of objects. We set up a policy for a server back in the section "Creating and Managing Server Policies." Now we're going to set up a mailbox store policy.

Find and right-click the System Policies container for your organization in Exchange System Manager. Select New ➢ Mailbox Store Policy from the pop-up menu. This opens the New Policy dialog box, shown in Figure 12.41. From the dialog box, select the property pages that you want the policy to apply to, and click OK.

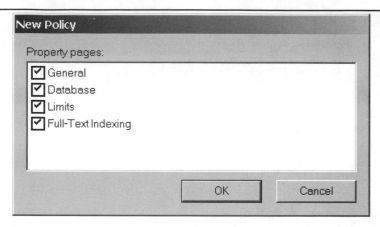

The dialog box for the policy opens (see Figure 12.42). You can now bop around the various property pages and set the properties as you wish. You can set all properties that make sense when you remember that this policy will apply to a group of mailbox stores. For example, you can set a generic maintenance interval on the Database page, but you can't set the database paths, set startup mount status, or determine whether restores overwrite the databases. That makes sense because you really have to set these policies on a store-by-store basis.

Set properties for the policy the same way as you set them for your new mailbox store. When you're finished selecting properties for your policy, click OK to create the policy.

To add a mailbox store to the policy, follow the instructions in the section "Creating and Managing Server Policies," earlier in this chapter. You should see two mailbox stores that you can add to the policy: the default mailbox store and the mailbox store that you just created. For fun, add the default mailbox store to the policy. Then open the Properties dialog box for the store and look at the various property pages (see Figure 12.43). Note how much is grayed out, meaning not only that you can't change the properties, but also that the properties were set simply because you added the store to the policy. Now, imagine that you had 10 or 20 Exchange servers, each with multiple mailbox stores. Even if you had to set up two or three policies to cover all the mailbox stores, the job of setting properties for the stores would be so much simpler with policies than without them.

Now, tab over to the Policies property page for your default mailbox store. You should see the policies that you just added the mailbox store to. You should also check the subcontainer for the policy that you just created in the System Policy container. Because it was added to this policy, your new mailbox should be in the subcontainer. Check out the previous section "Creating and Managing Server Policies" if any of this is a bit murky.

FIGURE 12.42

*Setting properties for a
mailbox store system
policy*

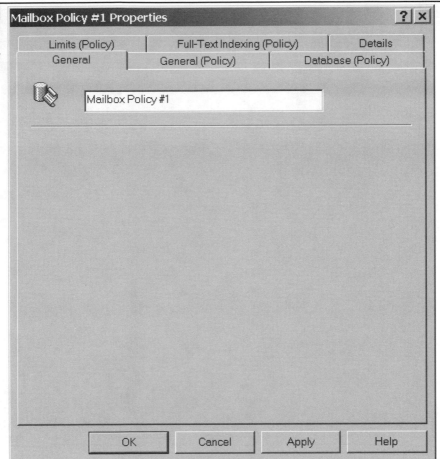

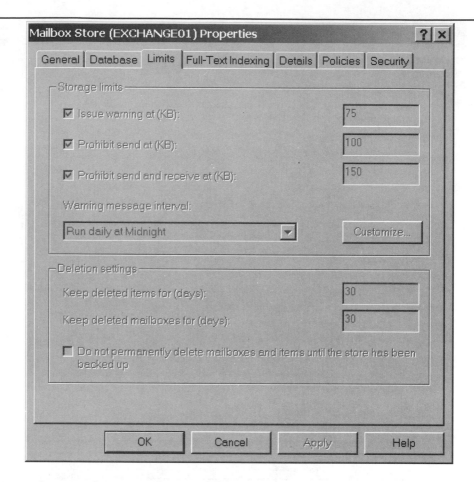

FIGURE 12.43

The Properties dialog box for mailbox store after the store has been added to a policy

Creating and Managing Public Stores

Public stores are a lot like mailbox stores, so I'm going to either very quickly discuss these or skip over issues that I covered in the section "Creating and Managing Public Stores."

Creating a Public Store

Before you can create a new public store, you need to understand how public stores and what are called *public folder trees* relate to each other. You absolutely will not be able to use public stores without this understanding.

Each public store is directly linked to a public folder tree. The default public folder tree on an Exchange server, Public Folders, is linked to the default public store, Public Folder Store (SERVER_NAME) on the server. In Figure 12.44, you can see my default public folders tree, Public Folders, and, the default public store, Public Folder Store (EXCHANGE01). A public store can link to only one public folder tree, and vice versa. You cannot link any more public folder trees to the default public folder store.

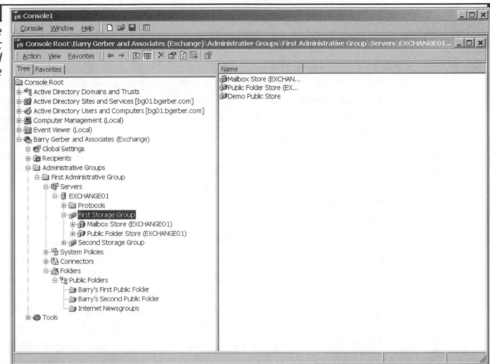

The default public folder tree and store are unique: They are the only tree/store combination that is MAPI-enabled. If you create additional tree/store combinations on a server, they cannot be MAPI-enabled. This means that the default tree/store combination is the only one that can be accessed by MAPI-aware (and IMAP4) e-mail clients such as Outlook.

When you look at public folders in Outlook, you're looking at the default tree/store combination associated with the mailbox store containing your mailbox. Think back to the section "Creating a Mailbox Store," when you had to associate a mailbox store with the default public store on an Exchange server. That's how you told Exchange which public folders (tree/store combination) to present when a client such as Outlook opened a mailbox in your new mailbox store.

If clients such as Outlook can see only the default tree/store combination on an Exchange server, of what use are additional tree/store combinations? Good question.

The answer is simple. You can access additional tree/store combinations using any of the following clients:

- Exchange 2000 Server's IFS client
- An enhanced Internet standard WebDav client
- An Internet standard NNTP client

Huh? *IFS* stands for Installable File System. IFS maps a drive on an Exchange 2000 server to the mailbox and public stores on the Exchange server. I'll show you how to use IFS later in this section. Web Distributed Authoring and Versioning (WebDav) clients are implemented in Web browsers. Microsoft has enhanced the WebDav Internet draft standard to allow it to work seamlessly with Exchange 2000 Server. WebDav is at the heart of Outlook Web Access, which lets you access your Exchange mailbox and public folders with an Internet browser and additional tree/store combinations can be made available through a Windows 2000/Exchange 2000 NNTP server. Network New Transfer Protocol (NNTP) clients can access Internet news servers.

Now you can create a public store. Before you can do so, however, you must create a public folder tree to associate it with. To create a new public folder tree, find and right-click the Folders container for your administrative group; then select New ➤ Public Folder Tree from the pop-up menu. The public folder tree Properties dialog box opens. Enter a name for the tree. I'm going to call mine Demo Public Folder Tree. When you're done, click OK. You should now see your tree in the Folders container.

Now you can create your public store. Right-click on either your default storage group or the storage group that you created earlier in this chapter. Then select New ➤ Public Store from the pop-up menu to open the public store Properties dialog box, shown on the left side of Figure 12.45. Name your new public store on the General properties page. Next, click Browse in the Associated Public Folder Tree field and select the public folder tree that you just created, as I'm doing on the right side of Figure 12.45. You worked with the last two fields on this Property page back when you created a new mailbox store.

PART

IV

FIGURE 12.45

The public store Properties dialog box, with its General properties page and Select a Public Folder Tree dialog box exposed

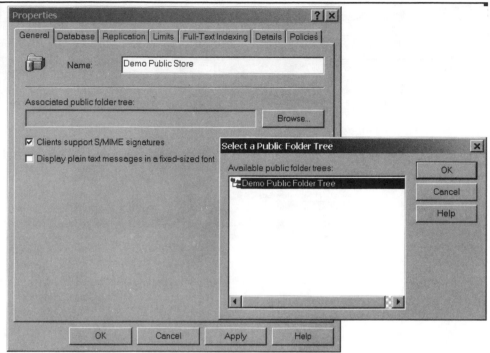

The Database property page looks and works exactly like the same page on the mailbox store Properties dialog box. We'll talk about the Replication page in Chapter 15, when we have at least one more server to replicate public folders to. The Limits page has a Deleted Items field, but it doesn't have a Retention field for mailboxes, for obvious reasons. Public stores don't hold mailboxes. The Limits page also has an additional field, Age Limits for All Folders in This Store. Use this field to set a default number of days before an item in any public folder in the store is deleted. You can override the default using the Limits page for any public folder, as you saw in the section "Creating a Public Folder." The Full-Text Indexing and other pages look and work just as they do for mailbox stores.

When you're done creating your public store, click OK on the public store dialog box. Your MMC should look something like the one in Figure 12.46.

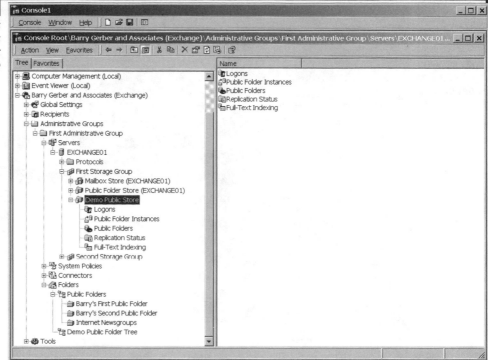

Now, you should create a public folder in your new tree/store. We'll use the folder later. Call the folder Test. To create the folder, follow the directions in the earlier section "Creating a Public Folder."

Managing Public Stores

Based on your experience with it when creating a public store, you should have no trouble using the public store Properties dialog box to manage your new public store. I won't discuss the dialog box any further here; instead, I'm going to discuss three aspects of public store management in this section:

- Use of public store management containers
- Mail-enabling public folders in a nondefault public folder tree
- Providing access to public folders in a nondefault public folder tree

Use of Public Store Management Containers

As you can see in Figure 12.46, a public folder store has a range of subcontainers, just like a mailbox store. As with mailbox stores, these subcontainers are used for managing the store. Many of the subcontainers are used in the same way that they're used for mailbox stores:

Logons   Works just like the Logons subcontainer for mailbox stores.

Public Folders   Shows resource usage and other information for all public folders in the store, in a manner similar to the Mailboxes subcontainer for mailbox stores. These are folders that originated in the store or, to put it another way, that are local to the store.

Full-Text Indexing   Works just like the same subcontainer for mailboxes. In fact, you set up full-text indexing for public stores exactly as you set it up for mailbox stores.

Public store subcontainers with no parallel in mailbox store subcontainers include the following items:

Public Folder Instances   Shows information for all public folder instances in a public store. This includes not only the folders in the Public Folders subcontainer, but also folders that have been replicated to this server from other Exchange servers.

Replication Status   Shows progress when replicating folders across Exchange servers. I'll cover this subcontainer in Chapter 15.

Mail-Enabling Public Folders in a Nondefault Public Folder Tree

As I noted in the section "Managing Public Folders," when you create a public folder in the default public folder store, it is automatically mail-enabled. It can send and receive messages. Public folders created in other public stores can send and receive e-mail messages, too, but you have to mail-enable them before this is possible. Let's mail-enable the folder Test that I asked you to create at the end of the section "Creating a Public Store." To mail-enable a public folder, right-click it and select All Tasks ≻ Mail Enable from the pop-up menu.

After a few seconds, select Refresh from the Action menu and open the Properties dialog box for the folder. Miracle of miracles, the folder now has an E-mail Addresses property page and a set of e-mail address, to boot. Open your Outlook client and notice that the folder is in the Address Book. You can send messages to it. Don't close your Outlook client, we're going to use it in the next section.

Providing Access to Public Folders in a Nondefault Public Folder Tree

Just to prove that nondefault public folder trees are unavailable to Outlook clients, look at the public folder hierarchy in your client. You see the default public folder tree, Public Folders. However, you don't see the new tree that you just created.

As I mentioned earlier, you can access nondefault public folder trees using three types of clients:

- Installable File System (IFS)
- Web Distributed Authoring and Versioning (WebDav)
- Network News Transfer Protocol (NNTP)

Let's focus on IFS here. When Exchange 2000 Server is installed, the server's Information Store is mapped to the M: drive on the server. In Figure 12.47, you can see the M: drive on my Exchange server as viewed in Windows 2000's My Computer file browser. The folder MBX contains all the mailboxes in all the mailbox stores on my server. I'll leave it to your imagination to come up with neat ideas for using the MBX folder. The folder PUBLIC FOLDERS includes all public folders on my server. And, of course, the folder DEMO PUBLIC FOLDER TREE is the public folder tree that I created earlier in the section "Creating a Public Store."

FIGURE 12.47

Viewing the IFS-enabled M: drive on an Exchange server, and choosing to share a public folder tree on the M: drive

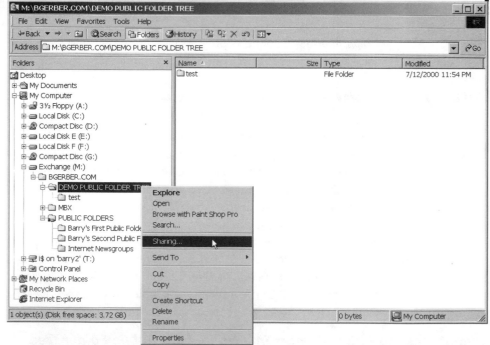

Like any other disk-based directory (folder), you can share one or more of the folders or subfolders on the M: drive. You control access to such shares as you control access to any Windows 2000 share: through the Windows 2000 security system, not the Exchange 2000 system.

In Figure 12.47, I've right-clicked on the folder that represents my new public folder tree, and I'm selecting Sharing from the pop-up menu. In Figure 12.48, I've chosen to share my new folder tree. Among other things, I can set the name that users will see when using the share, and I can control access to the tree by clicking Permissions. Notice that Web Sharing tab. Yes, like all disk-based directories, you can also share this folder through your Internet Information Server for access with a Web browser such as Microsoft's Internet Explorer. Pretty neat.

FIGURE 12.48

Sharing a public folder tree

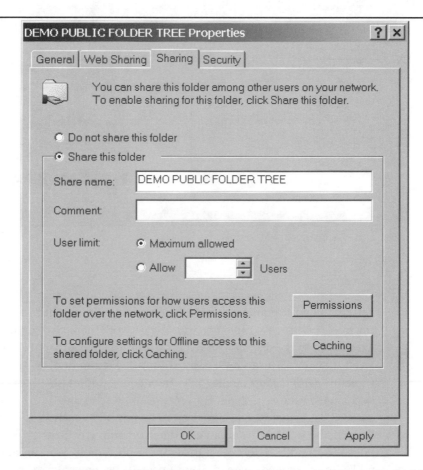

When you've shared your public folder tree, users can access it using a standard Windows file browser such as My Computer or My Network Places—assuming, of course, that they have permissions to do so. In Figure 12.49, a Windows 2000 Professional user is using My Network Places to view the contents of the folder Test. That's the folder that I asked you to create in your new public folder tree back in the section "Creating a Public Store." Notice how the public folder tree share is extracomputer. That is, you don't have to drill down to the server EXCHANGE01 in the network hierarchy to see the tree; it's right at the top of the network hierarchy.

FIGURE 12.49

Using Windows 2000 Professional's My Network Places to view the contents of a public folder in a public folder tree, and preparing to create a new item in the folder

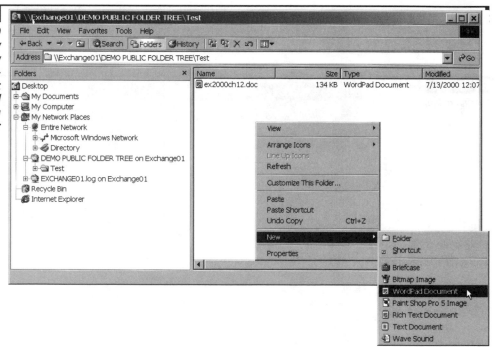

You can map the public folder tree share or any folders in it to a drive letter. To map the tree, you have to drill down into the network hierarchy and find it on your Exchange server. You can map folders within the tree either at the extracomputer level, shown in Figure 12.49, or by drilling down and finding the folder on the server.

Because nondefault public folder trees don't support MAPI content, you can't post Exchange messages in them. However, you can send messages to them if they're mail-enabled, and you can drag and drop Exchange items such as messages from an Outlook client into them. You can also drag and drop any file that you want into them, as I did with the Word document in Figure 12.49. Finally, you can right-click in the folder and choose to begin creating a new file using whatever applications are supported on your computer. In Figure 12.49, I'm about to create a new WordPad document in the folder Test.

WARNING   Be careful when you share a public folder or a public folder tree. Initially, the Windows 2000 group Everyone has pretty near total control over the folder. The group can add items to the folder and delete any item in the folder. It can't delete the folder, but you may not want Everyone to have such wide-ranging access to all folders.

Before we leave public stores and public folder trees, take a moment to think about what's going on here. By every method, from e-mail to drag-and-drop, you can store anything in Exchange 2000 public stores and access it in a variety of ways through public folder trees. The stores are essentially mountable file systems protected by Exchange 2000 Server's powerful online backup and offline restore capabilities, and they are supported by such services as full-text indexing. Remember how Exchange 5.5 was the developmental model for major Windows 2000 Server components such as Active Directory, organizational units, and routing sites? Could Exchange 2000 Server be the model for the next generation of the Windows server operating system?

The Routing Engine

The Routing Engine is involved in moving messages in and out of an Exchange 2000 server, both within an Exchange organization and between an Exchange organization and foreign messaging systems. Because we have only one server that's not connected to any foreign messaging system, it's too early to discuss the Routing Engine. We'll devote lots of time to the management of Exchange message routing in Chapters 13, 15, and 16.

The System Attendant

As I noted in Chapter 4, the System Attendant (SA) performs a number of housekeeping tasks. The SA is assigned some of its tasks when Exchange is installed, such as triggering the generation of e-mail addresses for foreign messaging systems for Exchange recipients, or building interrouting group tables for its server. You turn on other SA tasks when setting up a particular Exchange object, such as when you turn on message tracking for a mailbox store. The good news is that your main worry with the SA is that its service remains up and running. The service can be monitored like any other Exchange service, so even that worry is manageable.

Summary

This chapter dealt with two key elements of Exchange 2000 Server: the Exchange 2000 Server hierarchy and Exchange 2000 Server core components.

The Exchange 2000 Server hierarchy consists of the Exchange organization, administrative groups, servers, and recipients. Exchange organizations are largely containers that hold all the objects that make up an Exchange system. We dealt with a number of these objects in Chapter 11 and this chapter, and we'll continue to deal with them in later chapters. However, when it comes to directly managing your Exchange organization, there is little that you can or need to do to. One of the most important organizational management tasks is delegation of control over your organization to Windows 2000 users and groups. That's how you parcel out responsibility for managing the wide range of objects in your Exchange organization.

Exchange administrative groups are key organizing and security control objects. They enable you to bring together Exchange servers, system policies, connectors, and folders in such a way that you can delegate management responsibilities to Windows 2000 users and groups at a more refined level than the Exchange organization. A default administrative group is created when Exchange is installed. You must enable display of the group. As you add new Exchange servers, they can be part of an existing administrative group, or you can create new groups for them.

You create system policies for servers, mailbox stores, and public stores within the System Policies folder in an administrative group. Essentially, system policies are templates that enable you to automatically fill in the property pages for a group of objects, thus customizing the object to behave as you want. This saves time when you need to configure a number of servers, mailbox stores, or public stores at the same time. It also enables you to ensure that objects are configured appropriately. When a policy has been created, you add objects, such as servers, to the policy, and thus apply the policy to the objects.

More than anything else, Exchange servers are home to Exchange storage groups. Servers are so vital to the operation of an Exchange system that monitoring them and ensuring that they are up and running should be considered a task of major importance. You can create a wide range of server monitors and manually or automatically (through e-mail or scripted notifications) keep tabs on them.

We dealt with all the Exchange recipients but public folders in the last chapter. If they have permissions, users can create public folders in their Outlook clients. Exchange managers can also create public folders in Exchange System Manager. Rights to public folders can be controlled either from Exchange System Manager or by folder owners in their Outlook clients. You can set storage, deleted item retention, and automatic item deletion properties for public folders.

Exchange 2000 Server core components include the Information Store, the Routing Engine, and the System Attendant. The Information Store consists of storage groups. Storage groups contain mailbox and public stores. Mailbox stores contain user mailboxes. Public stores hold public folders. Public folders are organized in public folder trees. Management of both mailbox and public stores is quite similar. As with individual mailboxes and public folders, you can control storage limits and deleted item retention. You can also control automatic deletion of items from public folders. When you set these parameters at the store level, they become the defaults for newly created mailboxes and public folders.

Public stores and their related public folder trees are an interesting pair of items. Only the public store and the public folder tree created when Exchange is installed on a server are fully MAPI-enabled and capable of being seen by Outlook and IMAP4 clients. Any tree/store combinations that you create cannot be accessed through these clients. They can be accessed only through the Windows 2000 Server file system, an enhanced Web browser, or an Internet news (NNTP) client. All kinds of public folders can be replicated to other Exchange servers. We'll talk more about this in Chapter 15.

The Routing Engine is an important component of Exchange 2000 Server. We'll spend considerable time on message routing in later chapters. The System Attendant is a silent but key participant in an Exchange system. It does a range of housekeeping chores and requires no management other than ensuring that it is functioning properly.

Now you're ready for one of the most interesting and exciting pieces of Exchange 2000 Server architecture: Internet messaging. In Chapter 13, we'll add and manage an e-mail link to the Internet. In Chapter 14, we'll set up support on our server for a number of Internet protocols.

PART V

Expanding an Exchange Server Organization

So far, you've been working within some pretty narrow confines: one Exchange 2000 server on a network that is isolated from all others, whether private or public. Now comes the really fun part of the Exchange 2000 experience: connecting to world outside of your one-and-only server.

In the next two chapters, we'll focus on the Internet. In Chapter 13, "Managing Exchange 2000 Internet Services," you'll learn about the Internet and then you'll connect your Exchange server to it. Chapter 14, "Managing Exchange 2000 Services for Internet Clients," will give you a firm grounding in key Internet protocols and their management: Post Office Protocol Version 3 (POP3), Internet Message Access Protocol Version 4 (IMAP4), Hypertext Transfer Protocol (HTTP), and Lightweight Directory Access Protocol (LDAP).

In Chapter 15, "Installing and Managing Additional Exchange 2000 Servers," you'll add additional Exchange 2000 servers to your Exchange organization. You'll add a new server in the same routing group as your current server. Then you'll add a server in a new domain and routing group.

Finally, in Chapter 16, "Connecting to Foreign Messaging Systems," you'll connect your Exchange organization to other, non–Internet-based, foreign messaging systems. We'll concentrate on X.400 and Microsoft Mail systems.

CHAPTER 13

Managing Exchange 2000 Internet Services

I n today's networked world, among all the foreign messaging system options available, you're most likely to have to implement Internet messaging support. The Internet is the most widely used conduit for the exchange of e-mail messages between a wide range of messaging systems. The Internet is based on a set of standards for the content of messages and for moving messages between messaging servers and between messaging servers and clients.

In this chapter, we'll look at the inner workings of Internet messaging. We'll focus heavily on the Transmission Control Protocol/Internet Protocol (TCP/IP), the Domain Name System (DNS) service, and the Simple Mail Transfer Protocol (SMTP), and we'll explore how these support worldwide Internet messaging. We'll also spend some quality time with the Windows 2000/Exchange 2000 SMTP Virtual Server Connector, the engine that moves Internet messages into and out of your Exchange organization and the Exchange 2000 SMTP Connector that enhances SMTP Virtual Server functionality. Finally, we'll look at some of the things that you need to do to ensure that your Internet connection stays up and running.

How Internet Messaging Works

Internet messaging depends on TCP/IP, DNS, and SMTP. Without any one of these, Internet messaging can't work.

As it does inside Windows 2000 local area networks, the TCP/IP protocol supports communication between computers connected to the Internet. It provides a way of both packaging data and moving it reliably between computers, and it provides an addressing scheme so that one computer can precisely specify the computer to which it needs to send data. TCP/IP serves not only Internet messaging, but also a number of other Internet protocols. We'll talk about these in a bit.

DNS is a client/server service. A computer that needs to communicate with another computer to send an Internet message, for example, uses DNS to figure out the Internet address of the receiving computer. DNS translates English-language domain-based addresses such as `barrywin2k.bgerber.com` into number-based addresses that computers can use.

SMTP, another client/server protocol, defines a range of messaging standards. These include message content and specific protocols for computers to use when sending or receiving Internet messages to other servers. It is at the heart of both Exchange 2000 server's internal interserver routing system and its services for Internet messaging. SMTP also plays a major role in POP3 and IMAP4 client/server communications by relaying messages that are sent by POP3 and IMAP4 clients to recipients on the Internet.

This section focuses on Internet messaging from a conceptual and descriptive perspective. In the section "Internet Messaging: Getting and Staying Connected," I'll talk very specifically about how you set up TCP/IP, DNS, and SMTP.

Where to Go for More on TCP/IP, DNS, and SMTP

Throughout this section, I'm going to assiduously avoid interesting, though diverting, treatises on TCP/IP, DNS, and SMTP. Instead, I'll present enough practical information so that you can set up and operate your Exchange Internet messaging system. For lots more on these topics, see *Mastering Windows 2000 Server*, by Mark Minasi, et al. (Sybex Inc., 2000), or *Microsoft Windows 2000 Server Administrator's Companion*, by Charlie Russel and Sharon Crawford (Microsoft Press, 2000). Also take a look at the Windows 2000 Server and Exchange 2000 Server documentation. Other sources of DNS information include the documentation that comes with your DNS software (if you're not using Windows 2000 Server's DNS), and the books *sendmail, 2nd edition,* by Bryan Costales and Eric Allman (O'Reilly & Associates, 1997), and *DNS and BIND in a Nutshell, 3rd edition,* by Paul Albitz & Cricket Liu, (O'Reilly & Associates, 1998).

TCP/IP: The Backbone of Internet Networking

TCP/IP is the information superhighway's data packaging and cargo service. Programs based on the protocol assemble data into standardized packets and ship the packets from computer to computer. It supports the smooth movement of data across bridges and routers from subnetwork to subnetwork. And, all of this happens more or less at the speed of light.

TCP/IP's Transmission Control Protocol describes how data packets are to be organized and reliably delivered from one computer to another. The Internet Protocol (IP) defines how Internet addresses are formed (the familiar xxx.xxx.xxx.xxx format) and specifies that every computer on the public Internet must have a unique address.

TCP/IP is not just for Internet messaging. It also supports such Internet services as ping, File Transfer Protocol (FTP), whois, finger, and the Web's Hypertext Transfer Protocol (HTTP). Essentially, almost any time that a packet needs to move across the Internet, TCP/IP does the work.

TCP/IP is implemented in software on networking hardware. TCP/IP software prepares and drops packets into network adapter, bridge, and router hardware environments. This hardware supported by more software moves the packets to their next destination and finally to their target destination. The next time you browse over to your favorite Web site, think about all this and marvel at the speed and accuracy with which everything happens. You've got TCP/IP to thank for a great deal of this experience.

 NOTE There are two types of IP addresses: public and private. Public IP addresses are the ones that you use when connecting to the Internet. You must obtain these addresses from a valid supplier of public addresses, such as an Internet Service Provider (ISP). There can only be one instance of a public IP address on the entire worldwide Internet network. Private addresses are addresses in a certain range that are never exposed to the Internet. They are defined in the Internet Task Force's RFC 1918 and range from 192.168.0.0 to 192.168.255.255. Private addresses are used on internal networks. If you have Internet connections, you must hide private addresses behind routers or network address translation (NAT) devices that allow many computers with private IP addresses to reach the Internet through one public IP address. Many modern network routers and firewalls include NAT capabilities. Check out RFC 1631 for more on NAT.

DNS and SMTP: The Dynamic Duo of Internet Messaging

When you address a message, to bg@bgerber.com, for example, how does that message get from your computer to BG at bgerber.com? Everything starts with a service called an *SMTP host*. SMTP hosts are responsible for sending and receiving Internet mail.

Let's take a simple example assuming that you're using a simple POP3 e-mail client such as the one available in Outlook Express. When you send your message, the POP3 client contacts the SMTP host that you've specified as the SMTP (outgoing mail) server in your e-mail client. I won't go into detail on how the POP3 client finds the SMTP server because all of this is covered in detail a bit later in this section. If the SMTP server hasn't been barred from relaying messages for you, it takes the message and puts it into its send queue.

Before it can relay your message, the SMTP host must translate the e-mail address bg@bgerber.com from human-friendly to computer-friendly. To start this translation process, the SMTP host parses the address into two parts:

- The domain name (bgerber.com)
- The addressee or mailbox (bg – short for *Barry Gerber*)

Next, the sending SMTP host needs to find the IP address of an SMTP host that serves the domain specified in the e-mail address (the *receiving SMTP host*). To do this, it queries a DNS server (called a *name server*) in the receiving domain for the IP address of the receiving SMTP host. You'll remember from Chapter 7, "Installing Windows 2000 Server," that DNS servers contain, among other things, the names and matching IP addresses of computers in one or more domains. I'll get into the process involved in finding the IP address of an SMTP host in just a bit. For now, accept that the DNS finds the match.

When the IP address of a receiving SMTP host in the domain bgerber.com, for example, has been found, the sending SMTP host uses the address to contact the receiving host. When contact has been made, the sending SMTP host tells the receiving SMTP host that it has a message for the addressee *bg*. The receiving SMTP host checks to see whether the addressee exists; if it does, the host accepts the message. With the message now inside the local messaging system, local services take over and deliver the message to the proper mailbox.

Now let's look more closely at the role of DNS in all of this. The Domain Name System is an interesting combination of centralization and decentralization. A specific DNS server doesn't have to know about all the domain names and matching IP addresses in the world. It can query other DNSes for matches.

A query starts with a group of servers managed by an organization called *InterNIC*. These servers contain the name servers for all the registered .com, .net, .org, and .edu domains that exist and referrals to servers that support other domains such as .mil. When you apply for a domain name, you must supply the names of at least two name server computers for your domain. These can be part of your domain or external to your domain, as long as they are the place to go to get authoritative information about the computers and services in your domain.

You can find the name server information for any domain at http://rs. internic.net/. Find and click the Whois hotlink, and enter the name of the domain. Here's the current name server information for my domain bgerber.com from InterNIC:

```
Whois Server Version 1.1


Domain names in the .com, .net, and .org domains can now be registered
with many different competing registrars. Go to http://www.internic.net
for detailed information.


Domain Name: BGERBER.COM Registrar: NETWORK SOLUTIONS, INC. Whois
Server: whois.networksolutions.com
Referral URL: www.networksolutions.com
Name Server: NAMESERVER.CONCENTRIC.NET Name Server:
NAMESERVER3.CONCENTRIC.NET Name Server: NAMESERVER2.CONCENTRIC.NET Name
Server: NAMESERVER1.CONCENTRIC.NET
Updated Date: 07-apr-2000
```

Notice that the name servers for bgerber.com are operated by the Internet Service Provider that supplies my Internet connectivity, Concentric Networks. I plan to take on management of DNS services for my domain soon, now that Windows 2000 Server provides such excellent and well-integrated DNS support. Perhaps by the time you read this, you'll find that the concentric name servers have been replaced by two bgerber.com name servers.

DNS Servers Are Far from Dumb

DNS servers are born knowing that they should go to the InterNIC servers to get a list of name servers for a particular domain. You don't have to tell them; they just do it. So, as long as your DNS is set up properly, as in Chapter 7, and as long as your server is connected to the Internet, your DNS will automatically hit InterNIC's name servers.

As soon as the sending SMTP host has secured a list of name servers for the receiving domain from the InterNIC servers, it asks one of the name servers for the name of the SMTP host for the domain. The name of the SMTP host is contained in what is called an *MX record*. (*MX* stands for *mail exchanger*.) A mail exchanger server is an SMTP host for the domain. I'm sure I don't have to say it, but I will: The *exchange* in *mail exchanger* has nothing to do with Exchange server. It's a concept and reality in the Internet messaging arena.

Here's a sample MX record:

```
bgerber.com. IN MX 10 exchange01.bgerber.com.
```

For our purposes right now, this MX record has two key parts:

> bgerber.com   Specifies the domain name used in addressing e-mail (bg@bgerber.com)

> exchange01.bgerber.com   Is the name of the SMTP host for bgerber.com

You'll learn more about MX records later in this chapter in the section "Setting Up and Managing DNS," when you actually set up your DNS service for Internet messaging.

"Wait!" you exclaim. "The sending SMTP host still doesn't have an IP address to send the message to." You're right. Now it must query the receiving domain's DNS one more time for the IP address of the SMTP host (the mail exchanger server), exchange01.bgerber.com in my case. As you might imagine, this requires another DNS record, an Address or *A* record that exposes the IP address of the receiving SMTP host for bgerber.com exchange01.bgerber.com. Here's an example of this record:

```
exchange01.bgerber.com. IN A 216.112.83.228
```

In this A record, the following is true:

exchange01.bgerber.com The name of the SMTP host

216.112.83.228 The IP address of the SMTP host

I'll talk more about A records later in this chapter in the section "Setting Up and Managing DNS."

Okay, now let's pull it all together. Figure 13.1 shows how TCP/IP, DNS, and SMTP all work together to enable Internet messaging.

TCP/IP, DNS, and SMTP, the lynchpins of Internet messaging

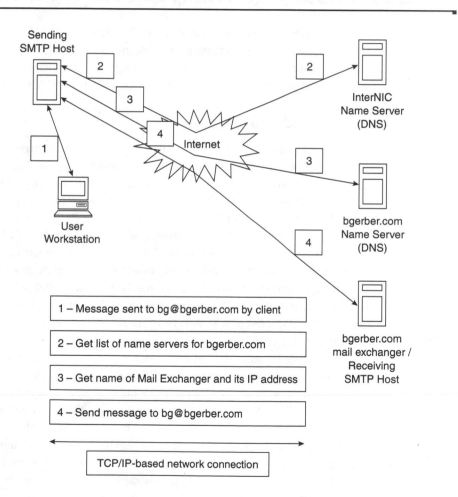

1 – Message sent to bg@bgerber.com by client

2 – Get list of name servers for bgerber.com

3 – Get name of Mail Exchanger and its IP address

4 – Send message to bg@bgerber.com

TCP/IP-based network connection

TIP InterNIC is not just a place for servers to go to find a domain's name servers. It's also a great place to find out about getting a domain name. Go to `http://rs.internic.net/regist.html` for more information and a list of authorized domain name registrars, companies that can sell you a valid domain name.

Internet Messaging: Getting and Staying Connected

Now that you have a basic grounding in TCP/IP, DNS, and SMTP, you're ready to connect your Exchange organization to the Internet and manage that connection. You perform both tasks by setting up and managing your good friends TCP/IP, DNS, and SMTP, for and on your Exchange server. Let's get started. TCP/IP is our first "victim."

Setting Up and Managing TCP/IP

As an Exchange 2000 server administrator responsible for Internet messaging, your task is to ensure that those of your Exchange servers that will support Internet messaging are assigned valid public Internet addresses. Additionally, of course, you need to ensure that the correct hardware (a modem or one or more network adapters) is installed in your server and that your server is physically connected to the Internet.

"Did you say 'modem?'" Yes, modem. There are two kinds of TCP/IP connections: continuous and noncontinuous. A continuous TCP/IP connection is always on. Continuous TCP/IP connections ride on top of networking topologies such as Ethernet, Asynchronous Transfer Mode (ATM), Frame Relay, and Digital Subscriber Line (DSL). Noncontinuous connections require a connection before they become active. Asynchronous dial-up, serial port-based connections are the most prevalent type of noncontinuous connections.

The SMTP mail system runs most naturally on continuous networks. When an SMTP host needs to contact another SMTP host to send it a message, the receiving SMTP host must be available to receive the message within a particular time window. As you'll see in a bit, SMTP host contacts aren't predictable. They happen when a message is available and then at specific but fairly long intervals thereafter until a timeout period has been reached, typically two to three days. When the timeout period has been reached, the SMTP host returns the message as undeliverable. All this means that you can't just connect your modem-based SMTP host to the Internet at a particular time and expect to receive messages from all SMTP hosts that happen to have messages for you.

SMTP can still work with noncontinuous networks. However, things must be set up so that a continuously connected SMTP host sends and receives messages for a noncontinuously connected SMTP host. Let's call the continuously connected SMTP host a *smart host*. Then the noncontinuously connected host can contact the smart host on a regular basis to pick up new messages and send outgoing messages that have queued up since the last contact. Usually you go to your Internet Service Provider (ISP) for smart hosting. You can also use this approach within your own organization for connects by smaller remote offices.

 TIP The use of smart hosts isn't limited to noncontinuous TCP/IP connections. Your Exchange server can use smart hosts even if it is continuously connected to the Internet. For example, you might choose to isolate all or part of your Exchange server environment from direct Internet access by installing only one of your Exchange servers as a smart host and having other Exchange servers send and receive messages through that smart host.

In Windows 2000 environments, dial-up noncontinuous TCP/IP links are built on the Remote Access Service (RAS). If you need to operate an internal smart host for other internal SMTP hosts to dial into, you also use RAS on the continuously connected host.

If you're going to use RAS for a noncontinuous Internet link, don't forget to set up RAS with dial-out capabilities. Also, remember to create a RAS phone book entry for the ISP to which you'll be connecting. For more on RAS, check out the Windows 2000 Server books referenced in the sidebar "Where to Go for More on TCP/IP, DNS, and SMTP," at the beginning of this chapter.

I strongly suggest that you try really hard to use a continuous connection for your SMTP host or hosts. Back in Chapter 5, "Designing a New Exchange 2000 System," I touted the wonders of modern continuous connect technologies for linking to the Internet. I spoke especially fondly of DSL technology. It's fast (up to T1 speeds), reliable, and inexpensive (I pay less than $200 for 384Kbps of business-level, multi-IP address DSL bandwidth). Setting up a continuous-connect link to the Internet is easier, and, with a good provider, continuous links are less prone to problems than noncontinuous links. Higher-speed continuous links buy you quick and easy access to other Internet services such as Web browsing, chat, and FTP. I strongly suggest that you go for a continuous link, unless you're really cost-constrained.

If the default network adapter in your Exchange server uses private IP addresses, as defined in the previous section "TCP/IP: The Backbone of Internet Networking," then you'll need a second network adapter to link your Exchange server to the Internet.

The adapter must have a valid public Internet address. See Chapter 7 and the references in the sidebar "Where to Go for More on TCP/IP, DNS, and SMTP," at the beginning of this chapter, for more on setting up TCP/IP on a network adapter in Windows 2000 Server.

Setting Up and Managing DNS

More than anything else, DNS is a repository for information about computers on your network. You set up DNS when you installed your Windows 2000 Server domain controller back in Chapter 7. In this section, you'll learn how to create specific DNS entries (records) to support Internet messaging on your Exchange server.

Creating Key DNS Records for Exchange

You need to create two DNS records. These are the Address and Mail Exchanger records that I discussed briefly in the section "DNS and SMTP: The Dynamic Duo of Internet Messaging."

Creating an Address Record

An Address or A record associates the name of the Exchange server that serves as an SMTP host with its IP address. My server is called exchange01.bgerber.com, and its IP address on the Internet side is 216.112.83.228. Although I haven't installed an SMTP connector on the server yet (that comes in the section "Setting Up and Managing SMTP"), it will soon become the SMTP host for my Exchange organization. The A record should look like this:

```
exchange01.bgerber.com. IN A 216.112.83.228
```

IN means that this is an Internet record.

 WARNING The period after "com" in exchange01.bgerber.com. is *required*, as are all the periods in the DNS records listed in this chapter.

If this is the name and address that you gave your Exchange server back when you installed Windows 2000, you don't even have to make this DNS entry. The entry should already have been made when DNS was installed. If not, here's how to create the Address record in your Windows 2000 DNS.

Find and right-click your domain in the DNS snap-in in your Microsoft Management Console, and select New ➢ Host. Fill in the New Host dialog box, shown on the right side of Figure 13.2. The PTR record is a reverse lookup record that lets a DNS client query the DNS server not for the IP address associated with a particular host, but for the host associated with a particular IP address. PTR records are created in the Reverse Lookup Zones container shown on the left side of Figure 13.2. See one of the Windows 2000 or DNS books referenced in the sidebar "Where to Go for More on TCP/IP, DNS, and SMTP," at the beginning of this chapter, for more information.

FIGURE 13.2

Using the New Host dialog box to add a new Address record to DNS

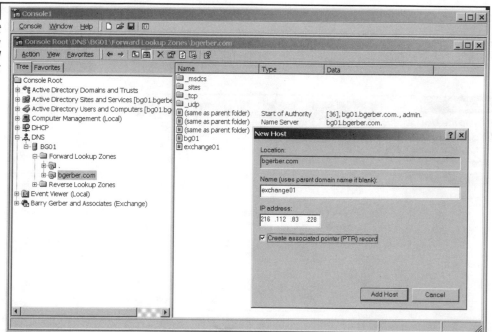

 TIP You can associate any computer name that you want with any IP address. I could have named my Exchange server mickeymouse.bgerber.com, if I wanted to. As long as the name is used consistently, the specific name that you choose doesn't matter.

Creating a Mail Exchanger Record

Now you need to set up an MX record to provide DNS with the name of a computer that functions as an SMTP host for your Exchange organization. As I noted in the previous section on DNS, the MX record for my domain bgerber.com looks like this:

```
bgerber.com. IN MX 10 exchange01.bgerber.com.
```

This record says that mail bound for the domain named `bgerber.com` should be sent to the DNS-defined SMTP host `exchange01.bgerber.com`. The number *10* is a preference value. If there are multiple MX records for mail delivery to a given domain, an external SMTP host will first attempt a delivery to the internal receiving host with the lowest preference value.

To add an MX record, follow the instructions in the previous section for creating an Address record, but select New Mail Exchanger from the menu that pops up when you right-click your domain. In Figure 13.3, I've already filled in the Properties dialog box for my new MX record. Because my SMTP host will support the parent domain `bgerber.com`, I've left the Host of Domain field blank.

FIGURE 13.3

Using the New Resource Record dialog box to add a new Mail Exchanger record to DNS

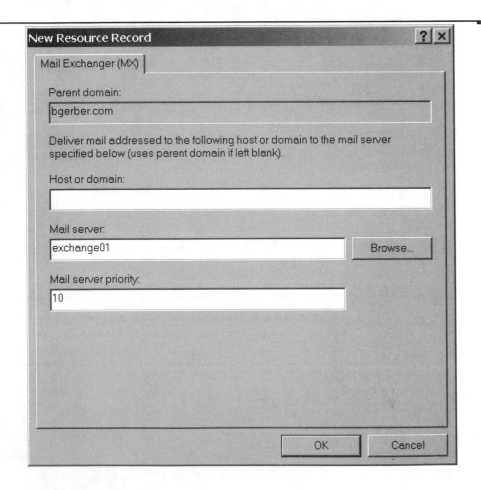

There's one neat thing that you can do with MX records: You can set up domain aliases. For example, if people in the Barry Gerber and Associates consulting department want to use the domain name consulting.bgerber.com on their business cards (instead of the simple bgerber.com), I can add an MX record to direct mail sent to consulting.bgerber.com to exchange01.bgerber.com. The record would look like this:

    consulting.bgerber.com. IN MX 10 exchange01.bgerber.com.

This record says that mail bound for consulting.bgerber.com should be sent to exchange01 at bgerber.com.

Of course, if you're going to use addresses such as JoeJones@consulting.bgerber.com, you'll need to be sure to add that SMTP address to Joe Jones' list of SMTP addresses, as per my instructions in Chapter 11, "Managing Exchange Users, Distribution Groups, and Contacts."

We Get Letters

You might have noticed that my e-mail address is included in the Acknowledgments section at the front of this book. Since the publication of the first edition of *Mastering Microsoft Exchange Server*, I've received hundreds of e-mail messages from readers. Most of those messages are about Internet access, and most of the Internet access questions are about using SMTP mail. The rest are predominately about Outlook Web Access—getting to an Exchange mailbox with a Web browser. I'll talk about troubleshooting OWA in the next chapter. Right now, if only to save a few million future electrons, I'll talk about two key DNS/SMTP messaging issues raised by readers. I'll also sprinkle other questions and responses throughout the rest of the book, as appropriate.

First, if your SMTP host is going to send and receive messages through a smart host using a noncontinuous connection, special care is required in setting up DNS records. The DNS entries must be for that host, not for your Exchange server. For example, if your SMTP connector is going to pick up and send messages through a proxy SMTP server operated by your Internet Service Provider, the DNS entries must be for the smart host. Your ISP will make the DNS entries for you in its DNS. All you need locally is a DNS or hosts file entry for the IP address and the name of your ISP's SMTP host. I'll show you how to set up a noncontinuous SMTP link later, in the section "Installing and Managing the Exchange SMTP Connector."

Second, if you want to operate your own SMTP host but you don't want to expose your Windows 2000 DNS to the outside world, you can use an external DNS operated, for example, by an Internet Service Provider. If you decide to do this, then your ISP needs to put the A and MX records that I talk about in this section into its DNS.

Finally, if you opt for either of the options discussed here, you need to turn name serving for your domain or domains over to the ISP. That is, the InterNIC must have the ISP's name servers, not your Windows 2000 name servers in its name server database.

Setting Up and Managing SMTP

SMTP in an Exchange 2000 Server environment is not one pack of services all neatly managed under one user interface roof. To set up and manage SMTP services for your Exchange organization, you have to focus on two different sets of services:

- Windows 2000 SMTP services
- Exchange 2000 SMTP Connector services

SMTP services are installed when you install Microsoft's Internet Information Server (IIS) on a Windows 2000 computer. You did this back in Chapter 7, when you installed Windows 2000. You work with SMTP services through what is called an *SMTP virtual server* (SMTPVS). SMTP virtual servers are SMTP hosts.

One SMTP virtual server is installed by default when you install IIS. This is usually enough to cover the messaging requirements of most organizations. However, if you need more SMTP virtual servers, you can create as many as you like. You would add SMTP virtual servers, for example, if you needed to provide different users with different levels of security or to send messages of markedly different sizes through different SMTP virtual servers.

When you install Exchange 2000 Server, Exchange hijacks the SMTPVS and makes it its own. This fact is most obvious in the way that you manage SMTP virtual servers before and after you install Exchange 2000 on a Windows 2000 server. Before Exchange 2000 is installed, you manage SMTP virtual servers through the IIS interface. After Exchange is installed, you manage SMTP virtual servers through the Exchange System Manager.

Under the covers, the most significant change that comes with installation of Exchange 2000 is that users of the standard Outlook client can send and receive Internet messages without enabling an Internet messaging client such as a POP3 client. Your Exchange server communicates with SMTP hosts to send and retrieve messages for Exchange mailbox-enabled users. These users view and compose messages to or from Internet correspondents using Outlook in exactly the same way as they do for messages to or from Exchange mailbox-enabled users. When an Outlook client connects to an Exchange server, as I described in Chapter 10, "A Quick Overview of Outlook 2000," the client sends all its messages to and receives all its messages from the Exchange server, whether those messages are from internal Exchange server users or from external Internet mail users. The Exchange server becomes the only point of contact that a user needs to access the electronic messaging world.

In taking over the Windows 2000 SMTPVS world, Exchange changes the directories that the SMTPVS uses to manage message traffic. When you install IIS, a set of directories is created for the default SMTPVS under IIS's `Inetpub` directory in a directory called `mailroot`. When you install Exchange 2000, another set of directories is created for SMTPVS use. The Exchange installation program places these directories in the directory structure used by Exchange: `...\Exchsrvr\Mailroot\vsi 1\Mailroot`. Subdirectories of Mailroot include these:

`Badmail`   Holds messages that cannot be sent and that cannot be returned to their senders

`Pickup`   Holds outgoing messages created as text files in standard RFC 822 format; Exchange moves properly formatted messages in this directory to the `Queue` directory

`Queue`   Holds messages for delivery, whether to other SMTP servers (outgoing) or to the Exchange mailbox store structure (incoming)

Exchange hijacks the SMTPVS in another way. Upon installation, an Exchange server is ready to use the SMTPVS to move messages between itself and other Exchange servers in its routing group.

As you can see, the SMTPVS is at the heart of Exchange Internet messaging. The Exchange 2000 SMTP Connector (SMTPC) is important, too, although its role is to supplement the functionality of the SMTPVS.

The SMTPC links your Exchange 2000 Server environment to the Windows 2000 virtual server environment, allowing you to select the SMTPVS that will support its activity. The SMTPC also enhances your SMTPVS in several ways, adding such features as enhanced security and connectivity. If you don't need these enhanced services, the SMTPVS will perform all the SMTP host functions for your Exchange server environment.

Now let's look at the SMTPVS and SMTPC in detail.

Need a Dial-up SMTP Host Link for Your Exchange Server?

If you want to run your Exchange-based SMTP host in dial-up (noncontinuous) mode, I'll have to ask you to be patient for a little while. I need to explain how both the SMTPVS and SMTPC work. I promise we'll get to dial-up options before the end of this chapter.

Managing SMTP Virtual Servers

An SMTPVS behaves like the generic SMTP host that I described in the section "DNS and SMTP: The Dynamic Duo of Internet Messaging," earlier in this chapter:

- The SMTPVS can be used with a connection to the Internet or to your organization's own TCP/IP local or wide area network.
- The SMTPVS operates in continuous connect mode.
- The SMTPVS can operate in noncontinuous connect mode.
- The SMTPVS attempts to send outgoing messages whenever it has a spare moment without a fixed delivery schedule.
- The SMTPVS keeps trying to send a message until a preset timeout period is reached, returning the message to the sender when the timeout period has been reached.

You manage the SMTPVS with a nice graphical user interface. The interface, which we'll look at in just a bit, gives you considerable control over your Internet messaging environment. It lets you do the following:

- Limit the number of simultaneous server connections
- Log server activity
- Set up a range of security controls
- Control absolute message size as well as message traffic per connection
- Specify how undeliverable messages are to be handled
- Set message delivery timing and timeout options

To open the SMTPVS management user interface, find your Exchange server in Exchange System Manager, and click it open until you see the container labeled Default SMTP Virtual Server. See the left side of Figure 13.4 for help in locating the virtual server. If you don't like the name given to your virtual server when IIS was installed, you can change the name by right-clicking the server and selecting Rename. To open the Properties dialog box for your virtual server, right-click the virtual server and select Properties from the pop-up menu. The dialog box is shown on the right side of Figure 13.4.

FIGURE 13.4

*Exchange System
Manager with the
default SMTPVS
exposed and the SMT-
PVS Properties dialog
box opened*

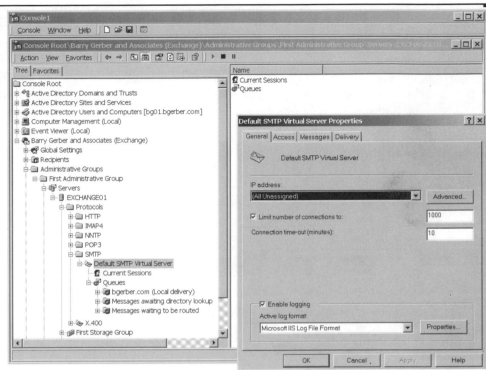

As you can see in Figure 13.4, the virtual server Properties dialog box has four property pages: General, Access, Messages, and Delivery. Let's look at each of these in order.

General

You use the IP Address field on the General property page to specify which IP address will be used by your SMTPVS. This refers to the IP addresses assigned to network adapters installed in your Exchange server. If you have one adapter in your server, that is your only IP address option. If you have two or even more adapters in your server, you have multiple options for this field.

In a simple Exchange environment, your Exchange server is likely to have two adapters. One adapter is set up to support connectivity to the server by workstations and servers on your internal networks, and the other adapter is set up to support your Exchange server's connection to DNS servers and SMTP hosts on the Internet. The main purpose for the internal network adapter is to support user access to the Exchange server. It could also be used to give users access to the SMTPVS on your

Exchange server, allowing them to use clients other than Exchange server-connected Outlook clients. Here's a good rule of thumb: Unless you have good reason, don't allow users to send messages from any client but an Exchange server-connected Outlook client.

Back to the IP address field. Accept the default IP address option All Unassigned to provide SMTPVS services to internal users and to your Exchange server. Select only the IP address of your Internet-connected network adapter to limit SMTPVS services to only your Exchange server.

You're not through yet. That little button labeled Advanced is a humdinger. You can do some really neat stuff with it. Let's check it out. Click Advanced to open the Advanced dialog box, shown in Figure 13.5. You can use this dialog box to change the TCP port on which other computers contact the SMTPVS, and you can set filters to prevent specific external users from sending messages to the SMTPVS.

FIGURE 13.5

Using the Advanced dialog box to change the SMTPVS TCP port and to set filters to reject messages from specific e-mail addresses

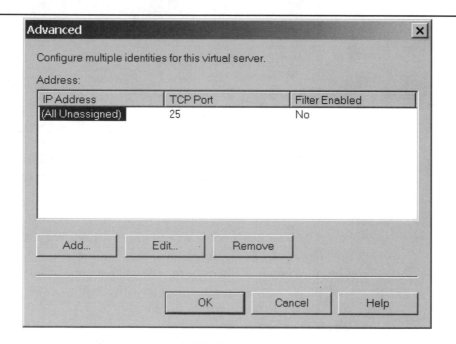

TCP port 25 is the default port for SMTP services. When other computers try to contact your SMTP host, they normally do it on port 25. If you change the port number, they won't be capable of contacting the host. So why would you change the port number? The answer: usually for security purposes. As long as SMTP-oriented client or server applications know that they should contact the SMTP host through the new port number, the host is considerably safer from hackers than a host using port 25. For now, leave the port number as it is.

If you ever do need to change the port, select the appropriate row in the Address field on the Advanced dialog box, and click Edit (see Figure 13.5). This opens the Identification dialog box, shown in Figure 13.6. Just change the TCP port number and click OK.

FIGURE 13.6

Use the Identification dialog box to change the SMTPVS TCP port and apply filters

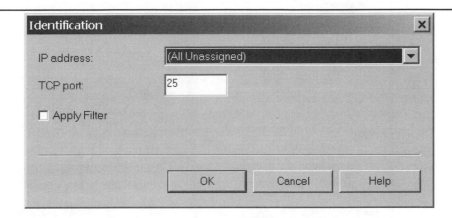

"So, what's all this filters stuff?" you say, eyeing Figures 13.5 and 13.6. Filters prevent the flow of messages into your system from specific external e-mail addresses. You obviously apply them by selecting Apply Filter on the Identification dialog box in Figure 13.6. But how do you create them?

To create filters, we have to sidestep a bit. Find and right-click the Message Delivery container in the Global Settings container in Exchange System Manager. Select Properties from the pop-up menu to open the Message Delivery properties dialog box shown on the right side of Figure 13.7. Tab over to the Filtering property page. The page is pretty self-explanatory. To add a filter, click Add. Enter the address of an Internet-based sender that you want the SMTPVS to reject messages from, and click OK. You can archive messages that are filtered. Archived messages go into a file. The file can get large, so archive with care.

You'll notice that I've asked that messages with a blank sender be filtered. That's a nice way to cut back on your daily intake of spam messages. If you don't want to send a message to the filtered sender informing them that messages aren't getting through to recipients in your system, check the last option on the dialog box.

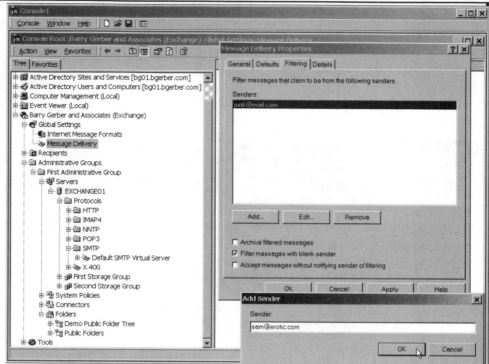

Okay, now we can sidestep back to SMTPVS management. The next field on the SMT-PVS dialog box (back to Figure 13.4) lets you control how many connections your SMTVS will accept. One SMTP host can open multiple connections to another SMTP host. So, it's not just a matter of how many hosts may try to connect to your SMTPVS at once, but how many connections each might open. There's no hard and fast rule on settings here. Be sure that the default value of 1,000 is set. I suggest that you monitor your SMTPVS using Windows 2000's Performance Monitor. Reduce the number of connections, if the SMTPVS seems to be struggling to meet demand or if your server's processor or disk drives are getting overworked. Up the number if message delivery drags and other components of your system aren't significantly taxed.

The Connection Timeout field on the SMTPVS dialog box allows you to set the number of minutes after which an inactive client will be disconnected from the SMT-PVS. The default setting of 10 minutes is as low as you should go.

Select Enable Logging to record SMTPVS events. You can select the type of log that you'll use. Unless you are sure that you have an application that allows you to read a file in any other format, select Microsoft IIS Log File Format from the drop-down list labeled Active Log Format. You can read files in IIS log file format as text files or through IIS. By default, SMTPVS log files are stored in the directory \WINNT\SYS-TEM32\LOGFILES\SMTPVSx, where x identifies each existing SMTP virtual server (for

example, log files for the default SMTPVS are stored in the directory \WINNT\SYS-
TEM32\LOGFILES\SMTPVS1). See the Exchange 2000 documentation for file formats,
file-naming conventions, and additional information. Click the Properties button to
specify how frequently a new log file is created (such as every day), how many log
files can accumulate before older ones are deleted, and where the log files are stored.
Log files can get big, so be sure that you have lots of disk space to hold them and that
you don't allow too many to accumulate before older files are automatically deleted.

Access

As you can see on the left side of Figure 13.8, the Access property page focuses on the
limits that you can place on intranet or Internet access to this SMTPVS. At times you
may find yourself using Access property page features to control access by other SMTP
hosts. However, you're more likely to use these features to control access by external
users of POP3 or IMAP4 e-mail clients who want to relay messages out to the Internet
through your SMTPVS. You need to control use of your SMTPVS by these folks both to
limit the load on the SMTPVS and to prevent e-mail spoofing. E-mail spoofing is the
transmission of an e-mail message in such a way that it appears to have been sent by
someone in your e-mail domain when that someone is actually not a member of the
domain.

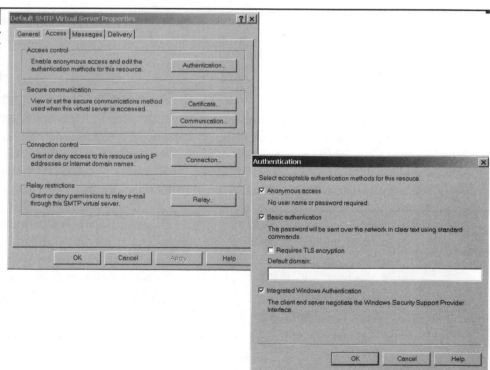

FIGURE 13.8

*The Access property
page of the SMTPVS
Properties dialog box,
with the Authentication
dialog box open*

You can control authentication, the security of communications, access based on IP address, and use of the SMTPVS by others to relay outgoing messages. Access control is both an important and often confusing area. Let's take a close look at your options on the Access page.

Authentication

Click Authentication to open the Authentication dialog box shown on the right side of Figure 13.8. Three authentication methods are available:

Anonymous access   Other computers may access this SMTPVS without providing a username or password.

Basic authentication   Other computers may access this SMTPVS, sending their passwords in without encryption.

> *Requires TLS encryption*   Transport-layer security encrypts usernames, passwords, and message content; if selected, clients that don't support TLS will not be capable of connecting to the SMTPVS. You must generate a key certificate if you're going to use TLS (see the next section "Secure Communication,"). The next version of the Secure Sockets Layer (SSL) protocol will be replaced by TLS.

> *Default domain*   When basic authentication is selected, specifies the Windows 2000 domain used to match client-submitted usernames and passwords; clients in a trusted domain can submit username as domain_name\username.

Integrated Windows authentication   Standard Microsoft Windows-encrypted usernames and passwords are accepted; message content is not encrypted.

By default, all three authentication methods are selected. This means that a client can access the SMTPVS using any one of the methods. For standard SMTP host functionality, anonymous access is required. Remember that any SMTP host in the world could potentially contact your SMTPVS with a message. By default, SMTP hosts do not use any authentication method. On the other hand, if your SMTPVS is going to operate only in a tightly controlled environment where contact is limited to a few password-protected SMTP hosts, you'll want to turn off anonymous access and select basic authentication or integrated Windows authentication, as appropriate.

If you want to control access to your SMTPVS outgoing message-relaying functionality, this isn't really the place to do it, unless you're going to dedicate this SMTPVS to relaying outgoing Internet-bound messages. Later in this section, I'll discuss a better way to control relay access.

Secure Communication

As I mentioned in the previous section, if you're going to support TLS secure communications, you'll need a security certificate. You'll also need to specify that a secure channel should be opened using the certificate.

Security certificates can serve two purposes. They authenticate the certificate owner, and they provide a public key for encryption of data transmitted between computers operated by the certificate owner and other computers.

If your Web browser has ever initiated download of software from a certificate-bearing Web site, such as Microsoft's site, you've seen the authentication function of security certificates in action. I'm talking about that little dialog box that pops up stating that what you're about to download and install on your computer is indeed coming from the source shown on the dialog box.

Public key encryption involves the use of public and private keys to scramble (encrypt) and unscramble (decrypt) communications. As I noted previously, the public key comes with the certificate. A server and its client may have and use pre-existing private keys, or private keys may be generated during a communication session. I'll talk more about public key encryption in Chapter 17, "Advanced Exchange Server Management," when I discuss the use of public key encryption to support internal Exchange server messaging.

Certificate creation and management is based in Internet Information Server. If someone has already secured a certificate for your Internet Information Server, you can use it for TLS communications. In the alternative, you can create a new certificate.

Where Do I Get a Certificate?

You secure certificates from certificate authorities (CAs). Windows 2000 has its own CA, which is used to issue internal certificates and which you must set up on a Windows 2000 server. This CA is used for Exchange internal messaging security. We'll talk about it in Chapter 17.

For communications with the outside world, you want a certificate from a neutral third-party CA. One of the better known CAs is VeriSign, at www.verisign.com. At the time of this writing, VeriSign certificates ranged in price from around $350 to $900 per server, depending mostly on the services included and whether 40- or 128-bit encryption is used. You can also get a 14-day free trial certificate from VeriSign.

Here's how to create a new certificate or use an existing certificate. When you click Certificate on the SMTPVS Properties dialog box (see Figure 13.8), the Web Server Certificate Wizard opens. On the second page of the wizard, the Server Certificate page, you can choose to create a new certificate, assign an existing certificate to your SMTPVS, or restore a certificate from a backup. Select the appropriate option.

Using an existing certificate is very easy. Select the certificate that you want to use from the list on the next wizard page, and follow the online instructions. That's it. Now move to the last paragraph in this section.

If you chose to create a new certificate, you'll be asked on the next wizard page if you want to prepare a certificate request to be sent later or to send the request immediately. Basically, the wizard prepares a text file whose contents are used by a certificate authority when it generates your certificate. The prepare-now-send-later option lets you interact with the certificate authority. The Send Request Immediately option is grayed out unless you have a Windows 2000-based certificate authority running on your network. Even if you have such an authority on your network, you don't want to use it to generate a new certificate, for the reasons noted in the sidebar "Where Do I Get a Certificate?" The bottom line is this: Be sure to *prepare the request now, but send it later*.

The next wizard page asks for a name for the certificate and the bit length of the encryption key, and lets you choose to a special cryptography feature, Server Gated Cryptography, if you have an export version of IIS. The name is used to identify your certificate in the IIS user interface. Use a descriptive name such as Exchange Default SMTPVS. You have two choices for encryption key bit length: 512 and 1024. The best choice from a security point-of-view is 1024 bits. However, the longer-length key can significantly slow encryption and decryption. So, I suggest that you start with 1024 bits and see how your SMTPVS performs. Drop down to 512 bits if incoming and outgoing message delivery is slow. Server Gated Cryptography allows lower-security 40-bit encrypted products, mainly those exported to other countries from the United States, to negotiate 128-bit encryption after an initial 40-bit handshake. You need to use it only if you're working in an environment outside the United States or Canada and you must work with a version of Internet Information Server limited to 40-bit encryption.

You input a name for your organization and an organizational unit on the next wizard page. Here you're striving for a unique identifier. Generally, using your corporate name and a departmental identifier works fine. For example, I might use Barry Gerber and Associates as my organization name, and Exchange Messaging as my organizational unit name.

On the next wizard page, you enter your organization's common name, a fully qualified domain name for the Exchange server running the SMTPVS. Use the server's DNS name. For example, I would use exchang01.bgerber.com.

The next wizard page is a bit tricky. All it wants is your country/region, state/province, and city/locality. You select the country/region from a drop-down list, so that's no problem. However, you must type directly into the other two fields, even though they are ostensibly drop-down lists. Type the full name of your state or province. Abbreviations are not acceptable to certificate authorities. Therefore, it's *California*, not *CA*, and *Los Angeles*, not *LA*.

You enter the name of a file in which the certificate request with all the stuff you've entered should be saved. Unless you want to change the location of the certificate request file, accept the default. Whatever you do, be sure to note the location of the file and its name.

That's about it. The final two wizard pages summarize your earlier choices and offer a field that you can click to get a list of external certificate authorities. When you're all done, click Finish.

Now, to get your certificate, you go to the Web site of a certificate authority (see the sidebar "Where Do I Get a Certificate?") and follow the directions on the Web site. At some point, you will be asked to paste the certificate request that you just created into a field on your Web browser. Just open the certificate request file in Notepad, select its entire contents, copy the selected text, and paste the copied text into the field on your browser.

After you've completed the certificate request process at the certificate authority, you'll receive your certificate in an e-mail message. Copy the certificate and save it to a new file on the same directory on Exchange server as you saved the certificate request. You don't have to save the certificate here, but it helps to standardize the location of certificate requests and the certificates themselves.

To install the certificate, restart the IIS Certificate Wizard. It will remember that you have a request pending and will ask you if you want to install the certificate. Reply in the affirmative, and follow the onscreen directions. That's it. You now have a certificate to support your SMTPVS's TLS-based security functionality.

Remember that your certificate supports both authentication and encrypted (secure channel) communications. If you want to use the latter functionality, you must tell your SMTPVS to use a secure channel for communications. To do so, direct your attention back to Figure 13.8. Click Communication and select Require Secure Channel. If the option is available, you can also choose to use 128-bit encryption. That's it. You're done with installing and activating your security certificate.

For more on certificates, including references, see Chapter 14, especially the section "Enabling Secure Sockets Layer Support for LDAP."

Connection Control

For security purposes, you can limit the computers that can connect to your SMTPVS. Limits may be based on the following:

- The IP address of a single computer
- The subnet IP address of a group of computers
- A DNS domain name

Under most circumstances, you wouldn't want to limit access to your SMTPVS because doing so means that any SMTP host on the Internet wouldn't be capable of sending e-mail to your messaging domain. However, connect limits do come in handy in some situations:

- You want to shut out certain sending SMTP hosts to prevent spamming or other undesirable communications.
- Your SMTPVS will contact a smart host to send and receive messages through it.
- You need to run a tightly controlled private messaging system over the Internet, and one or more of your SMTP hosts is registered in the public DNS namespace.

To set connection limits, click Connection on the Access property page for your SMT-PVS (look back at Figure 13.8). This opens the Connection dialog box. As you can see in Figure 13.9, you can limit access to a specific list of computers or allow access to all computers but those listed.

FIGURE 13.9

Using the Connection dialog box to limit access to an SMTPVS

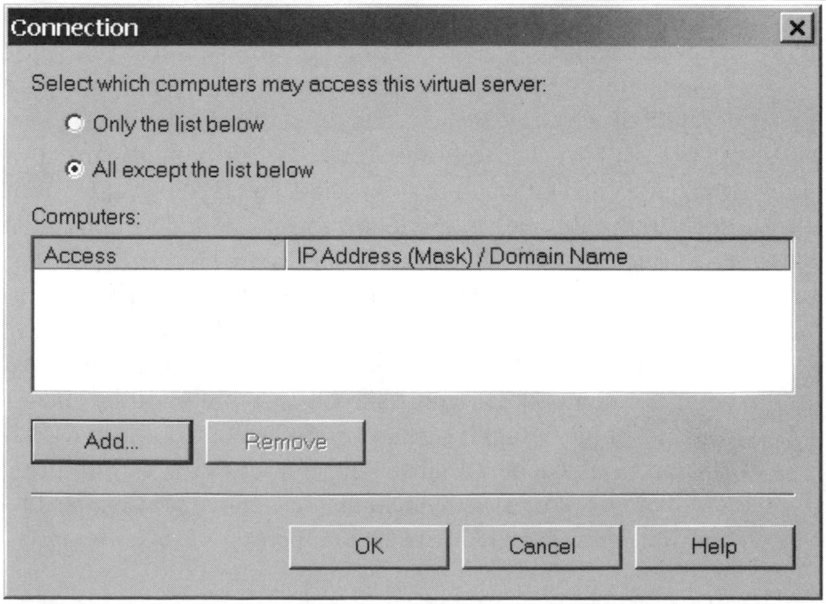

To add a new computer, subnet, or domain, click Add to open the Computer dialog box shown in Figure 13.10. Here's a brief list of your options and how to use them.

Single computer   Enter the computer's IP address, or click DNS Lookup to search for the IP address by inputting the computer's name.

Group of computers   Enter the starting IP address of the subnet that you want to reference and the subnet mask for the IP address. This is the easiest way to limit internal user access to the SMPTVS.

Domain   Enter the name of the domain that you want to reference.

You can add as many computers, subnets, and domains as you need.

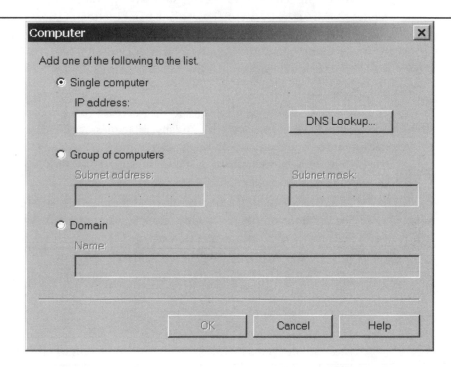

FIGURE 13.10

Using the Computer dialog box to select computers, subnets, and domains to be used in limiting access to an SMTPVS

Relay Restrictions

If you want to control who can use your SMTPVS to send outgoing messages, the Relay button on the Access property page of your SMTPVS's Properties dialog box (see Figure 13.8) is your friend. As I mentioned earlier in this section, letting just anyone on the Internet use your SMTPVS to send messages can create both server load and security problems.

The Relay Restrictions dialog box, which you open by clicking the Relay button, looks a lot like the Connection dialog box in Figure 13.9. It has one additional field,

Allow All Computers Which Successfully Authenticate to Relay, Regardless of the List Above. If anonymous authentication is permitted as per the dialog box shown in Figure 13.8, leaving this option checked means that any e-mail client or SMTP host on the Internet can send messages through your SMTPVS. So, if this is your main SMTP host, deselect the Allow All Computers option.

To control who can use your SMTPVS to relay messages, you need to be sure that the Only the List Below option is selected on the Relay Restrictions dialog box, and you need to add subnets or one or more domains to the Computers list on the dialog box. The Computer dialog box that you use to set relay restrictions looks just like the dialog box shown in Figure 13.10. Use the Computers dialog box to add the internal subnets that this SMTPVS will serve. Alternatively, you can add the DNS domain names that are used by internal users, or a combination of subnets and domain names. Of course, the Computers list on the Relay Restriction dialog box can refer to both user computers and other SMTP hosts, including internal SMTPVs that use this SMTPVS to relay messages to the Internet for them.

Messages

You use the Messages property page shown in Figure 13.11 to control message traffic and to specify what happens with undeliverable messages. This is an important page because it lets you control both the load on your SMTPVS's CPU and disk drives, and the amount of network traffic that it generates. Here's a quick look at the options on the Messages property page:

Limit Message Size To   Sets the maximum size of messages sent through the SMTPVS; the default is 4MB including any attachments. Some SMTP hosts cannot receive messages greater than around 3MB, so if users report a lot of rejected messages, you might want to reduce this value to 3MB.

Limit Session Size To   Sets the maximum amount of data that can be relayed though the SMTPVS during a session (connection). The default is 10MB. Use this setting to control server load.

Limit Number of Messages Per Connection To   Sets the maximum number of messages delivered by the SMTPVS per connection to other SMTP hosts. Assuming adequate CPU power, a smaller number speeds up message delivery by using multiple connections. The default of 20 should work fine in most situations.

Limit Number of Recipients Per Message To   Sets the maximum number of recipients for any message sent through the SMTVS. The default of 64,000 should be adequate for most environments. Set the value lower to improve message delivery time.

Send Copy of Nondelivery Report To   Sets an address to which nondelivery reports (NDRs) are sent. By default, a message is sent only to the originator of an undeliverable message. Enter an address here that will also receive nondelivery reports. In busy environments, this can result in an overwhelming number of nondelivery messages, so use the option with care. I recommend having NDRs sent to the postmaster for your domain. I'll explain how you set up a postmaster in the upcoming section "Setting the Address for the Domain Postmaster."

The Badmail directory holds undeliverable messages for possible review by Exchange administrative staff. By default, this directory is located in the SMTPVS's Mailroot directory. You can change its location here. The directory must be periodically manually emptied.

The Forward All Mail with Unresolved Recipients to Host option forwards undeliverable messages to another SMTP host (SMTPVS or non-SMTPVS) that might be capable of resolving unresolved recipient names. Don't set this option on the other host as well, or a game of performance-degrading e-mail ping-pong will ensue.

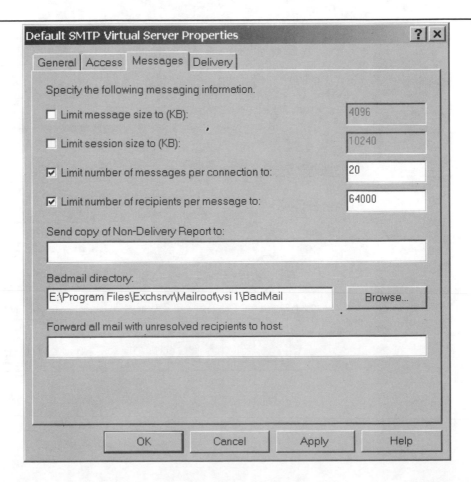

FIGURE 13.11

Using the Messages property page to set limits relating to messages and to specify how undeliverable messages should be handled

Delivery

You use the Delivery property page shown in Figure 13.12 to set message retry intervals, specify how long before a sender is first notified that a message has yet to be delivered, and set a period after which a message that has not yet been delivered is returned as undeliverable. You also use this property page to set security options for outbound message delivery, to set limits on connections that your SMTPVS uses to deliver messages, and to set up some pretty neat advanced options. We'll start by examining the fields on the Delivery page itself. Then we'll look at what's behind the three buttons at the bottom of the page.

FIGURE 13.12

Using the Delivery property page to set limits regarding messages yet to be delivered

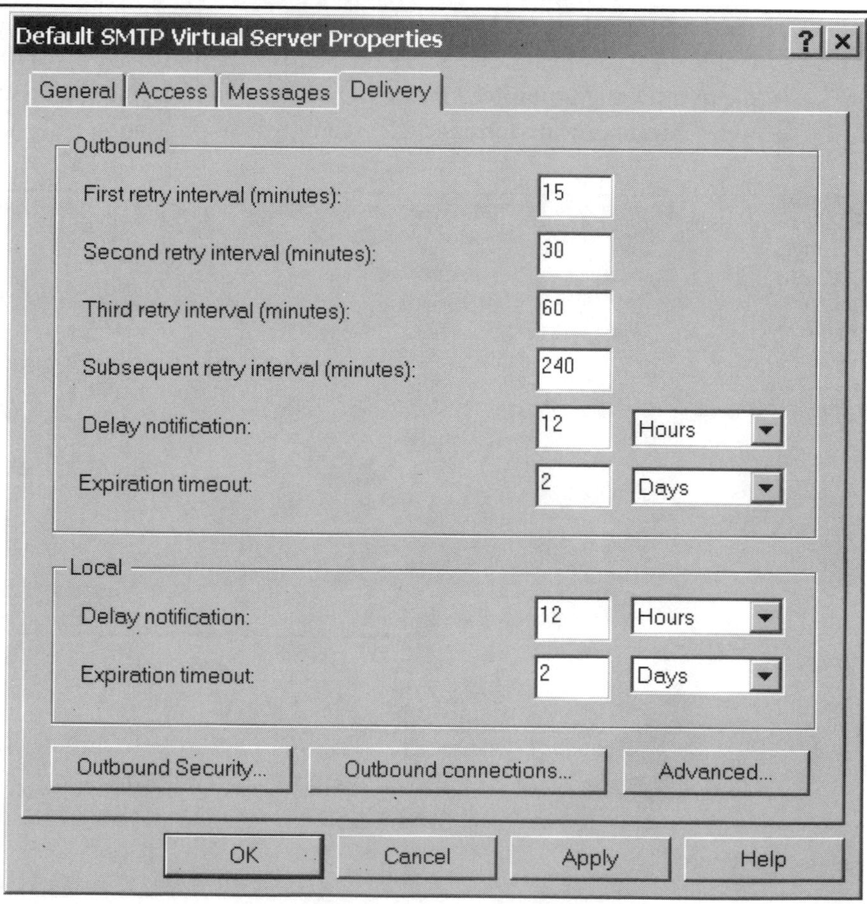

Fields on the Delivery Property Page

As you go through the following list, be sure that the parameters on your Delivery property page match the ones in Figure 13.12. In the late prerelease versions of Exchange 2000 Server that I worked with for this book, the default settings were too short for some options.

Outbound   Applies to messages destined anywhere but an internal Exchange server mailbox store

> *First Retry Interval (Minutes)*   The number of minutes to wait before trying to send an as yet undeliverable message.
>
> *Second Retry Interval (Minutes)*   The number of minutes to wait before making a second attempt to send an as yet undeliverable message.
>
> *Third Retry Interval (Minutes)*   You guessed it; I won't say any more.
>
> *Subsequent Retry Interval (Minutes)*   The number of minutes to wait before each subsequent attempt to send an as yet undeliverable message.
>
> *Delay Notification*   Time in minutes, hours, or days before the sender is notified that a message is as yet undeliverable.
>
> *Expiration Timeout*   Time in minutes, hours, or days after which attempts will no longer be made to deliver the message. The message will be forwarded to another SMTP host, assuming that one was specified on the Messages property page, or a nondelivery message will be issued.

Local   Applies to delivery of messages by the SMTPVS to an internal Exchange mailbox store.

> *Delay Notification*   See "Delay Notification," under "Outgoing," earlier in this list.
>
> *Expiration Timeout*   See "Expiration Timeout" under "Outgoing," earlier in this list.

Outbound Security

Click Outbound Security on the Delivery property page to bring up the Outbound Security dialog box. As you can see in Figure 13.13, this dialog box is used to configure the security options that your SMTPVS will use when contacting other SMTP hosts. You can pick only one of the three authentication options on the dialog box: Anonymous Access, Basic Authentication, or Integrated Windows Authentication. See the subsection "Authentication," earlier in this chapter, for more on these three options and on the TLS encryption option.

FIGURE 13.13

Using the Outbound Security dialog box to select the authentication method that an SMTPVS will use when contacting other SMTP hosts

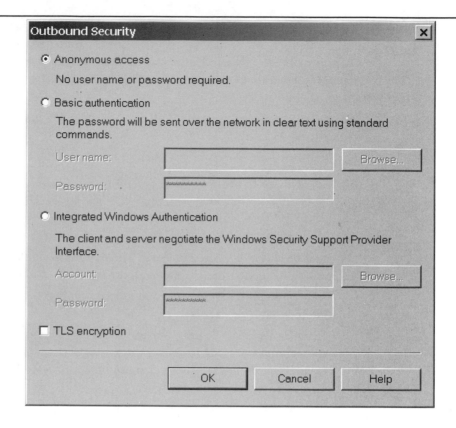

Of course, you must be sure that the SMTP hosts that your SMTPVS will be contacting *all* support the method of authentication and encryption you've chosen. You can enter only one username/password (basic authentication) or account/password (integrated Windows authentication) combination, so this severely restricts the SMTP hosts that your SMTPVS can connect to. The nonanonymous access outbound security options are best used for connecting to internal SMTP hosts or to a single SMTP host that will act as a smart host sending and receiving messages for your SMTPVS.

TIP As noted previously, the outgoing authentication option that you set for an SMTPVS applies to all communications initiated by the SMTPVS with other SMTP hosts. If you need authenticated communications with one or a few SMTP hosts and you still need connectivity to the rest of the world's SMTP hosts, try this option. Disable outgoing authentication (select Anonymous Access) for the SMTPVS. Then use an Exchange SMTP connector to set up a specific connection for each SMTP host that requires authentication. As you'll see in the section "Installing and Managing Exchange SMTP Connectors," one of the ways that SMTP connectors enhance your SMTPVS is by allowing you to send messages to specific domains with specific authentication and connectivity requirements.

Outbound Connections

You learned how to limit connections by other SMTP hosts to your SMTPVS in the previous subsection "General," which dealt with the General property page of the SMTPVS Properties dialog box. Now I'll show you how to limit your SMTPVS's connections to other SMTP hosts.

Click Outbound Connections on the Delivery property page, shown in Figure 13.12, to open the Outbound Connections dialog box (see Figure 13.14). As you can see for inbound connections, you can limit both the total number of outgoing connections and the period in minutes before a connection closes after an SMTP host stops accepting messages. The defaults should be fine. Remember that the real SMTP-based connections-based load on your server is the sum of inbound and outbound connections. Be sure to use Windows 2000's performance monitor to monitor your SMTPVS to ensure that messages are moving with adequate speed and that SMTP message transfer isn't placing undue strain on your Exchange server's CPU or disk drives.

FIGURE 13.14

Using the Outbound Connections dialog box to set limits on connections used by an SMTPVS to deliver messages |

The Outbound Connections dialog box adds a new kind of connection limit, a per-domain limit. This enables you to limit the load that you place on any other SMTP host that you connect to.

You can also change the default TCP port from the standard 25 on the Outbound Connections dialog box. You should never do this if your SMTPVS will be a generic SMTP host sending messages to and receiving messages from any and all Internet-connected SMTP hosts. TCP port 25 is the standard port for SMTP host communications. If you change the port, your SMTP host is dead in the water. For more on this option and why you might use it, see the previous subsection "General."

Advanced Delivery

You can set a variety of options on the Advanced Delivery dialog box of the Delivery property page (see Figure 13.15). Because the options are so diverse, I won't summarize them. Instead, I'll discuss each briefly.

FIGURE 13.15

Using the Advanced Delivery dialog box to set a range of special options for an SMTPVS

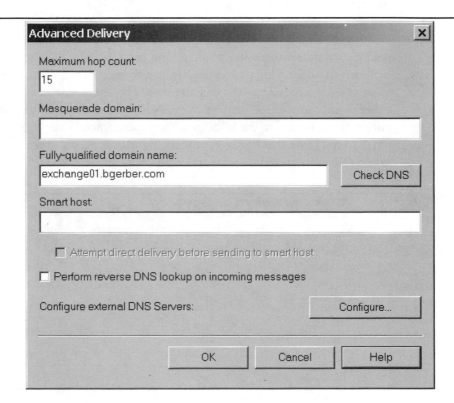

Sometimes it takes several SMTP hosts to relay a message to its final destination. Each time another SMTP host participates in relaying a message is called a *hop*; the host adds a line to the message, which is how a host knows the current number of hops. To limit Internet traffic, a maximum hop count limit is set. When this limit is reached, the message is treated as nondeliverable by an SMTP host, and a nondelivery message is sent to the originator of the message. When the hop count for a message grows large, it is usually because of an addressing error. A maximum hop count of 15 is reasonable, except in certain networking topologies in which a larger number of hops could legitimately be required to deliver a message.

A masquerade domain is an alternate domain to which other SMTP hosts to send their nondelivery reports.

The fully qualified domain name is the full DNS name of the SMTPVS. By default, the fully qualified domain name of my SMTPVS is the name of the server that it's running on—in my case, `exchange01.gerber.com`. You can provide any name here as long as it is registered in your DNS as associated with the IP address of the computer. Click Check DNS to ensure that the name is indeed in your DNS.

When you specify a smart host on the Advanced Delivery dialog box, you're specifying a computer that will receive mail from your SMTPVS and send it out. There is no way with the SMTPVS to also specify that incoming messages received by the smart host for your SMTPVS should be sent to the SMTPVS. To do this, you'll need to set up an SMTP connector. We'll do that in the section "Installing and Managing the Exchange SMTP Connector," later in this chapter. If you want to use the limited smart host functionality offered here, enter the fully qualified domain name of the smart host. If you use a smart host, you can specify that the SMTPVS first try to deliver messages directly to the recipient before sending them to the smart host. This lets you send internal messages directly while using the smart host for Internet messages.

If you want to know the domain from which each inbound message comes, select Perform Reverse DNS Lookup on Incoming Messages. Then your SMTPVS will use DNS to convert the IP address of the mail originator into a fully qualified domain name. This can be helpful in troubleshooting.

You can set up the addresses of external DNS servers to be used by your SMTPVS when resolving addresses for Internet-bound messages. This allows you to use your internal DNS servers only for resolving internal addresses.

Readers Ask About Internet Security for Exchange Servers

Earlier in this chapter, I noted that I get lots of e-mail from readers. One question that a number of readers ask involves putting an Exchange server running an SMTPVS behind a proxy server or firewall. Here's what I tell those readers.

A proxy server, such as Microsoft's Proxy Server, is designed to protect workstations and servers placed behind it from malicious Internet hackers. When your network is behind a proxy server, there are two ways to make an Exchange server's SMTPVS accessible to e-mail clients and SMTP servers on the Internet. You can put the Exchange server on the same Windows 2000 server as your proxy server, or you can make the proxy server look to the outside world like it's an SMTP host.

Depending on the proxy server product that you use, if you locate your Exchange server with SMTPVS on a proxy server, you must make sure that packet filtering is set correctly, or the SMTPVS will still be invisible. For the details, especially as they apply to Microsoft

Continued

CONTINUED

Proxy Server, see article Q176771, "Using Packet Filters with Exchange Server," in Microsoft's Knowledge Base, accessible at http://support.microsoft.com.

If your Exchange server with SMTPVS is behind a proxy server, you need to set parameters to support access by e-mail clients from and to SMTP hosts. Two Knowledge Base articles address this sort of configuration: article Q181847, "How to Configure Microsoft Exchange Server with Proxy Server," and article Q178532, "Configuring Exchange Internet Protocols with Proxy Server." Firewalls are an alternative to proxy servers for securing Internet-connected Exchange servers. Be sure that the firewall is set up to pass packets to your Exchange server(s) on all relevant SMTP TCP messaging ports. Check out the book *Firewalls 24seven*, by Matthew Strebe and Charles Perkins (Sybex, 1999), for more on these helpful adjuncts to network security.

That's it for the SMTPVS's Properties dialog box and friends. Now, before we tackle the SMTP Connector, I need to show you how to set a passel of other SMTP messaging options.

Managing SMTP Virtual Server-Related Functionality

You can set a variety of SMTPVS-related options outside the SMTPVS Properties dialog box shown in Figure 13.8. These options include setting the address of your domain postmaster and setting a range of Exchange organization-wide formatting and other properties relating to Internet messages. I'll talk about these options and where you set them in this section.

Setting the Address for the Domain Postmaster

At times, both humans and SMTP hosts need a standard address within your Internet messaging domain with which to communicate about matters relating to the domain. Here are some key situations in which this address is used.

Your SMTPVS sends nondelivery reports from your domain with postmaster@[your_domain] in the From field. Anyone needing to contact a human being about a nondelivery report replies to the postmaster address.

As I noted previously, your SMTPVS will send a copy of each nondelivery report that it sends to the originator of a message to an e-mail address that you enter on the Messages property page of the Properties dialog box for your SMTPVS. This helps you track nondelivery problems. The postmaster address is a good one to use here.

By common agreement, people contact the postmaster address to find the e-mail address of a particular person in an Internet messaging domain. Whether the human behind the postmaster address sends the address or not is a matter organizational policy, but it's nice to know that the option is there.

Of course, the postmaster is just an e-mail address. It can be any valid SMTP address, so it can be any type of Exchange recipient: a mailbox-enabled user, a mail-enabled user, a distribution list, a contact, or a mail-enabled public folder. (See Chapter 11 and Chapter 12, "Managing the Exchange Server Hierarchy and Core Components," for more on setting up and using Exchange recipients.) The postmaster address can even be an SMTP address outside your Exchange organization. Most people add the address `postmaster@[your_domain]`—mine is `postmaster@bgerber.com`—to the SMTP addresses for a specific Exchange mailbox. But you can do anything you want, from creating a new Windows 2000 account and Exchange mailbox for a postmaster, to sending NDRs to your best friend (or, more likely) your worst enemy in Antarctica.

Whatever you do, the key is to monitor this account. It can provide you rich information on the configuration and performance of your SMTPVS—and it is, after all, a piece of your organization's presence in the outside world.

Setting Global Internet Message Formatting and Other Properties

Up to now, I've talked almost exclusively about setting a wide range of properties for a single SMTPVS on a single server in your Exchange organization. By and large, the properties we've talked about so far have related to SMTPVS security and Internet message delivery and receipt. You can also set Exchange organization-wide parameters that control the format of messages and attachments to them, and that control whether certain automatically generated message content, such as out-of-office responses, is permitted. Settings for most of these parameters can apply to messages sent to all or to specific Internet domains, meaning that you can use different message formatting and automatic message content-generation parameters for different Internet domains. Let's look at these properties and how they function in the SMTP messaging environment.

Setting MIME Content Types

Internet-bound messages and attachments to them cannot be in 8-bit binary format. They must be encoded into 7-bit ASCII text format. When this happens, all or part of the original look, feel, and behavior of messages and attachments can be lost. To preserve these characteristics, encoding schemes and content type identifiers are used. I'll talk about message encoding later in this section. I'll talk first about content type identifiers.

The Multipurpose Internet Mail Extension (MIME) protocol specifies content types for various kinds of files and documents when those files and documents enter the Internet environment. Content types enable a specific helper application to open when an encoded message attachment is accessed using a MIME-compliant POP3 or IMAP4 e-mail client, or a Web browser. Content type identifiers provide information that makes it possible for an attachment to be opened in a related helper application.

If you use Windows, you're very likely familiar with the concept of helper applications. When you double-click a Word file in My Computer or Windows Explorer and Word opens, displaying the file, Word is the helper application. You may have had a similar experience when using Microsoft's Internet Explorer: You clicked on a URL for a Word document in your browser, and the document opened either in a separate copy of Word or, perhaps, with help from OLE2, in Word right inside Internet Explorer.

A content identifier specifies only the file extension associated with an attachment. It doesn't specify the helper application that should be used for the extension. That information must be present on the computer running the POP3 or IMAP4 e-mail client or the Web browser that is accessing the attachment. This is the same information used to open any application associated with a file extension. You manage file extension associations in Windows Explorer under View ➢ Options ➢ File Types, or in My Computer under Tools ➢ Folder Options ➢ File Types.

If there is a file extension association for the file extension, and if the helper application exists on the computer, the attachment opens in the application. If the application doesn't exist, the user sees the same standard error message that would be seen if that user tried to double-click to open a file in Windows Explorer or My Computer.

Okay, that's enough about MIME content type identifiers. Now let's see how they're used in Exchange 2000. By default, Exchange 2000 Server adds MIME content type information when it prepares an attachment for transmission over the Internet through your SMTPVS. That way, assuming that there's a MIME-compatible client on the receiving end, the message recipient can open any attachments and view them as the sender intended.

You can view and add MIME content types and associated extensions. MIME content types are set for your entire Exchange organization, so you work with them in a subcontainer of the Global Settings container in Exchange System Manager. To access MIME content types, open the Internet Message Formats Properties dialog box by right-clicking Internet Message Formats (see the left side of Figure 13.16) and selecting Properties from the pop-up menu. This opens the Internet Message Formats dialog box, shown on the right side of Figure 13.16.

FIGURE 13.16

*Using the General
property page of the
Internet Message
Formats Properties
dialog box to view
and set MIME
content types*

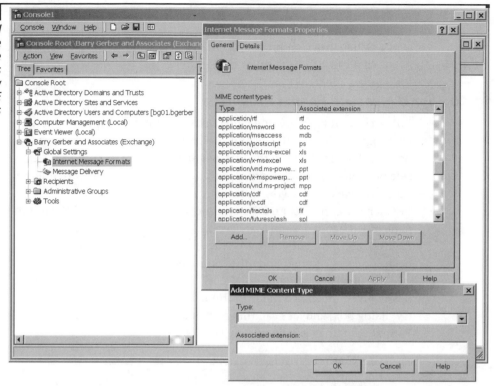

As you can see in Figure 13.16, Exchange 2000 Server comes with a large number of
MIME content types built in. Figure 13.16 shows some of the application-related
MIME content types. Other content types include text, audio, and video. These content types use generic extensions that could be associated with any of a number of
applications. For example, one of the text content types is text/plain, which is associated with the file extension TXT. An attachment with a TXT file extension opens in the
application associated with the extension TXT on the user's computer. That application may be Microsoft's Notepad, or it may be any other application that can handle
ASCII text files.

Now let's take a very quick tour of the buttons on the Internet Message Formats
dialog box's General property page. You use the Move Up and Move Down buttons to
position a content type where you want it. Content types are processed in the order
that they appear in the list. To add a content type, click Add on the General property
page, and use the Add MIME Content Type dialog box, which is also shown in Figure
13.16. You'd add a new content type only when both of the following statements are
true:

1. You need to support a new application or other content type, such as text, audio, or video.

2. Others with whom your Exchange users communicate have messaging clients that can handle the new content type.

Setting Additional Message Format Properties

MIME content types are one kind of message format property—there are others, and we'll explore them in this section. To set these properties, you must work with SMTP policies that are stored in the Internet Message Formats container, shown on the left side of Figure 13.16. We worked with the properties of this container in the last section; now we need to work in the container.

Click the container and then right-click the object labeled Default in the right pane of Exchange System Manager; then select Properties from the pop-up menu (use Figure 13.17 to orient yourself). This opens the Properties dialog box that contains default message format and other property settings for your Exchange organization (see the right side of Figure 13.17). As far as I've been able to determine, Microsoft hasn't given much of a name to this dialog box. Let's call it the Domain Message Policy dialog box, and let's call things such as the Default object in the Internet Message Format container *domain message policies*.

FIGURE 13.17

The dialog box for default domain message policies, with its General property page exposed

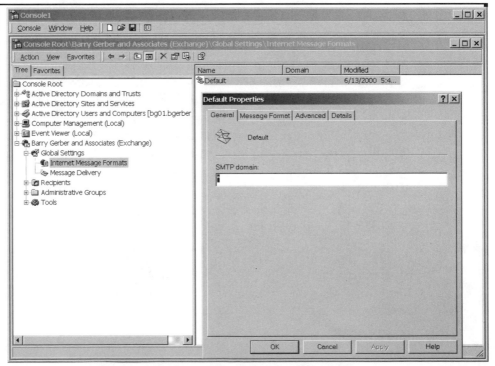

The property settings on the Domain Message Policy dialog box labeled Default apply to all SMTP domains in the world. I know that because there's an asterisk in the SMTP Domain field on the General property page in Figure 13.17. An asterisk in an SMTP Domain field in Exchange means that whatever a particular dialog box does, it does that for all domains that SMTP messages can be sent to.

You can create new domain message policies. These policies apply to specific domains. This is neat because it enables you to customize the way messages are formatted and handled, depending on the domain for which they're destined. To create a new domain message policy, right-click the Internet Message Formats container and select New ➢ Domain from the pop-up menu. Just be sure to specify the SMTP domain that the message settings apply to on the General property page for each new domain message policy.

 WARNING   Don't confuse the external specificity of domain message policies with the internal ubiquity of the same objects. You can create different domain message policies that apply to messages going to different external domains, but all the domain message policies that you create are used by all the SMTP virtual servers in your organization.

Okay, let's go back to the default Domain Message Policy dialog box. Tab over to the Message Format property page, shown in Figure 13.18. Track along on Figure 13.18 as we move through the rest of this section.

FIGURE 13.18

The Message Format property page of the default message policy dialog box

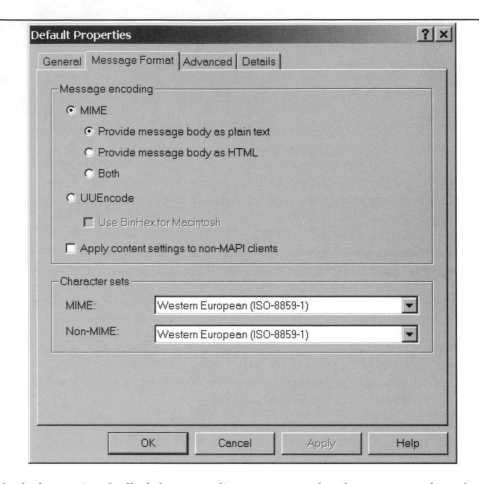

In the last section, I talked about encoding messages so that they can move through the 7-bit ASCII world of the Internet. As you can see in Figure 13.18, you have two options for encoding outbound messages: MIME and UUEncode (Unix-to-Unix Encode). You can't have it both ways, so you need to be sure that those who will receive messages from your Exchange client can read messages encoded according to the protocol that you choose. Whichever option you choose, both messages and attachments will be encoded in the format. You can't choose to encode messages in MIME format and attachments in UUEncode format.

You can send MIME-encoded messages as plain text, in HTML format, or both. Plain text is straight 7-bit ASCII text, which is recognizable by any SMTP mail client. HTML encoding is now quite popular for Web browsers and is growing in popularity for e-mail message content. Among other things, HTML supports such things as bold, italic, and colored text as well as different fonts. I'll talk more about HTML encoding in the next chapter. Choose plain text unless you're sure that recipient e-mail clients can handle HTML encoding.

UUEncode is an older encoding standard that doesn't support the rich text capabilities that MIME supports. You should select this option only if you're sure that clients receiving SMTP messages sent from your Exchange server cannot handle MIME encoding. The incapability to handle MIME encoding is growing increasingly rarer. Of course, if recipient clients that can't deal with MIME are isolated in identifiable Internet messaging domains, you can create a special domain message policy for them. This is exactly why Exchange lets you create domain-specific message policies.

If you choose UUEncode encoding, you can choose to have attachments sent in BinHex format, which is compatible with the Apple Macintosh computing environment. Be careful here: All messages are sent in BinHex format. Non-Mac users won't be capable of opening the attachments unless they manually decode them using a BinHex decoder that runs on their particular operating system.

The Apply Content Setting to Non-MAPI Clients option is both interesting and maybe just a bit esoteric. If you check this option, messages from Internet e-mail clients will first be translated from their MIME or UUEncode formats into Exchange's native MAPI format. Then they will be encoded in the format that you've chosen in the Message Encoding section of the Message Format property page. You'll probably have to read this over a couple times and refer to Figure 13.18 more than once, but I guarantee that you'll finally figure out what's going on here. You use this option to ensure that all Internet-based messages are stored in a consistent format. If this sort of consistency is important to you, then, by all means, check the box. Do remember, though, that this dual-translation process has a cost in CPU and disk access cycles, so use it with caution.

You use the Character Sets section to select the character set that's used for outbound Internet messages. There's a drop-down list for MIME and UUEncode. Select carefully: If a receiving client isn't set up to handle the character set, your sent messages will be, at best, difficult to read and, at worst, unreadable. You can use a separate domain message policy to apply different character sets to outbound messages for different Internet messaging domains.

Setting Other Properties

Now tab over to the Advanced property page of the Domain Message Policy dialog box (see Figure 13.19). This page contains two more options related to text formatting and options to activate or deactivate different kinds of automatically generated message content. Let's look at each of these in turn.

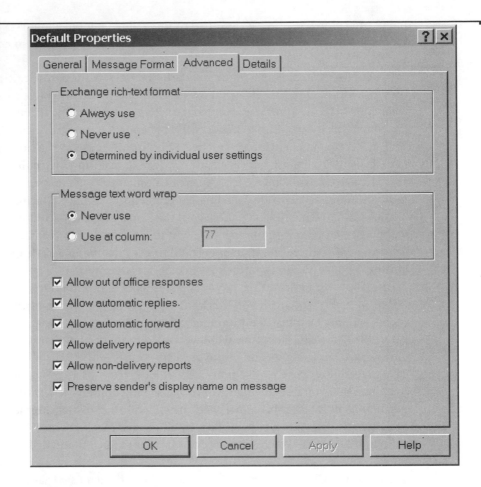

FIGURE 13.19

The Advanced property page of the default message policy dialog box

More Text Formatting Options

You can send messages in Exchange's native rich-text format. Exchange rich-text format supports such features as bold, italic, and colored text; bulleted and numbered lists; centering; right, center, and left alignment; as well as Exchange-specific attachment encoding. Messages and attachments that are sent out of Exchange in this format are still encoded in MIME or UUEncode and must be decoded by the receiving host. If you choose this option, all message recipient e-mail clients must be capable of handling Exchange rich-text messages. Those that can't could have difficulty reading the message, and attachments will show up in an unreadable file called winmail.dat.

You can choose to always or never use Exchange rich-text formatting. You can also leave it to individual users to set the option in their Outlook clients. I strongly recommend against allowing users to set this option, however. If they leave the default, Exchange rich-text format, and if you've selected the Determined by Individual User Settings option, then all outbound Internet messages will be sent in Exchange rich-text format. If users change the default to plain text or HTML, then internal Exchange messages lose rich-text formatting.

If Internet recipients need to see messages in Exchange rich-text format, your best bet is to create a separate domain message policy for them, being sure to select Always Use for Exchange rich-text formatting. That way, whatever format your users have set in their e-mail clients, outbound messages to those who need Exchange rich-text format will be sent using as much of Exchange rich-text formatting as is possible, given the settings on the originating e-mail client.

Unlike messages composed on a typewriter, with computer-generated text, you don't have to press the Enter (Return) key at the end of each line. Text is automatically wrapped at whatever the current window size is set to. Some older e-mail clients can't wrap text, leaving you, at best, with text that runs on in one long line until the end of a paragraph is reached. If you expect to be sending messages to domains with these older e-mail clients, select Use At Column. The default, 77, means that an end-of-line marker will be inserted in the text after the space character, which is closest to but not more than 77 characters.

Automatically Generated Message Content

The limits that we're going to deal with here aren't about message length and such. They're about automatically generated message content. These limits are listed in the bottom half of the Advanced property page, shown in Figure 13.19. By default, all of them are selected. Here's what they're all about:

Allow Out of Office Responses   Enables or disables out-of-office messages set up by users in their Outlook clients (see Chapter 10)

Allow Automatic Replies   Enables or disables automatic replies to incoming messages set up as rules by users in their Outlook clients (see Chapter 10)

Allow Automatic Forward   Enables or disables either Outlook client-initiated or administrator-initiated forward of messages to another e-mail address

Allow Delivery Reports   Enables or disables outgoing reports that a message has been received by your SMTPVS

Allow Nondelivery Reports   Enables or disables sending of nondelivery reports by your SMTPVS

Preserve Sender's Display Name on Message   Enables or disables user's Windows 2000/Exchange 2000 display name, in addition to e-mail address in outbound messages

Being able to turn off these message content-generating features is a godsend, especially if you're responsible for security or SMTPVS/network performance, or if the business folks in your organization want to limit the amount of information that is sent to the Internet world, such as display names. And what's so neat is that, depending on the Internet domain that you need to communicate with, you can create different domain message policies with different rules about which automatic content-generation features are enabled and disabled.

Managing SMTP Virtual Server-Related Connections and Queues

Take a look at Figure 13.4, back at the beginning of this chapter. Notice the two containers and their subcontainers below your default SMTPVS. You use these containers to manage SMTPVS connections and queues.

The Current Connections container shows the SMTP hosts and user clients that are connected to your SMTPVS. You can terminate any or all of these connections by right-clicking the Current Connections container (all connections) or any connection in the container).

You can troubleshoot problems with incoming and outgoing SMTP messages in the Queues container. In Figure 13.4, the Queues container currently has three subcontainers:

bgerber.com (Local Delivery)   Holds inbound messages to be delivered to a mailbox on the Exchange server.

Messages Awaiting Directory Lookup   Holds inbound messages whose recipients have not yet been looked up in Active Directory. (This includes messages whose distribution groups haven't been expanded.)

Messages Waiting to Be Routed   Holds outbound messages whose next destination server has not been determined. (When the next destination server is determined, the message is sent.)

A subcontainer is temporarily created in each of these containers for every destination server for which at least one message currently exists. When all messages have been sent to a particular destination server, Exchange deletes the subcontainer, only to re-create it when new messages for the destination server become available.

Two other containers are created as needed:

Final Destination Currently Unreachable   Holds outbound messages for which a destination server can't be determined

Presubmission   Holds messages accepted by the SMTPVS but that are not yet being processed

Okay, now check out the introduction to the next section, which deals with the SMTP connector. If you don't need the functionality of an SMTPC, then you can move on to the last section of this book, "Did It Work?" to test out your SMTPVS.

Installing and Managing the Exchange SMTP Connector

The Exchange 2000 Server SMTP Connector, or *SMTPC*, as I called it earlier in this chapter, is very different from earlier Exchange SMTP-related services. Exchange 5.x's Internet Mail Service (IMS) was a full-blown SMTP host. It could do pretty much anything that Exchange 2000's SMTPVS can do, and more. In Exchange 2000 Server, most of the *more* is provided by the SMTPC.

You can use the SMTPC to do the following:

- Control how messages are routed to SMTP hosts or smart hosts through an SMTPVS
- Set additional limits on the types and sizes of messages that can be sent through an SMTPVS
- Prevent Windows 2000 mailbox-enabled or mail-enabled users from sending Internet-bound messages
- Connect Exchange routing groups

In this section, I'll concentrate on the first three items in this list. I'll touch on the fourth use of the SMTPC in Chapter 15, "Installing and Managing Additional Exchange 2000 Servers."

Dial-up Send and Receive SMTP Smart Host Access: We're Getting Close

Those of you who need send and receive dial-up access to a smart host should pay close attention here. I'll cover about three-quarters of what you need to know to set up dial-up access. For the other quarter, you'll have to wait until the next section on demand-dial interfaces.

You might be wondering how the SMTPC interacts with the SMTPVS. Essentially, the SMTPC sits in front of one of more SMTP virtual servers, providing specialized message-routing functionality. Its most important feature is its support for highly customized connectivity between Exchange SMTP virtual servers and specific external or internal SMTP hosts—including, of course, other SMTP virtual servers. Even though SMTP virtual servers and SMTP connectors work together to move messages, from here on, I'll use the term *SMTPC* if the SMTPC is controlling the action.

If you're having trouble grasping this description of SMTPC/SMTPVS interaction, the best way to clarify matters is to install and configure an SMTPC. So, let's get right to it.

Find and right-click the Connectors container in the Exchange System Manager (see the left side of Figure 13.20). Then select New ➢ SMTP Connector from the pop-up menu. This brings up the SMTPC properties dialog box shown in the right side of Figure 13.20.

FIGURE 13.20

Creating a new SMTP connector starting with the General property page

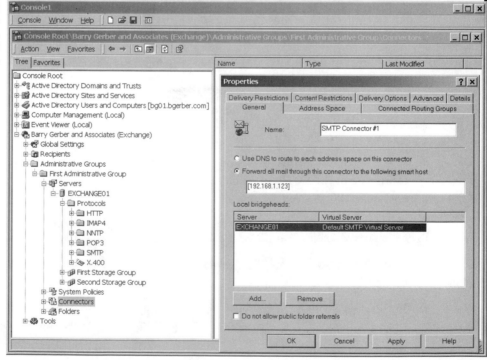

Right now we need to explore the General, Address Space, Delivery Restrictions, Content Restrictions, Delivery Options, and Advanced property pages. I'll discuss the Connected Routing Groups page in Chapter 15.

General

The General property page is an important one. On it, you name your SMTPC, specify how it will function in transferring SMTP messages, set the SMTPVS that it will function through, and set a parameter relating to how public folder information is handled when the SMTPC is used to connect Exchange routing groups. We'll look at all but the last of these here, saving public folder referrals for Chapter 15.

Name your new SMTPC anything that works for you. It will show up in the Connectors container under this name.

Your SMTPC can use DNS to route messages, or it can forward messages through a smart host. If you choose the DNS method, your SMTPC finds and accesses other computers just like the SMTPVS. If you choose to use a smart host, the SMTPC connects to the smart host and only to the smart host to do its business.

If you choose to use a smart host, the name that you enter here overrides any entry that you may have made on the Advanced Delivery dialog box of the Delivery property page of the Properties dialog box for your SMTPVS. (Whew, that's a mouthful!) Take a look at Figure 13.15 for a quick visual refresher on the Advanced Delivery dialog box.

The SMTPC lets you do something with your smart host that you can't do with the smart host that you set on the Advanced Delivery dialog box for your SMTPVS: The SMTPC lets you set things up so that the smart host is asked to send messages that it has received for your Exchange Internet domains. If you need full dial-up send and receive smart host services, this is a key piece of the puzzle. I'll show you how to set up this puzzle piece in just a bit.

You'll notice that I've specified an IP address for the smart host rather than a fully qualified domain name. You can do this as long as you enclose the IP address in brackets. Do note, however, that if you enter an IP address here, you'll have to change it if the IP address of the smart host changes. Another approach would be to use a fully qualified domain name that is maintained in an external DNS, or to create an Address record for the smart host in your internal DNS.

You must specify at least one bridgehead server. This is the server that provides the SMTPVS services to make the connection to the DNS or smart host computers that you specified in the Use DNS or Forward All Mail Though fields. You'll notice that I've chosen (actually been forced) to use my one and only SMTPVS.

NOTE Connectors live in a routing group inside of an administrative group. You can't see the routing group in Figure 13.20 because we haven't yet turned on the display of routing groups. We'll do that in Chapter 15. Routing groups are not based on a specific Exchange server such as SMTP virtual servers. SMTP virtual servers are processes that run on Exchange servers. SMTP connectors refine the functionality of SMTP virtual servers. They aren't processes that run on servers. Rather, they live in Active Directory, and their particular refinements are invoked by associated SMTP virtual servers as the need arises.

Address Space

The Address Space property page is shown on the left side of Figure 13.21. This is a fairly simple page. You need to add at least one address space: Click Add to do so. This opens a little dialog box from which you can pick the kind of address space that you need. You're offered several options, including SMTP, X.400, and Microsoft Mail. Select SMTP to open the Internet Address Space Properties (see the right side of Figure 13.21).

You'll remember the asterisk from our discussion of domain message policies. This means that, with the exception of any parameters set elsewhere on this dialog box, this SMTPC should function for all SMTP domains in the world. If you want this SMTPC to service one or more domains, but not all domains, you can specify a single SMTP domain here. Then you can create additional address space objects to cover the other domains that you want this SMTPC to service.

FIGURE 13.21

Using the Address Space property page to create a new SMTP address space for an SMTPC

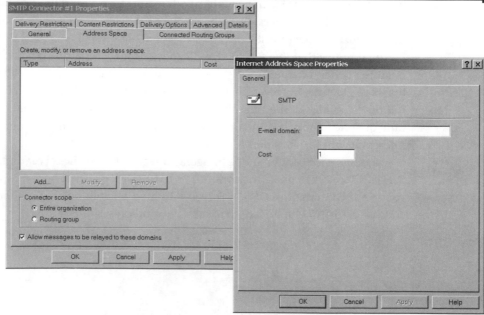

You use the Cost field to set the relative time or dollar cost of using this connector to process messages for this address space, as opposed to using a different connector to process messages for the same address space. You need this feature only when you set up multiple connectors. You usually set up multiple connectors when you connect two Exchange routing groups to ensure redundant links between the routing groups. When routing, Exchange server always attempts to use the lowest-cost route (which might very well be a higher-cost but also higher-speed route) before attempting to use a higher-cost route.

Connector scope lets you specify which servers can use your SMTPC. You can allow your entire organization to use the SMTPC, or you can restrict use of the SMTPC only to servers in the routing group where the SMTPC resides. You might use this feature to control security in your organization, but its most important functions are in the area of cost. Say that you've established an inexpensive or high-performance route from the SMTPVS supported by this SMTPC to whatever external computers you plan to connect to. But, say also that this route is inexpensive or fast only for servers in the SMTPC's Exchange routing group, which are servers linked by higher-speed network connections. Other servers in other routing groups in your organization may have their own least expensive routes and fastest routes to the servers supported by this SMTPC. Limiting use of the SMTPC to servers in the SMTPC's routing group ensures that servers in other routing groups will use their own best routing options, not options that aren't optimal, given their location.

The last field on the Address Space property page enables you to disable the relaying of messages bound for the address spaces that you've defined. Users and computers that can authenticate using Basic or Integrated Windows authentication can relay messages even if Allow Messages to Be Relayed to These Domains is deselected. If this SMTPC supports a direct connection to the Internet, you'll probably want to disable this function so that not just anyone with an SMTP client or just any SMTP host can relay messages.

Delivery Restrictions

You use the Delivery Restrictions property page, shown in Figure 13.22, to select the Exchange recipients that can send messages using the SMTPC. If your organization doesn't want everyone to have access to Internet messaging, you use this property page to create a list of users who are not allowed to use this SMTPC to send messages. To prevent an Exchange recipient from receiving SMTP messages, just remove the SMTP address or addresses on the E-mail Addresses property page of the recipient's Properties dialog box (see Chapters 11 and 12 for more on this property page).

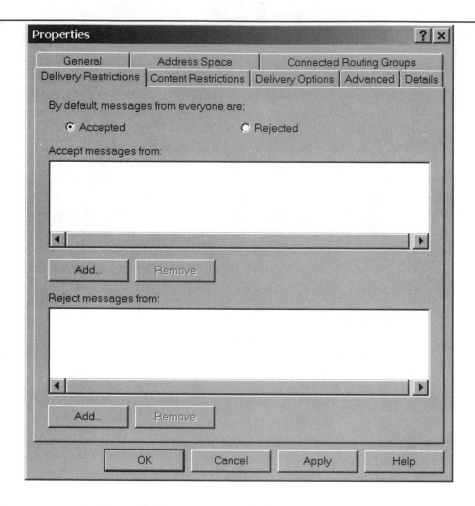

As you can see in Figure 13.22, you can simply choose to accept or reject messages from everyone, or you can create lists of Exchange recipients from whom messages may or may not be accepted. You can use only one of the list or both lists. Click the appropriate Add button to add recipients to a list, and then select the recipients from the Select Recipients dialog box that opens.

Content Restrictions

The Content Restrictions property page lets you specify whether messages with certain characteristics may be delivered through the SMTPC (see Figure 13.23). Here's a quick take on the options on the Content Restrictions property page.

FIGURE 13.23

*Using the Content
Restrictions property
page to specify the
kind of messages that
can be sent through
an SMTPC*

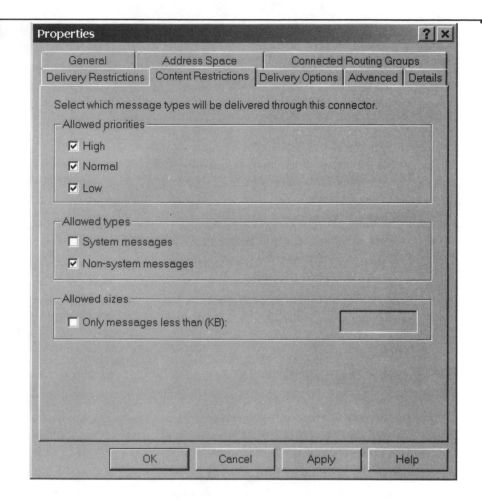

Users can specify a priority for each message that they send. Messages with deselected priorities are not sent.

Exchange uses system messages for such things as public folder replication. Windows 2000 uses messages to support such things as Active Directory replication. If you deselect System Messages, only standard user-originated messages will be sent. If your SMTPC is going to be used to contact a smart host, you should deselect System Messages.

You use the Allowed Sizes field to set the maximum size in kilobytes of messages that can be sent through your SMTPC. The default is no size limit.

ESMTP, TURN, and ETRN

Before we jump into the last two property pages on the SMTPC dialog box, let's clarify some key terms. The next two sections will make a lot more sense if you have a clear understanding of what ESMTP, TURN, and ETRN are all about. All three of these terms identify specific parts of the overall SMTP specification. They are key to message retrieval from an SMTP smart host.

By default, your SMTPC uses the Extended SMTP (ESMTP) command set when contacting other SMTP hosts. This command set includes extensions to the original SMTP protocol's command set. Extensions cover such things as advanced, more secure message interchange; longer TO and FROM fields; and preannounced message length limits so that an SMTP host doesn't try to send messages that are longer than the receiving SMTP host allows.

The TURN command essentially reverses or turns around the communication roles between two SMTP hosts. At the start of communications, the contacted SMTP host is expecting the contacting SMTP host to send it messages for domains under the contacted host's control. The TURN command tells the contacted SMTP host that the contacting host wants the contacted host to send messages to it for domains under its control—in other words, "At first you thought that I contacted you to send you messages, but now I want you to send messages to me."

The TURN command can be authenticated. The SMTPC will issue the command only if it has a valid username and password to send to authenticate the command. Additionally, the SMTPC will not accept TURN requests from SMTP hosts that can't or won't send a valid username and password.

The ETRN (Extended TURN) specification doesn't allow for password-protected command authentication. However, it does require that the SMTP host issuing the ETRN command also provides the fully qualified domain name of the SMTP host that supports the domain for which messages need to be picked up. The smart host then initiates a new session with the SMTP host specified in the ETRN command. This can be done on the same link that the original ETRN command was issued on, including an existing dial-up connection. This allows for a fairly secure link between the SMTPC and its smart host.

Delivery Options

Okay, now on to the Delivery Options property page, shown on the right side of Figure 13.24. You use this page to specify when and how messages are sent through your SMTPC.

FIGURE 13.24

*Using the Delivery
Options property page
to specify how and
when messages are
sent through an
SMTPC*

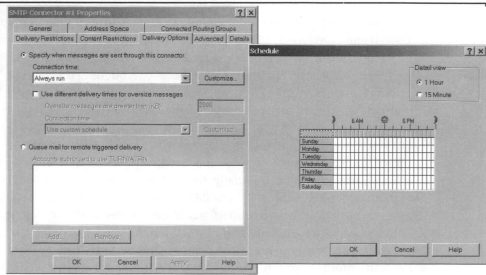

Either the SMTPC can send messages on its own, or an SMTP host can contact it to pick up outbound messages. To implement the first option, select Specify When Messages Are Sent Through This Connector. You can then specify the schedule for connection by selecting from a limited set of choices on the Connection Time drop-down list or by clicking Customize and setting any schedule you'd like on the Schedule dialog page, shown on the right side of Figure 13.24. You can then go one step further and set another delivery schedule for large messages.

This may come as a surprise, but if you need to set up a dial-up send and receive link to a smart host, you should accept the Always Run connection time option. You'll see why when I discuss demand-dial interfaces in the next section.

Your second delivery option is Queue Mail for Remote Triggered Delivery. If you select this option, you're telling your SMTPC that another SMTP host will contact it to pick up messages ready for delivery. The other SMTP host will issue the ETRN or TURN command. The TURN command will be accepted only if the other SMTP host sends the account name and password of a Windows 2000 account listed in the field

Accounts Authorized to Use TURN/ATRN. Whoever manages the other SMTP host must enter information required for the host to contact your SMTPC, including the Windows 2000 account name and its password. If no accounts are entered in the Accounts Authorized to Use TURN/ATRN field, only ETRN requests will be accepted. For a quick refresher on TURN and ETRN, check out the sidebar "ESMTP, TURN, and ETRN," just before the start of this section.

You're probably wondering about ATRN in "TURN/ATRN." ATRN (Authenticated TURN) is another version of TURN that can also be authenticated. At this writing, and very like at the first release of Exchange 2000 Server, ATRN won't be supported. When it is, there will be two authenticated methods for requesting that your SMTPC send waiting messages.

To use the remote triggered delivery option, you need another SMTP host whose administrator is willing to initiate a connection to your SMTPC. This isn't impossible, but you're more likely to find that kind of willingness inside rather than outside your organization. For example, few Internet Service Providers (ISPs) are likely to agree to initiate communications, especially dial-up connections with your SMTPC to pick up outbound messages. However, most ISPs are more than willing to let you initiate connections, including dial-up connections, to one of their SMTP hosts so that you can send messages through it in smart host fashion. All this means that you're most likely going to use the first option on the Delivery Options page, Specify When Messages Are Sent Through This Connector. Enabling dial-up from another SMTP host would be most useful when two or more Exchange servers are set up to connect to each other through a dial-up connection.

Advanced

Up to now, we've spent most of our time moving messages from our SMTPC to other SMTP hosts. Now we're ready to tackle the Advanced property page, shown in Figure 13.25, which lets us reverse the process and get messages from another SMTP host.

FIGURE 13.25

*Using the Advanced
property page to spec-
ify how an SMTPC will
retrieve messages for
the domains it
supports*

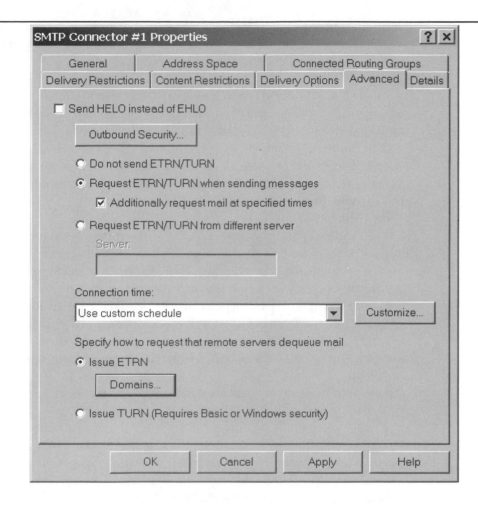

When an SMTP host contacts another SMTP host, it first issues either a HELO or an EHLO command. The HELO command is a request to communicate using standard SMTP commands. The EHLO command tells the other SMTP host that the contacting host wants to use ESMTP commands.

Today, most SMTP hosts can handle ESMTP, so you're pretty safe accepting the default and leaving the Send HELO Instead of EHLO option unselected. Of course, if you've designed this SMTPC specifically to contact an SMTP host that doesn't support EHLO, you can select the option. Note, however, that if you choose to use standard SMTP commands, all the other options on the Advanced properties page are grayed out, meaning that standard SMTP commands don't support these options. This means that, among other things, dial-up retrieval of messages from a smart host is not possible. Here's the bottom line: If you need the kinds of capabilities on the Advanced property page, find an ISP that supports ESMTP.

The rest of the Advanced property page is about setting up your SMTPC so that it asks another SMTP host to send it messages. If you need to contact a dial-up send and receive SMTP smart host, pay close attention to this section. If you have no need for this feature, then select Do Not Send ETRN/TURN, and you're done.

Click Outbound Security to open the Outbound Security dialog box, if you need to set up an authentication method, username, and password for your SMTPC's connection to its remote host. (Check out Figure 13.13 and related text for more on using the Outbound Security dialog box.) I'll talk a little more about this option at the end of this section.

If you've already set up your SMTPC so that it can send messages through a smart host, and if you want it to ask the smart host for new messages for the domains that your SMTPC supports, then select Request ETRN/TURN When Sending Messages. You specify whether you want to use ETRN or TURN at the end of the Advanced property page. With this option selected, every time your SMTPC contacts its smart host to send messages, it will ask the smart host for new messages. If you also want your SMTPC to ask the smart host for messages on a schedule of some sort, then select Additionally Request Mail at Specified Times. I'll show you how to set the schedule in a moment.

If you want to use a different smart host to pick up messages than the one that sends messages, select Request ETRN/TURN from a Different Server. Again, you specify whether you want to use ETRN or TURN at the end of the Advanced property page. Be sure to enter either an IP address for the server, in brackets, or the fully qualified domain name of the server. This option lets you send messages through one smart host and receive them through another. If you pick this option, you can set the schedule for connections to the smart host. Join me in the next paragraph to see how.

You use the Connection Time field to set the schedule for contacts with the smart host that you selected previously. You can pick from a limited number of options from the drop-down list, or you can set a custom schedule. See the right side of Figure 13.24 for the Schedule dialog box.

The last section of the Advanced property page enables you to specify whether the ETRN or TURN command is used to request that an SMTP smart host send messages. You can also set whatever security parameters are available for whichever command you choose. If you need clarification regarding the ETRN and TURN commands, check out the sidebar "ESMTP, TURN, and ETRN" a few pages back.

If you select ETRN, you need to specify the local Internet messaging domains that ETRN should be issued for. The SMTPC uses this information to form the fully qualified domain name that it needs to send with the ETRN command. As Figure 13.26 makes pretty clear, selecting a domain is very easy. Just click Domains, and then click Add and select the domain from the Add ETRN Domain dialog box.

FIGURE 13.26

Using the ETRN Domain property page to specify the domains that an SMTPC will retrieve messages for when using the ETRN command

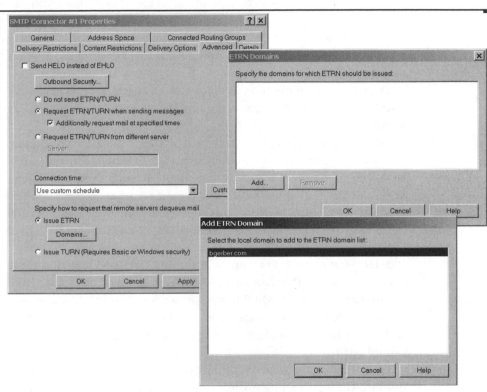

If you select TURN, of course, you need to enter a username and password using the Outbound Security dialog box. To do this, open the Outbound Security dialog box near the top of the Advanced property page by clicking Outbound Security. Then select either Basic Authentication or Integrated Windows Authentication, and enter a valid username and password.

If you've tracked through this section, you probably need a send/receive dial-up link to an SMTP smart host. That's exactly what's covered in the next section. Go there if you need dial-up connectivity. If not, you're ready to test your SMPTC. Skip down to the last section of this chapter, "Did It Work?"

Installing and Managing Demand-Dial Interfaces

Demand-dial interfaces are a bit magical. In the SMTP messaging world, whenever a connection is needed to a specific IP address and a demand-dial interface exists for that interface, the connection is automatically made through the demand-dial interface to the IP address. If you tracked through all the sections of this chapter and you need a send/receive dial-up connection to an SMTP smart host, you should just have had the following epiphany: "If you set up an SMTP connector to connect to a specific IP address and that IP address is supported by a demand-dial interface, connectivity just happens." That's it! So now all that remains is for us to set up a demand-dial interface.

Demand-dial interfaces are Windows 2000 objects, not Exchange 2000 objects. They're created and managed within the Windows 2000 routing and remote access world.

We'll be setting up a telephone-based interface, so before you do anything else, you need to be sure that a functioning modem is installed in your Exchange server. Next, you need to enable routing and remote access on your server. We're going to move through setting up routing and remote access at breakneck pace, so hold on to your hat. If you need more information, see the books on Windows 2000 referenced in the sidebar "Where to Go for More on TCP/IP, DNS, and SMTP," at the beginning of this chapter.

Select Start menu ➢ Programs ➢ Administrative Tools ➢ Routing and Remote Access. This opens the Routing and Remote Access snap-in, shown in Figure 13.27. As an alternative, you can add this snap-in to your Microsoft Management Console. Find and right-click your Exchange server and, from the pop-up menu, select Configure and Enable Routing and Remote Access. The Routing and Remote Access Server Setup Wizard opens.

Click Next on the wizard's introductory page to access the Common Configurations wizard page, and then select the Network Router option. On the Routed Protocols wizard page, verify that TCP/IP is included in the Protocols list. If it's not there, add it. On the Demand-Dial Connections wizard page, select the Yes option so that the routing and remote access service will support demand-dial interfaces. Use the IP Address Assignment wizard page to specify whether you want the routing and remote access server to automatically assign IP addresses to incoming connections or to get the addresses from a list. If you select the former option, you're done. Select the latter option if you expect incoming calls, and then enter the IP address range that you want to use on the next wizard page—then you're done.

FIGURE 13.27

*The Windows 2000
Server Routing and
Remote Access snap-in*

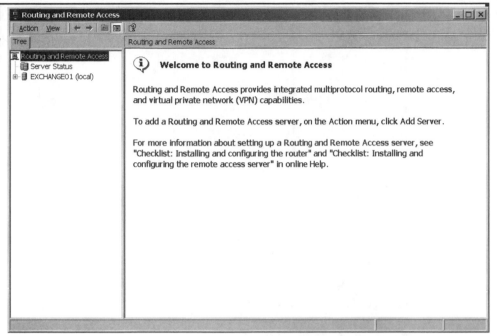

You can change the settings that you made with the Demand-Dial Connections wizard. Right-click your server in the Routing and Remote Access snap-in, and select properties from the pop-up menu. This opens the Properties dialog box for your server's Routing and Remote Access service (see Figure 13.28). I'm not going to take you through all the property pages on this dialog box; if you need to tinker with your settings, check out the books that I mentioned previously in this section.

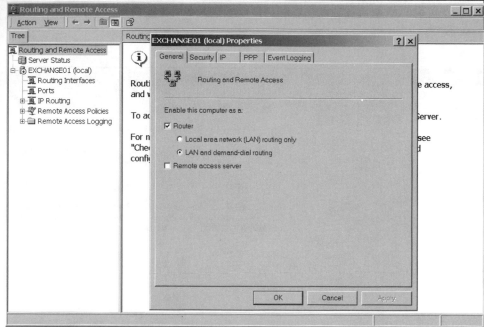

Okay, now let's set up a demand-dial interface. Find and right-click the Routing Inter-faces container in the Routing and Remote Access snap-in (see Figure 13.28). It's the container just below the server name in the snap-in. Then select New Demand-Dial Interface from the pop-up menu. This opens the Demand Dial Interface wizard. We're going to slow down here just a bit because it's very important that you get this part right.

Click over to the Interface Name wizard page, shown in Figure 13.29. Enter an intelligible name for your demand-dial interface. I've named mine ISP Smart Host.

FIGURE 13.29

*Naming a demand-dial
interface on the
Interface Name page
of the Demand Dial
Interface Wizard*

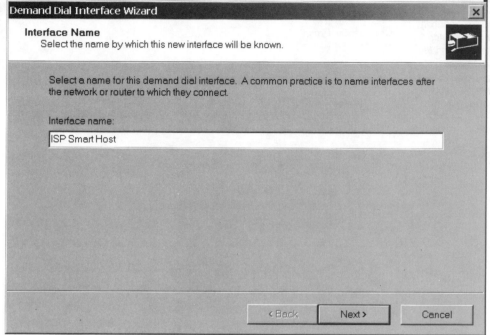

The Connection Type wizard page offers you two connectivity options (see Figure
13.30). Be sure that the Connect Using Modem, ISDN Adapter, or Other Physical
Device option is selected. Next select a physical device on the Select a Device wizard
page, shown in Figure 13.31.

FIGURE 13.30

Selecting a connectivity option for a demand-dial interface on the Connection Type page of the Demand Dial Interface Wizard

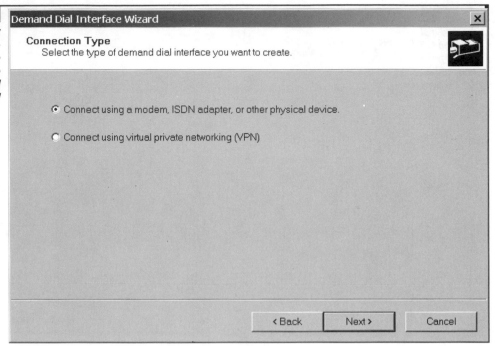

FIGURE 13.31

Selecting a physical device to be used by a demand-dial interface on the Select a Device page of the Demand Dial Interface Wizard

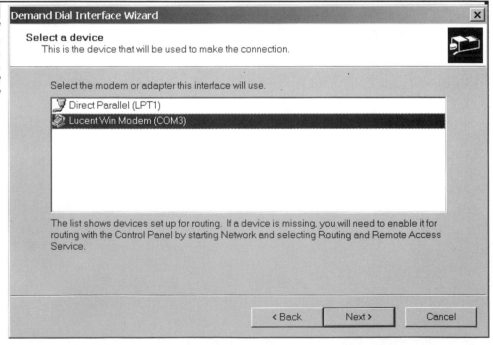

Use the Phone Number wizard page to enter the phone number or numbers of the computer that you want to connect to (see Figure 13.32). Make sure that this number or these numbers are appropriate for reaching the remote SMTP host.

Next set the networking protocols to be supported on your demand-dial router and security options using the Protocols and Security wizard page, shown in Figure 13.33. Be sure that Route IP Packets on This Interface is selected. Although it should be taken care of in the setup of your SMTPC, you can also select the option that ensures that a plain-text password will be sent if that is the only way to connect to the dial-up system.

FIGURE 13.32

Entering a phone number for a demand-dial interface on the Phone Number page of the Demand Dial Interface Wizard

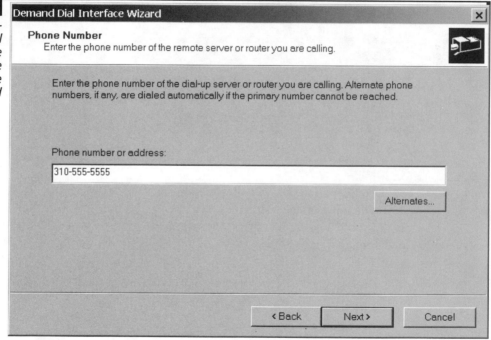

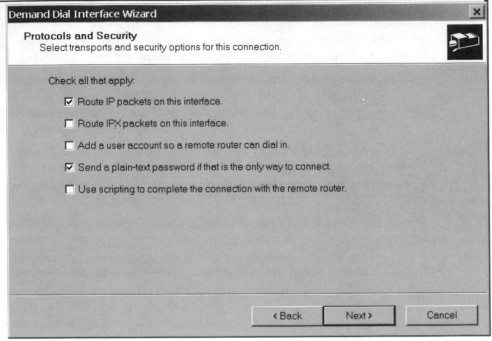

You need to enter the security information expected at the remote site. As per Figure 13.34, you must enter a username and a password on the Dial Out Credentials wizard page. If you're logging into a Windows network, you may also need to enter the Windows domain name.

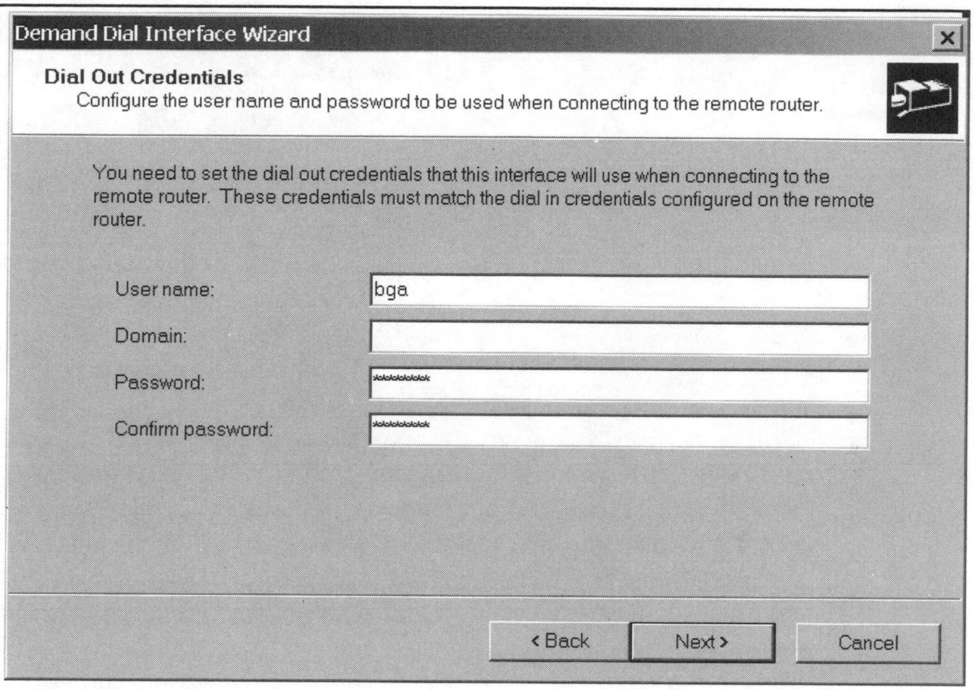

FIGURE 13.34

Entering security information for a demand-dial interface on the Dial Out Credentials page of the Demand Dial Interface Wizard

Demand Dial Interface Wizard ⬛ ✕

Dial Out Credentials
Configure the user name and password to be used when connecting to the remote router.

You need to set the dial out credentials that this interface will use when connecting to the remote router. These credentials must match the dial in credentials configured on the remote router.

User name: bga

Domain:

Password: ✱✱✱✱✱✱✱✱✱

Confirm password: ✱✱✱✱✱✱✱✱✱

< Back   Next >   Cancel

That's it for the Demand Dial Interface Wizard. Now you need to do one more thing to enable the interface: You need to link it to the IP address of the smart host that you specified when you set up you SMTPC. You do this by setting up a static route.

Expand the IP Routing container in your Routing and Remote Access snap-in. Then find and right-click Static Routes and select New Static Route. This opens the Static Route dialog box, shown in Figure 13.35. Select the demand-dial interface that you just created from the Interface drop-down list.

FIGURE 13.35

Using the Static Route dialog box to set up a static route for a dialup connection

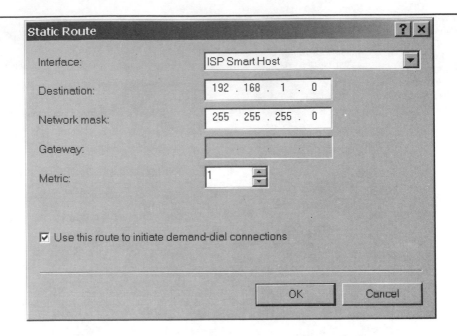

Next enter the IP address of the network that you want to connect to. This should include the IP address of the smart host that you entered on the General property page of the Properties dialog box for your SMTPC (see Figure 13.20). My smart host has the address 192.168.1.123. I've entered 192.168.1.0 to indicate that any address in the 192.168.1.0 through 192.168.1.255 range can be reached through the demand-dial interface. If you need to be more specific, you can enter a narrower address range, even one address. Be sure to enter a mask for the address. The mask that I entered is appropriate for the IP address that I entered. You'll have to change the mask if you need to enter a narrower address range.

Leave the metric setting at 1. Be sure that Use This Route to Initiate Demand-Dial Connections is selected.

When you've finished configuring your static route, you can test you demand-dial interface. Open a command prompt on your Exchange server and enter the command ping [IP_address]. Here, [IP_address] is any IP address in the range that you set for your static route. Your computer will attempt to ping the address and fail, but you should hear it dialing the phone number that you set for the demand-dial interface. After the connection is made, you should be able to reissue the ping command and get a valid response.

Don't worry about the delay in connecting to the smart host's network affecting your SMTPC. The SMTPC will keep trying to connect to its smart host until the dial-up connection is completed. But why should you take my word for it? You're now ready to test your SMTPC, and the next section of this chapter is exactly the place to do so. See you there. Oh yeah, take a look at the sidebar "More E-mail Questions from Readers," if you want to use an SMTP mailbox to receive messages for your Exchange organization.

More E-mail Questions from Readers

Many reader problems with SMTP arise from a misunderstanding about the difference between Internet mailboxes and SMTP hosts when it comes to noncontinuous SMTP mail connections. An Internet mailbox—a mailbox supported by an ISP's own SMTP host computer—usually holds messages for one user. To access those messages, a user runs a POP3- or IMAP4-compliant Internet e-mail client, connects to the ISP's SMTP host, and reads the messages. On the other hand, an SMTP host is a collection of Internet mailboxes. SMTP hosts connect to each other to send and receive messages; as noted above, users connect to their Internet mailboxes to access the messages in them.

Internet mailboxes are incapable of receiving or sending messages on their own. They require the services of an SMTP host to receive messages for them. Internet e-mail clients, not Internet mailboxes, send messages through SMTP hosts.

Some readers want to set up noncontinuous connections, not between their Exchange server's SMTPC and an SMTP host, but between their SMTPC and a specific Internet mailbox residing on an SMTP host. With one exception that I discuss next, this isn't possible.

The exception? Microsoft, probably in response to messages similar to the ones that I get, devised a way for Exchange Server to use one or more POP3 Internet mailboxes sort of like an SMTP host. However, this solution, called Microsoft Exchange Connector for POP3 Mailboxes, is available only for Microsoft's Small Business Server version 4.5 or later, which supports up to 50 users. For more information on the Connector, check out the Web site http://www.microsoft.com/smallbusinessserver/deployadmin.

Did It Work?

Assuming that your SMTPVS or SMTPC can connect to the Internet by whatever means you configured, you can now test your setup. First, try sending mail to your Exchange mailbox from outside your Exchange system—for example, from an account that you've set up with an Internet Service Provider. Use a POP3 or IMAP4 mail client. Next, ask someone on the Internet to send mail to your Exchange mailbox's Internet mail address. For the record, it does no good to send a message from your Exchange mailbox to your Exchange mailbox's Internet address. The address is resolved inside your Exchange server and is delivered directly to your mailbox. The message never gets out to the Internet.

 TIP I have an e-mail account with an ISP. One of the main things that I do with it is test new SMTP virtual servers and SMTP connectors. I use an IMAP4 mail client connected to the ISP's network to send messages to myself on a new SMTPVS or SMTPC, and to receive messages that I send through the new SMTPVS or SMTPC from an Exchange client. For more on using IMAP4 clients, see the next chapter.

If everything works, you're home-free. If you have problems, make sure that all your SMTP-based DNS entries are correct. Use the `ping` command to `ping` key IP address and fully qualified domain names. Check to be sure that your SMTPVS or SMTPC is connecting to the Internet properly. If all else fails, track back through all the settings that you made for your SMTPVS or SMTPC. If you're working with an SMTP smart host, check with the smart host provider to be sure that all is well on its end. With a little perseverance, everything will fall in place and you'll be movin' mail on the Internet with the best of them.

Summary

TCP/IP, DNS, and SMTP are at the heart of Internet messaging. TCP/IP moves information within local area networks and across wide area networks. IP addresses are at the core of TCP/IP communications. IP addresses identify networked computers so that other computers can connect to them using TCP/IP and other Internet protocols. IP addresses such as 192.168.10.221 are not the stuff of good human communications. DNS allows humans to refer to IP addresses by warm and fuzzy names such as `mycomputer.fuzzyname.com` or `sendmymailherestupid.upodunk.edu`. SMTP hosts are the engines that move inbound and outbound Internet messages between SMTP e-mail clients and SMTP host computers. DNS helps SMTP hosts find the TCP/IP addresses of the SMTP hosts for specific Internet domains.

Internet messaging administrators are responsible for properly setting up TCP/IP, DNS, and SMTP within their Internet domains. This involves configuring IP addresses for computers exposed to the Internet, ensuring that SMTP hosts are correctly registered in DNS and are accessible to the outside world, and setting up internal SMTP host services so that SMTP messages can move smoothly and rapidly between internal and external hosts. When everything is working well, Internet messages flow around the world like the best Vermont maple syrup in the summer.

Exchange 2000 Server implements Internet messaging through SMTP virtual servers. SMTP virtual servers are SMTP hosts. When an SMTPVS is connected directly and continuously to the Internet, SMTP host services pretty much just happen. When continuous connectivity isn't available, an Exchange SMTP connector may be required.

SMTP virtual servers can be configured in a variety of ways, both at the Exchange server and at the Exchange organizational level. At the server level, security can be extensively controlled through a set of authentication, certification, and external domain name-based connection and service access limits. Size limits can be set for inbound and outbound messages. Additionally, limits can be set to control the traffic on both inbound and outbound connections between the SMTP virtual server and its fellow Internet-based servers.

At the Exchange organizational level, a number of parameters can be set that affect the operation of SMTP virtual servers. These parameters include a range of options for formatting messages and attachments to them, and determining whether certain types of message content can be generated by SMTP virtual servers in the organization.

The SMTP connector's major strength lies in the way that it adds the capability to connect an SMTP virtual server to specific SMTP hosts in very tightly controlled ways. More than anything else, the connector supports the use of SMTP smart hosts, SMTP hosts that send and receive Internet messages for other SMTP hosts. With a properly configured SMTP connector in place, it is possible for an SMTP virtual server to send its messages out through an SMTP smart host and use the smart host to retrieve messages sent to the smart host in the name of the SMTP virtual server. The SMTP connector can be configured to provide secure interaction between the SMTP virtual server and the smart host.

In addition to this functionality, the SMTP connector can be used to add valuable features to any SMTP virtual server. It can be used to limit access to SMTP services based on Windows 2000 accounts, and to limit the types and sizes of messages that can move though an SMTP virtual server.

Finally, Windows 2000 Server demand-dial interfaces, which are a part of Windows routing and remote access services, can be used to implement dial-up (noncontinuous) links to an SMTP smart host. With a properly set up SMTP connector, dial-up interface, and static route, a dial-up connection with the smart host is initiated whenever the SMTP virtual host has outbound messages to send or is ready to receive inbound messages.

Well, by now you should have Exchange SMTP host services up and running, or you should at least know how you're going to get them up and running. When everything is working as advertised, why not send me a message celebrating the event? You can find my e-mail address at the end of the Acknowledgements section at the front of this book.

Whew! That was a long chapter, and we still have one Internet-oriented chapter to go. In the next chapter, we'll continue our focus on Internet messaging as we look at Exchange 2000 Server's support for the POP3 and IMAP4 e-mail protocols, as well as Exchange's support for Outlook Web Access, Web browser-based access to Exchange mailboxes. We'll also devote some time to two other Exchange-relevant Internet protocols: the LDAP directory access protocol and the NNTP network news protocol.

CHAPTER 14

Managing Exchange 2000 Services for Internet Clients

This is one of the most exciting chapters in this book. Windows 2000 Server and Exchange 2000 Server come with a set of Internet-based client-server protocols that, taken together, raise it from a fairly tightly controlled, proprietary client/server product to an open and flexible electronic messaging system.

Each of the protocols that I'll discuss in this chapter is a client/server protocol. For each protocol, I'll cover both the server and client aspects of the protocol, in that order. However, before we tackle these protocols, let's spend some time talking about Exchange 2000 virtual servers and what Microsoft calls *front-end/back-end server configurations*.

Virtual Servers and Front-End/Back-End Servers

You can't effectively implement the Internet client/server protocols that I discuss in this chapter without an understanding of two key concepts:

- Exchange virtual servers
- Front-end/back-end servers

Virtual servers, upon which SMTP host services are built, also support the protocols that we'll be discussing here. Front-end/back-end servers allow users to access the Exchange 2000 environment with POP3, IMAP4, and and HTTP (Web browser-based) clients without having to reference the specific Exchange server where their mailboxes or public folders are located. They also relieve mailbox servers of authentication loads and can make enhanced firewall-based security easier to implement.

Exchange 2000 Virtual Servers Are Not Just for SMTP

Exchange 2000 Server implements the Internet protocols in the previous list using virtual servers that are quite similar to the SMTP virtual servers that we explored in the last chapter. If you haven't read last chapter's section "Setting Up and Managing SMTP," on SMTP virtual servers, I suggest that you do so now.

Computer and networking managers are constantly worrying about system uptime, and for good reason. Their jobs depend on reliable, available systems. You can do several things to ensure that your Internet virtual servers remain up and running 24 hours a day. You can manually monitor the services using the monitoring tools that I talked about back in Chapter 12, "Managing the Exchange Server Hierarchy and Core Components," and then do what you can to expediently restart stopped services. You also can supplement manual monitoring with a server-based self-monitoring system based on features of the Windows 2000 Server operating system.

To do this, find and right-click the service in the \Computer Management\Services and Applications\Services container. This opens the Properties dialog box for the service (see Figure 14.1). Tab over to the Recovery property page of the dialog box. You can use the Recovery page to tell the computer to do anything from attempt to restart the virtual server service to reboot itself. As you can see in Figure 14.1, you can specify a different action for each of three successive recovery events. You can also set other parameters, including a message that is sent to users informing them when a restart is about to occur.

FIGURE 14.1

Using the Recovery property page of the Properties dialog box for a service to set actions to be taken when a service is no longer available

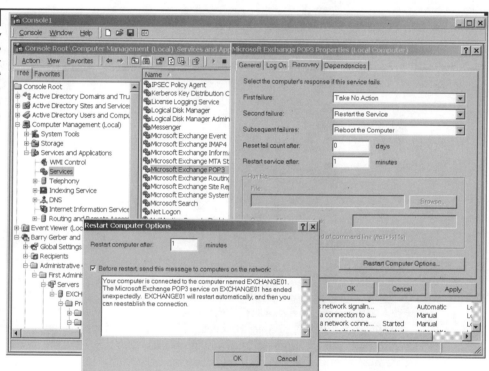

If you don't want to offer one of the services discussed in this chapter, you need to disable the service. On the General property page of the Properties dialog box for a service (see Figure 14.2), click Stop to stop the service and then select Disable from the Startup Type drop-down list. You can reset the Startup Type to Automatic at any time if you decide that you want to offer the service to your users.

FIGURE 14.2

Using the General property page of the Properties dialog box for a service to disable the service

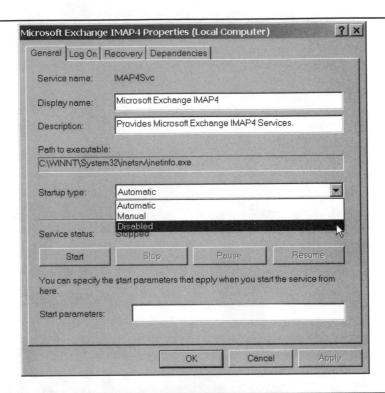

How Not to Disable an Internet Service

You can pause, stop, and start a virtual server that supports POP3, IMAP4, HTTP, NNTP, or SMTP services by right-clicking the virtual server in Exchange System Manager and selecting Stop, Pause, or Start. However, this isn't a good way to turn off a service. The service will remain stopped until you restart it, assuming that you didn't set restart parameters for the service on the Recovery property page of the Properties dialog box for the service (see Figure 14.1). However, the service will start right back up when the computer is rebooted.

Front-End/Back-End Exchange Server Configurations

In multiserver Exchange 5.5 environments accessing POP3, IMAP4, and HTTP services could be a royal pain. Generally, users had to point their e-mail and Web browser clients at the Exchange server that contained their mailboxes, so there was no way to provide a single fully qualified e-mail server domain name or Web server URL that worked for everyone in an organization. Instead, you had to give each user the specific fully qualified domain name or URL for the Exchange server where their mailboxes were stored. And, if you added or removed a server or moved a mailbox to a different server, you had to give the user a new e-mail server domain name and Web server URL.

With Exchange 2000, all has changed. You can configure an Exchange 2000 server to act as front-end server that all users contact for POP3, IMAP4, and HTTP services. The front-end server then relays or proxies requests from the user's client to the back-end server that contains the user's mailbox. The front-end server makes an LDAP query to determine the user's Exchange server.

Users are authenticated on both the front-end and the back-end server using either basic clear text or integrated Windows authentication. It's best to set authentication on the front-end server for all three supported protocols to basic clear text. That way, pretty near all POP3 and IMAP4 clients and Web browsers will work. Of course, if you know that all clients that will hit your server will be capable of authenticating using Windows 2000 security, select integrated Windows authentication for better security.

The front-end server's Information Store can remain, but the three protocols do not access it. For better performance, Microsoft recommends eliminating unnecessary components such as storage groups and routing groups, and disabling unnecessary services on front-end servers such as the Information Store service.

Exchange 2000 Server front-end/back-end topologies have two other advantages. You can use them to position back-end servers behind firewalls and to offload Secure Sockets Layer (SSL) encryption and decryption from back-end servers. The front-end server sits in front of the firewall and is configured so that the front-end server is the only computer that can contact back-end servers. SSL encryption/decryption is required for HTTP access to Exchange mailboxes and public folders. You can optionally use SSL encryption/decryption with POP3 and IMAP4 clients. When a client requests SSL encryption/decryption, your front-end server performs these tasks for back-end servers, letting back-end servers focus their energies on Information Store access.

Of course, front-end servers make sense only in multiserver Exchange environments with sufficient resources to dedicate a computer to front-end services. If you have but one Exchange server, you don't need to worry about front-end services, unless you want to put your servers behind a firewall or to reduce message SSL encryption/decryption loads on the server. If you have multiple Exchange servers and can't afford to dedicate a separate server to front-end services, you can do as we did with Exchange 5.5 and provide each user with a separate domain name and URL for their particular server.

Enabling a front-end server is easy. Find and right-click the server in Exchange System Manager, and select This Is a Front-End Server from the pop-up menu. (This option is available only when there are at least two Exchange servers in your Exchange organization.) Next restart the server; after it is up and running, remove all private and public and public stores.

At this point, we've installed only one Exchange server in our organization, so we can't implement a front-end/back-end server system right now. Just keep this very nice and most user-/administrator-friendly Exchange 2000 enhancement in mind as you read through this section. In the next chapter, "Installing and Managing Additional Exchange 2000 Servers," we'll get into implementing a front-end/back-end system.

Managing Post Office Protocol Version 3 (POP3) Messaging

Exchange Server includes full support for POP3. POP3 is a simple but effective way for a client to pull mail from an e-mail server. There's no fancy support for access to folders other than your Inbox or all the fine bells and whistles that you'll find in the Outlook 2000 client. However, if you're looking for a simple lightweight client that can function readily over the Internet, POP3 isn't a bad choice.

 NOTE IMAP4 is implemented in Exchange 2000 Server in much the same way as the POP3 protocol. I'll cover IMAP4 in the next section. I strongly suggest that you read this section even if you're not planning to implement POP3, though, because in the section on IMAP4 I'm going to discuss only the areas where POP3 and IMAP4 differ.

POP3 Setup: The Exchange Server Side

When you install Exchange Server, a default POP3 virtual server is installed. After installation (and assuming that you want to support POP3 e-mail client access to your Exchange Information Store), your job is to decide whether you need to change a set of default parameters to customize your POP3 environment to the needs of your organization and users.

You customize POP3 default parameters at the server level. You can override some POP3 defaults at the individual mailbox level.

Setting Up POP3 at the Server Level

The first step in setting up POP3 for your server is to find the Protocols container for your server (see Figure 14.3). The Protocols container includes six protocol containers.

Five of these are Internet protocols. We worked with SMTP in the last chapter, and we'll tackle X.400, the only non-Internet protocol, in Chapter 16, "Connecting to Other Foreign Messaging Systems." We'll cover the other protocols in this chapter. In addition, we'll talk about the Lightweight Directory Access Protocol, which is no longer an Exchange server component—it's part of Windows 2000 Server, but it is such a key piece of the electronic messaging puzzle that it deserves coverage in a book on Exchange server.

FIGURE 14.3

The server Protocols container and its six protocol subcontainers with the HTTP, IMAP4, NNTP, POP3, and SMTP default virtual servers exposed

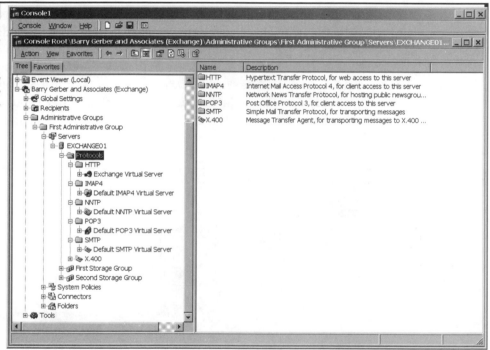

 NOTE I'm not going to extensively discuss the Default POP3 Virtual Server dialog box, and I'm going to include screen shots of dialog box property pages only when required for clarity. Why? Well, as I noted previously, Microsoft used the SMTP virtual server model to implement POP3 services. I already discussed SMTP virtual servers in Chapter 13, "Managing Exchange 2000 Internet Services." So, I just want to talk here about what's unique in relation to POP3 virtual servers. I'll discuss the POP3 virtual server property pages and call your attention to the appropriate explanatory text and figures in the section "Setting Up and Managing SMTP," in Chapter 13.

Right-click Default POP3 Virtual Server, and select Properties to open the Properties dialog box for the default POP3 virtual server. Except for the absence of the Message and Delivery property pages, the Properties dialog box for POP3 virtual servers looks a lot like the Properties dialog box for SMTP virtual servers (see Figure 13.4, back in Chapter 13). The POP3 dialog box includes a property page labeled Message Format. This page is shown in Chapter 13 in Figure 13.18, which deals with global SMTP virtual server message format settings.

General

The General property page of the POP3 dialog box is shown in Figure 14.4. You can link the virtual server to all unassigned IP addresses or to a specific IP address. You can also set advanced properties for your connection using the Advanced dialog box (see Figure 13.5 and related text in Chapter 13). On the POP3 Advanced dialog box, the SSL Port field replaces the Filter Enabled field (see Figure 14.4). The SSL port supports the encrypted transfer of logon information and messages between your Exchange server's POP3 virtual server and its clients. The SSL port is set automatically. For more on SSL, see the next section, "Access."

FIGURE 14.4
The General property page of the Default POP3 Virtual Server dialog box, with its Advanced dialog box exposed

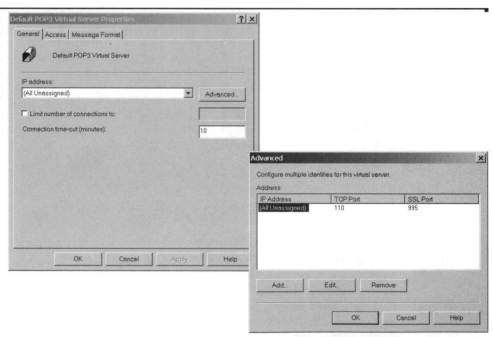

As with SMTP virtual servers, you can also limit the number of connections to your POP3 virtual server and set the number of minutes after which an inactive POP3 client connection times out and is disconnected. I suggest that you leave the default, which is no limit. Monitor POP3 activity with Windows 2000 Server's performance tool (Start menu ➤ Programs ➤ Administrative Tools ➤ Performance). If you see heavy POP3 activity, start by limiting the number of connections to some number less than that shown by the Performance tool. The default timeout setting of 10 minutes is really about as low as you should go, and idle clients really don't require much of your server's resources. Don't depend on timeouts to help you much with load problems.

 TIP You can manage connections to POP3 virtual servers using the Current Sessions subcontainer of the POP3 virtual server container. Within this subcontainer, you can view and terminate connections. This feature is also available for SMTP, IMAP4, and NNTP protocol services.

Access

The Access property page is the spitting image of the SMTP virtual server Access property page, shown in Figure 13.8, except that it doesn't include the Relay button because message relaying is a unique feature of SMTP hosts. The Authentication dialog box, also shown in Figure 13.8, doesn't include the anonymous authentication option because we're talking here about somebody's private mailbox, not a public SMTP host. The Authentication dialog box also lacks the TLS (advanced SSL) encryption option. You set up SSL for POP3 on the server side by installing a key certificate using the Certificate button in the Secure Communication area of the Access property page. You don't have to check anything in a check box. For more on SSL and certificates, see the section "Secure Communication" in Chapter 13.

You manage SSL in exactly the same way for IMAP4 clients as you do for POP3 clients. The other three protocols discussed in this chapter—HTTP, LDAP, and NNTP—also support SSL, but you configure SSL differently for these protocols. I'll talk about differences when I discuss these each of these protocols later in this chapter.

Message Format

You use the Message Format property page to set default message-encoding parameters and the type of character set to be used in messages, and to tell Exchange Server whether to send documents in Exchange's rich-text format. Except for two differences, the POP3 Message Format property page looks just like the one for SMTP virtual servers shown in Figure 13.18. The field Apply Content Settings to Non-MAPI Clients, and the MIME and non-MIME character set fields, neither of which makes sense for a POP3 server, are absent on the POP3 Message Format property page. As you'll see in the next section, "Customizing POP3 Support for a Mailbox," you can change the defaults that you set here on a mailbox-by-mailbox basis.

How Do Internet Clients Send E-mail?

POP3 clients (and IMAP4 clients, for that matter) pull incoming messages from POP3 (IMAP4) servers. However, POP3 and IMAP4 servers do not provide outgoing messaging services for their clients. SMTP hosts provide this service. In the last chapter, I talked about how Exchange 2000 SMTP virtual servers can provide outgoing SMTP host services (relay services) to Internet e-mail clients such as POP3 and IMAP4.

Customizing POP3 Support for a Mailbox

To customize POP3 support for a specific mailbox, find and right-click the user in \Active Directory Users and Computers\Users, and then select Properties from the pop-up menu. This opens the Properties dialog box for the user (see Figure 14.5). Tab over to the Exchange Advanced property page, and click Protocol Settings. The Protocols dialog box opens. Click POP3 and use the POP3 Protocol Details dialog box to change the POP3 settings for the mailbox. In Figure 14.5, I'm viewing POP3 properties for my mailbox.

FIGURE 14.5

Using the POP3 Protocol Details dialog box to manage POP3 properties for a mailbox

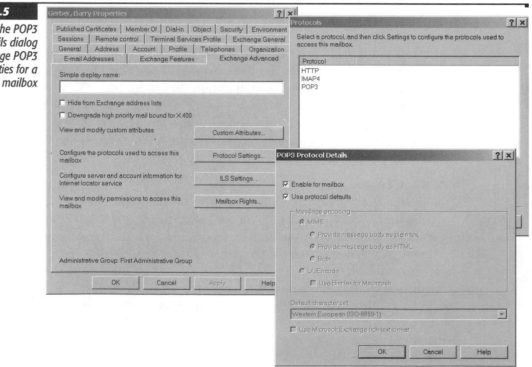

To disable POP3 services for a mailbox, deselect Enable for Mailbox. To change the default message formatting information, which you can see even though it's grayed out, deselect Use Protocol Defaults and set the encoding, character set, and rich-text format options that you want to use for the mailbox. You've seen all the options on the POP3 Protocol Details dialog box, and you should be clear on what they are and when you might want to change them. So, that's all for managing POP3 protocols at the mailbox level.

POP3 Setup: The Client Side

I've always thought of POP3 clients as one of life's little miracles. You set some basic parameters and tell the client to check for mail on your POP3 server, and your mail shows up. I'm sure that building sophisticated POP3 servers and clients is quite a task, but using them is a snap. Let's get some clients configured so that you can experience the miracle.

Start with Microsoft's Outlook Express Client

Although you can use any POP3-compliant Internet mail client to access your Exchange Server's POP3 server, you'll find that Microsoft's Outlook Express client is not only one of the best, but it's also enabled to support all the Internet protocols that I cover in this chapter. I strongly suggest that you use the Outlook Express client for the exercises in this book, even if you plan to use another one later.

The Outlook Express client comes with Microsoft Internet Explorer versions 4 and 5. You can download the latest version of IE from Microsoft's Web site, www.microsoft.com.

Getting Connected to an Exchange Server-Based POP3 Server

First you need to set up your POP3 client to connect to an Exchange Server-based POP3 server. Before you start, you'll need to gather the following information:

- Name of the sender to be displayed in the From field of POP3 messages
- Your Windows 2000 account user logon name
- The password for your Windows 2000 account
- Your Exchange mailbox alias name
- Your Windows 2000 or pre-Windows 2000 domain name
- Your POP3 e-mail address, which is your Exchange Server Internet mail (SMTP) address

- The IP address or name of your POP3 server (for incoming messages)
- The IP address or name of your SMTP server (for outgoing messages)

Let's take a look at how each of these is used to set up a POP3 client.

Outlook Express makes it pretty easy to set up a POP3 client; follow along in Figure 14.6. Open Outlook Express's Tools menu, and select Accounts. On the resultant Internet Accounts dialog box, tab over to the Mail page and click Add. Select Mail from the little menu that opens. This brings up the Internet Connection Wizard, which takes you through the steps of adding a POP3 or IMAP4 Internet mail account.

FIGURE 14.6

Entering a name to be displayed in each sent message as the message's sender

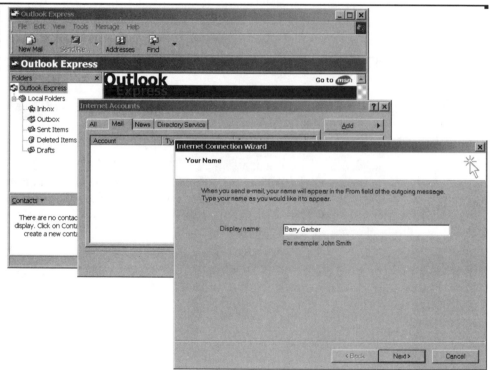

As you can see in Figure 14.6, the first thing you need to enter is the name of the sender that is displayed in the From field of each message that you send. I've cleverly chosen Barry Gerber. Click Next, and you're asked to enter your Internet e-mail address (see Figure 14.7). This is the Internet address for your Exchange server mailbox. Mine is bgerber@bgerber.com.

FIGURE 14.7

*Entering the SMTP
e-mail address for an
Exchange mailbox*

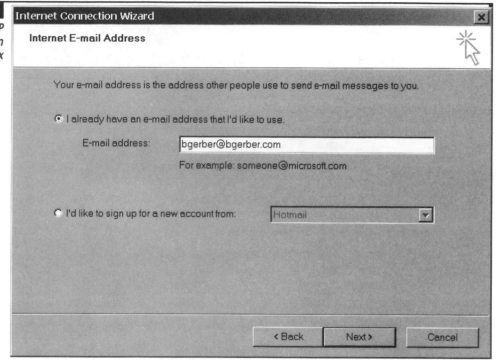

Click Next to select the kind of incoming mail server that you're setting up an account for (POP3 or IMAP4), and to enter names of the servers that will handle incoming and outgoing mail for your client (see Figure 14.8). Your incoming mail server name is the IP address or Internet domain name of the Exchange server where your mailbox resides. POP3 server services must be running on this server. Your outgoing mail server name is the IP address or Internet domain name of a server running SMTP mail services, a server that can send your mail out to the Internet for you. Although you could use any SMTP mail server, if you're running a Windows 2000 SMTP virtual server, you need look no further.

FIGURE 14.8

Selecting an e-mail server type (POP3 or IMAP4) and entering e-mail server names

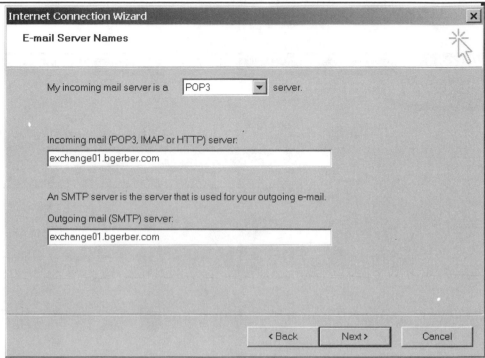

Note in Figure 14.8 that I've entered the fully qualified domain name for the Exchange server exchange01.bgerber.com that runs both POP3 services and Windows 2000 SMTP virtual services. You can use a different name for the SMTP server side of things—for example, I could have used mail.exchange01.bgerber.com. Just be sure to register the name with an accredited registrar. Check out http://www.internic.net for more information.

In Figure 14.9, I've moved on to the next Internet Connection Wizard page, where I've entered my POP account name and password, which are my Windows 2000 logon username and password. It's this simple if you've accepted the default when mailbox-enabling your Windows 2000 account and allowed your mailbox alias to be set to the same value as your logon username. If your Windows 2000 logon username is different from your mailbox alias, you need to enter your POP3 username in the following format: Windows_2000_user_account_name\mailbox_alias_name. You can find your logon account name on the Account property page of the Properties dialog box for your Windows account, which is in the \Active Directory Users and Computers\Users container. Your mailbox alias is on the Exchange General property page of the same dialog box.

FIGURE 14.9

*Entering information to
log onto a POP3
mailbox*

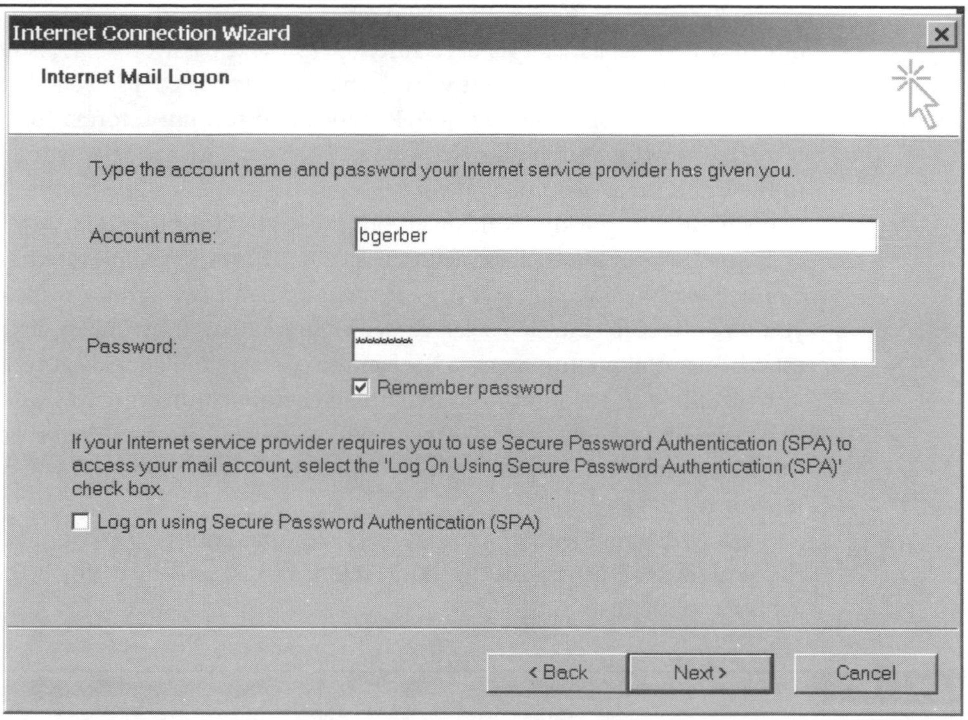

How Exchange 2000 Server POP3 Authentication Works

You're authenticated to access your Exchange mailbox with a POP3 client in a number of ways. First, Exchange Server attempts to authenticate your use of your mailbox just as it would if you were using a standard Outlook client. That is, it attempts to authenticate you through the Windows 2000 security system. It needs to find your Windows 2000 domain and account name, and finally to validate that you've entered the correct password for that account. To speed up the authentication process if your Windows 2000 system includes a large number of domains, you can add the name of the domain where your Windows 2000 account resides in the form Windows_2000_domain_name\POP3_account_name (for example, bgerber.com\ bgerber). Next Exchange Server needs to check to be sure that your Windows 2000 account is authorized to access the mailbox. Finally, it must verify that your mailbox is enabled for POP3 services.

Secure Password Authentication (SPA) refers to a set of authentication protocols, any one of which can add a level of security to clear-text passwords. SPA is not the same as SSL. You don't need it to access your Exchange server's POP3 server.

When you finish entering the POP3 server and account information, click Next to move to the wizard's Friendly Name page. Here you enter the name that is displayed in the list of mail accounts that you've set up. As you'll see in a minute, the friendly name helps you quickly locate an account that you want to modify.

If you haven't set up a connection option for Internet Explorer, the next Internet Connection Wizard page you'll see is the one that lets you tell Outlook Express how you'll connect to your POP3 server (see Figure 14.10). If by LAN or an already-established dial-up link to an ISP, select that option and click Next to move to the last wizard page. If you want to dial up just before connecting to your POP3 server, select the first option, and the wizard will guide you through the process of setting up the parameters for your dial-up session. Finish that page, and you're on to the last wizard page.

Click Finish on the last wizard page. Notice that your new account is now listed on the Mail page of the Internet Accounts dialog box. Leave the dialog box open; we'll get back to it in a minute.

FIGURE 14.10

Selecting the type of connection to be used to access a POP3 server

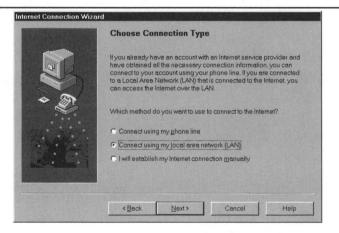

Other POP3 Client Settings

Various POP3 clients enable you to set a range of other parameters. One of the most important involves whether you leave copies of your messages on the POP3 server. To better understand this option, you need to understand that POP3 clients download each message that is on the server. If you don't leave copies of messages on the POP3 server, they aren't available when you access them with a different client on the same or a different computer.

Your POP3 server is also your Exchange server. If you don't choose to leave a copy of all messages downloaded by your POP3 client on the server, you won't be able to access them with another POP3 client or with the Outlook client. Whether you leave copies depends on how you work. If you're going to work from one place with the POP3 client, you can suck all your messages down into that client and deal with them there. If you're going to use a POP3 client when you're away from the office and an Outlook client when in the office, you'll want to be sure to leave a copy on the server.

To leave a copy of messages on your Exchange server, you'll need to turn back to the Internet Accounts dialog box that you left open a bit ago (see Figure 14.11).

Highlight the friendly name of your account—mine is exchange01.bgerber.com— and click Properties to bring up the (POP3) Properties dialog box, shown in Figure 14.12.

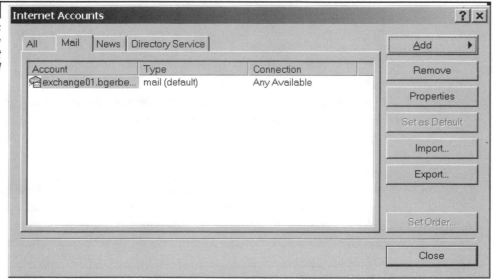

FIGURE 14.11

The Internet Accounts dialog box, with a newly created account listed

FIGURE 14.12

The (POP3) Properties dialog box, with the Advanced property page displayed

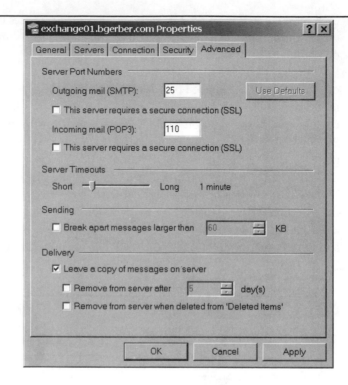

The first three pages of the dialog box contain information that you entered with the Internet Connection Wizard. You use the Security page to install certificates for digitally signing messages and for encrypting them. The Outlook Express docs do a pretty good job of explaining certificates or directing you to Web sources for more information.

In Figure 14.12 down in the Delivery area, I've told Outlook Express to leave a copy of my messages on my Exchange server when it downloads messages to my POP3 client. Because I want to control what happens to my messages with my regular Outlook client when I'm connected in the office, I didn't check either of the Remove options in the Delivery area.

I'll leave it to you to explore these and other client settings offered by Outlook Express or your favorite POP3 client.

Did It Work?

Figure 14.13 shows the rewards of all the server- and client-side configuring that we've been through. As you can see, we're looking at a message sent to me by Barry Gerber and Associates money maven, Jane Dough. It was sent from her standard Outlook client and includes a couple fonts that I can see in my Outlook Express client because, in this case, my Exchange server's POP3 server is configured to send me messages in HTML format. Very nice.

FIGURE 14.13

Viewing an HTML-formatted message with Microsoft Outlook Express

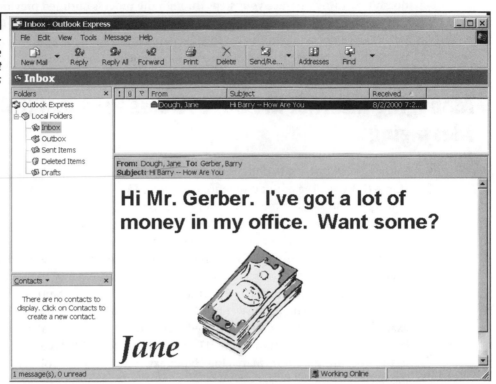

 WARNING Don't confuse the POP3 Sent and Deleted Items folders with the folders of the same name on your Exchange server. The POP3 versions of these folders contain only messages that you've sent and received with your Outlook Express POP3 client. Because POP3 lets you access only your Exchange server-based Inbox, messages sent with or deleted from your standard Outlook client don't show up in your POP3 client's Sent and Deleted Items folders. If you want that kind of fancy stuff, then consider IMAP4.

I'm going to leave it to you to figure out how to send and retrieve messages with your POP3 client. It's easy and, hey, what's life without new things to learn?

Troubleshooting POP3 Problems

Generally, I've found POP3 to be one of the easiest and least vexing protocols of all to use. If you do have trouble, ensure that your network connection is working; if that doesn't fix things, retrace your steps through the process outlined previously. If you still can't get POP3 to work, there are three major troubleshooting tools for POP3 connections: protocol logging, event logging, and counters for NT's Performance Monitor. See the Exchange Server documentation for help using these.

Managing Internet Message Access Protocol (IMAP4) Messaging

Exchange 2000 Server includes support for the Internet Message Access Protocol version 4 (IMAP4). The major difference between IMAP4 and POP3 is that IMAP4 lets you access messages in folders in your Exchange mailbox and in Exchange public folders by subscribing to specific folders. With both protocols, you can permanently download messages to your local computer and view them. IMAP4 also lets you view messages without permanently downloading them, much like the standard Outlook client. In fact, the main attraction of IMAP4 lies in its capability to provide users with access to messages in folders in a manner very much like the standard Outlook client. The IMAP4 client isn't an answer to all standard Outlook client users' dreams. For example, it doesn't give users formatted access to their Outlook calendars or journals. For that, you'll have to turn to the HTTP-based Outlook Web Access client discussed in the upcoming section "Managing Hypertext Transport Protocol (HTTP) Web Browser-Based Messaging."

IMAP4 setup is very much like POP3 setup on the server and client sides, so I'll just call your attention to the differences between the two protocols as I discuss IMAP4.

IMAP4 Setup: The Exchange Server Side

As with POP3, we'll look at your IMAP4 configuration options at the server and individual mailbox levels. As I promised earlier, I'll discuss only differences between POP3 and IMAP4 setup.

Setting Up IMAP4 at the Server Level

In Exchange System Manager, find the default IMAP4 virtual server in your Exchange server's Protocols container, and double-click it. Select Properties to open the Properties dialog box for the virtual server (see Figure 14.14). Only two of the property pages on the dialog box are significantly different from the POP3 pages. Let's take a quick look at these two pages, the General and Message Format property pages.

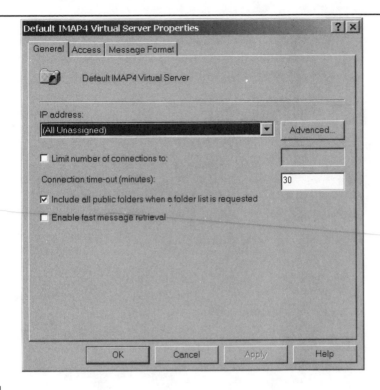

FIGURE 14.14

The General property page of the Default IMAP4 Virtual Server Properties dialog box, one of two pages that differ from the pages for POP3 setup

General

Just like the POP3 General property page, the IMAP4 General page, shown in Figure 14.14, lets you specify IP addresses, advanced settings, connection limits, and a time-out value for inactive connections for your virtual server. Because of the nature of the IMAP4 protocol, however, the IMAP General page has two additional options.

Because they can access all the folders on an IMAP4-compatible server that a user has rights to, IMAP clients need information about available folders. To get this information, the clients make requests for lists of folders. Some IMAP4 clients suffer from performance problems when receiving lists with large numbers of public folders. If you're using such a client, to access your Exchange server, deselect Include All Public Folders When a Folder List Is Requested to eliminate public folders from folder lists sent by the IMAP4 server to the client.

An IMAP4 server also sends information about messages in folders to its clients. To speed up this process, Exchange Server's IMAP4 server can estimate message size. Some clients require exact message size information. If your IMAP4 client is one of these, ensure that Enable Fast Message Retrieval is deselected so that the IMAP4 server sends exact message sizes to its clients.

Message Format

IMAP4 supports only MIME encoding. Unlike POP3, it doesn't support the older UUencode standard. That explains the absence of the UUencode option on the IMAP4 Message Format property page (see Figure 14.15).

FIGURE 14.15

The Message Format property page of the IMAP4 (Mail) Site Defaults Properties dialog box

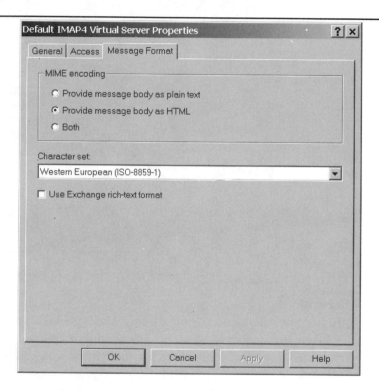

Customizing IMAP4 Support for a Mailbox

I've already discussed the IMAP4 options that you can set for mailboxes. So, let me close this section on server-side IMAP4 setup by noting that you can adjust for some of the differences in IMAP4 clients that I mentioned at the mailbox level. For example, if specific users are running a client that demands precise message size information, you can deselect the Fast Message Retrieval option on the mailboxes of those users.

IMAP4 Setup: The Client Side

With the exception of choosing IMAP4 in the drop-down list on the E-mail Server Names page of the Outlook Express Internet Connection Wizard (see Figure 14.7), the initial setup of an IMAP4 account is no different from the setup of a POP3 account.

The only difference on the account Properties dialog box is on the IMAP4 property page. As you can see in Figure 14.16, you can do the following:

- Set a root folder path for the folders that you access with your IMAP4 client
- Choose whether your IMAP4 client should ask its IMAP4 server to check all folders for new messages
- Specify whether two special folders, Sent Items and Drafts, and their contents are to be stored on your IMAP4 server

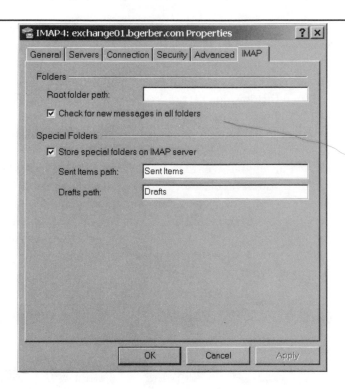

An IMAP4 client can tell an IMAP4 server where in your folder hierarchy it should begin accessing folders. For example, if I entered {exchange01.bgerber.com}INBOX into the Root folder path field shown in Figure 14.16, Outlook Express would display only my Exchange Server Inbox, and I wouldn't even see any of the other folders on the server. If you want to see all those folders, leave this field blank.

A new message is any message that shows up in a folder, whether it was received there as a new e-mail message or you dragged it to the folder. To be sure that you see new messages in all folders, ensure that the option Check for New Messages for All Folders is selected.

You want to see the same items in your Sent Items and Drafts folders whether you are using your IMAP4 or Outlook client. To keep these in sync, be sure to select the option Store Special Folders on IMAP4 Server.

 WARNING A limitation in the IMAP4 protocol prevents you from accessing folders with forward slashes (/) in their names. The only fix is to rename any folders with the "offending" character.

When you're finished setting up your new IMAP4 client, click Finish on the wizard. Next you're asked whether you want to download a list of folders on your IMAP4 server. Responding in the affirmative initiates a connection to your IMAP4 server and a download of available mailbox and public folders.

When the download is finished, you'll see a dialog box like the one in Figure 14.17. You use this dialog box to view the folders to which you've subscribed. By default, you have subscriptions to only your Inbox and the Sent Items and Drafts folders. That's why these folders have a little icon in front of them in Figure 14.17. You can always tab over to the page labeled Visible in Figure 14.17 to see the folders to which you have subscribed. To subscribe to a folder, select it, as I've selected Public Folders in Figure 14.17, and click Show. You must click each folder that you want to subscribe to and then click Show. Clicking the folder Public Folders and then clicking Show subscribes to only the folder Public Folders, not to any of its subfolders. Click OK when you're done, and Outlook Express opens with your IMAP4 connection in place (see Figure 14.18).

FIGURE 14.17

Using the Show/Hide IMAP Folders dialog box to subscribe to specific Exchange server folders

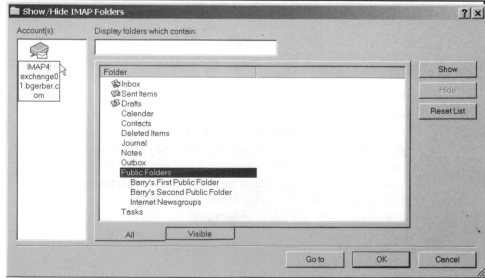

Did It Work?

Notice in Figure 14.18 that both my POP3 and IMAP4 client connections are available, with POP3 in the top half of the left pane and IMAP4 in the bottom half of the left pane. If you set up your POP3 and IMAP4 clients in the same copy of Outlook Express, your Outlook Client should look a lot like the one in Figure 14.18.

Also take a long look at those nice buttons and the drop-down list at the top of the right pane in Figure 14.18. The buttons allow you to do the following:

Synchronize button   Initiate a synchronization of folders on your IMAP4 client with folders on your Exchange server (based on parameters set using the Settings drop-down list)

IMAP Folders button   Subscribe to folders on your Exchange server (opens the dialog box shown in Figure 14.17)

Settings drop-down list   Select a synchronization option for each folder (Don't Synchronize, All Messages, New Messages Only, Headers Only)

FIGURE 14.18

Outlook Express includes features that make it easy for users to manage their IMAP4 clients.

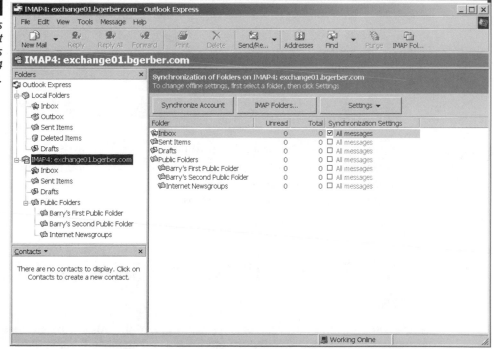

In Figure 14.19, you can see my favorite message from Jane Dough in all its HTML-enhanced glory.

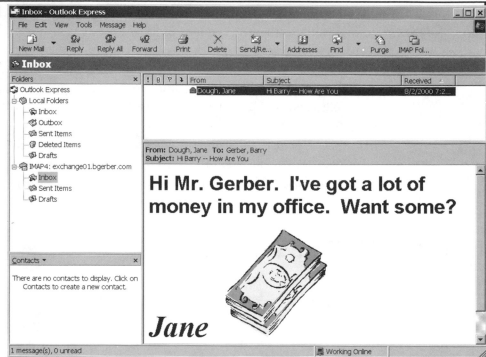

FIGURE 14.19

Using IMAP4 client support included in Outlook Express to view a message stored in an Exchange Server Inbox

Now, go ahead and play around in your IMAP4 folders. Note that all the folders are a direct reflection of the folders on your Exchange server. If you have any problems with IMAP4, take a look at the little troubleshooting section in the previous discussion of POP3 clients in the section "POP3 Setup: The Client Side."

That's it for IMAP4. I leave the rest to you, your brain, your eyes, and your fingers. Have fun.

IMAP4 and My Palm Vx PDA

My current PDA is a Palm Vx unit. It's connected to the Internet by a wireless Minstrel modem. When I'm away from the office or my home, I use the IMAP4 functionality of Palm, Inc.'s MultiMail Pro to read and send e-mail using my Palm Vx. Although the modem runs at 9.6Kbps, most of the time performance is good enough for the majority of the messages that I work with on the road.

Managing Hypertext Transport Protocol (HTTP) Messaging

Exchange 2000 Server's Web browser-based technology for accessing mailboxes and other folders is very different from the technology used in Exchange 5.x server. This is so even though both the 5.x and 2000 versions of the technology answer to the name *Outlook Web Access* (OWA). The good news is that Exchange 2000's new technology is more stable and reliable, and capable of handling larger numbers of users. So far, there doesn't appear to be any bad news.

Exchange 5.5 was cobbled together using Microsoft's HTML-oriented Active Server Pages (ASP) for communications between a client and an Exchange server's Internet Information Server (IIS). Exchange 5.5's OWA used Microsoft's Messaging Application Programming Interface (MAPI) and Collaboration Data Objects (CDO) to communicate with the Exchange server's information store. In essence, OWA was a part of Internet Information Server. MAPI-based access was slow, and it limited the number of users who could use the service at the same time.

Exchange 2000's OWA implementation takes a very different approach. Clients still use HTTP, although not ASP, to communicate with an IIS. However, the IIS accesses Exchange information stores directly, without help from MAPI or CDO. If the store is on the same server as the IIS, access is direct and fast. If the store is on a back-end computer and the IIS computer is serving as the front-end computer, communications are still quite fast and use HTTP.

OWA 2000 allows users to access their mailboxes and public folders using an Internet browser that is compliant with the HTML 3.2 and JavaScript standards. Both Microsoft Internet Explorer 4 and later, and Netscape 4 and later, meet this specification. Internet Explorer 5.x (IE 5.x) and later supports Dynamic HTML and Extensible Markup Language (XML), which allows for faster client-side performance and such very cool features as expandable folder hierarchies, drag-and-drop capabilities, HTML composition, right-click menu options, toolbar tips, and Kerberos authentication. Kerberos authentication is available only when IE 5.x runs on Windows 2000.

The newest OWA client doesn't support a number of features included in the standard Outlook client. For example, it doesn't include support for offline use, tasks, the Outlook journal, Outlook rules, copying between private and public folders, auto-dialing of contact phone numbers, spell checking, and reminders. Still, OWA does provide enough functionality to make Web browser-based e-mail access both easy and fun. You could do worse than to standardize on OWA as your users' one and only remote e-mail access client. If you can live with its limits, you might even go one step further and make it your local standard as well.

Support for OWA is installed when you install Exchange 2000 Server. As with support for other Internet services, OWA is one of the basic Exchange 2000 Server, messaging and collaboration services. Unlike with Exchange 5.5 Server, OWA is installed automatically, and you can't choose not to install it or to install it later.

OWA 2000 User Connectivity Is a Dream

If everything I've said so far about Exchange 2000 Server's OWA has failed to excite you, I know that this will. Based on my experience to date, the security and related mailbox access problems that plagued OWA 5.5 have been eliminated in OWA 2000. From a connectivity perspective, OWA 2000 works as advertised right out of the box. For example, there is no need for users to have rights to log on locally for the Exchange server where their mailboxes are located.

Outlook Web Access Management: The Server Side

Outlook Web Access just works. There's nothing you have to do to set it up, although you do have some configuration options at the server and mailbox levels. Unlike the other Exchange virtual servers, you can perform most OWA setup functions with either Exchange System Manager or the Internet Information Server administrator.

Setting Up OWA at the Exchange 2000 Server Level

The default HTTP or OWA virtual server is different from other Exchange virtual servers. Look at Figure 14.20 for a graphic indicator of this difference. First, notice that the default HTTP virtual server is labeled Exchange Virtual Server and sports a different icon than the other virtual servers. That's just the cosmetics. Try to right-click the server's icon and select Properties from the pop-up menu. A dialog box opens telling you that you have to administer the virtual server's settings using Internet Information Server's administrator.

"Huh?" I can hear you saying. There is a method to Microsoft's apparent madness, but it will take a while to explain.

FIGURE 14.20

The HTTP virtual server (Exchange Virtual Server) with the General property page of the server's Exchange virtual directory exposed

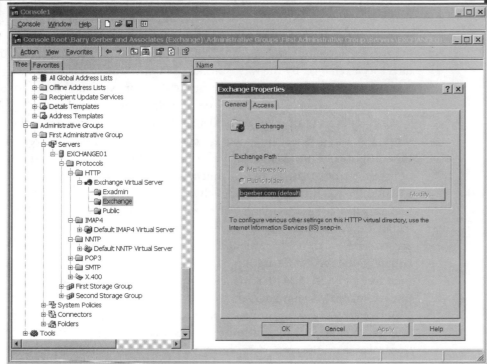

The default HTTP virtual server supports Web browser access to mailboxes, public folders, and certain administrative functions on your Exchange server. Take a look at the virtual server's virtual directories in Figure 14.20. They're labeled Exadmin, Public, and Exchange. These virtual directories represent the three basic types of Web browser access that you have to your Exchange server:

Exadmin   Used by Exchange System Manager itself to access mailboxes and public folders (can also be used by custom applications)

Public   Provides access to public folders

Exchange   Provides access to mailboxes

The three virtual directories are not Exchange 2000 Server virtual directories; they are Web server virtual directories that are part of the Internet Information Server environment. Web server virtual directories map physical directories, shares on other computers, or URLs on a server in such a way that Web browser users can include virtual directory names in URLs. For example, to get to an Exchange server mailbox, you use the URL `http://SERVER_NAME/Exchange/MAILBOX_NAME`, as in `http://exchange01.bgerber.com/Exchange/bgerber`. *Exchange* refers to the virtual directory Exchange. By the way, you can use upper or lower case, so *exchange* is as good as *Exchange*. I'll show you how virtual directories work in the section "Managing OWA at the Internet Information Server Level," later in this chapter.

Although you must manage the default HTTP virtual server using the IIS administrator, you can perform some management tasks on the default server's virtual directories (right-click on a virtual directory and select Properties). At first glance, it may not seem that you can do all that much. As you can see on the right side of Figure 14.20, there's nothing that you can change on the General property page for the virtual directory labeled Exchange. The Exchange Path field was set and locked down on installation of Exchange 2000 Server. The Exchange virtual directory is for mailbox access, so the path is set for mailboxes in my domain, bgerber.com. The Exadmin and Public virtual directories are similarly locked down and point to paths that support their functionality. I'll talk more about these paths in the section "Managing OWA at the Internet Information Server Level."

Tab over to the Access property page of the Exchange virtual directory dialog box (see Figure 14.21). Okay, you control freaks, here's something to control. The Access Control area on the property page lets you select rights that enable or disable what can be done within the virtual directory. Rights include these:

Read   Users can read or download files or directories and their properties.

Write   Users can upload files and their properties, or change content in write-enabled files.

Script source access   Users can access the source code for scripts (read or write permissions must be selected).

Directory browsing   Users can see a list of files and subdirectories, but they must name the file or subdirectory because they do not get full browsing rights to the virtual directory and all its subdirectories.

As Figure 14.21 shows, all access rights are granted as they are required for OWA to function properly.

FIGURE 14.21

The Access property page of the HTTP virtual server's Exchange virtual directory

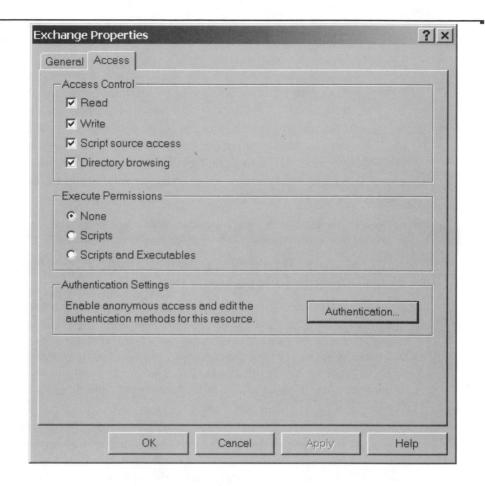

Execute permissions determine the kinds of files that do something that a user can access. Here's a quick look at execute permissions:

None   Users can access only HTML or image files.

Scripts   Users can access JavaScript, ASP, and other types of scripts.

Scripts and Executables   Users can access scripts and standard executable files (such as DestroyMyComputer.EXE).

OWA requires only access on the user's part to HTML and image files, so the option None is selected.

By default, the Authentication methods for access to virtual directories are basic clear text and integrated Windows authentication. You can enable anonymous authentication—although you should do so only if you really know what you're doing—by clicking Authentication and selecting the option from the Authentication Methods dialog box. For more on anonymous authentication and the anonymous account, see the section "NNTP Setup: The Server Side," later in this chapter.

You can change access settings on the Public virtual directory's dialog box. However, you can't modify access settings on the dialog box for the Exadmin virtual directory. Administrative access to mailboxes and public folders is something to be tightly guarded, so no changes are allowed, although, as you'll see in a bit, you can change these settings on the Internet Information Server side.

General Rule: Don't Mess with Default HTTP Virtual Server Virtual Directory Properties

I decided to discuss virtual directory properties in this section not because I want you to dash off and change them, but for three other reasons. First, I want to show you what is available in Exchange for accessing and managing HTTP virtual servers and their virtual directories. Second, I want to prepare you for what you're going to see in a minute or so as we move into the IIS side of OWA. And, third, I want you to know something about managing virtual directories in Exchange in the unlikely event that you need to create additional HTTP virtual servers.

Notice that nowhere here do I say anything about changing default HTTP virtual server properties. Unless you know Exchange 2000 Server and Internet Information Server like you know the back of your hand, you can only mess things up. For example, granting anonymous access to the Exchange virtual directory enables anyone to access any mailbox on your Exchange server.

Customizing OWA Support for a Mailbox

You have only one configuration option at the individual mailbox level. You can disable OWA for a mailbox. By default, OWA is enabled.

Managing OWA at the Internet Information Server Level

Now let's look at HTTP virtual server management through the IIS manager. If you're working on your Exchange server, you can find the IIS administrator snap-in in the container \Computer Management (Local)\Services and Applications\Internet

Information Services. You can also find the snap-in at \Start menu\Programs\
Adminstrative Tools\Internet Services Manager. If you want to manage your
Exchange server's IIS from another computer that is running IIS, you can add the
Internet Information Service snap-in and then connect to your Exchange server's IIS.
To do this, right-click Internet Information Service and select Connect from the pop-
up menu. Then enter the name of your Exchange server in the resultant Connect to
Computer dialog box.

Figure 14.22 shows a basic view of my IIS administrator. Notice the three virtual
directories Public, Exchange, and Exadmin. These are the same virtual directories that
you saw in Exchange System Manager under the default HTTP server.

FIGURE 14.22

*An Exchange HTTP vir-
tual server's virtual
directories, as seen in
the Internet
Information Services
plug-in*

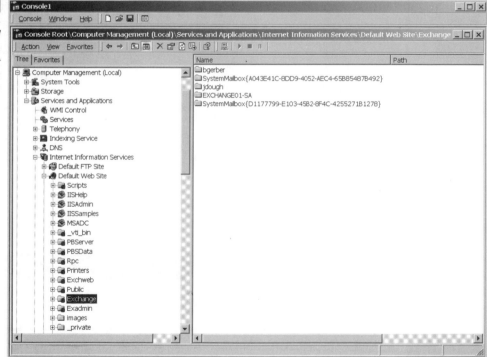

In Figure 14.23, you can see an expanded view of the three OWA virtual directories.
Notice all the stuff that's in those directories. It's everything you'd see if you looked
into the Information Store on your server using Exchange System Manager. That
shouldn't come as too much of a surprise, given that these virtual directories are
designed to provide Web browser access to the Information Store.

Figure 14.23 makes it easier to see why `http://exchange01.bgerber.com/exchange/bgerber` takes me to my mailbox via my Web browser. In a similar vein, `http://exchange01.bgerber.com/public/barry's first public folder` lets me access my first achievement in public folder creation. And, if I'm in an administrative mood, `http://exchange01.bgerber.com/bgerber.com/mbx/bgerber` lets me manage my mailbox.

FIGURE 14.23

An expanded view of an Exchange HTTP virtual server's virtual directories

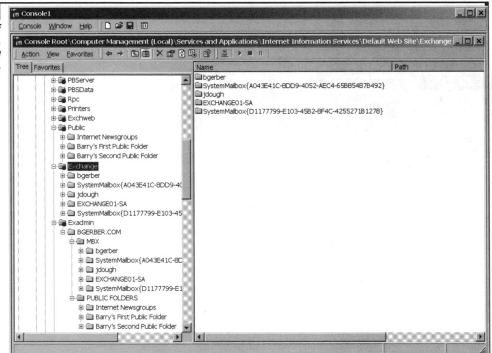

 NOTE Notice the virtual directory labeled Exchweb in Figures 14.22 and 14.23. That's where key OWA support files reside. You don't have to worry about it; I just want you to know what it's for because its name implies that it has something to do with Exchange Server.

Okay, now let's look at the properties for these virtual directories. I'm going to move pretty quickly through these properties because there's a lot more here than an

Exchange administrator needs to worry about and because Windows 2000 IIS management is the stuff of long and winding books. If you want to get into IIS management, you'll find just what you're looking for in Microsoft's *Internet Information Server 5.0 Documentation* (Microsoft Press, 1999). *Mastering Windows 2000 Server*, by Mark Minasi, et al. (Sybex, 2000), also contains a good basic section on IIS 5.0.

Let's open the Properties dialog box for the Exchange virtual directory. Right-click the virtual directory labeled Exchange, and select Properties. In Figure 14.24, you can see how, on the Virtual Directory property page, the virtual directory name is tied to a physical directory on an Exchange server. The local path points to the physical directory on my Exchange server named M:\bgerber.com\MBX. Remember the M: drive. It's a special mapping that Exchange server creates on installation so that you can access mailboxes and public folders in My Computer's file browser or even using a command prompt. Take a moment to look at the M: drive on your Exchange server using the My Computer file and folder browser.

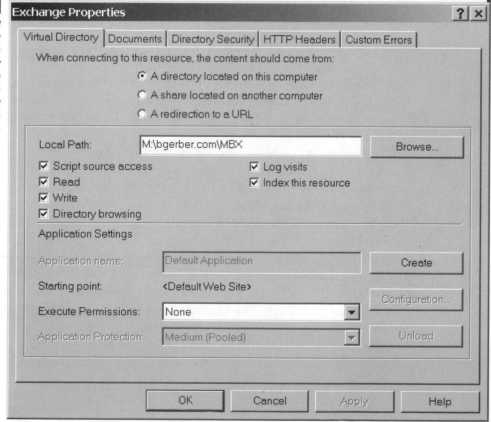

FIGURE 14.24

The Properties dialog box for the Exchange virtual directory, with its Virtual Directory property page exposed, as seen in the Internet Information Services snap-in

It should come as no surprise that the virtual directory Public ties to the physical directory M:\bgerber.com\Public Folders. The virtual directory Exadmin ties to \\.\BackOfficeStorage, which, in my case, ties to M:\bgerber.com, the root of my Exchange server's mailbox and public folder store.

If you need a refresher on the M: drive, check out the section "Backing Up Exchange 2000 Server," in Chapter 8, "Installing Exchange 2000 Server," and the section "Managing Public Stores," Chapter 12.

Except for a few fields, the rest of the Virtual Directory property page should look familiar to you. It includes the access control and execute permissions that you saw on the dialog box for this virtual directory in Exchange System Manager (see Figure 14.21). Yep, you can set these properties here or in Exchange System Manager. Authentication settings aren't on this page; they're over on the Directory Security property page. That's also where you enable SSL encryption.

Each virtual directory and subdirectory that you see in the Internet Information Services snap-in has a Properties dialog box just like the one in Figure 14.24. Just for fun, you might want to roam around the IIS snap-in and check out the permissions that are granted and the directory mappings for some of the virtual directories.

Outlook Web Access (HTTP) Setup: The Client Side

Client-side setup is a breeze. Just fire up your Web browser and specify that you want to connect to the Internet Information server or front-end server that supports your Exchange server plus /exchange. I use the URL http://exchange01.bgerber.com/exchange to connect.

When you run IE 5.x on Windows 2000 and you're logged into the Windows 2000 domain/account that has access to your Exchange mailbox, you're automatically authenticated for access to your Exchange 2000 server. The Exchange user interface opens right up. If this is not true, you'll see the Enter Network Password dialog box, shown in Figure 14.25. In Figure 14.25, I've entered my Windows 2000 user logon name and password, along with the name of my Windows 2000 domain. As long as my logon name is the same as my mailbox, entering the previous URL works fine. If the two were not the same, then I would need to add a forward slash and the name of my mailbox to the URL, such as http://exchange01.bgerber.com/exchange/gerber.

In Figure 14.26, I'm using the Microsoft Internet Explorer Web browser to look at my favorite message from Jane Dough, complete with HTML text formatting. Notice the Options icon on the left side of Figure 14.26. You can use it to set up an out-of-office message, set time and date formats, set calendar and contacts options, and change your password.

FIGURE 14.25

Logging into an Exchange mailbox using the Enter Network Password dialog box

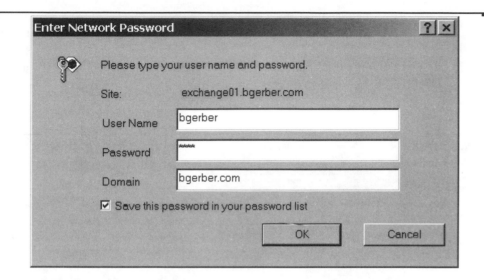

FIGURE 14.26

Viewing an Exchange message with a Web browser

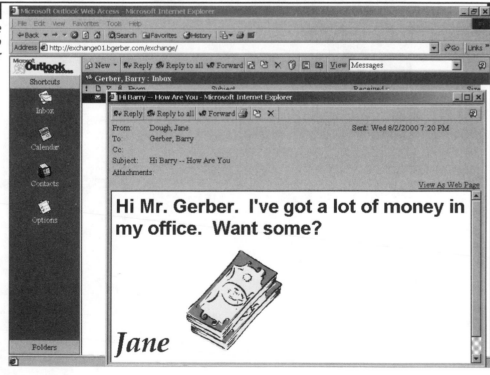

The Calendar and Contacts icons in Figure 14.27 let you work with your Exchange server-based calendar and contacts almost as if you were using a standard Outlook client. Figures 14.27 and 14.28 offer graphic proof that OWA really supports these two key Outlook/Exchange Server features. Yes, you can even check the availability of those you want to include in a meeting just as you can with the standard Outlook client.

FIGURE 14.27

Creating a new Calendar appointment with a Web browser

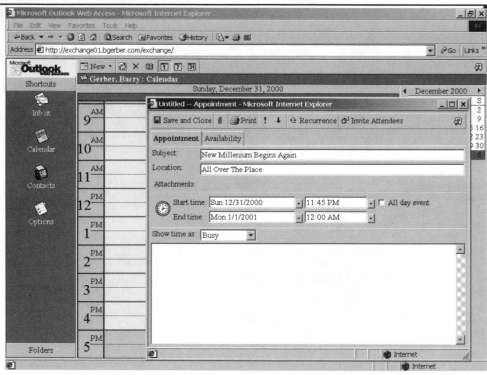

FIGURE 14.28

*Creating a new contact
with a Web browser*

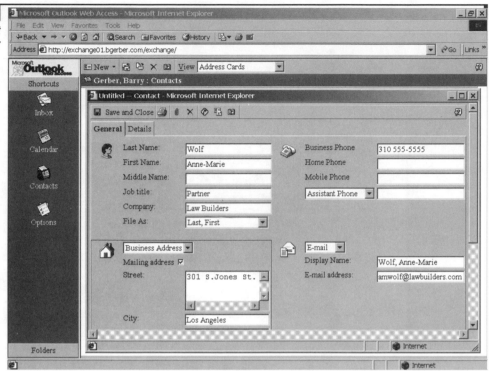

Just to be sure you're clear on what's happening, check out Figure 14.29, which shows the contact that I just created using OWA in the standard Outlook client. Fantastic!

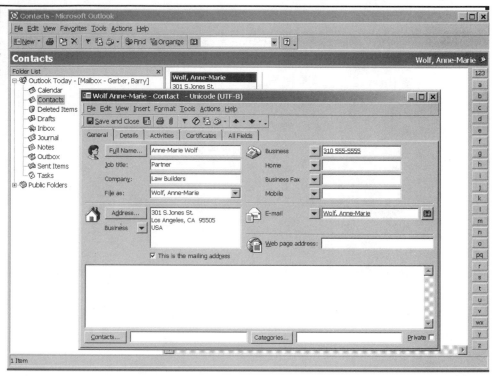

FIGURE 14.29

Viewing a contact created in a Web browser using the standard Outlook client

Some Interesting OWA URLs

You can access a number of items on an Exchange server using a set of special URLs. Here are just three of them:

To access the calendar in a user's mailbox:

/EXCHANGE_SERVER_NAME/exchange/MAILBOX_NAME/calendar

Example: /exchange01.bgerber.com/exchange/bgerber/calendar

To start composing a new message in a user's mailbox:

/EXCHANGE_SERVER_NAME/exchange/MAIBOX_NAME/?Cmd=new

Example: /exchange01.bgerber.com/exchange/bgerber/?Cmde=new

Continued

CONTINUED

To open a public folder:

/EXCHANGE_SERVER_NAME/public/PUBLIC_FOLDER_NAME

Example: /exchange01.bgerber.com/public/barry's first public folder

A New Era for Exchange-Oriented Web Application Developers

Although it's beyond the scope of this book, I must say something about the fantastic new programming options enabled by Microsoft's exposing Exchange 2000 Server's Information Store through the Windows 2000 file system and the Web. Using a variety of built-in and custom file system, HTML, and other commands, it's possible to program sophisticated custom applications with third-party products and proprietary products ranging from Microsoft Word to Visual Basic and C++. For an excellent introduction to this exciting new development opportunity, see *Programming Collaborative Web Applications with Microsoft Exchange 2000 Server*, by Mindy Martin (Microsoft Press, 2000).

Managing Windows 2000 Support for the Lightweight Directory Access Protocol (LDAP)

The Lightweight Directory Access Protocol (LDAP) is a client/server protocol that lets you browse, read, and search for information stored in an electronic directory. It was developed at the University of Michigan to allow access to an X.500 directory using TCP/IP and without the overhead required by the original X.500 Directory Access Protocol.

Microsoft's first implementation of LDAP was in Exchange Server 5. LDAP services were implemented to provide access to the Exchange directory, which, of course, served as the model for Windows 2000's Active Directory. So, it should come as no surprise that today LDAP services are central to Windows 2000 Server and Active Directory. As I pointed out in Chapter 3, "Two Key Architectural Components of Windows 2000 Server," LDAP is one of the four naming conventions used in Windows 2000. Key tools for access to Active Directory by administrators and developers rely on LDAP services and protocols. LDAP support is installed when you install Windows 2000.

From a messaging standpoint, LDAP plays a key role. The Exchange 2000 Active Directory Connector, used to migrate from Exchange 5.5 to Exchange 2000, communicates extensively using LDAP protocols. An LDAP interface is used to select filtering rules that define Exchange recipient policies. LDAP is also important in migrations from other messaging systems to Exchange Server.

From an electronic messaging perspective, LDAP clients and Windows 2000's LDAP server work together to give users access e-mail address and other information independently of the standard Outlook client. This allows POP3, IMAP4, and OWA clients to look up e-mail addresses almost as easily as if they were using the standard Outlook client, no matter where on the Internet or an intranet they happen to be,

Windows 2000 Server's LDAP server accesses Active Directory, which, as I'm sure you're aware by now, contains user-related data attributes such as recipient display names, phone numbers, and e-mail addresses. Upon request, the LDAP server returns directory data to LDAP-compatible clients. Server-to-client data transmissions are limited by the user authentication rules and directory attribute permissions that are in place for the LDAP server on your Windows 2000 Server.

LDAP Setup: The Server Side

You can set up LDAP at the server level in four different areas:

- Set limitations
- Hide Active Directory attributes from users
- Create and modify users, distribution groups, and contacts
- Set up support for Secure Sockets Layer encryption

I'll discuss each of these in turn.

Setting Limitations

LDAP is chock full of limitations. As with POP3, IMAP4, and OWA, these limits help you control computer and network resource usage. You can set limits on such things as connections to the LDAP server, the number of active queries at any given time against the server, how long a query can take, and the maximum size of a returned results set.

Server-side support for POP3, IMAP4, and OWA is a piece of cake when compared with the same thing for LDAP. At this writing, the tools for accessing and managing LDAP security and other settings are, to put it mildly, cryptic.

You don't manage LDAP limits and other attributes in Exchange System Manager. Instead, because LDAP is a Windows 2000 service that accesses Windows 2000's Active Directory, you have to manage it in Windows 2000. There is no simple MCC snap-in that you can use to view and change LDAP server properties. You have to edit

Active Directory entries directly, using a program such as Active Directory Service
Interface (ADSI), which I discussed back in Chapter 11, "Managing Exchange Users,
Distribution Groups, and Contacts," in the section "Setting the Default Format for
Display Names."

Figure 14.30 shows just how deeply you have to dig into Active Directory with
ADSI to find and modify LDAP's administrative limits. How do you modify a specific
limit? Why, it's simple: Just delete the old one and add a new one. Yuk!

FIGURE 14.30

*Using the Active
Directory Service
Interface (ADSI) to
view LDAP administra-
tive limits*

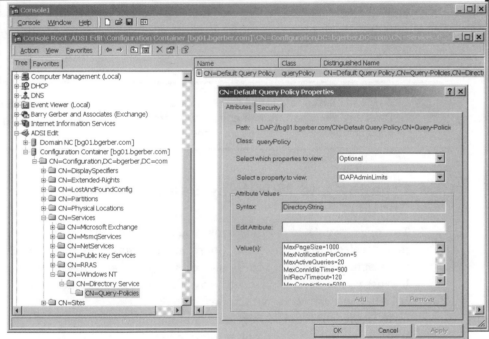

Because of these complexities and the dangers of editing the Active Directory schema
without a complete understanding of what you're doing, and because LDAP is a Windows 2000 component, I'm going to forgo discussing LDAP server-side setup here.
Instead, I'm going to direct you to a very helpful book on Active Directory and LDAP:
Microsoft Consulting Services' *Building Enterprise Active Directory Services, Notes from
the Field* (Microsoft Press, 2000). This book rings true because it's based on real-world
experiences. Chapter 5, "Designing a New Exchange 2000 System," should prove
especially helpful for those responsible for LDAP configuration.

Hiding Active Directory Attributes from Users

Hiding Active Directory object attributes, such as the telephone numbers of all Windows 2000 users, is even more challenging than messing with LDAP limitations. I fact, it's so challenging that I'm going to punt and defer to someone far more knowledgeable about Active Directory security than I: Alistair Lowe-Norris. Alistair lives in England and works at Leicester University. He was a member of the Windows 2000 rapid deployment team at the university, and he has written a book on Active Directory that picks up where most others leave off, *Windows 2000 Active Directory* (O'Reilly and Associates, 2000). His Chapter 10, "Active Directory Security: Permissions and Auditing," brings together theory, concept, and practice in a masterful way. You're in good hands with Alistair.

 TIP In relation to this and the previous section, keep your eyes open for better Active Directory management and editing tools from Microsoft and third-party vendors. It shouldn't be too long before we see them.

Creating and Modifying Users, Distribution Groups, and Contacts

This one's easy. As you already know, you create and modify mailbox-enabled users, mail-enabled users, distribution groups, and contacts using the Active Directory Users and Computers snap-in. You should be an old hand at using this snap-in by now because you've been using it since way back when you installed Windows 2000. For a refresher, you can check out Chapter 11.

In Figure 14.31, I'm adding some information to my own user object. You'll see some of it again when we look at information about me in Active Directory about me using an LDAP client.

FIGURE 14.31

*Adding information
about a user in Active
Directory Users and
Computers*

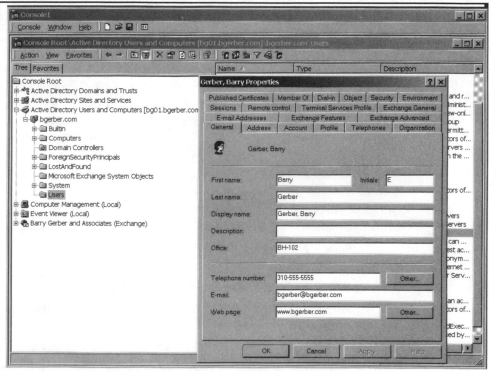

Enabling Secure Sockets Layer Support for LDAP

Like everything else about LDAP, setting up SSL support is not simply a matter of
selecting an Enable SSL check box. The process is rather convoluted, but I'm going to
cover it here because I think it's especially important to protect LDAP servers, which
have access to everything in your Active Directory, from prying eyes on the Internet
or on an intranet.

To secure internal LDAP client/server communications, you use Windows 2000
Server's certificate authority to generate both server and client certificates. Don't
worry that setting up SSL support will prevent access by LDAP clients that aren't
enabled for SSL. You're enabling SSL as an option. If a non-SSL client tries to connect,
the LDAP server will still service it. The good news is that, by default, a client must
supply a standard Windows 2000 username and password over a secure channel to
access an LDAP server. So, non–SSL-enabled clients can't just march in and get whatever they want from Windows 2000 LDAP servers. SSL adds another layer of security
to user authentication by encrypting data packets.

Here's how to set up SSL for LDAP servers and clients:

Installing and Managing a Windows 2000 Certificate Authority

Installing a certificate authority is pretty simple. First, you have to install the software on a Windows 2000 domain controller. To do this, put the Windows 2000 Server CD-ROM into your CD-ROM drive. When the Windows 2000 Server menu appears, select Install Add-On Components. Then use the resultant Windows 2000 Components Wizard to select the Certificate Services option. You'll be told that once the certificate services are installed, the computer can't be renamed or moved to another domain. Consider this message, and click OK if you can live with this reality.

Next select the Enterprise Root CA option on the Certification Authority Type Selection property page, and click Next. Then fill in the information on the CA Identifying Information page of the wizard. All you need to fill in are the first two fields on this page, and you should fill in the third field. Here are some suggestions:

CA Name   An acronym for your organization (for example, BGA for Barry Gerber and Associates); shows up as the issuer of each certificate

Organization   The full name of your organization

Organizational Unit   Optional, but you might want to set it to CA, for Certification Authority

On the next wizard page, accept or change the certificate database and certificate database log file options, and click OK. Agree to let the wizard stop Internet Information Server services, and then installation and configuration of your certificate authority begins.

When installation is complete, you need to add an instance of the Group Policy snap-in to your Microsoft Management Console (MMC) on your domain controller. On your MMC, select Console ➤ Add/Remove Snap-in. Click Add on the Add/Remove Snap-in dialog box. Then find and double-click the Group Policy snap-in on the Add Standalone Snap-in dialog box. On the Select Group Policy Object dialog box, click Browse, select Default Domain Policy, and click OK. Then click Finish on the Select Group Policy Object dialog box. Click Close on the Add Standalone Snap-in dialog box, and click OK on the Add/Remove Snap-in dialog box.

You should now see a snap-in in your MMC labeled Default Domain Policy, followed by the name of your domain controller, in parentheses. You need to create an automatic certificate generation policy for the domain controllers in your domain. Then all domain controllers will request a security certificate and will be capable of supporting secure communications, including those involving SSL.

Here's how to set up the policy. Using the Default Domain Policy snap-in, find and right-click \Computer Configuration\Windows Settings\Security Settings\Public

Key Policies\Automatic Certificate Request Settings. Select Properties from the pop-up menu, and then select New ➤ Automatic Certificate Request. The resultant wizard will quickly guide you through generation of the policy. On the Certificate Template wizard page, select Domain Controller. On the next wizard page, select the certificate authority that you installed earlier in this section; click Next and Finish on the last wizard page. At this point, LDAP will respond to requests for non-SSL and SSL communications sessions.

 NOTE   You manage your Certification Authority using the Certification Authority snap-in. Go ahead and install it in your MMC. For help, see the instructions for installing the Group Policy snap-in earlier in this section.

Now you're ready to move on to the client side.

Requesting and Installing a Client Security Certificate

The certificate authority that you installed in the last section is ready immediately after installation to support client requests for security certificates. The easiest way to obtain a certificate for Internet services is with Microsoft's Internet Explorer Web browser (IE). Open IE and enter the URL **http://DOMAIN_CONTROLLER _NAME/certsrv**; the URL for my Windows 2000 network is http://bg01.bgerber.com/certsrv. When you've connected to your domain controller, complete the following steps:

1. Log on to the server. Use your Windows 2000 user logon name and password.
2. On the first IE page that you see after logging in successfully, accept the option Request a Certificate.
3. On the second IE page, accept the option User Certificate Request.
4. On the third IE page, submit the request for a certificate.
5. On the fourth IE page, select Install This Certificate.
6. On the fourth IE page, you're informed that the certificate was installed.

To see your certificate in IE, select Tools ➤ Internet Options. Then tab over to the Content property page of the Internet Options dialog box, and click Certificates. You should see your certificate on the Personal page. The certificate should have been issued to your Windows 2000 user logon name by the certificate authority that you set up earlier.

As we move through the rest of this chapter, I'll show you how to enable SSL security on the client and server side. You can test out your certification setup by following my instructions.

This was the quickest of passes through the subject of security certificates. For more, see Microsoft Corporation's *Windows 2000 Server Resource Kit* (Microsoft Press 2000); *Microsoft Windows 2000 Security Technical Reference*, from Internet Security Systems (Microsoft Press, 2000); and *Configuring Windows 2000 Server Security*, by Thomas W. Shinder, M.D., et al. (Syngress, 2000).

Windows 2000's LDAP Server Is Not the Right Choice for a Public LDAP Server

By default, Windows 2000's LDAP server does not allow anonymous access. That makes good sense because we're talking here about the crown jewels of the Windows 2000 operating system. You certainly could manipulate Active Directory permissions to make anonymous access less of a threat, but it would be a significant challenge. If you're thinking about operating a public, anonymous access LDAP server, Windows 2000 is not the way to go. There are other LDAP servers out there, including the one that comes with Microsoft's Site Server (http://www.microsoft.com/siteserver/), that are more appropriately designed for public LDAP access.

LDAP Setup: The Client Side

In this section, I'll show you how to set up and test LDAP functionality in Microsoft Outlook Express.

Setting Up an Account for an LDAP Directory Service

We need to set up an account to access Windows 2000's Active Directory using the LDAP protocol. So, select Accounts from Outlook Express's Tools menu. When the Internet Accounts dialog box opens, tab over to the Directory Service page. As you'll notice, Microsoft has already set up a bunch of LDAP servers for you to play around with. If you installed Internet Explorer and Outlook Express on a computer that is a member of your Windows 2000 domain and if you are logged into your domain, you should see a directory service called Active Directory. You can use this service immediately. It points directly to the Global Category for your Windows 2000 Active Directory, using a special non-SSL-TCP port number of 3268 instead of the standard port 389 for non–SSL access or 636 for SSL access.

Now let's install our new directory service, one that connects to our LDAP server using standard port numbers. On the Internet Accounts dialog box, click Add and select Directory Service from the menu that pops up. This starts our old friend, the Internet Connection Wizard, shown in Figure 14.32.

FIGURE 14.32

Adding a new directory service with the Internet Connection Wizard

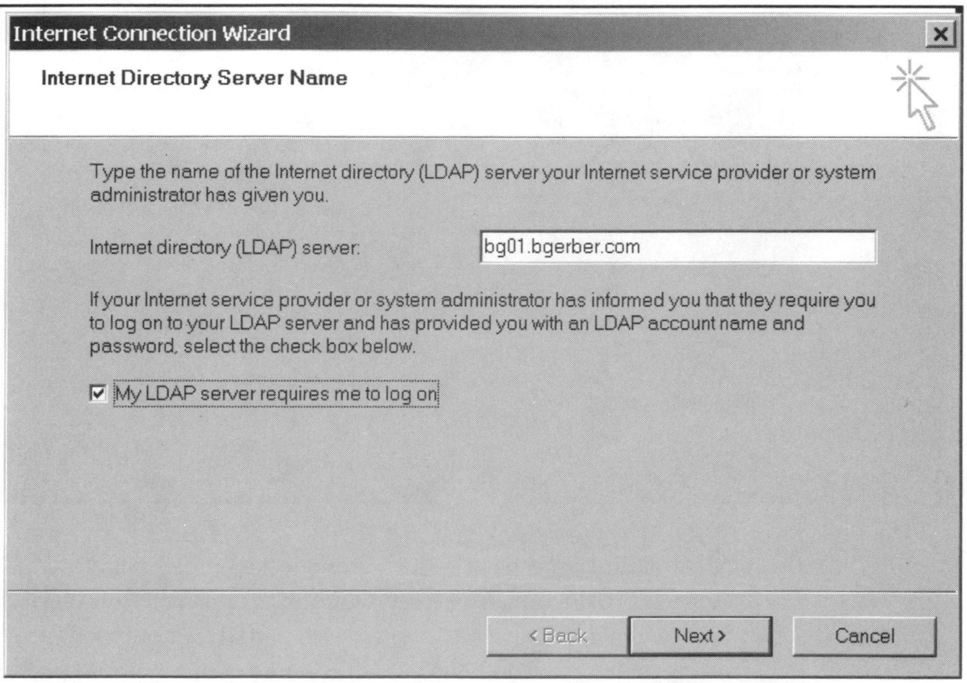

Fill in the IP address or domain name of your LDAP server (domain controller), and check the box labeled My LDAP Server Requires Me to Log On. The next wizard page lets you enter an LDAP account name and password, and indicate that you need to log onto your LDAP server using Secure Password Authentication (see Figure 14.33). Enter your Windows 2000 user logon name and password, and check the secure password authentication box. Remember, I mentioned earlier that, by default, LDAP server requires secure logons. If you don't check the box, you won't be able to connect to your LDAP server.

FIGURE 14.33

Entering information required for logging onto a directory server

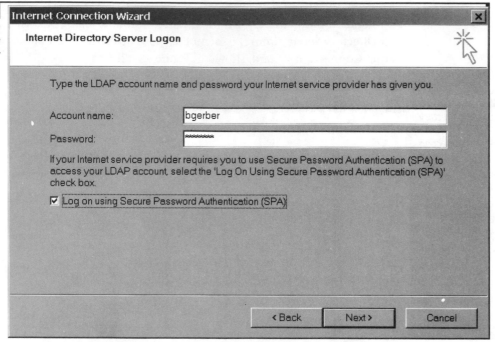

On the next wizard page, be sure that Yes is checked in the field Do You Want to Check Addresses Using This Directory. Outlook Express will now check your LDAP server to find e-mail addresses associated with partial names typed into the To or Cc fields of a new message. You'll see how that works in just a bit. When you're done with this page, click Next and then click Finish to complete configuration of your new directory service.

As with POP3 and IMAP4 accounts, you manage your LDAP account by opening the Properties dialog box for the account. You need to open the Properties dialog box to set at least one additional parameter for your LDAP client. To do so, in Outlook Express, select Tools ➢ Accounts, and then find and double-click your new directory service. You don't need to change anything on the General property page, so tab over to the Advanced page, shown in Figure 14.34.

FIGURE 14.34

*The Advanced prop-
erty page of the
Properties dialog box
for a newly created
directory service*

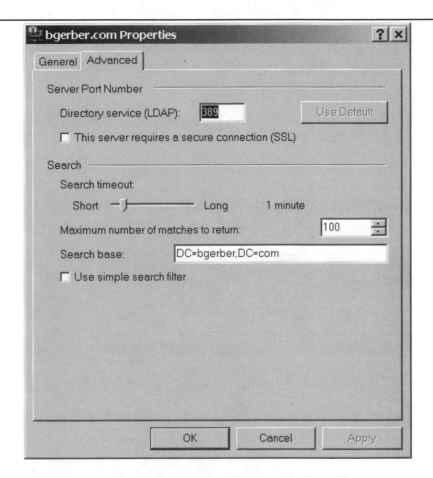

As you can see, you need to enter some information in the Search Base field at the bottom of the property page. The search base is the location in the directory where a search begins. We want to start at the top of the directory at the domain level. So, first you need to break your Windows 2000 domain name into separate components at every dot (period). My domain name is bgerber.com, so I wind up with two components, bgerber and com. Then, starting with the leftmost component in your domain name, enter **DC=** followed by the name of a component. Separate components by commas. As Figure 14.34 shows, DC=bgerber,DC=com is my Search base entry.

If you didn't enable SSL for your LDAP client and server, you're done with the Advanced property page. If you enabled SSL, select This Server Requires a Secure Connection (SSL). When you do this, the LDAP port changes from the nonsecure 389 to the SSL secure 636, and SSL security is enabled for your LDAP client.

Did It Work?

First, let's try to find a name in Active Directory using Outlook Express's basic Find function; track along on Figure 14.35. On the Outlook Express main window, click Address Book on the toolbar. This brings up the Address Book dialog box. Click Find to bring up the Find People dialog box. Select your LDAP account from the Look In drop-down list at the top of the dialog box, and type all or part of a name in the Name field. You can just type in your first name here. Click Find Now, and in a flash the LDAP service returns information on all matching entries in Active Directory. In Figure 14.35, I've found the only Barry in my Active Directory. If there were five people in my Active Directory with the name Barry, all five would have shown up in the Results field. The search works for all unhidden users, distribution groups, and contacts in the Active Directory Users and Computers container.

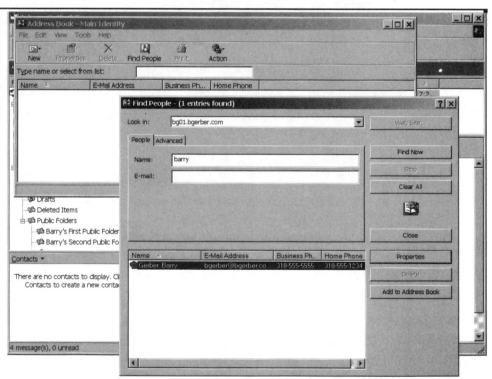

FIGURE 14.35

A list showing the one user who meets the criteria for an LDAP search using the Outlook Express client's Address Book

Double-click one of the entries in the Results field in Figure 14.35. I double-clicked Gerber, Barry. This opens the Properties dialog box for my Active Directory entry (see Figure 14.36). Notice the information on the first property page. As you'll remember, I entered most of it back in the section "Creating and Modifying Users, Distribution Groups, and Contacts." Some of the information in Figure 14.36 was entered on other property pages for my user object.

FIGURE 14.36

Use the Properties dialog box for a returned directory entry to view other information about the Active Directory object.

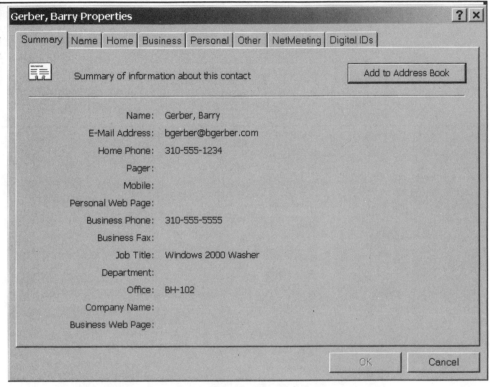

All those tabs on the dialog box open worlds of possibilities. If information is available on an LDAP server, it will be displayed in appropriate fields on each of the six pages of the dialog box. The Home and Business pages have room for lots of contact information, including business and personal Web site URLs. The Other page provides space for general notes and information about group memberships. The NetMeeting page is for information used in initiating network-based conferences, and the Digital IDs page contains information about the Digital IDs associated with this person.

This LDAP directory searching stuff is a lot of fun, especially on a cold winter night. If you're connected to the Internet, try some of the directory services that Microsoft provides with Outlook Express. See if you can find an old acquaintance, friend, or enemy.

Okay, now let's try composing a new message and using LDAP to find the e-mail addresses of the folks we want to send it to. Click Compose Message on the Outlook Express toolbar. This opens a new message window (see Figure 14.37). Type all or part of the name of one of your Exchange Server recipients into the To or Cc field, and click the Check Names icon right next to the Address Book icon on the message's toolbar. Assuming correct spelling and such, the name that you typed in should be resolved into e-mail addresses by your LDAP client and server. You know that an address has been resolved when the name is underlined in the To, Cc, or Bcc field, as it is in Figure 14.37. If you want to know more about this recipient, double-click one of the resolved addresses to open the Properties dialog box, shown back in Figure 14.36.

FIGURE 14.37

A new message with an e-mail address that has been resolved using LDAP against Windows 2000's Active Directory

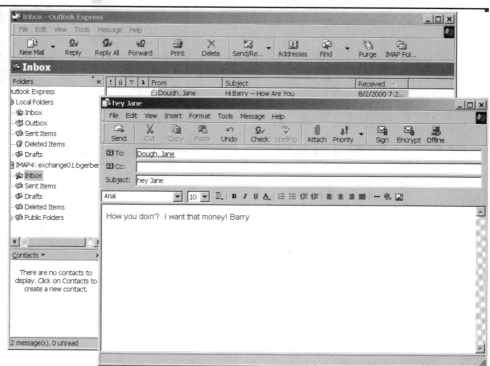

Go ahead and send your message. If it got through to the recipients that you intended, all is well in the world, and you can take a break or move on to the next section on the Network News Transfer Protocol and the newsgroups that it supports. If nothing has worked, make sure that your network connection is working, ensure that your network security settings are in sync on your LDAP client and server, and, if that doesn't help, go back over the previous steps. If things are still not working, take a look at the troubleshooting section under the section on POP3.

 NOTE If you don't need to send or receive messages and just want to browse Active Directory with an LDAP client, the Address Book is available in on Windows 2000 computers as a separate application. To run it, select Start menu ➢ Programs ➢ Accessories ➢ Address Book. The standalone Address Book application uses the same settings as the Outlook Express Address Book, so you don't have to set up LDAP server access twice.

Managing Exchange Server Support for the Network News Transfer Protocol (NNTP)

Aren't these advanced Internet protocols fantastic? Well, we're not finished with these wonders yet. We've got one more to go, the Network News Transfer Protocol (NNTP). Many people think of NNTP as the protocol that supports those wild, woolly, and sometimes useful public Internet newsgroups that are home to everything from the infamous and sometimes offensive alt groupings to the fairly staid German-language zer groupings. However, my goal in this section is to show you how to implement newsgroups internally. I'll spend a little time talking about linking up to external groups and making all or some of them available to your Exchange users, but I really want to show you how you can use newsgroups and the threaded conversations that they enable to improve productivity in your organization.

Like SMTP, NNTP is a Windows 2000 service based in Internet Information Server. Also like SMTP, a default NNTP virtual server is installed when Windows 2000 is installed. However unlike SMTP, NNTP isn't installed automatically when you install Windows 2000; you must choose to install it. When you installed the Windows 2000 server that was to become your Exchange server back in Chapter 7, "Installing Windows 2000 Server," you may remember that I asked you to be sure that NNTP was selected for installation.

As with SMTP services, when you installed Exchange, it sort of hijacked NNTP and brought it under its control. In this case, in addition to adding the NNTP virtual server to its Exchange System Manager Protocols container, Exchange installed a public folder called Internet Newsgroups, which is the default home for NNTP newsgroups on your default NNTP virtual server. The neat thing about this is that users can view newsgroups with MAPI clients such as the standard Outlook client and or with an IMAP4 client.

Exchange public folders aren't the only place you can store newsgroups. Newsgroups can also be stored in the Windows 2000 file system. When newsgroups are stored in the file system, of course, they're not visible as public folders.

When setup is done, your Exchange server's NNTP virtual server acts just like any other NNTP server. Anyone who can get to the Internet Newsgroups public folder by use of the standard Outlook client, the Outlook Express IMAP4 client, or the OWA client can get to the newsgroups on your Exchange server. In addition, your NNTP server fully supports standard newsreader clients such as FreeAgent, WINVN, or the news client built into Microsoft's Outlook Express.

By whatever means users get to your Exchange NNTP server, if they have the rights to do so, they can post new or reply messages to any newsgroup, or they can respond directly to the original sender of a news message by e-mail. Your server will see to it that those messages and postings are available not only locally but, if you want, to users of the newsgroup outside your Exchange site or organization.

If all this isn't enough, your NNTP server can also feed its newsgroups to other NNTP servers. Couple all this good stuff with the kind of user-friendly interface that you've come to expect from Exchange Server, and you've got it all NNTP-wise. Let's get right to NNTP setup.

NNTP Setup: The Server Side

Unlike most of the other virtual servers that we've looked at, the default NNTP virtual server is chock full of subcontainers whose functions are not obvious from the names of the containers. So, before we look at these containers in more detail, let's start with a quick overview of each. As you read this list, follow along on the left side of Figure 14.38.

Default NNTP Virtual Server   Holds subcontainers

Newsgroups   Holds a couple default newsgroups and all the newsgroups that you create for this virtual server

Feeds   Holds links to other NNTP servers that either send newsgroup articles to or receive newsgroup articles from your virtual server

Expiration Policies   Holds policies specifying when articles stored in the file system (not in Exchange public folders) should be deleted from newsgroups managed by your virtual server

Virtual Directories   Holds specifications for other locations (Exchange stores, file system directories, or shares) where newsgroups managed by your virtual server can be stored

Current Sessions   Shows connections to your virtual server and allows for termination of selected or all connections

FIGURE 14.38

The default NNTP virtual server with its sub-containers and Properties dialog box exposed

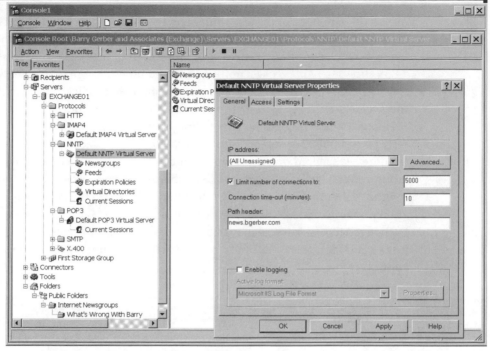

NNTP Virtual Server Properties

As with the other Internet protocols, you can set a range of properties for your default NNTP virtual server. These include general properties, access properties, and a number of other settings. Let's take a closer look at these properties.

General

Open the Properties dialog box for your server by right-clicking it and selecting Properties from the pop-up menu. You can see the dialog box and its General property page on the right side of Figure 14.38.

The only field that you haven't seen elsewhere in this chapter is the Path Header field. You need to enter into this field the fully qualified domain name of the Windows 2000/Exchange server that is supporting this virtual server. I entered news.bgerber.com, which I associated in my DNS with the IP address of my Exchange server using a host record. The path header is included in newsgroup articles from your NNTP server. It's used to prevent the sending of multiple copies of a message (looping) when an NNTP server is connected to other NNTP servers through multiple Internet providers.

Access

As you do with most of the other Internet protocols that we've looked at in this chapter, you use the Access property page of the Default NNTP Virtual Server Properties dialog box to control who can access your server and how they can access it. Figure 14.39 shows the Access page; nothing here should be foreign to you. However, the Authentication Methods dialog box, which you open by clicking Authentication on the Access property page, is a little different. Figure 14.40 shows the Authentication Methods dialog box. First, note that anonymous access is supported for your NNTP server. Most public newsgroup servers allow anonymous access at least to users with IP addresses serviced by the operator of the server. If this is to be an internal newsgroup server, you'll probably want to disable anonymous access. If this is to be an internal server that is connected to the Internet, you'll very likely want to disable anonymous access. As you'll see in a bit, you can control access to newsgroups on the Exchange server side, so enabling anonymous access isn't absolutely necessary. It's just a good idea, at least until you've been able to get more specific newsgroup access controls in place.

FIGURE 14.39

The Access property page of the default NNTP virtual server Properties dialog box

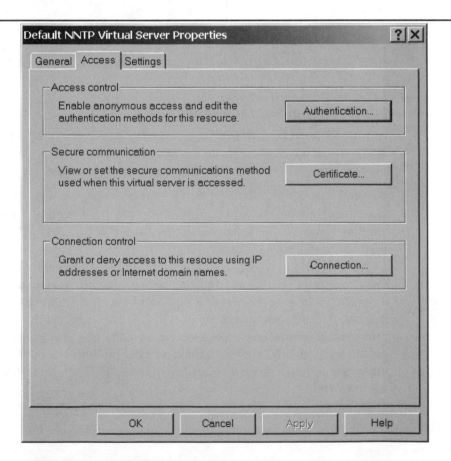

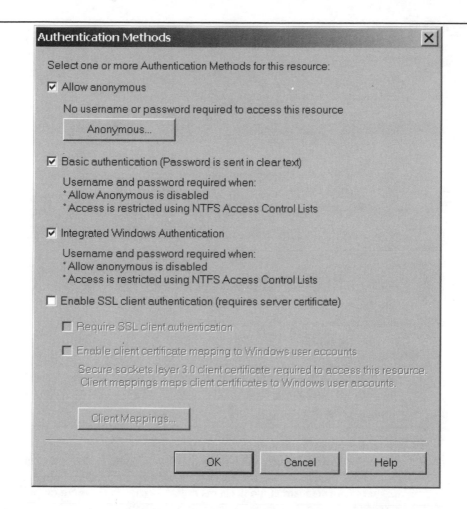

FIGURE 14.40

*The Authentication
Methods dialog box*

The Anonymous button on the Authentication Methods dialog box lets you select the
Windows 2000 account that is used to connect to your NNTP virtual server when a
user connects anonymously. Clicking the button opens the Anonymous Account dialog box, shown in Figure 14.41. You use this dialog box to set the name of the
account and its password. Unless you have a good reason to do so, you can leave the
default settings. If you change the password of this account in \Active Directory Users
and Computers\Users, be sure to change it on the Anonymous Access dialog box, or
anonymous access will stop working. You can check Enable Automatic Password Synchronization on the Anonymous Account dialog box to ensure that a password
change in one place leads to an automatic change in the other.

FIGURE 14.41

*The Anonymous
Account dialog box*

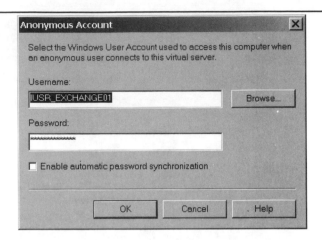

To enable SSL encryption select Enable SSL Client Authentication (requires server certificate) on the Authentication Methods dialog box in Figure 14.40. After you've selected to use SSL encryption, if you select Require SSL Client Authentication, users will be able to access your news server only if they've enabled SSL in their newsgroup clients and if they've installed a key certificate. You can even go one step further down the security trail and map specific client certificates on a Windows 2000 certificate authority to a specific Windows 2000 user logon account. If you select any of the SSL options, don't forget to install a certificate back on the Access property page.

 WARNING Remember that when you've secured your NNTP virtual server from NNTP clients, you've completed only half the job. If your NNTP newsgroups are stored in Exchange public folders, you also have to secure those folders from users who can access them with standard Outlook clients or IMAP4 clients. For more on public folder security, see the section "Managing Public Folders," in Chapter 12.

Settings

The Settings property page is heavily laden with property fields, as you can see in Figure 14.42. However, most of the fields on the page are pretty easy to understand and manage. Let's take a quick tour of the Settings property page.

FIGURE 14.42

*The Settings property
page of the default
NNTP virtual server
Properties dialog box*

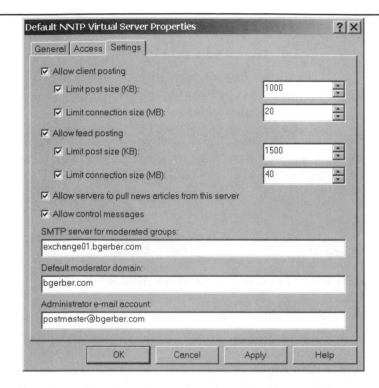

When you allow users to post messages to your NNTP server, you need to set some
limits on the largest single article that users can post and on the total size of all articles posted during one session (connection). The defaults of 1MB and 20MB, respectively, are a bit large for my tastes, but I'll leave it to you to determine whether you
have adequate bandwidth and disk storage to handle such settings.

Other NNTP servers can be allowed to connect to your NNTP server and feed it
news articles. As with user posting, if you select this option, then you can limit the
maximum size of any single article that can be posted and the total size of all articles
posted during one session.

If you want other servers to connect to your NNTP server and get news articles
from it, be sure to check the option Allow Servers to Pull News Articles from This
Server. Don't worry that NNTP servers will just start connecting to your server; you
still have to create a feed for any pull NNTP server. We'll talk about feeds in the section "Setting Up Feeds to or from Other NNTP Servers."

Before I explai~~n~~ ~~~~ ~~co~~ntrol Messages field, let's talk a little about what control messages ~~~~ ~~~~e types of control messages:

Ca~~~~ ~~~~ NNTP client to delete a specific news article

~~~~ ~~~~ usually from an NNTP server, to create a newsgroup

~~~~ ~~que~~st, usually from an NNTP server, to delete (remove) an existing ~~new~~sgroup

On your NNTP server, there is a newsgroup for each type of control message. Someone must process each control message. If Allow Control Messages is selected, your NNTP server queues control messages and treats them in a way that makes processing easy. If this option is not selected, control messages show up in their respective newsgroups as nothing more than standard news articles. I'll talk a bit more about control messages in the next section, "Managing Newsgroups."

Sometimes you don't want a new article to show up in a newsgroup before someone, a moderator, reviews and approves the articles. You can designate any newsgroup as a moderated newsgroup, and you can specify a different moderator or the same moderator for any moderated newsgroup. New articles are sent to the moderator by e-mail, so you need to set an SMTP server that your NNTP server will use to send articles to the moderator. In Figure 14.42, I entered the fully qualified domain name of my old reliable Exchange server, exchange01.bgerber.com.

You can also set a default moderator domain for your NNTP server. This one's a little tricky. When you specify that a particular newsgroup should be moderated, you can specify the e-mail address of the moderator. If you've entered a default moderator domain, as I have in Figure 14.42, and you choose to use the default address, the address is constructed from the default moderator domain that you enter here and the name of the newsgroup. Say there was a newsgroup called Stuff, and I chose the default, the moderator address would be stuff@bgerber.com. Of course, I would also have to create a mailbox on my Exchange server with an SMTP address of stuff@bgerber.com.

Now that we've got our NNTP virtual server configured, we're ready to tackle newsgroups.

Managing Newsgroups

Newsgroup management includes the following:

- Maintaining, creating, and deleting newsgroups
- Creating virtual directories
- Setting expiration parameters for news articles
- Administering NNTP server connections
- Setting up feeds to or from other NNTP servers

I discuss each of these tasks in the sections that follow.

Maintaining, Creating, and Deleting Newsgroups

You create, maintain, and delete newsgroups in the Newsgroups container of your NNTP server. You can see the Newsgroups container for my default NNTP virtual server in Figure 14.43. Notice the three special newsgroups for control messages in right pane. They're created automatically on installation of your NNTP virtual server.

Before I do anything else, let me tell you about the Find Newsgroups dialog box, on the left side of Figure 14.43. You open it by right-clicking your Newsgroups container and selecting Limit Groups Enumeration from the pop-up menu. You use this dialog box to limit the newsgroups displayed in the right pane. Right now, with only three newsgroups, who needs limits? The asterisk in the Newsgroups field of the dialog box ensures that I'll see all newsgroups. But, imagine that I had thousands of newsgroups to manage. Seeing all of them in my Newsgroup container could make it very difficult to find and work with a specific newsgroup. So, I can use the Find Newsgroups dialog box to specify search criteria that show me only certain newsgroups or a maximum number of newsgroups. For example if I entered `control.c*` in the Newsgroups field and clicked OK, I'd just see the newsgroup control.cancel.

FIGURE 14.43

The Find Newsgroups dialog box

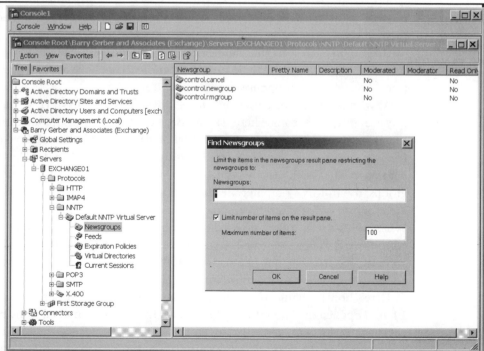

PART

V

Expanding an Exchange Server Organization

We'll create a new newsgroup in just a bit, but first we need to secure our control message newsgroups. We don't want just anyone going into the control message newsgroups and accepting the creation or deletion of groups or the deletion of messages. There are three ways to secure your control message newsgroups:

- Set each of the three control message newsgroups as moderated
- Limit access to the newsgroup server where you administer newsgroups
- Set permissions on the directories for the message control newsgroups so that only newsgroup administrators can access the newsgroups

You can implement any one or all three of these options. I'm partial to the third option because, as you'll see in a bit, it hides the control message newsgroups from the NNTP clients of all but those who need to access the newsgroups. Here's a quick take on each of the three options for restricting access to message control newsgroups.

If the control message newsgroups are set as moderated, messages are e-mailed to each message control newsgroup's moderator for action before they're displayed in the newsgroup. When the moderator acts on the messages, the messages disappear from the newsgroup, so there's no way anyone will see them. You can set any newsgroup as moderated by right-clicking it and selecting Properties from the pop-up menu. On the resultant dialog box, select Moderated and set the e-mail address of the moderator.

Controlling access to your newsgroup server works best when anyone who might see the control messages can be trusted to ignore them. Take a look at the earlier section "Access" for your options on access control.

As with the HTTP virtual server, virtual directories on the NNTP server point to physical directories somewhere. The message control newsgroups are stored in a virtual directory named Control. This virtual directory points to a subdirectory of the Internet Information Server's Inetpub directory, specifically `\Inetpub\nntpfile\root\control`, which usually resides on the C: drive. To secure your control newsgroups, use the My Computer file and directory explorer to set permissions on the directory for only those who absolutely must access the message control newsgroups. When you set security on the subdirectory in this manner, users won't even see the control newsgroups in their NNTP clients unless they log in with a Windows 2000 account that has adequate permissions on the subdirectory. Even users who connect anonymously won't see the message control newsgroups.

Here's how to change permissions on the directory named Control. In Figure 14.44, I opened the Properties dialog box for the directory named Control by right-clicking the directory and selecting Properties from the pop-up menu. Next I gave full permissions on the directory named Control to the Windows 2000 security group, Administrators. I deselected Allow Inheritable Permissions from Parent to Propagate

PART

V

Expanding an Exchange
Server Organization

to This Object. That removed the default permissions that the Windows 2000 group Everyone has on the directory. That's all there is to it. You don't have to set permissions on the subdirectories of the directory named Control.

Just for the record, I could have created a new Windows 2000 security group just for NNTP administrators and given that group full permissions on the directory named Control. Then I could allow users to administer the NNTP server by adding them to the group. If I did this, I'd still grant full permissions to Administrators, just so that they could retain control of the directory.

You have one more task to complete before this permissions setting will work. You have to tell your NNTP server that you want to restrict the visibility of the virtual directory named Control. To do this, find and right-click the virtual directory named Control in your NNTP server's Virtual Directory container. Then select Properties from the pop-up menu. The Properties dialog box for the virtual directory opens. Select Restrict Newsgroup Visibility, and click OK.

FIGURE 14.44

Limiting access to the physical directory mapped to the virtual directory for message control newsgroups

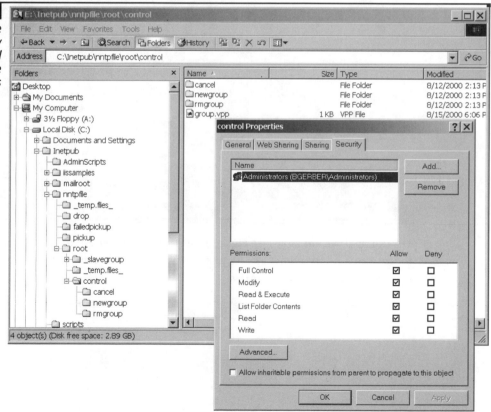

Okay, we're ready to create a newsgroup. This really is simple. First right-click on your Newsgroups container and select New ➤ Newsgroup from the pop-up menu. This opens the New Newsgroup Wizard, shown in Figure 14.45. Enter the name you'd like to use for the newsgroup. Newsgroups are structured hierarchically, from highest to lowest component. Components are separated by periods. In Figure 14.45, I'm creating a newsgroup to hold articles containing discussions about proposals that Barry Gerber and Associates has submitted for funding. As you can see, the newsgroup is named BGA.Discussion.Proposals.Pending.

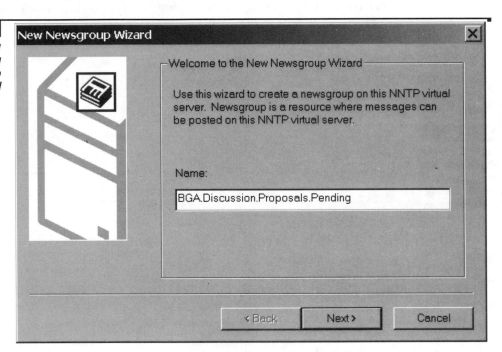

FIGURE 14.45

Entering a name for a new newsgroup using the New Newsgroup Wizard

On the next wizard page (see Figure 14.46), you enter a description of your new newsgroup and a pretty name. What's a pretty name? It's the name that's displayed whenever possible for us mere mortals.

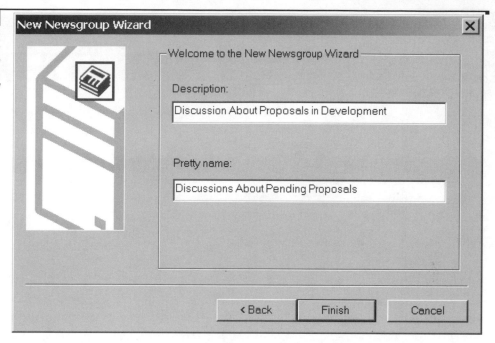

FIGURE 14.46

Entering a description and pretty name for a new newsgroup using the New Newsgroup Wizard

When you're done, click Finish on the last wizard page and take a look at your Exchange System Manager, which should look something like the one in Figure 14.47. Not only should your new newsgroup appear in the right pane of System Manager along with your message control newsgroups, but you should also see a new public folder under Internet Newsgroups (see the lower-left corner of Figure 14.47). If you don't see the new public folder, right-click Internet Newsgroups and select Refresh. That should bring the new folder into view. Notice that while the new public folder has the pretty name you entered for your newsgroup, the newsgroup itself has the ugly name.

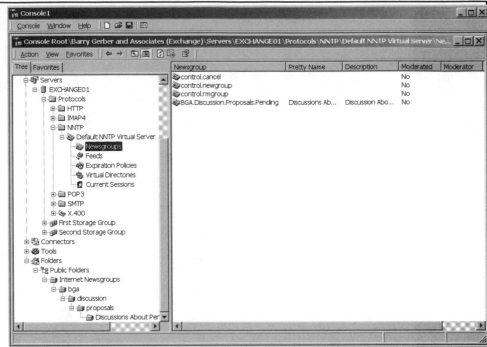

Now I want to make sure that you understand what's going on here. Not only have you created a newsgroup that users can access with NNTP clients, but you've also created a public folder that any user can access as a public folder with a standard Outlook client or any IMAP4 client. That is very cool.

Just for fun, I added some more newsgroups to the newsgroup hierarchy BGA.Discussion. You can see them in Figure 14.48, along with the public folders created to support the newsgroups. To create each of these newsgroups, I just entered the full newsgroup name that you see in Figure 14.48 into the Name field on the New Newsgroup Wizard. My NNTP server, with help from Exchange, created the public folder hierarchy.

FIGURE 14.48

The default NNTP virtual server, with several newly created newsgroups and their supporting Exchange public folders displayed

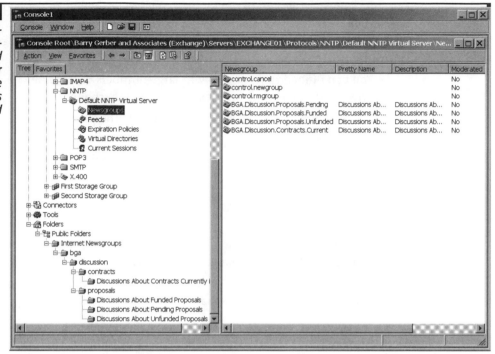

Deleting newsgroups is very easy. Just right-click the newsgroup and select Delete from the pop-up menu. My experience to date with Exchange 2000 Server indicates that although a newsgroup's parallel public folder is created automatically, you must delete the parallel public folder manually. You delete the public folder in the same way as you delete the newsgroup.

Creating and Using Virtual Directories

Newsgroups and the articles that they contain are stored on virtual directories. Virtual directories can map to an Exchange public folder, a file system directory local to your NNTP server, or a network file share. Double-click the virtual directory named Default in the Virtual Directory container of your default NNTP virtual server. Then click Contents on the directory's Properties dialog box. Notice that the virtual directory named Default is mapped to the Exchange public folder Internet Newsgroups. By default, all newly created newsgroups are stored in that public folder.

Aside from functioning as repositories for the default newsgroup store on an NNTP virtual server, virtual directories enable you to place selected newsgroups on storage media other than the media that contains the server's default store. For example, you can store some newsgroups in the Internet Newsgroups public folder and other newsgroups in directories on one or more disk drives.

There are several advantages and some disadvantages to storing newsgroups outside your Exchange public folder system. On the positive side are these:

- You can offload newsgroups with large numbers of large news articles to disk drives and tape backup units external to your Exchange system.

- NNTP client users see all the newsgroups, whether they're stored in Exchange or on the file system.

- You can still manage your NNTP servers from inside Exchange.

Negatives include these:

- You have to back up Exchange-based and file system-based newsgroups separately.

- Exchange users with standard Outlook and IMAP4 clients can see only newsgroups stored inside Exchange public folders.

- You have to manage the files that support file system-based newsgroups separately from the public store that supports Exchange-based newsgroups.

Here's how to set up file system-based newsgroup storage using NNTP virtual directories. First open your My Computer file and directory browser. Then create a directory on one of the disk drives on your Exchange server. You can name your directory anything you want and nest it as deeply as you want. In naming your directory, let clarity rule. The subject matter of the newsgroups that will be created in the directory should be clear from the name that you give to your directory. Also, for clarity's sake, I strongly suggest that you name the root of the directory \Newsgroups. I've chosen to name my directory \Newsgroups\BGA\SWDev because I'll be storing newsgroups in this directory that are related to software developed by my consulting group, Barry Gerber and Associates.

Okay, now we're ready to create that virtual directory. Find and right-click the Virtual Directories container for your default NNTP virtual server. Then select New ➤ Virtual Directory from the pop-up menu. This opens the New NNTP Virtual Directory Wizard, shown in Figure 14.49.

You enter a name for the root-level of the newsgroup tree that you want to create. You're not going to store anything in a newsgroup with the name that you enter here. You're going to create newsgroups by appending newsgroup names to this root level.

I'll show you how in just a minute. As you can see in Figure 14.49, I've entered BGA.Software as my root-level newsgroup tree name. You can't enter anything here that would duplicate the newsgroup structure that you already created in the Internet Newsgroups public folder. So, I couldn't enter BGA.Discussions.Clients here because I already have a BGA\Discussions tree in my Internet Newsgroups public folder. Getting root levels right is a little tricky. As with almost everything else, practice is the best teacher.

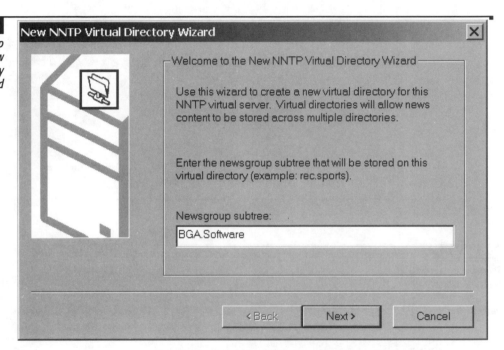

FIGURE 14.49

Entering a newsgroup subtree using the New NNTP Virtual Directory Wizard

When you're done entering the name of your root-level newsgroup tree, click Next. On the next wizard page (see Figure 14.50), select the File System option. Then on the next page, browse to and select the lowest level of the disk directory that you created above (see Figure 14.51). Click OK and then Finish on the wizard, and you're done creating your virtual directory. Figure 14.52 shows my NNTP virtual server with its new virtual directory, BGA.Software, in place.

FIGURE 14.50

Selecting a path where newsgroup content should be stored using the New NNTP Virtual Directory Wizard

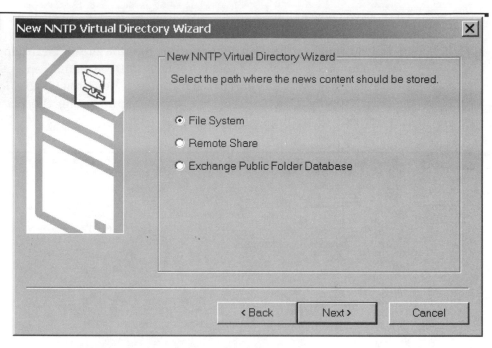

FIGURE 14.51

Selecting the disk directory to which a new virtual directory should be mapped

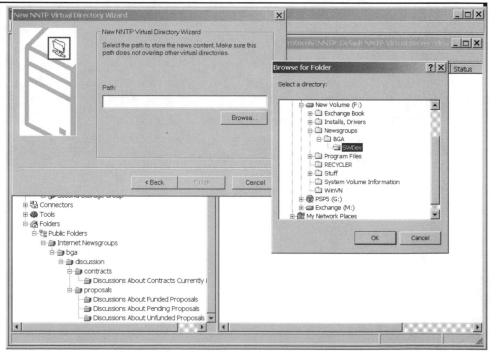

FIGURE 14.52

*An NNTP virtual server
with a newly created
virtual directory*

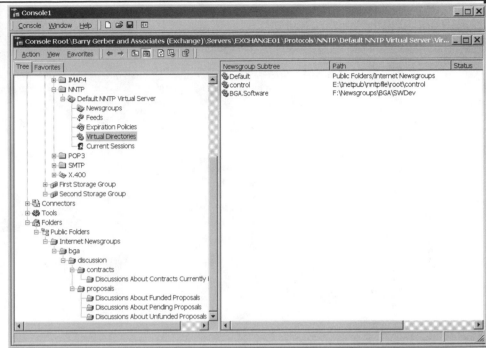

Now you need to create your new newsgroup. In Figure 14.53, I'm creating a news-group named BGA.Software.GS.Code. In Figure 14.54, you can see that this news-group will hold discussions among BGA staff about software that we are developing for a hospital named Good Samaritan.

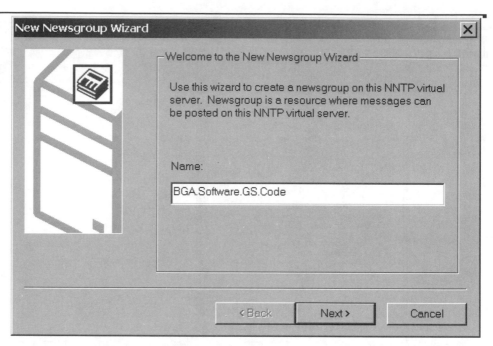

FIGURE 14.53

Entering a name for a new newsgroup using the New Newsgroup Wizard

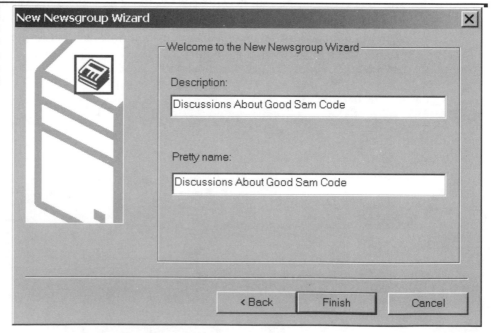

FIGURE 14.54

Entering a description and pretty name for a new newsgroup using the New Newsgroup Wizard

Now go back to My Computer, and take a look at the disk directory that you created a bit ago. Notice that it's now got subdirectories for the new newsgroup that you created. My directory is shown in Figure 14.55, with its two new subdirectories, gs and code, which parallel the last two components of the name of the newsgroup that I just created, BGA.Software.GS.Code. The BGA.Software part of the newsgroup name is already taken care of as the newsgroup subtree name associated with the virtual directory.

FIGURE 14.55

Viewing new disk directories created by an NNTP virtual server to support a new file system-based newsgroup

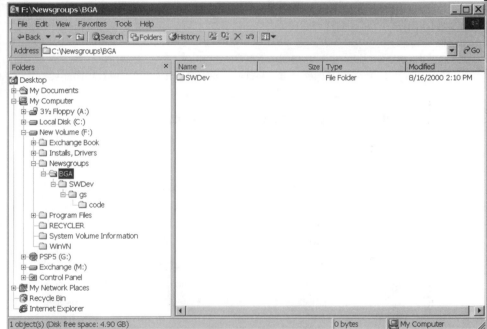

Now click Refresh and look at your Internet Newsgroups public folder. You shouldn't see any subfolders in the folder for the new newsgroup that you just created. That's because this newsgroup's news articles will be stored on the file system, not in your Exchange server's public store.

That's about it for virtual directories. Remember that you can create new NNTP virtual servers and plop their newsgroups anywhere you like in new Exchange public stores, Windows 2000 files systems, or Windows 2000 file shares. You can mix and match these three storage options. The possibilities are endless, although I'm sure your time isn't.

Setting Expiration Parameters for News Articles

If you expect users to add lots of articles to all or some of your newsgroups, you'll want to be sure to set rules for automatic deletion of articles after the passage of a certain amount of time. You set rules for newsgroups stored in public folders differently than for newsgroups stored in the file system.

For newsgroups stored in the Internet Newsgroups public folder, you set the number of days that a news article may remain in a public folder before it's deleted. This is no different than the way you handle autodeletion in any other public folder. For more on public folder item expiration, see the section "Creating and Managing Public Folders," in Chapter 12.

If you're working with newsgroups stored on the file system, you set an expiration policy. You do this in the NNTP virtual server's Expiration Policy container. Just right-click the container and select Properties. Then set the number of days that a news article can remain in all or select folders.

Administering NNTP Server Connections

As with most of the other Internet protocols that I've discussed in this chapter, you manage connections to your NNTP virtual server in the server's Current Users container. You can review and see how many connections there are at any time. You can also terminate connections in this container. Users are connected only when they're doing something that downloads or uploads data. So, if you've got a lot of users who do nothing most of the time but keep their NNTP clients open all day, you won't see tons of connections in the Current Users container.

Setting Up Feeds to or from Other NNTP Servers

Newsfeeds allow one NNTP server to export some or all of its newsgroups and their contents to another NNTP server. You can think of newsfeeds as a newsgroup replication process. The NNTP virtual server that comes with Windows 2000 Server is not newsfeed-enabled. Installing Exchange 2000 Server adds this feature to the Windows 2000 virtual server.

Historically, newsfeeds have been used to replicate public Usenet newsgroups between news servers around the world. Usenet is a worldwide network of computers that supports sharing of news articles through the use of newsfeeds. However, that doesn't mean that there's no place for newsfeeds that synchronize newsgroups solely between the Exchange servers in your Exchange organization.

Within your Exchange organization, you *cannot* use newsfeeds to replicate newsgroups stored in the Internet Newsgroups public folder. That's because such a replication would have to create another instance of the newsgroup folder, inside the Internet Newsgroups folder, with exactly the same name as the newsgroup that you're trying to replicate. This would violate basic principles of both Active Directory naming and logic, so it can't be done. However, you can use newsfeeds to replicate news-groups that are stored in virtual directories other than the Internet Newsgroups folder. We created such a newsgroup earlier, and we'll soon use newsfeeds to replicate it on another Exchange server in our organization.

 TIP Although you can't use newsfeeds to replicate newsgroups stored in the Internet Newsgroups folder to other Exchange servers in your organization, you can replicate any newsgroup in the Internet Newsgroups folder as you would any other public folder. For more on public folder replication, see the section "Managing Public Folders," in the next chapter.

Key to setting up a newsfeed is an arrangement with the manager of the NNTP server that has the newsgroups that you want to replicate. You must arrange to either send newsgroup information to or retrieve it from the other server. When that agreement is in place, you can exchange newsgroup information with the other NNTP server within the limits that you and the manager of that server set. We'll explore those lim-its later in this section.

Newsfeeds are set up between two NNTP servers. A feed must be set up on each server. Exchange 2000 Server supports three different kinds of newsfeeds:

- Master
- Slave
- Peer

Master/slave newsfeed configurations enable you to distribute the load on a group of NNTP servers. Depending on your needs, you can set up one or more slaves. The mas-ter NNTP server can send news articles to or receive news articles from its slave servers. The master NNTP server assigns a unique ID to each news article that moves between it and its slaves. The master uses these IDs to keep track of the news articles on each slave. Using information in its news article ID database, the master sends only new news articles to its slaves. Master/slave configurations are generally used inside an organization.

Peer newsfeed configurations usually are used to support the exchange of news articles between two Usenet NNTP servers. IDs are not attached to news articles trans-mitted between peers. As news articles are received, the peer server adds IDs to them. Armed with its ID database, a peer NNTP server can be a master server.

The same NNTP virtual server can be a master server or a peer server, but not both. Either a master or a peer server can support slaves. In either case, the effect is the same. Peer and master servers interact with their slaves in exactly the same way, and you set up master/slave relationships in exactly the same way.

I could spend a good deal of time going over the range of possible newsfeed configuration permutations and combinations. Instead, I'm going to focus on a simple scenario and then let you take it from there, setting up whatever peer and additional master/slave configurations you need.

Rather than work with Usenet newsgroup feeds, I'm going to concentrate on setting up a master/slave newsfeed internal to your Exchange organization. This should give you enough exposure to newsfeeds that you can set up a Usenet feed if and when you need one. I'm going to set up newsfeeds to support the master/slave replication of the newsgroup that we created in a new NNTP virtual directory back in the section "Creating and Using Virtual Directories." This isn't a hollow and meaningless exercise. Newsgroup replication using newsfeeds is the only way that you can create a replica of a newsgroup stored in an NNTP virtual directory other than the one where the Internet Newsgroups public folder is stored.

Before we go any further, I have a little secret to tell you: While you weren't looking, I set up another Exchange server, EXCHANGE02. Well, actually, I set it up in the next chapter. Talk about time warps! Anyway, I'm going to use EXCHANGE02 as the slave server in my master/slave newsfeed configuration. Don't let your lack of a second Exchange server stop you cold. I suggest that you read through the rest of this section, while newsgroups are fresh in your mind. Then, after you've set up at least one more Exchange server in the next chapter, you can come back and complete the master/slave feed exercise that follows.

Before we start creating newsfeeds, you need to create a new NNTP virtual directory exactly as you did in the section "Creating and Using Virtual Directories." You must create this virtual directory on the server where you want to replicate your newsgroup. For me that's EXCHANGE02. *This is important: You must create the directory, but you must not create the newsgroup that you're going to replicate. Your newsfeeds will take care of creating the newsgroup and populating it with news items.*

Okay, assuming that you've created your new NNTP virtual directory, we're ready to go. First we need to create a feed to our slave server on the server that will function as our master NNTP server. This is the server on which you created your first NNTP virtual directory. For me, that's EXCHANGE01.

To set up a newsfeed, right-click the Feeds subcontainer of your NNTP virtual server and select New ➤ Feed. Then use the resultant New NNTP Feed wizard, shown in Figure 14.56, to create your newsfeed.

FIGURE 14.56

Entering the name of the remote newsfeed server on the first page of the New NNTP Feed Wizard

Enter the fully qualified domain name or IP address of the newsgroup server on the first page of the wizard (see Figure 14.56). You want to enter the name or IP address of the server that will become the slave NNTP server for this newsfeed. For me, that's exchange02.bgerber.com. Ideally, at this time, your master server should be capable of making a network connection to the slave server. If it can't, when you click Next, you'll see a dialog box telling you so and asking if you want to use the domain name or IP address anyway. If you know that the connection will be in place when you activate your master/slave configuration, click Yes. If not, then your master/slave configuration won't work, but at least you can get some experience setting up a master/slave newsfeed configuration. When you're done, move on to the next wizard page.

On this page, you specify the role that the remote server will play (see Figure 14.57). You're creating a newsfeed from what will be your master NNTP server to your slave NNTP server. The remote server will be a slave. Select the slave option.

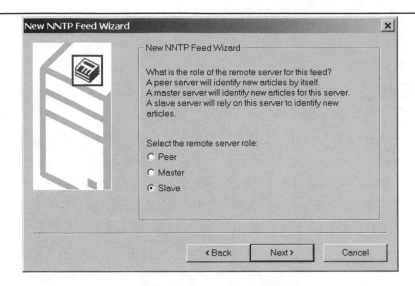

Now you must set the direction of this newsfeed. You do this on the next wizard page. You want your master NNTP server to send news articles to your slave NNTP server; this is the master side of the configuration, so you should select Outbound, as I have in Figure 14.58.

FIGURE 14.58

Specifying whether the newsfeed master server will receive (Inbound) or send (Outbound) news articles to its newsfeed slave on the third page of the New NNTP Feed Wizard

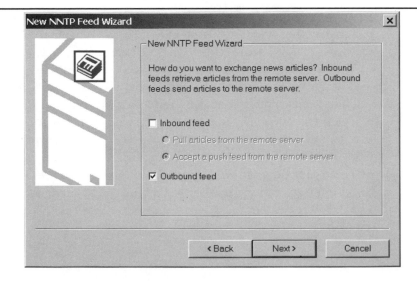

Finally, you must specify the newsgroup(s) to be sent to your slave NNTP server. When you first see the wizard page, shown in Figure 14.59, there's an asterisk in the Newsgroups field. You should delete that entry by selecting it and clicking Remove. Now you need to add an entry for the newsgroup that you want to replicate. In my case, this is the newsgroup bga.software.gs.com. Click Add to open the Add News-group dialog box. Enter the newsgroup's name and click OK to go back to the wizard page. Click Finish on the wizard page, and you should see your new newsfeed in the newsfeeds container on the server that is to be the master NNTP server for the newsfeed.

FIGURE 14.59

Specifying which news-groups will included in the newsfeed on the fourth page of the New NNTP Feed Wizard

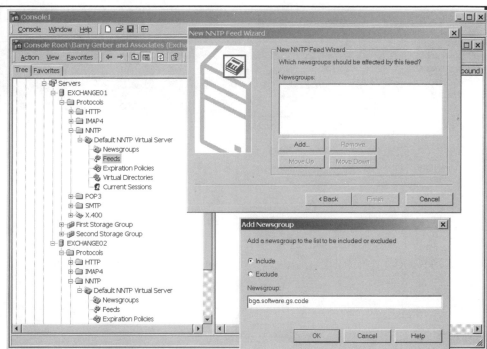

Now you need to create a newsfeed on what will be your slave NNTP server. Follow the directions that you used to set up the newsfeed for your master NNTP server, making only the following changes:

   First wizard page   Enter the domain name or IP address of your master NNTP server. (Mine is exchange01.bgerber.com.)

   Second wizard page   Select Master.

   Third wizard page   Select Inbound.

On the fourth wizard page, do exactly as you did when setting up the same page for your slave NNTP server. It should be clear why you filled in the master newsfeed wizard as you did. If not, review the explanatory text at the beginning of this section.

Master servers replicate only when a new news article shows up in a newsgroup, so until you post a news article in a newsgroup, nothing will happen. The master doesn't even send information about the newsgroup itself until a new item appears in the newsgroup, so you won't see the newsgroup until you post a new article in it. I'll show you how to post news articles in the next section, "NNTP Setup: The Client Side." Before you dash over there, however, I suggest that you finish this section. To satisfy your curiosity a bit, Figure 14.60 shows the newsgroups on my Exchange server after the master, EXCHANGE01, updated the slave, EXCHANGE02.

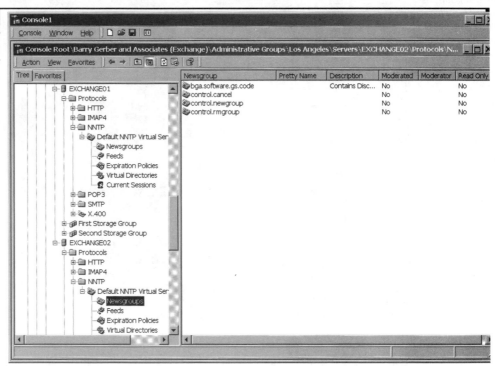

FIGURE 14.60

The newsgroup after it has been replicated to the slave NNTP server

Now we need to look at the dialog box that you use to manage newsfeeds. Find the
newsfeed for your slave NNTP server. Remember, it's on your master server, not on
your slave server. Double-click the newsfeed to open its Properties dialog box. The
General property page of dialog box is shown in Figure 14.61. On the General page,
you can see what kind of feed you're working with, enable or disable the newsfeed,
modify the name of the slave server, and change the TCP port used to link the master
and slave servers for this newsfeed. Both servers must use the same TCP port.

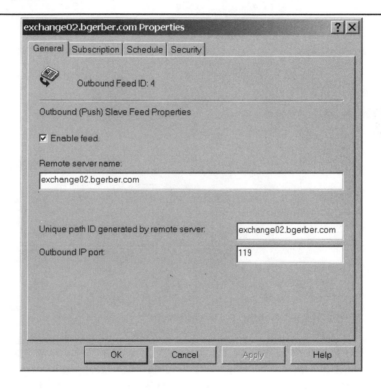

FIGURE 14.61

The General property
page of the slave
newsfeed, as created
on the NNTP master
server for the
newsfeed

You use the Subscription property page to add and remove newsgroups from a newsfeed. As you can see in Figure 14.62, the page looks pretty much like the New NNTP Feed Wizard page, shown in Figure 14.59. You use this page in exactly the same way to change the newsgroups that will be sent to your slave server.

FIGURE 14.62

The Subscription property page of the slave newsfeed as created on the NNTP master server for the newsfeed

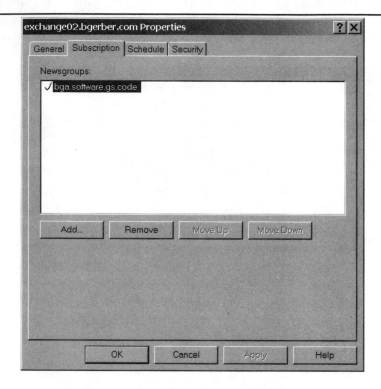

The Schedule property page in Figure 14.63 is a bit deceiving. As I noted earlier in this section, master NNTP servers send new newsgroup information when a new news article appears in a newsgroup, so this schedule isn't for initiating the sending of new news articles. Rather, it's for setting a retry interval and the maximum number of retries allowed, and for indicating when (if ever) the master should stop trying to connect to the slave to send queued newsgroup information. The defaults are okay for reliable network connections. For less reliable network connections, however, you should experiment to find a good combination of run interval and maximum number of attempts.

FIGURE 14.63

*The Schedule property
page of the slave
newsfeed, as created
on the NNTP master
server for the
newsfeed*

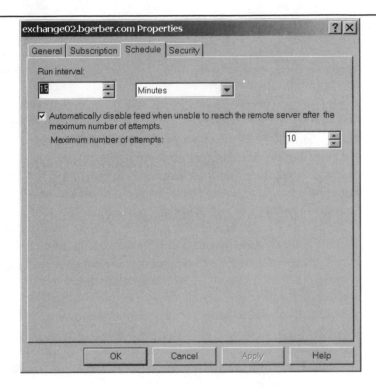

Except for the fact that it's for a slave newsfeed, the dialog box for a slave newsfeed
looks pretty much the same as the dialog box for a master feed. The only major difference is that the Schedule property page is grayed out, which makes sense because the
slave isn't doing any sending in the newsgroup configuration that we've set up. Of
course, you can set up slave configurations in which the slave sends outbound newsgroup information to a master, such as to provide the master with newsgroup postings made by users to the slave NNTP server. As you might expect, the Schedule
property page for a slave server so configured is not grayed out, meaning that you can
set retry interval, maximum retries, and other properties.

That's about all the time we have for newsfeeds. For more information, check out
the Exchange 2000 documentation and the book *Managing Usenet*, by Henry Spencer
and David Lawrence (O'Reilly and Associates, 1998).

NNTP Setup: The Client Side

If you use the standard Outlook client or a Web browser to access newsgroup folders, you don't have to do a thing. You access newsgroup folders just as you'd access any other public folder.

If you use a standard NNTP client such as FreeAgent, WinVN, or Outlook Express, you'll have to do a bit of configuring. You'll need to enter the Internet domain name or IP address of the Exchange server that supports your NNTP server. You'll also have to enter appropriate security information, if required.

Each NNTP client has its own unique user interface, and all of these are pretty straightforward. So, unless you're using Outlook Express, I'll leave it to you to figure out how to set up and use your favorite client.

Here's how to set up a news account in Outlook Express. Select Tools ➢ Accounts. On the Internet Accounts dialog page, click Add and select News from the pop-up menu. When the Internet Connection Wizard opens, enter your name; on the next wizard page, enter your e-mail address. Use the next wizard page to enter the fully qualified domain name or IP address of your news server; my server is news.bgerber.com. If you've turned off anonymous access to your news server, select My News Server Requires Me to Log On, and click Next. If you don't need to log onto your NNTP server, you're done. If you need to log on, enter your logon name and password on the next wizard page, and select Secure Password Authentication, if it's required. Then you're done.

Next you'll be asked if you'd like to view a list of available newsgroups. Answer in the affirmative. Outlook Express' news client then downloads a list of newsgroups, and the Newsgroup Subscriptions dialog box, shown in Figure 14.64, opens. Select the accounts that you want to subscribe to, and click Subscribe. When you're done, click OK and take a look at Outlook Express. Your new news account and the newsgroups that you subscribed to should now show up in the left pane of Outlook Express (see Figure 14.65). Notice in Figure 14.65 how I'm also viewing my Exchange public folder-based newsgroups using my IMAP4 account. Finally notice that the one newsgroup that isn't stored in my public folders, BGA.Software.GS.Code, shows up in my news account, but not among the public folders in my IMAP4 account. Yahoo! Everything works as advertised.

FIGURE 14.64

*Subscribing to news-
groups using the
Newsgroup
Subscriptions
dialog box*

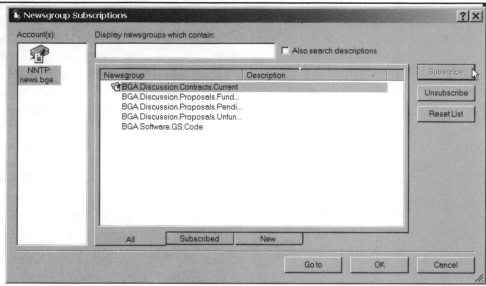

FIGURE 14.65

*Viewing newsgroups in
Outlook Express and
composing a news
article*

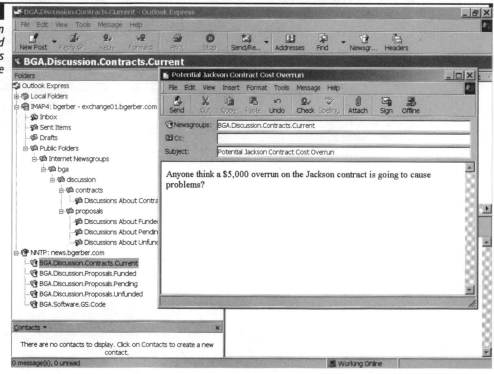

In Figure 14.65, I'm composing a news article that I want to post to the BGA.Discussion.Contracts.Current newsgroup. I just selected the newsgroup and clicked New Post in the top-left corner of Outlook Express. That opened the window that I'm using to compose a message about cost overrun on a BGA contract. Actually, I'm asking a question that I hope others will respond to. To post the message, I click Send. The message goes into my Outlook Express outbox. To send it, I click Send/Receive on the Outlook toolbar. Actually, all you can see in Figure 14.65 is Send/Re.

To view the news article that I sent, I need to synchronize my newsgroups. As Figure 14.66 shows, Outlook Express newsgroup accounts have an account management bar in the right pane that is much like the one for IMAP4 accounts. After clicking the synchronization check box for each newsgroup, I simply clicked Synchronize to download from my NNTP virtual server all available articles in the newsgroups to which I subscribed. Notice that there's one unread news article in the BGA.Discussion.Contracts.Current newsgroup. That's the one that I posted back in the last paragraph. I can also read the article in the public folder Discussion About Contracts Currently in Force.

FIGURE 14.66

Synchronizing news-groups using the Outlook Express news account management bar

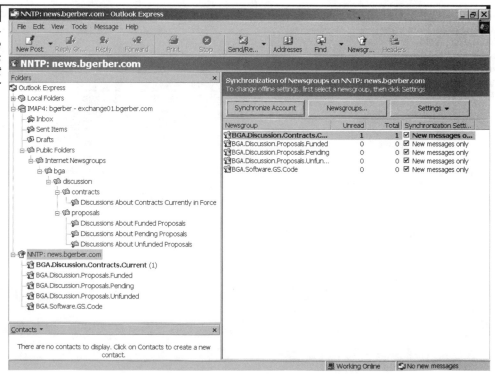

Okay, it's a little later now, and as Figure 14.67 shows, Jane Dough and I have been carrying on a conversation about the Jackson cost overrun. Notice that the conversation is displayed in threaded format. Each response is linked to the specific news article to which the response was made. In this case, Jane responded to me, and I responded to her response. Conversation threading is very nice. You can also view news articles in threaded format using the standard Outlook client by selecting View ➢ Current View ➢ By Conversation Topic. This is not some special feature for newsgroups. You can view the contents of any Outlook folder in threaded format. By the way, in IMAP4 clients, threaded views aren't available for Exchange public folders or any other folders, for that matter. You can verify this for yourself by checking out your public folders in the IMAP4 client.

FIGURE 14.67

Viewing a threaded newsgroup discussion in Outlook Express

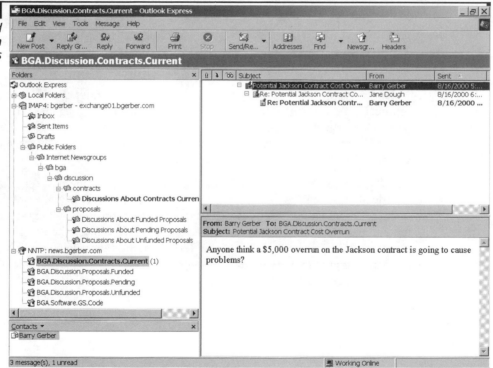

What About Those Other Exchange 2000 Server Internet Services for Internet Clients?

Exchange 2000 supports two additional services for Internet-based clients, Chat Server and Instant Messaging Server, as well as one service that partly uses Internet protocols, Conferencing Server. Instant Messaging Server is part of the Standard and Enterprise editions of Exchange 2000 Server. Chat Server is available only in the Enterprise edition. Conferencing Server is a separate product.

To cover the Internet-based services I discussed in this chapter, I had to forgo discussing these three services in detail. Here's a quick run-through on the services so that you can at least see what they might do for your organization. For more information, see the Exchange 2000 Server online documentation.

Exchange chat service enables real-time, text-based interaction between users through the Internet Relay Chat (IRC) and Extended Internet Relay Chat (IRCX) protocols. Microsoft developed the latter protocol.

Instant messaging is based on the Microsoft-designed Internet-oriented rendezvous protocol (RVP), which Microsoft is working to make a full-fledged Internet protocol. Instant messaging also uses the HTTP, LDAP, and WebDAV protocols. A user can find out whether another user in his or her Exchange contacts is online and then, if the user is online, attempt to open a text-based conversation.

Conferencing Server is a separate product that uses Exchange-based messaging and scheduling capabilities to support real-time multisite audio/visual interaction. By default, Conferencing Server uses IP multicasting to enable multi-image interaction among many users at different sites. As an alternative, it can use the non-Internet H.323 standard developed by the International Telecommunications Union (ITU), but only two site interaction is supported. Conferencing Server clients use the ITU's T.120 protocol. Microsoft's preferred Conferencing Server client is its NetMeeting product.

Summary

In this chapter, I focused on configuring and using five advanced Internet client/server protocols: the Post Office Protocol version 3 (POP3), the Internet Message Access Protocol version 4 (IMAP4), the Hypertext Transfer Protocol (HTTP), the Lightweight Directory Access Protocol (LDAP), and the Network News Transfer Protocol (NNTP). POP3, IMAP4, and NNTP can be configured and managed entirely through Exchange 2000 Server. HTTP requires occasional forays into the world of Internet Information Server. LDAP is based in Windows 2000 Server, which is at the heart of that operating system's Active Directory and must be managed entirely on the Windows 2000 side.

POP3, IMAP4, and HTTP (Outlook Web Access, or OWA) let users access all or part of the folders in their Exchange mailboxes with something other than a MAPI client, such as the standard Outlook client. IMAP4 and OWA also allow users to access Exchange public folders. POP3 and IMAP4 clients are available in a number of flavors for a wide range of computing platforms, from the smallest of personal digital assistants to Windows, Macintosh, and Unix computers. OWA enables access to Exchange mailboxes and public folders with a Web browser.

POP3 offers the least sophisticated but also one of the easiest routes to Exchange mailbox access on both the client and server ends. Users can download only the messages that are in their Inboxes. They can see neither the other folders in their mailboxes nor Exchange public folders. IMAP4 adds access to all available folders, both private and public. However, server and especially client setup and management are considerably more complex. OWA is the easiest way to gain non-MAPI access to Exchange mailboxes and the folders in them, as well as to public folders.

The LDAP protocol adds e-mail address and other Active Directory attribute lookup functionality to POP3, IMAP4, and OWA message access. The Windows 2000 LDAP server interacts with Active Directory to find and return information based on queries from LDAP clients. LDAP server management is the least user-friendly of all. Only those well schooled in the intricacies of Active Directory should attempt to alter its settings. By default, the LDAP server is tightly secured to protect the rich and highly sensitive data that is maintained in Active Directory. Generally, it is very good practice to leave security as it is.

Exchange NNTP support brings Internet newsgroups to Exchange public folders while preserving newsgroup access from standard NNTP clients. This functionality enables threaded discussions that are accessible through standard MAPI and NNTP clients. Although NNTP services are generally associated with public news servers operated by Internet Service Providers, organizations should also seriously consider using NNTP to support Intranet communications.

As with the SMTP service, virtual servers support POP3, IMAP4, HTTP, and NNTP services. Multiple virtual servers can be created for any of the four protocols. This allows for the dedication of different servers to different organizational or user needs.

Implementing each of these protocols involves setting limits that protect computers and networks against overloading. These limits revolve around such things as total number of connections to the protocol server, and the amount of data moved in one operation or during a single connection.

Additionally, each protocol allows for tight or loose security, at both the user authentication and the packet encryption levels. Security is enough of an issue when Internet protocol communications take place on an intranet. It is critical when sensitive data must travel the Internet. The strongest security available from Microsoft for these protocols is based on Windows 2000 account-based authentication and Secure Sockets Layer (SSL) encryption. Some POP3 and IMAP4 clients support client-side digital signatures for additional user authentication.

The POP3 and IMAP4 protocols also support different kinds of message formatting. This includes plain-text and MIME formatting, as well as choices of character sets. The IMAP4 server even supports Microsoft's Exchange rich-text format.

None of the Internet protocols supported by Windows 2000 Server/Exchange 2000 Server offers the rich set of features available with the standard Outlook MAPI client. However, in certain circumstances, such as for home and on-the-road use, a simpler, easier-to-install, and lighter-weight client could very well be the right choice.

In the next chapter, we'll add another Exchange server to our domain. Then we'll add a new domain and an Exchange server in that domain. This will give us a chance to explore a range of Exchange server features, from front-end/back-end server configurations to folder replication.

CHAPTER **15**

Installing and Managing Additional Exchange 2000 Servers

FEATURING:

Okay, we're ready to add new Exchange servers to our Windows 2000 domain and to a new domain in our Windows 2000 forest. We'll start by adding a new server to our first domain and its default administrative group. Generally, you add new servers in an administrative group to handle the load created by additional users or to provide local area network connectivity for a group of users with slower wide-area links to other Exchange servers in the group. We'll be moving pretty fast in this chapter, so fasten your seat belts.

Adding an Exchange Server to a Domain's Default Administrative Group

You've already installed one Exchange server in your administrative group. Installing another is a pretty basic task. You'll need a second Windows 2000 server on which to install Exchange Server. Instead of going through the second installation in detail, I'll just call your attention to any differences that you'll encounter when installing another server in your domain. You'll find full details on installing Windows 2000 Server in Chapter 7, "Installing Windows 2000 Server," and Exchange 2000 Server in Chapter 8, "Installing Exchange 2000 Server."

Installing an Additional Windows 2000 Server

For our purposes here, you should install your new server in your existing Windows 2000 domain, the one that you used for your first installation. (For me, that's my bgerber.com domain.) Like your first Exchange server, it's better that your second Exchange server not be a domain controller. Don't forget to name the server according to the naming conventions that you've set up. (Mine will be called EXCHANGE02.) When you're done and your new Windows 2000 server is up and running, ensure that you can see it from your first server. Try pinging the server by name: `ping exchange02.bgerber.com`, for example. This will work just fine if you follow the directions in Chapter 7 for installing a Windows 2000 server that is to become an Exchange server.

Installing an Additional Exchange 2000 Server

Installing another Exchange server in a domain is about the easiest thing you'll ever do. First, insert the Exchange Server CD-ROM into the CD-ROM drive of your new

Windows 2000 server. When the setup program starts, click Exchange Server Setup, agree to the licensing information, and select the Exchange components that you want to install. That's it! Because there can be only one Exchange organization in a domain, the installation program simply uses existing information about your Exchange organization to install your second Exchange server. No questions asked.

When the installation program is finished, to prove that all is working properly, open the Exchange System Manager program on your first server. You should now see two servers under your administrative group (see Figure 15.1). Now go over to your new server, and set up a Microsoft Management Console with Exchange System Manager and other relevant snap-ins. You should see the same two servers in exactly the same format as on your first server (see Figure 15.2). In fact, things look so much the same that I opened the Properties dialog box for each computer's Computer Management (Local) container just to prove that two different Exchange servers are involved here.

FIGURE 15.1

A newly installed Exchange server, viewed through the Exchange System Manager, running on an already-installed Exchange server

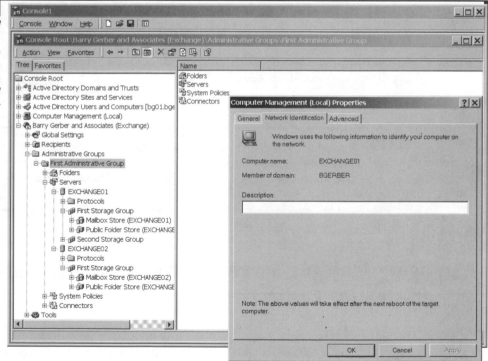

FIGURE 15.2

A newly installed Exchange server, viewed through the Exchange System Manager, running on the new server

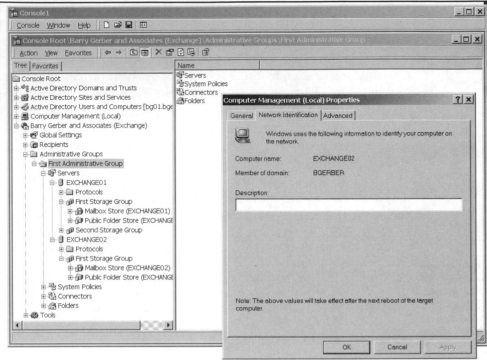

 TIP Throughout this chapter, if you make a change in Exchange System Manager on Server A and don't see the change on Server B, right-click the container on Server B where the change should be visible, and select Refresh. You should then see the change on Server B.

Managing Multiple Servers in a Domain's Default Administrative Group

For most Exchange server features, managing multiserver administrative groups is no different than managing single server administrative groups. Exchange servers in an administrative group write configuration information to and read it from the same

Windows 2000 Server Active Directory. They communicate automatically so that such tasks as cross-server monitoring or public folder replication can take place without any intervention on your part, other than setting up a particular monitoring or public folder replication scenario.

Exchange System Manager is central to multiserver management. It was designed to let you manage a whole Exchange organization from one server or workstation. It works far more transparently and smoothly than Exchange 5.5's Administrator program. You usually don't have to manually connect to a server to manage it, and you don't have to do anything to switch focus from one server to another, other than clicking on that server or one of its containers.

In addition to managing an Exchange server locally or from another Exchange 2000 server, you can manage Exchange servers from a non-Exchange Windows 2000 server or from a Windows 2000 Professional workstation. To do so, you need to install the Exchange management tools on the server or workstation. For information on installing the Exchange management tools under these circumstances, see the sidebar "Running Exchange System Manager Remotely," in the section "Setting Up Microsoft Management Console for Exchange 2000 Server" in Chapter 8.

By and large, when managing one Exchange server from another computer running Exchange System Manager, you can pretty much follow the directions in Chapter 11, "Managing Exchange Users, Distribution Groups, and Contacts," and Chapter 12, "Managing the Exchange Server Hierarchy and Core Components." However, multiserver administrative groups do offer some opportunities and challenges that are not present in single-server groups. I'll focus on these in this section. In multiserver administrative group environments, opportunities and challenges arise in the following areas:

- Creating mailbox-enabled Windows 2000 users
- Enhancing Exchange server monitoring
- Using system policies
- Implementing full-text indexing
- Creating Information Store databases
- Working with public folders
- Moving a mailbox from one Exchange server to another
- Backing up Exchange databases
- Implementing front-end/back-end server topologies

Let's look at each of these in more detail.

Creating Mailbox-Enabled Windows 2000 Users

The only difference between creating a new mailbox-enabled user when you have multiple Exchange servers and creating a new mailbox-enabled user with a single Exchange server is that you have the opportunity create the mailbox on a mailbox store on any of your Exchange servers. You already know how to create new users, so I'll walk you through this scenario quickly. If you need a refresher on new user creation, see the section "Managing Exchange Users" in Chapter 11.

In Figure 15.3, I'm creating a new user. I'm setting a password for the new user in Figure 15.4, and in Figure 15.5 I'm choosing to create the new mailbox on my second Exchange server, EXCHANGE02. As soon as I make this choice, Exchange automatically selects the default mailbox store on the server that I've selected. That is, First Storage Group/Mailbox Store (EXCHANGE01) automatically changed to First Storage Group/Mailbox Store (EXCHANGE02) as soon as I selected Barry Gerber and Associates/First Administrative Group/EXCHANGE02.

FIGURE 15.3

Creating a new Windows 2000 user

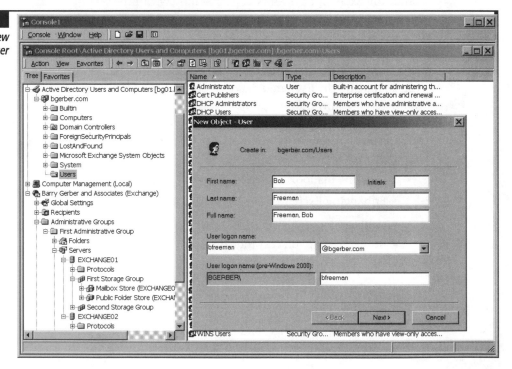

FIGURE 15.4

Entering a password for a new Windows 2000 user

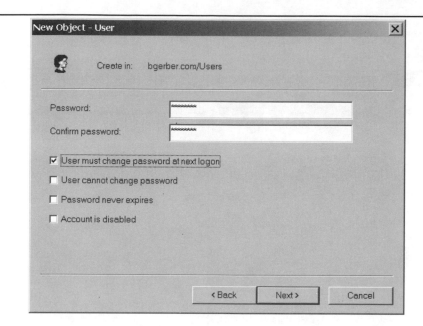

FIGURE 15.5

Choosing to create a new mailbox on a second Exchange server

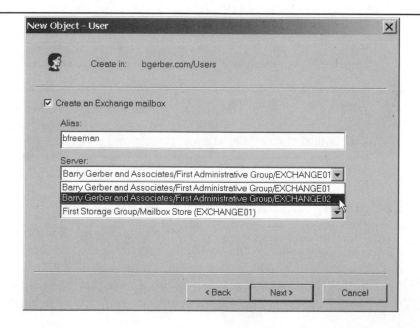

PART

V

Expanding an Exchange
Server Organization

Now check out Figure 15.6. Notice that Bob Freeman's new mailbox is indeed on the default mailbox store on my new server, EXCHANGE02.

FIGURE 15.6

A new mailbox is stored on a second Exchange server.

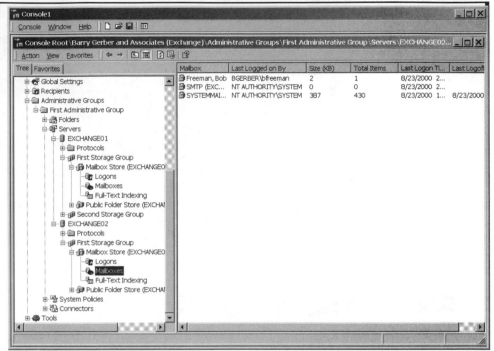

 TIP A new mailbox doesn't show up on a server until it has been accessed at least once. To make a mailbox visible, send a message to the mailbox, or open the mailbox with an Outlook client or Internet e-mail client.

Enhancing Exchange Server Monitoring

Back in Chapter 12, I discussed server monitoring in the section "Monitoring." As you'll remember, you can monitor any service on an Exchange computer. You can also monitor such things as available virtual memory, CPU utilization, free disk space, and SMTP queue growth. When monitors are in place, you can set up your Exchange server so that e-mail or scripted notifications are sent when a monitored resource reaches a particular state. Scripted notifications allow you to send a message to a pager, for example.

In single Exchange server environments, it's possible for services or other resources on the server to deteriorate to such a level that the server can no longer send a notification. In multiple-server environments, one server can monitor another server, increasing the possibility that a notification will be successful.

In Figure 15.7, I'm setting up an e-mail notification in which EXCHANGE01 monitors EXCHANGE02. I'm setting up the notification on EXCHANGE01. I opened the Custom List of Servers dialog box by clicking Customize on the Properties dialog box for the e-mail notification. Note that the notification will be sent to my mailbox, which is on the monitoring server. It doesn't make a lot of sense to send a notification to a mailbox on the monitored server because that server could enter a state in which it would be incapable of receiving messages.

PART

V

Expanding an Exchange
Server Organization

FIGURE 15.7

Setting up an e-mail notification in which one server, EXCHANGE01, monitors another, EXCHANGE02

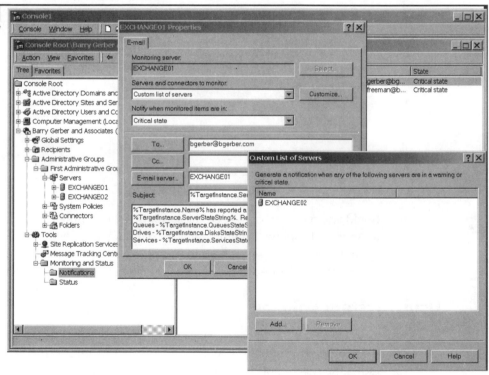

I also need a notification for EXCHANGE01. I'm setting up that notification in Figure 15.8. Notice that notification will be sent to bfreeman@bgerber.com, the mailbox that we created on EXCHANGE02 in the last section.

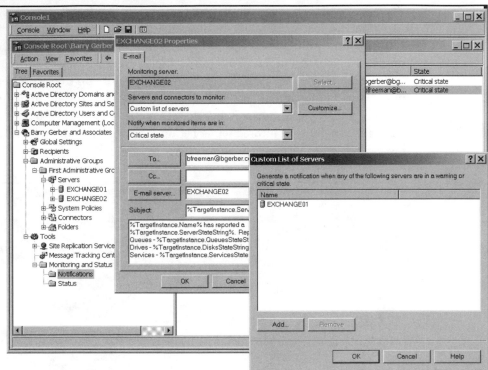

FIGURE 15.8

Setting up an e-mail notification in which one server, EXCHANGE02, monitors another, EXCHANGE01

You should also run notifications on the server being monitored. This protects against a situation in which network failures prevent one Exchange server from seeing another, but in which the server with problems can still be reached by an e-mail client or can still access resources required to send a scripted notification.

Using System Policies

System policies enable you to create a template that specifies how certain properties will be set for servers, mailboxes, and public stores in an administrative group. Figure 15.9 shows the system policy that we created back in Chapter 12 in the section "Creating and Managing Server Policies." Remember that server policies cover only a server's General property page. When I created my server policy in Chapter 12, I added EXCHANGE01 to the policy and then applied the policy. After installing EXCHANGE02, I added that server by right-clicking the policy, selecting Add Server, and then selecting the server from the resultant dialog box Select Items to Place Under the Control of This Policy. Then I applied the policy by right-clicking the policy and selecting Apply Now.

FIGURE 15.9

A server policy for the servers in an administrative group

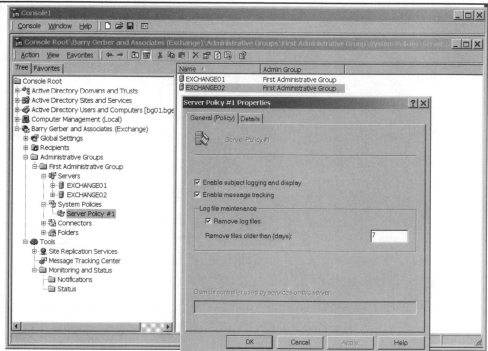

In Figure 15.10, you can see the General property page of the Properties dialog box for each of my Exchange servers. You can tell that the policy is in effect on each server because the properties designated in the policy in Figure 15.9 are grayed out and therefore unchangeable on each server's respective Properties dialog box.

This little exercise should make it clearer how helpful system policies can be when you need to install and manage multiple servers in an administrative group. First, you don't have to set key properties for the servers or their Information Stores. Second, you can lock down certain settings so that they can't be changed inadvertently.

FIGURE 15.10

A server policy applied to both servers in an administrative group

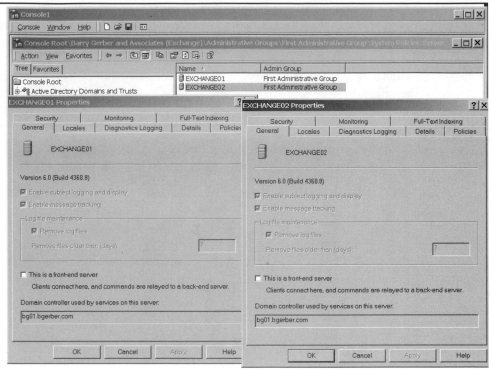

Implementing Full-Text Indexing

Exchange 2000 Server supports full-text indexing of items stored in mailbox and public stores. This significantly speeds searches for specific content in stored items. I discussed full-text indexing in Chapter 12, in the sections "Implementing Full-Text Indexing on a Mailbox Store" and "Use of Public Store Management Containers."

As in Figure 15.11, you can see and manage mailbox stores and information stores on any Exchange server in an administrative group from any computer running Exchange Systems Manager. When you create full-text indexing using an instance of Exchange System Manager that is running on a computer other than the one on which you want to create indexing, you will run into one easily resolved problem.

The catalog for a full-text index is stored on a local drive on the Exchange server where indexing runs. When you try to turn on full-text indexing from another computer, Exchange System Manager selects a local path on the Exchange server where you want to run indexing on which to place the catalog. If you accept the path or change it, Exchange System Manager then tells you that it can't be sure that the local path is valid (see Figure 15.11). This happens because Exchange System Manager isn't running on the target Exchange server. If you're satisfied that the path is correct, you can respond Yes and the index will be created.

As an alternative, you can run Exchange System Manager on the server where you want to create full-text indexing. You can still take advantage of cross-computer management of full-text indexing after the index is created.

FIGURE 15.11

Full-text indexing can be managed from any computer running Exchange System Manager, but indexes should be created with care when Exchange System Manager isn't running on the target Exchange server.

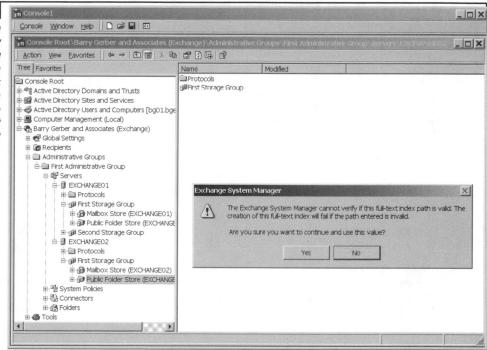

That's all I need to tell you about full-text indexing in multiserver administrative groups.

Creating Information Store Databases

When you use Exchange System Manager on one computer to create a new mailbox or public store on an other Exchange server, you'll run into the same issue as you do with full-text indexes. Exchange System Manager won't be able to verify that the database and log paths that it has chosen for the store's database are valid.

As with full-text indexing, if you're sure about the path, or if you've changed it to one that you know is correct, click Yes, and the database will be created. As an alternative, you can create new mailbox and public stores by running Exchange System Manager on the Exchange server where they will reside.

See the sections "Creating a Mailbox Store" and "Creating a Public Store" in Chapter 12 for more information.

Working with Public Folders

In this section, we'll talk about three issues relating to public folders in multiserver administrative group Exchange Server environments:

- Public folder hierarchy replication
- Public folder replication
- How to access segments of the default (organizational) public folders tree stored on different Exchange servers

Let's look at each of these in a bit more detail.

Public Folder Hierarchy Replication

You can create public folders on any Exchange server that has a default public store (called Public Folders Store). Public folders can contain items in the form of messages, forms, files, and so on. A public folder hierarchy is a list of public folders and their subfolders that are stored in the default public stores on the Exchange servers in an organization. The hierarchy also includes the name of the server on which a copy of each folder resides. The hierarchy does not contain the actual items in the folders. There is one organization-wide public folder hierarchy.

In a single Exchange server environment, the hierarchy exists and is stored on the Exchange server. In multiserver administrative groups, each Exchange server has a copy of the public folder hierarchy. Exchange servers work together to ensure that each Exchange server in an administrative group has an up-to-date copy of the public folder hierarchy. This process, called *public folder hierarchy replication*, is automatic.

Exchange System Manager uses the public folder hierarchy to appropriately display public folder objects in various containers and to retrieve information about public folders, whether that information is stored in the hierarchy or on the server where the public folder physically resides. E-mail clients use the hierarchy to display a list of public folders available on all servers in the organization and to access items in a specific folder. Security limits associated with a given public folder, of course, limit actual access by Exchange System Manager and e-mail clients.

Public Folder Replication

By default, Outlook and Outlook Web Access clients look first for a public folder on the user's public folder store, which may or may not be the same Exchange server where the user's mailbox is located. The default public store is configured on the General property page of the Properties dialog box for a mailbox store. If a specific public folder doesn't exist in the default public folder store, the client is directed to a server where the public folder resides. As you can imagine, when many pubilc folders are accessed over a lower-bandwidth network, server and network loads can get pretty heavy as users access public folders on one or a limited number of Exchange servers. So, if you want, you can replicate folders on one Exchange server to other Exchange servers in an administrative group. This is most useful in two situations:

- When you need to balance public folder access loads on your Exchange servers
- When an Exchange server or group of Exchange servers is separated from other servers by lower-bandwidth links

Additionally, IMAP4 clients see folders only on the Exchange server to which they connect. This includes public folders. If you want an IMAP4 client to see public folders on other Exchange servers, you must replicate the folders to the IMAP4 client's Exchange server.

Having whetted your appetite regarding public folder replication, I'm going to ask you to wait a bit before tackle the subject. We'll get into replication later in this chapter in the section "Managing Public Folders."

Accessing Segments of the Default (Organizational) Public Folders Tree Stored on Different Exchange Servers

You'll remember from the section "Creating and Managing Public Folders," in Chapter 12, that you can create and manage public folders in Exchange System Manager. For the most part, public folder management is straightforward in multiserver Exchange Server environments. There is one gotcha, which I'll get to in a bit. First let's look at the straightforward side.

Figure 15.12 shows the public folders on my server EXCHANGE01. Most of those folders should look quite familiar. We created them at various points in our passionate pursuit of that occasionally elusive little animal Exchange Server. You can double-click any of these folders and see its Properties dialog box. Refer back to Figure 12.21 for a view of that dialog box.

FIGURE 15.12

Public folders stored on the Exchange server EXCHANGE01

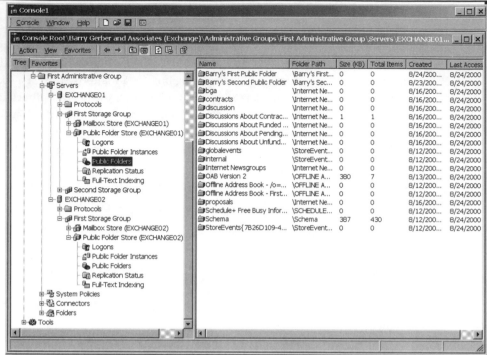

Now look at Figure 15.13. It shows the public folders on EXCHANGE02. First notice that none of the public folders that I created on EXCHANGE01 exist on EXCHANGE02. Refer to Figure 15.12 to substantiate this claim. Also note that EXCHANGE02 has a public folder that I created on EXCHANGE02 that is called Folder on EXCHANGE02. This folder doesn't exist on EXCHANGE01. All of this should demonstrate that the Public Folders container in each Exchange server's Public Folder store contains only folders created on the server itself.

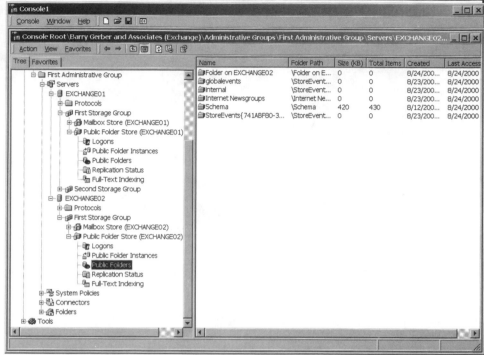

FIGURE 15.13

*Public folders stored
on the Exchange
server EXCHANGE02*

Now we're ready for the gotcha. Let's say that I want to create a new public folder on EXCHANGE02. First I need to locate the Public Folders container that holds the default public folder tree for my organization. I've selected that container in Figure 15.14. To ensure that I'm working in the public folder store on EXCHANGE02, I need to right-click the Public Folders container and select Connect To from the pop-up menu. Then I need to select EXCHANGE02\Public Folder Store (EXCHANGE02) from the Select a Public Store dialog box, and click OK (see Figure 15.14). Now I know that I'm working on the correct public folder store, and I can manage and create public folders to my heart's content.

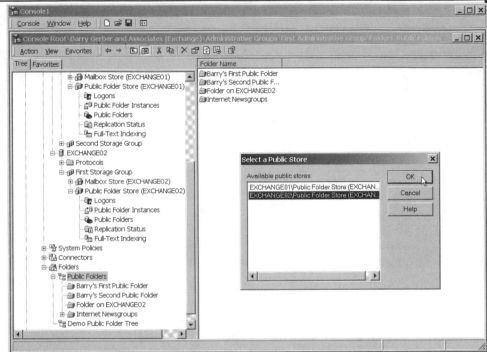

Note that you can't be sure that you're connected to the correct public folder store by the folders that are displayed in the Public Folders container. This display is based on the organization-wide public folder hierarchy. So, you see all public folders in your organization, regardless of whatever server they are stored on in the Public Folders container. In Figure 15.14, I'm connected to EXCHANGE01, but I still see the folder named Folder on EXCHANGE02.

Moving a Mailbox from One Exchange Server to Another

You may need to move an Exchange mailbox to another server for a couple reasons:

- A user moves to a new physical location where a different Exchange server is used to hold user mailboxes

PART

V

Expanding an Exchange
Server Organization

- You need to balance the load on the processors or disks of your Exchange servers, or the load on your networks, by changing the distribution of mailboxes across your Exchange servers

Mailbox moves are quite easy. Find and right-click the user in the Users subcontainer in the Active Directory Users and Computers container. Then select Exchange tasks from the pop-up menu. This opens the Exchange Task wizard. Click over to the Available Tasks wizard page, and select Move Mailbox (see Figure 15.15). Click Next, and select the new location for the mailbox, as I have done in Figure 15.16. Click Next, and the wizard initiates the mailbox move. When the move is complete, close the wizard by clicking Finish. The mailbox should now show up in the mailbox store on the server to which the mailbox was moved.

FIGURE 15.15

Using the Exchange Task Wizard to move a mailbox to a different server

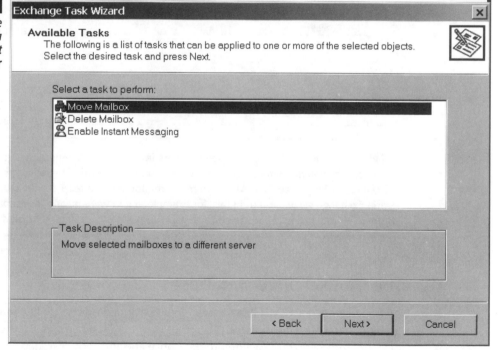

FIGURE 15.16

Using the Exchange Task Wizard to specify the server and mailbox store to which a mailbox should be moved

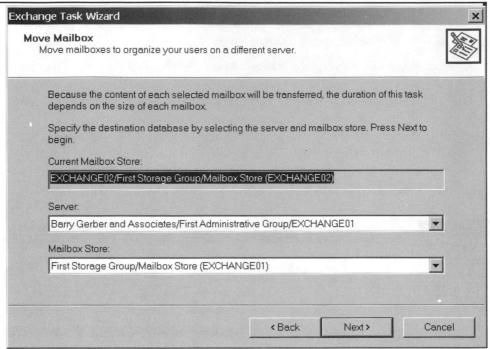

 TIP You move mailboxes between servers in different administrative groups in the same way as you move them between servers in the same administrative group. You can also use the Exchange Task Wizard to move mailboxes between mailbox stores on the same Exchange server. You'd do this, for example, if you were having disk capacity or performance problems and had created a new mailbox store on a different disk drive.

Backing Up Exchange Databases

Any backup product worth its salt will let you back up and restore Exchange Information Store databases, regardless of the server they may reside on. As Figure 15.17 indicates, the Windows 2000 backup program once enhanced by installation of Exchange Server can indeed back up mailbox and public stores, regardless of their home server.

This remote backup capability is a mixed blessing. Centralized backup is generally easier to administer. You can save some dollars on backup hardware and might save on support staff. However, if your Information Store databases are likely to grow significantly, you might find that you lack the network bandwidth required to centrally back up all your Exchange servers in a given time period. Switched Gigabit Ethernet backbones might help, but their cost and maintenance are still relatively high compared to the cost of local backup for each server.

Third-party backup products from a variety of vendors also support multiserver Exchange database backup. For more on third-party options in specific and Exchange Server backup in general, see the section "Backing Up Exchange 2000 Server" in Chapter 8.

WARNING Windows 2000 Server's backup program cannot back up either registry or system state information on remote servers. Third-party backup products are usually capable of backing up these two vital Windows 2000 components.

FIGURE 15.17

Preparing to back up Information Store databases on different Exchange servers using the Windows 2000 backup program, as enhanced by installation of Exchange 2000 Server

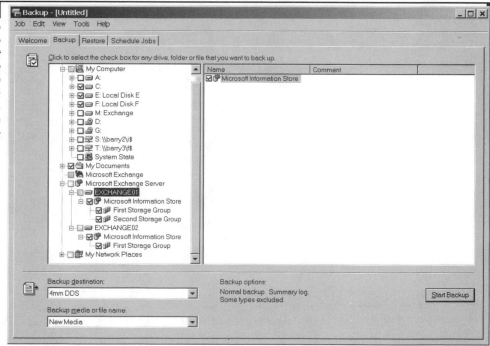

Implementing Front-End/Back-End Server Topologies

I introduced you to the notion of front-end/back-end servers in Chapter 14, "Managing Exchange 2000 Services for Internet Clients," in the section "Front-End/Back-End

Exchange Server Configurations." Basically, when using a POP3, IMAP4, or HTTP (Outlook Web Access or OWA client), a user contacts a front-end server. The front-end server then relays or proxies requests from the user's client to the back-end server that contains the user's mailbox and public folder hierarchy information. The front-end server makes an LDAP query to determine the user's Exchange server. The front-end server also handles Secure Sockets Layer (SSL) data encryption tasks.

Setting up a front-end/back-end configuration is very easy. Select the server that is to function as your front-end server, and open the server's Properties dialog box by right-clicking the server and selecting Properties from the pop-up menu. I've decided to make EXCHANGE02 my front-end server. In Figure 15.18, I've done the one and only thing that I need to do to accomplish this end: I selected This Is a Front-End Server. Then all I had to do was to stop and restart the default POP3, IMAP4, and HTTP virtual servers on EXCHANGE02, and my new server was up and running.

FIGURE 15.18

Turning an Exchange server into a front-end server

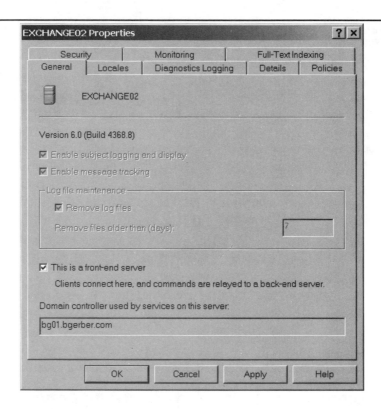

To make things easier, I added some host records to my DNS. As you can see in Figure 15.19, I added records for POPMAIL, IMAPMAIL, OWAMAIL, and SMTPMAIL. All but the last record points to EXCHANGE02, my front-end server. SMTPMAIL points to my other Exchange server, EXCHANGE01. Now when users need to enter a URL or a POP3 or IMAP4 server name or OWA URL, they can just enter the appropriate name based on these host records. Now let's see how this all works.

FIGURE 15.19

New DNS host records make it easy for users to take advantage of a front-end server.

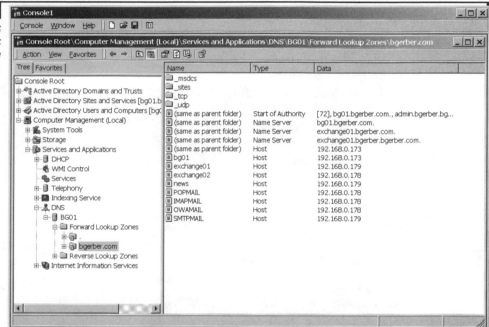

In Figure 15.20, you can see the login dialog box that opens when I enter the URL `http://owamail.bgerber.com/exchange` in my Web browser. I'm trying to access my mailbox, which resides on EXCHANGE01. I don't need to point to EXCHANGE01; my front-end server, EXCHANGE02, takes care of communications between my Web browser and EXCHANGE01, where my mailbox and public folder hierarchy information reside. In Figure 15.21, I'm reading a "very informative" news article about a new contract.

FIGURE 15.20

Logging on to an Exchange server through a front-end server to use Outlook Web Access

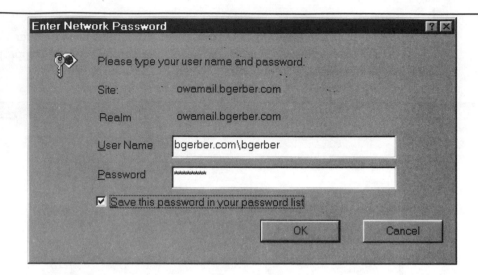

FIGURE 15.21

Accessing an Exchange mailbox and public folders through a front-end server using Outlook Web Access

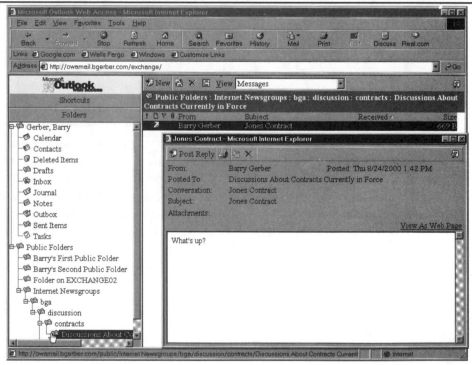

Finally, take a look at Figure 15.22, where I'm setting up my Outlook Express IMAP4 client to access my IMAP4 and SMTP servers using the new host records that I created. Again, even though my mailbox and public folder hierarchy information are located on EXCHANGE01, my front-end server, EXCHANGE02, will handle communications between my IMAP4 client and EXCHANGE01 in a way that's totally transparent to me.

FIGURE 15.22

Setting up an IMAP4 client to access an Exchange server through a front-end server

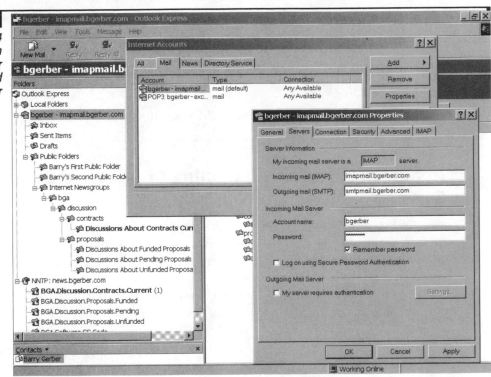

I really like front-end/back-end server topologies. They make it easier for users to access key Exchange Internet access protocols on back-end servers, and they significantly reduce the security-related load on back-end servers.

Adding an Exchange Server to a New Administrative Group in a Domain

I introduced you to administrative groups in the section of Chapter 12 called "Managing Administrative Groups." I talked about how you use administrative groups to distribute management of an Exchange organization based on such criteria as geography or organizational hierarchy. In this chapter, I'll extend that discussion to multiadministrative group Exchange organizations. In this section I'll cover these topics:

- Handling administrative groups, routing groups, and Exchange 5.5 Server sites
- Adding a new administrative group to an Exchange organization
- Installing an Exchange server in a new administrative group

Let's get right to these three very interesting topics.

Administrative Groups, Routing Groups, and Exchange Server 5.5 Sites

In Exchange Server 5.5, you created a new site by installing the first Exchange server in the site. As you installed a new server, you designated either that it would join an existing site or that a new site should be created when the server was installed. Servers could not be moved between sites.

Exchange 5.5 sites served two major purposes. First, they served as a means of controlling management of a specific set of servers. You could give management rights for different sites to different Windows NT groups or users. Sites also served as a place to corral a set of servers linked by reliable, higher-bandwidth networks and as the management locus for intersite message routing. By setting up connectors between sites, you enabled the routing of e-mail and Exchange server administrative messages between sites, and you specified the network services to be used for routing. To enhance reliability, you could also set up multiple redundant routing links between any pair of sites.

In Exchange 5.5, administrative and routing functions were coterminous with the site. Administrative control was granted over the entire site. All servers in the site were linked to other sites and the servers in those sites by the same set of connectors.

With Exchange 2000 Server, administrative and routing functions are separated. Administrative groups work like sites in that you can delegate control over an entire administrative group to Windows 2000 groups or users. Also, as with Exchange 5.5 sites, Exchange servers join an administrative group upon installation of Exchange

Server and cannot be moved between administrative groups when installation is completed.

Routing is handled differently in Exchange 2000 than it was in Exchange 5.5. It's done through routing groups, which reside inside Routing Groups containers within administrative groups. Visualize it this way: \Exchange Organization\Administrative Group\Routing Groups Container\Routing Groups. A Routing Group container can hold many routing groups. A routing group holds information on both the Exchange servers that belong to the routing group and the connections that will be used to connect the routing group to other routing groups in an Exchange organization.

Routing groups work differently, depending on whether an Exchange organization is operating in mixed or native mode. You'll remember from Chapter 12 (in the section "The Exchange Server Hierarchy") that, upon installation, Exchange servers run in mixed mode. This means that they can connect to and communicate with Exchange 5.5 servers using the Exchange version of Active Directory Connector. To retain compatibility with Exchange 5.5 sites, Exchange 2000 administrative groups and routing groups are coterminous in mixed mode. A Routing Group container is installed when the first Exchange server is installed in an administrative group. The servers in an administrative group must all reside in one of the routing groups in the administrative group's Routing Groups container. They cannot reside in routing groups in other administrative groups.

When an Exchange organization is switched to native mode, any administrative group can contain a Routing Groups container, whether it contains Exchange servers or not. Exchange servers can be moved to any routing group in any Routing Groups container in any administrative group in an Exchange organization. This enables you to delegate control of message routing for a set of Exchange servers to a group of managers other than the managers who handle other administrative tasks for those servers (for example, management of system policies or public folders). Assuming that you've actually changed a server's physical network connection, on the software side, you can move an Exchange 2000 server to any routing group in any administrative group with a simple drag and drop or cut and paste. The server stays in its administrative group's Servers container, as it must because, as I've already said, servers can't be moved from the administrative group in which they were created.

 WARNING Before you even think about switching to native mode, please read the warning note in Chapter 12 in the section "The Exchange Server Hierarchy." Key point: You can't return to mixed mode after changing to native mode.

Adding a New Administrative Group to an Exchange Organization

Unlike in Exchange 5.5, in which a new site is created when the first Exchange server is installed in it, in Exchange 2000, you have to create a new administrative group before you install your new server. I love simple tasks, and this is one of the simplest. To add a new administrative group to your Exchange organization, right-click the Administrative Groups container in your Exchange organization and select New ➢ Administrative Group. Use the resultant dialog box shown in Figure 15.23 to give your administrative group a name. You can name the group anything you'd like, and you can change the name at any time, so don't be too concerned about how you name it right now. When you're done, click OK. You should see your new administrative group in the Administrative Groups container (see Figure 15.24).

FIGURE 15.23

Using the new administrative group Properties dialog box to create a new administrative group

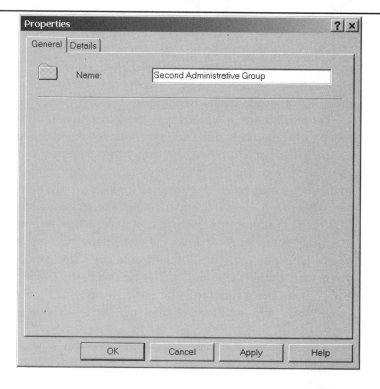

PART

V

Expanding an Exchange
Server Organization

FIGURE 15.24

A new administrative group displayed in Exchange System Manager

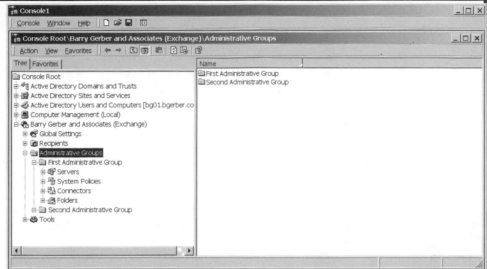

Now let's move onward and install a new Exchange server in our new administrative group.

Add Administrative Groups Only When You Need to Distribute Management Responsibilities

The title of this sidebar may seem a bit redundant, given the discussion of administrative groups in this chapter and Chapter 12. However, I want to make it clear that Exchange 2000 organizations of significant size can exist quite happily with only one administrative group. Because you can create as many routing groups as you need in an administrative group, you can handle a wide range of server location/networking topology issues within a single administrative group. If you determine that one administrative group is enough, you'll still find the following discussion useful as it deals with cross-routing group communications.

Installing a New Exchange Server in a New Administrative Group

This is another very simple task. Follow the directions in the earlier sections of this chapter, "Installing an Additional Windows 2000 Server" and "Installing an Additional Exchange 2000 Server." The only difference is that the Exchange Installation Wizard now shows you a drop-down list from which you can pick the administrative group in which you want to install your new Exchange server (see Figure 15.25). Select your new administrative group, and your new server will be installed in the group. Figure 15.26 shows my new server, EXCHANGE03, installed in my new administrative group. Yesssssss!

FIGURE 15.25

Selecting the administrative group into which a new Exchange server will be installed

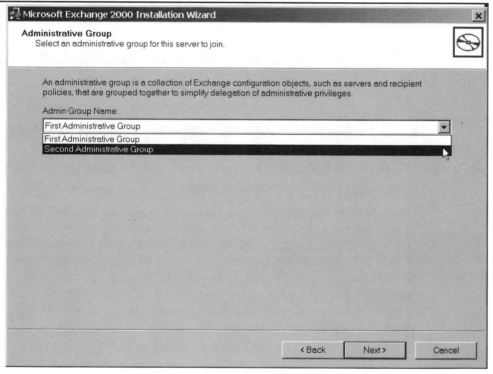

FIGURE 15.26

*A new Exchange server
after it has been
installed in a new
administrative group*

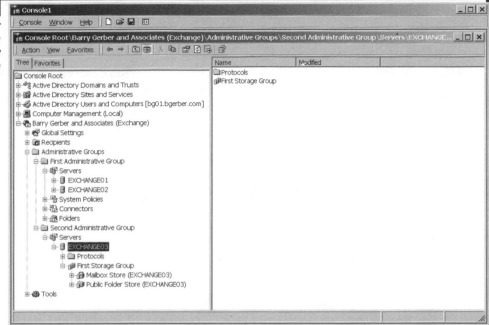

For some of the exercises we'll be doing from here on, you need to switch your
Exchange organization to native mode. Before you make the final move to native
mode, let me remind you once again that this is bridge-burning time. After you've
switched to native mode, you can't go back without reinstalling your entire Exchange
organization. So, think before you leap. If you can't switch to native mode, you can
still track through the remaining sections of this chapter. I'll point out those tasks
that require native mode. Furthermore, if it's possible to do a particular task in some
form in mixed mode, I'll tell you how.

To switch your Exchange organization to native mode, right-click your organization (at the top of Exchange System Manager) and select Properties. On the General
property page of the resultant Properties dialog box for your organization, select
Change Mode and then click Yes to confirm your choice. That's it—your bridges are
burned.

Before we leave this section, I'm going to rename my two administrative groups.
*You can change the name of an administrative group only when your Exchange organization
is running in native mode.* I'm going to call the first administrative group Los Angeles
and the second group New York. This will add a little realism to some of the tasks that
we're going to do in the next section and will make it easier for you to see what's

going on than if we used the original and less-than-informative administrative group names: First Administrative Group and Second Administrative Group.

To rename an administrative group, right-click it and select Rename from the pop-up menu; then change the group's name. Figure 15.27 shows my newly named administrative groups. You can also change an administrative group name by clicking it, and then waiting a second or two and clicking it again. When you do this, the old name is highlighted and you can then type in the new name just as you can with directory and file names in the My Computer directory and file browser.

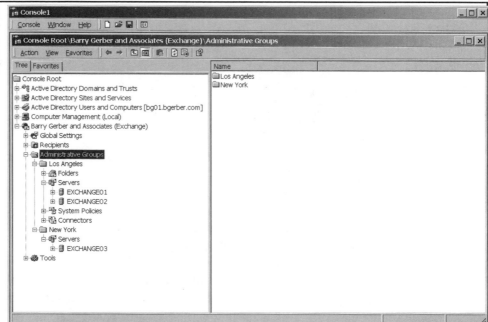

FIGURE 15.27

Two Exchange Server administrative groups after they have been renamed

Managing Multiple Administrative Groups in a Domain

Now that you've installed a new Exchange server in a new administrative group, you have to manage that server and its relationship to other Exchange servers. We'll talk about a number of management tasks in this section:

- Delegating control of an administrative group
- Adding subcontainers to administrative groups

- Using routing groups and connectors
- Managing public folders

The first three of these tasks relate directly to the management of administrative groups and routing groups. You'll most likely need to perform the last management task in this list in multirouting group environments, whether one or more administrative groups is involved. I've chosen not to go into specifics on single-administrative group/multiple-routing group environments (see the sidebar "Add Administrative Groups Only When You Need to Distribute Management Responsibilities"). So, it turns out that this section is the best place to discuss public folder management. I'll also point you back here when I discuss management of Exchange servers that you install in new Windows 2000 domains.

Delegating Control of an Administrative Group

In Chapter 8, in the section "Granting Permission for the Exchange Administration Group to Manage Exchange Server," I showed you how to delegate control of your Exchange organization to the Windows 2000 group Exchange Admins. That delegation gave anyone in the Exchange Admins group permission to fully manage your Exchange organization.

Now let's say that you want to give a different Windows 2000 security group permission to manage each of your administrative groups, which are subcontainers of your Exchange organization. *Except for the fact that your administrative group names will have the standard names in mixed mode, you delegate control over administrative groups in exactly the same way, whether your Exchange organization is operating in mixed or native mode.*

First you need to create your security groups. I need two security groups, one for each of my administrative groups, Los Angeles and New York. As you'll remember, you create users and groups using the Active Directory Users and Computers snap-in. Find and right-click the Users container, and select New ➢ User from the pop-up menu. Enter the name of the group on the New Object – Group wizard, shown in Figure 15.28, and ensure that Global and Security are selected. On the next wizard page, accept the default (do not create an Exchange e-mail address). Then click Next and Finish on the last wizard page. Now follow these same instructions to create a group to manage your other administrative group.

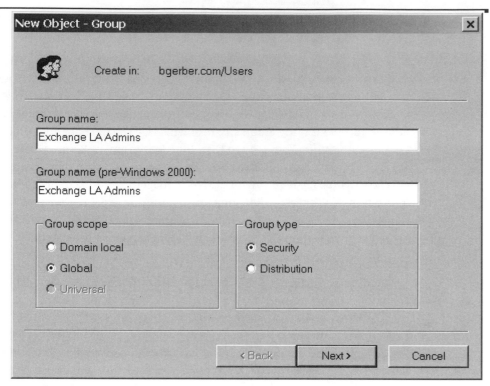

To delegate control of an administrative group to a security group, right-click the administrative group and select Delegate Control from the pop-up menu. In Figure 15.29, I'm delegating control of my Los Angeles administrative group to the security group that I created in the last paragraph, Exchange LA Admins. I clicked Add on the Users or Groups page of the Exchange Administration Delegation Wizard. This opened the Delegate Control dialog box. I selected Exchange Full Administrator on the dialog box and then clicked Browse so that I could select the group Exchange LA Admins from the Select Users, Computers, or Groups dialog box in the bottom-right corner of Figure 15.29. For more on the role options on the Delegate Control dialog box, check out the section "Granting Permission for the Exchange Administration Group to Manage Exchange Server," in Chapter 12. After selecting the appropriate security group, I selected OK until I was out of the two dialog boxes; then I clicked Next on the wizard and then clicked Finish.

FIGURE 15.29

*Delegating control of
an administrative
group to a Windows
2000 security group*

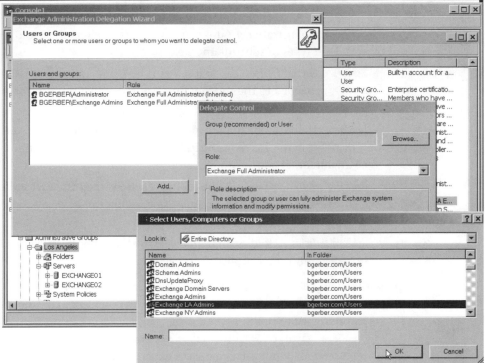

Note in Figure 15.29 that on the Users or Groups page of the Exchange Administration Delegation Wizard, the security group Exchange Admins has Exchange Full
Administrator permissions on the administrative group by virtue of inheritance.
Exchange Admins has permissions on my entire Exchange organization, and these
permissions pass down to subcontainers in the organization. The only way to remove
this group's control over this administrative group is to remove its control at the
Exchange organization level. You can do this if it makes sense, but do leave your
domain administrator in control of your organization, or there will be no way to
manage organization-wide Exchange functionality. Additionally, if you don't leave
your domain administrator in control only the group(s) delegated control over your
administrative groups will be capable of delegating (adding or removing) control for
those groups.

Be sure to delegate control over your other administrative group to your other
security group. Then add the appropriate users to each security group using the Members property page of each group's Properties dialog box.

Adding Subcontainers to Administrative Groups

As you know, administrative groups can have subcontainers that hold a variety of useful objects. Four types of subcontainers exist:

Servers   Created when the first server is installed in an administrative group; servers are added to the subcontainer upon installation into the administrative group.

Folders   Holds public folders (public folder trees); created when the first server is installed in the first administrative group. A subcontainer must be manually created in other administrative groups.

Routing groups   Holds routing groups; created when the first server is installed in the first administrative group. A subcontainer must be manually created in other administrative groups.

System policies   Holds system policies; subcontainer must be manually created in an administrative group when needed.

Only one of any of the four types of subcontainers can exist in an administrative group. Each of the four types of subcontainers can contain one or more of the objects that it was designed to hold.

You've already worked with the server, system policies, and folders subcontainers. In the next section, you'll get a chance to experiment with routing groups; in the section "Default Public Folder Tree Management," you'll use the folders subcontainer to control management access to the organization-wide public folders tree.

Upon installation of the first Exchange server in your organization, your first administrative group was populated with three subcontainers: Servers, Folders, and Routing Groups. The Routing Groups container doesn't show up in Exchange System Manager until you tell Exchange System Manager to display routing groups. We'll do that in the next section of this chapter. When you create a new administrative group in mixed mode, the group has no subcontainers. The new administrative group is populated with a Servers subcontainer and a Routing Groups subcontainer when you install the first Exchange server in the new administrative group. The server is placed in the Servers group and in the Routing Groups container of the new administrative group.

As in mixed mode, when you create a new administrative group in native mode, the group has no subcontainers. When you install the first Exchange server in your new administrative group, only a Servers subcontainer is created. The new server is placed in the new administrative group's Servers container. However, unless you manually create a Routing Groups container and a routing group, and then select this new routing group during installation of an Exchange server, the new server is placed in the Routing Groups container of your first administrative group.

This difference in the way administrative groups are populated with subcontainers in mixed and native mode makes sense. In mixed mode, administrative and routing functionality must reside in the same administrative group to make Exchange 5.5 sites happy. In native mode, it really doesn't matter in which administrative group's Routing Groups container a server is placed on installation because, security willing, it can be dragged into any routing group in any Routing Groups container in any administrative group in an Exchange organization.

In either mixed or native mode, you add subcontainers to an administrative group by right-clicking the group and selecting New ➢ SUBCONTAINER, where SUBCONTAINER is the kind of subcontainer that you want to add. In the next section, we'll add a routing groups container to our new administrative group.

Using Routing Groups and Connectors

Routing groups containers hold routing groups. Routing groups contain connectors and members. Connectors support network links between the Exchange servers in a routing group and Exchange servers in other routing groups. Members are the Exchange servers that are included in a routing group. An Exchange server can exist in one and only one routing group at any given time. Figure 15.30 should help make all this clearer. It shouldn't surprise you that all three of my Exchange servers are in my Los Angeles administrative group's first routing group, even though, as you can see in Figure 15.30, the server EXCHANGE03 was installed in my New York administrative group. As I mentioned earlier, unless you take action to the contrary, a server installed into an administrative group other than the default administrative group is placed in the default administrative group's default routing group.

FIGURE 15.30

An administrative group's Routing Groups container and its subcontainers

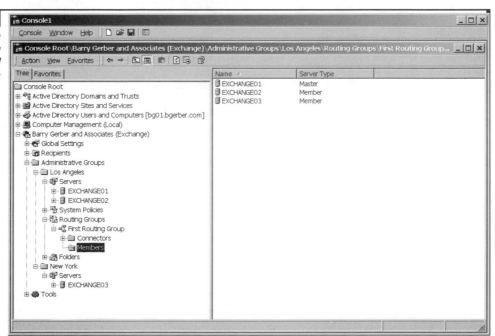

You can use routing groups and connectors in a variety of ways. Here are two examples, each of which I'll expand upon in this section.

If you have two or more administrative groups, each with its own routing group and set of Exchange servers, you can set up routing between the two groups with one or more connectors. If you like, you can delegate control over your administrative groups to different Windows 2000 security groups, thus restricting management of routing in each routing group to a specific group of individuals.

If your Exchange server is running in native mode, you can create one or more administrative groups that contain no servers and then create a Routing Groups container and routing groups in your new administrative group or groups. Then you can drag appropriately connected servers from their original routing group or groups to your new routing groups and create connectors between these routing groups. You can delegate control of message routing to a group or groups entirely different from the group or groups that manage other functionality on your Exchange servers.

By default, routing groups are not displayed in Exchange System Manager. Before we start, I'd like for you to turn on the display of routing groups for your Exchange organization. To view routing groups, right-click your Exchange organization and select Properties from the pop-up menu. Then select Display Routing Groups on the Properties dialog box for your organization, and click OK.

Connecting Exchange Servers in Two Administrative Groups, Each of Which Has Its Own Routing Group

To connect the Exchange servers in two administrative groups, you need to do two things:

- Ensure that each of your Exchange servers is in the appropriate routing group
- Create connectors between your routing groups

Each of these two tasks is relatively simple. Let's tackle them in order.

Ensuring That Each Exchange Server Is in the Appropriate Routing Group

As I noted earlier when I installed the Exchange server EXCHANGE03 in my second administrative group (renamed New York), the server was installed in the Servers container in the administrative group. However, because there was no Routing Groups container in my New York administrative group, the server was placed in the first routing group in the Routing Groups container in my first administrative group, (renamed Los Angeles). Check out Figure 15.30 for a refresher. If I had been in mixed mode, both the Servers and the Routing Groups containers would have been created in my second administrative group, and my new Exchange server would have been placed in those containers.

The problem is that EXCHANGE03 is not linked to my Los Angeles servers on a high-bandwidth, highly reliable network, so it doesn't belong in the same routing group as these servers. I need to place EXCHANGE03 in a separate routing group, either in my Los Angeles administrative group or, if I want to ensure that only the administrators of my New York administrative group can manage message routing on EXCHANGE03, in my New York administrative group.

I want routing for New York servers to be managed by the New York administrators. So, I need to create a Routing Groups container in my New York administrative group. To do this, I right-click the New York administrative group and select New ➤ Routing Groups Container from the pop-up menu. The container immediately shows up in the New York administrative group. Then I need to create a new routing group in the new routing groups container by right-clicking the container and selecting New ➤ Routing Group. This opens the Properties dialog box for the new routing group. As you can see in Figure 15.31, I've chosen to call my new routing group First Routing Group.

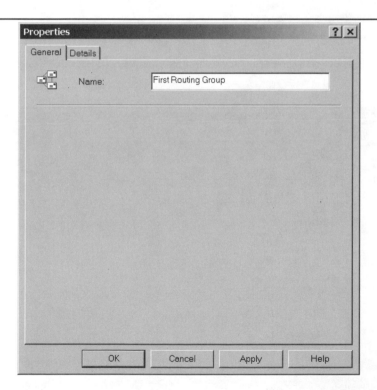

In Figure 15.32, I'm dragging EXCHANGE03 from the routing group in my Los Angeles administrative group into the routing group that I just created in my New York group. Figure 15.33 proves that the drag-and-drop method indeed worked.

FIGURE 15.32

Dragging an Exchange server to a new routing group

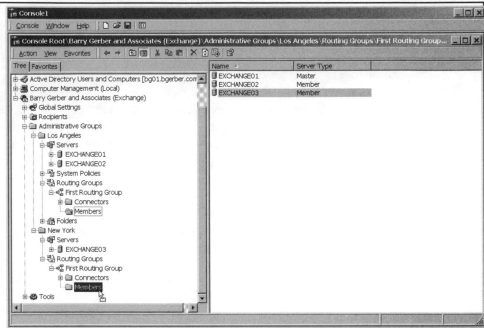

FIGURE 15.33

An Exchange server in its new routing group

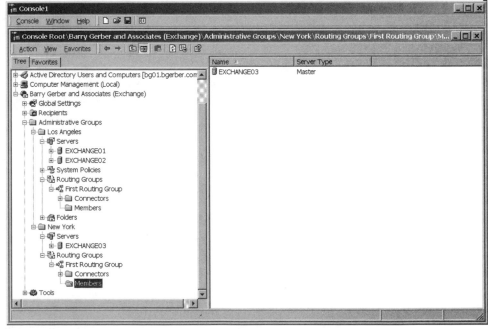

NOTE If your Exchange organization were operating in native mode and you had added a Routing Group container and a routing group to your new administrative group before installing your new Exchange server in the administrative group, you would have been able to select the routing group during installation. Here, I just wanted to show you that you can create and populate routing groups after the fact.

Masters and Members

Notice in Figure 15.32 that EXCHANGE01 is a master, while my other two servers are members. There is one master server in a routing group. This server keeps up-to-date information on the status of all connectors in the routing group. It receives link state information directly from various sources, including member servers. The master then propagates this information to member servers. Knowing the latest link state information limits the number of tries by servers in a routing group to use currently unavailable routes.

Connecting Routing Groups

Now that I've got servers in routing groups in each of my two administrative groups, I can link them with a connector. I have three options:

- Routing group connector
  - Is the simplest of the three connectors to set up
  - Has the fewest parameters to set
  - If security permits, you can automatically connect two routing groups by configuring properties for one of the two routing groups
  - Uses an SMTP connection
  - Requires a continuous connection
- SMTP connector
  - Is similar to a routing group connector, but more parameters must be set
  - Involves manually setting up a connector for each routing group to connect two routing groups
  - Also supports Internet SMTP mail services in conformance with RFC 821

- Works with a continuous or noncontinuous (TCP/IP) connection (for example, a PPP dial-up connection)
- Allows for custom authentication and encryption, remote triggering of e-mail delivery, and message size limits
- X.400 connector
  - Requires understanding of X.400 services
  - Involves manually setting up a connector for each routing group to connect two routing groups
  - Also supports X.400 messaging services in conformance with 1984 and 1988 CCITT X.400 standards
  - Works with a continuous (TCP/IP) or noncontinuous connection (for example, an X.25 connection)

You can create one or multiple connectors to link a pair of routing groups. You create multiple connectors to support redundant links between the routing groups. If you want to set up redundant connections, be sure that each link uses a different physical connection. For example, don't set up a routing group connector and an SMTP connector that both use the same physical network connection. Instead, use different connections, such as a wide-area T1 on a Frame Relay connection for your routing group connector, and a dial-up link for an SMTP connector.

Because of its simplicity and the availability of a continuous TCP/IP connection between my Los Angeles and New York administrative groups, I'm going to use a routing group connector here. You would use an SMTP connector here for the same reasons that you would use one for Internet messaging, mainly to control dial-up links between Exchange routing groups. For more on the SMTP connector, see the section "Installing and Managing the Exchange SMTP Connector," in Chapter 13, "Managing Exchange Internet Services." The X.400 connector is most useful in organizations in which X.400 is already known and used for messaging connectivity. For example, although it has been replaced by SMTP in many venues, X.400 still has a presence in Europe, especially in the world of electronic document interchange. I'll talk more about X.400 connectivity in Chapter 16, "Connecting to Other Foreign Messaging Systems."

To set up an Exchange routing connector, right-click the Connectors container in one of your two administrative groups, and select New ➢ Routing Group Connector. In Figure 15.34, I'm going to create a routing group connector in the first routing group in my Los Angeles administrative group.

FIGURE 15.34

Preparing to create a routing group connector in an administrative group

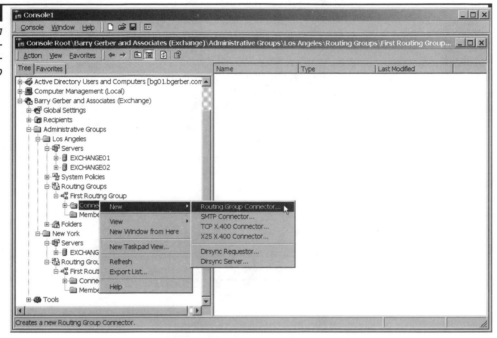

Figure 15.35 shows the Properties dialog box for my new routing group connector. Let's look more closely at the property pages on the dialog box.

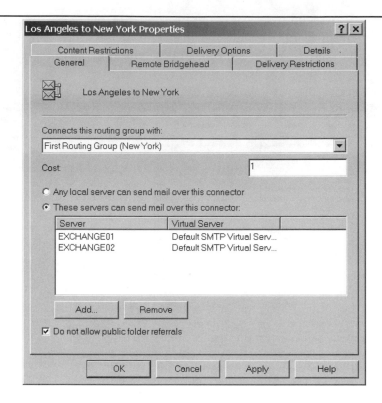

FIGURE 15.35

The Properties dialog box for a new routing group connector, with its General property page exposed

General

Because this connector will link my servers in Los Angeles and New York, I've named the connector Los Angeles to New York on the General property page. The drop-down list presents me with the only choice that I have right now for the routing group to which I want to connect, First Routing Group (New York). This is very nice because I don't have to type in anything. If I had set up a number of routing groups in my Exchange organization, the drop-down list would offer me a choice of all of them.

The Cost setting is useful for establishing usage priorities for multiple connectors between the same two routing groups. For example, if I had both a routing group connector and a dial-up SMTP connector, I would give the routing group connector a cost of 1 and the dial-up SMTP connector a cost of, say, 10. That way, the routing group connector would always be used unless its link became unavailable. Then the dial-up SMTP connector would be used. Costs are also used to determine the closest server when multiple copies of a public folder exist on different servers. Costs can range from 1 to 100.

You can choose whether all servers in the routing group can send mail over the connector or whether just selected ones can. In Figure 15.35, I've chosen to include both of the servers in the routing group. I could have accomplished the same end by select Any Local Server Can Send Mail over This Connector. I made the choice I did because I wanted to hammer home the point that those good old SMTP virtual servers are sending those messages. If I had more than the default SMTP virtual server on one or both of my servers, I would have been offered an opportunity to pick the one that I wanted to handle this traffic. Remember that different virtual servers can serve different IP addresses. So, you could use different virtual servers connected to different networks to provide redundant routing group connector links. That's pretty spiffy.

A public folder referral tells an Outlook client which Exchange servers have a copy of a public folder. The client looks first on its home public folders server, which may or may not be its mailbox server. If the public folder isn't on that server, the home public folder server provides public folder referrals for the public folder. The Outlook client uses these referrals to search other servers for the public folder. If you plan to replicate public folders that exist in other routing groups to at least one Exchange server in the routing group that you're creating, then you probably don't want to forward public folder referrals. If you forward referrals, an Outlook client could try to find a public folder on a distant Exchange server before looking on a local server.

Remote Bridgehead

A bridgehead server is an Exchange server in a routing group that communicates with bridgehead servers in other routing groups. Bridgehead servers receive messages for themselves and other servers in a routing group. They process their own messages and route messages for other servers to those servers. One or more of the Exchange servers in a routing group can be set as a bridgehead server. For fault-tolerance, it's a good idea to set up multiple bridgehead routers, if you have them. In Figure 15.36, I've designated the only server in my New York administrative group as the remote bridgehead server.

You can choose which SMTP virtual server on an Exchange server will act as a bridgehead server.

That grayed-out stuff about Exchange 5.x credentials is used when you're connecting to an Exchange 5.x server. By default, Exchange 2000 cross-routing group communications use Windows 2000 Server-based authentication. When you're connecting to an Exchange 5.x server, the fields aren't grayed out, and you can override this default by entering a Windows NT 4 domain name and account to be used to authenticate this connector.

FIGURE 15.36

The Remote Bridgehead property page of the Properties dialog box for a new routing group connector

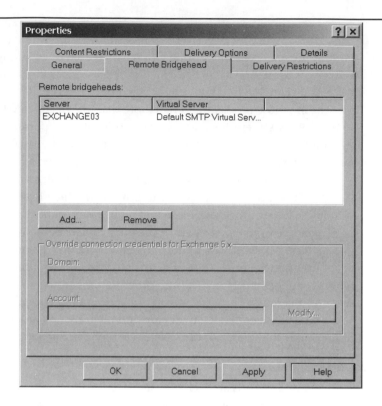

 NOTE Only routing group connectors allow multiple bridgehead routers. SMTP and X.400 connectors can communicate with only one bridgehead router. So, to create multiple Exchange server-based fault-tolerant connections with SMTP and X.400 connectors, you have to set up multiple connectors.

Delivery Restrictions

You can limit message transmission through your connector based on the sender. As you can see in Figure 15.37, you can tell the connector which Exchange recipients to accept messages from and which recipients to reject messages from. When you click either of the two Add buttons, you're offered a list of recipients from which to choose. This page should be somewhat familiar from earlier chapters, so I'll let you take it from here.

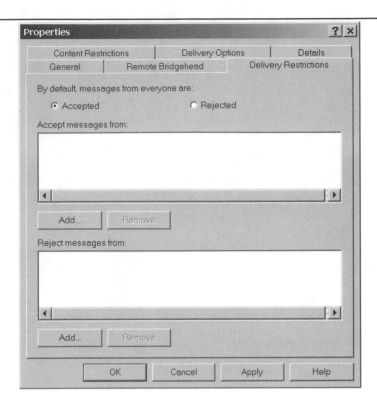

FIGURE 15.37

*The Delivery
Restrictions property
page of the Properties
dialog box for a new
routing group
connector*

Content Restrictions

Figure 15.38 shows the Content Restrictions property page. You can allow or disallow transmission of messages based on the priorities set by their senders. The default is to allow messages of all priority levels through the connector.

Everything that travels between Exchange servers by way of a connector moves as SMTP messages. Nonsystem messages are the e-mail messages that users, contacts, and distribution groups send. System messages are messages from the Exchange or Windows 2000 system. These include public folder replication messages, delivery and nondelivery reports, and Exchange monitoring tool messages. You can dedicate a connector to system or nonsystem messages, or to both.

You can also limit the size of messages sent through your connector. The default is no limit. You might want to do this if the routing group connector you're setting up rides atop a slower network link than another routing group connector.

FIGURE 15.38

The Content
Restrictions property
page of the Properties
dialog box for a new
routing group
connector

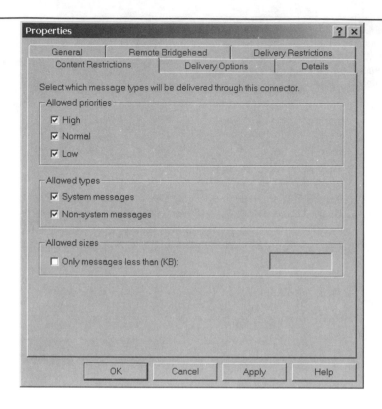

Delivery Options

You use the Delivery Options property page (see Figure 15.39) to specify when your connector should run and whether larger messages should be delivered on a different schedule than smaller messages. You've seen pages like this one before, so I'll leave it to you to work out the details.

FIGURE 15.39

*The Delivery Options
property page of the
Properties dialog box
for a new routing
group connector*

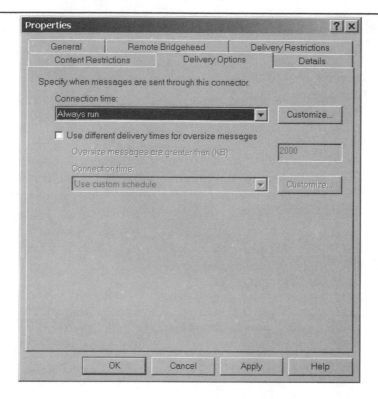

When you've finished with the Properties dialog box for your new connector, click OK. You're immediately offered the option to create the routing group connector for your other routing group (see Figure 15.40). This is that wonderful feature of routing group connectors that's not available with SMTP or X.400 connectors. Based on the information that you entered for your routing group connector, after it creates your local connector, Exchange creates a connector for your other routing group. Click OK to accept Exchange's most gracious offer, and your second connector is created in a flash.

WARNING You must have Exchange Full Administrator permissions for an administrative group to create a new connector in the administrative group. Automatic creation of a remote routing group connector works only if you have such permissions for both administrative groups. If you don't have Exchange Full Administrator permissions for the remote administrative group, someone with such permissions can manually set up the connector for the remote routing group.

FIGURE 15.40

Exchange offers to automatically create the routing group connector for the second of two connected routing groups.

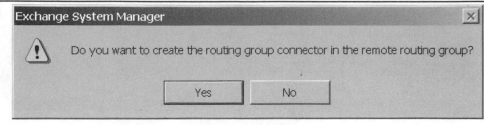

In Figure 15.41, you can see the two connectors that support two-way communication between my two routing groups. Exchange automatically created the connector in my New York administrative group. The connector received the same name as my Los Angeles connector. I renamed it to reflect the fact that it is a connector from New York to Los Angeles. Figures 15.42 and 15.43 show the General and Remote Bridgehead property pages of the dialog box for my New York routing group connector as they were configured automatically by Exchange. That's not bad for a Microsoft product, he said tongue-in-cheek.

FIGURE 15.41

Two newly created routing group connectors link two routing groups in two different Exchange administrative groups.

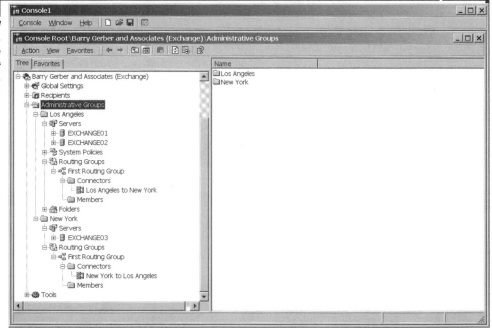

FIGURE 15.42

*The General property
page of the Properties
dialog box for an auto-
matically created rout-
ing group connector*

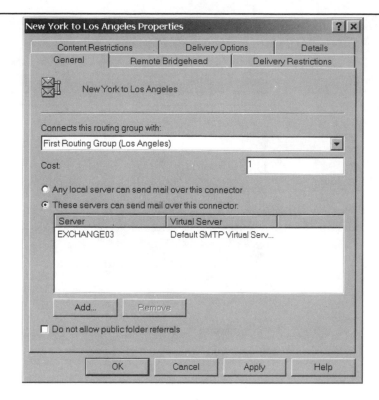

FIGURE 15.43

The Remote Bridgehead property page of the Properties dialog box for an automatically created routing group connector

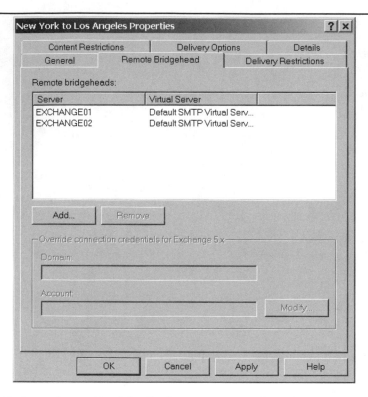

Figure 15.44 shows the status of the Exchange servers and routing group connectors in my Exchange organization. In Figure 15.45, I'm creating a new e-mail notification that will inform me when there is a problem with the connectors in EXCHANGE01's routing group. For more on notifications, see the section "Setting Up Notifications," in Chapter 12.

FIGURE 15.44

Two new routing group
connectors are up and
running.

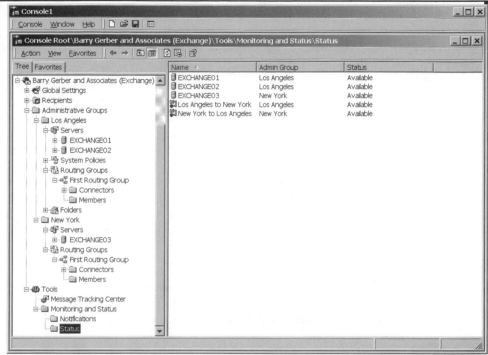

FIGURE 15.45

Creating an e-mail
notification for the
routing group connec-
tors in a routing group

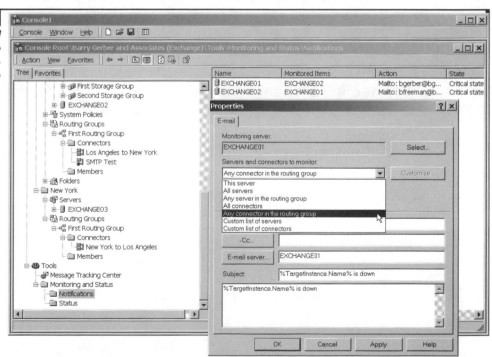

Using Parallel Windows 2000 Organizational Units and Sites

When you've decided to delegate control of Exchange tasks to multiple administrative groups, it might also make sense to similarly delegate control of Windows management tasks. This requires the use of Windows 2000 organizational units (OUs), which work a lot like administrative groups. OUs are created in the container \Active Directory Users and Computers\DOMAIN_NAME, where DOMAIN_NAME is the Windows 2000 domain name; mine is bgerber.com. Right-click the domain name and select New ➢ Organizational Unit from the pop-up menu. Give the OU a name and click OK; your new OU shows up in the DOMAIN_NAME container. You can then delegate control over the OU to any Windows 2000 security group or user, or combination thereof. When the OU is in place, you can then add a new Computer, User, or other subcontainer to the OU, and drag objects from other similar containers and drop them in the new subcontainer.

There is also a Windows 2000 parallel to Exchange 2000 routing groups. They're called *sites*. Sites group together well-connected servers and are the locus for intersite Windows 2000 message routing. You create sites in the Active Directory Sites and Services container. Sites are somewhat more complicated than OUs, so I'll leave it to you to further understand and implement them.

You can find out more about OUs and sites in the book *Mastering Windows 2000 Server* (Sybex, 2000), by Mark Minasi, et al., and the book *Microsoft Windows 2000 Server Administrator's Companion* (Microsoft Press, 2000), by Charlie Russel and Sharon Crawford.

Connecting Exchange Servers Using Routing Groups in Administrative Groups That Have No Exchange Servers

I'm not going to take too much of your time here. Basically, to set up routing groups in administrative groups without Exchange servers, you do the following:

- Ensure that your Exchange organization is running in native mode.
- Create one administrative group or more.
- Delegate control to your new administrative group or groups.
- Create a Routing Groups container in your new administrative group or groups.
- Create routing groups in your new Routing Groups container or containers.
- Add each of the Exchange servers for which you want to manage routing to the appropriate newly created routing group.

- Install connectors between your routing groups.
- Establish appropriate notifications.

Based on your experience in this chapter, you should be able to take it from here and create a very sophisticated routing group setup. Go to it and have fun.

Managing Public Folders

All of what I said about public folders in single administrative group environments in an earlier section of this chapter ("Working with Public Folders") applies to public folders in multiadministrative group environments. Look to that section for more conceptual discussions of public folder hierarchy replication and public folder replication, as well as accessing the organizational public folder tree from different Exchange servers using Exchange System Manager.

Public folder management gets to be more complex as additional administrative groups are created and connected by routing groups. Two issues come immediately to mind.

First, an Exchange organization's one and only MAPI-based default public folder tree can remain in the first administrative group where it was originally created, or it can be moved to another administrative group. In either case, when the default public folder tree has been move to a new administrative group, control of its management can be delegated to a specially constituted Windows 2000 group. Thus, from a security perspective, folders containers and the default public folder hierarchy are somewhat analogous to routing groups containers and routing groups.

Second, as Exchange organizations grow in size and complexity, nothing becomes more important on the public folders side than the location of public folders and replicas of public folders. You can significantly reduce network traffic and decrease folder access times by replicating heavily accessed public folders to Exchange servers in different routing groups with relatively low-bandwidth links to the Exchange servers where the public folders currently reside.

Let's take a closer look at public folder tree management and public folder replication.

Default Public Folder Tree Management

As I noted in the introduction to this section, you can control management access to the default public folder tree by moving that tree to other administrative groups than the one in which the tree was originally created. To do this, you must create a new Folders container in an administrative group, and then drag and drop the default public folder tree to the new Folders container.

In Figure 15.46, I'm dragging my default public folders tree from its default location to a new administrative group and Folders container created just for public folder management. Managers of that administrative group can both view and change the properties of all public folders in the tree and create new folders in the tree. I've delegated control over my administrative group Public Folders Management to a Windows 2000 security group that includes only those users whom I want to be able to manage my Los Angeles and New York administrative groups. Now, the managers of my Los Angeles and New York administrative groups who are not members of the new security group have limited control only over the public folders in their administrative groups through the public folder stores on the Exchange servers in their administrative groups. Check out Figure 15.47 for an illustration. Managers of my Los Angeles and New York administrative groups who aren't included in the security group delegated control over my public folders administrative group can no longer create new public folders. That's because administrative creation of public folders can be done only on the default public folders tree to which they no longer have access.

FIGURE 15.46

Dragging the default public folders tree from its default location to a newly created Folders container in a newly created administrative group

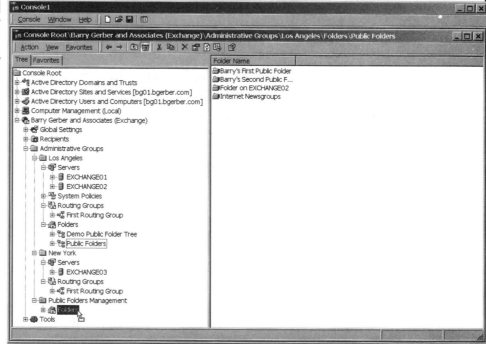

PART

V

Expanding an Exchange
Server Organization

FIGURE 15.47

*Public folder manage-
ment options are lim-
ited to the default
public folder store in
other administrative
groups after the
default public folders
tree for an organiza-
tion is moved to its
own administrative
group.*

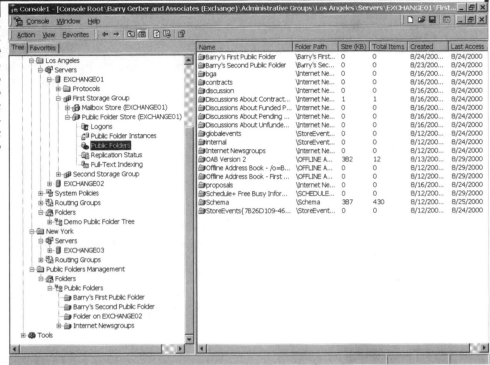

Just for the record, if I needed to do so for security reasons, I could also have created
the Folders container in my New York administrative group and dragged the default
public folders tree to that container. This would give the managers of my New York
administrative group control over my organization-wide public folder hierarchy.

For more information on managing public folders using the default public folders
tree, see the section "Accessing Segments of the Default (Organizational) Public Folders Tree Stored on Different Exchange Servers," earlier in this chapter.

TIP You can limit all administrative access to public folders in administrative groups
that contain Exchange servers (Los Angeles and New York, in my case). You do this by creating an administrative group and installing Exchange servers that support only public
stores into the new administrative group. Then you delegate control over the new administrative group to a Windows 2000 security group that includes only those Windows 2000
users whom you want to be able to manage public folders.

Public Folder Replication

Technically, all copies of a public folder, including the one on the Exchange server where the folder was originally created, are called *replicas*. There's good reason for this. After a folder has been replicated, users will place items into it on the replica on their own default public folders server, or on the nearest server as calculated using connector costs. So, no replica of the folder can be considered a master copy. The replicas of a folder update each other on a regular basis, reinforcing the idea that there is no master copy.

You can set up replication of a public folder on either the server that will provide the folder or the server that will hold the new replica of the public folder. To replicate a folder, right-click the folder in either the Public Folders subcontainer of the Public Folders Store or the default public folders tree. Then select Properties from the pop-up menu. This opens the Properties dialog box for the public folder. Tab over to the folder's Replication property page. In Figure 15.48, I'm setting up a replication of Barry's First Public Folder from EXCHANGE01 (in my Los Angeles administrative group) to EXCHANGE03 (in my New York administrative group). I clicked Add on the Replication property page to open the Select Public Store dialog box. Clicking OK on the Select Public Store dialog box adds EXCHANGE03 to the list of public stores to which the folder's content will be replicated.

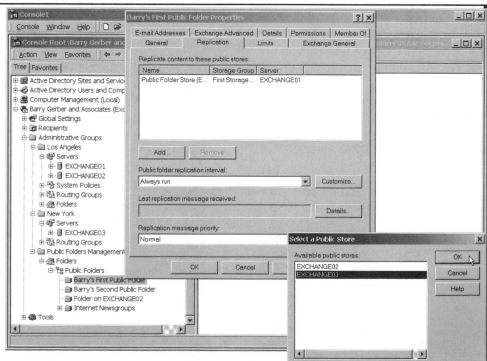

FIGURE 15.48

Setting up replication of a public folder from one server to another

Let's look quickly at some of the other properties that you can set on the Replication property page. The public folder replication interval is based on a schedule that you can set. Depending on the importance of the contents of the folder and available network bandwidth, you can accept the default Always Run, or select other options from the drop-down list or create your own custom schedule for replication of this folder.

When replication has started, the Last Replication Message Received field shows the latest replication status message. We'll look at this field later, after replication has occurred. You can give replication messages for a folder more or less transmission priority. Options include Not Urgent, Normal, and Urgent. Select Normal or Urgent for folders with contents of some importance to your organization; select Not Urgent for messages of lesser importance.

When replication has taken place, you should see the folder in the Public Folders container of the public folders store on the server on which the new replica was created. Figure 15.49 shows the replica on the original server, EXCHANGE01. In Figure 15.50, you can see that a replica of the folder Barry's First Public Folder does not exist on EXCHANGE02, as it shouldn't. Finally, the replica that I just created does indeed show up on EXCHANGE03 (see Figure 15.51).

FIGURE 15.49

The original replica of a public folder on EXCHANGE01

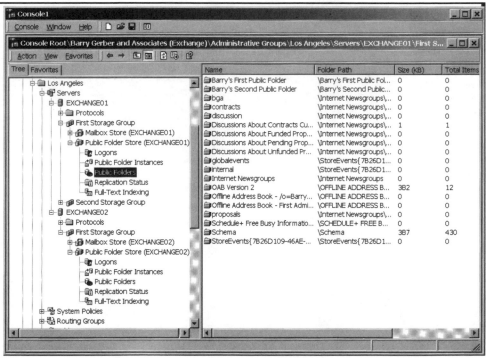

FIGURE 15.50

*There is no replica of
the public folder on
EXCHANGE02.*

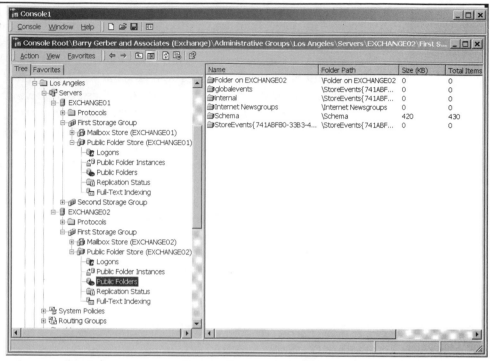

FIGURE 15.51

*The new replica of the
public folder on
EXCHANGE03*

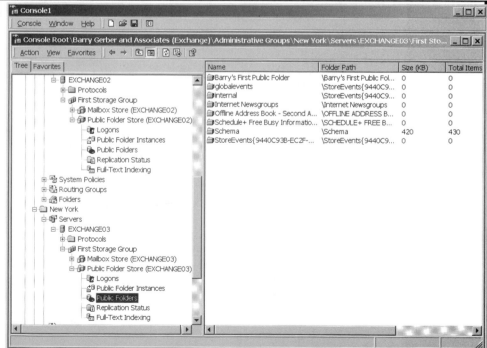

Finally, as Figure 15.52 shows, the synchronization between the two replicas of the public folder is current. That's really all there is to public folder replication. Monitoring replication is a matter of attending to the dialog box shown in Figure 15.52 and, of course, ensuring that the connectors between your routing groups are up and running.

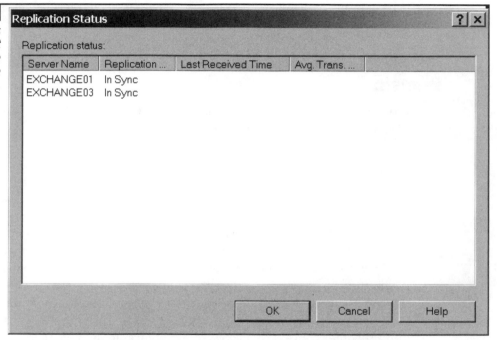

 TIP You can set replication scheduling and message size defaults for public folders. You set them for each public folders store. To do so, right-click a public folders store and select Properties. Then set a replication schedule or maximum replication message size limit. The defaults are Always Run and No Message Size Limit.

Don't forget that newsgroups are public folders that you can replicate like any other public folder. Everything works as it does with other public folders.

Installing an Exchange Server in a New Domain in the Same Windows 2000 Forest

In this section, we need to start by setting up a new domain. That means we have to install a new Windows 2000 Server domain controller for the new domain. Then we need to install Exchange 2000 Server. As with our previous installations, it's best if the domain controller and Exchange aren't installed on the same computer.

Installing a Domain Controller for a New Windows 2000 Domain

A Windows 2000 forest is the boundary of an Active Directory namespace. Two types of domains can be set up in the same Windows 2000 forest:

- A child domain of an existing root domain tree
- A new root tree

As you read on, you may find it useful to refer to the section "Namespaces," in Chapter 3, "Two Key Architectural Components of Windows 2000 Server."

I might add a new child domain to my bgerber.com root domain tree for one of the subdivisions of Barry Gerber and Associates, my consulting department, for example. I'd likely name the child domain consulting.bgerber.com. The domain consulting.bgerber.com sits below the parent domain, bgerber.com. As you may remember, this sort of domain structure is called a *single contiguous namespace*. From a security perspective, all domains in a single contiguous namespace trust each other. Logging into a subdomain gives a user access to all resources in the single contiguous namespace except those resources to which the user has been specifically denied access.

When you install Windows 2000 server in any child domain in a single contiguous namespace, you don't have to do anything special to create a basic security link between the parent and child domains. An irrevocable two-way trust is set up between the parent and the child domain, meaning that users in either domain can access resources in the other domain as long as they have the appropriate security permissions. The trust is transitive, meaning that if domain A trusts domain B, and domain A trusts domain C, then domain B trusts domain C, and vice versa.

In multiroot tree or noncontiguous namespaces, you add a new root domain that is parallel to other root domains in your Windows 2000 forest. I might add a new root domain to support a new venture by my consulting group, such as selling frozen vanilla yogurt. Hey, that's not so far-fetched. I've certainly spent some time in recent years thinking about such a business (well, actually, any business other than consulting). I'll call this new root domain bgyogurt.com.

As with child domains, when you install an Exchange server in a new root domain, you don't have to worry about a basic security link. Irrevocable two-way trusts are created between the root domains.

In this section, we're going install an Exchange server in a new root domain. When you've done this, you shouldn't have any problems installing an Exchange server in a child domain. As we go through the Windows 2000 and Exchange 2000 installation processes, it should be clear how you'd do an install in a child domain.

By creating a new root tree, we're violating the rule that you should try to build single-domain tree forests with as many child networks as needed, but with no parallel root trees. However, I think from a business perspective that my new frozen yogurt enterprise merits its own root tree. More importantly, we get to work with the more challenging of the two intraforest domain creation scenarios.

You install Windows 2000 Server just as you have in the past. I'll leave it to you to perform that task. For help, check out the references in the first paragraph of the section "Adding an Exchange Server to a Domain's Default Administrative Group," earlier in this chapter.

While installing Windows 2000, or immediately thereafter, be sure to set DNS server addresses for your new server to the IP addresses of your existing Windows 2000 DNS servers. Promoting your new server to a domain controller for a new root domain in an existing Windows 2000 forest requires that your new server contact a domain controller in the forest to authenticate its right to join the forest. The DNS entries are the only thing that the server needs to find a domain controller. You could rely on simple NetBIOS if there are no routers between your new server and at least one of your Windows 2000 domain controllers. If there are routers, you must rely on WINS. However, DNS feels so right and is, after all, the name resolution tool of choice for Windows 2000 networks.

After you've installed Windows 2000 Server, you're ready to promote the server to domain controller status. There are a few tricky steps in this process, so I'm going to walk you through the installation process. Select Program Menu ➤ Run, type in **dcpromo**, and click OK. You'll soon see the Active Directory Installation Wizard. Click Next. On the Domain Controller Type wizard page, select Domain Controller for a New Domain, as I have done in Figure 15.53. Don't worry; you'll get a chance later to tell the wizard that you want your new domain to live in an existing forest.

FIGURE 15.53

Using the Active Directory Installation Wizard to create a domain controller for a new domain

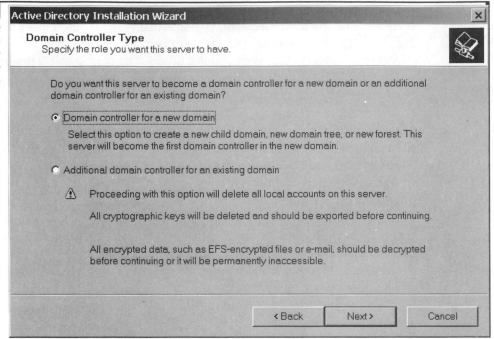

On the next wizard page, select Create a New Domain Tree (see Figure 15.54). You don't want to create a child in an existing domain tree, so the first option is the correct one. Click Next to move on to the Create or Join Forest wizard page, shown in Figure 15.55. Be careful here. You don't want to create a new forest. If you did that, you'd have a totally independent domain existing in a separate Active Directory. Select Place This New Domain Tree in an Existing Forest, and click Next.

FIGURE 15.54

*Using the Active
Directory Installation
Wizard to create a
new domain tree*

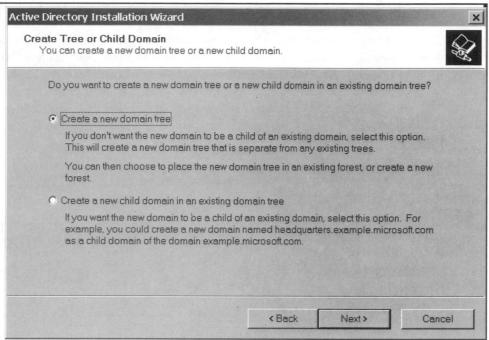

FIGURE 15.55

*Using the Active
Directory Installation
Wizard to place a new
domain tree in an
existing forest*

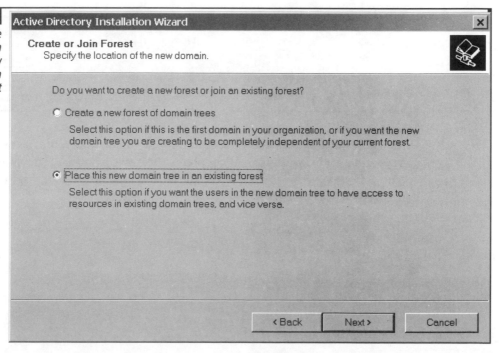

You enter a Windows 2000 username, password, and domain name on the Network Credentials wizard page (see Figure 15.56). You need to enter a username from your existing domain that can be used to authenticate the creation of a new domain in the forest. The administrator account will work fine unless you've altered its permissions. Notice that I've entered the domain name bgerber.com. I can do that because of the steps I took relating to DNS servers a few paragraphs back. If I were relying on Net-BIOS or WINS, I'd enter the pre-Windows 2000 or NetBIOS name of my domain, BGERBER.

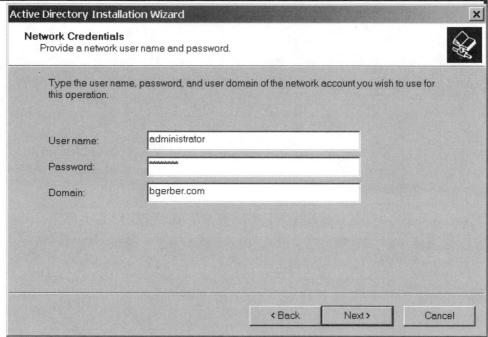

FIGURE 15.56

Using the Active Directory Installation Wizard to enter information required to authenticate creation of a new domain in a forest

You enter the full DNS name of your new root domain tree on the next wizard page. As you can see in Figure 15.57, I've entered the name bgyogurt.com. Enter the pre-Windows 2000 NetBIOS name of your domain on the next wizard page (see Figure 15.58). My new domain's NetBIOS name is BGYOGURT.

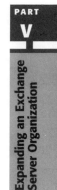

FIGURE 15.57

*Using the Active
Directory Installation
Wizard to enter the
name of a new root
domain tree*

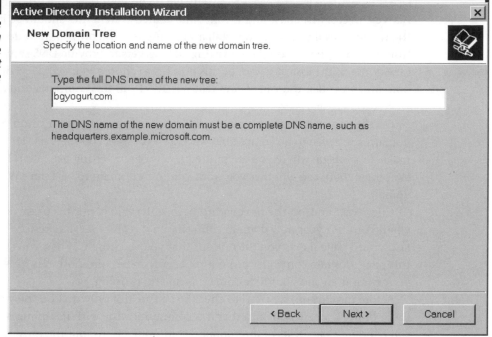

FIGURE 15.58

*Using the Active
Directory Installation
Wizard to enter the
pre-Windows 2000
NetBIOS name of a
new root domain*

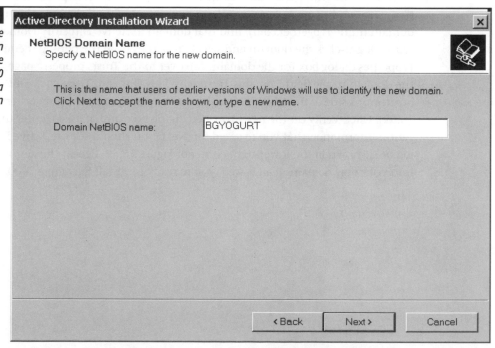

Use the next two wizard pages to specify where on your new domain controller the Active Directory database and log files and shared system files should be located. Next the wizard asks if you want to install and configure DNS on your new domain controller. Although you could use existing DNS servers to provide DNS services for your new domain, the easiest choice at this point is to choose to install DNS on your new domain controller. You can always remove DNS from this computer and use other DNS servers later.

On the next wizard page, you're asked whether you want permission on your new domain controller to be compatible with pre-Windows 2000 servers. This choice you make depends on where you are in the process of converting existing NT servers to Windows 2000, and whether you want your new domain to be a pure Windows 2000 domain.

Click Next and, on the next wizard page, enter and confirm a password to be used when you start your new domain controller in directory services restore mode. The last wizard page shows you the options that you've chosen. When you click Next on this page, domain controller promotion begins. When promotion is finished, reboot your computer, and your new domain is up and running.

Before moving on, we need to check to be sure not only that our new domain is functioning properly, but also that it is communicating with its sibling domain. You can conduct many tests of interdomain communications, but the most useful is to verify the trust relationships between the two domains.

You use the Active Directory Domains and Trusts snap-in to perform the verification. Here's how you do it; follow along on Figure 15.59. While logged into your first domain (mine is bgerber.com), find that domain in Active Directory Domains and Trusts. Right-click the domain and select Properties from the pop-up menu to open the Properties dialog box for the domain. Tab over to the Trusts property page, and select the domain in the field Domains Trusted by This Domain. Then click Edit. The dialog box for this side of the trust relationship opens (see the upper-right corner of Figure 15.59). Click Verify on the newly opened dialog box, and, if asked, enter the authentication information that you're asked for. Next, you should see the Active Directory dialog box, shown in the lower-right corner of Figure 15.59. Repeat this test while logged into your new domain. If all is well, you're ready to install Exchange 2000.

FIGURE 15.59

Verifying a trust relationship between two root tree domains

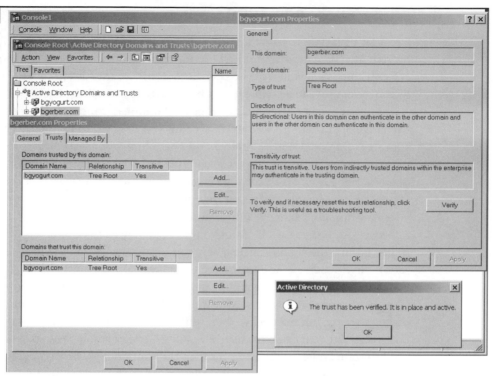

If you have problems installing your new root domain, I suggest that you take a look at William Boswell's *Inside Windows 2000 Server* (New Riders, 2000). His chapter on deploying Windows 2000 domains is the best that I've seen on more complex installations of Windows 2000 Server. Don't be thrown off by the fact that a good deal of the chapter deals with upgrades from NT 4 to Windows 2000. Boswell has done a fine job pointing out where you can apply upgrade-related theory and practice to brand new installations.

NOTE   While you're playing around with trusts, you should try another experiment. Click on either of the trust relationships on the Trusts property page. Notice that the Remove button remains grayed out. That's because, as I mentioned earlier in this section, these trusts are irrevocable. A basic security pipeline is in place between your two domains, and there's no valve to close the pipeline. You must rely on delegation of control and security settings for individual objects to expose and protect cross-domain resource access.

Installing Exchange 2000 Server

Okay, let's get right to installing Exchange in our new domain. Be sure that you're logged into the Administrator account for your new domain or its equivalent (any account that is a member of the Domain Admins security group). As always seems to be true, you must do a couple things before actually installing Exchange.

First, you need to delegate Exchange full administrator permissions to your Exchange organization to whatever account you're going to use to install Exchange in your new domain. I suggest that you use the Administrator account for your new domain. Here's how to set up those permissions. On an Exchange server in your first domain, right-click your Exchange organization and select Delegate Control. Then use the Exchange Administration Delegation Wizard to assign the administrator for your new domain Exchange full administrator permissions.

Second, unless you want to put your new Exchange server in an existing administrative group, you should create a new administrative group in your Exchange organization. Right-click the Administrative Groups container, select New ➤ Administrative Group, enter a name for the group, and click OK. I called my new administrative group Barry's Yogurt Business. Now wait for five minutes or so to be sure that the changes you've just made have been fully established in Active Directory.

If you want, you can also create a Routing Group container in your new administrative group and a new routing group in the container. If you do, you'll be offered the opportunity to have your new server placed in the new routing group. If you don't do this now, after installing Exchange, you can create the routing group and drag your server from whatever other routing group it was placed into upon installation to your newly created routing group. I will need a routing group because, although my yogurt business is in Los Angeles, it's located some distance from my consulting business and is linked by a relatively low-speed and somewhat unreliable DSL connection. I decided to create a new routing group before installing Exchange Server. I called it BGYogurt – Los Angeles.

Installation of your new Exchange server should be pretty uneventful. You will need to select the administrative group and, if you created one, routing group where your new server is to be installed (see Figures 15.60 and 15.61).

FIGURE 15.60

Selecting the administrative group into which a new Exchange server will be installed

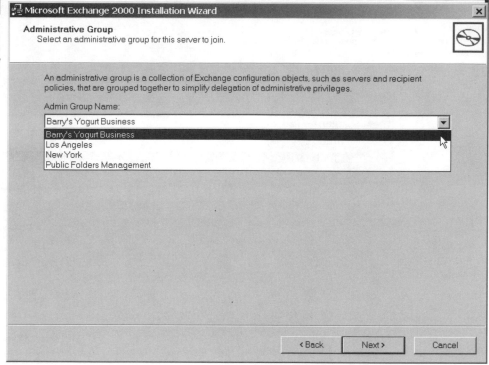

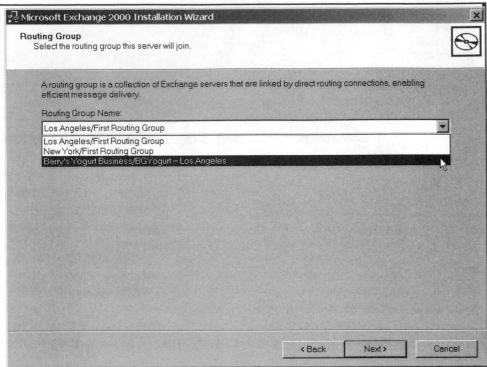

As soon as your new Exchange server is up and running, you're ready to begin managing it and your new Windows 2000 server. Join me in the next section, where we'll take on these tasks.

Managing Servers in Multidomain Environments

Windows 2000 Server includes an impressive array of cross-domain management functionality. With the appropriate permissions, you can manage Active Directory and individual Windows 2000 servers from any server in any domain in a forest. Exchange Server works very much the same, again with appropriate permissions, enabling you to manage your Exchange organization from any workstation or server in a forest on which at least the Exchange management tools are installed.

Interestingly, managing both Windows 2000 and Exchange 2000 servers in multidomain environments is pretty much like managing these servers in a single-domain, multiadministrative group environment. So, in this section, I'm going to talk a little about cross-domain permissions that you might need to put in place and about some of the Windows 2000 and Exchange 2000 tasks that you might undertake in a cross-domain environment. Let's start with Windows 2000 Server.

Cross-Domain Management of Windows 2000 Servers

With the right permissions, you can manage anything in Active Directory from any computer on which the Windows 2000 management tools have been installed. It doesn't matter in which domain in the forest the computer resides. In Figure 15.62, I'm logged into the Administrator account on my first domain, bgerber.com. Without changing the permissions in place after my new Windows 2000 domain, bgyogurt.com, was created, I am able to manage Active Directory components in my second domain from my first domain as though I were logged into my second domain.

Here's what's going on in Figure 15.62. First, in Active Directory Domains and Trusts, I right-clicked my new domain and selected Manage from the pop-up menu. That opened a separate instance of Active Directory Users and Computers for my new domain. In Figure 15.62, I'm adding a new mailbox-enabled user to my new domain, bgyogurt.com. And I'm doing all of this while logged into my first domain, bgerber.com.

FIGURE 15.62

Managing a new Windows 2000 domain using a new instance of Active Directory Users and Computers, while logged into the first Windows 2000 domain created in a forest

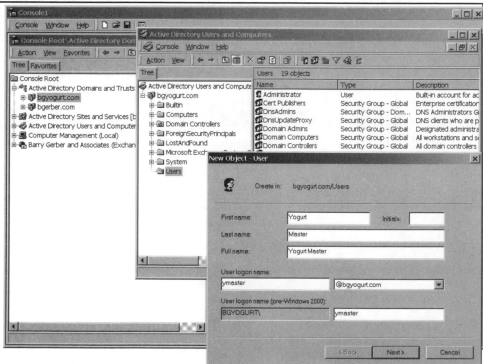

You can also manage another domain by right-clicking Active Directory Users and Computers and selecting Connect. Next select Browse from the resultant Connect to Domain dialog box, and then select the domain to which you want to connect from the Browse for Domain dialog box (see Figure 15.63). Click OK to exit the various dialog boxes, and your Active Directory Users and Computers snap-in should look something like the one in Figure 15.64.

FIGURE 15.63

Connecting to a Windows 2000 domain that will be managed using the existing Active Directory Users and Computers snap-in

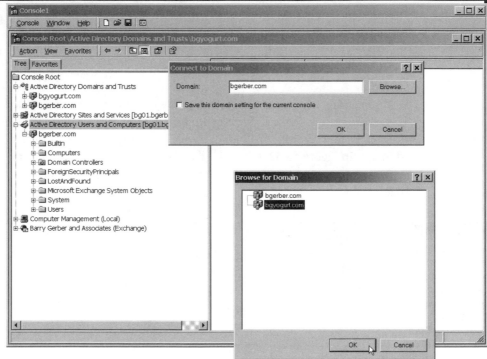

FIGURE 15.64

*Managing a new
Windows 2000 domain
using the existing
Active Directory Users
and Computers snap-
in, while connected to
the new domain and
logged into the first
Windows 2000 domain
created in a forest*

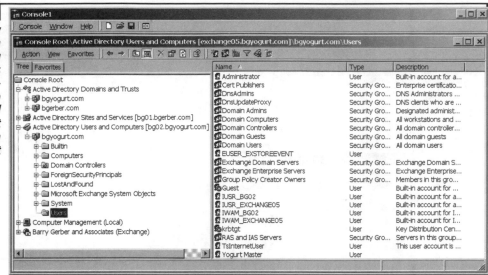

If you try to do what you just did from your new domain, you'll be able to see objects,
but you won't be able to modify or create them. So, you wouldn't be able to create a
new user in your first domain from your new domain. That's because a Domain
Admins security group in the first domain created in a forest always has full control
over objects subsequently created in the forest, including new domains and the
objects that they contain. The Administrator account for a domain is a member of
Domain Admins security group in the first domain, so it has full control over all
domains.

The reverse, however, is not true. Users or groups in other domains must be delegated full or partial control over the first domain. You do this while logged into your
first domain using an account that is a member of the domain's Domain Admins
group. Right-click your domain in the Active Directory Users and Computers container, and select Delegate Control. This opens the Delegation of Control Wizard. In
Figure 15.65, I'm about to delegate control to the Domain Admins security group in
bgyogurt.com.

FIGURE 15.65

Delegating control over users and other objects in the first Windows 2000 domain created in a forest to a group in a new domain

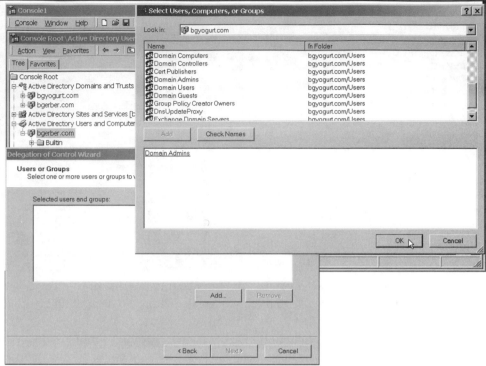

Move to the Tasks to Delegate wizard page, select Create a Custom Task to Delegate, and Click Next. On the next wizard page, select For This Folder, Existing Objects in This Folder, and Creation of New Objects in This Folder, and then move to the next wizard page. The Permissions page offers many options. If you know exactly which permissions you want to delegate, select them. If not, select Full Control, but be aware that you're giving away the keys to the kingdom to members of the Domain Admins group in your new domain. When you're done with the Permissions page, click Next and then Finish on the final wizard page. The permissions that you've selected are then applied to your first domain.

Now, while logged into your new domain, open an existing user or create a new user in your first domain. All should work fine.

I want to tell you about one other cross-domain (really cross-server) management tool. You can add a Computer Management snap-in to the Microsoft Management Console for any Windows 2000 server for which you have management permissions. Use the Add/Remove snap-ins dialog box to add a computer management snap-in. Select Another Computer on the Computer Management dialog box, and then browse to select the remote computer that you want to manage. When you finish using the Add/Remove Snap-in dialog box, you'll find a new snap-in for the computer that you selected in your Microsoft Management Console.

In Figure 15.66, I'm looking at the application log for my new Exchange server, EXCHANGE05, which resides in my new domain, bgyogurt.com. I'm doing this from another Exchange server, EXCHANGE01, while logged into my first domain. Sure, you could do this with NT 4's Server Manager, but could you get to almost everything on an NT server with Server Manager or the other remote management tools such as DHCP Manager? No way! And, there were lots of things that you couldn't do remotely in NT 4, such as disk management. Life is definitely better for systems administrators with Windows 2000.

FIGURE 15.66

*Viewing the applica-
tion event log on a
remote Exchange
server*

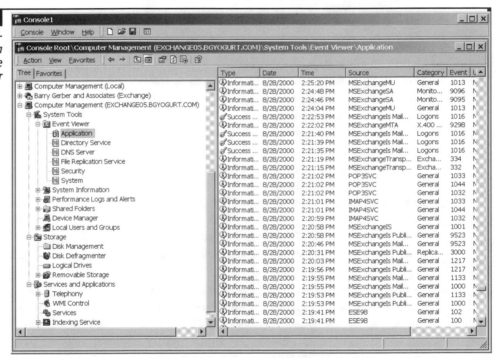

As you work with a remote Computer Management snap-in, you'll discover that you can view and manage some of the objects on the computer and that you can't do a thing with others. This is a permission problem. Usually you'll be told what needs to be changed to open access to you. For example, if you try to manage a DNS server on a remote computer and you don't have adequate permissions to do so, you'll see a message specifying the permissions that you need.

I'll leave it to you to explore the rest of the wonders of multidomain Windows 2000 management.

Managing Exchange 2000 Servers in Multidomain Environments

One of the first things that you might want to do on the Exchange side is to add users or security groups in your new domain to the Exchange Admins security group that you created when you set up your first Exchange server. If you did as I suggested in Chapter 8 and granted Exchange full administrator permissions to Exchange Admins, then users or security groups from your new domain that are added to this group will be capable of fully managing your Exchange organization. If you need a refresher on the Exchange Admins group, see the section "Component Management Security," in Chapter 8.

As an alternative, you might want to limit Exchange management for users and security groups in your new domain only to the new administrative group into which your new Exchange server was installed. To do that, you delegate control at the administrative group level.

You might be wondering how that new mailbox-enabled user that I created in the last section came out. Figure 16.67 shows the E-mail Addresses property page for my friend Yogurt Master. Notice that her address suffixes are the same for as everyone else in my Exchange organization. For example, her SMTP address is ymaster@bgerber. com, not ymaster@bgyogurt.com. The fact that Yogurt resides in a Windows 2000 domain named bgyogurt.com doesn't have any effect on her e-mail addresses, which are controlled inside Exchange. Yogurt's Windows 2000 user logon name *is* based on her Windows 2000 domain. Take a look back at Figure 16.62, where you'll see that her logon name is ymaster@bgyogurt.com.

To give Yogurt a bgyogurt.com e-mail address, I would have to publicly register the domain name bgyogurt.com and ensure that the correct host and MX records were set up in my DNS or another public DNS, if my DNS wasn't exposed to the Internet. Then I'd have to add a new SMTP address for her on the E-mail Addresses property page, in Figure 16.67. If I wanted all e-mail addresses for all new and existing users who reside in the domain bgyogurt.com to be automatically set using the @bgyo-gurt.com suffix, I would have to create and apply a recipient policy for that domain. I'll talk about how you do this is Chapter 17, "Advanced Exchange Server Management."

FIGURE 15.67

Without special inter-vention, mailbox-enabled users in a new Windows 2000 domain receive e-mail addresses with the same suffixes as Exchange users in other Windows 2000 domains.

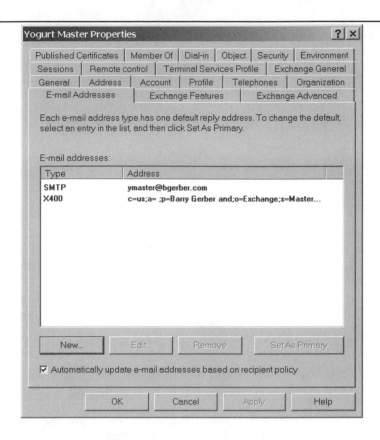

As I mentioned earlier, managing Exchange servers in multidomain environments isn't all that different from managing them in single-domain environments. You use the same tools in the same way, and, with the appropriate permissions in place, cross-domain management is transparent. Want an example? Take a look at Figure 15.68. I set up the new message routes between my new routing group BGYogurt – Los Angeles and the routing groups in my Los Angeles and New York administrative groups in exactly the same way as I would set them up in a single-domain environment. I didn't have to use any new tools or use existing tools in any different way. And, I could have set up routing from any Exchange server in my Exchange organization.

FIGURE 15.68

Viewing a new set of multidomain Exchange Server message routes in Exchange System Manager

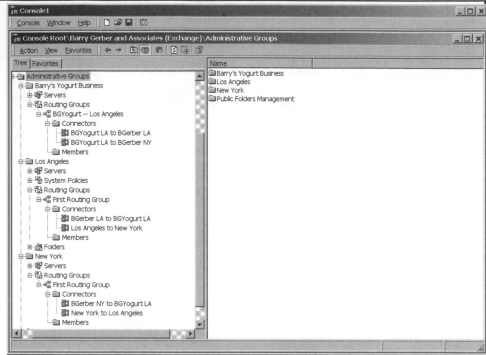

Having read this and previous chapters, you should now have a number of Exchange 2000 Server building blocks at your disposal. Now it's your turn. Go ahead, mix and match these building blocks to create a customized cross-domain Exchange organization that meets your needs.

What About Cross-Domain/Cross-Forest Exchange Organizations?

Because this section is about multidomain Exchange systems, you might be wondering about Exchange 2000 organizations that live in other Windows 2000 forests. You can't directly incorporate such organizations into your current Exchange system, and you can't manage them from your current system. Moving Exchange 2000 Server users from one forest to another is a subject that is beyond the scope of this book, and Microsoft has said little about the process as of this writing. Users in different Exchange organizations, of course, can send SMTP- or X.400-based messages to each other, just as they'd send such messages to users on any other SMTP- or X.400-enabled mail server in the world. To give users in different Exchange organizations access to directory information,

Continued

CONTINUED

you can manually export directory information from each Windows 2000 forest's Active Directory and import it into Active Directories in other forests. I'll talk a little about Active Directory exports and imports in Chapter 17.

Summary

An understanding of Exchange 2000 Server administrative groups is central to the installation of additional Exchange servers in an Exchange organization. Not only are administrative groups for the servers in an Exchange organization, but they also contain system policies, routing groups, and public folders. In addition, administrative groups are central to distributed management in Exchange 2000 organizations. Administrative access can be delegated to specific Windows 2000 users or security groups on an administrative-group-by-administrative-group basis.

Every time a new Exchange server is installed in an Exchange organization, it is installed in an administrative group. The server cannot be moved from that administrative group to another administrative group.

Routing groups support the movement of system messages and user e-mail messages between the Exchange servers in an organization. Routing groups enable connectivity between groups of Exchange servers linked by higher-speed, more reliable networks. Routing groups can be connected using SMTP- or X.400-based protocols. Multiple connections can be set up between a pair of routing groups for reliability enhancing redundancy.

Administrative groups and routing groups are tightly coupled in Exchange 2000 Server mixed-mode environments. This allows Exchange 2000 Server to integrate with Exchange 5.5 Server sites. To an Exchange 5.5 server, an Exchange 2000 administrative group, and the routing groups that it contains appears to be an Exchange 5.5 site. Exchange 2000 servers see an Exchange 5.5 site as a contiguous administrative group/routing group.

In Exchange 2000 Server, native-mode administrative groups and routing groups can be decoupled. An Exchange 2000 server must remain in the administrative group into which it was installed. However, it can be placed in any routing group in any administrative group in an Exchange organization. Special administrative groups can be created that contain only routing groups. This allows for the decentralization or consolidation of message routing administration. Administrative groups also allow for similar handling of public folder and system policy management.

Additional Exchange servers can be installed in an Exchange organization that exists in a single-root tree Windows 2000 domain. Exchange servers also can be installed in child domains in single-root tree domains. Finally, Exchange servers can be installed in Windows 2000 forests with multiple-root domains. All such installations are relatively easy to do because the installation process is guided by good graphical user interfaces.

Managing multiple Exchange servers, whatever the Windows 2000 domain topology used, is also quite simple when the correct permissions are in place. The same tools are used in the same way, whether two or hundreds of computers are being managed.

CHAPTER <u>16</u>

Connecting to Other Foreign Messaging Systems

n Chapter 13, "Managing Exchange 2000 Internet Services," I showed you how to configure Exchange to communicate with the most popular foreign messaging system, the SMTP-based Internet messaging system using SMTP virtual servers, and, when required, the Exchange SMTP connector. In this chapter, I'll discuss Exchange 2000 connectors for other messaging systems.

In addition to the SMTP connector, Exchange 2000 Server comes with five connectors for external messaging systems:

- *X.400 Connector,* which links X.400 messaging systems or can be used to link Exchange 2000 routing groups

- *Connector for MS Mail,* which links Exchange to Microsoft mail systems and lets you keep using MS Mail 3.*x*–compatible gateways with Exchange 2000 Server. This connector also comes with a directory synchronization component for synchronizing Exchange and MS Mail address lists.

- *Connector for cc:Mail,* which has the same functionality as Connector for MS Mail.

- *Connector for Lotus Notes,* which has the same functionality as Connector for MS Mail.

- *Connector for Novell GroupWise,* which has the same functionality as Connector for MS Mail.

I'll cover the X.400 Connector and the Connector for MS Mail in some detail. Then I'll briefly discuss the other connectors. My focus in this chapter is more on setting up a connector than giving a detailed presentation of the history, purpose, and use of a particular messaging system. I assume that if you need a particular connector, there is sufficient conceptual and practical experience in your organization that I don't need to go into detail about each messaging system.

Using the X.400 Connector

X.400 connectors ride on top of a service transport stack (STS). You have three options:

- TCP/IP X.400 Service Transport Stack
- X.25 X.400 Service Transport Stack
- RAS X.400 Service Transport Stack

As their names imply, the first STS is based on TCP/IP networking protocols, the second relies on the X.25 packet-switching protocol, and the third STS uses Windows 2000's Remote Access Service. A TCP/IP STP will run on any TCP/IP network. For an

X.25 STS, you need an X.25 device, such as an Eicon port adapter. For a RAS STS, the
Remote Access Service must be installed.

To set up a service transport stack, find the X.400 container in the Protocols container on one of your Exchange servers, and right-click it. Then select New and
whichever of the STSs you want to install. We're going to install a TCP/IP X.400 Service Transport Stack, so select that option to open the Properties dialog box for your
new STS. You don't have to modify anything on the dialog box (see Figure 16.1),
unless you don't like the default name, or, more importantly, if services that communicate with an X.25 service are installed on your Exchange server. If an X.25 service
already exists on your server, use the OSI address information to ensure that the existing X.25 service and the TCP/IP STS don't clobber each other. The Hex or Text option
determines the format in which the T, S, and P selectors are shown. Click OK when
you're done. You should now see your TCP/IP STS in your server's X.400 container.

FIGURE 16.1

*Setting up a TCP/IP-
based service
transport stack*

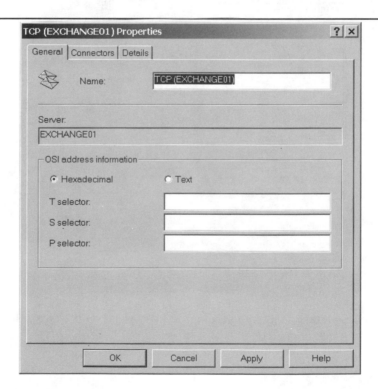

Now that you've created an STS for your X.400 connector to ride atop, you're ready to
create the X.400 connector itself. Find and open the routing groups container for the
Exchange server on which you just created the TCP/IP STS. Find and right-click the

Connectors subcontainer, and select TCP X.400 Connector from the pop-up menu to open the Properties dialog box for your new connector (see Figure 16.2).

Here, I'm setting up a link to a public X.400 service provider, Public X.400 Corp. Connecting to this provider will give Barry Gerber and Associates Exchange users direct access to external users of X.400 systems. Of course, we could just as easily have sent mail to X.400 users through publicly available TPC/IP-to-X.400 gateways, but we consultants at BGA need to keep our skills well honed in the X.400 department to keep our clients happy.

FIGURE 16.2

Using the General property page of the dialog box for a new X.400 connector to begin setting up a connection to a public X.400 service provider

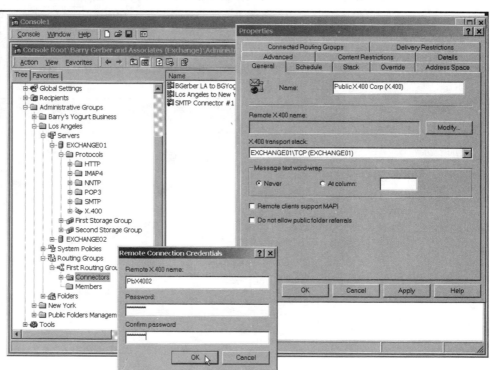

Let's take a closer look at key property pages on the Properties dialog box for the X.400 connector.

On the General property page, I entered a meaningful display name for the connector. This is the name that will show up in the Connectors container. The Remote X.400 name is the name that your Exchange server must send to the X.400 service provider's system, along with a password to authenticate a connection. I obtained the correct name and password from my service provider. Click Modify, and enter the name and password on the Remote Connection Credentials dialog box shown in Figure 16.2.

Because I can't be sure that users on the other side of my link to Public X.400 Corp will have clients capable of text wrapping or MAPI, I have set Message Text Word-Wrap to Never and have deselected Remote Clients Support MAPI. Because I'm not using this connector to link Exchange sites, I've also deselected the option Do Not Allow Public Folder Referrals.

Both your server and the foreign system can contact each other to exchange messages, or one system can contact the other at all times for message exchange. If your server will be contacting the foreign X.400 system, then use the Schedule page to set that schedule. If the foreign system will contact your server exclusively, set the schedule frequency to Never.

You must enter addressing information on the Stack property page that your Exchange server can use to find the remote X.400 computer system. You can enter a DNS domain name or an IP address (in brackets, for better performance) or an OSI address in the standard OSI T selector, S Selector, P selector format. You must enter an address in one of these formats to complete your X.400 connector.

The Override property page is used to manually reconfigure default service transport stack parameters such as connection retry values, transfer timeout values, and so on. The changes that you make on the Override page apply to this X.400 connector only.

You'll need to get pertinent X.400 addressing information from the manager of the target system. Enter that information on the Address Space property page.

The Advanced property page is used mostly to set parameters for X.400 conformance and links, message body part, and the global domain identifier (GDI) for the foreign system. Follow along with Figure 16.3 as we cover the parameters on this page.

Let's start with the X.400 conformance area on the property page. The default, 1988 normal mode, should work with most foreign X.400 systems; see the Exchange documentation for details on these options.

FIGURE 16.3

The Advanced property page for an X.400 connector

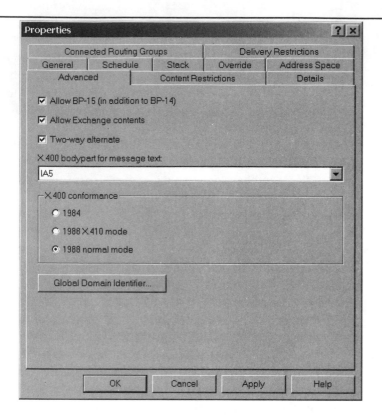

Now let's pop up to the fields at the top of the Advanced property page. Conformance with 1988 normal mode supports the Body Part-15 (or BP-15) standard, which includes specifications for such things as the encoding of binary message attachments and the handling of Electronic Data Interchange (EDI) body parts. The more limited BP-14 standard is specified in the 1984 X.400 standard and is supported in the 1988 X.400 standard. If you're sure that the foreign system supports BP-15, then select this link option. If you don't select BP-15, binary parts will be sent in BP-14 format, which can still be handled by any X.400 system that conforms with 1988 normal mode.

Select Allow Exchange Contents if you're using this connection exclusively to link two Exchange sites indirectly, or if you know that all users at the receiving foreign system (or systems) have clients capable of Extended MAPI. (Check to be sure about the latter condition—you don't want those foreign users to be confused by an extra body part containing Exchange stuff that doesn't map to the X.400 standard.)

Under the Two-Way Alternate option, two X.400 systems take turns transmitting and receiving messages, speeding transmission somewhat. The X.400 Connector supports this option; if the foreign system also does, select the option.

Leave the X.400 Bodypart for Message Text option set at IA5, unless you're communicating with systems that support foreign languages and their accents and other special characters. Other options on the drop-down list include versions of IA5 that are specialized for languages such as German, Norwegian, and Swedish, as well as some other standards.

The global domain identifier is a portion of the X.400 address of the target system. It is used to prevent message transfer loops that involve outgoing messages. Check with your X.400 provider for help with these settings.

You've worked with the Content Restrictions and Delivery Restrictions property pages before. For more on these two pages, check out the sections "Content Restrictions" and "Delivery Restrictions" in Chapter 13.

When you're done configuring your X.400 connector, click OK. The connector shows up in your Connectors container.

Using the X.400 Connector to Link Exchange Routing Groups

If you absolutely can't use a routing group connector or Internet connector (for example, if X.400 is your organization's major protocol), you can link routing groups with an X.400 connector. To link a pair of Exchange routing groups with an X.400 connector, create a new X.400 connector. Then fill in the General property page, entering the name and password of a Windows 2000 account authorized to contact the other Exchange server, such as Administrator. On the Stack page, enter the domain name of the other Exchange server. Then tab over to the Connected Routing Groups property page and select Add. Next select the routing group to which you want to link with this connector from the drop-down list on the resultant Properties dialog box, and click OK. Exchange will automatically create the addressing information that you would normally have to enter on the Address Space property page of your X.400 connector. Repeat the same process for the other routing group. That's it! You've linked your two routing groups using X.400 connectors. For more information on connecting routing groups, see the section "Using Routing Groups and Connectors" in Chapter 15, "Installing and Managing Additional Exchange 2000 Servers."

Using the Connector for Microsoft Mail

If your organization is using Microsoft Mail (MS Mail) for PC Networks, you can transparently link MS Mail and Exchange users with the Connector for MS Mail (CMM). Exchange also comes with software for migrating (moving) MS Mail users to Exchange; I'll discuss this software in Chapter 17, "Advanced Exchange Server Management."

Migration is a pretty big move. As you start building your Exchange system, the CMM lets you maintain communications between Exchange users and MS Mail users. With Exchange-to-CMM links in place, you can then take a more leisurely approach to migration.

You can also use the CMM to let Exchange users take advantage of gateways that are not available for Exchange Server and to give MS Mail users access to Exchange's more powerful and stable connectors and gateways. For example, you can use Exchange's SMTP host services and the CMM to move Internet mail in and out of MS Mail environments, dumping Microsoft's weak SMTP gateway for Microsoft Mail for PC Networks (MS Mail PC) in the process.

Here's how the CMM works. A shadow MS Mail PC network and post office are created on the Exchange server running the CMM. Then a Windows 2000 service runs on the Exchange server that essentially emulates the functions performed by MS Mail PC's EXTERNAL.EXE program. This service moves messages between the Exchange shadow post office and the MS Mail PC post office, just as EXTERNAL.EXE does for a group of real MS Mail PC post offices.

The CMM runs on top of standard Windows 2000 local area network protocols or using NT's Remote Access Service (RAS) asynchronous or X.25 connections. You can use one or all of these links; network links should be set up before you configure the CMM. You can run only one instance of the CMM per Exchange routing group, but you can connect to multiple MS Mail PC post offices through a single CMM. And one CMM can serve some or all of the administrative groups in an Exchange organization.

You must install the CMM before you can use it. If you installed it when you installed Exchange Server, you're ready to go. If not, you'll need to run the Exchange 2000 Server setup program and install the CMM. After that, you can move on to the configuration discussion that follows. Figure 16.4 should help refresh your memory regarding installation of Exchange 2000 Server components. If you need more information on component installation, see the section "Running the Exchange 2000 Server Setup Program" in Chapter 8, "Installing Exchange 2000 Server." Just for the record, you can't install a new Exchange 2000 Server component until you set the Action for Related Existing Components to Change, as I have in Figure 16.4.

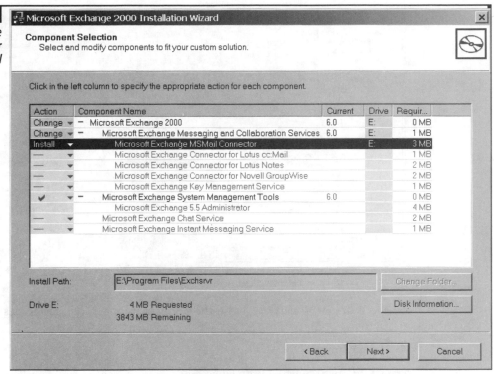

FIGURE 16.4

*Installing the Exchange
2000 Server Connector
for Microsoft Mail*

You access the CMM in the Connectors container in the administrative group that holds the Exchange server on which you installed the CMM. It's in the Routing Groups\Connections container for that administrative group. To start configuring the CMM, find and double-click the Connector for MS Mail. The Connector for MS Mail Connector Properties dialog box will pop up (see Figure 16.5).

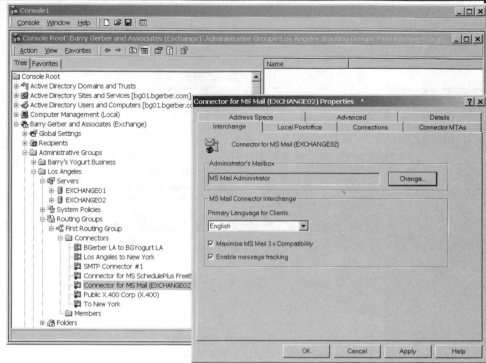

Let's look at key property pages on the Connector for MS Mail Properties dialog box.

Interchange

The CMM opens on the Interchange property page (see Figure 16.5). The first thing that you need to do is add an administrator's mailbox. Click Change and select an Exchange recipient from the resultant dialog box.

If the primary language for clients isn't English, select the correct language from the drop-down list. Select the Maximize MS Mail 3.*x* Compatibility check box to let MS Mail users view and save OLE-embedded objects sent from Exchange clients. When this option is selected, the CMM creates a second version of the embedded object that's compatible with the earlier version of OLE supported by the MS Mail PC

Windows client. Compatibility is costly in terms of storage because the second version can be quite large (up to 1 MB), so choose this option with care and forethought.

I strongly suggest that you enable message tracking. It is especially helpful in debugging problems with the Connector for MS Mail.

Local Postoffice

The Local Postoffice property page, shown in Figure 16.6, is for the CMM shadow post office. The network name is drawn from the first 10 nonspace letters in your Exchange organization's name. Mine is Barry Gerber and Associates, leading to the MS Mail PC network name BARRYGERBE. The post office name is the first 10 nonspace letters of the administrative group into which you installed your Connector for PC Mail. Exchange uses the original name of the administrative group, First Administrative Group, ignoring any changes that you later make to the name, which leads to the post office name of FIRSTADMIN.

I strongly suggest that you not change the shadow post office's network or post office name. They are used in generating MS Mail addresses for Exchange users. If you must modify the network or post office name, you need to do two things after making the modification. First, you must regenerate the MS Mail address type. This is easy: Simply click Apply on the Local PostOffice property page. Second, you should carefully read the Exchange documentation for information on the steps that you must take to modify the default recipient policy and any other policies that reference MS Mail addresses to reflect the new MS Mail address. These modifications are made in the Exchange organization-wide Recipient Policies container.

You can change the Sign-on Password on the Local Postoffice property page. However, you need a password for Async or X.25 connections only. See the next section for more on these two types of connections.

You'll need information on the Local Postoffice page when you set up links on the MS Mail PC side so that they can access the shadow post office. Write down the network and post office names as well as the Sign-on ID and, if you entered one, the Sign-on Password.

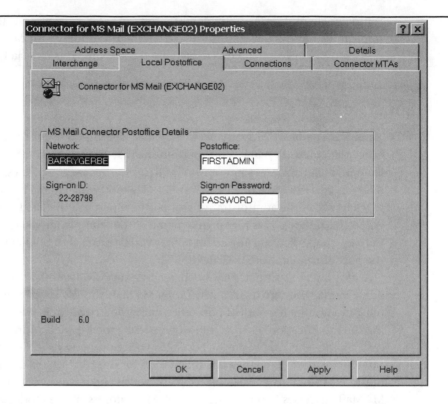

Connections

Tab over to the Connections property page (see Figure 16.7). This is where you add and maintain the MS Mail PC post offices serviced by the CMM. Notice in the figure that the connection to the Exchange shadow MS Mail PC network and post office—BARRYGERBE\FIRSTADMIN, in my case—is already there; the link is created automatically.

FIGURE 16.7

The Connections property page of the MS Mail Connector Properties dialog box

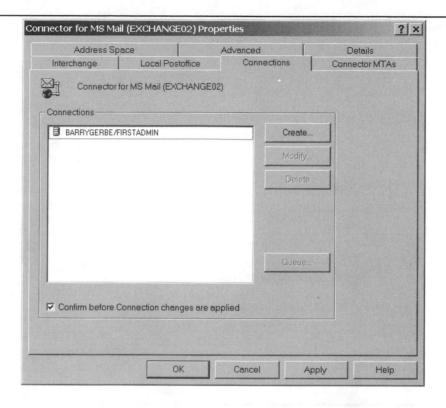

Now we have to create links to other real MS Mail PC post offices. From the Connections property page, click Create to bring up the Create Connection dialog box, shown in Figure 16.8. We're going to create a link based on a local area network, so be sure that LAN is selected under Connection Parameters. Next, we have to tell the CMM where the post office is located on the LAN.

FIGURE 16.8

Setting up a new connection to an MS Mail PC post office

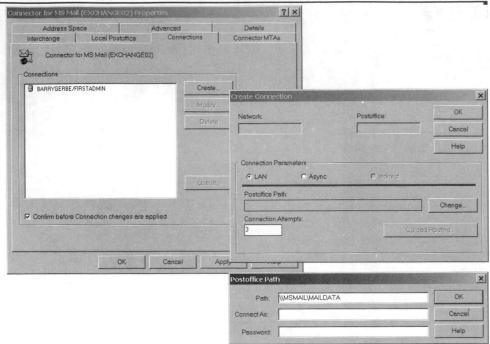

 NOTE If we had chosen the Async or X.25 option, we would have been asked for appropriate information to make the connection. If you've set up a modem connection between two MS Mail PC post offices, you should have no trouble filling in the information for Async or X.25 connections.

Click Change to enter the post office location. This brings up the Postoffice Path dialog box, shown in the lower-right corner of Figure 16.8. The path must be entered in Universal Naming Convention (UNC) format, which doesn't use disk drive letters and allows computers to connect without drive mappings. For the UNC path to work, you need to ensure that the MAILDATA directory (or whatever directory name you used) is shared on the computer where MS Mail PC runs. Generically, the UNC format is \\Computer_Name\ShareName. My MS Mail PC post office is on a Windows NT 4 computer named MSMAIL in the share MAILDATA. (MS Mail PC administrators will immediately recognize MAILDATA as a standard data directory for MS Mail PC post office installations.) So, the path shown in Figure 16.8 is \\MSMAIL\MAILDATA.

Use the Connect As field to enter a network logon account name for the server that's holding the MS Mail PC post office. Enter the password for the account in the Password field. You need to fill in these fields only if the Windows 2000 account under which the CMM runs doesn't have standard Windows 2000-based security access to the MS Mail PC post office server.

After you've entered the path to and logon credentials for the MS Mail PC post office, click OK in the Postoffice Path dialog box. If you've entered the correct path, and if security is properly set, you're returned to the Create Connection dialog box (see Figure 16.9). If something doesn't work, make sure that the path and security are set correctly.

Notice that I didn't have to manually enter the names of the MS Mail PC network (GCMSMAIL) or post office (LA). The Exchange server automatically retrieved this information from the post office.

Change the Connection Attempts default if you want the CMM to attempt to deliver messages more than three times before returning them to the sender on the Exchange side. Click the Upload Routing button to get routing information on MS Mail PC *indirect* post offices. These are post offices that have mail routed to them by the MS Mail PC post office that you're connecting to now. This routing is set up at the MS Mail PC post offices. The CMM can reach indirect post offices through its connection to the routing post office. With routing in place, you don't have to create a CMM connection to each of the indirect post offices.

PART

V

Expanding an Exchange
Server Organization

FIGURE 16.9

The connection to the MS Mail PC post office has been established.

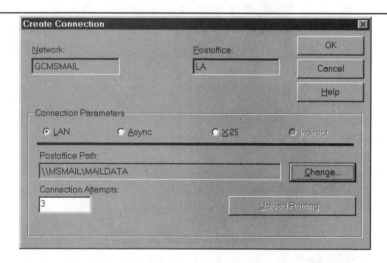

Click OK on the Create Connection dialog box when you're done, and then click OK on the Apply Changes Now dialog box that pops up next. This finalizes the creation process and adds the newly created MS Mail PC post office link to the Connections area of the Connections property page.

Tab over to the Address Space property page. Notice that an MS Mail address type has been automatically added to the list for the MS Mail PC post office (see Figure 16.10). Note that you can specify that this Connector for MS Mail should apply to the current routing group or to your entire Exchange organization.

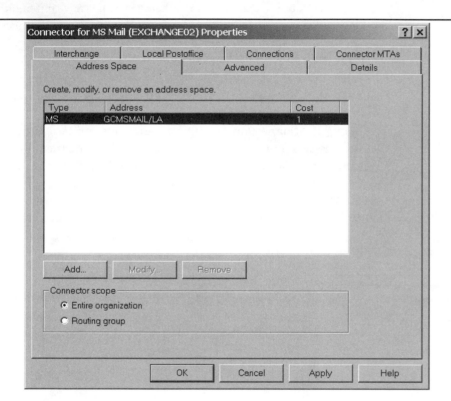

FIGURE 16.10

A new address space is added for the CMM connection.

Connector MTAs

A message transfer agent (MTA) must be created to serve your newly established MS Mail PC post office connection. The MTA is a Windows 2000 Server service. You manage it just like any other Windows 2000 service, such as the services for the Exchange components.

Tab over to the Connector MTAs property page and click New. This brings up the New MS Mail Connector (PC) MTA Service property page (see Figure 16.11). Give the service a name. You'll see this name when you look at services running on this computer with the Microsoft Management Console snap-in Computer Management.

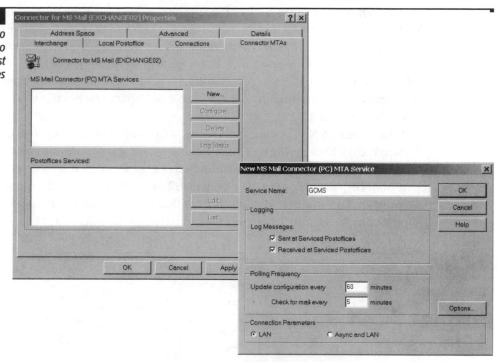

FIGURE 16.11

Setting up an MTA to support connections to MS Mail PC post offices

Use the fields on the Log Messages area to indicate whether you want sent or received message traffic to be logged. Log files will be placed in the shadow post office's LOG directory. These can be awfully verbose. As with any logs, you should generally turn them on only when you're diagnosing a problem.

Leave the polling frequency settings at their default levels. The value that you set in the Update Configuration Every field determines how fast the MTA will get changes in parameters set in the Options dialog box. Remember, the default is 60 minutes. You can change the frequency at which the PC MTA checks for mail in the Check for Mail Every field.

Use the Connection Parameters area to select the means by which the MTA will connect to the real MS Mail PC post offices that it supports. Three options are available, two of which are shown in Figure 16.11: LAN, Async and LAN, and X.25 and LAN. The Async and LAN option supports both asynchronous-modem and LAN connections, and the X.25 and LAN option supports LAN as well as X.25 connections.

The Async and LAN, and the X.25 and LAN options show up only if appropriate hardware and supporting software are installed. All three options support LAN connections. More on this in a bit.

Click Options to bring up the MS Mail Connector (PC) MTA Options dialog box (see Figure 16.12). If you want, you can use the Maximum LAN Message Size field in the Options dialog box to set a maximum size for messages moved in both directions by this MTA over a LAN-based link. If the space on a target MS Mail PC post office falls below the value in the Close Postoffice If field, the MTA will stop transmitting messages to the post office until the available disk space reaches the value set in the Open Postoffice If field.

Select NetBIOS Notification to have the MTA notify MS Mail PC users on the same LAN that they have new mail. Check Disable Mailer if you want to stop the MTA from distributing messages to the LAN-connected post offices that it serves. Selecting Disable Mail Dispatch stops the MTA from distributing directory synchronization messages to LAN-connected post offices. (I'll discuss MS Mail PC directory synchronization in the section "Directory Synchronization with Microsoft Mail Systems.")

FIGURE 16.12

Setting options for the MS Mail Connector (PC) MTA

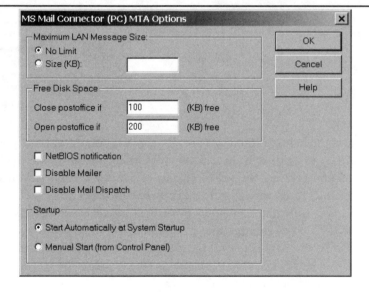

Finally, select the start-up mode for the MTA service from the Startup area of the Options dialog box. The default starts the service when Windows 2000 starts. This is usually the appropriate choice. If you want to start the service manually using the Services container in the Computer Management snap-in, choose the somewhat misnamed option Manual Start (from Control Panel).

When you're done configuring options, click OK to return to the New MS Mail Connector (PC) MTA Service dialog box shown in Figure 16.11.

Close the New MS Mail Connector (PC) MTA Service dialog box by clicking OK. Your Connector MTAs property page should look something like the one in Figure 16.13.

Now you can assign the post office that you set up on the Connections property page to your new MS Mail Connector MTA. Click List in the MTA Service dialog box to bring up the Serviced LAN Postoffices dialog box (see Figure 16.14).

FIGURE 16.13

A new MS Mail Connector MTA service has been created.

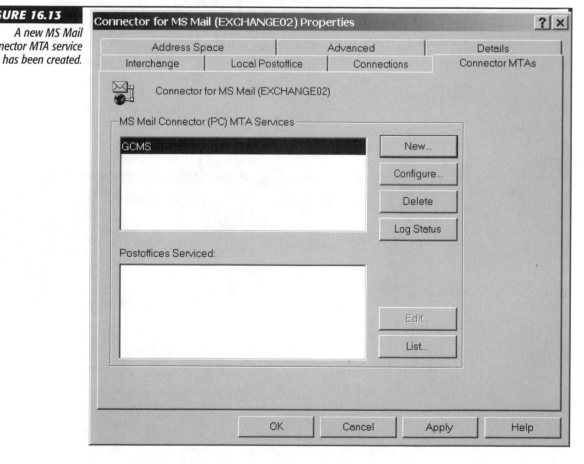

Select the post office that you want to service. Click Add and then click OK. Your Connector MTAs property page should look like the one in Figure 16.15.

If a CMM will be handling a lot of message traffic and will be using multiple connection methods (LAN, Async and LAN, X.25 and LAN), it's best to create at least one CMM MTA for each method. Just be sure to assign LAN-linked post offices only to the MTAs that support such links exclusively, not to MTAs that support Async and LAN or X.25 and LAN. This will leave the MTAs connected by the latter two methods free to handle only the message traffic that isn't based on LAN links.

FIGURE 16.14

Adding a LAN-linked post office to the list of serviced LAN-linked post offices

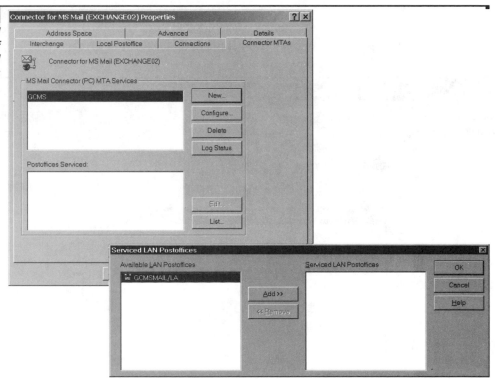

FIGURE 16.15

The post office will now be served by the newly created MS Mail Connector MTA service.

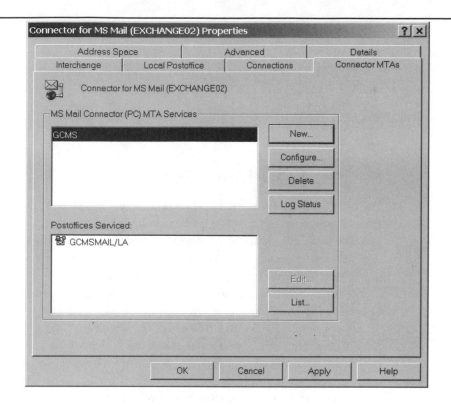

Advanced

Use the Advanced property page to set message size limits for the CMM. As with other message size limits that you've set in other chapters of this book, go with unlimited messages size unless you're concerned about two issues:

- That your Exchange or MS Mail post office computer lacks sufficient space to store such messages

- That network performance will be compromised by transmission of large messages

Starting the MTA Service

Find and click the Services container in the Computer Management snap-in. Find the new CMM MTA service that you created. As you may remember, the service that I created is called GCMS. Click Start to bring up the service. Also, make sure that the MS Mail Connector Interchange service is running. If you've indicated that you want the CMM MTA service to start automatically in the future, you won't have to do this again.

MS Mail PC Post Office Setup

The next thing that you need to do is tell the real MS Mail PC post offices about the shadow post office. In a DOS session, start up MS Mail PC's ADMIN program and log in as someone with MS Mail PC Admin rights. You or someone in your organization should know how to do this. When ADMIN is up and running, you'll see a DOS screen that looks something like the one in Figure 16.16.

Use the right arrow key to select External-Admin, and then press the Enter key. This brings up the External-Admin screen shown in Figure 16.17. Make sure that the Create option (on the menu at the top of the screen that starts out "Create Modify Delete") is selected, and press Enter. Fill in the information about the CMM shadow post office here. Use the network and post office names that you wrote down just a bit ago.

The route type should be Direct. Be sure to pick a connection type—MS-DOS Drive, Modem, or X.25—that matches the LAN, Async, or X.25 configuration for this post office on the CMM MTA that serves it. When you're finished entering the configuration information, you're asked whether you want to create the post office. Be sure that Yes is selected, and press Enter.

Your CMM's shadow post office and your real MS Mail PC post office(s) are now communicating with each other through the CMM MTA. All we need to do now is test the link.

FIGURE 16.16

MS Mail PC's ADMIN program is up and running.

FIGURE 16.17

Creating an external post office entry for the CMM shadow post office

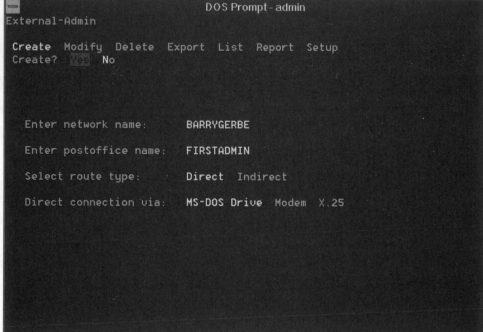

Did It Work?

You test the CMM link by sending messages from the MS Mail PC side to the Exchange side, and vice versa. Addressing these messages will be a bit primitive because we haven't yet synchronized directories between our MS Mail PC and Exchange systems. We won't be able to select the addresses from the address list, so we'll have to enter them manually.

Let's start on the MS Mail PC side. The following example assumes that you're using the MS-DOS MS Mail PC client. With the To field selected as you compose a new message, press Enter. This brings up the Postoffice Address List. Press the left arrow key to bring up the list of Address Lists, from which you select Postoffice Network List and press Enter. The Network List now pops up. Select the name of your CMM shadow post office's network (BARRYGERBE, in my case), and press Enter.

If there is more than one post office (that is, Exchange administrative group) in your network (Exchange organization), a list of post offices will be presented. Pick the post office that you want to send test mail to; you'll then see a little box for entering the mailbox's name (see Figure 16.18).

FIGURE 16.18

Addressing an MS Mail PC message to an Exchange mailbox

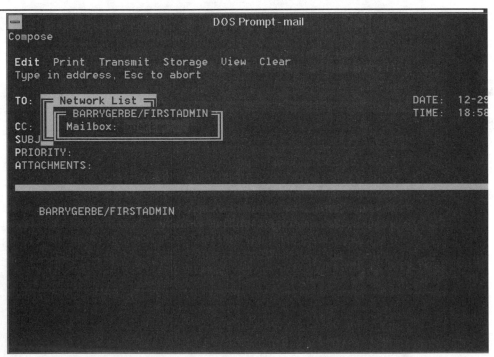

Here's where the magic happens. Notice that I'm addressing mail to BARRYGERBE/ FIRSTADMIN, which represents the name of my Exchange organization and administrative group and the name of the CMM shadow post office. The mailbox name that I type in at this point is that of an Exchange mailbox, so the mail will be sent to that mailbox. To an MS Mail PC user, it looks as if the message will be sent to a real MS Mail PC post office on a real MS Mail PC network. When we've got directory synchronization going, the illusion will be even better.

After you type in the Exchange mailbox name, press Enter, and then compose the message and send it off. In a few minutes, the message will show up in the Inbox of the mailbox owner's Outlook client.

TIP If DOS clients aren't your cup of tea, you can enable access to an MS Mail post office from an Outlook client. In your Outlook client, select Tools ÿ Services. Then click Add on the Services dialog box, and select Microsoft Mail from the Add Service to Profile dialog box. Finally configure your connection using the Microsoft Mail dialog box.

To send a test message from an Outlook client connected to the Exchange Server to an MS Mail PC network mailbox, start composing a new message. Follow along on Figure 16.19 for the rest of the steps in setting a Microsoft Mail address. Click To and then click New in the Select Names dialog box. This opens the New Entry dialog box, which isn't shown in Figure 16.19. Ensure that Contact and In This Message Only are selected, and then select Microsoft Mail Address from the list labeled Select Entry Type. Click OK. To enter the address, use the New Microsoft Mail Address Properties dialog box that pops up (see Figure 16.19).

When you're finished, click the little To button in the lower-left corner of the dialog box. The display name for the address will now appear in the To field of your new message. Complete the message and send it off. After the CMM MTA has done its thing, the owner of the MS Mail PC mailbox can access the message using any of the MS Mail PC clients.

If your test fails, go back and be sure that you've done everything that I've indicated. This is one of the more complex Exchange connectors to set up, so it's not inconceivable that everything won't work the first time.

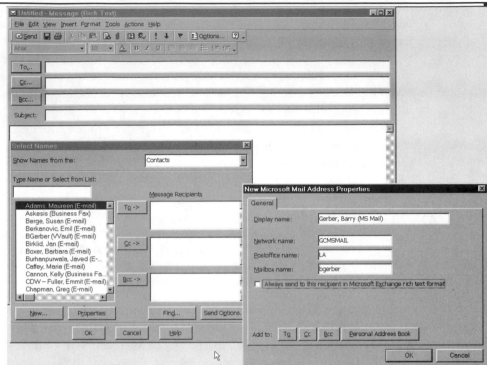

The Connector for MS SchedulePlus Free/Busy

When you install the CMM, a connector is also installed for synchronizing legacy Microsoft SchedulePlus systems with the Exchange calendar system. You'll find the connector in the same Connectors container as the CMM in Exchange System Manager. The connector is very easy to set up and administer. If you need any help with it, check out the online Exchange Server documentation.

Directory Synchronization with Microsoft Mail Systems

- Understanding Dirsync
- Adding an Exchange organization to a Dirsync system
- Administering and managing the Exchange Server directory synchronization service

In the last section, using the Connector for Microsoft Mail, we enabled mail interchange between our Exchange and MS Mail PC systems. As you'll recall, when we tested the CMM, we had to enter addresses for the other system manually. In this chapter, we'll use directory synchronization (*Dirsync*) to remove that annoying inconvenience. Using Dirsync, we'll import Exchange addresses into MS Mail PC, and vice versa. Then, when they compose messages, users of Exchange and MS Mail PC will be able to pick addresses for the other system from address lists just as they do for their own systems.

Understanding Dirsync

Let's start by talking about Dirsync, which is a component of MS Mail PC. Each MS Mail PC post office has a directory database that includes those recipients whose mailboxes reside in the post office. *Dirsync* is the name of the process that keeps the recipient directories in a group of MS Mail PC post offices synchronized. This ensures that the address lists for any post office will include the current recipients at all the post offices that participate in the Dirsync process.

One MS Mail PC post office is set up to be a *Dirsync server*. All other post offices that participate in the Dirsync process are set up to act as *Dirsync requestors*.

The Dirsync requestor in each post office sends directory change updates for its post office to the Dirsync server. Each Dirsync requestor asks the Dirsync server for directory updates for all the other post offices, and the server sends them out. Requests and their responses are moved between MS Mail PC post offices as messages.

WARNING The Dirsync server performs the equivalent of the Dirsync requestor functions for its own post office. So, a post office that is a Dirsync server cannot also be a Dirsync requestor. This is a key piece of the Dirsync puzzle. Forget it, and you'll do an Escheresque meltdown trying to figure out how the Dirsync server gets updates for and sends them to its own post office.

Dirsync is amazingly simple, yet when I first incorporated my Exchange system into an existing MS Mail PC Dirsync process, I managed to do just about everything wrong in spite of having been involved with MS Mail PC and Dirsync for years and years. Why did I screw up? I had set up the Dirsync process on the MS Mail PC side eons ago, and I thought I remembered how it worked. I didn't. The consequences? The Dirsync-Exchange link failed, and it took hours to fix it.

To save you from the miseries that I suffered, here's a list of several key rules of the Dirsync road, some of which I repeat for emphasis from the previous Dirsync basics.

- A single MS Mail PC post office—including an Exchange Server shadow MS Mail PC post office—can function as either a Dirsync server or a Dirsync requestor. It *cannot and need not* function as both. The Dirsync server performs requestor duties for its own post office.

- There can be only *one* Dirsync server for a group of Dirsync requestors. One Dirsync server can serve multiple MS Mail post offices, whether they are on the same or different MS Mail PC networks. Here's where I went wrong in my first effort to include my Exchange system in the Dirsync process. I'd already established the Dirsync server on the MS Mail PC side. My one and only Dirsync server was already running on one of my MS Mail PC post offices. I then created a Dirsync server on one of my Exchange servers, and all hell broke loose—or, more precisely, *nothing* broke loose. Trying to keep the requestors happy, the two Dirsync servers got into deadlock battles of epic proportions, and I never saw an updated address list on either side. Things returned to normal when I got rid of the Exchange Dirsync server.

- There can be only one Dirsync requestor per CMM and, you'll remember, only one CMM per Exchange routing group.

- Because Dirsync uses messages to exchange requests for updates and the updates themselves, the CMM must be installed and running between your Exchange and MS Mail PC systems.

- As is true without Exchange in the mix, you must run DISPATCH.EXE on the MS Mail PC side to perform whichever Dirsync server or requestor tasks are assigned to real MS Mail PC post offices. There is no need for (or equivalent of) DISPATCH.EXE on the Exchange Server side; these tasks are performed by the Exchange Server's directory synchronization service.

Adding an Exchange System to Dirsync

Throughout this section, I'll assume that you've got Dirsync running on the MS Mail PC side. If not, the MS Mail PC *Administrator's Guide* provides detailed instructions.

Because the Dirsync system is up and running on the MS Mail PC side, a Dirsync server is already in place. That means that we need to install a Dirsync requestor only on the Exchange side.

To set up a Dirsync requestor on the Exchange server where you installed the CMM, find the Connectors container that holds your CMM, right-click it, and select New ➢ Dirsync Requestor from the pop-up menu. This brings up the New Requestor dialog box, where you select the Dirsync server that the requestor will use (see Figure 16.20). My Dirsync server is on the MS Mail PC network GCMSMAIL in the post office named LA, so I've selected the only MS Mail PC network/post office option, GCMSMAIL/LA.

Click OK in the New Requestor dialog box when you've chosen the Dirsync server post office. Next you'll see the Properties dialog box for the requestor (see Figure 16.21). Let's take a quick tour of the dialog box's property pages.

FIGURE 16.20

Selecting the Dirsync server post office

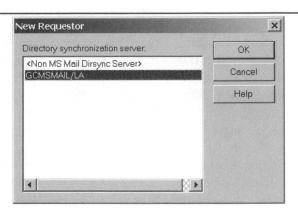

FIGURE 16.21

The Dirsync requestor's Properties dialog box, with the General property page exposed

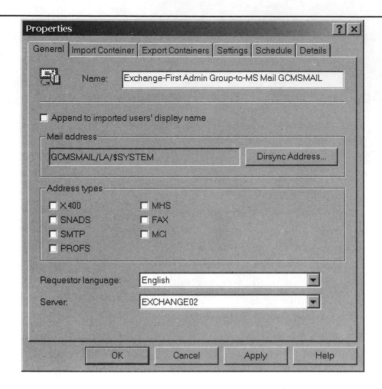

General

Follow along on Figure 16.21 as I discuss the General property page. Give your connector a name that clearly indicates its function. If you want the name of the requestor to be appended to each imported MS Mail PC display name to make it easier to see where the address came from, check the box next to the Name field. Generally, however, you won't want to do this. It's usually better if MS Mail PC addresses look just like standard Exchange addresses.

The Dirsync address is set automatically, based on the choice that you made in the New Requestor dialog box; don't change it. Use the Address Types box to select the types of addresses that you want to request from the Dirsync server. The Requestor Language drop-down list contains the primary language used on your mail system. Use the Server drop-down list box to select the server that the requestor is assigned to. The drop-down list includes only Exchange servers with the CMM installed.

Import Container

Use the Import Container property page to tell the requestor where to put incoming address updates (see Figure 16.22). Click Modify, and pick the container that you want from the Active Directory Users and Computers container that pops up (see Figure 16.23). Notice in Figure 16.23 that import container choices are presented by Windows 2000 domain. I have two domains, bgerber.com and bgyogurt.com, so I get a containers tree for each. Notice that I'm selecting the container BGA-LA in the domain bgerber.com. This is an Active Directory for Users and Computers container that I created just for imported MS Mail addresses. If you import MS Mail addresses into the Active Directory Users and Computers Users container, these addresses will be exported back to your MS Mail post office(s) when you set up export containers in the next section.

To set up a new container into which MS Mail addresses will be imported, create a new organizational unit. You must do this on a Windows 2000 domain controller. In Active Directory Users and Computers, find and right-click the domain where you want to create the new organizational unit, and select New ➤ Organizational Unit from the pop-up menu. Then fill in the name of your new organizational unit on the resultant dialog box, and click OK. You can pick only one import container. That's not a problem because imported addresses will be added to the Exchange global address list, making them available to all users in your Exchange organization.

When an address is imported for which there is no Windows 2000 account, it can be set up as one of three different types of mail-enabled Windows 2000 users:

- A disabled Windows 2000 account with a mailbox
- A Windows 2000 account with a mailbox
- A Windows 2000 contact

You select this option in the field on the Import property page labeled When Replicating a Mailbox Whose Primary Windows Account Does Not Exist in the Domain. The default Windows 2000 Contact is best unless you want to use the Dirsync process to begin creating Windows 2000 accounts and mailboxes for a future migration of MS Mail PC users.

FIGURE 16.22

The Import Container property page

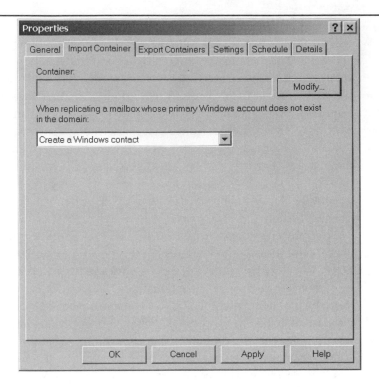

FIGURE 16.23

Selecting the Active Directory Users and Computers container to receive incoming MS Mail PC addresses

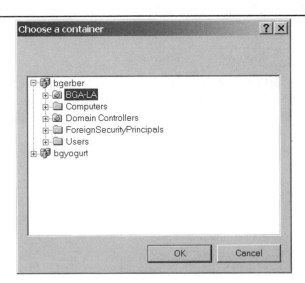

Export Containers

On the Export Containers property page (see Figure 16.24), click Add and use the same interface as shown in Figure 16.23 to select the Exchange Active Directory Users and Computers containers whose addresses will be exported to the MS Mail PC system. Here, your best choice is the Users container. The neat part of this process is that you can add any or all containers that are available. For example, I could select the Users container in my bgyogurt.com domain. Thus, through one requestor, you can export all the addresses in your Exchange organization. But, don't pick the container that you selected for MS Mail address imports in the last section, "Import Containers." If you do, you'll wind up exporting those addresses back to MS Mail post offices.

FIGURE 16.24

Users in the Users container for the domain bgerber.com will be exported to the MS Mail PC side.

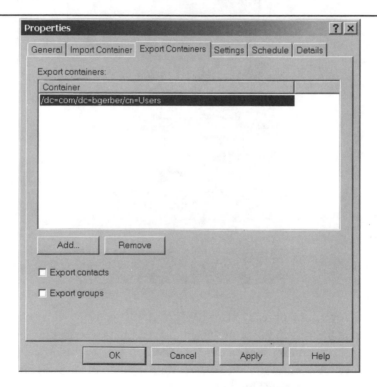

Use the Export Contacts and Export Groups fields to choose whether you want to export either of these two Exchange recipients, along with addresses for mailbox-enabled users and public folders.

Settings

If you want to add security to your Dirsync process, enter a password on the Settings property page (see Figure 16.25). This password is unique to Dirsync and has nothing to do with other passwords used with the CMM. In just a bit, we'll tell the Dirsync server about this password.

FIGURE 16.25

The Settings property page

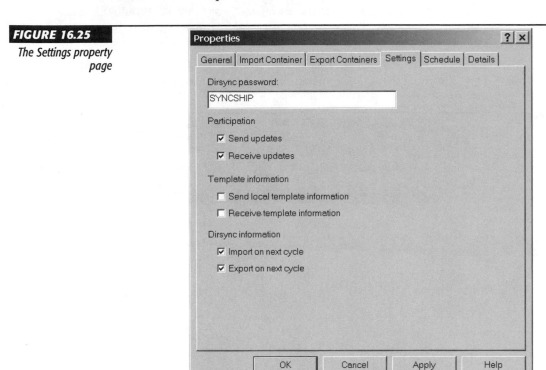

If you expect really heavy Dirsync traffic, you can set up two Exchange-based Dirsync requestors to the same Dirsync server. Each requestor must be on a different Exchange server and must use a different CMM. If you do this, select Send Updates for one requestor and Receive Updates for the other. If you're going to have only one requestor, select both options.

If your MS Mail PC post offices use address templates, you can select to send Exchange templates to MS Mail and receive MS Mail templates in Exchange here. Check both Import on Next Cycle and Export on Next Cycle to force the requestor to perform both tasks on its next scheduled run.

Schedule

Set the schedule for the requestor using the Schedule property page (see Figure 16.26). Notice that the page has no Always or Never options. This is because directory synchronization is generally run once a day; in fact, on the MS Mail PC side, you can't schedule it to run more often than once a day. Leave the default schedule time as it is.

FIGURE 16.26

Setting a schedule for the Dirsync requestor

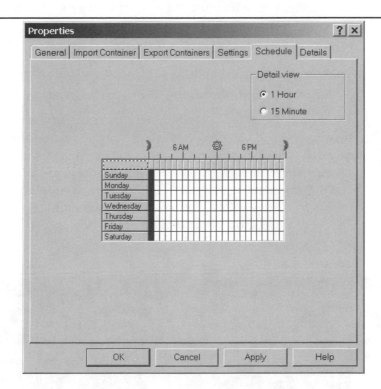

When you've finished setting the requestor schedule, you're done. Click OK to finalize the creation of the requestor. From now on, you'll find the requestor in the Connectors container for the routing group where you created it.

Now you need to start the directory synchronization service using the Services container in the Computer Management snap-in for the server on which you installed the requestor. While you're at it, be sure that directory synchronization is set to start automatically.

Dirsync Server Settings

Now you need to tell the Dirsync server, which I'm assuming is already running on the MS Mail PC side, that it will be contacted by the Dirsync requestor that you just set up. This is a security measure. Using MS Mail PC's DOS-based ADMIN.EXE program, do the following:

1. Select Config from the first menu that you see, and press Enter.

2. Select Dirsync from the next menu, and press Enter.

3. Select Server from the next menu, and press Enter.

4. Select Requestors from the next menu, and press Enter.

5. Select Create from the next menu, and press Enter.

Use the resultant input screen to add the name of your Exchange MS Mail PC shadow network and post office (see Figure 16.27). If you've included a password in the Settings tab of the Dirsync Requestor object in Exchange for extra security, enter the same password that you set up when creating the requestor.

Now simply restart DISPATCH.EXE. That's it—well, almost. Remember to get out of the MS Mail PC ADMIN.EXE program. When it's running it locks a file that DIS-PATCH.EXE needs to access during directory synchronization, thus preventing synchronization.

FIGURE 16.27

Giving an Exchange Server-based Dirsync requestor access to an MS Mail PC-based Dirsync server

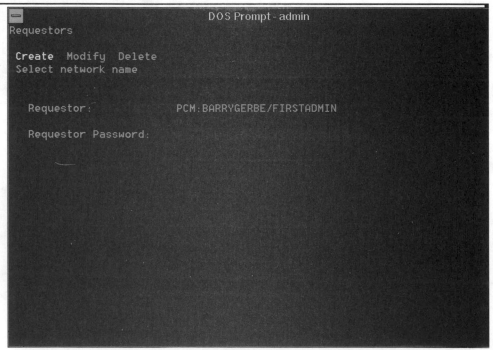

TIP You manage your Dirsync requestor using the Dirsync object in the same Connectors container where your Connector for MS Mail resides. The dialog box looks exactly like the one that you used to set up your Dirsync requestor.

Did It Work?

You'll have to wait until a full Dirsync cycle has completed to find out whether the process was successful. This can take a day or so. You'll know that everything worked as advertised when your Exchange recipients show up on the MS Mail PC side, and vice versa.

After the first Dirsync cycle, create a few new test mailboxes on both sides. If everything is okay, Dirsync will update the directory databases on the Exchange and MS Mail PC sides to reflect these additions.

 NOTE When testing, you can speed up the Dirsync process on the MS Mail PC side by running a bunch of programs normally handled by DISPATCH.EXE. The *Administrator's Guide* for Microsoft Mail for PC Networks includes detailed instructions for doing this. On the Exchange side, you can schedule the requestor to run hourly (using the requestor's Schedule property page) and then select both the Send Updates and Receive Updates options on the requestor's Settings property page. This will force a full Dirsync cycle on the Exchange side at the top of the hour. If you don't want to wait until then, just reset the server clock to the top of the hour.

You Can a Run Dirsync Server on an Exchange Server

You may have noticed that on the same pop-up menu where you choose to create a Dirsync requestor, you can choose to set up a Dirsync server. You'd do this if you never installed a Dirsync server in your Microsoft Mail PC environment—that is, on a DOS-based PC. Dirsync server installation is pretty easy, so I'm going to let you work out the details. The MS Mail PC documentation will help fill in whatever details are lacking in the Exchange 2000 online docs. *Remember that you don't have to install a Dirsync server in your Exchange environment if one is already set up and running on the MS Mail PC side.*

Administering and Managing the Exchange Directory Synchronization Service

The Exchange directory synchronization service (DX) is the real power behind Dirsync. It's similar to the program DISPATCH.EXE on the MS Mail PC side because it does a lot of the real work of directory synchronization.

You don't have to worry much about the DX. Still, because the service is an Exchange object, you can use a dialog box to manage it. The DX object that you want is in the container for the server on which you installed your Dirsync requestor or server. It is labeled *Directory Synchronization*.

Find and right-click the directory synchronization object, and select Properties from the pop-up menu. You'll see a dialog box like the one in Figure 16.28.

FIGURE 16.28

The dialog box for administering and managing the Exchange Server directory synchronization service

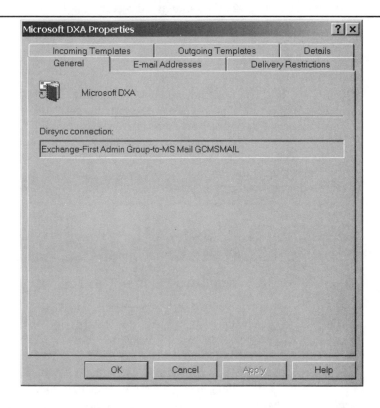

The only property pages that won't be familiar to you are those pertaining to Incoming Templates and Outgoing Templates. By default, only two pieces of information about each recipient are included in the Dirsync process: mailbox name or alias (JSmith, for example), and display name (Smith, John). As you'll remember, Exchange Server provides a large number of additional recipient information fields—including home address, office phone, fax, and department—and it lets you define up to 10 additional custom attribute fields. To add recipient information fields on the MS Mail PC side, you must define a template that will hold that information.

Exchange users can view Exchange recipient information fields when running an Outlook client, and MS Mail PC users can see MS Mail PC recipient information when running an MS Mail PC client. So how do you allow users on one system to see information about recipients on the other system? You use the Incoming Templates and Outgoing Templates property pages.

Each Exchange Server recipient information field has a name, as does each field in an MS Mail PC template. You set up mappings or links between Exchange Server's and MS Mail PC's field names on the Incoming Templates and Outgoing Templates property pages. Mapped fields are exchanged along with the two standard recipient information fields and, voilà, information about recipients on both systems is available to users of either system.

Mapping is easy as long as you have the field names for your MS Mail PC template in hand. Setting up MS Mail PC templates is also a breeze; the Microsoft Mail PC *Administrator's Guide* provides very clear instructions. I'll leave the rest to you.

A Brief Overview of Other Exchange Foreign Messaging System Connectors and Exchange Gateways

Exchange 2000 Server includes connectors for other messaging systems. In addition, third parties offer gateways to a range of foreign messaging systems. Let's take a very quick look at these.

Other Exchange Connectors for Foreign Messaging Systems

Exchange 2000 Server comes with connectors for the following:

- Lotus cc:Mail
- Lotus Notes
- Novell GroupWise

If your legacy system is Lotus's cc:Mail, Microsoft has a way for you to link your users to Exchange Server. The Connector for cc:Mail links cc:Mail post offices and Exchange Server sites. Like the Connector for MS Mail, it passes messages between cc:Mail and Exchange Server, and it synchronizes addresses between the two systems. Conceptually, the Connector for cc:Mail is much simpler. It's also considerably easier to configure, lacking things such as shadow post offices.

The connectors for Lotus Notes and Novell GroupWise work similarly to the connectors for MS Mail PC and cc:Mail. Message transfer and directory synchronization are supported on both connectors. The Notes connector handles Notes document links and letterheads and supports cross-system exchange of calendar and schedule information. In addition to messages, the GroupWise connector enables GroupWise users to share appointments, tasks, notes and phone messages with Exchange users, and enables Exchange users to share tasks and meeting requests with GroupWise users.

Our work with Connectors and the Exchange 2000 online docs for the cc:Mail, Notes, or GroupWise connectors should be all you need to succesfully set up and install one of these connectors.

Exchange Server Gateways

A wide variety of vendors provide gateways for electronic messaging systems and devices such as PROFS, SNADS, CompuServe, fax machines, pagers, and voicemail. Check with Microsoft for information on products and vendors. You install, administer, and manage these gateways pretty much like the connectors that we covered in this chapter.

As you plan for links to other electronic messaging systems, keep in mind the wide range of connectivity options available via the Internet. You can reach a number of electronic messaging systems through Exchange Server SMTP hosts—AOL, CompuServe, and MCI Mail are three examples. So, you don't really need special gateways to these systems. You can even reach X.400 systems through the Internet, making the X.400 Connector desirable only if you need to support functions such as the X.400 flavor of electronic data interchange. Of course, you can reach the Internet through most X.400 systems, so if X.400 is your electronic messaging protocol of choice, you can pretty much get along on it alone.

Exchange's SMTP host environment is a powerful, robust, and stable link to the Internet. As a general rule, don't add gateways that you don't need. Every gateway is another administrative and management headache. Save the gateways for electronic messaging systems that you can't readily reach through the Internet, such as fax, pagers, or voicemail. Even in this area, things are changing every day. For example, faxing and paging are getting more Internet-capable every day. Can voicemail be far behind?

Of course, sometimes specific gateways may be the best choice. If performance is key, a direct gateway between two disparate systems, such as Exchange Server and SNADS systems based on IBM mainframes, is your best choice. Without the conversion steps required by an Internet middleman, mail can move more quickly between different systems. Gateways can also make message tracking and directory synchronization easier because no Internet messaging baggage must be taken into account.

Summary

Exchange 2000 Server includes connectors to a number of foreign messaging systems. These include Internet, X.400, Microsoft Mail for PC Networks, Lotus cc:Mail, Lotus Notes, and Novell GroupWise. At a minimum, these connectors support message interchange and directory synchronization between Exchange systems and the foreign systems.

The X.400 connector supports both direct links to other X.400 messaging systems and links between Exchange 2000 routing groups in the same Exchange organization. X.400 connectors ride atop service transport stacks, which support TCP/IP, X.25, and Remote Access Server-based asynchronous connections. Configuring the X.400 connector for links to external X.400 messaging systems requires an understanding of X.400 messaging standards. Connecting Exchange routing groups with an X.400 connector is simple and straightforward. X.400 connectors should be used for routing group links only after it is clear that neither routing group connectors nor SMTP connectors are appropriate for connecting routing groups.

The Connector for MS Mail is used to connect Exchange administrative groups and organizations to Microsoft's legacy MS Mail for PC Networks systems. The connector allows for the interchange of messages between the two systems. A shadow MS Mail PC post office is installed on an Exchange server, and it is linked with MS Mail PC post offices by processes that run on DOS-based MS Mail computers and Windows 2000-based Exchange servers. The synchronization of e-mail addresses between the two systems is supported by the Dirsync process, which is native to the MS Mail PC environment. A separate connector is used to synchronize schedule information between legacy SchedulePlus implementations and Exchange 2000 systems.

Connectors for Lotus cc:Mail and Notes and Novell GroupWise function similarly to the Connector for MS Mail, moving messages and directory information between these foreign systems and Exchange. The Notes and GroupWise connectors have been enhanced to allow for the interchange of information unique to these systems.

PART VI

Exchange and Outlook: The Next Level

With this section, our tour of Exchange 2000 Server comes to an end. We've been over a lot of flat and gently sloping territory in the past 16 chapters. Now it's time to head up into the mountains for a look at some of Exchange Server's advanced features. In Chapter 17, "Advanced Exchange Server Management," we move into the heights of advanced Exchange Server administration and management. We'll cover all those topics that I earlier promised to get to. You're ready now, and we're gonna have fun! In Chapter 18, "Building, Using, and Managing Outlook Forms Designer Applications," we'll reach for the peaks of Exchange application development, focusing on one of the easier and more interesting options—Outlook 2000's Forms Designer package and how it integrates with Exchange 2000 Server.

CHAPTER 17

Advanced Exchange Server Management

FEATURING:

As you've probably realized, Exchange Server is loaded with fancy and fantastic features. Although we've covered a lot of these already, a number of Exchange Server and Exchange-related Windows 2000 Server advanced features remain to be explored. We'll tackle these features in this chapter. I think you'll be pleased to see that a number of these features are really quite easy to use.

Setting Up Exchange Advanced Security

Exchange Server is pretty secure in and of itself. User message stores and the use of the Exchange System Manager are protected by Windows 2000 Server security. Internal Exchange server-to-server system and e-mail messaging is secure, and you can protect Internet-based messaging using secure authentication methods and Secure Sockets Layer encryption.

In addition to all of those, a level of advanced security is available in Exchange: digital signatures and data encryption based on the RSA public key cryptography system. A digital signature assures a message's receiver that the contents of the message haven't been altered since it was digitally signed, and that the message was truly sent by the indicated originator. Data encryption with public and private keys virtually guarantees that only authorized recipients can read a message.

You must enable advanced security on a mailbox-by-mailbox basis. Each enabled Exchange mailbox has two pairs of keys, each consisting of a public and a private key. One pair of keys is for digital signing, and the other is for encryption.

When a user chooses to sign an outgoing message, the user's Exchange client uses the private signing key of her or his mailbox to add a digital signature to the message. The message recipient's Exchange client verifies the signature using the public signing key of the sender's mailbox.

To encrypt an outgoing message, an Exchange client uses the unique public encryption key for the mailbox of each recipient of the message. When a user receives an encrypted message, the user's Exchange client uses the private encryption key for his or her mailbox to decrypt the message.

Public keys are stored in Active Directory as attributes of each advanced security-enabled mailbox. Private keys are stored on each user's private disk space in an encrypted file with the extension .EPF.

To run advanced Exchange Server security, you'll need to install a special *Key Management Service* program, or simply KM Service, or more simply (KMS). Among other things, KMS does the following:

Certifies public signing and encryption keys to ensure their authenticity.

Creates public and private encryption keys. (Public and private signing keys are created by Exchange clients.)

Holds backups of private encryption keys and public signing keys.

Generates tokens that are used only once to enable digital signatures and encryption or to recover lost or forgotten keys for a user.

Maintains the original copy of the list of users whose rights to advanced security have been revoked.

The KMS database itself is encrypted for additional security.

You can install one KMS per Exchange administrative group. The same KMS can support multiple administrative groups.

You can enable advanced security across Exchange organizations. You can then send secure messages to those in other organizations using Internet standard security algorithms.

 WARNING Virus programs can't scan encrypted messages. So, any virus program that operates on message attachments before they have been decrypted (for example, as they come in from the Internet or as they are stored on Exchange server) won't catch viruses in encrypted messages. A workstation-based program that watches for viruses as applications and files are opened should catch viruses in previously encrypted message attachments.

Installing Key Management Server and Supporting Software

Windows 2000 Server's Certificate Server is required to install and run KMS. I showed you how to install Certificate Server in Chapter 14, "Managing Exchange 2000 Services for Internet Clients," in the section "Installing and Managing a Windows 2000 Certificate Authority." If you installed a Certificate Server, then you're ready to install KMS. Join me in the next section. If you haven't installed a Certificate Server, then go back to Chapter 14 and install one. When you're done, meet me in the next section.

Installing KMS

Before you can install KMS, you need to install three Exchange certificate templates on your Certificate Server. If you are running multiple certificate servers, you need to install the certificates on only one of your certificate servers. To install the three certificate templates, you will use the Certification Authority snap-in for Microsoft Management Console. You should have installed the snap-in when you installed Certificate Server back in Chapter 14. Open the Certificate Authority snap-in, and right-click the Policy Settings subcontainer (see Figure 17.1). Select New ➢ Certificate to Issue. On the resultant Select Certificate Template dialog box, hold down the Ctrl key and select Enrollment Agent (Computer), Exchange User, and Exchange Signature Only; then click OK. The templates are now installed, and you can proceed to the installation of KMS.

Installing the three certificate templates required before the Exchange Key Management Service can be installed

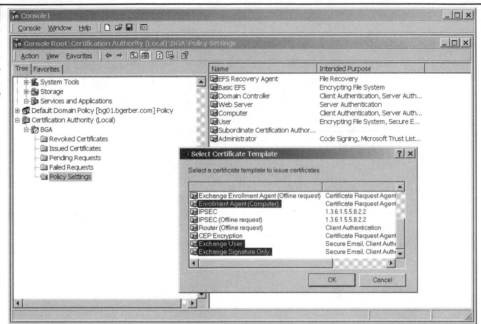

KMS software is installed on an Exchange server. For maximum security, the server should be set up on a disk formatted for the NT File System (NTFS).

KMS is at the heart of your advanced Exchange security system. Be sure to locate the computer that runs it in a physically secure place. KMS access doesn't generate much network traffic, so it makes little difference on which of your Exchange servers you put it.

To install KMS, insert the Exchange 2000 Server CD-ROM and select Exchange Server Setup from the dialog box that opens. On the Component Selection page of the Exchange 2000 Installation Wizard (see Figure 17.2), select Change as the action for the components Microsoft Exchange 2000 and Microsoft Exchange Messaging and Collaboration Services. Then select Install as the action for Microsoft Exchange Key Management Service. On the next wizard page, select the administrative group where you want to install KMS (see Figure 17.3).

FIGURE 17.2

Using the Exchange 2000 Installation Wizard to set up installation of the Key Management Service

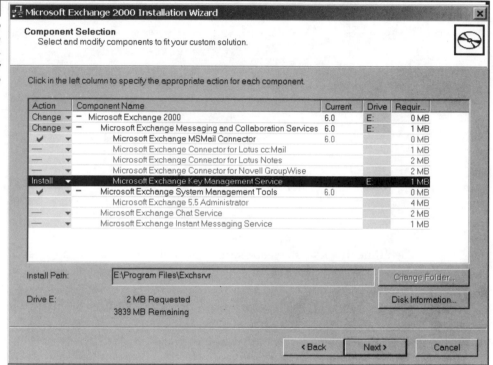

FIGURE 17.3

*Selecting the adminis-
trative group into
which the Key
Management Service
will be installed*

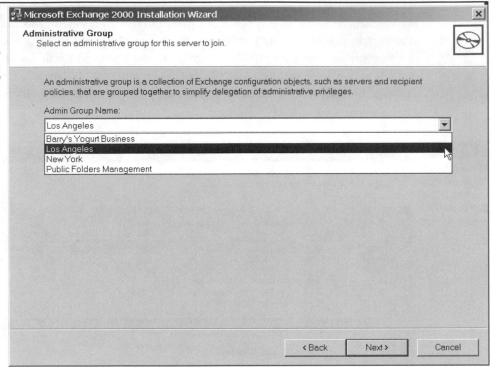

Each time that KMS starts up—usually at bootup of your Exchange server—a special password must be entered, or the program won't run. You choose how you want to enter that password on the next wizard page. As you can see in Figure 17.4, you can choose to enter the password manually or to have KMS look for it on a diskette or a hard disk.

Entry at bootup is obviously the most secure approach, but that means someone must be present when the server boots. The most convenient method is to store the password on a hard disk on your Exchange server with a backup on a diskette. Storing on hard disk is new to Exchange 2000. In the past, disk-based startup was possible only with a diskette, meaning that someone with access to the diskette had to be present when the server booted up. The diskette password entry approach had its drawbacks. Sometimes Exchange managers left the password diskette in the drive, and the server couldn't boot with it in place. Some Exchange managers prioritized bootup so that the server would boot up first from hard disk. Leaving the password diskette lying around severely compromised security. Although it's still not perfect, hard disk-based password entry is probably the best option for most organizations. With the password stored on the hard disk, KMS will start without need for an onsite keeper of the KMS password and without need for an exposed password diskette.

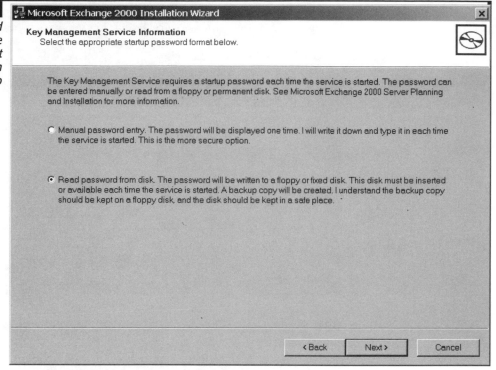

FIGURE 17.4

Selecting the method to be used to enter the Key Management Service password on startup

If you choose to enter the KMS startup password manually, the next wizard page shows you the password and asks that you write down the password and carefully preserve it. If you choose disk-based password entry, the next wizard page shows you your options for storing the password (see Figure 17.5). The default options are for two disks, one for the master copy and one for a backup copy. You can change the location of either copy. I've set the options for my KMS so that the master copy is stored on the C drive of my Exchange server. If either of the options you've chosen includes a diskette, when you click Next, you'll see the dialog box in Figure 17.5 asking you to insert a diskette. Do so and click OK, and the password file will be written to the diskette.

FIGURE 17.5

*Selecting the drives
where a master and
backup copy of the
password file will be
stored*

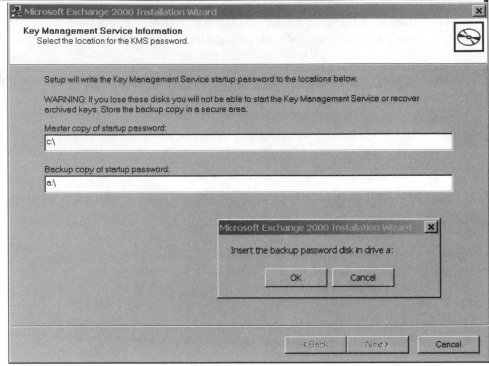

The final wizard page shows you the component options that you've chosen. Click Next, and installation begins.

After installation, the Key Management Service is set to start up manually. You can use the Services container in the Computer Management snap-in to set KMS to start up automatically with the rest of the Exchange Server components. Before you leave the Services container, start the Key Management Server.

Before you can move on, you need to grant KMS some rights on your new certificate server. Follow along on Figure 17.6. Find and right-click the certificate server in your Certification Authority snap-in, and then select Properties from the pop-up menu. Tab over to the Security property page on the Properties dialog box for your certificate server, and click Add. On the Select Users, Computers, or Groups dialog box, find the computer on which you just installed KMS. (I installed KM on EXCHANGE02.) Select this computer, and click Add and then OK. Next you'll see a dialog box like the one in Figure 17.7. KMS needs to manage this certificate server, so select Manage (Enroll will be selected automatically), and click OK. If you have multiple certificate servers, be sure to do this task on each of them.

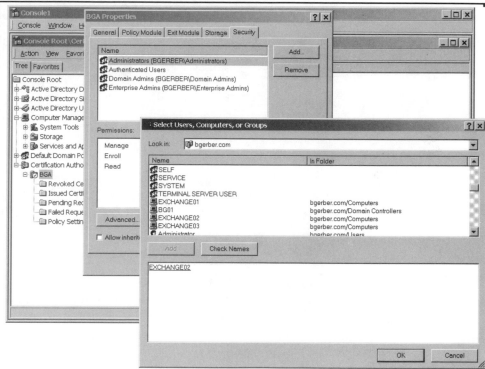

FIGURE 17.7

Granting a KMS server management rights on a certificate server

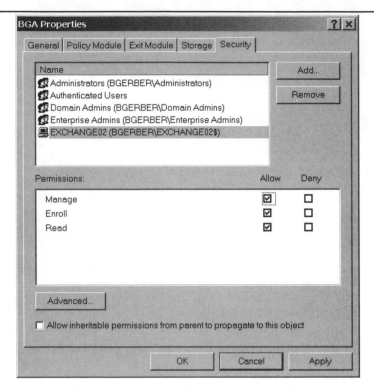

Now you need to add the snap-in that you'll use to manage KMS to your Microsoft Management Console. It's called Exchange Advanced Security. To add it, in your MMC, select Console ➤ Add/Remove Snap-in. Then click Add on the Add/Remove Snap-in dialog box, find and select the Exchange Advanced Security snap-in in the Standalone Snap-in dialog box, and click Add. Finally, work your way out of the dialog boxes.

Now expand the Exchange Advanced Security snap-in. You'll see all your administrative groups that have mailbox stores in them. As you can see in Figure 17.8, the administrative group that I created back in Chapter 15, "Installing and Managing Additional Exchange 2000 Servers," to hold my default public folder tree doesn't show up in the Exchange Advanced Security snap-in. That's because the administrative group has no mailbox store.

Take a look at the administrative group into which you installed KMS. Notice that there are two objects in the group (see Figure 17.8). One is named Encryption Configuration, the other Key Manager. You use the encryption configuration object to set encryption parameters for an administrative group. You'll find an instance of this object in every administrative group with a mailbox store. The key manager object is used to administer KMS. An instance of this object is placed into an administrative group when you install KMS in that group. Because I installed KMS only in my Los

Angeles administrative group, the Key Manager object exists only in that administrative group.

FIGURE 17.8

The Exchange Advanced Security snap-in with the Encryption Configuration and Key Manager objects, which were installed into the administrative group where the Exchange Key Management Service was installed

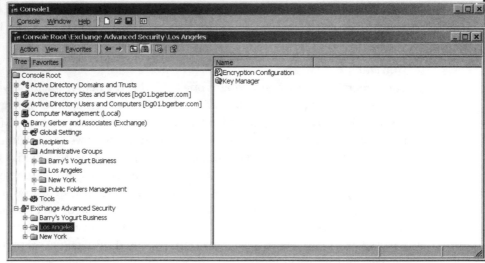

 TIP You can also manage Exchange advanced security for any administrative group from within the Advanced Security subcontainer that exists within the administrative group itself. Upon installation of KMS, this container is added to each administrative group with at least one mailbox store. The container includes the same objects that you'll find in the Exchange Advanced Security snap-in for each administrative group.

Managing the Key Management Service

There are three distinct KMS management tasks:

Setting encryption algorithms

Setting KMS's own security and other properties

Enabling advanced security for mailboxes

We'll cover each of these tasks in order. To start, be sure that you're logged on to a Windows 2000 account with Exchange full administrator privileges. In the Exchange Advanced Security snap-in, select the administrative group where you installed KMS (see Figure 17.8).

Setting Encryption Algorithms

As I mentioned earlier, you use an administrative group's Encryption Configuration object to administer and manage encryption algorithm settings. Open the Encryption Configuration Properties dialog box by double-clicking the Encryption Configuration object. The dialog box has two property pages, General and Algorithms. Let's look at each of these in more detail.

General

The General property page contains one field, the Key Management Service location. You use this field to select a KMS for an administrative group into which you haven't installed KMS. The field is grayed out in administrative groups where KMS is installed, indicating that the KMS can't be changed. Because you're working right now in the administrative group where you installed KMS, the KMS location field is grayed out.

To enable Exchange advanced security in administrative groups where a KMS isn't installed, you need to select a KMS server (actually administrative group) using the General property page of the Encryption Configuration dialog box for that administrative group. For example, when I set up advanced security for my New York and Barry's Yogurt Business administrative groups, I used the General property page in each administrative group to select the KMS in my Los Angeles administrative group. Figure 17.9 should make this clearer.

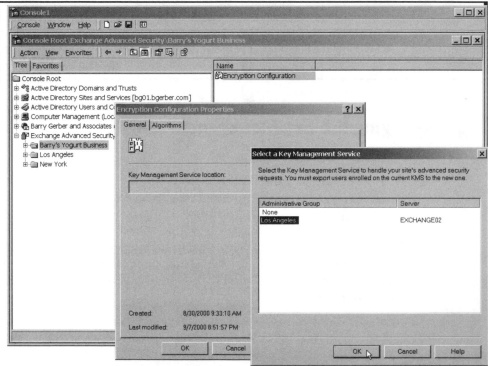

FIGURE 17.9

Selecting the administrative group KMS server to be used in an administrative group without a KMS server

Algorithms

Before I talk about the Algorithms page, I need to give you a quick tutorial on encryption algorithms. Two general encryption options are available to Exchange Server clients: the Exchange Server and S/MIME options.

The proprietary Exchange Server encryption option uses standard encryption algorithms. It is designed for Outlook 97 and earlier clients, which do not support S/MIME. The S/MIME option is based on the Secure MIME Internet standard. It, too, uses standard encryption algorithms.

The Exchange Server encryption option gives you a choice of three encryption algorithms: Data Encryption Standard (DES), CAST-40, and CAST-64. (*CAST* stands for the initials of *C*arlisle *A*dams and *S*tafford *T*avares, who developed the algorithm at Northern Telecom.)

Both DES and CAST-64 use 64 bits for keys, while CAST-40 uses only 40 bits. Because it produces a shorter and more easily broken key, CAST-40 is less secure than either CAST-64 or DES. Because the U.S. government allows exportation of 64-bit or higher encryption only to a specific list of countries, however, only CAST-40 encryption is available for Exchange Server software shipped to countries not on the list. You can set the encryption algorithm used for each administrative group separately. Exchange Server knows what encryption algorithm to use for messages to an administrative group, so if you have administrative groups both inside and in countries not on the U.S. government's legal 64-bit and higher encryption list, you don't have to use the less-secure CAST-40 algorithm across your entire Exchange organization.

Like the Exchange Server encryption option, the S/MIME option lets you choose from three encryption algorithms: Triple Data Encryption Standard (3DES), DES, RC2-128, and RC2-40. (*RC* stands for either *R*on's *C*ode or *R*ivest's *C*ipher, in honor of the inventor of the algorithm, Ron Rivest.)

3DES encrypts the regular DES key three times, meaning that there are really three keys. Microsoft's 3DES is a 112-bit implementation of the algorithm. RC2-128 encrypts at 128 bits. RC2-40 is the 40-bit algorithm for use outside the United States and Canada. 3DES is considered the most secure of the three S/MIME algorithms.

Okay, now for the Algorithms property page (see Figure 17.10). The default settings for Exchange and S/MIME encryption use the strongest algorithms available, so don't change them unless you have good reason to do so.

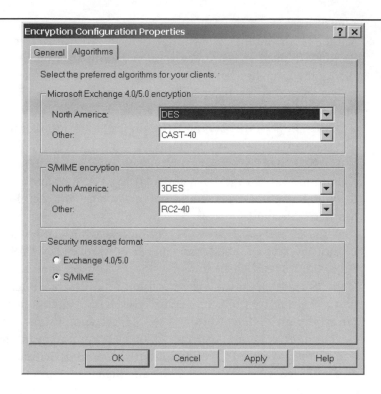

You set the default message format in the Security message format area. The default is
set in the user's Outlook client when Exchange advanced security is enabled. KMS can
use either Exchange Server or S/MIME encryption when sending a message, so you're
not setting the one-and-only encryption method to be supported by KMS. Users can
change the default in Outlook 98 and later clients. Set the default to support the
majority of Outlook clients in the administrative group or your organization.

Setting KM Server's Own Security and Other Properties

If you have Exchange full administrator rights on an administrative group container, you can change encryption options using the Encryption Configuration
Properties dialog box shown in Figure 17.10. However, to change KMS's own security, you must have some very special rights. You must be a Key Management Server
Administrator (KMSA).

As a KMSA, among other things, you can change your KMS password, add and
remove other KMSAs, and enable and disable advanced security for mailboxes. When
you've enabled advanced security for a mailbox, the mailbox's owner can use digital

signatures and data encryption. As you can see, KMSAs are very powerful, so you should assign KMSA rights with great care. To start with, the default KMSA is the account that installed KMS. That is often the Windows 2000 administrator account for the domain where KMS was installed, but for reasons of security, you can use any account that you want. If you used another account, just substitute it for "administrator" in the discussion that follows.

To modify KMS's own security for the first time, be sure that you're logged in under the account that installed KMS. Then double-click the Key Manager object in the administrative group subcontainer of the Exchange Advanced Security container (see Figure 17.8). Before you can run Key Manager, you need to enter the special KMS password for the domain administrator (see Figure 17.11). This is not the password of the account that installed KM Server. It's a special password for use when the administrator runs Key Manager. The default password is *password*, in lowercase. In a bit, I'll show you how to change the default.

FIGURE 17.11

Entering the KMS password for the administrator of the domain where KMS is installed

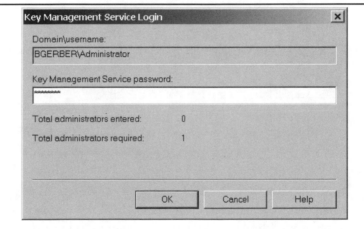

When you're done with the password dialog box, click OK to open the Key Manager Properties dialog box shown in Figure 17.12. Let's take a look at the property pages on this dialog box.

General

You can view information about the certificate server that supports the KMS on the General property page. Select a certificate server, and click View Details to open the Certificate Detail dialog box. As you can see in Figure 17.12, the General property page of this dialog box tells you about the certificate server's own certificate, which it issued to itself because it is a root certificate authority. The other Certificate Detail property pages tell you more about the certificate, including whether it is currently okay. If the certificate isn't okay (for example, if it has expired), the certificate server can't issue other certificates, so you should be sure to keep your certificate server certificates in good order.

The Key Manager Properties dialog box, with its General and Certificate Detail (General) property pages exposed

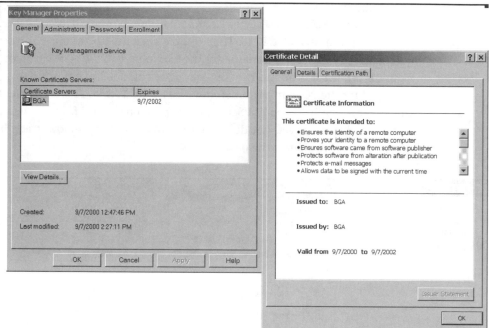

Administrators

When you try to tab over to the Administrators property page, that pesky Key Management Service Login dialog box (see Figure 17.11) pops up. That happens every time you tab to any of the four property pages except the General page. This is to protect the Exchange advanced security system. In earlier versions of Exchange, you could tell Key Manager to remember the password for five minutes. That little security hole has been plugged, much to the chagrin of anti-carpal tunnel syndrome groups around the world. Remember that the default KMS password is *password*.

If you need to add or remove KMSAs, use this page. In Figure 17.13, I'm adding the administrator in my bgyogurt domain—where the administrative group Barry's Yogurt Business is located—to the list of KMSAs. Each KMSA has its own special KMS administrator password, so when you're adding a new KMSA, you'll be asked to enter a password for the new KMSA. You can change a KMSA's password by selecting the

KMSA, clicking Change Password, and filling in the information on the resultant Change Password dialog box. You can change a password only if you know the current password. So, if you're a cross-organizational KMS administrator, you'll want to keep a record of administrator passwords and require that password changes be reported to you.

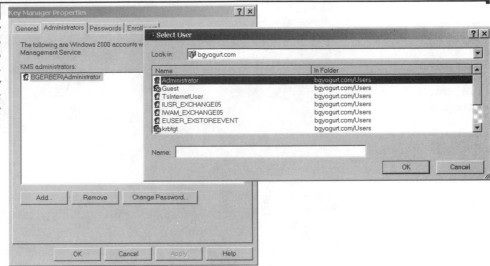

FIGURE 17.13

Adding a Key Management Service administrator using the Administrators property page of the Key Manager Properties dialog box

 TIP A user granted KMSA status must be delegated at least Exchange administrator permissions on the administrative group that contains the Key Manager. Without these permissions the user won't be able to do KMSA tasks.

Passwords

If you want to increase security, you can use the Passwords property page (see Figure 17.14) to require that multiple KMSAs authorize specific advanced security tasks. For example, if you've defined five KMSAs, you can require that any number of them from one to five must enter their Windows 2000 usernames and KMSA passwords for any of the tasks shown in Figure 17.14 to complete.

The Add/Delete Administrators, Edit Multiple Password Policies option sets the maximum number of KMSAs required to add or delete administrators and to change the rest of the items on this property page. We'll talk about these other items in a bit. The number of KMSAs that you selected for the Add/Delete Administrators, Edit Multiple Password Policies option must be greater than or equal to the number that you select for the other options on this page. So, if you have three KMSAs and you require that all three authorize addition and deletion of administrators and editing of multiple password policies, you can require that one, two, or three KMSAs authorize any of the other options on the property page.

FIGURE 17.14

Use the Passwords property page of the Key Manager Properties dialog box to increase security when using Exchange Server's advanced security.

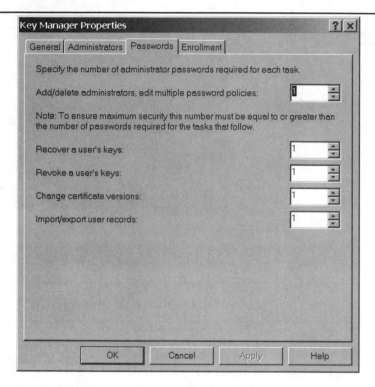

Be careful with all this multiple password authorization stuff. If you involve too many cooks in this particular concoction, the day might come when you find yourself in a bowl of alphabet soup without a spoon.

 NOTE You can't specify which KMSAs must consent to the completion of a task, just the number of them that must consent. If you have five KMSAs and require consent from three of them, any three of the five can authorize the task.

Enrollment

Use the Enrollment property page to set some policies to be applied when advanced security is enabled on an Exchange mailbox. As Figure 17.15 notes, when advanced security is enabled for an Exchange mailbox, KMS generates a token. The mailbox owner must enter the token using an Outlook client as part of the process of enabling advanced security. I'll show you how the key is used a few pages down the road.

You can pass the key to the mailbox owner manually in a face-to-face meeting, or you can have KM Server mail the key to the mailbox to be enabled. The e-mail option is disabled by default. For utmost security, leave the option disabled.

When the key is sent by e-mail, it is accompanied by a message. You can change the message by clicking Customize Message.

FIGURE 17.15

Manage the security certificate creation and distribution process using the Enrollment property page of the Key Manager Properties dialog box.

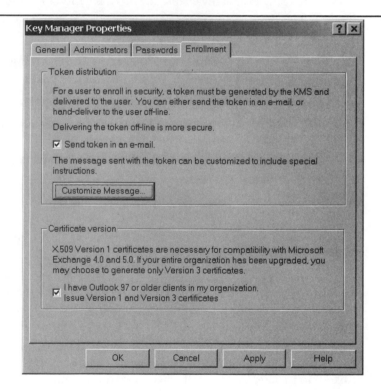

Outlook 97 and earlier clients use version 1 X.509 certificates to bind users' public keys to their mailbox. S/MIME-compatible clients support version 1 and version 3 certificates. Version 3 certificates are preferred. KMS issues X.509 version 1 certificates. For version 3 certificates, it turns to Microsoft's Windows 2000 Certificate Server.

That's why Certificate Server must be installed in your Windows 2000 environment before you can install KMS.

If your organization uses Outlook 97 or earlier clients, you must select Issue Version 1 and Version 3 certificates in the Certificate Version area of the Enrollment property page. If your organization uses only Outlook 98 or later S/MIME-compatible clients, you need not select this option, and only version 3 certificates will be issued.

When you're done setting up Key Manager, click OK. Your old friend the Key Management Service Login dialog box pops up. Enter your password (still *password*, unless you changed it on the Administrators property page), and your changes are saved.

Enabling Advanced Security for Mailboxes

Now we're ready to actually enable advanced security for mailboxes. This is a two-step process that's done partly on the Exchange Server side and partly on the Exchange client side. We'll start with Exchange Server.

Enabling Advanced Security for Mailboxes: The Exchange Server Side

As a KMSA, you can enable advanced security for mailboxes in three ways:

By enrolling mailbox-enabled users one at a time in Active Directory

By enrolling mailbox-enabled users in groups, selecting specific users from the Exchange global address list

By enrolling all mailbox-enabled users with mailboxes in a specific mailbox store

If you need to enable advanced security on only a few mailboxes, the first option should work just fine. However, if you've got a bunch of mailboxes that need enabling, one of the latter two options is a better choice, depending on whether you need to enable some of the mailboxes in your organization or to enable all the mailboxes in a particular mailbox store.

To enroll mailbox-enabled users in advanced security one at a time, find and double-click the user in \Active Directory Users and Computers\Users. Then tab to the Exchange Features property page and double-click E-mail Security. This function is part of KMS, so you must enter the KMSA administrator password. After you've entered the password, you'll see the Exchange Security dialog box, shown in Figure 17.16. Click Enroll, and you'll see a dialog box asking you if you want to send the key (token) to the user by e-mail. If you choose this option, the user receives a special key message in his or her Outlook client Inbox. If you choose not to e-mail the key, a dialog box opens showing the key. You can copy the key and paste it into a Notepad file along with the name of the user so that you can give the key to the user in a secure manner. The token is also written to a file. I'll tell you where the file is a little later in this section.

Don't worry about the Recover and Revoke options on the Exchange Security dialog box right now. I'll talk about them later in this chapter.

FIGURE 17.16

*Enabling Exchange
advanced security for
mailbox-enabled users
in Active Directory one
user at a time*

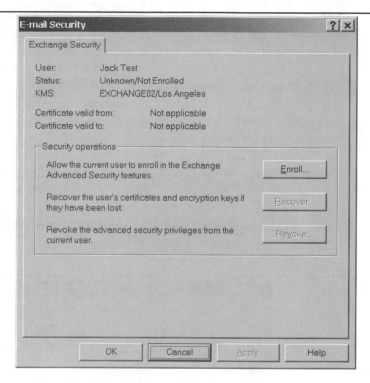

This may seem like a laborious way to enable advanced security for a user. It's a bit easier if you send the key by e-mail, but you're right. This is no way to run an advanced security system in a large organization. That's where the other two options for enabling advanced security come in. They let you enable advance security for groups of users.

To use one of these options, right-click Key Manager and select All Tasks ➢ Enroll Users. This opens the Enroll Users Selection dialog, box shown in Figure 17.17. The first option lets you choose as few or as many users as you want to enable from the global address book. The second option lets you choose to enable *all* of the mailboxes on as many mailbox stores as you want.

FIGURE 17.17

*Using the Enroll Users
Selection dialog box to
choose an option for
enabling Exchange
advanced security for
a group of
mailbox-enabled users*

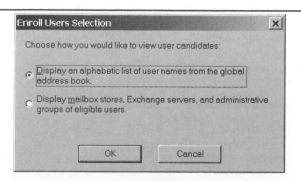

If you select the first option, after you enter the KMSA password, the Enroll Users dialog box shown in Figure 17.18 opens. Mailbox-enabled users that can be enabled for advanced security are shown in bold. Other objects and mailboxes already enabled are shown in grayed-out text. Select the users for whom you want to enable advanced security, click Add, and then click Enroll. That's it.

If you choose to have tokens sent to users by e-mail back on the Enrollment property page of the Key Manager Properties dialog box, you're done. The tokens will be automatically sent to each advanced security-enabled user. If you choose not to send tokens by e-mail, you'll have to give tokens to each user. Tokens, whether or not they're sent by e-mail, are recorded along with the name of the user to whom they are assigned, in the file \PROGRAM FILES\EXCHSRVR\KMSDATA\ENROLL.LOG. This is the same directory into which you installed Exchange Server. If you didn't accept the default installation directory, you'll find the file in the EXCHSRVR\KMSDATA directory, wherever you had it placed by the Exchange setup program.

FIGURE 17.18

Enabling Exchange advanced security for mailbox-enabled users selected from the Exchange global address list

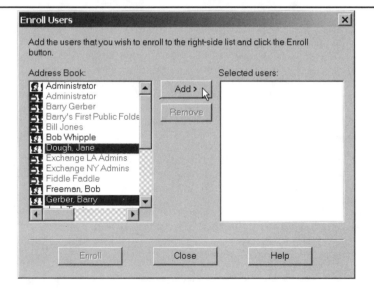

Figure 17.19 shows what happens when you choose to enable advanced security at the mailbox store level. In Figure 17.19, I'm about to enable advanced security for all the mailbox-enabled users whose mailboxes reside on the default mailbox store on the server EXCHANGE03 in my New York administrative group. Well, that's quite a mouthful, but I'm sure that you can appreciate the value of this option. It lets you kill a lot of birds with one stone, assuming that you want to do what it does. As with the previous option, token delivery is by e-mail or hand delivery.

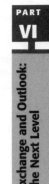

FIGURE 17.19

Enabling Exchange advanced security for all mailbox-enabled users whose mailboxes are stored on a particular mailbox store

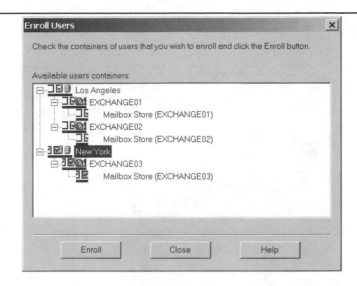

Enabling Advanced Security for Mailboxes: The Outlook Client Side

Open a client for the mailbox for which you want to enable advanced security. In the example presented here, I'm using an Outlook 2000 client. If you enabled the KMS's e-mail option, you'll find an e-mail message from the Exchange Server's System Attendant that includes your security token. Open the message to see the token (see Figure 17.20). To simplify matters, highlight and copy the token.

FIGURE 17.20

A message including an advanced security token and instructions for its use sent by the Exchange System Attendant

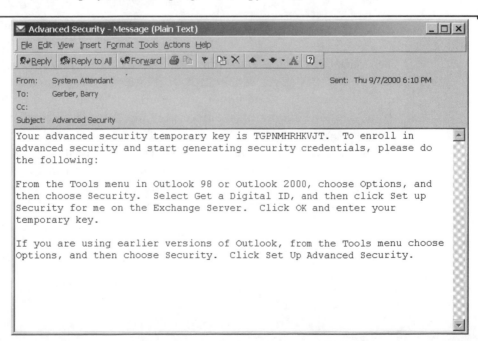

Next, select Options from the client's Tools menu to open the Options dialog box, and then tab over to the Security property page (see Figure 17.21).

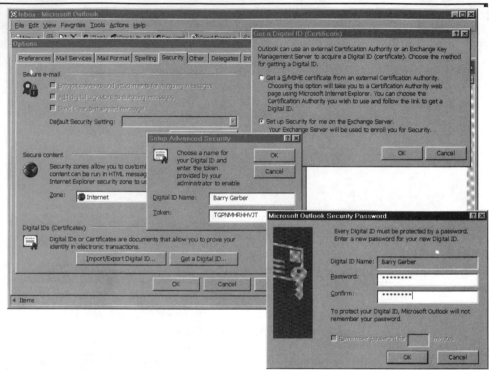

Then, click Get a Digital ID to bring up the Get a Digital ID (Certificate) dialog box (see Figure 17.21). As you can see in Figure 17.21, you can get an S/MIME certificate from an external certificate authority or a certificate through your Exchange Server. The first option is for one-off external certificates. Select the second option, remembering that your Exchange KMS can broker the issuance of an S/MIME certificate.

When you click OK on the Get a Digital ID (Certificate) dialog box, the Setup Advanced Security dialog box opens (see Figure 17.21). Paste the token into the Token field, or type it in and click OK. When the Microsoft Outlook Security Password dialog box opens, enter and confirm an advanced security password that will be used when you generate or try to open a digitally signed or encrypted message. (The password must be at least six characters long.) When you're done, click OK.

Click OK in response to the next dialog box, which tells you that your request to enable security has been sent to the Key Management server and that you'll be notified when the request has been processed. This feature is pretty impressive. Communications between clients and KM Server are all by e-mail messages, so the client can be linked to the Exchange server environment by anything from a dial-up connection to a hard-wired WAN or LAN link.

After the time required for a round-trip mail cycle, a message from the System Attendant will appear in your Outlook Inbox. The subject of the message will be Reply from Security Authority. This is a very special message. When you open it, you won't see a standard message window. Instead, you'll see the Microsoft Outlook Security Logon dialog box, which looks a lot like the Microsoft Outlook Security Password dialog box in Figure 17.21. Enter your password (the one that you just created) and, if you want, set the length of time in minutes that Outlook will remember the password after you've entered it. This is a nice feature. With it, you don't have to type in your password every time you create or open a secure message. I suggest that you select this option, or you'll have to re-enter your password at least once more before you're done enabling Exchange advanced security. When you're done with this dialog box, click OK.

Next you're asked if you want to add the certificate to the root store, which is part of your certificate server's database. Click OK, and then hit OK to make your way through the remaining dialog boxes. In a bit, you'll receive a message from the System Attendant telling you that advanced security has been successfully enabled.

Finally, you'll see the contents of the message from the Exchange System Attendant that you just opened. The message tells you that security has been successfully enabled for your mailbox.

 NOTE After you've enabled advanced security for a mailbox, you can tell Outlook to digitally sign and encrypt *all* messages by selecting these two options on the Options dialog box (see Figure 17.22). The option Send Clear Text Signed Message ensures that the recipient can use the Outlook preview pane to view your messages.

FIGURE 17.22

Enabling digital signatures and encryption for all messages

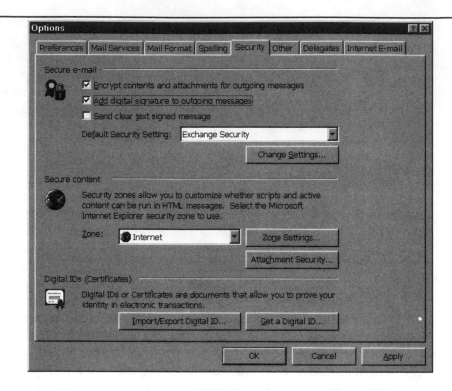

After a while, take a look at the E-mail Security dialog box for your mailbox (see Figure 17.23). Because the mailbox is now fully security-enabled, the Certificate Valid From and Certificate Valid To fields are filled in. By default, security keys are valid for a year. New keys will be automatically generated at the end of this time period.

FIGURE 17.23

The valid life span of a mailbox's security keys has been set.

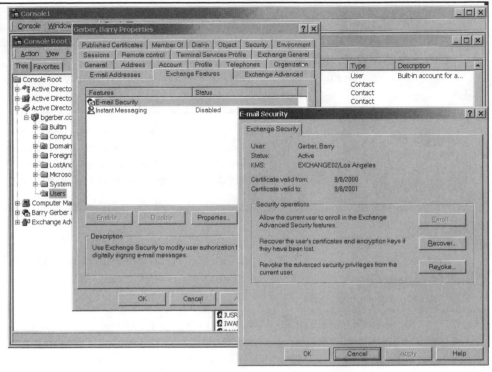

When a mailbox's Security property page looks like the one in Figure 17.23, advanced security is fully enabled, and the mailbox user can send and receive digitally signed or encrypted messages. The mailbox's public keys are part of the mailbox definition in Active Directory.

 TIP You can keep track of advanced security activity in Exchange by keeping an eye on the Windows 2000 Event Viewer's Application log.

Sending and Receiving Digitally Signed and Encrypted Messages

Because this book doesn't focus on Exchange clients, I'll just give you a quick overview on the topic. When using the Options dialog box, if you asked to have all messages digitally signed and encrypted, you'll be led through any required steps for each message. If you've chosen to sign or encrypt messages individually, then while composing a message in your Outlook client, click Options on the message's Standard toolbar. On the Message Options dialog box, select Encrypt Message Contents and Attachments and/or Add Digital Signature to Outgoing Message. When you send the message, you'll be led through the steps required to give it advanced security.

 TIP You can also set security options for a message by selecting Properties from the message's File menu and then selecting Security from the resultant Properties dialog box. This option not only lets you select encryption and digital signing for the message, but it also lets you pick from alternate security settings (S/MIME, as opposed to Exchange Server, for example).

Additional Advanced Security Management Options and Issues

The E-mail Security dialog box for a mailbox-enabled user has two options that we didn't talk about earlier: Recover and Revoke (see Figure 17.23). We're now ready to tackle these options. I also want to talk to you about some of the options on the Key Manager All Tasks menu that I haven't discussed yet and about incorporating security certificates from external sources into your Exchange advanced security environment. Finally, I want to leave you with a caution regarding backing up your KMS databases.

Recovering Certificates and Encryption Keys

The Recover option on the E-mail Security dialog box is useful in the following situations:

> When users lose a temporary key before using it to set up advanced security on the client side
>
> When users lose an advanced security password
>
> When users corrupt or remove local security information from their computers
>
> When users imported from other KMS servers need new keys to generate and read new messages

Click Recover to start the recovery process. When it's finished, a Microsoft Exchange Administrator dialog box pops up to give you a new key. This key will be different from the original one; when the user reinstalls advanced security, whichever of the first three problems needed fixing will be fixed. I'll talk about exporting and importing users in a bit. Recovery is the final step in the import/export process.

Revoking Advanced Security Privileges

Click Revoke to remove advanced security rights for a mailbox. If you ever want to re-enable these rights, just generate a new key for the mailbox and ask the mailbox user to enable advanced security on the client side. To revoke a certificate, the KMS must have Manage permissions on the certificate server that issued the certificate. I talked about granting these permissions earlier in the section "Installing KMS."

 TIP You can also perform recovery and revocation functions for multiple mailbox-enabled users. Right-click Key Manager and select All Tasks ➢ Revoke Certificates, or All Tasks ➢ Recover Keys from the pop-up menu. Exchange System Manager provides you with familiar interfaces for selecting mailbox-enabled users for revocation or recovery.

Exporting and Importing Users

Sometimes you may need to move users from one KMS server to another, such as when you retire an Exchange server where KMS is installed. The process of moving users between KMS servers was complex in Exchange 5.5, requiring users to decrypt their e-mail before the move, because keys from the old KMS server could not exist side by side with keys from the new server. As you'll see later, Exchange 2000 fixes these limitations and makes moving users between KMS servers relatively easy.

The export/import process is tightly secured. You can't export users until you specify the KMS server that will import the users. Users can't be imported until they have been exported from another KMS server. All information in the export file is encrypted using the certificate of the importing KMS server.

The export process involves the following:

> Saving the KMS certificate on the importing server (Key Manager All Tasks menu item: Save KMS Certificate)
>
> Exporting users (Key Manager All Tasks menu item: Export Users)
>
> Importing users (Key Manager All Tasks menu item: Import Users)
>
> Recovering keys (Key Manager All Tasks menu item: Recover Keys)

I'll leave it to you to implement export/import processes as you need them. The wizards that support exporting and importing include good documentation. The online docs aren't bad, either.

WARNING You should back up your source and target KMS databases before moving users. See the upcoming section "Backing Up KMS Databases" for the location of the databases.

Changing the KMS Startup Password

The only item on the Key Manager All Tasks menu that I haven't discussed is Change Startup Password. When you choose this item, you'll see a dialog box with the same startup password options that you saw when you installed KMS (see Figure 17.4). If you need to change your KMS startup password, check out the section "Installing KMS," earlier in this chapter.

Cross-Trusts

You can add certificates from sources that are external to your Windows 2000 environment. This enables internal users to trust such certificates and thus expands the range of secure interaction. This arrangement is called *cross-certification*.

You add external certificates to certificate trust lists (CTLs). All Windows 2000 Server computers have CTLs. If you add a certificate to the CTL on a domain controller, it is published to a CTL that applies to the entire domain. If you add a certificate to a nondomain controller, the certificate applies only to that computer and the services that run on it. So, if you add a certificate to an Exchange server running KMS, Exchange advanced security users will trust the certificate.

To add a certificate, install the Certificates snap-in in your Microsoft Management Console on the Exchange server running your KMS. During installation, select the Computer Account and Local Computer options. After the snap-in has been installed, expand its tree so that you can access \Certificates (Local Computer)\Trust Root Certification Authorities\Certificates. Right-click Certificates and select All Tasks ➤ Import. This opens the Certificate Import Wizard. Click Next and, on the File to Import dialog box, type in the name of the file containing the external certificate (you get the certificate from the external source). Click Next, affirm your choices, and click Finish.

For more on certificates and certificate servers, see *Microsoft Windows 2000 Server Administrator's Guide*, by Charlie Russel and Sharon Crawford (Microsoft Press, 2000), especially Chapters 18 and 19.

Backing Up KMS Databases

According to Microsoft, KMS databases must be backed up locally. You can't back them up from another computer running Windows 2000 Backup or any other

Exchange 2000-compatible backup program. The databases are located in the directory \PROGRAM FILES\EXCHSRVR\KMSDATA. The KMS service must be stopped to back up the files.

Tracking Messages

One of the biggest pains in the management of electronic messaging systems comes from lost (or *allegedly* lost) messages. With Exchange Server's message-tracking capability, you can get information on the status of messages in your Exchange system. This includes those between Exchange users, those generated by Exchange system components, and messages sent through Exchange connectors for foreign messaging systems, such as the Connector for MS Mail. You can track an outgoing Internet message up to the point at which the message is handed to an SMTP virtual server. Beyond that, you have to use the message logging features of the SMTP virtual server. For incoming SMTP messages, message tracking begins where an SMTP virtual server hands the message to Exchange.

You'll remember that in earlier chapters, I always suggested that you turn on message tracking for whatever Exchange server or other messaging component we were working with. This is because Exchange Server's message tracking system relies on logs created when tracking is turned on. So, if you haven't already done so, I suggest that you go back and turn tracking on. You can enable message tracking on:

> Exchange server mailbox and public stores (enable on server's General property page)

> Connectors to foreign messaging systems, such as the Connector for MS Mail (enabling property page varies—for Connector for MS Mail, enable on connector's Interchange property page)

You can track both user messages and system messages. Let's begin with user messages.

Tracking User Messages

Start up Exchange's Message Tracking Center (or, as we'll call it here most of the time, the *tracker*). To do so, find and right-click the Messaging Tracking Center subcontainer in the Tools container in Exchange System Manager. Then select Track Message. This opens the Message Tracking Center dialog box, shown in Figure 17.24.

FIGURE 17.24

The Message Tracking Center dialog box

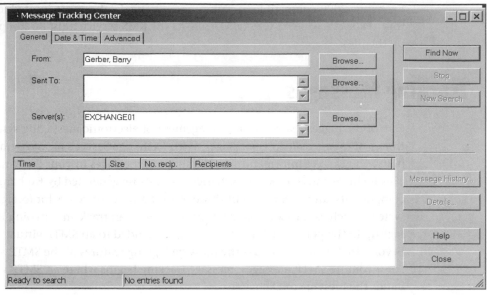

In Figure 17.24, I'm preparing to find messages that I sent to others. I clicked Browse to the right of the From field and used the Select Recipient dialog box to find and select my mailbox. You can leave the From field blank, in which case you're asking the tracker to find messages from all senders. (We're not using the Sent To field, but if you want to narrow your search for messages, you can select one or more specific recipients using this field.) After filling in the From field, I browsed in the Server(s) field for the server where my mailbox resides and selected EXCHANGE01. You can select one or more Exchange servers in the Server(s) field. Next I tabbed over to the Date & Time property page (see Figure 17.25) and entered zero in the During the Previous field. This tells the tracker to select only messages sent on the current day. I could also have selected the On field, which by default is set to the current date. Finally, I tabbed back to the General property page and clicked Find Now.

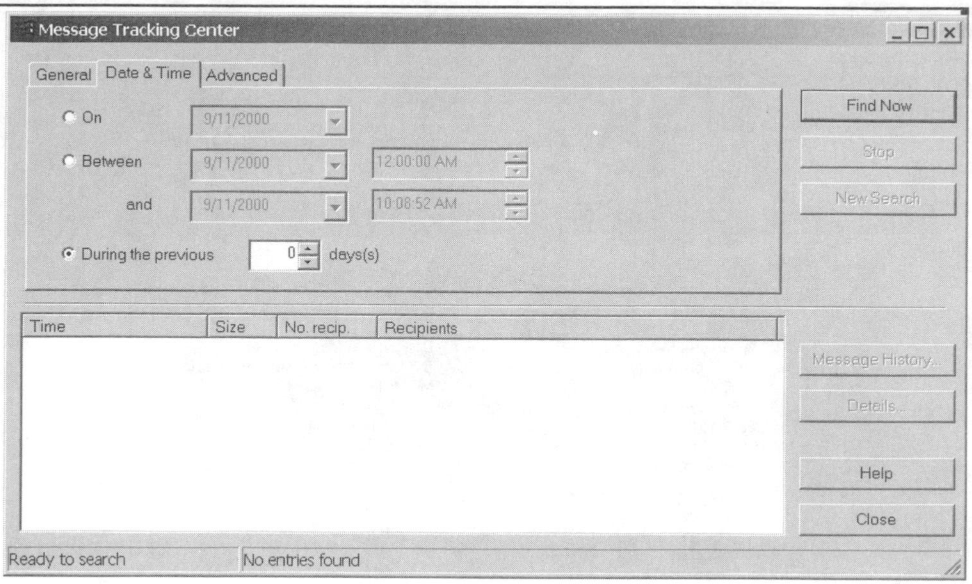

FIGURE 17.25

Selecting the time period over which the tracker should search

As you can see in the Message History dialog box on the left side of Figure 17.26, the tracker found seven messages sent by me on September 11, 2000. To find out more about a message, double-click it. I double-clicked the first message in Figure 17.26, the one sent to Jane Dough and Yogurt Master. This brings up the Message History dialog box (see Figure 17.27). Jane Dough's mailbox is on EXCHANGE01. Yogurt Master's mailbox resides on EXCHANGE05, the Exchange server that I set up for my yogurt business back in Chapter 15.

The first seven lines in the Message History field show how the message moved to Jane Dough's mailbox, finally being delivered in the seventh line, which reads "SMTP: Store Driver: Message Delivered Locally to Store." Right after the message was delivered to Jane Dough, delivery to Yogurt Master on EXCHANGE05 began. The tracker found all of this information in the log files for EXCHANGE01.

Delivery completed when the message was delivered to Yogurt's mailbox, as documented in the last line in the Message History field. The tracker found this information in the log files for EXCHANGE05.

If you need a permanent record, you can save the tracking history for a message to a text file. To do so, click Save on the Message History dialog box and select the file where you want to store the history.

You can click any line in the Message History field, and then click Details to see additional information about the message. This opens the Message Properties dialog box. On the right side of Figure 17.27, I'm looking at details for the last line in the Message History field.

FIGURE 17.26

Viewing message tracking results for selected e-mail messages

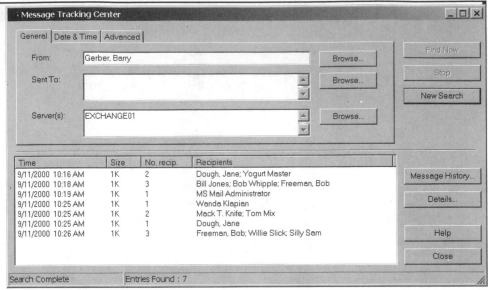

FIGURE 17.27

Viewing the detailed history of a message's trip through an Exchange server system

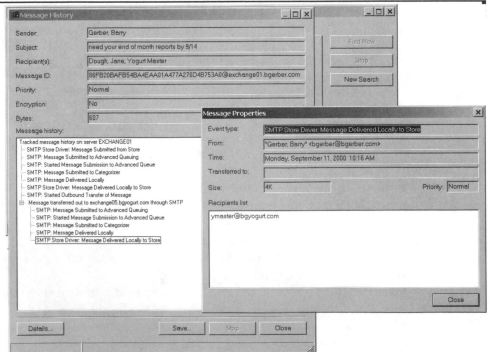

Setting up another search is easy. Click New Search on the Message Tracking Center dialog box (see Figure 17.27). Click OK when the tracker tells you that your existing message history will be deleted, and enter the new search criteria.

 TIP Message tracking logs are text files. A separate log file is created for each day that message tracking is enabled on a server. The logs for an Exchange server are located on the server in the directory \PROGRAM FILES\EXCHSRVR\SERVER_NAME.LOG, where SERVER_NAME is the name of the Exchange server being logged. For easy identification and sorting, the logs are named using the convention YYYYMMDD.LOG. You can process log files in your own programs, extracting information about message flow, quantity, and so on from them. See the Exchange online documentation for information on the structure of log files.

Before we leave user message tracking, take a look at the Advanced property page on the Message Tracking Center dialog box. You can find a message by its ID and choose to include nonsubmission events in your search. The latter option tells the tracker to include messaging information that is unique to mixed-mode (Exchange 2000 and 5.5) environments. Searches by message ID require more discussion.

Every Exchange message has a unique identifier that includes the address of the originating organization, the name of the originating Exchange server, the date, and a series of digits. Here's an example of an Exchange message ID:

    c=us;a= ;p=Barry Gerber and;l=EXCHANGE02-000908011010Z-2

Can you pick out the date and time (09/08/00 11:01 AM) in the digits just after the server name? The date is in reverse order.

The ID is one of the properties of a message; you can use it to track a message using the Message Tracking Center. But how do you find the ID? First you must find a copy of the message. If you're trying to figure out why a message never arrived at its intended location—which is generally why you'd use the tracker—you'll want the copy of the message stored in the Sent Items folder for the originating mailbox.

Using an Exchange client, find and open the message. Then select Properties from the message's File menu. Tab over to the Message ID property page in the resultant message Properties dialog box for the message. There, in all its lengthy glory, is the message ID (see Figure 17.28). In fact, the message ID is so long that you can't even see all of it in the Message ID field. When you have the message ID, you can enter it on the Message Tracking Center's Advanced property page. Be sure to enter a server or set of servers to search on the General property page, and a date/time range that covers the date and time when your message was sent. Click Find Now, and you'll see any information on the message that is available in your messaging tracking logs.

FIGURE 17.28

Finding an Exchange message's ID

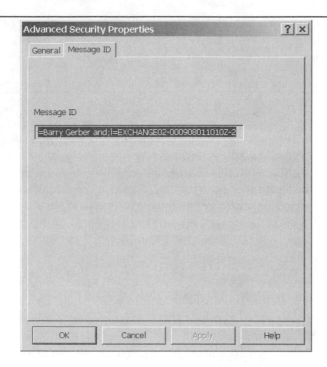

That Message ID Is Awfully Long!

Worried about accurately typing in that long message ID? Relax. If you're running an Outlook client and Exchange System Manager on the same machine, you can use Ctrl+C to copy the ID from the Message ID property page, and then use Ctrl+V to paste it into the Message ID field. If you're running the client and the Exchange System Manager on different servers, you can paste the ID into a message and send it to yourself. Or, you can drag the original message into a new message and send it to yourself as an attachment to the new message. When you open the attachment in the new message, you can look at all the properties, including the ID, just as if it were the original message. If you need to track the message for a user, this last approach is especially useful. Users don't have to know anything about message IDs—all they need to do is send you the message that needs to be tracked.

Tracking System Messages

If you're interested in messages generated by key Exchange Server components such as information stores or the System Attendant, don't enter anything in the From field on the tracker. You must still enter one or more servers and ensure that an appropriate date/time range is set on the Date & Time property page. Leaving the From field blank tells the tracker to find all messages that moved through the selected Exchange server or servers. You can't pick the system components that send messages from the Select Recipients list that pops up when you click the From field's Browse button. And, unlike with Exchange 5.5, you can't choose to see system messages. The only way to see system messages is to leave the From field blank. Unfortunately, you'll also see ordinary user e-mail messages.

Figure 17.29 shows the results of a search with a blank From field covering all of my Exchange servers. The highlighted line in Figure 17.29 is for the replication of some items in a public folder. The folder exists on four servers. In Figure 17.30, you can see that the replication is taking place from my EXCHANGE01 to the three other servers, EXCHANGE02, EXCHANGE03, and EXCHANGE05.

You can't tell for which public folder the replication is taking place. That's sort of a bummer. But even this limited amount of information is useful for testing purposes. For example, if a server participating in the replication of a public folder wasn't getting updated, you could force replication by placing a new item in another replica and then checking tracking information for a clue as to where the problem might be. Of course, before turning to message tracking, you'd check to ensure that the Exchange services on the server and its replication partners were running. Then you'd be sure that any network links and Exchange connectors between the troubled server and its replication partners were up and running.

FIGURE 17.29

Viewing message tracking results for selected e-mail and Exchange system messages

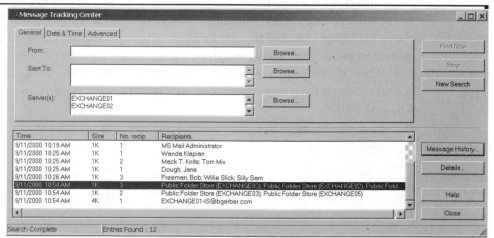

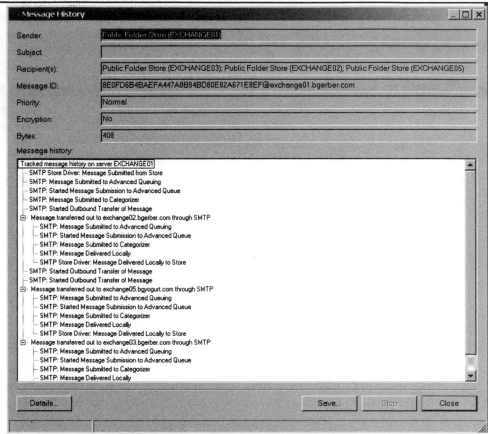

Want to see a system message involving the Exchange System Attendant? Figure 17.31 shows the tracking history for an automatic reply from me to a message sent to me by the Exchange System Attendant on EXCHANGE02. The reply was sent after I set up Exchange advanced security for my mailbox (see the section "Enabling Advanced Security for Mailboxes: The Outlook Client Side," earlier in this chapter). Notice that the message moves from my mailbox's home server, EXCHANGE01, to the server where Exchange server's Key Management Services are running, EXCHANGE02.

FIGURE 17.31

*A system message sent
to the Exchange
System Attendant on
an Exchange server*

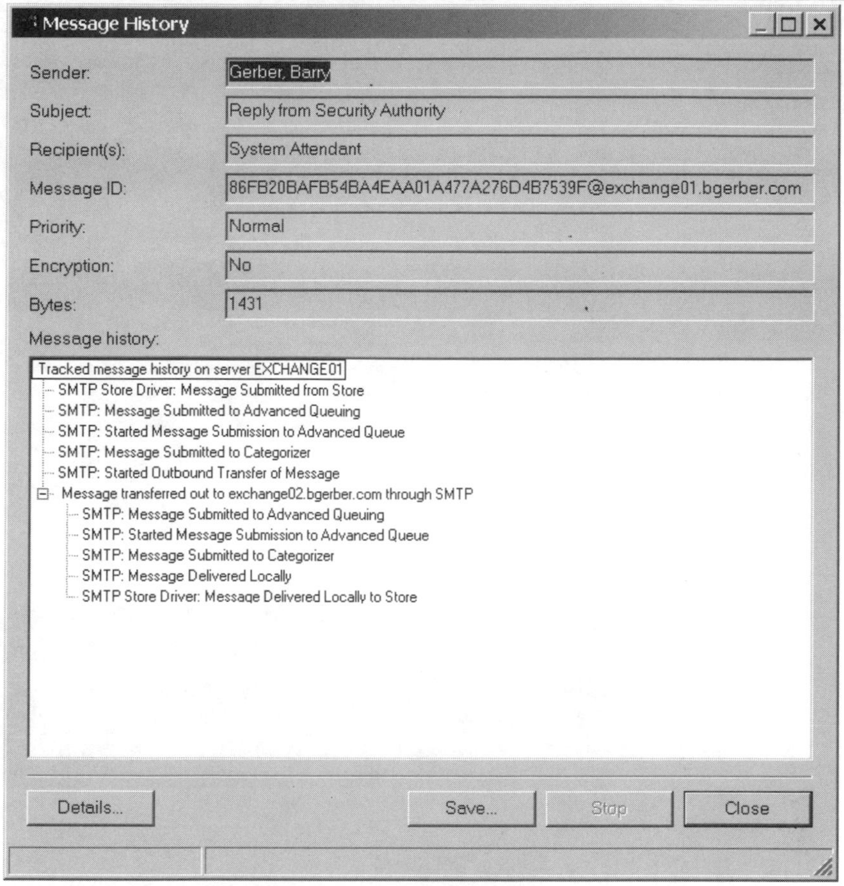

Message History

Sender:	Gerber, Barry
Subject:	Reply from Security Authority
Recipient(s):	System Attendant
Message ID:	86FB20BAFB54BA4EAA01A477A276D4B7539F@exchange01.bgerber.com
Priority:	Normal
Encryption:	No
Bytes:	1431

Message history:

Tracked message history on server EXCHANGE01
- SMTP Store Driver: Message Submitted from Store
- SMTP: Message Submitted to Advanced Queuing
- SMTP: Started Message Submission to Advanced Queue
- SMTP: Message Submitted to Categorizer
- SMTP: Started Outbound Transfer of Message
- Message transferred out to exchange02.bgerber.com through SMTP
    - SMTP: Message Submitted to Advanced Queuing
    - SMTP: Started Message Submission to Advanced Queue
    - SMTP: Message Submitted to Categorizer
    - SMTP: Message Delivered Locally
    - SMTP Store Driver: Message Delivered Locally to Store

[Details...]   [Save...]   [Stop]   [Close]

Adding Proxy Addresses to a Mailbox

Back in Chapter 11, "Managing Exchange Users, Distribution Groups, and Contacts,"
in the section "E-mail Addresses," we looked briefly at the E-mail Addresses property
page of the mailbox dialog box (see Figure 17.32). I promised then to talk more about
how you can add new addresses for a mailbox. Well, you're now ready for all the gory
details, so here we go.

FIGURE 17.32

The E-mail Addresses property page of the user Properties dialog box for a mailbox

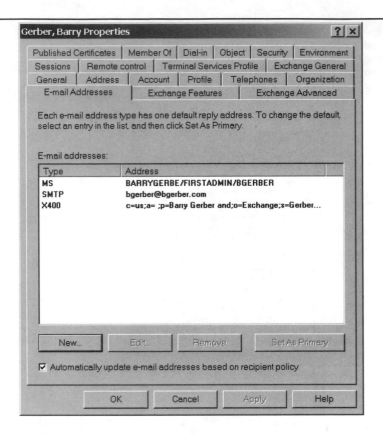

Creating Proxy Addresses

First, why would you want to add a new address for a mailbox? Well, maybe your default Internet address is jjones@monster.com. Now, that's okay, if you don't mind getting lost among the millions of employees at good old Monster Corp. Let's say that you're in Sales at Monster Corp., and you'd at least like to have that recognized in your e-mail address: jjones@sales.monster.com. The first step is to add what's called a proxy address to your mailbox.

Open the dialog box for your user account in \Active Directory Users and Computers\Users, and tab over to the E-mail Addresses property page. Click New on the E-mail Addresses property page. This brings up the New E-mail Address dialog box, shown in Figure 17.33. As you can see, you can create secondary proxies for all the address types supported by Exchange Server. Select Internet and click OK. The new Internet Address Properties dialog box pops up (see Figure 17.34). Type in the new address and click OK; as you can see in Figure 17.35, the new address is created.

FIGURE 17.33

*Selecting the type of
proxy address to
create*

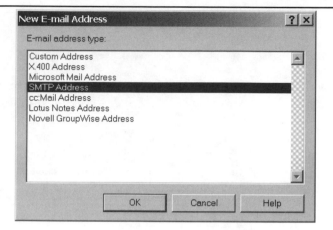

FIGURE 17.34

*Entering the new proxy
address*

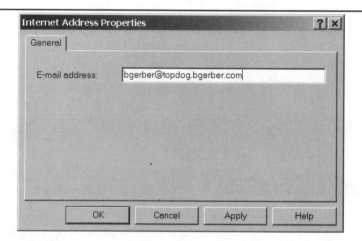

Notice in Figure 17.35 how "smtp" in the new address is in lowercase. That tells you immediately that this address is a secondary proxy address. You can make it the primary address by clicking the Set As Reply Address button. After you click Set As Reply Address, SMTP is displayed in lowercase for what was the primary proxy address (bgerber@bgerber.com, in my case), indicating that it has become a secondary proxy address for the mailbox.

New proxy addresses aren't limited to Exchange Server mailboxes. You can add a new proxy to any of the other Exchange recipient types: contacts, distribution groups, and public folders. Secondary proxy addresses can be very useful in a lot of places. Let your imagination roam. When you get the basics down, you can both help your organization and have great fun with secondary proxies.

FIGURE 17.35

The new proxy address is a secondary proxy address.

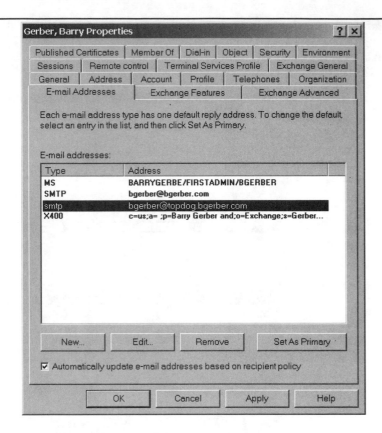

Telling DNS About New Proxy Addresses

When you've created the proxy addresses, Exchange Server is ready to receive mail addressed to them. However, before the mail can be received, you might have to make some changes in your Internet-connected Domain Name Service. For example, if a new Internet secondary proxy uses a new Internet domain name like the one in my example (bgerber@topdog.bgerber.com), you'll have to add host and MX records to your Domain Name Service, telling the world that you're now handling messages addressed to the new proxy. See the section "Setting Up and Managing DNS," in Chapter 13, "Managing Exchange 2000 Internet Services," for a refresher on DNS.

TIP One of my favorite uses for secondary proxies is to provide multiple SMTP addresses for a user for the same Internet domain. For example, my primary SMTP address is bgerber@bgerber.com. My secondary proxy address is bg@bgerber.com. The second address is quicker to write and somewhat easier to remember. Internet messages sent to either address come to my Exchange mailbox. Don't believe it? Send messages to both addresses. The really nice thing about this kind of proxy is that you don't have to enter any new information in your DNS because the Internet domain name (bgerber.com, in my case) is already registered.

Automating the Creation of New Proxy Addresses

If you have to add secondary proxy addresses to a bunch of mailboxes, you can use a recipient policy to do so. I'll show you how to do this in the next major section, "Managing Organization-wide Settings."

Managing Organization-wide Settings

Using Exchange global settings, you can do a number of quite interesting tasks. These include the following:

- Managing recipient policies
- Managing address lists
- Managing details and address templates
- Managing organization-wide mailbox message defaults

Let's take a look at each of these in turn.

Managing Recipient Policies

You use recipient policies to specify how e-mail addresses will be set for a set of Exchange users. In this section, I'll show you how to play some neat tricks with recipient policies and how to manage the recipient update service that ensures that recipient policies are applied as you set them. We'll cover two topics.

Setting different default e-mail addresses for different recipients

Managing the recipient update service

Setting Different Default E-mail Addresses for Different Recipients

In the section "Setting the Default Format for Organizational E-mail Addresses," in Chapter 11, I showed you how to change the default e-mail addresses for an organization using the default recipient policy for the organization. In Chapter 15, in the section "Managing Servers in Multidomain Environments," I noted that you could change default e-mail addresses for select groups of users. In that chapter, the focus was on recipients in a different Windows 2000 domain. I promised in that chapter to show you how to do this. In the last section, "Adding Proxy Addresses to a Mailbox," I also promised to show you how to set a secondary proxy address for specific users. Let's get to it!

In Chapter 15, I created a second Windows 2000 domain for my nascent yogurt business. I called the new domain bgyogurt.com and added it to my Exchange organization by installing an Exchange server, EXCHANGE05, in the domain. Although I didn't have to do so, I also decided to use bgyogurt.com as the Internet domain of my new company. Now I want to ensure that the default e-mail address for every user in the domain bgyogurt.com is set to EMAIL_ALIAS@bgyogurt.com, where EMAIL_ALIAS is the user's Exchange e-mail alias. Here's how you do that.

First, find the Recipient Policies container for your Exchange organization. Refer to the left side of Figure 17.36 for help in locating the container. Right-click the container and select New ➢ Recipient Policy from the pop-up menu. This opens the Properties dialog box for your new policy, shown in the middle of Figure 17.36. Give your policy a name. Now you have to add filters to ensure that the policy applies only to the recipients that you want. Click Modify on the Properties dialog box to open the Find Exchange Recipients dialog box (see the right side of Figure 17.36). Here you select the recipients to which you want to apply your new policy.

FIGURE 17.36

The dialog box for a new recipient policy, and the Find Exchange Recipients dialog box used to modify filter rules for a recipient policy

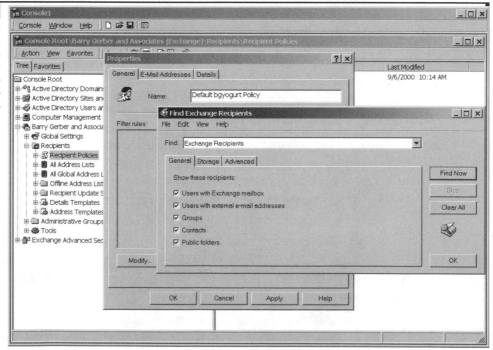

You use the General property page of the Find Exchange Recipients dialog box to select the types of Exchange recipients for this policy. In the case of my domain bgyogurt.com, I want to apply my new policy to all recipients, so I'll leave all of them checked.

In Figure 17.37, I'm specifying that my new recipient policy should apply to all mailboxes on the server EXCHANGE05. This is the only Exchange server in the domain bgyogurt.com, and I want the policy to apply to all recipients in the domain. So, selecting EXCHANGE05 is all I have to do to ensure that my new recipient policy will do what I want. You can select only one specific Exchange server per policy. So, if I were to add a new Exchange server to bgyogurt.com, I would have to add a recipient policy for it.

FIGURE 17.37

Specifying the Exchange servers to which a new recipient policy should apply

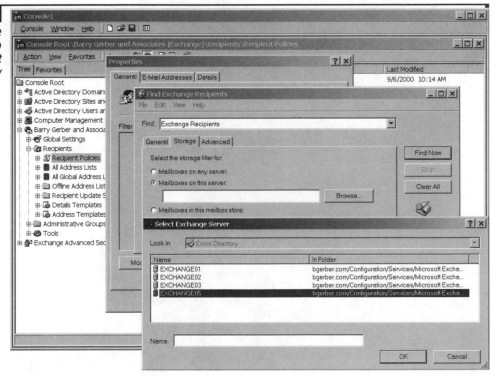

After selecting an Exchange server and clicking OK on the Select Exchange Server dialog box, click OK on the Find Exchange Recipients dialog box. A warning dialog box opens (see Figure 17.38). This dialog box tells you that the policy you're creating won't apply until you take the necessary action to apply it. You need to do one more thing before you're finished, so don't worry about applying the policy yet. Click OK to clear the warning dialog box.

FIGURE 17.38

A dialog box warns that a recipient policy must be applied when its filter changes.

Next you must set the e-mail defaults that you want to use for this recipient policy. You do that on the E-mail Addresses property page of the Properties dialog box for your new recipient policy. In Figure 17.40, I'm changing the default SMTP address format from @bgerber.com to @bgyogurt.com. Now all recipients on the server

Figure 17.39 shows the script that will be used to select the Exchange recipients to which your new policy will apply. The script was generated from the choices that you made earlier. As you can see in Figure 17.39, the script is pretty easy to read.

FIGURE 17.39

The filter that is used to select the recipients to which a recipient policy applies

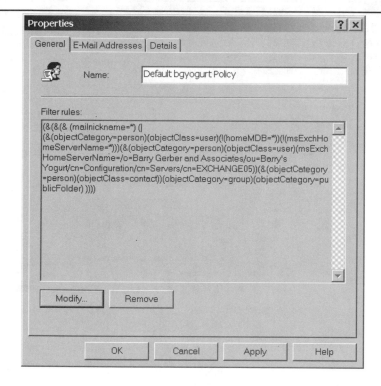

Next you must set the e-mail defaults that you want to use for this recipient policy. You do that on the E-mail Addresses property page of the Properties dialog box for your new recipient policy. In Figure 17.40, I'm changing the default SMTP address format from @bgerber.com to @bgyogurt.com. Now all recipients on the server

EXCHANGE05 will receive an SMTP e-mail address EMAIL_ALIAS@bgyogurt.com
instead of the organization-wide EMAIL_ALIAS@bgerber.com

FIGURE 17.40

*Setting default e-mail
address formats for a
recipient policy*

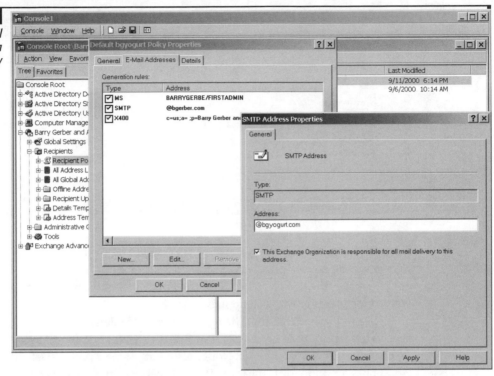

When you close the Properties dialog box for your new recipient policy, you'll see the
dialog box shown in Figure 17.41. Click Yes, and all existing e-mail addresses that
meet the criteria of the filter that you created will be updated to the e-mail addresses
that you set in your new recipient policy. You should now see a new recipient policy
in the Recipient Policies container (see Figure 17.42).

FIGURE 17.41

*A dialog box that initi-
ates updates of all
e-mail address
affected by a recipient
policy*

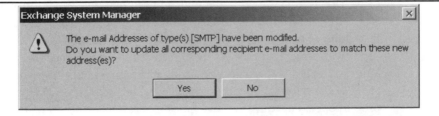

FIGURE 17.42

*A new recipient policy
in the Recipient
Policies container*

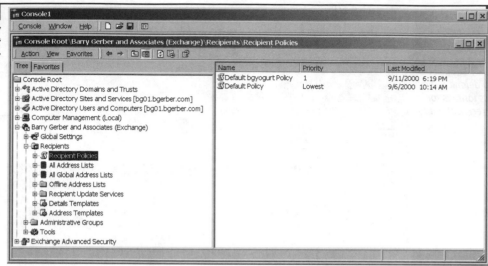

FIGURE 17.42

*A new recipient policy
in the Recipient
Policies container*

To apply your new policy as you were instructed to do in the warning dialog box, right-click the policy and select Apply This Policy Now. Any time you change a recipient policy, be sure to reapply it. Okay, the policy will now affect existing and newly created recipients to whom it applies.

Notice in Figure 17.42 that the organization-wide default recipient policy (Default Policy) has a priority of Lowest. This means the default policy will apply only when no other policy exists for a user. Notice also that my new policy (Default bgyogurt Policy) has a priority of 1, meaning that it supersedes the organization-wide default policy. Newly created recipient policies are assigned a priority number that is one higher than the highest existing priority. A priority of 1 is the highest priority. If you have multiple policies that might apply to a user or set of users, set priorities to ensure that the correct policy applies.

Policies are listed in descending priority order in the Recipient Policy container. To change a policy's priority, right-click it and select All Tasks ➤ Move Up, or All Tasks ➤ Move Down from the pop-up menu. You can't change the priority of the default recipient policy, although you can delete it. Before deleting the default policy, ensure that other policies you've created cover your organization.

Okay, now let's set up a policy to give certain users a secondary SMTP proxy address. I'm going to set up a policy to give Barry Gerber and Associates executives an SMTP address format of @topdog.bgerber.com. Because you've been through this process once, I'm going to move quickly here. Open the dialog box for a new recipient policy. Select the recipient types to which you want the policy to apply on the

General property page. I want this policy to apply only to users with an Exchange mailbox, so I'll pick that option.

Next tab over to the Advanced Property page. You can select fields for Exchange recipients, by recipient type, and then specify what should appear in the field for the recipient policy to apply to a recipient. These fields are set on the various property pages of the dialog box for a recipient (user, contact, distribution group, or public folder). In Figure 17.43, I've selected the Department field and specified that a user must have a value of Executive Management in the field for the filter to apply to the user. You can select from among a number of operators, including Starts With, Ends With, Is Not, Present, and Not Present. You can set multiple filter criteria for the same or different recipient types. Click Add to add the filter to the list of filters.

Next, on the E-mail Addresses property page on the Properties dialog box for my new recipient policy, I added a secondary SMTP proxy address @topdog.bgerber.com. Finally, I applied my new recipient policy. Now every existing and newly created mailbox-enabled user whose department is set to Executive Management will receive an SMTP primary e-mail address formatted as EMAIL_ALIAS@bgerber.com and a secondary SMTP address formatted as EMAIL_ALIAS@topdog.bgerber.com.

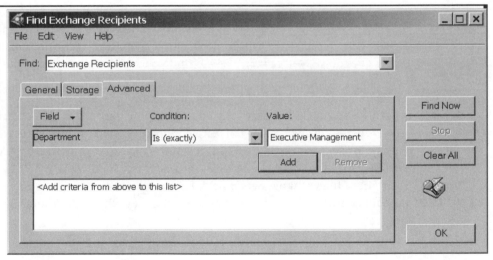

FIGURE 17.43

Using the Advanced property page of the Find Exchange Recipients dialog box to set a recipient policy filter based on the department to which a user belongs

Managing the Recipient Update Service

Among other things, the recipient update service is responsible for applying recipient policies to Exchange recipients. When a recipient or recipient policy is created or altered, the service creates or modifies recipient e-mail addresses based on recipient policies. The recipient update service doesn't always do its thing immediately. Try this: Right after you create a new mailbox-enabled user, tab over to the user's E-mail Addresses property page. I'll bet that the addresses aren't there yet. Wait 30 seconds or so, and then right-click the E-mail Addresses page and select Refresh. The addresses should appear.

The recipient update service runs on Exchange servers. The recipient update service updates information in Active Directory, which, of course, exists on Windows 2000 domain controllers. An Exchange server running the recipient update service can update one and only one domain controller. A domain controller can be updated by one and only one Exchange server. So, you can have multiple recipient update services in a domain only if you have multiple domain controllers.

For redundancy, you should have at least two domain controllers in a domain. That means that you can also have redundant Exchange servers running the recipient update service. If portions of your network are linked by slower, less reliable connections, you should place Exchange servers that run the recipient update service on both sides of such links.

Two types of recipient update service servers exist. One of these updates the Active Directory for a Windows 2000 domain. The other updates Active Directory for an entire Windows 2000 forest of Exchange servers.

Most of the time, you don't have to worry a bit about the recipient update service. However, if you add a domain controller, or if an existing recipient update service server goes down, you're very likely to find yourself messing with recipient update services.

Here's a quick overview of recipient update service management.

The Recipient Update Services container appears on the left side of Figure 17.44. The Properties dialog box for the recipient update service in my Windows 2000 domain bgerber.com is on the right side of the figure. As you can see, it currently runs on EXCHANGE01. I can change the server any time by clicking the Browse button to the right of the Exchange Server field. I can also use this dialog box to change the domain controller being serviced by the recipient update service and the update interval.

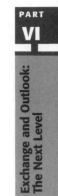

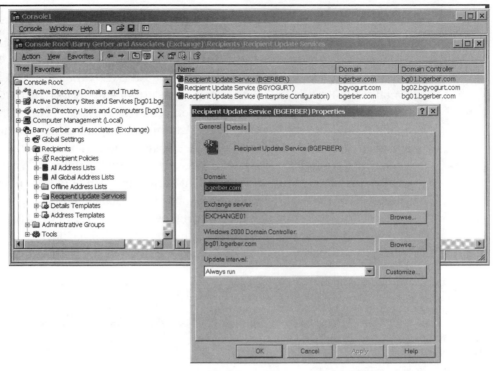

FIGURE 17.44

The Recipient Update Service container and the dialog box for an instance of the recipient update service that runs on a specific Exchange server

To create a new recipient update service, right-click the Recipient Update Services container and select New ➢ Recipient Update Service. Use the resultant dialog box to create the new service.

To force an update of recipients by a service, right-click the service in the left pane of Exchange System Manager and select Update Now. To force a service to re-create all e-mail addresses under its control, right-click the service and select Rebuild. A rebuild can take several hours in a domain with a large number of recipients. Exchange System Manager kindly warns you of this possibility and asks whether you want to continue.

Managing Address Lists

Exchange 2000 supports a range of address lists. These include both global and narrower address lists. You can see these lists on the left side of Figure 17.45. You can create your own address lists in either the All Address Lists or the All Global Address Lists container. In Figure 17.45, I'm creating a new list for employees of Barry Gerber and Associates who work in the Los Angeles office. I right-clicked the All Address Lists container and selected New ➢ Address List from the pop-up menu. On the Properties dialog box for the list, I named it BGA Los Angeles and clicked Filter Rules to open the same Find Exchange Recipients dialog box that we used in the section "Setting Different Default E-mail Addresses for Different Recipients," earlier in this chapter. First, I selected Only Users with Exchange Mailbox on the General property page of this dialog box. This ensures that other recipient types won't appear in the list. In Figure 17.45, on the Advanced property page I'm specifying that recipients should be included in this list if the field City equals Los Angeles.

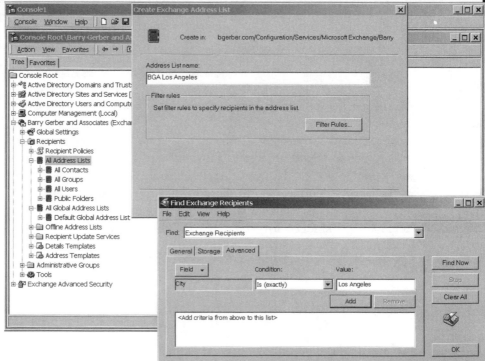

FIGURE 17.45

Creating a new address list using the Create Exchange Address list dialog box

That's it, after I click OK to exit the two dialog boxes, my list is created. Figure 17.46 shows the membership of the list. To view a list's membership, find and right-click the list object, and select Properties from the pop-up menu. Then click Preview on the resultant Properties dialog box for the list. In Figure 17.46, the Preview button is hidden by the Address List Preview dialog box. The new address list shows up in an Outlook client's address book (see Figure 17.47).

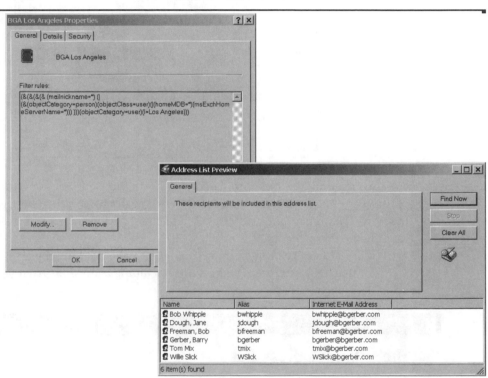

FIGURE 17.47

Viewing a new address list in an Outlook client's address book

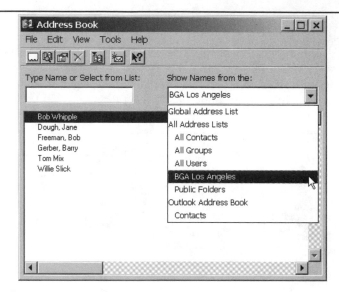

You can create address lists within address lists. In this way, you can create hierarchies of lists. For example, I could create a BGA Los Angeles list but then set its filters so that it will never have any addresses. Then I could create address lists inside that list for different departments.

How are address lists kept current? You might have guessed it by now. The recipient update service keeps address lists, including address lists that you create, up-to-date.

The Offline Address List

Back in Chapter 10, "A Quick Overview of Outlook 2000," I briefly discussed the use of the Exchange offline address list in the section "Synchronize." The offline address list is copied to a mobile computer so that a user can address and compose e-mail messages while disconnected from the Exchange Server environment. You manage the offline address list in the Offline Address Lists container (see the left side of Figure 17.45). There is a default offline address list. You can create additional offline address lists (right-click the Offline Address Lists Container, and select New ➢ Offline Address List). The default offline address list draws its recipients from the default global address list. You can change this option by adding or removing address lists using the address list's Properties dialog box (right-click the list and select Properties). Offline address lists are not kept up-to-date by the recipient update service. A specific Exchange server is assigned responsibility for keeping each offline address list current.

Managing Details and Address Templates

The only subcontainers in the Recipients container that I haven't covered are the Details Templates and Address Templates subcontainers. There's little that you can or have to do with these objects, but it does help to understand them a bit.

Outlook clients use details templates to display the properties of a recipient or to perform other Outlook client functions, such as a search for a specific recipient. Address templates are used when an Outlook client user creates a one-off address for a foreign messaging system. Templates exist for a wide range of languages. You can add to or modify these templates. See the Exchange Server documents for more information on template management.

Managing Organization-wide Mailbox Message Defaults

You can set global maximum inbound and outbound message size limits, as well as limits on the number of recipients that a message may contain. These limits apply to user mailboxes. Message size limits apply to messages entering or leaving a mailbox. Recipients per message limits apply to messages sent from a mailbox. If a message exceeds any of these limits, it is returned to its sender. The default for all three of these limits is No Limit.

You can set inbound and outbound message size limits on a mailbox-by-mailbox basis (see the section "Delivery Restrictions," in Chapter 11). The default for a mailbox is No Limit. If a mailbox has no limit and if you've set global limits, the global limits apply. You can't set maximum recipients per message limits on a mailbox-by-mailbox basis. The only way that you can set mailbox-based limits of this kind is by establishing global limits.

You set global message size and recipients limits using the Message Delivery Properties dialog box, shown in Figure 17.48. Open the dialog box by right-clicking the Message Delivery container, selecting Properties from the pop-up menu, and tabbing over to the Defaults property page. In Figure 17.48, I've changed the limits.

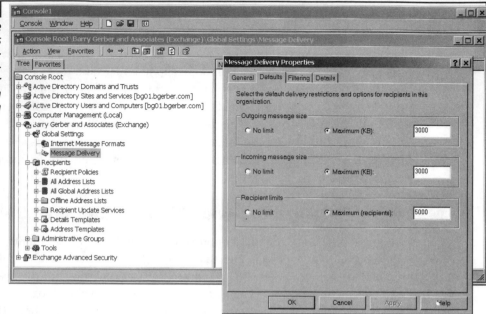

In Chapter 13, in the section "Messages," I discussed setting incoming and outgoing message size and per message recipient limits for an SMTP virtual server. You might be wondering how these limits relate to the global limits discussed in this section. SMTP virtual server limits apply to messages passing through that server. Global limits apply to messages entering and leaving a mailbox. If a user tries to send a message that meets mailbox limits but that doesn't comply with SMTP virtual server limits, the message is returned by the SMTP virtual server. If the SMTP virtual server attempts to pass an incoming message that doesn't meet global limits to a mailbox store, the mailbox store rejects the message. The virtual server then sends a nondelivery report to the sender of the message.

Looking at Figure 17.48, you might be wondering about the Filtering property page on the Message Delivery Properties dialog box. I discussed this page in Chapter 13 in the subsection "General," in the section "Managing SMTP Virtual Servers." In a few words, filters let you screen out SMTP messages from specific e-mail addresses, enabling such things as junk e-mail control.

Monitoring Exchange Connectors

I discussed Exchange server monitoring in some detail in Chapter 12, "Managing the Exchange Server Hierarchy and Core Components," in the section "Monitoring," and in Chapter 15, in the section "Enhancing Exchange Server Monitoring." You can also monitor Exchange connectors. I held off talking about connector monitoring until now because we just finished installing Exchange connectors in the last chapter. We installed these connectors:

- SMTP Connector (Chapter 13)
- Routing Group Connector (Chapter 15)
- X.400 Connector (Chapter 15)
- MS Mail Connector (Chapter 16)

Now we're ready to look at connector monitoring.

As Figure 17.49 shows, you monitor connectors in the same place that you monitor servers, in the \Tools\Monitoring and Status\Status container. On the right side of Figure 17.49, you can see that, while the X.400 connectors between my Los Angeles and New York Exchange servers are fine, there is a problem with the routing group connectors between those servers.

FIGURE 17.49

Using the Status container to monitor servers and connections

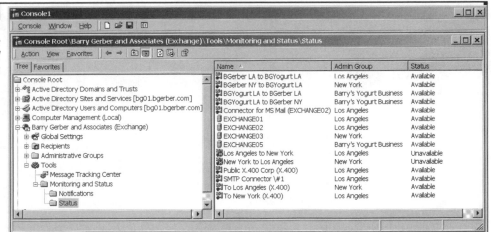

The problem with my routing group connectors is confirmed in Figure 17.50, which shows an e-mail notification sent to me noting that my connector from Los Angeles to New York is down. To set up the notification, I right-clicked the Notifications container shown in Figure 17.49 and selected New ➤ E-mail Notification from the pop-up menu. I then filled in the resultant Properties dialog box, as shown in Figure 17.51. The key here is selecting Any Connector in The Routing Group in the Servers and Connectors to Monitor field. You set up connector notifications in the same way that you set up server notifications. For more information, check out the section "Setting Up Notifications," in Chapter 12.

FIGURE 17.50

An e-mail notification that a connection is down

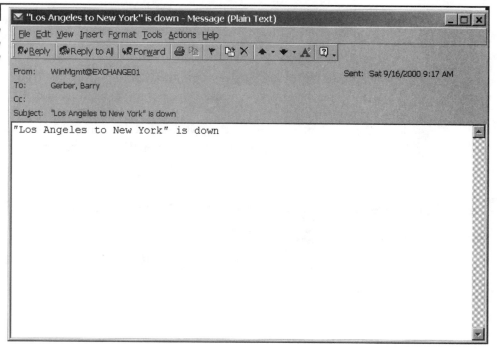

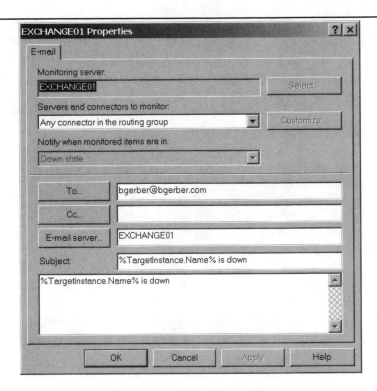

FIGURE 17.51

Settings for an e-mail notification for a routing group connector

In this case, it's clear that the problem is with the routing group connector circuit between my Los Angeles and New York servers. The X.400 connector between the servers is up and running, and all of the servers in Los Angeles and New York are available. All I need to do is figure out where in the routing group connector circuit the problem exists. That's not easy, but at least I don't have to worry about the Exchange servers that support the connectors being out of commission. If servers are missing along with connectors, resolving the problem becomes a bit more challenging. You need to rule out a problem with servers before moving on to debugging connector links.

Active Directory Imports and Exports

Wouldn't it be nice if you could move information into and out of Active Directory? For example, then you wouldn't have to worry about manually creating users and their mailboxes. The good news is that you can import information into and export it from Active Directory. The bad news is that this is not a task for someone who lacks a sophisticated understanding of Active Directory.

In this section, I'm going to point you to a Windows 2000 Server tool for doing Active Directory imports and exports. I'll show you how to use it to do a basic export so that you can see how Active Directory exports and imports are structured. Then I'll point you to some books that you can use to gain the understanding that you'll need to become competent at Active Directory importing and exporting.

The tool is LDIFDE.EXE. It comes with Windows 2000 Server. *LDIF* stands for *LDAP Data Interchange Format*, which is a draft Internet standard for a file format that can be used to move data into and out of a database compliant with Lightweight Directory Access Protocol (LDAP). Active Directory is LDAP-compliant. *DE* in LDIFDE.EXE stands for *data exchange*.

To run LDIFDE.EXE, open a command prompt (Start menu ➤ Programs ➤ Accessories ➤ Command Prompt). Type **LDIFDE -?** for a list of command-line switches. To export Active Directory information on users, type the following: ldifde -f OUT-PUT_FILE_NAME -s DOMAIN_CONTROLLER_NAME -d "dc=DOMAIN_NAME_1-x" -p subtree -r objectclass=user. Here, OUTPUT_FILE_NAME is the name of the file to which output from LDIFDE.EXE should be sent, DOMAIN_CONTROLLER is the name of the Windows 2000 domain controller with the Active Directory from which you want to export, and DOMAIN_NAME_1-x is a portion of your Windows 2000 domain name, starting with the lowest level (for example "dc=bgerber,dc=com").

Figure 17.52 shows the LDIFDE command line that I entered to export user information from the Active Directory on my domain controller, bg01.bgerber.com. In Figure 17.53, you can see some of the information about my user account and mailbox that was exported.

FIGURE 17.52

Running LDIFDE.EXE

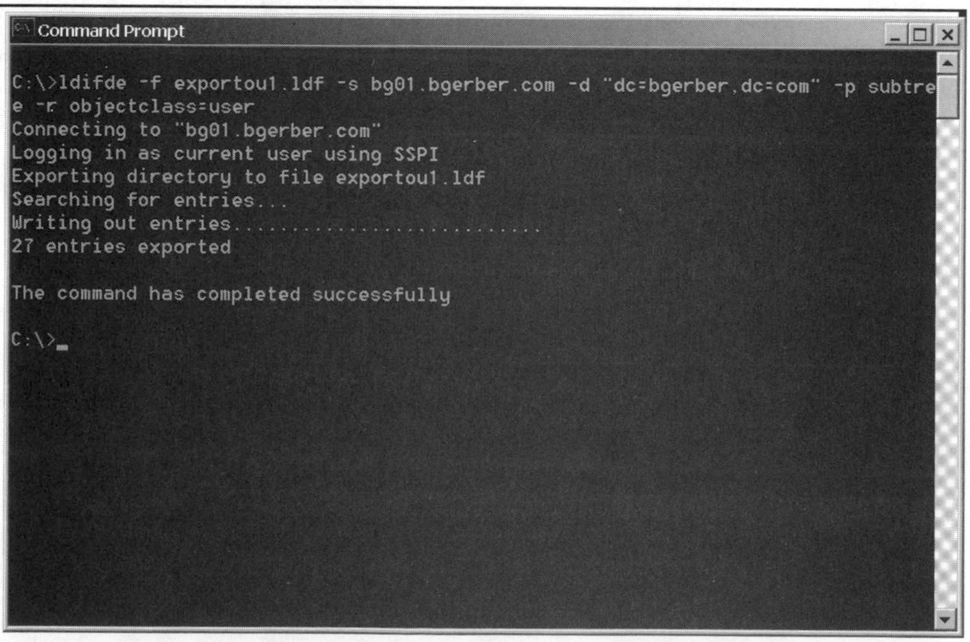

```
C:\>ldifde -f exportou1.ldf -s bg01.bgerber.com -d "dc=bgerber,dc=com" -p subtre
e -r objectclass=user
Connecting to "bg01.bgerber.com"
Logging in as current user using SSPI
Exporting directory to file exportou1.ldf
Searching for entries...
Writing out entries..........................
27 entries exported

The command has completed successfully

C:\>_
```

I hope that Figure 17.53 instills in you just enough awe to prevent you from going much further without boning up on Active Directory. These references should help: Microsoft Knowledge Base article Q237677, "Using LDIFDE to Import/Export Directory Objects to the Active Directory" (available at www.microsoft.com); *Windows 2000 Active Directory* by Alistair G. Lowe-Norris (O'Reilly and Associates, 2000); *Building Enterprise Active Directory Services, Notes from the Field*, by Microsoft Consulting Services (Microsoft Press, 2000); and *Active Directory Developers Reference Library Volumes 1-5* David Iseminger, editor (Microsoft Press, 2000).

FIGURE 17.53

A small portion of the output from running LDIFDE.EXE in Figure 17.52

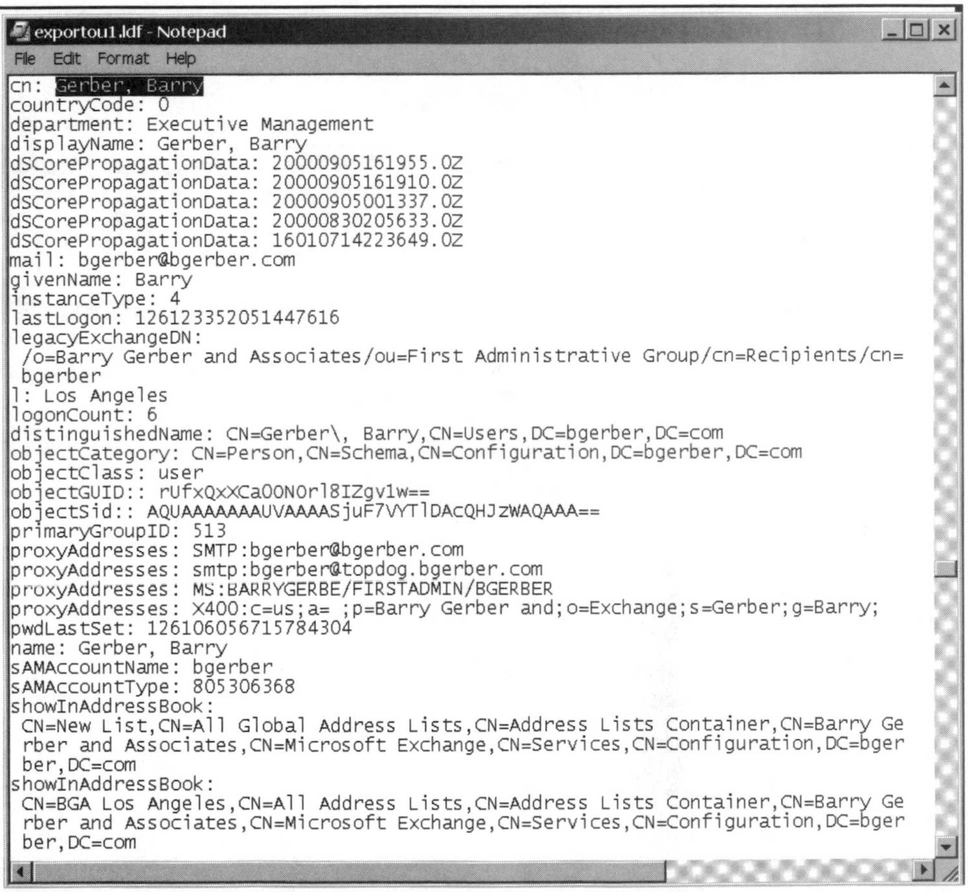

```
exportou1.ldf - Notepad                                          _ □ ×
File  Edit  Format  Help
cn: Gerber, Barry
countryCode: 0
department: Executive Management
displayName: Gerber, Barry
dSCorePropagationData: 20000905161955.0Z
dSCorePropagationData: 20000905161910.0Z
dSCorePropagationData: 20000905001337.0Z
dSCorePropagationData: 20000830205633.0Z
dSCorePropagationData: 16010714223649.0Z
mail: bgerber@bgerber.com
givenName: Barry
instanceType: 4
lastLogon: 126123352051447616
legacyExchangeDN:
 /o=Barry Gerber and Associates/ou=First Administrative Group/cn=Recipients/cn=
 bgerber
l: Los Angeles
logonCount: 6
distinguishedName: CN=Gerber\, Barry,CN=Users,DC=bgerber,DC=com
objectCategory: CN=Person,CN=Schema,CN=Configuration,DC=bgerber,DC=com
objectClass: user
objectGUID:: rUfxQxXCa00N0rl8IZgv1w==
objectSid:: AQUAAAAAAUVAAAASjuF7VYTlDAcQHJzWAQAAA==
primaryGroupID: 513
proxyAddresses: SMTP:bgerber@bgerber.com
proxyAddresses: smtp:bgerber@topdog.bgerber.com
proxyAddresses: MS:BARRYGERBE/FIRSTADMIN/BGERBER
proxyAddresses: X400:c=us;a= ;p=Barry Gerber and;o=Exchange;s=Gerber;g=Barry;
pwdLastSet: 126106056715784304
name: Gerber, Barry
sAMAccountName: bgerber
sAMAccountType: 805306368
showInAddressBook:
 CN=New List,CN=All Global Address Lists,CN=Address Lists Container,CN=Barry Ge
 rber and Associates,CN=Microsoft Exchange,CN=Services,CN=Configuration,DC=bger
 ber,DC=com
showInAddressBook:
 CN=BGA Los Angeles,CN=All Address Lists,CN=Address Lists Container,CN=Barry Ge
 rber and Associates,CN=Microsoft Exchange,CN=Services,CN=Configuration,DC=bger
 ber,DC=com
```

Troubleshooting Exchange Server

Sometime in 2001, Sybex, the publisher of this book, will release an update to what was already a great book, *Exchange Server 5.5 24seven* (1999). The book's author, Jim McBee, is an Exchange professional with lots of experience fixing broken Exchange servers and clients. So, my first tip on troubleshooting Exchange Server is that you buy Jim's book. Even the 5.5 version will help with a lot of Exchange 2000 troubleshooting.

My second tip is that you make Microsoft's Internet-based Knowledge Base your home away from home. In a world paced by the clock of Internet immediacy, things change very fast. Microsoft's Knowledge Base does a respectable job of keeping up with the frenzied pace of the company's development teams.

As of this writing, you can get to Knowledge Base through the URL `http://www.microsoft.com`. On the site's home page, select the Knowledge Base option from the Support menu (see Figure 17.54). Select Exchange 2000 Server from the My Search Is About drop-down menu. Then select from the available options and type in your question in the My Question Is field. Click Go and sift through the answers presented to you.

FIGURE 17.54

Accessing Microsoft's Internet-based Knowledge Base

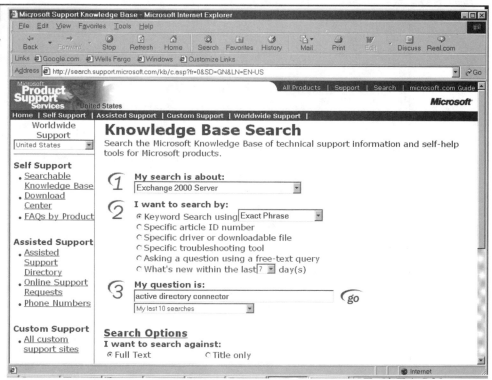

There's an art to posing Knowledge Base questions. Basically, you should keep your questions simple. If you are trying to solve a problem about an error message, search for all or part of the error message. If your question is really about another Microsoft product, select that product from the drop-down menu. Be sure to follow any promising links to other Knowledge Base articles. Finally, make sure that you look for the latest and greatest information on any subject that you're concerned about.

My third tip is that you get, test, and install all service packs for Exchange Server and Outlook and other clients. Many of the problems that you'll experience with Exchange Server are recognized in Knowledge Base articles and, if they're deemed significant enough, are fixed in service pack releases.

My fourth tip is that you stay in touch with the Exchange community. Microsoft supports a set of newsgroups at www.microsoft.com/exchange/support/ Newsgroups.htm. *Windows 2000 Magazine* offers a set of Exchange newsgroup-like forums as well as many other useful resources at www.winntmag.com. The print edition of *Windows 2000 Magazine* offers excellent articles on Exchange Server (subs@win2000mag.com). You should also subscribe to the Exchange and Windows 2000 e-mail newsletters offered by the magazine. Duke Communications International, publisher of *Windows 2000 Magazine*, also offers a high-powered, no-nonsense, no-advertising monthly publication called *Exchange Administrator* (exchange@win2000mag.com).

Tip no. 5? Consider paid support from Microsoft and others. It can be pricey, and the best support services cost the most. However, this is often the best way to get your problems solved fast. Check out http://support.microsoft.com/directory/ for Microsoft's options. The Microsoft consulting operation can put you in touch with Microsoft staff or independent consultants who can help.

Armed with Jim McBee's book, access to Microsoft's Knowledge Base and other information sources, the latest Exchange Server and client service packs, and a modicum of paid support, your life as an Exchange administrator will be, if not a vacation in Maui, at least far less harried than it would be without these useful troubleshooting aids.

Controlling E-mail–Based Viruses

Nothing strikes terror in the heart of network administrators like computer viruses. Viruses are bad enough when carried from computer to computer on disks. But, store files containing them on a network file system for all to access, or send them to one and all by e-mail, and computer viruses become true threats to mission-critical systems. I've done quite a bit of work in public health, and I can tell you that there's more than a little similarity between computer viruses and those that cause influenza and other menaces to health.

There are two ways to deal with e-mail–borne viruses. You can catch them while the files that contain them are still inside your e-mail system, or you can catch them when users try to run the files containing them. I prefer to implement both options. However, if I had to make a choice, I'd rather shoot down viruses while they're still inside my e-mail system.

A number of third-party Exchange Server-based virus control products are on the market. Appendix A, "Cool Third-Party Applications for Exchange/Outlook Clients and Exchange Server," lists several worthy products. My current favorite is Trend Micro's ScanMail for Microsoft Exchange.

ScanMail includes information on virtually all known viruses. The virus list can be updated automatically over the Internet on a regular schedule. The product also uses a set of rules and pattern recognition to help it find suspicious new viruses.

ScanMail operates on messages in both the mailbox and public information stores of an Exchange server. It automatically scans messages as they come into the stores, and it can be scheduled to make regular passes on all Exchange folders. You can even scan all or selected mailboxes manually.

When ScanMail finds a virus, it can send notifications to the sender, the recipient, and the Exchange administrator. When ScanMail can't clean a virus, it can be configured to remove the infected file and send the virus to Trend Micro's Virus Hospital for further analysis and, hopefully, a virus-cleaning solution.

I use ScanMail in league with Trend Micro's network-aware, real-time, workstation-based virus product, Office Scan, and the company's server file scanner, Server Protect. I can say without fear of contradiction that my own network and a number of clients' networks have been totally virus-free since I implemented this three-pronged virus management system. Check out Trend Micro's products at http://www.antivirus.com.

 TIP Be sure to keep both your virus software and virus signature files up-to-date. If you don't, having virus software in place is like taking a flu shot using an out-of-date vaccine.

Supporting Remote and Roving Clients

Aside from ensuring that remote users install and set up their e-mail clients properly—as well as providing Windows 2000 Remote Access Service (RAS) dial-in services and the modems and phone lines to support them—you don't have to do much else to support remote users on the server side. For more on the RAS, see *Mastering Windows 2000 Server*, by Mark Minasi, et al. (Sybex, 2000).

Installing the Outlook client for remote access is easy. The installation software specifically asks if the client will be used for remote access. If you answer yes, then each time you start up your Exchange client, you'll be asked if you want to connect to your Exchange server or work offline. Aside from a proper installation, the user needs to understand how to dial in to the network and use the Exchange client's folder synchronization capability.

Linking Exchange Clients to Exchange Server over the Internet

You can connect Exchange clients to your Exchange Server without the benefit of RAS services. You can connect directly over the Internet through an Internet Service Provider (ISP). All you have to do is log into your ISP as usual. You'll have to create an entry for the server in the HOSTS file on the computer on which you're running the client. The entry must be for the Exchange server name only, not the fully qualified domain name of the server—that is, EXCHANGE01, not EXCHANGE01.BGERBER.COM. For more on the HOSTS file, see *Mastering Windows 2000 Server*, by Mark Minasi, et al.

The remote procedure calls that support Exchange client-server communications must be capable of passing over the ISP-based link between your client and server. Technically, this requires that TCP/IP port 135 is enabled on all firewalls and routers between the client and the server. You can test to see whether this is the case by using a program developed by Microsoft called RPCPING.EXE. This program comes with Exchange 2000 Server; it's part of the support file package on the CD-ROM.

To connect your client to the server, you need to get to the MS Exchange Settings Properties dialog box. To do this, right-click the Microsoft Outlook icon on your desktop, and select Properties. Double-click Microsoft Exchange Server on the MS Exchange Setting Properties dialog box. Type in the name of your Exchange server as named in your HOSTS file. Then type in your mailbox's display name or alias, and click Check Name. You'll know that all is well if the display name for your mailbox shows up underlined. Click OK to exit the various dialog boxes and open your mailbox. It takes a while the first time, but when your client is capable of talking to the server directly over the Internet, you will be able to do virtually anything that you can do locally or with a RAS connection.

Some users sit at the same desk all day, every day. Others are moving around all the time, often not even having a computer of their own. These users are often referred to as *roving users*. Basically, you want all roving users to have a directory on a server where they can pick up their Exchange and other settings every time they log into the network, whatever workstation they use to log in.

The Exchange settings that you're interested in are those for home server and mailbox name. You want a roving user to get the same server and mailbox name no matter what workstation he or she chooses to log in on.

Supporting a roving Exchange user is no different from supporting a roving user who is working with any other software, such as Microsoft Word. With Exchange, you want to present the same server and mailbox name. With Word, your goal is for the user to get the same default template, window-size settings, and so on. The specific procedures that you must follow to support roving users depend on the workstation (and sometimes network) operating system that you're using.

Fortunately, Microsoft has a tool for simplifying the job of setting up correct profiles for roving Exchange users. This tool, PROFGEN.EXE, can be found in the Exchange Resource Kit. You can also download the program for free from Microsoft's Exchange Web site.

A third-party product, Profile Maker, is easier to use and more comprehensive in scope than PROFGEN.EXE. Check it out at the site of its manufacturer, AutoProf.com (http://www.autoprof.com).

Migrating Foreign Messaging System Users to Exchange

You can move users from foreign messaging systems to your Exchange system. In some cases, Microsoft provides specific migration tools, while in others it provides more generic tools. Remember that your primary goal is to import data from your legacy messaging system into Windows 2000's Active Directory and Exchange's information stores.

Migration is a complex process. Rather than describe it here in detail, I just want to make sure that you know it's available. Most of the documentation for migration is provided only online and on the Exchange Server CD-ROM, in the Migrate directory. Let's take a quick look at your options.

Exchange Server ships with comprehensive migration tools for the following foreign messaging systems:

- Microsoft Mail for PC Networks version 3.x
- Lotus cc:Mail database versions DB6 and DB8
- Lotus Notes versions 3.x, 4.0, 4.1 and Lotus Domino server versions 4.5 and 4.6
- Novell GroupWise versions 4.x and 5.x
- Collabra Share versions 1.x and 2.x (forums to public folders)

Migrations for all the systems listed are done entirely using the Microsoft Exchange Server Migration Wizard, which is installed along with Exchange Server. To start the wizard, select Start menu ➤ Programs ➤ Microsoft Exchange ➤ Migration Wizard. Migrations move most available directory and message data to the Exchange 2000/Windows 2000 environment, and both also assume a live network link between your Exchange system and the foreign messaging system. If everything is running properly, these migrations are a piece of cake.

You can also migrate from the following foreign messaging systems by extracting data from the old system into a file using a Microsoft-supplied source extractor and then importing it into Exchange using the Migration Wizard:

- Microsoft Mail for AppleTalk networks
- IBM PROFS
- NetSys (formerly Verimation MEMO)
- Digital ALL-IN-1

If that's not enough, Microsoft provides information on building your own migration source extractor to produce data that can be imported into Active Directory using the Migration Wizard.

Finally, and this is very neat, using the Migration Wizard, you can migrate directory information from any LDAP-compliant directory. And, if your legacy messaging system supports IMAP4, you can move mailbox data from it to Exchange mailbox stores using the Migration Wizard.

 NOTE Whichever route you take, be sure that someone on your migration team fully understands both the foreign electronic messaging system that you're working with and the computer operating system that it runs on top of. Without this expertise, you can get into some very hot water. If no one in your organization qualifies for this distinction, consider getting help from the vendors of your electronic messaging system and operating system, or think about hiring a knowledgeable consultant or two.

Summary

This chapter covered a number of advanced features of Exchange 2000 Server and Exchange-related features of Windows 2000 Server. These features enable Exchange administrators to do everything from enhancing message security to modifying e-mail address formats to migrating foreign messaging system users to Exchange.

Exchange advanced security enables users to strongly encrypt the messages that they send and to digitally sign them, better assuring recipients that the messages were really sent by the name in the From field. The Exchange Key Management Service (KMS) is at the heart of advanced security. KMS enables advanced security for mailboxes. It uses Windows 2000 Server's certificate services to obtain the security certificates required to extend advanced security to mailboxes. KMS interfaces are themselves tightly secured to further protect the integrity of Exchange advanced security.

KMS creates an advanced security-enabling token for each mailbox. The mailbox user must enter the token and select a password that is used each time a message is encrypted or digitally signed. KMS can send the token to each mailbox by e-mail, or Exchange administrators can manually deliver the token to each mailbox owner. When advanced security is enabled on a mailbox, Outlook client users can easily encrypt and sign individual messages. They can even require that all messages be encrypted or signed.

The Exchange Message Tracking Center is used to follow a message through an Exchange organization. Messages can be tracked as they move across Exchange servers and connectors, right up to the point that they leave an Exchange organization. Both e-mail and system messages can be tracked. Message tracking is useful both to prove to users that a message did indeed reach its destination and for troubleshooting Exchange system problems or apparent problems.

Exchange managers can modify the default e-mail address formats used to create e-mail addresses for Exchange recipients. One of the most interesting and often-used modifications involves the creation of secondary SMTP proxy addresses for a user. Secondary proxies enable a user to have multiple Internet addresses. When secondary proxies are created that involve domains not already registered in an Internet-connected DNS server, MX and host records for the domain must be created in the DNS, or other SMTP hosts won't be capable of sending messages to the new secondary proxy address.

Several Exchange features are implemented at the global or Exchange organization-wide level. Using recipient policies, Exchange managers can set up differently formatted default e-mail addresses for different Exchange recipients. A variety of selection criteria is available for specifying the recipients covered by a recipient policy. Exchange managers can also set up address lists using similar filters. Address lists are visible to users in their Outlook address books. The Exchange recipient update service, running on an Exchange server, keeps recipient e-mail addresses and address lists current as selection criteria change and new recipients are added to recipient policies and address lists. Multilingual details and address templates, respectively, support Outlook client features and one-off address creation in Outlook. Exchange administrators can set Exchange organization-wide message size and recipients per message limits for Exchange mailboxes.

Manual creation of Windows 2000 users and Exchange 2000 mailboxes and other recipients can be very labor-intensive. It is possible to import information into Windows 2000 Active Directory and export it from Active Directory. The program LDIFDE.EXE is used for Active Directory imports and exports. The program is run at a command prompt and is not very easy to use. Exchange administrators must possess a good deal of knowledge regarding Active Directory and the format of LDIFDE.EXE import files, as well as the format of individual entries in LDIFDE.EXE import files, before they can safely undertake Active Directory imports.

Exchange server troubleshooting is a constantly moving target. The best tools are an advanced Exchange server management book; use of online support from Microsoft and others, ensuring that the latest Windows 2000 and Exchange 2000 service packs are installed on servers; and, if all else fails, use of paid Microsoft or other consulting support.

Computer viruses borne by e-mail can be controlled on an Exchange server or after the user opens an attachment with a virus. Ideally, both Exchange server-based and user workstation-based virus software should be in place. Both virus software and virus signature files should be kept up-to-date.

Supporting both remote and roving clients is quite easy with Exchange. Remote clients can be supported using either Windows 2000's Remote Access Service or through an Internet connection. Roving users are most easily supported using a product such as Microsoft's PROFGEN.EXE.

Exchange 2000 Server comes with a variety of tools for migrating users from foreign messaging systems to Exchange. The Exchange Migration Wizard simplifies migration from a number of messaging systems, supporting live links to these systems during migration. For other foreign messaging systems, Microsoft provides source extractors to pull data from the systems and place it into files. The files can then be imported using the wizard.

CHAPTER 18

Building, Using, and Managing Outlook Forms Designer Applications

FEATURING:

Nobody likes filling in forms, right? Well, the answer probably seems obvious—until you consider the alternative: a blank piece of paper. Imagine doing your taxes without all those wonderful IRS and state forms. Imagine trying to process tax reports formatted every which way but clearly. Done right, forms—especially electronic forms—make it easier for users to get through complex or repetitive data-entry tasks with minimal pain. In addition, these forms help their creators collect data in a uniform manner and process it easily.

There are two major ways to create electronic forms for your Exchange Server environment: Microsoft Exchange Forms Designer (EFD) and Microsoft Outlook Forms Designer (OFD). EFD forms can be used with any Exchange or Outlook client for Exchange Server 4, 5, 5.5, or 2000. OFD forms can be used only with 32-bit Outlook clients. The 16-bit Windows 3.*x* Outlook client is really the old Exchange client in disguise, so you can use only EFD forms with it. Clearly, your choice of forms design environments depends on the mix of Exchange Server clients in your organization.

EFD comes with pre-Exchange 2000 versions of Exchange server. OFD is built into the 32-bit Outlook clients designed for Exchange Server. The two products offer very similar visual forms design environments. EFD forms are compatible with Microsoft Visual Basic, so if you're familiar with VB, you'll find the EFD development environment familiar. OFD lets you use Microsoft Office's Visual Basic Scripting Edition, as well as ActiveX and OLE controls, so Visual Basic skills are not wasted with OFD.

Overall, I find OFD a bit easier to use. Beware, however, because you can't build very interesting applications without some form of programming, whether in Visual Basic (EFD) or in Visual Basic Scripting Edition (OFD).

When you start working with EFD and OFD, you'll find yourself waking up at night with fantastic ideas for forms. Here are some examples:

- *Request forms,* used to ask for something:
    - Purchase orders
    - Computer program modifications
    - Computer hardware maintenance
    - Travel requests
    - Vacation or sick-day requests
- *Data collection forms*, used to gather information:
    - Data for line-of-business applications such as patient management or product/services purchasing
    - Employee feedback on health insurance plans
    - User feedback on products or services
    - Employee participation in company picnics

- *Report forms*, used to provide required information:
  - Employee status reports to supervisors
  - Employee travel and mileage reports
  - Department head reports on success in staying within budget allocations
- *Other forms*, used for a variety of purposes:
  - Standardized communications forms (for example, telephone notes, while-you-were-out memos)
  - Forms for playing multiuser tic-tac-toe, chess, and other games

The decision to create a form should be informed by a clear understanding of the process that you're automating and the people involved in that process. If this is the case, you'll be a winner, reducing paper shuffling and increasing the productivity and satisfaction of everyone involved. On the other hand, if you don't study processes and people carefully, you'll frustrate your bosses and users alike to the point that your forms will hinder rather than help the work flow that you're trying to automate.

The Outlook/Exchange Application Design Environment

As I indicated way back in the first chapter of this book, EFD and OFD aren't the only way to design applications. The Exchange application design environment includes the following:

- *Forms design tools*:
  - Exchange Forms Designer, used to make your own forms
  - Outlook Form Designer, used to make your own forms
- *Folder design tools*:
  - The Exchange or Outlook client, used to create, organize, and set actions to take place within folders
- *OLE-2–based applications*   A word-processing document, a spreadsheet, or another element from an OLE-2–capable application such as Microsoft Word or Excel is pasted or inserted as an object into an Exchange message. The message becomes the application.
- *Exchange Application Programming Interfaces (APIs)*   APIs are used to develop custom-coded applications using Visual Basic, C++, J++, or any other compatible programming language.

- *Exchange 2000 Server file- and Web-based data access* Use file- and Web-based access to Exchange private and public stores to create applications using end-user applications such as Word or programming languages such as Visual Basic, C++, or J++.

Creating OLE-2 apps is just a matter of pasting or inserting the appropriate application object into an Exchange message. You don't need my help with that. To do justice to API-based and Exchange 2000 file- and Web-based application design, I'd need to write another book at least the size of this one. That's why I'm focusing this chapter on form design—and even then, as you'll see, we'll be able to just touch the surface of this fascinating topic.

I'll focus here on OFD. OFD and EFD are quite similar in a number of ways. If you need to use EFD, check out my book *Mastering Exchange Server 5.5, Third Edition* (Sybex, 1998) for a detailed discussion of EFD.

Although OFD is fairly easy to use, it is a full-featured application, and I can't possibly teach you everything that you need to know about using it. My goal here is to show you how easy forms design can be and to get you started doing a simple form with OFD. For more details, you'll need to look at the OFD documentation and, if you want to get into serious programming, a good book on Visual Basic. In addition, take a look at *Mastering Microsoft Outlook 2000*, by Gini Courter and Annette Marquis (Sybex, 1999 standard edition, 2000 premium edition), and Thomas Rizzo's *Programming Microsoft Outlook and Microsoft Exchange* (Microsoft Press, 1999). Both books provide an excellent grounding in OFD and Visual Basic.

Installing Outlook Forms Designer

OFD is part of the Outlook 98 and 2000 client. The Outlook Visual Basic help files and Microsoft Script Debugger are part of the Outlook Development Tools package. Install these when you install Outlook on your computer, or add them with the Add/Remove option on the Control Panel.

We'll start with a firm grounding in OFD basics. Then we'll actually build a form. Don't run too far ahead, or you just might build a form that doesn't work very well, if at all.

Outlook Forms Designer Basics

Begin by opening the OFD environment. In your Outlook client, from the Tools menu, select Forms ➤ Design a Form. The Design Form dialog box opens (see Figure 18.1). In Figure 18.1, I've clicked the Details button to show information about each form type at the bottom of the dialog box.

As you can see in Figure 18.1, you can create a form using a variety of Outlook message types from appointments to tasks. You use the drop-down menu at the top of the form to select the container or location from which to choose forms. The Design Form dialog box opens with the Standard Forms Library selected. Forms can be stored in a personal forms library unique to each user, in any Outlook private or public folder, and in other special storage locations. Take a look at the drop-down menu for all the options.

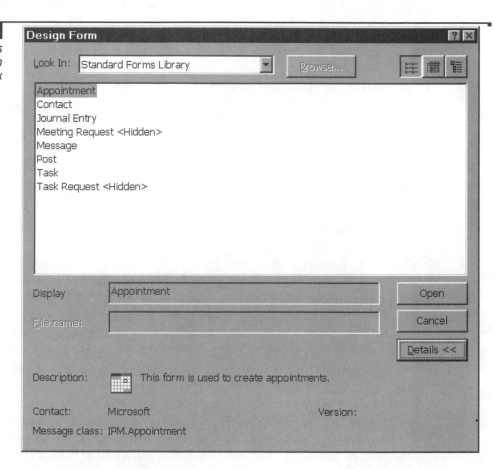

FIGURE 18.1

The Outlook Forms Designer Design Form dialog box

Outlook Message Forms

We're going to design a message form, so double-click Message in the Standard Forms Library on the Design Form dialog box. This opens the Form Designer environment, as shown in Figure 18.2. For all intents and purposes, the Form Designer environment is nothing more than an Outlook object—in this case, a message. You can work on it, save it to disk, and come back and work on it some more at any time.

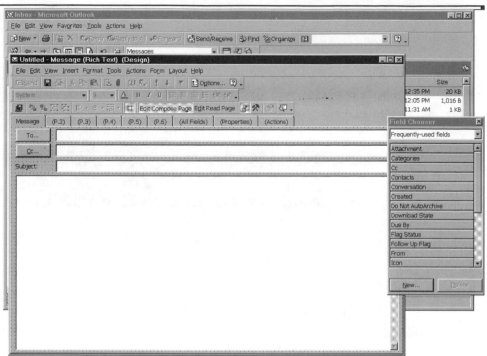

Before we actually start developing a form, let's take a quick tour of the Outlook Forms Designer environment. Keep your eyes on Figure 18.2.

Notice the tabs on the form. They're labeled Message, (P.2) through (P.6), (All Fields), (Properties), and (Actions). These delineate specific property pages on the form. When a form's tab label is in parentheses, the property page is hidden when the end user opens the form. Generally, you hide unused property pages and pages where you don't want users to know what's going on. For example, if you don't want an end user to know where a reply to a form is being sent or to be able to change the subject of the reply, you hide the property page with the To and Subject fields on it.

Messages have two basic kinds of pages: compose pages and read pages. Note the two buttons just above the property page tabs labeled Edit Compose Page and Edit Read Page. You use compose pages to create new Outlook items, such as messages. You use read pages to view composed items that have been processed by Outlook or Exchange Server. Outlook e-mail messages offer a good example of these two types of pages. When you click the New Message button in Outlook, a compose form opens. You enter addressing information, a subject line, and a message using the compose form. After you send the message, you can view it with a read form by double-clicking it in your Sent Items folder.

Any customizable page on a form can have compose and read pages. This option is enabled by default on the Message page. You must enable the option on all other pages by selecting Form ➢ Separate Read Layout when on the page. You can also use Form ➢ Separate Read Layout to disable the compose/read page option on the Message page. When a message form page has no separate read page, users see data in the same format whether composing or reading a message. If a field is editable, it can be edited whether the message is being read or composed.

 WARNING Create message pages without read pages with care. You could be courting disaster if you let readers edit the content of messages that they receive. Be sure that recipients of filled-in forms without read pages are trustworthy and have no reason to alter the data in messages.

By default, you start out editing the compose page of the Message page (see Figure 18.2). Click Edit Read Page to see what a read page looks like (see Figure 18.3). Default read pages have From, To, and Cc fields that are read-only. Users can't enter data into these fields. The Subject and Message fields on a read page are editable.

FIGURE 18.3

The Outlook Forms Designer environment editing a read page

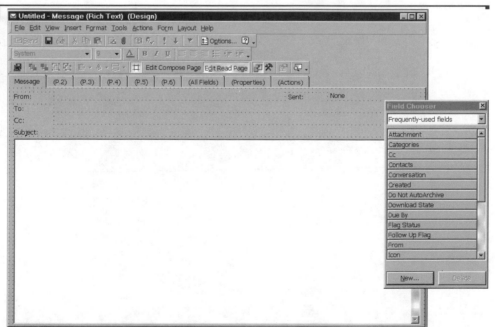

The Field Chooser and Control Toolbox

You use two key dialog boxes when you design forms: the Field Chooser and the Control Toolbox. The Field Chooser is visible in Figures 18.2 and 18.3. You can drag and drop any Exchange Server field, including fields that you design yourself, from the Chooser to your form. For example, if you wanted to include the size of your message on your form, you'd drag a message size field onto the form. You use the drop-down menu at the top of the Chooser to select the kinds of fields to be displayed. By default, you see the most frequently used fields. Among others, you can also see only address fields, only date/time fields, only the fields that you created, or only the fields in other forms. Open the drop-down list to see all your options.

We're done with the Field Chooser for now, so click the Field Chooser button to close the Chooser. Then click the Control Toolbox button to open the toolbox. See Figure 18.4 for the location of these buttons.

Figure 18.5 shows the Control Toolbox. With the exception of the button with an arrow on it, each of the buttons in the toolbox creates a different control for your form. You drag and drop controls onto your form.

Controls define data input and viewing fields, or provide additional means for managing activity on the form. Figure 18.5 includes the names of each of the controls.

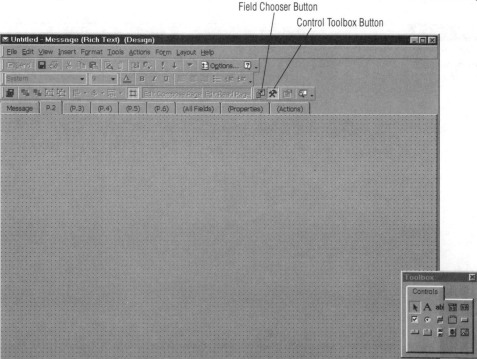

FIGURE 18.4

The Outlook Forms Designer ready for action

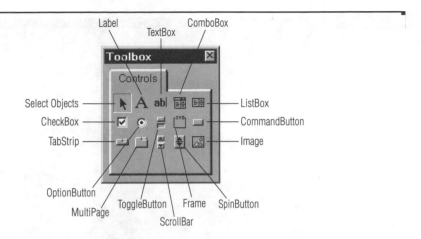

FIGURE 18.5

The Outlook Forms Designer Control Toolbox

Figure 18.6 shows the key OFD controls as they appear in a real Outlook message. Here's what each is for:

TextBox   Is a place to enter one line or multiple lines of text

CheckBox   Is for options that can be toggled on or off

ToggleButton   Is similar to CheckBox, but the button is either pushed in (on) or not (off)

ComboBox   Lets you create a drop-down or drop-list box where users can type responses or select from a choice of optional responses

Frame   Frames or groups other fields

Image   Displays a graphic image

Label   Provides text labels where needed

OptionButton   Is for multiple-choice options; users cannot select multiple option buttons on the same frame field

ListBox   Lets you create a drop-down or standard list box where users can select from a choice of optional responses but not type in their own responses

TabStrip   Is a multipage control where you add additional controls; the controls on each page are the same

MultiPage   Is a multipage control where you add additional controls; each page is a separate form with its own unique controls

FIGURE 18.6

Key controls that can be used on an OFD form

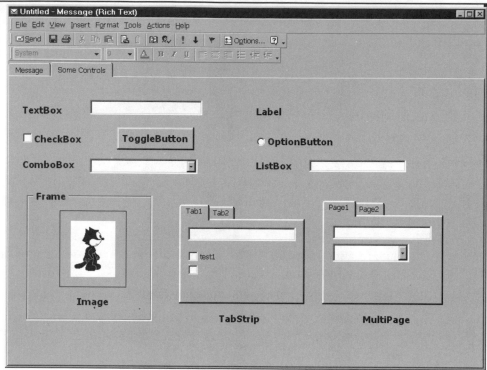

Other controls, such as the CommandButton, ScrollBar, and SpinButton controls, are used to manage activities on the form. For example, to build a data input field in which the user can move through a set of numbers and select a specific number, you'd use a SpinButton. We'll work with a SpinButton later in this chapter.

Form and Control Properties

Forms and controls have properties. To look at the properties of a form or a control that you have dragged onto your form, right-click anywhere on the form (the gray dotted area of a form or control) and select Properties or Advanced Properties.

Take a look at the Properties and Advanced Properties of the To control on the Message page of your form. You can change the properties of a To control to make it read only or read/write. To do so, open the control's Advanced Properties dialog box, as indicated previously. Then find the Read Only property in the Properties dialog box and click it to change the property from True to False, or vice versa. If a control doesn't have a read only property, it is a fixed read/write control. The Subject control is a fixed read/write control.

By the way, the colors of a control have nothing to do with whether it is editable. Control colors are simply properties of the control. You change them as you do any other property.

The Difference Between Controls and Fields

What's the difference between controls and fields? You use most OFD controls to build fields for entering and viewing data. You can refer to a specific control on a form as a *field* when it has been bound to a data field in an Exchange Server database. Until then, it's only a control. We'll talk more about data binding in a bit.

Building the Picnic Form

Okay, we're ready to begin building our first form. This form is to collect information from Barry Gerber and Associates (BGA) employees about an upcoming picnic, so we'll call it the Picnic Form. Be sure that the OFD environment is open and ready for you to create a message form. If you've closed the environment, refer back to the beginning of this chapter for details on opening it.

Among other things, you can customize the To and Subject fields for your message on the Message page. We're not ready for that yet, though. We need to start on one of the blank form building pages, so tab over to page two (P.2) on your form.

Working with Properties

First, let's change the form's background color. Right-click your form and select Advanced Properties from the pop-up menu. This opens the Advanced Properties dialog box for the form page (see Figure 18.7). You can use this dialog box to set all kinds of attributes for the window itself; I'll leave it to you to explore all its great features. To change the background color, double-click the first item in the Properties dialog box, BackColor. Use the Color dialog box to select a new background color for your form page. In Figure 18.7, I'm choosing white as the background color for my page.

Adding Controls

Now we're ready to add controls. As we move along, I'll show you how to do lots of neat stuff. Virtually everything you learn when adding one type of control can be used when you create other types. I'll tell you how to do a particular task as we set up a particular control; after that, I'll assume that you know how and when to use what you've already learned in creating other controls. As we go along, refer back to Figure 18.5 if you need to look for the location of buttons on OFD's Control toolbar.

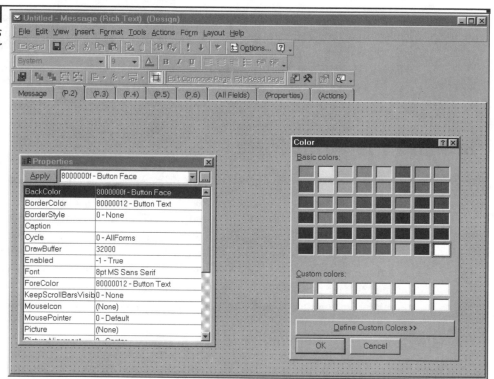

FIGURE 18.7

Changing a form's background color

Let's start by adding a label that will serve as the title of our form. Click the label button on the Control toolbox with your left mouse button. The label button is the one with the large capital letter *A* on it. Continuing to hold down your left mouse button, drag your mouse pointer over to the general location where you want the label to appear—I'm putting mine at the top of the message. Let go of the left mouse button. This brings up a little rectangular box with the word Label1 inside.

Click inside the box until it's surrounded by a dark rectangle with eight small white boxes and one large gray rectangle around it. You use the small boxes to change the size of the label control. Just put the pointer on one of the small white boxes, hold down the left mouse button, and drag the box to make the control larger or smaller. Resize your label control until it's about the size of the one in Figure 18.8.

To move your label control, put your mouse cursor anywhere on the control, hold down the left mouse button, and drag the control to the desired location on the form. By default, controls are snapped to a grid when they are moved. If you'd rather have very fine-grained control over where your control is placed, select Snap to Grid from the form's Layout menu. This toggles Snap to Grid off. Select Snap to Grid again to turn it on. Fine-grained control is great in some circumstances, but it can be a pain when you want to line up your controls in an aesthetically pleasing manner. You can use the Align options on the Layout menu to help tame unruly non–Snap to Grid controls.

Those little dots on your form show the grid that things are being snapped to. If they bother you, select Layout ➢ Show Grid to toggle off grid visibility.

FIGURE 18.8

Creating a title label for a form

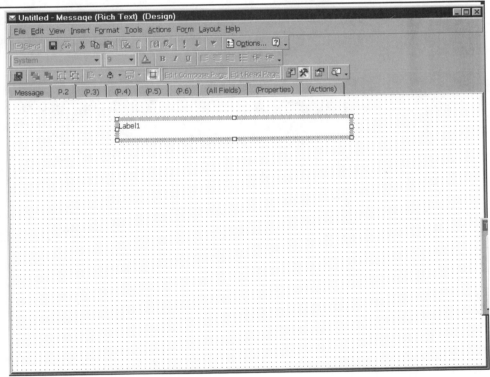

Next, right-click the label field and select Properties from the pop-up menu (see Figure 18.9). Type the text for your label into the Caption field on the Properties dialog box. My label is "The BGA Picnic Is Coming Soon." Next, change the font size to 10 and make it bold. Then click OK. If the field is too small for the text that you've added, resize it and drag the label field around the form until it's attractively placed (see Figure 18.10). To make the rectangular box with the little resizing boxes disappear, simply click the form anywhere outside the field.

FIGURE 18.9

Changing the text of a title label for a form

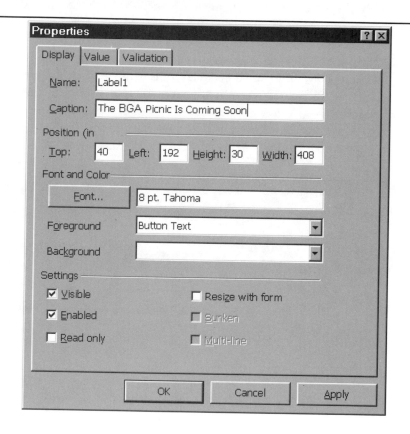

FIGURE 18.10

A label field resized to become the title of a form

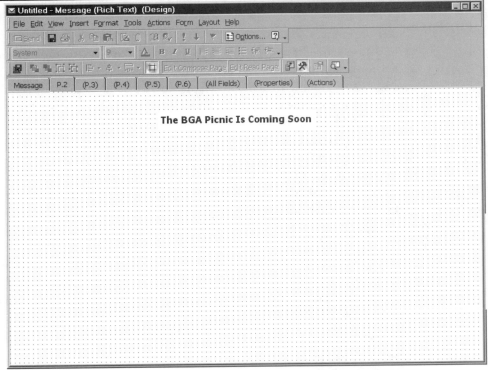

We took a lot of time fiddling around with sizing and placement on that first field. From here on, I'll leave it to you to do that kind of stuff on your own. Let's add another field.

WARNING Be sure to save your form to disk on a regular basis. As with any other Windows application, use the File ➤ Save As, and File ➤ Save options. To reopen your form to work on it at a later date, you have to use the Outlook main window Tools ➤ Forms ➤Design a Form. Then select User Templates in File System from the Design Form dialog box that pops up, and browse to the location of your form.

For planning purposes, we need to find out what people will want to drink at the picnic. Let's create a set of multiple-choice options and a control for people to enter other preferences.

Because people should be able to select more than one drink option, we'll use CheckBox fields grouped in a frame field to represent the options. (If we used options button fields grouped on a frame, people would be able to select only one option in the group.) First, drag and drop a frame control from OFD's Control toolbar; check out Figure 18.5 if you need a refresher on the Control toolbar buttons.

We'll be offering four picnic drink options—coffee, tea, milk, and beer—so we'll need four CheckBox controls. Drag and drop four CheckBox controls onto the frame that you just created. Place the four CheckBox fields in a vertical line (see Figure 18.11). Next, as shown in Figure 18.11, add a text box and label controls for users to enter drink preferences other than the four that you offered in the CheckBox controls.

 NOTE When you place fields on a frame field and then drag the frame, its associated fields stay in place and move with it. This makes it easy to properly locate a frame field and its associated fields.

Next you need to set the captions for each of the four controls. The captions on the four controls in Figure 18.11 are Coffee, Tea, Milk, and Beer. You set these captions just as you did for the title label that you created. Right-click the first control and select Properties from the pop-up menu. The Properties dialog box opens on the Value property page. I'll explain why later. For now, tab over to the Display property page and type **Coffee** in the Caption field. Click OK, and your first control now has the label Coffee. Go ahead and do the other three controls; then we'll move on.

FIGURE 18.11

Creating a set of drink options for a company picnic

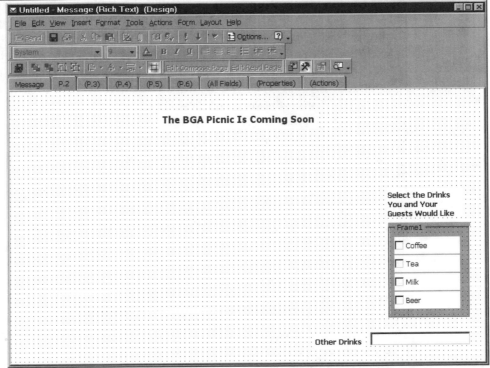

Binding Controls to Exchange Server Data Fields

Now we're going to do something that is absolutely vital to the working of Outlook forms. We're going to bind each of the four data controls to a field in the Exchange Server database. If you don't do this, data entered into a form won't be available for viewing or manipulation after the form has been filled in and sent back to you. Think of it this way: Controls aren't data. They don't store data. They're just a way to enter data, but if they aren't bound to Exchange Server database fields, the data entered into them dies when a message containing an Outlook form is sent to someone or posted in a folder.

Remember the sidebar earlier in this chapter in the section "Form and Control Properties," where I discussed the difference between controls and fields? Well, this is where a control earns the right to be called a field.

You can bind controls to standard Exchange fields, or you can create new fields and then bind controls to them. We'll be binding our controls to new Exchange fields.

Here's how to bind the Coffee CheckBox control to an Exchange database field. Open the Properties dialog box for the control. The dialog box opens by default on the Value property page, just as it did when you entered captions for the four drink controls. This is the cyberworld equivalent of a nagging spouse. Microsoft doesn't want you to forget to bind each control to an Exchange Server database field. Until you do, the Properties dialog box always opens on the Value page.

Click New on the Value page. This opens the New Field dialog box. Type in a name for the new Exchange Server database field. I like to use a combination of the form name and a meaningful name for the field. In Figure 18.12, I'm using the name PicnicCoffee.

Before you close the Properties dialog box, you need to change the type for this field. Set the Type to Yes/No. CheckBoxes and ToggleButtons must be set to type Yes/No. If you don't do this, when people select a CheckBox or depress a ToggleButton, values that they check will not be in the form when they send it back to you. When you've selected the Type Yes/No, notice that the format changes to *Icon*, meaning that the actual graphic image of the button is saved. Set the format to Yes/No or True/False. That way, data from this field will be saved in the Exchange Server database in a format that is easy to manipulate.

While you're at it, take a look at the other Type options that are available. The lineup is very rich, including (in addition to text) number, percent, currency, date/time, and formula. Each field includes formats appropriate to its content. For example, the Date/Time field includes a number of ways of displaying day of the week (such as Monday, Tuesday), month, day of the month (such as 1st, 20th), year, and time.

Now back to the task immediately before us. Click OK, and you've created your new field and bound your control to it.

 TIP You're very likely to create a number of bogus fields while experimenting with Outlook forms. It's easy to get rid of unwanted fields—maybe too easy. To remove a field, open the Field Chooser, click the field that you want to remove, and click Delete at the bottom of the Chooser. Then you need to delete the field from the current form. Tab over to the All Fields page on the form, and delete the field. This probably goes without saying, but I'll say it anyway: Be careful not to delete valid fields, especially after lots of forms have been filled out and their fields are snugly stored in your Exchange Server database.

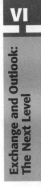

FIGURE 18.12

*Binding an Outlook
form control to a
new Exchange
database field*

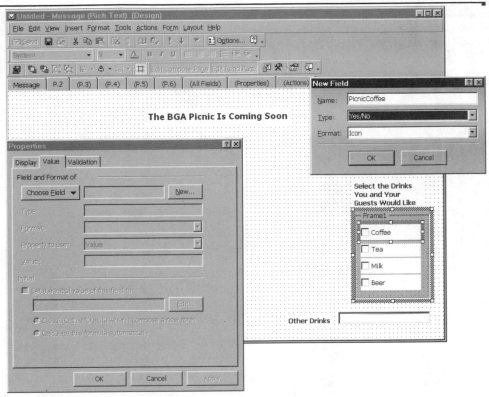

Setting Initial Values for Controls

Figure 18.13 shows the Properties dialog box again. Notice the frame with the caption Initial at the bottom of the dialog box. This is where you set the value that will
be seen by a user when the form is first opened. You don't need to set any initial
values for a CheckBox. However, you might want to set a specific initial value for
other fields. For example, you could set the initial value of a ComboBox to one of
the possible values for the ComboBox. More about ComboBoxes, possible values,
and such in a bit.

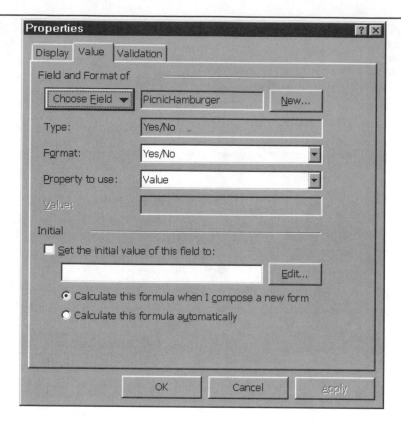

Now go ahead and create and bind new fields for the other three drink CheckBox controls. Don't forget to set the Type for each field to Yes/No. When you're done, we'll add some more controls to the form.

Testing an Outlook Form

You can run a form anytime while you're creating it. Just select Form ➤ Run This Form on the form itself. In the case of a message form, a standard Outlook message is displayed that looks just like your form (see Figure 18.14). You can just look at the form to admire your work, or you can fill in the form and send it to yourself to see how it works.

Whoops! Notice that caption on the frame. It says Frame1. We really don't need a caption on the frame. To eliminate it, close the test message and go back to your form. Open the Properties dialog box for the frame and delete the caption. That's it.

The capability to run a form at any time is a fantastic capability of Outlook Forms Designer. As you can see, it makes format checking and debugging extremely easy.

FIGURE 18.14

Testing an incomplete Outlook form

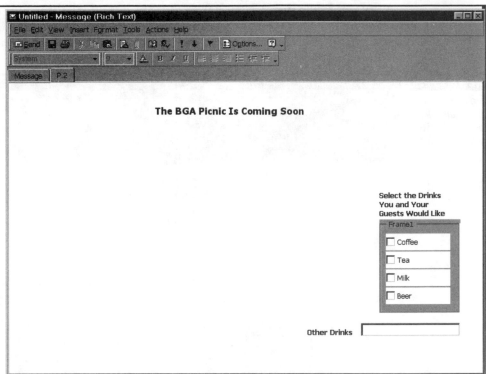

Adding More Controls to the Picnic Form

Okay, we're ready to continue developing our Picnic form. I'm going to move much more quickly now that you have the basics of forms design under your belt.

Add a label above the frame for your Drinks CheckBox fields. "Select the Drinks You and Your Guests Would Like" seems to be a good choice for my form.

Now we need to add a control so that people can type in other drink choices. Add a TextBox and label as shown in the lower-right corner of Figure 18.11.

Next we'll add a set of CheckBox fields so that people can pick the main dishes that they want. We'll also provide an entry field to indicate a preference for other main-dish options.

Well, we're certainly not about to go through all the steps that we just went through to create this new set of fields; we'll just copy and paste. Put your mouse pointer an inch or so to the left and above the Select the Drinks You and Your Guests Would Like label. Hold down the left mouse button and drag your mouse pointer until the select rectangle includes everything up to and including the Other Drinks control (see Figure 18.15). Release the left mouse button. All the controls within the rectangle should be highlighted. Select Copy from the form's Edit menu (or use the keyboard shortcut, Ctrl+C). Then choose Paste from the Edit menu (or press Ctrl+V).

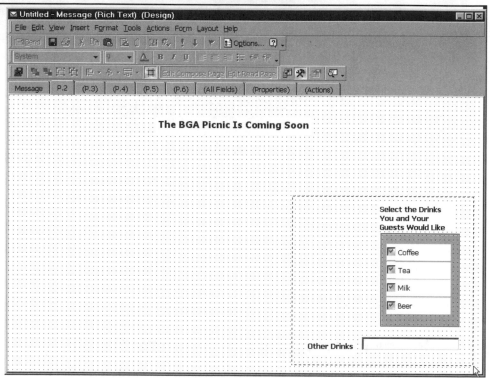

FIGURE 18.15

Selecting a set of controls that will be copied and pasted elsewhere in a form

If you don't see the new frame and its associated CheckBox fields, they've probably been pasted right on top of the old frame. In that case, just move the top frame with your mouse, and you'll see the original frame underneath. You now have two identical frames and CheckBox buttons. Move the copy to the left of the original.

Now edit the leftmost Drinks frame and its associated CheckBox fields. Change the Coffee, Tea, Milk, and Beer captions to Hamburger, Turkey Burger, Veggie Burger, and Hot Dogs. Next add new database fields for the four new controls, and set their types to Yes/No. Then edit the Drinks label and the Other Drinks entry field so that they are appropriate for a main dish. When you're done, your form should look something like the one in Figure 18.16.

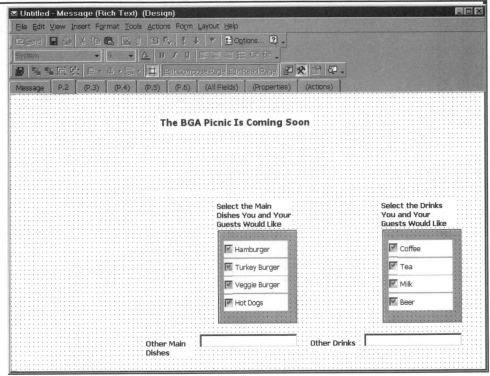

We'll need to know how many guests each person plans to bring and what kinds of games people will want to play. So, we need to add a TextBox for the number of guests, plus a label and two ComboBoxes for favorite games (see Figure 18.17).

We're going to set up a fancy TextBox for entering number of guests. Create the TextBox control and bind it to a new field, setting the Type for the Number of Guests TextBox to Number. Don't worry about the format. Next, drag and drop a SpinButton onto the right edge of your TextBox, just as you see in Figure 18.17. Then, bind the SpinButton to the same field as you bound the TextBox.

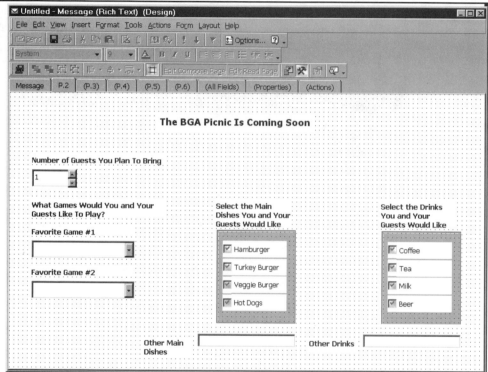

FIGURE 18.17

The picnic form now collects information on the number of guests and favorite games.

Run your form, and you'll see that you can use the spin button to pick whatever numeric value you want. The problem is that you can spin up to some pretty grand numbers of guests or down to negative numbers of guests. We don't want to bankrupt my little company, so let's set the minimum and maximum values that you can spin to. Right-click the SpinButton and open the Advanced Properties dialog box. Find the Max and Min properties, and set Min to 1 and Max to 8.

Now run your form. The initial value is 1, even though you didn't set an initial value. That's because you set Min to 1 for the SpinButton. And, you can spin only up to 8. Pretty nifty, huh?

Validation

You've probably noticed the Validation tab on the Properties dialog box. You use this tab to require that users enter data into a field or to ensure that data entered by users meets a specific set of criteria. For example, we could have required that the value entered into our Number of Guests field should be greater than 0 and less than 9. We could even have put in a message that would be shown to users if they put in a number outside the range of acceptable values. In this case, the SpinButton works much more elegantly than any set of validation checks. So, validation isn't needed here, but I'm sure that you can imagine a number of scenarios in which validation would help ensure the quality of data entered into a form.

Now, go ahead and create the two ComboBoxes for favorite games. The ComboBoxes start out blank. At this point, if form users opened the drop-down list, they'd find nothing to select from. To add some options, right-click the first games ComboBox and select Properties from the pop-up menu. Then enter some games in the Possible Values field. If you want one of the values to show in the ComboBox when the form is first opened, type that value into the field named Set the Initial Value of This Field To. Check out Figure 18.18 for the details.

Notice in Figure 18.18 that I set the initial value for the ComboBox to Baseball. That way, the field shows the value Baseball when the form is initially opened.

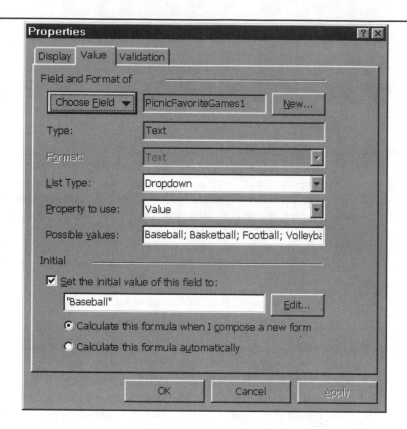

We need to do two more things before we finish. First, we need to rename the second page on our form from P.2 to something else, such as maybe Please Fill In Survey Here. Click the tab for P.2 and select Form ➢ Rename Page. Enter a new name in the Rename Page dialog box, and click OK.

Second, we need to set a subject for our message. That way, all messages sent to us will have a standard subject line. The initial value of my subject field is Survey for BGA Picnic. Tab over to the Message property page of your form, right-click the form's Subject field, and select Properties. When the Properties dialog box for the field opens, tab over to the Value property page and type in an initial value.

That's it. We've finished creating our form. Be sure to save it.

Now we need to publish our form.

Publishing a New OFD Form

You can publish an OFD form in a number of locations:

- An Exchange Server organizational forms library
- Your own personal forms library
- Your own Outlook folders
- Exchange Server public folders

Exchange Server organizational forms libraries reside on an Exchange server and are available to all users by default. Forms in your personal forms library are available only to you when you're logged into your Exchange Server mailbox, as are forms in your own Outlook folders. Exchange Server public folders are available to any user granted permissions to use them.

As you'll see in a bit, the form that we just created will be invoked when a user replies to a message from a specific individual. The user receives a message, opens it, and replies to it. The reply is the form. When the user is finished filling in the form, he or she sends the reply back to the original sender.

The form needs to be available to the recipient of the message, so we can't publish it in a personal forms library or private folders. To accomplish the end outlined in the previous paragraph, the form must be published in an Exchange Server organizational forms library. Even a public folder won't do. I'll show you why in a short while.

Creating an Organizational Forms Library

So, you're probably asking, where is this Exchange Server organizational forms library thingie? Right now, it's nowhere. You must create an organizational forms library on one of your Exchange Servers. That means that you have to shift gears, go over to your Exchange Server, and open your MMC and go to the Exchange System Manager, your constant companion since way back in Chapter 8, "Installing Exchange 2000 Server."

To create an organizational forms library, right-click your Public Folders container and select View System Folders from the pop-up menu. Your public folders will disappear, and in their place you'll see a bunch of folders. Right-click the one named EFORMS REGISTRY and select New ➢ Organizational Form from the pop-up menu. This opens the organizational forms library Properties dialog box, shown in Figure 18.19. Fill in the form, being sure to select the correct language so that accents and other characteristics of the language are supported. You can create multiple organizational forms libraries in an administrative group. The only requirement is that there can be only one library per language.

FIGURE 18.19

*Using the organiza-
tional forms library
Properties dialog box
to create a new
organizational
forms library*

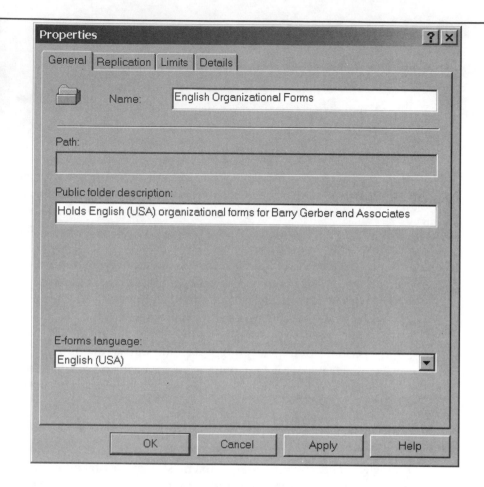

When you're done with the dialog box, click OK, and your new organizational forms library shows up in the EFORMS REGISTRY system folder (see Figure 18.20). Double-click the form in the left pane of your MMC to open its full Properties dialog box. Notice that this folder has all the property pages that any other public folder has. You can assign access permissions just as you would for any other folder. For more on public folder management, take a look at Chapter 12, "Managing the Exchange Server Hierarchy and Core Components."

FIGURE 18.20

*A newly created orga-
nizational forms
library in the* **EFORMS
REGISTRY**
system folder

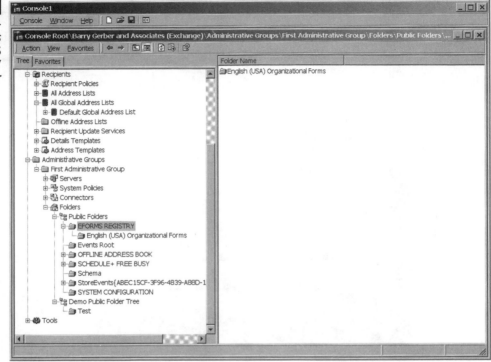

To publish your form, on the form itself, select Tools ➤ Forms ➤ Publish Form or
Tools ➤ Forms ➤ Publish Form As. Then select the location where you want to store
your form from the drop-down list on the Publish Form or Publish Form As dialog
box (see Figure 18.21). Zip up and down the options in the drop-down list. You'll see
every private and public storage area available to you.

In Figure 18.22, I'm publishing my picnic form in the organizational forms library.
I've chosen to name the form BGA Picnic Form.

When the form is saved, we're ready to move on to the next step. Yes, there is a
next step.

FIGURE 18.21

Selecting the forms library where the form will be stored

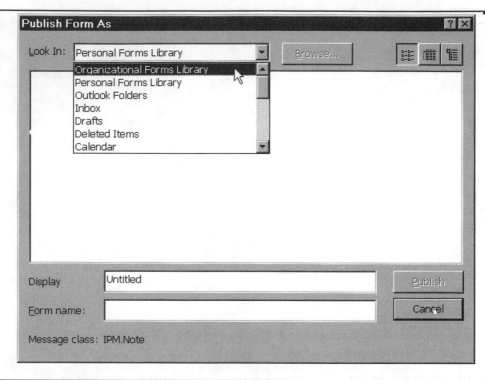

FIGURE 18.22

Storing a form in the organization forms library

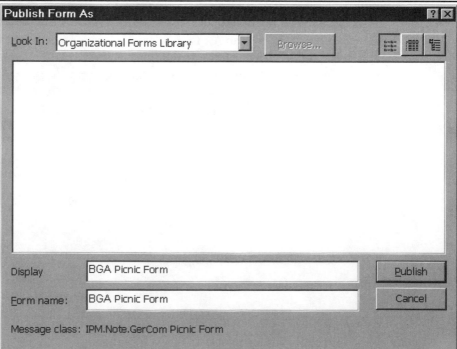

Creating the Message Form Used to Send the Picnic Form

I'll bet you thought we were done. Nope. The form that we just created is, for all intents and purposes, a reply form, not a send form. If you run the form, you get a Message tab to address the message and show its subject, and you get the Picnic Survey tab. If you send this form to someone and that person clicks the Reply button on the message, all that person will get is a standard reply message. The Survey tab won't be there.

You can provide users with a reply version of the form in two ways.

1. Attach your saved form to a message. In the message, tell users to double-click the attachment to open it and then to fill in the survey and send it back. In this case, you might want to make your mailbox alias or display name the initial value in the To field of the message. Then users won't have to enter your e-mail address to send the form back.

2. Create a message with a reply that is itself your form.

Although the first option is easier for you to pull off, it requires a lot more work for the user than the second option. There's also more room for error. So, we're going to take the more elegant approach of option two.

Our second message is very simple. You've already done everything required to create it. Here's what to do:

1. Select Forms ➢ Design a Form from Outlook's Tools menu.

2. Select Message from the Design a Form dialog box.

3. Add the same subject line that you created for the original message "Survey for BGA Picnic."

4. On the Properties page of the form, click the CheckBox labeled Send Form Definition with Item.

5. On the Actions page of the form, double-click the row with the action name Reply.

6. On the Form Action Properties dialog box, on the frame labeled This Action Creates a Form of the Following Type, use the drop-down to change the form name from Message to the name of the form that you just published in your organizational forms library (BGA Picnic Form, in my case).

7. Repeat the steps 5 and 6 for Reply to All.

8. Save your form, and publish it in your personal forms library under a name such as Message with BGA Picnic Form as a Reply.

Okay, that's it. Now, we're ready to put our forms to use.

NOTE When you selected the form BGA Picnic Form in step 6, you were offered only three containers from which to select the form: Standard Forms Library, Organizational Forms Library, and Personal Forms Library. Those are all the choices there are. Now do you see why a public folder wouldn't do here? Public folders are not a choice because they might not have been replicated across an entire Exchange organization. Organization forms libraries are cross-organization by definition, meaning that they are replicated to all Exchange servers in an Exchange Organization.

 TIP Like fields, you just might wind up with a bunch of useless forms in a library or folder. You delete forms from folders just like any other item in a folder. To delete forms from libraries, from the Outlook main menu, select Tools ➢ Options ➢ Other. Next, click Custom Forms, and then click Manage Forms and use the resultant Forms Manager dialog box to delete and otherwise manage your forms.

Using Forms

To use the form we just created, select New ➢ Choose Form from the File menu of Outlook's main window. Use the Choose Form dialog box to find your personal forms library and double-click the form that you created in the previous section (Message with BGA Picnic Form as a Reply, in my case).

In Figure 18.23, I'm sending a message off to an Outlook distribution list that includes all BGA staff. Note that there is no sign of the form at this point. In Figure 18.24, a member of BGA's staff (me again) has clicked Reply on the original message and has just finished completing the picnic survey form that opened as part of the reply message. When I click Send, the message with the form is sent to the original sender (me, yet again).

FIGURE 18.23

Sending a form to an Exchange recipient

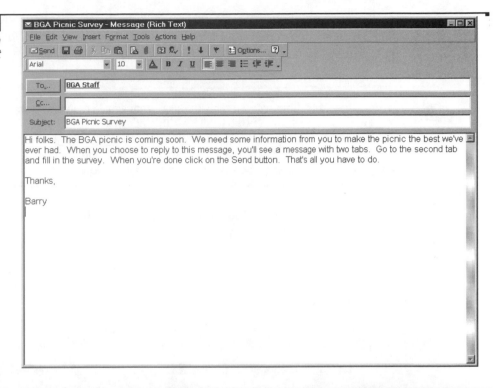

FIGURE 18.24

The data in a completed form ready to be returned to the form's sender

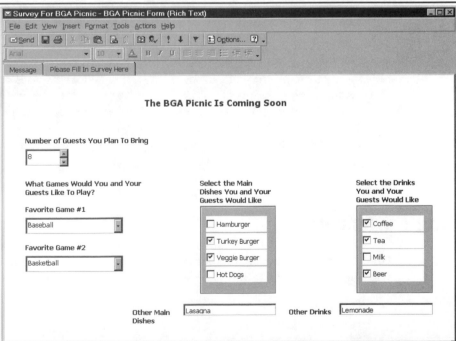

To be fancy, I could show you the form as it looks to the original sender when the reply is received. However, it would be anticlimactic because the form looks just like it does in Figure 18.24.

 TIP Do you find the two-tab reply message annoying? I mean, why should someone have to tab over to the survey tab to fill it in? This little aesthetic nightmare is easy to fix. All you have to do is cut the To and Cc fields from the Message page and paste them on the survey page. Then hide the Message page. Now your reply form is a beautiful single page. If you do make this change, be sure to save and republish your results.

Just one thing before we conclude this section: All those fields that you created are available in the Outlook client. You can open the Field Chooser in the client and drag and drop any of these fields onto the field bar (the one with From, Subject, Received, and so on) your Inbox. For example, if you drag the Number of Guests field to the field bar, you will then see in your Inbox, for every form that has been returned, how many guests the sender plans on bringing to the picnic.

The Difference Between Save, Save As, Publish, and Publish As

Outlook Forms Designer is full of ways to save and publish your work. As you're building a form, it's a good idea to save or republish it frequently, just be sure that you know where things go when you use all the save and publish options that OFD provides.

Save and Save As don't work like they do in other applications such as Microsoft Word. Save saves your form into your Outlook client's Drafts folder. Save As is more traditional and saves your work to a disk file of your choice. If you want to save or resave your form to a file, use Save As. Publish As lets you choose the forms library or folder where you want to publish your form. Publish republishes your form in the forms library or folder where you opened the form, or anywhere you chose with Publish As.

Don't Stop Here!

Unfortunately, we have to stop our exploration of OFD here, but don't let that stop you from exploring OFD further on your own. You can do so many great things with

OFD, such as creating forms for posting in public folders, for setting group meetings, or for collecting key line-of-business information.

Also look into and get into Visual Basic scripting. You'd be amazed at what you can do when you combine Outlook forms and VB scripting. You can do simple tasks such as collating responses from Outlook forms, all the way up to complex applications that help your organization sell its products or services, maintain its inventory, or manage its customers, clients, or patients.

OFD has a very good user interface. Combine that with its fine online help, and you can usually have a project based on newly discovered OFD features up and running in minutes. As with any piece of technology—Outlook and Exchange Server included—your OFD watchwords should be *plan*, *do*, *test*, and *have fun*.

Where to Get Sample Forms and Help with Forms Development

Exchange Server comes with a number of sample forms-based applications, and you can download more of both the EFD and the OFD persuasions at Microsoft's Web site. These apps support such functions as customer tracking and help desks. They're worth looking at both because they may help you understand how to build multiform applications and because they use Exchange's public folders to organize apps, as well as deliver them to users throughout an Exchange organization.

Check the shelves of your favorite bookstore for weighty (5 pounds at least) tomes on EFD and OFD. And take a look at Microsoft's Web site, which has some fairly good stuff. For example, a search for FORMSHLP.EXE on the site will reward you with a nice add-in help file on OFD for use with your Outlook client.

If you expect to get into forms programming, get a hold of one of the books out there on Office 97 or Office 2000's Visual Basic Scripting Edition. You might even want to buy Microsoft's Visual Basic learning package. It sells for less than $100 and comes with a minimal feature set version of VB, a very nice introductory VB training manual, and lots of examples. This little gem will not only familiarize you with visual forms development, but it will also give you some basic training in VB scripting.

Oh, yes, don't forget those books I mentioned way back at the beginning of this chapter.

Summary

There are a number of ways to develop applications in the Exchange 2000 Server environment. This includes using electronic forms, customized Exchange folders, OLE2-based applications, Exchange API-based applications, and Exchange 2000 file- and Web-based applications. Electronic forms are a fairly easy way to create quite sophisticated applications that elicit information from Exchange users. They can be used to fulfill a wide variety of corporate tasks, from issuing purchase orders to submitting monthly expense information.

Outlook Forms Designer is one of the best form design interfaces around. You create forms in a logical, intuitive, object-oriented visual environment. You can add controls to a form that support everything from labels to text, to checkboxes and radio buttons, to drop-down lists. You can modify the properties of forms and of the controls that you place on them to alter the function and look and feel of both. And, you can create send and reply forms, combining the two into seamless messages in which the reply form with all its controls pops up when the recipient clicks Reply.

You bind controls to fields stored on your Exchange server. So, data from each recipient of a message is stored in Exchange and is available for analysis using a range of tools, including Visual Basic or C++ programs.

You can store Outlook Forms Designer forms in a variety of places, including private and public folders. However, for ease of access within an Exchange organization, organizational forms libraries make the most sense. Organizational forms libraries are public folders with all the characteristics and capabilities of public folders, including the capability for replication and easy management of user access.

Well, folks, this is the last chapter of *Mastering Exchange 2000 Server*. For me, researching and writing the book has been a lot of fun and relatively painless. I hope that your experiences with Exchange Server are as positive and rewarding.

APPENDIX **A**

Cool Third-Party Applications for Exchange Server and Outlook Clients

I never appreciated the meaning of "cool" until I started playing with Exchange Server and its clients, and some of the fantastic applications that third-party vendors have created to extend the reach of an already-great set of products. Here I'll tell you some of my favorite products at the time of this writing.

Products are listed by category, along with information on how you can contact the vendors. If a particular contact method isn't listed for a particular vendor, I could find no information about that contact method for the vendor. Some vendors provide live demos or even trial versions of their products that you can download over the Internet.

Most of the vendors listed here either have begun shipping or have committed to shipping Exchange 2000 versions of their products. Contact the vendor for more information.

Remember, I can't take responsibility for the workability of these products in your Exchange Server and organizational environments. That's up to you.

Workflow

The great promise of electronic messaging systems such as Exchange Server lies in their capability to help manage the flow of documents to complete a specific task among the various persons who need to be involved in the task. Lotus Notes has long been considered one of the better workflow applications. As Exchange Server grows with each release, it gets closer and closer to Notes in its capabilities. The third-party products noted here help fill in the gaps that remain.

Document Management Extensions for Microsoft Exchange

Document Management Extensions for Exchange enable users to share files with full document-level security, version control, check-in/check-out, and full-text indexing. This product enables serious Exchange-based groupware applications. Contact: 80-20 Software, phone (425) 739-6767; World Wide Web www.80-20.com.

Sales and Project Tracking

Sales and Project Tracking uses Exchange Server public folders to support sales force automation and project tracking, especially for organizations with long sales and project development cycles. The product includes a searchable knowledge base; task assignment and monitoring capabilities; corporate calendaring, resource allocation, and contact information. Contact: PortalSoft Technologies, phone (505) 346-0507; fax (505) 346-0509; World Wide Web www.portalsoft.com.

Transform Response

Transform Response is a tool for developing group inbox applications. The product can be used to support such applications as a customer service center for a Web site, an e-mail extension to a call center, or a corporate or customer help desk. Contact: Transform Research, phone (613) 238-1363; fax (613) 237-9221; e-mail info@tran-sres.com; World Wide Web www.transres.com.

Backup Software

The key here is support for Exchange Server. Windows 2000 Server's own backup program backs up the Exchange mailbox and public information stores while they're open and in use. That's really nice, but Windows 2000 Server's Backup isn't the most full-featured backup product around. For example it doesn't backup either the registry or system state on remote computers. Still the Windows 2000 backup program can work well for small networks, especially if each server is backed up locally. For more features, turn to third-party backup solutions that include Windows 2000 Server's Backup's open information stores backup capability. The products listed here include this capability, although usually as an add-on.

ARCserve

ARCserve has been around for a long time and is a good package. It has very good backup scheduling capabilities. Contact: Computer Associates, phone (800) 243-9462; fax (800) 225-5224; World Wide Web www.cai.com.

Backup Exec

Like ARCserve, Backup Exec has been around for eons and is a good backup product with nice backup scheduling capabilities. See also Veritas's Remote Storage for Exchange, which archives message attachments to a secondary storage device such as tape and then seamlessly returns the attachment when a user tries to access it. Contact: Veritas, phone (800) 327-2232; fax (407) 531-7770; World Wide Web www.veritas.com.

CommVault

CommVault's focus is on backup and restoration of the contents of individual Exchange Server mailboxes. It also handles the full Exchange information store. Contact: CommVault Systems, phone (732) 870-4104; World Wide Web www. commvault.com.

Legato NetWorker

Well known for the excellence of its Unix backup products, Legato also supports the Windows NT 4 and Windows 2000 Server environments with its NetWorker backup product. An optional module for Exchange Server extends support to Exchange Server 5.5 and Exchange 2000 Server. Contact: Legato, phone (650) 812-6000; World Wide Web www.legato.com.

UltraBac

UltraBac.com's backup entry sports very nice backup setup and scheduling interfaces. Contact: UltraBac.com, phone (425) 644-6000; World Wide Web www.ultrabac.com.

Exchange Server Administration and Management

Three of these products either display existing Exchange or Windows 2000 performance monitoring data in a different form, or extend the range of monitoring options available. The fourth product adds list and reply server capabilities to Exchange Server.

AppManager

AppManager has modules for the whole BackOffice suite. It lets you monitor the health and performance of an entire distributed Exchange system. Contact: NetIQ, phone (408) 330-7000; e-mail info@netiq.com; World Wide Web www.netiq.com.

Argent Guardian for Exchange

Argent Guardian monitors Exchange Server environments. Monitoring includes response time tracking, SMTP connectivity, top senders and receivers of messages, and mailboxes over storage limits. Contact: Argent, phone (860) 674-1700, World Wide Web www.argent.com.

bv-Control for Microsoft Exchange

bv-Control checks for potential security holes, analyzes mailboxes and public folders, scans mailboxes for viruses and inappropriate material, provides server traffic reports, monitors performance, supports drag-and-drop moving of mailboxes, and documents Exchange environments. Contact: BindView, phone (877) 230-9787; World Wide Web www.bindview.com.

EXMS

EXMS does such wonderful tasks as automatically maintaining distribution lists and synchronizing the Exchange directory with other databases. For example, the product can be used to create new Exchange mailboxes based on new or changed entries in an organization's human resources system. Contact: Discus Data Solutions, phone (212) 279-9090; fax (212) 290-8066; e-mail info@discusdata.com; World Wide Web www.discusdata.com.

Internet Marketing Manager

Internet Marketing Manager adds list and reply services to Exchange Server. You can use it to create automatically maintained distribution lists and to deliver automated replies. Contact: NTP Software, phone (800) 226-2755; fax (603) 641-6934; e-mail info@ntpsoftware.com; World Wide Web www.ntpsoftware.com.

List Manager

List Manager brings automatic list server capability to Exchange Server. Users can subscribe to and unsubscribe from lists. The product also includes an archive option that allows users to retrieve past postings. Contact NTP Software, phone (800) 226-2755; fax (603) 641-6934; e-mail sales@ntpsoftware.com; World Wide Web www.ntpsoftware.com.

Network Documentor Service

Network Documentor is a pay-by-the-server service that automatically builds comprehensive documentation for an Exchange Server organization. Users can select the Exchange components to be documented. Contact: Encora, phone (877) 923-2672, World Wide Web www.encora.com.

Profile Maker

Profile Maker helps Exchange managers build and support common Outlook/Exchange Server profiles. It allows for configuration of local file paths, message retention settings, addressing, delivery, and folder options. If a user changes his or her profile, that profile is replaced the next time the user logs into the network. Contact: AutoProf.com, phone (603) 433-5885; World Wide Web www.autoprof.com.

RoboMon

RoboMon monitors Exchange Server environments, including everything from CPU usage to end-to-end connectivity. This utility provides extensive reports. Contact: Heroix, phone (800) 229-6500; World Wide Web www.heroix.com.

STM for Exchange

Among other things, SRM for Exchange automatically discovers Exchange servers and components, monitors space in mailbox and public stores, identifies unused mailboxes and old messages that might be deleted to increase storage capacity and reduce backup time, and generates historical reports for information store planning. Contact: HighGround Systems, phone (800) 395-9385; World Wide Web www.highground.com.

TS.E-Mail

TS.E-Mail does extensive end-to-end performance analysis and reporting for Exchange Server and other messaging systems. The product, which goes several steps beyond Exchange Server's own monitors, has some very nice graphical presentations. Contact: Tally Systems, World Wide Web www.tallysystems.com.

Veranda

Veranda is a very cool product. Among other things, it lets you analyze Exchange Server message activity; plan for computer and network upgrades; audit for security problems; and charge back costs by sites, departments, and employees. Contact: Tally Systems, World Wide Web www.tallysystems.com.

Wireless Messaging

If your users need to stay in touch on the road when no phone line is available, these products are what you're looking for. Some support specific wireless options such as packet wireless networks. Others support everything from standard cellular phone to satellite service links.

Mail on the Run!

Mail on the Run! software adds very complete support for remote Exchange Server access, using wire-based, cellular, and wireless packet networks such as ARDIS. Contact: River Run Software Group, phone (203) 861-0090; fax (203) 861-0096; World Wide Web www.riverrun.com.

OnAir Mobile

OnAir Mobile software provides high data-throughput support for a range of wireless and wired options. Contact: Telesis North, World Wide Web www.telesisnorth.com.

PageMaster/ex Pager Gateway

With this utility, you can add pagers to Exchange address lists. It sends messages to alphanumeric or numeric pagers through Exchange Server using modem or Internet connections. Contact: OmniTrend, phone (860) 673-8910; World Wide Web www.omnitrend.com.

Fax Servers

Generally, fax servers enable users to send and, in some cases, receive faxes through a central server instead of their own workstations. Fax servers that integrate with Exchange Server add a new address type for faxing. To send a message to an e-mail user, select the user's e-mail address from an Exchange address book. To send a message to a fax user, select the fax "address" from an Exchange address book.

FACSys Fax Connector

FACSys Fax Connector operates like any other connector on an Exchange server, but it sends faxes. Contact: FACSys, phone (732) 271-9568; fax (732) 271-9572; e-mail sales@facsys.com; World Wide Web www.facsys.com.

Faxcom

Faxcom runs as a Windows service. Contact: Biscom, phone (800) 477-2472; fax (978) 250-4449; e-mail sales@biscom.com; World Wide Web www.biscom.com.

Faxination

Faxination provides full Exchange Server integration and supports a range of languages. It allows for off-hours scheduling and least-cost routing. Contact: Fenestrae, Inc., e-mail info@fenestrae.com; World Wide Web www.fenestrae.com.

FAXmaker

FAXmaker runs as a Windows 2000 Server service and allows faxes to be sent from an Outlook client. It includes call cost accounting. Contact: GFI, phone (888) 243-4329; fax (919) 388-5621; e-mail sales@gfiusa.com; World Wide Web www.gficomms.com.

Fax Resource

Fax Resource installs and works as an Exchange Server connector. Contact: IMECOM Group, phone (603) 569-0600; e-mail igisales@imecominc.com; World Wide Web www.imecominc.com.

Fax Sr.

Fax Sr. is a sophisticated fax server that works with a wide range of higher end messaging platforms including Lotus Notes and Exchange Server. Contact: Omtool, phone (800) 886-7845; fax (603) 890-6756; e-mail asksales@omtool.com; World Wide Web www.omtool.com.

LanFax

LanFax operates as an Windows service, and supports Outlook clients as well as other MAPI-compatible clients. Contact: Esker, phone (405) 624-8000; fax (405) 624-3010; e-mail sales@esker.com; World Wide Web www.esker.com.

MsXfax

MsXfax operates as an Exchange connector. Contact: BSN Group, World Wide Web http://www.bnsgroup.com.au.

Security, Virus Protection, and Antispam

What scares users more than the boss? Security breaches, viruses, and junk mail! These products let you catch security breaches, mail-borne viruses, and spam messages in their natural habitat: your Exchange server. Most of these products automatically download and install virus updates.

Antigen for Exchange Server

Antigen for Exchange Server does real-time virus scans and repairs of inbound and outbound messages. It also does scheduled scans and fixes. Contact: Sybari Software, phone (516) 630-8500; fax (516) 630-8555; e-mail sales@sybari.com; World Wide Web www.sybari.com.

Anti-Virus Software for Exchange Server

Anti-Virus Software for Exchange Server, like most of its competitors, scans mail on an Exchange server for viruses, including attachments and zipped files. As most similar products do, this one sends notifications about found viruses. During virus outbreaks, the software's virus-scan frequency automatically increases. Contact: Nemx Software, phone (613) 831-2010; fax (613) 831-1898; World Wide Web www.nemx.com.

Global Virus Insurance

Global Virus Insurance does most of the Exchange Server-based virus scanning and cleaning tricks performed by its competitors. Contact: Panda Software, phone (818) 553-0599; fax (818) 553-0590; World Wide Web www.pandasoftware.com.

Mail Essentials for Exchange/SMTP

Mail Essentials for Exchange is an all-in-one package that does virus and spam control. It also handles encryption, addition of disclaimers to outgoing messages, and automatic replies. Contact: GFI, phone (888) 243-4329; fax (919) 388-5621; e-mail sales@gfiusa.com; World Wide Web www.gficomms.com.

Nemx Power Tools for Exchange Server

Nemx Power Tools monitor messages and attachments for violations of corporate policy, offensive language, viruses, and spam content. The product also adds signatures to outgoing Internet messages, enabling the insertion of corporate disclaimers in all messages. Contact: NEMX Software, phone (613) 831-2010; World Wide Web www.nemx.com.

Norton Anti-Virus for Exchange

The pioneering Norton line of antivirus solutions includes an offering for Exchange Server. The product provides full-service virus scanning and cleaning. Contact: Symantec, phone (408) 253-9600; fax (408) 253-3968; World Wide Web www.symantec.com.

Praetor

Praetor is one of that new breed of spam e-mail filters. It uses lists of banned or approved text as its first line of defense. The product also includes proprietary technology developed through the analysis of techniques used by spammers. Contact: Computer Mail Services, phone (800) 883-2674; fax (248) 352-8387; e-mail info@cmsconnect.com; World Wide Web www.cmsconnect.com.

ScanMail

ScanMail looks for viruses on an Exchange server, even in encoded and compressed items. The product also handles spam e-mail. Contact: Trend Micro Inc., phone (800) 228-5651; fax (408) 257-2003; e-mail sales@trandmicro.com; World Wide Web www.antivirus.com.

Exchange Server/Telephony Integration

Unified messaging, the linking of a variety of messaging tools from pagers to telephones to e-mail clients, has long been a dream of forward-looking communications types. As these products indicate, the tools for accomplishing unified messaging are finally beginning to emerge.

Internet PBX

Internet PBX is a client/server telecom manager. The server part runs as a service on NT Server. The client runs on a Windows workstation and lets you manage voicemail, digital conferencing, phone switching, dialing, faxing, and even e-mail (using voice input). The whole product is integrated with Exchange Server. Contact:

COM2001.com, phone (858) 314-2100; fax (858) 314-2002; e-mail
sales@com2001.com; World Wide Web www.com2001.com.

OnePoint Messenger

OnePoint Messenger supports voice, fax, and e-mail messaging in Exchange Server
environments. Contact: Baypoint Innovations, phone (408) 562-3400; World Wide
Web www.bayptin.com.

Unified Messenger

Unified Messenger is a high-end product that integrates with Exchange Server It
stores voicemail messages inside users' Exchange mailboxes. You can reply to voicemail with e-mail. and vice versa. More real coolness! Contact: Octel, World Wide Web
www.octel.com.

INDEX

Note to the Reader: Throughout this index **boldfaced** page numbers indicate primary discussions of a topic. *Italicized* page numbers indicate illustrations.

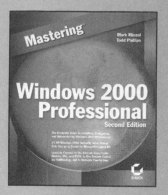

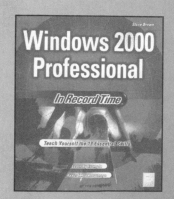